Comparative Politics

Comparative Politics

INTEGRATING THEORIES, METHODS, AND CASES

THIRD EDITION

J. Tyler Dickovick

Washington and Lee University

Jonathan Eastwood

Washington and Lee University

New York   Oxford
Oxford University Press

Oxford University Press is a department of the University of Oxford.
It furthers the University's objective of excellence in research, scholarship,
and education by publishing worldwide. Oxford is a registered trade mark of
Oxford University Press in the UK and certain other countries.

Published in the United States of America by Oxford University Press
198 Madison Avenue, New York, NY 10016, United States of America.

For titles covered by Section 112 of the US Higher Education
Opportunity Act, please visit www.oup.com/us/he for the latest
information about pricing and alternate formats.

Library of Congress Cataloging-in-Publication Data

Names: Dickovick, James Tyler, 1973– author. | Eastwood, Jonathan, author.
Title: Comparative politics: integrating theories, methods, and cases /
    J. Tyler Dickovick, Washington and Lee University, Jonathan Eastwood,
    Washington and Lee University.
Description: Third Edition. | New York: Oxford University Press, [2018]
Identifiers: LCCN 2018015555 (print) | LCCN 2018017028 (ebook) |
    ISBN 9780190854874 (ebook) | ISBN 9780190854867 (Paperback) |
    ISBN 9780190854935 (Looseleaf)
Subjects: LCSH: Comparative government.
Classification: LCC JF51 (ebook) | LCC JF51 .D53 2018 (print) | DDC 320.3—dc23
LC record available at https://lccn.loc.gov/2018015555

9 8 7 6 5 4 3
Printed by Marquis, Canada

Brief Contents

Contents

PART I: Comparative Political Analysis

CHAPTER 1

The Comparative Approach: An Introduction   1

CHAPTER 2

Theories, Hypotheses, and Evidence   24

PART II: The State, Development, Democracy, and Authoritarianism

CHAPTER 3

The State   47

PART III: Institutions of Government

PART IV: Politics, Society, and Culture

PART V: The Comparative-International Nexus

PART VI: Country Profiles and Cases

Insights

The field of comparative politics is changing, not only in how it's studied but in how it's taught. We set out to write this textbook because we saw the need for a new approach—one that is truly comparative, that goes beyond a litany of facts or abstract ideas. In the process, we had to rethink what a book for this course should look like. We started with a central aim: to get students to think like comparativists. Toward that end, we have integrated theories and methods with a range of country case applications to address the big questions in comparative politics today.

Many undergraduates take a course in comparative politics because they are broadly interested in world affairs. They want to understand issues such as democracy and democratization, economic and social development, transnational social movements, and the relationship between world religions and conflict around the globe, just as we did as students (and still do!). This book focuses squarely on these big issues and offers a framework for understanding through comparison.

Our job is to teach students how to think critically, how to analyze the world around them. We want our students to do more than just memorize facts and theories. Ultimately, we want them to learn how to *do* comparative politics. This course is successful if students can use the comparative method to seek out their own answers. We are successful as educators if we give them the analytical skills to do so.

What's New in This Edition?

We have updated this edition of *Comparative Politics* to reflect feedback we received from numerous readers, instructors, and students, not to mention our own experiences of teaching with the book. We are truly grateful to those who have shared their perspectives with us, and we have made the following revisions throughout the book:

- Amplified and enhanced discussions on the United States, Russia, China, and North Korea to incorporate the most current developments
- Updated information on international elections and the Trump administration in the United States, with further coverage on the growth of populist and nationalist movements across the globe
- Revisions and updates to the Country Profiles and Thinking Comparatively features
- New Case Studies and Insights, and revisions, where necessary, to existing ones
- Broad revisions to figure and table data, as well as maps.

An Integrative Approach

One of the distinctive features of this book is the *way* we have integrated theories, methods, and cases. Rather than focusing on either country information or themes of comparative politics, we have combined these approaches while emphasizing application and analysis. By providing students with the tools to begin doing their own analyses, we hope to show them how exciting this kind of work can be. These tools include theories (presented in an accessible way), the basics of the comparative method, and manageable case materials for practice, all in the context of the big questions.

We thus take an integrative approach to the relationship between big themes and country case studies. This text is a hybrid containing sixteen thematic chapters plus linked materials for twelve countries of significant interest to comparativists. The country materials following the thematic chapters include both basic country information and a series of case studies dealing with specific thematic issues.

We link the country cases to the thematic chapters via short "call out" boxes—**"Cases in Context"**—at relevant points in the chapters. For example, a "Case in Context" box (titled "Democracy's Success in India: What Can We Learn from a Deviant Case?") in a discussion of theory in chapter 6, "Democracy and Democratization," points students to a full **case study** on democratization in India, included at the back of the text.

CASE IN CONTEXT

Democracy's Success in India: What Can We Learn from a Deviant Case?

PAGE 466

India is a major anomaly for modernization theories of development. In essence, the relationship between its political and economic development has been the inverse of what modernization theory would predict. India is the world's second largest society and its largest democracy—consider, therefore, the share that Indian citizens hold in the world's broader democratic population. This anomaly has potentially serious implications and makes the puzzle of Indian democratization all the more intriguing.

For more on the case of democratization in India, see the case study in Part VI, p. 466. As you read it, keep in mind the following questions:

1. What, if anything, does Indian anti-colonial resistance have to do with the country's democratization?
2. What, if anything, does Indian democratization suggest about the importance of individual actors, leadership, and institutional design?
3. Can you think of a way to "save" modernization theory in the face of the case of India?

Indian Voters, 2017, in Uttar Pradesh state. India is the world's largest democracy.

CASE STUDY

Democracy's Success in India: What Can We Learn from a "Deviant Case"?

CHAPTER 6, PAGE 136

How does modernization theory account for low-income democracies such as India? As discussed in chapter 6, modernization theory predicts that economic development will lead to democratization and democratic consolidation. Indeed, this relationship generally holds. More often than not, increasing economic development increases the probability that any given society will have democratic politics. India, however, poses a major anomaly for some versions of modernization theory. Given that India's population is approximately one-seventh of the world's population, this anomaly is not easily dismissed.

Why does India constitute an anomaly or "deviant case" for modernization theory? India only recently began to see notable economic development; and for most of the twentieth century, the country was profoundly poor. Modernization would lead us to suspect authoritarian governance under these conditions. Yet after decolonization, India defied pessimists and built the world's largest democracy, one that has now endured for decades. There are several conclusions that one could draw from this. We could decide that this anomaly disproves or

refutes modernization theory, and turn to some other theory of democratization. For example, we could turn to institutional theories of democratization as an alternative. Perhaps something about the parliamentary form of government rather than presidential government contributed to India's rather successful democracy (as is discussed in chapter 10); one could consider the Indian case to test this hypothesis. For example, has the parliamentary system with its multiparty coalitions and governments that are accountable to the legislature resulted in more power-sharing and less "winner-take-all" politics? Has it resulted in a prime ministerial "style" that is less centralized than in presidential systems? There is evidence both for and against the argument that parliamentarism has been a cause of India's democratic success.

Another alternative, though, would be to use a deviant case like India's democracy to amend or clarify the nature of the original theory. What if modernization theory is not making the law-like generalization that development leads inevitably to democratization, but rather a "weaker" claim that economic

development *facilitates* democratization and democratic consolidation? Why would this be different? Because the theory would now say that it is *unlikely* that India could successfully democratize without first achieving a higher level of economic development, but not that it is *impossible*. A more flexible theory of modernization might be compatible by including insights from other theories. For example, perhaps modernization theory could be linked to institutional theories, like the one on parliamentarism mentioned previously. Maybe parliamentarism is particularly called for as a form of institutional design when the society in question has a relatively low level of economic development. We are speculating here for the sake of argument and not proposing this theory; India's history of development and democracy does not and cannot prove this assertion. Rather, it might suggest this hypothesis, which we could then test through the examination of other well-selected cases. In general, deviant cases are useful. We should be pleased when we find them, as they help us to critically assess existing theories, modifying or rejecting them as appropriate.

Another "Case in Context" box in chapter 6 (titled "Is China Destined for Democracy?") invites students to consider whether democratization in China is inevitable. Other boxes in that chapter focus on issues of democracy and democratization in Brazil and the United States.

Using these short "linking" boxes has enabled us to integrate a complete set of case materials without interrupting the narrative flow of the chapters. The kind of reading we suggest with the structure of this text is similar to following hyperlinks in online text—something students do easily. This flexible design feature also caters to the diversity of teaching styles in today's political science. Instructors can choose to have students follow these links to case studies as they go, using all or just some of them, or they can choose to teach thematic chapters and country materials separately.

The text integrates theories, methods, and cases in other ways as well. **"Insights"** boxes make connections by briefly summarizing important scholarly works representative of the major schools of thought.

INSIGHTS

Nationalism: Five Roads to Modernity
by Liah Greenfeld

Greenfeld argues that nationalism is fundamentally *cultural* and needs to be understood as an imaginative response to social conditions. To understand nationalism's emergence and growth, we must understand why the idea spread that humanity is divided into distinct "peoples" who are "sovereign" and "equal." For Greenfeld, the key preconditions for the development of national identity are problems in *stratification systems* through which societies hierarchically divide themselves, such as the class structure. Elite *status inconsistency*—a condition present when the stratification system breaks down and elites are no longer sure of their status—leads some groups to seek to transform identity, and national identity often seems to such groups to serve their interests well. Greenfeld examines this hypothesis against a number of cases (including England, France, Russia, Germany, and Japan), finding pronounced status inconsistency in each case in the key groups that are most central in redefining their societies as nations. At the same time, Greenfeld acknowledges the importance of institutions like the state prior to national identity's emergence in helping to shape the type that develops in any given case. Scholars working with this theory also note that political institutions play an important role in spreading and preserving national identity.

Liah Greenfeld, Nationalism: Five Roads to Modernity. *Cambridge, MA: Harvard University Press, 1992.*

Each chapter after the introduction chapter (chapter 1) closes with a **"Thinking Comparatively"** feature, which focuses on *a* case or set of cases to illustrate how students can apply the theories discussed in the chapter.

Why Did Zimbabwe Become and Remain Authoritarian?

THINKING COMPARATIVELY

Authoritarian regimes come in many varieties, and they come from many different origins. We have emphasized that there is no single thing called "authoritarianism" that one theory can explain. Rather, authoritarian regimes have distinct features and exhibit many different types of transitions (and non-transitions). Scholars have developed a number of explanatory models to account for these. Some of the main general factors in most cases, though, include (1) historical relationships between contending groups, (2) the strength and form of existing institutions, (3) a country's level of economic development, (4) political-cultural traditions and tendencies, and (5) the strategic situations and choices of key actors. Of course, as we have seen in other chapters, it is not enough to merely list such contributing factors; we must figure out how such factors interact and which are most important. What do you think? And how could we test your ideas empirically?

KEY METHODOLOGICAL TOOLS

Evidence and Empirical Critiques

One reason that many theories continue to endure in different areas of comparative politics is that most of the major theories have some empirical support. This makes it challenging to determine which theory is the most accurate. In reality, most theories will not be accurate under all circumstances, but rather each will explain some outcomes better than

In these features we highlight important methodological tools or strategies, such as the use of deviant cases and the most-similar-systems (MSS) design. We then model for students how to use these analytical tools in practice.

Organization

The sixteen thematic chapters of this book are divided into five parts:

- Part I (chapters 1 and 2) focuses on basic methods in comparative politics, covering conceptualization, hypothesis testing, the formation of theories, and the use of evidence. The goal in these first two chapters is not to focus on the details of methodology, which can be taught in more specialized courses, but on the overarching logic of comparative inquiry.
- Part II (chapters 3 through 7) focuses on the state (chapter 3), political economy (chapter 4), development (chapter 5), democracy and democratization (chapter 6), and the various forms of authoritarian regimes (chapter 7).
- Part III (chapters 8 through 11) focuses on the analysis of political institutions, giving students the tools to analyze institutional design in constitutional structures and judiciaries (chapter 8), legislatures and elections (chapter 9), executives (chapter 10), and political parties and interest groups (chapter 11).
- Part IV (chapters 12 through 15) focuses on issues that link comparative politics to political sociology, such as the study of revolution and other forms of contention (chapter 12), national identities and nationalism (chapter 13), race, gender, and ethnicity (chapter 14), and religion and ideology (chapter 15).
- Part V consists of a single chapter, 16, which links comparative politics to international relations, emphasizing how global politics has produced new sets of problems that both comparativists *and* international relations scholars must analyze. As such, the book points to another kind of integration, pushing students to see connections between comparative politics and other courses in political science.

After chapter 2, the thematic chapters follow a common format. They are divided into three main sections:

- Concepts: covers basic definitions and develops a working vocabulary.
- Types: discusses useful typologies, such as the major types of dramatic social change that interest political scientists.
- Causes and Effects: walks students through the major theories that aim to explain causes and effects, ending with the "Thinking Comparatively" feature to model analysis.

The final part of the book, Part VI, comprises country "profiles" and in-depth "case studies." We selected twelve countries after surveying more than

CASE STUDY

The French Revolution

CHAPTER 12, PAGE 289

The French Revolution took place amid major structural problems in eighteenth-century French society (Furet 1995; Doyle 2003). In this period, France, like much of early modern Europe, remained an "estate society," divided into three groups: a nobility with special privileges, the clergy, and commoners. The social status of the nobility, however, was weakened by the ongoing efforts of the centralizing, absolutist crown. As the monarchy and its state grew stronger, the nobility felt increasingly marginalized. At the same time, the French absolutist state, largely through its involvement in foreign wars (especially the American Revolution), faced major fiscal difficulties (Doyle 2003). Indeed, by the late eighteenth century, it was nearly bankrupt. Meanwhile, periodic problems in food distribution and rural poverty ensured that much of France's rural population felt discontent. Finally, the spread of the Enlightenment and of nationalism provided the bases for an intellectual critique of the old regime (Greenfeld 1992; Bell 2001).

The revolution began as a series of efforts to reform the French state. The crown called an "Assembly of Notables," but the assembly declared that the Estates General, which had not met since the early seventeenth century, needed to be called. When the Estates General convened, it was divided in the customary manner into the three estates mentioned previously. However, before long, politics and propaganda forced representatives of the first two estates to join the latter one, the core idea being that the French nation shouldn't be divided by estates because all of its members should be equal. The third estate *was* the nation, as Sieyes declared (Furet 1995: 45–51). In other words, the Estates General was reinterpreted as being something like a modern, national legislature (though the leaders of the Estates General remained bourgeois and nobles, along with some clergy, and not "popular" actors).

Reform quickly devolved into a novel form of collective behavior that was surprising even to its most central participants and those who attempted to lead and control it. Street actions began, and mobs attacked the Bastille prison on July 14, 1789, wishing to destroy a reviled symbol of the arbitrary authority of the monarch to imprison opponents at will. By 1792, the monarchy had fallen amid increasing violence—much perpetrated by mobs known as the "sans culottes"—opening a period known as the "Terror" in which perceived enemies of the revolution were murdered in large numbers. Robespierre was a key figure in this period, perpetrating the paranoid violence that ultimately consumed him. This was followed by a period of relaxation known as the "Thermidorian reaction," and, finally, by the rise of Napoleon. On one hand, Napoleon appears a conservative figure, since, for example, he declared himself emperor. But on the other hand, he can be viewed as a revolutionary whose mission was to spread the French Revolution to the rest of Europe, through an imperial war.

What struck so many contemporaries was the Revolution's *destructive* nature. It seemed intent on an eradication of the old society and the replacement of all of its forms by new, "revolutionary" ones. This included the creation of a new, revolutionary calendar, the efforts to destroy the Church and its teachings, the war on the nobility, the destruction of many architectural sites, and so forth. The French revolution subsequently became the model for many later revolutionaries and its ideals inspirational for nationalists and republicans everywhere. At the same time, it surprised nearly everyone involved, and those who attempted to control it quickly learned that they had helped to unleash social forces beyond their ability to lead (Arendt 1963).

150 instructors of comparative politics to see which they considered most crucial for inclusion. The cases are Brazil, China, France, Germany, India, Iran, Japan, Mexico, Nigeria, Russia, the United Kingdom, and the United States. This selection offers broad coverage of every major world region, democratic and authoritarian polities, every major religious tradition, highly varying levels of economic and social development, and quite different institutional designs.

For each country, we first provide a "profile": an introduction with a table of key features, a map, and pie charts of demographics; a timeline and historical overview; and brief descriptions of political institutions, political culture, and political economy.

Following each profile is a set of case studies (five or six for each country) that we reference in the thematic chapters as described earlier (via the *"Case in Context"* boxes).

The case sets end with research prompts to help students get started as comparativists.

Flexibility in Instruction: Ways of Using This Text

The chapters are arranged in a logical order yet written in such a way that instructors might easily rearrange them to custom fit a course. Some instructors, for example, may wish to pair chapter 3 (on the state) with chapter 13 (on nationalism and national identity). Others might wish to assign chapter 15 (on religion and ideology) alongside chapters 6 and 7 (on democratic and authoritarian regimes). We have written the book with the flexibility to facilitate such pairings. Indeed, while we strongly suggest beginning with chapters 1 and 2, students will be able to follow the text even without reading them first.

Similarly, the book's structure supports a range of options for using the country materials. Some instructors may wish to teach selected country materials at or near the beginning of a course. Some may wish to make reference to country materials as the course proceeds, assigning students to read them as they are clearly and visibly "called out" in the text. One approach could require all students in a course to familiarize themselves with only a subset of the countries detailed here, rather than all twelve. Another might require each student to select three or four countries, following rules or categories of countries as laid out by the instructor.

The book also works with or without supplemental materials chosen by the instructor. The "Insights" boxes throughout the text provide indications of excellent options for further readings. Many other choice readings are noted in the "References and Further Reading" section at the back of the text, organized by chapter. A companion book of classic and contemporary readings is available, in addition to a reader on current debates (see Packaging Options, p. xxv). In short, instructors can use this text alone or link it seamlessly to other readings.

Summary of Features

We have built a number of useful features into the text, some of which we have already mentioned:

- *"Case in Context"* boxes tie in to the narrative of the main chapters, pointing students to full case studies in the book's final part.
- *"Insights"* boxes illustrate causal theories by describing the work of key authors in the field, making this work accessible to introductory students.

- **"Thinking Comparatively"** sections at the end of every chapter (after chapter 1) model the application of theories and the testing of hypotheses. Each "Thinking Comparatively" section includes a **"Key Methodological Tools"** feature, which introduces key skills and strategies for doing comparative political analysis and reinforces lessons learned in the first two chapters.
- **"Thinking It Through"** questions close every chapter. These help students test their ability to apply comparative politics theories to cases.
- Every section of case studies offers a series of **"Research Prompts"** that can be used to develop comparative projects and papers, applying what students have learned as they start to do comparative analysis.
- Every chapter ends with a **"Chapter Summary,"** enabling students and instructors to review the main points at a glance.
- At the back of the text, we include **"References and Further Reading"** by chapter that students can use to dig deeper into the issues raised or as they begin their own research.
- A **running glossary** in the margin of the text highlights the meaning of key terms as they appear and serves as a quick study reference.

Supplements

Oxford University Press offers instructors and students a comprehensive ancillary package for qualified adopters of *Comparative Politics: Integrating Theories, Methods, and Cases.*

Ancillary Resource Center

The Ancillary Resource Center (ARC) at https://arc2.oup-arc.com/ is a convenient, instructor-focused, single destination for resources to accompany this book. Accessed online through individual user accounts, the ARC provides instructors with up-to-date ancillaries while guaranteeing the security of grade-significant resources. In addition, it allows OUP to keep instructors informed when new content becomes available.

The ARC for *Comparative Politics* contains a variety of materials to aid in teaching:

- Instructor's Resource Manual with Test Item File—The Instructor's Resource Manual includes chapter objectives, detailed chapter outlines, lecture suggestions and activities, discussion questions, video resources, and Web resources. The Test Item File includes more than eight hundred test questions selected and approved by the authors, including multiple-choice, short-answer, and essay questions.

- Computerized Test Bank—Using the test authoring and management tool Diploma, the computerized test bank that accompanies this text is designed for both novice and advanced users. Diploma enables instructors to create and edit questions, create randomized quizzes and tests with an easy-to-use drag-and-drop tool, publish quizzes and tests to online courses, and print quizzes and tests for paper-based assessments.
- PowerPoint-Based Slides—Each chapter's slide set includes a succinct chapter outline and incorporates relevant chapter graphics.
- CNN Videos—Offering recent clips on timely topics, this collection includes fifteen films tied to the chapter topics. Each clip is approximately 5–10 minutes, providing a great way to launch your lectures.

Course Cartridges

For qualified adopters, OUP will supply the teaching resources in a course cartridges designed to work with your preferred Online Learning Platform. Please contact your Oxford University Press sales representative at (800) 280–0280.

E-Book

E-book for Comparative Politics: An eBook version of this text (9780190854874) is available online at RedShelf (www.redshelf.com), Chegg (www.chegg.com), or Vitalsource (www.vitalsource.com).

Companion Website

Comparative Politics is also accompanied by an extensive companion website at www.oup.com/us/dickovick. This website includes a number of learning tools to help students study and review key concepts presented in the text. For each chapter, you will find learning objectives, key-concept summaries, quizzes, essay questions, web activities, and web links.

Packaging Options

Adopters of *Comparative Politics: Integrating Theories, Methods, and Cases* can package *ANY* Oxford University Press book with the text for a 20% savings off the total package price. See our many trade and scholarly offerings at www.oup.com, then contact your OUP sales representative at (800) 280-0280 to request a package ISBN. In addition, the following items can be packaged with the text for free:

- *Oxford Pocket World Atlas, Sixth Edition*—This full-color atlas is a handy reference for political science students. Please use package ISBN 978-0-19-046231-4.

- Very Short Introduction Series—These very brief texts offer succinct introductions to a variety of topics. Titles include *Nationalism, Citizenship, Global Economic History, Fascism,* and *Democracy,* to name just a few.
- *The Student Research and Writing Guide for Political Science*—This brief guide provides students with the information and tools necessary to conduct research and write a research paper. The guide explains how to get started writing a research paper, describes the parts of a research paper, and presents the citation formats found in academic writing. Please use package ISBN 978-0-19-046160-7 to order.

Acknowledgments

We are very grateful to a number of individuals who have been helpful to us as we worked on this project. At Washington and Lee University, we thank our respective provosts, deans, and department chairs who have supported our work. This includes June Aprille, Bob Strong, Daniel Wubah, Marc Conner, Larry Peppers, Rob Straughan, Hank Dobin, Suzanne Keen, Mark Rush, Lucas Morel, David Novack, Krzysztof Jasiewicz, and Sascha Goluboff. We are very grateful to the many friends and colleagues, both at Washington and Lee and elsewhere, who read and commented on chapters or country profiles, including Francoise Fregnac-Clave, Rachel Beatty Riedl, Tim Lubin, Dan Kramer, Christian Jennings, Robin Leblanc, Ayşe Zarakol, Rich Bidlack, David Bello, Ken White, and Alessandra Del Conte Dickovick. We also thank Hardin Marion for his excellent close reading of the first edition and the comments he generously shared with us. We have many other colleagues and friends who have given us intellectual and moral support for which we are grateful. Numerous students have been extraordinarily helpful as well. We are particularly grateful to Miranda Galvin, Ali Greenberg, and Anna Milewski. Other students to whom we wish to express our appreciation include, but are not limited to, Samara Francisco, Morten Wendelbo, Maya Reimi, Linnea Bond, Natasha Lerner, Amy Dawson, Justine Griffin-Churchill, David Razum, John Twomey, Lauren Howard, Kate LeMasters, and Maren Lundgren. We are also thankful to students in numerous iterations of Politics 105 (Global Politics), many of whom offered insightful questions on a "prototype" of this text (in early years) and on the first and second editions (more recently), as well as students who read the book in Eastwood's International Comparative Sociology course. We owe thanks to Washington and Lee for support for the work of some of the students mentioned previously through the Summer Research Scholar Program, and our own work through the Lenfest Sabbatical Grant, and the Glenn Grant, Lenfest Grant, and Hess Scholars programs for summer research.

Our families have been characteristically supportive and gracious throughout the years that we worked on this project. Their collective patience has been extraordinary. We owe eternal gratitude to our spouses, Maria Emilia Nava and Alessandra Del Conte Dickovick. We are also grateful to (and for) our wonderful children: Gabriela Eastwood, Carolina Dickovick, Gabriela Dickovick, Samuel Eastwood, and Alexander Eastwood. We owe much gratitude to our parents and extended families as well, of course.

We are grateful as well to the fine editorial staff at Oxford University Press. We particularly appreciate the excellent ideas and efforts of Jennifer Carpenter, Lauren Mine, and Thom Holmes. All of them improved this text substantially with their insights and hard work over several years. We have also benefited from the work of Jane Lee, Barbara Mathieu, David Bradley, Maegan Sherlock, and Brianna Provenzano, among others. We are also grateful to Andy Blitzer and Alison Ball for their work with us on the 3rd edition.

We owe gratitude as well to those who developed our passion for (and understanding of) comparative politics. With the standard caveat that any errors of fact or interpretation in this text are solely our own, we want to thank first our earliest teachers of comparative politics. Above all, we wish to thank Kent Eaton and Liah Greenfeld. We also owe great thanks to Jeffrey Herbst, Deborah Yashar, Chuck Lindholm, Scott Palmer, John Stone, and Evan Lieberman; as well as Nancy Bermeo, Atul Kohli, Lynn White, and Claudio Véliz, among others.

Finally, we thank the external evaluators of this edition, who gave generously of their time and expertise:

Lauren Balasco
Pittsburg State University

Elizabeth Carter
University of New Hampshire

Anastasia Kuz-Grady
University of North Carolina, Wilmington

Lydia Lundgren
Clemson University

Joseph H. Moskowitz
New Jersey City University

Kristoffer Rees
Indiana University East

Gunes Murat Tezcur
University of Central Florida

Cheryl Van Den Handel
Northeastern State University

We also thank the many reviewers of the previous editions, whose insights helped shape the book:

Dauda Abubakar
Ohio University

Despina Alexiadou
University of Pittsburgh

Michelle Allendoerfer
George Washington University

Jason Ross Arnold
Virginia Commonwealth University

Andrew Appleton
Washington State University

Tanya Bagashka
University of Houston

Karolyn Benger
Georgia Institute of Technology

Anna Brigevich
The University of North Carolina at Chapel Hill

Diane Bulpett
Northeastern University

Joel R. Carbonell
Kent State University at Stark

Ryan Carlin
Georgia State University

Luis F. Clemente
Ohio University

Howard Cody
University of Maine

Jeffrey Conroy-Krutz
Michigan State University

William Crowther
The University of North Carolina at Greensboro

Ian Down
University of Tennessee—Knoxville

Glen Duerr
Cedarville University

Matthew Fails
Oakland University

Ronald A. Francisco
University of Kansas

Nathan W. Freeman
University of Georgia

Joseph J. Foy
University of Wisconsin—Parkside

John D. Granger
University of Central Florida

Ivy Hamerly
Baylor University

Keisha Haywood
Ramapo College of New Jersey

Tobias Hofmann
National University of Singapore

Jennifer Horan
The University of North Carolina at Wilmington

John Hulsey
James Madison University

Eunsook Jung
Fairfield University

Peggy Kahn
University of Michigan—Flint

Katherine H. Keyser
Drew University

Stephen Juan King
Georgetown University

Natalie A. Kistner
James Madison University

Lada V. Kochtcheeva
North Carolina State University

Gallya Lahav
Stonybrook University

Eric Langenbacher
Georgetown University

Ricardo Rene Laremont
Binghamton University

Jeffrey Lewis
Cleveland State University

Rahsaan Maxwell
University of Massachusetts Amherst

Mary M. McCarthy
Drake University

Gregory J. Moore
Eckerd College

Katarina Moyon
Winthrop University

Anna Ohanyan
Stonehill College

Sanghamitra Padhy
Davidson College

Vanja Petricevic
Florida Gulf Coast University

Juris Pupcenoks
Washington College

Laura Roselle
Elon University

Dietmar Schirmer
University of Florida

James Seroka
Auburn University

Hootan Shambayati
Florida Gulf Coast University

Oxana Shevel
Tufts University

Tracy H. Slagter
University of Wisconsin Oshkosh

Marcus Stadelmann
University of Texas at Tyler

Jeffrey K. Staton
Emory University

Emmanuel Teitelbaum
George Washington University

Anca Turcu
University of Central Florida

Rollin F. Tusalem
Arkansas State University

Cheryl Van Den Handel
Northeastern State University

Adryan Wallace
University of Hartford.

Meredith Weiss
University at Albany—SUNY

Aubrey Westfall
Virginia Wesleyan College

Jennifer J. White
University of Georgia

Fiona Yap
University of Kansas

Gamze Cavdar Yasar
Colorado State University

Jiangnan Zhu
University of Nevada—Reno

The field of comparative politics is always changing, and a book of this sort covers a huge array of research areas. As such, we anticipate a need to update this text in the future. We are very eager for suggestions, corrections, and other comments that instructors or students might make. We have established an e-mail address specifically for these inquiries, and all comments will go to and be read by the authors. The address is **comparative.politics@oup.com**. So if you have any suggestions for future issues, or find any errors or omissions, please let us know. We hope you enjoy the book.

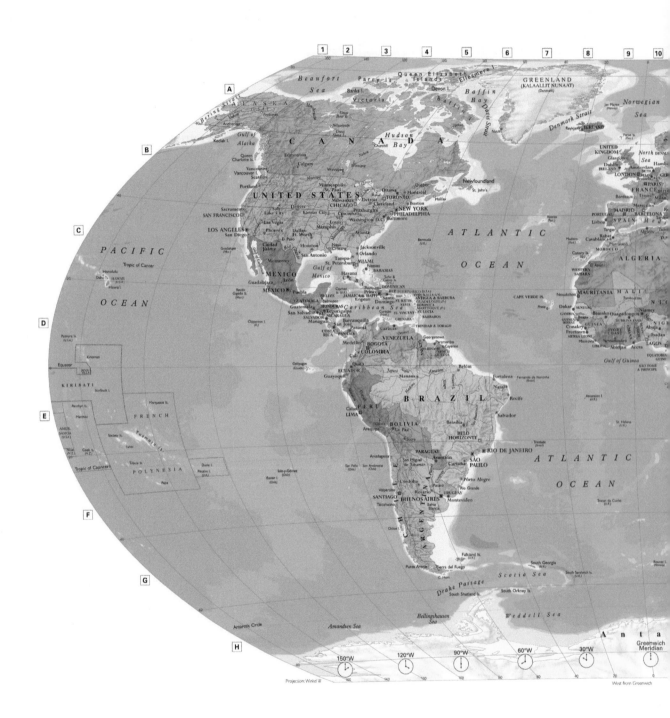

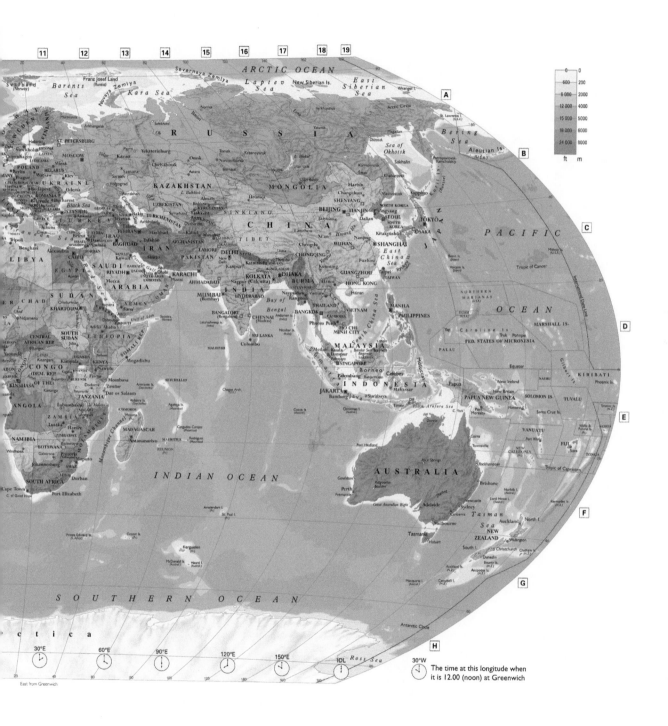

11 **12** **13** **14** **15** **16** **17** **18** **19**

ARCTIC OCEAN

Svalbard (Norway) · Franz Josef Land (Russia) · Novaya Zemlya · Severnaya Zemlya · Laptev Sea · New Siberian Is. · East Siberian Sea · Wrangel I.

Barents Sea · Kara Sea · Bering Sea · Aleutian Is. (U.S.A.)

NORWAY · SWEDEN · FINLAND · Murmansk · Arkhangelsk · Norilsk · Arctic Circle · St. Lawrence I. (U.S.A.)

Oslo · Stockholm · Helsinki · ESTONIA · ST. PETERSBURG · R U S S I A · Yakutsk · Petropavlovsk-Kamchatskiy

Copenhagen · LATVIA · Sekehard · Yenisey · Magadan

GERMANY · Gdansk · LITHUANIA · Vologda · Yekaterinburg · Tomsk · Krasnoyarsk · Okhotsk · Sea of Okhotsk

POLAND · Warsaw · BELARUS · MOSCOW · Perm · Kazan · Chelyabinsk · Omsk · Novosibirsk · Barnaul · Sakhalin · Khabarovsk

Prague · Kiev · UKRAINE · Samara · K A Z A K H S T A N · Ulan-Ude · Amur · Vladivostok · Sapporo

Vienna · Budapest · ROMANIA · Odessa · Saratov · Volgograd · Astrakhan · L. Balkhash · Almaty · M O N G O L I A · Ulan Bator · Changchun · Harbin

MOLDOVA · Black Sea · GEORGIA · Tbilisi · UZBEKISTAN · Bishkek · SHENYANG · NORTH KOREA · TŌKYŌ

Naples · GREECE · BULGARIA · TURKEY · ARMENIA · Baku · Tashkent · KYRGYZSTAN · SINKIANG · BEIJING · TIANJIN · Dalian · SEOUL · SOUTH KOREA · OSAKA

Athens · Izmir · Ankara · AZERBAIJAN · TURKMENISTAN · Samarkand · Dushanbe · TAJIKISTAN · Taiyuan · C H I N A · Kitakyūshū

Tripoli · SYRIA · Damascus · IRAQ · TEHRAN · Mashhad · Kabul · Ürümqi · Lanzhou · Xi'an · Huang · Nanjing · East China Sea

Benghazi · Alexandria · Beirut · Jerusalem · Amman · BAGHDAD · I R A N · AFGHANISTAN · T I B E T · Chengdu · WUHAN · SHANGHAI

LIBYA · CAIRO · JORDAN · Kuwait · Esfahan · LAHORE · DELHI · Kathmandu · CHONGQING · Fuzhou · Taipei

EGYPT · KUWAIT · BAHRAIN · PAKISTAN · New Delhi · NEPAL · Kunming · GUANGZHOU · TAIWAN

Aswan · SAUDI · RIYADH · QATAR · UNITED ARAB EMIRATES · KARACHI · AHMADABAD · KOLKATA (Calcutta) · DHAKA · HONG KONG · Hainan

Mecca · ARABIA · OMAN · Muscat · MUMBAI (Bombay) · I N D I A · HYDERABAD · BANGLADESH · MYANMAR · Rangoon

SUDAN · CHAD · N'Djamena · Khartoum · YEMEN · Sana'a · Gulf of Aden · Socotra (Yemen) · Nagpur · HYDERABAD · BURMA · Naypyidaw · NORTHERN MARIANA IS.

CENTRAL AFRICAN REP. · SOUTH SUDAN · E T H I O P I A · Addis Ababa · DJIBOUTI · Lakshadweep (India) · BANGALORE (Bengaluru) · CHENNAI (Madras) · Andaman Is. (India) · BANGKOK · Phnom Penh · CAMBODIA · VIETNAM · MANILA · GUAM (U.S.A.)

SOMALIA · SRI LANKA · Nicobar Is. (India) · HO CHI MINH CITY · PHILIPPINES · Yap · Caroline Is. · Truk · Pohnpei · MARSHALL IS.

CONGO · UGANDA · KENYA · Mogadishu · MALDIVES · Colombo · MALAYSIA · Medan · Kuala Lumpur · PALAU · FED. STATES OF MICRONESIA

GABON · Yaoundé · CONGO (DEM. REP. OF THE) · RWANDA · Nairobi · SINGAPORE · Bandar Seri Begawan · BRUNEI · SARAWAK · Celebes · Equator · NAURU · KIRIBATI

KINSHASA · BURUNDI · Dodoma · Mombasa · SEYCHELLES · Palembang · Banjarmasin · Borneo · Makassar · PAPUA · New Ireland · Gilbert Is. · Phoenix Is.

TANZANIA · Dar es Salaam · Chagos Arch. (U.K.) · JAKARTA · I N D O N E S I A · New Britain · SOLOMON IS. · TUVALU

ANGOLA · ZAMBIA · Lusaka · Aldabra Is. (Seychelles) · Agalega Is. (Mauritius) · Bandung · Java · Surabaya · Timor · Arafura Sea · PAPUA NEW GUINEA · Port Moresby · Honiara · Santa Cruz Is. · Tokelau Is. (N.Z.)

Lubumbashi · Blantyre · COMOROS · Cocos Is. (Austral.) · Christmas I. (Austral.) · Darwin · Honiara · WALLIS & FUTUNA IS. (Fr.) · SAMOA

ZIMBABWE · Harare · MALAWI · MADAGASCAR · Cargados Carajos (Mauritius) · VANUATU · FIJI

NAMIBIA · BOTSWANA · Bulawayo · Antananarivo · MAURITIUS · Rodrigues (Mauritius) · Cairns · Port Vila · NEW CALEDONIA (Fr.) · Suva · TONGA

Windhoek · Gaborone · Pretoria · MOZAMBIQUE · RÉUNION (Fr.) · Townsville · Nouméa

Johannesburg · Maputo · SWAZILAND · Port Hedland · Rockhampton · Lord Howe I. (Austral.) · Norfolk I. (Austral.) · Kermadec Is. (N.Z.)

SOUTH AFRICA · LESOTHO · Durban · Amsterdam I. (Fr.) · Alice Springs · AUSTRALIA · Brisbane · Newcastle · Sydney

Cape Town · C. of Good Hope · Port Elizabeth · St. Paul I. (Fr.) · Geraldton · Kalgoorlie · Great Australian Bight · Adelaide · Canberra · Tasman Sea · Auckland · North I.

Prince Edward Is. (S. Africa) · Crozet Is. (Fr.) · Perth · Fremantle · Melbourne · NEW ZEALAND · Wellington

INDIAN OCEAN · Kerguelen (Fr.) · Tasmania · Hobart · South I. · Christchurch · Chatham Is. (N.Z.)

McDonald Is. (Austral.) · Heard I. (Austral.) · Dunedin · Bounty Is. (N.Z.) · Auckland Is. (N.Z.) · Antipodes Is. (N.Z.)

SOUTHERN OCEAN · Macquarie I. (Austral.) · Campbell I. (N.Z.)

Antarctica · Antarctic Circle · Ross Sea

PACIFIC OCEAN

East China Sea · South China Sea · Bay of Bengal · Mozambique Channel

Midway Is. (U.S.A.) · Wake I. (U.S.A.) · Volcano Is. (Japan) · Bonin Is. (Japan) · Tropic of Cancer · Tropic of Capricorn

International Date Line

A **B** **C** **D** **E** **F** **G** **H**

ft   m
0   0
600   200
6 000 2000
12 000 4000
15 000 5000
18 000 6000
24 000 8000

30°E · 60°E · 90°E · 120°E · 150°E · IDL · 30°W

East from Greenwich

The time at this longitude when it is 12.00 (noon) at Greenwich

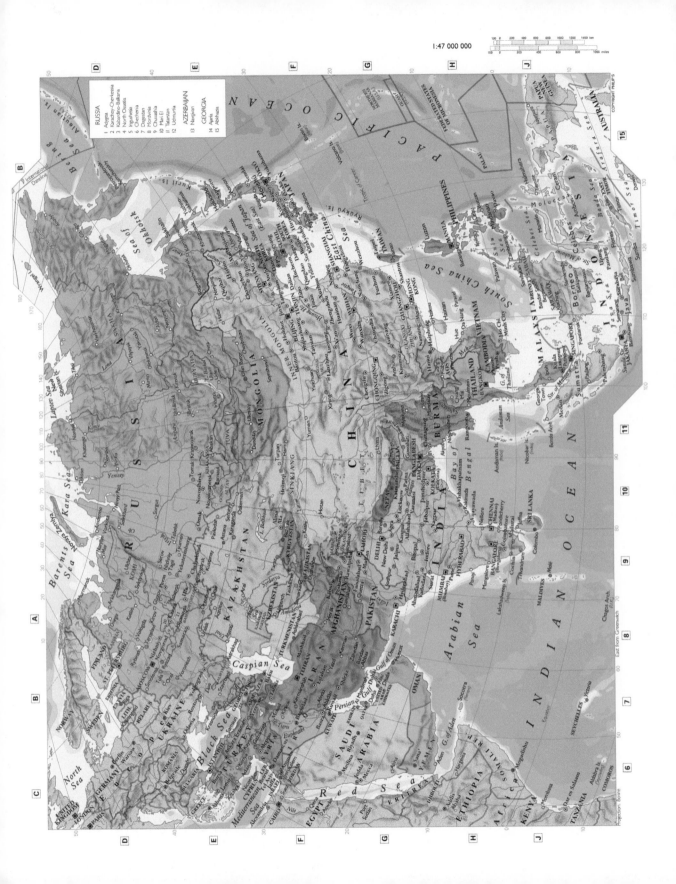

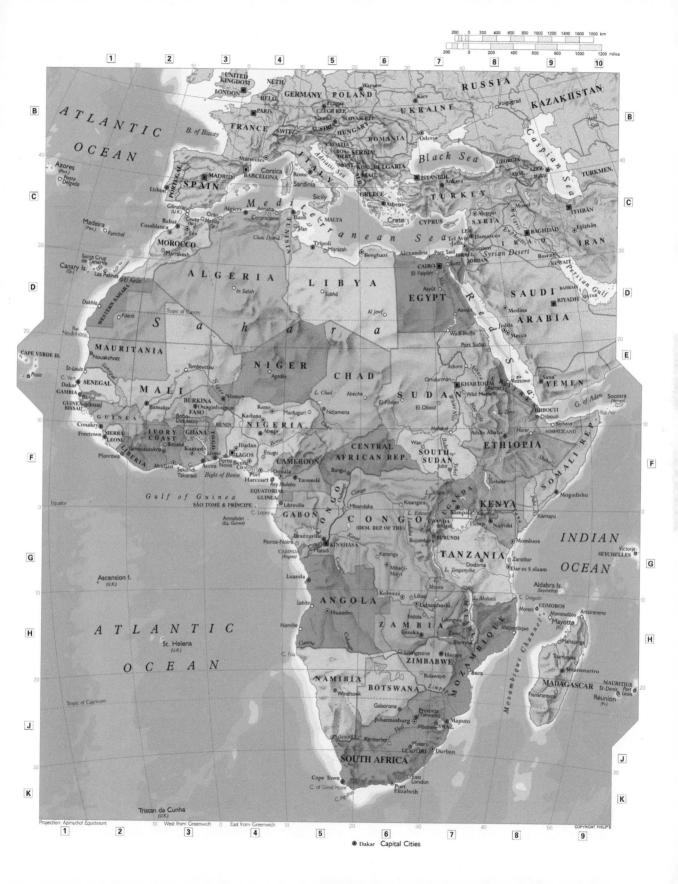

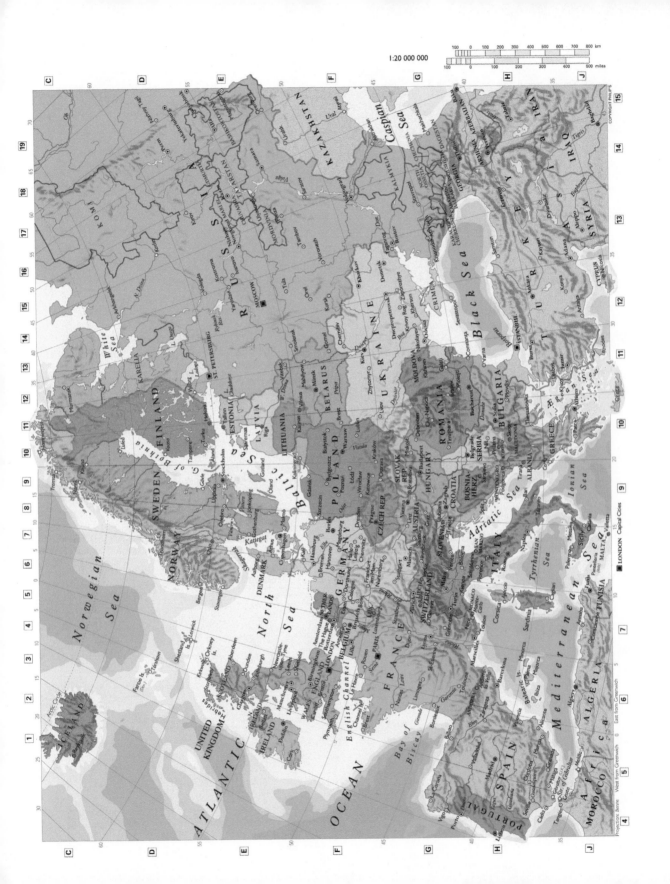

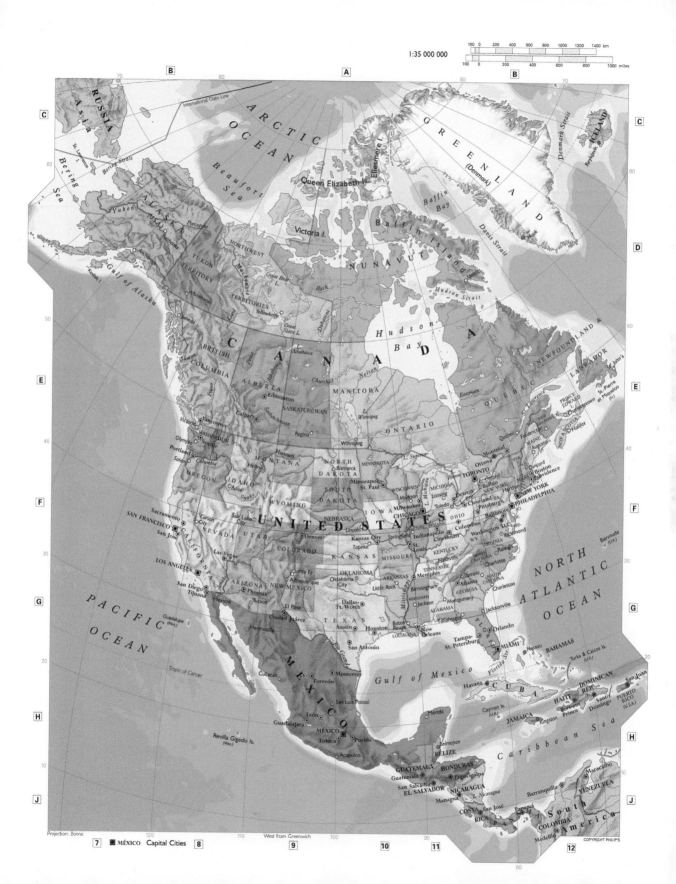

1:35 000 000

100 0 200 400 600 800 1000 1200 1400 km
100 0 200 400 600 800 1000 miles

ARCTIC OCEAN

RUSSIA
ASIA
St. Lawrence I.
Bering Strait
Bering Sea

International Date Line

GREENLAND
(Denmark)

ICELAND
Reykjavik

Denmark Strait

ALASKA
(U.S.A.)
Yukon
Porcupine
Anchorage
Kodiak I.
Gulf of Alaska
Juneau
Whitehorse

Queen Elizabeth Is.

Ellesmere I.

Beaufort Sea

Victoria I.

Baffin Bay

Baffin Island

Davis Strait

YUKON TERRITORY
Arctic Circle
Peel
NORTHWEST TERRITORIES
Great Bear L.
Yellowknife
Great Slave L.
Mackenzie
Hay

Back

NUNAVUT

Hudson Strait

BRITISH COLUMBIA
Skeena
Fraser
Victoria
Vancouver
Seattle
WASHINGTON
Olympia
Portland
Salem
Columbia
OREGON
IDAHO
Boise
Snake

CANADA

ALBERTA
Edmonton
Calgary
Peace
Athabasca
L. Athabasca
SASKATCHEWAN
Saskatchewan
Regina

Churchill

Nelson

MANITOBA

L. Winnipeg

Winnipeg

Hudson Bay

ONTARIO

Eastmain

QUÉBEC

LABRADOR

NEWFOUNDLAND

St. Lawrence
St-Pierre et Miquelon (Fr.)
St. John's

PRINCE EDWARD I.
NEW BRUNSWICK
Charlottetown
Fredericton
NOVA SCOTIA
Halifax

MONTANA
Helena
WYOMING
Salt Lake City
UTAH
NEVADA
Carson City
Sacramento
SAN FRANCISCO
San Jose
CALIFORNIA
LOS ANGELES
San Diego
Tijuana
Las Vegas
ARIZONA
Phoenix
Tucson

Missouri
NORTH DAKOTA
Bismarck
SOUTH DAKOTA
NEBRASKA
Lincoln

MINNESOTA
Minneapolis-St. Paul
L. Superior
WISCONSIN
Madison
IOWA

UNITED STATES

COLORADO
Denver
KANSAS
Topeka
Kansas City
OKLAHOMA
Oklahoma City
Santa Fe
Albuquerque
NEW MEXICO

El Paso
Ciudad Juárez
Hermosillo
Mexicali

MICHIGAN
L. Michigan
L. Huron
Lansing
MILWAUKEE
CHICAGO
ILLINOIS
Springfield
St. Louis
MISSOURI
ARKANSAS
Little Rock
Memphis
Nashville
TENNESSEE

Toledo
Detroit
Cleveland
OHIO
Columbus
Cincinnati
Indianapolis
INDIANA
KENTUCKY

TORONTO
Buffalo
Pittsburgh
Hartford
NEW YORK
Ottawa
Montreal
Québec
MAINE
Augusta
Concord
Boston
Providence
NEW YORK
PHILADELPHIA
Baltimore
Washington D.C.
W.V.
VIRGINIA
Richmond

NORTH ATLANTIC OCEAN

Bermuda (U.K.)

PACIFIC OCEAN

Guadalupe (Mex.)

Revilla Gigedo Is. (Mex.)

MÉXICO

Rio Grande
Dallas-Ft. Worth
TEXAS
Austin
San Antonio
Houston
LOUISIANA
Baton Rouge
New Orleans
Jackson
MISSISSIPPI
ALABAMA
Montgomery
Birmingham
GEORGIA
Atlanta
Columbia
SOUTH CAROLINA
NORTH CAROLINA
Raleigh
Charlotte
Charleston

Tallahassee
Jacksonville
FLORIDA
Tampa-St. Petersburg
Orlando
MIAMI

Gulf of Mexico

Florida Keys

Havana
CUBA
BAHAMAS
Nassau

Tropic of Cancer

Culiacán
Torreón
Monterrey
San Luis Potosí
León
Guadalajara
MÉXICO
Toluca
Puebla
Acapulco

Mérida

BELIZE
Belmopan
GUATEMALA
Guatemala
HONDURAS
Tegucigalpa
EL SALVADOR
San Salvador
NICARAGUA
Managua
L. Nicaragua
COSTA RICA
San José
PANAMÁ

Cayman Is. (U.K.)
JAMAICA
Kingston

HAITI
Port-au-Prince
DOMINICAN REP.
Santo Domingo
PUERTO RICO (U.S.A.)
San Juan

Turks & Caicos Is. (U.K.)

Caribbean Sea

Maracaibo
Barranquilla
VENEZUELA
Medellín
COLOMBIA

South America

Projection: Bonne
West from Greenwich

■ MÉXICO Capital Cities

COPYRIGHT PHILIPS

1:35 000 000

| 100 | 0 | 200 | 400 | 600 | 800 | 1000 | 1200 | 1400 km |

| 100 | 0 | 200 | 400 | 600 | 800 | 1000 miles |

Tropic of Cancer

NORTH

Havana
BAHAMAS
CUBA
Turks & Caicos Is.
(U.K.)

ATLANTIC

HAITI
DOMINICAN
REP.
San Juan
Virgin Is. (U.S.A. - U.K.)
Anguilla (U.K.)
St. Martin (Fr. - Neth.)
MEXICO
JAMAICA
Kingston
Port-au-
Prince
Santo
Domingo
PUERTO
RICO
(U.S.A.)
ST. KITTS
& NEVIS
ANTIGUA &
BARBUDA
Basse-Terre
GUADELOUPE
(Fr.)
DOMINICA
Roseau
MARTINIQUE
(Fr.)

OCEAN

BELIZE
GUATEMALA
HONDURAS
Tegucigalpa
Caribbean Sea
Fort-de-France
Castries
ST. LUCIA

Guatemala
San Salvador
EL SALVADOR
NICARAGUA
Managua
ST. VINCENT
Kingstown
BARBADOS
Bridgetown

COSTA
RICA
San José
Panamá
GRENADA
St. George's
Port of
Spain
TRINIDAD &
TOBAGO

I. del Coco
(Costa Rica)
PANAMA
Barranquilla
Maracaibo
Cartagena
Aruba
(Neth.) NETH.
Oranjestad
Willemstad
ANTILLES
Barquisimeto
Caracas
Valencia

Medellín
Bucaramanga
Cúcuta
San Cristóbal
Orinoco
Ciudad Guayana
Georgetown
Paramaribo

I. de Malpelo
(Colombia)
Cali
BOGOTÁ
VENEZUELA
GUYANA
Cayenne
C. Orange

COLOMBIA
Quito
SURINAME
FRENCH
GUIANA

Galapagos Is.
(Ecuador)
ECUADOR
RORAIMA
AMAPÁ

Guayaquil
Putumayo
Japurá
Equator
Marajó
I.
Belém

G. of Guayaquil
Napo
Iquitos
Amazon
Santarém
São Luís
Fortaleza

Marañón
AMAZONAS
Madeira
Amazon
PARÁ
MARANHÃO
Teresina
CEARÁ

Chiclayo
Juruá
Purus
Tapajós
Xingu
Parnaíba
RIO G.
DO NORTE
Natal

Trujillo
ACRE
Pôrto Velho
Campina Grande
PARAÍBA

Chimbote
Madre de Dios
PERU
RONDÔNIA
PIAUÍ
Recife

PERNAMBUCO
BRAZIL
ALAGOAS
Maceió
SERGIPE

Callao
LIMA
Cuzco
TOCANTINS
São Francisco
BAHIA
Aracaju

Titicaca
Arequipa
La Paz
MATO GROSSO
Cuiabá
GOIÁS
DIS. FED.
Brasília
Salvador

BOLIVIA
Cochabamba
Santa Cruz
Goiânia
MINAS GERAIS

Sucre
Belo
Horizonte
ESPÍRITO
SANTO

Iquique
MATO GROSSO
DO SUL
Ribeirão
Prêto
Vitória

Antofagasta
Paraná
PARAGUAY
SÃO PAULO
Juiz
de Fora
Campos

Salta
Pilcomayo
Asunción
Campinas
SÃO
PAULO
RIO DE
JANEIRO

San Miguel
de Tucumán
PARANÁ
Santos
Niterói

San Félix
(Chile)
San Ambrosio
(Chile)
Resistencia
Corrientes
Curitiba

Iguazú
SANTA CATARINA

ARGENTINA
Uruguay
RIO GRANDE
DO SUL
Pôrto Alegre

PACIFIC
Córdoba
San Juan
Santa Fe
Paraná
Pelotas

Viña del Mar
Valparaíso
SANTIAGO
Mendoza
Rosario
URUGUAY

Arch. de Juan Fernández
(Chile)
Robinson
Crusoe
BUENOS AIRES
Montevideo

Talca
La Plata

Concepción
Bahía
Blanca
Mar del Plata

OCEAN
Valdivia
Colorado
SOUTH

Negro
Viedma

Puerto Montt
CHILE

ATLANTIC

Comodoro Rivadavia
Gulf of San Jorge

Gulf of Penas
OCEAN

Magellan's Str.
FALKLAND IS.
(U.K.)
West Falkland
Stanley
East Falkland

Punta Arenas
Tierra del Fuego
South Georgia
(U.K.)

C. Horn

Projection: Lambert's Azimuthal Equal Area

COPYRIGHT PHILIP'S

West from Greenwich

LIMA Capital Cities

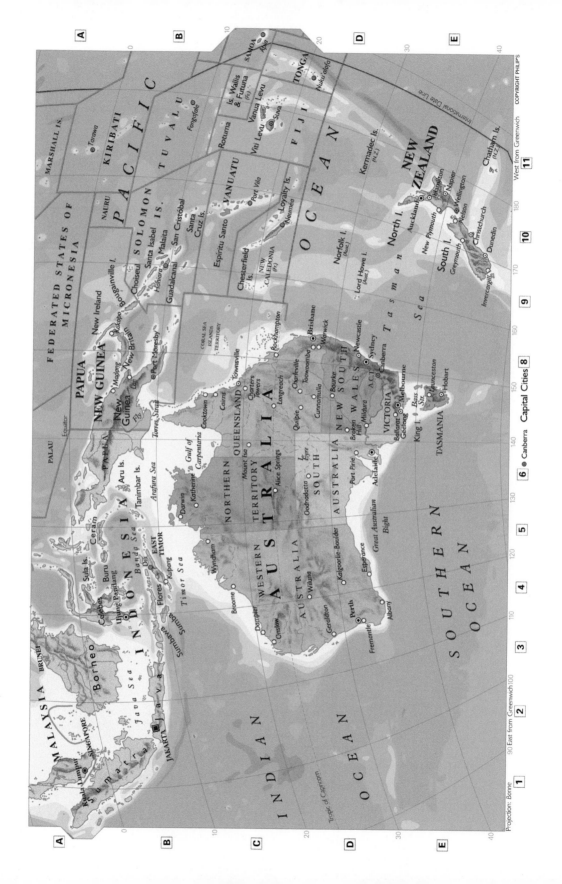

CHAPTER 1

The Comparative Approach: An Introduction

Germany's Angela Merkel and Russia's Vladimir Putin converse at the World Cup in Brazil, July 2014.

Pop quiz. Fill in the blank in the following sentence:

In _____, Columbus sailed the ocean blue.

A large proportion of American students who have completed elementary school will be able to answer correctly: *fourteen hundred ninety-two*.

This recollection from childhood illustrates the ways we first begin to learn about societies and their histories. We learn important events and the dates, names, and places associated with them. We learn simple facts: that Columbus set sail in 1492 and "discovered" the New World. For many of our formative years, this is what we think learning means in our courses on social studies, history, world affairs, or current events.

Scholarship is not defined, however, by knowledge of facts alone, and the learning we do as adults must be different: it must be based on more than just description and recall. The task now, at the collegiate level, is to develop analytical skills. In this book, we examine the similarities and differences in politics within and between countries around the world, using comparisons and contrasts as our central tools. We cover more than just facts about the politics of China, or India, or France. We *analyze* politics *comparatively*.

• • •

Asking Why: Research Questions in Comparative Politics

To illustrate the type of learning this book promotes, we turn to another mnemonic device from primary school:

List the "Five W's" used to ask questions.

You may easily recall the answer (or be able to reconstruct it):

Who, What, Where, When, and *Why. (And to this list we often add "How.")*

Now ask yourself about the relative merits of these "Five W's." Which of these questions are the most profound and lead us to learn the most? Are we likely to gain a deep understanding of the social and political world from questions of the general form "Who did this?" or "Where did this happen?" or "When did this happen?" For the most part, these relatively simple questions lead us to answers based on simple facts, such as prominent historical figures (*Who*), or places (*Where*), or dates (*When*). Consider how most of the "Five W's" are answered in the sentence *In fourteen hundred ninety-two, Columbus sailed the ocean blue*. Who is the subject? Columbus. Where did this event occur? The ocean blue. When did it happen? 1492. What did the subject do (or how did the event happen)? He sailed. Within one easily remembered rhyme, we have answers to a host of basic questions. And, of course, the same is true for more contemporary politics. For instance, saying "In 2017, Emmanuel Macron was elected president of France" also provides answers to *who*, *where*, *what*, and *when* questions.

Even if we don't know certain facts, we can often find them easily in modern life, and we do not need rhymes, other mnemonics, or even reference books. Online search engines (e.g., Google) provide virtually free access to basic facts (though they can also provide access to inaccurate information). Smartphones, laptops, and other devices make basic information accessible almost anywhere. Try typing some basic questions using the "Five W's" into a search engine. Who is the president of Brazil? Where (or what) is the capital of Estonia? When did Tanzania become a free and independent nation? For these questions, the correct and complete answer is available almost instantly. Some knowledge of basic facts is obviously important, but this is not the type of question that interests us in this text. We will not focus simply on *descriptions* of *who* did *what* and *when*, nor on *where* things happened.

Now try searching for "*Why* did Columbus sail the ocean blue?" or "*Why* did Tanzania gain independence from its colonizer?" or "*Why* was Emmanuel Macron elected president of France?" Your search will probably lead to an essay full of reasoning and argumentation as well as facts. Of course, the essay may or may not be reliable, and more comprehensive searching—using scholarly articles and book chapters—could provide you with other essays that offer contrary perspectives. These *why* questions lend themselves to richer discussions and debates than *who/what/when/where* questions. We cannot answer many *why* questions in one or two sentences. Answering *why* correctly requires more research, more reasoning, and more debate than the preliminary factual questions about who did what, where, and when.

We can debate the correct answer to *why* questions. You may think you have a simple answer to why Columbus set sail: he was an explorer by nature, intellectually curious, and seeking adventure. But a classmate may offer an equally compelling answer: the exploration westward across the Atlantic was promoted and financed by the Spanish crown (King Ferdinand and Queen Isabella), who were forced by geopolitical rivalries and strategic concerns to extend and expand their territories. Who is correct? In your answer, you focus on Columbus himself, whereas your classmate makes reference to impersonal factors (such as geopolitical strategy) that push individuals toward certain actions. Both of you include facts in defending your answers, such as the relevant actors (who), the period in which this took place (when), and the country from which Columbus set sail (where). But the debate is not easily resolved, even with these basic facts. We can respectfully disagree on the primary cause of why something happened. We construct **arguments** by supplying evidence in a logical form in support of positions or claims, and the relative merit of our arguments depends on who has the better supporting evidence.

argument The placement of evidence in logical form in support of a position or claim.

Generally, we do not debate at great length about *when* an explorer set sail, *who* he was, or *where* he left from and where he went.[1] We either know these facts or don't. Anyone who has watched *Jeopardy!* or played trivia games will notice that such games almost never ask *why* something happened. The answers would surely be too long and almost certainly too debatable. Basic factual knowledge may earn you points on a game board, but it alone cannot be the route to a deeper understanding of the social and political world.

Questions that begin with that little word—*why*—are often not answered with a simple fact; rather, the answers begin with another deceptively powerful word: *because.* Note that the root of the word *because* is *cause. Why* questions give rise to answers that talk about the causes of events, and they turn basic facts (who, what, where, when, and how) into evidence supporting a claim about cause and effect.[2] This is the core pursuit of **comparative politics**: We seek to develop strong claims about cause and effect, testing various *hypotheses* (i.e., possible answers to our questions) using factual evidence and developing larger theories about why the world operates the way it does. Through most of this book, we will provide some basic information necessary to speak the language of comparative scholars, but our emphasis is on asking and trying to answer *why* questions.

We do not ignore factual information when we ask questions. Indeed, some knowledge of a particular case usually makes us interested in a topic and motivates the questions we want to ask. We find some set of facts that do not fit with our intuition, and we pursue it further. We are intrigued by facts that present us with puzzles. The number of such puzzles is virtually infinite, but certain major questions take center stage in comparative politics. Many are easy to ask but challenging to answer. As we note later, some may be phrased as *how* questions, but the logic behind them is the same: We seek to understand causes and effects to comprehend the world around us.

Few political phenomena are *monocausal*, or caused by just one thing. Often many factors combine to produce an outcome. Explaining something does not amount to simply naming one or another of these factors. Rather, we try to explain by identifying not just the *necessary* conditions to produce an effect but those that are *sufficient* to produce it. For example, the fact that a given community is divided into different groups might be a *necessary* factor of civil war. But because most such divided countries are not engaged in civil war most of the time, the condition of being divided is clearly not *sufficient* to produce this effect by itself, and thus probably cannot be said to be the main cause of war.[3]

Major Questions in Comparative Politics

Comparative politics focuses on certain key questions that researchers have debated for years. Some important questions that we examine in this book are listed in Table 1.1. All of these are about causes and effects and we can attempt to answer them, at least partly, by comparing and contrasting the politics of different countries. Some such questions, like the last two in the table, may also imply research on relations between countries as well as politics within countries.

The questions in the table are very general, and we would likely begin research by asking a more specific version of such questions about one or two countries. Rather than "Why do countries go to war?" we might ask, "Why did France opt

comparative politics The subfield of political science that aims to analyze multiple cases using the comparative method.

TABLE 1.1 **Prominent Questions in Comparative Politics**

Why are some countries democratic and others not?
Why are some countries rich and others not?
Why do countries have different institutions and forms of government?
Why do countries have different policies in a variety of areas?
Why do some social revolutions succeed and endure while others fail?
Why do some countries develop strong senses of statehood and nationhood and others not?
Why do countries go to war or establish peace?
Why are some societies subjected to terrorism and others not?

not to support the Iraq War in 2003?" This question is more specific but also open-ended enough to have many possible answers. In scientific terms, this question can have several competing hypotheses we can test out using evidence, as we discuss later in this chapter and in the next. Possible answers may be based on France's strategic interests and calculations, its position in global affairs, French attitudes or culture with respect to war, and/or other possibilities.

Contrast this question with a more leading one, such as "How did French defeat in World War II lead to France's decision not to support the Iraq War?" In this version, the questioner presumes he or she knows the answer to why France decided not to support the war. The researcher is entering the research expecting to confirm one particular answer.

Given our own human biases, this researcher may well choose evidence selectively, neglecting that which does not fit that researcher's assumptions and preconceptions. It is highly unlikely that someone asking this leading question will answer with "France's defeat in World War II had no effect." Moreover, the leading question may imply that the analyst should ignore or fail to consider potential alternative explanations. This type of question can therefore lead to a biased argument.

Forming questions with *why* is a good rule of thumb, but good questions may also begin with other words, such as *how*. The questions in Table 1.2 also lead to debates about cause and effect. The first question asks about "consequences," which is just another way of asking about the effects of certain causes (in this case, the causes would be institutions). The question is also **open-ended**; that is, no hunch or expected answer is built into it, so the researcher can remain open to what the evidence reveals. The second question is just a bit more specific, identifying a certain consequence and a certain institution, but it is also open-ended. As we get more specific, we must take care not to commit the error of building the answer into the question or assume that what we are researching is the only answer. In this case, we would not want to assume that a presidential versus a parliamentary system of government is the main factor that shapes education policy.[4] The next question asks "under what conditions" democracies form, which is just another way of asking about the causes of democracy, if we compare and contrast where and

open-ended question A question that, in principle, is open to numerous possible answers.

Students in Paris, France, protest the Iraq War in 2003. Why did France opt not to support the Iraq War?

when and how it happens. So too does the final question in Table 1.2 ask about cause and effect, as shown by the verb *affect*. These are all valid research questions, even if they don't begin with *why*.

Some questions that begin with *why* may be poor questions, or at least they may be ill-suited to cause-and-effect research. Contrast the following two questions in which the *how* question is a more open-ended and better question than the *why*:

- Why did the United States foolishly invade Iraq in 2003 for no good reason?
- How did the decision to initiate military action against Iraq come about?

It is perfectly legitimate to ask "why the United States invaded Iraq" as an open-ended social science question, but the tone of the *why* question here suggests

TABLE 1.2 Additional Research Questions About Cause and Effect

What are the consequences of different kinds of institutions for policy?
What are the consequences of presidential versus parliamentary systems of government for education policy?
Under what conditions will democracies emerge and consolidate?
How do major social revolutions affect subsequent political developments in their respective countries?

that it is focused more on the issue of right and wrong than on cause and effect. That leads to a different kind of question, one focused on the ethical evaluation of policy decisions (discussed further in the next section).

In any case, while there are many ways to ask good questions in comparative politics, the key to most of them is keeping our minds open to the possibility that any of several hypotheses may have the power to explain what we want to explain.

Empirical Arguments Versus Normative Arguments

The issue of right and wrong relates to the issue of *causal* or *empirical* arguments versus *normative* arguments. In this text, we mainly address **empirical** arguments: arguments that link cause and effect, uncovering answers to why the political world operates as it does. **Normative** arguments, by contrast, emphasize the way things should be. The following pair of questions highlights the distinction:

- Why are some countries democratic and others authoritarian? (causal/empirical)
- Why is democracy preferable to authoritarianism? (normative)

> **empirical** Drawn from observations of the world.
>
> **normative** Concerned with specifying which sort of practice or institution is morally or ethically justified.

Comparativists answer questions like the first more often than the second, though we care about the answers to both types of questions. We are not primarily concerned in this book with resolving normative arguments about what is right and wrong. This is not because comparativists are indifferent to moral concerns. To the contrary, most social scientists hold strong convictions, indeed probably *stronger* normative views about politics than the average citizen, given their choice of career. Comparativists would overwhelmingly express a preference for democracy over authoritarianism if asked, though some might point to some limitations of democracy or argue that authoritarian rule has sometimes coincided with economic growth. Yet, as comparativists, we do not usually spend our intellectual energy coming up with new arguments for why democracy is morally superior to authoritarianism. Rather, we spend this energy trying to solve the puzzle of why democracy and authoritarianism arise in the first place.

So the point of analyzing politics comparatively is not to come up with good arguments in favor of democracy, or greater wealth, or peace. Rather, our job is to find what causes these things, and we can assume that a commitment to uncovering the causes comes from some interest in the outcome. Comparativists are like doctors diagnosing social problems: instead of explaining why it is better to be healthy, we focus on understanding how we can be healthy as a political society (which, in the terms discussed in this chapter, often involves explaining why preferred political outcomes happen when they do). Comparative political scientists often have an ethical or moral passion that drives research, as we may wish to make government and society more effective, efficient, equitable, just, responsive, and accountable. Yet our principal role in that process is to describe what is and explain why rather than proclaim what ought to be.

Solving Intellectual Puzzles: A Contemporary Analogy

Social science is a process of problem solving. By way of analogy, we can glimpse the sort of intellectual puzzles we solve through the mirror of pop culture. Among the most successful TV shows in the world today (apart from reality shows) are those in which researchers, academics, and scientists are presented with a puzzle that they must solve, usually within a short period. Medical dramas, legal dramas, and crime dramas all fit this mold. The researchers may be doctors trying to diagnose a potentially fatal disease, detectives trying to solve a murder using forensic evidence, or attorneys trying to prosecute a case against a presumed perpetrator. Examples are legion: *NCIS*, *The Mentalist*, *Sherlock* (or the Sherlock Holmes adaptation *Elementary*), and the long-running *CSI: Crime Scene Investigation*, among others.

What these shows have in common is the basic approach to puzzle solving used by the experts. The protagonist will typically be presented with a puzzle early in the episode and will then begin gathering evidence and formulating hypotheses. Usually, some of these hypotheses will be inconsistent with the evidence, or new evidence will emerge that contradicts a hypothesis. In such shows, this development is deliberate, of course, to build suspense and mislead the viewer. We may find, for example, that the person we were supposed to think was the killer had an alibi and was somewhere else on the night of the murder. By the latter part of the show, the protagonist usually comes across some piece of evidence that pulls the case together and gives it a logical interpretation. The episode typically concludes when a hypothesis is confirmed, sometimes signified by a criminal's confession or maybe by a medical treatment that succeeds.

Social scientists operate in a similar fashion to these puzzle-solving professionals, but comparativists face some additional constraints. (If we really want to solve our puzzles, we have to be even more clever than the people on TV.) The most obvious constraint is the lack of laboratories in comparative politics.[5] Whereas physicians, forensic scientist, and prosecutors often have recourse to physical evidence such as blood samples or DNA or cell phone records, scholars of comparative politics often rely on evidence of a more qualitative and historical nature. The evidence used by social scientists is often subject to interpretation. For example, one political scientist may deem Mexico a democratic success story since 2000 because an opposition party won a presidential election, and multiple parties now compete successfully for power. Another may argue that Mexico is not a democratic success story because the country still suffers from high levels of social and economic inequality and from unequal political participation.[6]

Many academics and other professionals rely on evidence and logic and reason to make persuasive arguments, even in the absence of absolute proof. Returning to our pop culture analogy, the detective Sherlock Holmes often rules out many options by process of elimination, gathers evidence that is consistent with a certain interpretation of the facts, and builds a hypothesis. Sometimes, Sherlock will have a particular hypothesis that is shown to be wrong by some new bit of evidence. In those instances, he must generate a new hypothesis to solve the case. Typically, at the end of a detective story, proof comes with a confession that reveals the full story. In courtroom dramas, to use another example, there may not be "proof" that someone committed a crime, but the jury may be convinced "beyond a reasonable doubt" that the accused is guilty. Again, in some instances, there may eventually be a confession by the perpetrator that does lead to "proof," once the hypothesis is backed by substantial evidence and the perpetrator is informed of the strength of the prosecution's case. Medical dramas are similar in that the doctors must diagnose complicated cases using the evidence available to them. The solution usually takes the form of a treatment that cures or saves the patient. In all of these cases, the common theme is the need to solve a puzzle using a combination of evidence, logical reasoning, and educated guesses.

Unfortunately for social scientists, the world never confesses its secrets like some TV criminal, and we cannot typically administer some pharmaceutical in a controlled fashion to cure a body politic. The best social scientists can do is make the strongest and most persuasive case possible by using and interpreting the available evidence. Many social scientists who use statistical methods—including sociologists, political scientists, and most economists—even formalize standards for what is a persuasive finding. Some use 95 or 99 percent "confidence" in their ability to reject a claim of "no effect" as a crucial benchmark in examining hypotheses.[7] Much of comparative politics, though, deals with smaller numbers of cases and is less amenable to statistical analysis. However, even in these instances we seek evidence, examine hypotheses, make arguments, attempt to responsibly gauge the confidence we can have in those arguments, and contribute to theoretical debates.

We address theories and hypotheses in greater detail in chapter 2. First, however, we turn to the concepts, variables, and causal relationships.

Concepts

Social science works with **concepts**, abstract ideas that we formulate to ask and answer our questions. Examples of concepts are numerous, and major concepts of comparative politics include freedom, democracy (as well as liberal democracy, electoral democracy, delegative democracy, and many other subtypes), justice, nationalism, constitutionalism, federalism, identity, gender relations, special interests, and social movements, among many others. Working with concepts helps us think about the social world, which is too complex to analyze without them. We must be very careful in defining them, because bad concepts make for bad analysis.

concept An idea comparativists use to think about the processes we study.

Logically, concepts are categories. In some areas, such as physical and natural science, certain categories are relatively clear.[8] The elements of the periodic table are an example. Concepts like "helium" and "oxygen" describe things in the real world that have certain numbers of electrons and protons. Yet there are few such clear-cut categories in social and political life. Concepts like "democracy" and "revolution" do not define phenomena the same way that "hydrogen" refers to an atom composed of a single proton and a single electron. Social and political concepts like democracy and revolution shade into each other by degree. Thus, conceptual definitions typically do not capture exact boundaries between social and political phenomena in the real world, but we use them so that we can get a handle on that world. Reasonable concepts and categories help us make sense of all the events that take place.

Features of Good Concepts

What makes a concept worthwhile? Good concepts have several features, including clarity, coherence, consistency, and usefulness. The concept of "democratization" when used correctly is an example of a concept that is worthwhile on all these counts.

First, concepts must be clear and coherent.[9] Maybe you begin a research project because you are troubled by differences in levels of democratization across different countries. At the beginning, you have a common-sense understanding of democratization. To do good comparative work, however, you must make the meaning of the term explicit and clear. What do you mean by democratization? What is it you are studying? You cannot say "democratization consists of all the positive things that happen when a society changes." This is neither clear nor coherent. A clearer and more coherent statement would be "democratization is the process by which civil liberties and political rights are extended to all adult citizens in a nation." We begin with common-sense concerns about specific problems, but we need to define our key concepts precisely.

Second, concepts must be logically consistent, both internally and from one to another. For example, one cannot conceptualize democratization in terms of "expansion of liberty and equality" without addressing the possibility that increasing liberty may lead to some degree of inequality. The issue here is whether our concept of democratization is *internally* consistent. Likewise, one cannot conceptualize democracy as being about a "set of institutional arrangements," such as elections, while viewing democratization as being about a "sort of political culture or set of values and norms." This is an issue of logical consistency *between* the concepts of democracy and democratization, which we presume are related, but which seem to point in different directions here.

Third, concepts should be useful. They must be specific enough that they allow you to draw distinctions in analyzing examples. The concept of democratization can be useful because we can meaningfully distinguish between countries that have democratized and those that have not. Our use of concepts is pragmatic because we identify concepts based on how they help us answer research questions.[10] For comparative analysis, concepts must allow us to identify *variations* between times and/or places, which the concept of democratization does: it allows us to differentiate and examine the variations between places that have undergone democratization and those that have not. To be useful, concepts must also allow us to measure variables, which we examine further later.

Conceptualization

Using concepts may be creative because social scientists need to develop their own in many cases. The process of making up and defining concepts is called **conceptualization**. It is often necessary to come up with new ideas and definitions, though we must be self-conscious and thoughtful in how we conceptualize. In comparative politics, a good practice is to look at how scholars have already conceptualized major ideas in books (including textbooks) and articles. We should not coin a new phrase just for the sake of it, and we do not want to end up with a thousand different definitions of a concept like "democracy" when there are already several good and accepted definitions available. Too much creation of concepts could generate confusion and make discussion more difficult. Nonetheless, no concept is perfect, and you may need to conceptualize in novel ways on your own, depending on your specific projects.[11] Doing so can be part of an intellectual contribution as long as your concepts are clear, consistent, and useful.[12]

Some concepts are very general, while others are very specific. To take "nationalism" and "national identity" as an example, we might see the concept of collective identity (an individual's sense of belonging to a group) as being quite general.[13]

conceptualization The deliberate process through which we create and select social-scientific concepts.

The Concept of Freedom

In societies such as the United States, freedom is seen as a core value. Virtually everyone is a supporter and defender of freedom, and popular images present the American nation as the "land of the free." Yet what it means to be free is not so clear, and the term has multiple, distinct, and perhaps even contradictory meanings.[14] Some view freedom in "negative" terms: people are free to the extent that nobody impinges on their ability to act in accordance with their will. Others view freedom in "positive" terms: One is free to the extent that one can engage in particular sorts of acts or ways of life. Others may view freedom in mystical terms, suggesting that one is free to the extent that one experiences transcendence through service to others through participation in collective action, or through spiritual contemplation. There are also Marxist-inspired interpretations of freedom holding that one is free to the extent that one is not *alienated* from others, from one's work, and from a sense of purpose or meaning. (And, last but not least, Janis Joplin sang that "Freedom's just another word for nothing left to lose.")

All of these understandings take freedom to be a quality of an individual. Yet many also speak of the collective freedoms of groups. For instance, many societies, in seeking independence from colonial powers, produce *authoritarian* regimes that do not promote individual freedoms. Often, the members of these societies nevertheless celebrate them as distinctively *free*. Note that all of these meanings of the term (and we could list many more) resonate with millions of people in the world today.[16]

Libyan women celebrate liberation from Qaddafi's rule. Tripoli, September 2011.

Greater specificity comes with adding more attributes to the concept, maybe by specifying that we are interested in those collective identities that are political or that have major implications for politics. More specific still, one can divide *political* identities into more specific subtypes, for example, political identities that say that everybody in your country is like you and that they are all equal. Some questions require more general concepts and others more specific concepts. This issue is sometimes referred to as **"Sartori's ladder of abstraction."**[15] The ladder ranges from general concepts at the top to very specific concepts at the bottom, and the rung one stands on depends on the specific questions being asked and the cases being examined.

Sartori's ladder of abstraction The idea that we can organize concepts on the basis of their specificity or generality.

Operationalizing: From Concepts to Measures

Once we have a clear notion of a concept, we need to be able to measure it; that is, we need to **operationalize** our concept. To operationalize a concept is to make it workable, mainly by making it measurable (which often means either being able to say whether the phenomenon in question is present or how much of it there is in a given case). When a concept is operational—or we have an operational definition—we can begin to explain what we are studying. We can start to explain cause and effect only when we have clarified what we are talking about and can measure it.

operationalization The process through which we make a concept measurable.

TABLE 1.3 Possible Operational Definitions of Democratization

---

A case of democratization occurs when …

- a country holds a free and fair multiparty election
- two turnovers of government at the ballot box have occurred, in which the ruling party loses an election and peacefully steps down from power
- free and fair elections are held, and a constitutional law is in place guaranteeing the rights of freedom of speech, press, assembly, and religion to all citizens
- there is no verifiable suppression of political participation and expression
- more than two-thirds of citizens in a survey express values that reject authoritarian rule

---

There may be many ways to operationalize a certain concept, as shown by the example of democratization in Table 1.3. All of these may be valid ways to operationalize democratization so long as the operational definition matches up with the concept. If we conceptualize democratization in terms of elections, we should measure it in terms of elections (not, for example, by values people hold). As we begin to measure our concepts, we move more toward the "real," or empirical, world we observe.

Empirical Evidence

Questions demand answers. Social scientists do not ask questions just to ask them but to attempt to answer them. So how do social scientists answer their questions? In short, they couple empirical evidence with theory. In comparative politics, *empirical* means those observations we can make from looking at the real world rather than using abstract theories or speculation. We look at how theory and evidence interact in chapter 2. For the moment, we only highlight the forms of evidence most often used in comparative politics, since this is necessary for understanding the method. A key is the distinction between facts and evidence.

Facts and Evidence

Facts—understood here as simple statements about what is or is not the case—are abundant, but evidence is more precious. As noted previously, online sources such as Wikipedia and Google provide almost costless access to a massive set of facts (though a lot of information found online is inaccurate). **Evidence** consists of facts used in support of a proposition or hypothesis. Notice something built into these definitions: evidence is indeed based on facts. So a point of view or an opinion, whether your own or someone else's, is not evidence. The fact that someone else believes something does not mean there is evidence for it, even if that opinion has been published by a prominent scholar or public figure. Evidence should be available for the reader to gather as well and not be simply based on hearsay, though research sometimes requires anonymity of sources. Wherever possible, research should be replicable by someone else.

To use a simple example of varying qualities of evidence, say we ask two students to make a simple claim about whether Saudi Arabia is a democracy and to back

evidence A set of facts or observations used to support a proposition or examine a hypothesis.

this claim with evidence. In the two examples in Table 1.4, the difference between the two students is not the correctness of the claim, which is the same. Nor is it the facts, which are true on both sides. Rather, the difference is in how well evidence is used to back the claim. Successful comparativists are mostly known not for the correctness of their assertions but for the ways they empirically support their claims.

Strong evidence has several characteristics. Most obviously, it must be relevant to the issue at hand. If you are arguing about Saudi Arabia's democracy, the fact that the country is Muslim, or an oil exporter, is not an indicator of democracy. We may debate whether these factors help *cause* democracy or a lack of democracy, but they are not measures of democracy itself the way free and fair elections and civil rights are.

The evidence often should be at the same **level of analysis** as the claim you are making—that is, at the individual, organizational, or societal level, for example. We can ask good research questions at many levels of analysis: individuals, groups within a country, whole countries and societies, regions of the world, and the world as a whole. But we need to be careful that our evidence reflects our level of analysis, or at least that we deal with levels of analysis in a way that makes logical sense. Countries are made up of individuals, but individuals are not countries, and there are important differences between individuals, groups, and societies at large. We need to carefully ask ourselves which units (individuals, federal regions, countries, parties) our questions are about and make sure that our evidence comes from appropriate units.

For example, it is appropriate to try to study how individual and regional differences in preferences about some policy question may influence policy adoption at the national level, but it would be a mistake to think that policy adoption simply reflects individual majority opinion in all cases. The same is true the other way around: if you are talking about an individual or a small group, you cannot assume you know everything about them just because of what country they come from; this is essentially stereotyping (and in social science is often called the "ecological fallacy," mistakenly attributing a contextual characteristic to all of the individuals who inhabit that context). Analysts risk committing logical mistakes if they do not pay attention to levels of analysis.

level of analysis The level (e.g., individual, organizational, societal) at which observations are made or at which causal processes operate.

TABLE 1.4 Examples of Strong and Weak Use of Evidence

Student 1	Student 2
Claim: *Saudi Arabia is not democratic.*	Claim: *Saudi Arabia is not democratic.*
Evidence: Saudi Arabia has not held free and fair elections for its national government. Women do not have the same political and social rights as men.	Evidence: Saudi Arabia is an Islamic country whose economy is based on exporting oil. It is a long-time ally of the United States and is led by King Salman and a large royal family.
Claim: strong *Facts: correct* Evidence: ***strong***	*Claim: strong* *Facts: correct* Evidence: ***weak***

Cases and Case Studies

case In comparative analysis, a unit or example of a phenomenon to be studied.

Cases are the basic units of analysis in comparative politics. In many instances, our cases are countries, usually for a certain period. We may seek, for example, to explain North Korea's lack of democracy versus the (imperfect) progress of democracy in South Korea; the cases here are the two countries we are comparing, and perhaps our time frame will be the period after the Korean War of the 1950s.

A case is not always a country, however. To start with, we could consider other geographical units: we may be interested in the social history of the state of California or Texas, or in comparing the two. Or we may be interested in the state of Gujarat in India or in the city of Caracas, Venezuela. We may be interested in contrasting the European Union with the African Union or the "majority Catholic nations of southern Europe" with the "majority Protestant nations of northern Europe." In this instance, the case for study would still be a geographic area but not a country.

Cases can also take other forms. They may be political groups, organizations, specific institutions, historical processes, eras, or even discrete events. The civil rights movement in the United States may be a case of a social movement. To do a comparison, one might examine the "civil rights movement of the 1960s" in juxtaposition to the "women's suffrage movement of the early 1900s." Or one might examine the "presidency of John F. Kennedy" and the "presidency of Barack Obama" as two cases for comparison. The French Revolution may be a case of a social and political revolution, and so too may the "Revolutions of 1848" (which took place across many countries in Europe) be treated as a "single case" of social and political revolution. Finally, we may also look at comparisons over time within a single country. An example might be comparing "the politics of health care in 1960s America" with "the politics of health care in twenty-first-century America." The key is delineating one's case as a unit that can be usefully understood as a cluster of events or attributes.

Comparative politics studies vary considerably in terms of how many cases they handle. Some studies focus on a single case.[17] Most scholars feel that single cases can be illuminating but that they are not sufficient for testing all hypotheses. At the other end of the spectrum, some studies deal with *large-N* comparisons in which many cases are analyzed through statistical searches for common features (this is discussed further in chapters 2 and 13). In between these approaches, at the heart of traditional comparative politics, we find *small-N* comparisons of two or more cases.

The Comparative Method

Comparative politics—unlike, say, the study of American government or international relations—is defined by its method. It makes arguments about cause and effect through structured and systematic comparing and contrasting of cases.

Variables and Comparison

variable An element or factor that is likely to change, or vary, from case to case.

The causes and the outcomes we are trying to measure are called **variables** because they vary from one case to another. For instance, if we were to argue that the African country of Ghana has a high level of democracy because it was colonized by the British, while the neighboring country of Togo has a low level of democracy because it was colonized by the French, then both the supposed cause and the effect vary from one country to the other. The effect (or **outcome**) is the level of democracy, which is high in one case and low in the other. The cause we would be proposing is the colonizer, which is British in one case and French in the other.

We will typically be seeking to explain a certain outcome or result or consequence. In the cause-and-effect story of X → Y, our research will center on investigating the various possible causes (you might think of them as "X factors") to explain "the Y." Since outcomes depend on the causes, a social science convention is to call the outcome the **dependent variable**, while the cause(s) is (are) called the **independent variable**(s). Many terms are used, but for our purposes, all of the expressions in each column in the following table are nearly synonymous.

Cause	→	effect (or result or consequence)
independent variable	→	dependent variable
explanatory variable	→	outcome
X variable	→	Y variable

If we compare or contrast two or more cases to make a causal argument, we will be looking for similarities and differences (also called **variations**) between the cases. Using just two countries for the moment (to keep it simple), we may look to explain why two countries have different outcomes, or we may look at variations in outcomes between two countries. We may ask why one country is wealthy but a neighboring country is poor. Or, conversely, we may ask why two very different countries had very similar outcomes, such as becoming democracies around the same time.

outcome Typically used as a synonym for "effect," something that is produced or changed in any social or political process.

dependent variable In hypothesis testing, the dependent variable is the effect or outcome that we expect to be acted on (or have its value altered) by the independent variable.

independent variable In hypothesis testing, an independent variable is one that we expect to "act on" or change the value of the variable.

variation Difference between cases in any given study of comparative politics.

The city of Nogales straddles the border between Mexico (left) and the United States, divided by a three-mile fence completed in 2011. Why do these neighboring countries have such striking differences?

To address such questions, we can use two simple tools as points of departure: *most-similar-systems* analyses and *most-different-systems* analyses.[18] These approaches use comparison for the same fundamental purpose: ruling out plausible explanations for certain phenomena as we attempt to build causal theories. That is, quite similar or quite different cases are used as comparative checks to see what arguments cannot account for a certain outcome. Ruling out these other arguments allows the researcher to narrow down the research process by focusing on the possible causes that remain and testing evidence supporting these causes. It is important to note that these designs work best for case comparisons in which we are expecting fairly deterministic, rather than highly probabilistic, relationships between "predictors" and "outcomes." If we anticipate "probabilistic" relationships between some predictor and some outcome (e.g., as members of a population become more educated, they will tend to become more tolerant), ruling out theoretical arguments based on single cases will not help us.

Most-Similar-Systems Design

most-similar-systems (MSS) A research design in which we compare cases that are similar with respect to a number of factors but with distinct outcomes.

The **most-similar-systems (MSS)** design is predicated on the logic that two cases (such as two countries) that are similar in a variety of ways would be expected to have very similar political outcomes. Thus, if two cases have variations in outcomes, we would look for the variations that can explain why the countries are dissimilar.

While Table 1.5 may make the analysis appear formal, people actually do this type of analysis informally all the time. Consider discussions you have with others about things seemingly as simple as why we like certain movies. Virtually all feature films released in cinemas are of similar length, are filmed for large screens, use professional directors and producers, have a plot with a protagonist (often a big star), use carefully

TABLE 1.5 Most-Similar-Systems Design

REGIME TYPES IN AFRICA

Variable	Case 1: Togo	Case 2: Ghana
Similarities		
Climate	Hot	Hot
Income	Low	Low
Ethnic Demography	Heterogeneous	Heterogeneous
Largest Religion	Christian	Christian
Other Religions	Islam, Traditional	Islam, Traditional
Outcome		
Regime Type	Authoritarian	Democratic
Cause		
Hypothesis: Colonizer	France	United Kingdom

chosen music as a soundtrack, and elicit emotion from the audience (or at least are intended to). Yet we all have preferences for some films over others. Amid these significant similarities among all films, we can identify—through comparison—the certain factors that lead each of us to appreciate or dislike a film.

If we can demystify the process of comparison by realizing that we use it subconsciously all the time, it is just a half step to how this might be done in practice when analyzing political questions. Consider the presentation in Table 1.5 of two African countries, neither of which you are assumed to know a great deal about.

We are wondering why one country (Ghana) is a democracy and another (Togo) is not. The table notes several similarities between the two countries, making the variation in outcomes a true puzzle. If we were to hypothesize a cause, we might argue that the colonial legacies of the countries mattered: Togo was colonized by France (and previously Germany) and Ghana by Britain. As we look for the cause of variations in outcomes, we can essentially cross out the many variables on which the countries are similar, as they are unlikely to cause differences. For instance, the hot climate of Togo cannot explain why it is more authoritarian than Ghana, because Ghana is hot as well. Eliminating these similarities as potential causes leaves us looking for other possible causes where the countries vary.

So "colonizer" might fit the bill, as Table 1.5 suggests. Does this mean we have proven that colonizer is the answer? Not at all. We would need to do several

People wait to vote in Accra, Ghana, in 2004. Despite many similarities with its neighbor Togo, Ghana is a democracy, while Togo is not. Why?

things to make this case, as we shall see going forward. First, we would consider alternative hypotheses. Instead of colonizer, we might just as easily have said that the economic performance of each country was the key factor that shaped regime type, or that the nature of the military command was the key cause, or that the ideology of the founding fathers of each country mattered most. Only by examining and weighing these various causes could we gain real insight into why one country is democratic and the other is not. Thus, our second caveat is that we would need to find plausible evidence and have a strong argument linking the cause to the outcome. We would want to explore the ways in which colonization affected politics in these West African countries. We would assess the evidence to determine whether it had an impact, and we would make sure there is a plausible story that allows us to connect the dots between the cause and the effect.

One potential source of initial confusion is that MSS designs place a premium on identifying the differences between cases, not the similarities. You might think of it this way: If two cases are most similar, what is remarkable about comparing them? What is remarkable is where most similar cases differ. Differences in outcomes between similar cases are noteworthy, and differences in possible causes are what will help us explain them. We invert this logic when using the other tool that serves as a basic point of departure in comparative politics: most-different-systems designs.

Most-Different-Systems Design

most-different-systems (MDS)

A research design in which we compare cases that differ with respect to multiple factors but in which the outcome is the same.

The **most-different-systems (MDS)** design uses a logic that mirrors that of the MSS. In this approach, the researcher identifies two cases that are different in nearly all aspects yet are similar on a particular outcome. This puzzle leads the researcher to develop hypotheses to explain the peculiar similarity. See Table 1.6, which presents an example of two major revolutions in world history that happened in very different geographical and historical contexts.

Just as MSS designs place a priority on identifying differences between cases, MDS designs place a premium on identifying the similarities that can give us analytical leverage. Again, the name is revealing: in an MDS design, what variables are noteworthy and telling? Those that are *not different*. If France in 1789 and China in 1949 are so different, what accounts for both having major social revolutions? In the interest of cultivating your habit of building comparisons, we leave it to you to insert your own hypotheses. Might both countries have had populations facing extreme deprivation at these times? Or perhaps in both countries new actors emerged at these moments in history to lead a revolution? We will not answer these questions here; but since several major variables differ between these "most different" cases, we may surmise that similarity in revolution will be attributable to one of the relatively scarce number of other similarities we can find.

As noted previously, MSS and MDS are probably most appropriate for theorizing about causal relationships that are deterministic. In other words, it is not always the true that finding a case in which a hypothesized relationship between some x and some y is *not* observed invalidates the theory that x causes y. For example, this book will later make reference to the classical "modernization theory" of democracy, which asserts that as societies become wealthier, they tend to become more democratic.[19] We may find examples of wealthy countries that are authoritarian and of poor

TABLE 1.6 **Most-Different-Systems Design**

MAJOR SOCIAL REVOLUTIONS

Variables	Case 1: France (1780s)	Case 2: China (1940s)
Differences		
Continent	Europe	Asia
Population (approx.)	< 30 million	> 500 million
Century	Eighteenth	Twentieth
Regime	Monarchy	Nationalist Party
Outcome(s)		
Social Revolution	Yes	Yes
Cause		
[Insert Your Hypothesis Here]	???	???

countries that are democratic. A handful of such examples would hardly invalidate the theory since many other factors also affect the probability that a country will be democratic. Even in such cases, though, MSS and MDS designs can often help us to develop clearer theories that we can later test with other sorts of research design. They exemplify a classic approach to building theories in comparative politics.

Comparative Checking

While the MSS and MDS designs are the foundation for initial comparisons, they do not complete our analysis. Analysts must constantly remain aware that one pair of cases does not "prove" a hypothesis to be true everywhere, any more than one case study can prove a hypothesis. Rather, we must constantly engage in **comparative checking**, or examining the conditions under which certain arguments hold. This checking sometimes involves mixing MSS and MDS designs to test our hypotheses further and to give us a sense of how **generalizable** they are, or how applicable to a wide number of cases.

Return briefly to Table 1.5, the MSS table using Togo and Ghana as examples. That MSS analysis provided us with a glimpse of the possibility that colonizer or colonial legacy may affect regime type. From that table, we might think we have found that being colonized by France leads to authoritarian rule, while the good fortune of being colonized by Britain leads to democracy. However, even just a bit of comparative checking beyond these two cases will reveal that the story is not so simple, as Table 1.7 shows.

Table 1.7 illustrates that a simplistic explanation of African regime types based on colonizer is insufficient. Benin, which neighbors Togo, was colonized by the French and is now democratic, in counterpoint to our simplistic view from the MSS table (Table 1.5). The fact that a single case does not correspond to this theory's prediction does not "prove" that colonizer is irrelevant to regime type,

comparative checking The process of testing the conclusions from a set of comparisons against additional cases or evidence.

generalizability The quality that a given theory, hypothesis, or finding has of being applicable to a wide number of cases.

TABLE 1.7 **Comparative Checking**

Variable	Case 1: Togo	Case 2: Ghana	Case 3: Benin
Similarities			
Climate	Hot	Hot	Hot
Income	Low	Low	Low
Ethnic Demography	Heterogeneous	Heterogeneous	Heterogeneous
Largest Religion	Christian	Christian	Christian
Other Religions	Islam, Traditional	Islam, Traditional	Islam, Traditional
Outcome			
Regime Type	Authoritarian	Democratic	Democratic
Cause			
Colonizer	France	UK	France

any more than our first MSS "proved" that colonizer is relevant to regime type. Rather, it shows that a more sophisticated examination of the causes of democracy is needed. How might we proceed?

In looking for other possible causes, we have many strategies to pursue. We can look to a larger number of cases to see if other hypothesized arguments might still hold. We should also dig in to our original cases once again to see if there are any variations or hypotheses that we may have overlooked. We can also revisit the scholarly literature—a strategy underutilized by many beginning comparativists—digging in to see how scholars explain the outcome that interests us. We may find new hypotheses, or refine the hypothesis we have already worked with. In this case, perhaps we would find from the literature that colonialism has impacts on regimes but that it takes shape over time differently in different cases; maybe colonialism is something that matters but needs to be understood in a more sophisticated fashion and not as simply either "French" or "British." Finally, we could use a strategy that focuses attention on how politics happens over time, called *within-case comparison*.

Within-Case Comparison

within-case comparison The comparative analysis of variation that takes place over time or in distinct parts of a single case.

Within-case comparison means looking more carefully within one's own case(s) to examine the variations there. For instance, to use the Togo/Ghana example, we might find that there are certain pieces or moments within the Togo case where there was some democracy. Maybe people in certain cities or regions of the country gained more rights, while people in other cities or regions were left without.[20] Or maybe Togo democratized (somewhat) at certain moments, such as the early 1990s, only to backslide to an authoritarian regime. Looking at different moments in time or in space may allow us to dig deeper into a case to better understand our evidence.

To use another example, consider why hopefulness about the future may have been relatively high in the United States in the 1990s but is lower today. Many variables are similar across these two periods: the basic governmental structure of the country and certainly the geography of the country are quite stable, for instance. In other words, a country at an earlier period (call it Time 1) is "most similar" to the same country at Time 2. Yet some things do change over time, and those variables are good candidates to explain changing outcomes. The economy may change, for instance, or the composition of the workforce, or international events, the successes and failures of one or another political candidate, or the political mood. Many other examples can also illustrate the virtues of comparing periods within a country. The takeaway point is that comparison does not end with simple charts listing attributes of different countries, but instead is a way to delve systematically into the evidence case studies provide.

Is the Study of Politics a Science? The Limits of the Comparative Method

We speak of *political science* even though in comparative politics, we rarely find a "proof" of the kind found in geometry, for example. Some scholars view the common methods for the study of politics to be inherently scientific in nature. Some even think the study of politics is (and should be) a science that aims to uncover general laws about political and social life. Others think it is a science but one that shows *probable* relationships between variables rather than showing general laws.[21] Others outside the discipline (including some natural and physical scientists) may view the study of politics in a more skeptical fashion, arguing that the term *science* is more aspirational in nature: for them, politics is not yet a science, though it may aim to be. Still others may argue that politics is not a science and should not be. It may be more interpretive and may relate more to the humanities than to other sciences.

To be sure, for many questions, social scientists cannot use one of the major tools that drives knowledge in the natural and physical sciences: the controlled experiment. We cannot subject individual countries to precise conditions to examine the effects the way we can in a chemistry lab, although many social scientists do look for so-called "natural experiments" in which real-world events mimic laboratory conditions in key ways.[22] In general, truly definitive proof is hard to come by in the social sciences. The sorts of comparative designs we have discussed in this chapter comprise one way to make up for our inability to do experiments everywhere. When we observe countries that are quite similar in the MSS design, we are approximating the controlled experiment of the laboratory: we hold many variables constant, and vary one or two key variables to see if we can measure their impact. However, the analogy is imperfect. As we will see in chapter 2, noting that some x correlates with our y of interest, even if this is true in *all* observed cases, is not enough to draw strong conclusions about causality.

Given the complexity of the world and the many factors that affect political life, hypotheses that are confirmed "beyond a reasonable doubt" are generally the best we can aim for. In addition, we can try to gauge how much doubt a reasonable person would have in our conclusions. Physicists have described the "law of gravity," but social scientists do not typically uncover fully analogous "laws" that appear to hold everywhere. We instead rely on theories that give more or less powerful explanations about how the world operates. The strongest theories persist over long periods, even if they do not explain each and every possible case or circumstance. We elaborate on this point in chapter 2.

In this book, we take the approach that comparative politics can aspire to scientific inference, even if it has certain limitations.[23] Some argue that mathematical approaches focusing on many cases are the gold standard in political science because with large numbers of cases, researchers are liberated from the idiosyncrasies and complexities of individual cases. In one version, political science could replace "proper names" with variables.[24] We do not, however, presume that we must always follow the models of *quantitative* research designs (which we will discuss further in chapter 2). There are many ways in which detailed studies of smaller numbers of cases can show us things obscured from view in quantitative studies of many cases. *Qualitative* analyses—such as deep historical probing of individual cases and detailed descriptions of social contexts—can be as scientific as white-coated lab work. Moreover, quantitative and qualitative methods complement each other, a point that seems to be increasingly recognized in political science.

Comparative work may contribute to knowledge in many ways. These include conceptualization, refining the basic ideas and terms we use, and categorizing cases. Other contributions come from theoretical critiques, which can highlight inconsistencies of certain explanations, allowing researchers to develop a better theory. And, of course, many good critiques will also be empirical, pointing out cases that do not fit with favored explanations. Each of these forms of contribution is consistent with the scientific method, even if it does not always involve direct testing of hypotheses. In chapter 2, we explore how these aspects of the comparative approach help us build theories in comparative politics.

Chapter Summary

Asking Why: Research Questions in Comparative Politics

- For scholars of comparative politics, the key questions are about *why* something happens, or about cause and effect, even though we are often also interested in normative questions about right and wrong.
- Research in comparative politics addresses questions on such major issues as economic development, political regimes and institutions, and a range of social outcomes.

Concepts

- Concepts are the ideas we use to categorize the world and enable us to measure and compare observations.
- Good concepts are clear, coherent, consistent, and useful.

- Social scientists often must do their own conceptualization, or develop their own concepts, and must operationalize their concepts to enable measurement.

Empirical Evidence

- Comparative politics relies heavily on facts and evidence to support arguments about cause and effect.
- One of the main empirical approaches is the use of case studies and comparisons between cases.

The Comparative Method

- Variables are features that vary from one case to another and enable comparison between cases.
- Two approaches to comparison involve the

most-similar-systems design and the most-different-systems design, both of which examine variations and similarities between cases to assist in testing hypotheses.

- Good comparative study requires more than just brief examination of similar and different variables; it often involves further examination through steps such as comparative checking and within-case comparison.

Is the Study of Politics a Science? The Limits of the Comparative Method

- While the study of politics aspires to scientific conclusions, it is rarely able to prove its conclusions with absolute certainty.

Thinking It Through

1. Imagine you are going to do a project that tries to explain why democracy has been relatively successful in the United States. What sort of conceptual work would you need to do before you could complete this study?

2. If you were to conceptualize democracy as a political system in which (1) certain individual rights are respected, (2) elections are periodically held, and (3) political transitions are peaceful, what would you have to do to operationalize this concept for the purposes of a comparative study?

3. What are the five most interesting *why* questions about comparative politics that you can think of? What are the main concepts they imply?

4. Take one of the questions you have formulated in response to question 3. Now think of how you could construct a most-different-systems (MDS) design to compare cases and answer your question.

5. Take one of the questions you have formulated in response to question 3. Now think of how you could construct a most-similar-systems (MSS) design to compare cases and answer your question.

CHAPTER 2

Theories, Hypotheses, and Evidence

A medical worker undergoes Ebola response training during the outbreak that began in 2014.

n 2014, a deadly outbreak of the Ebola virus struck several countries in West Africa. Guinea, Liberia, and Sierra Leone were especially hard hit. Medical professionals from around the world came to the region in an attempt to contain the outbreak. Some villagers, however, did not welcome them; and in fact, at least one youth group mobilized to fight off the doctors because they noticed something: soon after the doctors arrived, people in a village began to die. As *The New York Times* reported, some villagers reached a simple conclusion: the doctors bring death, and the way to stop Ebola was to stop the doctors.[1]

This kind of faulty logic almost certainly proved deadly to some. Examples like this show how important it is to have good theories that can help us understand—not misunderstand—how the world works. Such an example also shows how important it is to interpret evidence correctly. In this story, it was the case that the disease was claiming lives despite the doctors' best efforts, not that the doctors were doing the killing. Villagers were confusing *correlation*—observing factors that accompany each other—with *causation*, or an argument that one thing causes another.

In this chapter, we discuss how theories work. We discuss how to form *hypotheses*, or educated guesses about what will happen under certain circumstances, and how to avoid certain pitfalls in testing those hypotheses. All this will prepare you better for examining the issues of comparative politics that make up the rest of the book.

Introduction to Theories, Hypotheses, and Evidence

Social scientists look for convincing answers to important questions about why things happen: why are some countries democratic and others not, or why do revolutions occur, or why do some countries have two main political parties while others have many parties in their legislatures? The first step in comparative politics is asking good research questions about the causes and effects of political events. Chapter 1 gave us an approach—the comparative method—to begin to answer those questions by comparing and contrasting cases, most often different countries or specific events in different countries. We may examine the political party systems of Germany and France, or the communist revolutions in Russia and China, for instance. To do so, we juxtapose the facts of the different cases to make an argument about the similarities and differences between them.

In this chapter, we talk about the tools we need to *answer* questions, with a focus on two elements that help us to formulate possible answers: theories and hypotheses. We discuss what theories and hypotheses are and how they differ from one another. We then discuss how evidence is used to test hypotheses and theories.

Theories

theory A general set of explanatory claims about some specifiable empirical range.

Theories are general explanations of empirical phenomena, or explanations about how the world operates. A theory aims to explain more than just one or two cases or examples, and it is typically backed by a considerable number of supporting facts. An explanation or framework in the social sciences will rarely earn the right to be called a theory if we cannot find considerable support for its arguments in the real world.

This may not be the only way you hear the word *theory* used. There is also a more casual everyday usage to describe a hunch or idea. For instance, imagine a friend who says, "The Chicago Cubs are going to win the World Series this year, that's my theory." From a social scientific point of view, this is a prediction, not a theory. It may be a good or a bad prediction, but it is speculative at best, a hopeful guess. Without some logical argumentation and backing in facts, it is not really a theory based on reason and evidence. If, on the other hand, the friend offers a detailed explanation that shows how the team with the strongest pitching routinely wins the World Series, and proceeds to detail how Chicago's pitching is stronger than that of other teams, then the friend is approaching a general theory about the relationship between two variables: pitching and championships. In this theory, pitching is the cause and winning the championship is the consequence, which is also called the effect or the outcome.

In political science, there are two different types of theory, typically referred to as normative theory and empirical (also known as positive) theory. Normative theory deals with questions of values and moral beliefs. An example might be the question "What is the best kind of political system we could construct?" This is a matter of morals and ethics. Empirical theory, by contrast, deals with empirical questions. An example is "Which factors are most likely to produce a preferred political system?" This is about the factors and variables that cause things to happen. In this book, we are mostly focused on empirical theories: we discuss theory as a *general* explanation of why things happen.

Hypotheses

hypothesis A specific prediction, derived from a theory, that can be tested against empirical evidence.

Hypotheses are *specific* proposed explanations for why an outcome occurs. To answer research questions, we may generate or formulate hypotheses that we think can explain a set of facts upon further research. Hypotheses are not explanations already backed by lots of evidence. Instead, they are possible answers to a question, which we plan to test out by applying them to data, looking at specific observations (or "cases") to see if there is evidence to support the idea. Informally, you can think of them as hunches. If the hypothesis receives that support from the evidence, it may become a thesis in an argument.[2]

Developing hypotheses requires us to make imaginative leaps from unanswered questions to possible explanations. Hypotheses can be generated from existing theories in a **deductive** fashion: starting with general ideas and then testing whether they work on specific examples. For example, say we are asking about why an anti-colonial revolution happened in a certain African country in the 1950s. We may begin our research with a major theory that holds that social revolutions (such as the French Revolution, Russian Revolution, or Iranian Revolution) are caused by the social upheavals produced by modernization. We seek to apply this theory to the African country we are studying. Using the theory as our general model, we might hypothesize that the anti-colonial revolution in the African country was produced by a history of modernization. Another way to think of this sort of approach is to consider it an effort to test an *observable implication* of the starting theory.[3]

> **deductive reasoning** The process of moving from general claims or theories to specific observations or predictions about a phenomenon or set of cases.

Not all hypotheses are deduced from general theories, of course. Some can also come from looking at a case that deviates from a particular theory. We can learn a great deal from so-called **deviant cases,** or "**outliers,**" that do not do as we might expect. For instance, in many international comparisons, the United States is a deviant case. It has both higher income inequality and greater differences in life expectancy between racial groups (to name just two variables) than one might expect based on its level of economic development. By focusing on some characteristics that make the United States different from other cases, we might sometimes understand general relationships better. For example, perhaps it is not a country's overall level of economic development that predicts the life expectancy of its people, but individual life chances. By this thinking, U.S. income inequality may help us to account for the fact that high development does not lead to high life expectancy for all U.S. groups.

> **deviant case (outlier)** A case that does not fit the pattern predicted by a given theory.

We often formulate a hypothesis with some initial knowledge of the topic at hand, but we do not want to presume we already know the answer to the questions we are asking. We do not normally aim to create a hypothesis in an **inductive** way—moving from specific observations to general claims. That is, we don't do the research, find the answer, then go back and propose our hypothesis (although sometimes our analysis does suggest new hypotheses, and inductive approaches to theory generation do exist). Instead, we formulate our hypothesis with an open mind toward what answers we may find. Our hypotheses may be supported or rejected by the research we do, so there is always the possibility that they are wrong. In fact, most hypotheses are wrong, and rarely if ever can we fully confirm or disprove a hypothesis with limited research.[4] The goal is not to pick the correct hypothesis at the outset but rather to learn something from the study we undertake. In fact, many social scientists believe that our knowledge advances more from refuting hypotheses than from defending or supporting them.

> **inductive reasoning** The process of moving from specific observations to general claims.

Hypotheses and theories inform one another. Theories help guide us in formulating hypotheses, and confirming hypotheses may either support or undermine theories. In general, hypotheses are more tentative and speculative than theories. A specific hypothesis is generated for each research question and is put on the line to be tested in each case. While the evidence from testing a specific hypothesis may support or oppose a particular theory, it usually is insufficient to reject or confirm a theory by itself. Generating a theory is a more elaborate, long-term process than generating and testing a single hypothesis.

thesis A statement for which one argues on the basis of evidence.

After testing hypotheses for a specific study, scholars will typically offer a **thesis**, a claim to argue on the basis of evidence from research. One can think of a thesis statement that usually appears near the beginning of a well-written scholarly paper. In comparative politics, a thesis is an argument supported by the research evidence that comes from testing a hypothesis. (It is no coincidence that the word hypothesis—with the prefix "hypo"—roughly means something "less than" or "not yet" a thesis.) While a thesis has evidence supporting it, that does not mean it is a full theory. Before achieving the status and prestige of being called a theory, an idea requires ample evidence to support it, typically based on research by many scholars. For the most part, students of comparative politics test hypotheses, make specific claims in the form of theses, and are expected to use evidence to argue in support of their theses, taking account of existing theories. We are informed by theory and can contribute to debates by theorizing, but we rarely craft or falsify entire theories alone.

How Theories Emerge and Are Used

Theories emerge and are used all the time to explain the world around us. Let us take a prominent theory from beyond comparative politics that has long featured prominently in social and political debate: the theory of evolution. First, we offer a very abridged version of the theory, followed by one specific hypothesis derived from the theory.

> *Theory (abridged):* The origin and development of species are based on a process of natural selection in which organisms with a genetic advantage in a given natural environment thrive and propagate their genes, whereas organisms at a genetic disadvantage will fall out of the gene pool over the long term.
>
> *Hypothesis (example):* The theory of evolution accounts for humans' walking on two legs. Human ancestors first began to walk on two legs in African savannahs where grasses grew tall; those walking on two legs had an advantage over similar four-legged mammals because they could better see and more easily flee predators.

In testing this hypothesis—that humans first walked upright to flee predators—a scholar will examine whether the evidence is consistent with such an explanation. The evidence uncovered may include fossils and archaeological evidence. As part of the work, the scholar may note that other prominent arguments are inconsistent with one or more substantial pieces of evidence, thereby making this hypothesis relatively more capable of explaining the observed facts.

Of course, even if the scholar finds that the evidence is consistent with the hypothesis, a single study will not be the end of the story. Counterarguments will emerge. Indeed, the existence and progress of the social sciences depends precisely on the common efforts of the scholarly community to question existing explanations and to provide alternative ones. In our example, some scholars who accept the evolutionary perspective may argue that humans first walked upright to conserve energy while foraging for food. Scholars who reject the theory may also contribute arguments to the debate, and even non-scientists may do so, as long as their arguments are tested empirically. We can pursue the scientific endeavor by further testing related hypotheses to see how the theory changes as a result.

We narrow in on good explanations by finding increasing evidence that certain hypotheses are consistent with the evidence while others are inconsistent with the evidence. We can rarely, if ever, confirm a hypothesis or prove it fully true; rather, we can find that a hypothesis is increasingly viable as we find more and more evidence to support it. Ideally, much like a courtroom lawyer that has the evidence on his or her side, we will make our case "beyond a reasonable doubt" as we defend our claim.

Theories have facts and evidence supporting them, but these are not proof that a theory is valid and correct in all circumstances. Often, a wrong theory will hold sway for a long period of time until it is supplanted by a stronger theory. For example, the earth was long believed to be situated at the center of the universe, and this appeared consistent with many facts, such as the sun and moon rising and falling beyond the horizon each day. However, this theory eventually came into conflict with observations that suggested that the earth revolved around the sun. Both theories persisted for a time until it became clear that the heliocentric (sun-centered) theory best explained the structure of our solar system. Thus, competing theories may coexist, and there may simultaneously be facts and evidence that support a theory and other facts and evidence that contradict the theory. Theories may ultimately fail and be rejected, but ideally theories only "die" when replaced by new ones that better explain existing evidence.[5]

Theories in political science explain tendencies and help us understand many cases, but there are almost always exceptions to the rules. Nothing in political science works in all cases the way the laws of physics work everywhere on earth. For example, as you will read in chapter 6 (and as briefly mentioned in chapter 1), there are several competing theories to explain why countries become democracies. There is considerable evidence that wealthier countries are likelier to be democratic than poor countries, but this does not mean every rich country will be a democracy and every low-income country will be under authoritarian rule. Rather, the theory of the link between wealth and democracy posits a tendency, much as eating healthy foods and not smoking will *tend to* increase one's life expectancy. Not everyone who eats well and avoids smoking will live to old age, and not everyone who smokes and eats junk food will die young. Cause-and-effect relationships in the social sciences are general patterns, not absolute laws. As a result, building theory is an intensive process over an extended period of formulating and testing hypotheses, gathering and examining evidence, and understanding and synthesizing debates. Theories are imperfect but can be improved over time.

Since theories compete with one another as the best explanations of social phenomena, it may be natural to think of scientists competing with one another to come up with the best theory. This is true in part, but the social sciences are

also a collective endeavor. In this sense, when a theory is rejected, it represents an advance of our understanding. Even critiques of one scientist's effort by another scientist are part of the process of testing and contesting the best explanations.

Types of Evidence

For most students being introduced to comparative politics, the dominant form of evidence will be **qualitative**, meaning it comes from accounts of historical or contemporary events. For instance, if I wish to examine the hypothesis that the French Revolution of 1789 was caused by the emergence of a self-conscious middle class (*bourgeoisie*), then I may look to accounts of that class and its attitudes and involvements in political life in the years leading up to 1789 in France, perhaps comparing it to other countries where a revolution did not take place. In this case, my data are not numbers and figures inserted into a spreadsheet but rather the detailed accounts of historical record. I may examine my hypothesis using the facts of who did what, when and where they did it, and how. Qualitative evidence may come from many sources such as written works like constitutions and laws, historical or journalistic accounts or reports, and interviews or surveys of people.

Social scientists also use **quantitative** data such as statistics and figures as they aim to make **inferences**, or conclusions based on evidence, about cause and effect. Examples include measures of average incomes or average life expectancies across countries. Such quantitative comparisons may be undertaken using national statistics from government agencies, numerical data from surveys, or data collected by researcher observations. Various data sources may be used to compare and contrast outcomes in different countries. At a more advanced level, such descriptive statistics can be used to formulate and begin to test hypotheses about the causes and effects of differences between countries. Other quantitative research in comparative politics focuses on the construction of formal mathematical models of the strategic behavior of individuals and groups in political situations. Quantitative data differ from qualitative data in their presentation, but both types are used to generate and test hypotheses. While the details of statistical methodologies and formal mathematical modeling are beyond the scope of this book, we work from the premise that both qualitative and quantitative work may be used to categorize and describe differences across cases, but they can also be used to examine hypotheses about the causes of those differences.[6]

In comparative politics, you will use historical accounts and data more often than you will make predictions about the future. This is because we have real evidence only for things that have happened and not for what might happen. Of course, the past may give us expectations about the future, which is why we hear that those who fail to learn about the past are doomed to repeat it. But in terms of concrete evidence, we cannot know what has yet to happen. For this reason, we work with existing cases to develop hypotheses and theories. For instance, we may hypothesize that China, which is not currently a democratic country, will move toward democracy as it grows wealthier. This hypothesis may come from observations about what has happened in other countries as

qualitative A form of analysis that aims to discern relationships between events or phenomena as described in narrative form, such as an account of a historical process.

quantitative A form of analysis that aims for the mathematical discernment of relationships between variables, typically involving a large number of cases or observations.

inference The process through which we aim to test observable implications (often, though not always, about cause and effect) of any given theory; also refers to conclusions reached through this process.

The Qualitative–Quantitative Debate

The increasingly sophisticated use of statistics in social science has generated considerable debate about the best methods and types of data for research. Qualitative (non-mathematical) research often closely examines a few cases. Such approaches, as mentioned in chapter 1, are often called *small-N* studies, with *N* meaning the number of cases. Quantitative approaches often handle many cases, using mathematical techniques to measure the degree of association between a set of variables that cut across each case. Some scholars who prefer quantitative work maintain that qualitative studies of one, two, or three cases are susceptible to reaching conclusions that only work for those selected cases and not a larger number of cases (some people call this the *small-N problem* or the *sample size problem*). According to this perspective, qualitative arguments may not "travel well." On the other hand, scholars who advocate strongly for qualitative work may argue that quantitative research is sometimes unpersuasive because it neglects the context and detail needed to make arguments meaningful. From this perspective, quantitative arguments that travel too far miss the real causes in a case as they unfold over time. Despite this debate, qualitative and quantitative research are increasingly interdependent in contemporary social science, and they complement each other in important ways. The perspective of this text is that extreme views of one or another sort are ill-advised. In general, quantitative work has the potential to make strong empirical claims about large numbers of cases and general associations between variables, and some would argue that qualitative work has the ability to reveal causal mechanisms or processes at the case-specific level (even if it typically cannot demonstrate which mechanisms really determine outcomes, it can help us to sketch better causal theories that could, in turn, be tested statistically). It has been argued that a common logic underpins any good social science work.[7] While this position is controversial, much of political science relies on formulating research questions and then using available data to test hypotheses about answers to these those questions.[8]

they have grown wealthier. Well-regarded theories may strongly suggest that China will democratize, and we may expect that it will do so, but to test the hypothesis we will have to await future events. Evidence comes only from events that have happened.

Spring Festival travel rush in Shenzhen City, China, 2012. Will China move toward democracy as its middle class grows larger? We address this question in the discussion of democratization in chapter 6.

Hypothesis Testing

The core of comparative politics is examining hypotheses about cause and effect between two or more variables, using observations from different cases. We defined variables in chapter 1 as some measure that can vary from one observation to the next. Examples range from a country's average income or average life expectancy, to whether a revolution occurred in a given country, to the most prominent religion in a particular state, to the religion of a particular person.

In social science, cause-and-effect arguments are based on examining different variables and how those variables relate to one another and may depend on one another. If country A is wealthy and country B is poor, what does country A have that country B does not that makes it so?[9] An explanation will hinge on identifying what variable might cause A to have become rich and B to remain poor. Our goal will be to identify what other variables go alongside wealth that are lacking in countries that are poor and to examine whether those variables made the difference. Our first key distinction here is between correlation and causation.

Correlation

correlation A relationship between two variables in which they tend to move in either the same direction (positive correlation) or in opposite directions (negative correlation).

Correlation measures the association between two variables. When two variables correlate, they are related to one another (or, to separate the words, they "co-relate"). To use a simple example, the temperature in many places will correlate with the month of the year: when it is February in much of the Northern Hemisphere, the temperature will be relatively cold; whereas in July, the temperature will be relatively hot. This does not mean it is impossible to have a hot day in February or a cold day in July, just that there is an association in general. There is thus a correlation between the variable "month of the year" and the variable "temperature."

If two variables have a positive correlation, they tend to increase together. One increases as the other increases. An obvious example is the income of a person and the amount the person spends on luxury goods. People with low incomes cannot afford to spend money on luxury goods, while the wealthy may spend a large amount on luxury goods. These two variables are positively correlated. A negative correlation is just the opposite and means that as one variable tends to increase, the other tends to decrease. An example might be the number of cigarettes one smokes per day and one's life expectancy.

Just as we can find a positive correlation between wealth and democracy, we can conversely find a negative correlation between another pair of variables: poverty and democracy. Consider the number of people in a country living on an income below $2 per day (call this variable the absolute poverty rate) and the level of democracy. In this case, the rich countries have relatively low levels of poverty and high levels of democracy, while many countries in Africa have high levels of poverty and low levels of democracy. When we look at the nearly two hundred or so countries in the world today, these correlations are apparent, even though it should be noted that there are some countries that are rich but not democratic and some that are low-income yet are democratic.

Correlation: Wealth and Democracy

Wealth and democracy of nations appear to be *positively correlated*. This correlation can be easily observed on a world map that shows which countries are wealthy and which are poor, set alongside a map that shows which countries are democracies and which are not. Europe, the United States, Australia, Canada, Japan, and several other countries are highly democratized and are quite wealthy. Many countries in Africa, on the other hand, have low incomes and low levels of democracy. Where "incomes" are high, "democracy" is high; and where "incomes" are low, "democracy" is likely to be low.

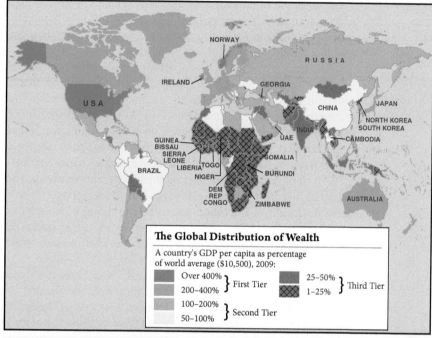

The Global Distribution of Wealth

A country's GDP per capita as percentage of world average ($10,500), 2009:

- Over 400% } First Tier
- 200–400% } First Tier
- 100–200% } Second Tier
- 50–100% } Second Tier
- 25–50% } Third Tier
- 1–25% } Third Tier

(a)

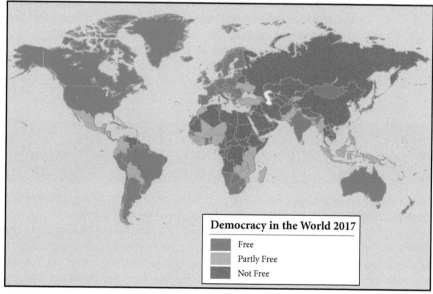

Democracy in the World 2017

- Free
- Partly Free
- Not Free

(b)

Map 2.1
(b) Courtesy FreedomHouse.org

Causation

Causation exists when one variable causes another. This helps us answer the fundamental questions raised in chapter 1, such as "Why are some countries democracies?" Recall that *why* questions are often best answered with *because* answers. As the word *because* implies, answering *why* involves explaining causes. Without causal arguments and theories, correlations are just patterns in search of an explanation. When we have causation, we usually have correlation, but the opposite is not true. Failing to distinguish between correlation and causation can lead to a variety of problems, as we will show.

Does the correlation between wealth and democracy prove that getting rich causes democracy to happen? Not necessarily. It may be that this correlation points in the direction of a causal argument, such as wealth → democracy. Or maybe the other way around: democracy → wealth. On the other hand, it may be that the correlation exists, but there is no causal reason for it. It may be simply due to chance that rich countries happen to be democracies. Or there may be other factors that result in both wealth and democracy, so called "confounding variables."

As it turns out, one of the central theories of comparative politics suggests that countries that grow wealthy *are* likely to become democratic for specific reasons we detail in chapter 6. The causal argument, beginning with the positive correlation between wealth and democracy, finds that historically, countries have developed a middle class as they have grown wealthier. This middle class, rather than the elite, ends up being a central force that pushes for more rights for all citizens. In poor countries without a middle class, democracy is unlikely to succeed, but growing middle classes in countries that are growing rich have helped bring democracy with them. While the correlation here does have a causal explanation, notice that the correlation needed an argument and logic to bring the story together and to make the fact of the correlation into evidence that supports an argument. Note also that the presence of a causal story here does not mean that the proponents of this view have *established* that this is the correct causal story.

We cannot assume that all correlations between two variables (call them X and Y) mean that X leads to Y. We will use various examples to illustrate possible relationships between variables. The first of those was the causal argument that X leads to Y (Figure 2.1).[10]

Causation: Legislative Elections and the Number of Political Parties in Legislatures

While almost no arguments in social science get "proven," the argument linking district-based electoral systems and political systems with few parties has substantial support. In countries like the United States, electing a single representative from each Congressional district means that small parties like the Green Party, Reform Party, and Libertarian Party end up with virtually no members of Congress, even in years when they have 5 percent or more support from voters nationwide. This is clearly because (note the use of *because*) such parties get a small percentage in many districts, which may result in winning no seats if Republicans and Democrats get higher percentages; by contrast, if the whole country voted in one big district, and Congressional seats were distributed in proportion with the vote received, these small parties would win more seats. In this sense, the structure of the elections is at least one of the causes of the two-party system.

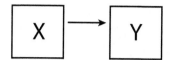

Figure 2.1 Causal Relationship Between Correlated Variables (X and Y)

But there are many other possibilities. Figure 2.2 shows some possible relationships between variable X and variable Y that are not the simple causal relationship
where X → Y. If we assumed X → Y in each of these cases, we could run into a
number of analytical problems.

We discuss each of these problems in order.

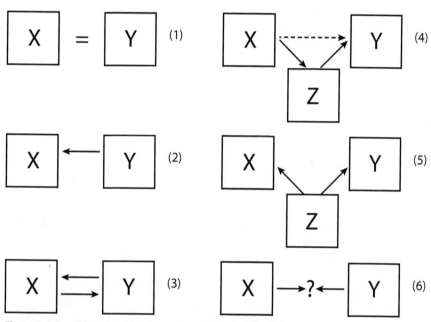

Figure 2.2 Possible Problems with Causal Arguments About Correlated Variables (X and Y)

(1) Definitional problems and falsifiability problem

The first problem is one that is rarely noted because it apparently involves
arguments that are "too correct." In reality, one common problem is confusing
cause and effect between two variables with two variables that are the same by
definition. If X is measuring the same thing as Y, they will correlate perfectly. But
this is not because X → Y, but rather because X = Y.[11] A common problem for
comparativists is defining two variables that are so nearly the same that the causal
argument is meaningless, or tautological. This definitional problem relates to the

falsifiability The testability of a theory or hypothesis. A good hypothesis could be logically demonstrated to be false by evidence.

problem of **falsifiability**, which is the idea that for an explanation to be meaningful, it must be contestable. To argue that something is true means something only if there is a chance it could at least possibly be incorrect and could be proved wrong. For instance, say we are asked why a baseball team won a game, and our "analysis" is that the winning team "just scored more runs" than the losing team, or "just got it done." This argument is correct, in the narrow sense that it is not inaccurate, but it is also meaningless, precisely because it can never be otherwise: scoring more runs over the course of a game and winning the game are one and the same, by definition. By contrast, if we say that none of the world's democratic countries will ever again succumb to dictatorship, then that argument is falsifiable because a contrary example is possible.

(2) Reverse causality problem

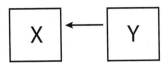

The reverse causality problem is rather simpler to understand. Our story at the beginning of the chapter held that villagers noted that contagious epidemics brought doctors into villages and people in the villages began to die, and they concluded that doctors were causing the illness rather than the illness bringing the doctors to the village. In this case, two variables are correlated, but the causal argument linking the two may be the opposite of what we anticipate. Instead of

Definitions and Falsifiability: Dictators and Dictatorships

In trying to explain why countries become dictatorships, we may often be drawn to the actions of certain key individuals. Say we argue that North Korea is a dictatorship because North Korean people have no practical rights under Kim Jong-un. The cause is Kim Jong-un's rule and the consequence is dictatorship, as defined by a lack of political rights for citizens. We may then note that Kim Jong-un, like his father, Kim Jong-il, is a dictator who does not allow free and fair elections, tramples civil liberties, and rules with an iron fist. But if we say that these aspects of Kim Jong-un's rule are the *causes* of North Korea becoming a dictatorship, we are conflating cause and effect. We are characterizing the rule of Kim Jong-un as a dictatorship more than we are giving a real cause for why dictatorial rule in North Korea came about. Arguing that individuals like Kim Jong-un cause dictatorships may work as long as we are careful in our causal argument and separate it from our definition; but in this case, our cause and our effect are the same.

Kim Jong-un, General Ri Yong Ho, and Kim Jong-il of North Korea in 2010. When Kim Jong-il died in 2011, his son Kim Jong-un took over the dictatorship. Why has this authoritarian regime persisted despite international isolation and poor economic performance?

Reverse Causality: Cancer Rates and Longevity

For much of the twentieth century, cancer rates were higher in countries with long life spans than they were in countries where the average life span was shorter. Given this correlation between the variables, one (wrong) conclusion might be that cancer causes people to live longer. This would, of course, have the causal relationship backward. Cancers are diseases that affect the old more often than the young, so where people live longer they are likelier to suffer from cancer. Because many people in countries with short life spans (such as some African countries, unfortunately) do not live to old ages, cancer is infrequent. Understanding "which way the causal arrow goes" is crucial: In this case the arrow goes longevity → cancer, rather than cancer → longevity.

X leading to Y, perhaps Y leads to X. Getting the "causal arrow" pointed in the right direction is essential, and reversing causality has the potential to lead to disastrous consequences.

(3) Endogeneity problem

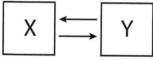

The **endogeneity** problem is about circularity: It happens when two variables exhibit mutual or reciprocal effects. You may know of a simple expression such as "the chicken and the egg" problem, though endogeneity arises any time variables mutually affect one another. If X and Y correlate and seem to go together, we may be left trying to figure out whether X caused Y to happen or Y caused X to happen. Reasonable people may disagree about which direction the causal arrow goes.[12] Endogeneity problems are common in the real world. When we talk of vicious circles (of, say, poverty and dictatorship) or virtuous circles (of, say, economic growth and human development), we are describing a situation in which many important variables are endogenous. Indeed, endogeneity as such is not a problem but a feature of many social and political phenomena. It becomes a problem when we mistakenly claim one variable causes another when the two variables are, in fact, endogenously linked. Even so, social scientists don't want simply to identify multiple variables

endogeneity The name given to any circumstance in which two variables exhibit mutual or reciprocal effects.

Endogeneity: Education and Health

Children's health and children's education seem to correlate positively: When one improves, so does the other. So, do improvements in education lead to better health, or do improvements in health lead to better education? Both are plausible. Healthier students will be more likely to have good attendance at school and will be better able to thrive in their work there, making improved health a cause of improved educational outcomes. Conversely, better education may lead to more knowledge about healthy practices, including nutrition and sanitation. So education may make for less frequent visits to the doctor. In this case, the two variables are endogenous.

as endogenous but to understand more precisely the *ways* endogenously linked variables interact over time. One of the leading strategies for resolving this dilemma in qualitative research is closely tracing the historical sequence. Where we have good information about when and where things happened, who did them, or how events unfolded, we may be able to determine whether X leads to Y or Y leads to X. If we can identify clearly whether the chicken came before the egg (or vice-versa), we may be able to address this problem. This is not, however, always possible, as the box on education and health shows.

In addition, there are statistical strategies for dealing with this problem that we cannot explore here, but you could learn about them by taking a more advanced social science methods course.

(4) Intervening variable problem

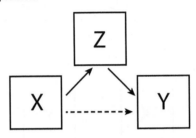

Intervening variables are another potential problem, though they are not always problematic. The situation here is that X leads to Y, but indirectly: the effect of X on Y is mediated through another variable, Z. This is not always a problem. An example is eating fatty foods and having a higher risk of heart disease. Eating lots of fatty foods leads to an accumulation of cholesterol in the arteries, which leads to higher risk of heart disease. Even though there are intervening steps between the actual eating and the risk of heart disease, we can still say eating fatty foods causes a higher risk of heart disease. As long as we can specify the argument and its steps, we do not have an intervening variable problem. The potential problem arises when we miss an intervening variable and this leads us to a wrong interpretation (or, alternatively, if we control for the

Intervening Variables: Communism and Democratization

In 1989, many of the countries of central-eastern Europe became democracies as they left the communist bloc dominated by the former Soviet Union. An amateur analyst might be tempted to conclude that communism therefore caused democracy. The communist regimes must have encouraged the citizenry to demand their rights, and then they agreed to hold elections to fulfill those rights. This is nonsense. In reality, the democratization of the region came about as a reaction and response to years of communist rule, generated by civil society and civic groups, and directed at the authoritarian regimes. Communism cannot meaningfully be said to have caused the democratization. Rather, intervening variables, such as citizens' long, pent-up frustrations, combined with some particular trigger events, brought on the fall of communism. An interpretation of the democratic wave of 1989 as a consequence of communism would have the argument quite wrong if it lacked the key intervening variables.

intervening variable in a statistical model we are using to examine the effect of X on Y). The previous box example illustrates the problem of failing to consider intervening variables (or "causal pathways").

(5) Omitted variable problem

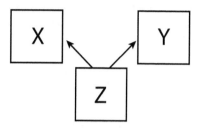

We frequently miss or omit variables that should be in our analysis. We observe an empirical relationship between X and Y and assume this means that one creates the other, when in fact both are attributable to a third factor, sometimes also called a confounding or "lurking" variable, because though it is there in the background, we might not see it. If X and Y are positively correlated, it may not be that $X \rightarrow Y$ or $Y \rightarrow X$ at all. Instead, some factor Z may lead to both X and Y, thus giving rise to the correlation between them. That is, $Z \rightarrow X$ and $Z \rightarrow Y$. This is a very common problem, and one of the great difficulties of social science involves ruling out likely Z variables of this sort. If you take a course in statistics, you will learn how to deal with this problem *if Z is measured*. But if Z is not measured, or if we don't even know to look for it, its presence can "bias" our estimate of X's effect on Y.

(6) Spurious correlation problem

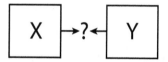

Finally, there are many variables out there in the world, and some are bound to correlate with one another even in the absence of any causal relationship. Many problems that seem to be of this sort will actually be omitted variable problems

Omitted Variables: Ice Cream Sales and Murders

There is a peculiar correlation between ice cream and murder rates, often cited in methodology textbooks.[13] Let's say a study gives convincing evidence of a positive correlation between increases in ice cream sales and increases in murder rates. What's more, the analyst claims to have a causal argument. What could such a causal argument be? Does eating ice cream lead people to murder? Unlikely. Murdering someone gives a craving for ice cream? Probably not. The answer is a missing variable: the temperature outside. This omitted variable affects both ice cream sales and murder rates, both of which increase in the summertime. Failing to account for omitted variables can lead to dangerously flawed causal arguments.

Spurious Correlation: Stock Markets and Butter Production in Bangladesh

According to an accomplished statistician now at the University of California, Berkeley, the variable most highly correlated with the performance of American stock markets for several decades was not U.S. corporate profits, or rates of inflation or unemployment in the United States, but rather butter production in Bangladesh.[14] If this is true, surely it is so by coincidence. It is highly improbable that some factor happens to affect only American stock prices and butter production in Bangladesh but not any of the other variables that might also be expected to link the two (such as the overall performance of the global economy). With the seemingly boundless number of variables we might observe in the world, some are bound to correlate even when there is no real relationship between them.

upon further investigation, but there are examples of correlations where simply no meaningful causal relationship exists. Lucky superstitions are examples where two variables seem to correlate, but there is no plausible relationship between them. Perhaps your college's sports team always seems to win when you put your lucky hat on for the game. This correlation may continue for some time, but there is no reasonable scientific explanation linking your hat-wearing tendencies to victory, and no reason to expect that you putting on your hat will lead your team to win the next game. Though the variables "hat wearing" and "victory" may correlate, there is no causation. (Sorry. You can take off your hat now.)

Critiques: Using Theories and Evidence

Evidence can be used to support an argument, but it can also help us counter an argument, and this too is a meaningful contribution to advancing our understanding and knowledge. Evidence can enhance our knowledge by providing a helpful critique of the conventional wisdom. Accordingly, empirical critiques have a prominent place in comparative politics, as do the theoretical critiques they enable.

Empirical Critiques: Using Deviant Cases

In testing hypotheses, we often hope to find evidence that supports a particular theory. Specifically, we want to find cases that confirm or reaffirm our theory or support our hypothesis. But many interesting advances come from empirical evidence that does not fit a theory well. Deviant cases—those that do not fit a theory or are exceptions or outliers—are very important in advancing social science theory. These cases help us test out why a theory doesn't work and understand what improvements need to be made to our knowledge. They allow us to make an **empirical critique** of a theory because the cases do not support it. Much like getting a bad result on a certain test can encourage us to do better where we fell short, so too a deviant case forces us to think about how to improve our arguments.

empirical critique An effort to point to important evidence that does not support a conventional version of any given theory.

Theoretical Critiques: Improving Theories and Hypotheses

theoretical critique An effort to show that a given theory has logical limitations.

Theoretical critiques are new ideas that improve on the logic or reasoning of existing theories. Theory and empirical evidence constantly interact, and where deviant cases help provide an empirical critique, these can help us improve our theories.

Empirical Critique: Ghana and Modernization Theory (see chapter 6)

Ghana is a low-income West African country that defies expectations by having a robust democracy. This presents an intriguing challenge to the theory of modernization, which we present further in chapter 6. Modernization theory holds that democracy can be expected as a consequence of economic development, industrialization, education, and urbanization—all of which contribute to the emergence of a middle class.[15]

While Ghana is advancing on some of these criteria, the country clearly is poor, with a limited industrial base, low levels of education, and only some recent urbanization. Yet it is a rather successful democracy with free and fair elections and protections for citizens' rights and liberties. Ghana thus becomes a very interesting case to examine, precisely because it facilitates an empirical critique of a prominent theory about democratization.

They often provide the impetus for improvement of the theory. Empirical critiques allow us to advance social science by pointing out anomalies, inconsistencies, and deviations from a theory. Theoretical advances can also come from critiques of the theory itself, through reexaminations of the logic, assumptions, or arguments underpinning it. The following box gives an example of how a theoretical critique emerged from empirical evidence that didn't fit a theory.

Critiques help us craft better arguments and theories. First, they can improve our understanding of **scope conditions**, or the conditions under which an argument works. Identifying and examining cases that do not fit an argument is a good potential avenue for further research. Second, critiques based on empirical evidence can help improve our concepts and lead to a clearer understanding of what exactly we are studying. For instance, the tiny, oil-rich country of Equatorial Guinea has grown rapidly to become one of the wealthiest countries in Africa, but much of its wealth goes just to the dictator's family. Studying this empirical example might give us more insight into what exactly a country's "economic development" means. By identifying weaknesses in arguments and offering alternative explanations, critiques give us better understandings of why things happen.

scope conditions The conditions or range of cases for which an argument works.

Theoretical Critique: Dependency Theory in Latin America (see chapter 5)

From the 1940s to the 1960s, many leading scholars of Latin America argued that the continent suffered from economic dependency relative to the world's industrial powers. This "dependency theory" suggested that poor Latin American countries essentially lost money, resources, and power to the wealthy and powerful countries of the world. The image was of exploitation of the poor countries on the world's periphery by the rich "core" countries. However, empirical evidence after World War II challenged this theory, as countries such as Brazil managed to grow, develop, and industrialize with some success. As a result, dependency theory received a theoretical critique from other scholars, including Peter Evans and Fernando Henrique Cardoso and Enzo Faletto. (Cardoso, incidentally, later became president of Brazil in the 1990s.) This next generation of dependency theorists characterized the relationship between Latin America and the core countries as one of "dependent development" in which the continent could develop and grow, but still in a subordinate position that furthered its dependence on capital from the wealthy countries. This theoretical critique came from the recognition that the original dependency theory had a failing: it could not explain or account for growth or progress in Latin America.

The Challenges of Measurement:
Biases, Errors, and Validity

The challenges of garnering and wielding evidence are multifaceted. Beyond determining how to gather evidence and which pieces to use, we must pay attention to measures and **indicators** (elements or features suggesting underlying factors). Without careful and thoughtful measurement, we may accidentally introduce biases and errors into an analysis. **Bias** is a preference for one idea or perspective over another, especially a preference that may result in unbalanced use of evidence or in analytical error.

Bias aside, it is possible to simply make **measurement errors**, such as by typing the wrong number in a spreadsheet. This kind of error happens more often than you might expect and sometimes in consequential ways. As a well-known example, a spreadsheet data error in work by Harvard economists Carmen Reinhart and Kenneth Rogoff produced erroneous results in highly influential research about government debt and economic growth (note that this error was discovered by a graduate student!).[16] Less obvious might be how a measurement cannot fully reflect what it is trying to measure. Most college students have taken standardized tests such as the SAT or ACT, which attempt to measure overall competence in math and language. Scores for most students will fluctuate from one test to the next depending on the specific questions. Whatever their merits, the tests thus have a degree of measurement error in conveying competence. Many social science measures are imperfect, and we should keep this in mind when carrying out our analyses.

A second measurement problem is **measurement bias**. One example of bias comes from respondents in a survey who are untruthful, whether consciously or subconsciously.[17] Another would be if the questions we ask people are interpreted differently by different groups of respondents. Perhaps the most serious form of bias for beginning researchers is seeking to confirm one's favored hypothesis. This can include a tendency to believe things are a certain way that we want to see them. Imagine that a very ideological capitalist student wants to show that countries with free markets have performed better economically than countries that have more active government involvement in the economy. The eager student knows that the United States performed better than the U.S.S.R. in economic growth rates in the 1980s and uses these cases to "prove" the hypothesis that less government involvement in the economy is better for the economy. Subconsciously, the student may have chosen those cases because he knew what he would find, and that it would support his preference. But looking at the same question in other cases (say, Scandinavia or Canada vs. African countries) might show very different results. The point is not that the student is wrong—in fact, he may be correct—but that the student's preconceptions biased the research. We must ask research questions and test hypotheses fairly by ensuring the answer is not predetermined.

Even when researchers are careful not to bias their measures, we must consider the problem of **measurement validity**—that is, whether a given measure effectively captures or represents what is being researched. Indicators that are valid accurately reflect our concept. Informally, validity means measuring what we claim we are measuring. In some cases, this is straightforward, and our measures may be perfectly valid. To measure the "total number of political parties represented

indicator An element or feature that indicates the presence of an underlying factor.

bias A preference for one idea or perspective over another, especially a preference that may result in unbalanced use of evidence or in analytical error.

measurement error Either an episodic error, such as improperly recording data, or a systematic error, meaning that a measurement does not fully reflect what it is designed to measure.

measurement bias A measure is biased if it will not produce comparable results for all observations.

measurement validity Whether a given measure effectively captures or represents what we are researching.

Measurement Validity: Nationalism in Latin America

Complex concepts like those in comparative politics have real potential for problems of validity, and this is especially true of cultural phenomena that are less subject to precise measurement. For example, Miguel Angel Centeno aimed to measure levels of nationalism in several nineteenth-century Latin American societies.[18] For obvious reasons, nineteenth-century Latin Americans cannot be surveyed (and there may be limitations to what surveys can reveal about identities in any case). Therefore, Centeno needed to select indicators of national sentiment. Among others, he chose the presence (or relative lack) of national monuments. Is the presence of national monuments a valid indicator of "nationalism" or "national sentiment"? To say yes, we must suppose there is a relationship between national sentiment and the construction of national monuments. Is this assumption correct? If not, does this mean that we should disregard such imperfect indicators? There is often a tension between measurement validity and our desire to have measures that are objective and precise. The construction of monuments is relatively easy to measure, but it may not fully capture national sentiment; on the other hand, measuring national sentiment by more extensive accounts (say, from diaries and newspapers of the time) may give us greater validity, but the measure may be fuzzier than the measure using monuments. We often must use necessarily imperfect indicators, but we must remember their limitations and search for the best available measures.

in a legislature," we may simply find a record of every member of the legislature, note which party each member is from, then count the number of distinct parties to which legislators belong. On the other hand, consider the challenge of trying to measure overall health outcomes of a given country. Is life expectancy the right measure for this? Or infant mortality rates (the percent of infants that die before the age of two, for example)? Or rates of asthma, malaria, or HIV/AIDS? In truth, each of these is a valid measure of something specific, but none precisely measures "overall health."

Several guidelines can help promote measurements that are accurate, unbiased, and valid. We should strive for valid measurement to the greatest extent possible, but sometimes, when dealing with certain questions and sets of data, we will have to work with imperfect indicators of the concepts that interest us. We should explicitly state our reservations about our measures (and potential biases) when we present our work. This allows others to make their own judgments. In addition, we should be mindful of how our measured variables relate to our concepts and questions. In your own research, you should ask yourself what can actually be measured and whether the measurements actually correspond to the concept you are trying to study.

Qualities of Good Analysis and Argumentation

THINKING COMPARATIVELY

Comparative politics tests hypotheses and builds theories by using evidence and identifying causal relationships. Careful use of theory and evidence allows a researcher to give a hypothesis a good test. The results of that test and that research will lead to a thesis that can be well substantiated and compelling. Good argumentation will avoid, or at least address, the problems of causal inference and measurement shown in this chapter. We conclude the chapter with some guidance for high-quality analysis in comparative politics.

THINKING COMPARATIVELY

Step 1: Asking Good Questions: Why?

Good arguments are generally good answers to good questions. It is nearly impossible to have a good answer to a bad question. For this reason, we begin with asking good questions. Good questions have a number of characteristics, among them the following. First, good questions can be answered with evidence. The question of why human beings form political societies is not a bad question for political philosophers, but it is not an especially good question for comparative politics because it is virtually impossible to answer using empirical evidence. Second, good questions are interesting. Questions can be interesting in several ways. They may produce knowledge that is relevant to making policies and laws, for example. But especially important is that they somehow contribute to existing theories. Related to this, they should elicit curiosity, both from a potential audience and from you, the analyst. Third, good questions can be answered, at least in a preliminary but meaningful fashion, given the time and resources at your disposal. (Keep in mind that a research paper for the end of the semester in an undergraduate course cannot typically have the same ambition as a doctoral dissertation that may require many years of research and writing to complete.) Finally, good questions ask for causal explanations. They do not just ask for descriptive accounts of processes, but they push us to explain why some phenomenon or phenomena has (or have) come to pass.

Step 2: Hypothesis Testing: Generating Good Hypotheses and Testing Them Fairly

The second set of issues for beginning comparative political analysis is formulating an appropriate hypothesis and testing it with as little bias as possible. A hypothesis should be based on clearly defined variables and concepts. To explain why country X became a democracy, for example, we need a good definition for democracy and how we know country X is a democracy. A good hypothesis will typically be rooted in some existing theory from comparative politics. For example, can modernization theory (see chapter 6) offer a hypothesis for why country X democratized? Good hypothesis testing often involves reading theories and arguments about cases other than the one we are interested in. Generating a hypothesis about democratization in country X may require us to read theories and arguments not just about country X itself but also about other countries. Good hypothesis testing will not mean the researcher goes looking to prove his or her own pet argument, picking and choosing evidence to make the point. Once a hypothesis is formulated, it should receive a fair test from the researcher, who can and should use the available evidence to weigh the proposed argument and how well it works or does not.

Step 3: Balancing Argumentation: Evidence, Originality, and Meaningfulness

A final key to good comparative analysis is making meaningful claims and avoiding trivial arguments. If you are developing your own argument, you should offer your own distinct hypothesis and then your own original claim based on your research. Self-evident and obvious arguments contribute much less to social science than arguments that are memorable. Ideally, you would like those hearing your argument to think it is one "only this person would make in this way" while also thinking you have defended your argument well. Another way to put this is to see that your argument produces new knowledge rather than reproducing old knowledge. You do not want to replicate, copy, or transcribe others' ideas; you want to generate and defend your own.

Originality matters, but it must be balanced with a respect for existing knowledge. Originality does not mean developing ridiculous and goofy arguments or ignoring previous research. Serious evaluation of existing evidence is as important in formulating one's argument as it is in testing the hypothesis. Good comparative analysis means more argumentation than pure description and more attention to evidence than pure opinion. It is neither an opinion piece nor a book report about a country. It represents a middle ground in which you have an argument where original claims and interpretations are backed with evidence. Basing your argument on significant reading and research will be the likeliest route to success. There is no substitute for this research work. Indeed, original research is original precisely because it contributes in helpful ways to an existing research tradition.

One challenge from extensive research is that there will frequently be multiple variables that can be shown to have some impact on a particular outcome. For instance, a country's economic growth may be shown to depend on the following: geographic location, relationship to the dominant powers in the world economy, policies, leadership, culture, institutions, histories of colonialism, chance and luck, and many other variables. It is important, however, to do more than make a "laundry list" and simply say "all of these matter." The challenge is to prioritize the variables that have the most important impact on the outcome. In the jargon, we call this being parsimonious, selecting the most important variables and giving them pride of place in the argument.

Doing all of this will enable a researcher to engage with the larger scholarly literature and the central debates in comparative politics. The strongest works of comparative politics—the major books and articles in the field—are the products of years of research work and refined thinking, but the basic process can be emulated by those new to the field. The best student work comes from analyses that draw on diverse sources, including theoretical sources, to weigh the validity of different claims, show competent understanding of relevant literature, build on relevant concepts and theories, and highlight the individual's unique synthesis and contribution. This asks a great deal, and it requires practice, but our guidance boils down to the suggestions in Table 2.1.

Comparative research requires considerable thought and planning, but it is also best learned by doing. This comes from reading in the field to see how scholars analyze politics and by conducting one's own research for papers, presentations,

THINKING COMPARATIVELY

TABLE 2.1 Guidelines for Comparative Research

Guideline	Step 1: Ask Good Questions	Step 2: Test Hypotheses	Step 3: Write Your Argument
Do the basics	Ask open-ended *why* questions about cause and effect.	Define concepts and variables clearly.	Read and use the scholarly literature on your topic.
Be original and informed	Ask questions you do not know the answer to before starting your research.	Use theories from scholarly books and articles to help form hypotheses.	Aim for meaningful, original claims, and avoid laundry lists of factors that just "matter."
Consider the evidence	Ask questions for which evidence is available to test a hypothesis.	Be aware of your biases and work from the evidence, not assumptions.	Use evidence and not opinion to make your claims.

THINKING COMPARATIVELY

exams, or other outputs. The remainder of the book will help provide you with this practice. In the next chapters, we turn to the major themes of comparative politics and use these to work on the process of formulating and generating questions, hypotheses, arguments, and theories. We provide some of the requisite knowledge of these topics, and examples of quality research, while pushing you to analyze comparative politics on your own.

Chapter Summary

Introduction to Theories, Hypotheses, and Evidence

- Social scientists use theories, hypotheses, and evidence to build arguments about how the world operates. Theories are general explanations of how empirical phenomena operate across a range of cases. They are typically backed by some evidence. Hypotheses are potential explanations of cause and effect for specific cases. They are designed to be tested using evidence and are often derived from theories.

Hypothesis Testing

- The central practice in comparative politics is testing hypotheses about causal questions using empirical evidence. This involves measuring variables and seeing how variables correlate across cases.
- Variables that correlate with one another may have a causal relationship, but not necessarily.
- There are several fallacies and logical traps to avoid when making causal arguments about correlated variables, to include reverse causation, omitted variables, intervening variables, and spurious correlation.

Critiques: Using Theories and Evidence

- Political science can advance by developing critiques of existing theories and arguments. Critiques can be empirical, based on demonstrating cases that do not fit a theory, or can be more purely theoretical by using reason and logic to show problems with a theory.

The Challenges of Measurement: Biases, Errors, and Validity

- Measurement is a leading challenge facing comparative political scientists. Comparativists aim to avoid measurement errors and biases and seek to ensure that measures are valid, or measure what they claim to measure.

Thinking Comparatively

- Good practices in comparative politics include asking causal "Why" questions, developing unbiased hypothesis tests, and making arguments that are original yet informed by an understanding of existing theories and findings.

Thinking It Through

1. Considering the examples of problems with causal arguments in Figures 2.1 and 2.2, come up with your own examples of omitted-variable problems in the real world.

2. Considering the theory of modernization, which holds (among other things) that wealth is likely to lead to democracy, what sorts of countries would you seek out if you wanted to test the theory on deviant cases? Think of some examples, or do some preliminary research online that will help you identify some.

3. What are some examples of measurement problems that you could foresee if you were to conduct a study of how a country's culture affects its wealth?

4. What beliefs do you have about politics that you think are rooted in a theory? For example, do you have beliefs about how politicians tend to behave, the media's role in politics, or the likelihood that student activists can "change the world"? If so, consider what you think the theory is, and contemplate it in light of this chapter. What are the achievements and shortcomings of the theory?

5. Ask yourself what puzzles you about politics or social life in a certain country (perhaps including the United States). Now try to develop a hypothesis for a possible answer that would explain the puzzle. How could you develop a research plan that would allow you to gather evidence and test your hypothesis?

CHAPTER 3

The State

Egyptian police and soldiers outside a voting center in 2011. The military and police shape the development and functioning of the state in critical ways.

n the years just after World War II, many observers thought of the Western European state system as fairly settled. The idea of modern states had first developed in this region. The consolidation of states' power was high, even in cases like Germany and Italy, which unified only in the late nineteenth century. And despite the 1945 split of Germany into East and West, followed by its reunification several decades later, the European states on the whole seemed likely to persist into the distant future.

But at least two recent developments have called into question the stability of the Western European system of nation-states. The first is the movement over the second half of the twentieth century toward European integration, beginning with the European common market and culminating in the creation of the European Union (EU). Some have wondered whether a European "super-state" might form, and others have made arguments for and against this possibility.[1] Still others, though, have become pessimistic about the prospects of the EU after the United Kingdom voted to leave and Euroskeptics became more prominent in several other countries. The second development is the presence of secessionist and sub-state nationalist movements in the region, perhaps most notably in Catalonia (an area on the Mediterranean coast of Spain that includes the city of Barcelona) and Scotland (which is part of the United Kingdom). In the fall of 2014, Scotland held a referendum on becoming independent from the United Kingdom. The referendum failed, but some of its supporters are undaunted. Similarly, many in Catalonia are hopeful of forming an independent state in the future; and in 2017, a referendum on Catalan independence, declared illegal by the Spanish government, was carried out: the supporters of secession won the vote amidst a boycott by those who opposed secession. Though relatively few commentators, at the time of this writing, expect Catalan independence, it is unclear what the future holds. Could such developments gather steam? If Catalonia or Scotland successfully forms a new state, will others in the region follow in its wake? To answer such questions, we may benefit from better understanding the characteristic features of modern states and the processes through which previous states have been formed.

It is impossible to understand modern politics without understanding the state. It is states that we judge to be authoritarian or democratic, and it is states that exhibit the institutional features such as executives and legislatures that we discuss later in this book. States are the most powerful organizations on which most political actors make claims. States are key factors in economic development; and they shape the experiences of citizens, residents, and still other individuals. Finally, states are the central characters in the story of international politics: Even in this rapidly globalizing world in which nonstate and transnational actors seem increasingly important, the state remains fundamental.

But what *is* the state? Where do states come from, and what does this tell us about their character and likely future? What do states do? How do they differ from one another, and why are some strong and others weak or even failed states? These are the questions we begin to answer in this chapter and those that follow.

. . .

Concepts

Analysts of comparative politics do not always agree completely on the definitions of words such as *state* or *development* or *democracy*. Often, though, there is a sort of lowest common denominator, an agreed-on general idea about what a concept covers. With respect to the state—and here we focus on the modern state that evolved over the last several centuries[2]—this lowest common denominator is the classic definition posited almost a century ago by Max Weber: the state is the central political institution that exerts a "monopoly on the legitimate use of physical force within a given territory."[3] Note that by "legitimate" Weber means recognized by members of the society in question as generally justified. Political scientists do not themselves decide what is or is not "legitimate."

What does Weber's definition mean? Definitions work, in part, by telling us what something is *not*. What is a state not? Well, it is clear from this definition that a political arena with many distinct actors using legitimate force would not be a **state**. Consider a scenario of anarchy, for example, the infamous "war of all against all." If a society has no central authority that can use force, then perhaps anyone can. In such a society, individuals need to either acquire the ability to use force themselves or make arrangements with someone who can. If they do not, they remain vulnerable to potential harm from others; and without some higher authority, they have no one to turn to. Yet the diversity of political societies is not limited to the extremes of anarchic systems and modern states. Indeed, there are many intermediary types.

The Modern State

We begin by comparing the **modern state** to *another* sort of political society that was not anarchic but in which a nonstate order was present: European feudalism in the medieval era.[4] In the feudal political order, hierarchical ties linked peasants, at the bottom, to kings, who at least nominally sat at the top (in tenuous balance with the church), with a nobility mediating between them. In the feudal order,

state The most important kind of political organization in modern politics, which, in its ideal form, is characterized by centralized control of the use of force, bureaucratic organization, and the provision of a number of public goods.

modern state A concept used to distinguish states in the modern world from earlier forms of political centralization; it includes features such as extensive bureaucracy, centralization of violence, and impersonality.

however, kings were understood to be the greatest among nobles, and their rule over the population of their kingdoms was mostly indirect. There was little standardized taxation, there were few standing armies, and the king's administration did not provide meaningful public services. Peasants in such a system were unlikely to find recourse against local nobles by petitioning the king.[5] Achieving such recourse was not impossible in principle, but the organizational capacity of the system typically made it unfeasible. Most people traveled very little, and the authority to which they were subjected was local, and often arbitrary. Law was present, but **rule of law**, referring to a political system in which the law is consistently applied equally to all, was not. No single, centralized authority could claim to control the legitimate use of force.[6] Indeed, it was considered legitimate for a variety of actors to exert force, and not just because such authority had been delegated to them.[7] The king's authority was rivaled by both the authority of the church and the nobility.

Now think about the state you live in (and by this, of course, we mean your country). Imagine an incident of violence taking place within this state. Is that violence considered legitimate or illegitimate? This will depend on who is doing it and why. If it is your neighbor, and he or she holds no official position, chances are the violence is illegitimate. What about a police officer subduing a violent suspect? What is critical here is that all of the use of force considered legitimate in a society ultimately traces its legitimacy back to the state. In other words, in a society with a state, violence is tremendously concentrated in the military and law enforcement agencies.[8] This means that in well-functioning states, interpersonal violence is likely lower than in other systems: states with high capacity limit and control interpersonal violence, to the extent that citizens of well-functioning states are often able to ignore what little interpersonal violence is present.[9] This does not mean, though, that states with high levels of capacity are nonviolent. Rather, they represent the greatest concentration of the capacity to exert force that the world has ever known.[10]

So far, we have used a fairly minimal definition of the state. It is worth noting that there are other important features of modern states, which we discuss further later in the chapter, including their bureaucratic type of organization, their impersonality, and above all the fact that they claim sovereignty. Moreover, states aim to *do* many things, and as time passes, these actions of the state get incorporated into our idea of what a state is.

State Capacity

State capacity is the measurement of a state's ability to accomplish its goals.[11] In general, today we would say that a state has high capacity when (1) it has established a monopoly on the use of force; (2) it has a properly functioning bureaucracy, with relatively low levels of corruption and irregularity, accomplishing tasks such as coordinating defense, maintaining infrastructure, and managing projects in education and public health; and (3) rule of law is maintained, producing a predictable and manageable environment for citizens as they go about their business. To do this it must successfully generate revenue, usually by taxing its population, a task more difficult than you might imagine.[12]

As we will see later, the goals that states have taken on have increased over time.[13] Because the list of states' necessary activities is a moving target, so is the definition of "state capacity": a state that would have been considered to have high

rule of law A system that imposes regularized rules in a polity, with key criteria including equal rights, the regular enforcement of laws, and the relative independence of the judiciary.

state capacity The ability of the state to achieve its objectives, especially the abilities to control violence, effectively tax the population, and maintain well-functioning institutions and the rule of law.

capacity in the late seventeenth century, such as the English or French state of that time, would today be considered weak or to have low capacity. For example, seventeenth-century France—unquestionably a strong state with high capacity in its historical context—did not provide (or aim to provide) public education, but today this is considered a key function of states. A state that fails at doing so is now considered to have lower capacity than a state that succeeds.

Another way to think about this would be to see states as moving along a continuum of stateness.[14] In other words, rather than thinking of state or nonstate as a dichotomous ("yes" or "no") variable, we could think of stateness as a quality of a given political order that has a range of possible values: state capacity, from this point of view, is the degree to which a political order has achieved stateness.

Fragile States

As with many other concepts, scholars do not always agree about how to precisely define and measure **failed or fragile states**, but, put simply, states become increasingly fragile when their capacity declines to a certain point. So a fragile state is one that cannot or does not do what states are conventionally supposed to do. Perhaps the clearest example in recent years has been Somalia, where the state as such is just one power among many. Rival groups, essentially large gangs, control their own territory and battle over it where territories meet. Public service provision is minimal where it exists at all. We will examine failed and fragile states at greater length in chapter 4 on political economy.

fragile state A state that cannot or does not perform its expected functions, referred to by some scholars as a "failed state."

The State–Society Relationship

We have said that the state is fundamental to understanding modern politics. At the same time, it is important to remember that the state is part of society. It does not exist outside or above the society but is one among many organizations. "Society" can be thought of as the large and complex set of ties that connect people to each other. In other words, it can be thought of as a space created by lots of different overlapping social networks. So society is composed of webs of friendships, professional linkages, voluntary groups and religious organizations, media ties, and many other structured systems of relationships. In these patterns of overlapping networks, power is distributed. In modern societies, formally organized power is, as we have seen, concentrated in the state. But in most modern societies, despite the state's concentration of *formal* power, there is a great deal of political activity that is not controlled by state actors. We need to be able to take this activity into account.

When political scientists speak of the state–society relationship, they imply that the modern state is partially autonomous and is situated in relationships with other actors, and that these relationships are important to study. Why? Because sets of relationships with other actors affect the state's goals and constrain its policy options and, thus, its actions. These relationships also have implications for those other actors, and especially for participants in "civil society," which we discuss further later in the chapter. When we say that the state is partially autonomous we mean that it is not subject to the total control of other organizations. Instead, it tends to serve as a base to control those other organizations. For example, before the creation of modern states in Europe, the political institutions that preceded them (confusingly, also often called "states") existed in dynamic tension with the

Catholic Church. In essence, these organizations shared sovereignty in complicated and even contradictory ways. Modern states, though, tend to be more autonomous from religious organizations, as we explore more fully in chapter 15.

So the state is part of society more broadly, but in many modern societies, it assumes a directing role, coordinating key forms of collective action. In well-institutionalized states, nonstate actors do not declare wars, for example, or otherwise usurp the state's roles and functions. And when crises emerge, populations often turn to states, demanding that they address those crises and often holding them accountable if they do not. Societal actors can also attempt to remake aspects of the state itself. Democratic states institutionalize mechanisms that aim to allow for the regular and peaceful participation of the citizenry in coordinating state action. When this does not work, as we shall see in chapter 12, social movements, insurgencies, and even revolutions can emerge from society to constrain or transform the state and its activities. Many analysts believe, though, that revolutionary transformation is very rare in strong states, and in particular in strong democratic states.[15]

The quality, strength, and type of state are not the only important factors in this connection. Many scholars think that countries have different degrees and types of **civil society** with different organizations; networks of social actors; media; and customs and habits of organizing, talking, and meeting. Scholars do not all agree about how precisely to define civil society, but most use this term to mean something like a space relatively autonomous from state coercion within which people can deliberate and strategize about matters that have political implications. Organizationally, civil society can be thought of as housed in labor unions; in social clubs and other voluntary groups; in churches, mosques, and synagogues; and in many other such sites. From a networks perspective, we can see civil society as dependent on the existence of ties that are not fully embedded in the arms of the state. In other words, civil society depends on the possibility of lots of us being able to know and communicate with each other without those exchanges being predominantly coordinated (or limited) by state actors.

civil society A space in society outside of the organization of the state in which citizens come together and organize themselves.

These civil society organizations and networks allow groups of citizens to analyze politics and make claims on the state.[16] According to many scholars, strong civil society accompanies strong states with well-institutionalized democracies, but it is more problematic for authoritarian states, which will often seek to co-opt or even eliminate citizen activities of this sort.[17] This is intuitive: an authoritarian state's position is strengthened to the extent that potential rivals do not have the organizational capacity to challenge it. For this reason, many political scientists believe that proponents of democratization would do well to invest in civil society: for example, by subsidizing a diverse array of organizations or by trying to help lay the infrastructure for interpersonal networks to form. Moreover, this is not just a theory, but a policy that has been put in practice by many groups and organizations, including the (U.S.-government-funded) National Endowment for Democracy, the World Bank, and the United States Agency for International Development.

Other scholars take a different view, seeing "strong societies" as potential obstacles to the formation of strong states.[18] Why might this be so? Think again for a moment about the key characteristics of modern states described previously. States concentrate power, enforce laws, and distribute resources. As such, the creation of modern states almost always produces considerable struggle, particularly between state-builders and other actors who are relatively well off (in terms of power or other resources) in a pre-state or weak-state environment. Well-organized networks or clusters of actors in society can often resist state-building efforts by leveraging their power to avoid taxation, the full application of the rule of law, or the extension of rights and privileges to other groups. However, proponents of the view that civil society leads to stronger, more democratic states would argue that these sorts of groups are not what they mean by "civil society." This realization may lead us to develop our concept of civil society a bit further. Perhaps the concept applies only when there is a certain amount of openness. If isolated and exclusive organizations resist the state for the sake of their minority interests, perhaps that's not "civil society," which may be found only when participation and public deliberation is broad based and egalitarian.

In general, we could say that strong, democratic states tend to be relatively autonomous from civil society but nevertheless responsive to citizens. Paradoxically, many of the strongest states might be those that are self-limiting in a lot of key ways. Weak states are often simultaneously less autonomous and less responsive to the broader citizenry. Weak states do not necessarily refrain from intervening in economy and society: rather, they tend to intervene often but irregularly and unpredictably. And strong states sometimes help societies solve problems of collective action, providing "public goods" that would be impossible for individuals in large-scale societies to produce on their own.[19] Nonetheless, a debate continues about whether having a "strong society" that is influential and wields political power correlates with a "strong state" or a "weak state."[20]

Types

As noted earlier, states have many other characteristics besides exerting a monopoly on the legitimate use of force. In the discussion that follows, we focus first on several key characteristics of states and then on state functions.

Characteristics of Modern States

States are defined in part by characteristics such as a bureaucratic mode of organization, impersonality, and the claim of sovereignty. Here we discuss each of these in turn.

BUREAUCRACY

When you read the word *bureaucracy* you might think of the Department of Motor Vehicles (DMV) or maybe even one of the offices at the college or university where you are taking this course. There is a pretty good chance that the word does not conjure up images of efficiency, rationality, and precision but rather of frustration, delay, and inefficiency. Yet social scientists think of at least some bureaucracies as ideal—typically efficient and rational.

Organizations are **bureaucratic** when they have a rational, universally applicable system, administered on the basis of rules and by officeholders.[21] Bureaucracies are, in their ideal form, impersonal and transparent. In other words, in a well-functioning bureaucracy, those rules are available for all to see. Think about the DMV. There is a good chance that you, or at least people you know, have a driver's license and had to pass through bureaucratic channels to acquire it. Your receipt of your license was probably not dependent on, for example, who you are related to, the whims of

bureaucracy A form of organization that, in its ideal form, has individuals operating and working under established, specified, and complex rules.

your examiner, or the paying of a bribe. And you probably couldn't just go to your friend the mayor and ask that person to give you a license rather than dealing with the appropriate bureaucratic authority. Instead, there is a clearly stipulated set of rules governing who can and cannot receive licenses and also governing who can and cannot make judgments about who has satisfied the appropriate conditions. Of course, the individual who takes you out for your practice test has the ability to exercise a bit of personal judgment—perhaps you roll ever so slightly through a stop sign and he or she is feeling generous and lets it slide—but this personal judgment is sharply delimited: The examiner cannot declare that since you are so nice you get a special license that also allows you to fly a plane, for example.

Now, why would anyone want a bureaucratic system? Going to the DMV is notoriously painful and frustrating, and working there is probably not much better. Ironically, our common perception that bureaucracies are inefficient is partly a consequence of their working well. Granted, sometimes this perception is true—sometimes bureaucracies really are poorly run and inefficient—and even well-functioning bureaucracies will often lead to frustration. But the key issue is the ends or goals toward which bureaucracies are oriented. When we say that bureaucracies are efficient, we mean that they can be a highly efficient way to *coordinate behavior in pursuit of common projects*. Think of the military as an example. Wars are not conducted on the basis of the whims of individual troops but rather through their bureaucratically organized action. A well-functioning bureaucracy is like a system of levers linking a leader or group at the top of an organizational hierarchy to a large number of individual actors lower down (see Figure 3.1). Bureaucracies turn the people who hold offices into *instruments* for the realization of goals set higher up in the organization. If this mode of organizing collective action still seems inefficient to you, imagine administering a welfare program or a health care system, or waging a war, through non-bureaucratic channels.

Modern states are simply more bureaucratic than other, older, political organizations. This feature of modern states—combined with their unprecedented abilities to extract resources (in the form of taxes) from the populations subjected to their control—helps explain their efficacy and power. Note that states with less functional bureaucracies necessarily have far lower state capacity.

IMPERSONALITY

impersonality A quality attributed by some scholars to modern states, which are presumed to be less likely to be identified with the personalities of their leaders.

Modern states are also more **impersonal** than many other political organizations.[22] This feature is related to their bureaucratic character but not reducible to it. When we say that they are impersonal, we mean that they are not closely identified with the personality of an individual.

You might find this a bit confusing. Don't we pay an awful lot of attention to our presidents and prime ministers? And haven't there been some societies with modern states in which cults of personality center on individual dictators, such as Kim Jong-un of North Korea? Indeed, both of these things are true, and the impersonal character of the modern state is a matter of degree. Think of the difference, though, between the type of legitimacy accorded a president of the United States and that accorded a king in a premodern kingdom. Imagine what would happen if the President of the United States, for example, were to declare that the Constitution is just a manifestation of the President's will, or that the country is a personal possession. The point

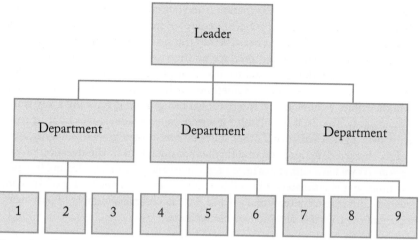

Figure 3.1 This is a simplified model of how a bureaucratic structure can achieve the coordination of complex tasks carried out by individual officeholders. Imagine that this organization's mission requires the coordinated performance of nine complex tasks. How difficult might it be to accomplish these tasks in the absence of bureaucratic organization?

is not that a modern state has never had such a leader but that such claims are rare and typically regarded as illegitimate.

This same impersonality is extended to the treatment of the general population. The ideal-typical modern state treats members of the population as **citizens**, meaning that it regards them as essentially equal in terms of their political role and rights. Modern states tend to offer fewer special privileges to individuals based on *who they are*. Of course, there are still elite cliques in modern states, and the mere fact that these states formally treat citizens impersonally does not eradicate preference or discrimination based on personal characteristics.

citizenship A form of relationship between the state and individuals subject to its control in which citizens have certain basic rights and are in some way represented in the state.

SOVEREIGNTY

The third key dimension of modern states that we consider here is **sovereignty**. The concept of sovereignty has several overlapping meanings. The two most important, though, are (1) sovereignty as the control over some territory and (2) sovereignty as the *source* of legitimate authority.[23] Of course, these two meanings are related, and they derive partly from the basic feature of the state—that it exerts a monopoly on the use of force.

sovereignty The key way the authority of the modern state is conceptualized: states are understood to be the ultimate authority within their specifically demarcated territories.

Historically, as states developed, the relationship between political organizations and territory changed in important ways. Before modern statehood, boundaries tended to be very permeable. For example, the Pyrenees Mountains (which separate France and Spain) were once a kind of informal division, a shared space across which people easily moved back and forth, blurring the differences between subjects of the French and Spanish kings. After the rise of modern states, however, the frontier was redefined as a formal boundary, and the population became fixed as citizens of either France or Spain.[24] Today, the boundaries between state territories are sharply delineated.

Related to this territorial distinction is the notion that the state holds ultimate authority within its territorial zone. States are sovereign not only because they can exercise constraining force but because they can act in other ways as well. They can tax, organize the citizenry, and produce a variety of public services. Territoriality is a key principle in doing so, and territorial disputes have been quite common in the history of the state system. Sometimes such disputes are settled by violence and other times by diplomacy. International recognition is typically a key feature of sovereignty. That is, it is difficult for a state to maintain claims about its sovereignty over a given territory if other states do not recognize its sovereignty.

This characteristic leads us to a further consideration of the question of what states *do*. As we have said, states have a tendency to acquire more roles and functions over time, so it is ultimately impossible to construct an exhaustive list of the state's activities. But in the contemporary world, we can observe a number of particularly important ones, several of which we discuss next.

Traditional Functions of States

States provide defense against external threats, police internal threats, tax their citizens, and document and sort populations, in addition to managing the economy. (We discuss additional key functions of modern states in the domain of political economy in chapter 4.)

DEFENSE

A first key function of states is the coordination of military action, ostensibly, at least, to protect the citizenry against potential foreign threat. As we shall see later, this feature of states, like taxation, was a key component in their emergence. Moreover, it is one of the most visible tasks of states. Modern states tend to have highly organized, bureaucratized, permanent military organizations. How the military is positioned within the state varies. As we shall see in later chapters, in some instances, military officials are key players in state decision making. In others, civilian control is well institutionalized.[25] This is often very important, because if civilian control is not well institutionalized, one often sees a higher incidence of coups d'état, and the political instability generated by such events can have important short- and long-run effects. Even in societies with relatively well-established civilian control of the army, however, the military remains a potentially important actor within most modern states.

POLICING

States do not just establish and maintain militaries for use in conducting foreign policy. They also establish organizations to police their societies internally. States that do this effectively have well-institutionalized rule of law and transparent judicial procedures.[26] Again, this characteristic of states is related to the core aspect of their definition discussed previously: policing is one of the key mechanisms through which the monopoly on force is maintained. Sometimes this role is shared with the military. For example, a number of states use national guards to provide internal security. More generally, the organizational and administrative arrangement of policing varies a lot, and how these functions are organized has much to do with how a country's specific political institutions are structured, as we discuss in later chapters.

CASE IN CONTEXT
The Mexican State and Rule of Law

PAGE 507

Mexico is a country that has had varying success in terms of state-building. In recent years, rule-of-law issues have been of special concern. The Mexican government has made an effort to crack down on organized crime, leading to high levels of violence. The causes of this violence, and the policies that might reduce it, are subject to much debate.

For more on rule of law in Mexico, see the case study in Part VI, pp. 507–508. As you read it, keep in mind the following questions:

1. Is Mexico really likely to become a "failed state," as some have worried, or is this fear hyperbole? Why or why not?
2. Does the United States play a role in Mexico's recent difficulties in maintaining rule of law? If so, how?

States also create and maintain systems of punishment linked to the police and judicial systems. Some states continue to use physically violent forms of punishment, such as the death penalty. States typically use incarceration as a key strategy, though they vary quite considerably in the frequency and extent of imprisonment. The United States, for example, incarcerates an astonishingly high percentage of its population, in relative terms.[27] States also vary considerably in the quality of their prison systems. Some scholars have emphasized the centrality of systems of policing and incarceration in creating the modern state.[28]

TAXATION

To perform the basic functions just discussed (defense and policing) among other responsibilities, states need money. Taxation is thus among the key roles of states. The state's very existence is dependent on taxation, and strong states tend to be those that tax their citizenry successfully and efficiently.[29] The reason is perhaps obvious: in many societies, at least, the state is not mainly in the business of producing goods for sale on the market, and therefore it is dependent on revenues generated by economic activity that takes place *outside* of the state.

Although funding their own activities is crucial for states, efficient taxation serves other purposes as well. States with high capacity often encourage citizens to feel that they are contributors to the state's collective projects via paying taxes. Without effective taxation, citizens may feel disconnected from the state, regarding it as an alien organizational force or seeing it simply as a distributor of resources. Of course, inefficient and arbitrary taxation—or taxation perceived to outweigh individual and collective benefits—can likewise generate alienation and opposition.

The processes through which the earliest modern states established systems of effective taxation were arduous and often violent. A number of early social and political revolutions were, at least in part, responses to centralizing states' efforts to extract more resources.[30] Today, many societies in the developing world continue to experience taxation difficulties, and the situation is often a catch-22: weak states have trouble taxing their citizenry, but they cannot become stronger until they do. These problems are sometimes exacerbated in developing states that are rich in natural resources. In such instances, leaders may avoid the political conflicts involved in trying to increase taxes because they can instead rely on revenues from exports of those resources. This situation, sometimes called the "resource curse," is seldom good for the long-term development of state *or* society.[31]

ORDER, ADMINISTRATION, AND "LEGIBILITY"

Modern states also carry out some less obvious ordering practices. Given the challenges of administering complex societies, most states gather considerable information about their territory and about their population. Both state and private actors invest heavily in maps and in the demarcation of different types of territory. For example, public lands might be administered by the state, private lands regulated, and other forms of land ownership (e.g., communal land ownership, in a number of historical and contemporary cases) transformed into one or the other. The use of private property is often subjected to considerable regulation. Sales and purchases of lands, houses, and businesses are tracked, and zoning laws proscribe certain uses of each.

States also go to great expense to learn about their populations. Public services are often contingent on government registration, and states often try to bestow services on some and withhold them from others (this includes access not just to the state's resources but, in the case of migrant populations, to its territory). In the process, various statuses (e.g., citizen, legal resident, migrant, and so forth) are bestowed on different individuals. Population surveys and censuses enumerate residents, document their characteristics, and sometimes even catalog their beliefs and values. Scholars like James Scott have referred to this as the process through which states render their populations "legible," by which they mean knowable and, as such, amenable to centralized administration.[32] Some scholars emphasize that these efforts to render populations "legible" sometimes lead to the creation and perpetuation of consequential social and political categories, for better and worse.[33] On one hand, being able to categorize and know about the populace may make it possible to deliver needed public services more efficiently. On the other hand, the process of viewing society through certain categories (which Scott called "seeing like a state") can lead to states micromanaging society in ways that are intrusive and counterproductive. A state that knows more about who people are (and where they are) may be more capable of serving them and their many needs, but it may also be more capable of controlling, defining, or even repressing them.

Causes and Effects: Why Did States Emerge and Expand?

In this section, we consider a core explanatory question about the rise of the modern state: why did states emerge in the first place and become the dominant form of political organization around the world? In other words, why do we live in a world dominated by states? In 1500, there were few if any strong states, and none that had the capabilities of contemporary states. Today, all large-scale societies *try* to have states, and therefore at least nominally do. This is perhaps the most important change in modern global politics and is in need of causal explanation.

Several major theories of the modern state concentrate on trying to explain the rise of states as such, while others seek to explain the rise of the **state system** and its global diffusion from early modern Europe to the rest of the world. We begin with the first set of theories, which include political/conflict theories, economic theories, and cultural theories of the state.

state system The condition that many of the most important actors in international relations are states, which can be understood as systemically linked to one another.

Political or Conflict Theories

Political or conflict theories of the state argue that the state's rise was a consequence of conflict. One set of such explanations, rooted in classical political theory, tries to explain the state as essentially a compromise between warring factions.[34] These theories tend to be abstract, and they may be influenced by their close linkage to political theories that aim to *justify* the state. You may have heard of Thomas Hobbes's idea that a strong state, manifested in "the sovereign," is needed to keep internal conflict at bay.[35] Some scholars see the state as having developed as a sort of predatory institution through which stronger actors asserted their dominance and extracted resources from others.[36] Some, in turn, focus on predation as a case of state failure: in these cases, what we need to explain in the rise of strong states is how predation is minimized or restrained.[37]

The authors of some of these theories of the state have tried to trace the actual historical development of the state as an organization. A much-cited version of this theory is the "**bellicist theory** of the state," which holds that states are created by war.[38] The core idea is that for states to rise, they have to figure out how to do three things. First, political administration must be at least partly centralized.

bellicist theory Theory associated with scholars such as Charles Tilly, who argued that interstate wars were decisive in the creation of the modern state.

The Arrival of Napoleon Bonaparte at Schloss Schönbrunn, engraved by Aubertin, c. 1820. According to conflict theories of the state, under certain conditions, war making can help states grow stronger. It encourages the state's ability to extract revenue, its ability to mobilize the population, and its capacity to exert the Weberian monopoly on legitimate force.

CASE IN CONTEXT
The State in France   PAGE 435

France was one of the earliest strong states in Europe and came to be the region's great power in the seventeenth century. Indeed, under the Bourbon kings in the seventeenth and eighteenth centuries, it was the foremost example of royal absolutism. As such, it figures prominently in many accounts of the state's rise. It is a central case in most of the major theories of the state's emergence discussed in this chapter.

For more on the French state, see the case study in Part VI, pp. 435–436. As you read it, keep in mind the following questions:

1. What would the bellicist theory say about French state formation?

2. What are some of the distinctive features of the state in France?

In the first states that emerged in Europe, this meant that feudalism had to go. Second, extraction of revenues from the underlying population must be dramatically enhanced. Administering a modern state costs lots of money, and until the state gets good at taxing its citizenry, it cannot do very much. Third, the state must develop the ability to mobilize the population in collective endeavors.

According to proponents of the bellicist theory, warfare is particularly useful for all three tasks, particularly once innovations in military technology changed conflict so as to make large armies necessary.[39] If frequent foreign warfare takes place, states need to increase their revenue generation and to mobilize important elements of their populations to win. The threat posed by total warfare also presumably helps to convince otherwise unwilling individuals to make these sorts of sacrifices. In the process, such warfare undermines the power of nonstate actors like a military nobility. In medieval Europe, where knights were the main combatants, the upper nobility's control of related resources ensured them great power. But military innovations like advanced archery and gunpowder "democratized" warfare in a certain sense, also rendering it far more costly, requiring large-scale collective efforts and revenue extraction.[40]

Essentially, the bellicist theory argues that warfare forges strong states. One of the virtues of the theory is that it seems able to account for the particular historical trajectory of Europe in the global comparative context. For many scholars, the fact that strong states developed first in Europe is a mystery, precisely because of the relative backwardness of Europe in preceding centuries when you compare it to great civilizations like China or the Islamic world.[41] Indeed, these other civilizations had developed complex, bureaucratic, imperial structures that in many respects looked like modern states. But according to the bellicist theory, the very dominance of these organizations helps explain why strong modern states did not first develop in Asia or the Middle East: These large empires did not face frequent interstate "total wars" against their rivals, though they did face plenty of conflicts. Europe's backwardness—the fact that it was internally divided with small, petty kingdoms endlessly fighting each other—meant that for several centuries, the forming European states were essentially constantly at war. As a result, according to this theory, they developed into powerful war-fighting machines, and their rulers

INSIGHTS | Coercion, Capital, and European States
by Charles Tilly

Tilly is the most famous exemplar of the bellicist theory of the state, as epitomized by his phrase from an earlier book: "War made the state and the state made war."[42] He explains why modern states replaced previous structures, as well as why the form of this change differed across cases. Tilly finds that warfare is the critical driver of state-building because war demands extraction of resources from the population and complex administrative systems. Modern state development took three forms. "Coercion-intensive" formation came in Russia, an agrarian society with little commercial development and little concentrated capital, where the Czars used coercion to force their population to fund wars by producing agricultural surplus. "Capital-intensive" state-building in the Netherlands and some Italian city-states came as monarchs borrowed funds from merchants and paid for mercenary armies. "Capitalized coercion" came in Britain and France and was based on capital accumulation in large towns like London and Paris, combined with large rural populations that could also be coerced to produce rents. According to Tilly, this last model produced the strongest modern states.[43] Competition eventually produced modern states in all of these cases because states proved better at fighting wars than other forms of government.

Charles Tilly, Coercion, Capital, and European States, AD 990–1992. *Oxford: Blackwell, 1992.*

effectively established the ability to tax and mobilize the population, marginalizing their rivals in the process. Some proponents of this theory have even used it to try to explain relatively weak state structures elsewhere. For example, one has argued that the allegedly weak states of Latin America may be due to the fact that Latin American states almost never fight foreign wars.[44] The theory has also been used to try to explain Africa's relatively weak states.[45]

Economic Theories

Economic theories of the state don't ignore the role of geopolitical conflict, but their proponents think that economic modernization is the fundamental cause of the rise of modern states. Karl Marx was an influential proponent of this idea. For Marx, the modern state simply represents the interests of the bourgeoisie, the owners of capital.[46] These capitalists create the state as an organization so that they can manipulate the circumstances that will maximize their profits, which ultimately, from this point of view, means exploiting labor. Of course the actual historical processes through which this happened, according to Marxist scholars, is more complex than this formulation suggests and requires understanding the specific mechanisms through which these changes happen in given places at given moments in time.

Not all proponents of economic theories of the state have a Marxist or left-wing perspective, however. Others see states as products of elite coalitions responding to new economic circumstances. From this point of view, the best way to explain the rise of any given state is to trace the process through which elite coalitions were formed and maintained. A good example is the work of North, Wallis, and Weingast (see the "Insights" box on *Violence and Social Orders*).

Critics of economic theories of the state note that they often treat the state merely as a reflection of underlying interests rather than an autonomous actor.[47] You might think about whether this criticism applies equally well to both Marxist and non-Marxist versions of this theory. And how might proponents of economic theories answer such criticisms?

Cultural Theories

Some scholars argue that structural factors like geopolitical conflict and economic change are not enough to explain the rise of states. For these scholars, we must include cultural factors such as changing beliefs and values in the explanation.[48] Among the most persuasive reasons for including such factors is the notion that state-building involved a dramatic disciplining in the daily life of individuals.[49] Could state-building really have been fully coerced from the center of society? Or, perhaps, did cultural changes increase people's willingness to do things like accept state scrutiny, pay taxes, comply with regulations, face periodic conscription, and accept more extensive policing?

How could such "cultural factors" have played a role in the rise of states? One possibility is that nationalism and national identity (discussed further in chapter 13) may have contributed to the willingness to accept these impositions in emerging states.[50] The core idea here is that national identity is closely bound to the state. If I consider myself a member of a nation, I might see the state as the expression of that nation, and I might accept its legitimacy. Moreover, nationalists might have been able to justify projects of state expansion on the grounds of national interest or national pride. A second idea is that religion might have played a role in early modern state formation. In particular, some scholars have argued that the rise of Calvinism was key to the success of early modern European state-building (see the "Insights" box on Gorski's *Disciplinary Revolution*).

We should note that few analysts of comparative politics view cultural factors such as religion or nationalism as the sole explanation for the emergence of states. These factors may, however, be critical, as they *interact* with the economic or political processes discussed previously.

INSIGHTS

Violence and Social Orders: A Conceptual Framework for Interpreting Recorded Human History
by Douglass North, John Wallis, and Barry Weingast

North, Wallis, and Weingast aim to explain the emergence of what they call "open access orders" versus "natural states." Open access orders are relatively democratic, with a powerful state, a well-established rule of law, and other rule-governed, autonomous organizations to which everyone in principle has access. "Natural states" are still personalized, with a weak rule of law and less autonomous organizations. Prior to the development of the modern state, "natural states" were the rule, as powerful landowners served their own material interests by forming and shifting alliances. Actors were constrained mainly by their power positions vis-à-vis competitors and the monarch. These authors argue that the rule of law and open access orders emerged when important coalitions had an interest in giving up their prerogatives in exchange for protection. Specifically, when elites judged that they would be better off with rights than with special privileges, open access orders were able to emerge.

Douglass North, John Wallis, and Barry Weingast, Violence and Social Orders: A Conceptual Framework for Interpreting Recorded Human History. *New York: Cambridge University Press, 2009.*

| INSIGHTS | The Disciplinary Revolution: Calvinism and the Rise of the State in Early Modern Europe |
| | *by Philip Gorski* |

Gorski argues that states develop not just because elites create organizations but also because populations become increasingly willing to follow their commands.[51] Gorski asks *why* anyone would be willing to accept the increasing *discipline* of life under a modern state.[52] He answers that Calvinism—an influential and austere form of Protestant Christianity—paved the way in Europe. Calvinists created "disciplined" societies of hard work, chaste sexual relationships, and systematic relief for the poor, among other things. Moreover, because political conflict became linked to religious conflict in the sixteenth and seventeenth centuries, early modern states often became partners in this endeavor. Not surprisingly, "disciplined" populations were easier to govern than populations with other cultural influences.[53] Calvinists were not the only religious actors to emphasize these modes of discipline, but they set the standard.

Philip Gorski, The Disciplinary Revolution: Calvinism and the Rise of the State in Early Modern Europe. *Chicago: University of Chicago Press, 2003.*

Indeed, all major theories of the state's emergence focus on both political/conflict and economic factors, and most ascribe at least some importance to culture. For example, even proponents of the bellicist theory note the importance of economic factors, and many proponents of economic theories of the state acknowledge that frequent warfare in early modern Europe played an important role in state-building projects there. As you will see in later chapters, theoretical advances in comparative politics are often made not by replacing old theories with completely new ones but by synthesizing existing theories, considering them against new evidence, and adding new dimensions or features to them.

Diffusion Theories

Not all theories of the state begin by trying to explain the rise of states in Western Europe. Indeed, some theories are more interested in explaining **diffusion**, or the global spread of the state as a form of organization. Why and how, these theories ask, did the state come to be the dominant way of doing politics *everywhere*?

diffusion The process through which a practice or idea spreads locally, nationally, and globally.

CASE IN CONTEXT

The State in the United Kingdom

PAGE 550

Some analysts see in early modern England one of the earliest strong states, and at least one major theorist sees the early formation of a modern English state in the late medieval era.[54] Others see in the United Kingdom a historically minimal state. Could both views be correct? If so, *how* could they both be correct? What circumstances might favor the juxtaposition of early state development with a relatively limited state?

For more on the state in the United Kingdom, see the case study in Part VI, pp. 550–551. As you read it, keep in mind the following questions:

1. What evidence is assembled by those who argue for strong, early state-formation in the United Kingdom?
2. Was the United Kingdom ever a fully absolutist state? Why or why not?

Of course, such theories are not incompatible with those that we have considered so far. Indeed, often they are based on implicit or even explicit answers to the prior question about the state's origins.

When a social or political form like the state appears to spread, there are at least three logical explanations. One is that its development is purely coincidental. Given the extent of the spread of the state, however, this seems unlikely. The second is that common underlying features present in all cases explain each individual case. For example, maybe over the course of the twentieth century—when many modern states were created—we merely saw a repeat of the same processes that had been witnessed in early modern Europe, such as increasing interstate warfare. But the evidence does not seem to fully fit this picture. A third logical possibility is that the spread of the state had *systemic* qualities.[55] In other words, there is some sort of international system through which it diffused globally. Here we will try to distinguish three basic models for how this might have happened. Note that these are not necessarily incompatible or mutually exclusive.

The first version of this theory has an affinity with the bellicist theory of the state's emergence. Once states are formed as war-making machines, we might expect them to rapidly out-compete rivals because of their skill in making war. Proponents of this sort of theory would point to the extent to which state forms were bound up with colonialism: the European states, over just a couple of centuries, extended political control over most of the world, bringing state forms of organization with them. Their military and technological capacity allowed them frequently to achieve relatively easy victories over civilizations that often judged them to be barbarians (not without justification, some would say).

Not all versions of this theory focus exclusively on the state's military prowess, however. Instead, some variations note that the state can produce social and economic gains that, in turn, reinforce it (see the "Insights" box on Spruyt's *Sovereign State and Its Competitors*).

The second version of this theory has a still greater affinity with economic theories of the state. This version says that states spread to serve the interests of the international capitalist class. Building on the Marxian idea that the state represents capital's interests, and Lenin's idea that capitalism turned to imperialism to protect itself from

CASE IN CONTEXT
What Is a Weak State, and Can It Be Changed? The Case of Nigeria   PAGE 521

One major state where boundaries were created by colonial powers is Nigeria, which is also perennially cited as a problematic or weak state. Some argue that state weakness in Nigeria is a consequence of oil, others that it is a function of ethnic and religious differences. Finally, some think state weakness there and elsewhere might be caused by the legacies of colonialism.

For more on the Nigerian state, see the case study in Part VI, pp. 521–522. As you read it, keep in mind the following questions:

1. Is colonialism responsible for Nigeria's relatively weak state?
2. What is the relationship between the state's strength, corruption, and economic development in Nigeria?

INSIGHTS   The Sovereign State and Its Competitors
by Hendrik Spruyt

Spruyt focuses on the development of states in early modern Europe, but his theory is about the spread of the state as an organizational form, and the resulting emergence of the *state system*. The state had several rival types of organizations, including the feudal order, city-states, and leagues of merchant cities like Germany's "Hanseatic League," yet the modern state survived while these other forms essentially disappeared. Why? Spruyt argues the state rose up as a product of both economic changes and political conflict. States became formidable fighting machines, so their relative success might be partly explained through a kind of "survival of the fittest," but Spruyt says this is not a sufficient explanation because other formations (such as city-states) were often as good at fighting wars. Rather, states did other things that helped them out-compete their rivals. In particular, states did things that were good for their long-term economic development, such as standardizing currencies and measures and establishing clearer territorial boundaries. Spruyt also notes that states won out in part by "mutual empowerment," as they preferred to deal with other states and encouraged the emergence of one another's organizational and institutional forms.

Hendrik Spruyt, The Sovereign State and Its Competitors. *Princeton: Princeton University Press, 1994*

internal "contradictions,"[56] proponents of this version argue that colonialism aimed to create new markets for European goods and also sources of raw materials and exploitable labor of certain kinds. From this point of view, colonial subjugation was one way to achieve capitalism's desired ends, but not the only one: Indeed, ongoing neocolonial exploitation can take place perfectly well via a division of core and peripheral states in the international system.[57]

Yet there is a third strategy in which some scholars try to explain the spread of the state, one that has more of an affinity with cultural theories of the state's emergence. Here the notion is that organizational forms like the state are themselves cultural phenomena or ideas, and that ideas about how organizations should be structured play an important role in determining the organizational forms adopted by others. **Organizations** in a given field very often take on the same or at least a very similar structure, a phenomenon known as **isomorphism**.[58] For example, it used to be that universities did not have specific registrar's offices, financial aid offices, and so forth, just like political organizations once did not have professional, standing armies. When organizational forms spread, there seem to be two main sources of their spread: efficiency with respect to the organization's chosen ends *and* fit with cultural models and expectations for how such organizations are *supposed* to be organized.[59] In the first case, a university might develop a registrar's office because increasing complexity requires an office to coordinate classrooms, meeting times, and so forth. In the second case, anyone who starts a university already "knows" that a university is "supposed to" have such an office: A cognitive map or template for the organization already exists. According to **world society theory** (sometimes called "world polity theory"), the state is very much like this: it became an institutionalized part of modern politics and is therefore replicated culturally even when causes that might have been operative in its initial emergence are not present.[60]

organization Institutionalized group such as a state, corporation, political party, social movement, or international body.

isomorphism In institutional theory, the quality that two or more organizations have by virtue of being structurally very similar.

world society theory A theory associated with scholars such as John Meyer who argue that basic organizational features of the state system are cultural and have diffused globally.

INSIGHTS

World Society and the Nation-State
by John Meyer, John Boli, George M. Thomas, and Francisco O. Ramírez

John Meyer and his co-authors are proponents of a "world society" or "world polity" theory focused on "cultural" factors. The "world society" school treats the spread of such organizations as not entirely coercive, pointing out that people in many societies willingly and even eagerly adopt existing models of the state. The authors propose a thought experiment. They tell us to imagine a new island society discovered by the global community. The society would, within just a couple of years of contact with the global order, likely define itself as a nation-state, establish a government, a currency, a taxation system, boundaries, provisions for its defense, and so forth. A thought experiment is not proof, but there is also empirical evidence in the overlap in structure between states and other national-level organizations and institutions. Global organizational norms are spread through several channels, including international organizations like the United Nations, the World Bank, and the International Monetary Fund, as well as NGOs (non-governmental organizations). Indeed, social science itself—including comparative politics—probably plays a role in these developments. When political scientists attempt to find ways to measure and combat corruption, for example, or even to define features of strong or successful states, they publicize their results and thus contribute to global organizational convergence when changes are implemented.

John Meyer, John Boli, George M. Thomas, and Francisco O. Ramírez, "World Society and the Nation-State," 1997. American Journal of Sociology, Vol. 103, No. 1, pp. 144–181.

THINKING COMPARATIVELY

Great Britain, the United Kingdom, or Neither? State and Nation in England and Scotland

KEY METHODOLOGICAL TOOL

Thinking through Case Studies

Political scientists use case studies for a variety of purposes. In later chapters, we will formally specify hypotheses and methods for testing against them, but here we begin by using a basic case study to think about general theories. In this example, we consider three of the major theories of state-building discussed in this chapter and ask what each would say about the development of the state (and nation) in the United Kingdom. Although all three theories seem capable of explaining the general outlines of this case, they are not necessarily equal. Political scientists concerned with these problems must come up with strategies to get leverage over the competing theories.

Perhaps the simplest tool in comparative politics is the single case study (often a country, as noted in chapter 2). Through this type of examination, we can gather information to develop hypotheses that cut across other cases. Case analysis can help us identify key mechanisms and define general relationships. Debates in comparative politics are seldom ended on the basis of a single case study, but this approach nonetheless has much to contribute. Here we will consider how looking at the single case of the United Kingdom (from England to Great Britain) might help us think about theories of state formation.

The island now known as Great Britain was long made up of distinct kingdoms (Map 3.1). For much of their political history, state-building projects were specific to these kingdoms. The most influential of these in political history has been England, which comprises a large share of the island's territory (with Wales to the west and Scotland to the north).

A number of scholars have considered the *English* state-building project to be a paradigmatic case. To some extent, the nobility's power to rule over the inhabitants of the countryside was curbed as early as the 800s; but with the Magna Carta of 1215, the crown also took on some limitations. After Henry VIII in the sixteenth century, the state was independent of the Roman Catholic Church, having separated from Rome and created its own church with the monarch at its head. Over the course of the seventeenth century, despite—and perhaps because of—civil conflict, parliamentary power grew, and nationalism and national identity were stoked. By the close of the century, a truly "constitutional monarchy" was established. Slowly,

England developed the characteristics of a full-fledged modern state: effective local administration developed[61] into a centralized bureaucracy, which resulted in a standing army and the authority to collect taxes regularly after 1688.[62] The country went through many fluctuations in royal power, but the rough balance of power between the crown and the parliament progressively shifted toward the latter.

England's political history merged into a single state with the other parts of the modern United Kingdom. At different stages, this took place in different ways.

THINKING COMPARATIVELY

(a)

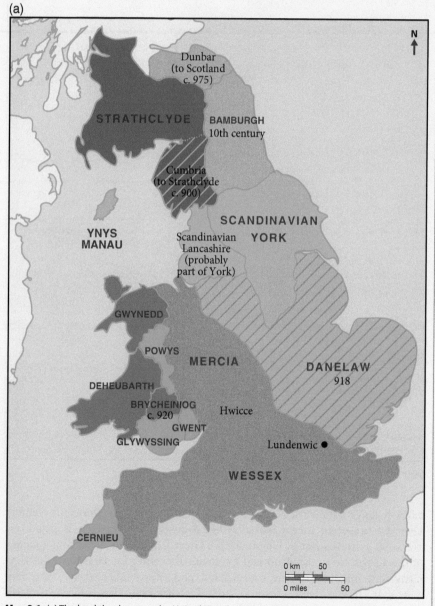

Map 3.1 (a) The land that became the United Kingdom, circa 900.

(b)

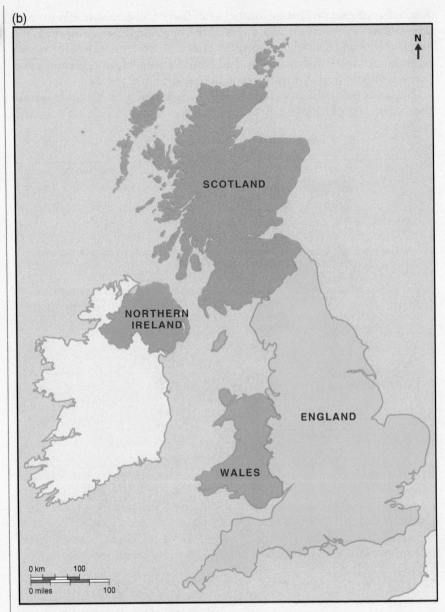

Map 3.1 (b) The United Kingdom today.

English kings conquered Wales and governed it from the thirteenth century. Dynastic ties often meant partially shared governance between England and Scotland. With the Act of Union (1707), Great Britain was born from a merger of the Kingdoms of England and Scotland. Thereafter (at least until our day), many state institutions were consolidated, and efforts undertaken—for a time seemingly successful—to create a "British" rather than "English" or "Scottish" national identity.[63] Interestingly, this does not mean that English or Scottish (or Welsh) identities disappeared. Rather, they co-existed with an overarching sense of Britishness, perhaps more in some regions than others. Meanwhile, over the course of centuries, Ireland had been, in good measure, incorporated by force; even after the secession of the Republic of Ireland in 1922, Northern Ireland remained part of the "United Kingdom of Great Britain and Northern Ireland."

We can find evidence in this case study for all of our major theories of state-building—bellicist, economic, and cultural. Let's consider briefly how each of these might view this single case:

THINKING COMPARATIVELY

Bellicist: In the early modern period, like the rest of Europe, the British Isles were often involved in interstate war. The imperatives of war and continental alliances meant that the state had to be prepared for conflict, which meant taxation and, as time went on, greater investment in the military.[64] There is little doubt that this military preparation contributed to state-building.

Economic: At the same time, the giving up of privileges in exchange for the rule of law (as analyzed by North, Wallis, and Weingast) probably saw its earliest expression in England. And it was Britain that, according to institutional economists, first saw the emergence of sustained economic growth. Proponents of the economic state-building theory argue that these developments were probably linked. They see state growth as a consequence of the extension of the rule of law, the protection of property, and the establishment of a well-functioning state.

Cultural: Both the culturalist theories focusing on Calvinism (Gorski) and nationalism (Greenfeld)[65] also find ample evidence in the English/British case. Calvinism in a variety of forms was influential there, and according to some, this case is one of the earliest instances of modern nationalism.

What should we make of this evidence? It shows us several things. First, it shows us what a case study can and cannot do. Typically in comparative politics, a case study cannot fully adjudicate between rival theories of general processes. In looking only at the United Kingdom, we will probably be unable to decide among the theories considered in this chapter. But this case also shows us that existing theories may be too simple. If all of the factors these theories emphasize are operative, we could use a new theory that addresses how those factors fit together. Thinking along these lines might help you create a better model of state- and nation-building in general.

Such questions are not just matters of historical interest. State- and nation-building might settle into equilibrium at various times, but they are not really static phenomena. Several decades ago many would have been skeptical that a strong Scottish independence movement would emerge, that a referendum would be held (as happened in September 2014, when 55 percent of voters chose to remain part of the United Kingdom), and that there would be talk of a possible written constitution for the United Kingdom as well as a distinct English Parliament. In the aftermath of the Brexit referendum in summer, 2016, questions about the future of both national identity and political representation in the United Kingdom seem more pressing than ever. It remains to be seen how these issues might be resolved, but there is no denying that both the state and the nation are in potential flux in the United Kingdom today. As you think about ongoing processes of nation- and state-building, consider whether the major comparative-historical theories discussed in this chapter have something to say to us about twenty-first-century politics.

Chapter Summary

Concepts

- The state is the most important form of political organization in modern politics and is characterized in ideal form by control of the use of force, bureaucratic organization, and the provision of public goods.
- The related ideas of the modern state, state capacity, and failed states are some of the core concepts in comparative politics.

Types

- Major features of modern states include bureaucracy, impersonality, and sovereignty.
- States are coordinators of collective projects, such as taxation, defense, and policing.

Causes and Effects

- Theories about why modern states emerge focus on political conflict, economics, culture, and processes of global diffusion.

Thinking Comparatively

- We considered some of the uses of the single "case study," noting that the case of the United Kingdom seems to offer some support for several of the major theories of state-building discussed in the chapter.

Thinking It Through

1. In the "Causes and Effects" section of this chapter, we considered the causes of state formation. Since the map of the world is now covered with states, do you think these theories are of purely historical interest? Or do they still matter today? Think in particular of countries recently in the news—such as Afghanistan, Iraq, Sudan, or Syria—where commentators and policymakers still talk about a need for "state-building." Do theories of state formation have any relevance today in those countries?

2. Test the theories of state formation considered here against your knowledge of U.S. history. Which of the theories seems to explain the formation of the American state best, and why? What were the major steps in state formation in the American state, and how well can each theory address these stages?

3. Consider whether you think the presence of a strong civil society will tend to make a state relatively strong or relatively weak, in the sense of the state being a powerful decision maker that affects lots of social and political activity. Do civil society and the state compete and divide a fixed amount of power, or do they reinforce each other, each making the other more powerful? Think of a case study that might help you examine this question.

4. Return to the opening paragraphs of this chapter, which discussed the possibility of the formation of new states in contemporary Western Europe. After reading the chapter, what do you now think about the likelihood of this happening? Ground your answer in the theories of state formation you have learned.

5. Many people agree that our world is rapidly "globalizing." This globalization can be economic; can involve social norms, customs, and institutions; or it can involve organized force (e.g., international organized crime, terrorist groups, and imperial powers). If the globalization of organized force gets carried very far, what implications, if any, might this have for the utility of the Weberian definition of the state? Would a radically (politically) globalized world be one in which new types of states were observed? Or would it be a world of weak states?

CHAPTER 4

Political Economy

Japan. Sharing tomorrow.

Published in November 2017

ABENOMICS

For future growth, for future generations, and for a future Japan that is robust.

"I will break down any and all walls looming ahead of the Japanese economy and map out a new trajectory for growth. This is precisely the mission of Abenomics."

— Prime Minister Shinzo Abe

JAPANGOV THE GOVERNMENT OF JAPAN

A booklet about "Abenomics," the approach to political economy pushed by Japanese Prime Minister Shinzo Abe. AP Images

The subject of this chapter is **political economy**, which can be loosely defined as the ways politics and economics interrelate and affect one another.[1] Our emphasis is on politics and public institutions that affect the economy, though we will also note ways that economic change affects politics. In chapter 5, we consider the political economy of so-called developing countries specifically (especially those in Africa, Asia, and Latin America), while the emphasis in this chapter is on what are sometimes called the "advanced, industrialized countries."

As a subject area, political economy has a rich heritage. You are probably reading this textbook for a course in a department called "political science," or possibly "politics," "government," or "international affairs." But two hundred years ago, the academic study of "political science" in its modern sense didn't really exist. Prominent philosophers and thinkers who considered questions of political organization and public action had another name for their area of study: *political economy*. Implicit in this name was the idea that politics and economics were deeply intertwined. To political thinkers of the eighteenth and nineteenth centuries, including Adam Smith and Karl Marx, what happened in the economy would affect politics in almost any country, and vice versa.

Later on, the disciplines of "politics" and "economics" became separate (along with sociology, among other fields), as the social sciences underwent a division of labor. Political scientists focused especially on issues such as the state (see chapter 3), types of governing regimes (chapters 6 and 7), and government institutions (chapters 8 through 11). Yet the study of politics has remained deeply concerned with questions about society and the economy. Many chapters in this text address these intertwined issues. Chapters 12 through 15, for instance, examine questions related to social institutions, identification, organization, and action. In this chapter, we explore the enduring linkages between politics and economics. Our particular emphasis here is on the political economy of so-called advanced, industrialized countries, such as those in most of Europe, plus other economically powerful countries such as Japan, Australia, Canada, and the United States.

. . .

IN THIS CHAPTER

THINKING COMPARATIVELY

CASES IN CONTEXT

United States • United Kingdom • Japan • Germany

political economy The interaction or interrelationship between politics and the economy in a given country or internationally, to include how politics affects economies and how economies affect politics.

Concepts

To better understand political economy, we should define several of the key measures and indicators that help characterize a country's economy. Which statistics can tell us something about its overall level—that is, its sophistication and advancement? Is it a large economy, is it wealthy on average, and how is wealth distributed? Apart from the level of a country's economy, how is it performing? A country may be rich and successful, but its economy may be declining and performing poorly, just as a country may be relatively poor but performing well. (We examine this question of performance in low-income countries more in chapter 5.)

The most common ways of measuring a country's economy involve the **gross domestic product (GDP)**, or similar measures such as **gross national income (GNI)**. Each of these provides a composite measure of a country's total economy but measures it slightly differently. GDP is the total market value of all goods and services produced within a country's borders, usually in a year's time. In other words, the gross domestic product is the total (or gross) amount of goods and services produced (i.e., the product) in a given country (hence, domestic) in a given year. GNI is the total income from all goods and services earned by a country's producers, regardless of where they operate. So a German company operating in India that earns profits would be counted in the GDP of India but in the GNI of Germany. We will refer to GDP as our most common basic measure of a country's economic activity.

We often wish to compare the average wealth of individuals in different countries, not just the total wealth of each country. Economists therefore turn to *per capita* measurements of GDP, which represent average income per person. Relatively wealthy countries (such as the United States, Japan, and many in Western Europe) may have annual GDP levels of $30,000 per capita or more, while the poorest

gross domestic product (GDP)
The total value of goods and services produced in a given country or territory; per capita GDP is divided by the population.

gross national income (GNI) A measure of the total income of all of a country's citizens, whether living in their home country or abroad.

CASE IN CONTEXT

Did Free Markets Help the United States Get Rich? Will They in the Future?

PAGE 566

The idea of economic strength has been important for many years in the United States. The country has had an extremely powerful and dynamic economy for some time, but now there is considerable worry and handwringing about the future of American economic performance. Income inequality has reached alarming heights, and a host of social indicators for some populations resemble those usually seen only in the "third world." There have been troubling declines in labor force participation, and the cost of living is prohibitively high in some places where "good jobs" are located. Though unemployment is now low at the time of this writing (in 2018), the economy did not recover quickly from the recession induced by the financial crisis of 2008. Finally, the U.S. government faces serious,

long-term fiscal problems. Perhaps even the "most developed" countries are never *fully* developed and continue to face development hurdles.

For more on political economy in the United States, see the case study in Part VI, pp. 566–567. As you read it, keep in mind the following questions:

1. In what sense should we think of the United States as a "developed" society? What does this case reveal to us about the notion of "development"?

2. What specific development dangers are likely to emerge in post-industrial societies? How, in cases like this, might aspects of development itself prove potentially risky for later-stage development?

countries have GDPs per capita of less than $500 per year, and "middle-income" countries are in the range of a few thousand dollars per year. One benefit of this approach is that it standardizes GDP across countries of different sizes, dividing production by the population size. Otherwise it would be very difficult to compare the economic performance of large and small countries.

The overall GDP and GDP per capita measure the overall size and income level of an economy, and *GDP growth* from year to year is the simplest measure of economic performance. Very high GDP growth, such as in China over the last twenty years, is in the neighborhood of 7 percent to 10 percent. Such rates of growth are possible in low-income countries that are starting from a low economic base, where many people are not employed to their full potential. In advanced, industrialized countries, however, which tend to be wealthier, 5 percent growth would be very strong, and a growth rate of about 3 percent a year or lower is more typical. Some countries also have negative GDP growth rates. This happens in times of recession in advanced economies, and it has happened frequently in poorer countries, such as many in Africa or, in recent years, Venezuela.

GDP is a simple concept, but the value of a person's income also depends on how much money can buy. That is, the cost of living matters. An income of $30,000 per year goes much further in a country where rent is $250 a month, and a week's groceries cost $50 than in a country where rent is $1,000 a month, and a week's groceries cost $200. Because prices are frequently lower in low-income countries, a dollar (or local currency) can go farther. The adjusted measure scholars often use is income based on **purchasing power parity (PPP).** In many instances, in countries where average incomes are very low (such as in Africa), a GDP/capita of about $400 may correspond to a GDP/capita at PPP of over $1,000. Conversely, in countries where prices are very high (such as Japan and Scandinavia), a GDP/capita may be *reduced* by adjusting for PPP; for instance, someone earning $50,000 in one of these countries may only be able to buy as much as an average person earning $40,000 in the United States (see Table 4.1).

purchasing power parity (PPP)
An adjustment made to income measures to account for differences in cost of living.

The measurement of economic performance may extend beyond the economic indicators discussed previously. Measures also include a range of social outcomes including such factors as standards of living, quality of life, and cultural change. The section on "Types" outlines several important ways of measuring development besides economic growth.

Inequality

Measures of income such as GDP do not provide much information about how income is distributed among people. An average GDP per capita of $30,000 can result in a country where half the people earn $60,000 and half earn nothing, or it can happen in a country where everyone earns $30,000 exactly. The first country would obviously have a more unequal distribution of income and would have half of its population in grave poverty. Measuring poverty and inequality is thus important to many who study development.

Income inequality measures how earnings are distributed. Some societies have incomes that are distributed very equally across people, while other countries have incomes that vary dramatically between different people. Imagine two societies. In the first, the average income for someone in the richest 10 percent is $150,000,

inequality In the social sciences, the differential distribution of access to goods like power, status, and material resources.

TABLE 4.1 **Economic Measures Around the World**

Country	GDP/Capita (2016) ($)	GDP Growth (2016) (%)	Consumer Inflation (2016) (%)	Absolute Poverty Rate*	Gini Index**
Brazil	8,649.9	−3.6	8.7	4.34	51.35
China	8,123.2	6.7	2.0	1.85	NA (estimated 33.97 in rural areas and 36.69 in urban areas)
France	36,855.0	1.2	0.2	0	32.26
Germany	41,936.1	1.9	0.5	0	31.39
India	1,709.4	7.1	4.9	21.23	35.15
Iran	4957.6 (2015)	−1.5 (2015)	8.6	0.25	38.78
Japan	38,894.5	1.0	-0.1	0.35	32.11
Mexico	8,201.3	2.3	2.8	3.04 (alternative estimate 5.65)	48.21 (alternative estimate 49.14)
Nigeria	2,178.0	−1.5	15.7	53.47	42.97
Russia	8,748.4	−0.2	7.0	0.02	37.73
South Korea	25,538.8	2.8	1.0	0.34	31.56
United Kingdom	39,899.4	1.8	0.6	0.24	34.07
United States	57,466.8	1.3	1.3	1.0	41.04

Sources: Columns 1–3, World Bank, World Bank Open Data (https://data.worldbank.org); columns 4–5, World Bank PovcalNet, (http://iresearch.worldbank.org/PovcalNet/home.aspx); accessed November 4, 2017.

*Note: Poverty rate is measured as percent of the population living on less than $1.90/day (PPP in 2011 dollars) in the most recent year for which data are available (ranging from 2008 for Japan to 2015 for Brazil and the Russian Federation).

**Note: Estimates for the Gini index are from most recent year for which data are available on the World Bank's PovcalNet site (ranging from 2008 for Japan to 2015 for Brazil and the Russian Federation).

and the average income for someone in the bottom 10 percent is $12,000. In the second, the average income for someone in the top 10 percent is less (say, $75,000), and the average income for someone in the bottom 10 percent is higher (say, $16,000). We might say the first country is more unequal because the ratio of the incomes between those at the top and those at the bottom is much larger.

To use specific examples, the United States has a more unequal distribution of income than the countries of Scandinavia. The most commonly used measure of inequality across an entire population is the **Gini coefficient,** which measures how much of a society's wealth or income is held by what percentage of the population. The number ranges between 0 and 1, with 0 being absolute equality with everyone

Gini coefficient The most common measure of income inequality in any given population, usually expressed as a number between 0 and 1, with 0 being total equality and 1 being maximal inequality.

A poor neighborhood, or favela, in Rio de Janeiro, Brazil. Notice the wealthier neighborhood off in the distance. Brazil has often been held up as an example of high income inequality.

having the same amount of wealth or income, and 1 being a scenario in which a single person owns all wealth.[2] Rough Gini coefficients can be calculated using deciles or quintiles of the population (each tenth or fifth). There are quicker measures of inequality one can calculate as well. As noted previously, one may simply examine the incomes of the top 10 percent versus the bottom 10 percent of the income range, for example. Inequality is a pressing concern in many countries, from the United States to Brazil. Information about Gini coefficients and other measures of inequality and economic performance of this sort can be easily found online. See, for example, the Human Development Reports provided by the United Nations.

Employment and Inflation

Other economic measures relate to how people experience the economy on a daily basis. **Employment** and **unemployment** are especially important because of their impact on people's well-being and on a country's overall economic health. Employment can be measured by the total number of jobs created or lost, or as a percentage of the population with or without paid employment. **Underemployment** is another factor being tracked, signifying the degree to which members of the labor force are employed less than they wish to be (e.g., part-time instead of full-time) or are in jobs "below their skill level." In many developing countries, analysts draw a distinction between formal and informal employment as well; and most consider formal employment preferable because it tends to offer more benefits, rights, and support. In developed economies, far fewer people are informally employed (say, as unofficial and unlicensed street vendors) than in much of the developing world.

    Inflation is a measure of how quickly prices are rising. Prices affect the cost of living, and people find it more difficult to plan for the future when they are uncertain what prices will be in the future. Inflation can ruin people's savings by

employment Ongoing, regular access to paid work.

unemployment The lack of ongoing, regular access to paid work.

underemployment When workers are employed less than they wish to be or below their skill level.

inflation Increase in the prices of goods and services.

making the amount they have saved worth less in terms of what it can buy. As a result, high levels of inflation have brought about the collapse of many regimes. In the worst cases, countries have slipped into **hyperinflation**, in which prices rise by as much as several thousand percent per year, or more. Conversely, **deflation** (or declining prices) is also a significant problem that arises in economic crises, as people stop buying to await lower prices in the future, and the values of homes and other assets decline. Finally, it is worth noting that inflation and employment, though distinct, are related in ways that you might find surprising. Indeed, central banks and other policymakers often face trade-offs when they try to keep both unemployment and inflation low. An emphasis on keeping inflation low at all costs is associated by many with higher levels of unemployment.

> **hyperinflation** Exceedingly high inflation, which dramatically erodes the value of money over time.

> **deflation** Decline in the prices of goods and services, often associated with depressions or serious slowdowns in economic activity.

Fiscal measures—that is, measures of the government's revenues and expenditures—of a country's economic health, such as total indebtedness, may also be taken as indicators of a country's economic well-being. In many circumstances, poor fiscal indicators will imply economic challenges in the future, as debts come due. By the same token, some argue that an excessive focus on fiscal balance sheets can hamper governments' ability to engage in countercyclical spending, evening out the business cycle and avoiding recessions. Indeed, one of the great debates of political economy pits those who favor fiscal conservatism and "Keynesians," who favor higher levels of government spending. This distinction often aligns with another that pits those who favor policies designed to reduce inflation with those who favor policies conducive to "full employment." As you can see, thinking about the indicators of a healthy political economy leads directly to what is probably the field's central debate, which concerns the role of the state in economic life.

> **fiscal measures** Measures of a government's revenues and/or expenditures.

Types

In this section, we will think about the respective roles of the market and the state in modern economies. We first look at market-led and state-led economies as two main types, and we consider the intellectual arguments for why each might enhance economic performance. We then consider the types of state activities in an economy.

Markets and States in Modern Economies

Perhaps the most meaningful way to consider the different types of political economies around the world is to think about how the role of the state plays out differently across countries. We addressed the concept of the state in chapter 3, focusing on how it originated and on the basic features of a functioning state, especially with respect to national defense and the administrative ordering of the polity. However, it is clear that modern states do far more in this day and age than simply exercise a "monopoly on the legitimate use of force in a given territory." In the process of governing in the modern world, states act in ways that affect the political economy. States provide a range of public services and public goods, perhaps with a view toward creating opportunities for the citizenry and toward protecting the vulnerable. Of course, the role of the state in the economy is limited in most countries. In modern economies, private actors (from individuals to corporations) play an important role, and many economic decisions are made not by governments but by these private actors.

Think about buying lunch from a sandwich shop. This is largely a private transaction. The government doesn't set the price of the sandwich (in most countries), although it may levy a tax on the sale of the sandwich. Rather, the seller sets the price based on a couple of considerations. One is the cost of making the sandwich, which factors in not only the cost of the ingredients but also the shop's rent and the sandwich maker's pay, for example. Another consideration is how much potential buyers might be willing to pay. In turn, the potential buyer has to decide whether a sandwich at a given price is worth it. (Maybe some days it is and other days not.) In general terms, we might call this a "market" transaction, even if it doesn't take place in an actual marketplace. We say this because the transaction is between two or more private actors, based on prices set by what a seller is willing to charge and a buyer is willing to pay.

Many people studying political economy would argue that a "market-based" economy relying on private actors is more efficient and will perform better than a "state-led" economy. For example, imagine the government mandated that an egg salad sandwich must be made in a particular way. The sandwich business's ability to meet buyers' preferences would be reduced, potentially resulting in reduced sales of sandwiches. On the other hand, many observers would note the important roles states play in making economies work and in promoting economic performance. If the government guarantees the contract between the sandwich shop owner and the bank, or helps the owner access capital, this may help the business and, indirectly, the customers. Political economists have different estimates of the relative merits of market-led and state-led economies' results.

MARKETS AND ECONOMIC PERFORMANCE

A central debate in political economy, then, in recent years has been over what should take the lead in promoting national economic advancement: private markets or the state. Which is more likely to foster development: governmental intervention in the economy, or freely functioning markets with no governmental intervention? Of course, a range of factors can condition how a country performs economically, ranging from geography, to how political institutions are organized, to technological advancements, to the strategies of businesses, to a range of cultural factors that may vary from one place to another. However, the most significant debate in political economy has to do with the role of the market and the role of the state in guiding economic decision making. We consider the idea that a country with a market-led economy will perform well and will follow that with a consideration of how an economy with significant state intervention might perform well.

A leading argument in political economy is that free markets are the basis for creating wealth. This argument has a long and fruitful history, famously beginning with Adam Smith's publication of *The Wealth of Nations* in 1776. The free-market perspective spawned the field of economics, whose modern school of market-oriented thought is nowadays often called **neoliberalism**. Smith's idea of the "invisible hand" offered the marvelous conclusion that through the individual efforts of people seeking only their own well-being, society as a whole is made better off. Society benefits not from generosity and kindness but from the economic efficiency and expansion that takes place when everyone pursues their own gain. This logic of market is expected to promote economic advancement within any given country,

neoliberalism An ideological tendency that favors liberal democracy and market-led development.

CASE IN CONTEXT
Political Economy of Britain

PAGE 551

The United Kingdom is one of the most interesting cases for the comparative analyst for several reasons. First, it was the first major industrializer and is considered to have been one of the first societies to establish a modern, growth-oriented economy. Second, it has developed over many centuries, moving from being a predominantly agrarian society to an industrial economy to a post-industrial one, so it allows us to ask long-term questions about such a sequence. Third, it was the country from which some of the leading theories of political economy we are considering here were first conceived and, to some extent, transformed into policy.

For more on development in the United Kingdom, see the case study in Part VI, pp. 551–552. As you read it, keep in mind the following questions:

1. Which major theories have been used in efforts to explain the economic development in the United Kingdom, and what are their strengths and limitations in relation to this case?

2. What does this case suggest about the relationship between the political economy of development and the social-scientific construction of *theories* of development?

and it also extends to the world economy as a whole, with the idea that free trade between countries makes all countries better off.[3]

Advocates of free-market economics are influential in policymaking today and argue that the "invisible hand" should operate largely unrestrained, without government interference. The proper role of government, in this logic, is largely to establish a rule of law that protects property rights and enforces contracts.[4] Beyond this, the theory is that government should leave most economic activity to the market.[5] This means that government should not be doing things such as creating and financing companies, running factories, or setting wages. Where government has been doing these things, the pro-market perspective holds that economic activity should undergo **privatization**, or transfer of control from public to private. Such a pro-market perspective has informed policy recommendations to developing countries for many years, as we discuss in chapter 5.

privatization Transfer of control (of a business, industry, or service) from public to private.

The argument in favor of markets is that markets promote economic well-being, and also that states do not. Neoliberal economists commonly hold that government intervention in the economy results in inefficiencies and losses to society as a whole. They argue that this is because only markets are able to coordinate complex information about values and goods that state planners simply cannot master.

"Public choice theory" supplements these arguments by characterizing public officials as self-interested actors who often get in the way of markets. Public officials may claim they promote the public good, but they are human beings, all with their own self-interests, their own agendas, and their own failings. Just because someone chooses to go into public service does not mean they will truly be willing to set aside their own needs for the good of the people. One founder of this school of thought called this view of public service "politics without romance."[6] To begin with, public officials are susceptible to bribery, influence peddling, and corruption. Even in the absence of outright corruption, public officials will typically focus first and foremost on their own incentives. Elected officials will look to the next election, and appointed bureaucrats will look to move up the career ladder. They all will try to maximize their

The Australian Stock Exchange. "Markets" in large-scale industrial and post-industrial economies are often highly complex phenomena, difficult even for experts to understand.

own power and influence, often at the expense of the public they are nominally serving, and giving officials authoritative control over economic resources will lead to poor outcomes. Governments can be expected to "fail," with damaging results.

Neoliberal approaches lead to a relatively clear set of policy recommendations, many of which center on "getting the state out" of the economy. They also have the powerful backing of many in the highly reputed field of economics. This contributes to the wide adoption of market-led approaches to development, in countries ranging from the United States to Poland to Chile.

STATES AND ECONOMIC PERFORMANCE

As a central institution in public life, the state takes a very active role in the economy in many countries. Whereas free-market theorists expect this activity to lead to

---

INSIGHTS | Capitalism and Freedom
by Milton Friedman

Milton Friedman was arguably the leading academic proponent of free-market economics in the twentieth century. Friedman was a Nobel Laureate based mainly at the University of Chicago. Friedman's prominence was reflected in his leadership of the "Chicago School" of economic thought and in his influence on prominent public officials. Friedman argued that government intervention—other than in a few limited areas—generally had unintended negative consequences for economic growth. In the 1980s, the thinking of scholars such as Friedman influenced the policies of President Ronald Reagan in America and Prime Minister Margaret Thatcher in Britain. A bit earlier, in the 1970s, a market-based economic strategy for a developing country was implemented by the dictatorial regime in Chile, whose economists had been trained at Chicago under Friedman and who came to be called the "Chicago Boys."

Milton Friedman, Capitalism and Freedom. *Chicago: University of Chicago Press, 1962.*

economic decline and poor performance, other scholars argue that state intervention can be instrumental in supporting good economic outcomes. Proponents of **state interventionism** hold that markets are unlikely to generate national wealth on their own. According to this argument, where states function well, they have an ability to coordinate the behavior of various economic actors, stimulate needed investment, and promote human capital and advanced industrial production. Many state policies can promote successful industry. These policies may include various ways of protecting local businesses from foreign competition,

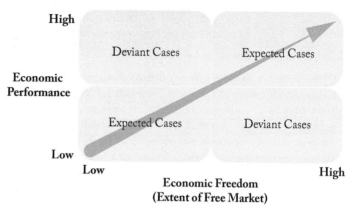

Figure 4.1 Markets and Development: A Prediction from Neoliberalism

especially in the early stages of development when a country is trying to build up its "infant industries." They may also involve direct state investment in important industries (such as steel), or incentives or advantages provided to private businesses (such as low-interest loans to build factories). Governments may also actively intervene to make their currency cheaper and their exports thus more desirable to foreign consumers; as any American who has bought inexpensive Chinese goods at Wal-Mart can attest, this policy has been used successfully by several countries at their early stages of development.

Advocacy for state interventionism in **economic management** grew in the twentieth century, with governments taking on much larger economic roles than they previously had. Around the mid to late 1800s, European countries such as Germany and Italy unified and consolidated into nation-states. Some new government roles came in terms of social welfare provision. A landmark change was the establishment of social insurance programs (such as a state-supported old-age pension and disability insurance) in Germany under Chancellor Otto von Bismarck in the late 1800s (see "Case in Context" box). Soon thereafter, the world went through major events that led to increased central state power: countries mobilized militaries in the lead-up to the horrors of World War I (1914–1918), and the subsequent Great Depression (mainly in the 1930s) gave rise to much more active state involvement in the economy. Pushes for more government involvement in economic and social life ranged from Franklin Roosevelt's New Deal in the United States (which included the establishment of the pension program known as Social Security) to Adolf Hitler's National Socialism (Nazism) in Germany, to the collectivization of economic activity and centralization of economic decision making of the Soviet Union. Each of these resulted in states that took on larger roles in societies and their economies, in very different ways that ranged from simply increased social services in liberal democracies to state-dominated overhauls of the economy in totalitarian systems.

As states took on more prominent roles in the economy, a major debate emerged about the best institutions to promote economic performance, with views reflecting the pro-market and pro-state perspectives noted previously. To represent this debate, consider Table 4.2. As Table 4.2 shows, the statist argument is not simply the opposite of neoliberalism or market-led approaches. The neoliberal

state interventionism An approach to economic management in which the state plays a central role, not just through enforcing contracts and property rights but through active interventions such as coordinating investment, supplying credit, and, in many instances, through the establishment and running of state-owned enterprises.

economic management States' efforts to shape the economic performance of their societies, especially in fiscal and monetary policy.

INSIGHTS	Embedded Autonomy: States and Industrial Transformation
	by Peter Evans

Evans looked at countries with very different states, many of which were developing countries. These included South Korea, Brazil, Zaire (now Democratic Republic of Congo), as well as India. Considering the first three countries, Zaire supported the pessimistic view of state action offered by public choice theorists: the state was staffed with self-interested actors, and individual interests took precedence over public interests. On the other hand, South Korea (like Japan) had a state with very different structures and personnel with different networks and work expectations. The South Korean state successfully collaborated with industry while still remaining independent of interest groups. They did so by supporting selected companies

that met targets for promoting industry and development. Brazil was "in between" these two cases, with a state that had some segments acting like South Korea's (such as the effective bureaucracies that promoted heavy industries) and some segments acting like those in Zaire. Evans attributes the performance of the three countries in industrialization—South Korea at the top and Zaire at the bottom, with Brazil in between—to these variations in the state. These issues of the role of the state in developing countries receive further treatment in chapter 5 on the topic of development.

Peter Evans, Embedded Autonomy: States and Industrial Transformation. *Princeton, NJ: Princeton University Press, 1995.*

approach generally expects states to hinder economic performance where they intervene, but statism does not expect states to promote the economy in every possible way. Rather, success depends on the *quality* of states and the decisions they make. Actions by states may promote or may hinder the economy, depending on whether the state is strong or weak and makes good or bad decisions. In chapter 5, we will see that this argument has continued application to developing countries when considering regions such as East Asia (note South Korea in Table 4.2) and much of Africa. In considering the evidence in Table 4.2, we put a question mark by the United States and list it as possible evidence for both the pro-market and pro-state arguments. To see why, consider the "Cases in Context" box on the United States and its political economy: you may think of the United States as the paragon of market economics, but it is not clear that this was always so.

TABLE 4.2 The Market–State Debate: An Overview

Perspective	Market	State
Does policy matter?	Yes	Yes
What causes economic success?	Free markets	Strong states/Quality state interventions
What causes poor performance?	Too much state involvement	Weak or low-quality state/Poor state interventions
Testing the Theory: What countries provide good evidence?	United Kingdom United States?	South Korea United States?
Testing the Theory: Why has China been successful? (see chapter 5)	After 1979, opening up to the market has led to economic success.	Even after 1979, strong state remains active in managing economy.
Main Policy Recommendation	*Reduce* the size of the state and its role in economy.	*Build* the capacity of the state to intervene well.

Social scientists increasingly recognize that both the market and the state can play important roles in promoting and facilitating economic performance.

Especially since the collapse of global communism at the end of the Cold War, most would argue that economies are best built on the principles of private property and through the use of markets to set most prices and allocate many resources. At the same time, there is also substantial agreement that states are needed to provide some **public goods**—ranging from law and order to defense to public health and other investments in human capital and physical infrastructure—that may not be provided by the market. States are also presumed necessary to correct certain market failures and to protect the most vulnerable. They must provide a positive environment in which individuals and private enterprise will have incentives to invest in themselves and in their society over the long run. Despite some consensus, the market–state debate rages, renewed by changing events and challenges to existing interpretations and existing evidence. We might find some role for both markets and states, and some scholars attribute successful development to a proper balance between the two. This logic extends to contemporary developing countries, as discussed in chapter 5.

public goods Goods or services, often provided by a government, for use by all members of a society and for which one person's use of the good does not compromise anyone else's use of the good. Examples include national defense, basic infrastructure, and a healthy environment.

Economic Functions of Modern States

Having explored the key conceptual distinction between market economies and statist economies (while acknowledging that most countries blend elements of both), we turn now to consider some specific roles states play in modern political economies: states commonly engage in economic management, invest in human capital, and build infrastructure. They also intervene in the economy to support those who might be vulnerable, such as the poor, or the elderly who may no longer be able to engage in as much economically productive work. This last category of state action can be called the provision of welfare state services, efforts to ensure a degree of social well-being.

STATES AND ECONOMIC MANAGEMENT

Citizens also typically hold their states responsible for economic management. This does not mean that all modern states play the same economic role: some states intervene greatly in the economy, holding ownership of firms in key economic sectors, for example, while others intervene less. However, even the least interventionist states participate in considerable economic management. Typically, poor economic performance on the part of a *government* leads to declining legitimacy. Sustained and extraordinarily poor economic performance can undermine the state itself.

States endeavor to manage the economy in several main ways. As we mentioned, some take ownership of key industries. Additionally, all states regulate the economy, though the extent and form of regulation vary. They perform basic functions such as enforcing contracts. They establish and enforce rules about the banking system, helping structure the ways in which capital is accumulated and invested. States create rules that govern labor and its contractual relationships with employers, codifying rules about strikes, collective bargaining, and minimal conditions: such as safety protections, work hours, and, in some cases, wages. States also often regulate commercial products: for example, a number of states regulate the nature of advertising claims, ban toxic products such as lead paint, and impose controls on pollution from factories.

Equally important, modern states carry out economic management through attempts to influence the business cycle. States try to engender economic growth and to avoid or at least mitigate periodic economic downturns. The two main tools states have in this connection are fiscal policy and monetary policy.

Fiscal policy essentially involves taxing and spending. States can attempt to produce economic growth during downturns by increasing their spending (or by cutting certain taxes), which essentially adds to existing demand in the economy. This practice is often called fiscal stimulus or countercyclical spending because it aims to counter the business cycle, evening out economic performance and producing steady growth over time. Also important to fiscal policy is the management of the state's balance sheets: a certain amount of debt is normal, but excessive debt can produce crises that can threaten economic performance and the political viability of regimes holding power.

Monetary policy involves the government's efforts to shape how much money is in circulation and the value of a state's currency. Governments have a variety of specific tools that help manage how the prices of goods and services rise and fall. Some states will try to reduce the value of their currency in relation to other countries' because this policy will favor their exports. Others will aim to establish and maintain a strong currency. Inflation (or rising prices) and deflation (or falling prices) are frequent worries; and although governments cannot completely control the rising and falling value of prices and currencies, modern states are typically considered responsible for this sort of economic management.

fiscal policy Budget setting, which is dependent on generating revenue followed by government spending.

monetary policy States' efforts to shape the value of a society's currency, often through the use of a central bank in the case of a modern state.

INVESTMENTS IN HUMAN CAPITAL: EDUCATION AND HEALTH

As mentioned previously, the modern state has periodically taken on new roles over the course of its history. One such role is coordinating the provision of

A public school classroom in Myanmar. States do not just make wars and police their territories, but they also provide numerous public services like education.

education, public health, and other investments in human capital. Of course, education is in some societies provided partly by private organizations; but even in such instances, the state is usually involved, through regulation and often through subsidies. Public education has really existed only over the last couple of centuries, and some states still have difficulty providing it.

Historical research shows that states initially endeavored to use public education to help create citizens.[7] This is still an important function of educational systems, which teach people about the rights and duties attached to their status as members of the society subject to the state's authority. Above all, though, policymakers view education as a way for a state to enhance the long-run global economic competitiveness of its society. An educated workforce has more skills than an uneducated one, and as a result becomes more attractive to prospective employers. Higher education has expanded globally as states have developed; and states often heavily subsidize higher education, both because they hope to educate their workforce and because they view institutions of higher education as sources of technological innovation that they hope will be economically beneficial.

The modern state is also held responsible for many aspects of public health, such as coordinating and regulating vaccination, overseeing food distribution and safety, and managing infectious diseases. Indeed, the expansion of state-managed public health, along with economic growth, has produced the lion's share of global health advances in recent years, including rising life expectancies and declining rates of infant mortality. States in most advanced industrial or post-industrial societies often aim to take on for themselves the task of paying for health care services, or at least contributing to this effort. Many developing countries, too, have established public health care systems, though the quality and reach of these programs vary considerably. States have come to provide these services because important constituencies have demanded that they do so, bolstered by the expanding perception over several decades that this is simply part of what states do. At the same time, as with education, these initiatives can be viewed as the state's investment in human capital. Healthier populations tend to be more productive as labor forces and to possess higher skills. Even something as simple as ensuring that children have a healthy diet can potentially produce long-term gains.

CASE IN CONTEXT
State-Led Development in Japan

PAGE 493

Japan's modern state began to develop in the late nineteenth century and grew in the twentieth, alongside the country's rapid economic development. For this reason, it is often cited as a rapid modernizer. This case also shows that states can play a key role in successful economic performance, as we discuss further in chapter 5.

For more on the state in Japan, see the case study in Part VI, p. 493. As you read it, keep in mind the following questions:

1. How, historically, has the Japanese state been involved in the economy?
2. How has this involvement changed in recent years?

INFRASTRUCTURE AND OTHER PUBLIC GOODS

States are also typically responsible for the establishment and maintenance of a variety of forms of infrastructure of common life. States license and regulate media infrastructure, controlling, for example, radio, television, phone, and Internet systems. States typically create and maintain civil engineering infrastructure as well, particularly highways. They are also often involved in at least the regulation and often the administration of ports and airports; and many play a role in the establishment and maintenance of rail systems as well. These things matter a lot, and not just because of the convenience afforded private citizens by having functional highways, railways, and airports. Commerce depends on reliable and efficient transportation; and states that neglect investment in these areas often handicap their societies' economic performance, and, therefore, ultimately their own strength.

As with all of these typical activities of states, there is considerable variation in the style and level of a state's involvement. Some states centrally plan the construction and maintenance of infrastructure and ensure that these activities remain 100 percent public (which means carried out and controlled by the state). Others aim to work via partnerships with private contractors: A state may allow a private firm to maintain a toll highway or a rail system, the firm generating its own revenues by charging consumers for services, or a state may indeed hire an outside firm to provide some such service. There are major philosophical differences about the degree to which services like education, transportation infrastructure, health care delivery, and even prisons should be "public" or "private." These concerns link to broader debates about the future of the welfare state mentioned earlier. Over the course of the twentieth century, the advanced industrial and post-industrial state came to be one that robustly served the roles we have discussed in this section, one that did so while aiming to reduce inequality, defend workers' rights, and ensure a minimal standard of living, all while maintaining a mixed capitalist economy.

WELFARE STATE FUNCTIONS

In the period after the Second World War, advanced industrial societies converged, to some extent, on the idea that the state should serve certain broad economic and social functions, and they were to some extent followed in this, where possible, by developing-world states. The model that was constructed is often referred to as the **welfare state**, meaning that the state should have as a key task the maintenance of its population's welfare. As we shall see in the "Causes and Effects" section in this chapter, scholars try to explain the development of the state's expanding role in a variety of ways. Before exploring the reasons behind the emergence of the welfare state, we note what some of the basic functions of welfare states are.

While welfare states do many different things, their key tasks include providing social insurance or pensions that protect the elderly and disabled, unemployment insurance that protects those who cannot find work, and health care for their citizens. They vary widely in their ambition in this respect, and in their efficacy. Some would argue that the United States has shown a more modest commitment to the welfare state model, whereas the Scandinavian countries are often held up as exemplars of strong and successful commitment to welfare state goals. We would

welfare state A state that aims to provide a basic safety net for the most vulnerable elements of its population, often accomplished through social insurance, public health care plans, and poverty relief.

stress that all welfare states provide benefits to a range of citizens and residents, not just the poor. In the United States, for example, societal members are eligible for Social Security and Medicare. Also key to most welfare states is the idea that citizens are entitled to certain basic *social* rights that go beyond narrow political freedoms. As you can see, welfare state functions were marked departures from modern states' historical roles in the period of their early formation, which were more centered on war making and internal policing (though the state's effort to manage the economy goes back a long way).[8]

Although most advanced industrial and post-industrial societies have welfare states, this should not lead us to suppose that they are all the same. Indeed, they vary in terms of how they collect most of their taxes, how much tax they collect, and the extent and form of their social spending. Today some argue that the welfare state is in crisis. At least since the 1980s, it has been subjected to the critique that it is inefficient and not well suited to the competitive environment of today's global economy. Indeed, many welfare states currently face fiscal difficulties, in part because of demographic trends. As "Baby Boomers" age, social insurance and health care provision will grow more costly. On the other hand, supporters of welfare states point out that these fiscal problems have often been exacerbated or even caused by tax cuts and other actions carried out by the welfare state's opponents. It would not be an exaggeration to say that the question of what will happen to the welfare state will be one of the most important issues in global politics in the coming years.

Causes and Effects: Why Do Welfare States Emerge?

One of the leading questions raised in this chapter is "What explains economic performance?," with the role of the market and that of the state being important hypotheses to explain variations in outcomes across countries. This hypothesis shapes the debate in both advanced, industrial economies (the subject of this chapter) and lower-income, developing countries (the subject of chapter 5). We address these hypotheses in chapter 5 on development. As a result, we turn now to another important (and related) question about the political economy in advanced, industrialized societies: *Why are states as economically active as they are?* In a sense, this section bridges the various discussions about the state and the economy, as seen in the key causal question in chapter 3 (Why did states emerge?) to the key causal question in chapter 5 (Why do economies perform as they have?). We ask here why states have gone from having been relatively minimal economic actors in the nineteenth century to having larger roles as more robust "welfare states" in the world's most advanced economies in the twenty-first century.

As we noted earlier, the modern welfare state began to develop in the nineteenth century, when a number of states, notably France and Germany, experimented with "social insurance."[9] The major causal question we address here is why the economic functions of the state have changed over time. In particular, we consider the expansion of the state's role in regulating or even providing for the welfare of its citizens. In other words, why have states increasingly taken on tasks like

CASE IN CONTEXT
The German State: Unification and Welfare
PAGE 451

Germany is a country of perennial interest to political scientists, among other reasons because it achieved political unification only in the late nineteenth century and shortly thereafter began to develop some limited welfare state functions. Its process of change was thus highly compressed. Whereas some other modern states existed as such for decades or even centuries before coming to take on welfare state functions, Germany did so only very briefly.

For more on the German state, see the case study in Part VI, pp. 451–452. As you read it, keep in mind the following questions:

1. What, if anything, is the relationship between Germany's later unification and its early partial welfare state development?
2. Why did the conservative Bismarck adopt welfare functions for the German state?

providing health care, social insurance, and other social safety-net features over the course of decades?

Note that this question should not imply that all movement is in one direction on this issue. Countries have often moved toward reducing the role of the state in providing social welfare services. Prominent examples include the United Kingdom under Margaret Thatcher in the 1980s and the former Communist countries of Central and Eastern Europe after 1989. Nonetheless, a major research question has been why states have generally gone from entities with limited economic functions to ones that have larger roles over time. To address this question, we look at several prominent theories about the emergence of welfare states.

Cultural Changes

Some scholars have argued that welfare states emerge because of changing values and norms.[10] From this point of view, earlier states did not develop a social safety net because nobody really wanted them to. One can argue that this is because other institutions were regarded as more suitable to the provision of welfare: for example, religious organizations or workhouses before the late nineteenth century. Another argument is that something in the post-Enlightenment world made people start to think that formerly intractable social problems could be solved and that the state should play a role in solving them.[11] One classic theory of the welfare state focuses on changing ideas of *citizenship* in this connection, as argued most influentially by T. H. Marshall.

Industrial Capitalism

Another important theory, though, has been that industrial capitalism creates welfare states. This makes sense, given that the welfare state is typically described as a state that responds to problems produced by capitalist development. Industrial capitalism has, without doubt, led to massive economic growth, but it has also generated social and economic changes that have proved dislocating to many people and many societies. At a very fundamental level, capitalist societies (with their more advanced economies) have more complex divisions of labor in the economy. For example, a few centuries ago, the vast majority of working people in the world were farmers, but today in the industrialized nations only a small fraction work in agriculture. This economic change—however much opportunity and growth it brought—disrupted long-standing social institutions. Thus, in "traditional" agrarian societies, families played many roles in providing what we may think of today as government social services: support to the elderly and some form of education to the young (with the latter often coming in the form of experience in farming practices or a trade learned from a family member or close associate). Meanwhile, religious institutions and norms about charity or almsgiving would have been the primary means of providing protection to the unfortunate in some places; self-organized mutual-aid associations and community institutions might have supported the indigent, rather than the state. In more complex economies, as the prospects for growth took off, things changed: more people went to factories or offices to work, families became more nuclear, and so on. In this process, institutions such as the family and the church lost some of their roles to a state that emerged as an important agent in managing the complexity of the economy. In this general sense, capitalism and the attendant complexity of modern society may itself account for the rise of the welfare state.

There are several very distinct theories about how capitalism leads to welfare states. Some are more Marxist and emphasize a *critique* of capitalism. Some of these theories see the welfare state as essentially reactionary. Marx thought that capitalism would inevitably undermine itself because it would produce larger groups of impoverished suffering workers who would eventually overthrow the state. However, some Marxists argue that welfare states involved the co-optation of workers by the state and the owners of capital, such that "immiseration" did not proceed as Marx had predicted. In general, the position most closely associated with Marx on these questions has been that the welfare state as such cannot, in the end, do away with exploitation, which can only happen with a revolution.[12] At the same time, though, many self-described Marxists and others on the left have been strong proponents of expanding the welfare state on humanitarian grounds.

Scholars with a different ideological orientation have seen a very different causal relationship between capitalism and the welfare state. Those who lean more to the right have tended to view the welfare state not as a bulwark against socialist revolution, but as creeping socialism itself.[13] From this point of view, in societies outside the orbit of the Soviet Union, proponents of socialism have needed to use the institutions of democratic society to achieve their aims. The welfare state is, from this point of view, the creation of social actors disaffected with capitalism and who would end capitalist development if they could.

Finally, another view holds that the welfare state is neither capitalism's effort to save itself nor the work of its enemies but rather a response to the social dislocations that industrialization generates. Perhaps it would be better to think of this position as a range of possible theories or views holding as follows: industrial capitalism is indeed central to the development of the welfare state, but this is not a simple story either of capitalism's co-optation of the poor or of the poor's co-optation of capitalism. Rather, some scholars argue that industrial capitalism more generally produced such dramatic changes that a new sense of order was needed.

INSIGHTS — Capitalism, Socialism, and Democracy
by Joseph Schumpeter

Schumpeter, an iconoclastic economist, agreed with Marx that capitalism would inevitably undermine itself. However, he thought this would happen in a very different way than Marx had forecast. Schumpeter regarded the essence of capitalism as residing in the entrepreneurial activity of capitalists. Progress is made because of the "creative destruction" that such activity unleashes as old modes of economic activity are replaced by productivity-enhancing new ones. However, according to Schumpeter, this could not last indefinitely because capitalism is so successful that it generates powerful social actors who are interested in undermining it. Intellectuals in particular, he argued, would seek to reduce inequality of condition as a way of satisfying their envy of society's allegedly most productive members. From this point of view, the welfare state is a key mechanism through which non-capitalist actors could be expected to impose socialism on capitalist societies, through regulation, redistributive taxation, and related strategies.

Joseph Schumpeter, Capitalism, Socialism, and Democracy. *3rd ed. New York: Harper, [1942] 1962.*

Both of the views highlighted in the "Insights" boxes (Schumpeter's and Polanyi's, following) have an affinity with an ideological position. Schumpeter's view is essentially critical of the welfare state from the right. Its proponents would likely advocate shrinking or dismantling the welfare state in the interest of expanding entrepreneurial activity and the scope of the free market. Polanyi's view is more supportive of the welfare state, regarding it as an institution that helps to make industrial capitalism manageable and livable. (Of course, it is also possible to offer a critique of the welfare state from the left, with many on the left supporting the expansion of welfare state functions and more redistribution, or arguing that the state does not do *enough* to help the less fortunate.) It is very important to recognize here that while different theories might have ideological implications (or policy implications), as comparative political analysts, we should not let these implications drive our research. In other words, the fundamental causal question here is not "What should we do about the welfare state?" but "Why did it emerge?" We may be motivated by policy outcomes or ideology, but we benefit from being able to distinguish these from our causal analysis.

Mobilization and Political Action

A number of scholars who are interested in the welfare state are critical of both sorts of theories mentioned so far (cultural changes and industrial capitalism). The first focuses on ideas in the creation of welfare states, the second on the impact of social structures. Where, one might ask, are the actors in these theories? Those searching for an alternative approach might focus on trying to identify the key actors in the creation of welfare states and seeing how they are interested. The main relevant ones to consider would, in the opinion of many scholars, be more concrete groups that claim to represent economic classes, such as labor unions and business groups, and the state itself.

In essence, this third theory sees the state as a product of negotiation and conflict among different interest groups.[14] Imagine, for example, an industrial society with a minimal state. In this society, business leaders exert a strong influence on politics, using that influence to ensure that the state does not regulate their management of labor.

INSIGHTS

The Great Transformation: The Political and Economic Origins of Our Time
by Karl Polanyi

Polanyi argued that economic relationships are always "embedded" in society more generally. He meant, in essence, that people's economic behavior could not be fully understood without understanding its social and cultural context. Economic behavior is never neutral but is always organized around ideas about the good life and what society ought to ultimately value. However, industrial capitalism aimed to "disembed" itself from ordinary social relations. Changing habits and tastes, rural-to-urban migration, social mobility, the breakdown of old local and religious ties, as well as the loss of traditional methods of economic self-support (and social support) accompanied the dizzying growth and potential improvement in living standards that industrial capitalism yielded.

Polanyi's supposition is essentially that human beings cannot live like this. That is, an economy that is truly "disembedded" from social relations is impossible. Industrial capitalism destroyed old social relations, but the tendency to establish social relations is resilient, and new ones would be rebuilt. A strong welfare state linked to liberal democracy was one such strategy. However, it was not the only one, and Polanyi also thought that the fascist movements of the twentieth century were efforts to reimpose a sense of community and embeddedness in the wake of the dislocations provoked by capitalism.

Karl Polanyi, The Great Transformation: The Political and Economic Origins of Our Time. *2nd ed. Boston: Beacon Press, [1994] 2001.*

Imagine also that a strong labor movement develops. Further, some members of the labor movement are proponents of "seizing the means of production" (e.g., taking over factories) and destroying the position of business leaders, while others wish to expand their influence and pursue their interests within the context of the state itself. Finally, imagine that some political leaders, or perhaps a political party, declare themselves the representatives of labor. Think about the strategic position of the different actors we have identified in this simplified story. In narrow terms, the laborers want to expand their interests, seeking basic rights, higher pay, safer conditions, and perhaps monopolistic access to certain jobs. The business leaders wish to maintain their interests in the face of those demands. Political leaders wish to acquire office or stay in office.

To oversimplify a bit, we could say that laborers have two options: to push for radical social change or to compromise. Business owners face the same sort of choice: either compromise and accept a moderately redistributive and regulatory state (but one that is unlikely to dramatically impinge on their interests), or hold on in efforts to preserve a more minimal state. It is not hard to see how such a situation could present at least the possibility of a welfare state compromise.

One of the greatest advantages of this general theoretical approach is that it can potentially explain variation in types of welfare regimes.[15] Not all welfare states are the same. Scandinavian welfare states have been very robust and have retained high popularity with their citizens. Welfare states in France and Germany have been somewhat more modest, though they too have survived retrenchment (efforts to cut back the welfare state) fairly well. The United States stands out for having a relatively weak welfare state in comparative terms,[16] with less generous transfers and a more individualistic orientation: retrenchment has been relatively strong in the United States.[17] Moreover, much of the state's welfare functioning targets the middle class and has been "submerged," in the sense that its action is partly hidden from the view of the average citizen.[18]

わたしたちの声をきいてください

Experts on the welfare state in Japan discuss its structure and efficacy. Even as welfare states experience some difficulties in long-standing industrial and post-industrial economies, some newly industrializing societies are building their own. Will they look to Japan and Europe as they do so or develop their own models?

INSIGHTS

Three Worlds of Welfare Capitalism
by Gøsta Esping-Andersen

Esping-Andersen's modern classic is best known for two of its many features. First, it emphasizes "de-commodification" as the key goal of welfare states. This draws on Polanyi's ideas discussed previously and certain arguments of Karl Marx: under capitalism, the individual becomes "commodified"—because workers sell their labor for wages in the labor market—and this is thought to be dehumanizing. Esping-Andersen argues that welfare regimes, through providing for basic human needs, push back against the commodification of persons.

Esping-Andersen's second contribution is to argue that three main types of welfare regimes developed in the twentieth century: (1) liberal regimes in places like the United Kingdom and the United States, (2) corporatist regimes as developed in continental Europe, and (3) social democratic regimes as developed in Scandinavia. They vary in the extent to which they successfully resist the commodification of citizens, with social democratic regimes being most successful. Further, he

tries to explain *why* these different regimes developed, and he focuses on "the nature of class mobilization" as well as "class-political coalition structures" and "the historical legacy of regime institutionalization."[19] Early welfare state development, he argues, depends in part on the class position of farmers. In Scandinavia, small farmers developed a coalition with urban workers. In mature welfare state development in the post-war period, the position of the middle class is key. In Scandinavia, the middle class emerged as part of the welfare state coalition. In some other societies, it was more ambivalent. Moreover, these processes are path dependent. The type of welfare state created in Scandinavia not only owed its success to middle-class support, but it was structured in such a way as to retain that support. Other welfare states might have been institutionally designed in ways that would later produce political weaknesses.

Gøsta Esping-Andersen, The Three Worlds of Welfare Capitalism. *Princeton: Princeton University Press, 1990*

Any fully satisfactory theory of the emergence of the welfare state should be able to account for these sorts of variations. The theories just discussed can *try*, if they can show that the independent variables they are interested in vary in ways that match the pattern. For example, such a theory could potentially explain the varied paths of welfare states by talking about different forms of capitalism or different timing of industrialization. But actor-centered theories are poised to offer detailed accounts of variation in welfare state regimes. They can point to differences in, for example, (1) the relative power, size, and interests of actors such as labor and business interests; (2) different institutional features of the state that can facilitate or impede certain types of compromise; or (3) different organizational methods for aggregating interests, such as parties or labor unions, with varying capacity to mobilize.

Another advantage of actor-centered theories is that they seem more capable of handling contingencies and exogenous shocks to political development. A critical juncture in the creation of European welfare states was the dual shock of the Great Depression and the Second World War. Think about how these events might have changed (1) the willingness of key groups, such as the middle class, to participate in a welfare-state-supporting coalition and (2) the ability of the welfare state, once created, to maintain such a coalition by maximizing middle-class interests. Note that structural factors from industrial capitalism are not missing from this account, and that ideas can be brought into such theories as well. For example, many analysts see Keynesian economics and its focus on government management of the business cycle as having an affinity with the welfare state. The rise of Keynesian policies in the post-Depression world also likely contributed to the welfare state's institutionalization.

International Learning Effects

A final theory that should be considered may be especially useful for understanding how and why welfare states have proliferated, expanded, and propagated across the world. We will not fully understand how welfare states emerged and took shape around the world if we think about countries operating in a vacuum. Rather, countries may alter their welfare states based on experiences they observe elsewhere because other countries may provide examples of good practices or cautionary tales about what not to do. From the beginnings of the welfare state in the late 1800s, countries have looked to other countries' experiences, sometimes emulating them, sometimes avoiding them, and sometimes adapting international experiences to local realities. In recent years, states in Asia have been taking on many of the functions performed by welfare states in the world's wealthiest regions such as Europe; in so doing, the Asian states may be building in a matter of perhaps a decade what took "Western" countries many decades to construct.[20]

This idea that countries "learn" from one another is not to imply that late-developing welfare states like those in Asia simply mimic what happened in Europe or other advanced, Western economies. First, countries may adapt the form and functioning of the welfare state to local realities. For instance, there is evidence that Japan's welfare state gave a greater role to the family than was the case in Western Europe, and that Asian countries attempted to adapt the welfare state to respond to the decline in the size of families and households (given the importance of these foundational social units in Asia, as elsewhere) during a period of rapid industrialization after World War II.[21] Similarly, international "learning" can flow from successful experiments in lower-income developing countries; it is not simply a matter of the poor countries learning from the rich. A recent example is seen in the experiences with so-called conditional cash transfers in Latin America, which are cash payouts to citizens (often low-income citizens) that are conditional on the citizen undertaking certain actions. In Brazil, a program known as *Bolsa Familia* provides cash to low-income Brazilians as long as they keep their children in school and up-to-date on vaccinations. Such policies have also flourished in Mexico, among other countries. In addition to some evidence of poverty reduction, initial experiences with these programs have generated policy interest in other countries across Latin America and in other regions of the world as well that have considered "learning" from existing programs.

As is the case with many theories, this one about international learning effects can be combined with other theories discussed in this chapter. For instance, the rapid emergence of welfare states in Asia in recent years may be linked to the rise of industrial capitalism in that region, or it may be a response to the mobilization of important political actors in Asia, or changing notions of citizenship in that part of the world. The emphasis is not on one theory to the exclusion of others but on learning how each might contribute to our overall understanding of the emergence of the variety of welfare state programs observed around the world today.

Welfare States in the Nordic Countries: What Can We Learn and How?

KEY METHODOLOGICAL TOOLS

Formulating Hypotheses

Formulating a hypothesis is one of the most important steps in comparative analysis. Usually, analysts generate hypotheses *deductively* from a theory. This means teasing out specific and testable claims that logically follow from the theory and that can be judged in relation to empirical evidence. Sometimes, though, analysts proceed *inductively*. This means thinking about how a theory could potentially account for observable features of a case or set of cases. But the method of formulating a hypothesis is less important than the rigor of efforts to test that hypothesis.

For many social scientists, the goal of a research project is to test a hypothesis and, using evidence (often from case studies), to reach a conclusion. Ideally, that conclusion will help inform more general theories about the way the world works. However, not every good piece of research will result in a clean test of a hypothesis. In many instances, good research will delve into the particular experience of a case study, noting factors that seem relevant in understanding that case. This process may generate a hypothesis for future use rather than be a full hypothesis test itself.

In formulating hypotheses about causation, it is important to keep your focus on the evidence from the cases you examine. As an example, let's consider what we might learn from investigating Nordic countries such as Denmark, Norway, and Sweden. The welfare state is reasonably large and sophisticated in these countries. We will consider how to move from that basic empirical observation toward hypothesis generation, hypothesis testing, and theory building. Let's say you read Esping-Andersen's account (see the "Insights" box on *Three Worlds of Welfare Capitalism*) and focus on Sweden. You learn that Sweden has a relatively robust welfare state of the "social democratic" variety; according to existing theory, this is due to the nature of class coalitions at certain key moments in the country's history. Consider a few options for how one might develop a research project from this observation, and think about which ones add the most value.

Option 1: You discover that a different country Esping-Andersen didn't consider (say, Finland) has a robust welfare state that seems consistent with the "Scandinavian" model. You consider the author's argument ("class coalitions help explain welfare states") and seek evidence to test the hypothesis about the role of class coalitions on this new case of Finland.

Option 2: You study further on Sweden, reading the entirety of Esping-Andersen's analysis. You follow the footnotes and bibliographic resources. Through this considerable work, you discover ample confirming evidence for the author's argument. You then declare that you have rigorously tested Esping-Andersen's hypothesis using the Swedish case.

Option 3: You discover that another country (say, Brazil) has a growing welfare state, but you notice that a major factor in its creation seems to be a desire to promote rapid economic growth. You treat this as a hypothesis that could be tested in Sweden (and other countries) to rival Esping-Andersen's "class coalitions" hypothesis.

Do any of these options make more or less sense to you as a research agenda? Each may be a good learning exercise. Certainly option 1 sounds like a good opportunity to use a case study to examine a hypothesis you have drawn from the academic literature. Now look at option 2 more carefully, and see what is limited about it. Are you really "testing the hypothesis"? It sounds as if you generated a hypothesis based on the case of Sweden and then proceeded to test that hypothesis using the case of . . . Sweden. You are really using the same evidence to replicate the analysis that Esping-Andersen did. (To be sure, being able to "replicate" existing studies is important, but option 2 is quite different from rigorously testing a hypothesis or examining a case afresh using *new* evidence.) To contribute toward building a theory of the causes of the welfare state, it might be more helpful to see if hypotheses generated from the Swedish case work in other cases (option 1). Conversely, you might see if hypotheses generated from other cases can help explain the Swedish case. This latter possibility leads us to option 3—a good and promising avenue for research. By looking at Brazil, you might discover a new factor that seemed to contribute to welfare state development in that country. This in turn might help in re-examining or rethinking the original Swedish case, which could help build a better theory of the welfare state overall.

Let's look at option 3 a bit more. Ask yourself, would it be fair to say you "tested the hypothesis" that the desire to promote economic growth leads to the growth of the welfare state, using Brazil as your case? Not really. This is the same logic behind what limits option 2: you can't really say you are *testing* a hypothesis using the same evidence from which the hypothesis is *generated*. If one case study leads you to a certain argument, that can *generate* a hypothesis for testing on future cases. That is different from a true hypothesis test in which you make a prediction before knowing the empirical realities of the case.

We want to emphasize here that generating hypotheses can itself be a contribution to the advancement of political science. That is, not every contribution in the discipline takes the form of a hypothesis test or theory building; it is sometimes useful to make empirical observations that generate hypotheses for future testing (perhaps helping us redefine our terms as well). One or more well-done case studies that generate hypotheses for future testing can represent an important contribution and step forward.

Chapter Summary

Concepts

- Key concepts and measures from political economy include gross domestic product (GDP), gross national income (GNI), inequality and the GINI coefficient, employment, unemployment, underemployment, inflation, deflation, hyperinflation, and fiscal measures.

Types

- There are two major contrasting perspectives on how political economy works: one that emphasizes the importance of free markets, and one that emphasizes the actions and powers of states in promoting economic growth. Many scholars argue that both markets and well-coordinated state action are the keys to political economic success.

- States perform a number of key functions in the economy, including but not limited to economic management, investment in education and health, and welfare state provision.

Causes and Effects

- Three main theories of the rise of welfare states emphasize (a) cultural changes, (b) industrial capitalism, and (c) mobilization and political action.

Thinking Comparatively

- We considered the Nordic welfare state model in thinking about how to develop a research agenda.

Thinking It Through

1. Consider the various political economy indicators offered in the "Types" section of the chapter. Do you think some of these are more relevant than others? If you were "ranking" countries' political economies, which of these would take precedence for you in evaluating how countries are performing? Noting that GDP per capita and GDP growth are the most commonly used indicators, are there any reasons to argue for an alternative indicator, on economic, political, or moral grounds?

2. One of the central debates in political economy and development (as seen in chapter 5) is about the relative roles of the "market" and the "state" in promoting growth and economic performance. Which of those arguments is the more intuitive to you? What evidence supports that argument, and what evidence have you seen that challenges it?

3. Test the theories of the establishment of welfare states against your knowledge of U.S. history. Which theory best explains the development of the welfare state in the United States, and why? What, if any, are the special features of welfare state development in the United States that need to be explained, and how well can each theory address these features?

4. Some argue that the welfare state is now in crisis. What would each of the theories of the welfare state's emergence suggest about the likelihood of the *survival* of welfare states?

5. Given that welfare state functions became common in advanced industrial societies in the middle of the twentieth century, do you think that these functions ought to be incorporated into the concept of strong states? In other words, can a contemporary state be strong without performing welfare state functions, or does failure to provide welfare benefits make a state relatively weak by definition?

CHAPTER 5

Development

The military border between North and South Korea. These two countries vary markedly in their political, economic, and social development. Why might this be so?

The countries of North and South Korea are separated by a "Military Demarcation Line" that is heavily fortified and tense. Yet the peoples of these two states are separated by more than this: dramatic differences in health, life expectancy, infant mortality, levels of education, prospects for advancement, access to information, and the freedom to participate in political life. North of the line, indicators of all these good things are very poor, and south of the line, astonishingly good. What makes this comparison still more interesting is how recently this profound divergence occurred.

The comparison of North and South Korea is potentially instructive in its own right, but it is just one example of a general situation that interests scholars of comparative politics who focus on development: Some countries are incredibly rich and give their citizens high "capability" to achieve the ends they set for themselves,[1] and others are poor, leaving their citizens with far fewer resources and opportunities. The hope of comparative political analysts is that we can help explain why, and that in doing so, we will help citizens and policymakers maximize their own chances.

North and South Korea are clearly different on various indicators, ranging from economic growth to poverty levels to citizens' opportunities. In this chapter, we examine the differing ways development can be understood. We begin by looking at the concept of "development," focusing on the most commonly used definition of the term, which is overall income. The subsequent section, "Types," highlights the many other forms and definitions of development, including other economic outcomes, more social indicators, and even measures of cultural values and ecological sustainability. The "Causes and Effects" section then explores the various theories that seek to explain why development happens. In the "Thinking Comparatively" section at the end, we return to this example from the two Koreas to illustrate how we might use comparative case studies to test hypotheses about why development happens.

Concepts

Development is a complex concept, and there is heated disagreement about what counts as development and what does not. For example, would you say an oil-rich country such as Saudi Arabia is experiencing development if its economy is growing rapidly, but nearly all of the benefits of that growth are going to a small number of elites? Would you say that a country is developing if people are not getting wealthier but are living longer, healthier lives? What about a country like China, where wealth is increasing for many people, and poverty is declining fast, but the environment is being damaged severely? The indicators of development outlined in this section range from narrow macroeconomic indicators, such as economic growth, to social indicators, such as cultural development, that are more difficult to measure. As you read them, consider which best captures for you the idea of development.

The first and most straightforward sort of development to consider is economic growth, or increases in a country's overall level of economic activity. Beyond growth of the overall economy, development may also be evaluated using other economic and social indicators, including income inequality, poverty levels, and the standard of living. We could even define development in political terms, saying a country is more developed when it becomes more democratic, though we will leave this topic to chapter 6.

The simplest indicator of a country's economic development is how much the economy produces, or how much income its people earn. As noted in chapter 4, this can be measured using such indicators as gross domestic product (GDP) or gross national income (GNI). Here we will not discuss all of the various *economic* indicators that could be used to evaluate development, since several were explored in the "Concepts" section of chapter 4. However, in the next section, we consider some major ways that development has been evaluated in lower-income countries, beyond the economic indicators already examined and including a number of social and political measures. These include questions of poverty and inequality, such as whether people of different races and genders have comparable access to economic and social opportunities, and overall well-being. We consider measures of well-being and "human capital" (such as health and education) and how or whether development can be compatible with environmental sustainability and respect for distinct cultural values in an age of global interactions.

development A process by which a society changes or advances, often measured in terms of economic growth, but also sometimes measured in terms of quality of life, standard of living, access to freedoms and opportunities, or other indicators.

Types

As noted previously, there are many ways of understanding and measuring development beyond income per capita, and we examine some of these here. We still consider some economic measures related to how income is distributed in a population. Yet we also look at other possible ways of understanding development. One is to focus on more social indicators, such as those based on health, education, and other measurements of quality of life or standard of living. Another is to think about whether a society treats different groups equally (such as men and women, or majority and minority ethnic groups). Finally, we will consider the relationship between development and issues such as environmental sustainability and cultural autonomy.

CASE IN CONTEXT

What Explains India's Recent Growth?

PAGE 465

India is a country that in recent years has achieved consistently strong growth but that nevertheless still has a large population suffering from extreme poverty. In many ways, India's development story has been idiosyncratic, above all because the country became the world's biggest democracy decades before achieving strong growth. Ordinarily, as we discuss in chapter 6, the opposite is the case, and economic development precedes democratization.

For more on Indian development, see the case study in Part VI, p. 465. As you read it, keep in mind the following questions:

1. Why was India's performance so poor for so long, and why did it finally take off?
2. Was democracy bad for India's economic development?
3. What are the prospects for India's poor in the coming years?

Poverty

poverty The state of being poor, as measured by low income, deprivation, lack of access to resources, or limited economic opportunities.

poverty line A specified threshold below which individuals or groups are judged to be in poverty.

absolute poverty A conception of poverty that involves setting a certain line below which people will be defined as poor, typically understood in terms of the inability to purchase a certain set of basic goods or services.

Poverty is usually measured with respect to an established **poverty line**, a basic level of income needed to maintain a reasonable standard of living in a given country. Traditionally, major international agencies such as the World Bank and the United Nations Development Programme used about one dollar or $1.25 per day (per person) as the **absolute poverty** threshold worldwide, though in recent years many have turned to a two dollars per day threshold (or, often, $1.90/day in 2011 dollars at purchasing power parity). There has also been an effort to expand the criteria for measuring poverty, taking into account additional indicators such as access to public services and public goods. Poverty may be understood as an income measure but also as a measure of whether people have access to health care and education.[2] The number of people facing absolute poverty is about one billion worldwide, though in relative terms, this number has declined in recent years.[3]

Poverty lines may also be measured by individual countries, and each country may do so in different ways.[4] In the United States, for example, the poverty line is defined for households and families of different sizes, and is recalculated on a regular basis to reflect the cost of living. The U.S. poverty line for 2015 was $12,060 for a single person under the age of 65.[5] However, looking at only the poverty line does not indicate poverty *depth*, or how far someone is below the poverty line. It is simple just to count the number of people living below the line, but a person with income of $12,059 will be counted the same as someone with $8,000 or less, even though there is clearly a difference in how deeply someone is in poverty in the two cases.

Social Outcomes and Human Development

life expectancy The average age until members of a society (or some group within society) live.

Several indicators of an individual's overall well-being and standard of living are not based only on income and macroeconomic performance. They may be termed *human capital* because they represent the accumulated skills and investments people have made in their own capacities (or, indeed, that others have made in their capacities). Health is perhaps the most fundamental aspect of human capital. It can be measured by a number of instruments. One is **life expectancy**, or the age to which a given person may expect to live, depending on the circumstances into which they were born. Another is **infant mortality**, often measured as the percentage of children who do not survive to the age of one. Other health measures include infection and morbidity rates for different diseases, and accessibility of health care and health insurance coverage. Education is a second major aspect of human capital. The most important and commonly used measures are **literacy rates** and school enrollment and completion (often thought of as "educational attainment," frequently measured in terms of years of schooling). The quality of education is important as well, as the standardized scores of youth on math and science tests are often compared across countries, for example.

Some analysts who want to define development broadly have aimed to capture the "standard of living." These often use some of the indicators just discussed. One of the most commonly used measures of standard of living around the world is the United Nations' annual **Human Development Index (HDI)**. This brings together income with life expectancy and educational measures (literacy and school enrollments) in a single index to give a broad view of development and well-being.

Standards of living often go along with (or are positively correlated with) other indicators of development. Yet the evidence suggests that inequality actually *increases* as income increases at certain stages of economic development, specifically in moving from low-income stages of development (where nearly everyone is poor) to middle-income stages (where a fraction of the population grows wealthier and the remainder does not see much increase). Conversely, some societies (such as Cuba and the state of Kerala in India), have aimed to increase access to education and health *without* necessarily doing so via increasing the personal incomes of their citizens.[6] There are many routes to improving standards of living and reducing poverty, but many countries remain behind. In many African countries, such as Nigeria, for example, standards of living and human development remain lower than in wealthier countries (see the "Case in Context" box "Why Are Natural Resources Sometimes a Curse? The Nigerian Case").

Gender Relations and Racial and Ethnic Identities

In recent years, scholars have begun to break down statistics by groups, and a leading example is gender. We now recognize that a society with large differences in life expectancies between men and women, for instance, may be seen as a less-developed society than one where life chances are more equitable. Likewise, if women and men have radically different educational or professional opportunities, we might consider this a development challenge. We examine gender and politics in depth in chapter 14, but we note here that gender matters for development in two major ways: it is both a *means* to development and one of the *ends* of development.[7] In terms of *ends*, we might define development to say it occurs when economic and social opportunities are available to women and men alike. Regardless of how well a country's economy does, that society might not be considered developed if its women are not allowed to own property, or hold jobs outside the home, or voice their opinions.[8] In terms of *means*, gender also matters because empowering women in particular helps advance other aspects of development. Well-known examples include the benefits of extending education and small business loans (sometimes as little as $25 or less) to women in low-income countries. These small changes often have the effect of increasing women's incomes, which

infant mortality A major public health indicator, which typically measures the number of infants per 1,000 born that do not survive until the age of one year.

literacy rate The percentage of a population who can read.

Human Development Index (HDI) A composite measure developed by the United Nations to provide a broad view of annual development and well-being around the world, based on income, life expectancy, and literacy and school enrollments.

PAGE 522

CASE IN CONTEXT
Why Are Natural Resources Sometimes a Curse?
The Nigerian Case

Nigeria has some of the largest oil deposits in the world. So it must be a rich country, right? Actually, Nigeria remains one of the poorest countries in the world. Although the Nigerian economy is one of the most important in Africa, historically, it has performed poorly. Perhaps surprisingly, this may be *because* of the oil. A number of scholars have argued that countries like Nigeria suffer from what is sometimes called the resource curse, as oil or other high-value commodities can potentially produce corruption, distort the formation and functioning of key institutions, crowd out investment in other areas, and affect a country's currency in negative ways.

For more on Nigerian economic development and the resource curse, see the case study in Part VI, pp. 522–523. As you read it, keep in mind the following questions:

1. How has oil helped, and how has it hurt, Nigerian development?

2. What policies might the Nigerian case suggest to the leaders of a country that has just discovered large oil deposits?

3. If oil is so bad, why is Norway not poor like Nigeria? (Or does this indicate that other factors are involved?)

Natural gas burns as oil is welled in the Niger Delta region in Nigeria. Nigeria is a major oil producer, and yet its population remains among the world's poorest.

in turn typically results in households making more resources available for nutrition, family health care, and children's education. Indeed, evidence suggests that women, on average, are more likely than men to invest scarce resources in their families (and, thus, in human capital).

Major differences in development levels of other population groups may also be an indicator of development (see Table 5.1). If certain racial or ethnic minorities are systematically deprived of the opportunity to participate equally in the economy, we can argue that development is incomplete. This gap between groups may not always be captured by economic statistics like GDP, inequality, and poverty, and it may go beyond political rights as well. South Africa under the official racism of *apartheid* (1948–1994) was one example. Blacks certainly had lower incomes than whites, and no political rights to speak of, but they also suffered from separate and inferior systems of education, health care, and housing. Under apartheid, South Africa had higher average social indicators than most other African countries, but its inequalities were especially shocking. Unfortunately, however, disparities in development due to discrimination on the basis of race, ethnicity, and gender are not only found in extreme cases like apartheid-era South Africa.

TABLE 5.1 Measures of Human Capital

Country	Life Expectancy (at Birth, for males; in years) (2015)	Infant Mortality (per 1,000 live births) (2016)	Literacy Rate (%)	Human Development Index (HDI) Rank, 2016
Brazil	72	14	90.4	79
China	75	9	95.1	90
France	80	3	> 99	21
Germany	79	3	> 99	4
India	67	35	62.8	131
Iran	75	13	85.0	69
Japan	81	2	> 99	17
Mexico	75	13	93.5	77
Nigeria	52	67	51.1	152
Russia	65	7	> 99	49
South Korea	79	3	> 99	18
United Kingdom	80	4	> 99	16
United States	76	6	> 99	10

Sources: Life expectancy and infant mortality, World Bank Open Data, https://data.worldbank.org, accessed November 4, 2017; Literacy Rate, United Nations Human Development Report, 2014; HDI Rank, United Nations Human Development Report 2016, http://hdr.undp.org/en/composite/HDI, accessed November 4, 2017.

Satisfaction and Happiness

For many people, development is really about each person's satisfaction or happiness in life. Understanding development in these terms recognizes that income is a means to an end and not an end in itself. People usually seek higher incomes because it gives them access to other things they desire, or the opportunity to consume things they like, such as good food, or better housing, or access to higher education, or luxury items, or a vacation. The most fundamental concept in economics for measuring people's ability to fulfill their preferences is not income, but **utility**. Utility gives a notion of the value people derive from consuming or having access to that which pleases them. If I like Coca-Cola more than Pepsi Cola, I will "derive more utility" from drinking a Coca-Cola, while a friend who prefers Pepsi to Coke "gets more utility" from a Pepsi.

Others have argued that utility is insufficient as a measure of people's well-being or happiness. Utility captures people's preferences. To say that I get more utility from one thing than another is, in essence, to say that I will select the former rather than the latter if I have to choose between them. But people may not always choose the things that make them happier. Indeed, people may sometimes choose

utility The value that people derive from resources to which they have access.

things that leave them in a worse state of subjective well-being (think, for example, of an addict who chooses to continue to use drugs). Motivated by such cases, some scholars have tried to measure happiness by asking people to rate their own level of happiness, life satisfaction, and related concepts. Other scholars, though, argue that people's self-perceptions may be less reliable than studying their "utility" through analyzing their behavior.

Happiness comes from more than just consuming goods and services. It may come from having free time, or social status, or strong ties to family and friends, or from living a spiritually fulfilling life. Social scientists face major challenges in trying to measure human happiness, but they continue to make efforts. In recent years, the mountainous nation of Bhutan (in the Himalayas) made a splash internationally by publishing its own measures of "Gross National Happiness." Increasingly, more countries and more scholars are following suit; and even China, Canada, France, and the United Kingdom have recently begun to think about how to measure their peoples' happiness.

Cultural Development

For many people around the world, part of development might mean retaining and deepening one's own culture. In this view, economic modernization does not necessarily improve a society: if economic growth brings commercialization and cultural disintegration, some people(s) will wish to have none of it and will prefer to define development as exercising the right to self-determination, living autonomously from the rest of the world, and enjoying the rich cultural traditions they hold dear. Perhaps an indigenous group will wish to protect its own language and traditions while avoiding the influences of Hollywood and "Western values." For many people, "development" might not even be a positive word but might instead signify a push by outsiders—intentional or unintentional—to undermine local practices.[9] Increasingly, many researchers, sensitive to these concerns, argue that citizens of the countries we study should play a central role in defining development goals. The desire to protect traditional cultures is not limited to small and remote indigenous groups but can also be seen in many large, post-industrial nations wrestling with questions of growth and development, such as France (as seen in the case study on globalization in chapter 16).

Sustainability

environmental sustainability The quality that one or another practice has with being compatible with the long-term health of the environment.

Finally, **environmental sustainability** is an important aspect of development. With increasing attention to the issue of climate change, many scholars argue that if an approach to development is not sustainable, it won't work. Sustainable development can be defined as development that conserves resources to respect the needs of future generations. Only by stewarding its resources effectively and not depleting them too rapidly will any society remain viable over the long run. To incorporate sustainability into development discussions, some scholars have even proposed replacing GDP with new measures that account for the use of resources. They note that cutting down a tree increases GDP, as do many pollution-causing activities, even though these activities may be "using up" a society's natural endowments.[10] We discuss the concept and the challenge of sustainability in chapter 16. Among the main political challenges in promoting sustainable development are the difficulties of securing collective action between many countries when each country has incentives to "freeride" on the efforts of others.

Causes and Effects: Why Does Development Happen?

To examine the causes of development, we focus mainly on GDP growth per capita, for two reasons. First, as noted earlier, these measures are the most commonly used in studies of development. Second, GDP growth per capita often goes hand in hand with several other indicators of development listed previously. In particular, countries that grow in terms of GDP per capita often also advance on other social indicators, with improved health, more education, higher levels of happiness, and reductions in poverty. Of course, this is not true in all cases, and rising GDP is not the only determinant of these other indicators, but it is true quite often. For this reason, and since it is more comprehensive than many of those other indicators, development scholars often use it when they're seeking a single measure. That said, there can be trade-offs between GDP growth and other indicators, such as inequality, as we have noted; and GDP/capita certainly does not capture every dimension of development. These strengths and limitations of the measure should be kept in mind.

The central question here is why economies grow, diversify, and become more productive and successful. What allows countries to essentially liberate people from their small farming plots to work in cities, factories, law offices, research labs, banks, and hospitals? Why have people and societies been able to accumulate capital that they can use to foster even more productive economic activity? The answers to these questions are debated extensively, and several theories have arisen to explain them. We group the focal points of these theories into four categories:

1. the role of the market and the state in promoting development, a topic we explored in the previous chapter in the context of "developed" countries;
2. institutions such as legal rules and social norms that shape the behavior of economic actors;
3. cultural values; and
4. the domestic and international structures that condition development, including a country's place in the international system.

Institutions: The Market–State Debate, Revisited

A leading institutional argument about the causes of development reflects a major debate in political economy, which we emphasized in chapter 4. The issue is the relative merits of **market-led development** versus **state-led development**. According to the pro-market argument, individual decisions of free and independent economic agents will lead to a more efficient allocation of resources. As people try to maximize their own gains, the society as a whole becomes better off. Allowing the market to work freely leads to prosperity.

On the other side of the debate, advocates for state-led approaches argue that development requires an actor capable of coordinating disparate agents, planning for the long term, and supplying capital for big development pushes in

market-led development An approach to economic management in which the state aims to control economic behavior as little as possible.

state-led development An approach to economic management in which the state plays a prominent role in coordinating the behavior of economic actors and intervening in the economy.

low-income countries. The argument goes that the state is uniquely suited to performing this task. This perspective was especially prominent immediately after World War II, when Europe was reconstructed and new states emerged from colonialism around the globe. Development scholars envisioned a "big push" in development in the world's poorer countries, where massive state-led investment would generate a virtuous circle of self-sustaining growth.[11] In subsequent years, East Asia was the most rapidly growing region in the world. Statist scholars argued that the success in that region was due to timely and constructive state involvement in the economy, not free markets. Beginning with Japan immediately after World War II—and then extending to South Korea, Taiwan, and elsewhere into East and Southeast Asia—the "Asian Tigers" offered compelling evidence. In these cases, active involvement by well-organized and capable states helped direct investment to productive enterprises. Effective states helped propel these economies to growth rates that sometimes exceeded 8 percent to 10 percent per year. Similarly, statists might attribute China's current growth to a state that maintains a steady hand in the economy.

State-led approaches to development were popular from the 1950s to the 1970s, but the arguments for market-led development returned to prominence in the 1980s and 1990s. For several decades after World War II, the state played a leading role in the economies of many developing countries, from Japan to India to Brazil to much of Africa. In some countries, this role was inspired or encouraged by the apparent economic, military, and technological success of the Soviet Union in the 1950s and 1960s and by the easy availability of loans in the 1970s. In the early 1980s, however, many Latin American countries in particular suffered from economic crises driven by accumulated debts. Less than a decade later, communism collapsed in Central Europe, and the Soviet Union broke apart (see the country profile on Russia). These events led to a sense in many advanced capitalist countries that communism and state planning as an economic model had been discredited.

At this time, many prominent institutions advocated for economic liberalization in developing countries, or moves toward free-market economics. Major proponents of this approach included the International Monetary Fund (IMF) and the World Bank, based in Washington, DC. These organizations arranged loans to many developing countries that faced economic difficulties. The loans were conditional upon those countries opening up to freer trade and flows of capital, and often to reductions in the role of the government in the economy. The 1980s and the 1990s were times when many developing countries moved toward more free-market systems, with the main questions being how far and how fast these changes would be made.

In more recent years, the debate has shifted once again for a couple of reasons. First, the turn toward free-market economics led to critiques of how the free market performed. In many countries, reducing the role of the state in the economy was associated with the losses of formal jobs (or increases in unemployment and underemployment), a rise in inequality, and even crises such as hyperinflation. Second, evidence began to accumulate that "state-led" or "state-directed" development had worked effectively in certain places, namely, where the quality and professionalism of the state was high. Thus, a theory emerged that the *quality* of the state

CASE IN CONTEXT

How Did China Become an Economic Power?

PAGE 421

China's development has been dizzyingly rapid in the last forty years. The country's economic performance was largely quite poor through most of the twentieth century; but after a series of reforms beginning in 1978 and 1979, the Chinese economy took off. The country is now often referred to as the "global factory," and it now rivals the United States for the title of the world's largest economy.

For more on Chinese development, see the case study in Part VI, pp. 421–422. As you read it, keep in mind the following questions:

1. What factors—political, institutional, and cultural—likely contributed to poor growth in China in the years when Mao Zedong held power?
2. Is China's recent success in development a simple story of the state getting out of the way and letting markets do their work, or is it more complicated?
3. How might we explain the emergence of the reforms that began in 1978 and 1979? In other words, *why* did China reform?
4. What sorts of challenges does the Chinese economy face in the medium-term future?

might matter more than the *quantity* of the state in determining how an economy develops. High levels of performance in several East Asian countries over several decades—and by China in the 2000s and 2010s—showed that some of the strongest performing economies may exhibit relatively high levels of state involvement.

As noted in chapter 4, the discussion about the role of markets and states is generally a matter of degree. Even most strong advocates of market-led development would prefer the existence of a state that is capable of ensuring rule of law, enforcing contracts between private actors, and providing basic order. (For instance, almost no one would favor a situation of stateless "anarchy" as recently existed in Somalia.) And even strong advocates of state-led development frequently acknowledge that free markets can be a very useful feature in part of the economy. (Most statists would not favor totalitarian state control of all economic activity, as might be most approximated in North Korea.)

Finally, as you consider this key debate, keep in mind that many scholars of development will have different outcomes in mind. Many may be focused on economic growth, while some may be focused on explaining the degree of poverty reduction in a country. Others will look at inequality, still others at human opportunities more broadly, and yet others at the environmental sustainability or cultural appropriateness of "development." Consider whether different measures of development might influence one's evaluation of different development strategies—and if so, how.

Institutions: Beyond the Market–State Debate

Development takes place over long periods of time, and the state and the market are not the only things that make it happen. Other institutions also matter. By **institutions**, political scientists mean the many features of a society that shape peoples' behavior and actions, as discussed in chapter 4 and later chapters. The **new institutional** framework focuses on a broader set of institutions.

institution A regularized or patterned activity that shapes the behavior of individuals and groups, including formal organizations like the state or political parties, as well as more informal institutions such as norms and values.

new institutionalism The name given to the turn to institutional theory in the last several decades in economics, political science, and sociology.

To use an example, consider the institution of property rights. In societies where an individual's right to private property is well established and secure, people are likely to behave in ways that promote development. On the other hand, if property rights are not secure, development may be hindered. Imagine you have a house and a few acres for growing crops. If the government can seize your house at any time, or if squatters can simply take over your land, then you will be unlikely to invest a lot of money in your house, or in making your land more productive. Were private property secure, on the other hand, you might be likelier to make those investments. And so too might your neighbors. This would lead to a society that is more economically secure. According to this argument, the institution of strong property rights would promote investment because it allows individuals to reap the rewards of their investments in the long run.[12]

The institution-based approach to comparative politics, or **institutionalism**, has several strains. **Rational institutionalism** holds that political and economic outcomes are best explained in terms of individuals' responses to their institutional environments. Rational institutionalists emphasize economic logics, and many of these scholars would be found engaging the debate about states and markets mentioned previously. **Historical institutionalism** also finds that institutions matter but traces these consequences through time, showing how historical changes shape future events. For historical institutionalists, the timing and sequencing of events matters, as do specific circumstances that may arise at "critical junctures" in time, when a country may take any number of different paths.[13] The reason historical trajectories are so important is that changes are **path dependent**: the farther a society goes down a certain path, the less and less likely it is to diverge from that path. For example, if a country develops by privileging a number of state-linked businesses, it will be hard for the government to change this without some sort of crisis. History is "sticky" and cannot be easily reversed. Historical institutionalists also tend to focus on how institutions produce collective actors and organize interests, in contrast to the individualist tendency of rational institutionalism. Institutionalists argue that development is shaped by the institutions in place, by how

institutionalism An approach to theorizing in comparative politics and related fields that places emphasis on the power of institutions to shape the behavior of individuals.

rational institutionalism An approach to theorizing in comparative politics and related fields that places emphasis on the power of institutions to shape the behavior of individuals, one that often focuses on implications of institutions for individuals' strategic choices.

historical institutionalism An approach to theorizing that places emphasis on the power of institutions to shape the behavior of individuals, and how this operates over time.

path dependent The name given to historical processes in which future developments are shaped or partially determined by events at previous stages in those processes.

INSIGHTS

State-Directed Development: Political Power and Industrialization in the Global Periphery

by Atul Kohli

Atul Kohli works to overcome the "state–market divide" by explaining successful economic development as a function of both the public sector and private capitalist enterprise. Kohli has argued for the importance of understanding state capacity (as defined in chapter 4) and the importance of constructive state intervention, and places the state prominently in the title of the book, but not to the exclusion of private actors. He uses the metaphor of a chariot pulled by two horses—the state and private business—and notes that where these pull in the same direction, development occurs; but where the two horses pull in opposite directions, the chariot will not move (or may topple). Kohli uses the case of Korea to show success and Brazil as a moderate success, but highlights the African case of Nigeria as a failed economy where the state does not work to promote private enterprise.

Atul Kohli, State-Directed Development: Political Power and Industrialization in the Global Periphery. Cambridge: Cambridge University Press, 2004.

institutions are created, and by how they evolve over the long run. The preceding example of property rights could be seen as involving both rational institutional and historical institutional approaches, and a major recent work provides another example (See box on page 110).

Culture and Development

The approaches just discussed characterize institutions as the protagonists of development, yet there are other approaches to development that emphasize deeper features of a society itself—features that reflect commonly held customs, norms, habits, and values. That is to say, for many trying to understand development, culture matters. Many scholars are interested in *both* culture and institutions as predictors of development, and the links between these factors are not always clear.

CIVIL SOCIETY, SOCIAL CAPITAL, AND TRUST

A society where people can cooperate and work together is likelier to thrive than one filled with distrust and lacking organization. One of the earliest and most prominent modern proponents of this view was Alexis de Tocqueville, in his classic *Democracy in America*. Tocqueville attributed America's economic vibrancy in part to a variety of cultural characteristics (including hardy frontier mentalities and inventiveness), reserving special mention for the degree to which Americans constructed an active civic life, noting famously that "Americans of all ages, all stations of life, and all types of disposition are forever forming associations."[14] Rich associational life—which may itself be a consequence of *institutions*—can generate the values and complex structures needed for a diversified economy.[15]

It is very difficult to imagine a modern economy without complex organizations, such as corporations or cooperatives, that either are relatively large or have rich linkages to many other organizations. Researchers find that **civil society**—often thought of as a space in which people can engage in social exchange and public deliberation not fully controlled by the state—links directly to economic outcomes (see, e.g., the "Insights" box on Fukuyama's *Trust*). Societies with extensive and/or beneficial social networks in political and economic life are said to have the virtue of high levels of **social capital**, advantages held by virtue of relationships.

Social capital can build on itself and help reinforce a society's development. It is said to work in several ways. First, density of network ties, as already mentioned, may generate **trust**, or confidence in the reliability or good conduct of others. This is because shared ties help people build and maintain reputations; and in dense networks in which those you know already know each other, people have a lot to lose from behaving in untrustworthy ways. It is also because in dense networks, information tends to flow rapidly, which has many economic benefits. The notion of "bonding capital" is based on the density of ties and the idea that deepening these ties has benefits for the economy. Another form of social capital is sometimes called "bridging capital," which is the set of benefits that come from networks extending out to reach new people and places.[16] Sometimes these benefits are beneficial for the group, such as when trade between previously disconnected subgroups becomes possible. Sometimes benefits accrue mainly to the relatively small number of people who are themselves the "bridges" and who can act and profit as "brokers" (of information or contacts, for example).

civil society Public space or zone of social life, at least partially autonomous from the state, in which individuals are free to engage in deliberation and social movement activity, for example.

social capital Advantage that individuals or groups hold by virtue of their social relationships.

trust The extent to which an individual has confidence in the reliability or good conduct of others.

INSIGHTS   The Colonial Origins of Comparative Development
by Daron Acemoglu, Simon Johnson, and James A. Robinson

This article traces differences in economic development around the world today to the varying historical paths of different world regions. Colonialism and geography played especially important roles, with the impacts playing out over more than a century. Colonizers such as Britain established different types of states in the different regions of the world. Where mass settlement was not possible (for reasons of geography and endemic disease), colonizers set up states that worked primarily to extract resources with little investment. This happened in tropical Africa, for instance. Places that were easier to "settle," such as North America, ended up with stronger state structures. Over time, these institutions evolved into colonial states and later into independent states in the nineteenth and twentieth centuries. States that were originally designed to extract resources tend to continue that way today (with negative consequences), whereas countries actively settled by colonizers tended to develop into systems more capable of promoting development. The historical development of the state as an institution (from decades or centuries ago) still casts a long shadow over development today.

Daron Acemoglu, Simon Johnson, and James A. Robinson, "The Colonial Origins of Comparative Development," American Economic Review 91 (2001): 1369–1401.

RELIGION

Some argue that religious differences between groups and between nations may also explain differences in development.[17] Theories of this kind gained prominence early in the twentieth century and have remained part of the discourse about economic and social change ever since. In contemporary development studies, scholars have attempted to explain the relative success of different world regions on the basis of religious beliefs. For some time, scholars theorized that Confucian values hindered the economic performance of East Asian countries, relative to Europe and the United States. They posited that cultural expectations of obedience and respect for authority could limit the creativity and entrepreneurial spirit that capitalistic growth requires. Paradoxically, as East Asia has flourished in recent years, scholars have found advantages in Confucian values, emphasizing how a strong belief in order and authority, respect for the state, and respect for education may all facilitate growth.

Similarly, some scholars hypothesize that features of Muslim faith may have hindered development in the Arab world. For instance, the Qu'ran restricts lending on interest, which may make large investments difficult (though it should be noted that many modern Islamic states have developed "Islamic bonds" and other financial instruments). Muslims show high rates of opposition to globalization, which may imply an unwillingness to participate in the global economy.[18]

Finally, the *degree* of religion may matter more than the *type* of religion. Religious institutions of many kinds can bind people together and may therefore increase trust and cooperation, which in turn can lead to positive political, social, and economic outcomes. In any event, many arguments linking religion and development operate through *intervening* or *mediating* variables. That is, religious beliefs affect certain behaviors or institutions that in turn affect economics, perhaps with several steps in between. This was one of the original lines of thinking pioneered by Max Weber, a founder of modern sociology and political science, in his book *The Protestant Ethic and the Spirit of Capitalism* (1958; first published, in German, in 1905).

INSIGHTS | Trust: The Social Virtues and the Creation of Prosperity
by Francis Fukuyama

The argument that civil society matters did not exist only for Tocqueville's nineteenth-century America. Francis Fukuyama argues that economic modernization in many countries around the world has been rooted in the cultivation of **trust**. Societies with high levels of trust have been able to move beyond the small, family-owned economic units that dominate low-income economies, creating major corporations that can take advantage of their size to increase productivity.

Insofar as a division of labor and specialization are central to economic expansion, the emergence of such strong institutions in the high-trust societies accelerates growth. Fukuyama thus traces economic development ultimately to a fundamentally cultural value.

Francis Fukuyama, Trust: The Social Virtues and the Creation of Prosperity. *New York: Free Press, 1995.*

VALUE SYSTEMS

Cultural factors that shape development may include values other than those associated with religious beliefs. Prominent candidates for values that favor development are those that allow people to orient their behavior toward the future rather than toward the present, to engage in long-term planning rather than the day-to-day. The virtue of thrift, or a propensity to save, can matter here, as successful societies are those in which people can defer gratification from today into the future in the hopes of using savings to invest and build more wealth. Work ethic may also be important; this can possibly link back to the religious values but find its roots elsewhere in a culture. At the same time, some scholars may be skeptical of the claim

A group baptism among Evangelical Christians in El Salvador. Evangelical Christianity is prominent in Central America and a number of other countries, notably in many parts of the developing world. Scholars debate religion's relationship with economic development.

that these things are all "cultural," if we mean they are disconnected from the structural factors that often shape people's lives. For example, whether someone engages in long-term planning may be less "cultural" than just a matter of whether their life is sufficiently free from stress, danger, and constant labor to allow that planning.[19]

Individualism is also often considered important, as it may allow those who accumulate wealth to build with it rather than feeling compelled to distribute it to friends, acquaintances, and hangers-on. According to these theories, notions of individual accountability and responsibility, rationality and pragmatism in some places contrast with the lack of such progress-promoting virtues in societies where people spend everything they earn, leaving little on which to build.

Systems and Structures: Domestic and International

Institutionalist approaches generally hold that development is determined largely by the actions and decisions of individuals, as shaped by institutions and the incentives and constraints they create. Culturalist approaches generally see people's behavior in the economy as shaped and constrained by beliefs, values, norms, and habits. In the case of statist and neoliberal approaches, the domestic forces that matter are the extent and nature of states and their involvement in the economy. But there are other approaches as well. Some scholars—most notably Marxists—have traced economic outcomes to fundamental underlying structures in an economy, such as the basic form of economic production, and the system of social classes generated by these forms of production.

DOMESTIC ECONOMIC STRUCTURES AND CLASS INTERESTS

Several schools of development scholarship emphasize the impediments and traps confronting societies as they attempt to promote development. In this view, certain powerful groups may block development by seeking to perpetuate their own advantages at the expense of the populace at large. Even where the institutions of democracy seem to be functioning well, interest groups or lobbies may demand special treatment from the government that prevents the reforms needed for economic growth. Scholars on both the right and the left of the political spectrum may adopt this view regarding the importance of domestic structures and vested interests. On the right, some scholars have argued that democracy itself can undermine capitalism, because in democracies special interests will often seek preferential treatment from the government.[20] The most important scholar on the left was the intellectual founder of one of the twentieth century's most important ideologies: Karl Marx.

INTERNATIONAL ECONOMIC STRUCTURES AND CLASS INTERESTS

Karl Marx's ideas were made the official ideology in the Soviet Union (U.S.S.R.) after that country was created out of the Russian Revolution of 1917. And while Marx's ideology was eventually considered a recipe for "socialism in one country" by the dictator Joseph Stalin, some Marxist schools of thought also foresaw an internationalized crisis of capitalism. Many early Marxists hoped for a "permanent revolution" around the world and diagnosed the global inequalities that capitalism had engendered. (Vladimir Lenin, leader of the Russian Revolution and the U.S.S.R.'s first head of state, led the charge with a book entitled *Imperialism: The Highest Stage of Capitalism.*)[21] Over time, however, many Marxist approaches in social science shifted from emphasizing prospects for global socialist revolution to offering critiques of how politics operates within capitalist economies.

According to Marxian arguments, the structure of the international economy will place some powerful countries in the favorable position of capitalist accumulation. Meanwhile, other countries and world regions are subjected to serving the role of providing low-wage labor and resources, though a small number of elites residing in the low-income countries may be complicit with the interests of the rich countries. For example, a select number of rich Nigerian businesspeople and politicians may work with the international business community to ensure capitalist investment in Nigeria, which will result in profits for the international capitalists and their local "collaborators," but the Nigerian people as a whole will not benefit.

Many scholars adopted such perspectives to account for underdevelopment in the "global south," the "Third World," or the "less developed countries." In the views of many of these scholars, the international economy has been a zero-sum game in which one person's gain is another person's loss: for some to be rich, others in the world must be poor.[22] One of the leading concepts has been **dependency**, which holds that low-income countries will remain in a subordinate economic position relative to wealthy countries, depending on markets in the rich world as a place to sell their low-value goods while importing high-value goods from those rich countries. In its earliest versions, dependency theory held that low-income countries faced deteriorating terms of trade relative to the capitalist countries at the center of the world economy, which would make the goods from the dependent countries ever less valuable.[23] The theory was revised

dependency A theory that argues that developing countries cannot simply embrace free trade because this will lead to ever-increasing wealth disparities between them and the advanced economies.

CASE IN CONTEXT

Does the Global Economy Help or Hurt Developing Nations like Brazil?

PAGE 408

Brazil is a country that has had a mixed economic record since independence. Its fortunes have varied dramatically from year to year. After many years of rapid growth, it recently endured one of the worst recessions in its history. Nonetheless, in the past two decades it has seen some progress in relation to two of its traditional scourges: income inequality and poverty (though much work remains to be done). Brazil still has a long way to go to realize its ambition to become a hemispheric power, and perhaps, ultimately, a global power.

For more on Brazilian development, see the case study in Part VI, p. 408. As you read it, keep in mind the following questions:

1. How might income inequality and economic underdevelopment interact? In the Brazilian case, historically, does one cause the other, are they independent, or are they mutually reinforcing?

2. Why has the Brazilian economy taken off in recent years? Did the social programs of the Lula da Silva and Rousseff governments simply siphon off economic surplus for other (humanitarian) ends, or could they be thought of as further investment in the Brazilian economy and its medium- to long-run prospects?

when it became clear that some developing countries experienced "partial" development, moving from the world's "periphery" to its "semi-periphery."[24] The revised version of dependency theory thus acknowledges that development is possible for low-income countries, but argues that their circumstances necessitate the state's active involvement in the economy to promote industrialization.[25] The early version of dependency theory that argues that developing countries will always be disadvantaged has been discarded, but this revised version of the theory continues to inform the debate about development today through its discussion of the state's role.[26]

GEOGRAPHY

Another set of structural variables that may condition development is geography. The location that a country or region inhabits is largely unchangeable and may shape economic opportunities. One major geographic factor is whether a country has access to the sea; landlocked countries rely more on relations with their neighbors if they want to trade with the rest of the globe, and the distances to global markets and logistical challenges associated with being landlocked might hinder growth.[27] By a similar logic, development might be favored in areas with good natural harbors, or in countries that have oceans as barriers to would-be attackers. One might say, then, that North America was relatively *favored* by geography as it grew. More controversially, location in the tropics has long been posited as a hindrance to development.[28] The logics here range from the plausible to the blatantly racist; a recent plausible view is presented in the "Insights" box on the work of Jared Diamond. Geography's impact on development may not be constant over time. In other words, geographic factors may prove advantageous or disadvantageous only when coupled with certain technologies or institutions.

When the World Values Survey, a massive, ongoing project being carried out by an international network of social scientists, polled tens of thousands of people in more than eighty countries about the most important issues they face, the topic of economic growth and development stood out above all others.[29] A strong economy can lead to a better quality of life and greater satisfaction for most people,

---

INSIGHTS   The Modern World System
by Immanuel Wallerstein

Wallerstein developed a theory of international politics in which each place on the globe would fit into a certain role in the global economy. Known as world systems theory, this approach broke the world into categories of states: core, periphery, and semi-periphery. The core countries constitute the economic and technological center, accumulating the preponderance of profits from global production. The peripheral areas are those poor locations destined to supply basic inputs to the world capitalist system, mainly raw materials (including minerals and foodstuffs) and cheap labor. Semi-peripheral areas—roughly the "middle-income" countries—would have their own particular structural role as well, perhaps "allowed" or "encouraged" to industrialize to a certain degree to keep the global system functioning.

Immanuel Wallerstein, The Modern World System. Berkeley: University of California Press [1974] 2011.

while a weak economy can severely restrict social improvements and make politics more divisive. Since people care so much about this issue, development is not exclusively an academic concern. It matters to policymakers and everyday citizens as well. For instance, imagine you are the top economic official in a poor African country, and you want to know how best to raise people out of poverty in your country. Comparing South Korea to Brazil, you may examine why **export-led growth** (an economic strategy based on selling natural resources or products in foreign markets) seemed to work in South Korea, and import-substitution worked for a time in Brazil, and you may ask under what conditions each can work.[30] Whether a policymaker or a citizen, can you draw practical lessons for your country from development successes and failures?

export-led growth A strategy for achieving economic growth dependent on sending natural resources or agricultural or industrial products for sale in foreign markets.

The issue of development involves many substantial questions. Why do some countries advance and grow while others do not? Why do countries grow at some times and not others? Why does poverty increase or decline? Why does education improve, or why do health outcomes decline? Why is inequality on the rise in some places and declining in others? These are only a subset of the questions that may be asked about the topic of economic and social development. Even if we consider mainly economic growth, as we did through much of this chapter, scholars debate fiercely about the strongest and most successful explanations. With the intent of developing your skills as a comparativist, we will not conclude by saying which answer is "correct." Instead, we offer two observations.

First, there is likely some truth to each of the arguments we have presented about why development happens. Markets can help, states can help, institutions can matter, culture can matter, and international and domestic structures can matter. It is possible and appropriate to combine elements of these different approaches—for example, noting that culture, geography, and the role of the state all affect development. The reason these theories have earned mention in the chapter is that they have been supported by some evidence in the real world.

INSIGHTS   Guns, Germs, and Steel: The Fates of Human Societies
by Jared Diamond

Jared Diamond sought to answer a question once posed to him by a friend from the poor nation of Papua New Guinea: Why do some people have more "cargo" (i.e., "stuff") than others? Diamond found answers in nature and geography. In Africa, the poorest continent in the world today, people faced natural disadvantages from their environment. For instance, none of the large resident animals—zebras and rhinos, for example—could be domesticated, which held back advances in farming and precluded the development of African cavalries. In Europe, by contrast, farming and militaries both advanced with the use of the horse, an animal that could not survive in Africa due to endemic parasites. In Eurasia, people could also expand their populations along the continent's long east–west axis, which allowed migration and growth, while African peoples were prevented from migrating and expanding by the varying climates along the continent's north–south axis. Diamond argues that geographic and climatic forces led European peoples to develop the powerful societies that colonized and dominated the rest of the world.

Jared Diamond, Guns, Germs, and Steel: The Fates of Human Societies. *New York: W. W. Norton, 1997.*

Second, as we noted in chapter 2, it is also important to make meaningful arguments that do not simply say that "everything matters." Rather, through close examination of empirical evidence in specific case studies, we can find for ourselves what factors matter under what conditions, and *how* different factors might work together. For example, one might discover that both geography and culture partially shape economic institutions in a particular case—and that these institutions, in turn, both directly and indirectly shape development.

Since development is a process that unfolds continuously over time, an especially useful comparison can be of the same country at different points in time. For example, why was the import-substitution model successful in Brazil for a time, and why did it seem to fail at a later point in time? Using the theories from this section, you can formulate hypotheses to explain such successes and failures.

KEY METHODOLOGICAL TOOL

Most-Similar-Systems (MSS) Design

As noted in chapter 1, one way to set up a useful comparison is to choose two cases that are very similar on several criteria yet different on a key outcome. The comparison of the two Koreas and their differences in economic development is an example. Choosing two countries that have much in common allows the analyst to isolate the variables that are likely to cause the different outcomes. In this case, geography and many aspects of culture are similar, which means these variables are unlikely to explain the major differences in outcomes. Comparative political scientists do not have laboratories to work with the way natural scientists do, so "most similar" cases are as close as one can get to controlling for many variables the way one does in a laboratory. In fact, some MSS designs come from what is called a "natural experiment," such as when a country is divided into smaller parts and analysts can observe the subsequent outcomes across the different parts of the country.

Explaining the Development of North and South Korea

At the beginning of this chapter, we noted that the neighboring countries of North and South Korea have had radically different experiences with development. South Korea went from being one of the poorest countries on earth in the late 1950s to one of the richest by the 1990s. It has seen its incomes skyrocket and its economy transform into an industrial powerhouse, while the population has gone from having a majority illiterate and in poverty to one in which less than 5 percent of people fit in those categories. North Korea, of course, started in roughly the same position as the south. Yet today, it remains extremely poor, as noted at the beginning of this chapter. It experiences periodic famines and frequently depends on foreign aid that its leadership extorts through creating international crises. As shown in the following table, South Korea's estimated per capita GDP is almost sixteen times North Korea's—an astonishing economic divergence. Explaining such differences over time between economically successful and unsuccessful countries is one of the classic questions in development studies. In fact, a major book in this area (*Why Nations Fail*, by Daron Acemoglu and James A. Robinson) addresses this precise divergence between the Koreas and others like it.

Country	Per Capita GDP (CIA World Factbook)
North Korea	$1,700 (estimate as of 2015)
South Korea	$37,700 (estimate as of 2016)

Here we walk through how a comparative analyst might try to explain this difference. We would note right away that we don't aim to offer a definitive "answer" to this question that focuses on one theory over another, though some might argue that this is a relatively straightforward comparison with an obvious answer, as we note a bit later. We want to emphasize that we use basic thought experiments here for the sake of simplicity; these are not full hypothesis tests using substantial amounts of evidence. As you read this section, focus on the *logic* of hypothesis testing and the general strategy we use to apply theories to these real-world cases. Note that for more definitive results, we would need to consider much more evidence and carefully measure each of the variables we consider.

One reason this is an interesting comparison is that North and South Korea are very similar in terms of several variables we might expect to affect development, including culture and geography, but these countries vary dramatically in terms of the dependent variable (development). Table 5.2 summarizes some similarities and differences between the two cases, noting how much or how little variation there is on the key variables.

South Korea's political and economic institutions are based much more than North Korea's on capitalism and the use of domestic and global markets, as well as democracy in more recent decades. (In fact, for Acemoglu and Robinson, the comparison of the Koreas is a prime example of the importance of political institutions in shaping economic outcomes. You might see this as the "leading candidate" theory to explain the divergence, though we would emphasize the logic of considering different theoretical perspectives.) In terms of external influences, the country followed a model established by Japan, in two ways. First, Korea was a Japanese colony before World War II, and Japanese colonialism brought economic linkages to Japan and a powerful state, along with an emphasis on educating the workforce.[31] Second, Japan's economic success served as a model in terms of policy. South Korea's state adopted a pro-business strategy that included some state intervention, but with strict rules: Companies receiving state support had to meet

KEY METHODOLOGICAL TOOL

(continued)

Examples include comparisons of East and West Germany after the country was partitioned, or comparisons of India and Pakistan after the partition of British India. Another pair of countries with similarities is the Dominican Republic and Haiti, which are located on two halves of the same island. Of course, in each of these instances, the two cases will have developed quite differently over time. Setting up a MSS design is not enough to definitively demonstrate which variables cause an outcome, as that requires exploring the evidence, but it can help rule out unlikely causes of variations in outcomes.

TABLE 5.2 Possible Explanations for Variations in Development

SOUTH KOREA AND NORTH KOREA

Variable	Case 1: South Korea	Case 2: North Korea	Extent of Variation
Independent Variables for Hypothesis Testing			
Culture	Korean heritage (with minority Christian population)	Korean heritage (with negligible Christian population)	Limited
Geography	Korean peninsula Coal and mining resources	Korean peninsula Coal and mining resources	Limited
Economic and Political Institutions	Mixed state/market economy Capitalist orientation Influenced by Japan, United States Export-led growth for decades Use of markets Democracy (in recent years)	Command economy Communist Rule Influenced by China, U.S.S.R. Inward-looking economy Almost no use of markets Autocracy for decades	Major
Dependent Variable			
Development	High development and growth Advanced economy	Low development and growth Poor economy, major poverty	Major

targets for production and exports, or they would be cut off.[32] Thus, the South Korean case was interpreted by some as a constructive form of state intervention and by others as a country where the state did right by "emulating" the rules of the market.

Even the East Asian financial crisis of the late 1990s and the global economic crisis that began in 2008 did little to dent South Korea's long-term achievements. In fact, South Korea has served as a model for other Asian economies, much as Japan had served as a model for South Korea.[33] Indeed, several features of China's current economic approach appear to have drawn from South Korea's experience in promoting export-led growth. This has had interesting implications for the different theories mentioned previously: the focus here is on political and economic institutions, but there is also renewed interest in cultural theories of development because development has spread so convincingly across East Asian countries in particular.

North Korea differs quite dramatically from South Korea in its political and economic institutions, while it shares a similar geography and a common cultural background from the period before the two countries were divided. The country was pulled into the Soviet orbit after the end of World War II, while South Korea was aligned with the United States. Eventually, a major conflict broke out, the Korean War, in which North Korea was supported by China under Mao Zedong and South Korea was supported by the United States (with numerous American troops) and its allies. Eventually, the conflict was halted without satisfactory resolution for either side, and as a result we are left with the two countries, each of which claims to be the legitimate government of all of Korea. North Korea still employs a Soviet-style "planned economy." This means that all key decisions about production and funding are made by the state; and to the extent that market forces govern exchange, they do so only informally. In essence, the two countries vary not just in terms of their development histories but also in terms of the nature and extent of their states' involvement in the economy.

How would each of our theories explain the relative economic fortunes of North and South Korea in recent decades? (See Table 5.3.) Notice that the institutional arguments are promising for the reasons noted previously. At the same time, while we note that the cultural arguments might not work at first glance, that does not mean "culture" is irrelevant. A scholar doing a deeper exploration of the two countries might find ways to show that political cultures changed over time between the two countries in ways that affected the economy as well. In short, both countries may be culturally "Korean," but that does not mean they are identical in terms of culture: the North Korean political culture is certainly different from the South Korean political culture after decades of separation and such different experiences.

As you can see here, our thought experiment does not definitively establish that one of these theories is right, but it demonstrates how we would initially proceed in applying these general theories of development to the basic outlines of these two cases. This helps us think about what types of arguments might work and which might not in explaining variations in outcomes by country.

TABLE 5.3 Hypothesis Testing: North Korea and South Korea

Theory	Hypothesis: What Explains Variation?	Thought Experiment and Hypothesis Test	Next Steps for Theory
Institutions (market institutions)	Different enforcement of property rights and contracts South: Strong enforcement North: Weak enforcement	Promising	Bring in additional cases and examine these cases further. Consider how to account for South Korea's practice of state-led development.
Institutions (states and state policy)	Different qualities of state and state policy South: High quality (with robust industrial policy) North: Low quality	Promising	Account for why North Korea has failed with statist strategy. Examine South Korea's mix of state involvement and market forces in state-led development.
Culture	Different cultural backgrounds, including values, religion, and habits	Not promising (Despite some differences, countries have similar cultural backgrounds)	Adapt hypothesis to include values and habits along with other variables. Develop more complex hypothesis on how institutions change national economic cultures over time, for example.
The World-System	Different positions in "world system" South Korea: American and Japanese influence North Korea: Soviet and Chinese influence	Somewhat promising but incomplete (Positioning in the global system likely mattered by influencing institutions)	Adapt hypothesis to include world-system along with other variables. Develop more complex hypothesis that also draws on institutional theories, for example.

Chapter Summary

Concepts

- Development is a topic of pressing interest to billions of people around the world, and it can be measured in many different ways.
- The most common ways of measuring development are economic, most notably the level and growth of per capita GDP, but also the extent of poverty and economic inequality.

Types

- Development can be measured by social indicators (such as health and education), standards of living, satisfaction and happiness, equity across societal groups, cultural change, and environmental sustainability.

- Cases from around the world show that many of the indicators of development positively correlate with one another, but not always.

Causes and Effects

- Using economic growth as an outcome, scholars have theorized about many important factors that lead to development. An important debate is about whether the economy should be led by the market or by the state. The current consensus is that both market and state play important roles in a modern economy.
- Institutions such as property rights play key roles in development and may link to the market and the state.

- Culture may shape development as well. It may be manifested in levels of trust and social capital, or in norms, ethics, and cultural tendencies that emerge in different places at different points in time.
- A final category of explanations for development can be found in "structural" or "systemic" factors, where the backdrop of the world economic and political order can either support or hinder economic advancement.
- There is surely some truth in each of these approaches, but these must be investigated with respect to specific cases.

Thinking It Through

1. The "Causes and Effects" section of this chapter focused on growth, but can you use at least one theory from that section to propose why some developing countries have more or less inequality (as defined in chapter 4) than others?

2. The so-called "BRIC" countries—Brazil, Russia, India, and China—all boomed at points in the 2000s. Does this correlation suggest they are all following similar development patterns? Does this timing provide evidence to support one theory about the causes of development more than others? Does it mean something "global" was causing growth and not something specific to each country?

3. Many countries have more and less successful economic periods over time. Which of the theories in this chapter does this fluctuation support? Does it "disprove" any theory based on culture because a country's culture is relatively "stable"? Does it "prove" that development depends on things that change over time, like a government's policies?

4. Many prominent developing countries are (or have been) major exporters of oil. Why have the resource-rich countries not benefited from consistent, rapid growth? To what extent are natural resources beneficial for development, and to what extent are they a "curse"?

5. Why do countries go through economic boom and bust cycles in their development? If countries are "most similar" (see chapter 2) to themselves, should economic performance be relatively consistent over time, unless there are major changes in policy (as was the case in China)?

CHAPTER 6

Democracy an
Democratizatioı

The bright umbrellas of protestors in Hong Kong, August 2017. They marched to show solidarity with several democracy activists jailed for previous protests.

Imagine a country where less than half of the population can vote, half have very limited basic rights, and social roles are allocated on the basis of ethnic or racial affiliation, so that members of some groups have virtually *no* rights and are the property of other people. Imagine still further that elections are periodically held but that to stand any chance of election one must be from the elite class, meaning: (1) a wealthy landowner; (2) a wealthy businessman; or (3) a doctor, lawyer, clergyman, or other professional whose social networks intersect with those of wealthy landowners or businessmen. If we told you that this situation were true of a given developing country, would you consider it fully democratic? Probably not, and yet the country we are describing is, of course, the United States of America in the years after its founding.

Our point is most emphatically not to deny the democratic status of the United States. It was, at the time, in spite of the conditions we have just listed, one of the most democratic large-scale societies the world had ever known. Rather, our point is that deciding whether a given country is democratic is more complicated than it appears at first glance. Democracy changes over time, meaning that its benchmarks and criteria are moving targets. Moreover, the line between more and less democratic regimes is somewhat gray.

Many people reading this chapter have lived only in democratic societies. Democracy is, for much of the Anglophone world, part of the backdrop of politics: it is simply assumed to be present (yet, as the preceding example demonstrates, this has not always been the case, and even today there are democratic deficits in this world). Where regimes are democratic, individuals and groups can freely contest their ideas and try to shape political life, with the winners of fair elections having greater opportunity to craft their preferred policies and laws through the democratic process. The losers typically accept the principle that in a democracy, it is possible one will lose a political battle, a debate, or an election; they continue to support the system or the *regime*, even if they oppose the particular government administration of the moment. They don't claim, if they lose, that the system is corrupt and needs to be overturned.

In much of the world, however, authoritarianism is the rule, and the very existence of democracy itself is a fundamental political issue. Only in recent decades has the world reached the point where over half of its citizens live under democracy. Understanding whether a country is democratic is a prerequisite for further discussions about politics, whether we are interested in legislatures and executives, or the power of interest groups and political parties, or religious politics and gender politics. While the precise definition of democracy is debated—and many will disagree on which countries are democratic—most political scientists will concur that prominent countries such as China, Iran, Saudi Arabia, North Korea, and Cuba are not democracies; and that many more countries, such as Russia, fall far short of full democratic practice, even if elections are held on schedule. We discuss authoritarian regimes in chapter 7.

In this chapter, we begin by addressing two central and related concepts: democracy (or democratic regime) and democratization, the process through which authoritarian polities become (more) democratic. We then discuss subtypes of democratic regimes using a number of our case studies to exemplify them. Finally, we turn to political science debates about the causes of democratization and democratic consolidation. Why do they happen where they do, in some places and not others? And why do they happen when they do, at some times and not others? We present several possible explanations. We close with a critical examination of whether the United States should be treated by political scientists as a model for democracy elsewhere.

. . .

Concepts

Democracy is one of the most fundamental concepts in politics, and given its importance, scholars have contested and reworked the concept and causes of democracy over the years.[1] As with many constructive debates in political science (in contrast with the dynamics of debates in electoral politics and campaigns), contestation over the definition is not a disagreement to be lamented but rather an important part of the study of democracy.

democracy A form of regime associated with "rule by the people" that signifies rights and liberties for citizens, including political rights to participate in elections and civil liberties such as freedom of speech.

Democracy and Democratic Regimes

Despite disagreement over exactly what democracy means, there is broad agreement on two salient points. First, many political scientists would share an intuitive sense of which geographic units in the world are relatively more or less democratic. Second, even in the midst of some disagreement, political scientists commonly accept definitions of democracy that emphasize two main types of rights, which we discuss further a bit later in the chapter: **political rights** to participate in

political rights Rights of individuals to participate in political life, including the right to political speech, the right to vote, and the right to join political associations.

FREEDOM IN THE WORLD 2017

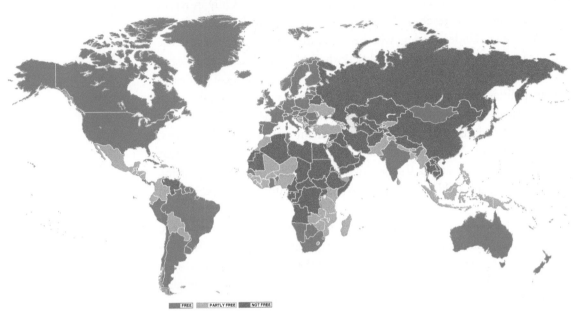

FREE   PARTLY FREE   NOT FREE

Map 6.1 Democracy in the world, 2017

Courtesy FreedomHouse.org

civil rights Rights of individuals to participate in civic life, including freedoms of assembly, speech, access to information, and equal access to institutions, among others.

electoral processes, and **civil rights** and related freedoms. The prominent NGO Freedom House, which monitors democracy in countries around the world, explicitly builds both elements into its assessment (Map 6.1). Leading works in recent years emphasize the distinction between mere electoral democracy and a more genuine democracy that also includes civil rights protections. To define democracy, most scholars use what is called a procedural, or minimal, definition. This approach emphasizes the minimal standards that a country should have in place—procedures or rules that govern political life—as contrasted with a variety of *substantive* issues noted later.[2]

regime A form or type of governmental system, with an emphasis on institutions and rules.

democratic regime A regime with predominantly democratic institutions, including basic civil rights and regular, free elections.

By using the term **regime**, political scientists are referring to a form or type of governmental system, with an emphasis on institutions and rules. The most significant distinction is between democratic and authoritarian regimes. You can think of a **democratic regime** as one with democratic institutions and rules. Similarly, an authoritarian regime has authoritarian institutions, structures, or rules. The regime is conceptually distinct from any particular democratic *government*. Thus, Iran has had an Islamic Republic as its regime since 1979 but has had several different governments under presidents such as Mohammad Khatami, Mahmoud Ahmadinejad, and Hassan Rouhani. The United States has had its constitutional republic since 1788 but many different governments in its regime.

Note that one's definition of "democratic regime" depends on one's definition of "democracy." For instance, some might classify Mexico or Nigeria as democratic regimes because they have relatively free and fair elections and protections for civil liberties. But others might consider these countries not to be fully democratic on the grounds that they fail to provide sufficient levels of security and opportunity for citizens.

PROCEDURAL (MINIMAL) DEFINITIONS OF DEMOCRACY

Procedural definitions of democracy say that what makes a country democratic is that it follows certain procedures, or rules and methods. Yet most leading procedural definitions of democracy view it as more than just elections every few years; they also include the civil rights and civil liberties that should be guaranteed to every citizen on an ongoing basis. Thus, even when political scientists speak of minimal, or procedural, definitions of what democracy is, they mean more than elections. Consider the following lists of political rights and civil liberties, which many political scientists agree are central to democracy[3]:

Political Rights:

- Elections are free and fair, and most individuals can vote.
- Elections are regularly scheduled or held periodically.
- Elections have multiple political parties, or some choice.
- Elections are open to most any individual to run for office.

Civil Liberties:

- Freedom of speech and expression
- Freedom to access sources of information/freedom of the press
- Freedom of assembly/to join interest groups and parties

Note that all of these are essentially measures of whether certain rules or procedures are followed. Also, note that the first four of these (the political rights) may be seen as directly related to electoral processes, and they presume that peaceful transfers of power do take place in accord with electoral decisions. The latter three (the civil liberties) are about political action outside of the realm of electoral processes and center on the rights of the public not to be harassed by the state. Important civil liberties can be found in the U.S. Constitution's first ten amendments. Passed together in 1791, this Bill of Rights set an international standard for civil liberties.

To illustrate the importance of both categories of freedoms, consider a thought experiment in which a country has regular free and fair elections but allows no protest, controls the press, and represses free speech. This would be less a true democracy and more a competitive authoritarian or electoral authoritarian regime.[4] Conversely, a system in which people have relative freedoms to voice their grievances but no right to elect their government officials would also be non-democratic. Only by fulfilling the basic requirements on both counts will a country earn a reputation for democracy.

Other criteria could conceivably be added. For instance, some leading scholars have proposed adding the following two additional criteria in determining whether a country is democratic:[5]

- Democracies are not overruled by an outside power (such as a colonizer).
- Democracies must maintain a clear distinction between civilian and military rule.

These two additional features further clarify the requirements for a democracy, ruling out the likes of countries that look like democracies internally but that systematically overrule the will of the populace. These may include locations such as

procedural definition of democracy A conception of democracy, contrasted with a substantive definition, that emphasizes the minimal standards, procedures, or rules that a country should have in place to govern political life.

the so-called independent homelands under South Africa's apartheid government before 1994.

SUBSTANTIVE DEFINITIONS OF DEMOCRACY

substantive definition of democracy A conception of democracy, contrasted with a procedural definition, that views a polity's democratic status as dependent on the satisfaction of certain substantive ends, such as the extension of broad rights or the reduction of income inequality.

While procedural definitions long dominated the debates about democracy in political science, recent years have seen an increasing turn to more **substantive definitions of democracy**. This range of definitions examines the notion of democratic depth and quality, suggesting that democracy is not just about certain rule-governed procedures being followed but rather about certain outcomes, in particular, the coordination of a certain kind of collective action. Proponents of a substantive definition of democracy often argue that countries can always undergo further democratization and that the question of democracy is not restricted to whether countries meet a minimum threshold.

Elements of a substantive definition may include the following:
- Participation, social inclusion, and civil society involvement
- Equity/equality by gender, race, or other groups
- Accountability (including lack of corruption) and institutional performance
- Public knowledge and awareness
- Poverty, inequality, and other economic outcomes

Obviously, these criteria rarely lend themselves to yes/no evaluations. Even the world's most established democracies can always make progress toward greater democratic depth or quality. In the United States, for instance, the percentage of citizens who vote in Congressional elections ranges from about 40 percent in years without a presidential vote to about 60 percent in years when a presidential election is held. This contrasts with much higher voter turnout in most of Europe, leading some to suggest that the United States falls short on certain substantive aspects of democracy. With respect to the economy, the American political and economic systems from the 1980s to the 2000s were characterized by higher levels of inequality than Europe (thus suggesting a substantive shortcoming in the American model relative to the European), but also generated lower levels of unemployment in most years (thus possibly suggesting a substantive advantage of the American model over the European).

regime change Any major change of regime type, including democratization, democratic breakdown, or certain types of authoritarian persistence in which one type of authoritarian regime gives way to another.

regime type The form of a political regime, such as democratic versus authoritarian, as well as subtypes, such as personalistic dictatorships or totalitarian regimes.

democratization The process of a regime becoming more democratic, including both democratic transition and democratic consolidation.

democratic breakdown The process through which a democratic regime partially or completely loses its democratic status.

Questions of substantive democracy lend themselves to some of the most intriguing research questions in comparative politics. In fact, as the number of democracies in the world has risen in the democratic wave since 1989,[6] questions of substantive democracy have taken an increasingly important position in comparative politics relative to procedural democracy. Of course, studying procedural democracy and studying substantive democracy are not mutually exclusive, as a country's reaching the procedural/minimal threshold may be related to improvements in the substantive elements just listed. For students interested in researching democracy, either or both of these definitions may be useful, but it is important to distinguish between them.

Regime Change and Democratization

The history of democracy and authoritarianism is one of change from one **regime type** to another. **Democratization** is the process that leads from authoritarianism to democracy, while changes in the opposite direction are commonly called **democratic breakdown** (and not "authoritarianization")[7]. We discuss the latter in the next chapter.

Democratization may be seen as a process that a country completes once it transitions from authoritarianism to a basic minimum democratic threshold, or it may be a more indefinite, ongoing process that continues to consolidate even after a country has reached a basic level of political and civil freedoms. Democratization itself can thus be a rich and diverse area for study. Two additional concepts that are central in the literature on democratization highlight the different stages of the process: transition and consolidation.

Transition is the movement from an authoritarian regime to a democratic one. This can happen through revolutionary means. A clear example is the wave of democratization that accompanied the end of the Soviet Union's dominance of Eastern Europe in the 1980s. Another possible example, the Arab Spring uprisings of 2011, *might* eventually lead to successful democratization, and a number of the effected countries have clearly taken some steps in this direction; but in some respects, this democratization seems to have stalled, and indeed, in most cases, authoritarian persistence seems to be the medium-term outcome. Transition can also happen through more gradual and negotiated means, such as the transition from the Augusto Pinochet dictatorship to Chilean democracy in 1990.

transition The movement from an authoritarian regime to a democratic one.

Consolidation refers to the process through which the new democratic order becomes institutionalized and therefore more likely to endure. For example, in the Chilean case, many might consider the elections and peaceful transfers of power from the left-leaning president Michelle Bachelet to the right-leaning Sebastián Piñera in 2010, back again to Bachelet in 2014 , and to Piñera once more in 2018, as signs of just how successfully consolidated Chilean democracy was after only two decades.

consolidation The process through which a new democratic order becomes institutionalized and therefore more likely to endure.

Chilean presidents Michelle Bachelet and Sebastián Piñera in 2017. Some view the peaceful and democratic alternation in power of these two very ideologically different leaders as a sign of the consolidation of Chilean democracy.

Types

As noted earlier, not only are there varying ways to define both democracy and authoritarianism (as we shall see further in chapter 7), but democratic and authoritarian regimes come in a variety of forms, with major implications for life in political society. Here we discuss representative versus direct forms of democracy before moving on to consider major forms or elements of transition to democracy.

Types of Democracy

Democracies—and ideas about democracy—come in multiple forms, with one of the most important contrasts being that between less direct (or representative) democracy and direct democracy. The heart of the difference lies in the degree and form of *mediation* between voters and the state.

REPRESENTATIVE DEMOCRACY

constitutional republic A polity without a monarch in which the basic rules of politics are laid out in a constitution.

constitutional monarchy A political system in which a monarch such as a king, queen, or emperor plays a role as a head of state but has powers limited by a constitution.

representative democracy A conception of democracy in which politicians and institutions are understood to represent the electorate, who nevertheless can constrain their behavior through periodic elections and other forms of participation.

Much of what we consider democracy is actually a representative form of government that is either a **constitutional republic** or a **constitutional monarchy**. Democracy, in the original sense of the term, signified direct rule by the people, through mass assemblies or legislation by direct vote of the masses. Clearly, modern nation-states do not typically govern on this basis, but democracies instead rely on elected representatives who vote for legislation on behalf of the populace as a whole. This form of government has come to be called **representative democracy** when it meets several criteria that show government is based on the people.

Foremost among the criteria for being considered a representative democracy is constitutionality, which guarantees rights to citizens. Constitutional rights limit the powers of government and also limit the power of the political majority, so that those who lose an election need not fear that their rights will be "alienated" by the "tyranny of the majority." The United States is a constitutional republic, while the United Kingdom is a constitutional monarchy in which the monarch is little more than a national figurehead and elected officials do the business of governing. Both can be considered representative democracies. We will refer to representative democracies to identify these modern nation-states where the population elects representatives democratically and citizens are guaranteed constitutional rights. These regimes are thus characterized by the citizenry having two broad categories of rights, both of which are necessary for a country to merit being called a democracy: political or electoral rights, and civil rights or civil liberties.

Political rights relate directly to electoral processes and include what is often considered the most fundamental of all democratic rights: the freedom to vote in free and fair elections. Also understood in the definition of political rights are various features that underpin and extend this simple consideration of electoral freedom. All citizens who have reached the age of majority (such as eighteen years) should have the right to vote; the franchise should not be restricted to one sex, one race, one ethnicity, or one religion. Elections should be held with some reasonable frequency (and not, say, every fifty years). Citizens should also have the right to present themselves as candidates for office and should be allowed to join different political parties in their running for office; they should not be required to join an official single party. Democracies may differ on many criteria, but all that are worthy of the name **multiparty democracies** will fulfill the preceding.

Civil rights or civil liberties are those that guarantee citizens the ability to participate in civic life *outside* of elections. They are coequal with political rights in determining whether a country is democratic. Some of the key civil rights are usefully summarized in the First Amendment to the United States Constitution: "Congress shall make no law respecting an establishment of religion, nor prohibiting the free exercise thereof; or abridging freedom of speech or of the press, or of the right of the people peaceably to assemble, and to petition the government for the redress of grievances." All elements here suggest the freedom of an individual's conscience with respect to his/her own beliefs. Freedom of religion is noted first, in the so-called Establishment Clause. Freedom of speech follows and includes an individual's right both to speak and to obtain information from multiple sources of information via access to an independent press. Freedom of conscience and speech is also linked to the freedom to assert one's belief that government should change its laws or policies. Such assertions may take place through peaceful assemblies, such as rallies or protests, or public statements.

Of course, democracies differ in both political rights and civil liberties, and these rights are rarely absolutes. To take the case of the civil liberties surrounding free speech, the oft-cited example is that "freedom of speech does not give you the right to yell 'fire' in a crowded theater." More formally, we may consider that freedom of speech may be bounded by the need to protect others' freedoms as well. Hence, even democracies that stand firmly on the principle of free speech will wrestle with questions of what sorts of speech may be illegal, including libel and slander, and hate speech or provocations to violence (such as calling for the assassination of a head of state). The principle of free speech does not stop debates about whether making campaign contributions should be a form of protected speech, or whether such contributions may be limited to prevent donors from buying undue political influence. Likewise, while most democracies allow some freedom of religion (an issue closely related to freedom of speech), how they manage the relationship between religion and public life varies considerably, a topic that will be discussed further in chapter 15.

Similarly, other civil liberties have reasonable limits that are shaped by interpretation of constitutions and the law. For instance, a democratic free press may not be allowed to report nuclear secrets that could compromise national security, and freedom of religion may not extend to allowing murderous cults to engage in human sacrifice. The right to bear arms, found in the United States Constitution's Second Amendment, may be interpreted in various ways, including giving individuals the right to possess a range of firearms; but it clearly does not give private citizens the right to possess their own weapons of mass destruction.

Political rights are also shaped differently in different countries. Many of these variations simply reflect the number of possible ways of crafting democratic institutions. Elections may come at fixed intervals (maybe every five years, or every seven), or on a more flexible schedule. Exercising the vote may be mandatory or optional. Elected officials may switch parties freely when in office or they may be required to resign their seat if they change parties.

multiparty democracy A democracy in which at least two parties compete for power.

Some arrangements are touted as democratic but seem to call the process into question. For instance, many systems with questionable (or worse) democratic credentials have made the case that all political discourse can be contained within one single unifying national party, such as China's Communist Party.[8] While this clearly violates the principle of multiparty democracy, it nonetheless seems clear that some single-party countries are more democratic than others. An example that shows the complexity of the debate is the African nation of Uganda from the 1980s to the mid-2000s. There, a generally popular president maintained that the best system for governance in Africa was "no-party democracy" because in too many African countries political parties tended to reflect and reinforce volatile ethnic divisions. This argument was plausible but dubious since the president sat atop the so-called National Resistance Movement, which was not officially a party but represented the state. Without any political parties, the state itself (and its president) may wield control that looks rather anti-democratic.

In short, representative democracies include a range of debates about the specific nature and extent of civil liberties, and there are numerous ways to set up the political institutions of such systems. As it is often said, not all democracies follow the American model, or the British model, or any other. They do, however, share in common the basic features discussed in this section.

Ugandan president Yoweri Museveni in a victory parade following his fifth reelection, in 2011. How democratic is Uganda?

DIRECT DEMOCRACY

The challenges of understanding democracy do not end with reaching the democratic threshold. As noted previously, many of the world's most powerful democracies today continue to deal with the challenges of deepening democratization. Among the controversial issues in these polities are some options that may be seen as taking democracy closer to the people yet sidestepping elected representatives. **Referenda** (or plebiscites)—in which specific issues are put to popular vote—are prominent here. These feature in individual countries in the European Union (perhaps the most notable example being the 2016 "Brexit" referendum in the United Kingdom), as well as in American states, most notably California, with its possibilities for citizens to place initiatives and propositions on the statewide ballot and to recall elected officials.

referendum A popular vote on a specific issue.

The increasing use of referenda, plebiscites, or ballot initiatives may be considered an increasing use of **direct democracy**. That is, at least the votes themselves might be considered examples of direct democracy, though there are questions and debates about which items should be placed before the people in these forms, and who should place them there. Moreover, some evidence suggests that referenda can be used to promote anti-democratic outcomes. While democracies may be increasingly using direct democratic initiatives, they are not a necessary feature of representative democracy.

direct democracy A conception of democracy that places great emphasis on direct citizen involvement in politics, especially involving plebiscites and/or citizen assemblies.

Direct democracy can also take the form of citizen assemblies, community councils, and similar forms of association. Often, proponents of direct democracy also favor some representative democratic institutions, seeing these as complementary. Some people, though, see direct or "participatory" democracy as an alternative to representative forms. Some worry that such "participatory" forms do not always include sufficient safeguards for individual voices and that they can give rise to collective decisions that do not protect the rights of political minorities very well.

Types of Democratization

In this section, we discuss two different aspects or stages in the process of democratization. You can think of them as types of democratization, but only in a certain sense. A fully successful case of democratization will involve *both* democratic transition and then the consolidation of the emergent democracy.

DEMOCRATIC TRANSITIONS

Democratic transitions are changes from one regime type (authoritarianism) to another (democratic rule). In some countries, these may be relatively rapid processes, taking only several days. By contrast, some countries go through long, slow transitions from authoritarian rule to democracy. Brazil in the 1980s and Mexico in the 1990s are examples of slower-motion transitions in which it became increasingly clear over time that the authoritarian system was being replaced by a more democratic regime. The variation in the duration of transitions was expressed in a statement by historian Timothy Garton Ash. In the midst of the cascading transitions to democracy in Central Europe in 1989, he described the events by saying, "in Poland it took ten years, in Hungary it took ten months, in East Germany it took ten weeks, perhaps in Czechoslovakia it will take ten days."[9]

democratic transition The process through which a non-democratic regime becomes democratic.

Transitions are also diverse in their causes and impacts. Some are relatively controlled by the authoritarians who are on their way out of power, while others come from the collapse of the previous power structure. In Latin America in the 1980s, many countries (such as Brazil and Chile) had slow transitions to democracy in which the military built in advantages for itself to ensure that its policies and preferences would influence democratic politics for some time. Other democratic transitions have happened in more revolutionary fashion in countries ranging from the Philippines to the West African nation of Benin.

DEMOCRATIC CONSOLIDATION

democratic consolidation The process through which, after a transition from authoritarianism, a polity strengthens its democracy.

Democratic consolidation is typically a longer-term process than transition.[10] It may be seen as the process by which democracy and its political and civil rights become normal or habitual for citizens. The term "consolidation" has been characterized as happening when democracy is "the only game in town."[11] That is, a democracy may be seen as consolidated when there are no major political groups advocating for a return to authoritarianism or for the overthrow of the democratic system. Related to this, consolidation may have happened when the populace as a whole has rejected the idea of authoritarianism and supports the democratic regime. Compared with these ideas or values, a more mechanical indicator of consolidation may be when a country has "turned over" its government two or more times; that is, the people who used to govern lose an election and step aside, and then the people who replaced them eventually lose and step aside. When and where this happens, it is a good sign that democracy is accepted by all the major political actors and has become routine.

Consolidation is challenging even in leading democracies. Many countries that have made the transition to free and fair elections and civil liberties will face difficulties in guaranteeing these for the citizenry. Even the world's longest-standing democracies, such as the United States, have not fulfilled all of the promises often associated with democracy. Consolidation is a long-term endeavor because delivering full democratic rights to all citizens (and indeed developing a full notion of who is a citizen) is a historically complex process. To look at the American example, note that rights may be progressively extended to more groups (often beginning with relatively wealthy male property holders and slowly incorporating others) and not offered to everyone at once. It is also a process that can suffer setbacks as countries fail to consolidate or revert to authoritarian rule.

For those interested in the minimal, procedural definition of democracy, democratization may be most associated with transition, a process in which a formerly non-democratic (i.e., authoritarian) regime is liberalized and attains democratic credentials. On the other hand, consolidation may require consideration of how robust a democracy becomes, as well as questions about whether a country will maintain its basic standards of political and civil rights over time. For those political scientists interested in understanding broad patterns of levels of democracy around the world, a transition above a certain threshold may be sufficient for the purposes of a given study, while those interested in understanding a democracy's quality and depth may necessarily be examining its process of consolidation.

CASE IN CONTEXT
Democratic Consolidation in Brazil

PAGE 409

For years Brazil alternated between authoritarianism and transitory attempts at democracy. In recent decades, though, its democracy has achieved noteworthy consolidation, and despite concerns about corruption and high levels of political cynicism, relatively few now fear the imminent return of Brazilian authoritarianism. Given that Brazil is one of the world's largest countries, and an increasingly influential one, this is a very positive development. But how did it happen? And what lessons does Brazil offer to other countries interested in democratic consolidation?

For more on this case, see the case study in Part VI, p. 409. As you read it, keep in mind the following questions:

1. How does Brazil's recent economic performance relate to its democratic consolidation?
2. How, and to what extent, has Brazilian democracy come to include poorer Brazilians?
3. Are there risks to Brazil's democracy in the widespread perception that the political class is highly corrupt?

Causes and Effects: What Causes Democratization?

Uncovering what causes and sustains democracy is a central challenge facing political scientists. Here, we combine the debates about democracy and democratization to ask why democracy varies both across countries and over time. In other words, we consider both *where* democracy happens and *when* it occurs. Note that both of these considerations get at the underlying question of *why* regime types emerge, consolidate, and shift. Although we cannot capture the entire debate, we highlight five prominent lines of theory:

1. *modernization theory*, which traces democracy to broad social changes, especially economic development and the changes that accompany it;[12]
2. *cultural theories*, which attribute democratization and democratic consolidation to cultural variables that may predispose some countries to democracy and prevent or hinder democracy in other places;[13]
3. *systemic or structural theories*, which situate countries in an international environment where major powers or global trends may condition whether democracy emerges or not;[14]
4. *domestic institutional theories*, which find that the advent and success of democracy depend on the forms of political institutions within a country (such as political parties and interest groups, or the ways branches of government are shaped);[15] and
5. *agency-based theories*, which argue that individual actors, or small groups of actors, are the drivers of changes in regime types (whether democratic or authoritarian).[16]

We consider these five perspectives in turn.

As noted in the previous chapters, different theoretical perspectives are not entirely mutually exclusive, but they do offer different arguments about political behavior and what causes it. While good arguments may draw from multiple perspectives, it is important that comparative political scientists understand both

CASE IN CONTEXT

Is China Destined for Democracy?

PAGE 422

One of the most important questions in contemporary global politics is whether China will democratize in the coming years— and, if so, how. In certain respects, since reforms began there in the late 1970s after the death of Mao Zedong, we have seen some limited democratization at the local level. But China remains an authoritarian state dominated by a single party, and virtually no political scientists would consider it democratic.

For more on authoritarianism and potential democratization in China, see the case study in Part VI, pp. 422–423. As you read it, keep in mind the following questions:

1. What would each of the theories from the chapter predict about the prospect of China's democratization?
2. Which of these predictions do you find most plausible, and why?
3. If Chinese economic growth slows in future years, how do you think this might affect the prospects for democratization in China?

what they are arguing and how they might be arguing *against* some other perspective. Fundamentally, arguments are based on efforts to test specific hypotheses— derived from theories—against empirical evidence.

Modernization

modernization theory A theory that traces democracy to broad social changes, especially economic development and the changes that accompany it.

Perhaps the most central debate in modern comparative study of democracy centers on elements of **modernization theory**. Advocates of a modernization approach examine the relationship between economic development and democratization. With respect to the causes of democratization, an extensive literature finds changes in economic structure to be a key to democratic change; in these analyses, economics drives much of politics. Modernization scholars argue that economic change drove democratization through the emergence of such factors as a middle class (or *bourgeoisie*) and a literate population. Urbanization over decades and centuries was key in turning former lords and peasants into small businessmen who demanded greater political say without being either reactionary or revolutionary. More recently, the link between modernization and democratization finds new support (with modifications and revisions) for the idea that democracies become more stable and secure when they are relatively wealthy.

Conversely, poor countries that lack the stabilizing force of a robust middle class will tend toward authoritarianism. In the absence of the modernization process outlined previously, no democratic push can emerge. Societies divided between a small, wealthy elite and impoverished masses will be prone to reactionary, noninclusive politics dominated by the former, or to revolutionary mobs where the latter can seize power. Neither group has an interest in leaving political power to the other. Only economically modernized societies, with their relatively moderate middle classes, can strike the balance between these extremes.

Modernization theory includes a variety of different approaches. According to some versions, the economic and social forces of modernization that shape democracy do not only occur at one point that triggers a democratic transition. Rather, economic development may also support the persistence of democracy, once democracy is established.

INSIGHTS	Political Man: The Social Bases of Politics *and* Some Social Requisites of Democracy: Economic Development and Political Legitimacy
	by Seymour Martin Lipset

As discussed in this chapter, one of the most consistent findings in comparative politics has been that economic development often "goes with" democracy and democratization. In other words, having a highly developed economy increases the likelihood of stable democracy. Classical theorists drew attention to this connection, but the political sociologist Seymour Martin Lipset was the first scholar to demonstrate the relationship with strong empirical evidence, showing that a range of development variables correlated with democracy.

Recall from chapter 2 that correlation is not the same as causation. The mere fact that there is a relationship between two variables does not mean that one necessarily causes the other. Maybe democracy causes economic development, after all.[17] Modernization theory *predicts* that causality will move from economic development to the creation and consolidation of democratic institutions. It does so by trying to specify causal mechanisms through which growth might be expected to promote democracy. Lipset pointed to numerous potential mechanisms, such as literacy and education, but his main idea was that economic development leads to the creation of a strong middle class; and that this middle class, in turn, promotes democratization and democratic stability. If Lipset is right, proponents of democracy should be very attentive to social and economic factors such as increasing income inequality, since a decline of the middle class might weaken democratic institutions.

Seymour Martin Lipset, Political Man: The Social Bases of Politics. *Garden City, NY Doubleday and Co., 1960; and "Some Social Requisites of Democracy: Economic Development and Political Legitimacy."* American Political Science Review 53, *no. 1 (1959): 69–105.*

Modernization theory faces the challenge that there are exceptions it has trouble explaining. For example, India is the world's largest democracy, and it remains quite poor. Moreover, it democratized well before its recent years of economic growth. Can modernization theory explain India's democratic success? And how can modernization theory explain the fact that democratization often happens rapidly and in waves?

Different versions of this theory specify different hypothetical mechanisms linking economic development to democracy. Remember, what we mean by "causal mechanism" is the process through which something produces something else, according to a theory.[18] Scholars can agree that two variables—like economic development and democracy—are related without necessarily agreeing about how they are linked, as discussed in chapter 2. As we have seen, classic versions of modernization theories of democracy point to the intervening variable of a strong middle class.[19] Some more recent versions of modernization theory suggest a different intervening variable: Economic development might produce democratic values such as the value of "self-expression."[20] We return to this issue later in the chapter.

Culture and Democracy

Economic development is just one of many conceivable causes of democratization. Other significant contributions have emphasized new factors, especially as the regional emphasis among democratization theorists has shifted from historical changes in Western Europe to those in Latin America, Africa, and Asia. Cultural arguments may be able to provide substantial leverage on understanding political trajectories in different countries.[21]

CASE IN CONTEXT

Democracy's Success in India: What Can We Learn from a Deviant Case?

PAGE 466

India is a major anomaly for modernization theories of development. In essence, the relationship between its political and economic development has been the inverse of what modernization theory would predict. India is the world's second largest society and its largest democracy—consider, therefore, the share that Indian citizens hold in the world's broader democratic population. This anomaly has potentially serious implications and makes the puzzle of Indian democratization all the more intriguing.

For more on the case of democratization in India, see the case study in Part VI, p. 466. As you read it, keep in mind the following questions:

1. What, if anything, does Indian anti-colonial resistance have to do with the country's democratization?

2. What, if anything, does Indian democratization suggest about the importance of individual actors, leadership, and institutional design?

3. Can you think of a way to "save" modernization theory in the face of the case of India?

Indian Voters, 2017, in Uttar Pradesh state. India is the world's largest democracy.

One prominent cultural argument is the "Asian values" argument, as articulated by certain non-democratic leaders in Asia who argued why Asia is not conducive to democracy like the "West" is.[22] According to this argument, Asian cultures value stability and harmonious social relations over individual rights, and are comfortable with respect for authority and deference to the state. Accordingly, democracy is not a priority but is secondary to ideas of order, hard work, and social progress. An additional caveat is in order here: a country's "culture" may be defined in many different ways and by different individuals or groups. The assertion by a Malaysian or Singaporean prime minister (or anyone else, for that matter) about what his country's culture is should not be taken as the definitive word on the subject. Indeed, political cultures may be deliberately shaped by states and governments—especially in non-democratic countries—for a number of purposes. Many Malaysians and Singaporeans may differ with the former prime ministers Lee Kuan-Yew or Mahathir Mohamed about their own societies' compatibility with democracy. Not all culturalist arguments are so transparently self-serving for authoritarian leaders, however. Some scholars have tried to explain authoritarian persistence in Latin America as rooted in alleged cultural tendencies toward "corporatism" and "authoritarian centralism."[23] Still others have argued that religion makes a difference in shaping the likelihood that a country will be democratic.[24]

While arguments like these have had some influence, political scientists rarely demonstrate that such-and-such a country or continent is not democratic because of some fixed cultural element that is static and unchanging, and sophisticated approaches to cultural explanation do not attempt to do so. To take Africa as an example, political scientists would rarely rest on an argument such as, "Africa is

Democracy in America
by Alexis de Tocqueville

Tocqueville's analysis of American democracy is complex and multifaceted. Scholars influenced by his work, however, have often focused on one of its key aspects. He believed that the protection of liberal rights and the functioning of democratic institutions depended in good measure on *mores* or values and feelings held in the population. In other words, democracy depends partially on "political culture." Above all, he was impressed by the degree of participation in democratic politics he witnessed in the United States: people got involved and seemed to *enjoy* their involvement.

Tocqueville didn't think of political culture as some unchanging thing attached to a group. It wasn't that Americans were intrinsically disposed to democracy. Rather, these tendencies were shaped by social and institutional factors. For example, the pattern of immigration and the nature of inheritance in the United States had led to relatively higher levels of preexisting equality: the country had no real hereditary nobility, at least not like in Europe at the time. He also felt that American political institutions at the national level were largely well designed, singling out the country's administrative decentralization. Perhaps more important, particularly in New England, local townships had established political institutions that depended on participation. These institutions, Tocqueville famously wrote, inculcated certain "habits of the heart" in those who participated in them, awakening a desire for deliberation.

The critical idea here, therefore, is not that some countries are culturally destined for democratization and others for authoritarianism, but that social and institutional conditions do influence political culture, which can then help constrain politics.

Alexis de Tocqueville, Democracy in America, *trans. Harvey Mansfield and Debra Winthrop. Chicago: University of Chicago Press, 2002 (first published, in French, in 1835 and 1840).*

not very democratic because its people don't want it," or "Africa has lots of authoritarian rule because people belong to tribes." Besides sounding judgmental (in ways that can border on racism, when some wrongly assume Africans are less capable of sophisticated political calculations), the conception of culture here is too thin. Cultural scholars recognize that values, norms, and customs are shaped and reshaped, defined and redefined over time. Culture is dynamic rather than static. While cultural differences among countries may help explain some continuities over the course of years, ideas and values are also constantly shifting. For instance, cultural arguments may note that Latin America was long deemed to have male-dominated polities, but they may also note the increasing empowerment of women in many countries in Latin America that may have played a role in the processes of democratization there, as with the case of the Mothers of the Disappeared (*Madres de [la] Plaza de Mayo*) in Argentina.

The International System

For any country, the prevailing tendencies in the international system are likely to affect the chance of democracy. To use just the twentieth century as an example, it may seem sensible to suggest that the period between the two World Wars (including the Great Depression), the Cold War, and the post–Cold War era were three very different time periods with respect to the question of how widespread democracy would be. Looking at snapshots of the global situation at certain moments in time can convey the importance of the international environment.

During the Cold War, for example, the countries of Eastern and Central Europe (the so-called Second World) were obviously kept under authoritarian rule by the power of the Soviet Union. Less obviously, but just as truly, the poorest countries of the "Third World" also languished under dictatorships sponsored by both the

Soviet Union and the United States. In a time period when the major international powers prioritized security and influence over democratic rights in Asia, Africa, and Latin America, military leaders found it relatively easy to retain power over civilians. To use a slightly earlier historical example, colonial rule was non-democratic. For many of the peoples of the world, the political and economic system of the colonial era—when Britain, France, Spain, Portugal, and Holland dominated much of the globe—was one of non-democratic rule by distant powers.

As seen in the examples of post-war Japan and Germany, the international system can promote democracy as well as hinder it. After the collapse of communism from 1989 to 1991, democratic ideas were transmitted and propagated around the world. Samuel Huntington's work, for instance, includes an emphasis on the "learning" different countries could do from one another, with populations worldwide witnessing democratization in other countries and, in effect, concluding that "if they can do it, so can we."[25] The positive "demonstration effects" of watching neighboring countries change surely helped propel a wave of democratization that spread globally.

As with the other theories noted earlier, there is actually a variety of possible versions. There is no question that global patterns of democratization are real. The important question is what causes those patterns. One possible answer is to point to common conditions of the sort identified by other theories (e.g., perhaps waves of democratization are products of shared or global economic development). Another is to focus on the *structural* features of the global system, as in the example of Soviet and U.S. influence during the Cold War noted previously. A third approach combines the international system and cultural perspectives, such as Huntington's idea of democratic learning and "demonstration effects"[26] or in the notion that certain prestigious ways of organizing politics diffuse globally and exert cultural influence because they are perceived by "world society" to be legitimate.[27]

Domestic Institutions

Whether a democracy is sustained or collapses, whether transitions to or from democracy happen, and how well a given democracy functions may depend on the institutions in a given society. To review the concept from earlier chapters, we mean by *institutions* those features of a political system that shape the behaviors of actors. These can include organizations and groups, rules and patterns, and norms and values. Some arguments about the effects of domestic institutions are best addressed in later chapters: does federalism or unitarism work better to hold countries together (chapter 8);[28] do parliamentary and presidential forms of government affect the likelihood of democracy (chapters 9 and 10);[29] and so on. But the possible impacts on democracy are noteworthy here.

To use an example familiar to many students of American history, the first attempt at self-government in the American colonies was the loose confederation established by The Articles of Confederation of 1781, and it was a political failure that imperiled the security of the young, post-Revolutionary nation. It was only with the passage of the Constitution (in 1787 and 1788) that the foundations of the new nation were secured, owing to a new institutional framework that gave greater power to the central government. The success of the latter charter (and the failure of the former) might be attributed not to major economic development or cultural change in a few short years in the 1780s but rather to the more enduring

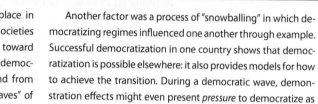

INSIGHTS | The Third Wave: Democratization in the Late Twentieth Century
by Samuel Huntington

Huntington observes that democratization takes place in "waves," or historical periods in which lots of societies democratize and others in which societies tend more toward authoritarianism. He identifies three major waves of democratization: from 1828 to 1926, from 1943 to 1962, and from 1974 until the 1990s. Between these came "reverse waves" of increasing authoritarianism. Huntington's interest was in explaining the contemporary "third wave" of democratization. Huntington pointed to multiple factors but drew particular attention to two types of external or systemic factors. One was the role of "external actors" such as the European Union, the United States, and the Catholic Church under John Paul II in fomenting democratization. For example, the United States changed its policies in the late 1970s under Jimmy Carter, arguing that a respect for democracy and human rights needed to be emphasized alongside national interests. In the early 1980s under Ronald Reagan, the National Endowment for Democracy was established, designed to assist global democratization.

Another factor was a process of "snowballing" in which democratizing regimes influenced one another through example. Successful democratization in one country shows that democratization is possible elsewhere: it also provides models for how to achieve the transition. During a democratic wave, demonstration effects might even present *pressure* to democratize as authoritarian forms come to seem less legitimate.

Perhaps the fundamental question to be asked of theories like Huntington's is *how much* factors like demonstration effects and international system pressures explain. Are they more, less, or equally important to factors internal to democratizing societies, like institutional reforms or economic development? And how can they explain the variation in patterns of democratization across cases?

Samuel Huntington, The Third Wave: Democratization in the Late Twentieth Century. *Norman: University of Oklahoma Press, 1991.*

design of the formal and legal framework for the union—that is to say, to a more suitable institutional design.

Dysfunctional political institutions can also undermine a regime, whether it is democratic or authoritarian. Chile's longstanding democracy collapsed in 1973, for many reasons, at least some of which were electoral; in elections in 1970, electoral rules split the center and right parties, allowing leftists to obtain the presidency with the support of only about one-third of the country. This likely contributed to some middle-class support for the overthrow of the democratically elected regime by the military. The Weimar Republic in Germany between the two World Wars was hobbled by similar institutional issues in the electoral system, as well as by an unclear division of power between the President as head of state and the Chancellor as head of government. One might not attribute Germany's democratic collapse and the rise of Nazi rule to institutional factors alone, but these surely contributed to dissatisfaction with the democratic regime that undermined its support. So too can authoritarian regimes fail partly for lack of functional institutions, as when Mexico's PRI finally lost power in 2000 after seventy-one years; again, the reasons were numerous, but institutional factors range from the fragmentation of the leading party, to the development of opposition at local and state levels, to increasingly competitive elections, to the increasing recognition of the government's inability to provide services.

Agents and Actors: The Role of Individuals and Groups

There is little doubt that many political outcomes are ultimately traceable to actions by major individual decision makers, that is, powerful individuals in positions of leadership. The question is whether these decisions are shaped and conditioned by other factors—such as economic development or institutions— or must be understood primarily in terms of individual choices.[30] A prominent example from recent years was from South Africa in the 1990s, where national hero Nelson Mandela had a prominent role in the process of democratization. Like other "Founding Fathers" in the United States and elsewhere, Mandela seemed "uniquely" capable of making difficult decisions and compromises, leaving open the question about what would have happened in his absence. In the South African case, there were many other individuals—both prominent political figures and lesser-known negotiators—who also had significant individual roles. Can individuals and groups make democracy happen?

The emphasis on specific individuals and groups tends to be focused more on specific transitions in certain countries than on broad patterns of democracy around the world. Analytically, we might *expect* individuals and other actors to matter more when the question at hand is about specific changes at a certain historical moment. Looking at the world map and trying to understand where democracies are found might naturally lead us to consider broad forces, such as geography and the large sweep of world history, or perhaps cultures. Looking more closely at a single country at its particular moment of democratization might push us in the direction of more "proper names."[31] Much as looking through a telescope gives a sense of large-scale natural and environmental forces and looking under a microscope gives a sense of the detailed actions of individual organisms, so too might looking "cross-nationally" give a sense of broad scope and looking "within a country at a given moment in time" give a sense of individual action.

This approach is about more than just great individuals—the Mahatma Gandhis, George Washingtons, and Nelson Mandelas of history. Groups and coalitions matter. For instance, the transitions from the 1970s and 1980s (which included southern Europe, Latin America, and central-eastern Europe, as well as some countries elsewhere) highlighted the importance of divisions within authoritarian leadership as a cause of democratization. In particular, some leading scholars (discussed further in the "Insights" box on *Transitions from Authoritarian Rule: Prospects for Democracy*) argued that democracy comes about when splits within an authoritarian regime lead to the emergence of "softliners."[32] These softliners interact with pragmatists in the opposition to form a powerful coalition for moving toward democracy. This movement comes at the expense of hardliner authoritarians and to the disappointment of those "maximalists," or radicals, in the pro-democracy movement who oppose any cooperation or negotiation with elements of the authoritarian regime. The bottom line in Table 6.1 pushes democratization.

Important interest groups or pressure groups can exercise their collective power in ways that facilitate democratization or democratic breakdown. Trade or labor unions might call a strike and immobilize a country and its economy, helping to bring down a regime. Or business groups or investors may boycott a regime, refusing to invest and ruining the economy to push politics to the breaking point. Powerful religious movements and representatives of the clergy might help to bring down a regime from their positions within their churches, mosques, or temples. And many other mobilized groups in civil society—from human rights campaigns, to ethnic solidarity movements, to university students (yes, you), to revolutionaries—have helped keep regimes in place and helped bring them down.

TABLE 6.1 **Actors in Democratic Transition**

	Authoritarian Regime	Pro-Democratic Forces
Extreme	Hardliners	Maximalists/radicals
Moderate	Softliners	Minimalists/pragmatists

Combining Arguments and Theories: Multiple Causes

It is not always necessary to pick one and only one of the preceding categories to explain why democratization succeeds or fails. Many scholars of democratization will acknowledge the importance of multiple causal factors. Arguments can recognize causal complexity: most important outcomes, like democracy, will be the result of multiple factors.

To use just two of the aforementioned perspectives, for instance, cultural change and economic development can affect one another, and both can condition democracy. Or, as noted previously, Samuel Huntington documented a "wave" of democratization in the 1980s and highlighted five causes.[33] In addition to *economic modernization* came the *declining legitimacy of authoritarian regimes*, the role of the *Catholic Church*, and two external factors: *demonstration effects* (or the effect of watching your neighbors become democracies) and *greater international support for democracy* from the United States and other large powers.

The argument by Inglehart and Welzel discussed in the "Insights" box incorporates elements of more than one theory discussed in this chapter. But, importantly, it does more than simply make a list of all the possible arguments and say they are all valid. It would not be very analytically powerful to say, "Democracy comes from a whole range of cultural values, economic modernization, and a whole bunch of

---

INSIGHTS   Transitions from Authoritarian Rule
by Guillermo O'Donnell, Philippe C. Schmitter, and Laurence Whitehead

Unlike the accounts produced by modernization theorists, *Transitions from Authoritarian Rule* stresses the uncertainty of democratic transitions. According to these scholars, transitions are extremely complex and indeterminate, meaning that producing a general theory of transitions is a challenging if not impossible task. Nevertheless, they draw some important general conclusions. First, they judge international systemic factors to be important, but *less* important than the jostling of domestic actors. Second, they stress that the uncertainty in question is above all the uncertainty faced by those very domestic actors. In other words, they frame the question from the perspective of actors *within* transitioning societies.

O'Donnell, Schmitter, and Whitehead, in their summary of the project's conclusions, note that governing coalitions in authoritarian regimes tend to divide into two camps: "softliners"

and "hardliners" (see Table 6.1). At the same time, one tends to see a division in the opposition between "radicals" who want no compromise with the existing regime and "pragmatists" who are willing to work with the existing regime if they see the chance for a democratic transition. Successful transitions tend to involve collaboration between softliners in the authoritarian regime and pragmatists. Critical here is that these softliners need to feel as if they are able to initiate and partially control the process: in other words, they are unlikely to cooperate if they expect to be persecuted in the aftermath of a transition. Likewise, the dynamics internal to the opposition is important. Pragmatists must be able to ensure sufficient buy-in on the part of other opposition actors such that agreements can be honored.

Guillermo O'Donnell, Philippe C. Schmitter, and Laurence Whitehead, eds., Transitions from Authoritarian Rule *(4 vols.). Baltimore, MD: Johns Hopkins University Press, 1986.*

INSIGHTS

Modernization, Cultural Change, and Democracy: The Human Development Sequence
by Ronald Inglehart and Christian Welzel

Inglehart and Welzel use survey data to analyze the relationship between economic development, cultural tradition, and democratization in more than eighty countries.

The fundamental difference separating their work from earlier modernization theory is that they posit a distinct mechanism. Recall that Lipset argued that economic development produced democracy fundamentally through creating a vibrant middle class. Inglehart and Welzel think of economic development as shaping political institutions *through* culture, as reflected in the values and aspirations of individuals. They find that societies with low levels of development tend to have people who are focused on "survival values." For example, they may place a lot of stock in family authority, presumably because the social bonds of the family are critical to survival in the context of material scarcity. Societies with higher levels of development, however, show higher levels of "self-expression values,"

meaning higher valuation of individual-level autonomy and freedom. According to the authors, any society achieving increasing economic development is expected to see increasing "self-expression values." They find that religious and cultural traditions shape the timing and extent of this change, but that economic development is the *cause* of the change.

So how do they get to democracy? They find that higher levels of self-expression values correlate with democratic institutions. They presume that the individual's culturally induced demand for greater autonomy is the source of political-institutional change. In other words, Inglehart and Welzel's model looks like this:

Economic development → Cultural change → Democratization

Ronald Inglehart and Christian Welzel, Modernization, Cultural Change, and Democracy: The Human Development Sequence. *Cambridge: Cambridge University Press, 2005.*

structures and institutions." As suggested in chapter 2, this may be *correct*, but it is not much of an argument. One can take a stronger and potentially more informative stand by showing how different theories and factors inform one another. Notice the steps in the chain of logic in the sketch at the end of the Inglehart and Welzel "Insights" box. To use this example, showing that economic modernization precedes changes to cultural values in a particular sequence is more powerful and informative than simply listing both and saying, "They both matter."

CASE IN CONTEXT

Is American Democracy in Trouble?

PAGE 567

There is no doubting that the United States has been one of the most important and influential democracies in the world. Virtually all political scientists continue to regard it as a democracy even still. However, some scholars have expressed concerns about declining levels of public trust and civic association, increasing partisan polarization and fragmentation of the media landscape, and increasing levels of income inequality, among other worries.[34]

For more on the question of whether American democracy may be in trouble, see the case study in Part VI, pp. 567–568. As you read it, keep in mind the following questions:

1. What are the implications for this issue of the major theories of democracy and democratization discussed in this chapter?

2. How does this question relate to procedural versus substantive definitions of democracy?

3. If, indeed, income inequality and declining trust (in institutions and in others) suggest that we have reason to be concerned, what could be done about it?

Is American Democracy a Model?

The central question in the study of democratization is why democratization happens or does not happen. This necessarily involves an understanding of the dates and time periods at which democratization may occur. As we noted at the beginning of this chapter, from an American perspective, this may seem like a relatively straightforward proposition, but this is an illusion. Consider the following multiple-choice question:

In what year did the United States of America achieve democracy?
1. 1776
2. 1787
3. 1791
4. 1863
5. 1920
6. 1965
7. None of the above

At first glance, the most obvious answer might appear to be A, the year of the signing of the Declaration of Independence. Similarly, one may argue that the signing of the Constitution in 1787 was the crucial moment, as this established a representative republic. The year 1791 witnessed the ratification of the Bill of Rights, a moment indispensable to democratization if democracy is understood to require civil liberties as well as political rights. Although the years at the founding were pivotal moments in American democracy, these are not the only possible correct answers to the question. The year 1863 saw President Abraham Lincoln issue the Emancipation Proclamation, a declaration recognizing that upon the end of the Civil War, America would end slavery, its most conspicuous and infamous source of "unfreedom." The year 1920 may be an even less obvious date, but one whose consequences for democracy were direct and massive: it is the year in which women were first provided with constitutional guarantees of the right to vote. This dramatic extension of voting rights not only enshrined the principle of universal suffrage but also had the effect of increasing the electorate by a huge percentage. The year 1965 may seem, to most eyes, to be too recent to count as part of America's democratization process, but it is the year of the passage of the Voting Rights Act, a culminating step in the American process of guaranteeing the vote to all of its adult citizens.

Yet one may also argue with some validity that "None of the above" is the best response to the question of when America achieved democracy. This would be true particularly for those who view the *quality* and *depth* of democracy in America as halting or subpar. Notice here that the criterion is not one that is easily reached through passage of a law guaranteeing the right to vote. Rather, it depends on the degree to which individuals exercise their rights and the degree to which each individual has an equal ability to influence the society's political life. The difference here is significant, and most political scientists would agree that it makes sense to measure democracy both according to a basic threshold and relative to an ideal. Few political scientists disagree about the importance of the aforementioned procedural definition of democracy that takes into account basic political rights

THINKING COMPARATIVELY

KEY METHODOLOGICAL TOOLS

Within-Case Analysis

Not all comparison in comparative politics is about comparing multiple, distinct cases. That is, sometimes we make comparisons and conduct analyses *within* cases. Typically, we do so for different reasons than when we compare cases. When we compare multiple cases, we are often trying to get "leverage" on some key variation.

Within-case analysis, in contrast, is often used for tracing causal processes.[35] In the case at hand, we are interested in comparing different junctures in the process of democratization in the United States. This is useful precisely because comparing different aspects or stages of that process might reveal a more complex and realistic pattern of causality.

So, when would you use this? Ideally, within-case analysis is used in the context of broader, comparative analysis.[36] A comparative politics researcher might use the within-case analysis we describe in this section as part of a broader comparative project that looks at long-run democratization in the United States in comparison with other cases.

to vote and the presence of fundamental civil rights. The question is whether this definition sufficiently covers all of the characteristics of a democracy. By these criteria, the United States is clearly above an international democratic threshold, and has been at most of the historical moments discussed previously, today along with most of the other advanced, industrialized countries in the world (and a healthy number of lower-income countries).

On the other hand, democracy in the United States has been characterized by different scholars in less favorable light, according to other plausible criteria: low voter turnout, low levels of voter knowledge and interest, disproportionate influence of certain interest groups and lobbies, excessive polarization, and under-representation of women and minorities in elected office, among other issues. You may deem some of these to be problematic, or all of them, or none. But for the purposes of our discussion, does this mean that democratization in the United States is incomplete? If one adopts a minimalist or procedural definition of democracy, then by nearly all accounts the United States is a democracy. If one adopts a substantive definition, however, then the United States has shortcomings, as do all other countries that meet the procedural definition of democracy.

The causes of transitions to democracy are numerous, and the United States is no exception. Analysts may find that one or more of the broad categories of explanation account best for democratization. In other words, there may be a need to disaggregate the concept of democratization, which may be a name that we give to a sequence of distinct processes. It is not a foregone conclusion that the same factors that produced initial democratization in the United States are responsible for the end of slavery or the extension of suffrage. Just the same, we can attempt to explain different aspects of stages of democratization via the theories we have considered in this chapter. Moreover, if different theories are more or less effective at explaining different aspects or moments in U.S. democratization, this might tell us something useful about those theories for broader comparative purposes. For instance, understanding the extension of suffrage to women and the civil rights achievements of the 1960s (most notably the Civil Rights Act of 1964 and Voting Rights Act of 1965) may lead some in the direction of social actors and groups including the women's suffrage movement (such as Elizabeth Cady Stanton and the Seneca Falls Convention) and the leaders of the civil rights movement (such as Dr. Martin Luther King, Jr., the Southern Baptist Convention, and the NAACP). Others may focus on the economic and social factors at the time that drove the country toward change. Within-case findings about this can then be brought back to comparative analysis, as we can ask whether similar processes are also visible at similar junctures in other cases.

Table 6.2 demonstrates how our different theoretical approaches might be used to explain a variety of democratizing moments in American history. These are not definitive statements but are simply illustrative of how scholars in different theoretical "schools" or "traditions" might approach the same question. We choose three different moments since America's movement toward independence: the American Revolution; the Emancipation Proclamation and the abolition of slavery; and the extension of civil and political rights to women and to blacks in the twentieth century. Notice the research question and the outcome at the top, and then consider the cells of the table as possible ways different scholars might address these questions and explain these outcomes.

TABLE 6.2 Causal Interpretations of American Democracy and Democratization Across Time Periods

	Eighteenth Century	Nineteenth Century	Twentieth Century
Dependent Variable	Independence and Constitution	Emancipation/Abolition of Slavery	Universal Suffrage
Research Question	Why did American colonists push for independence and establish a democratic republic?	Why did President Lincoln and Congress end slavery during/after Civil War?	Why did unrepresented groups (women and African Americans) at last attain voting rights?
Modernization (Economic/Social Change)	Merchants and small businesses of colonial economy seek to establish independence from British Crown	Decline of slave-based economy and economic conflict between industrial North and agricultural South	Growing demand for labor necessitates greater political inclusion of excluded groups
Culture	Frontier culture and settler groups (Puritans, etc.) incompatible with distant monarchy; local institutions encourage democratic norms	Changing perceptions of African Americans among national elites; religious culture nurtures abolitionism	Declining tolerance for prejudice on the basis of sex or race
Structures/Systems (International)	French–British rivalry creates opportunity for colonists to succeed in battle against Crown	International trade and relations with great power Britain (including blockade and question of Britain recognizing Confederacy)	American power and "arsenal of democracy" necessitate full domestic inclusion for global leadership
Institutions (Domestic)	Fractured thirteen colonies attempt loose Articles of Confederation and learn need for stronger union under Constitution	Congressional and constitutional impasse between Southern "nullification" and states' rights advocates versus Northerners	Evolution of congressional majority in populous regions of country in favor of change
Agency/Actor	"Founding Fathers" have formative role in Revolution and shaping new nation	Abolitionists drive political debate; extremist groups generate reaction	Women's suffrage movement and civil rights movement central to creating demand for change

Regarding our earlier point about why you might use within-case analysis, note that it is perfectly possible that the best explanation of the eighteenth-century sequence is derived from the theory that focuses on structures/the world system; that the nineteenth-century sequence is best explained by the theory that focuses on culture; and the twentieth-century sequence is best explained by modernization theory. Or some other such combination may be the strongest. The payoff here is that if we were to find this, it would bring nuance to our general theory in a useful way, and we could bring this insight back to comparative analysis.

Chapter Summary

Concepts

- The word *democracy* has numerous meanings.
- One major distinction is between procedural and substantive definitions of democracy.
- Regime change can include both the development of democracy and also the breakdown of an existing democratic regime.

Types

- Types of democracy include both representative and direct forms.
- Democratization can be thought of in terms of both democratic transition and consolidation.

Causes and Effects

- Scholars have developed a number of theories to explain why democratization takes place when and where it does. Perhaps the most famous is modernization theory, which predicts that economic development increases the likelihood of democratization.
- Another theory is that political culture shapes the possibilities for democracy and democratization, and that some political cultures increase the possibility of the establishment and persistence of authoritarian regimes as well.
- Systemic and structural theories say that democratization is more a function of factors operative at the level of the international system than things happening within societies. They focus, among other things, on waves of democratization and also of democratic breakdown.
- Some theories place more emphasis on contingency, agents, and institutional *design*.

Thinking Comparatively

- We looked at several key sequences in the history of democratization in the United States, and we introduced the concept of within-case analysis.

Thinking It Through

1. As we have noted in this chapter, India is somewhat unusual for having achieved a robust democracy *before* achieving economic modernization. What might modernization, cultural, structural, institutional, and actor-centered theories say about this case? Which of these theories do you think could make most sense of the Indian case? Why?

2. We have noted in this chapter that democracy can take a variety of forms, with one major distinction being between "representative" and "direct" democracy. But what is the relationship between these forms? Are they ultimately compatible? Do gains in one involve trade-offs in the other? Think about this question in relation to case examples.

3. In recent years there has been much discussion among politicians and public intellectuals about whether democracy can be engineered or even imposed. Some think that if the appropriate conditions are established, democracy can flourish anywhere. Others think that societies need to come to democratization organically and on their own. What would each of the theories we have considered have to say about this question?

4. "American Exceptionalism" has long held that the United States is different from Europe in that it did not establish a robust socialist tradition. More generally, we could say that, since Alexis de Tocqueville, some have viewed the United States as exceptional in its long-standing liberal democracy. Critics, of course, have argued that this democracy has been limited and indirect. Recently, we have seen two notable trends that bear on democratic practice in the United States: (a) increasing levels of income inequality, and (b) declining public trust in major institutions. What, if any, are the implications of these trends for the future of American democracy? What would each of the major theories of democratization and democratic consolidation say about these issues?

5. Imagine that the leader of a poor country with low levels of rule of law and dysfunctional political institutions asks you to help design a new democratic system for their polity. What would each of the theories considered in this chapter say about the possibility of your doing so? Now imagine that you were asked to help institutionally engineer increasing democratization in the United States. Ask the same question of this project. Are the implications the same? Different? Why?

CHAPTER 7

Authoritarian Regimes and Democratic Breakdown

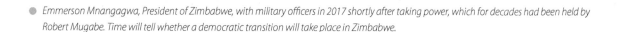

Emmerson Mnangagwa, President of Zimbabwe, with military officers in 2017 shortly after taking power, which for decades had been held by Robert Mugabe. Time will tell whether a democratic transition will take place in Zimbabwe.

In the 1960s, there was a country in Africa called Southern Rhodesia. It was a British colony that asserted its independence and was ruled by a white minority descended from colonial settlers. This country granted few rights to the black African majority and concentrated economic and political power in white hands. By the 1970s a resistance movement emerged to overthrow the white regime, led by a charismatic rebel leader who vowed to bring democracy to the black African majority. After a long struggle, this movement for democracy finally overthrew the repressive white regime in 1979, and a negotiated settlement with the support of Britain gave rise to a freer society in 1980. The transition even set in motion some much-needed land reform that would reshape the terrible inequalities between poor blacks and rich white farmers, and the new president set to work.

The name of the charismatic liberation hero was Robert Mugabe, and he renamed the country Zimbabwe. After an initial burst of enthusiasm with Mugabe's rule (as he invested in causes such as girls' education, a policy and idea well ahead of its time in sub-Saharan Africa), however, things turned quickly. Beginning in the 1980s, his regime was responsible for massacres of opponents and innocent victims in the region known as Matabeleland. By the 2000s, he presided over a brutal and repressive regime that encouraged so-called war veterans from the liberation war to occupy white-owned farms and frequently kill the owners and anyone loyal to them; the fact that many of these alleged "war veterans" were just teenagers, and thus born after the liberation war, was not lost on many observers. In the midst of the killing and disorder, Zimbabwe's economy collapsed into hyperinflation, and the agriculturally rich country once known as "the bread basket of Africa" came instead to be known as the continent's basket case. As of late 2017, more than thirty years later, Mugabe has just been displaced from power, with Emmerson Mnangagwa, a longtime collaborator of Mugabe, assuming the presidency. Early signs suggest that the transition will be an example of "authoritarian persistence," though some observers are hopeful that it might pave the way for eventual democratization.

It was not obvious from the start that Zimbabwean independence would end up with a persistent authoritarian regime, but Mugabe's regime was widely reviled in recent years—around the world and by many Zimbabweans—as one of the most abusive and despotic dictatorships in Africa. Time will tell whether this will change. You can use the theories described in this chapter as you think about the prospects for democracy or authoritarian persistence in Zimbabwe and other countries.

How does this happen? What gives rise to such brutal regimes, and what allows them to persist even as they preside over ruination? Whereas chapter 6 sought to explain democracy and democratization, this chapter turns the question around to look at authoritarian regimes. These sorts of regimes were for a long time the majority of all governments. They cast a specter over the entire twentieth century, and they still exist in many forms today.

· · ·

Concepts

In chapter 6, we looked at democratic regimes and transitions to democracy. In this chapter, we focus on two main concepts: authoritarianism (along with authoritarian regimes) and authoritarian transitions.

Authoritarianism and Authoritarian Regimes

At first glance, **authoritarianism** might be viewed simply as the absence of democracy as outlined in chapter 6, but the concept is in fact much more complex. It can be thought of as a characteristic of some ideologies (e.g., fascism and some varieties of socialism) or even as a behavioral tendency, as in so-called authoritarian personalities.[1] In general, we characterize an ideology or behavioral tendency as authoritarian to the extent that it is favorable to hierarchy and to closed, concentrated processes of decision making.

authoritarianism A form of government or regime that is non-democratic.

Authoritarian regimes are those that exemplify, to one degree or another, this authoritarian ideal. While many of us have had the good fortune to grow up in democratic societies, we should recognize that in many places and times authoritarian regimes have been the norm. Indeed, if we were to take a historical view of political regimes, we would see that most different types (e.g., oligarchies, empires, monarchies, and sultanates) fall into the general authoritarian category.[2]

authoritarian regime A non-democratic regime.

While we are interested in modern regimes here, there is still a lot of variation to explore. Modern authoritarian regimes vary in several respects. One is the extent to which the regime centers on an individual, as opposed to a ruling elite clique, *junta*, or bureaucracy. Personalistic regimes may invoke the names of history's greatest villains: Hitler, Stalin, Pol Pot in Cambodia, and even as far back as Caligula in the Roman Empire. Of course, these personalistic rulers relied on institutions such as political parties, militaries, or secret police to support their rule, but their rule was quite different from that of the nondescript generals and admirals who ruled Brazil or Argentina in the 1970s. Another distinction is the degree to which the regime expounds an overarching ideology, such as communism or fascism, as opposed to governing without attempting to socialize the citizenry in such ways. A third major difference is the extent to which and the way in which the regime constrains or violates human rights. Most theorists would recognize all authoritarian regimes in the contemporary world as violating some basic rights, such as the right to self-determination and basic political freedoms. However, some authoritarian regimes are willing to leave individuals alone, in relative freedom, so long as they accept the regime's authority and stay away from politics. Others aim to control almost every aspect of their citizens' lives. The subtypes of authoritarian regimes described in the "Types" section express some of these distinctions.

Transitions to Authoritarian Regimes

Regime change is not a one-way street from authoritarianism to democracy; on the contrary, democracies can break down and collapse, and authoritarian regimes can persist and solidify their rule. Although the end of the twentieth century witnessed a wave of democratization in Central and Eastern Europe, Latin America, Asia, and Africa, more recent years have recalled that authoritarianism persists and even grows in some places.[3] Reversion to authoritarianism in democratic countries has a long history, from the breakdown of the Weimar Republic and the rise of Nazi Germany in the 1930s to the many coups in Latin America and Africa in the 1960s and 1970s. Consolidation may stop or be reversed. Transition may fail, or a country may retransition from democracy back below the threshold to authoritarianism. Political scientists do not use the word *authoritarianization*, but we do examine these processes of **democratic breakdown** and **authoritarian persistence**.[4] We also need to consider the various paths to the establishment of **hybrid regimes** (which combine authoritarian and some democratic elements).[5]

Types

As noted previously, authoritarian regimes vary in important ways. In this section, we discuss the key subtypes of authoritarianism, as well as the variable forms that transitions to authoritarian regimes can take.

Types of Authoritarianism

Some of the most important types of authoritarian regimes are totalitarian regimes, theocracies, personalistic dictatorships, and bureaucratic-authoritarian regimes. We discuss each of these in more detail in this section.

TOTALITARIAN REGIMES

Totalitarian regimes represent the most notorious form of authoritarian rule, epitomized by the communist and fascist regimes of the twentieth century that sent millions of people to their deaths, especially in Nazi Germany and the Soviet Union, particularly during the years of Joseph Stalin's leadership in the latter case. Many would consider today's North Korea to be another example of a totalitarian regime. Totalitarian regimes deny civil rights to citizens and do not hold free and fair elections, but their manipulations and machinations go far beyond those of many other authoritarian regimes.

democratic breakdown The transition from a democratic to a non-democratic regime.

authoritarian persistence The ongoing continuation of an authoritarian regime, such that democratic transition does not take place.

hybrid regime A class of regime that appears to be neither fully democratic nor fully authoritarian, such as electoral authoritarianism, delegative democracy, and illiberal democracy.

totalitarian regime A form of authoritarian regime that aims to control everything about the lives of its subject population, such as in the Soviet Union and Germany under the Nazis.

Totalitarianism gets its name from the attempt to overhaul or control the totality of a society, most notably through propagation of an official governing ideology to which all people are expected to conform.[6] Totalitarian regimes will go to great lengths to preclude freedom of thought and conscience, often using secret police, spies, and informants to report on suspected dissidents; freedom of thought is antithetical to the ambitions of totalitarian leadership. There is usually one official governing party, often led by a dominant figure who is the subject of hero worship or a cult of personality. State control over the economy is common and prevents any economic actors from building up a power base that might be used to challenge the total domination the state has over public life. Many totalitarian regimes use prisons, work camps, and mass executions in an attempt to re-educate society and to eliminate supposedly undesirable elements, especially ethnic minorities. The Soviet Union under Joseph Stalin and Nazi Germany under Adolf Hitler are the most horrific examples, with each responsible for millions of deaths in the mid-twentieth century.[7] To a large extent, the history of that century was the story of the struggle between liberal democratic regimes and totalitarian regimes.

Totalitarianism may be a modern phenomenon. There certainly are precedents for totalitarianism in historical societies, such as ancient Sparta. But for the most part, the relative weakness of premodern states precluded the possibility of true totalitarian regimes, despite *efforts* that look quite totalitarian, such as medieval European states' efforts to censor literature and to enforce Christian orthodoxy by force.

Some analysts argue that the concept of totalitarianism was an artifact of the Cold War, or even a propaganda tool for the liberal-democratic West, used to demonize the Soviet Union and its allies.[8] There is no doubt that totalitarianism was most associated with the atrocities committed by both the Nazis under Hitler and the Soviets. It is important as a concept, however, as it allows us to describe important variation between forms of authoritarianism that aim to control everything in the lives of their people and those that allow greater latitude. Contemporary Russia and Venezuela, for example, although not totalitarian states, as some of their critics contend, clearly exemplify one type of authoritarian regime; whereas contemporary North Korea and even, to some extent, Cuba go much further in their restrictions on personal freedoms and might be labeled "totalitarian." Finally, some scholars argue that totalitarian regimes are so distinctive in terms of the characteristics we have discussed here to deserve their own category, rather than to be thought of as a type of authoritarianism.[9]

THEOCRACIES

Some authoritarian regimes are closely linked to religions and religious institutions. If religious leaders control an authoritarian state, or if a state imposes very strict religious restrictions and uses religion as its main mode of legitimation, we refer to it as a **theocracy** or theocratic regime. In the premodern world, many if not most states were theocratic; and the monarchies of Western Europe, for example, had strong theocratic features. Today there are fewer theocratic regimes, but some stand out as particularly noteworthy, such as Saudi Arabia and Iran. Many states, though, continue to involve religion or to impose religious restrictions, a subject to which we return in chapter 15.

theocracy An authoritarian state controlled by religious leaders, or a state with very strict religious restrictions that uses religion as its main mode of legitimation.

PERSONALISTIC DICTATORSHIPS

Not all authoritarian regimes are totalitarian or theocratic. Indeed, many contemporary authoritarian regimes are not. Some simply allow little role for the population in political decision making, but the state does not aim to control every aspect of their lives. Among more limited authoritarian regimes we find the classic forms of dictatorship that have been particularly common in modern political history. The terms **personalistic dictatorship** and the more antiquated "sultanism" refer to domination of a political system by a single individual.[10] This individual concentrates power and governs as he (or she, but usually he) sees fit. Autocracy, despotism, dictatorship, or tyranny can be used to express similar ideas, though some of these terms can sometimes refer to domination by a clique of more than one leader. As distinct from totalitarian rule, the sultan/autocrat/despot may not aim to establish an overarching ideology. In other cases, an ideology may be promoted but does not come to be implemented to the extent that it would be in a totalitarian regime. As distinct from theocratic rule, while a personalistic dictator might support religion, repress religious minorities, and use religion as a tool of the state, it is the dictator—and not the religious system in question—that is the highest authority.

The justification for rule in personalistic dictatorships may be based on the assertion of the public interest, such as the ability to promote economic success, or the need to combat subversives. Sometimes, dictatorships of this sort are explicitly framed as temporary. On other occasions, they have been presented as likely "necessary" for a long time. The idea of "democratic Caesarism" has sometimes been used to justify them, the suggestion being that some societies on the path to democratization are not yet ready for democracy but, rather, need a strong leader to help them get ready, or even to maintain order over the longer term.[11]

Conveniently, though, such self-appointed leaders are often slow to judge the countries they rule to be *actually* ready. Some authoritarian rulers of this sort argue

personalistic dictatorship A form of authoritarianism in which the personality of the dictator is highlighted.

CASE IN CONTEXT
Democratic Features of Authoritarian Systems? The Case of Iran   PAGE 478

In 1979, Iran underwent a social revolution that brought a radical and religious government into power. Some regard this government as totalitarian, as it imposes strict controls on public expression, religion, and issues of "morality." Religious leaders at the top of the hierarchy have ultimate control, and thus we would be justified in considering it theocratic. Interestingly, though, in this context, Iran still has some quasi-democratic features as well. Elections are still periodically held, and they are actually contested, though not always fairly. In short, there is some debate within the Iranian state, but within a rather narrow band policed by religious authorities, and in a broader context that most would regard as highly authoritarian.

For more on authoritarianism and democracy in Iran, see the case study in Part VI, pp. 478–479. As you read it, keep in mind the following questions:

1. On what grounds does Iran claim to be democratic? What criteria do social scientists use in judging it not to be so despite some clearly democratic features?

2. What are the implications of Iran's totalitarian and theocratic approach for the long-term viability of its regime? Does totalitarianism help the regime stay in power or create vulnerabilities?

that democracy is not right for all countries, and some hold that a country needs a strong leader to keep people in line. There have been a number of personalistic dictators in Africa, among other regions of the world, and several of them are unfortunately memorable. They include the tyrants Mobutu Sese Seko of the former Zaire (now the Democratic Republic of the Congo), Jean-Bedel Bokassa of the Central African Republic (who declared himself emperor), and Idi Amin of Uganda.[12]

BUREAUCRATIC-AUTHORITARIAN REGIMES

Personalistic dictatorships and related forms of autocracy shade into a form of authoritarian regime that became very common in parts of the developing world in the mid- to late twentieth century: the **bureaucratic-authoritarian regime**. These regimes are usually focused less on a single individual than in personalistic dictatorships, instead relying on an organized bureaucracy (often, though not always, the military) to run the country.

Though less often associated with particular historical figures, such regimes are not necessarily less brutal than personalistic regimes. The Argentine military in the 1970s, for example, was infamous for torture and for methods of execution that included throwing dissenters out of helicopters into the Atlantic Ocean.[13] Bureaucratic-authoritarian regimes in Asia and Latin America used a range of justifications for assuming rule, including the political impasses and economic failures of civilian regimes in their countries.[14]

Like most personalistic dictatorships, bureaucratic-authoritarian regimes tend to be less ideological than totalitarian regimes, or more pragmatic. They can be right-wing or left-wing, but the fundamental rationale they typically use in trying to garner legitimacy is the alleged need to establish order or economic progress. They tell their societies they can achieve full modernity only through a strong hand and technical administration. Yet these regimes, which were very common in the 1960s and 1970s, typically viewed their role not as displacing civilian regimes to call new elections, but as governing their countries for extended periods. In other words, bureaucratic-authoritarian regimes seldom view themselves as merely brief caretakers.

Some would consider the category of "party dictatorships" to overlap with that of bureaucratic-authoritarian regimes. For example, some would argue that the Mexican government during the period of the *Partido Revolucionario Institucional*'s (PRI) dominance shaded into bureaucratic authoritarianism (see discussion in the "Case in Context" box titled "Mexico's 'Perfect Dictatorship' and Its End"). Party dictatorships are distinguished from personalistic dictatorships most clearly by the fact that it is a party, rather than a single individual, that aims to hold onto power. In the contemporary world, China might be considered a good example of this.

HYBRID AND SEMI-AUTHORITARIAN REGIMES

Sometimes regimes are hard to classify as either democratic or authoritarian. Indeed, this seems to be a growing problem. This is especially true after the third wave of democratization (discussed in chapter 6), which led to stronger democratic international norms with which regimes wish to appear compliant.[15]

bureaucratic-authoritarian regime A type of authoritarian regime, common in Latin America and elsewhere in the mid to late twentieth century, that was associated with control of the state more by a group of elites (often military) than by a single individual leader.

Accordingly, regimes developed techniques and learned from one another about how to appear to comply with these norms while nevertheless remaining in power. Over the years, the range of variations among different types of regimes has led to a proliferation of names for regimes that fit somewhere in between full democracy and complete authoritarianism. Some scholars have urged caution about coming up with new names, noting that while there are many subtypes of democratic or authoritarian regimes, we want more than simply "democracy with adjectives."[16] Nonetheless, these terms have resonance and have become prominent.

illiberal democracy A polity with some democratic features but in which political and civil rights are not all guaranteed or protected.

delegative democracy A hybrid form of regime that is democratic but involves the electorate "del-egating" significant authority to a government.

electoral authoritarianism A name applied to situations in which authoritarian regimes nominally compete in elections.

competitive authoritarianism A form of government or regime that allows some political competition but not enough to qualify as fully democratic.

The notion of **illiberal democracy** emerges from the many experiences where countries have reasonably fair elections but then do little to hold elected leaders accountable.[17] While these countries are described as democracies, largely due to reasonably fair elections, they may share more in common with authoritarian regimes. Several regimes in Latin America have been characterized as **delegative democracies**,[18] while the term **electoral authoritarianism** has been used to describe hybrid regimes elsewhere.[19] More recently, some of these regimes have been labeled as examples of **competitive authoritarianism**, meaning that they do allow some political competition but not enough to qualify as fully democratic.[20] Note that these terms are not perfect synonyms. A delegative democracy is considered at least partially democratic. Competitive authoritarianism blurs the line in this connection, the key idea being that the regime is not truly democratic but that it exerts control through elections that are at least nominally competitive. The incomplete nature of democracy in many hybrid regimes was described by the Peruvian scholar Hernando de Soto, who once discussed politics in his country in the 1980s and 1990s by saying, "we elect a dictator every five years."[21]

Types of Transition (or Nontransition) to Authoritarianism

As mentioned previously, many forms of regime change can end in authoritarianism. These include the replacement of one form of authoritarian regime with another, as well as democratic breakdown and transitions to hybrid regimes. We discuss these here, but first we take a look at authoritarian persistence.

AUTHORITARIAN PERSISTENCE

Authoritarian persistence is a pressing issue in light of the many non-democratic regimes in the world today that seem enduring, perhaps including China, Cuba, and North Korea, among others. In discussing democratic transition and consolidation in chapter 6, we noted that these processes may not always be completed. Such a case may suggest partial democratization, but the flip side of the coin is the persistence (and therefore apparent "success") of an authoritarian regime. At some level, this distinction may seem to be merely semantic, but we must take care not to assume that all countries are destined to become democracies in the end.[22] Indeed, questions about the persistence of authoritarianism become more interesting if an authoritarian regime persists despite predictions that it should not.

Authoritarian regimes have their own characteristics and attributes, which may contribute to their stability. For instance, the Chinese Communist Party—which was an economic failure for its first thirty years in power—has very successfully presided over that country's decades of economic growth since it undertook reforms beginning in 1979. This economic success is undoubtedly part of why

Daniel Ortega, president of Nicaragua, as he is sworn into the presidency for his third term, in 2012 (he was re-elected in 2016). Ortega's supporters claim that his policies aim to reduce inequalities and poverty, while his critics charge that his government is not fully democratic.

the authoritarian regime has endured and democratization has not gained steam after the brutal crackdown on protestors in Tiananmen Square in 1989. In short, to understand regime types and regime changes, we must recognize that they depend not only on the details of how a transition goes but also on the features of authoritarian regimes.

Moreover, it is worth noting that there are at least two main kinds of authoritarian persistence. The first is the persistence of a single authoritarian regime, as suggested earlier. Often this persistence is accompanied by major internal changes to the regime. An example, again, is the rule of the Chinese Communist Party. Today's Communist Party embraces very different policies and a different style of rule than it did, say, under Mao Zedong in the 1960s. Yet the same party and the same basic state have remained in place, and thus most political scientists would consider this a case of a single authoritarian regime's persistence. In other words, the reforms of Deng Xiaoping and his successors, while radical, did not constitute an institutional break in regime type but rather a slower transition that leaves the regime firmly in the authoritarian category.

Let's consider a different sort of pattern: the substitution of one authoritarian regime for another. Whereas the first type of authoritarian persistence that we considered has no punctuated regime change, this type does. Some authoritarian regimes give way to other authoritarian regimes, often of very different types. One example is modern Iran. In 1979, millions of protestors backing the Islamic Revolution succeeded in overthrowing the longtime ruler, the Shah Reza Pahlavi, a U.S.-supported authoritarian leader (see extended discussion in the Country Profile and Case Studies for Iran in Part VI). The result was a very different type

CASE IN CONTEXT

Oligarchy, Democracy, and Authoritarianism in Russia

PAGE 537

For decades, Russia was the center of the Soviet Union, which, like virtually every modern state, claimed to be democratic, though in this instance quite dubiously. Then, between 1989 and 1991, the Soviet Union fell apart, more quickly than almost anyone had anticipated, leading to the emergence of a hybrid regime under Boris Yeltsin. A period of economic and political instability followed until Vladimir Putin, aided by an oil boom, began to impose political order. He did this, in part, by developing a hybrid of electoral politics with strong authoritarian features, considered a classic case of competitive authoritarianism.[23] The state has been used to repress his opponents, and his 2012 re-election to the presidency was denounced by many for its irregularities and was the source of much popular protest. Putin could conceivably alternate between holding the presidency and governing indirectly through others in the coming years, or he may find ways to continue to hold the presidency

himself, though his ability to hold onto power over the long term remains to be seen.

For more on Russia as a competitive authoritarian regime, see the case study in Part VI, pp. 537–538. As you read it, keep in mind the following questions:

1. If Russia is a competitive authoritarian regime rather than a democracy or a fully authoritarian regime, when did it become one? What does the case suggest about how we can distinguish hybrid from democratic and authoritarian regimes?

2. How much of Russia's authoritarian character is due to the state's ability to make use of oil wealth? Given the prolonged downturn in the market for oil, how, if at all, has the hybrid regime model changed? What tactics has Putin used to try to maintain power?

of regime: The Islamic Revolution was theocratic (i.e., led by religious clerics), conservative, and nationalistic, as opposed to the secular, modernizing, and pro-Western rule of the Shah. Yet both were authoritarian and both opposed liberal democracy. Indeed, what is particularly interesting about this case is the question of which of the two authoritarian Iranian regimes in question is *less* democratic, a subject Iran scholars debate. From Cuba to China to Ethiopia, there is a long history of regimes that change in style, type, or ideology, substituting one flavor of authoritarianism for another.

Authoritarian regimes use a number of techniques and strategies in their efforts to persist. These are sometimes called strategies of "regime maintenance." One such strategy is to produce economic benefits for citizens. This can take the form of efforts to produce growth (as in Singapore or, more recently, China) or in the form of patronage and clientelism, which involve the state using its own resources to benefit supporters.[24] Authoritarian regimes also often use repression.

This can take the form of using police to stifle protest activities and, in its most egregious cases, the use of large-scale violence against civilians. Authoritarian regimes also typically try to limit the access of political opponents to resources like information, media, and public space. We return to some of these issues in chapter 12.

DEMOCRATIC BREAKDOWN

The decline of democratic regimes may be the most iconic type of regime change leading to authoritarianism. Examples abound, such as the collapse of Germany's Weimar Republic in the 1930s leading to the rise of the Nazis (see "Case in

CASE IN CONTEXT
Mexico's "Perfect Dictatorship" and Its End

PAGE 508

Mexico was once called "the perfect dictatorship." The PRI, the party that governed from 1929 to 2000, won every election in that period through a combination of inducements and repression, and by incorporating most of the major political actors in society, such as business and labor unions, into a standing relationship with the regime. In 2000, the PRI lost for the first time in seventy-one years, and Mexico's regime changed. The story was one of the most compelling regime changes of the late twentieth century. In 2012, Enrique Peña Nieto was elected, returning a PRI politician to the presidency, but very few observers think this signaled a return to the old system. At the time of this writing, Peña Nieto is historically unpopular, and many observers expect the PRI to again lose the presidency in summer 2018.

For more on Mexico's regimes, see the case study in Part VI, pp. 508–509. As you read it, keep in mind the following questions:

1. What mechanisms and tactics did the PRI use to maintain its authority and control for so long?
2. What explains the eventual decline of a party that was able to govern for so long? What variables or historical changes contributed to democratization?

Context" box on "Democracy and Authoritarianism in Germany") and the coup d'état against the Allende government in Chile in the 1970s that led to the Pinochet dictatorship. Democratic reversals and returns to authoritarian rule are also diverse in form, much like democratization and authoritarian persistence. Some countries may "authoritarianize" (i.e., witness a democratic breakdown) in fits and starts, perhaps with partial losses of freedom and increasingly suspect elections interspersed with moments of continued political participation by the citizenry. A clear case of this is Venezuela under Nicolás Maduro in recent years, with a regime that virtually no political scientist would now consider to be democratic. Other democratic breakdowns may be abrupt and dramatic, with a military force overthrowing a democratic regime in a coup, or an elected ruler declaring a state of emergency and martial law; examples are numerous in the history of the developing countries of Africa, Asia, and Latin America.

As is the case with democratization, these democratic breakdowns may also reverse (in this case with a return to democracy), sometimes indefinitely and other times only temporarily, or stop somewhere in between democracy and authoritarianism. One democratic breakdown that stopped, for instance, was in Ukraine in 2004, when hundreds of thousands of citizens took to the streets in the Orange Revolution to protest a fraudulent and manipulated election. While Ukraine was a flawed and partial democracy before the Orange Revolution, the movement undoubtedly prevented further movement in the direction of authoritarianism at that time. Sadly, weak institutions contributed to a renewed crisis in Ukraine in 2014, leading to violence, further weakened institutions, and the loss of some of the country's territory to Russia.

Several patterns of democratic decay and collapse are worth special attention. First, democratic regimes sometimes collapse because voters elect authoritarians. This may sound surprising. Why would people vote for an authoritarian when they have democracy? One reason is that they may not know they are voting for an authoritarian. A political candidate who promises law and order, economic

Orange Revolution Protestors in Ukraine in 2004.

development, and the end of corruption may give no indication that he or she intends to close the parliament and the court system and to declare martial law as means to this end. Another reason is that in some societies where democratic consolidation is incomplete, democracy may appear to have weaknesses as well as strengths, and voters might have different trade-offs to calculate than do citizens in well-institutionalized democracies. Consider a democracy that has produced painfully poor economic performance, and one in which corruption is rife, and rule of law is only minimally established. Are you sure you would not be tempted to vote for an authoritarian who promised to end 80 percent annual inflation, extremely dangerous streets, and an obviously corrupt and thieving class of party leaders who drained the national treasury and deposited the funds in accounts in the Cayman Islands? Perhaps you would not (we believe that we would not), but you can probably understand why some people would.

Second, democratic regimes sometimes collapse because organized actors in society move against them. Organized labor can strike; middle-class individuals can demonstrate, marching, setting up barricades, or banging pots (a form of protest common in Latin America called the "*cacerolazo*"); businesses can withdraw capital; and, perhaps most dangerous, the state bureaucracy itself can refuse to comply with the orders of civilian leaders. This is most dangerous when the military, or segments of the military, lose faith in democracy or in the given democratic regime. When this happens, a coup d'état becomes more likely. In the view of most analysts, coups d'état are intrinsically anti-democratic when brought against democratic regimes. They can, however, issue in different sorts of outcomes, including democratizing effects. Indeed, coups against authoritarian regimes sometimes happen, and sometimes for the sake of establishing democracy. Many coups,

PAGE 452

CASE IN CONTEXT
Democracy and Authoritarianism in Germany

Germany is a country that has seen a number of major regime changes over the course of its modern history. As such, it is a sort of laboratory for scholars interested in questions of democracy, democratization, and democratic breakdown. It has seen failed democratic consolidation; emergent authoritarianism; the splitting of the country after military defeat, with parallel authoritarian (East Germany) and democratic (West Germany) polities; and, finally, successful reunification with a well-consolidated democracy.

For more on this case, see Part VI, pp. 452–453. As you read it, keep in mind the following questions:

1. Why did Germany see so many transitions in the twentieth century?
2. Does the German case help us understand why transitions happen more generally, or is it idiosyncratic?
3. These transitions occurred back and forth in the same country. What are this fact's implications for theories about why regime change happens?

though, involve the military acting against a civilian (and often democratic) regime and substituting an authoritarian regime in its place.

Third, as we discuss in greater detail in chapter 12, sometimes regime change takes the form of revolution. These revolutions can in some instances be democratizing, but in many other instances, they actually lead to greater concentration of power under an authoritarian regime. The history of France in the nineteenth century, after the French Revolution, shows the ambiguities of such outcomes, as the country went through both democratizing and dictatorial periods.

TRANSITION TO HYBRID OR SEMI-AUTHORITARIAN REGIME

Hybrid regimes can emerge out of either democratic or authoritarian regimes, as we discuss in further detail in the "Causes and Effects" section later in the chapter. Partial democratic breakdown can lead a formerly democratic polity to fall into semi-authoritarian status. A traditionally authoritarian regime can enter into the same hybrid status as a result of partial and limited democratization—or else superficial efforts to appear compliant with international norms and expectations. Here we will sketch a fictitious but roughly representative example of each scenario. Polity A involves a transition from a more democratic regime to a hybrid regime, and Polity B involves a transition from a more authoritarian regime to a hybrid regime.

The citizens of Polity A achieved notable democratization several decades ago, against the odds. Similar countries in their region remained authoritarian or reverted to authoritarianism in subsequent years, but Polity A remained democratic. Of course, there were problems. Ongoing poverty and inequality were major issues. Political parties became bureaucratic and prone more to elite corruption than to representing the populace. Those parties came to dominate political life: you could not access state resources or services without going through the parties. Then, a major regional crisis struck. The country's debt expanded dramatically, and as a result, it had to make major cuts in public spending. Polity A's state could no longer do the kinds of things its citizens expected the state to do, such as

Authoritarian Persistence in Nineteenth-Century France

PAGE 436

We think of France as one of the world's leading democracies, and it is. However, for many decades, France dealt with a serious case of authoritarian persistence. Unlike the United Kingdom or the United States, which experienced gradual but steady democratization, France swung sharply between republican and imperial forms of government in the nineteenth century. Even in the twentieth century, the Vichy government was authoritarian. Of course, it owed its position to the Nazis' quick military victory over France, followed by France's collaboration, and should not be thought of as having emerged organically from French political life. At the same time, it was not without its French supporters.

France is a good case for the analysis of authoritarian persistence. Why, after all, did authoritarianism keep coming back in spite of the strong republican tradition that developed after the revolution of 1789?

For more on this case, see the case study in Part VI, pp. 436–437. As you read it, keep in mind the following questions:

1. Why did the French Revolution not lead to uninterrupted democracy?
2. What major features of nineteenth-century French society might have contributed to its cycles of authoritarianism?
3. What lessons, if any, does nineteenth-century France offer to democratizers of contemporary authoritarian states and to those undergoing slow processes of democratic consolidation?

(more or less) effectively policing, providing some minimal health care and food and housing assistance for the poorest, and managing the business cycle through effective government spending when times were tough. A political candidate came along promising to change all of that by throwing the corrupt elites out of office. Once elected, this leader began to argue that the very institutions of representative democracy were part of the problem because they were inherently elitist, that the existing legislature and judiciary were full of representatives of the old parties. The leader used this argument to justify the constitutionally questionable transformation of these institutions. Soon, the legislature and judiciary were filled with loyalists of the new leader, as were the electoral authority and the military. Elections continued, but in many ways the deck was stacked against the regime's opponents. As the country entered into severe economic problems, the regime's authoritarianism grew, and it increasingly repressed political opponents.

The citizens of Polity B lived for many decades under an authoritarian regime. That authoritarian regime collapsed, however, and savvy politicians rushed to fill the ensuing political vacuum. These political entrepreneurs quickly (maybe even recklessly) embarked on major political and economic reforms, ostensibly creating a brief and limited democracy. The result was that the publicly owned resources the state had amassed during its many decades of authoritarianism quickly fell into the private hands of a small, highly concentrated group. At the same time, living standards for the majority of the population fell dramatically, and social problems such as crime and drug addiction soared. Within a few years, a leader arose promising to restore the country's glory and the people's old standard of living, blaming the new elites for Polity B's problems. This leader, like the leader in

Polity A, continued to allow regular elections to be held but practiced intimidation of the press, selective prosecution, and occasional fraud to remain in power.

Both Polity A and Polity B underwent transitions to hybrid or semi-authoritarian regime status. You may call them "Venezuela" and "Russia," if you like, though with those two countries, there may still be some disagreement about whether they are competitive authoritarian or fully authoritarian regimes.[25] The first started from a position of relatively robust democracy and the second from long-standing authoritarianism. These are only two of numerous possible patterns through which such regimes can emerge.

Causes and Effects: What Causes Authoritarian Regimes to Emerge and Persist?

In this section, we consider four major theories of the emergence of authoritarian regimes: those that focus on class coalitions at critical junctures, those that focus on poverty and inequality, those that focus on weak states, and those that focus on political culture. We also discuss some special causal circumstances surrounding hybrid regimes.

Historical Institutionalist Theories

As discussed in chapter 5, historical institutionalist theories look for critical junctures in which institutional patterns become set.[26] In explaining the emergence of authoritarian regimes, these theories look for junctures where either authoritarian institutions are formed or coalitions supportive of authoritarian rule are established. Why might these events happen at certain key moments in the development of a polity? Well, first of all, there are in many societies at many times certain groups that would be better off without democratization, or believe that they would be. Such groups might include (1) representatives of organizations who receive special treatment under an existing authoritarian state—perhaps religious organizations or, in some circumstances, military actors; (2) economic actors who want to control the state to use it as a tool against those who wish to redistribute wealth or to expand economic rights; or (3) individuals or groups who fear that democratization will lead to the confiscation of their wealth or the reduction of their privileges—possibly wealthy economic actors such as landlords or business owners and/or nobles, depending on the circumstances. If elite actors have reason to fear democratization, they might try to form and maintain non-democratic institutions and to assemble a coalition supportive of such institutions.

A historical institutionalist theory tries to explain how institutions get set in a particular pattern and then explains subsequent development as a consequence of the institutional path that has been established. Such a theory would thus mainly try to explain why authoritarian institutions were established in the first place. It may further argue that the coalitions of actors supporting the institutional arrangements must remain present to account for the persistence of those arrangements.[27]

Let's imagine another fictitious society. It undergoes a transition from one type of authoritarian regime—an absolutist monarchy with an agrarian economy and an economy based on estates—to a more modern dictatorship. The following actors are present at the transition:

- the existing state, which is authoritarian to the extreme;
- the representatives of the old nobility, who fear revolutionary change, having read about those ghastly rebellions in France;
- landowners, some of whom are noble and some not, who make their living from collecting rents from peasants on their land;
- a relatively small but increasingly powerful group of industrial entrepreneurs;
- a relatively small but growing group of industrial workers;
- a large religious organization that has exerted a monopoly with the support of the old state; and
- a large mass of peasants.

The old state had bankrupted itself and then had begun imposing heavy taxes on the rents acquired by agricultural elites (including the dominant church, which owned a lot of land). It had also taxed its own exporters heavily, arguing that manufacturing should serve the interests of the crown by producing goods for sale only to the king's subjects. It had cut all military spending. Under such circumstances, a coalition has formed among four elite groups: landowners, the military, the church, and the industrial entrepreneurs. While these groups' interests are not identical, they all are being hurt by existing policy. If this coalition brings about regime transition, though, that regime might be authoritarian, because each of these groups wants to protect its existing privileges. Now let's imagine further that this coalition successfully creates new institutions: we might expect those institutions to endure and for authoritarianism to persist until some new crisis emerges later in the country's history. The importance of such coalitions is central to the classic argument by Barrington Moore about why authoritarian and democratic regimes emerge (see the "Insights" box on *Social Origins of Dictatorship and Democracy*).

Some might say that Moore's argument is not really historical institutionalist because he places so much emphasis on class relations (which, in terms of the state–society schema discussed in chapter 3, fall on the society side of the ledger) and democratic or authoritarian outcomes. A key question here is the extent to which the persistence of a given democratic or authoritarian regime is a consequence of (1) ongoing class coalitions or (2) institutional inertia. Moore, despite being criticized for not being sufficiently state-centric,[28] seems to have assumed that once the conditions for democratic or authoritarian regimes are established, they are largely set for the foreseeable future. Some other, rational-choice institutionalist accounts differ in this respect.

Poverty and Inequality

If we accept modernization theory's explanation of democratization—that economic development causes societies to become more democratic—we would expect the obverse to be true as well. Economic collapse, increasing poverty, and increasing income inequality likely predict a turn toward authoritarianism, and ongoing economic stagnation and poverty likely predict authoritarian persistence.

INSIGHTS

Social Origins of Dictatorship and Democracy: Lord and Peasant in the Making of the Modern World
by Barrington Moore

Moore is essentially the intellectual grandfather of one variety of contemporary historical institutionalism. He offers a modified Marxist account of why some societies ended up with liberal democratic, fascist, or communist/socialist regimes by the twentieth century; and he finds his answer in the class structures of the societies he studied as they made the passage to modernity. While Moore's book is nuanced, the *key* variable he notes is the presence or absence of a "bourgeoisie" or "middle class." If a strong middle class was present when a society passed to political modernity, it was likely to end up a liberal democracy.

Conversely, countries without a strong and large middle class present during the passage to modernity were likely to result in coalitions averse to democracy. There are lots of ways that this can happen. An existing agrarian elite might join forces with the small middle class to outcompete peasants; or the middle class might form an alliance with the peasants themselves, producing a revolution that tends toward authoritarianism. Moore argued that the first scenario tends to produce right-wing authoritarianism and the second, left-wing authoritarianism.

Think for a moment about the relationship between Moore's argument and that of S. M. Lipset discussed in chapter 6. Each is interested in the presence or absence of the middle class as a key determinant of whether a regime is likely to be democratic or authoritarian, yet there are important differences between their arguments. Can you identify them?

Barrington Moore, Social Origins of Dictatorship and Democracy: Lord and Peasant in the Making of the Modern World. *Boston: Beacon Press, 1966.*

This theory is intuitive. If you are worried about where your next meal is going to come from, or how to access health care for your seriously ill children, you are probably less likely to devote your energy to demanding the right to vote, engaging in political speech, protesting, reading political newspapers, and the like. As a result, all else being equal, we would expect pressures in poorer societies to link more directly to the satisfaction of basic economic and social needs than political liberties. This most emphatically does *not* mean that poorer people do not value political rights and liberties, as has sometimes been asserted, but rather that some needs will tend to strike us as more immediate than others, depending on our circumstances.[29] International survey research that tracks political attitudes supports this finding: as economic development increases, prioritization of political freedoms tends to increase; whereas in poorer societies, "survival values" score more highly.[30] Again, people in poorer societies would, all else being equal, likely *prefer* democratic regimes in many instances, but they may be less likely to successfully *press* for democratization and/or the maintenance of democratic institutions.

Economic factors of this sort might matter not just in how they affect citizens' attitudes but also in how they shape the institutional environment. While historical institutionalists argue that paths are set at critical junctures, determining long-run outcomes, rational-choice institutionalists are more interested in how institutions relate to the ongoing interests of groups and individuals in the polity. Further, rational-choice institutionalists look at how shifting configurations of interests and institutions change the bargaining positions of those groups and individuals.

Income inequality, in addition to absolute poverty, is another likely factor contributing to the establishment of authoritarian regimes. Societies with high levels of income inequality seem more likely to be authoritarian than those with low levels of income inequality. The relationship between these variables is complex, however. One source of the association between authoritarianism and inequality may be that authoritarian regimes sometimes promote social and economic inequality in addition to obvious political inequality. In an authoritarian regime, there is not open access to the state.[31] Rather, some elites are privileged, and other citizens are excluded from connections and decision-making power. This discrepancy is clearest in cases where dictators amass property for themselves and their associates, such as the infamous Somoza family, which held power in Nicaragua from 1936 to 1979 and came to hold an absurdly high percentage of Nicaraguan territory as its personal property.[32] If a large segment of the population has limited access to resources, we would expect that segment to be less involved in democratic participation or in pressing for democratization.

Income inequality may help favor authoritarianism in another way as well: it may engender envy and social division of the sort that potential authoritarian leaders can exploit. Many authoritarian regimes will present themselves as avengers of injustice. Populist leaders who tend toward authoritarianism can claim to represent disenfranchised poor people and can promise to redress visible inequalities. Interestingly, this seems to be a characteristic of both left- and right-wing populism.[33]

INSIGHTS   ## Economic Origins of Dictatorship and Democracy
by Daron Acemoglu and James Robinson

Like the arguments discussed in the previous section, Acemoglu and Robinson's account of the determinants of regime type is also "institutionalist," but it falls closer to the rational choice framework. To simplify the argument, Acemoglu and Robinson argue that political modernization exhibits one of several main paths. The first is mostly unproblematic and steady democratization, like in the United Kingdom and the United States. The second is a see-saw pattern of alteration between authoritarianism and democracy, as in parts of Latin America. The third is authoritarian persistence based on shared prosperity and relatively good governance. The fourth is authoritarian persistence based on repression.

Their game-theoretical approach views institutional arrangements as products of different actors pursuing their interests. On one hand you have elites, who want to maintain their elite status, which means privileged access to power and other resources. Then you have the general population, which has an interest in democratization. Elites hold power prior to democratization, and they can be expected to preserve as much of it as possible. So what determines the pattern of political modernization is the relative situation of elites and the general population. Elites can choose repression or can try to placate the general population in one of two ways: they can make "pro-citizen" concessions and try to run a polity that keeps the population rich and happy, or they can make the "credible commitment" of institutionalizing citizen control through democracy. Acemoglu and Robinson suggest that they will choose democracy only if they have to and if they expect that they can hold on to more resources through doing so than through choosing another path. However, if elites cannot implement pro-citizen policies, and if democracy is likely to lead to a dramatic decline in their privileges, they are likely to choose repression.

Daron Acemoglu and James Robinson, Economic Origins of Dictatorship and Democracy. *New York: Cambridge University Press, 2006.*

State Weakness and Failure

Another theory focuses on state structures, arguing that weak or failing states are more likely to yield authoritarian politics.[34] This may be related to economic theories of authoritarianism. While some forms of authoritarianism go with strong states (e.g., totalitarian forms), many tend to be linked to weak states or to those shading toward state failure. Even the major totalitarian polities emerged from states that faced serious difficulties, such as late-Czarist Russia in the 1900s or Weimar Germany in the 1930s.

As noted in chapters 3 and 4, one of the key features of strong states is that they are well institutionalized. Well-institutionalized states tend to be less personalistic and more resistant to the efforts of private actors to co-opt them for their own gain. "Predatory states" or regimes, however, are those in which one group in society is able to capture the state and use it for the group's own benefit.[35] In some of the worst cases, the boundary between the private property of the ruler's family and that of the state is unclear, and ruling elites use the military instrumentally against their opponents within society.[36] So we seem to have a kind of paradox. On one hand, well-institutionalized, strong states with high capacity may be less likely to fall into authoritarianism; but when they do, there is a higher chance that they will develop totalitarian forms of authoritarianism, which requires a strong state to begin with. Just the same, authoritarianism in weak states with predatory regimes can be very destructive as well.

Of course, state failure or state weakness can be an independent variable that causes authoritarianism, but it in turn is caused by something else. State failure or state weakness happens for a reason, as discussed in earlier chapters. It may be that low economic development leads to weak states, which in turn leaves a polity vulnerable to authoritarianism. If this is the case, low economic development can be thought to indirectly encourage authoritarianism *through* its impact on state weakness. In other words, causal sequences like the following simplified model are possible, with the arrows understood to represent *probabilistic* causality:

Low economic development → Weak state → Authoritarianism

An alternative theory might look like the following, also treating a weak state as a variable that intervenes between a more distanced cause and authoritarian politics:

Unstable class coalitions → Weak/poorly institutionalized state → Authoritarianism

This theoretical causal sequence rests on the assumption that strong states might be products of stable class coalitions. If this is true, and if weak states breed authoritarianism, then unstable class coalitions might be thought to indirectly raise the likelihood of authoritarian outcomes.

Political Culture Theories of Authoritarian Persistence

Other theories of authoritarian regimes hold that the beliefs, norms, and values of a country's citizens determine its regime type. The idea here is that people in societies that are culturally authoritarian are more likely to have and keep authoritarian regimes. Theorists have identified different types of authoritarian cultures, and some argue that certain countries or regions have inherently different values.

Not surprisingly, as noted in chapter 6, authoritarian rulers are sometimes happy to support this type of argument, such as Singapore's Lee Kuan Yew, who claimed "Confucian values" were not compatible with "Western" democracy.

Which values are hypothesized to matter depends very much on the theory in question. Some scholars have argued that certain types of national identity might be more conducive to authoritarianism than others.[37] Others have suggested that certain countries or cultural regions, like Latin America, have a generalized "centralist" disposition that increases the likelihood of accepting authoritarian regimes.[38] Others have noted that some societies establish "traditions" of authoritarianism and that the weight of tradition predicts a higher probability of future authoritarianism.[39] Still others have argued that what matters are not general cultural dispositions of this sort but rather the variation, observed through extensive survey research, in attitudes toward civic participation.[40]

Even those who are skeptical of the claim that political culture strongly predicts authoritarianism will often be more receptive to the idea that political-cultural variables can, under certain circumstances, increase the likelihood that certain *types* of authoritarianism will develop. This idea might be clearest in the case of modern totalitarian regimes. It is very difficult to explain the *path* taken by Soviet or Nazi totalitarianism without paying some attention to the ideas of Marxist and fascist thinkers and the ways in which these ideas influenced the thinking and strategic behavior of key actors in the establishment of those regimes.

INSIGHTS

The Civic Culture: Political Attitudes and Democracy in Five Nations
by Gabriel Almond and Sidney Verba

Almond and Verba's book is as much a theory of democracy as authoritarianism, but here we will draw out its implications for the study of authoritarian regimes. Almond and Verba base their analysis on survey research that was carried out in five countries: the United States, the United Kingdom, Germany, Italy, and Mexico. The research was conducted in 1959 and 1960, when Mexico was still an authoritarian system (with the PRI dictatorship) and when Germany and Italy had been liberated by the Allies from the Hitler and Mussolini governments in the relatively recent past.

Almond and Verba create a typology of political-cultural orientations with three main categories: parochial cultures, subject cultures, and civic cultures of participation. Parochial cultures are characterized by populations that are largely distant from politics and try to stay out of the government's way, trusting it and other actors outside of their local groups very little. Subject cultures have higher levels of investment and trust in the state than parochial cultures, but they have lower levels of trust than participatory cultures; and members of subject cultures are not optimistic about their chances to influence politics. Members of civic cultures of participation, though, have high trust in government and other actors and also believe themselves to be very capable of shaping political decisions through participation.

Almond and Verba recognized that institutions also shape public attitudes, but their work suggested that public dispositions and attitudes were important factors in determining whether a given regime would be democratic or authoritarian.

Gabriel Almond and Sidney Verba, The Civic Culture: Political Attitudes and Democracy in Five Nations. *Princeton, NJ: Princeton University Press, 1963.*

Barriers to Collective Action

Rational-choice and game-theoretical approaches constitute a major alternative to political culture theories in attempting to explain authoritarian persistence. Such approaches try to model the rational processes of decision making in which citizens and politicians engage.[41] They tend to presume that these actors know their own interests (or preferences) and have imperfect information about the likely behavior of others. According to these approaches, actors are unlikely to engage in **collective action** unless it becomes rational for them to do so, meaning the chances of success seem high, their contribution seems important to the desired outcome, and they are unlikely to face major costs for participating in such action.[42] These approaches constitute alternatives to political cultural theories of authoritarian persistence because they assume that most people want more democratization (regardless of their culture), but that sometimes there are major barriers to democratic transition such that it would be *irrational* for any individual actor to take the necessary steps to provoke a transition.

Imagine a repressive authoritarian state. It severely restricts rights, grants decision-making authority to a small elite, authorizes a police agency to use violence and torture as key tools for stifling dissent, censors media heavily (including social media), and reads e-mails and taps the phones of any potential democratic activists. Let us also assume that the regime's repression has been successful to date and that there is no viable resistance at present. Now imagine that you really want to topple this regime and usher in a democratic replacement. Unfortunately, you are unlikely to be able to accomplish this change on your own. You are going to need lots of people to participate in collective action with you. Now let's imagine the conversation you might have with your best friend as you try to convince him or her to help you in the struggle:

> YOU: Eh, hey, what do you say we try to topple the authoritarian state?
>
> FRIEND: . . . Umm . . .
>
> YOU: Aren't you tired of this repressive regime?
>
> FRIEND: Um, aren't they tapping the phones? Let's talk about this later.

[Later, in a safe place, the conversation resumes:]

> YOU: So I was saying, what if we . . .
>
> FRIEND: Are you crazy? They'll probably catch us, and if they do, who knows what they'll do? Anyway, there's no way it could work.

In essence, rational-choice theories of authoritarian persistence say that your friend is right in this scenario and that authoritarian persistence will likely last until events change your friend's calculations, along with the perceptions and calculations of many others.[43] This could happen in a number of ways. For example, imagine that the large foreign power that used to bankroll the repressive state's security apparatus has made human rights the new centerpiece of its foreign policy and has therefore cut off such aid. Or imagine that there is a change in leadership in the regime, and the new leaders reduce repression.

collective action Action undertaken by individuals and groups to pursue their ends in formally or informally coordinated ways, often in pursuit of some common or public good such as expanded civil rights or sustainable use of common resources.

INSIGHTS

Now Out of Never: The Element of Surprise in the East European Revolution of 1989
by Timur Kuran

Kuran tries to explain how rapid transitions from authoritarian rule could take place when previous data indicates support for the old regime. He is particularly interested in the revolutions that took place in 1989 in countries like Poland, Czechoslovakia, and East Germany. His key insight is that under certain circumstances *preference falsification* may be quite common. If it is risky or socially unacceptable to publicly state your preference for more democracy, you are unlikely to do so. In such an environment, people are likely to overstate their support for authoritarianism. This preference falsification is costly: it is psychologically unpleasant to have to pretend to like things that you do not like. Some people most opposed to the regime

are least willing to falsify their preferences and are the first to make their voices known. If they do so without major repercussions, more people begin expressing their true preferences. A cascading pattern then develops as it becomes safer for more people to speak out against the regime.

Many authoritarian states seem to implicitly understand this, which is why so many of them devote such resources to controlling discourse and public gatherings. Barriers to the collective expression of preferences for democracy are barriers to mobilization against authoritarian regimes.

Timur Kuran, "Now Out of Never: The Element of Surprise in the East European Revolution of 1989," World Politics 44, No. 1 (Oct. 1991): 7–48.

Or that governance and the economy get so bad your friend feels that he or she has nothing left to lose. In such circumstances, collective action becomes possible, and authoritarian persistence is at risk.

These factors can interact with political culture. Part of the information that rational actors take into account is the likely behavior of their peers. This information is largely gleaned from their public expression of their beliefs and attitudes (the same things students of political culture are studying), and sometimes populations under authoritarian regimes might appear to be more supportive of the regime than they really are. We return to these themes in later chapters on political parties, social movements, and revolutions (chapters 11 and 12).

Special Causal Circumstances Surrounding Hybrid and Semi-authoritarian Regimes

As noted earlier, in contemporary politics we have witnessed an increase in the number of hybrid regimes, a pattern of political change that has given rise to a good deal of new and productive theorizing. To some extent, explanations for the emergence of hybrid regimes differ from those for the emergence of more traditional forms of authoritarianism, though we would not want to exaggerate these differences.

Equally important, if we are interested in transitions *from* or persistence *of* hybrid or semi-authoritarian regimes, we need to be attentive to their special characteristics.

We should not draw the conclusion that the factors cited earlier to explain the rise of authoritarian regimes or authoritarian persistence are irrelevant to hybrid regimes, but we should note that a particularly important variety of hybrid regimes—the competitive authoritarian regimes of recent decades—seem to show their own, historically specific, causal factors of importance.

INSIGHTS	Competitive Authoritarianism: Hybrid Regimes After the Cold War
	by Steven Levitsky and Lucan A. Way

evitsky and Way are interested in understanding the sorts of transitions that are likely to develop out of "competitive authoritarian" regimes, a term that they have coined to label regimes that do allow (often problematic) elections alongside other non-democratic features. As they note, competitive authoritarian regimes should not be thought of as transitional: there is no reason to assume that competitive authoritarian regimes will become democratic or more fully authoritarian. However, certain characteristics do predict the likelihood of transition from competitive authoritarianism to democracy or full-blown autocracy. First, lots of linkages to the West predict a move toward democratization. If there are not so many linkages to the West, though, two main paths are possible. The first is ongoing authoritarianism in the context of a strong state. This path is most likely, the authors argue, when (a) the state is strong at the beginning of the process and (b) the party or other strongest organizational vehicle in the competitive authoritarian environment (which is the core of the competitive authoritarian regime) has lots of "organizational power." The second path is authoritarian persistence with lots of instability and turnover, which is more likely in the context of a weaker and less stable state.

Steven Levitsky and Lucan A. Way, Competitive Authoritarianism: Hybrid Regimes After the Cold War. *New York: Cambridge University Press, 2010.*

Why Did Zimbabwe Become and Remain Authoritarian?

Authoritarian regimes come in many varieties, and they come from many different origins. We have emphasized that there is no single thing called "authoritarianism" that one theory can explain. Rather, authoritarian regimes have distinct features and exhibit many different types of transitions (and non-transitions). Scholars have developed a number of explanatory models to account for these. Some of the main general factors in most cases, though, include (1) historical relationships between contending groups, (2) the strength and form of existing institutions, (3) a country's level of economic development, (4) political-cultural traditions and tendencies, and (5) the strategic situations and choices of key actors. Of course, as we have seen in other chapters, it is not enough to merely list such contributing factors; we must figure out how such factors interact and which are most important. What do you think? And how could we test your ideas empirically?

As we noted at the outset of the chapter, modern-day Zimbabwe is an authoritarian regime that is characterized by many of the features we have discussed. It is a "personalist" regime, the population of which is subject to many of the vagaries of authoritarianism. It is characterized by repression, a lack of secure political rights, seemingly arbitrary rule, and so on. Even after its recent transition, authoritarianism persists. Although this may change, in what follows, we treat the post-Mugabe regime as essentially continuous with the Mugabe regime, on the grounds that the overall distribution of power has changed very little, at least so far.

KEY METHODOLOGICAL TOOLS

Evidence and Empirical Critiques

One reason that many theories continue to endure in different areas of comparative politics is that most of the major theories have some empirical support. This makes it challenging to determine which theory is the most accurate. In reality, most theories will not be accurate under all circumstances, but rather each will explain some outcomes better than others. So how do you avoid simply making "laundry lists" (as noted earlier) and saying, "Everything matters"? In preparing to make theoretical arguments, it is of course important for any particular question to examine how the empirical evidence lines up with the theoretical predictions and the specific hypotheses you might offer.

THINKING COMPARATIVELY

(continued)

One very useful tool can be evidence that allows you to critique a particular argument.

In aiming to build arguments, there is one very important misconception: that the only valuable type of evidence is that which supports a hypothesis or theory. In fact, some of the most valuable evidence is that which allows you to critique or challenge one particular argument. This is useful especially when you are trying to determine the strongest argument among many that have some supporting evidence.

It is important to stress that not everywhere in Africa is like this, and Zimbabwe itself has not always been like this, so our research question might be "Why is Zimbabwe authoritarian? Why did it become so, and why has it remained so?"

We should expect theories of authoritarian rule to be able to account for an authoritarian regime like that of Zimbabwe in recent decades. Looking at the various causal theories of authoritarianism, we can consider how each might propose an explanation for the emergence and/or persistence of the regime. In the section on "Causes and Effects" in this chapter, we have looked at several such theories. We list them in Table 7.1, along with what the theory might explain is the cause of Zimbabwe's authoritarianism. We also list in the third column an example of evidence that we might find supports this theoretical proposition. Note that the examples of supporting evidence here are not proven but are simply plausible for this particular case.

Looking at the theoretical prediction and the examples of evidence to support the theory, we may see a problem: we can find some plausible evidence to support all of these theories! We can go right down the column and come up with decent evidence. The authoritarian regime has indeed received the support of some key coalition actors; it has appealed to many of the poor in a populist fashion; it is a poorly institutionalized predatory state; it has represented itself as a quintessentially African unit resisting Western influence; and it has seen many hundreds of thousands of its opponents flee the country rather than risk repression. Indeed, this discussion illustrates something often experienced in the study of comparative politics. Sometimes, at a certain stage in the development of research on a topic or question, we do not know *which* theory truly offers the best explanation for a given phenomenon, and multiple explanations seem promising.

Does this mean we are stuck? Or that we should assume that all theories work equally well and that we should list them all as the answers to our research question? No. On the contrary, it is common for many good research questions to have multiple possible answers. Indeed, it is often a sign of a good question that it can have many possible answers: it suggests that the question is open-ended, and not

TABLE 7.1 **Authoritarianism in Zimbabwe: Theories, Explanations, and Examples of Supporting Evidence**

Theory	Theoretical Explanation	Example of Supporting Evidence
Historical Institutionalist	Coalitions of powerful political actors emerge that favor elite domination.	The regime receives support of the military and key economic actors.
Poverty and Inequality	Poorer citizens seek economic security and allow authoritarian rule.	The regime appeals to some poorer citizens as populist.
State Weakness	Weak, poorly institutionalized, predatory state will be authoritarian.	The regime has engaged in predatory behavior and undermined institutions.
Political Culture	Cultural values shape type of authoritarian regime that emerges.	The regime has worked within bounds of top-down "tribalism."
Collective Action	Disapproval of the regime is impeded by repression.	The regime creates large numbers of exiles.

one with a foregone conclusion that is self-evident and therefore uninteresting. In the parlance of comparative politics from chapters 1 and 2, a good theory must be falsifiable, and the fact that multiple possible theories can address a question is often a sign that the question is well conceived. Furthermore, theories in comparative politics will not last if they get no empirical support, so we should not be surprised if more than one theory has evidence working for it. But the job of the comparativist is to analyze the relative merits of these different arguments and to find ways to adjudicate among them.

What can you do if several different theories each have some evidence going for them? Our most important tool here is looking for evidence that works *against* one theory or another. This disconfirming evidence that allows you to critique one or more theories can sometimes help identify which theory stands strongest. In fact, evidence that works against one theory can be just as valuable as an extra bit of evidence that supports a theory. It may be *more* valuable, since the implications of truly disconfirming evidence are stronger than the implications of some evidence that is simply consistent with a theory.

What might be examples of disconfirming evidence for the theories in our Zimbabwe example? Table 7.2 has the same theories and theoretical explanations as Table 7.1, except this time we consider evidence that might show that the regime in Zimbabwe does not follow what the different theories predict. Notice that we can actually come up with at least plausible examples of disconfirming evidence as well for any of the theories we noted previously.

Here we see examples of how each theory could have some evidence against it, just as each theory had some evidence for it. Comparativists can use evidence both to support and to critique different theories as they try to identify which theory is strongest. We should be particularly attentive to evidence that would post a strong challenge to a theory. For example, in Table 7.2, the evidence presented for the "political culture" and "collective action" theories might suggest real weaknesses in

TABLE 7.2 Authoritarianism in Zimbabwe: Theories, Explanations, and Examples of Contrary Evidence

Theory	Theoretical Explanation	Example of Contrary Evidence
Historical Institutionalist	Coalitions of powerful political actors emerge that favor elite domination.	The regime's economic policy alienated key economic actors, including industry and commercial farmers.
Poverty and Inequality	Poorer citizens seek economic security and allow authoritarian rule.	The regime is (or at least was under Mugabe) relatively unpopular among many peasants and poor urban dwellers.
State Weakness	Weak, poorly institutionalized, predatory state will be authoritarian.	Zimbabwe's state and Mugabe's party and military have exhibited considerable capacity in the past.
Political Culture	Cultural values shape type of authoritarian regime that emerges.	Zimbabwe's deep cultural values have little to do with tribalism, but instead have deep emphasis on human rights.
Collective Action	Disapproval of the regime is impeded by repression.	Zimbabwe's people have been relatively open to expressing dissatisfaction with the regime.

THINKING COMPARATIVELY

their ability to explain Zimbabwe's authoritarianism. We cannot say, for instance, that traditional Zimbabwean political culture is the source of the regime's authoritarianism if Zimbabwean political culture is not actually authoritarian. Likewise, we cannot say that the source of its authoritarianism is that dissidents cannot organize or speak if, in fact, dissent is widespread and organized.

On the other hand, some theories can be defended in the face of potentially challenging evidence, either because the evidence is being interpreted wrongly or the theory has been construed in a limited or wrong way. Imagine proponents of the historical institutionalist theory trying to make their argument. They might acknowledge the evidence that the regime has alienated many elite economic actors and that this has negative implications for the argument attributed to historical institutionalism in the table: "Coalitions of powerful political actors emerge that favor elite domination." They could point out, though, that commercial and farming elites are not the only important actors among whom coalitions could form, and that the Zimbabwean state under Mugabe created a *new* coalition of powerful actors from the military and masses of unemployed men. Theories cannot proceed by being adapted to deal with each individual case; but if a theory has been misconstrued or its implications not fully built into tested hypotheses, seemingly disconfirming evidence might still be compatible with the theory.

Authoritarianism remains one of the most analytically and morally pressing questions in comparative politics today. As it has become clear that democracy was not simply going to predominate all over the world after the Cold War, scholars have reengaged with urgency on the question of authoritarian rule. The types and causes of authoritarianism are numerous and complex, but young scholars who develop the analytical skills of comparativists will be in a position to shed real light on these issues in the years to come.

Chapter Summary

Concepts

- Authoritarianism refers to political systems that are hierarchically ordered and have relatively closed decision-making processes.

Types

- There are many different types of authoritarian regimes, including totalitarian regimes that attempt to control entire societies through ideology, personalist dictatorships centered around individual autocrats, and bureaucratic-authoritarian regimes centered around groups such as the military.
- There are also many different possible transitions (or lack of transitions) between regime types other than democratization: authoritarian regimes can persist, they can give way to other authoritarian regimes, or they can turn into hybrid

regimes, while democracies too can break down and move toward authoritarianism or hybrid regimes.

Causes and Effects

- There are many theories about the causes of authoritarianism and its persistence, including theories based on historical institutional factors, poverty and inequality, state weakness, political culture, and impediments to collective action.

Thinking Comparatively

- Theories about the causes of authoritarianism (like theories in other areas) may all find some supporting evidence, and a useful strategy for judging the power of theories for specific research questions is also to consider how evidence may disconfirm a theory.

Thinking It Through

1. We have discussed in this chapter the distinction often drawn by political scientists between democratic regimes and "hybrid" or "competitive authoritarian" regimes. Where, precisely, is the line between these sorts of regimes? Consider any two cases of democratic regimes and try to work out what combination of developments would lead you to reclassify them as "hybrid."

2. We discussed a number of different theories of authoritarianism. Note that the historical institutionalist theories, the economic theories, and the political culture theories all aim to explain both the emergence and the persistence of authoritarian regimes. Can these theories explain the emergence and persistence of hybrid regimes equally well? If so, demonstrate how. If not, what sorts of modifications might help them to do so?

3. Is authoritarianism simply the opposite of democracy? Is it best thought of as an absence of democratic freedoms and rights? Or is democracy best thought of as an absence of authoritarianism? Why?

4. Identify your preferred theory to account for the persistence of authoritarianism in Zimbabwe, Nazi Germany, or another country of your choosing. Consider yourself a theorist associated with this preferred theory. Now imagine you have been called in to consult with the U.S. State Department about the best way to deal with authoritarian regimes the United States deems dangerous, such as North Korea, Syria, or Iran. What would your theory imply as a policy recommendation for how to deal with authoritarian regimes?

5. Describe some of the incentives that would make an authoritarian ruler seek to hang onto power, even when that ruler senses the regime is unpopular and performing poorly.

CHAPTER 8

Constitutions and Constitutional Design

Leaders of the transition from apartheid at the adoption of South Africa's democratic constitution, May 1, 1996. From left to right in front row: F. W. de Klerk (president 1989–1994), Cyril Ramaphosa (current president), Nelson Mandela (president 1994–1999), and Leon Wessels.

Consider the following passage:

We, the people of South Africa,
Recognise the injustices of our past;
Honour those who suffered for justice and freedom in our land;
Respect those who have worked to build and develop our country; and
Believe that South Africa belongs to all who live in it, united in our diversity.
We therefore, through our freely elected representatives, adopt this Constitution as the supreme law of the Republic so as to
Heal the divisions of the past and establish a society based on democratic values, social justice and fundamental human rights;
Lay the foundations for a democratic and open society in which government is based on the will of the people and every citizen is equally protected by law;
Improve the quality of life of all citizens and free the potential of each person; and
Build a united and democratic South Africa able to take its rightful place as a sovereign state in the family of nations.
May God protect our people.
Nkosi Sikelel' iAfrika. Morena boloka setjhaba sa heso.
God seën Suid–Afrika. God bless South Africa.
Mudzimu fhatutshedza Afurika. Hosi katekisa Afrika.

This passage is the preamble to the South African constitution passed in 1996, which established the foundational laws and was intended to form the basis for democracy in the country after decades of racial discrimination and white-only rule known as *apartheid*. One of the functions of constitutions can be to express the values of a society, especially those relating to the unity and aspirations of the people. The South African charter was a major step in creating a "New South Africa" based on equality and respect for the dignity of the country's peoples (even if it certainly did not solve all the country's problems with racism and inequality with the stroke of a pen). The preamble addresses this aspiration and notably concludes with an

expression translated into six of the country's major languages. These aspirations may vary from place to place: the lengthy introductions to China's and Iran's constitutions, for example, document the history of the revolutionary movements that gave rise to the regimes currently in power. The United States too has a famous preamble in its Constitution of 1787: *We the People of the United States, in order to form a more perfect Union, establish justice, insure domestic tranquility, provide for the common defence, promote the general welfare, and secure the blessings of liberty to ourselves and our posterity, do ordain and establish this Constitution for the United States of America.*

The Constitution of the Republic of South Africa, and most others like it, also does more than express the country's ideals in writing. It is a very specific legal document that creates a design for the country's formal political institutions, including the legislative, executive, and judicial branches. It also addresses the division of power between a central government and the provinces (as they are called in South Africa, which are akin to the states in the United States). With regard to judiciaries in particular, the South African constitution established a very important power of constitutional interpretation: judicial review. Judges were given the authority to rule which laws are consistent with the constitution and which are not. The South African judiciary even ruled on whether the Constitution itself was constitutional, evaluating the text, determining what was adequate and proper and what was not. It accepted much of the text submitted in 1994 but sent the Constitution back to its drafting body, the Constituent National Assembly, to clarify some issues and rewrite others.

In this chapter, we examine constitutions, the questions of whether and how they separate power between levels of government, and whether they are interpreted by judiciaries. We leave the discussion of the constitutional roles of legislatures and executives to chapters 9 and 10, where we treat those two branches of government individually. The issues related to constitutions and constitutional interpretation matter because, in most modern societies, constitutions establish many of the formal organizational features of the state and thus are keys to understanding politics.

institution Social or political structure[1] or set of practices, including government organizations, that shapes the behavior of individuals and groups.

This chapter begins our examination of formal government **institutions**, which are the structures and organizations that shape political behavior. The most obvious among these are the branches of government, two of which we explore in depth in subsequent chapters (the legislative, chapter 9, and executive branches, chapter10), and we also include political parties and interest groups that are a regular part of political life. Because the very foundation of political institutions is usually located in constitutions, we focus on these basic charters in this chapter and on the question of constitutional interpretation. How is political power divided among different governing institutions? Who rules on whether a law is constitutional? We take a close look at these issues and discuss both federalism and judiciaries, which are key elements of what constitutions say and what they do.

· · ·

Concepts

We look first at concepts and definitions, outlining what we mean by constitutions, federalism and unitarism, and judiciaries. We then turn to types across different countries, to show how constitutions, constitutional design, and constitutional interpretation may vary from place to place.

Constitutions

Constitutions are the foundational charters and fundamental laws of most modern states. They elaborate the structure of government and express the founding principles of the regime. They are usually written documents passed by some sort of constitutional convention or constituent assembly that brings together many of a country's leading political figures to hammer out the rules, laws, and structures needed to establish the basis for political life. This may occur at the founding of a country, as in the case of the United States, or when a new political regime is established, as has happened in France many times with the creation of new republics.

Constitutions have come to symbolize the social contracts that societies make to "constitute" themselves in which "the people" confer authority to political actors in exchange for the establishment of order and a rule of law. The history of constitutions links closely to the idea of **constitutionalism**, or limited government, and is thus part and parcel of the story of the evolution of modern governance, and especially the emergence of democracy itself.

As the basic founding laws of a society, constitutions are the set of rules and norms on which all other laws are based. In the United States, for instance, the

constitution Fundamental and supreme laws, usually written in a charter, that establish the basis of a political system and the basis for other laws.

constitutionalism The limitation of government through a constitution.

French protestors against the constitution of 1958.

Constitution is the ultimate point of political reference: even the president, as head of state, must act in accordance with its principles. Military enlistees and new citizens swear an oath of allegiance not to the president or the Congress but to uphold and defend the Constitution "against all enemies, foreign and domestic." In a real sense, the Constitution is the foundation of the United States' entire political system. In other countries as well, constitutions provide the basis for political unity, defining who and what the state is. These sets of laws outline the basic structure of the state and its patterns of governance, noting which branches of government have which powers and which responsibilities. In many cases, constitutions recognize or grant the basic rights of a country's citizens, though these rights are not always guaranteed in every case. Indeed, even highly authoritarian regimes often make use of constitutions, regardless of whether rights are infringed in practice.

In most cases, constitutions are written down in a single document that is subject to change by a process of amendment. Constitutions will not attempt to include the massive amount of statutes or laws that are needed to govern the society and establish its policies but will rather outline how these laws and policies are to be established and who decides on whether they are legitimate. They are, in short, the law above all other law, and the basis for political life.

Constitutional Design

constitutional design Features of constitutions that shape the basic features of the political system, such as separation of powers and responsibilities between levels of government and branches of government.

Constitutional design refers to the features of the constitution that shape the powers of different political institutions. These features vary, though all constitutions define the basic structure of government. Constitutional design is important because it gives countries the chance to set up effective institutions. For example, countries such as Nigeria, Mexico, the United States, and India have all witnessed wrangling over how power should be established and how governments should be instituted. Starting out, it was unclear whether many new nations would survive or would prove vulnerable to disintegration, especially after the end of colonialism in these countries.[2] The U.S. Constitution happens to have lasted to this day, but due to a variety of causes, other countries have re-crafted their constitutions and their constitutional designs on multiple occasions. After establishing one of the world's earliest republics in the late 1700s, France has gone through numerous constitutions, with the current one dating only back to 1958.

federalism System of government with constitutional design of separation of powers between central government and subnational governments.

The question of **federalism**, or the separation of powers among different levels of government in a country, is often central to constitutional design. One of the key issues in the U.S. Constitution, for instance, was dividing powers between the central government and the states. Federalism is a political system in which multiple levels of government have some degree of autonomy in the same territory. Only in some countries do subnational governments (such as states, provinces, or regions) have constitutional protection or authority and a guarantee of autonomy from the central government. These may be called federal systems. For instance, the 27 states in Brazil or the nine provinces in South Africa have constitutional guarantees of their authority to govern and establish laws in their respective regions, even as the central government also has the right to do so. As the American president (and political scientist) Woodrow Wilson put it, "The question of the relation of the states to the federal government is the cardinal question of our constitutional system."

By contrast, the absence of federalism is unitary government or **unitarism**, in which the institutions and branches of the central government effectively wield political power. Most countries in the world are unitary. In these countries, local governments (such as towns, cities, or villages) will have some authority to shape local rules, but the laws made by these local governments are subject to central authority. As we shall see, federalism is not necessarily more or less democratic than unitarism, but its implications for how government works are numerous.

Constitutional design usually also involves establishing a **separation of powers** among distinct branches, each with its own responsibilities and duties. Constitutions frequently begin by establishing a legislative branch responsible for formulating and passing laws. This may be called a parliament, a congress, or an assembly, or may be given any number of other names, as we examine in the chapter on legislatures (chapter 9). The executive branch (chapter 10) is the other portion of the government that is usually elected, at least in democratic regimes, and the powers and functions of the executive branch are routinely outlined in a constitution as well. For both of these branches, constitutions will often outline the procedure by which representatives are chosen, in addition to the powers they hold and duties they must perform. Constitutions also often address the structure and power of the judicial branch as well as the structure of the administrative apparatus.[3] This delineates the separation of powers between the three "branches" of government: legislatures, executives, and judiciaries. We discuss legislatures and executives in full chapters (9 and 10, respectively, as noted previously), though these are also clearly elements of constitutional design.

Judiciaries are branches of government that have particular importance in how constitutions are interpreted. The principal duty of the judiciary is to preside over cases in courts. This implies the power to interpret the laws put into effect by the other branches of government, but the extent of the judiciary's power to interpret (and even strike down) laws varies from one country to another. In some countries, judiciaries have considerable powers of constitutional interpretation, while in other countries, they do not rule on whether laws are constitutional. The principal distinction is the strength of **judicial review**, which refers to the power of constitutional courts to determine the legality of laws.

These two features—the extent of federalism and the respective roles of the branches of government—are central to both constitutional design and constitutional interpretation. For the remainder of this chapter, we discuss variations in constitutions themselves, as well as the different ways constitutions are designed and interpreted. These variations are considerable, as we will see in the section that follows.

unitarism System of government in which central government is predominant and the powers of subnational governments are limited to those delegated by the center.

separation of powers The division of powers in a government system between branches of government or between levels of government.

judiciary The branch of government responsible for the interpretation of laws in courts.

judicial review System of constitutional interpretation in which judges rule on the constitutionality of laws passed by the legislature and the executive.

Types

As noted in the previous section, there are several ways countries differ in how their constitutions are designed and interpreted. In general, constitutions can be designed to be flexible and easily changed or rigid and difficult to change. A second issue is how the constitution is interpreted, and specifically whether the judiciary has the power to interpret the constitution. A third element is the degree of federalism in a constitution. Finally, we note that both democratic and authoritarian regimes have constitutions, and these may differ in some ways but may also look quite similar on paper.

Flexible and Rigid Constitutions

One of the central distinctions among different types of constitutions is how easily they can be changed. Many constitutions are designed to be relatively difficult to change. Amending them may require supermajorities in each chamber of the legislature (i.e., more than just a simple majority of votes) or approval by a number of the units of the federation—the states, provinces, or regions. Some constitutions, such as that of the United States, are even harder to change. An amendment to the U.S. Constitution requires a two-thirds vote in each of the two houses of Congress, followed by approval of three-fourths of the states' legislatures. It has been amended only twenty-seven times since its passage, and only seventeen times since 1791.

At the other end of the spectrum are highly flexible constitutions that are easy to change, at least nominally. The most obvious case is those that can be changed by a simple majority of the legislature. The Constitution of the United Kingdom is one of the most flexible, at least according to the law. This is because in the British system, the Parliament is sovereign, as discussed in the next section: if a majority of the legislature passes a law, that law is by definition constitutional.

This flexibility relates to another unique feature of the British constitution. Today, nearly all countries in the world have a single written document (which can be amended) that defines the parameters of the political system. The principal exception to the rule of written constitutional charters is the United Kingdom. The United Kingdom does not have a single constitutional text, but rather, several documents are deemed to have constitutional significance as the country has developed its political system over the course of many centuries. The major constitutional documents include the Magna Carta of 1215, but also a range of other laws of great significance and stature such as the Bill of Rights of 1689, which emphasized certain limitations on the power of the monarchy; and the Acts of Settlement of 1701, which established patterns of succession to the throne. In this sense, it may be said that the United Kingdom has a "written" constitution but one that relies on a range of written documents rather than a single one. What is considered constitutional in the United Kingdom is also determined by acts of Parliament and precedents in common law. This makes the constitution adaptable as laws and cultural practices change (New Zealand, a former British colony, similarly relies on a set of major acts of Parliament that established the constitutional basis for the country's governance). This does not, however, mean that the United Kingdom has no constitution; in fact, it has one of the longest traditions of constitutional government in the world.

Apart from the United Kingdom's constitution, which is based on many documents and traditions, and the U.S. Constitution, which is a brief framework with a handful of amendments over the years, there are many written constitutions that differ in style and form. As societies have grown more complex, constitutions in more recent years have often grown longer and more intricate as they attempt to balance a range of different interests, institutions, and ideas. The South African Constitution, mentioned at the top of the chapter, is an example. So too is the Brazilian Constitution of 1988, as noted in the concluding "Thinking Comparatively" section of this chapter.

Constitutions regularly recognize the rights of citizens or grant rights to the citizenry. In the case of the U.S. Constitution, many fundamental rights were actually passed as a set of amendments to the original document, known as the Bill of Rights. Since then, however, many contemporary constitutions (including the South African and Brazilian examples) have incorporated significant rights into the main text from the very beginning, which is likely one cause of constitutions becoming much lengthier over time. That is, articles in the original constitutional texts of many countries specify civil rights and civil liberties, political rights, and social rights (such as access to certain public services).

Of course, rights may be well protected or disrespected in practice, regardless of their inclusion in the document. For example, the Brazilian case is one where constitutional rights and protections have been promised, yet the government has been unable to deliver in some areas such as public services. In such cases, the constitutional guarantees may be more aspirational in nature, even in a democratic country. We return later in the chapter to the question of constitutional protections in practice when we look at how constitutions may be somewhat different for authoritarian systems.

Separation of Powers: Judicial Review and Parliamentary Sovereignty

In many (but not all) countries, courts have the power to decide some constitutional issues and rule on whether a law passed by the legislature is constitutional. If constitutional courts find that the law is not consistent with the constitution or basic laws of a society, they may strike down the law. In these countries, constitutional courts are usually separated from the civil and criminal court systems. In systems with separation of powers, this is the "check" that the judiciary has on the legislature. Constitutional courts are not the only type of courts. Local courts are for local disputes and for claims involving local laws, including arrangements over property (such as buying and selling houses), issues of marriage and divorce, traffic violations, and some criminal offenses.[4] Constitutional courts are reserved for major constitutional issues about whether a law passed by the government is valid.

As noted earlier in the chapter, the process by which national courts examine the constitutionality of law is called judicial review. Most constitutions provide for a process of judicial review in which constitutional courts have judges who rule on the constitutionality of law. Judicial review is the central political power of the judiciary, and it occurs when judges examine the constitutionality of a law passed by the legislature. In countries with judicial review, the constitution is seen as the supreme law of the land, and it is the role of the courts to verify that laws passed by the legislature are consistent with the constitution.

Judicial review generally operates with a high court or "supreme court" at the pinnacle of the judicial system that serves as the final arbiter of constitutional law. This may be built on top of a system that has "lower courts" in different states, provinces, or localities around the country.[5] The high court is composed of a select number of established jurists or justices. (In the United States, there are nine justices on the Supreme Court, nominated by the president and approved by the Senate for life terms.) In systems with judicial review, the decisions of such courts are often final and can be overturned only by subsequent judicial decisions or by legislatures amending the constitution itself. This system of constitutional interpretation by judges is regularly a source of debate and disagreement in many countries, as discussed in the "Causes and Effects" section later in the chapter.

The most prominent examples of countries without constitutional courts and judicial review are those where the constitutionality of law is determined by the parliament. In such cases, the judicial system is composed of courts that rule on the merits of specific cases in accordance with the laws that exist, without questioning the legitimacy of those laws. Of course, here too there may be some interpretation of what the laws mean, but the court is not empowered to strike down or alter laws passed by the legislature. The United Kingdom is the most noteworthy example. In the United Kingdom, there is no high court empowered to rule on most matters of law; the few minor exceptions relate to the question of how some powers have been decentralized to the regions of Scotland, Wales, and Northern Ireland, and this has been true only since 2009.[6]

parliamentary sovereignty
System in which the constitutionality of laws passed by legislature and executive are not subject to constitutional interpretation by judiciary.

As mentioned previously, constitutional interpretation in the United Kingdom generally follows the doctrine known as **parliamentary sovereignty**. This means that if the legislature—often called the Parliament—passes a law, that law is, by definition, constitutional. The legislating body is the highest political and legal authority in the land. In theory, the British Parliament could easily overturn long-standing parts of the British constitution at a moment's notice.

Delegates to Brazil's Constituent Assembly celebrate the passage of the country's constitution in 1988.

Why has this not happened? Why has there not been massive zigzagging in terms of what the constitution means, from one election to the next, as new parties take power and lose power? In reality, the British Parliament refrains from over-turning the founding laws of the polity because it follows national norms, values, customs, and traditions. Much as American political parties would probably not envision getting rid of major elements of the Constitution, even if they had the supermajority they would need, so too does the British system exhibit constitutional stability from one elected government to the next. It may seem self-evident that demanding procedures have kept the U.S. Constitution from being amended more frequently, but the United Kingdom shows that procedure is not the only determinant of how and when constitutions change. Consensus in the society matters, as do traditions, habits, customs, and values.

Federalism and Unitarism

The distinction between federal and unitary countries (and countries in between) is a fundamental difference in the way power is divided in a society. As discussed earlier, federal countries have a system in which power is separated between the central government and some subnational governments that are partly autonomous. In unitary systems, power is located at the center. In unitary states, the center may delegate certain powers to local, regional, state, or provincial governments, but it retains the constitutional or legal authority to reverse its decision at virtually any time.

FEDERALISM

The question of ruling large, complex territories is perennial, but the idea of federalism as a solution came more recently.[7] The United States was an early leader in establishing federalism (along with Switzerland). Led by James Madison, considered the "Father of the Constitution" and a principal author of *The Federalist Papers*, the nation's founders developed an intricate political compromise designed to satisfy both the larger and smaller of the thirteen original colonies that came together to create the new nation. As the colonies became states in the union, the American system reserved considerable rights to those states that the central government (called the "federal government") could not infringe on. They backed up these rights in the form of a Senate where each state was to have equal representation, regardless of population. This idea of compromise between central power and regional (or state or provincial) power came to appeal in a range of contexts. Other countries did not adopt the American system in its entirety, but many saw virtue in the general approach to reconcile national and subnational interests.

Today, many federal countries around the world have intricate sets of interacting institutions. Originally designed to unify diverse territories while preserving subnational autonomy, federal institutions now do more than simply offer a way to ensure that nations do not fall apart: they divide governing power and allow some laws and policies to vary from place to place within a country, even as some national laws (and the national constitution) take precedence everywhere inside the borders.[8] Federalism is now seen by some as a strategy to ensure more than stability and protection, as it may also promote democratic inclusion, as well as capture the benefits of economic unity. For these reasons, many of the world's largest countries either are federal or have prominent features that resemble federalism.

CASE IN CONTEXT

No Constitution? No Supreme Court? Constitutionality in the United Kingdom

PAGE 552

The United Kingdom has no single document that counts as its written constitution, and it also has no process of judicial review to interpret the constitution on most matters. It is the archetypal case of parliamentary sovereignty. The British constitution is thus one of the most flexible in the world. Yet there is considerable continuity in the system: the country has a long-standing set of traditions and values that seems to transmit the meaning of the constitution from one generation to the next. How does this system work, and what are its consequences?

See the case study on the United Kingdom in Part VI, pp. 552–553. As you read it, keep in mind the following questions:

1. In what ways does the doctrine of parliamentary sovereignty link together the various themes of this chapter: a flexible constitution, federalism versus unitarism, and judicial review?

2. Would this sort of constitution be feasible in a new country today, or is it feasible only in the relatively unique circumstances of Britain's history?

3. In what ways could one make a case that the U.K. system is more or less democratic than the U.S. system?

Although only about twenty of the nearly two hundred total countries in the world are considered federal, these twenty countries account for a large portion of the world's population. Many of the largest and most populous countries are federal, including the world's four most populous countries after China: India, the United States, Indonesia, and Brazil. Other federal countries include Nigeria, which has the largest population of any African country, and Pakistan, Russia, Mexico, and Germany, which are some of the largest countries in their respective regions of the world. Using a relatively inclusive definition designed to capture virtually any country that *might* be considered federal, we have constructed Map 8.1.

There are debates about whether many of the countries shaded in Map 8.1 are reliably federal (such as Spain and Pakistan). Several institutional elements and historical features may suggest otherwise, and federal countries do not always respect real autonomy for subnational units. Conversely, other countries may have some federal features yet remain unitary states, as is the case with China, where provinces have gained economic and political autonomy relative to the central government in recent years. China shows that some countries can seek the benefits of decentralized government without necessarily establishing federalism.

Federal systems may be defined as those where subnational governments have constitutional guarantees of some power and autonomy in their own jurisdictions, as well as constitutional protections from infringement on the part of the central government. In practical terms, virtually all federal countries share other characteristics: an upper legislative chamber defined in the constitution with territorial representation for the states/provinces/regions that provides them with political protection, and full legislative and executive branches at the subnational level.[9] While the specific definitions may vary, it is clear that federalism is intended to ensure representation for the subnational level in national decision making.

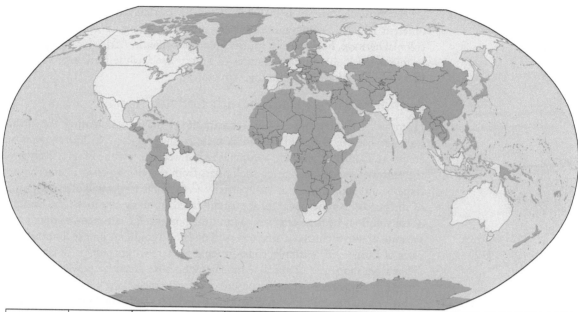

CONTINENT	AFRICA	ASIA	EUROPE	NORTH AMERICA	SOUTH AMERICA	OCEANIA
FEDERAL COUNTRIES	Comoros Ethiopia Nigeria South Africa	India Indonesia Malaysia Pakistan Russia United Arab Emirates	Austria Belgium Bosnia & Herzegovina Germany Spain Switzerland	Canada Mexico United States	Argentina Brazil Venezuela	Australia Micronesia

Map 8.1 Federal systems around the world (in yellow).

UNITARISM

Most countries in the world are unitary states, in which the central government is the only level of government specified in the constitutional charter. In unitary states, power is not constitutionally divided between layers of government but resides exclusively in the central government. This central government may then create (or allow for the creation of) more local levels of government, but these lower levels are dependent on the center and often accountable to the center. Municipalities, prefectures, counties, or other local governments may elect officials locally, but these will generally have little power. To use a translation from the French, the republic is "one and indivisible." Local governments may be able to elect officials, but the national government will make most significant policy. For instance, the center may establish the national school curriculum and may staff the offices of the health service, with relatively little scope for discretion at the local level.

Unitarism is especially prevalent in countries with certain characteristics. One is small size, as contrasted with the large size of most federal states. Most countries that are small are also unitary, with the exceptions being a handful of federal countries composed of a cluster of small islands.[10] Another tendency is for unitarism to hold in places where the population is ethnically, linguistically, and culturally homogeneous. Federalism seems to take root more where populations are linguistically diverse, as in Belgium and Switzerland, which are divided into different linguistic communities. Finally, unitarism may vary at least in part on colonial heritage. For example, former French colonies in Africa have long tended to follow the highly unitary features of France itself, while former Spanish and British colonies have varied in their structures.

Authoritarian and Democratic Constitutions

Historically, making government constitutional meant eliminating the divine right or absolute power of monarchs such as kings, queens, princes, sultans, or emperors. Constitutionalism, as established in western Europe progressively over the centuries, meant preventing such rulers from exercising power in an arbitrary fashion and holding them at least partially accountable to the will of at least some of the people. As the power of monarchs faded in many countries, the drafting of constitutions became one way to limit the power of government, to divide and separate power such that a single person or family could no longer dominate. In parts of Europe, for example, constitutional monarchy was seen as distinct from divine right monarchy or absolute monarchy, because executive power came to be derived by a mandate from the consent of the governed.[11]

Still, not all countries with constitutions exhibit the characteristics of democracy and limited government. In fact, the actors that demanded constitutionalism and the end of absolute monarchy were in many cases themselves elites, nobles, revolutionaries, or military leaders. They were not always interested in political rights and civil liberties for all, and they did not always represent the people. For many centuries, the rights established in constitutions were often restricted to a small subset of the population, such as property-owning males of a certain racial or ethnic background.[12]

Even today, not all political systems are perfectly constitutional, nor are all systems legitimate, fair, and just. Writing down a set of basic laws and rights on paper does not guarantee that those laws and rights will take effect or be enforced in practice; some countries that have constitutions fail to protect rights. Authoritarian regimes usually have constitutions, even where they deny political rights and civil liberties to their people. Such regimes may seek to establish their legitimacy on the basis of claims made in the constitution. For instance, a revolutionary socialist government may draft a constitution holding that the Communist Party is the sole entity capable of expressing the general will of the people. This would not seem "democratic" or "constitutional" to the minds of most people who value individual rights and liberties, but the document itself could nonetheless be recognized as a constitution. Other authoritarian regimes may place less importance on political parties (or may outlaw parties entirely) and instead vest the ruler(s) with the authority to determine what the population as a whole requires.[13]

Authoritarian constitutions will not typically declare dictatorial rule, however, and in fact may appear quite progressive in terms of the rights and powers they list. Even totalitarian regimes may formulate extensive sets of rights in their constitutions, at least on paper, whether they defend these in practice or not.[14] In some instances, authoritarian regimes may even outline some rights that a democratic constitution may not contemplate. For instance, the constitution of the Soviet Union established rights such as guarantees of education, access to health care, housing, and a pension in old age—none of which are listed in the U.S. Constitution. Some authoritarian regimes simply continue to govern under the constitutional charter of a previous democratic regime but will suspend or override certain elements of the constitution. Military regimes have been known to establish martial law or states of emergency, which sometimes extend for long periods of time and during which normal constitutional principles do not apply. This is often done using the justification that national security requires exceptional measures.

Some countries also base part of their judicial and legal system on another authority: official religious law. This tendency is most noteworthy in the Islamic world, where *sharia* law plays an important role in many countries, though the use of religious law is not limited to Muslim countries. *Sharia* law is based on the Qur'an (Koran), the Holy Book of Islam, and to a lesser extent on other core Islamic texts. Countries that follow *sharia* have judges and clerics that rule in conjunction with their interpretations of the Qur'an. Judiciaries in both Saudi Arabia and Iran are linked to the state religions, and they rule on the basis of religious law in many areas. Even interpretations of issues not treated directly in the Qur'an are reasoned by analogy with reference to the Holy Book or to the words and deeds (known as the *sunnah* and the *hadith*) attributed to the Prophet Muhammad.

Religious law is not necessarily authoritarian, nor does it characterize all Muslim countries. For instance, Turkey is a majority Muslim country with a formally secular state. Other countries, such as India and Indonesia, make partial use of Islamic law, such as applying it in certain kinds of legal cases between Muslims (such as family law about marriage, divorce, and parenthood between Muslims). Israel, the United Kingdom, and other countries make provisions for the use of religious law by Orthodox Jews and others, largely as an option for use by populations who wish to resolve such matters in religious courts. In fact, one leading scholar has argued that recent years have seen a rise in "constitutional theocracy" in which constitutional law is combined with recognition of an official state religion and some use of religious beliefs or texts as a foundation for law.[15]

Causes and Effects: What Are the Effects of Federal and Unitary Constitutions?

In the study of political institutions, political scientists often ask whether a given design is superior to others and whether the ideal institution depends on country contexts. For the purposes of this chapter, debate over the relative merits of different forms of institutions focus on constitutional design, and specifically the separation of powers along federal or unitary lines. We can consider at least three substantial questions about the consequences of federal versus unitary constitutions: (1) Which are best for social stability, (2) Which are best for protecting democratic rights, and (3) Which are best for the economy? While we will keep this question open to many possibilities, it is worth noting that much of the debate among political scientists has focused on the presumed advantages of federalism; this is reflected in the references to scholarship in the pages that follow, though we aim to give consideration to the various sides of the debate. We consider these questions about the possible advantages of federalism and unitarism here, as well as whether judicial review is necessary in protecting rights and upholding the law.

CASE IN CONTEXT
Constitutional Design: Theocracy in Iran
PAGE 479

In Iran (and in Saudi Arabia), clerics have considerable power, both at the pinnacle of the political system and at lower levels of government. Some analysts may see this power as emerging

Iran's Supreme Leader Ayatollah Ali Khamenei in Tehran in 2012. Behind him is a picture of his predecessor and leader of the Iranian Revolution, Ayatollah Ruhollah Khomeini.

from a dominant cultural feature and thus reflective of the norms of the people. Some may also see it as fitting that various societies have distinct systems reflecting their cultural differences. For others, basing law on a single religion (and a single religious text, as interpreted by clerics) constrains, by definition, the rights and liberties of those who are not Muslim or otherwise religious.

See the case study on Iran in Part VI, pp. 479–480. As you read it, keep in mind the following questions:

1. How is the judiciary an especially powerful branch of government in Iran, and what are its powers?

2. Are there checks on the judiciary's power, and if so, what are they? Or should the country be seen as a case of "judicial sovereignty" as opposed to parliamentary sovereignty?

3. Is it possible to conceive of religious law that is compatible with democracy—and if so, how?—or is separation of religion and the state a necessary feature of democracy— and if so, why?

What Constitutional Designs Support Social Stability?

To help answer the question of stability, we can start by looking at the origins of federalism and unitarism in different societies. A long-standing argument held that federalism was the result of disparate political units coming together for security, with the post-revolutionary United States being the classic example.[16] It may also be, however, that countries go federal to hold together; that is, they may devolve authorities to regions to prevent secession or division.[17] As for unitarism, here too the causes may be found in deep historical legacies, including efforts by monarchs long ago to consolidate power or to unify authority. As noted in chapter 3, the modern nation-states of Europe were created from the merging of much smaller units such as principalities, as well as the splintering of large empires.

From one perspective, federalism may be an institution uniquely capable of holding together a polity. By conferring powers to levels of government below the national, federalism may give more people a stake in the political system. If certain regions or groups feel they have greater autonomy, then they may be more willing to participate instead of demand independence. Movements demanding separatism, secession, or break-up of a country may gain less traction in countries where these groups have powers reserved to them by a federal constitution. One such approach has been taken by Ethiopia, where the constitution actually gives different regional groups the right to secede (though it is unclear how this would work in practice). The expectation is that by giving autonomy and power to the

INSIGHTS

Federalism: Origin, Operation, Significance
by William Riker

Riker's work is one of the leading arguments about what causes federal systems to emerge. In his examination of the creation of federal systems from the American Revolution up to the 1960s, Riker finds one commonality across diverse cases: federalism is the result of a bargain among regional actors and a prospective national government that is driven by external threats. Riker also notes that the American federal system is relatively centralized because most of the institutions of the national government do not serve the interests of the states, and the center prevails in most disputes involving the center and the states. The exception that keeps American government from being totally centralized is the system of political parties, which ensures that some power remains with local actors, due to how candidates are nominated, among other factors. Despite offering considerable explanation of the origin and operation of federalism, Riker surprisingly concludes that federalism is an institutional arrangement of relatively little significance, noting the fundamental similarities in governance between federal and unitary states.

William Riker, Federalism: Origin, Operation, Significance. Boston: Little, Brown, & Co., 1964.

ethnic groups, and by offering an out, the constitution will encourage compromise and enhance the recognition of the merits of unified government. By this logic, federalism enhances stability.

On the flip side, federalism might lead to exacerbating differences and undermining stability. By drawing significant lines (almost literally) between different groups, federal systems may end up encouraging different regions of the country to develop independent identities. This question emerges in Spain, where nationalism in Catalonia may have grown as the region's autonomy has increased. In other countries with more precarious economies and more fragile societies, such as Nigeria, ethnic minorities or regions that feel they are being treated unfairly by the central government are often critical of the federal system. In some such cases, they may increase demands for secession or separation, which may even explode into ethnic violence.

INSIGHTS

Federalism and Democracy: Beyond the U.S. Model
by Alfred Stepan

Stepan offers a corrective to the argument made by Riker, arguing that many instances of federalism in established countries are not the result of "coming together" but of central governments working on "holding together" different groups in a single country. Examples may include India, Belgium, and Spain. In addition, Stepan notes there are two other ways that many federal countries may be unlike the American model. First, federal systems may vary in how much power is given to the territorial chamber, such as a Senate. Some forms of federalism have powerful chambers that protect the interests of the states or provinces by giving voters in some areas a disproportionate number of representatives. Finally, Stepan notes that some instances of federalism are "asymmetrical," with greater powers given to some subnational regions than others. In addition to the three "multinational" countries mentioned previously, Canada also fits this model: its French-speaking province of Quebec has been recognized as a "distinct society" from the other provinces in majority anglophone Canada. In sum, Stepan notes the diversity of federal arrangements and argues that not all federalism follows the U.S. model.

Alfred Stepan, "Federalism and Democracy: Beyond the U.S. Model." Journal of Democracy 10, No. 4 (1999): 19–34

CASE IN CONTEXT

Federalism and the States in Nigeria: Holding Together or Tearing Apart?

PAGE 523

Nigeria is one of the most interesting cases in the world for the study of how federalism relates to secession and violence. The country began with three regions around the time of independence in 1960; and after a civil war broke out among the regions in the late 1960s, governments have created new states in an attempt to defuse conflict. Federalism is thus explicitly linked to the question of stability.

See the case study on Nigeria in Part VI, pp. 523–524. As you read it, keep in mind the following questions:

1. What is the nature of regional divisions in Nigeria, and along what lines are people in the country divided?
2. In what ways could expanding the number of states be expected to address the challenge of stability and violence between regions?
3. To what extent have the attempts to further federalism contributed to reducing conflict, and to what extent can we know how successful it has been?

What Constitutional Designs Support Democratic Rights?

Federal and unitary designs may affect democracy in ways similar to those discussed earlier: federal institutions may make government more stable and may facilitate democratic incorporation of the demands of many groups, or federalism may reinforce divisions. One main way in which federalism may affect democratic stability relates to a subject discussed in the previous section. If residents of one or another region in a country feel disempowered by political institutions, they may be more willing to use non-democratic means to achieve their objectives. Since federalism should contribute to the empowerment of regional groups, it may bind citizens together under democracy and encourage participation in democratic institutions.

Beyond the question of whether federalism or unitarism is likelier to make democracy persist, we may also consider which design better supports democratic rights. Consider a very heated cultural debate, such as abortion in the United States and many other countries, and how it relates to the question of federalism. The pro-life position holds that embryos and fetuses are people and therefore have a right to live (usually starting from the time of conception), implying that the biological mother may not choose to abort a pregnancy. The pro-choice position holds that a woman has a right to have control over her own body with respect to reproduction, and that the government may not dictate to her what she must do in terms of the decision to terminate a pregnancy.

There are many ethical, moral, and legal aspects to such a debate, but for the moment we ask only a question about federalism. One perspective on abortion has been a "states' rights" perspective, which maintains that different states in the United States (say, liberal Vermont and conservative Alabama) should be allowed to have different laws governing abortion, which would reflect the different sets of values and beliefs of the majorities in each place. This structure would allow different parts of a federal country to express their own views on rights and would be consistent with some of the perceived advantages of federalism.

Now consider another perspective. Whichever side of this debate you may come down on (pro-life or pro-choice), it is worth asking the following question with respect to federalism: should people have different fundamental rights in a country, depending on where they happen to be born or live? Let's say that Vermont adopted a more pro-choice set of policies and Alabama a more pro-life set of policies. If you favor the pro-life argument, should a human embryo or fetus in Vermont have fewer rights than one in Alabama? Should Vermont be allowed to adopt its set of policies because of federalism? If you favor the pro-choice argument, should a woman in Alabama have fewer reproductive rights and less choice than one in Vermont? Should Alabama be allowed to adopt its set of policies because of federalism?

It seems clear that different regions (such as states) should be allowed to pass their own preferred laws and policies to reflect the democratic wishes of their residents. On the other hand, it seems that some major debates get down to questions of constitutional rights that may need to apply everywhere in a society. This question is fundamentally about what is in a constitution and what federalism should be. The question about democracy and rights under federal constitutions is not straightforward, as this example shows.

What Constitutional Designs Support the Economy?

Federal or unitary systems of government may be good or bad for an economy, depending on one's point of view and on circumstances. On one hand, some see federalism as generating healthy competition among states or regions, which can be good for the economy. If state A sees that businesses are relocating to state B next door (maybe for reasons of lower taxes or better public services, for example), then state A may do its best to govern in a way more like state B (say, by lowering taxes or providing better services). Such situations will exert a form of positive peer pressure for good economic policies that will benefit the country over the long run. Federalism, by inducing economic competitiveness among states, approximates the kind of competition one sees in a market, which may be good for the economy. Of course, this idea of healthy competition implies that states will perform differently from one another, which may lead to significant differences in development and opportunities within a federal country, as the case of India shows (see the Case in Context, "Federalism and Differences in Development in India," box).

Along with inducing healthy competition, decentralizing power is theorized to have another advantage: it can allow people to sort themselves into different jurisdictions along with other people who share their policy preferences. Let's say town X and town Y are side by side. Town X has higher taxes and better-funded schools, while town Y has lower taxes and less school funding. Maybe a family with young children in school will wish to live in town X, and a retired couple with grown children will prefer to live in town Y. Decentralized government can accommodate both, whereas more centralized government would impose the same tax rate and the same amount of school funding for both families.[18] This example is more truly a question of decentralization than of federalism, since it deals with local communities, but the principle also extends to federalism and the roles of states, regions, or provinces.

CASE IN CONTEXT
Federalism and Differences in Development in India   PAGE 466

India is one of the world's fast-growing economic powerhouses, but it is also the country in the world with the largest number of people living in extreme poverty. Some of the dramatic differences in development in India can be understood by looking at differences across states. Some states have performed very well, while others have performed quite poorly. The country retains a politics that has a very regional flavor, despite decades of efforts at political centralization.

See the case study on India in Part VI, pp. 466–467. As you read it, keep in mind the following questions:

1. What are the positive and negative examples of development in India's states, and what lessons does each of these offer?
2. What factors can account for the variations in the performance of Indian states?
3. What lessons do you draw from the Indian case about whether federalism might contribute to poverty reduction or perhaps worsen poverty?

In federal systems, the state or provincial level of government often has a great deal of responsibility in many public services. In the United States, states have a major role in deciding on issues of health policy and in providing support to the poor, while local governments have the most significant responsibilities in primary and secondary education. Public schools are funded primarily from local taxes, and more Americans participate in local school boards than in any other type of elective office. In many countries around the world—federal and unitary alike—local governments commonly oversee such issues as local sanitation, local roads, and services such as the police, parks, and public lighting.

Although federalism and decentralization have many arguments in their favor, they can complicate economic performance in many circumstances. In countries such as Argentina and Brazil, states and provinces have acted irresponsibly, overspending and forcing the central government to bail them out.[19]

INSIGHTS
Fiscal Federalism
by Wallace Oates

Oates developed a "decentralization theorem" of the advantages of decentralized government and federalism under certain circumstances. First, Oates argued that federalism allowed for local governments that are closer to their constituents than the central government, and that this lets them have better information about what local residents need or want. They can use this information to better provide services. Oates also built on the argument that giving local governments the authority to offer different services would allow people to pick and choose where they want to live, based on the mixes of taxes and services they would get in each place.[20] While central governments would be needed to provide for truly national needs, such as defense and a common currency, the decentralized governments would be better equipped to make decisions about many local issues. The practice of decentralization raises many issues, including which services are local and which are national, but this theory served as a summary and basis for future debates over what should be the responsibility of central versus local or state governments.

Wallace Oates, Fiscal Federalism. New York: Harcourt Brace Jovanovich, 1972.

Situations like this make economic management difficult, because the states know there is always someone there to bail them out if they overspend; they have a soft budget constraint rather than a hard budget constraint.[21] We often see this problem in federal countries where states can exercise a lot of leverage over the national political process through representatives in the legislature, such as senators.[22] In general, federalism can create incentives for politicians to overspend and be fiscally irresponsible.[23]

Moreover, federalism can allow for inefficient resource allocation. One example may be that the Senates of Brazil and of the United States routinely allocate monies disproportionately to less populous, more rural states. In issues from farm policy to national security, smaller states are able to use their leverage in the federal system to guarantee for themselves certain benefits in the form of government funds. We cannot draw a firm conclusion, therefore, about whether federalism or unitarism is best for the economy (or for stability or democracy); as comparativists recognize, context and other conditions matter.

Judicial Review and Democracy

Along with the division of power between levels of government implied by the issue of federalism versus unitarism, another prominent feature of most constitutions is the division of power among branches of government. In particular, one major question is who is responsible for interpreting the constitution, as noted earlier in the section on judiciaries. A judiciary with constitutional powers of review can engage in an interpretation of the laws, and a question for many observers is whether this is appropriate and to what extent. In the United States, one of the biggest debates about the judicial system is over **judicial activism**, a term that has a negative connotation for many observers.[24] Judicial activism is a hot-button issue in the United States, and the phenomenon is also recognized and debated in other countries as well. According to critics, unelected judges and justices may take advantage of the power of judicial review to essentially legislate from the bench, as

judicial activism Term used, often pejoratively, to characterize judicial actions that actively reinterpret legislation and thus imply exercising powers typically reserved for the legislative branch.

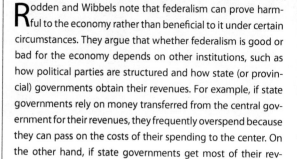

INSIGHTS

Beyond the Fiction of Federalism: Economic Management in Multi-Tiered Systems
by Jonathan Rodden and Erik Wibbels

Rodden and Wibbels note that federalism can prove harmful to the economy rather than beneficial to it under certain circumstances. They argue that whether federalism is good or bad for the economy depends on other institutions, such as how political parties are structured and how state (or provincial) governments obtain their revenues. For example, if state governments rely on money transferred from the central government for their revenues, they frequently overspend because they can pass on the costs of their spending to the center. On the other hand, if state governments get most of their revenues from their own taxes, they may spend more responsibly and not put the national economy at risk. Political parties matter because central government leaders that have political leverage over state-level officials can hold them to compliance with what the center wishes, while a political party system in which the center has little control over state-level actors is more problematic. Each of these scholars continues and develops related arguments in subsequent books, highlighting political incentives and the need for hard budget constraints for states if federalism is to work well.[25]

Jonathan Rodden and Erik Wibbels, "Beyond the Fiction of Federalism: Economic Management in Multi-Tiered Systems," World Politics 54, No. 4 (2002): 494–531.

opposed to situating lawmaking power with the representatives in the legislature. This practice may take some of the most heated and controversial debates out of the democratic process by removing them from the arena of elections, public debates, and protests and placing them in the arena of lawsuits, legal challenges, and the rulings of a small number of unelected judges in robes.

For some, judicial review is crucial to protecting rights and upholding the law.[26] By this argument, judges have the role of interpreting laws to ensure compliance with the letter of the constitution and legal precedent. Proponents of an active judiciary may argue that courts have often led legislatures (rather than followed them) in the recognition and expansion of fundamental rights. For this reason, proponents might argue, a judicial system has the task to interpret laws and guarantee that they are consistent with rights and obligations laid out in constitutions. One can witness both sides of this debate, for instance, in the question of whether judiciaries can and should require that a state offer marriage benefits to same-sex couples. Judges hold different perspectives on the role of courts in interpreting constitutions, as is evident in court decisions themselves—which are authored by judges—or in the writings of those judges and justices.

As a result of the political heat it generates, "judicial activism" is a term susceptible to unclear definition. For instance, critics of judicial activism in the United States have often been conservative critics of justices' rulings on social and cultural issues, such as the *Roe v. Wade* decision of 1973, which legalized abortion, and recent judicial decisions at the state level to expand civil union benefits and marriage rights to gay couples. However, studies in the 2000s showed that on the U.S.

A ceremony to install the new chief justice in France's Cour de Cassation, the country's highest judicial body for civil and criminal matters. France shows that not all judiciaries are structured the same: It has a separate constitutional council (*Conseil Constitutionnel*) to determine the constitutionality of laws.

Supreme Court, the justices who most frequently voted to overturn Congressional laws were the more conservative members.[27] Moreover, several of the rulings listed previously for the United States—including some widely acclaimed and unanimous rulings—may be seen as activist in retrospect. As you consider the case of constitutionality in the United States (see the Case in Context, "Is Judicial Activism in the United States a Problem?" box), you can use your own analysis to determine if any rulings fall under this definition.

There is one clear way to end judicial activism: end judicial review. This is not merely a thought experiment or hypothetical exercise. In fact, as noted earlier, one can look to the United Kingdom as a model. One argument against extensive use of judicial review is that judiciaries remove contentious issues from the public arena. According to this argument, debates about the most fundamental issues in a democracy are fought out by the strongest ideologically committed advocates in front of unelected judges. These issues are thus examined and decided on by small groups and powerful individuals, and they may not be reflective of broader public opinion. Those arguing against judicial activism would often prefer to have society's most contentious issues decided in legislatures rather than in courts. The United Kingdom prevents judicial activism by granting the legislative branch of government an unambiguously higher power than the judicial branch. One way to view opposition to judicial activism is to ask about the extent to which one would sacrifice judicial review. Put another way, judicial review and some degree of judicial activism are the flip side of the checks and balances between branches of government.

Most countries with written constitutions do have a constitutional court that is responsible for judicial review. By some accounts, the power of judiciaries has increased around the world over time. It should be noted that the debate is not limited to the United States and the United Kingdom but, rather, stretches around the world. Whether judicial review has been beneficial to democracy remains open to interpretation.

Whatever its causes, the debate persists between advocates of powerful judicial review processes who argue that judges often lead the law—asserting human rights that may take a long time to work through legislative channels—and those who see it as undue interference by unelected judges in major political issues. Both parliamentary sovereignty and separation of powers are compatible with democracy; they are simply different ways of understanding how constitutions should be interpreted.

CASE IN CONTEXT

Is Judicial Activism in the United States a Problem?

PAGE 568

For over two hundred years, the United States has enshrined the principle of judicial review of laws. Courts can strike down laws passed by Congress, if they deem the law to be in violation of the Constitution. The tension between the powers of Congress and those of the judiciary are not easily resolved.

See the case study on the United States in Part VI, pp. 568–569. As you read it, keep in mind the following questions:

1. What might be some of the challenges and problems of judicial activism?

2. Can you think of circumstances in which judicial activism would be appropriate and desirable?

3. What sorts of issues should be decided by the judiciary, and what sorts of issues should be decided by elected lawmakers?

INSIGHTS

Towards Juristocracy: The Origins and Consequences of the New Constitutionalism
by Ran Hirschl

Hirschl observes a move toward powerful judiciaries around the world in recent decades and asks about the causes and consequences of this change. He looks at the causes of greater judicial power—or "juristocracy," as he calls it—in Canada, Israel, New Zealand, and South Africa. For Hirschl, the decision to create strong judiciaries comes from strategic calculations made by some elites who believe that their interests will be better protected by judiciaries than by elected officials; that is, they believe that encoding certain principles as constitutional rights will protect their dominance. When these elites are under threat, a

coalition of economic leaders, political leaders, and members of the judiciary can combine to create a constitutional system where challenges to their power can be debated in terms of rights to be protected by the judiciary, and thereby removed from most public political debate. Hirschl argues that a consequence of increasing judicial review is not the progressive expansion of rights, nor enhanced democracy, but rather a protection of the interests of elites.

Ran Hirschl, Towards Juristocracy: The Origins and Consequences of the New Constitutionalism. *Cambridge, MA: Harvard University Press, 2007.*

THINKING COMPARATIVELY

KEY METHODOLOGICAL TOOLS

Most-Different-Systems Design

As noted in chapters 1 and 2, comparison can be based on two cases that are quite *different* in many ways and not just based on countries that are similar in many ways. Countries that are "most different" can make for very compelling comparisons where one finds a common outcome between them. Since the commonalities come from such different cases, it can give some confidence that they are attributable to some of the few similarities between dissimilar countries. In some cases, such as the prevalence of written constitutions discussed in this chapter, the reasons for the common outcome may be that lots of countries follow a similar logic. For the example here, the two countries of Brazil and South Africa established constitutions with several similar features, including strong judicial review and institutions to support federalism. This

What Explains the Similarities Between the Brazilian and South African Constitutions?

Contemporary Brazil and South Africa were quite different places in many ways when they both convened constituent assemblies to write new constitutions in the late 1980s (in Brazil) and early 1990s (in South Africa). South Africa was emerging from a long history of racial injustice and segregation in the system known as *apartheid* from 1948 to 1994. Conflict in the society was centered on the state's oppression of the black majority, and the responses of black South Africans to that oppression, though violence also erupted among and between ethnic groups. In South Africa, the transition to democracy in the early 1990s took place against the backdrop of attempts to move beyond a racially charged past, with the white-led National Party and the black-majority African National Congress (nominally headed by Nelson Mandela) taking the lead roles in negotiation. Brazil, by contrast, had no such legacy of legal, formal discrimination (though it certainly had a long history of "unofficial" racism and discrimination) in the twentieth century. It was a country coming out of two decades of military rule, with the military seeking a peaceable exit from power. We might thus expect them to come up with very different constitutions as their leaders formed conventions to establish a common framework for governance.

Yet the two countries' constitutions share many fundamental similarities. Most obviously, they both are based on a written constitution. Both constitutions expressed aspirational goals for the countries; but more important, they established basic political institutions, and the countries featured many similarities in their constitutional designs. Both established constitutional courts that would become powerful in interpreting the constitutions. Both also established a principle of shared power between the central government and state or provincial governments: that is, both had a degree of federalism.

Perhaps most noteworthy, however, is the sheer length of the constitutions. As of its adoption, Brazil's constitution of 1988 had 245 articles and filled a small book with all of its provisions. South Africa's (approved in 1996) had a very similar 243 articles, and took on a comparably huge number of issues: it instituted large numbers of rights beyond the freedoms of speech and liberty, specified rules for issues such as funding for political parties, introduced a variety of municipal structures, created a formal role for traditional leaders, established procedures for the division of revenue between the levels of government, and described the design of the national flag. Here, it can be useful to do a brief glance at another "shadow" case that we don't explore fully: these constitutions are both extensive, especially when contrasted with an American constitution that fits on just a few pages.

Why might such different countries have such similarly extensive constitutions, with features of judicial review and of federalism? We do not offer definitive statements about why constitutions vary in this way, but we illustrate how we can ask questions about the causes and consequences of institutions.

The reasons for the resulting similarities may be numerous. We might propose several hypotheses. Hypothesis 1 could be a matter of historical timing, in that both countries adopted their constitutions at a similar moment in history; this may have mattered more than geographic distance between them. Simply put, constitutions written in an era (like the 1980s and 1990s) may be extensive because countries have grown compelled to address more sets of rights and issues when drafting a new constitution (for a "new country"). Perhaps socially complex societies (whether due to multiethnic identities or complex economic systems, as both Brazil and South Africa have) require more negotiations between conflicting parties. This may result in extensive constitutions detailing the compromise. The American constitution in the late 1700s might simply not have envisioned all the issues that would emerge in modern societies, but those writing constitutions today may write more thorough contracts. For example, a constitution that receives input from both men and women of different races, social classes, and ethnic or linguistic backgrounds may necessarily involve more written agreements than one written by a more homogenous group operating on a shared set of assumptions.

Other hypotheses might also explain the extensive nature of these two constitutions. Hypothesis 2 might be less focused on historical background and more on the powerful actors in the constitution writing process, with an emphasis on the economic and political interests of the negotiators. The political parties in South Africa, and the politicians and military in Brazil, might have thought it necessary to make clear statements about the rights of all parties in the constitutional convention, with guarantees for both the new democratic governments and provisions that would provide some protection to the departing (non-democratic) government. Hypothesis 3 could be that the cases are not completely independent but are actually linked, in that the South African and Brazilian constitutions may have been modeled on certain aspects of other constitutions (whether in Germany or Mexico). Insofar as countries do not exist in vacuums, the South African and Brazilian constitutions may have been modeled in part on experiences elsewhere.

THINKING COMPARATIVELY

KEY METHODOLOGICAL TOOLS

(continued)

happened despite the fact that the two constitutions were created on different continents and in different social circumstances by rather different groups of actors. The fact that the countries are "most different" in many ways yet similar in outcomes makes it an intriguing pair of cases for hypotheses about why constitutions take the forms they do.

If research turns up evidence (as is the case) that South African and Brazilian constitution writers did explicitly look to other constitutions as models when writing their own, that would provide some support for Hypothesis 3.

Hypothesis 4 might identify other key similarities amid the differences between the countries, much as was discussed in chapter 1. South Africa and Brazil may have many differences, but there are also some key political and social similarities that may affect constitutional design. For instance, both are racially and ethnically diverse, and both have high levels of economic inequality. The constitutions were certainly attentive to potential inequities, which may be construed as evidence for this hypothesis. They are also relatively large countries with various identity groups living in different locations; this may favor a degree of federalism (which itself requires more extensive constitutional language than smaller, unitary states).

We will not explore the causality in detail, but as with previous chapters, we can simply think about what sort of evidence would support each hypothesis. Research can help determine which of the preceding hypotheses has the strongest support from the empirical evidence, and the findings from a specific comparison of these two cases will then have implications for broader research questions and other countries. Why do constitutions take similar forms in such different countries? Why do very different countries adopt federalism under disparate circumstances? These questions can be asked with respect to comparisons across many countries. Someone with expertise on the Brazil–South African comparison (or a similar

Pius Langa (left) and Dikgang Moseneke in 2005. Langa was the first black chief justice of South Africa's constitutional court.

comparison) will not have the final word on this for all countries but can contribute to thinking comparatively about important political questions such as constitutional design. The comparison can point to fruitful avenues for further research on the design and interpretation of constitutions. The comparative method we outlined in the beginning chapters and used in the previous chapters—including its use of the most-similar-systems design and most-different-systems design—can help us in the area of institutions as well.

Of course, we should note that these two constitutions are not completely similar. They have many differences that can also be the subject of further research. For one, the Brazilian constitution established a system with a president elected by popular vote; while in South Africa, the legislative chamber known as the National Assembly elects the president. The range of questions one could ask about these constitutions is thus considerable, and the same holds for the other major institutions explored in this chapter. Much as we can ask questions about federalism, we might look at seemingly similar countries and ask why one ends up being federal and the other unitary? Both Germany and Italy formed into coherent nation-states in the second half of the nineteenth century, and both have major regional differences internally, so why is one federal and the other unitary? Or, with regard to judiciaries, why have courts become so significant in constitutional interpretation even in former British colonies, given that Britain is the home of parliamentary sovereignty? These sorts of questions serve to show that institutions can be examined using the same comparative perspective developed and used in the earlier chapters. The possibilities of comparing institutions continue as we look at the branches of government in the next chapters.

> **THINKING COMPARATIVELY**

Chapter Summary

Concepts

- Constitutions are the basic charters of modern states, and they are written documents in most countries.
- Constitutions lay out the basic framework for government institutions in a country, and they are the foundational laws of that country.
- Two of the leading elements of constitutional design are federalism versus unitarism and the power of the judiciary to review for constitutionality laws passed by legislatures.

- Unitary countries are those in which the central government is sovereign and any subnational administrative units are subordinate to the national government.
- Countries with judicial review have constitutional courts that rule on whether laws passed by the legislature are in accordance with the constitution, and these courts have the power to strike down legislation as unconstitutional.
- Countries with parliamentary sovereignty do not have judiciaries that review the constitutionality of legislation.

Types

- Federal countries are those in which subnational units such as states or provinces have some constitutional protection and political autonomy from the national government.

Causes and Effects

- Federalism has been associated with enhancing national stability and democracy under some circumstances, and with conflict in other cases.

- Federalism has also been linked with improvements in economic growth and development, as well as economic difficulties.
- There is a long-standing debate about whether judicial review contributes to the protection of democratic rights or not.

Thinking Comparatively

- While many countries have written constitutions, these differ in many ways, and it is an open question whether one country's constitution is suited to other circumstances.

Thinking It Through

1. Imagine the U.S. Constitution were to be lengthened to add one hundred more articles, like many of the more extensive constitutions in the world today. What would be the likely content of these added articles? If the United States hosted a convention to write a new constitution today, do you believe the resulting document would be as brief as that formulated in the 1780s, or would the result likely be longer? Why?

2. What would happen if all copies (yes, including Internet copies) of the United States Constitution simultaneously disappeared? Would the rule of law break down? Or would the society remain robust and functional? What does your answer to this question imply about whether the text itself is of great import, or if social outcomes depend more heavily on customs and culture?

3. Imagine a country that has just achieved a ceasefire in a decades-long civil war. You have been asked by the government to accompany several constitutional experts to the country to advise the new "constituent assembly," whose job it is to write a new constitution that will ensure "stability, democracy, and prosperity." Under what circumstances would you advocate that the country adopt a federal structure?

4. Why has the U.S. Constitution survived for over two centuries? Do you believe it is because of the design of the document itself or because it happened to be implemented in a place with a certain history, geography, and cultural backdrop? Framed in a comparative sense, is the U.S. Constitution simply well suited to the conditions prevailing in the United States, or would it likely have enjoyed the same longevity elsewhere? Would it only work in large, heterogeneous societies, or only work in societies with our particular history of "coming together," or only in a society relatively far removed from most major foreign wars?

5. The United Kingdom is a country where a wide range of individual rights are respected, much like in other democracies. Given that many major rights are well protected, what are the problems with parliamentary sovereignty and a lack of judicial review? Are there any disadvantages of eliminating judicial review (and the potential for judicial activism) in well-established democratic societies?

CHAPTER 9

Legislatures and Legislative Elections

The home of New Zealand's Parliament, which features an interesting electoral system discussed in this chapter.

What can New Zealand teach other countries about how to run a democracy? At first glance, the country is so distinctive that one might say little. The island nation has just over four million people, and its greatest claim to fame may be its intimidating rugby team or that it was the setting for *The Lord of the Rings* movie trilogy. Its capital, Wellington, is the southernmost of any country on earth. Yet this former British colony has an electoral system for its legislature that many countries might wish to consider.

New Zealanders actually have two votes in their parliamentary elections. They have one for a specific individual to represent their district, and one for their most preferred party. When all the votes are tallied and computed, the winners in each district go to parliament, just as in many countries around the world, including the United States. But there is a catch: along with these representatives go a number of additional members chosen from lists made by the political parties. These "at-large" members of parliament are allotted to each party in a way that makes the overall composition of the parliament proportional to the vote each *party* received. The idea is to give each New Zealander his or her own representative for the local constituency, while making parliament more generally reflective of party preferences in the country as a whole.

New Zealand is not the only country to use this complicated approach to electing its legislature. In fact, the New Zealand model drew some inspiration from Germany's similar institutions, as we discuss later in the chapter. Whether the system is ideal or not depends on how one believes representation and legislatures should work, which we also discuss in this chapter. What is certain is that considering the relative merits of models like New Zealand's and Germany's, as contrasted with other models in countries ranging from the United States to the United Kingdom to Japan to Brazil, will provide insight into both representation and the legislatures that are designed to ensure it.

This chapter offers an introduction to the study of legislatures, with specific attention to the electoral rules and systems that shape them. We discuss how legislators are elected to represent the citizenry. In the two subsequent chapters (10 and 11), we elaborate on many aspects of representation and elections. Chapter 10 discusses the executive branch, but it must be noted that a discussion of executives cannot always be separated from that of legislatures. As a result, we discuss briefly in this chapter the relationships between legislatures and executives, but leave to chapter 11 the way in which many of the issues play out in parliamentary and presidential systems. Similarly, in talking about legislative representation in this chapter, we discuss political parties, but a fuller treatment of those important institutions is left to chapter 11.

· · ·

Concepts

Politics is about making laws to govern people, and legislatures are the most important bodies that shape the process of making and changing laws. Legislators legislate. While heads of state and heads of government in the executive branch may be the first *individuals* that come to mind when we think of *politicians*, the legislatures of the world are often what we will think of when we view politics as a whole process of governing.

What Legislatures Are

Legislatures are deliberative bodies composed of the decision makers who represent the population at large. Legislatures make laws and many political decisions, especially in democracies, but also even in personalistic dictatorships, which may rely on legislatures in their efforts to seem legitimate or to create the appearance of deliberative decision making. Legislatures are where debates take place about the fundamental values and preferences of voters. They are where interest groups and lobbyists often turn when they seek to influence the political process. They are where presidents and prime ministers often start their careers, and they are also typically the institution in government with the greatest responsibility for overseeing the conduct of the executive (an institution discussed in greater detail in chapter 10). In these bodies, legislators are of course important political figures, being leaders in major debates, whether in actual face-to-face settings in the legislature itself or through the use of the media.

> **legislature** Assembly or body of representatives with the authority to make laws.

The rise of legislatures, as opposed to executives, is part and parcel of the story of the emergence of constitutional and democratic regimes. For centuries, the history of representative government was the history of elected legislatures increasingly taking political authority from unelected executives. Parliaments, assemblies, congresses, and other legislative bodies asserted their rights to represent the populace, usually critiquing the unaccountable power of monarchs, such as kings, queens, or emperors. Of course, the earliest legislatures were not truly representative in most cases. The Parliament that asserted its authority over King John of England with the drafting of the Magna Carta in 1215 were not elected "commoners" but rather nobles in their own right. The French Estates-General revealed its inegalitarian character in its basic structure, with separate meetings for nobles, clergy, and commoners (the "third estate"). Even earlier, in the republics of ancient Rome, membership in the Senate was generally restricted to male property-holders or upper-class patricians. In many forms of colonial rule, as well, legislatures were initially chosen not by the people at large but rather by an elite subset of the population.

This existence of less-than-democratic legislatures can be found in authoritarian regimes today. In authoritarian systems, legislatures may be selected in a number of ways that exclude a free and open vote. For instance, the legislature may be comprised only of a subset of the population, such as being members of a certain dominant political party. This would be the case in Communist regimes such as China, where only members of the official Communist Party (or their close allies) are elected to office in practice. In other authoritarian regimes, legislators may be appointed by unelected executives. These are legislatures, even if the quality of representation is suspect.

Despite these non-democratic instances, if we take a longer-term view, many countries have moved toward more democracy over time, with more regular elections and the extension of the franchise to more people, most notably women, ethnic minorities, and men of lower social and economic status. Citizens in all contemporary democracies elect legislators, with the population at large having some choice among multiple political parties and/or candidates. The ability of those citizens to vote directly for the *executive* branch is not universal. While some democratic countries also have a direct election for the executive (such as a president), many others have an executive elected by the legislature itself, and that executive is nominally responsible to the legislature. In these systems, the people vote for their executives only in an indirect fashion, by choosing a legislature that in turn selects the executive branch of government. This makes the legislature of elected representatives the signature element of virtually any democracy.

What Legislatures Do

Representatives generally make law by proposing legislation and then organizing votes and bringing these to the floor of the legislature. Legislators who propose or favor a piece of legislation often undertake the necessary compromises and "horse-trading" that enable laws to get passed. The necessary trading and compromises may take place among the multiple parties in a governing coalition (as elaborated on in chapter 10 on executives) or within parties, as different legislators make specific demands of one another in exchange for "yea" or "nay" votes. Less commonly, legislation may be passed by members of two or more parties who share a common interest, even if they do not constitute a governing coalition. These bills are often called "bipartisan" (in two-party systems) or "multipartisan" (in systems with more than two major parties). There is some evidence that this is declining, certainly in the United States.[1] Depending on the power of party leaders to control the legislators, it may be necessary to make many concessions to specific legislators.

The specific process of legislation will vary from one legislature to the next. In some instances, a strong executive cabinet may be comprised of members of the legislature itself, and the rules governing legislative elections may make passage of the executive's favored proposals almost "automatic." In other circumstances, legislation may have to pass through multiple houses, or may have to work its way through votes of multiple committees just to get to the "floor" for a vote. Indeed, in some systems, the legislative process requires both these and more. In the United States, for instance, proposed legislation must often pass through committees in each of the two chambers of the legislature, then must pass votes in the whole body, then through a conference committee that reconciles any differences between the two chambers' bills, before going to the president for a signature.

The powers of legislatures are considerable in most democracies. In many countries, one of the main powers of the legislative branch is the so-called power of the purse. Legislatures typically have control over government budgets and are empowered to disburse funds to the executive branch and to the administrative agencies, or to cut off funding to certain initiatives that are unpopular or that it deems to be mismanaged. This power to allocate resources is one of the reasons executives must be attentive to the needs of legislatures, even in the absence of new laws being passed.

Legislatures often debate as part of the functions of representing the electorate and making legislation, and in doing so they also serve the function of focusing national discussion. Legislatures are where many public debates play out. The halls of the legislatures are designed for speechmaking, discussion, and debate, but this does not only happen in the chamber itself. Legislators also engage in less formal debate by shaping and responding to public opinion in the media and through interactions with citizens who have requests, complaints, arguments, suggestions, ideas, and new perspectives. Of course, not all such debate will be meaningful. Especially in authoritarian regimes, legislative debates may be reduced to displays of loyalty to the executive. In North Korea, legislators' most apparent role is to serve as an applauding audience for a dictator. In democracies too, not all legislators clarify and improve political discussion: they may also obfuscate or muddy the waters of political discussion, or may be beholden to special interests acting against the public good (though many such examples are matters of opinion). And they may—perhaps deliberately—spread misinformation or misleading information. In principle, however, elected legislators at the national level are expected to be opinion leaders that contribute to national discussions and propose solutions to public problems.

There are also several overlooked roles of legislatures. One is "socializing" politicians. Legislatures can be a "training ground" for future chief executives, such as presidents and prime ministers.[2] Another role is constituent service: citizens often contact their representatives' offices for assistance with a variety of concerns specific to local individuals or groups. Last but definitely not least, legislators often try to get re-elected.[3] Indeed, some scholars believe that the fundamental force driving legislative action is the push for electoral success.[4] Getting re-elected may not be part of the "job description" of being a legislator, but it is certainly one of the more time-consuming aspects of the job in many countries. This may involve extensive campaigning and fundraising in candidate-centered elections, or working to retain a spot on the political party's list of favored representatives in systems where electors vote by party.

Types

Legislative bodies may take a number of forms. They may have one or more houses or chambers, for example. In addition, the electoral processes that give rise to the legislators are numerous. Elections may involve voting for specific candidates, for political parties generally, or both. These different forms of legislatures and legislative elections give rise to different patterns of representation, as we shall see.

Sometimes legislative politics gets heated: Parliamentarians from opposing parties fight in Turkey, 2014.

Unicameral and Bicameral Legislatures

bicameral legislature Legislature with two chambers, which may have equal or unequal powers.

chamber An assembly or body of a legislature, often referring to one of two such bodies in a bicameral legislature.

lower chamber In a bicameral legislature, the house that typically has a larger number of legislators than upper chambers, and often represents the national vote either more proportionally or through smaller geographic constituencies.

upper chamber The chamber in a bicameral legislature that is usually smaller in number of legislators, often representing larger geographic constituencies such as states or provinces.

unicameral legislature Legislature with a single chamber.

Legislatures consist of one or more houses of assembly. **Bicameral legislatures**—those with two **chambers**, or houses—are common in democracies, especially in relatively large countries. This is the case in the United States and many nations in Latin America, for instance, where congresses consist of two legislative chambers, with each having its own name (such as House of Representatives or Chamber of Deputies). Many other countries exhibit a similar structure, using different names to signify the two chambers. In bicameral countries, the **lower chamber** is usually the one whose composition most closely reflects the population at large. Examples are the House of Representatives in the United States or the House of Commons in the United Kingdom. The **upper chamber** is usually smaller in size, and its composition is often less directly reflective of the population at large; it may represent territories such as states or provinces, as in the case of the Senate in many countries, or specific groups, such as in the House of Lords in the United Kingdom. The lower chamber has greater authority than the "upper chamber" in many countries. In countries such as Germany, the upper chamber is limited to voting on certain items that pertain to the states, and in other countries such as the United Kingdom, the upper chamber has even more limited (largely vestigial) powers. Here again, the United States is a bit of an exception in that its upper chamber—the Senate—has at least as much power as the lower chamber.

Unicameral legislatures are quite common in countries with small populations. For instance, unicameral parliaments are used in Scandinavia and are common in sub-Saharan Africa and some parts of the Middle East. Unicameral representation is usually most appropriate in unitary states and in countries that have relatively homogeneous populations; conversely, unicameral legislatures are uncommon where there are histories of different regional population groups with their own identities or in which regional minorities may demand special representation on the basis of territory. In addition to working in small, unitary democracies, unicameralism is also common in systems in many authoritarian regimes where a single political party dominates. In these cases, the governing regime may seek to minimize the "separation of powers" between national and regional interests that is implicit in bicameralism and prefer to channel all political demands through a single body dominated by the single party. The world's most populous country, China, fits the bill here, as it also has a unicameral legislature, despite its size.

Beyond the basic unicameral or bicameral structure, legislatures vary in another simple way: they have many different names, as noted earlier. For example, a legislature may be called a *congress* or *parliament*, an *assembly*, a *house*, or a *chamber*. Some of these terms have relatively specific meanings, or are most commonly used in certain ways to designate whether a legislative body constitutes the entire legislative branch or merely one part of it. Congresses and parliaments generally refer to the entirety of a legislative branch, which may include more than one chamber. Houses and chambers often refer to one of the component parts of the legislature, especially in the many countries with a bicameral (two-chamber) legislature. Assemblies may refer to either a legislature as a whole or one particular house or chamber within it.

Congresses and parliaments also have different connotations, as shown in Table 9.1. While the distinction is not a hard-and-fast rule, **congresses** are typically branches in a system with a separately elected head of government, while **parliaments** are often the name used for legislatures that choose their own head of government. In most congresses, the separately elected head of government—often called a president—does not depend on the congress for his or her position,

congress A form of legislature, typically associated with a presidential system in which there is a separation of powers.

parliament A type of legislature, often associated with systems in which the legislators vote on the leadership of the executive branch and the formation of a government.

TABLE 9.1 Common Attributes of Congresses and Parliaments

Type of Legislature	Congress	Parliament
Example	United States	United Kingdom
Head of Government	President	Prime Minister (or Premier, Chancellor, etc.)
Election of Head of Government	Separately elected by voters	Selected by Parliament
Independence of Head of Government	Executive does not depend on confidence of Congress	Executive depends on confidence of Parliament
Separation vs. Fusion of Powers	Separation of powers between Congress and executive	Executive fused with Parliament
Checks vs. Supremacy	Checks and balances between branches in constitution	Parliament supreme by constitution (but see next row)
Strong vs. Limited Executive	Executive limited by separation and checks	Executive *may* dominate lawmaking in practice
Bicameral vs. Unicameral	Either, but usually bicameral	Either

Chloe Smith, Member of Parliament from Norwich (U.K.) and a representative of the Conservative Party, and John Smith, of the Monster Raving Loony Party, whom she defeated.

but rather is accountable to the populace at large and to the constitution generally. These are usually systems designed with separations of powers and checks and balances between the legislative and executive branches. By contrast, parliamentary systems have executives that depend on parliament to legislate and even to retain their position. While the parliament is often the supreme lawmaking body, this does not mean the executive is weak: these systems may actually feature strong executive powers in practice, depending on whether executives can control their political party and its allies in parliament. We elaborate on this basic distinction further in chapter 10 when we discuss presidential and parliamentary executives, and we look at party systems in chapter 11.

Electoral Systems

Different legislative systems vary in how they organize elections. Among the various options, there are two basic categories of electoral systems used for legislatures, and any number of combinations of these two systems. The first is the district-based electoral system, and the second is proportional representation.

DISTRICT SYSTEMS

district system An electoral system in which voters select representatives from specific geographic constituencies.

constituency A group of voters or a geographic district that legislators or other elected officials represent.

District systems allocate one or more seats in the legislature to each of a number of districts in the country. These districts are usually territorial, with different geographic regions representing the different districts. These districts may be known as **constituencies**; and in most such systems, the district will have a single representative. The most common version is the single-member district (SMD).

Single-member district systems divide up a country into a number of territorial districts, with each district having the right to elect one legislator. This person is then expected to represent the interests of that district in the legislature. In most circumstances, political parties will run candidates for the seat in the legislature; and those representing major, well-known parties will have an advantage over those without such a party affiliation. Parties often have considerable discretion in how they choose their own candidates. In some countries, party leaders may exercise considerable control over who the candidates will be in each district. Another procedure is openly contested "primary" elections in which members of the same party run against one another for the party's nomination to a seat. While major parties have an advantage in name recognition and in communicating to voters what their candidates probably believe, "independent" candidates may also run if they meet the qualifications for getting their names on the ballot.[5] Ballot access is challenging in some countries but famously easy for candidates in others, especially for small local elections. Getting on the ballot is easy in the United Kingdom, for example, where the Monster Raving Loony Party has become a standby. Consider the SMD system in the United Kingdom in the "Case in Context" box entitled "The Mother of Parliaments" (which is not about the Monster Raving Loony Party).

Elections in SMD systems can have different features. A common approach is the **first-past-the-post**, or "plurality" system, in which the district holds elections and the candidate with the most votes wins. This may sound obvious, but note that in such a system, it may be common to have a winner with less than 50 percent of the vote, if there are many candidates who split up the vote between them. This can lead to surprising outcomes in some cases. For instance, consider an election in a relatively conservative district in which two conservative candidates run along

single-member district (SMD) Electoral system in which voters choose a candidate and the winner is elected by the most votes earned or through winning a runoff vote.

first-past-the-post Electoral system in which the candidate with the most number of votes is elected, regardless of whether a majority has been attained.

CASE IN CONTEXT

The Mother of Parliaments: The United Kingdom and the Westminster Model

PAGE 553

The British Parliament is often considered the "mother of parliaments" given its long history and the way it inspired legislatures around the world. It is the most famous example of a parliamentary system in which the legislature chooses and has constitutional powers over the executive; we explore this system further in chapter 10, contrasting it with presidential systems in countries such as the United States. While the British model, known as the "Westminster model," has been emulated often, it has rarely been adopted in its exact form by other countries.

See the case study of the British Parliament in Part VI, pp. 553–554. As you read it, keep in mind the following questions:

1. What features of the British Parliament seem especially "democratic" relative to the American model, and which less so?

2. What role does the notion of "parliamentary sovereignty" leave for the other branches of government, namely, the executive and judiciary? How can the Prime Minister and the executive be powerful when the Parliament itself is sovereign?

3. What is the effect of the single-member district voting system on the proportionality of Parliament? Will this type of system be an advantage or a disadvantage for small political parties?

with one liberal one. The liberal may only win 40 percent of the vote but take the election if the two conservatives split the remaining 60 percent. Accordingly, many SMD systems adopt other electoral rules, with a popular version being a **runoff** system between the top two candidates that ensures that the eventual winner will have received a "mandate" by winning a majority of the valid votes cast.

In general, first-past-the-post systems will often disproportionately favor larger parties that can gain a winning number of votes in many districts, even if these parties cannot win an outright majority of the votes cast. It can also disfavor slightly smaller parties that might get a solid fraction of the vote but not enough to gain a plurality in many districts. A well-known example of this is the United Kingdom, where the Conservative and Labour parties have often won majorities of parliamentary seats without winning a majority of votes cast. The third-largest party, such as the Liberal Democrats in the 2005 and 2010 elections, usually win a smaller proportion of seats than votes. In the 2010 election, neither of the two largest parties won a majority; but in the 2005 election, Labour won a majority of seats (over 55 percent) with a minority of votes in the country (35 percent), while the Liberal Democrats won only 9.6 percent of the seats for their 22 percent of the vote (Table 9.2).

Not all district systems are single-member districts. There are also **multi-member districts** (MMDs) in which more than one representative is elected from each district. These arrangements are less "winner-take-all" because they allow for multiple representatives and also multiple parties to have representatives in the same district.

What happens in these MMD systems often depends on the size of the districts and the number of representatives in each. Imagine if the United States had a system for its House of Representatives with two representatives in each district. Since the Republican and Democratic parties are usually the two leading parties in each district and are usually fairly close in polling, most reasonable calculations would result in the two parties each getting one seat in most districts around the country. But if districts were to have, say, ten representatives, the results might be significantly different. The two leading parties may split the seats between them. Or perhaps the two leading parties would each take four seats, and then a couple of smaller parties—say one on the far left and one on the far right—would win one seat each. This would change the composition of the legislature, encouraging more small parties to have representatives. Because MMD divides seats up according to the relative performance of different parties, this points in the direction of the next broad category of electoral systems: proportional representation.

TABLE 9.2 Results for Top Parties in United Kingdom General Election, 2005

Party	Total Votes	Percentage of National Vote	Number of Seats	Percentage of Seats
Labour	9,552,436	35.2	355	55.2
Conservative	8,784,915	32.4	198	30.7
Liberal Democrat	5,985,454	22.0	62	9.6

PROPORTIONAL REPRESENTATION (PR)

Many countries maintain that the most important factor in representation is not the district or geographic territory one represents, nor having an individual candidate to represent certain people, but rather the distribution of seats between parties. The logic is simple: If party X wins 44 percent of the vote in the country; party Y, 33 percent; party Z, 22 percent; and all other parties, 1 percent; then party X should have about 44 percent of the seats in the legislature, party Y about 33 percent, and party Z about 22 percent. **Proportional representation (PR)** can do a better job than SMD of making this happen.

Systems featuring an element of PR still face the challenge of allocating seats once the votes are tallied. There are many ways to allocate seats, but certain rules are common. First, in many PR systems, a threshold is often required to earn seats in the legislature. This may be 5 percent, for instance. With that threshold, any party with less than 5 percent of the vote would not earn a seat in the legislature because their vote totals were insufficient. This prevents PR systems from being dominated by lots of small parties—which would make complex coalitions necessary and likely not be conducive to stability—and can help ensure governability by restricting power to a handful of substantial parties. Second, the number of seats for each party cannot perfectly reflect the vote because there are always fewer seats than there are voters, and there will be some "remainders." In general, the number of votes a party gets is rounded off to a certain number of seats. For instance, if three parties contest an election for 12 seats, and all the votes for party A would suggest it earned 6.7 seats, party B earned 3.1 seats, and party C earned 2.2 seats, then one actual distribution might be 7 seats for party A, 3 for party B, and 2 for party C. A variety of calculation methods exists for sorting out the seats from votes in proportional representation systems.[6]

PR is designed (by definition) to offer proportionality in the vote for different parties, as we explore further in the "Causes and Effects" section. A leading example of a relatively "pure" PR system, albeit one where democracy is very suspect, is now found in Russia. South Africa also uses a model that features the classic form of PR for its lower house, the National Assembly. However, most countries using PR do not use it in its purest form. Rather, they blend it with district-based systems or make other modifications, as discussed in the section on hybrid systems later in the chapter.

Proportional representation may work in different ways, with different details. For instance, in the variant of PR known as **open-list proportional representation** (used in Brazil and many European countries), voters choose individual candidates; but the candidates' votes are combined together with the other members of their party, and then seats are allocated based on the parties' performances. This makes the legislature proportionally representative, yet the votes for candidates still influence which individuals are elected to the legislature: the candidates with the most votes within their party will have the highest priority for earning a seat. The system attempts to combine some of the features of PR with the right to vote for individual candidates (hence, "open list" rather than a "closed list" controlled by the party). It encourages candidates to seek individual support and can leave parties "less disciplined" than under forms of PR in which the party exerts greater control over its slate of candidates.

proportional representation (PR) In its pure form, an electoral system in which voters choose a preferred party and seats are allocated to parties according to the percentage of the vote the party wins.

open-list proportional representation Electoral system in which voters choose a candidate but votes are aggregated by political party to determine the allocation of seats across parties.

CASE IN CONTEXT

Electoral Rules and Party (In)Discipline in Brazil's Legislature   PAGE 410

The Chamber of Deputies in the Brazilian Congress uses open-list proportional representation. This system allows each voter to select a specific candidate and then attempts to achieve proportionality by aggregating the votes across parties. In Brazil, a consequence seems to have been weak political parties and a messy legislature, at least at some moments in time. For years, many scholars considered the electoral system to be the key item in Brazil's politics that could be changed to improve the quality of governance.[7]

See the case study on the Brazilian Congress in Part VI, p. 410. As you read it, keep in mind the following questions:

1. What do you think might be the reasons behind the adoption of open-list PR?
2. What are the consequences of this system for political parties, and why? Should this result be expected in all countries with this system?
3. If in fact the Brazilian Congress is becoming more coherent over time, yet the open-list PR system has stayed the same, what can explain the change?

Even with the distinction between PR and SMD, and the diversity of rules and mechanisms for each, there is additional variety in the types of electoral systems around the world. As suggested previously, many countries attempt to find a balance between the perceived advantages of PR systems and SMD systems. We might call these "mixed" or "hybrid" systems.

MIXED OR HYBRID

Many countries have sought to balance the advantages of SMD and PR systems and have invented a number of seemingly ingenious mechanisms for doing so, though these generally make the electoral system more complicated. These systems—which represent a hybrid between the two sets of systems already discussed—may have individual elected representatives but attempt to retain (or create) the proportionality among parties that PR systems provide. We return to the cases of Germany and New Zealand at the end of the chapter, but note here that it is possible in theory to elect representatives from districts, and then ensure proportionality of party representation in the legislature, mainly through the addition of supplemental "at large" seats to the legislature.

Other mechanisms ask voters to do more than choose their preferred candidate: they ask voters to *rank* candidates. The electoral system then uses this information about ranked preferences to determine winners. The **alternative vote**, also called the instant-runoff vote or preferential vote, is a simple version. All votes are counted to see voters' first choices. If no candidate wins a majority, the candidate with the lowest total is eliminated, and the votes for this last place candidate are redistributed according to those voters' second-choice picks. If there is still no majority, then the candidate with the next-lowest total is eliminated, and their votes are redistributed as well, and so on until one candidate has a majority of the vote.

A similar system is the **single transferable vote (STV),** which is used in some MMD systems where more than one candidate is elected. Under STV, the voter

alternative vote Voting system in which voters rank candidates and the votes of low-ranking candidates are reallocated until a winner is determined.

single transferable vote (STV) Electoral system in which voters rank candidates and the winners' surplus votes are reallocated to other, lower-ranking candidates until a slate of representatives is chosen.

TABLE 9.3 **Voting Procedures Under Different Electoral Systems**

Electoral System	Procedure for Voter
Single-Member District (SMD)	Choose candidate; top candidate is elected by most votes or runoff.
Proportional Representation (PR)	Choose preferred party; seats allocated to parties by vote percent.
Open-List PR	Choose candidate; votes aggregated by party for allocation of seats.
Mixed Systems/Hybrid Systems	Choose candidate and party (two votes), or other combination of above.
Single Transferable Vote (STV)	Rank candidates; winners' surplus votes reallocated until slate chosen.
Alternative	Rank candidates; votes of losers reallocated until winner found.

ranks candidates, just as in the alternative vote. But some winning candidates will have more than enough votes to win a seat, with some votes left over. The "surplus" votes for winning candidates are redistributed to voters' second choices (and third choices as necessary, and so on) until a slate of candidates is elected. Table 9.3 presents voting procedures under different electoral systems.

These ranking systems have a major advantage: they encourage voters to pick their most preferred candidate, thus reducing the need for **strategic voting**. Under strategic voting, many citizens may not vote for their favorite candidate because they fear he or she will not win, preferring instead to vote for a favorite (or a "least bad" option) among those who have a reasonable chance of winning. Ranking systems are used in Australia and for some local elections in the United States. And the applicability of these voting models is not limited to traditional politics: this vote procedure is also used to select the winners of the Academy Awards, or Oscars.

Indirect election is also a possibility for choosing legislators and is used most often for the upper chambers of bicameral parliaments. Legislators in the lower chamber (which in reality is the more powerful chamber in most bicameral

strategic voting Voting in a way that does not reflect a voter's ideal preference, so as to prevent a less-desired outcome.

indirect election Electoral system in which representatives are chosen by other elected officials rather than directly by the citizenry at large.

CASE IN CONTEXT

The Hybrid Electoral System of the Japanese Diet

PAGE 494

The Japanese Diet uses a mix of proportional representation and single-member constituencies. For much of the period after World War II, the country was dominated by the Liberal Democratic Party (LDP), but it now has a more competitive legislature. In the House of Representatives, 300 members are chosen in their districts, and 180 by proportional representation. The upper chamber, known as the House of Councillors, is also elected by a mixture of district-based systems and PR, but with subtly different rules. This is a simple example of a hybrid electoral system.

See the case study on the Japanese Diet in Part VI, p. 494. As you read it, keep in mind the following questions:

1. What might be the reasons for developing a hybrid system such as this?

2. What would be the expected consequences of this arrangement for the size and success of political parties?

3. Would there be advantages to adopting such a system in countries such as the United States that rely exclusively on districts?

countries) choose the members of the upper chamber in some countries. Alternatively, the members of the upper chamber of legislatures may be chosen by the states/provinces/regions of a federation. In Germany, for instance, the members of the *Bundesrat*, the upper chamber of the legislature, are chosen by Germany's state legislatures.

There is a virtually limitless number of conceivable electoral systems around the world. While certain trends predominate, this small selection of possible formats serves to illustrate the variety of options. The preferences for one system over another owes a great deal to national traditions and habits, as well as to the structure of the polity, to include population size and the importance of group identities and the extent of homogeneity in the population. Moreover, they are presumably "sticky" in the sense that parties and groups that do well within a given electoral system, and who therefore can potentially block changes, typically have an interest in preserving the system from which they benefit. For this reason, one seldom hears calls from the Republican and Democratic parties for the adoption of an alternative framework.

Executive–Legislative Relations

Legislatures routinely have responsibility for oversight of the executive branch. A classic example might be legislatures requiring testimony by military leaders on the conduct of a war, since the military may come under the authority of the executive branch, yet may be required to report to the legislature. Similar examples of such legislative oversight can occur in any number of policy areas, with cabinet ministers and executive officials regularly being required to submit reports and to undergo legislative questioning. This may entail the right to review executive appointees to major political positions (including those to the judicial branch in some instances, as well as appointees to some high-ranking executive offices in the administration). Oversight may also, in especially discordant situations, result in a motion of censure in which the legislature sanctions or scolds the executive for actions it deems inappropriate.

Beyond simply providing oversight, the legislature may be empowered to remove the executive from office if the executive "loses the confidence" of the people (or its elected representatives in the legislature). In parliamentary systems, the relationship between the executive and the legislature is relatively close because of the fusion of the two branches of government. The executive consists of a government elected by the members of the legislature, including a cabinet of ministers led by a prime minister (or equivalent). In these systems, the executive is "responsible" to the legislature and relies on the backing of the legislature for its continuation as a government. This fact confers power to the legislature to remove the executive from office, according to rules that vary from country to country. For instance, in many countries, a majority of the legislature voting "no confidence" in the executive will result in the government being disbanded and new elections being called. In Germany, however, bringing down the government requires a "constructive vote of no confidence" in which the vote of no confidence must be accompanied by a specific proposal for a new government that will take effect upon the completion of the confidence vote.

The German Bundesrat, which represents German states, or "Länder."

The parliamentary model allows the legislature to remove the government—making a call for new elections—without necessarily leading to a major constitutional crisis. In presidential systems, the procedure for removing a member of the executive is usually more elaborate, at least for the highest-ranking officials in the government. Legislatures can use processes of impeachment (or of demanding resignation) to remove the executive from office under relatively stringent conditions. In parliamentary systems, legislatures can remove executives at most any time for a lack of confidence in governing ability. In presidential systems, their power to do so is more limited by the fixed term of office given to the president.

CASE IN CONTEXT

Institutional Design: Germany's Bundestag and Bundesrat PAGE 453

Germany's legislative elections feature yet another wrinkle in the mix between district-based systems and PR. The elections for the *Bundestag* have constituencies but also aim to ensure overall proportionality to make the lower chamber reflective of voters' party preferences. The system is known as a mixed-member proportional system, and it allows (or requires) voters to vote twice: once for an individual and once for a party. Members of the Bundesrat, meanwhile, are selected by assemblies in the states (*Länder*).

See the case study on the German parliament in Part VI, pp. 453–454. As you read it, keep in mind the following questions:

1. What are the mechanics of how the size of the Bundestag is calculated?

2. Which sorts of political actors in Germany would be expected to like this system, and which would not?

3. Does the structure of representation in the Bundesrat affect the way one views the electoral system in the Bundestag?

Causes and Effects: What Explains Patterns of Representation?

Many heated debates center on the systems that elect legislative representatives. At question is how representation will be structured, and particularly how votes are translated into seats. Earlier in the chapter, we outlined the district-based representation and proportional representation approaches to legislative elections as well as hybrid forms. In general, district-based systems are more centered on the election of individual candidates and the latter more centered on the election of political parties, though we discuss a few caveats to that rule. A question for further consideration is "Which type of election is more representative?"

This, of course, depends on what "representative" means. When you consider what it means to have a legislature represent the people, what is essential? Is it necessary to have a single politician representing your district? If so, how do those who voted against that politician feel "represented"? Advocates of PR or party-based elections argue that political systems should come as close as possible to making sure each person's vote "counts" in representation. If you wish to vote for a smallish (but non-trivial) party because that party matches your beliefs, your vote should not be "wasted" simply because that party does not win a district seat. Rather, your vote should be reflected in the proportion of seats allocated to that party in the legislature.

Patterns of Representation

representation In legislatures, the process by which elected legislators reflect the interests and preferences of voters in their constituencies.

The first challenge with a causal argument about "what types of legislatures are more representative" is having an understanding of what **representation** means. In the terms of chapters 1 and 2, we have to define the dependent variable. It may be that no single, easily quantifiable indicator of "representativeness" exists, but this should not stop us from engaging in comparative analysis. In fact, the study of the consequences of different legislative forms is a leading example of how comparativists debate challenging concepts that are difficult to define.

INSIGHTS

Legislative Politics in Latin America

by Scott Morgenstern and Benito Nacif, editors

This edited volume looks at Argentina, Brazil, Chile, and Mexico in comparative perspective. The book makes reference to the U.S. system because much of the work on legislatures is based on studies of the U.S. Congress, but it explores how Latin American legislatures work differently from the U.S. system and from one another. Morgenstern and Nacif (and the numerous authors of the chapters in the book) show that many assumptions about legislatures are based on study of the U.S. Congress but do not hold in Latin America. First, while many scholars of Congress assume that getting re-elected is an ambition for Congresspersons, many legislators in Latin America

may actually be looking to move to other positions, including such state-level positions as governor. Second, legislatures in Latin America are generally more "reactive" than "proactive," responding to presidents in different ways. In making these arguments, the book examines three areas in detail: executive–legislative relations, the internal structure of legislative bodies, and the process by which policies are made. Through this approach, the authors develop a more nuanced comparative understanding of the variables that make legislatures differ.

Scott Morgenstern and Benito Nacif, eds. Legislative Politics in Latin America. Cambridge: Cambridge University Press, 2002.

The central function of legislatures is to represent citizens; a relatively small number of legislators represents the population at large, and individual legislators can never exactly represent the views of each and every citizen, but the process of election is seen to approximate the idea of "rule by the many." Electoral representation may take place on the basis of geography, identity group, or political party. In many countries, people in local or regional districts may choose one or more area residents to represent their constituency. In some other countries, specific seats may be set aside for women (as in the case of local assemblies known as the *panchayati raj* in India), racial or ethnic groups, or specific underrepresented castes or social groups, as is discussed further in chapter 14. Yet not all representation is based on individual representatives, as PR systems offer representation by political party, with citizens voting for parties instead of individual candidates. In this case, representatives appointed by the political parties staff the legislature, voting generally in accordance with the policy directives of the party as a whole.

Implicit in democratic elections is the fact that many citizens will not agree with their representatives some of the time. One may vote for a losing party or candidate, or one may be disappointed with a position taken by a representative one voted for. This raises the question of whether representatives should follow the public opinion of their constituents or their own consciences.

Ask yourself if you believe elected legislators should reflect the opinion of the public that elects them. It may seem obvious that legislators should follow public opinion. After all, representatives are there to represent the people who elected them and can reasonably be expected to reflect the preferences and values of their voting constituents. Incidentally, while Congresspersons in the United States exercise some independence from their constituents, one of the best examples of pure obedience to the majority's will comes from the United States: it is the case of the Electoral College, where the states appoint delegates for the presidential election who are presumed to vote in accordance with the popular vote in the state that delegated authority to them. This means that, as in a notable recent election, a candidate may win the presidency of the United States even while losing the popular vote by millions of votes.

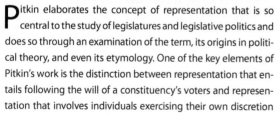

INSIGHTS　**The Concept of Representation**
by Hannah Pitkin

Pitkin elaborates the concept of representation that is so central to the study of legislatures and legislative politics and does so through an examination of the term, its origins in political theory, and even its etymology. One of the key elements of Pitkin's work is the distinction between representation that entails following the will of a constituency's voters and representation that involves individuals exercising their own discretion and judgment once they are elected. Calling this the "mandate–independence controversy," Pitkin argues that no clear rule can be established for whether representatives should follow the general wishes of the electorate or should follow their own counsel if they find these views incorrect. Rather, the essence of representation is acting on behalf of others, which implies that representatives should habitually be in harmony with the wishes of their electors but are also justified in voting independently where there are compelling reasons to do so on behalf of that same group. The rule for mandate versus independence must be examined on a case-by-case basis.

Hannah Pitkin, The Concept of Representation. *Berkeley: University of California Press, 1972.*

Contrasting with the argument of following public opinion, however, is an argument that legislators should be expected to exercise independence, and perhaps should even "think better" of the whims of the populace. In other words, voters do not expect to elect unthinking automatons that will do whatever the majority happens to prefer at any moment in time. Rather than simply being assigned to do the majority's bidding, representatives may be partially chosen for their thoughtfulness and reason, ability to foresee the consequences of legislative choices, and for their skill at compromise. They may be expected to exercise discretion, in other words. They may also be expected to "make the tough choices," even if the populace does not favor these.

Clearly, elections are the leading accountability mechanisms for legislators in democracies. If representatives vote in ways that are too far removed from the interests and preferences of their constituents, they can expect forceful challenges from political opponents (whether in other parties or in their own), and they can probably expect not to win re-election if they get too far "out of line." On the other hand, public opinion is fickle, and representatives need to cast votes not just on what is popular at a given moment in time but also with a view toward the future, both at the time of the next election and beyond. As noted in the preceding "Insights" box (on Hannah Pitkin's *The Concept of Representation*), there is no unambiguous answer to whether representatives should exercise independence from the voters who elected them or should follow those voters' wishes closely. But the distinction between these two goes to the heart of the challenging votes that representatives must make on a regular basis.

Electoral Systems and Representation

Some of the most fundamental questions about representation come from the electoral systems outlined previously: SMD, PR, and hybrid systems imply different forms of representation. Each has advantages in providing for a certain form of representation, and each faces challenges in providing representation by other definitions.

Where legislators are elected in districts, a large portion of the populace may not have voted for its representative. For instance, in an American district where a Democrat is elected with 52 percent of the vote versus 48 percent for a Republican (or vice versa), nearly half of the district may feel it is "not represented" by the chosen Congressperson. More strikingly, imagine an elected legislator who wins with less than half the vote. Consider a district with 65 percent of voters that say they are liberal and 35 percent that consider themselves conservative. Say the liberals split the vote, with a Democrat getting 33 percent and the Rent Is Too Damn High Party candidate getting 32 percent. The conservative Republican candidate squeaks out a win with 35 percent. This means that 65 percent of the district did not vote for the legislator that represents them, even though this group may agree that they would prefer a liberal. Of course, this can and has happened in reverse, with liberals winning conservative districts due to splits in the vote between conservative candidates.

In any electoral system, the question of how to divide up legislative seats is crucial, and SMD systems face challenges of **apportionment** and **districting** of seats. In lower chambers of most legislatures with district systems, the districts

apportionment The process by which legislative seats are distributed among geographic constituencies.

districting The process by which districts or other geographic constituencies are created for elections.

are often expected to be discrete geographic areas, but they are also expected to have comparable numbers of voters for the lower chambers of most legislatures. Of course, precise ratios of seats to the population of each district are not possible. For example, a district with 1,535,000 voters might be expected to have the same number of representatives as one with 1,536,000 voters. Yet as populations of different areas change, keeping districts at roughly the same population requires changing boundaries. This leads to processes of redistricting, as described in "The United States Congress" Case in Context box. One of the challenges of redistricting is that legislators themselves often have a role in the districting process, whether directly or through officials they have nominated, and this creates incentives for legislators to shape districts that favor them or their party. One consequence is **gerrymandering** in which districts are created in irregular shapes or of odd composition to achieve a desired political outcome. The term has the negative connotation of being deliberately designed by incumbents to protect their advantage, though it should be noted that districting has sometimes sought to shape boundaries in ways that favor historically underrepresented groups, such as racial minorities.

gerrymandering Creation of districts of irregular shape or composition to achieve a desired political result.

Malapportionment comes with imbalances in allocating seats to different districts. The extent of malapportionment varies tremendously from one country to another, but it is generally more common in upper chambers of bicameral parliaments, which are often designed to protect the territorial interests of states or provinces. Malapportionment can be defined as the extent to which a system gives some regions a higher ratio of representatives to voters than others. Would such countries be anti-democratic? Would this only apply in authoritarian regimes? Not unless you deem the United States to be anti-democratic or authoritarian, as it is one of the most striking examples of legislative malapportionment, at least in the Senate.

malapportionment Apportionment in which voters are unequally represented in a legislature, such as through relatively greater numbers of legislators per capita for low-population areas and lesser number of legislators per capita for high-population areas.

States, regions, or provinces are represented in Senates and "upper chambers" of legislatures. As might be suspected, federalism affects apportionment. Federal countries that wish to guarantee representation for smaller, less-populous regions will—almost by definition—create seats in the legislature that disproportionately favor those regions. In Brazil, for example, the smallest state (Roraima) has three senators for about 400,000 residents, while the largest state (São Paulo) also has three senators, but for over 41 million people. The relevant ratios are that Roraima has one vote in the Senate for every 133,000 residents, while São Paulo has one vote only for about every 14 million people. Similarly, differences in state representation are found in the United States, where Wyoming has one Senator for approximately every quarter of a million people, while California has a Senator for about every 18 million residents.

The consequences of apportionment and malapportionment are significant. In a theoretical sense, the question of apportionment is about nothing less than the basic principle of "one person, one vote." Put another way, malapportionment could be viewed as the degree to which an electoral system deviates from the "one-person, one-vote" principle: even if everyone has the right to vote, not everyone's vote "counts the same" if seats are malapportioned. It may have arisen for historical reasons and may be necessary to ensure national unity, but in a very real sense, one might say that the vote of a resident of a small state counts much more than the vote of a resident of a large state.

People in Wyoming have more representatives per capita in the Senate than Californians, and Vermonters more than Texans. Looked at through this lens, the residents of America's twenty-five lowest-population states comprise about 16 percent of the population and represent half of the Senate. In theory, these fifty Senators voting as a bloc could (with a vice presidential tiebreak) stop a policy favored in states representing 84 percent of the American population. (This phenomenon is made more striking by the Senate rule known as the filibuster, which in theory allows a bloc of only forty-one out of one hundred senators to stop legislation; see the Case in Context box: "The United States Congress: Dysfunctional or Functioning by Design?")

The advantage of small states in representation may have consequences that translate into political outcomes as well. The most obvious examples are those policies that favor low-population regions that are "overrepresented" by malapportionment, especially rural regions. In many instances, malapportionment may serve to prevent or impede implementation of a policy that will favor a majority of the population. In France, the Senate (*Sénat*) has long been known as the "agricultural chamber" because it provides an institutional bulwark to protect the interests of French farmers. The same may be said of farm policy in the United States. In Brazil, the military created additional new states at the end of authoritarian rule in the 1980s, and this was interpreted by some as a deliberate effort to ensure a larger number of Senators from pro-military regions of the country.

By contrast with SMD, elections in PR systems are often party-centered, rather than candidate-centered. For proponents of PR, one advantage of these systems is precisely the emphasis on parties, their platforms, and their policy proposals rather than the particular ideas and charisma of individual candidates. In candidate-based elections, charismatic and/or thoughtful individuals may communicate well with

CASE IN CONTEXT

The United States Congress: Dysfunctional or Functioning by Design?

PAGE 569

The United States is one of the inspirations for democracies around the world, but there are certain aspects of its system that stray from the "one-person, one-vote" ideal, at least in terms of how much representation each person gets per capita. Apportionment in the Senate and the pattern of districting in the House of Representatives are both areas that have been subject to criticism. The apportionment in the Senate means that residents of smaller states have more representatives per capita than residents of larger states. In the House of Representatives, a big question is how decisions are made to shape districts, and how this affects who is likely to be elected.

See the case study of the U.S. Congress in Part VI, pp. 569–570. As you read it, keep in mind the following questions:

1. If virtually all adults are allowed to vote, then in what sense could one say the U.S. electoral system is less "one- person, one-vote" than other possible systems? Is this characterization fair, and why or why not?

2. What is it about the U.S. electoral system that favors the status quo, whether in terms of policy or in terms of who gets elected?

3. What features of the U.S system, if any, would you alter?

voters, leading to successful election campaigns, yet these skills may matter less in the job of legislating and making policy decisions. Instead, what matters is which party has a majority, or which parties are in the coalition that makes up the governing majority. By ensuring that the whole of the legislature reflects the interests or preferences of the whole country, PR entrusts government to the largest party or leading parties that can make up a governing coalition. In theory, this can make government more capable of passing laws and enacting policies that "the people as a whole" want.

PR also tends to support multiple smaller parties, as contrasted with SMD systems, which favor large parties and accentuate the tendency toward two-party systems instead of multiparty systems. We explore the impacts of these electoral systems on party systems in chapter 11.[8]

Under SMD, smaller parties may earn a healthy minority of the vote (say, 10–15 percent) in many districts across a country yet still be largely shut out of the political process. Let's say the two largest parties—call them the Liberal and the Conservative parties—get an average of 40 percent of the vote each, ranging from about 30 percent to about 50 percent in each district, depending on the district's political leanings. Say also that two smaller parties (the Libertarians and the Greens) get about 10 percent of the vote in every district. Even if the country had five hundred districts (each with one seat in the legislature), it is very possible that the Liberals and Conservatives would split all the seats between themselves, while the Libertarians and Greens would have zero seats under the district system because the Liberals and Conservatives would outpoll them in every single district. Under PR, the Libertarians and Greens would not be shut out: in a five-hundred-seat legislature, they would each get about fifty seats, reflecting their support of 10 percent of the population each. PR would give these smaller parties leverage in political debate, as they may be able to swing to and from the larger parties, making the difference between the Liberals or Conservatives having a majority or not.

On the other hand, PR does not provide voters with a single identifiable legislator who "represents them." This can be troubling for several reasons. First, it can mean that voters do not know to whom they should direct their demands. It may be more challenging to participate and feel represented when one must contact an office of a political party rather than the office of one's district representative. This is especially true for voters who voted for a losing party and must go through a period of government in which they feel it will be very difficult to have someone who can speak on their behalf. Second, and related to this, PR can break the geographic link between citizens and their legislators. While political parties may have local offices and look to attend to local issues, they tend to respond to the overall national constituency in PR systems. By contrast, in district systems, the adage goes that "all politics is local," and citizens may feel more represented when it comes to getting political attention for local issues such as a need for bridge repair, sanitation, or other local issues.

Legislative Decision Making and Representation

Another source of questions about the quality of representation comes from how exactly decisions are made within the legislatures. For some time, a particular

INSIGHTS

Legislative Leviathan: Party Government in the House
by Gary Cox and Matthew McCubbins

Cox and McCubbins argue that the U.S. House of Representatives gets things done largely by the majority party operating as a "legislative cartel." As contrasted with other studies that argue that much of the work of policymaking is determined by committees, Cox and McCubbins note that committees are important but not independent of partisan forces. Majority parties in the House of Representatives routinely shape rules in ways that allow them to dominate the legislative process. In addition, because the majority party dominates decision making, much of the truly important negotiation goes on within the "cartel." In this model, there is little real debate on policy in the broader legislature itself, and this is not a model of representation that follows the ideal of a deliberative body of equal representatives. Instead, the system is reduced to an intraparty game in which the party leaders are key actors attempting to manage their majority party vote. Leaders of the parties create the structures that give rise to powerful committees and control the legislative agenda.

Gary Cox and Matthew McCubbins, Legislative Leviathan: Party Government in the House. *Berkeley: University of California Press, 1993.*

---

committee In a legislature, a body composed of a group of legislators convened to perform a certain set of tasks.

emphasis was placed not on individual members but on **committees** and their roles.[9] These organizations can take on the role of "legislatures within the legislatures," as a select group of parliamentarians or congresspersons shapes a policy and then presents it to the larger body with the expectation that it will be passed in the larger house. As politics has grown more complex and technical over time, legislators have tended to specialize in certain committees and defer to their party colleagues on others. If committees are powerful, then representation is less about each individual vote in the assembly and more about who is assigned to what committee and how this sets or shapes the agenda.

Political parties are some of the key actors in legislatures and are often more important than individuals. In terms of representation, parties are considered "disciplined" if their members vote together and less disciplined if their members vote differently from the party line. This party line is usually determined by the way the national party leadership would like the members to vote. Legislatures vary dramatically in the extent to which their parties exhibit discipline. One of the key factors in determining party discipline is the degree to which party leaders control the electoral fates of their members.[10] Dominance by party leaders may seem to be "less representative" than systems in which legislators vote more independently, but many systems—whether SMD, PR, or hybrid—rely on party discipline to get legislation passed.

Assume for the moment that most politicians would like to get re-elected or to continue their political careers. (While not always true, this shouldn't sound like too far-fetched an assumption.) This implies that politicians will be attentive to the people who nominate and select them. Now notice that who chooses the nominees and the representatives will differ from one electoral system to the next. In many party-centered systems, voters select parties and the party itself chooses who will be the representatives to the parliament. In practice, this gives a great deal of power to the leaders of the party, who can "set the lists" to determine who will become a member of the legislature. Where individual party members depend on party leaders for their nomination, they will typically adhere to the wishes of the leadership, currying favor with those who set the party list. On the other hand, many candidate-centered systems allow voters to choose party nominees, as is the case with party primary elections in the United States. In these instances, party leaders' leverage declines.

Differences in electoral rules should imply variations in the discipline of the political parties. Electoral systems that give more power to party leaders should lead to systems where parties vote in a disciplined fashion. Systems that encourage candidates to focus on district constituencies should lead to less-disciplined parties, with more representatives who have an "independent" streak or vote like "mavericks." Of course, these representatives will often be bucking the trend of their parties to conform to the preferences of the districts they represent. Even in such cases, parties have tools that they can use in their efforts to keep their representatives "in line." We examine these issues further in chapter 11 on political parties and party systems, but note its significance here for understanding how legislatures operate.

Legislative decisions may be shaped by committees or by political parties (and their leaders), but in either instance it is clear that decisions are not simply the result of adding up the preferences and the single vote cast by each representative. Other institutions within the legislature shape what issues get on the agenda and how they are presented to the legislature as a whole. These institutions ensure that legislatures have "structure" in how decisions are made: this is a different view of representation than is suggested by public and open debate on the floors of the voting chamber.

Executive–Legislative Relations and Representation

In most countries today, the power of legislatures and the nature of representation depend heavily on **executive–legislative relations**. At times, legislatures will have considerable powers over executives—some of which are noted in chapter 10, such as "votes of no confidence." On other occasions, legislatures will be relatively less powerful than executives. The balance of power between these two branches says a great deal about how politics plays out in any given country.

executive–legislative relations
The set of relationships between the executive and the legislative branches of government.

Executive–legislative relations are shaped by a number of underlying powers these institutions have vis-à-vis one another. A national constitution may be the ultimate source of *formal power* for legislatures and executives. Legislatures with formal powers to recall or bring down the government may see their leverage over the executive enhanced. This may be expected to make the executive more accountable to the legislature, and to make it more attentive to the legislature's demands. As important as these formal powers are *partisan powers*. Where party leaders in the executive have considerable powers to control the political fates of their fellow party members, they will be able to influence the so-called "rank-and-file" members of the legislature. This refers to the party discipline criterion mentioned previously. Where executives have control over party lists, executives will have considerable control in executive–legislative relations.

Executive–legislative relations are more complex than simple rules on paper of who has constitutional power. In many parliamentary democracies, legislatures have the nominal authority to remove the executive at any time with a vote of "no confidence" in the executive, but this does not necessarily mean that there will

Israeli Prime Minister Benjamin Netanyahu applauds with members of his Likud Party. In 2015, Netanyahu called a parliamentary election more than two years before it was required, in an attempt to reestablish and manage his governing coalition.

be constant turnover in the executive branch.[11] Similarly, in presidential systems, where executives are directly elected, there is most often a formally established balance of powers between the branches, but this can vary from time to time as the political fortunes of presidents fluctuates. Forms of executive–legislative relations shape the quality of representation as much as electoral systems and the internal functioning of legislatures; the exact ways it does so vary tremendously.

INSIGHTS   Divided Government
by Morris Fiorina

Fiorina examines the common phenomenon of divided government in the United States' two-party system in which American voters frequently elect an executive of one party and a legislature led by the other. For more than a century, Americans have often voted against the president's party in midterm elections—that is, in years when no presidential election is held—disrupting unified governments and "checking" presidential authority by supporting the opposing party. More recently, years with presidential elections have also seen an increase in ticket-splitting, where voters choose a president of one party and a Congressperson of the opposing party at the same time. Several conditions can contribute to divided government. Some are due to circumstances. For example, in the United States, the declining strength of political parties over time contributed, as voters became more attentive to individual candidates than to party labels. But other reasons may be more purposive or rational, as people may choose to divide government, whether consciously or unconsciously. For instance, ticket-splitting can make sense for moderate voters concerned that unified government by either party could be too far left or right; given this concern, divided government provides for a style of "coalition" government that requires cooperation and moderation between the parties.

Morris Fiorina, Divided Government. *New York: Macmillan, 1992.*

Comparative Legislatures
by Michael Mezey

This book offers a typology of legislatures according to two dimensions. The first is whether the legislature has strong or modest policymaking powers, and the second is whether it receives more or less support from elites and from the society at large. The two dimensions, and the types of legislatures that emerge, can be seen in the following table.

	Less Support	**More Support**
Strong Powers	Vulnerable	Active
Modest Powers	Marginal	Reactive

Where legislatures are empowered and supported, they can be *active* in setting the policy agenda; such is the case

with the U.S. Congress. The British Parliament, by contrast, is much more *reactive* because the Cabinet and Prime Minister have the power to set most policy in motion. Less-supported legislatures (as in some developing countries) are *vulnerable* to being dominated by the executive or other actors, even if they have strong powers "on paper." The most precarious situation is for constitutionally weak legislatures that are also ill supported: These are marginal. In addition, Mezey shows a fifth category of "minimal legislatures," which have very limited powers but some support from elites; these are often found in authoritarian systems such as the former Soviet Union. The key consequence of a given type is whether the legislature itself is forceful or weak in shaping policy.

Michael Mezey, Comparative Legislatures. *Durham, NC: Duke University Press, 1979.*

Altogether, many factors shape the nature and quality of representation. Electoral systems can give rise to candidate-centered politics, party-centered politics, or a mix of the two. How legislatures themselves operate then also shapes representation: sometimes parties and their leaders wield considerable control, sometimes certain committees wield power, and sometimes power is more open to all members of the legislature. Finally, the relationship between the legislature and the executive gives rise to different patterns of representation. All of these affect representation, as do many other factors. Representation itself is a hard concept to measure, but it is at the crux of most comparative questions about how legislatures matter.

Representation in New Zealand and Beyond

THINKING COMPARATIVELY

Can any electoral system plausibly claim to have the "best of both worlds" when it comes to representing the electorate? The debate between PR and district-based electoral systems often comes down to one common debate: is representation choosing a political party and its platform or voting for a specific candidate closest to one's views? It is likely that an observer will have a "gut reaction" to the advantages of one or the other, while acknowledging that the opposing side "has a point."

Party-based elections allow the electorate to focus on the issues and platforms that most interest them and then to hold the elected government accountable for acting on such issues. They also give a sense, of course, that the overall representation in the legislature actually reflects the will of the overall population rather than the will of specific subsegments of the population. Candidate-centered elections, on the other hand, give voters the sense that they have one or more people who represent their interests, and this allows the voters to hold their specified representative accountable for providing services to their constituency. On

KEY METHODOLOGICAL TOOLS

Hypotheticals and Counterfactuals

The approach to the question of representation here is designed to stimulate debate on the best model for an electoral system and whether countries might change these. This question involves taking political lessons from one country case, comparing these with another case, and then making a proposal based on an

THINKING
COMPARATIVELY

KEY METHODOLOGICAL TOOLS

(continued)

expectation of what would happen if an institution were changed. Of necessity, this means a degree of prediction and speculation, but based on inferences. Hypotheticals are questions designed to get at what likely *might happen* in a scenario under certain circumstances; notice that the root of the word is the same as "hypothesis." Counterfactuals are ways of considering what *would have* happened in a given case under different circumstances; an example might be "what would history have been like if the American colonies had lost the Revolutionary War?" Of course, it cannot be known with certainty what would have happened in a certain situation under other circumstances. In fact, this is why the comparative method—with its most-similar-and most-different-systems designs—is so helpful. But these thought experiments can help us think through the implications of changes in variables such as electoral systems.

Careful analysts will not be cavalier about using hypotheticals and counterfactuals. Predictions and policy recommendations are only valuable if based on considerable, careful study and thoughtful consideration of possible consequences. In the case here, there could be unintended consequences of any country switching its electoral system, and it is the duty of the analyst to think these through. Good comparative analysis should be based on evidence of things that have happened, not simply guesses about "what might happen if." Nonetheless, hypotheticals, counterfactuals, and thought experiments are used all the time by comparativists eager to play out of the logic of how outcomes might be different in countries with different institutions, social structures, and cultures.

the downside, district-based elections may result in disproportionate influence for certain parties—especially large parties at the expense of small parties—and proportional representation elections may sacrifice the identifiability of a specific legislator for a specific constituency. It may seem ideal if a country could have a political system that would have both of these characteristics: individual representatives for different districts of the country and also a legislature whose overall composition reflects the partisan preferences of the country.

So an ideal might be a system where each citizen would have a representative for their district, and the overall composition of the legislature could be guaranteed to be proportional. As noted before, countries such as Germany and New Zealand have done this. In fact, New Zealand switched its electoral system by national referendum in 1993, and the change brought about a German-style model that explicitly intended to bring greater proportionality into what was previously a first-past-the-post system. This makes the country an especially compelling case that illustrates how electoral systems change the proportionality of seats. In both Germany and New Zealand today, each voter has two votes: a vote for a candidate to represent the district in the parliament and then a vote for one's preferred party. Voters may vote for their favorite party and the local candidate from the same party, but no one is required to do so: one can "split" the ticket, picking one's favored candidate and then voting for another party. In each district, the candidate with the most votes is elected to the legislature, and there are a fixed number of such seats. The electoral commission also tallies all the votes for the parties and figures out how to make the legislature accurately reflect the proportion each party received.

For example, say the parliament has two hundred seats, of which one hundred are elected from districts and one hundred are available for allocation to the parties according to the party vote. If the Social Democratic Party won only twenty-five out of one hundred seats in the districts, but their party vote was 30 percent of the total, the system ensures them about sixty of the total two hundred seats (30 percent) in the parliament. Meanwhile, the parties that win more seats in the constituencies than their party vote are allowed to keep the extra seats they have won, and these are called overhang seats. So if the Freedom Party wins twenty-two seats in the districts, but only 10 percent of the overall vote, they are allowed to keep their twenty-two seats and are not limited to the twenty that their party vote would imply. A consequence of this is that the exact number of seats in the legislature is not constant. For example, the lower house of the German legislature (the Bundestag) does not have a fixed number of seats; while the parliament elected in 2009 had 622 legislators, the parliament elected in 2013 had 631, and the parliament elected in 2017 has 709.[12]

The intended result is both identifiable representatives for each district and overall PR. A sample of a ballot from such a system can be seen in Figure 9.1, which is from New Zealand. Notice that the candidates in the right-hand column represent some of the parties listed in the left-hand column.

Why might some argue for countries like the United States to adopt this sort of approach? One major challenge is a willingness to accept a totally new view of representation as both district-based and proportional, which is not how the country has operated historically. It would also require accepting that a computer will make the necessary adjustments to make the legislature proportional. But this process and its decision-making criteria would be quite transparent, being determined before the elections and visible to any and all observers. If you are living in a country that does not use this model, how would you attempt to explain to a German why your country should *not* change to such a model?

The idea of representation varies from country to country, with different countries having different patterns of representation and different ways that representatives are chosen. Ask yourself how and why you might object to the hybrid electoral system used in Germany and New Zealand (if in fact you do object). Entertaining these sorts of questions will lead to a deeper understanding of how legislative institutions work, as well as what is meant by the concept of representation that is so fundamental to politics.

THINKING COMPARATIVELY

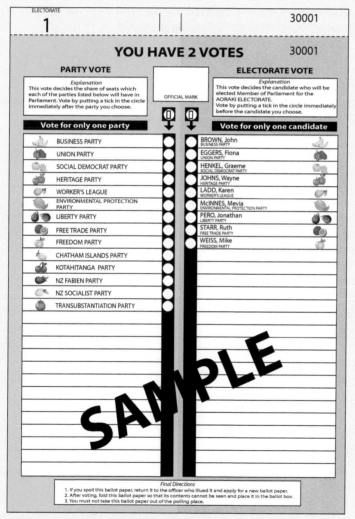

Figure 9.1 Sample Ballot from New Zealand.

(Source: New Zealand Electoral Commission)

Chapter Summary

Concepts

- Legislatures are deliberative bodies that are the foundation of modern governments.
- Legislatures pass laws and make policy, but they also lead public debate and have responsibilities for overseeing the executive, among other functions.

Types

- Legislatures can be bicameral (with two chambers) or unicameral (one chamber).
- Legislatures are elected by many different methods, including single-member districts (SMD), proportional representation (PR), and mixed or hybrid systems.

- There are several different patterns of interaction between legislatures and executives.

Causes and Effects

- A function of legislatures is representation, which can be conceptualized in different ways, and the nature and quality of representation are affected by several factors.
- Electoral systems can result in representation based on individuals, parties, or some mix of the two.
- Legislatures vary in the ways they function internally, and this too affects how they represent the populace.
- Executive–legislative relations also affect patterns of representation.

Thinking It Through

1. Imagine you are the leader of the Monster Raving Loony Party, a small party in the United Kingdom whose manifesto is posted at the following link: http://www.loonyparty.com/about/policy-proposals/. You are a big believer in the cause and are eager to win some seats in Parliament. Currently, you are at 6 percent in most opinion polls, but elections are not due for another couple of years. However, the government has called for public comment on a commission considering changing the electoral system in the United Kingdom. What would you propose the system should be for House of Commons elections? Considering political incentives, what do you expect would be the reaction of Members of Parliament from the three leading parties there: the Conservatives, the Liberal Democrats, and Labour?

2. Imagine you are an American, accustomed to (and approving of) the SMD system for electing congresspersons, and you are debating with a European who lives in a system that has always had PR. This European argues that the PR system offers chances to more political actors, saying that this enlivens debate and forces the legislature to take into account the interests of a broader

range of people. Can you convince your interlocutor that the American system is preferable to the European one?

3. What are the disadvantages, if any, of a system that requires ranking candidates and then calculates winners on the basis of voters' second or third choices?

4. There are several types of legislatures, according to Mezey and to Morgenstern and Nacif (see "Insights" boxes in this chapter). Can you see advantages in systems that feature "reactive" or otherwise weaker legislatures? Could this be a useful pattern of executive–legislative relations? Or are these sorts of legislatures simply less desirable than their stronger and more active counterparts?

5. Would you expect changes in institutional structures (such as a legislature or legislative elections) in a given country to reshape the political outcomes and policy decisions, or would these fundamental outcomes likely be shaped by cultures and other structures and thus be mostly independent of the institutional design? How could you find evidence or arguments to support your claim?

CHAPTER 10

Executives

Theresa May, Prime Minister of the United Kingdom, on her way to appear before parliament.

In 1776, a group of leaders from the thirteen American colonies signed a Declaration of Independence from Great Britain. Most of the document listed abuses perpetrated by King George III, Britain's monarch and head of state. Following the American Revolution, which ended with independence in 1783, the former colonists established a system of government strikingly different from that of Britain. Known as a republic, the United States had a written constitution, no monarch, powerful state governments, and several branches of government that were independent and designed to balance one another. The new republic arranged for an elected president as head of state and head of government.

Over the next two centuries, as both the United States and Great Britain became more mature democracies, the American presidential system and the British parliamentary system became two defining models for how governments could function. With its executive branch led by a prime minister, and a monarch who increasingly became a figurehead in a ceremonial position, Britain became the "Mother of Parliaments" around the world. Meanwhile, many other countries came to emulate the American system of a presidency with checks and balances.

In the United States and Great Britain, the executives have kept their same basic form over time, though their powers have shifted somewhat. Parliament formally retains political power and sovereignty in Britain, and the prime minister depends on retaining the legislature's confidence, yet the prime minister has considerable political leverage. The American president has become more influential over time as the United States has grown but still remains deeply entrenched in the same basic system of checks and balances that endures to this day. The two countries have been models for other countries for centuries, and they remain the points of departure today for understanding how executives work.

• • •

Concepts

Executives earn their name because they *execute* or administer policies and laws. In most countries, executives implement and administer the laws passed by legislatures, though in some authoritarian regimes the executive may act without a functioning legislature. Executives also contribute to the making of law. Legislatures (as examined in chapter 9) are usually authorized to initiate and pass laws in representative democracies, but executives play a major role in the public debate and decision making that leads to new laws. For example, executives may send budget requests to the legislature, or they may work with legislators to formulate a policy that the executive branch desires.

In most cases, executives have a substantial role in determining which laws and policies pass. In the United States, for instance, the president usually signs final bills as they become laws and has the power to veto (disapprove) bills, though the legislature can override the veto with a strong enough majority. In parliamentary systems, the executive shapes the agenda of the parliament to decide which initiatives will come to the floor for debate and also pressures parliamentarians to pass its desired policies. The relative power of the executive and legislative branches is one of the leading issues that determine how political decisions are made, and the relationship between the branches is a major theme running through this chapter.

The executive is the branch of government that runs the government **bureaucracy**, such as the Department of Defense or Department of Education in the United States, or the Ministry of Health or Ministry of Agriculture in a European country. These departments or ministries include large numbers of officials and civil servants that work for the executive branch. For this reason, the executive branch is often held to be responsible for the quality of government actions. When social services improve, executives may successfully claim credit, or when a war policy fails, the executive may take the blame. Legislatures have their portion of responsibility, since they typically pass the laws authorizing executive action and also expenditures, but executives are responsible for executing the laws on the books.

The executive can also refer to specific individuals who lead this branch of government. These "chief executives" are heads of state or heads of government. The distinction between these two—head of state and head of government—is significant. In brief, the **head of state** is a country's symbolic national representative, while the **head of government** is responsible for forming governments and formulating and implementing policies. **Prime ministers** are examples of heads of government. **Presidents** often combine the powers of head of state and head of government.

Monarchs, such as kings, queens, and emperors, are classic examples of heads of state. Traditional monarchs still wield political influence and power as heads of state in some contemporary societies, such as the sultanates and emirates of the Arab world and some small nations such as Swaziland. In Europe, traditional monarchies persist but are essentially figureheads with only symbolic power. In some other countries—usually where the nation-state is of more recent origin, such as India and Israel—a ceremonial president may be the nominal head of state, with political power again reserved for the head of government in the form of a prime minister.

executive The branch of government, or the individual(s) at the top of that branch, that executes or administers policies and laws in a country.

bureaucracy The organization of unelected officials, often considered part of the executive branch, that implements, executes, and enforces laws and policies.

head of state A person with executive functions who is a country's symbolic representative, including elected presidents and unelected monarchs.

head of government The top executive official responsible for forming governments and formulating and implementing policies.

prime minister A chief executive in a parliamentary system of government.

president An executive leader that typically combines the functions of head of state and head of government and is not directly responsible to a legislature.

monarch A head of state in a monarchy who usually inherits a position for life and may have either substantial political powers or very limited ceremonial powers.

The responsibilities and powers of the executive branch are extensive. By most measures, the executive could be the most powerful and dominant branch of government: it commands the bureaucracy and maintains nominal control over the military, and it is responsible for spending the budget approved to it by the legislature. In other words, the executive has powers of the pen and the pistol, and some control over the purse. Indeed, when democracies break down into authoritarian regimes, a typical result is the dissolution of the legislative branch and the loss of independence for the judiciary; it is often the executive's domination over other branches that distinguishes authoritarianism from the more balanced institutional arrangements of a democracy.

Executive branches of government consist of both a set of elected politicians and a more permanent bureaucracy or civil service. Elected officials will generally have discretion to make only a limited number of political appointments to allies, supporters, and copartisans. Beyond these, most of the bureaucracy is expected to remain neutral, executing the law regardless of election results. This ideal is not always upheld in practice, but bureaucrats are generally expected to implement and administer policies rather than to promote a political vision of what government should do.[1]

As a point of clarification, in many countries the elected executive officials and high-level political appointees are called the **government**. This is distinct from the entirety of public institutions in a country. For example, in parliamentary systems, when a "new government" is formed, this does not mean that the state bureaucracy changes, except perhaps at the highest level. Similarly, in the United States, the word **administration** can be used to refer to the top elected officials in the executive or to the broader bureaucracy that executes policy.

Understanding politics requires understanding how executives are selected. In turn, understanding executives depends on understanding legislatures, which we discussed in chapter 9. Especially in representative democracies (but also even in some authoritarian regimes), executives rely on legislatures or assemblies to pass laws that the executive will then implement or "execute." In this chapter, we begin by identifying what executives are and what they do. We then discuss the consequences of different patterns of executives. One of the main distinctions is between presidential and parliamentary forms of government. We use our cases to examine executives comparatively and discuss which forms are most likely to support democracy.

Types

There are two basic ways to structure the executive branch of government: presidential and parliamentary systems. The United States is an example of presidentialism, while the United Kingdom an example of parliamentarism. Some countries, such as France, have executive systems that combine features of presidentialism and parliamentarism, as do some less democratic countries, such as Iran. The relative power of the executive depends on a range of formal and informal powers, including the ability of the chief executive to discipline and manage their party and any other parties needed to comprise a governing coalition. Presidential and parliamentary systems thus have different kinds of **executive–legislative relations**. We discuss these variations throughout this section (and a summary view of types can be found in Table 10.1).

government In the context of executives, the set of top elected executive officials and high-level political appointees that shape and orient policy; also refers to the broader administrative apparatus of the state.

administration The bureaucracy of state officials, usually considered part of the executive branch, that executes policy.

executive–legislative relations The set of political relationships between the executive branch of government, which executes laws/policies, and the legislative branch, which often has the authority to pass those laws/policies.

TABLE 10.1 **Executive Structures**

Form of Executive	Features
Presidential	President is directly elected by population at large. President is ceremonial head of state and chief executive. Legislature is elected independently of executive.
Parliamentary	Prime minister is indirectly elected by parliament/legislature. Prime minister is head of government. Ceremonial monarch or president may be head of state.
Semi-presidential (hybrid)	President is directly elected by population at large. Prime minister or chief minister is responsible to parliament. President may have power to appoint prime minister, dissolve legislature, etc.

Executive Structures: Presidential and Parliamentary

Under the executive system known as **presidentialism**, the populace at large votes in elections for a chief executive, usually called a president, in a nationwide election.[2] This president is usually elected for a fixed term of several years and depends on the voting populace for their position, though the legislature or courts may have the power to remove the president in serious cases of criminal behavior, unconstitutional action, or other impeachable offenses. Most presidential systems in democracies feature **direct elections** in a nationwide popular vote, with particular electoral rules varying by country. In many countries (such as Mexico), the top vote-getter among all candidates wins, with or without a majority; in others (such as France, as seen in the Case in Context, "Electing the French President" box), there is a first round between all candidates and then a runoff between the top two vote-getters, unless one candidate receives an outright majority in the first round. The United States is actually an exception in its presidential electoral process, since election depends on winning a majority of the electoral votes allotted to the various states.

Presidential systems also have legislatures as another "branch" of government, and the issue of executive–legislative relations is important. In nearly all presidential systems, both the executive and the legislature are expected to abide by the rules of a written constitution, though these rules may be flouted by powerful presidents in less-democratic countries. Each branch of government has certain powers, rights, and responsibilities, with the legislature generally having the power to make most law. Presidents have the power to execute these laws, but they cannot make most laws themselves. They typically have the right to assent to a law proposed by the legislature, or to veto it; specific rules for what happens in case of a veto vary by country, but the legislature can often overturn the president's veto with an ample majority. The intricate dance that results between the executive and legislature in trying to get laws passed and instituted is known in the American system as a set of "checks and balances" between different political actors. Judiciaries also have a role in this set of checks and balances, as they have some authority to interpret the law and rule out provisions that conflict with the constitution or legal code. Checks and balances between independent branches of government may seem the most

presidentialism A system of government in which a president serves as chief executive, being independent of the legislature and often combining the functions of head of state and head of government.

direct election With regard to executives, an electoral system in which voters cast a vote directly for the head of government or head of state.

CASE IN CONTEXT

Electing the French President: What Do Runoffs Do?

PAGE 437

The French presidential election contrasts with the American presidential election. In France, the election is based on the nationwide vote and usually features two rounds. The first round is between a large number of candidates, whereas the second round is a "runoff" between the top two candidates from the first round. These electoral systems can produce different results because of the ways they encourage or discourage people to vote for compromise candidates.

See the case study on the French executive in Part VI, pp. 437–438. As you read it, keep in mind the following questions:

1. What are the advantages and disadvantages of the French runoff system?
2. Might any recent American elections have turned out differently if the electoral system were changed to follow the French model?
3. Would a change to such a system have any implications for smaller parties, or would the overall effect be not much change?

parliamentarism A system of government in which the head of government is elected by and accountable to a parliament or legislature.

indirect election With regard to executives, an electoral system in which most voters never cast a ballot directly for the individual who becomes head of government.

intuitive way to set up a democracy—at least to many Americans—but it is not the only way, as we see from parliamentary systems.

Parliamentarism works differently from presidentialism. The first step is an election of members of parliament (MPs) in which voters vote for a political party and/or elect a specific representative of a political party from their district. The second step is where these MPs select an individual as head of government and chief executive. This is an **indirect election** in which most voters never vote directly for the individual who becomes head of government. In most cases, each major party participating in the election has a prominent standard-bearer known to the public, so while individuals may not get to vote for this individual, there is often a leading face associated with the party. The leader of the party that wins the most votes is often selected by the parliament as the head of government, though

CASE IN CONTEXT

"The Most Powerful Person in the World"?
Checks on American Presidents

PAGE 571

The President of the United States is both the ceremonial head of state and the titular head of government, as well as the Commander-in-Chief of the nation's armed forces. Presidents are part of a system of formal checks and balances between executives and the other branches. The nature of these American-style checks and balances is the subject of much of the study of executives.

See the case study on the U.S. presidency in Part VI, p. 571. As you read it, keep in mind the following questions:

1. Why might the founders of the American constitution have insisted on checks and balances between the branches of government?
2. Are there negative consequences of checks and balances for making laws and making governments work, and are there examples where these have played out?
3. Before reading on parliamentarism, can you conceive of other ways to protect democracy that would not involve this style of checks and balances?

not always. Since many parliamentary systems have a quite a few large parties with none that is large enough to claim a majority of seats, the selection of the head of government depends on negotiations between the parties to see who can form a coalition big enough to govern; we discuss this later in the chapter. What heads of government are called in parliamentary systems varies by country and by language and include prime minister, premier, and chancellor.[3]

An indirectly elected head of government wields a form of executive power that is *fused* with legislative power. The fact that the executive and legislature come out of the same body gives rise to different kinds of executive–legislative relations than in presidential systems. On one hand, parliamentary systems often feature a high degree of party unity, with executives that can count on the "backbench" legislators in their party to support executive proposals. This is in part because legislators who do not vote along with the executive may create conditions for "no confidence" in the government, which can put legislators' seats at risk, as we discuss later. On the other hand, executives in parliamentary systems depend on the continued "confidence" of the legislature, since the legislature selected them and generally has the power to vote out the government. This is much easier to do in most parliamentary systems than in presidential systems that require complicated procedures to impeach presidents or force resignations. Parliamentary systems thus have back-and-forth exchanges between executives and legislatures, but "checks and balances" have different meanings than in presidential systems.

Other countries combine features of presidentialism and parliamentarism. These systems typically feature both a directly elected president as the head of state and a prime minister chosen separately as the head of government. In these **semi-presidential systems**, the prime minister and other government ministers or cabinet officials may be appointed by the president, but they are responsible to the legislature (or parliament) and can be dismissed by the legislature. France is a useful example of this system, as can be seen in the discussion of the political regime in that country (see Part VI, p. 432).

Many other configurations of executive power are possible besides the preceding three democratic examples. In Iran, for instance, the president may have some power in executive–legislative relations but is relatively powerless compared with the religious clerics. Whether the Supreme Leader in Iran is best seen as a judicial or executive authority (or both) is open to debate, but it shows that many executives often operate in an intricate web of institutions and cannot simply make decisions unilaterally.

Formal Powers

What executives can do depends on the **formal powers** they have, which are usually outlined in a country's constitutional charter or basic laws. One important formal power is the ability of some presidents to **veto** laws passed by the legislature. Depending on the country, the legislature may be able to override the veto with a majority or supermajority of greater than 50 percent. Veto power gives executives a chance to react to the legislature, but executives may also have more proactive formal powers.

An example of a proactive executive power is the ability in many countries to **dissolve the legislature**. In some countries, this may be exercised only on rare occasions or perhaps a limited number of times per presidential administration,

semi-presidential system A mixed or hybrid system combining aspects of presidentialism and parliamentarism.

formal powers The powers possessed by a political actor, such as a chief executive, as a function of their constitutional or legal position.

veto An act of executive power in which an executive rejects a law passed by a legislature.

dissolving the legislature The practice of a chief executive disbanding the legislature, often accompanied in a democratic regime by the calling for new elections.

while in others it may be exercised frequently when the executive deems it will improve governance or perhaps give the government a larger majority. In the United Kingdom, for instance, elections must be held at least every five years, but a prime minister and the government are entitled to call an early election—sometimes called a "snap election"—at a moment that may be most advantageous for the governing party. In some countries, this can be a major advantage to the incumbent, as governments can schedule elections at their convenience after big boosts of government spending, a phenomenon known as the political business cycle.[4]

decree An executive-made order that has the force of law, despite not being passed through a legislature.

Other formal powers in some countries include the power to pass certain laws or orders without the intervention of the legislature. For example, presidents may have the ability to issue **decrees**, which are orders that have the power of law despite not being passed through a legislature. These have been used extensively in more authoritarian regimes to limit political mobilization. Decrees have also been used by assertive presidents in relatively democratic countries such as Brazil in the 1990s when a president sought to halt an economic crisis. These may go into effect immediately and, in some instances, may only be overturned by restrictive votes in the legislature or by expiring after a certain period of time. Executives can also issue **executive orders** to the bureaucracy that shape the way the bureaucracy enacts and interprets the law. This can affect whether and how important regulations are enforced. In some situations, presidents may be empowered to declare a nationwide **state of emergency** that confers extraordinary powers to the president (and often to the military) to govern with less input from the legislature. The case of Russia shows that it is possible to centralize a great deal of decision-making power in the executive branch, whether as president or as prime minister.

executive order An order made by a chief executive or top official to the bureaucracy that determines how the bureaucracy should enact or interpret the law.

state of emergency A condition allowed by some constitutions in which guarantees, rights, or provisions are temporarily limited, to be justified by emergencies or exceptional circumstances.

It is also important to know what executives *cannot* do, because all democracies (by definition) have numerous checks on executive power. The first and most obvious restraints on executives are periodic *elections* for new governments. These ensure that an executive cannot remain in power indefinitely without popular support. Second are *constitutional limitations* on executive power, such as rights guaranteed to all citizens that the executive may not infringe. Third are *separations of powers*. This may include separating powers between levels of government, such as between central governments and state and local governments in a federal system. It also includes the ways the judicial and legislative branches check executive power and ensure oversight of the executive. Strict **term limits** on time in office may also be seen as a restriction on executive powers, as is the case with the American president, who may now serve a maximum of two terms and a total of eight years.

term limit Restriction on the number of times or total amount of time a political official can serve in a given position.

The other branches of government are responsible for ensuring that executives do not overstep their limits. Constitutional courts may rule that an executive has acted unconstitutionally or illegally. Legislatures may have even stronger mechanisms. One is public rebuke, such as the ability to censure or reprimand the executive. Legislatures may also be able to prevent executive action by withholding funds from executive agencies. In many instances, the legislature can also remove executives from office. In presidential systems, for example, this can occur after an **impeachment** process.

impeachment A process by which a legislature initiates proceedings to determine whether an official, often a top-ranking executive official, should be removed from office.

In parliamentary systems, the legislature chooses the executives, and the executive formally depends on the support of the legislature to retain office.

Executives in Russia: Formal and Informal Powers

PAGE 538

The dominance of the executive branch in Russia has become increasingly clear in recent years. Centralization has been especially accentuated under Vladimir Putin, who was president from 2000 to 2008, prime minister from 2008 to 2012, and became president again in 2012. Putin's role as head of state and head of government showed that some executives are capable of wielding authority through formal means and informal means. The powers of the executives have implications for the fate of democracy in Russia.

See the case study on the Russian executive in Part VI, pp. 538–539. As you read it, keep in mind the following questions:

1. What factors give rise to centralization by executives in countries like Russia?
2. Does the Russian case suggest that semi-presidential systems are likely to be unstable?
3. Does the power of Vladimir Putin say anything generalizable about the relative importance of formal and informal powers?

Vladimir Putin and Dmitry Medvedev at Putin's inauguration following the controversial elections of 2012. Even when Putin was prime minister and Medvedev was president, according to most observers, Putin remained in charge.

The legislature has the power to dismiss the executive if it no longer deems the government to be functioning adequately. This mechanism, the **vote of no confidence**, makes removing an executive much easier than in a presidential system. The vote of no confidence comes in many forms. In its simplest form, a confidence vote is simply called by members of parliament, and the government is voted out if a majority votes no confidence. The head of state then calls new elections for a new government. In Germany, on the other hand, there is a so-called constructive vote of no confidence, which is designed to ensure that there will always be a government in place. There, the legislative majority voting no confidence in a government simultaneously proposes a new government that will take its place.

More formal powers for the executive leads to greater influence over legislatures, while more checks on executive powers gives greater authority to legislatures.[5] Weaker formal powers may limit executives in their ability to promote their initiatives or agendas. It is relatively obvious that the ability to veto legislation enhances a president's power, for example, or that a legislature that can easily override a veto weakens the executive's power. However, as noted before, formal rules do not fully determine an executive's power, and it is not always clear how formal rules themselves matter. For example, Brazil's president used decrees a great deal in the 1990s, but most legislation of any significance ultimately had to be passed through the legislature.

vote of no confidence A vote taken by a legislature that expresses a lack of support for the government or executive, which, if successful, often results in the dissolution of the government and the calling of new legislative elections.

In parliamentary systems, one of the main issues with regard to formal powers is how confidence votes work. Where they are used, votes of no confidence are examples of the legislature exerting its control over the executive, but the existence of votes of no confidence is not proof of legislative power. In fact, legislatures can be powerful even without using confidence votes. Often, the mere threat of a confidence vote will be enough to force the executive to do the legislature's bidding. Actual votes of no confidence may rarely come to the floor of the parliament, and may succeed even more rarely, even where executives are weak.

Parliamentary countries are not all destined to have a merry-go-round of failed governments that last only a brief time before being voted down in confidence votes. Some countries have notoriously unstable systems while other countries rarely witness a confidence vote. Because prime ministers usually represent one of the largest parties in parliament, the executive in a parliamentary system will often have substantial support in the parliament. Parliamentarians who call for a no confidence vote place their own careers on the line, since these votes usually trigger new elections or shake-ups within the party.

Partisan Powers

partisan powers The powers accruing to a government official, such as a chief executive, by virtue of the official's leverage or power over members of a political party.

The formal powers of an executive are not the only factor that determines whether an executive has leverage over legislation. Formal powers are often less important than the **partisan powers** of the executive—that is, the president's leverage over same-party legislators and over parties in the governing coalition. Chief executives who can exercise such authority and can thus control the careers of other politicians will typically be able to pass a great deal of legislation.

The balance of power between the executive and the legislature depends partly on whether executive leaders can control the electoral fortunes of legislators. One of the most important forms of control is over the party's list of candidates for elections, as noted in the previous chapter. If the executive leaders can choose who will be on party's list of candidates, then those would-be candidates will be responsive to the needs of the executive. On the other hand, the executive's partisan powers are lessened if party leaders do not control the electoral fortunes of copartisans. Where party candidates are chosen by voters in primary elections, for instance, they will tend to be more loyal to their constituents than to their party leadership. This may result in legislators who vote against the wishes of their party leaders in the executive. In some parliamentary systems, a critique is that party leaders in the executive can "ram legislation through" and get it approved by a "rubber-stamp" parliament. Where executive leaders control the electoral fortunes of legislators and have a strong majority, the executive may be able to push its prerogatives through the parliament with ease, knowing that copartisans will support it. By contrast, a critique of certain presidential systems is that some executives may have too little partisan power and thus difficulty passing laws, as the case of Brazil shows.

Coalitions

coalition A group of two or more political parties that governs by sharing executive power and responsibilities.

The power of executive leaders also depends on whether a party governs alone or is part of a **coalition** of two or more parties. Governing coalitions form among parties in the legislature, but they determine the composition of the executive

CASE IN CONTEXT
Who Governs China?

PAGE 424

China's current political system is authoritarian, with a complex state administration interweaved with the single dominant party, the Communist Party of China (CPC). At present, Xi Jinping has consolidated power over the party, the presidency, and the military. How one becomes China's "paramount leader" is a study in the politics of party and state in China's intricate system.

See the case study on the Chinese executive in Part VI, pp. 424–425. As you read it, keep in mind the following questions:

1. How does a paramount leader consolidate power and emerge in China's system?
2. Why might an authoritarian regime such as China's require or desire to have any "checks and balances" between different actors?
3. Can we tell if strong, top-down authority of paramount leaders contributed to China's economic growth, held China back economically, or both?

Chinese leaders at the opening session of the National People's Congress in Beijing in March 2015. In the second row from the top stand five prominent leaders, with President Xi Jinping and Premier Li Keqiang second and third from the left, respectively.

and the government, so we consider them in this chapter. Coalitions usually arise when there are several major parties in a country and the party that won the most legislative seats in an election does not have the majority needed to pass legislation on its own. In parliamentary systems, where the executive depends on the confidence of the legislature, heads of government frequently need to hold together a coalition so as not to be voted out of office. This is especially common under systems of proportional representation (see chapter 9) where small parties are likelier to emerge and remain in existence. On some occasions, a governing party may have a majority but choose to form an alliance with another party for other reasons.[6] Coalitions are somewhat less common in presidential systems, where an election is held for a single chief executive that represents a certain party. In the United States, for instance, the party winning the presidency typically holds all the seats in the cabinet. Yet even in presidential countries like Brazil, presidents sometimes need to form a cabinet that represents various parties to have a coalition of parties that can get legislation passed.

In parliamentary systems, the largest party in the legislature has the advantage in forming a government and is usually the one from which the head of government emerges.[7] Parties with fewer seats are the "junior" members of the coalition but will demand some political reward for agreeing to participate in government. This comes from **cabinet** appointments to control ministerial **portfolios**. By controlling certain ministries, coalition members can reward their supporters with the ability to shape policy in the area where they control the cabinet position

cabinet The group of senior officials in the executive branch, including ministers, who advise the head of government or head of state.

portfolio The set of duties and tasks that correspond to a given ministerial office.

German chancellor Angela Merkel of the Christian Democratic Union (center) talks with then Foreign Minister Guido Westerwelle of the Free Democratic Party (right) and others as they negotiate to form a governing coalition.

and can help some of their top partisans with high-ranking appointments in the bureaucracy.[8]

Forming governing coalitions is a political art, especially in countries with many parties in the legislature. Not all coalitions are based on the largest party in parliament, for example. If a group of smaller parties gets together, they may be able to exclude the largest party or parties from the government. This may happen, for instance, if one extreme party (say, right-wing or left-wing radicals) gains the largest number of seats, but all other parties combine to prevent them from holding power. Substantial bargaining will take place over how cabinet positions will be distributed among the parties. Generally, the more seats a party wins, the more it can demand in ministerial portfolios and policy concessions.

There are several types of governing coalitions. Consider the following hypothetical example of the country of Santa Gabriela (Table 10.2). There are one hundred seats in the parliament, and the parties are arrayed along the political spectrum from far left (XL) and left (L) through the center (C) to right (R) and far right (XR). Imagine that each seat represents 1 percent of the vote, so that party R got 27 percent of the vote and therefore twenty-seven seats.[9] Many possible kinds of coalitions can be formed after this election. We give one example for several types of coalitions, listing the largest party first in each case, and encourage you to figure out other possible examples that fit each type of coalition. What different coalitions might form, and which parties might be represented in the executive branch?

TABLE 10.2 Hypothetical Distribution of Seats in Parliament of Santa Gabriela

Party	XL	L	C	R	XR
Seats	30	7	21	27	15

A **minimum winning coalition** has no "surplus" parties beyond those required to form a government. So, for instance, a coalition of the four parties C, R, L, and XR would not be "minimum winning" because parties C, R, and L could still have more than 50 percent of the seats even without the seats of XR. However, removing any one of the parties from the C-R-L coalition would give the coalition less than the 50 percent of seats needed. C-R-L is thus an example of a minimum winning coalition. There are several other possibilities in this election, such as an XL-XR-L coalition. A more restrictive version of a minimum winning coalition is **minimum connected winning**; this arrangement occurs when all parties in the coalition are "connected" to one another on the political spectrum. This prevents the example of the parties XL (far left) and L (left) forming a coalition with the party XR (far right), which would be improbable because there is no realistic "connection" linking these parties. There are other parties in between, namely, R and C. The logic is to include policy preferences as a factor in coalition formation. This rules out several minimum winning coalitions, but C-R-L is an example of a minimum connected coalition.

The **minimum size** coalition goes a step further and says the coalition that governs will be that closest to the threshold needed, usually 50 percent plus one seat. A coalition that includes only 51 percent of the seats is preferred to a coalition that includes a larger percentage of seats, because the participating parties will maximize their relative power within the coalition by not dispersing power. There will often be only one possible minimum size coalition, even when there are many possible "minimum winning coalitions." In Santa Gabriela, XL-C is the minimum size coalition.

Other logics can also shape the types of coalition that emerge (Table 10.3). One logic is to minimize the number of parties involved: two-party coalitions will be preferred to three- or four-party coalitions, even if the two-party coalition means more seats. Another option is that coalitions should contain the party holding the median seat in parliament or the "middle" parliamentarian on the political spectrum, because this echoes the will of the "median voter" or average citizen. In this case, party C is the median party. The median party coalition may or may not be "minimum winning." A final type of majority coalition will minimize the range or number of "spaces" on the political spectrum between parties. Between C and XR, for instance, there are two "spaces" (C to R, and R to XR). The same is true for L and R, while XL and R would have three spaces. Such coalitions prefer parties that are not too far apart, but there is no requirement that parties need to be "connected" or adjacent to one another. In Santa Gabriela, two spaces is the minimum possible. Sometimes this includes three parties connected to one another, and sometimes two parties with a space in between them.

minimum winning coalition A governing coalition that contains no surplus parties beyond those required to form a government.

minimum connected winning coalition A minimum winning coalition in which all parties in the coalition are "connected" or adjacent to one another on the political spectrum.

minimum size coalition A governing coalition that is closest to the threshold needed to govern, typically 50 percent of the legislative seats plus one seat.

TABLE 10.3 **Types of Coalition**

Type of Coalition	Definition of Coalition	Example	Seats (#)
Minimum Winning	No extra or surplus parties that are not needed to govern	XL – XR – L	52
Minimum Connected Winning	Minimum winning and parties are connected on policy spectrum	C – R – L	55
Minimum Size	As close as possible to minimum number of seats needed (often 50 percent)	XL – C	51
Minimum Number of Parties[i]	Fewest number of parties needed to form majority	XL – R	57
Median Party[ii]	Includes the median party in the middle of the political spectrum	XL – C	51
Minimum Range	Minimum number of spaces between parties on policy spectrum	R – C – XR	63

[i]Lijphart (1999) calls this coalition the "bargaining proposition" coalition.
[ii]Lijphart (1999) calls this coalition the "policy-viable" coalition.

grand coalition A governing coalition composed of two or more major parties that hold a supermajority of legislative seats and represent a supermajority of the electorate.

These coalitions all have a governing majority and all share a logic in which participating parties attempt to minimize the size or scope of the coalition. However, there are also two other major possibilities in coalition formation. A **grand coalition** may be made up of two or more parties that represent well over half of the electorate, and hold well over half the seats. One motivation for a grand coalition is national unity among the largest parties in a time of crisis. An example was the national unity government in Britain during World War II, when Conservatives, Liberals, and Labour all joined to support the war effort. Less dramatically, the "Grand Coalition" from 2005 to 2009 in Germany emerged after a closely contested election in which neither party came close to a majority but preferred a centrist coalition to another coalition that might have included parties on the left wing of the political spectrum.

Finally, not all governments necessarily have a majority of the seats in the legislature. In some parliamentary systems, the largest party (or a group of parties) may be able to form a government even with less than 50 percent of the seats. This happens where there are three or more major parties represented in parliament and no party gains a majority of seats. The government's ability to remain in power is tenuous in these cases, lasting until a vote of no confidence occurs or the next election is held. In Canada from 2008 to 2011, the Conservative government of Stephen Harper governed with only 46 percent of the seats in Parliament, since the next largest party was the Liberals (25 percent of the seats), followed by two other parties (the New Democratic Party and a regional Quebec-based party, the *Bloc Québecois*), with whom neither the Conservatives nor the Liberals could form a majority coalition. The Conservatives formed a government, which fell in 2011 when the other three parties agreed to vote no confidence and call new elections; the Conservatives then won an outright majority in the ensuing election.

In general, parties and their leaders decide to participate in a coalition because they prefer to be in government where they can affect policy rather than in opposition. Parties often have to compromise to join a coalition, and will prefer to form a government with those parties with which they agree on policy. In general, parties may prefer *not* to have a coalition that is very large and has well above 51 percent of the seats. The reason is relative power. A party that holds 33 percent of the seats (for instance) will

TABLE 10.4 Presidential Powers

Type of Power	Definition	Examples (Not in All Countries)
Formal Powers	Powers assigned to the office of the president by constitutional authority or by law	Dissolve the legislature Issue decrees and executive orders Veto legislation
Partisan Powers	Powers to control decisions and votes of legislators and other politicians through control of political party	Control lists of candidates for office Appoint party members to executive office Affect career paths of party members
Informal Powers	Powers of the president that are not official but come from informal ability to influence public policy	Influence public opinion and public debate Campaign for individuals or causes Patronage and clientelism

have most of the say in a coalition comprised of parties representing 55 percent of the seats in parliament but would only have a smaller fraction of the power in a coalition comprised of parties representing 70 percent of the seats. This is why we might expect coalitions to be relatively close to 50 percent of the seats, though it must obviously be above 50 percent to constitute a governing majority.

Informal Powers

Apart from formal and partisan powers, executives can have others that we simply call "**informal powers**" (see Table 10.4). These include the ability to influence public debate and public opinion. For instance, if the president of France wishes to force a public debate on immigration, he may bring up the issue in speeches and talk about it in the media. In the United States, we know this as the "bully pulpit of the presidency." There is nothing in most democratic constitutions giving the president legal authority to shape public opinion, but he is clearly free to use the podium and public position to shape politics. Indeed, one prominent scholar has referred to the most essential power of the American president as the "power to persuade," since formal authority alone will not work to control the legislature or the bureaucracy.[10]

In many countries, presidents can also use the government as a source of **patronage** or for the purposes of **clientelism**. This means providing jobs or other benefits to supporters, with the executive known as the patron and the recipients of this support known as the clients. Patron–client politics is generally seen as poor governance, but it is clearly a power that some presidents have.

Causes and Effects: What Explains Executive Stability?

One big question in the study of executives has been whether parliamentary forms of government are better for protecting democracy than presidential forms of government. While it may come as a surprise to American students, the debate has generally had presidentialism "on the defensive." Advocates of parliamentary forms of government have argued that parliamentarism better protects democracy. They point to evidence from Europe and several former British colonies around the world. These countries have a long history of parliamentarism and a stronger record of democracy than many presidential systems.

informal powers Those powers possessed by an office holder that are not "official" but rather based on custom, convention, or other sources of influence.

patronage The use of government favors, typically in the form of employment, to garner political support.

clientelism The practice of exchanging political favors, often in the form of government employment or services, for political support.

CASE IN CONTEXT

The Presidency in Nigeria: Powers and Limitations

PAGE 525

With its tendency for patronage and the need to balance the precarious relationship between North and South, Nigeria shows that social context greatly affects the environment in which presidents operate, regardless of constitutional powers. Given long-standing conflicts and challenges to governance in the country, the election of the executive in Nigeria takes into account the realities of ethnic divisions across the different regions of the country.

See the case study on the Nigerian executive in Part VI, p. 525. As you read it, keep in mind the following questions:

1. Would you consider the Nigerian presidency a strong or weak institution? Why?
2. What accounts for the similarities in certain features of the presidency across both military and civilian regimes?
3. What are the intended effects of the new constitutional rule shaping presidential election in a multi-ethnic country like Nigeria?

Stable and Unstable Regimes: Presidentialism, Parliamentarism, and Democracy

The debate has been whether presidentialism or parliamentarism affects the stability of democracy, not about whether parliamentarism is preferable to presidentialism in every respect. Presidential systems may have other advantages over parliamentarism, such as allowing voters to identify clearly with an individual candidate, giving voters a greater range of electoral choices, and providing the opportunity to "split a ticket" and cast a vote for one party in legislative elections and another party in the executive election.

Consider what is likely to happen in each type of system and how it will affect democracy. According to the argument in favor of parliamentarism, a parliamentary regime makes governments likelier to reach compromise and share power. There are often multiple parties represented in a parliamentary cabinet. Presidential regimes, on the other hand, generally have only one party represented in the cabinet and are less willing to compromise and share power. Moreover, if a parliamentary executive becomes unpopular, that executive can be easily removed by a no confidence vote. This means that a crisis in a particular government does not become a crisis of the whole political regime, whereas removing an unpopular elected president from office creates more of a constitutional crisis. (See the "Insights" box on the work of Juan Linz.)

Yet some scholars disagree that parliamentarism is better for democracy than presidentialism.[11] One critique introduces another factor into the equation: the political party system. In this critique, the argument is that parliamentary systems are not necessarily more inclined to power sharing. It depends on how legislators are elected and how many parties end up being represented in parliament. If a parliamentary system has just a couple of major parties, there will be few incentives for prime ministers to share power. (See the "Insights" box presenting Mainwaring and Shugart's critique.)

Another way to critique the argument in favor of parliamentarism is to examine specific empirical cases to see why democracy has succeeded in some places and

INSIGHTS

The Perils of Presidentialism *and* The Virtues of Parliamentarism
by Juan Linz

Juan Linz argues that parliamentary systems are better for democracy than presidencies, for five reasons:

1. *Competing vs. Clear Legitimacy.* Presidentialism divides power between the legislature and the executive, which makes it unclear who is responsible for public action. Parliamentarism makes clear that the executive heads the government.

2. *Fixed vs. Flexible Terms.* Presidential systems have rigid terms for presidents (such as four years), which makes changing an unpopular government difficult. Parliamentary governments may be replaced at any time upon losing the confidence of parliament.

3. *Winner-Take-All vs. Power Sharing.* Presidentialism allows a single party to lead the executive branch. Parliamentarism leads to more power sharing (via coalitions). This helps democracy by including more participants in decision making.

4. *Presidential vs. Prime Ministerial "Style."* Presidencies lead to more authoritarian, bombastic style than is found with the negotiating tendencies of prime ministers.

5. *Outsider vs. Insider Executives.* Presidents are likelier to be outsiders than prime ministers because parliamentary leaders have been in politics for decades.

Linz argues that these factors in the long run increase the likelihood that presidential systems will be taken over by authoritarians.

Juan Linz, "The Perils of Presidentialism." Journal of Democracy 1, No. 1 (1990a): 51–69; and "The Virtues of Parliamentarism." Journal of Democracy 1, No. 4 (1990b): 84–91.

not others. Parliamentarism has been predominant in Europe and presidentialism in Latin America and Africa, for example. We can see this by contrasting the stable democracy of the parliamentary system in the United Kingdom with the presidential systems of Brazil and Nigeria that have had periods of military rule. But Europe may have had successful democracies not because of parliamentarism but rather because it is rich. The less successful histories of democracy in Brazil and Nigeria may not be because of presidentialism but because those countries and others in their regions are lower-income. Close attention to the empirical cases chosen (the *when* and *where* of an argument) can affect our conclusions about *how* and *why* democracy persists.

To put it another way, remember that correlation is not causation (see chapter 2): just because parliamentary Germany is more democratic than Iran, and Iran has an elected president, this does not mean that parliamentarism *causes* Germany's democracy to succeed or that directly electing a president *causes* Iran's democracy to fail. The challenge is to document cause and effect rather than to assume it. This means that we need to try to anticipate and control for other, confounding variables—such as rich versus poor societies—when we look for causal relationships between outcomes such as parliamentarism and successful democracy.

The argument in favor of parliamentarism is a model for reasoning through the consequences of institutional design. Similarly, the response by critics exemplifies how thoughtful critiques can use both empirical evidence and theoretical argumentation to counter prominent theories. The argument that says party systems matter helps to specify further the conditions under which parliamentarism and presidentialism work well to support democracy. Both the theory and the critique are part of the constructive process of building scientific knowledge about the world.

INSIGHTS | Juan Linz, Presidentialism, and Democracy: A Critical Appraisal
by Scott Mainwaring and Matthew Shugart

Mainwaring and Shugart offer a two-part critique of Linz's argument. The main theoretical critique is that parliamentarism can be just as "winner-take-all" as presidentialism. In Britain, for example, a parliamentary executive may in fact have even more power than a presidential executive, if the prime minister tightly holds the reins of his or her own party. Where one party governs in a parliamentary system and the executive can dominate the legislature, parliamentary majorities are truly "winner-take-all." This article also offers an empirical critique that considers other factors. Presidential systems are most common in poorer countries (such as Latin America and Africa), while parliamentarism prevails in wealthy countries in Europe. It may be that wealth is actually causing democracy in Europe and poverty is causing authoritarianism in Latin America, and presidential or parliamentary government has little to do with these outcomes. Mainwaring and Shugart also note that parliamentary systems are more common in small countries (and islands) and in countries with a British colonial heritage, and that each of these factors may also increase the likelihood of democracy.

Scott Mainwaring and Matthew Soberg Shugart, "Juan Linz, Presidentialism, and Democracy: A Critical Appraisal." Comparative Politics 29, No. 4 (1997): 449–471.

In the debate over presidentialism and parliamentarism, it may be useful to consider examples such as India, which has long been one of the world's most surprising democracies: it is a relatively poor country (though growing rapidly), highly unequal, with more than a billion people from many different religious and ethnic backgrounds. Its parliamentary system is based on the British model. Parliamentarism may or may not have contributed to India's rather successful democracy, and you can consider the Indian case to test this hypothesis. Has the parliamentary system resulted in power sharing rather than "winner-take-all" politics, for example? Has it resulted in a prime ministerial "style" that is less centralized than in presidential systems? There is evidence both for and against the argument that parliamentarism has been a cause of India's democracy, as you will begin to see in the following box. Investigating further can allow a full hypothesis test of whether India follows the logic outlined by Juan Linz in the "Insights" box.

Stable and Unstable Executives: Styles of Presidential Rule

Looking beyond whether a democratic regime persists, there is also the question of how executives govern. Popularly elected leaders in a democracy are expected to work within a society that has rules and other institutions. For example, the legislature is expected to have some say as well as the president, and the president is not expected to be above the law. However, chief executives govern in very different ways, and there are some circumstances where elected executives wield considerable power. In many cases, even if a regime is formally a democracy, the president may assert more authority and centralize power considerably. One such type of regime is "delegative democracy," which confers substantial power to presidents. While the concept of delegative democracy was originally conceived for Latin American countries, you may consider whether the case of Russia under Vladimir Putin fits with the model.

Executives influence the economy as well as politics, and they may contribute either to good or to poor economic performance. Executive powers in the

INSIGHTS   Delegative Democracy
by Guillermo O'Donnell

O'Donnell argues that there is a kind of democracy called delegative democracy that differs from the normal representative democracy. In delegative democracies, a president is elected and then proceeds to govern however he or she sees fit. Power is concentrated in the single individual that runs the executive, and this executive sees himself or herself as having been delegated power for a period of time rather than seeing himself or herself as a representative of the people's interests. O'Donnell considers this a kind of democracy, because the president will respect certain limits, such as elections and limits on the term of office, but there are few checks on presidential power and little accountability of the president to other institutions. Courts and legislatures in particular have relatively little influence. O'Donnell finds this type of system to have existed in many parts of the developing world, from Latin America to parts of Asia and Africa. The existence of delegative democracy highlights the importance of executive power in determining the extent and nature of democracy in a country.

Guillermo O'Donnell, "Delegative Democracy." Journal of Democracy 5, No. 1 *(1994): 55–69.*

economy include proposing budgets for the legislature to approve, collecting taxes, and regulating the economy. Executives also make decisions about staffing key economic institutions, such as the central bank that controls the money supply. Finally, the executive in some cases will make major interventions in the economy. Examples include nationalizing companies or privatizing them, and perhaps bailing out important industries such as banks in a financial crisis. All together, these economic responsibilities mean that the executive branch has a great deal of leverage over the economy.

So how does a strong executive benefit or hurt the economy? One argument is that powerful executives can damage the economy through **populism**, a political

populism A political approach in which leaders, often heads of government and top executive branch officials, make direct appeals to "the people" and seek to develop direct political ties with the masses.

Juan and Eva Peron of Argentina in 1951. They are among the most important populist figures in the history of Latin America.

INSIGHTS

Neoliberalism and the Transformation of Populism in Latin America: The Peruvian Case
by Kenneth Roberts

Roberts examines the concept of populism, which is often associated with powerful and charismatic presidents, and argues that its most important characteristic is a leader who establishes personalistic links with the people. This happens when other institutions are weak, and the tendency of populist presidents to individualize power relates to the "delegative democracy" of O'Donnell noted in a previous "Insights" box. Historically, populism was most significant in the 1930s and 1940s in Latin America, when several charismatic presidents asserted personal power and spent large sums of government money in support for the working classes. This would suggest populist presidents are inclined to hurt the economy in the long run, but Roberts notes that populism can be consistent with more limited spending. In fact, some populist presidents in the 1990s, including Alberto Fujimori in Peru, Carlos Menem in Argentina, and Carlos Andrés Pérez in Venezuela, implemented free market neoliberal reforms (see chapter 4). This suggests to Roberts that populism is less about excessive economic spending and more about the chronic weakness of other institutions outside the executive.

Kenneth Roberts, "Neoliberalism and the Transformation of Populism in Latin America: The Peruvian Case." World Politics 48, No. 1 (1995): 82–116.

approach in which leaders make appeals to "the people" and seek to develop direct political ties with the masses (discussed in more detail in Chapter 15). With populist approaches, presidents often use the resources of the government to reinforce their personal power, making themselves into the symbolic embodiment of the nation and working to undermine other institutions. In many cases, such leaders literally hand out money as they go, spending large sums of government revenue to help their supporters and increase their own popularity. This propensity for populism will likely hurt the economy over the long run, if it results in excessive government spending. In a similar vein, executives can control patronage, as noted previously (under the "Informal Powers" section), and they may use control over government as a way to distribute favors to certain groups; this too can prove detrimental to the economy in the long run.[12]

On the other hand, strong executives may also make for a strong state, which is often associated with good economic performance, as seen in chapters 3 and 4. This may include decisive national leaders such as strong presidents, or strong bureaucracies in the executive branch. Examples would include ministries and government economic councils in East Asia that were responsible for major decisions that promoted economic development. To use a contemporary example, it is difficult to understand China's recent development without talking about the importance of decisions made by executive officials and leaders, from the president and premier to top officials at the central bank.

Stable and Unstable Executives: Patterns of Parliamentary Rule

A final set of causal questions about executives is what makes their *governments* endure or collapse. Most of the preceding "Case in Context" boxes point to relatively stable governments that last from one election to the end of a term of office, at least in the years from the 1990s to now. Other countries, however, are more notorious for executive instability due to coalitions that break down frequently. The case of Italy shows that governments in some countries are unstable while others endure. Italy has changed prime ministers nearly forty times since the end of World War II; during that time, the United States has had twelve presidents, only one of which resigned from office. This means a change of government has happened in Italy more than once every two years, though elections are only required to be held every five years. The turnover in the executive is even more dramatic if one counts a government as new every time a cabinet is reshuffled to accommodate various parties. By this criterion, Italy has had over sixty governments since World War II, leaving the average duration of a government at just about one year. This gives Italy perhaps the most unstable government among advanced democracies, though the constitution and the basic structure of government have persisted for some time. That is, Italy has seen unstable governing coalitions in a stable regime.

Despite the frequent turnover of governments, there are some ways in which Italian politics exhibits continuity. There are not necessarily new faces leading Italian politics every year or so. In fact, the very first post-war prime minister, Alcide de Gasperi of the Christian Democrats, led eight different cabinets in his eight years in office before finally losing the prime minister's chair. Several prime ministers, including recent Prime Minister Silvio Berlusconi, have been in the post three or more times. Moreover, there have been some time periods when prime ministers have been relatively secure, including Berlusconi from 2001 to 2006. Nonetheless, many governments have lasted less than a year, and very few last more than three.

A flip side of instability is the fact that many parliamentary systems are relatively inclusive of different parties and interests. This can be as a result of the electoral rules that favor multiparty systems (as discussed in chapters 7 and 9), or because cooperation happens where different groups in society have reasons to share power and build trust. For example, where countries are divided into different ethnic groups, elites and leaders may attempt to find mechanisms that will help govern without worsening conflict. However, these incentives are not limited to divided societies. In many European countries, political parties and interest groups have developed political systems that strive for consensus and inclusion of major actors in all big government decisions. These mechanisms are sometimes known as **consociational** arrangements, as discussed in the next "Insights" box.

consociational Systems that use formal mechanisms to coordinate different groups sharing access to power.

The debate about whether presidentialism or parliamentarism is "better" enters into this discussion of unstable coalitions and consociational arrangements. Note that in the next "Insights" box, by Arend Lijphart, the parliamentary systems are quite stable, while the presidential systems in Colombia and Lebanon have struggled more to prevent conflict. An argument in favor of parliamentarism holds that the flexible terms of office mean that a "crisis of government" does not become a "crisis of regime." That is, a government that fails and falls does not imperil the whole constitutional system. In a sense, Italy shows that. On the other hand, it is not clear that such instability in governments is desirable either. Certainly, the fixed terms of presidential systems at least theoretically provide the possibility that a government will adapt and respond to unpopular moves in time. Moreover, extreme instability in governments is likely to place many politicians in "permanent campaign" mode, which may compromise their focus on governing.

INSIGHTS

Consociational Democracy
by Arend Lijphart

This article shows that there are many ways for different groups and parties to share power in the executive branch, whether the system is parliamentary or presidential. In societies where reaching consensus is a priority and there are many political parties, one leading form of power sharing is the grand coalition cabinet that includes multiple parties. Another way to share power is for leading political elites to appoint powerful advisory councils and committees that reflect the interests of many major actors. Efforts such as these have featured in countries in central and northern Europe, such as the Netherlands, Austria, and Denmark. Presidential systems can find mechanisms for sharing power as well as parliamentary systems. At the time of Lijphart's writing, examples included agreements by the two leading parties to alternate the presidency in Colombia and between different religious groups to divide executive posts in Lebanon. This idea of consociational democracy suggests that executives need not be "winner-take-all" if there are other factors that push toward social consensus.

Arend Lijphart, "Consociational Democracy," World Politics 21, No. 2 (1969): 207–225.

Of course, whether a country has stability or instability in its governments depends on several features of political institutions: political parties and how they operate; electoral rules; rules about votes of no confidence; and whether party leaders can "discipline" the members of a party's rank and file. In addition, history and social realities contribute to these outcomes, and only further comparative research can point to the factors that cause these different outcomes.

THINKING COMPARATIVELY

KEY METHODOLOGICAL TOOL

Case Selection

One main lesson from the debate over presidentialism versus parliamentarism is the importance of case selection for comparisons. Cases are often (but not necessarily) countries that we select to study, and selecting the right ones is key. The disadvantages of presidentialism for democracy certainly appear to be greater in countries that are lower-income and have been democracies for only a short time, as noted by Mainwaring and Shugart in the "Insights" box earlier in the chapter. To make a causal argument, it is important to understand the background conditions that shape the likelihood of democracy.

Beyond the American and British Models

The United Kingdom and the United States are emblematic examples of the two basic ways of structuring the executive in a democracy, and the comparison of the parliamentary and presidential systems has become a central debate in the comparative study of executives. In both of these countries, democracy has persisted for a long time; and indeed both countries have increasingly extended the franchise and other democratic rights to more people over time. These two emblematic cases serve to show that both presidential and parliamentary systems are compatible with democracy, if social conditions are conducive.

As the chapter suggests, however, looking only at these two cases will tell us little about the variety of types of executives, much less give us a full understanding of the merits of different systems. Apart from executives that follow the two basic forms—presidential and parliamentary—there are hybrids and other models that combine features of both. From France to India to Switzerland to Uruguay, countries around the world have a huge variety of executive structures beyond the American and British archetypes.

In fact, the United Kingdom and the United States themselves are not static with respect to how executive power works. The United Kingdom's form of parliamentarism has usually been winner-take-all for the winning party, but a coalition between two parties governed from 2010 to 2015. Comparative research can help us to explain how executive power can change over time within a country, and not just in the United Kingdom. Why do some Italian coalition governments last longer than others, if the rules that shape elections of the legislature and the executive remain the same? Similarly, presidentialism is expected by some to lead to more "winner-takes-all" politics, but these systems also divide and share power in different ways over time. Some American presidents have asserted greater executive control over other branches. Prominent examples include Abraham Lincoln in the Civil War and Franklin Delano Roosevelt in World War II. Other presidents have followed Congress more. The extent of executive power—and why it varies from time to time—is thus an open question even after 230 years in a country like the United States. As with parliamentarism, this question is not only for the American case but also applies in countries such as Nigeria.

Consider Table 10.5, which includes a basic summary of the executive structure for the twelve countries profiled in this book. You will note a diverse array of executive structures, with some countries sharing certain features in common. You may detect patterns in the presidential and parliamentary experiences of the countries, and you can select cases for further comparison. The comparative method allows researchers to analyze why countries developed the executive structures they did, or what the consequences of these structures have been. It is also possible to do a comparison over time within one country, along the lines suggested previously for the United Kingdom or the United States. Why have executive structures changed or remained static over time? This question could be asked for any number of countries, including France, Iran, Nigeria, or Russia. Considering what you may know about these countries from this table and from other chapters, can you suggest what might be good test cases for studying the causes and effects of executive structures?

Selecting the right cases for comparative study can make the difference between an effective analysis and a weaker one. While we have referred to the United Kingdom and the United States as emblematic examples of parliamentary and presidential systems, the selection of cases for further study only begins with acknowledging these two models. The best cases to select will depend on the question being asked. Considering Table 10.5, a question about why ceremonial presidents have lost some of their powers over time might best be addressed by looking at countries such as Germany, India, Japan, or the United Kingdom. On the other hand, a question about the partisan powers of directly elected presidents might be well suited to a comparison of countries in the Americas, such as Brazil, Mexico, and/or the United States. A question about the informal powers of heads of state or chief executives might be able to draw on any number of the countries in the table. Russia and France might make for a useful analysis of the causes or consequences of semi-presidential systems.

Executives do not operate in a vacuum. They are affected by other structures and institutions. The legislative branch of government is a most important example, but the institutions of federalism and constitutional authority discussed in the previous chapters matter as well. Political parties (discussed in chapter 11) are equally important. Moreover, features of certain executives, such as populism, are partially shaped by factors that lie beyond political institutions, such as high income inequality, low levels of public trust, and perhaps even culturally rooted styles of leadership. Much of the discussion in this chapter cannot be isolated from how legislatures, political parties, and other institutions operate, and, ultimately,

TABLE 10.5 **Comparing Cases**

Case	Executive Structure
Brazil	Directly elected president chosen by national popular vote. Runoff election held between top two vote getters if none receives a majority in first round. President has weak partisan powers, but can issue decrees.
China	Executive structure includes president as head of state and chief executive. Two other top positions—often held by president—are head of the single (Communist) party and head of military. Premier is head of government in legislature.
France	Semi-presidential system combines presidentialism and parliamentarism. President is directly elected and appoints prime minister, but this appointment must be approved by legislature and government depends on confidence of National Assembly. President has power to dissolve legislature.
Germany	Parliamentary system with chancellor as the chief minister chosen by lower house of parliament (Bundestag), often at the head of a governing coalition of multiple parties. Ceremonial president has relatively limited powers.
India	Parliamentary system in which prime minister is head of government chosen by lower house of parliament (Lok Sabha) and depends on confidence of this body. President is also chosen by legislature, but has relatively minor powers.
Iran	President is elected and has authority vis-à-vis legislature, but real power lies with Guardian Council of top clerics and Supreme Leader, also a cleric (*ayatollah*). Other councils (Expediency Council, Assembly of Experts) also wield power.
Japan	Parliamentary system in which prime minister is head of government chosen by parliament (Diet), and depends on confidence of lower chamber (House of Representatives). Emperor is ceremonial head of state.
Mexico	President is directly elected by popular vote; top vote-getter wins even if no majority is attained. No re-election is allowed. For decades up to 2000, presidents in the dominant PRI party picked successors by "pointing the finger" (*dedazo*).
Nigeria	President is directly elected in national popular vote, separate from legislature. Prior to 1999, military leaders often led executive after coups. Largest party prior to 2015 elections (PDP) attempted to alternate northern Muslims and southern Christians in executive posts.
Russia	President is directly elected head of state. President appoints prime minister (chairman) as head of government, subject to approval of the legislature (State Duma). Vladimir Putin has exerted considerable authority both as president and as prime minister.
United Kingdom	Prime minister is elected by House of Commons, the lower chamber of Parliament. Executive has strong powers to set agenda and pass legislation, largely due to partisan powers. Monarch is ceremonial head of state, with no real political power.
United States	Directly elected president chosen by electoral college. Executive powers are separate from and checked by legislature. President has veto power, but cannot dissolve legislature. President has relatively weak partisan powers over legislature.

from political society more broadly. The ways all of these features interact will shape how executives perform.

With the concepts and arguments developed here, you should be able to investigate other executive structures around the world and form your own hypotheses and comparative arguments about them. There is much research to be done about the relative powers of executives in political systems and the consequences of these. This suggests that executive power will for a long time demand further study in countries around the world.

Chapter Summary

Concepts

- Executive branches execute and administer the laws proposed by legislatures in representative democracies.
- In non-democratic or authoritarian regimes, executives will often have a great deal of power.

Types

- Executives can be structured in two main ways—parliamentary and presidential—though there are also executives that combine features of both.
- The United Kingdom is the original and most famous example of a parliamentary system, and the British model is known as the Westminster model.
- Presidential regimes predominate in the Americas and in Africa, including in the United States.
- Like many other countries, France, Russia, and China combine some aspects of parliamentarism and some aspects of presidentialism.

- Executives have formal pow_____ powers that come from infl_____ other informal powers assoc_____ position of the executive.

Causes and Effects

- There is a debate about whether parliamentarism is better for democracy than presidentialism, because parliamentarism should lead to fewer outsiders and less radicalism, and it allows legislatures to remove unpopular executives.
- Presidential systems are most prevalent in lower-income regions and parliamentarism in Europe, so the advantage of parliamentarism may be due to other factors.
- Powerful executives have been associated with both centralization and populism, but also with promoting economic development.
- Parliamentary systems can operate in many ways and may have relatively stable or unstable governments.

Thinking It Through

1. Consider the "Insights" boxes on Linz and on Mainwaring and Shugart. Note that Mainwaring and Shugart disagree with only one of Linz's five theoretical arguments against presidentialism. What theoretical arguments can you offer defending presidentialism on the other criteria?
2. Considering the experiences of other countries described in this chapter and in Part VI, are there any institutional features you would advocate the United States should adopt? Why?
3. Do you think populism is possible under parliamentary rule? Why or why not?
4. We reproduce Table 10.2 here. Imagine yourself as the leader of each of the different parties and that you are interested in having an influence on government policy. What other parties would you approach in an attempt to form a coalition, and what would be your ideal coalition in each case? Why?

5. Consider Table 10.2 again. Identify the possible coalitions following the various criteria for coalition formation:
   a. Minimum winning
   b. Minimum connected winning
   c. Minimum size
   d. Minimum number of parties
   e. Median party
   f. Minimum range

TABLE 10.2 Hypothetical Distribution of Seats in Parliament of Santa Gabriela

Party	XL	L	C	R	XR
Seats	30	7	21	27	15

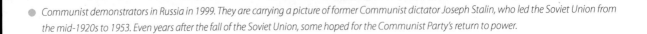

CHAPTER 11

Political Parties, Party Systems, and Interest Groups

● *Communist demonstrators in Russia in 1999. They are carrying a picture of former Communist dictator Joseph Stalin, who led the Soviet Union from the mid-1920s to 1953. Even years after the fall of the Soviet Union, some hoped for the Communist Party's return to power.*

Essa

Throughout the Cold War (1945–1991), the United States and the Soviet Union (or U.S.S.R.) were seen as political opposites in many ways. One of the key differences was between capitalist and communist economic systems, of course, but some of the other major differences were in how politics operated. The United States was a liberal democracy in which different political parties—mainly the Democrats and Republicans—competed for votes and in which citizens were free to join different interest groups to express their beliefs and opinions. The U.S.S.R. was a country dominated by a single party and state that claimed to be the sole legitimate representative of all the country's people. In political terms, the United States was a multiparty pluralist democracy, while the U.S.S.R. was a single-party totalitarian regime. This was a fundamental difference in the two countries. While most Americans believed that the right to freedom of association and to vote for multiple parties was based on individual rights, the leaders of the Soviet Union argued that the Communist Party alone—in collaboration with the state—could speak for the rights of workers.

The U.S.S.R. and its eventual collapse seemed to show that single-party rule was illegitimate, as were systems where the state plays a major role in deciding which organizations have a voice in politics. Yet many countries today remain dominated by a single party. As Map 11.1 shows, for example, the African continent has a large number of countries where a single party has been dominant since the 1990s—and many of these are even full-fledged democracies. The United States has only two major parties, far fewer than some other democracies in Europe and elsewhere that may have five or six major parties represented in the legislature. The number of major parties in a country thus continues to vary in the post–Cold War world.

Countries today also vary in how the state interacts with interest groups. Again, the U.S. model—in which different groups compete openly for influence in a "marketplace of ideas"—is not the only way a democracy can work. While few people openly advocate for Soviet-style authoritarian rule, many do advocate for much more structured interaction between major interest groups and the state than we see in the United States. For example, maybe major

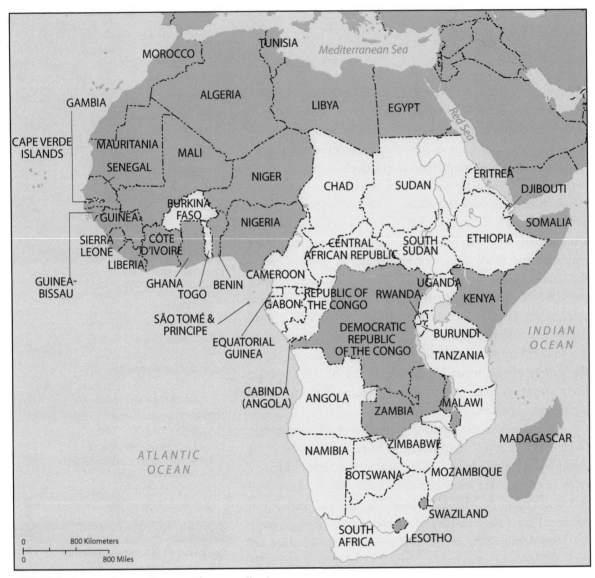

Map 11.1 Dominant-Party States in Africa (in yellow).

business groups and leading labor unions should have regular access to the top officials in government. Indeed, many people have argued that incorporating the preferences of all major groups into decision making will allow for more consensus and compromise, and in the end a better democracy. There is, in short, an ongoing debate about how the interests of citizens should be brought together and represented. That is the subject of this chapter.

· · · ·

Concepts

Most people will never be elected to or even run for public office, yet many will participate in politics in some way or another, beyond the act of voting. For example, many will be active in some type of organization with a political or public goal, whether to promote some cause or interest or just to support a candidate for public office. Politics is not exclusively the domain of elected officials and appointed judges; it also depends on citizens organizing and mobilizing to make their voices heard.

In considering institutions in the last several chapters, we have focused on the branches and structures of government itself: elected legislators and executives, as well as judges that may be elected or appointed. Yet many of the most important institutions that shape politics and policymaking in different countries are composed of groups of individuals who are not necessarily politicians themselves. Citizens do work in groups to have a profound impact on political life. They support their preferred candidates for public office and may join a political party to do so, and then they may volunteer time or contribute money to those parties. They also form interest groups that share common ideas or goals, and they may volunteer time or contribute money to those groups as well. In so doing, they bring together people with common interests in attempts to influence politics, policy, and the lawmaking process.

Political Parties

We consider **political parties** first because they are closely linked to the institutions of government we have examined so far. The main goal of political parties is the election of their candidates to public office. This goal is not only pragmatic but also ideological (related to ideas, ideals, and beliefs): parties want their elected representatives to make policy decisions the party supports.

Because elections channel party interests and ideas into the political process, parties must be responsive to what the electorate wants and demands. Being responsive does not mean, however, that they simply do or say whatever it takes to ensure the election of their candidates; rather, they are typically defined by a particular set of principles, which they try to stand by. Parties must often coordinate large numbers of voters around a common platform or set of ideas that the party takes as its basic principles. Platforms help parties distinguish themselves from other parties in competitive electoral environments. Because parties have a role in developing political ideas and in gathering voters around these ideas, it is often said that parties articulate and aggregate political interests.

political party A political organization that seeks to influence policy, typically by getting candidates and members elected or appointed to public office.

Party Systems

Countries have different numbers of major political parties, and the different patterns of party politics are called **party systems**. At one extreme, some authoritarian regimes outlaw political parties entirely, often on the grounds that they divide people into factions. Other countries are dominated by a single party, whether because voters prefer this party in reasonably free and fair elections, or because the dominant party has systematic advantages, or because other parties are outlawed. In most full democracies, the citizens' right to vote for different

party system Patterns of party politics characterized by the number of relevant parties in a country.

competing parties is seen as indispensable. Sometimes the result of exercising this right is a party system with two major competing parties, and sometimes it is a system with more than two major parties. We explore these different types in greater detail later in the chapter.

Interest Groups

The other main type of organization that has a major role in comparative politics is the **interest group**. These are organizations that make any number of demands in the political system on behalf of their constituents and members; such groups often have an active membership that pays dues to participate in and support the organization. Interest groups generally advocate for some policy position or political perspective, though they may not always seek to support specific candidates in elections. Like political parties, interest groups may endorse politicians in the hope of getting support for their causes, may contribute to or support campaigns, and so on; but they may also focus on petitioning or lobbying politicians to pass certain policies or laws. Interest groups want to see laws and policies that reflect their interests or views on the issues, so these groups often make public expressions of their political views.

Examples of interest groups are numerous and show the range of what such groups are and do. They include organizations of business owners and labor unions

interest groups Organizations that make demands in the political system on behalf of their constituents and members.

Members of the Mothers of the Plaza de Mayo marching in Buenos Aires, Argentina, in 2003, demand information about family members who were "disappeared" by the Argentine dictatorship between 1976 and 1983. While many interest groups correspond to economic interests, the Mothers are an example of an interest group based on shared commitments and beliefs about the rights of citizens.

of workers, for instance. In some circumstances, interest groups may be huge, as confederations of labor unions in some countries may represent a large fraction of all workers or households. Interest groups can also reflect the interests of a relatively smaller group of people and may serve different demographic groups. In the United States, prominent examples include the National Organization for Women (NOW), which advances causes on behalf of its many members, and the National Rifle Association (NRA), which represents the interests of many gun owners.

Some interest groups advocate on behalf of their members and also provide certain services or products to their members. For example, the AARP (formerly the American Association of Retired Persons) estimates that it has between 40 million and 50 million members, mostly senior citizens and people in or approaching retirement. It advocates on behalf of benefits for seniors, such as Social Security and Medicare, in addition to providing services such as supplemental health insurance for its members. The American Automobile Association (AAA) advocates on behalf of motorists and also provides members with travel discounts and access to tow truck services. For our purposes, interest groups are broadly defined but can include any organizations that advocate on behalf of a particular cause or in favor of certain legislation or policy.

The concept of interest groups is closely linked to the concepts of civil society and social movements. The first of these, **civil society** (also briefly discussed in chapter 3), is made up of many types of civic associations and social organizations, including volunteer organizations, neighborhood associations, and the like. Many of these are interest groups, though some may not take a political stand or advocate for a specific policy position, instead preferring to mobilize group members to take action on their own for improvement of their community, for instance. In chapter 12, we discuss another set of actors and organizations known as social movements, which are often distinct from interest groups in the ways they make their demands and the conditions under which they operate.

Interest groups and political parties are responsible for the functions of **interest articulation** and **interest aggregation**. Interest articulation is the process by which individuals and groups express their demands, needs, or wants in a political system. This is especially associated with interest groups, which publicly express their viewpoints, though parties do some interest articulation as well. Interest aggregation is especially associated with political parties and is the process by which individuals' preferences are brought together to make collective decisions. In most modern countries, it is not possible for those in government to govern by knowing each individual and taking his or her unique perspective into account. Rather, governments rely on citizens to express themselves collectively through mechanisms such as parties and interest groups. Citizens take on the responsibilities of making demands from their government, and doing so regularly involves the collective action of many people. Contrast what a single person working alone can achieve in politics with what people working together can achieve, and you will see the importance of interest aggregation and collective action.

civil society The set of organizations in civic life outside the state through which citizens associate and articulate and advance their interests; includes civic associations, interest groups, and volunteer organizations.

interest articulation The process by which political actors express their demands, needs, or wants in a political system, often through interest groups.

interest aggregation The process by which individuals' preferences are brought together to make collective decisions, often through political parties and the party system.

Types

Political parties can take on a variety of different forms, and political systems can have different numbers of parties. The number of different examples and types of interest groups are too numerous to mention, but we can outline how interest groups work in different countries by looking at something of great political importance: the structures of interest group representation.

Political Parties: Elite, Mass, and Catch-All Parties

For the average observer, the most distinguishing features of different political parties are the views they champion. For example, the Democrats and the Republicans in the United States can be distinguished by the parties' platforms on issues ranging from abortion to immigration to health care to taxes. Some parties are on the left of the economic spectrum, and others are on the right. In the United Kingdom, for instance, the Labour party has historically been associated with workers and unions, and the Conservative party is tied to business. Some parties—such as the "Green Party" in many countries—support environmental groups and are in turn supported by environmentalists. In many countries, there are parties that represent specific ethnic and racial groups, such as the Inkatha Freedom Party in South Africa that is strongly identified with the Zulu people. There are single-issue parties—such as those specifically opposed to immigration or favoring the legalization of marijuana—and there are even parties with no identifiable ideology whatsoever. Some obvious distinctions thus exist between political parties in the people they represent and the basis of their platforms.

Alongside differences in what the policies parties want, there are differences in how political parties are structured, an aspect that has changed over time. By most accounts, political parties first emerged as coalitions between individual legislators and politicians who shared common political interests and/or common beliefs; they formed their parties together to promote these common interests. These parties were known as **elite parties** because their membership and scope were largely restricted to a small number of political elites. By contrast, the twentieth century saw massive political mobilization of large numbers of citizens in larger parties. Communist and Socialist parties, for example, emerged as powerful groups in many countries; and they envisioned their structures as containing millions of workers and laborers who would pay dues, have membership cards, and become part of a broad movement. These came to be known as **mass parties**, and they were not restricted to leftist groups but became common among both fascists and more democratic groups attempting to include larger numbers of citizens in party politics. More recently, some major political parties have shifted to become **catch-all parties**, which are flexible on their ideological positions as they aim to attract support from a broad range of interest groups and voters.[1]

Proponents of the catch-all thesis have argued that when one party becomes successful as a catch-all party, it puts pressure on other parties to adopt the same approach and become more catch-all themselves.[2]

Other categories may exist as well, but this change over time describes many of the major shifts in the types of parties that exist. For some scholars, however, the distinctions between elite, mass, and catch-all parties can be overstated, because

elite parties Political parties in which membership and scope were largely restricted to a small number of political elites.

mass parties Parties consisting of large numbers of citizens as members and that undertake massive political mobilization.

catch-all parties Political parties that are flexible on their ideological positions and aim to attract support from a broad range of interest groups and voters.

all of these types are subject to common problems. One of the leading critiques of how parties operate—which we explore further in chapter 12, when we discuss social movements—was made by Robert Michels: it is that they tend to operate from the top down, having "oligarchical tendencies," regardless of their ideology and rhetoric.[3]

Party Systems: Dominant-Party, Two-Party, and Multiparty Systems

The many forms and structures of political parties shape the politics of different countries. But as important as the parties themselves are the party systems in which they operate. How politics plays out in a given country depends on which parties can get enough seats to have a strong voice and make a difference. A Green Party may be relatively inconsequential in policymaking if it never gains legislative seats because one or two other parties dominate, but it may affect policy more if it is routinely one of five or six parties that holds seats and is sought after as a partner in a governing coalition.

The most basic characteristic of party systems is how many major parties can be expected to compete meaningfully in elections to participate in government. Some countries have one party that is dominant, others have two, and yet others have more than two major parties that compete and jockey for position. Countries with only a single large party can be referred to as **dominant-party systems**. These occur in both authoritarian and quite democratic countries. Among democracies, South Africa is an example of a democratic country with a dominant party, the African National Congress (ANC). Many authoritarian regimes have dominant-party systems in which the governing party is in charge of politics. One particular

dominant-party system Party system in which a country contains only one large political party that predominates politically, often controlling the legislative and executive branches of government.

Cyril Ramaphosa, who in 2017 was elected leader of the African National Congress in South Africa, and became president in 2018

single-party system An authoritarian system in which parties besides the single dominant party are banned or disallowed.

type of system with a dominant party is the authoritarian **single-party system** in which parties besides the dominant one are banned or disallowed. Examples have come from around the world, including many communist regimes—especially during the Cold War, but also in countries such as China, North Korea, and Cuba today—as well as right-wing dictatorships such as Nazi Germany and right-leaning regimes in Asia—and many regimes with less clear ideologies in Africa up to the 1990s.[4]

Single-party regimes are often authoritarian, but they do have their defenders. Proponents of single-party regimes may say these are better suited to the needs of some countries. One such argument has been that liberal democracy is not equally well adapted to all cultures and regions of the world. This perspective was associated with, among others, Lee Kuan-Yew, the long-time prime minister of Singapore. Lee's argument in favor of single parties was based on a concept of "Asian values" that were argued to be distinct from "Western values," as noted in chapter 6.[5] This included an emphasis on community and deference to authority as opposed to a foremost emphasis on individual rights, and thus a cultural acceptance of dominant parties that may be most capable of delivering strong economic performance. A similar argument has been made more recently by the Chinese Communist Party.

Another argument has held that multiparty systems can be too divisive. This has featured prominently among leading parties in ethnically divided countries in Africa and countries divided along sectarian lines in the Middle East. In the African country of Uganda, for example, the president—who has been in power since 1986—long argued for "no-party" democracy on the grounds that political parties in Africa would simply split the vote along ethnic lines and give rise to tribalism or conflict. These lines of argument have been contested by many scholars, including African and Asian scholars who see the argument for dominant parties or restrictions on multiparty systems as an effort by elites to justify their own regime's continuation in power. Nonetheless, these examples feature prominently in discussions about whether dominant parties are appropriate or not.

While many single-party systems are not democratic, some democracies have single dominant parties as well. Examples include several countries in Africa

CASE IN CONTEXT

The Chinese Party System

PAGE 425

China is the most influential and important dominant-party system in the world today. The country is authoritarian and functions essentially as a single-party system. The various mechanisms for ensuring the dominance of the Communist Party are useful to understand, especially since the "Communist" in Communist Party has changed so dramatically with the many changes in China.

See the case study on the Chinese party system in Part VI, pp. 425–426. As you read it, keep in mind the following questions:

1. How has China's Communist Party developed and maintained its dominance?

2. What are some of the mechanisms it uses to maintain this system?

3. Do you find there to be any legitimate justifications for single-party rule, and on what does the Chinese Communist Party base its legitimacy?

PAGE 494

CASE IN CONTEXT
How Has Japan's Dominant Party Won for So Long?

Japan has been ranked as a free country by the independent organization Freedom House for every year since it began keeping track of democracy around the world. Yet for most of that period until 2009, Japan was dominated by the Liberal Democratic Party (LDP), and the LDP returned to dominance since 2012. How a dominant party can coexist with democracy is one of the key questions of Japanese politics.

See the case study on the Japanese party system in Part VI, pp. 494–495. As you read it, keep in mind the following questions:

1. What are the characteristics that distinguish a dominant-party system from a single-party system?
2. What accounts for the continued victories of the LDP over so many years?
3. Does the existence of repeated victories by the same party call democracy into question?

Japanese Prime Minister Shinzo Abe after another LDP electoral success in Fall 2017.

today, such as South Africa, which is dominated by the ANC. The major distinctions from the authoritarian regimes just discussed are that voting is relatively free and fair, and civil liberties are protected: it just happens that people elect and continue to re-elect the same party to govern, even though they could potentially make other choices. Some regimes have made the case that a single political party can encompass the many political debates in a country, but most observers in Western democracies argue that the right to choose from different parties (with their advocacy of different policies) is essential to democratic governance. A characteristic of dominant-party systems is a lack of competitiveness in national elections and, hence, a relatively certain outcome of those elections.

To many people living in advanced, industrialized democracies, the **two-party system** is more common and familiar than the dominant-party system. In two-party systems, there is a duopoly of power between two major parties that are seen as the main contenders for most major political offices. This duopoly usually

two-party system A political party system consisting of two significant parties that have a duopoly on opportunities to govern.

persists over multiple elections. The two major parties present different platforms, which often correspond to one more liberal and one more conservative party in terms of economic policy, though this is not always the main political distinction. Such a model can be seen in the United States with the Democrats and Republicans, for example, as well as in many other countries around the world. Until recently, another example would be Spain, with its left-leaning Socialist Workers' Party (*Partido Socialista*) and right-leaning People's Party (*Partido Popular*); but in recent years, other Spanish parties, especially the populist party *Podemos*, have emerged. As we discuss in the "Causes and Effects" section, the way elections work is a major factor in determining whether a democracy will have a two-party system. In particular, the presence of single-member districts in legislative elections (as discussed in chapter 9) contributes to the likelihood of two-party systems for reasons we explore later.

multiparty system A political party system consisting of more than two significant parties that have opportunities to govern.

Two-party systems may seem natural and stable to those who have lived their lives in them, but they are not the most common party system in a democracy. In fact, most democracies have more than two major parties. The scholar Arend Lijphart studied thirty-six long-standing democracies and found that **multiparty** systems with three or more parties were the norm in about half of these countries.[6] Some multiparty systems have two parties that are strongest year in and year out, but these compete against a handful of other parties that regularly win enough seats to influence the outcomes of elections. Whereas in two-party systems, one party or the other will typically win a given election by taking a majority of seats, multiparty systems quite often result in no party winning a majority because the vote is divided more ways. To recall some of the lessons of chapters 9 and 10, a no-majority win often happens when legislative elections are based on proportional representation, and it often results in executive branches that function with a coalition of multiple parties.

fragmentation (of party system) Contrasting with concentration, the extent to which political power and representation in a party system are characterized by relatively large numbers of relatively small parties.

concentration (of party system) Contrasting with fragmentation, the extent to which political power and representation in a party system are characterized by relatively small numbers of relatively large parties.

Within these different categories—dominant-party, two-party, and multiparty systems—the specific nature of the party system can still vary from case to case. For instance, a multiparty system can be considered relatively **fragmented**, with many small parties, or relatively coherent or **concentrated**, with a small number of larger parties.[7] Two-party systems may see frequent alternation of power between the two or may see one party that is stronger and wins more often for an extended period. Dominant-party systems may feature different degrees of dominance by the leading party, ranging from single-party regimes with 100 percent of the seats in a legislature to systems where a dominant party wins elections routinely but narrowly.

Counting the actual number of parties that matter is more challenging than it might sound. To determine the nature of a party system, assume one wants to consider only relatively serious parties that have a chance of winning a reasonable number of seats. As a hypothetical example, take the United States House of Representatives with its 435 members. If 434 were from the Republicans and Democrats, while one representative was a member of the Socialist Party or Libertarian Party, would it be reasonable to call this a multiparty system? Most would say it would remain a two-party system. What about the United Kingdom, where the Conservative and Labour parties have long been the two largest, but the Liberal Democrats sometimes command a substantial fraction of the seats

CASE IN CONTEXT
Consensus-Based Politics in Germany
PAGE 454

Germany, like many other countries, is a multiparty system in which it is common for a relatively small number of parties to wield most of the influence. The Social Democratic Party (SDP) and the Christian Democratic Union (CDU) have been the major players there for years, though several other smaller parties have retained influence and sometimes been in government coalitions.

See the case study on the German party system in Part VI, pp. 454–455. As you read it, keep in mind the following questions:

1. What factors might account for Germany having more than two important parties?
2. What does a multiparty system imply for the quality of governance?
3. Thinking back to chapter 9, what sorts of coalitions would you expect to emerge in a multiparty system, and which parties would you expect to enter coalitions together?

that is enough to prevent either of the other two from winning a majority? After the 2010 General Election, the Liberal Democrats were a necessary part of the Conservative-led governing coalition; but their electoral results have declined, and they are no longer part of the governing coalition. Was this a two-party or multiparty system? Could we call it a "two-and-a-half"-party system?

Perhaps surprisingly, the answer for many political scientists is yes, we can say a country has "two-and-a-half" major parties. There are a number of metrics used to measure the **effective number of parties**, and these are designed to get at how many major parties of consequence a system contains.[8] Another way to look at this issue is how fractionalized or fragmented a party system is, on a range between a perfectly concentrated, dominant-party system to a perfectly fragmented system in which each seat goes to a different party.[9]

We will not explore the formulas in great detail here, but a simple example can illustrate the difference between a more fragmented and a more concentrated party system. Table 11.1 gives some fictional countries, for which any resemblance to actual countries is coincidental. The middle columns reflect the proportion of legislative seats won by each of the five largest parties in descending order. So P1 is the largest party, and P5 is the smallest (if there is a P5; these systems have different numbers of parties). The formula for the effective number of parties takes the proportion of seats held by each party, squares each one, and adds these squares together. The result is a fraction, and the calculation then takes the inverse. So a system with two parties each having 50 percent of the seats would have $1/[(0.50)^2 + (0.50)^2] = 2$ as the effective number of parties. And a system with three parties each having 33.3 percent of the seats would have $1/[(0.333)^2 + (0.333)^2 + (0.333)^2] = 3$ as the effective number of parties. This formula generates the results in Table 11.1 for less clear-cut cases.

The effective number of parties calculated by this formula should be close to what one might expect from the proportions of seats won. There is a clear dominant-party system and a clear two-party system, even if other tiny parties compete in those two countries. In Duopolia, the two small parties matter more

effective number of parties A measure designed to capture the number of meaningful parties in a party system that weights the number of parties represented by their size.

TABLE 11.1 **Number of Parties**

	Proportion of Legislative Seats Won (%)					
Country	P1	P2	P3	P4	P5	Effective No. of Parties
People's Republic of Monopolia	99	1				1.02
United States of Duopolia	49	48	2	1		2.12
United Realm	40	40	20			2.78
Federation of Fragmentia	27	25	17	16	15	4.71
Coalitiastan	38	35	9	9	9	3.43

Note: P = Party.

than the small one in Monopolia because they can tip the balance of power from P1 to P2 or vice-versa. The United Realm looks like it should have about "two-and-a-half" or three parties: the third-largest is only half as powerful as the two largest parties, but it is also big enough to tip the balance of power once again. Fragmentia, meanwhile, has close to five meaningful parties, but we probably would not think of P3, P4, or P5 as being quite as important as P1 or P2. By contrast, Coalitiastan has two clear leading parties, and it looks more concentrated than Fragmentia, so it has a smaller effective number of parties but will also require governing coalitions for as long as this distribution of parties stands. As a result, it is more than just a two-party system. In fact, P3, P4, and P5 are all important, and either of the big parties would need at least two of them to make a coalition government; the effective number of parties is more than three.

A final aspect of party systems to consider is **party system institutionalization**, or the extent to which a party system is stable and remains so over time. It has several aspects.[10] One is the persistence and electoral success of parties over time. Do parties endure for a long time once they are established, or do they come and go, with old ones fading away and new parties emerging constantly? A more volatile party system is less institutionalized. Another aspect is the degree to which parties have stable ideologies, programs, or platforms. This relates to the question of whether a party is coherent and cohesive or not.[11] An additional aspect is the degree to which parties operate as institutions, as opposed to being focused on certain individuals. Where a party system is more institutionalized, a party's name has significance: it is likely to be around and to be associated with a certain set of ideas. By contrast, in less institutionalized party systems, a party's name (or brand) is less meaningful and more often subject to the whims of personalistic leaders.

Party systems are often more institutionalized in longstanding democracies and less institutionalized in less-established democracies, but this is not always the case. In France's well-established democracy, for example, the main party of the center-right has gone through many changes in name and structure in recent years, even as the right has won the presidency regularly for nearly twenty years. Conversely, other countries, such as Chile and Ghana, developed institutionalized party systems soon after becoming democracies in the 1990s.[12] Despite these exceptions, the tendency persists: substantial breakdowns of party system institutionalization are more common in fragile democracies, as the case of Russia showed from the 1990s to the authoritarian era dominated by President Vladimir Putin (see the next Case in Context box "Personalism and the Party System in Russia").

Interest Groups: Pluralism and Corporatism

Like political parties, interest groups are distinguished from one another by the specific ideas they hold as well as by their structure, which varies widely. Apart from the forms and functions of specific groups, there are also different patterns of how interest group representation works in politics. The most fundamental distinction is between countries where interest groups compete openly to influence government decision making—a pattern known as pluralism—and countries where there is a formal, established relationship between certain interest groups and state power: a pattern known as corporatism. The distinctions between the two forms of interest group representation can be summarized in terms of whether specific interest groups are identified as having a monopoly on the representation of a specific interest; both forms are ideal types, and many countries have had some mixture of the two forms.

Pluralism reflects the idea that interest groups compete in a "marketplace of ideas." Countries that have pluralist politics will often have large numbers of competing groups that strive to affect policy. Under a pure form of pluralism, none of these groups would have privileged access to the government or receive preferential treatment, even if they would sometimes win and sometimes lose arguments about what the government should do.

Under **corporatism**, on the other hand, certain major groups are designated as representatives of certain interests, and these have a more structured interaction with the government in power and with the state's administration (or bureaucracy). Advocates of corporatism sometimes assert that people "naturally" belong to certain interest groups—such as workers belonging to labor unions and business owners belonging to business organizations—and that organizing on this basis is thus important for political representation. Rather than an open competition among all interest groups, corporatist arrangements seek consensus based on regular interactions between designated groups and the state. Using the same root word as corporatism, one way to understand the phenomenon is that there is "incorporation" of specific interest groups into the decision-making structures of the state.[13]

Since many of the major decisions made in politics are about economics and economic policy, the most important interest groups in corporatist countries are usually organizations representative of business and those representative of labor. Business and organized labor confer with the state on issues such as wages, benefits, taxes, and policy toward foreign capital and international competition. At the national level, the bargaining between groups often involves **peak organizations**, which are top-level associations that bring together many like-minded organizations. Examples include national labor federations made up of many different unions, or business organizations representing many different companies or industries.

pluralism A system of interest group representation in which groups compete openly to influence government decisions and public policy and in which specific groups do not have official preferential access to decision making.

corporatism A system of interest group representation in which certain major groups are officially designated as representatives of certain interests and have a more structured interaction with the government in power and with the state's administration.

peak organization Top associations, such as labor federations and large business organizations, that represent common interests by bringing together many like-minded organizations.

CASE IN CONTEXT
Personalism and the Party System in Russia

PAGE 539

Russia illustrates the challenge and importance of party system institutionalization. The country has seen some major parties come and go while a single individual, Vladimir Putin, has accumulated more power. Even in the absence of single-party rule, a poorly institutionalized party system can facilitate authoritarian tendencies.

See the case study on the Russian party system in Part VI, pp. 539–540. As you read it, keep in mind the following questions:

1. Building on the observations of previous chapters, how do weak institutions in Russia facilitate the rise of a "strong man" like Putin?
2. What might account for the poorly institutionalized party system in Russia?
3. Which seems to have come first, the weak party system or the personalism of Putin?

Corporatism has been a major force in contemporary history. In fact, some have argued that the twentieth century was the "century of corporatism."[14] Over the course of the twentieth century, corporatism was influential across much of Europe and Latin America and in many parts of Asia and Africa. The geographic and historical reach of this phenomenon has led to many variants: some are more social and some more pro-market liberal in Europe, while some forms in Latin American have been more state led, others more led by labor, and yet others more inclusive of the peasantry.[15] Some analysts have advocated corporatism as a relatively successful and harmonious way to promote economic growth and development, while others have criticized it as favoring specific groups over individual rights and lending itself to exclusionary politics. Countries such as Mexico may provide evidence for either perspective.

INSIGHTS

Who Governs? Democracy and Power in an American City
by Robert Dahl

Dahl's work focuses on one city—New Haven, Connecticut—and documents how different sets of actors and interests have important roles in governing. It has become one of the foundational descriptions of how pluralism operates. Dahl finds that different aspects of policy and political decisions were influenced by quite different groups and not always by the same elites. The book argues that New Haven's social elite was not the same as its economic elite, and that the business community was not always the dominant player in decisions. Elected politicians wielded considerable power in shaping policy, but they were also responsive to interest groups and needed to sell their programs to voters at large. Among interest groups, the sets of actors that predominated differed. Dahl examined decisions about urban planning and development and education, as well as nominations for public office. While the business sector played a role in some aspects of decision making, the popularly elected mayor and appointed boards wielded significant influence. Dahl's work on the functioning and benefits of pluralism countered the view held by others that in a capitalist democracy, a single "power elite" dominates across the many aspects and areas of politics.[16] Some critics continue to argue that pluralist accounts understate the extent to which economic elites can shape politics.

Robert Dahl, Who Governs? Democracy and Power in an American City. *New Haven, CT: Yale University Press, 1961.*

CASE IN CONTEXT

The PRI and Corporatism in Mexico

PAGE 509

As noted in chapter 7, Mexico was once called "The Perfect Dictatorship." Part of the reason for this name was the ability of Mexico's PRI party to bring major interest groups under its banner. These included labor, business, and the state bureaucracy, as well as the armed forces. This broad-based form of corporatism made it very difficult for competitors to defeat the PRI, and the party governed uninterrupted from the 1930s to 2000.

See the case study on the Mexican party system in Part VI, pp. 509–510. As you read it, keep in mind the following questions:

1. How are interest group representation and the party system related in this case, and how did corporatism relate to the ability of the dominant party to retain power?
2. How was Mexican corporatism distinct from many other versions of corporatism?
3. What were some of the causes of the end of the prolonged period of single-party dominance in Mexico, and how do these relate to the corporatism that prevailed for so long?

It is possible to distinguish between more authoritarian and more democratic forms of corporatism.[17] In quite a few instances, corporatism has overlapped with dominant-party systems, and a single leading party undertakes the coordination of different interest groups. This has often been an authoritarian form of corporatism in which interest-group participation is highly regulated by the state. Versions of these circumstances can be seen in many single-party countries. Indeed, corporatism was especially noteworthy for part of the twentieth century as a strategy by which central governments could co-opt different groups, bringing them into the political system on terms set by the state or the leading party. Incorporated groups included workers and unions, business elites, peasants or farmers, and even students. This featured prominently in Latin American countries, for instance, where one of the leading examples is Mexico between the late 1930s and 2000 (see the Case in Context box, "The PRI and Corporatism in Mexico").

Corporatism happened under authoritarian regimes and dominant-party regimes in many cases; but it is not limited to dominant- or single-party systems, and in fact has featured prominently in many of Europe's multiparty systems, especially in social-democratic countries of northern Europe. This can be seen as a more democratic form of corporatism. Many of the political systems of northern Europe are consensus based and have been multiparty regimes in which corporatism has played a major role. We now examine the pros and cons of pluralism and corporatism.

Causes and Effects: Why Do Party Systems Emerge, and What Effects Do They Have?

There are many questions about cause and effect in the study of parties, party systems, and interest groups. Why do different party systems emerge? Why do some countries have greater party system institutionalization than others? Why do certain types of parties—such as Communist parties, social democratic parties, conservative pro-business parties, or fascist parties—emerge in some countries and not others? Why do some interest groups have greater impact in some places than others? We cannot address all of these here, but we encourage further research on this range of questions. We will focus on three questions: the causes of the emergence of party systems, the consequences of party systems on the quality of representation, and the consequences of different patterns of interest-group representation.

Party Systems and Representation

Party systems are closely related to how political representation works. In some senses, party systems are both a consequence of how representation works and a cause of how representation takes shape. We examine both sides briefly.

WHAT FACTORS SHAPE PARTY SYSTEMS?

Looking first at what causes different types of party systems to emerge, one main factor is the type of electoral system, as we discussed in chapter 9. Recall that a basic distinction among types of electoral systems is between district systems and proportional representation systems; in their simplest forms, the former has legislative elections within the geographic subdivisions of a country, while the latter allocates legislative seats according to the overall proportions of seats parties win in an election.[18] What would these different types of systems imply for whether two-party or multiparty systems will emerge?

In democracies that have single-member district systems, there is a pronounced tendency for two-party systems to emerge and persist, while multiparty systems are quite common in countries that use proportional representation. For many analysts, the electoral system itself seems to have an impact on the number of viable parties that emerge. The logic behind this is intuitive. Proportional representation, for example, is designed to accurately reflect the overall distribution of preferences for different parties, and the result is often many different parties winning legislative seats. District-based representation, by contrast, often favors relatively large parties that can win a plurality of votes and tends to result in fewer seats for small parties. The consequence of district systems as opposed to proportional representation was most famously associated with Maurice Duverger (see the "Insights" box on his book *Les Partis Politiques* [*Political Parties*]).

Of course, the electoral system is not the only cause of political party systems. Geographical, historical, social, and economic factors are also important; and certain political traditions or political cultures may lend themselves to more concentrated party systems or more fragmented systems.[19] Africa, for example, was home to a large number of one-party states from the 1960s to 1980s. The reason may be seen as geographical, because tendencies persist in certain regions of the world (with countries sometimes modeling their political systems on those of their neighbors), or as economic, because it applies to countries with certain levels of income. These tendencies in regions and in individual countries are also historical and social. Again in Africa, the historical context for many one-party regimes was the struggle for independence and freedom under a leading nationalist party, a phenomenon that can still be seen today with dominant parties even in relatively democratic countries such as South Africa and Tanzania. Yet we must also be careful not to generalize about regions, as we show in the "Thinking

Les Partis Politiques [Political Parties]
by Maurice Duverger

Duverger's work in this book and related articles discusses numerous features of political parties and party systems, but it is most renowned for its establishment of "Duverger's Law." The core result of this finding was that two-party systems tend to emerge where elections are based on a simple plurality vote. The logic is that parties on each side of the political spectrum (left and right) will recognize that they cannot afford to split the vote in a plurality system. To use an example, if six parties on the right each got 10 percent of the vote, their combined total would be 60 percent, but individually they would lose to the Communists if the Communists had, say, 40 percent of the vote. The parties on the right would therefore work together—to collaborate on selecting candidates and even to merge—to compete with the party on the other side. The left would do this as well, leading to a two-party system. By contrast, Duverger finds that proportional representation is conducive to multiparty systems because it encourages small parties; and other systems, such as runoff elections, have effects in between these two extremes. Duverger suggests that this is a virtual law of political life and is true in so many cases that it is often seen as one of the strongest findings in political science, though he and others do note occasional exceptions.

Maurice Duverger, Les Partis Politiques [Political Parties]. Paris: A. Colin, 1951.

Comparatively" section at the end of the chapter: all continents have mixes of party systems. Africa has two-party systems and fragmented multiparty systems as well as dominant-party systems, and the same goes for other continents.

A leading argument linking social and other political factors to the party system holds that which parties emerge and where parties stand depend largely on ideology and the beliefs of the citizens. This may sound obvious, but it is quite distinct from the argument that the electoral rules and other institutions determine what party systems will look like. Parties often have deep roots in an ideology or in a social base, and party systems will be shaped by the parties that emerge. A prominent example would be Communist parties around the world, which traditionally have had a strong ideological basis in Marxism and strong support

Parties and Party Systems: A Framework for Analysis
by Giovanni Sartori

In a major investigation of the origins, types, and functioning of different political parties, Sartori finds that different political party systems emerge due to differences in beliefs among groups in society and not just due to the type of electoral system used. He outlines a wide range of types of party systems that can be classified as one-party systems, two-party systems, and more limited and extreme forms of party "pluralism," with three to five or more than five parties. In Sartori's argument, ideological distance and "segmentation" between groups is a key variable. Where groups in society are rather close together on the political spectrum, a multiparty system emerges with a relatively small number of parties. By contrast, where people are deeply divided and fragmented by ideology, a more fractious multiparty system is likely to emerge. In one-party countries, Sartori sees several types of party systems that range from totalitarian regimes (like Nazi Germany or Soviet communism) to more pragmatic dominant parties; the "ideological intensity" of the dominant party again matters in the specific party system that takes shape.

Giovanni Sartori, Parties and Party Systems: A Framework for Analysis. New York: Cambridge University Press, 1976.

among members of the working class and labor unions (as well as intellectuals in some cases). The presence and strength of Communist parties on the left has also had the effect of shaping other parties on the right of the political spectrum. The link between the working class, Marxist ideology, and Communist parties shows that party systems are shaped not only by the electoral system but also by social realities and political culture. Other examples include Christian Democratic parties or other parties on the center-right in Europe and the Americas that are influenced by a degree of social conservatism. A prominent scholar who has worked on ideology and party systems is Giovanni Sartori.

HOW DO PARTY SYSTEMS SHAPE POLITICAL OUTCOMES?

In addition to being caused by various factors, party systems are themselves causes of political outcomes. In particular, they may shape whether politics are very moderate or more extreme. For example, one consequence of a two-party system under many circumstances is the tendency of the major parties to try to attract the hypothetical **median voter,** or the voter who is theoretically in the middle of the distribution of voters in a certain geographic area. If we assume for the moment that voters in a given district can be put on a spectrum from most liberal on the left to most conservative on the right, as in Figure 11.1, then the voter in the exact center is shown by the vertical line. In this example, the Conservative party will generally capture the votes to the right of center, and the Liberal party will capture the votes to the left of center. If both the Liberals and the Conservatives are strategic and rational, they will each do what they must to capture the entire half of the electorate that is on their side—plus a little more. Since the Liberals know that people on the far left are unlikely to vote Conservative, and the Conservatives know that people on the far right are unlikely to vote Liberal, the best strategy becomes trying to capture those represented by the median voter—the person right in the middle. In this case, the median voter is the swing voter (i.e., one who could go either way), and winning the swing vote is the key to getting a majority: 50 percent of the vote plus at least one person. The major parties will therefore propose policies that appeal to the median voter. Visually, you can think of this as the parties positioning their platforms where the vertical line is: both become relatively moderate and centrist.

median voter The voter who is theoretically exactly in the middle of the distribution of voters.

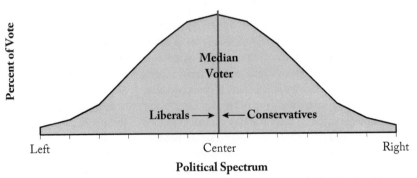

Figure 11.1 Voter Distribution and Political Party Strategy with the Median Voter.

Of course, parties must try to attract the median voter while still retaining the votes of the ideologues at their respective ends of the political spectrum. Yet those more extreme voters on the far left and far right also make their own rational calculations. They know that not voting for the large party on their side (when there are multiple parties on a side) may help tip the election to the other side. A very conservative voter, for example, has a reason to vote for a moderate Conservative party if doing so helps prevent the Liberal party from winning instead. This thinking discourages relatively extreme voters from voting for smaller and more extreme parties. Voters thus engage in **strategic voting**, or voting in ways that do not reflect their ideal position to prevent outcomes they think are even worse. Since swing voters are often the deciding factor in winning or losing an election, some analysts suggest that single-member districts and two-party systems draw candidates and voters alike toward the middle, in the direction of the median voter, therefore having a moderating impact on representation.

strategic voting The practice of voting in a way that does not reflect one's ideal preference to prevent electoral outcomes one thinks are worse, such as voting for a second-best candidate one thinks can reasonably win.

There are several reasons why a system with two dominant parties might not lead to moderation, however. In particular, one could imagine that the distribution of voters does not always look like what is shown in Figure 11.1. Perhaps it looks more like that in Figure 11.2, which is known as a bimodal distribution because it has two peaks: many voters who are fairly Liberal, and many voters who are fairly Conservative, but not many in the center or at either extreme. In this case, the Liberals might try to maximize their vote by offering platforms that appeal to voters on the left, about where the vertical line is shown. The Conservatives will do the same on the right. If they failed to do this, they would open themselves up to defeat by another new party that could claim more of the vote by positioning themselves strategically. For instance, if this country had exactly one hundred people, and the Liberals went for the center, then another party—call them the Left Party—could position themselves just to the left of the Liberals, and the Conservatives would position themselves just to the right of the Liberals. The Conservatives would sweep the vote on the right, and the Left would take the vote to the left.

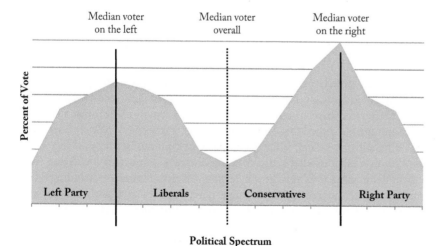

Figure 11.2 Bimodal Voter Distribution.

INSIGHTS   An Economic Theory of Democracy
by Anthony Downs

This work by Downs is known especially for its theorizing about the median voter. The book develops the logic noted in this section in which parties rationally adjust their platforms to appeal to the median voter. Downs does not, however, assume that all politics consists of appealing to the median voter. He notes the limitations to the median voter theorem and the conditions under which it will not hold. This work built on research in economics and political strategy and applied it to the study of elections and political parties. In addition to developing the specific median voter model, this form of research inspired much of the work in rational choice theory. According to this theory, most behavior of individuals or groups (such as political parties and interest groups) can be explained by actors attempting to maximize their economic or political gains.

Anthony Downs, An Economic Theory of Democracy. *New York: Harper Collins, 1957.*

The Liberals would thus be committing political suicide. More likely is that the Liberals and Conservatives would each go for the vertical line to capture the votes on their respective sides. In this case, a system with two dominant parties leads to polarization, not moderation.

We return to this example in questions at the end of the chapter. For now, though, you can imagine how such a political system might develop into a more competitive multiparty system, as new parties might emerge in an attempt to position themselves strategically. The key point is that this distribution of voters within this party system does not result in the two big parties going for the median voter if the parties are strategic and rational.

There are other reasons, too, why parties might not attempt to appeal to the median voter. Imagine a case where voters cannot simply be arrayed along a spectrum from right to left, and you will see that predicting their voting is much more complex.[20] Since people care about many different issues, such as religious or moral issues and the economy, it is not always clear what the left and the right will mean. Finally, it has been observed in the American context, for example, that there are essentially "safe seats" in many districts because certain parts of the country are quite liberal or quite conservative; parties as a whole are therefore less likely to move toward the center because each legislator responds to his or her own district's voters.[21]

It should be noted that the ways dominant-party and single-party regimes shape political outcomes is not as straightforward as it might seem; even in these systems, there are debates about the quality of representation. For over a century, many communists claimed that only a Communist Party could truly represent and speak on behalf of workers,[22] but the collapse of communism around the world seemed to discredit this alternative to the multiparty democracy associated with liberal individualism.[23] Similarly, single-party fascist regimes—including Nazi Germany—led to an association of single-party regimes with authoritarian and even totalitarian rule. The result was that prominent theories about democracy often assume multiparty competition to be the best form of political representation.[24] This did not, however, mean that all multiparty systems extend the principle of competition in the same way in the realm of interest groups. In multiparty democracies, interest groups may operate in relatively open competition under pluralism or in a more structured fashion using corporatist arrangements, as we discuss next.

Interest Groups and Representation

Pluralism and corporatism are each advocated by their respective proponents on the basis that they provide better and more effective representation. To start with pluralism, this theory describes how interest groups work in some countries, but it is also a theory about how interests *should* operate. Some theorists called "pluralists" openly advocate that this is the best approach for a government system: the government should listen to the competing arguments laid out by different social interests and mediate between them. This is closely linked to classical liberal ideas about democratic politics, which hold that government decisions should be based on respect for individual liberties. In the case of pluralism, an emphasis is on the equal opportunity for different groups to influence politics, with guarantees of rights to organize and assemble to petition the government. For instance, if workers in a given industry are seeking a nationwide increase in the minimum wage, but industrial capitalists fear this will harm profits and economic growth, it becomes the role of elected representatives to listen to the populace, process its demands, and respond accordingly.[25]

Yet there are also major critiques of the pluralist model. As is the case with presidentialism and other institutions in previous chapters, the model used in the United States is not presumed to be the best model for all democracies. The critique of pluralism can take at least two major forms that relate to interest groups. The first is that pluralism in essence gets bogged down due to the actions of special interest groups and is an inefficient way to make good decisions about effective policy.

One of the main challenges to assumptions about pluralism is the existence of the **collective action problem**. People do not necessarily participate in interest groups for all the beliefs they support. Rather, they consider the benefits of their own action and the costs of undertaking the action. This is especially true with public goods, where if a benefit for a certain person is small, then joining an interest group may not be worth the effort. The same is true if costs to the individual of joining the group are high. Achieving a desired result is rarely due to one more person's action, so people have an incentive to be free-riders: let others do the work and hope to participate in the collective reward.

The other critique of pluralism comes from the perspective that corporatism does a better job at integrating interests and ensuring the structured representation of major groups in society. The argument draws on a variety of empirical examples, ranging from economic growth successes in East Asia to harmonious social policies in Europe. In terms of economic growth, the likes of Japan and South Korea from the 1950s to 1980s were countries where scholars found that close linkages between the state and top business organizations (as well as labor) were important in setting national goals and reaching high levels of economic performance.[26] Meanwhile, in the context of long-established democracies in Europe, corporatist arrangements were argued to be a political solution that gave rise to consensus-based decision making. This was reputed to be useful in reducing

collective action The pursuit of political or social goals by members of a group.

INSIGHTS

The Logic of Collective Action: Public Goods and the Theory of Groups *and* The Rise and Decline of Nations: Economic Growth, Stagflation, and Social Rigidities
by Mancur Olson

Olson's early book, *The Logic of Collective Action*, is the basis of the field of study in how collective action occurs, as outlined previously. The logic of collective action applies to interest groups as well as other actors we discuss in chapter 12. Rather than assuming people will easily form interest groups to press for public demands, Olson noted the free-rider dilemma and the tendency of interest groups to function better when they provide specific benefits for their members. This is a critique of pluralism in the sense that interest groups cannot be assumed to form to represent diverse interests. Olson extended this critique in his later work, *The Rise and Decline of Nations* in which he argued that the accumulation of special interests over time slows down economic growth because governments respond to politically powerful actors rather than to the needs of the economy. One empirical example is striking: the United Kingdom, a victor in World War II, did worse economically for several decades than Germany and Japan, which lost the war. Olson attributes this to the continuity of special interests in the United Kingdom as contrasted with the elimination of many of those interests for the defeated countries.

Mancur Olson, The Logic of Collective Action: Public Goods and the Theory of Groups. *Cambridge, MA: Harvard University Press, 1965; and* The Rise and Decline of Nations: Economic Growth, Stagflation, and Social Rigidities. *New Haven, CT: Yale University Press, 1982.*

social tensions and in ensuring a relative political harmony between business and labor, since both were regularly integrated into political decision making.

Of course, corporatism can also have major disadvantages. It does not reflect an "arms-length" relationship between interest groups and the state. This raises the question about how the groups that participate in corporatist arrangements are chosen, and how this representation changes over time. What seems like useful collaboration at certain moments can seem like "crony capitalism" and favoritism at others. In addition, the structured relationships may favor some of the institutions that are powerful in the status quo. For example, who is more truly representative of American industry, Google or General Motors? While this may seem a minor issue, corporatism may tend to "calcify" relations between the state and certain actors. If the automobile industry and auto workers have close relationships with the state for decades, will they combine to support the General Motors of the world rather than the Googles? While corporatism has been seen by its proponents as facilitating policymaking, it may also be prone to make real reform more difficult. The economies of Europe in the 1990s faced a major challenge to economic growth as reform of labor and business relations became difficult. In situations where reform is needed, corporatist arrangements can impede economic adjustments by protecting the status quo for many workers and businesses.

Corporatism also tends to result in decision making by a relatively small number of elites, specifically those in government, business, and labor. In a more severe form, corporatism has been highly exclusionary and authoritarian. The idea of corporatism even contributed to totalitarian ideologies such as the early years of German Nazism in the 1930s and the period of Italian Fascism under Benito Mussolini from the 1920s to the 1940s. For many, this association with totalitarian regimes discredited corporatism as corporatist arrangements infringed individual rights in favor of groups and the state; totalitarian regimes provide the worst examples of this. To return to the school of thought favoring pluralism, James Madison and the authors of *The Federalist Papers* (1787/1961) argued that it is natural for people to form different "factions," and the best way to prevent any one of these from becoming too powerful and tyrannical was to encourage these different groups to compete. The debate between pluralism and corporatism is thus unresolved, with different empirical cases offering different lessons. Indeed, the debate may not be fully resolved because many countries feature elements of both models.

Party Systems in Sub-Saharan Africa

As noted at the beginning of the chapter, different political party systems have flourished at different times and in different places around the world. The United States has been a relatively stable two-party system for decades, while some countries in Western Europe have often had multiparty regimes, where parties that perform the best in elections often do not win a majority and thus need to make coalitions with other parties to govern.

Meanwhile, single-party and dominant-party regimes have rarely been found in Western Europe since the end of World War II, but have been much more common in Asia, the Middle East, occasionally in Latin America, and in Eastern Europe under Soviet rule. Africa is a final region of the world that has seen many single-party and dominant-party regimes. One may be tempted to reach some relatively straightforward conclusions about what shapes party systems: poorer regions and developing countries are likelier to have single-party systems. Leaders in Africa and scholars alike have at different times offered justifications and explanations for single-party dominance. The same has held in countries from Syria to Singapore. One might even hear (or make) arguments that these regions are culturally or politically unprepared for multiparty democracy.

However, one should not jump to such a conclusion. To take Africa as an example, the continent also has a number of other types of party systems, from multiparty competition in the tiny country of Benin to a stable two-party system in Ghana. Moreover, there is a major distinction between the quite democratic dominant-party systems in countries like Botswana or South Africa and the more authoritarian dominant-party systems in countries like Cameroon or Ethiopia.

This illustrates the importance of avoiding excessive generalizations that do not match up with the evidence. In particular, it is advisable to engage in a bit of "comparative checking" so as not to generalize from one or two cases. Indeed, the particular cases that do not fit the generalization would be useful ones to examine further, if they are "deviant cases" as noted in chapters 2 and 5.

There are several causes and consequences of different party systems and patterns of interest-group representation, and this area is still the subject of considerable research and debate. While it seems that electoral institutions do help shape party systems, these systems are also influenced by ideologies, cultures,

THINKING COMPARATIVELY

KEY METHODOLOGICAL TOOLS

Comparative Checking

Comparative politics will often be based on the examination of a small number of case studies. This allows the analyst to dig into the case in depth, but it also has the disadvantage of giving a "small sample size" of just a couple of cases. Unless one uses quantitative and statistical methods, one often does not subject the hypothesis to full testing across all the possible cases. A danger of this can be making inferences too quickly without keeping sight of whether the argument applies beyond the cases in the study. Ideally, we would like to make arguments that apply to more than just the cases we examine. A partial solution to this challenge is comparative checking, or relatively brief glances at other cases to see if the argument holds up or has obvious flaws. This does not mean doing a full study of more and more cases but rather briefly reviewing other cases to see if one's conclusions seem to work at a glance. In layman's terms, a bit of comparative checking can help tell if an argument "passes the sniff test." If so, one has greater confidence in the argument; if not, the comparative

THINKING
COMPARATIVELY

KEY METHODOLOGICAL TOOLS
(continued)

check can be useful in forcing the
analyst to revisit the argument to see
if it can be modified to make it more
applicable to other cases.

economics, histories, and many other factors. Similar factors also shape how plural or corporatist the state's relationship to interest groups is. In turn, the patterns that emerge in party systems and interest group representation affect what citizens do and how they vote and participate in politics. This chapter has thus begun to give a bigger role in politics to those citizens who may never consider themselves politicians. This focus on the actions and behaviors of groups of citizens will continue into our next chapters, where we look at the many ways people identify politically and express their interests and beliefs through different kinds of action.

Chapter Summary

Concepts

- Political parties are organizations that have the aim of nominating candidates and electing representatives to public office.
- Political party systems are different patterns in the number of major political parties and in the patterns of party politics.
- Interest groups are organizations that advocate for some policy perspective or political goal, and they may or may not support specific candidates.

Types

- Political parties have taken forms including elite parties, mass parties, and contemporary catch-all parties.
- Political party systems can be divided into dominant-party systems, two-party systems, and multiparty systems.
- Interest groups can compete with one another for political influence in a system known as pluralism, or they may

have more structured interactions with the state under corporatism.

Causes and Effects

- Political party systems are shaped by electoral rules as well as other factors such as ideology and social and historical influences.
- The political party system itself also affects politics by helping to determine whether major parties tend toward the center of the political spectrum or not.
- Pluralism and corporatism have both been argued by their respective advocates to result in stronger democracy.

Thinking Comparatively

- Certain types of party systems may be more prevalent in some regions of the world, but it is important to engage in comparative checking to avoid overgeneralizing.

Thinking It Through

1. Look back at the voter distributions in Figures 11.1 and 11.2. Imagine you are trying to start a third party called the Right Party to compete with the Liberals and Conservatives in a country that those two parties have dominated politically. You believe that the Conservatives are too moderate and would ideally like to position yourself as far to the right as possible. Strategically, what would be your best position on the political spectrum, keeping in mind that the height of the peaks in the figures reflects how many voters there are on that part of the spectrum? Would your strategy be different for Figure 11.1 as opposed to Figure 11.2?

2. Building on the last question, now place yourself in the position of the Conservatives. What would prevent parties from beating you? If the Right Party comes along, how could you prevent this other party from taking your place? What argument would you make to voters about why they should vote for you rather than a party that is farther out on the political spectrum?

3. The United States has long been associated with the ideas of pluralism. Are there any advantages that could be had from developing greater corporatist arrangements? What are some of the advantages that would be expected by advocates of corporatism in democratic societies? What would you expect to be the drawbacks of any such changes?

4. Thinking back to some of the comparative strategies from previous chapters, how would you determine whether a certain country's party system is shaped more by its electoral rules or by other factors? How can comparison help you answer this question, and what sorts of comparisons might you set up to distinguish between different causal factors?

5. This chapter has addressed both party systems and interest groups. Do you find one of these sorts of groups responds to the other more? Which set of organizations do you find more important in shaping how politics operates and what governments do? If you were given $100 that you were required to donate to either a party or interest group, which would you donate to and why?

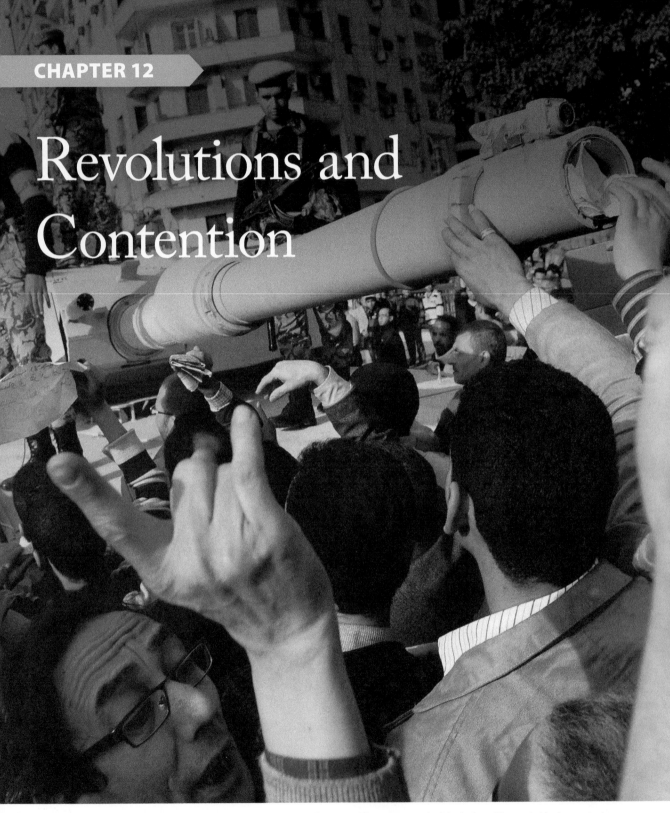

CHAPTER 12

Revolutions and Contention

Egyptian protestors restrain a tank in early 2011 during the "Arab Spring" uprisings. Throughout much of the Arab world, remarkable changes took place in this period and have continued since. Where will these revolutions—and their aftermath—lead?

In late 2010, in a small town in Tunisia, a policewoman insulted a street vendor and toppled his produce cart. This would normally have been an event of limited consequence, but what happened next made history. The vendor, Mohamed Bouazizi, went to the municipal offices to register his complaint. Rebuffed there, he set himself on fire in the street. He is believed to have done so to protest his humiliation and his lack of opportunity. His act galvanized protestors, seeming to indicate to many that "enough is enough" when it came to poor governance and a lack of social opportunities. The symbolic tactic of self-immolation would be repeated in Tunisia and elsewhere. Faced with continuous street protests, the Tunisian government—which did not use overwhelming force—fell by mid-January, not long after Bouazizi died of his injuries. By the end of the month, protests had spread to other Arab countries, notably Egypt. There, the state began to make strong efforts to quell protests. On one hand, it repressed protesters, among other places in the famous gathering point of Tahrir Square in Cairo. On the other hand, it became clear that there were limits to the army's willingness to repress the population. By mid-February 2011, the government of Hosni Mubarak had fallen. The uprisings then spread to other parts of the Arab world.

For years, many analysts and citizens had been skeptical about democratic opening and regime change in this region, and yet suddenly the air was full of excitement and a sense of opportunity. Outcomes have varied dramatically. Tunisia and Egypt ousted their old governments largely as a result of protests. Despite some serious challenges, the former case remains democratic. In the latter, post-revolutionary elections led to Mohammed Morsi and the Muslim Brotherhood briefly holding power, before they were displaced by a military coup in July 2013. Libya witnessed a NATO-supported insurgency that eventually dislodged the Qaddafi regime. Syria harshly cracked down on protestors, followed by insurgency, partial state failure, the de facto control of some parts of its territory by the Islamic State of Iraq and Syria (ISIS), intervention by multiple foreign powers, and humanitarian disaster.

Saudi Arabia has been mostly quiet (though at the time of this writing, there are stirrings of reform inside the regime). This process and these varied outcomes are in need of explanation. Why is this happening at all? Why in a "wave"?[1] Finally, why has contention been successful in some countries, less successful in others, non-existent in others, and led to massive destabilization and ongoing loss of life in a couple countries, above all Syria? Revolutions and related efforts remain an important part of the contemporary world, and they are among the most interesting and consequential subjects in comparative politics.

· · ·

Concepts

revolution A form of collective action in which some large-scale, structural change is either attempted or accomplished.

Students of comparative politics ask many questions about dramatic events like social movements and **revolutions**. Why do some instances of collective action achieve their apparent objectives while others do not? How do individuals and groups select different strategies and tactics for the pursuit of their interests? Why are some conflicts "reformist" and others "revolutionary"? Why are some violent and others peaceful? In shedding light on these and other questions, comparative political analysis can help to influence policy choices for governments and social movement organizers.

contention The name, most associated with scholars like Sidney Tarrow and Charles Tilly, referring to the pursuit of collective goods largely outside of formal political institutions.

Conflict is a near constant of political life because politics involves disputes over resources. These include not only material resources, such as housing, food, consumer goods, and access to services like medical care, but also less tangible goods like *status* and *power*.[2] All modern societies distribute resources unequally, though they vary considerably in the extent and form of this inequality. Politics can be viewed as an arena in which resources are distributed and one in which conflict takes place over *how* they are distributed. In this chapter, we consider some of the many forms that such conflict takes. Social scientists interested in studying conflict often refer to it as "**contention**."[3] They refer to the joint efforts of individuals to bring about a preferred outcome as "**collective action**."

collective action The name given by social scientists to joint efforts of individuals and groups to bring about a shared, preferred outcome.

What Is "Contention"?

formal institutions Institutions that are governed by formal rules and typically linked to complex organizations like the state or corporations.

Conflict can be peaceful or violent, and can happen inside **formal institutions** or outside of them. In democratic societies, conflict is very often channeled through participation in electoral politics, via the institutions discussed in chapters 8 through 11. For example, people can organize themselves into political parties and try to use these parties to gain office and work through the executive or legislative branches of the state. Constitutions, discussed in chapter 8, can from this perspective be viewed as the formal rules in terms of which conflicts in a society will be resolved. Non-democratic societies also sometimes have formal channels through which some conflict can be negotiated. For example, local councils or committees, as well as governmental organizations like the police, might be responsive to citizen inquiries in some such societies. However, even in democratic societies, formal politics is sometimes not sufficient to deal with conflicts.

Revolutionary and Non-Revolutionary Contention

What political scientists call "contention" is behavior that occurs mostly outside of formal political channels.[4] The category includes **social movements, social revolutions, insurgencies** and **civil wars**, and even **terrorism**, as well as so-called "**everyday forms of resistance**"[5] in which people without the resources needed to organize themselves for ongoing mobilization nevertheless resist power. Scholars try to understand both the nature of these different sorts of conflict and their *causes*.

Perhaps the most fundamental difference is between forms of contention thought of as "revolutionary" and those that are not. Social scientists debate the exact definition of revolutions, as we will see, but most agree that they either attempt to or succeed in *radically transforming* social, political, and economic relationships. Of course, other forms of contention also involve efforts to make change, but often more gradually or less radically.

Types

Not all forms of contention are as transformative as the "great social revolutions" of France, Russia, and China. As we shall see in this section, scholars have defined several distinct *types* of revolution according to actors' aims or accomplishments, and there are many important but non-revolutionary forms of social change.

Social Movements

Social movements are in some ways the most normal of the major forms of contentious action and are considered a healthy part of **civil society**, at least in democracies.[6] As discussed in chapter 3, "civil society" can mean different things, but the main idea is that modern, democratic polities allow for citizens to come together and debate questions of value and policy, ideally free from state coercion.[7] Thus civil society can be found in media sources like newspapers and the Internet but also in public gatherings and interactions between citizens, and above all in the social networks that make this kind of deliberation sustainable. Social movement organizing takes place in this space: That is, social movements (perhaps to varying degrees) have a kind of *autonomy* from the state.[8]

Social movements take place when citizens *organize over time* in the pursuit of common purposes. For example, movements have sought the expansion of suffrage rights to women or members of minority groups or movements to advance "pro-life" or "pro-choice" positions. In contrast, regardless of its goals, a spontaneous protest like a riot or a mob is not a social movement. However, social movements might use public demonstrations as a *tactic*. What would make a string of public demonstrations a social movement, then, would be their common underlying coordination.[9] Some group or connected groups of people, linked via **social networks**, work together on common goals and use protest activity as a way of achieving those goals. Other tactics might include community organizing, "consciousness-raising," educational or propagandistic work, and political lobbying. Since social movement activity is the most "normal" of the major forms of contentious action, most modern democratic societies have essentially reserved a place for it alongside formal politics. Former social movement leaders often enter into formal politics, perhaps most famously Congressman John Lewis, who was the Chairman of the

social movements Ongoing, organized collective action oriented toward a goal of social change.

social revolutions Revolutions that dramatically change social structures.

insurgencies Contention with formalized military conflict.

civil wars Sustained military conflict between domestic actors.

terrorism In the context of revolutions or insurgencies, a tactic used by some participants that involves violence directed at nonmilitary targets.

everyday resistance Efforts to resist or obstruct authority that are not clearly organized over time, such as work stoppages, slowdowns, and sabotage.

civil society A space in society outside of the organization of the state in which citizens come together and organize themselves.

social networks Structures of social ties and connections among individuals.

Protestors in Canada object to the Trump Administration's "travel ban" in January, 2017.

Student Nonviolent Coordinating Committee in the civil rights movement in the 1960s. Increasingly, social movement activity of this sort is becoming *transnational*, crossing the boundaries of the nation-state and taking place in what some call global civil society.[10] Think, for example, of protests against globalization like the World Social Forum, the Occupy Movement, or the demonstrations of the Spanish *indignados* ("indignant ones," including many unemployed and underemployed Spanish youth). These sorts of protests often deliberately seek to cross national borders and to protest forces that do so as well.[11] Another example would be global protests against the early 2017 efforts of the Trump administration to prevent migrants from some Muslim-majority countries to enter the United States.[12]

organize The ongoing coordination of collective action in the pursuit of common purposes.

social movement organization An organization that has been created to help maintain and lead social movement activity over time.

Social movements **organize**, or coordinate collective action, in many different ways. Organizations created to serve the purposes of social movements are called **social movement organizations**. While we must be careful to remember that movements do not reduce to such organizations, social movement organizations are often very important. Some are more elite led, and others more grassroots.

For example, the Solidarity movement in the 1980s in Poland that eventually triumphed over the communists had clear leadership, while social-movement organizing against the authoritarian regime in Iran in 2009–2010 was more decentralized, communicating via technology like texting, Twitter, and Facebook, and even involving activists literally calling to one another from rooftops. Some are highly unified, meaning that most activists agree and that there is not a lot of competition between different groups with their own aims. Others are more factious and divided. What seems to be true in most cases is that, for social movement

CASE IN CONTEXT
Brazil's Landless Movement

PAGE 411

Brazil has often been considered a country of elite-led transitions and non-revolutionary change, but in fact it has generated important examples of contentious action. One of the most interesting cases is the Landless Workers Movement, which organized to try to make landownership more equal in this very unequal society.[13] The movement has had some notable success and influenced the left-leaning governments of Luiz Inácio Lula da Silva (2003–2010) and Dilma Rousseff (2011–2016).

See the case study of the Landless Workers Movement in the Brazil country materials in Part VI, p. 411. As you read it, keep in mind the following questions:

1. Why would Brazilian society have important populations interested in land reform?
2. How did Brazilian activists organize to put land reform on local and national agendas? What sorts of organizational structures did they create to facilitate collective action?
3. Why might some people be worried about the potential co-optation of this movement?

activity to endure, *some* organizing must take place, and this often means that some individuals will be set off from other participants as *leaders*.

Some argue that social movement activity (like party organizing) eventually runs up against the "**iron law of oligarchy**."[14] According to this theory, organizational leadership necessarily creates its own interests, and every movement creates a new elite. It is worth noting that these concerns apply not just to social movements but also to other forms of contention discussed later.

Imagine that you and your classmates create a social movement. Your goal is to organize in favor of curricular changes at your university (maybe you don't want to have to take comparative politics!). If there is broad consensus among the students, there are clear and available mechanisms for communication (maybe on social media); and, most important, if your goals are clear and minimal and do not encounter sharp resistance, relatively little organization and complex coordination will be necessary. But what if the goals are less clear, or can only be accomplished in stages, or meet with strong resistance by the administration? For example, you want to take comparative politics but students have a number of conflicting suggestions about how it should be taught. Then the movement will need to achieve ongoing **mobilization**. In *this* instance, some individuals are going to have to assume positions of leadership, making decisions about what sorts of statements to issue, how to frame arguments and goals, and when to call for demonstrations. Otherwise, individual protest actions will be easily dispersed.

Typically, some individuals form groups and present themselves as strategic leaders. Once such groups are formed, the groups themselves, as well as the leaders within them, often get a vested interest in the group and the movement. Perhaps you were relatively unknown before the formation of the social movement, but now you have lots of status and a thousand friends (at least on social media). Do you, upon the movement's accomplishing its goals, really want to go back to being that kid in the back of the classroom to whom nobody pays attention? Something

iron law of oligarchy The idea, developed by Robert Michels, that collective action always produces new elites.

mobilization The engagement of individuals and groups in sustained contention.

of the same applies in "real world" social movements: leaders and their organizations often acquire status and power. This does not always lead to conflict with the movement's goals, but it can.

Moreover, in most major social movements, alternative groups claim the mantle of leadership. This can be seen clearly in the most famous social movement in U.S. history, the civil rights movement of the 1950s and 1960s, in which there were periods of tension and cooperation between the Southern Christian Leadership Conference (SCLC) and the Student Nonviolent Coordinating Committee (SNCC), as well as pre-existing organizations like the National Association for the Advancement of Colored People (NAACP) and more "radical" organizations like the Nation of Islam and the Black Panther Party, which presented itself as leading a distinct, if related, "Black Power" movement.[15] The point is not that the leaders of these different groups pursued only their own interests—they were all clearly devoted to the expansion of civil rights, and each played an important role in the movement's achievements—but that the interests of organizations and their leaders *matter* in social movements.

At the same time, the American civil rights movement offers cautionary evidence against simply associating social movements with their most visible leaders and leading organizations. Grassroots participation and organization and on-the-ground improvising were common. To take just one example, the Montgomery Bus Boycott of 1955–1956 depended heavily on the ingenious improvisational work of hundreds or even thousands of Black citizens not identified as social movement

Leaders and activists involved in the Montgomery Bus Boycott, which took place in 1955 and 1956 in Alabama.

"leaders" in the conventional sense.[16] While social movement organization depends on official leaders, it also depends on the initiative of grassroots activists.

Most important, movements are dependent on ongoing mobilization. A great deal of work in recent years has been devoted to tracing and explaining different patterns of mobilization. Two of the most important political scientists in this area stress several key "mechanisms of mobilization," including "diffusion, brokerage, and new coordination."[17] This means that when mobilization happens successfully, it spreads, often "shifting scales" (moving from the local to the state, national, or global level or else moving in the other direction from more macro levels to local activism); it involves individuals, groups, and organizations bringing previously disconnected actors together in pursuit of common goals; and it involves novel efforts on the part of those actors to work together.[18] We can think of this set of concepts as breaking down some of the elements of what is happening when a social movement achieves mobilization. An important part of explaining any social movement is explaining how such steps are traversed.

Social movements shade into other forms of contention. Since social movement activity has been normalized in contemporary democracies,[19] it shades into electoral politics. Social movements also shade into revolutions. We can distinguish revolutions from social movements based on differences in *goals* or in *consequences*, though there is perhaps no single clear line separating the two categories. Social movements tend to be viewed as reformist. They aim to make a society live up to some of its idealized values, or to extend rights associated with citizenship to groups to which those rights were previously denied. In other words, social movements aim to affect important social change but not dramatic *structural transformation*. Revolutions, in contrast, aim at the latter.[20]

INSIGHTS | Twitter and Tear Gas: The Power and Fragility of Networked Protest
by Zeynep Tufekci

In this recent book, Tufekci draws on extensive observation of numerous contemporary protest movements—in the Middle East, the United States, and elsewhere—focusing on the impact of social media on contention in the twenty-first century. Social media has mixed effects on collective action, she argues. On one hand, new technologies can help people solve coordination problems more readily than they once could have done. It may be easier to plan and organize a large protest than it used to be, for example. On the other hand, this increasing ease has some hidden disadvantages. Tufekci argues that the very difficulty of organizing in earlier eras helped social movements to build sustained relationships among their participants. Moreover, the ongoing engagement required for sustained participation may have helped to keep participants committed to the cause. Furthermore, twenty-first century communication technology may foster decentralized organizational structure, which poses leadership challenges as movements try to develop long-term strategies. Additionally, Tufekci suggests that the social meaning of large-scale protests may have changed. On her account, the power of twentieth-century protests was to show that their organizers had high capability and should be listened to. But if technology dramatically lowers the cost of large demonstrations, then they less effectively demonstrate a movement's capacity. In short, the challenges and opportunities faced by activists have shifted considerably.

How do these notions square with your experiences with online communication? Are there ways that participants in social movement activity could mitigate the challenges that Tufekci identifies?

Zeynep Tufekci. 2017. *Twitter and Tear Gas: The Power and Fragility of Networked Protest.* New Haven, CT: Yale University Press.

Revolutions

Most commentators agree that revolutions must be relatively sudden and must achieve dramatic social and political change. Beyond this, revolutions are challenging to define.[21] They must be *transformative*, at least in intent, and, depending on how narrowly we want to define "revolutions," in their actual consequences.[22] Thus, a reform program is not a revolution, though failed reforms can help produce revolutions.[23] They must involve, like social movements, some level of popular *mobilization*.[24] Given the difficulty in defining "revolution," one common strategy has been to enumerate *types* of revolutions. One basic distinction is between so-called social revolutions and more limited political revolutions.[25]

Social revolutions transform social and political structures. In other words, they make *major* changes in how power and other resources are distributed in society. For thinkers like Karl Marx, social revolutions more specifically transform the distribution of material resources among groups. Contentious action, according to this line of thinking, is only a social revolution if the **class structure** is transformed. Thus the Russian Revolution of 1917 would be considered a social revolution because it used the power of the state to transform the basis of economic activity, for example, by "nationalizing" industries, redistributing land from wealthy landowners to collectives comprised of peasants, and so forth. The same is true of the French Revolution, which essentially destroyed France's nobility and the social system on which it rested.

class structure The ongoing and patterned relationships between "classes," typically understood as groups of individuals linked together by economic interest or activity.

Political revolutions are probably more common than social revolutions. A political revolution changes *political institutions* like the state rather than transforming social structures like a class system or the basic features of an economy. It is important to distinguish political revolutions from other kinds of political change, however. Electoral transference of power between parties or groups would not be considered a political revolution because it would not actually change political *structures*. For example, when a new president is elected in the United States, no new constitution is written, and no radical changes to the structure of government itself are made: the new administration seeks only to use those structures somewhat differently than its predecessor and, perhaps, to gradually reshape them. Likewise, incremental changes in political structures through, say, consecutive constitutional amendments, would not be considered a political revolution because political revolutions are typically understood to happen suddenly.

political revolutions Revolutions for which the main effect is to alter political institutions rather than social and economic structures.

We might also like to distinguish coups d'état, which often present themselves as "revolutions," from revolutions themselves. For some scholars, what would distinguish a **coup d'état** from a revolution is that the former is elite driven (typically by the military and sometimes in alliance with civilian actors), whereas revolutions necessarily involve the mobilization of some other important groups besides elite actors holding formal power. However, sometimes military leaders respond to ongoing public mobilization by staging a coup. In such instances, depending on the outcome, scholars are more likely to consider the event a revolution.[26]

coup d'état The use of force or threat of force, typically by the military or a coalition involving the military, to impose a non-electoral change of government.

Other examples of political revolutions might include some of the Latin American wars of independence in the early nineteenth century and the wave of anti-Soviet revolutions in Central and Eastern Europe in the late 1980s and early 1990s. In these latter cases, far-reaching political transformations took place, and the satellite states of the Soviet Union were replaced with democratic republics.

These changes, in turn, gave rise to economic changes that impacted the class structure in these societies: most political scientists would still consider these "political revolutions," however, since such changes were not *direct* aims or consequences of the revolutions in question.

A third possible type is **anti-colonial revolutions**.[27] Most of the social and political revolutions discussed so far in this chapter are made against the state and/or the groups controlling the state before the revolution. But sometimes groups are subject to the domination of powers beyond their own nations and states. In such cases, those powers are sometimes the ultimate targets of the revolution. For example, in the middle of the twentieth century, numerous anti-colonial revolutions, typically motivated by *nationalism*, were made against colonial powers as well as local interests perceived to serve them. Their articulated goal was the *removal* of these powers so that the nation could "rule itself" independently. Whether anti-colonial revolutions should be considered a type of political revolution or their own category is open to debate.

> **anti-colonial revolutions**
> Revolutions brought by subjugated populations against colonial powers, typically with the purpose of removing them so that the society in question can achieve independence.

The fact that formal colonialism is now relatively rare has not stopped all scholars from treating "**Third World Revolutions**" as a distinct type.[28] According to such scholars, inequalities in the developing world depend for their enforcement not just on the states, armies, and police of those states themselves but on an *international* networks of more powerful states (e.g., the United States, Western Europe, Japan, perhaps now China) and international organizations (e.g., the World Bank and the International Monetary Fund). "Third World Revolutions," these scholars argue, therefore have distinct dynamics and should be analyzed separately. Just the same, this category overlaps with the broader distinction between social and political revolutions. A given case might, for certain purposes, be classified as both a political revolution and a "Third World" or anti-colonial one.

> **Third-World revolutions** A concept developed by John Foran holding that revolutions in the developing world have special characteristics.

Revolutions may take place "from below" or "from above." All revolutions involve elite and **subaltern** actors (those lower down the social hierarchy or with less power and status before the revolution), but some are more and some less elite driven than others. This distinction is complicated by the fact that, as we will see in the "Causes and Effects" section, different *theories* of revolution place greater or

> **subaltern** Occupying lower rungs in a hierarchical system.

CASE IN CONTEXT
The French Revolution

PAGE 439

The French Revolution might be the most iconic and well-studied revolution, and leaders of other revolutions have often looked to its history for guidance.[29] While not all scholars consider it the first modern revolution, most agree that it was seen as novel and that it dramatically influenced and still shapes revolutionary patterns.

For more on the French Revolution, see the case study in Part VI, p. 439. As you read it, keep in mind the following questions:

1. Why would the French aristocracy help bring about reforms that ended up undermining its group interests?
2. Why do some scholars see this as a "bourgeois revolution"?
3. How do causal factors like state weakness, status-order problems, and new, potentially revolutionary, ideologies like nationalism interact in this case?

The French Revolution has been a model for many revolutionaries ever since it took place, and it is a case that has been considered by virtually all theorists of revolution.

lesser emphasis on elite and popular participation in *explaining* revolutions. In any case, the categories of revolutions "from below" or "from above" cut across some of the other types of revolutions discussed in this section. For example, India's anti-colonial resistance included both elite and subaltern actors.

Insurgencies and Civil Wars

Insurgencies can be thought of as enduring, organized, armed actors contesting the power of the state. Insurgencies in some instances shade into revolutions, and many insurgencies claim to be *making* revolutions. Insurgencies also sometimes look like social movements, and they can often be tied to social movements carried out by civilians. We might distinguish insurgencies from revolutions and social movements, however, by the degree of *formalization* of military conflict.[30] One notable recent work defines insurgents as "nonstate armed actors that use violence to reformulate or destroy the foundations of politics in a given country."[31] Often, conflicts between groups of insurgents or between insurgents and the state are classified as "civil wars."

Sometimes it is difficult to distinguish revolutions from the civil conflicts to which they give rise.[32] For example, consider the U.S. Civil War. If it had turned out differently, it might have been subsequently defined as a political revolution, even though the goals of the Confederacy were conservative: most centrally, the preservation of slavery. Consider further the wars of independence in Latin America in the early nineteenth century. These were revolutions, though they did not achieve major social-structural change. They were led at first by civilians who aimed to create independent republics and to make citizens where there was before only the monarchy and its subjects. However, because Spain used its army to attempt to put down these revolutions, the conflict took military form. Different actors in these societies took sides. A number of groups were loyal to the crown and fought *against* the revolutionaries, and thus we might even think of these conflicts as "civil wars."[33]

Insurgencies might develop when several conditions occur. First, a government that oppresses the residents of a given region, class, or group, or one that otherwise seriously fails to fulfill their expectations, is likely to generate the desire for insurgent activity. Second, a political system that does not allow other avenues for the expression and resolution of grievances increases the likelihood of insurgency. Third, a weak state increases the chances of an insurgency developing. For an insurgency to endure, neither the insurgents nor the state can be strong enough to decisively win. **Guerrilla tactics** are designed to produce just this sort of situation.[34] This often leads to protracted conflicts spanning years or even decades.

Terrorism

Definitions of terrorism have been controversial. We can define it as broadly as the use or threat of violence for political ends, or as narrowly as the use of violence by non-state actors against civilians for reducing civilian support for one or another official policy. Some would argue that terrorism should be seen as a tactic or strategy rather than a distinctive type of contentious action.[35] If we view terrorism in this way, then it really is nothing more than a potential tool of individuals and groups participating in the other forms of contention discussed in this chapter. Yet terrorism is a concept that appears more complex when closely examined. It necessarily involves violence, or at least the threat of violence. Definitions of terrorism must all take into account the following issues: (1) who or what is perpetrating the violence; (2) who or what is the target of the violence; and (3) the goals, purposes, or consequences of the violence. Not all definitions give the same answer to each of these questions.

The broadest definitions of terrorism say that it makes no difference who or what is carrying it out.[36] Most important, they accept that *states* can be terrorist actors. This was the original meaning of the concept, which derives from descriptions of the violence of the French Revolution.[37] States like the former Soviet Union, Nazi Germany, or Chile under Pinochet (1973–1990), in executing thousands of citizens (or many more in the former two cases) without fair trials, employing torture, and so forth, were doing essentially the same thing as nonstate actors like al Qaeda or would-be state actors like ISIS. Narrower definitions seek to exclude state-led terrorism, or at least to designate a separate category ("state terrorism") for it.[38] The rationale for this is that the causes of organized violence perpetrated by a state and by a group of clandestine civilians are likely to be very different even if, for the victims, the effects are the same.

Broad definitions of terrorism say that the judgment of whether a given case of violence is terrorism does not depend on the status or identity of its victims. Narrower definitions tend to exclude violence directed toward certain classes of victims. For example, some would not consider violence directed at military installations or at military personnel, particularly in wartime, to be terrorism.[39] The question gets a bit fuzzier when we consider other functionaries of the state: is violence carried out against the police terrorism? What about bombing a government

guerrilla tactics Military techniques designed to produce an ongoing stalemate, usually employed in situations of asymmetric military capability.

building, such as a post office, when it is closed after working hours? The narrowest definitions assert that a distinctive feature of terrorism is that its victims are themselves civilians.[40] Broad definitions, again, say that the "purposes" of the violence are unimportant, or that they cannot even be reliably known.[41] Narrower definitions claim that, to be terrorism, violence must be intended to instill fear in a population.[42] Still narrower definitions assert that this intended fear must be part of a calculated strategy to bring about some major political change.[43]

As with revolutions, terrorism can be divided into types. For example, some terrorism—sometimes called "demonstrative terrorism"—seeks to make a show for publicity purposes, while "destructive terrorism" is oriented more directly toward coercion.[44] As with all conceptualization, the best definition of terrorism depends on the sorts of questions that a scholar is asking. If we are interested in the question of how terrorism affects civilian victims, we might want to include violence carried out by both nonstate actors and states in our definition (unless we have reason to believe that *who* does the violence makes a difference in how it is experienced by its victims). If we are interested, though, in explaining common patterns of civilian-on-civilian violence in places like Sri Lanka, Pakistan, and Israel/Palestine, we might opt for a narrower definition. In such cases we would probably exclude violence carried out by a state.

Some prominent examples of contemporary terrorism involve "terror networks," (see Insights box for Marc Sageman, *Understanding Terror Networks*). This way of viewing the phenomenon focuses on the structure of the organizations committing terrorism, often noting their decentralized design and the implications of this for both their capacity to act and the ability of authorities to combat them. Much of the attention in scholarship on terror networks has been on organizations like al Qaeda and related groups.

INSIGHTS — Understanding Terror Networks
by Mark Sageman

Researchers like Marc Sageman take a "social networks" perspective on these groups, meaning that they look at terrorist linkages as webs of relationships rather than as formal organizations or as ideological groups. According to Sageman, at least through the mid-2000s, al Qaeda was part of a "small world network" characterized by "dense interconnectivity."[45] This contrasts sharply with the structure of a formal military organization or even a typical social movement, which tend to be more fixed in structure and hierarchical.

As Sageman suggests, this network structure of many contemporary terrorist groups has important implications. Governments opposing such groups cannot just take out "the leader," whose importance may be mostly symbolic, since others can easily take that leader's place. The decentralized nature of the organizations means multiple actions can be carried out simultaneously and that not all participants have full knowledge of plans or even of the group's structure. Of course this carries certain disadvantages for such groups as well, particularly inefficiency. However, it helps to explain the resilience and endurance of such networks. Some terrorist groups, such as ISIS, have in recent years been engaged in quasi-state-building activities, though these efforts now seem to have failed, and they will likely return to a more decentralized structure. In any case, analysts should recognize that terrorist groups may vary significantly in terms of their organizational and network structures.

Mark Sageman, Understanding Terror Networks. *Philadelphia: University of Pennsylvania Press, 2004.*

"Everyday Resistance"

Some groups resist when they *don't* have the organizational resources to mobilize into social movements or revolutions. Banditry and other forms of resistance defined by the broader society as "crime" can often be understood in this way.[46] Subaltern groups employ what the political scientist James Scott has called "weapons of the weak" to practice "everyday resistance."[47] For example, they might struggle *symbolically* against inequality by telling stories that challenge prevailing power relations. They might struggle against it *materially* by engaging in tactics like work stoppage, slowdowns, boycotts, or even sabotage (some of these behaviors can be used as *tactics* in social movement organizing as well, of course). As Scott describes such efforts, "they require little or no coordination or planning; they make use of implicit understandings and informal networks; they often represent a form of individual self-help; they typically avoid any direct, symbolic confrontation with authority."[48]

Why would some individuals and groups resist inequalities in this way, rather than through formal political participation *or* joining social movements and revolutions? The short answer is that there are often barriers to participation in these sorts of activities. Subaltern groups likely to engage in "everyday resistance" are also likely to be excluded from formal politics. This may because of an autocratic state or simply a matter of their distance from formal political life. For example, a centralized authoritarian state might deliberately not extend *any* political voice to the rural poor. Or political parties in an established democracy may discover that there are no gains to be made in catering to marginalized constituencies, either because their numbers aren't sufficient, or they aren't perceived to be likely to vote, or no other parties are competing for their support.

But why wouldn't such people just join social movements or revolutions? At first glance, it may seem harder to understand why someone would engage in "everyday resistance" rather than other forms of contentious politics. Here we need to step back and think about what makes mobilization *possible*. In the case of resistance against totalitarian regimes like the Nazis, the answer is clear: a repressive state makes organizing too dangerous. But what about other circumstances?

Let us consider a fictitious (though fairly realistic) scenario. The residents of a rural region in a developing country live in small villages. Each village family has its own plot of land. They have traditional privileges to cultivate this land but no formal property rights, and the villagers share in farming some commonly held land. Villages are themselves separated by great distances, dangerous roads, and harsh mountain conditions. The state, aiming to increase agricultural production for export, establishes a company that will oversee the cultivation of non-traditional crops, say, pineapples and bananas. However, rather than organizing workers into a formal labor force on industrial plantations, this company keeps workers in their traditional villages, paying them piecemeal for their production of bananas and pineapples, and questions their claims to use the land traditionally allotted to them. The residents of these distinct villages may define their interests in similar terms: under ideal circumstances, they might want to organize to remove the company, or to gain a voice in its decision making, or simply for higher wages. However, their ability to do so depends on their ability to transcend the **individualization** of their behavior and goals. They need some mechanism of *communication* through which

individualization The treatment of problems as linked to the interests of individuals rather than as issues of common concern or interest.

they can agree about these goals and coordinate their action. In the circumstances described, this becomes very difficult. Individuals without the resources to resist collectively often resist in the only ways that they can. If communication between individuals with common interests is difficult and restricted to the local level, direct resistance and obstruction of perceived opponents rather than social movements and revolutions to dislodge or replace them are likely.

Thinking About Contention: Summary

Scholars have a variety of views on how distinct these different types of contentious actions are. Some decades ago, most of them were placed under the general category of **collective behavior**.[49] But now we often try to treat them separately (though, admittedly, many social scientists continue to focus on common features of different types of collective action). For example, some scholars specialize in explaining social revolutions, and others social movements, assuming that these are distinct phenomena with distinct causes. Some argue, though, that we can treat them as existing on a *continuum* of contentious action.[50] These phenomena—and their causes—can overlap. We divide them here—as ideal types—for the sake of clarity; but in reality, the lines separating different forms of contention are not always so clear.[51] Moreover, an instance of collective action can change form, moving, say, from everyday resistance to social movement organizing to social revolution.

Causes and Effects: Why Do Revolutions Happen?

There are a number of theories that have been used to explain contentious action. Here for the sake of clarity, we focus on explanations of *revolutions* specifically. It is worth noting, however, that each of the explanatory strategies discussed here have been applied (with differing levels of success) to many of the forms of contentious action discussed previously. As you go over these explanatory theories, think about how they might be modified and applied to other forms of conflict. Note that some theories try to explain why revolutions and other forms of contention are attempted and others try to explain why they are successful, a subtle but important difference.

Relative Deprivation

According to our first theory, relative deprivation can change people's psychology and increase the demand for social transformation. This family of theories attempts to explain revolutions as abnormal *deviations* from a normal status quo. The theory assumes that societies tend toward a kind of "equilibrium" state in which conflict is normalized or settled through formal political channels. However, sometimes certain conditions—for example, rapid economic growth, efforts to reform the state, or the intervention of a foreign power—produce *disequilibrium* to which revolution serves as a response. This theory goes by different names (as it has been presented in different forms) such as **strain theory**;[52] the "collective behavior theory";[53] "social psychological theories";[54] or even the **Tocqueville effect**.[55] Most theories of this kind specify a *social psychological* mechanism linking

collective behavior A paradigm for understanding various forms of contention, popular for part of the twentieth century, which emphasized the irrational, social-psychological dynamics of protest.

strain theory A theory suggesting that major social change causes social "strain" or conflict that increases demand for revolution.

Tocqueville effect The name given by some scholars to Tocqueville's observation that changing relative status positions were an important factor in some groups participating in the French Revolution.

CASE IN CONTEXT
The Russian Revolution

PAGE 540

You likely are already aware of the Russian Revolution of 1917, sometimes called the Bolshevik Revolution, which brought into being the Soviet Union. This was one of the most consequential revolutions in history, in part because its success contributed to the polarization of global politics throughout much of the twentieth century. The Russian Revolution is interesting, though, not just because of its consequences, but because of how it stands in relation to revolutionary theory. It was a Marxist revolution that didn't strictly follow Marx's template, in particular because of innovations made by Russian Marxists, especially Vladimir Lenin. Among other things, Lenin emphasized that revolution was possible in Russia even though it had not experienced the most robust capitalist modernization. He also emphasized that a small "vanguard" of organizers could lead a revolution, which some think contradicts Marx's idea that major structural forces,

rather than leaders and groups, produce revolution (an idea with which Lenin did not entirely disagree).

To learn more about this process, see the case study in the Russian country profile materials in Part VI, p. 540–541. As you read it, keep in mind the following questions:

1. What were the major factors that increased the probability of revolution in Russia?
2. What is a "Leninist party," and how important were Lenin and the sort of organization he championed to the revolution's success? More generally, what does the Russian case tell us about how much individuals and leaders matter?
3. Could the Russian Revolution have produced a different outcome, or was Soviet authoritarianism inevitable given the conditions of Russian society at the time?

changes in the social order to the desire for rapid social transformation. People's lives are disrupted, this produces tension, and they resolve that tension through reconstructing society and its political institutions.

There are certain surprising things about many revolutions that "disequilibrium theory" can help to explain. Some major revolutions have taken place during or just after periods of economic *growth* or some other sort of improvement in the lives of one or another group.[56] This seems surprising, as we might intuitively expect groups that are *suffering* to be more inclined to revolutionary behavior (and sometimes they are!). However, this theory suggests that dramatic upward *and* downward mobility raise the possibility of revolutions because they upset established conventions and status relationships and open up the possibility of a potentially revolutionary group experiencing **relative deprivation**.[57]

relative deprivation The state of having or feeling that one has less than other members of one's reference group (including one's own group over time).

Resource Mobilization and Political Opportunities

Theories of relative deprivation focus on explaining *demand* for revolution. By contrast, "resource mobilization" theories assume frequent or even constant demand for social change, often treating it as a consequence of **absolute deprivation** rather than relative deprivation. Proponents of this theory argue that what matters in producing a revolution are **political opportunities** or events that allow potential revolutionaries to "mobilize resources."[58] The most important political opportunity for revolutions is **state breakdown**, when a state loses its ability to carry out its core functions and to stifle dissent.[59] Other political opportunities that might facilitate contentious action would include elite conflict, military or other coercive

absolute deprivation A condition of being deprived of resources below some given threshold, as distinguished from *relative* deprivation.

political opportunities The availability of political options to redress grievances.

state breakdown Dramatic decline in state capacity.

forces becoming discontent with the prevailing order, the opening of a political system, or the creation of new groups or communication technologies that facilitate organizing.[60]

Another set of resources for would-be revolutionaries are preexisting patterns of mobilization. If we return to our previous example in the "Everyday Resistance" discussion, we would say that the villages described there had a low potential for mobilization. This is why we would expect the villagers to engage in "everyday resistance" rather than organized strikes, social movement activity, or revolution. However, some other environments provide patterns of mobilization that can facilitate organizing and collective action and can thus be thought of as resources. For example, in a heavily industrialized society, factory workers labor closely together and may have a history of mobilization via union organizing. In this instance, there is a preexisting pattern of mobilization, as well as potential *organizational resources*, which can be put to new uses.

In an industrial setting, the relevant organizational resources would be the labor unions themselves. However, organizational resources can take many forms. What is key to all of them is that organizational resources allow some central coordination, which can be especially important in early mobilization: it is very difficult for any given leadership to remain in control of a revolutionary process for long. Along similar lines, social networks and media access are important resources facilitating contentious action.

Finally, political opportunity and resource mobilization theorists are interested in access to *material* resources. Revolutions, like any other collective behavior, need to be financed. This doesn't mean that they have formal budgets and actors responsible for balancing them, of course; but especially in those many revolutions in which violence is a key tactic, revolutionary actors need access to weapons, meeting places, and supplies for the combatants.

INSIGHTS | Political Order in Changing Societies *and* Why Men Rebel
by Samuel Huntington and Ted Gurr

Here we jointly consider two classic works by different political scientists who shared partially overlapping perspectives. Huntington argued that revolution takes place when the development of the political system lags behind economic and social modernization. This process creates demands for broader incorporation of groups that previously were not involved in political life, but institutions are not able to accommodate those demands. As he put it, "ascending or aspiring groups and rigid or inflexible institutions are the stuff of which revolutions are made."[61] Revolutions are most likely when, during modernization, the alienation of a frustrated and growing middle class takes place at the same time as the alienation of the rural poor.[62]

While Huntington placed less emphasis on social psychological aspects of this process, others, like Gurr, focused attention on relative deprivation as the linkage between modernization, aspiration, and dissent. In other words, revolutions are explained by the social psychology of status differences. Both of these theories owe a good deal to the classic works of Alexis de Tocqueville and Crane Brinton. Critics of this theory assert that it is overly general and that it assumes that consensus rather than conflict is the normal state of affairs in society.

Samuel Huntington, Political Order in Changing Societies. *New Haven, CT: Yale University Press, 1968; and Ted Gurr,* Why Men Rebel. *Princeton, NJ: Princeton University Press, 1970.*

CASE IN CONTEXT

The Chinese Revolution

PAGE 426

In some ways, the Chinese Revolution imitated the Russian Revolution described in the previous section. Like the Russian Revolution, it was based on Marxism, and many of its leaders hoped to create a world of equality and social harmony. However, it evidenced some major differences, perhaps the most important being the centrality of peasant participation (Marx thought that peasants were not revolutionary; but Mao Zedong felt that in Chinese circumstances, the peasants were the most important revolutionary class).

This revolution raises two key questions that interest us, and you can consider them further by looking at the case study in the China country profile materials in Part VI, pp. 426–427. Those questions are the following:

1. When did the Chinese Revolution begin or end? Was the overthrow of the Qing Dynasty in 1911 and the establishment of the republic its own revolution or just a part of the broader revolution that led to the establishment of the (Communist) People's Republic of China in 1949?

2. Why did the communists, rather than their opponents, the "nationalists," triumph in the Chinese Revolution? Does this case show us that organizational resources and practices are key to successful revolutions?

INSIGHTS

States and Social Revolutions: A Comparative Analysis of France, Russia, and China

by Theda Skocpol

Skocpol's theory is a *structuralist* theory of revolutions. This means that she aimed to explain social revolutions by focusing on social structures (most importantly, states and social classes) rather than individuals and their beliefs, goals, and strategies. In concentrating on her three main cases of France, Russia, and China, Skocpol found two necessary conditions that she argued together *cause* social revolution. First, state collapse, provoked by foreign conflict, creates the possibility of revolt, dividing elites. Second, certain conditions facilitate revolt among the rural poor. According to this theory, if the potential for peasant mobilization accompanies "state breakdown," successful revolution will take place. Skocpol's emphasis on state breakdown was anticipated by scholars like Alexis de Tocqueville and Crane Brinton and has been carried forward by Jack Goldstone and others.

Critics of this theory worry that it is too mechanistic, that it leaves out human agency, and that it pays little attention to culture and ideology.[63] Others suggest that it only applies to a limited range of cases.

Theda Skocpol, States and Social Revolutions: A Comparative Analysis of France, Russia, and China. *New York: Cambridge University Press, 1979.*

Rational Choice

The rational choice theory of revolutions says that to understand revolutions we need to understand the conditions under which it becomes rational for people to engage in collective action.[64] Proponents of the rational choice theory of contentious action, including revolution, sometimes present it as a complement to resource mobilization and/or political opportunity theory.[65] It shares the general assumption that conflict is endemic to society and that individuals rationally pursue their own interests. However, it pushes these assumptions much further.

This approach focuses on individuals' rational analysis of costs and benefits for participation in contentious action. According to this theory, states hold together when they prevent individuals from making the choice to pursue dissenting interests through alternative organizations.[66] When states are successful in doing this, they hold together because the majority of individuals—even if they do not like the state or the regime that controls it—judge that it would not be in their own interests to engage in protest activity or revolution. Indeed, according to this theory, this is the state of affairs most of the time: it is seldom rational for the individual to join organized protest activity.

For example, imagine that you are disaffected with life in your society, frustrated that you have to take so many courses to get a college degree, and irritated that those who hold power get to decide what will happen in class and can coerce you into reading certain books (like this one). You meet someone who suggests that you should join their revolutionary group that will seek to overturn the academic hierarchy by force and award PhDs to everyone on the grounds that they have already learned a lot in the "real world." For the sake of argument, imagine that you agree with the beliefs and goals of their group and that you would really like to see such a social revolution take place (but please don't contemplate this *too* seriously!).[67] You have basically two choices: you can join the revolutionary group, or you can choose not to join. There are also two basic possible outcomes: the revolution might succeed, or it might fail. Chances are, your participation really isn't going to make the difference. So if you think in purely rational terms and value only your own interests and goals, you will likely conclude that the right thing to do is to abstain from joining and to just hope that the revolution succeeds. If you join and it fails you will likely face sanctions, like jail time or worse. If you abstain and it fails, there will be no cost and no benefit. If you abstain and it succeeds, there will be no cost and all of the benefits. If you join and it succeeds, you will reap these same benefits but will have to bear the costs of risk and participation. Table 12.1 illustrates a basic scenario of this sort in which it would be irrational to join a revolution.

free-rider Someone who benefits from a collective or public good without contributing to it.

In other words, the rational, self-interested thing to do is to be a **free-rider**: not join and hope others do the job for you. This is how rational choice theory explains the relative strength of states and the weakness and infrequency of revolutions despite the fact that they believe conflict is endemic to society. Most people make the rational choice to *not* participate in revolutions most of the time, *even* those people who have an individual interest in dramatic social change.

Efforts to explain revolution and related activities, from this point of view, should focus on conditions that alter the rational calculus of interest of potential revolutionaries, as illustrated in Table 12.2.

If a situation becomes so polarized that there will likely be costs brought to bear on individuals by *both* sides (the state and a revolutionary group), this increases the price of abstention. If this is coupled with a perceived weakness of the

TABLE 12.1 Is It Rational to Join the Revolution?

	Participate	Do Not Participate
Revolution Succeeds	Share in collective benefits	Share in collective benefits
Revolution Fails	Face personal costs	Face no personal costs

TABLE 12.2 One Scenario in Which Many Actors May Judge It Rational to Join the Revolution

	Participate	Do Not Participate
Revolution Succeeds	Share in collective benefits but also receive personal favors and special access to resources because I am a "revolutionary."	Share in collective benefits, but no personal favors or special access to resources.
Revolution Fails	Low likelihood of personal costs because the state is weak and so many people are participating in the revolution.	My group may be targeted for reprisal, so I may face personal costs even though I didn't participate.

state, this will likely increase the willingness of a number of individuals to join the revolution. Another example is if the revolution's success seems fairly likely, and its current participants can plausibly promise rewards to participants, this will also likely increase participation.

Cultural or "Framing" Explanations

Proponents of cultural or "framing" theories argue that previous theories like resource mobilization or political opportunity theory pay insufficient attention to variation in how social movement and revolutionary actors think about their participation, and the *causal* impact of differences in how movements' and revolutions' targets are "framed."[68] Others argue that contention itself has changed, becoming more focused on cultural issues like "identity."[69] Many are interested in "new social movements" like the global feminist movement or movements that mobilize around ethnic identities, a subject to which we turn in chapter 14.[70]

The core idea of **framing** is that every type of social action we engage in takes place via "discourse" or "stories" that we tell about ourselves, our behavior, and its context.[71]

framing The way in which a given problem or situation is described and understood, with implications for how it might be addressed.

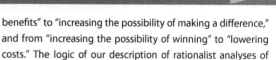

INSIGHTS	The Rebel's Dilemma
	by Mark Lichbach

Lichbach develops Mancur Olson's approach to the "logic of collective action" discussed in the last chapter, creating a powerful theory of dissent and pioneering the application of collective action theories to revolutions and related forms of contention. According to Lichbach, the analysis of revolutions and other forms of collective action involves discerning the *solution* to collective action problems arrived at in particular cases. In other words, we need to figure out the circumstances under which it would be rational for one or another individual to join in contention. Solutions run the gamut from "increasing benefits" to "increasing the possibility of making a difference," and from "increasing the possibility of winning" to "lowering costs." The logic of our description of rationalist analyses of revolutionary participation follows from his work in *The Rebel's Dilemma*.

Critics might charge that this theory makes the unrealistic assumption that human beings are always self-interested and rational. Some might also suggest that this approach is insufficiently attentive to social structures.

Mark Lichbach, The Rebel's Dilemma. Ann Arbor: University of Michigan Press, 1995.

Iran's Islamic Revolution and "Green Revolution"?

PAGE 481

In 1979, many observers were surprised when a revolution swept the Shah out of power in Iran, putting a religious regime in the place of his more secular dictatorship. Many revolutions seem to be "left wing," which in many people's minds means socialist and secular. Yet here was a conservative revolution that seemed, at least, to be countermodernizing. Of course, the reality on the ground was more complicated. The coalition that led to the Shah's downfall brought together many actors, from religious leaders like the Ayatollah Khomeini to secular Marxists to middle-class students. Just the same, the revolution has been taken by many to call into question existing theories of revolution.[72]

For more on the Iranian Revolution, see the case study in the Iran Country Profile materials in Part VI, p. 481. As you read it, keep in mind the following questions:

1. Was the Iranian Revolution "reactionary"? Is a religious revolution a contradiction in terms or just unusual when judged against the background of modern European revolutions?

2. What caused the Iranian revolution? How important were religious ideas? Does the Iranian Revolution enhance the plausibility of cultural/framing theories of revolution?

3. Why did this revolution take place in Iran but not in other Islamic countries at the time, like Egypt or Saudi Arabia?

Participants in all kinds of social behavior aim to construct narratives that make sense of their choices. Your act of reading this textbook might be "framed" in relation to a basic narrative about how you are a student enrolled in a college or university. Your long-term horizon probably includes some sort of job or advanced study (and hopefully a job after that!). Your act of reading is likely framed in relation to your role. As a student, you want or are expected to *learn*, and your act of reading the text is, at least officially, understood in this light. Note that these "frames" are more or less *collective* in character. In other words, you can reject them privately if you want to, but it is very difficult to do so publicly—say, by standing up in class and telling your instructor that you don't *want* to learn—without facing consequences.

According to these theories, the same is true in situations of social movements and revolutions. If you were to stand up in your classroom and declare that you are starting a social revolution, it is unlikely that this frame would "make sense" to those around you. More likely, they would have an alternative frame via which to interpret your outburst: you "are weird" or "have issues." Even if one thinks that common interests would suggest that some group, say factory workers, should organize or even revolt, if the appropriate frames are not in place, it is unlikely that they will be successful. The factory worker in the United States who stands on the shop floor and declares a social revolution is likely to be greeted with the same response as our fictional student doing the same in class.

So where do frames come from? They are part of *culture*. Different communities, practices, and walks of life exhibit shifting "frames" through which social problems and appropriate responses are constantly interpreted. The idea is the same, however: contentious action like revolution can only take place when participants have a frame for conceiving of it and talking about it. In many modern social revolutions, this language is provided by nationalism.[73] Some scholars have even argued that the very idea of revolution (sometimes called "revolutionism") is itself a prerequisite for revolutionary activity.[74] From this point of view, revolution cannot take place simply whenever there is inequality, anger, and frustration. Rather, revolution is only possible when the idea of revolution already exists as a model for addressing that discontent. Scholars increasingly emphasize that ideas about *how* to protest play an important role in contention.[75] Others stress the enduring influence of *ideologies*, a subject to which we turn in chapter 15.[76] One relatively recent theory of revolutions in the developing world, along somewhat similar lines, stresses the importance of "political cultures of opposition."[77]

As you approach the close of this chapter, you now know that scholars have a range of ways in which they conceptualize and explain contention, and that they do not all agree. In general, though, theories might lead us to expect that several conditions would increase the likelihood of successful contention:

1. Some preexisting grievances felt by one or more groups.
2. A weakening in the institutions that repress collective dissent, yet without sufficient political opening such that disputes can be resolved via formal political institutions.
3. The emergence of new methods or means of organizing and communication, whether these be technological (e.g., newspapers, social networking sites, enhanced transportation) or of some other form (e.g., semi-spontaneous organizing like the Montgomery Bus Boycott), or else new access to such means and methods.
4. Sufficient organizing success such that actors perceive some reasonable chance of further success.
5. The emergence of ways of talking and writing about underlying social problems that points toward contention rather than quiescence as the solution.
6. Organizational leadership that maintains the unity of contentious organizing rather than fracturing contention.

As you know, different theories place greater and lesser emphasis on each of these factors, and common sense tells us that they all matter. Drawing on the methods discussed throughout this book so far, think about how we might advance research from this point, determining with greater precision the relative weight of each of these factors and the precise ways in which they interact to produce successful organizing or revolt.

The "Arab Spring" of 2011 and Its Legacy

THINKING COMPARATIVELY

As discussed at the beginning of this chapter, beginning in Spring 2011, many authoritarian governments in North Africa and the Middle East witnessed a tremendous wave of contention. The protests began in Tunisia and spread quickly to a number of countries, with the most immediate consequence in Egypt, where hundreds of thousands of people crowded into Tahrir Square to demand change.

This truly momentous development encouraged further protests in other parts of the Arab world. Major protest action began, among other places, in Yemen, Libya, and then Syria. In the Libyan case, the dictator Muammar Qaddafi was quite willing to use massive force to repress protestors. Chillingly, authoritarian

KEY METHODOLOGICAL TOOL

Deviant or Negative Cases

Methodologically speaking, a "deviant case" is a case that has a notably different outcome from what one or

A Tunisian man casts a vote in elections in October 2011 made possible by the "Arab Spring."

dictators seem to have learned the lesson that repression is the way to preserve power. NATO intervened militarily in Libya, ostensibly to protect civilians, but ultimately to provide material assistance to rebels who eventually dislodged the Qaddafi regime. The outcomes in other cases have been mixed. The memory of the Arab Spring still inspires hope in many, but it would be a stretch to say that it democratized the region. So far, outcomes run the gamut from Tunisia's seemingly successful initial transition to democracy (still undergoing consolidation) to pronounced state weakness in Libya, considerable repression in Egypt, and major gains for terrorist groups in Syria as well as ongoing foreign intervention—not to mention great loss of life and massive displacement of people from their homes.

What would we want a theory of contention to be able to explain about these events? There are many interesting questions to be answered, but among the most central we would want to include the following: (1) Why did this wave of contention emerge?; (2) Why were the proponents of regime change successful in Tunisia and Egypt but not in Syria and only with NATO support in Libya?; and, finally, (3) Why has no significant contention been seen in Saudi Arabia, where a number of similar conditions can be found? In other words, any theory of what caused the revolts in Tunisia, Egypt, and elsewhere should be able to account for Saudi Arabia as a "negative case" in which at least some of the key factors in the other cases are present but in which the outcome is sharply different. These are not the only interesting questions one can ask about the Arab Spring revolts and their aftermath, but here we focus on them, largely restricting our discussion to the events of 2011.

To work toward establishing hypotheses, let us first think about what our theories would predict, and then we will briefly consider some of the common and varying conditions present in our cases. See Table 12.3.

As you can see from this table, not all of the hypotheses generated from these theories are mutually exclusive. Indeed, you can probably see ways in which they could be combined. This does not mean that the underlying theories are fully compatible: certain general theoretical issues cannot be glossed over. For example, some versions of rational choice theory says that demand for revolution is constant, while relative deprivation theory says it varies. Nonetheless, we can draw on different theories as we attempt to explain the complexities of a series of cases.

A number of factors may have contributed to the emergence and development of the "Arab Spring" and its aftermath. Many commentators have noted that demographic pressures produced discontent. These are societies with a comparatively high number of young adults and few economic opportunities for them. Another clear factor is the sense of frustration that many in the Arab world felt with their countries' nondemocratic status, particularly when judged against a world in which democracy seemed ascendant for several decades. Others point to social media, arguing that Twitter and Facebook helped protestors solve collective action problems, noting that some of the regimes have tried to restrict access to information technology.

What conditions were common in these societies before the wave began? Islam is the majority religion in all of them. Each began the sequence as an autocracy and, indeed, with a long history of authoritarianism. Each had relatively high poverty (though this varied in extent from case to case, as we shall see). Yet there were important variations along these dimensions. Note that the two cases where contentious action was most successful in the early years—Egypt and Tunisia—were not major oil exporters (Table 12.4).

This might suggest that *being* an oil exporter potentially thwarted this sort of contention, perhaps because oil export provided resources for the state to maintain legitimacy or even to repress opponents. Obviously, the lack of major government oil revenues was not a *sufficient* condition for successful contention, given that Syria also was not a major oil exporter, and its regime has, despite serious opposition, huge loss of life, mass emigration, and partial state breakdown, held onto power. To some extent, though, Syria's seemingly low oil export numbers need to be judged on the appropriate scale. In relative terms, the Syrian government, at least in years prior to the conflict, derived considerable resources from oil exports.

Another point of variation concerns the relationship between religion and politics. While, as noted earlier, they are all majority-Muslim countries, there are important differences in this regard. Perhaps the sharpest contrast here can be

TABLE 12.3 Contention: Theories, Hypotheses, and Evidence

Theory	Moving Toward Hypothesis *What does the theory predict causes contention?*	Possible Instance *What would a case look like if it followed the theory?*
Relative Deprivation	Increased discontent due to declining status of key groups	Demographic and economic trends mean poor job prospects for young adults, who mobilize against regimes they see as barriers to advancement.
Political Opportunities/ Resource Mobilization	1. Political opening (from democratic reforms *or* fiscal weakening of the state) 2. Preexisting mobilization capacity among key groups	1. Low willingness/capacity to repress protests leads to more successful contention. 2. More and larger preexisting political groups leads to more contention.
Rational Choice Theory	Changes in the strategic situations faced by key actors	Lack of repression of early protests changes actors' views on risks of contention. Weak state responses make victory seem more likely, producing cascade of participation.
Cultural or "Framing" Theory	Changing ideas or cultural change before or during the process	Contention emerges and strengthens as the very idea spreads that radical change is needed (e.g., the "Arab Spring" idea).

TABLE 12.4 Net Oil Exports, 2009, Barrels Per Day (in Thousands)

Tunisia	5
Egypt	−38
Libya	1,525
Syria	117
Saudi Arabia	7,322

Source: U.S. Energy Information Administration, http://www.eia.gov/countries/index.cfm.

found between Egypt and Saudi Arabia. Saudi Arabia is essentially a theocracy (though Islam in Saudi Arabia is Sunni Islam, meaning the clergy do not hold formal power, which is held by the royal family). The regime's legitimacy is maintained both by religious arguments and by lavish spending of oil revenues. Egypt has a long history of Islamic militancy, but for decades it was dominated by secular nationalists who attempted to marginalize political Islam. Framing theories of revolution might note that this could advantage the proponents of contentious action, since religious modes of dissent might be more readily used as a wedge in a society like Egypt than in Saudi Arabia. Of course, this could also produce problems for revolutionaries. The Arab Spring led the Muslim Brotherhood to power, but their overreach prompted resistance and their eventual fall, and Egypt has seen a return to authoritarianism under Abdel Fatah el-Sisi.

Another issue is the degree of poverty faced by these countries. If the relative deprivation theory is right, we would expect to find one or another group experiencing economically generated discontent. While these issues are complicated, for the sake of simplicity here, we will just look at per capita income (Table 12.5). Again, for the sake of simplicity, we will take these data to indicate that Tunisia,

TABLE 12.5 2010 Per Capita Income in Selected Countries (in U.S. dollars)

Country	GDP Per Capita (USD)
Tunisia	4,222
Egypt	2,654
Libya	11,321
Syria	2,931
Saudi Arabia	15,836

Source: UN Statistics Division, Social Indicators, http://unstats.un.org/unsd/demographic/products/socind/. Accessed on July 17, 2012.

Egypt, and Syria were likely to have a high degree of economically induced discontent, Libya a moderate degree, and Saudi Arabia a low degree.[78]

THINKING COMPARATIVELY

Finally, if we examine the sequence of contention in these societies, we see an important difference in the *process* of contention. In four of the five cases (Egypt, Tunisia, Syria, and Libya), strong contentious action developed; but in two of them (Egypt and Tunisia) the military was unwilling to fully repress the regime's opponents in the early stages of collective action (Table 12.6). This suggests that the military and its linkage to the existing regime—which we can take to be a function of state capacity—was critical to outcomes. Focusing on general judgments about just these variables, we can summarize the cases as shown in Table 12.6.

If we take our negative case—Saudi Arabia—out of the comparison, a clear hypothesis suggests itself: successful collective action may be due, in part, to the state's failure to repress. Other features are held constant, with the exception of the fact that Libya is an oil exporter, which is perhaps relevant only insofar as it *facilitates* the state's repressive capacity. In other words, factors like economic discontent and the religious versus secular character of the regime appear to be constants and thus may be causally unimportant. This is broadly consistent with our "political opportunity theory" discussed previously. However, when we bring Saudi Arabia into the comparison, this no longer appears to be the case. Rather, Saudi Arabia, where no major contention emerged during the period in question, varies from the other cases in two respects: (1) it is a religious regime, and (2) it does not seem to have witnessed dramatic, economically generated discontent. In other words, the inclusion of this case makes these factors relevant, which is critical to the hypotheses suggested by framing and relative deprivation approaches. Note that it does not *demonstrate* their causal force, however.

Indeed, we would not wish to push this exercise too far. As noted in earlier chapters, rejecting a theory or hypothesis because one or another case is not consistent with it presumes a deterministic model of explanation. Much of social science, though, including the study of collective action, does not result in hard-and-fast "rules" or "laws" that are true always and everywhere. Instead, it involves trying to understand probabilistic relationships or patterns in our data. In these

TABLE 12.6 Contention in the "Arab Spring": Five Cases

	Major oil exporter?	Theocratic regime?	Economically generated discontent?	State/military willing to repress protest?
Tunisia	N	N	Y (high)	N
Egypt	N	N	Y (high)	N
Libya	Y	N	Y (moderate)	Y
Syria	N*	N	Y (high)	Y (so far, to the extent possible)
Saudi Arabia	Y	Y	N	Y (presumably)

*As stated in the text, the Syrian state had in recent years derived considerable revenues from oil export, even though the country's share in the total international oil market is small.

cases, a single disconfirming instance does not prove a theory or hypothesis wrong.[79] What we have done here is to assess the extent to which several theories fit a handful of related cases, but it should not be thought of as demonstrating one or another of those theories to be correct or incorrect.

Of all of the cases we consider here, Syria has seen the most prolonged and violent conflict. As has been reported by major media, millions of refugees have been displaced in this violence. Foreign powers, including both Russia and the United States, have been involved; and Russia has provided military and diplomatic assistance to the Assad regime as it represses its opponents and those many civilians unfortunate enough to get caught up in the war. Moreover, these opponents have included ISIS, which for a time constructed a quasi-state in parts of Syria and Iraq, as well as coalitions of many other groups opposed to the Assad regime. Why has this conflict proven so enduring?

Two hypotheses suggest themselves. First, the very involvement of foreign powers may increase the conflict, as some political scientists have found that foreign intervention often draws out civil wars.[80] If parties to a violent conflict can turn to external powers for resources, perhaps they can fend off loss for longer periods of time, extending the duration—and thus the human costs—of the war. Second, one thing that makes Syria different from the other cases we have considered here is its pronounced religious heterogeneity. The society is strikingly divided into different religious groups, and many other social processes are organized via religious affiliation. As in Iraq, the conflict has split partially along sectarian lines. This does not mean that we should regard all of this violence as having religious motives. Indeed, religious affiliation can serve as a marker of group membership and a signal of whether someone is "with us" or "against us."[81] As such, members of one group might engage in anticipatory conflictual behavior with members of another group for no other reason than that they fear that the other group will otherwise victimize them. As we will see in chapter 13, empirical evidence suggests that in well-functioning economies with strong political institutions, cultural difference does not seem to meaningfully increase the probability of intergroup violence. But in the context of state breakdown, the results can be very different.

In any case, examples like Syria can be thought of as both humanitarian disasters and as cautionary tales about collective action that should be kept in mind alongside the triumphalist stories about earlier examples such as the French or American revolutions. Sometimes revolutions lead to the development of democracy and human rights. Other times they lead to repression. And still other times, they lead to state breakdown with no clear exit and to massive human suffering.

The purpose of this exercise is to get you thinking about how to make comparisons and not to fully explain variation in the "Arab Spring" and its aftermath. Indeed, this task will likely take years, both because we need to see how these processes play out and because scholarship in political science often depends on many efforts by many scholars to generate and test hypotheses. What you can see here, however, is one way in which we may begin to proceed if we wish to make sense of patterns following from the "Arab Spring." Note how much case selection matters. What would we conclude if Saudi Arabia weren't included? Can you think of other cases that might change our conclusions if we included them? Or cases that point to causal factors that we have not considered here?

Chapter Summary

Concepts

- Comparative political analysts are interested in how and why conflict sometimes takes place outside of formal institutions.
- There are a number of forms that such conflict takes. We were especially attentive to the differences between revolutionary and non-revolutionary strategies to create change.

Types

- Social movements are probably the most common form of organized conflict in advanced industrial democracies. Social movements are commonly regarded as organized collective action in the pursuit of social reforms of one or another kind.
- Revolutions are perhaps less common in advanced industrial societies but quite common in modern societies more generally. Revolutions are usually thought of as producing dramatic change rather than mere reforms.
- *Social* revolutions change structures like the class system.
- Political revolutions change the state.
- Anti-colonial revolutions create newly independent states after removing colonial powers.
- Insurgencies shade into revolutions. We can distinguish them by the degree to which insurgencies take protracted military form, often in the absence of large-scale civilian mobilization.
- Terrorism can be studied as a tactic employed by participants in social movements, revolutions, and insurgencies or as a particular form for the organization of resistance. In the latter case, much attention is placed on "terror networks."
- "Everyday resistance" is the name scholars give to the ways that groups resist and express discontent in the absence of the resources needed for complex organization and coordination.

Causes and Effects

- There are at least four general types of theories of revolution, and these theories can, with some modification, be applied to other forms of contention.
- Theories of "relative deprivation" and "social disequilibrium" try to explain revolutions through focusing on an increase in the *demand* for revolutions. It looks at the impact of modernization on existing political institutions and social hierarchies. It suggests that when modernization impacts these hierarchies, social equilibrium is broken, and important groups seek to produce a new equilibrium through revolution.
- Theories of political opportunities and mobilization try to explain revolutions through focusing on *supply* of mobilization opportunities rather than demand for revolution. It suggests that new political opportunities, such as state collapse and the presence of useful ways of organizing dissent, matter most.
- Collective action theories argue that collective action problems are the main barrier to revolution. When revolutions do take place, the best way to explain them is to show how collective action problems were solved.
- Framing or cultural theory says that other theories must be supplemented by a focus on ideology or culture. Material conditions are not enough to produce revolutions. Rather, people need to have ideas that "frame" their grievances in a way that suggests that revolution is the legitimate solution.

Thinking Comparatively

- The "Arab Spring" of 2011 presents a set of interesting and useful cases for these theories.

Thinking It Through

1. This chapter began and ended with a brief discussion of the "Arab Spring." Based on the theories and concepts discussed here, why do you think the protests described there have been successful and others unsuccessful? What do these cases tell us about contention in general?

2. The United States is a society in which wealth is unequally distributed and a number of groups feel aggrieved. Why is it that there has not been a strong revolutionary tradition in the United States? What would the theories we have considered say about this question?

3. In today's world, some groups claim to be making revolutions *through* democratic elections. In your view, is this possible? How would this change our definition of revolutions? Does it make

sense to broaden our concept so as to include such cases? Why or why not?

4. All of the major forms of contention discussed in this chapter are hard to control and to lead. They often give rise to unintended consequences and escape the grasp of those who began them. *Which* types of contention would be most difficult to lead and why? Which ones might be a bit easier to lead and why?

5. In this chapter, we considered numerous forms of contention, and then we focused on explanations of revolution. These explanations could potentially be applied to some of the other forms of contention as well. For which forms of contention do you think these explanations would be most successful? And for which do you think they would face the greatest difficulties? Why?

CHAPTER 13

Nationalism and National Identity

● *Rwandan refugees in 1994. This image is disturbing because it took place in the midst of the Rwandan genocide, one of the worst outpourings of ethno-national violence in recent years. Can comparative political analysis help us to understand and put a stop to such horrific events?*

The twentieth century witnessed some of the greatest atrocities in human history, from the Nazi Holocaust to the deaths of millions through violence, starvation, and famine in China, Cambodia, the Soviet Union, and Bangladesh, among many other places. As a response to the horrific events in Nazi Germany in particular, the international community declared that it would never again allow **genocide**, the mass murder of people of a particular racial, ethnic, or national group. Although mass killing continued around the world in subsequent decades, it was only in the late 1990s that much of the public realized that genocide had not been eradicated (though some observers were aware that it had never really disappeared). The genocides in both Rwanda and the Balkans were well documented, but the international responses to these crises were dramatically different. In the African case, the international community did very little, and peacekeepers stood by as the killing occurred, as their mandate did not authorize interference. In the European case, NATO mounted a joint military effort, bombing Serbia and forcing an end to formal hostilities, eventually bringing some of the leaders to The Hague for criminal trial.

In the twenty-first century genocide has continued, most notably in Sudan and now, many observers believe, in South Sudan and Myanmar.[1] In these and other instances the international community has largely remained divided and confused about how to proceed. To some extent this response may be due to a lack of sufficient will to intervene. But it may also be partially due to failure to truly understand violence linked to political identities. If this is true, policymakers may need to begin by understanding the nature and causes of national and ethno-national identities more generally. Comparative analysis of political identities and nationalism aims to help us better understand these issues. Why do some identity groups engage in violence against others? Is it mostly related to the identities themselves or to circumstances such as economic development or political institutions?

Comparative politics also aims to go beyond questions about violence to ask about political identities more generally. Why do modern societies

genocide Efforts to diminish or destroy a people and/or culture.

almost invariably define their populations as nations? Why do they approach citizenship and national membership differently? Why do some people seem to place so much emphasis on race and ethnicity as a basis for nationalism and others seemingly less so? What causes collective identities to change? In recent years, interest in identity and its political consequences has grown. As always, in this area of research, comparative analysis depends on clearly formulated concepts.

• • •

Concepts

We must begin by clarifying the meaning of the concepts of "identity," "the nation," and "nationalism."

Identity

identity The social label ascribed to an individual or group that locates the individual or group in political society more broadly.

social identity theory An important theory in social psychology that sees personal identities as linked to and partially derived from group identities and roles.

What *is* **identity**? Probably the simplest way to begin thinking about it is at the level of the individual. At the most basic level, your identity is your sense of self. You have a sense of who you are and of what makes you special and unique. You also participate in attributing identities to others. In other words, as **social identity theory** argues, even our own personal identities are constructed on the basis of social sources, and the ongoing acts of having an identity and labeling others are social.[2] Every day, we construct symbolic representations of the social world in which we live and our place in it. Thus our personal identities—our senses of ourselves as individuals—are drawn from roles linked to the role and group identities (e.g., student or professor, Brazilian or American, woman or man, brother or sister) that our society makes available to us.

The identities that matter most in politics are group identities. Group identities draw boundaries between in-groups and out-groups, though the *way* in which such boundaries are constructed varies a great deal. For example, sometimes group identities are very sharply bounded, and individuals are not allowed to pass from one group to another.[3] In other situations, group boundaries are permeable, and one can choose whether or not to belong to the group in question. Likewise, certain sorts of identities are compatible, such as being simultaneously Spanish and Catholic; whereas others are likely to be perceived by some people as incompatible, such as being simultaneously an anarchist and a fascist.

national identity An identity that locates one's social position in relation to national membership.

nationalism The view that the world is and should be divided into nations that are thought of by nationalists as sovereign and egalitarian.

nation A group thought of as sovereign and equal, typically comprised of a large, often geographically bounded population.

Identities are *cultural*, *historical*, and *political*. This means that they are created by human societies and expressed symbolically, that they change over time, and that they influence and are influenced by the ways that *power* is distributed in society. When we study them, we should be attentive to *how* they are constructed by different individuals and groups; how their forms change over time; and how different individuals and groups, with varying access to resources, struggle to identify themselves and one another for their own purposes. In short, identities are the social labels ascribed to individuals or groups, locating the individual or group in political society more broadly.

Nationalism, National Identity, and the Nation

In this chapter, we focus on what might be the most important form of political identity in today's world: **national identity**. As suggested at the beginning of this chapter, for some the idea of **nationalism** conjures up images of stringent restrictions on immigration, of discriminatory behavior, and, at its worst, of genocide. And yet while nationalism and national identity can sometimes be linked to exclusion and violence, this is not the whole story.[4] They are also linked in some cases to inclusive citizenship and democracy. Indeed, some scholars think that modern democracy would not have emerged without nationalism. In general, we could start by defining nationalism as the idea that nations should be the basic units of social and political life. **Nations**, in turn, are often defined as relatively large groups that think of themselves as *equal* and *sovereign*.[5] In other words, in modern politics, nations are thought of as the source of the state's legitimate authority. This is why all modern governments, even authoritarian ones, claim to speak on behalf of the "people" or "nation." To reiterate, nationalism is the view that we all have a national identity and that this identity is important. National identity says that we are members of nations and that these nations are sovereign and equal.

Scholars of nationalism typically follow Anthony Smith in dividing theoretical approaches to the subject into several main groupings: "primordialists," "perennialists," and "modernists."[6] **Primordialism** holds that all societies have something like nationalism, and that the main problem involves explaining why this is so. For these scholars, national identity is basically a strong sense of the group. Some use **sociobiology** or **evolutionary psychology** to try to explain the long history of group identities while others favor cultural explanations.[7] Proponents of **perennialism** disagree and think that not all societies have nationalism, but that some premodern societies *did* have it. For example, some scholars see several late medieval or early modern European societies as having had national identity.[8] **Modernism**, in contrast, takes national identity to be a modern phenomenon, which for most means from the late eighteenth century to today).[9] Whether you are a primordialist, a

primordialism The label applied by Anthony Smith to those theories of national identity that see it as continuous with prehistorical ("primordial") forms of identity.

sociobiology An approach to the study of societies that sees human society as governed by the same (evolutionary) principles as animal societies.

evolutionary psychology An approach to the analysis of human behavior that seeks to explain it almost exclusively on the basis of evolutionary theory (*see also* sociobiology).

perennialism The label applied by Anthony Smith to those theories of national identity that see it as neither exclusively modern nor continuous with prehistorical forms of identity.

modernism The label applied by Anthony Smith to those theories of national identity that see it as exclusively modern.

CASE IN CONTEXT
National Identity in the United Kingdom

PAGE 554

English nationalism is often considered one of the first, or perhaps the very first, case of the phenomenon. Interestingly, though, different scholars see it emerging in different historical moments: medieval times, the sixteenth century, the seventeenth century, and even the early twentieth century. Moreover, English national identity has coexisted with British national identity, and also with regional identities—to some, also national—like the Scottish, the Welsh, and the Northern Irish. All of this raises questions about how we define and empirically study the nation.

For more on the changing face of English/British national identity, see the case study in Part VI, pp. 554–555. As you read it, keep in mind the following questions:

1. How is it possible that different scholars date the emergence of English nationalism so differently?
2. How does English nationalism relate to British nationalism?
3. How does British nationalism relate to the identities of Scottish, Welsh, and Northern Irish residents of the United Kingdom?

CASE IN CONTEXT
Industrialization, Modernity, and National Identity in Mexico   PAGE 510

Many structuralist theories of nationalism and national iden-tity focus on industrial capitalism as a key cause. At first glance, structuralist theories focused on capitalism seem well prepared to explain the emergence of national identity in Europe, but they sometimes encounter trouble when applied to develop-ing world societies. Mexico is a case in point. One cannot begin to speak of modern industrial capitalism in Mexico until, at the very earliest, the late nineteenth century; and many would judge even this too early. Yet nationalism was an important force in Mexican politics from the early 1800s.

For more on the case of Mexican nationalism, see the national identity case study in Part VI, pp. 510–511. As you read it, keep in mind the following questions:

1. How would the approaches to nationalism discussed in this chapter treat the Mexican case? Which account seems to fit the case best?
2. If we consider Mexico against the background of Latin America more generally, what light does the compari-son shed on this question?

---

structuralism An approach to nationalism studies that sees big, difficult-to-change parts of society as determining what really matters about national identity.

constructivism In nationalism studies, the view that nations are symbolic constructs and so place greater emphasis on the creative efforts of individuals and groups to define and redefine their identities.

perennialist, or a modernist depends on how you conceptualize nationalism and the nation. Most contemporary scholars of nationalism are modernists.

One major point of disagreement among modernist scholars of nationalism separates those who are more "structuralist" and those who are more "constructiv-ist." **Structuralists** see big, difficult-to-change parts of society—such as major features of the economy—as determining what really matters about national iden-tity. **Constructivists** emphasize that nations are symbolic constructs, and so they place greater emphasis on the creative efforts of individuals and groups to define and redefine their identities.

An example of a structuralist theory is Ernest Gellner's linking of industri-alization to national identity (see Insights box on *Nations and Nationalism*).[10]

INSIGHTS   Nations and Nationalism
by Ernest Gellner

Gellner argues that industrial capitalism produces national-ism, in part through the instrument of the state. For Gellner, capitalism requires a homogeneous, interchangeable, socially and geographically mobile workforce as well as standardized language. Holding laborers in place by feudal ties or localism will be a major barrier to economic development; and capital-ism is facilitated by literacy, common language, and a mobile workforce compensated in wages. Gellner's theory is that these needs lead to nationalism because nationalism encourages the social characteristics that capitalism requires. Nationalism takes a language of "the people" and gives it high status. The national state standardizes its usage through official documents, the education system, and so forth. Likewise, nationalism says that

everybody in the nation is fundamentally equal, which breaks down hierarchical ties and gives rise to the interchangeability of modern workers. Critics worry that the theory doesn't clearly specify "causal mechanisms" through which the effect is pro-duced. Nationalism seems to "go with" capitalism, but we need a theory of *how* capitalism produces nationalism. If nationalism is created for the sake of capitalism, who are the "agents" who accomplish this, and what are their motivations and goals? Gell-ner's answer to this question is that the state coordinates the rise and maintenance of national identity, but that it does so *because* of underlying economic forces.

Ernest Gellner, Nations and Nationalism. *Ithaca, NY: Cornell University Press, 1983.*

INSIGHTS

Nationalism: Five Roads to Modernity
by Liah Greenfeld

Greenfeld argues that nationalism is fundamentally *cultural* and needs to be understood as an imaginative response to social conditions. To understand nationalism's emergence and growth, we must understand why the idea spread that humanity is divided into distinct "peoples" who are "sovereign" and "equal." For Greenfeld, the key preconditions for the development of national identity are problems in *stratification systems* through which societies hierarchically divide themselves, such as the class structure. Elite *status inconsistency*—a condition present when the stratification system breaks down and elites are no longer sure of their status—leads some groups to seek to transform identity, and national identity often seems to such groups to serve their interests well. Greenfeld examines this hypothesis against a number of cases (including England, France, Russia, Germany, and Japan), finding pronounced status inconsistency in each case in the key groups that are most central in redefining their societies as nations. At the same time, Greenfeld acknowledges the importance of institutions like the state prior to national identity's emergence in helping to shape the type that develops in any given case. Scholars working with this theory also note that political institutions play an important role in spreading and preserving national identity.

Liah Greenfeld, Nationalism: Five Roads to Modernity. *Cambridge, MA: Harvard University Press, 1992.*

An example of a constructivist theory is Liah Greenfeld's argument that national identity is an imaginative response to contradictory public claims about a group's status.[11] Greenfeld emphasizes social psychology, rather than economics, in analyzing the processes through which national identity emerges and thrives (see Insights box on *Nationalism: Five Roads to Modernity*).

These theories reveal just how different such structuralist and constructivist approaches can be, but simultaneously reveal points of similarity. For example, the group status inconsistency that Greenfeld emphasizes may often be due to "structural" changes in society such as shifting ways of organizing social and economic class or innovations in the ways that states recruit their staff. In other words, the fact that such a theory emphasizes social psychology and symbolic construction does not mean that it ignores structural characteristics of society.

CASE IN CONTEXT

Importing National Identity in Japan?

PAGE 496

Japan had a clear civilizational identity for centuries before modern nationalism. Indeed, under the Tokugawa regime, the country turned inward and sharply limited commercial and cultural contact with the outside world. Yet many scholars think that it only developed modern national identity in the late nineteenth century. One of the most striking things about the case of Japan is how quickly industrialization and economic growth followed the development of national identity.[12]

For more on Japanese nationalism, see the case study in Part VI, p. 496. As you read it, keep in mind the following questions:

1. What does Japan show us about the relationship between nationalism and other key aspects of modernization?

2. Are economy-centered, state-centered, or constructivist theories best suited to explaining the case of Japanese nationalism?

Types

Types of Nationalism

As discussed in chapter 1, political scientists can move up and down Sartori's ladder of abstraction in searching for more or less general conceptualizations of nationalism. At the level of greatest generality, scholars might look at the psychological preconditions of collective identity itself. A primordialist perspective might be useful in this case. At the same time, only modernist conceptualizations will offer sufficient specificity for asking questions about modern nationalism's *emergence*, since they are most able to draw clear qualitative distinctions between national identity and other identities out of which it might grow or that might otherwise resemble it in certain respects.

CIVIC AND ETHNIC NATIONALISM

To ask and answer more specific comparative questions about national identity and other variables, however, one needs still more specific conceptualizations. These typically take the form of *typologies* of nationalism. Most commonly, typologies posit a choice between two main forms of national identity (see Table 13.1). For part of the twentieth century, the distinction was between so-called **Western nationalism** and **Eastern nationalism**.[13] Note that these geographical distinctions were largely intended to capture an alleged difference between the nationalisms characteristic of Eastern and Western *Europe*. Western nationalisms, such of those of France and Britain, it was often alleged, were compatible with tolerance, liberal-democratic political institutions, and so forth. Eastern ones, however, like those of Germany or Russia, were based on the collective notion of the "volk," tended toward xenophobia, and were perhaps inhospitable to liberal-democratic institutions.[14]

Later, this distinction was developed and clarified into a distinction between **civic nationalism** and **ethnic nationalism**.[15] While different scholars parse these concepts in slightly different ways, the main issue here is a distinction between those societies who treat citizenship as technically open and as not based on ethnicity, and in turn take citizenship as the marker of national membership; and those that either have closed conceptions of citizenship (citizenship is and should be, according to such nationalisms, a biological inheritance) or that do not treat formal citizenship as a true marker of national belonging. France and Germany have been commonly taken as examples of these two kinds of nationalism. One might expect that societies characterized by civic nationalism could do a better job of incorporating immigrant communities and might even be less prone to interstate conflict, though this should be thought of as a hypothesis and not a fact.

Western nationalism An antiquated term for what is now often called "civic nationalism" (*see* **civic nationalism**).

Eastern nationalism An antiquated term for what is now often called "ethnic nationalism" (*see* **ethnic nationalism**).

civic nationalism A form of nationalism that says that you are a member of the nation if you are a citizen of its state.

ethnic nationalism A form of nationalism that says that you are a member of the nation because of your ancestry.

TABLE 13.1 Traditional Typology of Nationalism

"Western," "Civic," or "Territorial" Nationalisms	"Eastern" or "Ethnic" Nationalisms
France	Germany
United Kingdom	Russia
United States	Central and Eastern Europe
Australia	

Two foreign-born children take their oaths as citizens of the United States in 2011.

Sometimes this basic binary distinction takes on a slightly different form, such as in the distinction between "territorial" and "ethnic" nationalisms, though there is considerable overlap here with the civic–ethnic distinction.[16] **Territorial nationalism** is meant to refer to nationalism in which membership corresponds to residency in a territory, and civic nationalism to citizenship in a state, but these concepts are closely related.

Liah Greenfeld adds a further element to this civic and ethnic typological scheme, arguing that while ethnic nationalisms are always "collectivistic," civic ones can be either collectivistic or individualistic (for examples, see Table 13.2). This distinction can be rather difficult to understand.[17] The model of individualistic nationalism holds that nations are associations of individual persons.

territorial nationalism According to some scholars, a type of nationalism that closely resembles civic nationalism in that membership is fundamentally determined by where one is born or where one resides rather than one's ancestry.

CASE IN CONTEXT
Ethnic Boundaries of the German Nation?

PAGE 455

France is often presented as a quintessential "civic" nationalism. Germany is often juxtaposed to France as the quintessential "ethnic" nationalism.[18] Indeed, some go so far as to try to explain the rise of the Nazis as a function of this ethnic nationalism, a much debated and controversial claim.

For more on nationalism in Germany, see the national identity case study in Part VI, pp. 455–456. As you read it, keep in mind the following questions:

1. Why do many scholars consider German nationalism to be ethnic nationalism?

2. What would researchers have to show to *demonstrate* that long-standing patterns of Germany identity explain German atrocities in the twentieth century? What obstacles might such scholars face?

3. Has German nationalism changed in the post–World War II years?

TABLE 13.2 **Greenfeld's Expanded Typology of Nationalism**

CASE EXAMPLES

	Civic	Ethnic
Individualistic	United States United Kingdom	N/A
Collectivistic	France	Germany Japan Russia

This suggests that whatever the reality of the political community and the processes through which it is formed and maintained, it is conceived of by its members as voluntary or associative. Collectivistic nationalism, in contrast, sees the nation as having a kind of collective agency or will that transcends the agency or wills of individual members. According to Greenfeld, collectivistic nationalism increases the likelihood of authoritarianism. This is because authoritarian leaders can claim to represent the will of the united people.

JUS SANGUINIS AND *JUS SOLI*

A related distinction concerns the legal rules governing how a given society defines who is a citizen. As noted previously, citizenship is not always identical to national membership, but in the modern world one tends to go with the other. Different countries have different rules for how one acquires citizenship. The major distinction is between those who grant citizenship to anyone born in the country's territory (*jus soli*) and those that grant citizenship based on descent (*jus sanguinis*). These are not mutually exclusive possibilities, of course. Many countries' laws enshrine some version of both principles. For example, the United States practices both *jus soli* and a limited version of *jus sanguinis*. Neither are these two possibilities exhaustive, since most countries have some legal provisions for "naturalization," or the process through which someone can acquire citizenship years after birth, often after a period of residency in the country.

Scholars often see *jus sanguinis* as linked to ethnic conceptions of the nation.[19] Indeed, if proponents of ethnic nationalism believe that citizenship should reflect national membership, they almost certainly support *jus sanguinis* since they believe that the nation is ultimately a biological community rather than cultural or political one. In practice, this means that a right to citizenship can be transmitted over time to people who have little or no direct experience living in the country in question. For example, if two citizens of polity A move to polity B and have a child, that child automatically has citizenship in polity A. Now imagine that this child does not return to polity A but grows up and has children in polity B. In some cases, polity A citizenship would still be open to these children. Indeed, in some cases, such as Ireland, simply having grandparents who were citizens is sufficient. Other prominent examples of polities in which *jus sanguinis* is strongly operative include Italy and Hungary. In a number of such cases, an uninterrupted pattern of formal citizenship is not required. Rather, applicants for citizenship make their claim on the basis of biological descent from some past citizen, sometimes multiple generations removed.

Jus soli has been associated with civic nationalism. However, it is probably *most* closely associated with geography. A large majority of countries in both North and South America practice *jus soli*.[20] In most of the rest of the world's regions, full *jus soli* is rare. A limited form of *jus soli* is common (alongside *jus sanguinis*) in Western Europe and practiced in a number of other countries as well. Why is geography so strongly associated with jus soli? The answer is probably about immigration history. Most countries in the Americas have historically been societies of immigrants. In a number of societies, receiving many immigrants, officially embracing civic nationalism (however consistently or inconsistently), and taking a *jus soli* approach to citizenship go hand in hand. On the other hand, some scholars point out that *jus sanguinis* seems to be common in societies that *send* many migrants.[21]

LIMITS OF TYPOLOGIES IN THE STUDY OF NATIONAL IDENTITY

Some critics allege that typologies in the study of national identity, especially the distinction between civic and ethnic nationalism, are problematic because they appear to be linked to value judgments about different societies.[22] This concern deserves serious consideration. Typologies from political science exist to help us better analyze politics, but they may have other effects. If our categories too neatly sort the world in ways that make some actors appear to be more (or less) virtuous than others, we run the risk of creating damaging stereotypes.

Moreover, they may be misleading. In an important recent article, two sociologists study the types of national identity among a large set of American survey respondents.[23] What they find is that there are indeed multiple "types" of national identity that vary in key ways. Most important, they find plenty of individuals who correspond to traditional civic and ethnic types, though not everyone falls into one or the other group. Moreover, the variation they find is all *within* a single country, not *across* countries. Thus, there are empirical reasons to be suspicious of strong claims that one or another country simply reflects a single "type" of national identity.

If the strongest claims made by proponents of typologies of nationalism and national identity are true—if there are differences between civic and ethnic nationalisms that have implications for both domestic and international conflict—it would be hard for many social scientists, *as citizens*, to avoid making value judgments about them. But this critique should be a helpful reminder to us that *as social scientists* we should remain careful to avoid the projection of our own values onto the cases we study. Typologies of nationalism remain important in the literature, but they are controversial. One reasonable position is that so long as we treat such typologies as *ideal types*—and not as totalizing descriptions of specific identity groups—many critics' concerns lose some of their urgency. If we use categories thoughtfully, we may be less apt to simply label one country's nationalism as civic and another's as ethnic, but rather to see that strands of nationalism corresponding to both types pervade most polities. Considering the "civic" and "ethnic" ideal types might then be most useful as we track change within countries over time and not only in comparing between countries.

Causes and Effects: What Causes Ethno-National Conflict?

Much of the recent interest in nationalism and related forms of political identity—as noted previously—concerns the widespread perception that national and ethnic conflict and violence have increased since the end of the Cold War. Recent research has shown, however, that the growth of such violence began decades earlier, and that what appeared to be a spurt of such violence in the 1990s was a continuation of a long-run trend.[24] Moreover, most ethnically heterogeneous regions see very little intergroup violence.[25] Nevertheless, given the extent and seriousness of such violence—and the hope that policy based on social scientific knowledge can help us to reduce it—this is a particularly important area of research on political identities. There is relatively little theoretical consensus about how to explain ethno-national violence, and indeed what *ethnic* violence is.[26] We need to clearly conceptualize both "ethnicity" and "violence" (and, of course, to remember that not all conflict is violent).[27]

To begin studying such ethno-national conflict, the comparative political analyst must answer several questions. First, what makes a conflict national or "ethnonational"? Related to this, does a conflict being "national" or "ethno-national"

Late Yugoslav president Slobodan Milosevic on trial at the UN War Crimes Tribunal in 2001.

matter? In other words, can we understand a conflict better, or predict its likely course more effectively, if we know that it is linked to nationalism? Second, what type of conflict do we seek to explain? Third, what is the appropriate level of analysis to address the questions asked—for example, should our cases be distinct societies, localities, examples of group behavior, specific events, and so forth?

As for the first question, scholars take a variety of views. Some have suggested that there are multiple types of ethno-national identity, and that focusing on these different types might help us to account for variation in probabilities of violence.[28] A primordialist view of ethno-national identity, in contrast, might assume unchanging, irrational attachments to a given group. In addition, there are perspectives designated as constructivist (closely consistent with the "constructivist" view of nationalism discussed earlier) and as **instrumentalist**, meaning that the analyst assumes little significant affective attachment to the group but rather sees ethnicity as a product of political entrepreneurs seeking to manipulate populations for the pursuit of their own strategic ends. Finally, a number of scholars treat ethno-national identity as synonymous with "communal groups" more broadly for their research purposes:[29] For such analysts, it matters little whether a given group defines its boundaries in ethnic, racial, religious, or any other sorts of terms so long as the observable dynamics of conflict are the same.

> **instrumentalism** A type of explanation in social science that says that you can explain something by showing how its development or persistence is in the (usually material) interest of powerful individuals or groups.

Regarding the second question, about what type of conflict we seek to explain, some scholars have argued for a "disaggregation" of the concept of violence.[30] That is, there is more than one type of violence in need of explanation, and different kinds of violence might have different causes. The most fundamental distinction, perhaps, is between violence carried out by or via the state and violence that takes place between social actors independent of the state. Think of the difference between state-led efforts at genocide and, say, less centrally organized conflict between Hindus and Muslims in India. There are good reasons to suppose that the social and political conditions that underlie state-led genocide do not fully explain sectarian conflict outside the state, though they do have much in common. Much literature implicitly focuses on the former type, perhaps because state-led genocidal efforts have been so lethal and because they at least give the *appearance* of being preventable. However, genocide and other forms of intergroup violence, like periodic riots, can be analytically distinguished and likely require different explanatory approaches.[31]

Others note, importantly, that analysts must be attentive to *who* the parties to conflict are, since the "who" has great implications for the "why."[32] Lying behind such typologies are the analytical imperatives to (1) identify the major groups involved; (2) analyze their relative size and resources; (3) consider their relationship to the state and the society's stratification system; (4) take into account how they "frame" their own identities and those of other groups; and (5) understand the historical context of their relationships, given that these impact both how their identities and the potential for conflict are culturally framed and also the strategic calculations they are likely to make about the behavior of contending groups.

Ultimately, as with all of comparative political analysis, our goal is to provide *explanations*. There are several existing explanatory strategies in this area of research. It is worth noting that many scholars combine bits and pieces of these different explanatory strategies.

CASE IN CONTEXT

The Nigerian Civil War or Biafran War: Nationalism and Ethno-National Conflict in a Post-Colonial Society   PAGE 526

In much of the world, notably in Africa and the Middle East, as well as parts of Asia, European colonial powers created novel borders and boundaries. When these societies became independent in the mid to late twentieth century, they sometimes experienced problems of ethno-national tension and even violence, as groups without shared histories of long-standing political unification struggled over control of their new polities. A good example is Nigeria, where regional ethnic and religious tensions have been an issue since independence. The most extreme expression of these tensions manifested in the Biafran War (or the Nigerian Civil War) of 1967–1970, which caused tremendous loss of life.

For more on ethno-national conflict in Nigeria, see the case study in Part VI, p. 526. As you read it, keep in mind the following questions:

1. What would each of the major theories of ethno-national conflict we consider in this section say about this case? Each would find *some* supporting evidence. Does one or another theory, though, explain this case more fully?

2. How does ethno-national pluralism intersect with the resource-rich character of the Nigerian state? Would conflict be as much of a problem if Nigeria's oil wealth did not make the stakes so high?

3. Given what social-scientific theories of ethno-national conflict can show us about this case, what sorts of policies might mitigate further tensions and violence in Nigeria?

Primordial Bonds

You will recall from earlier in the chapter that primordialists tend to believe that national identity is essentially just another instance of a universal human tendency to form close (or "primordial") attachment to groups. The basic idea of primordialist explanations of ethnic conflict is that conflict takes place when preexisting groups feel that their group and/or their identity is under threat. For instance, perhaps "globalization" is causing a group to feel that its identity is being diluted. Or perhaps members of another group are perceived to be outcompeting them for jobs and other resources. Primordialist theories assume that these groups exist prior to the level of conflict, and that it is people's "passions" and "loyalties" that cause the conflict.

Let us consider a stylized example. Imagine a state called Pluria, controlled by a large group called the Plurals. But there is a region in the country of Pluria populated by two other groups known as the Alphas (Group A) and the Betas (Group B). The Alphas and Betas understand themselves (and each other) to be ethno-national groups. There are few Plurals in the region where the Alphas and Betas live. Members of group A (the "Alphas") tend not to trust members of group B (the "Betas"), and the Betas tend not to trust Alphas. However, both the Alphas and Betas have lived side by side for several generations without conflict. But some Alphas perceive the Betas to have closer ties to the Plurals, the large group that controls the state. These members of group A begin to speculate that group B plans to exploit these ties to dominate them. This perception of threat upsets the cooperative equilibrium that had been in place. Once group A feels threatened, and some of its members' hostility to group B is noticed by some members of group B, a counter-reaction among some members of group B develops. Some members of group A then take this counter-reaction as evidence in support of their prior belief that group B is opposed to their interests. Such a cycle could spin out of control and lead to conflict, and scholars have noted many cases that correspond roughly with this sort of pattern.

Some scholars who are sympathetic to elements of primordialist theories would argue that primordialist explanations alone are not fully satisfactory, as they need to be supplemented to explain conflict. Indeed, this may even be true of the stylized example considered in the previous paragraph. Since primordialist views of ethnic groups and nations seem to assume the permanent character of these groups *and* that these types of identities exist in all or virtually all human societies, they may have trouble explaining why in only certain cases ethnic conflict takes place. For example, if Hutus and Tutsis, Bosnians and Serbs, or Indian Hindus and Muslims lived alongside each other for many years, why did conflict suddenly erupt between them at particular historical junctures? To answer such questions, primordialists often need to invoke some other explanatory element, like economic crisis, political conflict, "modernization," and so forth. To this extent, as we have seen in other chapters, scholars may need to draw on distinct theories, creating a "hybrid" model of conflict to fully explain many cases.

Cultural Boundaries

Culturalist/constructivist explanations argue that conflict is the result of the distinct ways in which groups and their boundaries are constructed. In other words, some ways of drawing boundaries increase the chances that members of one group will attack members of another. At first glance, this theory might seem very similar to the primordialist theory noted previously. However, it differs in seeing high variability in the ways that different groups think about and represent themselves (and others) and sees this variability as key to explaining conflict. Often, such theories are rooted in accounts of "types" of nationalism like those discussed in the previous section.

Thus, some argue that ethnic nationalisms exhibit a higher probability of engaging in violence. Others similarly suggest that the likelihood of conflict is increased by "barricaded" identities, which construct sharp distinctions between in-group and out-group members and depict out-group members as threatening. This idea can be contrasted with "bounded" identities, which facilitate having multiple different associations.[33] As with primordialist explanations, however, other factors likely need to be invoked to explain why conflict actually takes place when it does, and why most "ethnic" or "barricaded" identities are not engaged in violence most of the time. Nations thought to construct boundaries in ethnic terms are not constantly at war; and even if it turns out that groups with "barricaded identities" are more likely to engage in violence, they are not constantly doing so, so some other variable must explain why violence emerges when it does.[34] Thus we might see a society constructing exclusive, impermeable boundaries as a condition that increases the probability of violence, but it is not a sufficient condition in and of itself.

Material Interests

Instrumentalist explanations make the assumption that people pursue "material" interests and that concerns like national pride or the dignity or "purity" of the ethnic group do not really matter much to them. The theory is called "instrumentalist" because it says ethno-national identities are just used as "instruments" for the pursuit of other purposes. Instrumentalists' explanatory strategy, therefore, involves hypothesizing that certain conditions in given cases make it politically expedient for some actors to deliberately foment ethnic boundaries and conflict. For example, if one group engages in violence toward another, perhaps the underlying reason is that the first group wants access to resources controlled by their victims. As with other theories noted so far, simple versions of such explanations taken alone are incomplete, begging questions about how ethnic boundaries could be useful manipulative tools to begin with if strategic action is paramount. In other words, if everyone is rational and self-interested, why are some people ethnic/national chauvinists to begin with? Why does it help politicians' chances, in some cases, to play to such sentiments?

One potential solution to this problem is to adopt George Akerlof and Rachel Kranton's idea of "identity utility."[35] Economists have long argued that people seek to maximize their "utility," or, roughly speaking, their satisfaction from different choices. We can recognize that people derive utility not just from material things but also from their identities. For example, it might be reasonable to assume that, on average, people prefer clear, dignified identities that are conducive to self-esteem. Then one can ask about the conditions under which people would turn to ethno-national chauvinism as they seek those ends. In this view, identity is thus shaped by preferences about both material and non-material payoffs.

Rational Calculation

Rational choice explanations—which have much in common with instrumentalist approaches—aim to model the strategic calculus of actors in situations of potential ethnic conflict. What distinguishes such approaches from ordinary instrumental explanations is (1) their typical use of mathematical models and (2) their focus on modeling the ability of members of a group to anticipate and thus make rational choices about how to respond preemptively to the behavior of members of the other group (and their own). The variables that must be considered in such models are many, including perceived likelihood of the other group perpetrating violence, perceived likelihood of victory if conflict breaks out, and perceived costs associated with *avoiding* violence. As noted earlier, rational choice models do not necessarily assume that material factors are central, and thus can be combined with any of the other perspectives mentioned here. For example, one could in principle combine a rational choice approach with a constructivist one, using constructivism to explain the exclusivist *preferences* of nationalist or ethnic chauvinist actors, and rationalism to explain the choices they make given those constructed preferences.

Let us try to imagine how such explanations work (see Table 13.3). It would not be rational, for example, for you to redefine yourself as the sole member of a group that nobody has ever heard of: there would be no actual group to offer benefits, and nobody else would recognize that membership. Likewise, if you were a

INSIGHTS

Nations, States, and Violence
by David Laitin

Laitin uses a "rational choice" perspective to explain why some ethnic and national groups attempt to assimilate, why others try to secede, and so forth. He notes that most ethnic and national groups get along with little violence, though they may have grievances with one another; and he argues that the rational calculation of interest explains why grievances sometimes result in violence. The spread of new identities depends on strategic decisions made by individuals about group affiliation, which in turn are shaped by the decisions of people around them. Individuals make choices about keeping or changing their own group affiliations based on three factors: economic benefit, "in-group status," and "out-group status." Group affiliation can impact one's income (as one's ethnic status can determine one's career prospects); it can influence one's standing within one's own group, and it can influence one's standing in the other group. For example, majority groups in some countries may condemn efforts by others to assimilate to the majority group, while the majority may encourage such efforts in other countries. Assimilation, secession, and other options are rational or irrational, depending on such factors.

David Laitin, Nations, States, and Violence. *New York: Oxford University Press, 2007.*

member of a minority group in a highly segregated society, trying to assimilate to the majority identity might not be rational, since you would likely face resistance from both majority and minority group members. However, as larger numbers of those around you take the assimilation path, it may become increasingly rational for you to do so (depending, of course, on your preferences). According to scholars like David Laitin (see Insights box on *Nations, States, and Violence*), these are the sorts of factors that shape the likelihood that someone will adopt a given ethno-national identity.

Somewhere along the line there is a "tipping point" beyond which it becomes more rational to assimilate than to persist in one's minority-group affiliation.[36] Of course, identification with an ethno-national group in most cases has no connection to violence. But a similar logic to the preceding applies to participation in secessionist movements. Scholars use this logic to try to predict whether participation in such movements will "cascade," or spread through a group.[37]

TABLE 13.3 Factors Influencing Ethno-National Identity: A Rational-Choice Approach

	Adopt the Majority Ethno-National Identity	Reject the Majority Ethno-National Identity
Few seek assimilation	Potential rewards if successful, but high risk is present, as potential costs include both in-group and out-group sanctioning.	No majority-group membership gains, but risks of in-group and out-group sanctioning minimized.
Many seek assimilation	Likelihood of group sanctioning goes down. Rewards are still present but with fewer potential costs.	No majority-group membership gains, and still no risk of in-group and out-group sanctioning.

Social Psychology

Social-psychological explanations come in a variety of forms.[38] On one hand, these approaches focus on common patterns of boundary construction and the ways in which social categorization structures our perceptions of those around us. Thus, they partially overlap with cultural constructivism. On the other hand, many stress the importance of status differences, and feelings of discontent and envy that these produce, in engendering conflict. The overarching idea, though, is that collectively held or group feelings and resentments lie behind conflict.[39]

In general, then, social-psychological theories focus on two things. First is the interactive process of the formation of group boundaries, the perception that "we are us" and "they are them." This relates to both the primordialist and constructivist approaches described previously (approaches that differ from each other most fundamentally with respect to the question of how such boundaries are established and how much they vary). The second is the relative social status of "us" and "them" in this connection. Many theories agree that some status configurations are more dangerous than others, and also that "status dynamics"—ways in which status systems change—can precipitate conflict. As such, social-psychological theories of group violence are "demand-side" theories, loosely analogous to the social-psychological theories of collective action discussed in chapter 12. In other words, they attempt to explain violence by assuming that it is a response to an increase in intergroup grievances. These theories view increased grievances (or the ways structural circumstances, such as a system of group rankings, can generate resentments) as key to explaining the likelihood of violence.

Of course, for most research questions, none of these ideal-typical explanations alone will suffice, but thinking through these general explanatory strategies is a good place to begin as we try to construct hypotheses to explain specific cases of ethnic conflict.

INSIGHTS | **Ethnic Groups in Conflict**
by Donald L. Horowitz

Horowitz's account of ethnic conflict emphasizes (among other factors) the social psychology of group resentment. Horowitz notes that ethnically diverse societies can be *ranked* or *unranked* systems. In a ranked system, at least one ethnic group is subordinated to another (as in India's caste system). In unranked systems, ethnicity might *correlate* with social class, but one group is not structurally subordinated to another. In ranked systems, conflict typically takes the form of class warfare or social revolution; whereas in unranked systems, conflict is often a drive to exclude, expel, or exterminate other groups. Among unranked systems, Horowitz further distinguishes between societies with many dispersed ethnic groups and those "ethnically centralized systems" with just a couple or several major groups. Major conflict centering on the state is likelier in ethnically centralized systems than in ethnically dispersed systems. While structural power relationships between groups matter, the driver of conflict is social-psychological: group resentment. Groups tend to compare themselves to other groups (a process exacerbated in many countries by colonialism) and often see themselves as entitled to higher status than other groups. Where differences in status persist, the potential ingredients for ethnic conflict are present.

Donald L. Horowitz, Ethnic Groups in Conflict. *Berkeley: University of California Press, [1985] 2000.*

Ending Ethnic and National Violence

In this chapter's "Thinking Comparatively" section, we consider how comparative research can influence policy. As noted at the beginning of this chapter, much of the practical "payoff" of research in this area, it is hoped, is that we may be able to reduce the probability of intergroup conflict.[42] Obviously, policy prescriptions should be strongly influenced by what empirical evidence about conflict shows us about theoretical explanations. If it seems that constructivist explanations of violence are correct, we may hope to use policy to influence the formation of ethnic and national boundaries. If rational-choice theories are correct, we can use them to alter the calculus of interests of leaders in potentially violent situations, perhaps by making clear that they will face consequences for their actions if they pursue violence. In general, there are at least four main proposed strategies for managing conflict suggested by social scientists, and comparative political analysis is being used to assess their reliability. These are open questions. Which of these views do *you* find most persuasive? What sorts of evidence could help us decide between them? Can you think of additional or supplementary approaches?

1. Institutional Approaches

By far the most influential proposal in political science has been that we may be able to reduce conflict by structuring institutions differently. There are several reasons for the popularity of this approach, among others that (1) political science in general in recent years has relied heavily on institutional analysis and (2) institutions—unlike, say, culture more generally—seem to be relatively amenable to engineering, at least in theory.[43] Typically, scholars propose one or another version of federalism or "**consociationalism**" as the solution to ethnic conflict.[44] Those who favor federalist solutions can be divided into two groups. Some wish to see decentralized political institutions cut *across* ethnic ties, the goal being to reduce the likelihood that leaders of such groups could harness political institutions in support of the interest and aims of their group. Others wish to see federation cut *along* ethnic lines. For example, some policymakers proposed a federated structure for Iraq that would have allowed considerable autonomy for Shiites, Sunni, and Kurds. In situations where formal ethnic federalism is not feasible (e.g., if the geographical settlement of different groups will not allow it), consociationalism calls for other methods for the systematic representation of ethnic groups as groups in the state.

2. Cultural and Civil Society Approaches

We have already noted that some suggest "peace building" initiatives, or efforts to foster "positive intergroup contact" as key.[45] In an important study, Ashutosh Varshney argues against excessive reliance on institutional solutions to intergroup conflict.[46] His analysis of group conflict in India reveals its local character and its roots in the structure of social networks. Conflict tends to take place in mostly urban areas and, indeed, in specific urban areas. Varshney's analysis led to the conclusion that the major variable that can explain the geographical distribution of conflict in India is the vibrancy of civic life: more specifically, in urban areas, the presence of civic associations that cut across ethnic lines protects against violence,

---

KEY METHODOLOGICAL TOOLS

Large-N Studies

Most of the comparative analysis discussed in this book involves trying to discern causal sequences in a relatively small number of cases. This approach has great utility. Sometimes, however, we need to compare lots of cases to make sure that our conclusions are not artifacts of case selection or bias.

This is exactly what James Fearon and David Laitin did.[40] They noted that much research on ethno-national bias selects cases *based on observed incidence of violence*. That research then finds links to patterns of ethno-national identity. But Fearon and Laitin chose a different tack, looking at a large sample including many cases of ethno-nationally diverse or heterogeneous societies. They found that ethno-national diversity was a *poor* predictor of intergroup conflict. This does not mean that ethnicity and nationalism have nothing to do with rates of conflict. Indeed, more recent work by Lars-Erik Cederman, Andreas Wimmer, and Brian Min has argued that ethnic conflict can be predicted more successfully when we take into account the role of the state. This work suggests that the key to explaining such conflict is to examine the ways in which access to state power intersects with ethnic and ethno-national distinctions.[41]

Large-N studies of this sort—which deal with a large number of observations—can often help us to distinguish between findings that only hold for a small number of cases and those that capture general tendencies or relationships.

consociationalism An institutional approach to managing potential conflict in polities with multiple groups, one that involves ensuring that each *group* has political representation.

which in India took place disproportionately in areas with low levels of associational activity. The major policy payoff here would be to find ways to strengthen non-ethnic associationalism. While in some ways this approach is presented as an alternative to institutional strategies, it is better regarded as a complement to such strategies. In other words, we are still talking about efforts to shape organizations rather than directly addressing networks, identities, or behavior.

3. Procedural and Judicial Approaches

Some scholars advocate using national and international judicial institutions to address problems of intergroup violence.[47] Rational choice and related forms of analysis draw important attention to the fact that the strategic considerations of both perpetrators and victims of violence shape outcomes over time. On one hand, it is important that potential perpetrators of violence have the reasonable expectation that there will be consequences if they harm others. On the other hand, once a cycle of violence has begun, it is important that at least some who have ties to such perpetrators do not so fear reprisal as to reach the judgment that ending violence would be too risky. Thus, some argue both for the importance of "individualizing responsibility" for the worst atrocities in ethnic conflict *and* for implementing forgiveness programs of one kind or another.[48] The de-escalation of South African conflict serves as a model for many proponents of this view.

4. International-System Approaches

More generally, international pressure can also reduce the violence carried out by states.[49] States and international actors can bring a variety of consequences to bear on transgressors of international human rights norms, and these may have an important deterrent effect. Such approaches are most likely to be successful, many scholars believe, when (1) the claim that other states or the international community are likely to act seems plausible and (2) the potential perpetrator of violence is not already isolated internationally, and thus has something to lose.

As you can see, these approaches are linked to the theories of conflict discussed previously. But how could we further test whether policies derived from theories will work? Theoretically, one approach would be to experiment with them, but for both practical and ethical reasons, this is not a real option. Therefore, we are largely dependent on comparing historical evidence from the real world, ideally when it exhibits "natural experiments" that mimic experimental comparison. As in other areas of comparative politics, we can examine existing theories of conflict through small groups of comparable case studies or through "large-N" studies. In the latter type of analysis, as discussed in the Key Methodological Tool box for this chapter, we would look for statistical correlations between predictors suggested by theory and cases of intergroup violence.[50] Truly identifying causal relationships without experiments is more difficult, but you can probably take a course on applied statistics at your university in which you will learn quantitative techniques for causal inference that do not rely on experimental data.

As with many of the areas discussed in this book, this is an ongoing research agenda with lots of questions left to debate and resolve. The hope is that we can come to more fully understand the ultimate sources of intergroup violence and, by doing so, the most efficacious ways to reduce or prevent it.

Chapter Summary

Concepts

- Comparative political analysts are interested in classifying and explaining major political identities.
- National identity is an important modern political identity emphasizing popular sovereignty and equality.
- Major theories of nationalism and national identity fall into the categories of primordialism, perennialism, and modernism.

Types

- Many scholars have identified so-called ethnic and civic forms of nationalism and national identity.
- A related distinction between *jus soli* and *jus sanguinis* characterizes differences in countries' laws about how citizenship is acquired or transmitted.
- Typologies of nationalism and national identity are increasingly controversial in the literature, with critics emphasizing both normative and empirical limitations.

Causes and Effects

- Scholars have produced a range of theories to explain ethnic and national violence. We considered five of them in schematic form.
- One theory holds that "primordial attachments" are responsible for collective violence. From this point of view, in other words, explanations of collective violence must account for the *emotional motivation* of perpetrators. Such theories often suggest that such emotional motivations are encoded in our biology, or in any case in our social nature, and threats to national identity (e.g., perceived imminent violence perpetrated by another group, or fears about cultural dilution in the face of globalization) prompt the behavior.
- Another theory holds that the nature of the cultural boundaries between groups strongly impacts the probability of conflict. Groups that define cultural boundaries as impermeable and essential are, according to this point of view, more likely to engage in violence.
- A third theory holds that material interests are the main determinant of collective violence. In other words, according to this theory, when groups claim to be engaging in violence because of group affiliation, they are actually interested in increasing their access to material resources like money, water, food supplies, or technology.
- A fourth theory holds that collective violence is best explained through modeling the rational decision-making processes of group leaders and/or members.
- A fifth theory holds that collective violence is the product of social-psychological processes that go beyond the ways that cultural boundaries are constructed.

Thinking Comparatively

- We thought about major policy proposals for reducing or eliminating intergroup conflict, and we linked these back to our earlier, causal theories of ethno-national violence.

Thinking It Through

1. In the "Causes and Effects" section of this chapter, we considered five major theories of intergroup/ethno-national conflict. These theories are not necessarily mutually exclusive. Sketch a hybrid theory that includes key elements of at least two of the theories discussed. Make clear (1) what is potentially gained through the linkage and (2) what, if anything, is lost about each of the theories included in the hybrid.

2. This chapter ends with a discussion of policy recommendations that have been made by political scientists who study ethno-national violence. We noted that they *related* to theories of ethno-national violence. However, some do not address "root causes," instead focusing on institutional solutions (like consociationalism) to problems that many theories would say are based on primordial, cultural, or material differences. Is this a contradiction? Why might someone who believes ethno-national conflict to have such geneses still prefer institutional solutions?

3. Pick a country you know well. Which of the three major perspectives on the historical origins of nationalism and national identity discussed in this chapter—primordialism, perennialism, and modernism—do you think would be most useful for the analysis of nationalism in this case? Explain the reasons for your selection.

CHAPTER 14

Race, Ethnicity, and Gender

Former U.S. President Barack Obama, former Chilean President Michele Bachelet, and Canadian Prime Minister Justin Trudeau in 2016.

In recent years, a number of countries have elected members of historically disadvantaged groups to the highest office. This trend has been especially notable in the Americas. Latin America, for example, has in recent years seen the election of several important women as president: Michele Bachelet in Chile (2006–2010, 2014–2018), Cristina Fernández in Argentina (2007–2015), and Dilma Rousseff in Brazil (2011–2016). The Americas have also recently witnessed the election of presidents from other disadvantaged social groups, such as Evo Morales in Bolivia (2006–present), Luiz Inácio Lula da Silva in Brazil (2003–2011), and Barack Obama in the United States (2009–2017). Some constituencies greeted these elections as a sign of political empowerment, and most observers would agree that this trend constitutes progress. But, as we shall see, it emphatically does *not* mean that race, ethnicity, and gender are no longer sources of political, social, and economic inequality.

Gender continues to strongly shape political representation, economic position, and social status, thus remaining a key and often under-examined feature of comparative politics. Race and ethnicity matter, too, perhaps especially given our increasingly global culture in which international migration is so common.[1] Possibly more than ever before, our societies are racially and ethnically diverse (to varying degrees, of course) and increasingly transnational, which yields both opportunities and challenges.[2] In this chapter, we consider identities linked to gender, race, and ethnicity in relation to efforts to achieve empowerment and political representation.

Despite the importance of gender, race, and ethnicity, with some notable exceptions, these subjects have often been minimized in the study of comparative politics. Happily, this tendency has started to change, in part because of **feminist theory** and **critical race** scholarship. In this chapter, we first focus on trying to clarify the concepts of race, ethnicity, and gender. We then move on to related concepts such as gender discrimination and gender empowerment. Then we turn our attention to how some women and members of minority groups have worked to enhance their participation and representation in formal institutions. As we shall see, while efforts to more fully

feminist theory An intellectual movement and approach to social and political theory that aims to ensure equal rights for women and to analyze ways in which gender and gender inequality relate to other important social and political phenomena.

critical race theory A movement in social, political, and legal theory that aims to discern the subtle effects of racism and related forms of prejudice.

boundaries Lines drawn symbolically between groups of people.

race The idea that human beings are divided into different groups, often thought of (erroneously) as biological categories.

ethnicity The quality that one has by identifying with or being ascribed membership in an ethnic group.

gender Culturally constructed roles or identities one has by virtue of being ascribed the status of male or female, to be distinguished from biological sex.

incorporate women and members of minority groups into formal political processes have a lot in common, they vary in important ways as well.

• • •

Concepts

Social scientists interested in the issues discussed in this chapter need to first define what we mean by race, ethnicity, gender, and sexual orientation. Though some of these concepts are related, they differ in important ways as well.

Race and Ethnicity

As discussed in chapter 13, all human societies construct collective identities, which vary considerably depending on their context. Among other things, these identities often involve **boundaries** between an "in-group" ("us") and an "out-group" ("them").[3] One strategy for trying to understand various types and instances of collective identity is to focus on the nature of these boundaries. Different types of identities depend on contrasting ways of drawing lines between groups of people. Identities based on **race**, **ethnicity**, and **gender** draw these lines in overlapping and yet distinct ways.

We shall begin to untangle the related concepts of race and ethnicity later in the chapter; for now we will just point to shared features of these categories of identity. Both suggest that people are divided into groups. Both treat group membership as important, and both can be sources of out-group discrimination and in-group pride. In some cases, the boundaries between groups are more permeable

Whip-toting riot police in South Africa's apartheid state in 1985.

than in others. Unequal relationships between ethnic and racial groups can be caused and reinforced by formal and legal differences. For example, think of explicit segregation under "Jim Crow" laws in the southern United States before the civil rights movement peaked in the 1960s or under South African apartheid. Alternatively, inequalities can be buttressed by more subtle forms of discrimination. Finally, as we discuss further in the "types" section following, some people think of race (and sometimes ethnicity too) as biological categories, though most social scientists reject this idea.[4]

As discussed in chapter 13, there is a range of social-scientific views on the nature of national, ethnic, and racial identities. Some accounts emphasize constructivism, others instrumentalism, and still others primordialism (see chapter 13 if you need to review these concepts and theories).

Gender

The first distinction that needs to be drawn here is between gender and sex.[5] People often conflate these two ideas, but they are not identical. From the point of view of many social scientists, *sex* is about being biologically male or female. *Gender*, in contrast, is *cultural*.[6] This means that it is essentially symbolic. One way to formulate this is to say that gender is the way in which human beings "make sense" out of sex. For example, think of ideas like "masculinity" and "femininity." We may link these ideas to ways of acting and even different sorts of bodies. For example, in some cultural contexts, maybe being very muscular is masculine, in others not; in some cultural contexts, femininity and athletic prowess may go hand in hand, while in others femininity may be linked to perceived physical passivity. But given all of these differences, we know that ideas about gender (like masculinity and femininity) cannot be reduced to underlying sex differences. Indeed, some individuals' experienced gender does not "match" their biological sex in the traditional sense, and some individuals have **transgender** identities.

Social scientists debate the precise relationship between sex and gender. The dominant view is **social constructionism** (or social constructivism), which holds that biological sex does not determine gender. From this point of view, biology is not destiny. **Biological determinism**, the other end of the spectrum, asserts that gender is just a reflection of sex. As far as we are aware, there are no serious social scientists that are true biological determinists in this sense. The main debate is really between "strong" and "weak" versions of social constructionism. The "weak" version holds that gender is indeed culturally constructed but that there may be some biological differences between women and men that limit or constrain this construction. For example, perhaps evolution has indeed encouraged some different tendencies in how people think about hierarchy or relationships or sexuality itself.[7] The "strong" version holds that any such tendencies are insignificant or do not exist at all.

In other words, social scientists largely agree that gender is not *determined* by biological sex. This premise has some important implications. Perhaps most important, if gender is socially constructed, it can change over time. Gender might have meant something different in 1950s America than it does today, for example. In other words, being a woman or a man decades ago was likely experientially different in some respects than it is in the twenty-first century (just think of the

transgender An identity in which one's gender does not conform to conventional matching with biological sex.

social constructionism An approach to analyzing social life that emphasizes the processes through which socially shared meanings and definitions are established and maintained.

biological determinism The view that a feature of social life, such as gender or ethnicity, is caused by underlying biology.

television show *Mad Men*). Note that if biological determinism is true, this change would be impossible. If gender can change over time, this means that (1) activists can try to shape it, at least to some extent, and (2) social scientists can try to map and explain the ways in which it has changed. Activities, identities, roles, jobs, even objects in the world can be seen as "gendered"; and regardless of one's sex, everyone can participate in such gendered activities, perform such gendered roles, and exemplify different gendered styles, in varying ways and to different degrees.[8]

Sexual Orientation and Gender Identity

When social scientists speak of sexual orientation in the most narrow sense, they refer to the fact that different people seek different sorts of sexual partners. Historically, in many societies, a heterosexual, or "straight," sexual orientation has been held up as the standard. People with other orientations, such as gays and lesbians, were labeled as deviant and, as a result, often faced serious discrimination. Some scholars refer to this view, which takes heterosexuality as "normal" and preferred, as "heteronormativity" or "normative heterosexuality."[9] It is important to recognize that sexual orientation and gender identity are not the same thing. According to Human Rights Campaign, a non-profit organization devoted to LGBTQ advocacy and education, "gender identity" refers, in part, to "how individuals perceive themselves and what they call themselves"; whereas sexual orientation is "an inherent or immutable enduring emotional, romantic, or sexual attraction to other people."[10]

Even today, people in same-sex relationships as well as people of diverse gender identities are subject to discrimination (and same-sex relationships are even illegal in some countries and territories), but social movements have led to decriminalization and widespread acceptance in numerous locations. These movements have also expanded civil rights in other ways, including, in some places, the extension of basic institutions like marriage. This has been accompanied by notable cultural change, captured by survey research, showing that public attitudes about these issues have shifted considerably in recent years in much of the world, fueled especially by the attitudes of younger cohorts.[11]

The process of extending rights and ending discrimination is far from over, and even in countries where the rights of LGBTQ persons have increased the most, discrimination remains a serious issue.[12]

Types

Different types of disadvantage and discrimination take place on the basis of race, ethnicity, and gender. At the same time, these categories may have different implications for potential empowerment.

Disentangling Race and Ethnicity

As with gender, some people imagine race to be a biological category. Scientifically, however, this way of thinking is inaccurate. As scholars have emphasized, there is far greater genetic variation within than between so-called racial groups.[13] The socially constructed (and thus non-biological) nature of race becomes even clearer when we look at the history of racial concepts. Categories such as "white" or "black" or "Asian" may appear to be stable and thus grounded in human nature, but they are not. Indeed, to take a particularly striking example, according to some scholars, in the nineteenth-century, U.S. Irish immigrants were sometimes defined as "non-white"; and even today in much of Latin America and other parts of the world, racial categories are far more fluid and permeable than they are in the United States.[14] Further, consider the racial typologies constructed in late-colonial Latin America, where elites asserted that some people of mixed-race parentage fell into categories such as "coyotes," "wolves," and "mulattos."[15] Very few people today would consider these categories to constitute anything but racist nonsense.

We can draw one of two possible conclusions from this set of successive and inconsistent categorizations. One possibility is that there are distinct and biologically real "races" but that most people have gotten them wrong for most of history, and that we now know what they really are. The other possibility is that they have been social constructions all along: in other words, that people have invented these ideas rather than discovering them in nature. Most scholars draw the latter conclusion.[16]

Scholars who study racial identity identify certain stages or periods of **racialization** and **racial formation**, meaning times in which social distinctions pertaining to the idea of "race" became more pronounced.[17] Typically, these processes have to do with one or another group having an interest in closing off competition for status or resources.[18] When individuals and groups compete for social status, they often seek to formally exclude others from competition, making it easier for themselves.[19] Race has often been used for this purpose.[20] For example, Europeans drew distinctions between themselves and "black" individuals from sub-Saharan Africa for centuries; but when European colonizers of the Americas sought to enslave those individuals on a mass scale and to exploit indigenous groups, they drew a clearer, "racialized" line between themselves, the indigenous population, and Africans, trying to justify their different forms of exploitation.[21]

In summary, most scholars believe that race is not a biological fact but is instead a social construction. An identity is a "racial" identity when people in a society *believe* that one or another group is significantly biologically different from other groups, and view these imagined differences through the race concept. For this reason, it is only a useful category for comparative analysis when we are studying societies who think about themselves and others in terms of race. In such cases, we aim to understand (1) how they think about race, (2) how ideas of race are constructed by different groups, and (3) whose interests are served by these different constructions. Some important comparative analysis aims to explain differences between societies' constructions and uses of race.[22]

The terms "ethnicity" and **ethnic group** are sometimes used as synonyms of race, but they are often applied more broadly. An influential conception of ethnic groups is as follows: "named units of population with common ancestry myths and historical memories, elements of shared culture, some link with a historic territory, and some measure of solidarity, at least among their elites."[23] Defined in this way, ethnicity is more conceptually general than race: "Common ancestry myths" does not necessarily imply that those myths are thought to be biological, even if they often are understood to be so. If one chooses this sort of conceptual approach, "ethnic group" is also a broader category of collective identity than more narrowly defined "national identity" discussed in the previous chapter.[24]

racialization The historical process through which social relations become interpreted in terms of racial categories.

racial formation A concept developed by Omi and Winant (1994) that describes the process through which ideas of race are constructed and develop over time.

ethnic group A group that identifies itself as having strong cultural commonality and a shared sense of long-run history, sometimes thinking of itself as a kind of kinship group.

Yet much work on questions of ethnicity and ethnic identity focuses not on the long-term past but on the nature of these identities and the roles they play in the contemporary world. Often, scholars of ethnicity think of it as an identity that is not necessarily bound to a state (though states often influence ethnicity in a variety of ways). For example, Irish Americans, Korean Americans, and African Americans might be called "ethnic groups" because while some members of these groups feel a sense of cultural belonging, they generally do not express a desire to form their own state. Ethnicity, as such, is perfectly consistent with membership in a broader civic or multicultural community in which individuals hold other collective identities besides their ethnicity.[25] Sometimes, in-group or out-group members think of ethnicity in biological terms. Most social scientists, though, think of ethnicity as based on cultural commonalities, ranging from shared rituals and practices to language. In the U.S. context, the national census considers categories such as Hispanic or Latino to be ethnicity rather than race. This has been somewhat controversial since categories such as Asian and African American are treated as race.[26]

Ideas such as ethnicity are constructed in very different ways in different societies.[27] Thus, identities deriving from tribal forms of organization in some parts the world, those deriving from distinct units in hierarchical stratification systems in some African societies or in India, and those of "hyphenated Americans" cannot for all research purposes be treated as instances of the same general phenomenon—yet social scientists will often treat all such identities as "ethnic." In modern societies, the following components are likely to be building blocks for how ethnicity is identified: the society's national identity and how it represents cultural difference, how the state deals with questions of citizenship and residency, formal and informal rules of national belonging and participation in public life, and the broader stratification system (which in most modern societies means the class structure).

The contemporary United States is an illustrative example. Its civic identity has been described as a "melting pot," but it is not hard to find contradictions to this idea. Examples include the indigenous population's forced relocation, clearly genocidal by today's standards; slavery and then segregation of African Americans; and discrimination against various waves of immigrants from the nineteenth century to the present. While the traditional model of assimilation has been hotly contested—both by scholars who argue that the United States has never been a melting pot and by those who argue that it should not be—the "melting pot" ideal has remained important among many Americans. Others, though, suggest that multiculturalism is an alternative view.[28] Here the core idea is that members of different groups do not need to leave their differences to the side: a meaningful political community can encompass diverse groups of people who maintain some degree of cultural difference. In a context like the United States, though, this is typically still linked to civic nationalism, since categories like citizenship and legal status are still seen by most the basis of many rights and as a qualification for full participation in politics.

In any case, widespread civic identity in the United States has not meant the denial of ethnicity, at least in recent decades. Rather, it has allowed for dual and multiple affiliations, as in the case of so-called hyphenated Americans. American culture has sometimes encouraged immigrants and their descendants to hold onto a reconstructed version of their old national identities, redefined as ethnicity.[29] This cultural aspect has sometimes been a matter of others labeling immigrants and sometimes one of proud internal identification (or both). Some societies, however, may seek to force immigrants to give up their traditional identities to assimilate.[30] More generally, the state plays a role in the ongoing construction of ethnicity, such as by making "official" decisions about how to use ethnic categories in the census or in laws and judicial decisions involving ethnicity.[31] It has made such decisions in cases involving questions of affirmative action in employment and in efforts by college and university admissions offices to ensure a diverse student body. The state also shapes ethnicity through the way it handles intergroup conflict, particularly in societies with multiple ethnic groups that sometimes experience pronounced differences, such as India or Nigeria.

Discrimination Based on Race and Ethnicity

Both ethnicity and race often serve as the basis for discrimination, which can be both explicit and implicit. In a country like the United States, racial and ethnic identities have a pronounced impact on one's prospects for income, assets, education, marriage, and incarceration, among other outcomes.[32] This impact is perhaps most notable in relation to assets and wealth, which is partly a legacy of historical inequalities.[33] Some discrimination is explicit and obvious: almost everyone recognizes the most virulent forms of racism. But while some people believe that racial and ethnic discrimination have declined across the globe—and indeed, in the United States, surveys show that explicit racism is less prevalent than it once was[34]—members of minority groups continue to experience high rates of discrimination.[35] A lot of inequality based on race and ethnicity is not obvious to most observers.[36] In the United States, **audit studies** (which use fieldwork to measure discrimination) confirm that equally qualified applicants with names stereotypically linked to some minority groups are less likely to be offered job interviews than applicants with stereotypically "white" names.[37] In short, social scientists who study race and ethnicity almost universally agree that even as explicit racism has declined in societies like the United States, racial and ethnic disparities remain a serious problem.

audit studies Research carried out by social scientists to measure the extent to which hiring practices are discriminatory.

Discrimination and its historical legacies take very different forms in different societies. Since race and ethnicity are socially constructed and because they intersect with other potential bases of cleavage in a variety of ways, there is no one set pattern of racial and ethnic discrimination. Brazil, for example, is often contrasted with the United States on this issue.[38] Many have asserted that Brazil does not face exactly the same problems of racism as the United States, since there is no *sharp* color line in Brazil. Yet it is clear to most observers that some groups in Brazil are nevertheless disadvantaged, leading to recent efforts at affirmative action and related approaches.

Demographic forces produce variation in how race and ethnicity are constructed, and they shape discrimination as well. Societies with long traditions as destinations for large-scale immigration can be expected to exhibit different dynamics than societies that have received little immigration. This observation might help explain why some countries in Western Europe, such as France, have faced challenges incorporating immigrant groups in recent years. Polities that presided over long histories of slavery may exhibit dynamics different from societies without such histories. Cultural traditions and beliefs likely matter as well. Finally, the principal actors involved vary from case to case. Actors that can be agents of discrimination include not just the state but other societal institutions, as well as groups and individuals within the society.

Gender Discrimination

The meaning of gender discrimination may seem fairly obvious. Many people are explicitly discriminated against on the basis of their gender. For example, a woman might be denied a job because she is a woman, or her work might be unpaid, or paid less than the work of an equally qualified man.[39] In a number of countries, as with racial and ethnic discrimination, political action over decades has resulted in laws offering some protection against discrimination based on gender and sexual orientation. Yet again, the protection offered does not fully resolve the problem, and in a number of societies explicit job discrimination remains rampant. Beyond this, other forms of discrimination, perhaps less obvious, happen in virtually all societies.[40] While both men and women experience sexual harassment, women are far more likely to encounter it.[41] Yet social-scientific data suggest that—in addition to persistent discrimination of this kind—women are systematically disadvantaged in somewhat subtler ways as well.

Women are often paid less than men.[42] In a number of places, this inequality is explicit, and it still happens with frequency in advanced industrial and postindustrial societies like the United States, despite efforts to curb the problem. But think about ways in which women suffer from pay differentials *beyond* such explicit forms of discrimination:

- First, cultural pressures still sometimes emphasize that women bear special responsibility for raising children. As a result, "work-life balance" issues tend to be especially acute for women; and, in just about any field, taking time off from the workplace means lower pay and slower ascent of the career ladder.[43] Women take time off not only to give birth but because in some cases they feel more pressure than male counterparts to stay home with children on an ongoing basis.[44]
- Second, employers may engage in anticipatory discrimination for these reasons. Women might be less likely to receive promotions—or even opportunities to demonstrate they deserve promotions or raises—because of expectations that their time may be divided between work and family.
- Third, discriminatory attitudes about women's abilities and competencies persist. For example, some people still believe, erroneously, that men are better at math and science and related technical subjects.
- Fourth, on a related note, some argue that the labor market itself is gendered.[45] Some jobs are considered by many to be stereotypically or characteristically male, and others stereotypically or characteristically female. Traditionally, jobs gendered as female have paid lower wages than those gendered as male. Thus women could, within these categories, receive "equal pay for equal work" and *still*, when we think about the broader society, be paid unfairly in the aggregate.

CASE IN CONTEXT
Gender in Post-Revolutionary Iranian Politics

PAGE 482

Many people think of post-revolutionary Iran as a country where discrimination against women is widespread. Indeed, this is accurate. However, as is so often the case with this country, the reality is more complex than many know. Iranian society is one in which women—despite structural and institutional obstacles and inequalities—do find ways to assert their agency.

For more on these issues, see the case study in Part VI, p. 482. As you read it, keep in mind the following questions:

1. What conditions did women face in Iran before the revolution?
2. How has the revolution impacted women's position in Iranian society?
3. How do some Iranian women resist coercion?

These are just some examples of mechanisms through which gender discrimination in the labor market might operate. Of course, they play out very differently in the wide range of contemporary societies.

In addition to pay inequality, women are often systematically disadvantaged because in many societies, parents invest more in the human capital of their sons than their daughters.[46] In these instances, women are not competing on a level playing field, as they have fewer resources. This tendency has been greatly reduced, however, in many advanced industrial and post-industrial societies. Indeed, in a number of countries, women consistently outperform men in the educational system.[47] Institutions of higher education increasingly have a hard time achieving gender balance between male and female students because women tend to have higher grades and better test scores.

Beyond serious, ongoing explicit and subtle discrimination in economic life, women continue to face discrimination in the political sphere in virtually all societies, though societies vary substantially in the *extent* to which this is true.[48] It is only over the last century that women have acquired the right to vote in most countries (including the United States), in some far more recently, and in a few not at all. And even in countries with long-established traditions of women's suffrage, women politicians rarely occupy top posts at parity with men. As we shall see later in this chapter, there is much debate about why this is the case and what its main consequences might be. Women are less likely than men to hold office at all levels of government. This disparity is perhaps most notable at the upper echelons of the executive branch. The systematic disadvantage of women in politics most likely reinforces other forms of disadvantage, since research indicates that women in political office are more likely than men to aim to eradicate discrimination and related problems.[49] Beyond these issues, keep in mind that globally, women are considerably more likely than men to experience poverty and sexual violence.

We wish to emphasize that while these claims are generally true, the global population of societies exhibits wide variation in the extent of observable gender discrimination and inequality. Some countries, such as the Scandinavian societies of Sweden, Norway, and Finland, stand out as especially progressive, although even these have not erased gender inequality.[50]

CASE IN CONTEXT

Gender Empowerment in Japan?

PAGE 497

Centuries ago, Japan was noteworthy, among other reasons, because it was sometimes governed by empresses. Yet contemporary Japanese politics has been regarded as a case in which gender discrimination is high. How and why is this the case?

For more on the subject, see the case study in Part VI, p. 497. As you read it, keep in mind the following questions:

1. On what grounds could someone claim that gender discrimination in Japanese politics is relatively high?
2. What are the major factors that have contributed to this tendency?

Empowerment of Women and Minority Groups

empowerment An increase in the social, political, or economic capabilities of an individual or group.

Empowerment is the expansion of the socially defined capability of a given group.[51] The simplest way to conceive of empowerment is as the opposite of discrimination. That is, you might think about women or minority groups becoming empowered to the extent that they overcome such discrimination. This idea is helpful but only partially defines empowerment, which could, in principle, extend beyond the achievement of parity. We think of empowerment as expanding women's and minority group members' capabilities in all spheres of life that relate to politics.

Empowerment can be economic.[52] For example, prohibiting or undoing economic discrimination (such as in the labor market) based on gender, race, or ethnicity is a

Leymah Gbowee and Tawakkol Karman, who, along with Ellen Johnson Sirleaf, shared the Nobel Peace Prize in 2011.

form of empowerment. Many agencies encourage economic development—another form of empowerment—by offering small loans specifically to women.[53] Similarly, many developing world societies, such as Brazil and Mexico, target women with "conditional cash transfers": that is, they disburse funds to those who comply with certain conditions, such as enrolling children in schools.[54] In part, this practice rests on evidence that women are more likely than men to invest such funds in the human capital of their families (i.e., health and education) rather than in personal consumption. Further, one can think of women's cooperatives—in which women not only pool resources but also create political structures that allow them to exert leadership—as potentially empowering. Government programs that provide services such as child care and medical care to women can also be empowering.

Empowerment can also be cultural or symbolic. One example of symbolic empowerment is a low-status group engaging in collective action to elevate its status. Of course, status often goes along with economic class and political power, but we should not assume that it always does so or that it is not independently important.[55] Lesbian, gay, bisexual, transgender, and queer (LGBTQ) rights activists in the United States and a number of other countries stand out for having aimed to shape the status position of the populations they represent and support. One aspect of the movement is working to expand the political representation of LGBTQ people. It also seeks to promote positive depictions of LGBTQ people, both in the media and in everyday life. This effort has involved lobbying media as well as more grassroots action such as gay pride parades and related events. Such actions aim to extend social benefits to in-group members, in addition to demanding broader social acceptance and elevated status. Symbolic empowerment may be an important component in achieving political and economic empowerment, since politics and economics are ultimately cultural.

Finally, empowerment can be directly political.[56] We can think of the women's movement and the civil rights movement in the United States as empowering, and we can think of participation in more specific social movement and protest activity as potentially empowering. Indeed, we would likely judge a movement or activity successful to the degree that it empowers group members. Political parties that aim to advance the goals of specific ethnic groups are also potentially empowering (for interesting reasons, as we shall see, political parties that represent women as a group are relatively rare[57]). Laws and interventions to ensure political opportunities for women and members of minority groups may be empowering as well. Perhaps most important, we can see empowerment in initiatives that increase women's and minority group members' representation in political offices.

On a related note, some scholars interested in women's empowerment have focused on "state feminism," which one political scientist defines as "the advocacy of women's movement demands inside the state."[58] This perspective reminds us that beyond social movement organizing and political competition for elected office, both elected and appointed office holders inside the state bureaucracy can contribute to the empowerment of women and other groups in myriad ways.[59]

In the "Causes and Effects" section that follows, we focus on political empowerment because it is fundamental. Once a group is politically empowered, it has an expanded capacity to shape agendas. As a result, it can then push for other forms of empowerment.

CASE IN CONTEXT

Gender and Political Representation in Brazil: Where Has Progress Come From?

PAGE 411

Historically, Latin America has been viewed, rightly or wrongly, as a region in which women face widespread discrimination. Yet in recent years, the women's movement has made notable advances in this region, such as in Brazil.

For more on the state of women's political empowerment in Brazil, see the case study on pp. 411–412 in Part VI. As you read it, keep in mind the following questions:

1. What have been the major successes of feminist activism in Brazil in recent years?
2. Why, according to political scientists, have gender-linked parties not been prominent in Brazil?
3. Why, nevertheless, has the Workers' Party tended to be more favorable to women's empowerment?

Causes and Effects: What Factors Influence the Political Representation of Women and Minority Groups?

In this section, we consider factors affecting political representation of women and minority groups. As noted previously, we are narrowing our focus a bit, as we will pay less attention here to questions of economic and symbolic empowerment, though these are not unrelated. We focus on social movement mobilization, the creation of political parties based on gender or ethnicity, and institutional design tools such as quotas. These potential causes of empowerment are not mutually exclusive but rather may go together.

Social Movement Mobilization

Perhaps the most important process through which women and minority groups can be empowered is through social movement mobilization.[60] Indeed, this process often underlies the two other main processes we consider in this section: political parties and policy responses.[61] As noted in chapter 12, social movements typically need to develop organizations to maintain their momentum and direction over an extended period: political parties are one such type of organization. The development of a political party out of a social movement is a step in the institutionalization of that movement's concerns.[62]

Social movement mobilization can also be effective in other ways. It can act in the form of symbolic empowerment to expand the interests of a group. Thus, social movement activity can aim to transform political culture or popular attitudes about a group, such as LGBTQ people (as we mentioned earlier). The civil rights movement in the United States is another clear example here. The movement's goals were many and included both the political and economic empowerment of African Americans; but one of its key aims was breaking down the symbolic barriers that facilitated many white Americans' support of or tolerance for discriminatory Jim Crow laws. Another example is activism on the part of minority groups in a number of European societies (such as the Scottish and Welsh in the United

INSIGHTS   American Indian Ethnic Renewal: Red Power and the Resurgence of Identity and Culture
by Joane Nagel

Nagel's book is an effort to explain a fascinating demographic pattern in the late-twentieth-century United States: the dramatic increase in the number of persons claiming an American Indian or Native American identity. This trend was not a product of an increased birthrate, but rather of more individuals claiming an identity that they would not have avowed previously. Nagel finds that, in part, this change was a consequence of social movement activity. In the civil rights era, a number of factors increased the likelihood of mobilization around an American Indian identity, and an important movement among persons of American Indian identity developed. Most notably, a group of "Red Power" activists seized Alcatraz Island in San Francisco in 1969. But this was only the most visible event in a much more widely dispersed process, which included additional takeovers, marches, and many other actions.

According to Nagel, part of what social movement mobilizing accomplished was a transformation in the status of American Indian identity. Movement activists redefined this identity from one that had been given little status in the broader American society to one seen as a source of pride. Nagel's account of this case highlights the importance of social movement

organizing in empowering groups symbolically, beyond just the expansion of economic position and political power.

Joane Nagel, American Indian Ethnic Renewal: Red Power and the Resurgence of Identity and Culture. *New York: Oxford University Press, 1996.*

In 1969, American Indian activists took over Alcatraz Island. This protest activity drew attention to their cause.

Kingdom and the Catalonians in Spain). These movements have sought symbolic empowerment in addition to expanded political power.

We looked at major theories of contentious action, including social movements, in chapter 12. One major cluster of social movement theories, prominent in Europe, claims that these movements have brought concerns of identity to the foreground in recent decades.[63] This assertion is debated, however, as some argue that identity concerns have always been central to social movements.

Whether or not social movement activity focusing on questions of [identity is] novel, there is no disputing that it can be an effective strategy f[or a] group. As noted previously, one way it can work is through he[lping to] support political parties that represent the interests of a group.

Political Parties Based on Gender or Ethnicity

So how do political parties help represent a group's interests? First, m[ost] electoral systems depend on political parties to organize political co[mpetition.] Parties bind political representatives together under common platform[s and] can strongly influence votes and thus political decision making. This in[fluence] varies from case to case, of course, and not all parties are equally capable of sha[ping]

INSIGHTS | The Power of Identity
by Manuel Castells

Castells considers the importance of identity movements in the contemporary world. He finds that identity issues prompt a great deal of contemporary social movement activity. The most important social transformations are cultural or cognitive, he argues, since "domination is primarily based on the construction of reality in the human mind."[64]

Castells argues that there are three main kinds of political identities. These are "legitimizing identities," "resistance identities," and "project identities." Legitimizing identities are tied to the nation-state, which Castells believes to be threatened by the rise of the global "network society." "Resistance identities" are tied to members of communal groups (like some ethnic groups) and are often oriented toward resisting the network society and globalization. Finally, "project identities" look forward rather than backward. They do not aim just to defend existing communities from larger forces but to construct new identities that transform society more broadly. Castells' favorite example here is the global feminist movement, which he calls the "movement against patriarchy." The core idea is that this movement has had success by changing women's identities, and that in the process it came to reconfigure key social institutions, such as the family. The reconfiguration of these institutions has changed gender identities more broadly.

Manuel Castells, The Power of Identity. 2nd ed. Malden, MA: Wiley-Blackwell, 2010.

the voting behavior of their members. Another reason that parties can matter is that in some political systems, parties exist as either an official (e.g., contemporary China) or de facto (e.g., Mexico in the heyday of the PRI) layer in institutional decision-making processes. As chapters 9 through 11 show, the nature of the electoral system and how the legislature and executive are structured also affect the ways in which parties organized around an ethnic group might exert influence. As we shall see, the nature of those systems also impacts the probability that an ethnic party will develop.

However party organization intersects with the state, parties are useful tools for pursuing group interests. When and why ethnic parties are formed is a somewhat complicated question. Several variables probably matter, but in interaction with one another.[65] In other words, none of them alone is likely sufficient to produce ethnic parties.

The first such variable is demographic.[66] How racially and ethnically heterogeneous is the society in question? This is not to suggest that there is an ideal level of ethnic heterogeneity for the formation of ethnic political parties but that some level of heterogeneity is key. The relative shares of the population divided into each group, as well as the number of groups and the geographical dispersion of groups, can influence the probability of the formation of ethnic parties. This demographic variable interacts with several other variables, the most important of which are likely (1) the society's culture of ethnic affiliation more broadly (e.g., how does the culture in general handle ethnic attachment?) and, equally important, what other bases for political mobilization are available that might crowd out ethnic party organizing; (2) the nature of political competition in the society in question; and (3) the historical and structural relationships between ethnic groups.[67]

The way a society handles questions of ethnic affiliation more broadly might also be relevant to ethnic party formation. For example, does the society define national identity in ethnic terms, or does it view national identity as attached to

Causes and Effects: What Factors Influence the Political Representation of Women and Minority Groups?

343

INSIGHTS	From Movements to Parties in Latin America
	by Donna Lee Van Cott

Van Cott seeks to explain how it came to be that Amerindian social movements in four Latin American countries successfully created parties pursuing their interests in the 1990s. Her four positive cases are Bolivia, Colombia, Ecuador, and Venezuela; and she notes that similar results did not take place in Argentina or Peru. This full set of both positive and negative cases allows her to compare societies in which there are large indigenous populations (Bolivia, Ecuador, and Peru) and those in which there are smaller indigenous populations (Argentina, Colombia, and Venezuela). This comparison shows that demographic variables alone do not explain the fate of ethnic parties but rather that demographic variables interact with other factors. There are two main factors that Van Cott considers especially important: institutional factors and social movement activity.

Within the institutional factors, Van Cott believes two to be particularly important. First, decentralization and related reforms (including reserved seats) in some of these countries allowed for opportunities for new political actors tied to ethnicity-linked organizing. In addition, the traditional left was weakened in the period of the "Washington Consensus," meaning that ideological space was opened up for new ways to frame resistance and to organize politically. In the successful cases, social movement activists seized on these opportunities as they created parties to pursue their group interests.

Donna Lee Van Cott, From Movements to Parties in Latin America. *New York: Cambridge University Press, 2005.*

citizenship?[68] Imagine a society that historically treats national identity in ethnic terms and where a large ethnic majority comprises this ethno-national group. We would expect this situation to affect the likelihood that either the majority group or any minority groups would seek political representation through parties.

Perhaps equally or even more important, other bases for social cleavage can crowd out ethnic attachment as a basis for forming political parties.[69] This is sometimes true of social class, for example. Sometimes a strong tradition of class-based organizing—think of a society in which people are mobilized as workers or as peasants—might reduce the likelihood of organizing around ethnicity.

CASE IN CONTEXT

Why Aren't There Major Ethnic Parties in Mexico?

PAGE 511

Mexico, like many countries, has had a long history of ethnic discrimination. As in the United States, we might expect to find a history of political parties forming there on the basis of ethnic cleavages. Yet again, as in the United States, we find little such history. This outcome, however, seems likely to be due to a different set of conditions, thus facilitating an interesting comparison.

For more on ethnic cleavages and political parties in Mexico, see the case study in Part VI, pp. 511–512. As you read it, keep in mind the following questions:

1. Why might one expect to find ethnic parties in Mexico?
2. What major features of Mexican political development might help us account for their absence?
3. How does this interesting case compare with the cases of the United States and India (discussed later)?

CASE IN CONTEXT
Ethnicity and Political Parties in India

PAGE 467

India stands out as a country where some ethnic-group-affiliated parties have seen success. What accounts for this success, and why have others failed? Political scientists in recent years have made advances in accounting for this variation.

For more on this question, see the case study in Part VI, pp. 467–468. As you read it, keep in mind the following questions:

1. What are the basic characteristics of those parties that have been successful?
2. How and to what extent might knowledge derived from the case of India be applied to other cases?
3. How does the development of ethnic parties in India compare with the cases of the United States and Mexico (discussed previously)?

The nature of political competition in a society seems to matter a lot as well. Ethnic parties seem to be more likely in parliamentary systems in which there is proportional representation because it is more likely that an ethnic party could win some seats and play a role in a coalition government in such cases.

Imagine a country in which 10 percent of the population falls into an ethnic group that has faced some discrimination, and members of this group seek to influence the political process to reduce this discrimination. A party could help in a system based on proportional representation, because if a high percentage of group members voted for the party, it could win parliamentary seats and bargain to join a governing coalition.[70] However, if the society has a first-past-the-post system (i.e., the winning candidate simply needs the most votes), there is little chance that group members would (rationally) pursue party organization. The reason is that if the party was perceived to be exclusively linked to the needs of a minority ethnic group, it would have trouble reaching the vote threshold needed to win seats. Of course, depending on how such an electoral system is structured, a minority ethnic party could achieve reasonable representation under some conditions. For example, if an ethnic minority is geographically concentrated, constituting a majority in some areas, it might be in the minority at the national level but still capable of winning a number of seats in the legislature.

Finally, the nature of the historical and structural relationships between groups, including their relative power, could matter greatly in influencing the likelihood of ethnic party development. For example, historical discrimination against a group may motivate them to form a party.

So far in this subsection we have been discussing political parties based on ethnic group membership. But what about gender? Interestingly, political parties based on gender are much rarer than parties based on ethnicity. Some scholars have investigated why this might be (see the Insights box on Mala Htun's work, *Is Gender like Ethnicity?*).

In short, several factors curb the formation of a women-only political party. The main reason may be, however, that women are institutionally linked to men: their interests as individuals and as members in other groups are tied in important ways to the interests of individual men and members of those other groups.[71]

Institutions for Promoting Women's and Minority Group Representation

One goal of many social movements and political parties is institutional design that will expand a certain group's political representation. While social movement organizing and political party formation can acquire a degree of permanence, institutional design can potentially shape outcomes in more enduring ways. In other words, this approach seeks to turn empowerment into an automatic feature of the political institutions of a given country. Of course, we could think of all legislation that is designed to empower women or members of minority groups as institutional design, since laws are part of the institutional fabric of the state. But what we have in mind here are efforts to ensure the participation of women and members of minority groups in formal political office.

The fundamental institutional design feature that has been used is a quota system, which reserves a certain number of candidacies or seats for members of a group.[72] This system has been implemented in a number of different ways. The biggest division is between "reserved-seat" systems and "candidate-quota" systems.[73] Reserved-seat systems are what they sound like: systems that reserve a certain number of seats for members of a particular group. For example, constitutions in some Latin American countries guarantee a specified number of seats for members of one or another indigenous community. Reserved-seat systems are the oldest form of quota system, and they tend to have only a limited impact on the representation of women's groups.[74] This limited impact may be due, in part, to the politics of implementing them: agreeing to set aside a high percentage of all seats for members of a particular group may meet with political opposition in many circumstances.

The other major types of systems are "candidate-quota" systems.[75] Here the idea is to guarantee that a certain number of female candidates—or members of other groups as the case may be—are running in elections. One major way this takes

---

INSIGHTS   Is Gender like Ethnicity? The Political Representation of Identity Groups
by Mala Htun

Mala Htun asks us to consider some key differences in the ways equitable political representation can be achieved for women and members of other groups. What she finds is that the nature of the group and its position in society matter greatly in achieving this representation. Gender groups seldom form political parties, and as a result, the preferred method to improve equity for women has tended to be candidate quotas (discussed further elsewhere in this chapter). In certain circumstances, however, ethnic groups have had greater success in establishing political parties.

The logic that Htun uses to explain this outcome is simple but powerful. Ethnic groups tend to "coincide" with other forms of group difference, whereas gender tends to "crosscut" them. For example, membership in a particular ethnic group might be related to the position of group members in the class structure, whereas women as a group tend to be found across the class structure of a given society (however economically empowered or disempowered they may be as a group). Since ethnic groups often "coincide," they can form parties and then seek reserved seats. But since women are a "crosscutting group," they have difficulty organizing via parties that represent the varied interests of women as a group.

Mala Htun, "Is Gender Like Ethnicity? The Political Representation of Identity Groups." Perspectives on Politics 2, No. 3 (2004): 439–458.

places is within political parties. Although gender-based political parties are relatively rare, political parties may still address issues related to gender, or they may position themselves to capture the votes of those who favor gender equality. Thus some parties will aim to formally or informally increase the number of female candidates within the party. When this is done formally, it is a party-level quota system. For example, a Social Democratic Party in country X might apply to itself the rule that 30 percent of its candidates for legislative office will be women. Imagine that they face a Christian Democratic Party as their main opponent. That party will now have to make a strategic choice: one possible option among others would be to apply a quota that matches or exceeds that self-imposed quota on the Social Democrats to demonstrate that, despite other ideological and policy differences, the Christian Democratic Party is progressive on issues of gender equality.

Party leadership may succeed in self-imposing quotas in systems where proportional representation is the norm, given that party leadership tends to have more power to select its candidates in such systems. If voters vote for parties rather than individual candidates, it is easier for the party to impose formal rules on itself as it selects candidates. How do you think such an approach would work in the United States, where many candidates are not selected by party leaders but in primaries where voters choose the party's nominee? What would happen if, say, the Republican Party leadership decided that it wanted to adopt a 40 percent quota for female candidates? Unlike in systems with centrally controlled party lists of candidates, this may be very difficult to achieve.

Another way quota systems can be adopted is through a law or constitution stating that *all* parties must meet certain quota thresholds.[76] But the adoption of such a system can be difficult to achieve as well and would require major changes in how elections are organized in a society such as the United States. More generally, the likelihood of a country's developing quota systems that apply to all parties depends on each party's calculation of its own electoral prospects if such reforms are carried out, as well as the parties' relative power. If a given party stands to benefit from new arrangements, it can be expected to support them; but if a party is either strongly ideologically opposed to the idea or stands to have trouble meeting quota requirements, it is likely to resist their universal imposition. Scholars debate which quota system is most effective.[77]

You can see the complexity of analyzing how, when, and why institutional design affects the representation of women or members of other groups. Two things, however, are clear. First, global efforts to expand political representation of women are increasing, and different quota systems have led to important gains. Second, social scientific interest in these issues is increasing as well—something to keep in mind for your next research project.

More generally, remember that the causes we have considered in this section are not mutually exclusive explanations of how empowerment takes place. Rather, these are potential tools for those who seek to empower minority groups, women, and other groups. In many cases of successful empowerment, these elements work together. For example, it is possible for social movement organizing to help produce both political parties and new institutional designs. However, parties and institutional design also influence the environment in which social movement organizing takes place. There seems to be no standard way in which these pieces fit together.

INSIGHTS

Quotas for Women in Politics: Gender and Candidate Selection Reform Worldwide
by Mona Lena Krook

Krook has developed an innovative approach to the study of empowering women through institutional design. She compares a number of cases of more and less successful adoption of reserved seat and candidate quota systems, and she draws the following general conclusions, among others:

1. The causal impact of a given variable is not universal, but rather depends on interaction effects with other variables. Thus, there is no "one size fits all" approach to institutional design in this area.

2. Institutional design can affect three major arenas: those of "systemic," "practical," and "normative" institutions. Different sorts of institutional design efforts affect these arenas in different ways. Not only do formal institutional changes matter, but moral arguments about issues such as justice and equity do too.

3. Processes of change differ in quality. The more successful ones are "harmonizing sequences" in which changes build on one another and actors adjust for unintended consequences of previous stages, while "disjointed sequences" are less successful.

4. Many actors with a variety of goals are involved in these processes. These actors include, at the very least, state-level actors like politicians, actors in "civil society" like activists, and "transnational" actors like certain NGOs. It is exceedingly difficult to predict how such actors will interact.

Mona Lena Krook, Quotas for Women in Politics: Gender and Candidate Selection Reform Worldwide. *New York: Oxford University Press, 2009.*

Measuring Gender Empowerment

Imagine that we wanted to evaluate how well the United Kingdom and some of its former colonies are empowering women. We will include Australia, Canada, New Zealand, the United States, and the United Kingdom in this set of cases. Suppose the idea is to build toward considering a hypothesis about a possible effect of traditional British culture on gender roles in politics and economic life. This may sound like a strange idea, but it is not implausible, given that gender is culturally constructed in different ways in different societies. Moreover, some research suggests that English colonialism had different impacts from other colonizers on the long-term democratic quality and stability in former colonies.[78] For the sake of our thought experiment, let us just imagine that this research has led us to hypothesize that former English colonies might show greater political empowerment of women than former Spanish colonies.

If we want to explore the possibility of testing a hypothesis, we cannot just spend time in these societies and see how people feel about gender and politics. Rather, we need to select specific measures of gender empowerment that allow us to study it in a rigorous way. Otherwise, we will likely project our own biases onto the social and political realities that we observe. If, though, we can settle on reliable and valid measures of gender empowerment, and if, in turn, we find that gender empowerment as measured by them is consistent with our hypothesis, we

KEY METHODOLOGICAL TOOLS

Selecting or Creating Measures

Measurement is about qualifying or quantifying the presence, amount, or degree of a variable you are researching. Good measures have to work effectively in at least two ways. First, they have to be true to the underlying concept you are researching. Second, they need to be defined such that any observer using the measurement technique will measure the phenomenon in more or less the same way. Another way to say this is that measures should be both "valid" and "reliable."

One measure that some have used for studying women's

THINKING COMPARATIVELY

KEY METHODOLOGICAL TOOLS

(continued)

empowerment is the GEM, or Gender Empowerment Measure, which was for some years prominently featured in UN Development Reports. The GEM seeks to measure the extent to which women have political and economic control of their lives and environments in different societies. It is a composite indicator based on underlying measures of women's and men's shares of (1) political positions, (2) prominent economic roles, and (3) overall income.[79] No measure is perfect, however, and some scholars have criticized the GEM on technical grounds.[80] We should also note that it has no way to account for symbolic and status-related components of empowerment. This raises potential concerns about measurement validity. Indeed, in part for reasons highlighted in this section, many analysts have in recent years turned to other measures, such as the Global Gender Gap Index, the Gender Development Index, and the Gender Inequality Index.[81]

could work toward examining whether and to what extent colonial legacy is a cause of any observed pattern.

One measure of the political empowerment of women was the Gender Empowerment Measure, which brings together several more specific variables (see "Key Methodological Tools"). This measure was used in a number of United Nations reports in the late 2000s and for some purposes, despite criticism, was considered by many the best single measure of gender empowerment at that time.

If we look at the Gender Empowerment Measure (GEM) ranks for 2009 for the Anglo colonies in which we are interested (see Table 14.1), we see results that seem consistent with our initial hypothesis. Australia ranks second, Canada fourth, the United States thirteenth, New Zealand twentieth, and the United Kingdom twenty-first. Ranks for former Spanish colonies are not this high, with only Spain being ranked higher than the *lowest* ranked British zone societies in this respect. Should we just conclude that former British colonies are clearly sites of higher levels of political empowerment for women? Not so fast. Since GEM is a composite measure, it captures economic empowerment as well. It may be that the strong showing of former British settler colonies (relative to former Spanish colonies) in terms of GEM is a consequence of higher levels of economic development in these societies.

Let's try a narrower measure. Remember that we are fundamentally concerned with *political* empowerment of women in this question. What if we look at the percentage of women holding legislative office? This could give us a clearer indication of *political* empowerment, given that it won't include information about the relative *economic* standing of women, which we may consider to be a different question (see Table 14.2).

Here, we see a very different pattern. In our set of comparative cases, Bolivia is on top, and the United States is on the bottom. New Zealand is the only former British settler colony in the top thirty, and Bolivia, Cuba, Ecuador, Spain, Nicaragua, Mexico, and Argentina all outperform *all* the other former British

TABLE 14.1 Gender Empowerment Measure (GEM) Global Ranks, Selected Countries

2	Australia
4	Canada
13	United States
15	Spain
20	New Zealand
21	United Kingdom
44	Chile
49	Argentina
50	Uruguay
51	Cuba

(*Source:* UN Human Development Report, 2009.)

TABLE 14.2 Ranking of Percentage of Women in National Legislature, Selected Countries

Rank	Country	% Seats in Lower/ Single House	% Seats in Upper House
2	Bolivia	53.1	47.2
4	Cuba	48.9	N/A
9	Ecuador	41.6	N/A
12	Spain	41.1	33.8
15	Nicaragua	39.1	N/A
17 (tied)	Mexico	38	33.6
22	Argentina	36.2	38.9
29	New Zealand	31.4	NA
44	Australia	26.7	38.2
49	Canada	25.2	38.6
57	United Kingdom	22.8	24.1
73 (tied)	United States	19.3	20.0

(*Source:* Interparliamentary Union 2015.)

settler colonies in our group (as do Costa Rica and El Salvador, though they do not rank as highly as the other Latin American countries listed in Table 14.2).[82]

Does this demonstrate that selected former Spanish colonies have higher levels of the political empowerment of women than former British colonies? Not necessarily. Can you think of some of the limitations of this measure? One would be that legislative representation is not the only form of representation. Another might be that empowerment of a group, even political empowerment, likely extends well beyond having members of that group hold office. Both of these are concerns about the potential *validity* of this measure of the underlying concept we are researching: political empowerment of women. What we see here is that a number of former Spanish colonies have achieved very high levels of legislative representation of women, outpacing former English settler colonies by this measure, which is interesting and deserving of comparative exploration.

The bottom line is that there is almost never a *perfect* measure. (Indeed, the United Nations has replaced the GEM with new measures of gender-adjusted development and gender inequality in recent years, in response to scholarly critiques.) All choices of measures involve trade-offs. You must be mindful of these trade-offs and remember that measures are only stand-ins for the underlying concepts you are researching. Measurement is crucial in understanding the extent to which women and ethnic and racial groups are empowered and active in politics, as it is for any question in comparative politics.

Chapter Summary

Concepts

- The meaning of concepts like race and ethnicity varies in relation to context. While some people think of race and sometimes ethnicity as biological, most social scientists view them as culturally constructed.
- Gender is distinguished from biological sex, and most social scientists think of gender as cultural rather than biological.
- In recent years, a number of societies have grown more pluralistic and tolerant with respect to sexual orientation and gender identity.

Types

- Race historically has almost always been linked to social actors' beliefs about biology, whereas ethnicity emphasizes cultural traditions. The concept of race in particular has been linked to exploitation.
- Discrimination based on both race and ethnicity is a common feature of many polities, historically and today. Discrimination has in some societies become more subtle over time; but its consequences, and the consequences of historical legacies of earlier forms of discrimination, are clearly visible.

- Discrimination based on gender is also a pervasive feature of polities. Again, a good deal of progress has been made, but gender discrimination remains a problem.
- Empowerment can be economic, symbolic, or political.

Causes and Effects

- One potential source of empowerment is social movement mobilization.
- Another is political parties, and parties tend to be more viable for ethnic groups seeking empowerment than for gender groups.
- Institutional design strategies like reserved seats and quotas can also be used in support of empowerment.

Thinking Comparatively

- A thought experiment about relative gender empowerment in the former colonies of Spain and the United Kingdom demonstrates the pros and cons of two major measures of political empowerment.

Thinking It Through

1. The theme of empowerment is much discussed in this chapter, including dimensions of empowerment and ways in which development is conceptualized and measured by social scientists. But what *is* empowerment? Develop your own conceptualization and link it back to the discussion in the chapter. What, if anything, is missing?

2. We discussed political, economic, and cultural or symbolic empowerment. How are these dimensions related? Is one more fundamental than the others, and if so, why? If a group wants to improve its position, would it be best advised to begin by focusing on one or another form of empowerment?

3. Imagine that you have been asked to consult with members of an indigenous group in a hypothetical country that wants to create a political party. How would you go about your work? What pieces of information would you seek to collect, and why? What major questions would you want answered, and why? How would the answers to these questions impact your recommendations?

4. Imagine now that you have been asked to consult with social movement activists that represent poor rural women of a particular ethnic group. They tell you that their ethnic, gender,

and class status compound each other and that their interests really are distinct from those of other groups. They would like your technical assistance as they aim to build a social movement. In particular, they would like your advice about how to "frame" that movement. What questions do you ask them, and how do you advise them? How is this case different from organizing around "women's issues" or the interests of a particular ethnic group?

5. Imagine once more that you are an "empowerment consultant." You have been contacted by the representatives of a political party that represents the interests of an ethnic group that has historically faced severe discrimination, one that is largely found in a particular area of the country and that constitutes about 10 percent of the country's population. They tell you that their country is going to write a new constitution and that they have a number of delegates in the constitutional assembly. They want your advice about what sorts of institutional designs they should push for as they aim to protect the interests of their people. What do you need to know to give them advice? How would your answer depend on their answers?

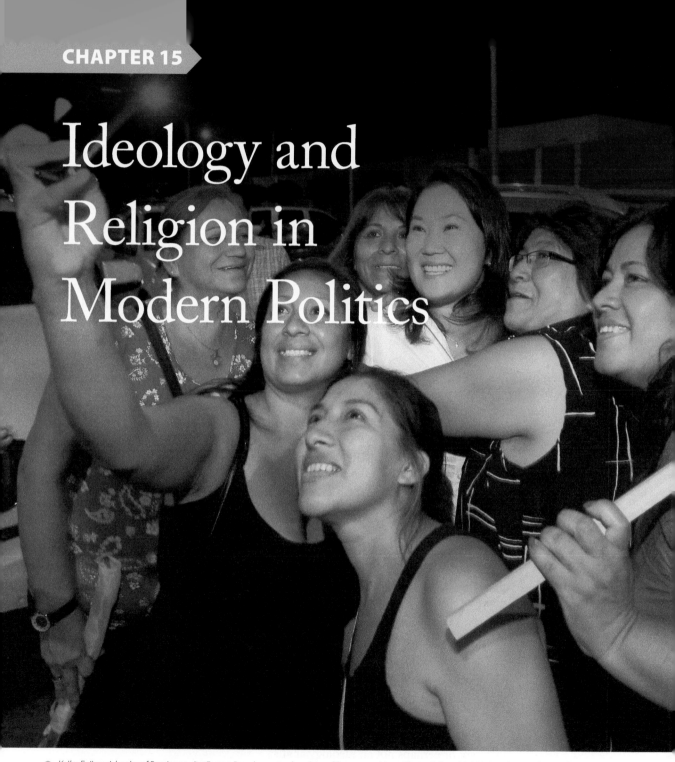

CHAPTER 15

Ideology and Religion in Modern Politics

● Keiko Fujimori, leader of Peru's populist Fuerza Popular party, daughter of former president Alberto Fujimori (1990–2000), poses for a selfie with supporters. Keiko Fujimori nearly won the presidency in 2016. There were protests against the Peruvian government's decision to pardon Alberto Fujimori, the populist former president, who governed from 1990 to 2000 and was later found guilty of human rights abuses and corruption. Fujimorismo lives on in Peru, represented by his daughter Keiko Fujimori and the Fuerza Popular party, which currently holds a majority in the Congress of the Republic of Peru.

In recent years, many commentators have been surprised by the rise of "populist" leaders and movements in Latin America, Europe, the United States, and elsewhere. Scholars do not always agree about what this populism is or why it emerged. However, many would say that the multicountry rise of groups opposed to globalization, immigration, and—in at least some cases—formal democratic institutions and the mainstream press is likely not a mere coincidence. Some of these populists present themselves as traditionalistic and religious. Others are secular and left-wing. Later in this chapter, we will ask what the rise of contemporary populism may or may not tell us about the position of religion and ideology in contemporary politics.

If you had told comparative political analysts in the 1960s that movements and candidates like these would proliferate in the early twenty-first century, most would likely have disagreed sharply. They expected modernization to render ideology and religion obsolete. Prominent scholars declared the "end of ideology," meaning that major political programs such as fascism, socialism, and communism had run their course.[1] Virtually all analysts agreed that religion would fade from public life in coming decades.[2] Yet both ideology and religion continue to exert a strong influence on modern politics. Scholars who study relationships between religion and the state find that in many countries, religious organizations and actors remain very much involved in the state.[3] Moreover, survey research shows that much of the world is quite religious.[4] Some demographers argue we should expect the world to grow *more* religious in coming years.[5]

The persistence of religion and ideology in public life has led analysts to ask a series of questions: What did the last generation of theorists get wrong? Did they misunderstand modernization? How has the role of religion in modern societies changed as societies have modernized? Why haven't ideologies such as fascism and socialism disappeared? Is twenty-first-century populism an echo of these earlier ideologies, a distinct type of ideology, or perhaps not an ideology at all?

· · · ·

Concepts

Both ideology and religion, when considered from the perspective of political science, are examples of what scholars call **political culture**. This means, essentially, that they are different types of *representations* that people hold about politics and things that affect politics. People have all sorts of beliefs, but ideological and religious beliefs tend to be deeply held and therefore may be highly impactful. This does not mean that religion and ideology are the same thing, of course, as we discuss in this chapter. Ideologies are explicitly political in their orientation, whereas religions might have political implications but are broader belief systems that extend well beyond politics.

Given that we are interested in understanding ideology and religion in *modern* politics, and since much analysis concerns the relationship between these phenomena and **modernity**, we start by discussing the controversial concepts of modernity and **modernization**. Note that you have already seen these concepts come up from time to time in earlier chapters.

Modernity and Modernization

"Modernity" is one of the most important labels in contemporary political life. Virtually nobody aspires to being "premodern." Rather, modernity constitutes a particular rung in the international status hierarchy, and as such has been a moving target for societies aspiring to "modern" status over the last several centuries.[6]

Modernity is a cultural construction; it has its origins in a particular time and place.[7] In other words, people created the idea of modernity, and like all ideas that affect competition for status and power, it served certain interests and did not serve others. Most fundamentally, the idea of "the modern" helped both motivate and justify European colonial projects in Africa, the Middle East, and Asia.[8] Indeed, this concept was perhaps one of the most formidable tools of those colonial projects' "soft power."[9] The European powers and some members of the Westernized classes in the subjugated, colonized populations agreed that such societies needed modernization. The watchwords of this vision were *technical efficiency, education, literacy, civilization*, and **secularism** (favoring secular—nonreligious—culture). It is not surprising, therefore, that anti-colonial resistance was, in its first generation, typically carried out using this same conceptual language:[10] rather than being the agents of modernization, colonizers were re-interpreted as barriers to it. Bound up with the notion, sometimes explicitly and sometimes implicitly, were the corollaries that modernization was a both a necessary and an inevitable process.

Transforming ideas like "modernity" and "modernization" into social-scientific concepts is a difficult task since we do not want to reproduce the biases implicit in the original concepts.[11] Despite this challenge, for this book we think the concepts are still worth using, partly because most of the world goes on talking about modernity and modernization. Political scientists and scholars in related fields generally mean several things by modernity and modernization, or they focus on several distinctive features of modern or modernizing societies.[12] First, they often characterize modernity by growth-oriented, or capitalist, economies, rather than stagnant or "traditionalistic" economic systems in which there is little accumulation of wealth over time. Second, they often characterize modernity by its open system

political culture The symbolically encoded beliefs, values, norms, and practices that shape the formal distribution of power in any given society.

modernity A contested term that refers to a type of society, typically one experiencing economic growth and with a relatively strong state, among other characteristics.

modernization The process through which a society becomes "more modern," which is typically understood to mean having an advanced economy and, sometimes, a democratic polity.

secularism The ideological complex that favors secular (nonreligious) culture.

of stratification, meaning that social position in modern societies is not fixed at birth: in "modern" societies, according to this view, social mobility is possible and legitimate. Third, they often characterize the chief political form of modernity as the modern, bureaucratic state; they see centralization and bureaucratization of power as hallmarks of modernity. Finally, as noted in chapter 13, some scholars see national identity as a distinguishing marker of modernity. As we discuss later, scholars increasingly note that modernization can take a variety of forms.[13]

Ideology

ideology A systematically coordinated and cognitively salient set of beliefs focused on politics.

Most comparative political analysts think of **ideologies** as highly organized and rationalized systems of ideas that directly bear on politics.[14] According to this way of thinking, your ideas about your tastes in music, fashion, food, and so forth are probably not ideological. But whether you know it or not, your thinking about politics is probably shaped, at least indirectly, by ideology. This ideology most likely contains ideas about what rights people should have and where these rights come from, ideas about whether individuals matter more than groups or vice versa, ideas about how the economy ought to be organized, and ideas about how collective decisions should be reached. Some people can be considered highly ideological, meaning that they are very focused on these things, or even that they are rigidly devoted to their views about them, but all of us are probably influenced by ideologies to some degree.[15]

Major political ideologies include liberalism, fascism, and socialism, each of which we discuss further later in the chapter. It is worth noting that these major political ideologies are largely secular. In other words, they oppose religion as a basis for organizing politics and present themselves as alternatives to it. Some scholars have gone so far as to argue that ideologies are like "secular religions."[16]

Religion

functional definition Definition that aims to define a given phenomenon by what it *does* or the "function" it serves.

substantive definition Definition that aims to define a given phenomenon by what it *is* rather than by what it does.

Social scientists tend to think about religion in two basic, contrasting ways: by using **functional definitions** and by using **substantive definitions**.[17] Functional definitions specify what religion *does*. They define religion by its ability to foster social integration, to give people a sense of order through creating and telling myths about history and the cosmos, or by its ability to motivate collective action. If we use a functional definition, we see lots of things—including modern ideologies—as religion. For certain research purposes, this view may be helpful.

More often, as we have seen throughout this book, when doing comparative analysis we want to make clear distinctions so that we can locate and explain variation. Substantive definitions of religion help make this possible. A substantive definition focuses on the content of religious belief or organization, its "substance" rather than just what it does. For example, a substantive definition might say, "Religions are systems of belief that grant a prominent place to God." For many purposes, though, this particular definition would not be helpful, since a number of religions (e.g., Buddhism) do not have gods, and many others (e.g., animism and Hinduism) have many gods or god-like entities. More commonly, though, substantive definitions of religion argue that what separates religion from other aspects of culture is that it gives prominence to some transcendent force (i.e., one beyond the normal or merely physical human experience).[18] This might be a deity, a goal such as Nirvana, or even the Platonic ideal of "the good."

A line of women waits for a bus in Tehran. Note the religious imagery on the building behind them.

Along these lines, some analysts define religion substantively as a cultural system or set of beliefs and organizations that are oriented toward the transcendent.[19] Note that this definition, unlike most functional ones, allows us to then pose empirical questions about religion's growth, decline, or changing features because we can track change about beliefs in the transcendent over time. However, it is worth remembering that some scholars have questioned whether "religion" is a universal category at all, suggesting it is a Western concept.[20] If this is true, we should be very careful about using it when making global comparisons.

Secularization, Religion, and Modern Politics

As noted previously, for a number of years comparative analysts thought that religion would decline in the modern world. They called this idea "**secularization**" or "secularization theory," and they came up with a number of reasons for their prediction.[21] Some noticed that as societies modernized, new religious groups emerged, giving people greater religious choice. For example, in the modern United States—unlike in, say, medieval France—one can choose from a wide variety of world religions, and in particular from a huge array of Protestant Christian denominations. Some scholars thought that this pluralism would undermine religious belief, because religious people would be less likely to have their beliefs constantly reinforced by like-minded people around them.[22] Others thought that modernization would cause religion's decline because of the importance of science and technology in the modern world. According to this point of view, "rational" explanations would replace "irrational" religious ones, leaving some people "disenchanted."[23]

Some scholars have argued, however, that this theory seems to describe only one small part of the world: Western Europe.[24] Much of the world is very religious, and some claim that over the longer term, societies like the United States have actually

secularization The process through which (according to some theories) societies become less religious as they become more modern.

become *more* religious, though there is little doubt that in recent decades many religious organizations have seen some decline in the United States.[25] Moreover, since societies with the highest birth rates tend to be more religious than societies with low birth rates, we may see continuing increases in global religiosity in coming decades.[26] In principle, this could happen even if societies are growing more secular as they grow wealthier.[27]

Comparative analysts continue to note some important changes in religion's role as societies modernize, however, and the old theories of secularization are not all wrong. Scholars today do not agree on whether we should call these changes "secularization," but they widely agree that we should distinguish between any change in religious belief itself and changes in religious *institutions* or *organizations*.[28] It seems that when societies modernize, religious institutions or organizations tend to become increasingly **differentiated** (independent) from the state, although, as we shall see, the extent of this varies.[29] Along similar lines, in some, but not all, modern societies, religious institutions and organizations become **privatized**.[30] This means that they become increasingly independent not just of the state but of the **public sphere**: They lose their power as a basis for public claims. For example, in societies with a strong tradition of privatizing religion, such as France, efforts by the church to influence major political decisions are typically viewed negatively. Much of the comparative analysis of religion and politics today involves mapping institutional or organizational changes and then trying to explain the different patterns that emerge. For example (as we discuss in more detail in the "Types" section), some societies separate church and state and then organize religions as denominations.[31] Some almost fully privatize religious institutions and organizations, while others allow the state to control them. Comparative analysis seeks to explain these variations.

differentiation The process through which institutions become increasingly autonomous from one another, including the reduction or other change in the linkages between religion and other institutions.

privatization In the context of the social-scientific study of religion, this refers to the process of religious practice being confined to the private sphere.

public sphere The space in which public life and deliberation take place (as opposed to the "private sphere").

Religious Conflict

Religious conflict is not surprising in a world with major ideological and religious differences, especially as religion's relationship to politics is in flux.[32] Many analysts assert that religion has served and will continue to serve as a motivator for international conflict, and we certainly have seen dramatic examples of religiously inspired violence across national boundaries in recent years. Others draw

CASE IN CONTEXT

Religious Difference and Conflict in Nigeria: Disentangling Ethnicity and Religion?

PAGE 527

The potential for intergroup conflict may become especially complicated in situations of religious diversity. The complication increases when religious difference creates tension and also overlaps with other potential bases of conflict, such as region and ethnicity. This is emphatically the case in Nigeria, which has struggled with problems of religious difference, including both inter-religious violence and elite bargaining within the state about regional, ethnic, and religious representation.

For more on religious difference in Nigeria, see the case study in Part VI, p. 527. As you read it, keep in mind the following questions:

1. How does the state manage religious difference?
2. How might Nigeria's federal system help?
3. What are the prospects for the development of a *denominational* approach to religious difference in Nigeria and other societies that face inter-religious conflict?

our attention to cases where pluralism within a polity coincides with great tension or even violence. Analysis of such cases is often complicated by the fact that religious difference tends to go along with other types of difference, such as regional and ethnic identity. As such, many of the theories discussed in chapters 12 and 13 are used to explain religious conflict as well.

Types

In this section, we begin by describing and providing examples of the major forms of ideology in modern politics. We then move on to do the same for major patterns of religious involvement in politics.

Modern Ideologies

As noted previously, the main families of modern political ideologies are liberalism, fascism, and socialism. This list is not exhaustive of the ideological universe, of course, but these are the most important major ideologies that political scientists have analyzed, and each was very prominent in the twentieth century.

LIBERALISM

Liberalism is probably the most widespread and influential of modern ideologies. Indeed, it is so widespread that sometimes analysts do not even notice that it is an ideology. Thus, scholars who declared that ideologies would disappear in modern society often did not include liberalism in this prediction.[33]

Like all complex ideologies, liberalism takes many forms, and not all of them are fully consistent. In general, though, the ideology of liberalism holds that (1) individuals are and should be more important than groups; (2) individuals' relationships with the state should be organized through democratic citizenship; (3) a democratic political system should be representative, and it should have constitutional limits that protect the rights of individuals; and (4) free-market capitalism is the best, and for many the most "natural," way of organizing the economy.

Our fourth point in the preceding paragraph is a generalization in that different variants of liberalism take different stances on the state's role in the economy. As noted in the Case Study "Liberal Ideology in the United Kingdom," many analysts consider **social democracy** to be a variant of liberalism, though it owes a great deal to socialism as well: it promotes state management of the economy as a means to preserve representative democracy. Broadly, liberalism is a continuum, from **libertarianism**—the view that the state's involvement in the economy and social life must be reduced to the minimal necessary level for the maintenance of order—to social democracy.

We should briefly mention "conservatism" in this context. In early nineteenth-century Europe, conservatism was a distinct ideology, one that aimed to restrain modernization processes, defend monarchy, and preserve religious organizations in their traditional positions. We can still today speak of conservatism as a strong cultural tendency in many societies. Indeed, in some societies, it could still be treated as a distinct ideology. Yet in many societies conservatism has come to constitute a form of liberalism. In the contemporary United States or Western Europe, few conservatives would go so far as to question liberalism's emphasis on

liberalism An ideology that emphasizes individual freedoms, representative democracy, and the market economy.

social democracy An ideological movement that favors both representative democracy with respect for basic individual rights and state action to promote relative economic and social equality, viewed by some as a variety of socialism but by many as a variety of liberalism.

libertarianism A form of liberalism, strongly opposed to social democracy, that is especially concerned with minimizing the role of government.

CASE IN CONTEXT
Liberal Ideology in the United Kingdom
PAGE 556

The United Kingdom was the birthplace of both orthodox liberalism and Keynesianism, two main views about the state's role in the economy that are central to modern ideological debate. Indeed, the society has also had strong social-democratic actors.

For more on liberalism in the United Kingdom, see the case study in Part VI, p. 556. As you read it, keep in mind the following questions:

1. Are both of these views varieties of liberalism?
2. If so, what makes them different from other ideologies, like socialism or fascism?

representative democratic institutions and markets. There may be some exceptions to this observation, however. As we will see in the Thinking Comparatively feature later, some variants of contemporary populism may share some characteristics with conservative ideology, such as a strong preference for in-group members and a distrust of representative institutions. Moreover, the growth of movements such as the so-called alt-right, including groups that identify as "neo-reactionary," may signal a resurgence in conservative ideology, at least at the fringe.[34]

As we shall see, liberalism is often suspicious of other ideologies. Indeed, some liberals present Nazism and socialism as more like each other than opposites. Rather than viewing ideologies on the standard "left–right" continuum, they see them on a continuum with liberalism at one end and totalitarianism at the other.

FASCISM

fascism An authoritarian ideology associated with regimes like the Nazis and that of Italy's Benito Mussolini, favoring authoritarianism, militarism, and right-wing nationalism.

The ideology (or family of ideologies) known as **fascism** was very prominent in the twentieth century, which saw fascist governments in Spain, Portugal, and Italy, among other places.[35] Some analysts also classify National Socialism (the ideology of the German Nazi Party) as fascist, while others see it as a distinct form given its totalitarian aspirations and more virulent, bizarre form of racism.

Fascism can be distinguished from liberalism in several ways. First, fascism does not share liberalism's respect for the individual. Rather, fascist ideology holds that the state, as the embodiment of the nation, is most important. In the paradigmatic case of Italian fascism under Mussolini, fascism was grounded in a nationalism that sought to recover the "glorious" history of Ancient Rome. Second, in line with fascism's lack of concern for the individual, the political programs associated with it typically do not make much effort to protect the individual's rights. Third, fascism is anti-democratic in that it views an authoritarian protector for the nation (e.g., Franco in twentieth-century Spain) as preferable to liberal democracy, which it argues can be co-opted by ideologies and actors hostile to the nation's interests. Finally, while fascists often embrace capitalist economics, they typically promote state capitalism in which the state has control of production and the use of capital.

Liberals criticize fascism not only for its lack of respect for individual rights but for the horrific human rights abuses that have been carried out in its name. Socialists critique it for these reasons as well and often add the critique that, in their

Fascists hold a flag honoring Benito Mussolini, Italy's notorious World War II–era dictator and ally of Adolf Hitler.

view, fascism is fundamentally about preserving the capitalist economy. Indeed, some socialists believe that capitalism will inevitably fall back on fascism as its ultimate defender.

For some time, the claim that fascism had been de-legitimated seemed plausible to many. However, a number of observers warn of fascist elements in some parts of the recent wave of populist politics. One may debate whether the term fascism is properly applied in those cases, but the very notion that such leadership styles could exist in advanced modern democracies would have seemed unlikely even a few years ago.

SOCIALISM

Perhaps the most widely discussed ideology (or family of ideologies) is **socialism**. Though there are many forms of socialism, by far the most influential socialist was Karl Marx, though the ideology predated him. Marx constructed his socialism as a critique of liberalism.

According to Marx, the freedoms promised by liberalism were illusory.[36] For example, Marx said, you might believe you can liberate people by giving them freedom of speech or religion, but this belief is based on a misunderstanding of freedom and the ways in which we are unfree. The main problem in modern society, from this point of view, is not that authoritarian regimes limit people's ability to make their own choices but that our economic system alienates us. In our ideal state, Marx says, we would experience fulfillment through labor. But capitalism, which divides our labor via assembly-line manufacture and the bureaucratic organization

socialism An ideology (or family of ideologies) that emphasizes economic equality as a key goal, to be pursued in large measure through state action.

CASE IN CONTEXT

Communist Ideology in Practice: Russia and the Soviet Union

PAGE 541

A number of socialist regimes developed in the twentieth century. The Soviet Union might have been the most important of these, if for no other reason than that it exported socialist ideology and used its influence to produce socialist revolutions in other states, with some success. But what would Marx have thought of the Soviet Union? Was it consistent with his socialist vision? Or did it embody some other form of socialism?

For more on this, see the case study in Part VI, p. 541–542. As you read it, keep in mind the following questions:

1. How did Lenin and Stalin change socialism?
2. Was the Soviet Union ideologically uniform, or were there ideological struggles within it?
3. Does the demise of the Soviet Union "prove socialism wrong"? Why or why not?

of office work, makes it impossible for us to find fulfillment in this way (if you have ever seen the movie *Office Space*, then you should have a good idea of what he had in mind). Marx further argued that capitalism impoverishes the majority as it enriches a parasitic minority. To solve these problems, socialists like Marx argued that revolution is necessary. The working class must seize the state and use it to take collective ownership of factories and other elements of the productive process, which are controlled by "capitalists." Once this happens, Marx hoped, socialism will eventually give way to *communism*, in which there will be no forced division of labor and, thus, no alienation.

These ideas inspired much of the world in the twentieth century, leading to the establishment of socialist or communist regimes in China, Vietnam, Russia, Cuba, and many other places. Many socialists, however, became disillusioned with these regimes. Some saw them as brutal and dehumanizing, with little likelihood of ever producing the promised world, free of alienation. Some of these disillusioned individuals turned to the ideology of liberalism. Within it, a subset attempted to construct a modified version—social democracy, which (as mentioned earlier) aims to preserve representative democracy and the respect for individual rights through active state management of the economy. Social democrats have been some of the most ardent supporters of the welfare state discussed in chapter 4. Moreover, there is not total consensus about their location within the typology of ideologies we have described in this chapter. Some see social democrats as liberals because of their emphasis on democratic institutions and freedoms. Others see them as socialists, since many social democrats emerged from the socialist tradition and because they tend to favor more state spending than do liberals. Finally, despite the emergence of social democracy in the twentieth century, there are still proponents of more traditional socialism in the world.

Modern Forms of Religion in Politics

Students in the United States are likely quite used to the idea of the "separation of church and state," given its prominence in U.S. political institutions and culture. Yet even in the United States, religion is politically important; and in much of the world, religious and political institutions are intertwined.[37] At the organizational level, this involvement can take many forms. Governments often regulate religions, stipulating what they can and cannot do. Governments also affect religious organizations financially. Many governments offer religious organizations direct financial support. Others give them tax advantages. Finally, numerous societies have **established religions**, meaning there is an official religion of the state.[38] Yet even in most such cases, we see some level of differentiation between religious and political institutions.

established religions Religions that are granted official status and support by the state.

LAY AND RELIGIOUS STATES

Most societies see increasing differentiation of religious and political institutions as modernization takes place. This does not happen in the same way everywhere, though there are several common patterns. A prominent one is the "laïcist" pattern in which the state seeks to completely dominate and privatize religion.[39] The core idea is that public life must be "**lay**" rather than religious: the state is seen as sharply antagonistic to religious organizations, as if competition between them were zero-sum. One of the most important examples of this pattern is France (see the Case in Context box on "Religion and Secularism in France"). In a society exhibiting this pattern, it is not just that the there is a separation between church and state but that, culturally, religion tends to be considered a matter of private conscience and nothing more. What this means will become clearer later, when we discuss denominationalism.

lay state State that establishes a formal separation of religion and public life.

We should note that laïcism sometimes goes along with socialism in ideology. There are liberals who favor a laïcist approach—and, indeed, the earliest architects of laïcism in both France and Latin America considered themselves liberals. However, most modern socialist regimes have been laïcist in their approach to religion, including the Soviet Union, Maoist China, and Cuba since soon after Castro came to power in 1959.

INSIGHTS   Why Muslim Integration Fails in Christian-Heritage Societies
by Claire L. Adida, David D. Laitin, and Marie-Anne Valfort

In this recent book, three scholars use both observational and experimental analysis to examine whether there is religiously based discrimination against Muslims in France, a society that formally proclaims laïcité, the principle that religion is solely a matter of private conscience. They present strong evidence that Muslim immigrants face more discrimination than Christian immigrants who, other than religion, are very similar to them (they focus on immigrants from similar regions of Senegal, using a purported "natural experiment" of the kind mentioned in chapter 2). Their research design draws on both qualitative and quantitative approaches.

Beyond showing evidence of religious discrimination in contemporary France, and somewhat more controversially, the authors argue that Muslim immigrants and the broader French

public are together stuck in a "discriminatory equilibrium." They suggest, in essence, that the following mechanism operates cyclically: Muslim immigrants respond to discrimination with behaviors that increase the probability of further discrimination. Some critics might charge that this involves "blaming" Muslim migrants for the discrimination they receive. The authors, though, would likely reply that they are not trying to assign responsibility but instead to answer the difficult empirical question of how and why such discrimination persists. They target a set of policy proposals in their concluding chapter, some of which are focused on individuals, others on secondary institutions, and still others on the state.

Claire L. Adida, David D. Laitin, and Marie-Anne Valfort. Why Muslim Integration Fails in Christian-Heritage Societies. Cambridge: Harvard University Press, 2016.

INSIGHTS

Public Religions in the Modern World
by José Casanova

José Casanova's *Public Religions in the Modern World* challenges conventional wisdom about secularization and the modern state. Casanova begins by a close analysis of what other scholars have meant by secularization. He comes to the conclusion that they have meant three things but have often confused them: a reduction in individuals' religious belief and practice; institutional differentiation; and religion's "privatization," or its eviction from public life. He places the first of these to the side and examines differentiation and privatization. Differentiation does indeed seem to be a core feature of modernization's impact on religion. Privatization, however, is an "option," not a *necessary* feature. In other words, according to Casanova, it is possible for a society to be both religious and modern, and even for religion to enter into public life in a modern society. Moreover, it is possible for the social position of religion to change, and some societies have witnessed religion's *de-privatization*.

José Casanova, Public Religions in the Modern World. *Chicago: University of Chicago Press, 1994.*

Somewhat more confusingly, some countries—particularly in Europe—have in recent years seen groups of citizens supporting what Rogers Brubaker has called "Christianist secularism."[40] These are people who are proponents of secularism but in a way that is not neutral with respect to religious traditions. Brubaker calls this "Christianist" rather than "Christian" to emphasize that these individuals are not necessarily religious Christians but nonetheless treat Judeo-Christian symbols and traditions as important cultural boundary markers and argue that these need to be protected. Many of these examples give strong evidence of Islamophobia.

CASE IN CONTEXT
Religion and Secularism in France

PAGE 439

France is often presented as the quintessential lay state. Religion is heavily privatized, and the population is, in comparative terms, fairly secular in its orientation. These issues have grown more complex in recent years, as evidenced by controversies over the use of Muslim symbols and traditional dress in public spaces in France. Recent experimental work by a team of social scientists (see Insights box for Adida, Laitin, and Valfort) strongly suggests that, in spite of the country's laicist tradition, non-Muslim residents of France tend to be alert to the religiosity of others and to discriminate against Muslims.[41]

For more on this, see the case study in Part VI, pp. 439–440. As you read it, keep in mind the following questions:

1. How is French secularism different from what is found in the United States?
2. Why did French secularism develop in the way that it did?
3. Are recent controversies over Islamic symbols qualitatively different from earlier episodes in the history of French religious politics?

Sisters who were expelled from their school in France in 2003 for wearing Islamic headscarves. The issue of public use of religious clothing and symbols has been a source of great controversy in France.

INSIGHTS

Secularism and State Policies Toward Religion: The United States, France, and Turkey
by Ahmet Kuru

Kuru examines the relationship between the state and religion in three countries: France, Turkey, and the United States. He makes a conceptual distinction between "assertive secularism" and "passive secularism." Assertive secularism is what we have called the "lay state." "Passive secularism" means that the state is mostly separated from religion, but religion is tolerated in public life: in other words, what we have called "denominationalism" in this chapter. Kuru wants to explain why assertive secularism is dominant in France and Turkey and why passive secularism is the norm in the United States. He notes that ideas and culture matter, arguing that ideas emerge in social and cultural contexts and that "ideological path dependence" helps explain the patterns. The key feature is whether a single, dominant religion is closely linked to an authoritarian government before the establishment of modern statehood. If so, it is likely that modernizers will embrace "active secularism." In France and Turkey, dominant religions were perceived to be closely allied with and inseparable from the enemies of a modern republic. In the United States, there was no such clear identification, and secularism took on the passive form.

Ahmet Kuru, Secularism and State Policies Toward Religion: The United States, France, and Turkey. *New York: Cambridge University Press, 2009.*

The broader point here is that in practice, laïcité may sometimes implicitly privilege some religions and more strongly oppose others.

In societies with laïcist systems, there are often minority groups and religious organizations that favor the inverse set of arrangements: a theocratic state, or at least one in which a single religion is given support. Moreover, sometimes these individuals triumph and overturn lay states.

We speak of polities such as Iran as "**religious states.**" Like lay states, their proponents often view competition between religion and a secular state as zero-sum. The difference is that they favor the religious side. Religious states vary a lot, and some are more tolerant of minority religions and of secular people than others. Saudi Arabia, for example, is fairly intolerant (though as of late 2017, there are some signs of initial efforts by the contemporary Saudi regime to reduce this intolerance). Costa Rica, which takes Roman Catholicism as the state's official religion, is fairly tolerant of religious difference.

religious state State in which religion is a key part of official politics, often involving religious establishment, religious legitimation of the state, and restrictions on religious minorities.

DENOMINATIONALISM

Scholars take full **denominationalism** to be somewhat exceptional. The main example of a fully denominational system is the United States. One could argue, though, that societies with growing **religious pluralism**, such as Brazil, might be moving toward a denominational model. In addition, *some* societies where established religions coexist with religious pluralism and high tolerance for religious difference share certain characteristics of the denominational model.

To fully understand denominationalism, we must first understand the concept of the denomination. If you live in the United States, you are probably used to hearing religious groups referred to as "**denominations,**" which are different from "churches" in the traditional sense and "sects."[42] A "church," as social scientists usually use the term, typically tries to make itself mandatory in a given territory and to link itself to the state (in other words, social scientists who study religion use this word in more restrictive sense than you probably do). A sect, in contrast,

denominationalism A system or set of beliefs that privileges denominational forms of religious organization.

religious pluralism The situation in which there are multiple religious organizations within a given society (the opposite of **religious monopoly**).

denomination A type of religious organization, prevalent in the United States among other places, that is voluntary and accepts the principle of religious pluralism.

CASE IN CONTEXT

Religion and Politics in Iran   PAGE 482

Iran is in many ways the polar opposite of France with respect to religion. Rather than privatizing religion, Iran elevates one religion and makes it the basis of the state's legitimacy, strongly favoring it and using it as the basis for law and politics.

For more on this, see the case study in Part VI, pp. 482–483. As you read it, keep in mind the following questions:

1. Why does Iran have a religious state when so many other Islamic societies have secular nationalist states?

2. Is the Iranian religious state a modern state? Why or why not?

often tries to turn *away* from the state and from public life and is typically defined as a group that removes itself from some other religious organization. Denominations are in a middle ground between churches and sects, engaging in public life but respecting pluralism (at least in principle) and considering membership to be voluntary.[43] Thus, a society in which religious difference is organized denominationally tends to see many different religious groups and organizations. Unlike in a laïcist society, however, denominations do not consider politics to be off limits. In a denominational society such as the United States, religious leaders of all persuasions routinely make pronouncements about public life. Majorities in denominational societies typically consider religious motivations to be appropriate in politics, as long as one or another religious group is not ultimately favored by the state, though sometimes this leads to controversy.

Some scholars have viewed denominationalism very positively as offering a good way to manage religious difference. As a result, there is some discussion about whether and to what extent it can be exported.[44] Views on this matter depend largely on explanations of denominationalism's origins. If its origins lie in institutional design, perhaps it is exportable. If they lie in difficult-to-change features of a society, such as levels of religious pluralism and diversity, it would be harder to export to countries without similar conditions.[45] If this is the case, however, perhaps denominationalism can develop spontaneously in different societies. We should note that denominationalism often coincides with the ideology of liberalism. At the same time, many proponents of liberal ideology are laïcist and worry that denominationalism can lead to states treating majority religious groups preferentially. Further, they worry that it may lead to failure to fully protect the rights of minority religious groups, depending on demographic factors and disproportionate political influence.

Causes and Effects: Why Does Ideology Remain Prevalent in Modern Politics?

As we have mentioned, neither ideology nor religion has ended, despite some analysts' predictions. Religion remains an important part of politics in most of the world; and while the bipolar order of the Cold War is no more, ideological difference is still plainly visible. Indeed, in the early twenty-first century, a wave of populist movements and political candidates has caused many to wonder whether decades of globalization and supranational political experiments such as the European Union will be weakened or even reversed. In this section of the chapter, therefore, we examine causal arguments about the changing role of ideology in modern politics.

Why Didn't Ideology (and History) End?

In the early years of the twenty-first century, scholarly attention to religion seemed, to some extent, to displace attention to secular ideologies. This trend was probably best explained by current events and contemporary history: religion has *seemed* to matter more in recent political conflict, especially after the attacks of September 11, 2001. Conservative evangelical Christianity and some conservative forms of Islam have been influential in a diverse range of societies (e.g., conservative evangelicalism has been influential in the United States while conservative Islam has been influential in Afghanistan, among other countries).

In recent years, however, there has been resurgence of both the left and the right around the globe.[46] Far fewer analysts today think that ideology doesn't matter. In many societies, right-wing actors, both religious and secular, have attempted to scale back or dismantle the welfare state. On the left, we have seen some actors turn to social democracy, which is consistent with the arguments of those who forecast an "end to ideology." Social democrats and liberals in general believe that some version of capitalism should be allowed and that liberal-democratic government is preferable to authoritarianism. Others on the left, however, seek an ideology that will stridently oppose liberalism, such as **"twenty-first-century socialism"** in the Venezuela of Hugo Chávez and Nicolás Maduro.

Efforts to articulate and foment "twenty-first-century socialism" have been notable. The idea here is to incorporate and respond to criticisms made of twentieth-century socialism—for example, that it was anti-democratic, allowed for the establishment of *new* oppressive bureaucratic hierarchies, and that it was often murderous on a

"twenty-first-century socialism" Ideology of government supporters in some contemporary societies (e.g., Venezuela, Bolivia) that aims to emphasize the allegedly more participatory and democratic features of these governments.

INSIGHTS   The End of History and the Last Man
by Francis Fukuyama

In this famous, controversial, and sometimes misunderstood book, Fukuyama argues that political conflict has been seen as ideological struggle since the beginning of modernity. Many different visions of the good life have contended with one another, from socialist to religious conservative. Liberalism was only one contender among many until the fall of the Soviet Union de-legitimized socialism. Then, no alternative to liberalism was left standing, and a consensus emerged about market relations in economics, liberal democracy in politics, and open stratification in society.

Many read Fukuyama's thesis as if he were simply arguing that the "good guys" had won, though his argument is more ambivalent, suggesting that the end of great ideological struggles may make it harder to find meaning and achieve great things. This argument has been the subject of major debates, most notably between its supporters and those of Samuel Huntington's "Clash of Civilizations" argument (discussed in a separate Insights box). Critics of Fukuyama say he fails to see other sources of division and conflict, that the fall of the Soviet Union does not invalidate all leftist regimes and ideologies, and that his account is *teleological*, meaning it assumes that history has a particular destination, or "end," toward which it is directed.

Francis Fukuyama, The End of History and the Last Man. New York: Free Press, 1992.

mass scale—without throwing out socialism's core aspirations. Proponents of twenty-first-century socialism, therefore, tend to accept the Marxist critique of capitalism as essentially exploitative and alienating and hope for a utopian future. They suggest that this can be achieved via a form of political decentralization that they call "participatory democracy."[47] To be clear, not all such regimes should be thought of as democratic. Indeed, in recent years, the Chavista regime has become increasingly authoritarian; and few political scientists would consider Venezuela (in 2018) to be a true democracy.

One might be tempted to dismiss "twenty-first-century socialism" as the utopian thinking of radical political activists, but those who have done so have been consistently surprised. As suggested by the chapter opening, in various parts of the developing world—especially in several Latin American countries in recent years, such as Venezuela, Bolivia, and Ecuador—these ideas have captured the imaginations of self-described revolutionary governments. Nicolás Maduro (and his predecessor, Hugo Chávez) in Venezuela and Evo Morales in Bolivia, and the many intellectuals and politicians associated with them, make strident claims that ideological conflict remains. That their governments constitute an alternative to liberalism cannot be missed (even if it's not always precisely clear what that alternative is or how sustainable these regimes' policies might be, particularly in Venezuela, now in the midst of a deep economic and political crisis).

Religious opposition to liberal/secular modernity and alternative ideologies such as "twenty-first-century socialism" share some things in common and are in other ways very different. Contemporary Venezuela and Iran have sometimes made common cause probably not only because they share some interests but because their ideological positions are sufficiently compatible, at least in the short run. What is shared? First and foremost, perhaps, is a clearly articulated opposition to the United States. But beyond this, they share a criticism of liberal

INSIGHTS — The Clash of Civilizations and the Remaking of World Order
by Samuel Huntington

Within political science, Samuel Huntington was one of the earliest voices claiming that religion would play an important, indeed resurgent, role in contemporary geopolitics. In *The Clash of Civilizations,* he famously argued that the world is divided into a set number of distinct "civilizations," and that these civilizations were built around different cultural traditions and often incompatible values. What would replace old ideological conflicts between the Soviet Union and the United States would be a clash between the world's civilizations, particularly between Islam and "the West." While many critics derided this analysis as simplistic and reductionistic, it gained wide currency, particularly after the terrorist attacks of September 11, 2001. For many public commentators and media figures, Huntington's model of opposed cultural traditions was a promising explanation. This and similar explanations have consequences and profound implications for policy. If Islam is by nature anti-democratic and pitted against "the West," and if civilizations are based on incommensurable moral and political beliefs, then conflict is largely inevitable and preparing for conflict the most prudent policy. But if this analysis is *incorrect*, these implications might be misleading, and such policies possibly even counterproductive.

Samuel Huntington, The Clash of Civilizations and the Remaking of World Order. *New York: Simon and Schuster, 1996.*

modernity as falsely universalizing a particular kind of experience *and* as hiding deeper alienation and exploitation. It is for this reason, in part, that Chávez and others like him could compellingly use religious discourse even as he and the Catholic Church remained in sharp conflict.[48]

INSIGHTS | Multiple Modernities
by Shmuel N. Eisenstadt

Many scholars have argued that contemporary ideological and religious conflict is less about "tradition" versus "modernity" and more about different "modernities," or different understandings of what modernity means. Seemingly conservative systems, such as the contemporary Iranian regime, incorporate elements of the "modern package." They revise the meaning of key terms, however, in relation to their indigenous cultural traditions *and* to the goals of those shaping the system: Iran's "democracy" may not be Europe's democracy.

According to scholars such as Eisenstadt, we can make sense of such cases by recognizing that there are *multiple modernities*. This label recognizes that the modernization processes witnessed in the United States and Western Europe are not the only available models, but rather that modernity might take different forms in other cultural contexts. The concept of modernity may have roots in the West, but it was carried globally via processes

of diffusion (especially, though not exclusively, via colonialism), and it has been re-framed and re-interpreted wherever it has gone.[49] Many scholars have understood the pairing of capitalism in economics and liberal democracy in politics as the core features of modernity. These are only forms, however, of the more general phenomenon of growth-oriented economics and political systems. Thus, early critical modernities arose in the competing alternative ideologies of the twentieth century: communism and fascism. From this point of view, the alleged "religious resurgence" of recent years should be considered another example of this process of emergent alternative modernities. While Eisenstadt's approach shares some common ideas with Huntington's assessment, it differs notably in pointing to common underlying features of modern societies.

Shmuel N. Eisenstadt, "Multiple Modernities." Daedalus 129, No. 1, Multiple Modernities (Winter 2000): 1–29.

Is Twenty-First-Century Populism an Ideology?

THINKING COMPARATIVELY

As noted at the outset of the chapter, the early twenty-first century has been marked by the rise of a variety of movements and political candidates that have been labelled "populist." Is this an ideology? "Populism" is a word that can mean different things to different people, but generally it signifies that these movements and candidates tend to identify themselves with "the people" and to claim that some set of institutions or groups have been damaging the interests of the people and need to be removed from power.[50] Often, those institutions and groups are perceived to be "foreign." For example, many populists in Europe are nationalists who are critical of the European Union and its policies. In Greece, the populist Syriza movement blames Europe for austerity programs that have been imposed. Populists in a number of other European polities blame the EU for policies that allow refugees and other migrants to enter their countries. In Latin America, many populists blame the United States for its history of intervention in the region. But some—like contemporary Venezuela—also blame international institutions like Human Rights Watch for criticizing their regimes' human rights abuses, claiming that these organizations are lackeys of the United States or of

KEY METHODOLOGICAL TOOL

Knowing When to Use a Typology

We could always construct types and subtypes of any complex feature of politics. A key methodological question is when and why to do so. Typologies draw distinctions that highlight some similarities and draw out some differences, but when we compare cases, there are many potential similarities and differences on which we could focus. The choice to use a typology, as well as which one to use,

KEY METHODOLOGICAL TOOL

(continued)

should depend on the research question at hand. If you are tempted to use (or create!) a typology, ask yourself which similarities and differences would be emphasized by that typology as well as which similarities and differences might be obscured.

Geert Wilders, a populist politician in the Netherlands best known for his outspoken criticisms of immigrants and Muslims.

European countries. Populists in the United States might simultaneously blame immigrants, globalizing trade deals, and the cultural attitudes of educated elites for their country's problems.

Jan-Werner Müller argues that populism can be identified by two characteristics. First, populists present themselves as opposed to "elites."[51] We can add that these elites may be foreign or domestic but either way are presented as distinct from the people. Second, populism is "antipluralist," meaning that populist leaders claim to represent the people in its entirety. According to Müller, this makes populism always potentially anti-democratic, since pluralism—the idea that there are multiple versions of the good and a variety of groups deserving to be recognized— is a key feature of democratic societies.[52] Another key scholar of populism, Cas Mudde, defines the phenomenon in a closely overlapping way, again emphasizing the opposition of populism to pluralism, but adding that it is also opposed to elitism. Mudde emphasizes that populism is a "thin" ideology, and as such can be mixed with other ideologies.[53]

To some extent, populism seems to upend traditional distinctions between "left" and "right."[54] There are populists most would locate on the right, such as Donald Trump in the United States or Geert Wilders in the Netherlands, and those that appear to be located much further on the left, such as Venezuela's *Chavistas* or, arguably and to a lesser extent, politicians like Bernie Sanders in the United States.[55] Indeed, there have been both right- and left-leaning varieties of *Peronista* populism in Argentina. Two scholars have recently argued that we should see left versus right and populist versus anti-populist as distinct ideological "dimensions."[56]

This raises the question of whether there are "types" of populism. Another way to put this is to ask whether, since populists vary so much, they fall into categories that we can use to better understand and predict their behavior.

Some scholars suggest that there is a big difference between "inclusive" populism, which they say is common in Latin America, and "exclusive" populism, which they say is common in Europe.[57] According to such arguments, the former type is distinguished by the fact that it aims to open up access to the state and its benefits to people—typically people with lower socioeconomic status—who previously had not been included. Thus, for example, the populism of Evo Morales in Bolivia can be thought of as "inclusive" because it presents "the people" as indigenous persons, rural populations, and others who have historically been marginalized. Those who promote this typology offer France's National Front as an example of "exclusive" populism. This is because they tend to define the native French population as "the people" and to treat historically marginalized groups like migrant populations as targets.

This distinction *does* seem to be meaningful. After all, the power and status of out-groups probably affect their vulnerability to populist regimes. So "exclusive populism" may be more damaging to already marginalized groups than "inclusive populism." And it may be possible, as some scholars have argued, that populism can be used to expand access to power and resources among disadvantaged persons in polities where many people have been largely ignored by the state.[58] Skeptics, though, would remind us that if populism undermines democratic institutions, any such gains might be temporary at best. Evidence from cases like Venezuela does suggest that even "inclusive" populism can lead to authoritarian regimes that ultimately make most people worse off.

At the same time, we should avoid letting the distinctions in our typologies blind us to commonalities. For example, the similarities among populist regimes and movements may for many purposes be more important than the differences. First of all, many of the "native French" supporters of the National Front may themselves feel disenfranchised and excluded from power. In a number of cases, working class populist supporters seem to be drawn from populations who once supported socialist parties or parties of "laborers." The decline of these parties in some countries and their transformation into "third way" parties in others may have left a number of these individuals feeling unrepresented by the institutions of traditional politics. There may still be a difference between a disenfranchised person in the developing world supporting a populist candidate who claims he will redistribute resources and a middle class person in a rich country who is anxious about the economy and increased migration who supports a xenophobic populist. But both may feel relatively disadvantaged in some way, and this may play a role in their shared receptiveness to populist ideas. If this is true, separating cases by this typology may make it harder to see common causal patterns.

The key point here is that whether a typology such as this will be useful depends very much on the reason one is making a comparison and the question one is asking. Any time that we distinguish or categorize, we highlight one or another characteristic in a set or subset of cases. We need to select the typology for our research purpose and be careful not to "reify" it, or treat it as more than a useful theoretical abstraction.

THINKING COMPARATIVELY

So, then, is populism an ideology? Most scholars could probably agree that populism impacts things in ways similar to how ideologies have in the past and that it has important implications for how our polities and economies may be organized in the future. It includes a series of ideas we can identity, as the definitions from Müller and Mudde cited previously show (emphasis on "the people," suspicion of "elites" and "foreigners"). Whatever one might think of these ideas, they seem to shape the behavior of many political actors in our world.

Chapter Summary

Concepts

- Religion and ideology are two major forms that ideas take as they shape politics.
- Ideology gets defined in lots of ways, but many scholars see it as systematically organized beliefs about how politics and society should be constructed.
- Religion, too, gets defined in numerous ways, but many scholars see it as a system of beliefs and accompanying organizations that posit a transcendental source of meaning.
- Scholars used to think that religion and ideology would both decline as societies modernize, but it now appears to most students of comparative politics that they continue to shape politics in meaningful ways.

Types

- The main modern ideologies are liberalism, fascism, and socialism. Much of twentieth-century international conflict was interpreted in the light of these ideologies.
- There is consensus that while religion may or may not decline when societies modernize, it does tend to undergo a process of *differentiation*. Scholars have tried to explain this in several ways.

- There are three main ideal-typical patterns of modern relationships between religion and politics: lay states, religious states, and denominationalism.

Causes and Effects

- Strong evidence indicates that religion and ideology have not gone away but are, rather, at least as important factors shaping comparative politics today as they were decades ago.
- Recent years have seen a seeming resurgence of ideological activity on both the left and the right.
- Some scholars argue that rather than seeing modernity and religion/ideology as opposed, we recognize that there may be a variety of modernities, many shaped by ideology and religious frameworks.

Thinking Comparatively

- The ideological landscape of contemporary populist movements points to the potential utility and limitations of typologies.
- When using typologies, we should be attentive to which similarities and differences they highlight and obscure.

Thinking It Through

1. As has been noted in this chapter, the United States is somewhat unusual in (1) its level of religious belief and practice given its development status and (2) the denominational way in which it organizes religious difference. Why might the United States be so different? What theoretical use can be made of this doubly "deviant case"?

2. Proponents of the "multiple modernities" approach think that modernization takes notably distinct paths in different cultural contexts. In contrast, traditional modernization theory says that modernization is always the same basic underlying process, though cultural context shapes how it happens. How could we design a comparative analysis to judge between these two

theories? Which cases would you select, and why? What questions would you ask about them?

3. In certain respects, lay states and religious states are mirror images of each other. One type of state tries to push religion out of the public square, and the other tries to firmly plant it there. Thinking about Ahmet Kuru's argument, analyze the nature of the relationship between these types of states. Why are they in certain respects so similar? How might we explain their differences?

4. We have seen that liberalism and socialism have been enduring political ideologies. The other major modern political ideology, fascism, has fewer proponents today, though some have attempted to revive variants of fascism. Has fascism likely disappeared? Why or why not? Under what circumstances might we expect to witness a resurgence of fascism?

5. Where does contemporary populism stand in relation to liberalism, socialism, and fascism? Is it more like one than another? Should it be considered a separate category?

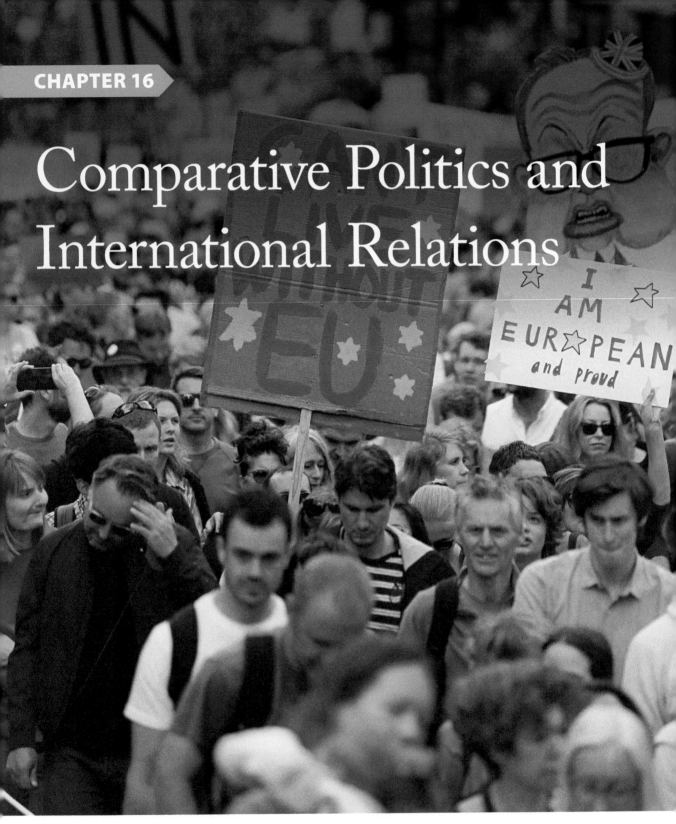

CHAPTER 16

Comparative Politics and International Relations

Signs from opponents of "Brexit," the United Kingdom's withdrawal from the European Union, approved in a referendum in 2016.

The years between 2009 and 2015 saw major economic upheaval across Europe as nineteen of the continent's economies struggled desperately to save their common currency, the euro, and as the region received large numbers of refugees. The economic crisis came after several years in which eurozone countries (European Union countries whose currency is the euro) in southern Europe faced high levels of debt. Greece ultimately required a bailout from European funds—and then a second one in 2012—sparking fear of contagion, since Portugal, Ireland, Spain, and Italy also risked defaulting on their debts. As Europe's largest economy and the center of the eurozone, Germany sought to hold the euro together without a massive bailout of the slower-growing economies. It pushed for strict controls on spending in the southern European countries, including requirements for austere budgets that would cut back on generous social programs and old-age pensions.

The complications were numerous: although Germany called for austerity in southern European countries, it had benefited from exports to those indebted countries, and banks in Germany, France, and abroad risked collapse if the euro fell apart. By 2012, the euro seemed to be hanging on by a precarious political and economic arrangement, one that involved a mix of cooperation and diplomatic fights among Europe's major allies. While the immediate economic crisis seemed to have passed in 2015, "Euroskepticism" persisted; and in 2016, the British population narrowly voted in the famous "Brexit" referendum to withdraw from the EU. At the time of this writing, negotiations about the form of that withdrawal are still ongoing, though it should take place in 2019.

In Europe, recent years have showed the challenges of reconciling international relations with domestic politics, yet the backdrop for this crisis is decades of remarkable European successes in creating a more unified continent. After the horrors of World War II, Germany and France (along with Italy, Belgium, the Netherlands, and Luxembourg) led a process designed to bring Europe together economically and politically.

It was clear that Europe wanted to avoid another cataclysmic war, and the continent's leaders felt that integration was the solution. The process began with a common market in coal and steel, which was symbolically rich in indicating shared sovereignty over the very materials needed for war.

Integration later expanded into a broader common market between these countries, and the European Community took on new members: the United Kingdom, Denmark, Spain and Portugal (after these two countries became democracies), and Greece. Integration then widened and deepened further, moving beyond **free trade** to free movement of peoples across many European borders, increasing the role of the renamed **European Union (EU)**. Alongside this process, the Berlin Wall fell in 1989, East and West Germany reunified in 1990, and the Cold War ended by 1991. The EU ultimately invited in most of the countries of central and eastern Europe, as well as countries in Scandinavia, and even Mediterranean island nations. It also created the euro in 1999 for the majority of its countries, deepening its integration further even as it expanded to include twenty-eight countries (see Map 16.1).

Yet throughout all of this integration, the countries of the EU have jealously guarded their sovereignty, and major decisions and treaties must

free trade A policy or approach in which a government allows foreign goods and services to compete freely with domestic production, as contrasted with protectionism, which favors domestic production.

European Union (EU) The political and economic union of many European states, numbering twenty-eight as of 2017 (though the United Kingdom is currently in the process of withdrawing from the EU, to be completed in 2019).

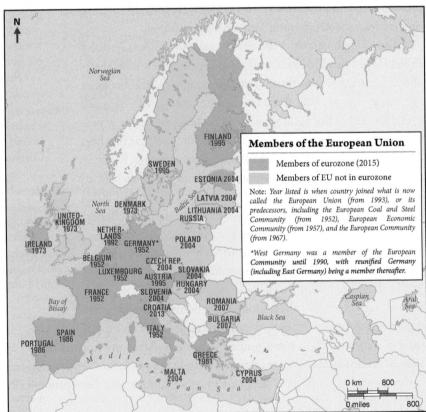

Map 16.1 Members of the European Union. The United Kingdom voted in 2016 to withdraw from the EU and is currently negotiating the terms of its exit, expected in 2019.

be approved unanimously. Meanwhile, some countries, such as Norway and Switzerland, have opted to stay out of the EU altogether.

European integration since World War II thus offers one of the world's greatest contemporary examples of international cooperation, while it also demonstrates the challenges of this cooperation and the reality that most states engage in international relations with a view toward their own national interests. Whether the ambitious and remarkable European project of post-war unification is in the process of foundering or flourishing, it is important to note how the comparative politics of different countries interfaces with international relations.

. . .

Concepts

Throughout this text, we have examined issues of comparative politics, which tends to focus on politics *within* different countries. In some instances, we have made reference to factors that cross borders, such as revolutions or processes of democratization that come in waves. Yet we have not focused directly on the many areas of **international relations** *between* countries, including war and peace and economic relationships. In discussing the actions of governments in international relations, we are often referring to decisions made in **foreign policy**.

> **international relations** The study of relations between countries and between actors in the international system.

> **foreign policy** The set of policies toward foreign nations made by a national government.

We consider two main areas under the topic of international relations: international security and international political economy. **International security** refers to issues of war and peace between nations and to issues of global security and conflict more broadly. As we discuss herein and have noted previously, these include terrorism and terrorist acts committed by nonstate actors. In addition, civil wars and conflicts may take place within a state and yet involve the relations between states. For example, a rebel group that is trying to take over the government in one country may seek refuge in a neighboring country. All of these issues of security and conflict fit in the domain of international relations, but they intersect with the comparative politics we have discussed throughout this book.

> **international security** The study of issues of war and peace between nations and global security and conflict more broadly.

Beyond security studies, the other principal area of study in international relations is **international political economy**, which examines how the economic relations between countries affect politics and how political relations affect economies. In the modern world, countries trade in goods and services, and money flows across borders, often in amounts reaching totals of trillions of dollars a day. Comparative politics and international relations intersect on political economy issues when it comes to questions of globalization, international trade, international finance, and efforts at integration or cooperation on economic issues.

> **international political economy** The study of how the economic relations between countries affect politics and how political relations affect economies.

International relations issues do not always fit neatly in one or the other of the two main categories we've set out here. Consider, for instance, efforts to stop flows of illegal drugs across borders. Is this a question of international security or of international political economy? A plausible answer is "both." Similar arguments could be made for questions of refugees fleeing violence in one country, or of immigration more generally. Many issues in the twenty-first century are

transnational Issues or institutions that cross international borders.

transnational in that they cross borders. The range of issues linking comparative politics and international relations is vast, and we explore them in this chapter.

We will briefly examine some of the leading issues where comparative politics and international relations overlap and affect one another. We look at how domestic politics affects international relations and how transnational issues affect the politics of different countries. Many of the issues we discuss are some of the great challenges and opportunities facing nation-states in the twenty-first century.

Issues

In this chapter, rather than address the "Types" we find in different social and political categories (such as types of revolutions, or types of development, or types of party systems), we focus on some of the leading issues in international relations that relate to comparative politics. These include economic globalization, immigration, transnational networks, and the global environment and sustainability.

Globalization and Trade

globalization The increasing interaction, both economic and cultural, among peoples and societies across national borders.

Globalization is one of the major trends in the world, a force shaping not only the economy but many aspects of everyday life. It refers to increasing interaction, both economic and cultural, between peoples and societies across national borders. Perhaps more than any other phenomenon, globalization epitomizes how international phenomena affect comparative politics. We begin with a discussion of the economic relations that come with flows of goods, capital, and people across borders.

What crosses borders? First, traded goods do, in the form of imports and exports. These can include cars or food, minerals or natural resources such as barrels of petroleum, textiles, or toys. Second, services are increasingly transnational. Examples include the now-famous customer service call centers located in India that serve a global clientele, or medical tourism that leads some residents of wealthy countries to seek out lower-priced surgeries in countries such as Thailand or Costa Rica.

capital A factor of economic production consisting of accumulated wealth or financial resources available for investment.

Third, money (or **capital**) crosses borders for a number of reasons. Many people and corporations have investments or own properties in other countries. Many immigrants living overseas send money home to their families or communities as well. And anything imported must be paid for, so money flows constantly. Finally, people cross borders, whether in search of opportunities for work or political freedoms, or to flee violence or strife in their home countries, or for recreation or business. With these transnational flows come challenges relating to the movements of goods, services, money, and people.

international trade The economic exchange of goods, services, and capital across international borders.

Turning first to **international trade** of goods and services, economic interactions between countries have increased significantly in recent years. Many people in advanced, industrialized countries are aware that an increasing number of goods come from overseas, but the extent is still impressive: the clothes on your back may have been tailored in Bangladesh or Pakistan; the cell phone in your hand may have been assembled in Brazil or China, with parts from Malaysia; and the apple you had at lunch may have come from Chile. Increasingly, this is true of services as well, especially as technology makes it easier and cheaper to communicate around the world. If you need an x-ray in the middle of the night in an American hospital, there is a growing chance that the image will be examined by a technician

A ship makes its way through the Panama Canal between the Pacific and Atlantic oceans.

in Australia, while a call to customer service in Europe may result in talking with someone in India.

This increase in international trade has given rise to many concerns in wealthier countries about job **outsourcing** (contracting abroad) and **offshoring** (basing some services or processes abroad). In some lower-income countries it has also created enthusiasm about the prospects for growth. As wealthy countries rely on goods produced in emerging economies, and as emerging economies rely on markets in wealthy countries, the world economy becomes more **interdependent** (in that individual economies are dependent on one another) and interconnected.[1] The trend of increasing trade has thus given rise to many clichés about globalization, some of which may indeed have a grain of truth to them: the world is "flat" or "shrinking," we are living in a "global village," and we have never been closer.[2] This is not to say globalization is brand new: by some measures, the end of the nineteenth century, when Great Britain was the leading power, was a time as globalized as any other time in history up to the last two decades.[3] Still, globalization is especially pressing today. Countries have increasingly reduced their barriers to trade with one another over recent decades. The importance of global trade in reshaping countries' economies is exemplified by the rise of China (see the Case in Context box in chapter 5 titled "How Did China Become an Economic Power?").

Trade between two or more countries—at least when it is voluntary—is based on the idea that the countries involved gain some advantage from trading. One of

outsourcing In international trade and business, the practice of an economic actor contracting out to other actors, often overseas. (*See* offshoring.)

offshoring In international trade and business, the practice of an economic actor basing some of its services or processes abroad rather than in its domestic market. (*See* outsourcing.)

interdependence A relationship in which two or more actors (such as countries) are mutually dependent on one another.

comparative advantage In international trade, the idea that different countries or territories will have different relative advantages in the production of different goods and services, which forms the basis for gains from trade.

the leading principles in international trade and political economy is **comparative advantage**. This principle holds that countries can benefit from trade by specializing in the goods they can produce with the greatest relative efficiency and by trading for goods they produce relatively less efficiently.

The following is a simple illustration to show the benefits of trade under the principle of comparative advantage. Imagine two countries, Pacifica and Atlantica, both of which have working populations that can produce shirts and phones. Pacifica is more populous, with 2,000 people to Atlantica's 500. On the other hand, it takes somewhat fewer people in Atlantica to produce a shirt or a phone than it does in Pacifica (see Table 16.1). It takes five Atlanticans to make a shirt as contrasted with ten Pacificans, and ten Atlanticans to make a phone as contrasted with fifty Pacificans. This is not necessarily because the skills of the workers differ by country but could perhaps be because there are more labor-saving machines in Atlantica, for example, which allow workers there to produce more rapidly. If Atlantican labor has advantages that allow it to produce more efficiently, how could these two countries gain from trading with each other?

For simplicity's sake, say Pacificans are interested only in buying more phones right now, and Atlanticans are interested only in buying more shirts. The strategy for each country without trade would lead to forty phones produced and purchased in Pacifica and one hundred shirts in Atlantica:

> *Pacifica:*   *Have 2,000 people produce 40 phones.*
>
> *Atlantica:*   *Have 500 people produce 100 shirts.*

But if the two countries can trade, the strategy for each country could be different. If the international price were four shirts to one phone, for example, the following is possible:

> *Pacifica:*   *Have 2,000 people produce 200 shirts, then trade to Atlantica for 50 phones.*
>
> *Atlantica:*   *Have 500 people produce 50 phones, then trade to Pacifica for 200 shirts.*

By specializing in the good they make relatively more efficiently and then trading, both countries are better off. Pacifica ends up with fifty phones instead of forty, while Atlantica ends up with two hundred shirts instead of one hundred.

TABLE 16.1 **Benefits of Trade Under Comparative Advantage**

Country	Population	Labor per Shirt	Labor per Phone	Possibilities Without Trade	Possibilities with Trade (Price: 4 Shirts =1 Phone)
Pacifica	2,000	10 people	50 people	Make 200 shirts or 40 phones	Make 200 shirts, trade for 50 phones
Atlantica	500	5 people	10 people	Make 50 phones or 100 shirts	Make 50 phones, trade for 200 shirts

The example would still work even if one country or the other wanted to trade only some of its product rather than all of it. And this example has two other noteworthy features. First, shirts require less labor to make than phones in each of the countries. Comparative advantage does not depend on countries differing on which product is easier to make than the other. Second, recall that a unit of labor (i.e., a person) in Atlantica is more productive than a person in Pacifica in making *both* shirts *and* phones, perhaps because of the machines they work with. Atlantica has an "absolute advantage" in both shirts and phones because both require less labor in Atlantica than in Pacifica. Yet comparative advantage still allows trade to benefit both countries, despite Atlantica's absolute advantage in both industries. This is the key lesson of comparative advantage, even though it is counterintuitive for many people.

As for the politics of trade, some groups will clearly benefit from trade while others will suffer, at least in the short run. Critiques of economic globalization often focus on those who are disadvantaged by trade and who may be politically important actors. The economic gains from comparative advantage are in aggregate; and while they may appear good for consumers and some producers, the benefits are not equal for all producers.

In the preceding example, opening up to trade might actually put workers out of a job in the Atlantican shirt industry as Atlantica imports shirts from Pacifica, and in the Pacifican phone industry as Pacifica imports phones from Atlantica. With exposure to trade, economic actors representing the relatively efficient sectors will benefit, and economic actors representing less efficient sectors may lose out. Free market economics may claim that these workers can simply move to the new industry (e.g., Atlanticans would move from making shirts to assembling phones), but this process is not simple: it can mean periods of unemployment and require retraining, for example. This change of industry can create economic, social, and political disruptions and uncertainty. Moreover, the more efficient phone making gets, the more dependent on technology (rather than human labor) its production might become, and it may be that those former shirt makers in Atlantica end up working in lower-level service jobs, such as warehouse processing or retail. Finally, we should note that the process of offshoring production, if not adequately regulated or monitored, can result in environmental damage to the locations where production takes place. It can worsen environmental degradation around the world if production becomes "dirtier" overall by moving to countries with lower environmental standards.

For example, say that building phones requires a lot of capital investment to build high-tech factories, while the shirt industry mainly requires labor and limited investment in some sewing machines. If Atlantica is relatively abundant in capital investment in the phone industry, and Pacifica is relatively abundant in labor for making shirts, then Atlantican capital owners will benefit from trade and Pacifican laborers will benefit.[4] Conversely, Atlantican laborers may not benefit as they find themselves competing with laborers in Pacifica, and Pacifican capital owners may not benefit as they find themselves competing with Atlantican capital owners. In an even simpler sense, ask yourself this: if you were the leader of Pacifica, would you want to have your economy based on producing shirts, or would

protectionism In international trade, the practice of a country protecting or giving favor to its own domestic producers.

you prefer to have your country produce higher-value and higher-tech goods like mobile phones? The answer to these economic questions often comes in the form of **protectionism**, or efforts by governments to protect domestic industries from foreign competition. The politics and demands of these different groups will influence the decisions made by governments. International trade is clearly an area where international politics affects the domestic and vice versa.

As noted in chapter 15, recent years have seen a global revival of populism. In countries like Hungary, Poland, Venezuela, the United States, and many others, leaders have arisen that are critical of globalization of one or another form. In some cases, this seems mainly to be about immigration; in others, the alleged perils of free trade. While all of these populist movements, candidates, and leaders are different—and respond to somewhat different conditions—in most cases they emphasize the alleged negative effects of global forces, including free trade, suggesting that these forces somehow undermine the nation's interest. Populism is not necessarily protectionist, but they often go together.

International Institutions and Integration

multilateral In international relations, the actions of three or more countries working together.

intergovernmental organizations (IGOs) The set of international organizations that push for cooperation between countries and work for the prevention or mitigation of international conflicts.

United Nations The most comprehensive global institution, which aims to prevent and manage conflict and to establish multilateral cooperation on matters of international law, economics, and human development and well-being.

international financial institutions (IFIs) Multilateral institutions, particularly the International Monetary Fund (IMF) and the World Bank, that have considerable leverage in international economy.

Since World War II, countries have increasingly collaborated on economic and policy matters. This too links comparative politics to international relations because individual nation-states have made conscious decisions about international relations that are often based on domestic politics. Collaboration began between the advanced, industrialized countries and accelerated after the end of the Cold War. At the **multilateral** level between many countries (i.e., when three or more countries participated), cooperation took the form of freer and more open trade in goods, greater movement of capital and finance, and greater cooperation in international law to bring some criminals to justice.

Several **intergovernmental organizations** push for cooperation between countries and work toward conflict prevention. The **United Nations** is the most comprehensive global institution. It was designed after World War II to provide a global forum for diplomacy and conflict prevention, and it encompasses a number of agencies with missions to enhance security and development; these include the development organization UNICEF, the World Health Organization (WHO), and the United Nations High Commission for Refugees (UNHCR).

Some multilateral institutions have had significant influence in the global economy and have been the source of much debate. This is especially true of the major **international financial institutions**, namely, the International Monetary Fund (IMF) and the World Bank. These two organizations have had leverage in international politics, especially in the 1980s and 1990s. During that period, these institutions pressured developing countries to follow a free market model rather than a model that featured protectionism, investments by the government in state-owned enterprises, and greater state intervention in the economy (as noted in chapter 5). This came to be known as the "Washington Consensus" because it reflected the policy recommendations of the World Bank and IMF, both of which are based in Washington, DC, along with the views of the U.S. government. The debate about the impacts of these reforms has raged, with advocates saying that these institutions helped developing economies make a needed shift to open up to market forces, while critics have argued that the draconian reforms hurt people and economies in developing countries and precipitated financial crises.[5]

Apart from these global, multilateral institutions are a range of regional organizations. At this level, there is sometimes economic and political **integration**, where countries agree to open up their economies to one another and shape common strategies toward other countries outside the regional bloc. There are many examples, including the North American Free Trade Association (NAFTA) and associations for free trade in South America, Pacific Asia, and regions of Africa; but the standout example is the EU, noted at the beginning of the chapter.

How the EU has achieved greater economic and political integration in a world of sovereign nation-states is one of the great questions of modern political economy. Over the decades from the 1950s to the present, much of Europe has transitioned from a region of long-standing suspicions and historical animosities (such as between France and Germany) to a more closely integrated set of countries. These share a supranational set of political institutions and interdependent economies. As noted at the beginning of the chapter, European integration began as little more than a trade zone involving six countries and a common market in coal and steel. Yet this cooperation expanded over time to include more members (see Map 16.1 at the beginning of the chapter) while also deepening its integration. The six original members formed the European Economic Community that established a common customs union for trade with other countries. Over time, the members reiterated a push for "ever closer union" between member countries. Subsequent treaties established the European Union, and its many member countries agreed to pool their sovereignty on some major issues. Besides the establishment of the euro, a notable example was the creation of the Schengen area, which eliminated internal border controls between the countries of the zone. The area encompasses the various EU countries on the continent (though not the United Kingdom or Ireland). The European Union now makes many of its decisions based on qualified majorities rather than on a "one country, one vote" principle.

We return to the example of the EU in the "Thinking Comparatively" section at the end of the chapter, but we note here that integration does not mean that nation-states have ceased to be important. In fact, even in the EU, major decisions about issues such as foreign policy or taxation require unanimous consent of the member governments, meaning that each nation-state effectively has a veto. As one of the world's most integrated supranational bodies, the EU shows that most integration is still deeply dependent on the nation-state. At the same time, globalization and integration have occurred alongside the emergence of many identities below the level of nation-state, such as ethnic groups and regional groups, in countries from Russia to Ethiopia to Mexico. Thus, even as China has integrated with the world economy, the Uighur ethnic group in the west of the country has tried to secure greater autonomy; and even as Spain has integrated with the EU, the Catalonian and Basque regions have sought guarantees of greater autonomy from the Spanish central government. Sometimes the groups seeking autonomy refer to themselves as nations. This combination of integration above the nation-state level and pressures from ethnic or regional groups below that level has put the nation-state under pressure, but it continues to be the central actor in international relations and comparative politics.

integration In international relations, a process by which countries agree to collaborate economically or politically, to make some decisions collectively, and to shape common strategies.

CASE IN CONTEXT

The United States and the World: A Love–Hate Relationship?   PAGE 572

The United States has been a leading nation in world affairs for over a century. It has been called the "indispensable nation" due to its dominant military, its economic significance, and its cultural power. The United States has exerted its power in many ways, including major and minor wars, but it has also at times been reluctant to engage in foreign entanglements.

For more on U.S. relations with the world, see the case study in Part VI, p. 572–573. As you read it, keep in mind the following questions:

1. When has the United States favored greater global integration, and when has it not done so?
2. What might explain the historical tendency for isolationism to recur in the United States?
3. What challenges are likely to be the most significant for the United States in the future?

Immigration

immigration The movement of people to foreign countries.

Another key area where domestic and international politics intersect is **immigration,** defined as the movement of people to foreign countries. Immigration is clearly an issue of international relations because it involves a country from which a person leaves (or emigrates) and a country to which the person migrates, or immigrates. It is also a matter of comparative politics because it regularly becomes a major domestic issue in the countries involved.

The details of immigration debates vary from one country to another, but immigration patterns can be compared. In many prominent examples, the pattern is for immigrants to move from lower-income countries with limited economic opportunities to wealthier countries. Immigration often induces conflicts or tensions between citizens of the receiving country and the newcomers, whom citizens often deride, claiming that foreigners harm the job prospects of "natives." For example, one of the leading political issues in the United States is the status of large numbers of migrant workers from Mexico, along with other Latin American countries (especially Central America) to a lesser extent. Immigration is a major issue across Europe as well, though patterns of immigrants' countries of origin differ from one European country to another. In France, many of the tensions are with respect to North African immigrants and their descendants. In Germany and northern Europe, there are larger numbers of immigrants from Turkey and the Middle East, particularly following Angela Merkel's decision in 2015 to accept hundreds of thousands of refugees, above all from Syria's devastating civil war.

assimilation The practice of being culturally absorbed by or integrated into another culture, especially with respect to immigration.

The issues surrounding immigration are numerous, contentious, and often blurred. One major issue is **assimilation** (being culturally absorbed by or integrated into another culture). Some immigrant groups prefer to merge with the "mainstream" of society, while others prefer to retain their cultural autonomy.[6] Moreover, there are major debates about how nation-states should accommodate immigrants. Advocates of assimilation often argue that immigrants must adapt to the cultural practices and conceptions of liberal values in the countries where they migrate. Immigrants, however, may wish to retain their own cultural traditions. They may argue that respect for different traditions is a basic tenet of modern liberal societies and that assimilation to a dominant culture is not required. Further, some scholars have claimed that positions in favor of assimilation are often based on misconceptions and simplistic notions about people of other backgrounds.[7] Other scholars note that a better goal might be "integration," of which assimilation is just one possible form. Here "integration" is understood as the successful incorporation of immigrant groups in the society. Immigrants might be considered "integrated" if they find stable housing and employment, and can imagine building lives in their new countries of residence, whether or not they have taken on all of the cultural practices of the "host society natives."[8]

Middle-ground views often favor multicultural notions of citizenship protected by a liberal state. Debates over multiculturalism are common in advanced, industrialized countries that have substantial numbers of migrants from the developing countries, and immigration has become a major issue in domestic and comparative politics. This is true across the European Union, as well as in the United States. In fact, German Chancellor Angela Merkel—as noted previously, a great champion of openness to refugees and other migrants—made a splash with a famous statement in 2010 saying that multiculturalism has "utterly failed."[9]

Sometimes immigrant communities are blamed for violent crimes committed by a handful of their members—a position that most social scientists view as unjustified. Indeed, on balance, social science scholarship on immigration and crime find that, if anything, they are negatively associated (i.e., controlling for other factors, more immigration predicts *less* crime), though findings on this question differ somewhat from study to study.[10] Sociologist Robert Sampson has found that, at least in some places, increasing the share of a neighborhood's residents that are immigrants is associated with *lower* levels of crime.[11] Yet in a number of countries, sizeable portions of the population seem to perceive immigrants as being associated with crime. This may be due to the efforts of politicians using immigrants as scapegoats, or may happen because of the so-called confirmation bias (i.e., we tend to see and remember the evidence that is consistent with our theories of the world.)

Some also blame immigration for terrorism. For example, the London bombings of 2005 were not reflective of the actions or beliefs of the Muslim population in Britain, despite arguments to the contrary. One controversial, arguably racist, perspective holds that Britain is now home to so-called Londonistan, a foreign population from Pakistan and other Muslim countries that is allegedly unassimilated to Western values such as tolerance and respect for individual rights, and that this is a threat to Western democracies.[12] An opposing perspective defends multiculturalism and argues that different communities and belief systems can and should be accommodated within tolerant and open societies.[13] While often defending multiculturalism and promoting tolerance, some social scientists are interested in exploring the relationship between the reception of immigrant groups and the development of extremist attitudes. Do discrimination and poor economic prospects fuel radicalism? From a social science point of view, this is a reasonable question.

Distinctions between types of immigrants matter, such as between those who are documented (have attained legal residence) and those who are undocumented (and are thus often considered "illegal"). A related distinction is between immigration patterns of different lengths of time. Some people leave their countries in search of temporary work (such as for a single growing season in agriculture), others seek permanent residence in a new country, and still others seek to become naturalized citizens of a new country. There are also distinctions between generations of immigrants: some groups consider themselves or are ascribed the status of immigrants even though they were born in the new country, and social scientists speak of first-generation and second-generation immigrants. Still another key distinction concerns the differences in cultural and material resources of various immigrant groups, which often relates to their reasons for migrating. Economic migrants are those who mainly seek economic opportunities. Others migrate to escape persecution and violence or environmental problems, and still others due to their values and beliefs. All of these distinctions are quite important, but these different groups of immigrants are often treated as if they were all the same in public debate.

Another issue is the tension between immigrants and descendants of immigrants from previous waves of immigration. Many countries—especially, but not exclusively, those with civic forms of nationalism, as outlined in chapter 13—have welcomed immigrants over time but face new challenges with each generation. Many Americans famously and proudly refer to the United States as a "nation of immigrants," while also calling for stricter limits on immigration and efforts to stop the flow of immigrants and deport those present. Pride in a history of immigration can thus coexist with **nativism**, which seeks to protect the interests of established groups of residents against the interests of immigrants. This position attempts to portray more recent immigrants as somehow different from previous waves. Sometimes even scholars make such claims, singling out groups like Hispanic or Islamic immigrants as being less open to assimilation,

nativism A political attitude that seeks to protect the interests of established groups of residents in a given country against the interests of more recent immigrants.

CASE IN CONTEXT
Globalization and Culture in France

PAGE 440

As we have noted in previous chapters, France gives us many examples of how cultural and economic challenges interact when questions of immigration arise. France experiences ongoing debate about its future in light of integration with the EU and the arrival of growing numbers of immigrants, especially from its former colonies in North Africa. It also has notable variation in how succeeding generations of immigrants are treated by and respond to French society.

For more on these issues in France, see the case study in Part VI, pp. 440–441. As you read it, keep in mind the following questions:

1. In what ways has France been ambivalent about the progress of globalization?
2. What might explain why France was once quite favorable to globalization but has more recently become uncertain about it?
3. In what ways has France tried to mitigate the perceived downsides of globalization?

less democratic, or less capable of economic integration.[14] Impartial reviews of the evidence, though, controvert such claims.[15]

Immigration thus brings together issues in the social, economic, and political domains. The social side involves cultural assimilation and competing conceptions of what it means to be part of a nation. Some of the hottest debates on immigration are as much about money as they are about identity. On the economic side, immigration raises issues of competition with native-born workers for jobs and for some public benefits. The political domain includes aspects of the social and economic sides but focuses on immigration as a policy issue, which is complicated because immigration is both a transnational and a domestic issue.

We should also note that just as immigration poses challenges, emigration—leaving a country to live in another—has some important economic implications for the countries left behind. One issue is the **brain drain**, or the fact that many times it is the most skilled and highly educated members of a population who leave. In some of these circumstances, relatively poor countries have invested heavily in preparing some of their top young people to build their country, only to see them leave for better opportunities elsewhere. On the flip side, emigrants are often huge contributors to their home countries through **remittances** of cash or resources sent back home to families and friends. Further, some emigrants who have left their home countries have gone into exile for political or economic reasons, because they are fleeing repression or lack of opportunity. This situation confronts the home country with the challenge of defining whether and how such emigrants should be reintegrated into their home societies, if and when they return. It can apply to short-term migrant workers who leave home temporarily for work, as well as to exiles who flee their homes indefinitely, leaving their property behind.

brain drain The departure or emigration of skilled and educated members of a population, especially with reference to developing countries in the international system.

remittances Cash or resources sent to a home country, often to family and friends, by emigrants.

Environment and Sustainability

Contemporary debates in comparative politics and international relations are not just about maximizing economic growth but also about the consequences of that growth around the world. A major worry is that the current consumption of resources and rates of environmental pollution are not **sustainable**, or capable of being sustained for future generations. At the local level, this has become a major issue in rapidly industrializing countries such as China, where environmental degradation has worsened dramatically through the pollution of air, water, and land. The result has been contamination and disease affecting many millions of people.

Environmental consequences from industrialization are horrific in many locations, yet the leading issue with respect to the environment at the global level is **climate change**. This is sometimes referred to in terms of global warming, though models of climate change predict a range of effects on the climate. Most climatologists and natural scientists agree that climate change is attributable in part to man-made causes and continue to collect more data that supports this well-established hypothesis.[16] The *extent* of humanity's impact on the climate is debated, but the prevailing current theory holds that mankind's effect on the climate has come mainly through **greenhouse gas (GHG) emissions**. Pollutants such as carbon dioxide and methane are emitted into the atmosphere and trap solar energy, warming the planet below, as in a greenhouse. Many of these pollutants come from fossil fuels used to produce energy, such as petroleum, coal, and natural

sustainability The notion, especially used with regard to the environment, that a resource is capable of being sustained for use or enjoyment by future generations.

climate change A set of changes to the earth's climate.

greenhouse gases (GHG) Emissions of gases such as carbon dioxide and methane from industrial activity and consumption of fossil fuels that contributes to climate change.

Environmental degradation accompanies rapid growth in China.

alternative energy Energy sources, such as solar or wind power, that are not derived from fossil fuels.

gas. This research is the origin of the call for **alternative energy** sources, such as solar or wind power.

Climate change estimates predict that global temperature averages will peak at two or more degrees Celsius above historic averages. This change is predicted to bring about other consequences, including melting of glaciers and ice sheets, rises in sea levels, flooding of coastal lowlands, increased numbers and severity of extreme weather events such as hurricanes and avalanches, desertification of marginal agricultural lands, and extinction of large numbers of animal and plant species. To the extent these events materialize, they will signify major, costly disruptions to peoples and societies across the planet. Droughts may lead to major conflict over food and water. Flooding may actually erase some cities.

Climate change and environmental sustainability present some of the most fundamental dilemmas in politics. One basic feature of pollution is that it is an **externality** from economic activity, meaning that the gains and costs from an activity do not accrue to the same actor. In the case of polluting, individual companies may gain profits from their production (or countries may grow economically from it), with the act of polluting as a by-product, but the costs of that pollution

externality An economic phenomenon in which the gains and costs from a given activity do not accrue to the same actor.

are passed on to others. Because polluters do not pay the costs to society associated with pollution, they do not have as much of an incentive to stop it. This condition represents the collective action problem and the "free-rider" problem outlined in previous chapters. One of the leading discussions about pollution is on the difficulties of managing resources that are shared among many people (or countries), when all actors have an incentive to freeride—to maximize their own benefit while passing the costs of their action onto others.

Climate change is thus more than a scientific challenge: it is also a political challenge both within and across national borders. Most efforts to halt climate change involve securing commitments by sovereign nations to reduce their greenhouse gas emissions over time. These agreements are not easily secured, as they require cooperation and agreement among large numbers of actors, and because there is little agreement on which countries should pay the costs of halting greenhouse gas emissions. In general, large developing countries such as China and India hold that the developed countries are responsible for most of the emissions to date and are thus primarily responsible for stopping climate change while lower-income countries catch up in development. Developed countries generally respond that climate change was unknown when many of the rich world's emissions occurred, and that much of the future damage will come from the developing countries.[17] Addressing climate change thus raises many of the central dilemmas in international politics. There have been successes in communities around the world in managing common resources, but scaling these efforts up to international levels through cooperation among nation-states is difficult.[18]

Transnational Networks

Many of the challenges facing nation-states in contemporary politics come from nonstate actors, and especially from **transnational networks** of different actors working across borders. Some transnational networks are particularly worrying because they are criminal or violent, and comparative politics matters here in part

transnational network A network of nonstate actors working across state borders.

INSIGHTS   The Tragedy of the Commons
by Garrett Hardin

Garrett Hardin's article is foundational in the study of common resources, and it has implications for many environmental challenges in the world today. The article focuses on the challenges of overexploitation of common resources by large and growing populations. Hardin's illustrative example of the tragedy is a pasture open to all herdsmen and their herds of animals. As each herdsman allows his herds to graze, the pasture is degraded a bit and its resources (grass) are used up, yet each herdsman has an individual incentive to encourage his livestock to continue grazing. This situation ultimately leads to a depleted common resource because benefits from using the commons are individual, but costs are shared by all. Hardin notes that this principle also operates with pollution in the atmosphere, except that users are not "taking out" natural resources but rather "putting in" contaminants and thus "using up" a resource shared by all. Possible ways to address the tragedy of the commons include assigning private property rights and requiring those who exploit natural resources to pay the costs associated with their use, or through cooperative institutions and practices.[19]

Garrett Hardin, "The Tragedy of the Commons." Science *162, No. 3859 (1997): 1243–1248.*

CASE IN CONTEXT
Resource Management in Japan

PAGE 497

To illustrate the challenge of managing common resources, we can look at the question of overfishing in Japan. This particular issue shows the difficulty of coordination in situations where each actor would like to maximize its individual benefit, yet all actors doing so would result in an unfavorable outcome for all.

For more on environmentalism in Japan, see the case study in Part VI, pp. 497–498. As you read it, keep in mind the following questions:

1. In what way does Japan contribute to the overfishing problem, and why does it not take action to stop it?
2. To what extent is it "rational" for any one country to limit its own role in depleting common resources?
3. What are some other examples of common resources that are difficult to manage politically?

because these networks thrive where states are weak, failed, or collapsed. Since September 11, 2001, one of the most notorious of these has been al Qaeda, the Islamic fundamentalist terror group. One of the distinguishing characteristics of al Qaeda and other terrorist groups like it, as discussed in chapter 12, is its decentralized structure, and the fact that its ideology spreads to other like-minded organizations.[20] Stopping or defeating the al Qaeda network is thus not as clear-cut as defeating a nation-state in a traditional war. We may see something similar with ISIS, which for some time had captured territory in parts of Syria and Iraq and seemed to be building a state or quasi-state. Now defeated "on the battlefield," it is expected to return to being a more decentralized organization. Similarly, although smuggling and trafficking rings may have hierarchical organizations, they may be more like networks than like nation-states. The "war on drugs" and the "war on terrorism" have pitted nation-states against much more amorphous and flexible enemies that do not have a capital city or even a fixed base of operations.[21]

Of course, not all transnational networks are criminal or violent; rather, globalization has generated a large number of transnational networks designed to leverage citizens' political voice. The emergence of transnational advocacy networks may be a key to facilitating greater governmental response to issues such as environmental protection and preventing violence against women.[22] In some circumstances, governments may not make needed changes unless pressured to do so by networks of advocates and activists that cross borders. The success of these networks may be due in part to their flexibility, which allows them to use strategies that are not available to governments.[23] Taking both terror groups and advocacy networks into account, it is both for better and for worse that transnational networks affect the politics and societies of countries around the world.

Nuclear Threats and Terrorism

The classic issues of international relations are those of war, peace, and conflict among nations. This may seem to be exclusively the domain of international relations and thus unrelated to comparative politics; but, as we will see in the section on "Causes and Effects," there is major debate about the role of domestic politics and domestic institutions in shaping international relations.

During the Cold War, the central issue in international relations was the war (or lack thereof) between the major powers: the United States and the Soviet Union. Weapons that created the possibility for mass casualties in civilian populations heightened the sense of urgency over war and peace. Some of these weapons are chemical, such as deadly gases and biological weapons that can spread infectious bacteria, viruses, and other deadly agents through a population. But the class of weapons that received and continues to receive the most attention is nuclear weapons, which can create massively destructive explosions capable of killing millions of people. The only use of nuclear weapons (then called atomic weapons) has been by the United States in the 1945 bombing of Japan at the end of World War II.

Nuclear weapons are currently known to be possessed by only a small number of countries: the United States, Russia, the United Kingdom, France, China, India, Pakistan, and North Korea. Israel is widely assumed to have nuclear weapons but has not declared its nuclear status; and in recent years Iran was widely presumed to be working toward nuclear status (see the Iran country Case Study box titled "Iran and the Politics of Nuclear Proliferation" on this topic). In many cases, countries have argued that developing nuclear weapons is a deterrent against attacks by other countries; this probably applies in many cases, such as the U.S.S.R. seeking a deterrent to the United States, or India seeking a deterrent to China, and Pakistan in turn seeking a deterrent to India (see the Case in Context box, "India in the Twenty-First Century"). Many current nuclear powers are hoping to prevent further **nuclear proliferation**—the spread of nuclear technology—to other states.

Terrorism is the other major concern in international security today. The definition of terrorism is greatly contested, as discussed in chapter 12, but in the context of international relations for this chapter, we may define it roughly as the use of violence to achieve political ends through psychological impacts on a civilian population. It is usually distinguished from acts of war in which militaries attack one another, but terrorism by this definition could occur during war when

nuclear proliferation The expansion of the number of countries and other actors possessing nuclear technology.

terrorism The use of violence to achieve political ends through psychological impacts on a civilian population.

INSIGHTS   The Five Wars of Globalization
by Moisés Naím

Naím notes five major "wars" of globalization that pit nation-states against flexible, decentralized criminal networks. Governments are waging wars against criminal activities in the areas of drug trafficking, arms trafficking, intellectual property theft (or piracy), human trafficking (alien smuggling), and money laundering. The criminal networks that mastermind these forms of trafficking and theft may be involved in more than one such area, and trends in these areas of criminality reinforce one another. Naím notes that nation-states will face considerable difficulty in defeating these networks,

for several reasons: these networks are not bound to certain geographic locations, are quite nimble compared with government bureaucracies, and are responding to strong incentives supplied by the market. Accordingly, Naím recommends that governments must adapt newer, more flexible international institutions to battle these networks while also preferring regulation of these ills over outright prohibition and criminalization.

Moisés Naím, "The Five Wars of Globalization." Foreign Policy 134, No. 1 (2003), 28–37.

CASE IN CONTEXT

Iran and the Politics of Nuclear Proliferation

PAGE 483

In recent years, Iran appeared to be developing the capacity to enrich and refine nuclear materials. The country is also an enemy of American ally Israel, and its regime is adversarial to the United States. The American government has sought to prevent Iran from developing a nuclear weapon, though Iran says its nuclear activity is for peaceful purposes. This led to considerable efforts at international diplomacy, culminating in a 2015 agreement between Iran and China, France, Germany, Russia, the United Kingdom, and the United States (JCPOA). This agreement may be called into question by the administration of United States President Donald Trump, who has been critical of it.

For more on nuclear power in Iran, see the case study in Part VI, p. 483. As you read it, keep in mind the following questions:

1. What might be the American and Iranian arguments against and for Iran's developing nuclear processing technology?
2. If we assume Iran will not stage a direct nuclear attack on the United States or Israel, in what ways does Iran illustrate the risks of proliferation?
3. How is nuclear proliferation linked to the prospects for terrorism?
4. What would the likely impacts on nuclear proliferation be if the United States government refuses to recertify the 2015 agreement with Iran?

nonstate actors In international relations, actors in international politics that are not nation-states; includes multinational corporations, transnational advocacy groups, and international criminal networks.

militaries target civilians. Often, terrorism is associated with **nonstate actors**, but countries such as the United States also declare other countries to be "state sponsors of terrorism."[24]

It has often been said that the world changed on September 11, 2001, when the Islamic fundamentalist group al Qaeda launched a terrorist attack on the United States. The attack killed nearly three thousand Americans in New York's World Trade Center, the Pentagon in Washington, DC, and on an airliner in Pennsylvania. This led to a United States response that began to shape the foreign affairs of the post-9/11 period. Yet terrorism began long before 2001, and movements around the world have been classified as terrorist organizations. Examples include the Irish Republican Army (IRA) in the United Kingdom and Ireland, whose stated aim was the end of British presence in Ireland, and separatist groups such as the Basque group ETA in Spain and the Tamil Tigers in Sri Lanka. States often define terrorist groups as those seeking to overthrow or replace an existing state structure. Showing the ambiguities of such definitions, the white apartheid regime in South Africa deemed the African National Congress a terrorist organization, but it was seen as a freedom movement by the majority of South Africans and ultimately by international public opinion. There have also been terror attacks committed in the United States by American citizens, such as the bombing of the Oklahoma City federal building in 1995 by Timothy McVeigh, which killed 168 people.

Terrorism is an international issue with significant domestic impacts, and a domestic issue with significant international impacts. To take one major example, the Palestinian group Hamas is deemed a terrorist organization by Israel, the

CASE IN CONTEXT

India in the Twenty-First Century: Domestic Politics, Identity, and Security

PAGE 468

It is commonly said that India and Pakistan have the world's "most dangerous border." The reasons for this assertion straddle the boundaries of comparative politics and international relations. Both countries are nuclear powers, and a range of domestic differences have resulted in long-standing tensions and conflict.

For more on these issues, see the case study in Part VI, pp. 468–469. As you read it, keep in mind the following questions:

1. How do domestic politics and international security interact in India and Pakistan?
2. How do national and religious identity and political institutions affect relations between the countries?
3. Are the issues raised here best seen as issues of international relations, comparative politics, or both? Why?

United States, and the European Union. Yet many Palestinians see it as a movement of freedom fighters seeking to liberate Palestine from Israeli occupation. Internationally, Hamas is also widely assumed to be supported by Iran and probably Syria. The actions of Hamas, which include rocket and mortar attacks into Israel, are central to Israeli domestic politics and to the foreign affairs of the United States in the Middle East. In turn, the decisions the Israeli government makes shape the international context of the region.

The issue of terrorism is of particular concern when it overlaps with the capacity for mass destruction, as highlighted by the cases of Iran, India, and Pakistan. For Iran, a concern is that it may distribute nuclear weapons to surrogate terror groups for an attack on its enemies rather than deploy them itself. For India and Pakistan, a major issue was the black market network led by Pakistani nuclear head A. Q. Khan, which resulted in nuclear technology making its way into the hands of numerous regimes and organizations. The prospects that a terror group may get its hands on nuclear devices, whether through state sponsorship or a black market, is one of the leading concerns in contemporary international relations.

Causes and Effects: What Are the Main Causes in International Relations?

Several major theories of international security offer different explanations for conflict and cooperation between states. To illustrate these, we will focus mainly how these theories work in the area of security, conflict, and peace rather than international political economy. We have addressed political economy in several other chapters (especially 4 and 5) and will return to it in the "Thinking Comparatively" section later in this chapter. The major theories we examine in this section are realism, liberalism, constructivism (which is generally seen as an approach rather than a theory), and, to a lesser extent, Marxism. We note how comparative politics fits into (or does not fit into) each of these theories. In each case, we look at the theory and how it explains in general the prevalence of conflict or peace in international relations.

Realism

realism In international relations, a theory that treats states in the international system largely as acting on the basis of national self-interest, defined often in terms of power, survival, and security.

Realism is probably the leading theoretical approach to international relations today, and the other major theories have emerged more recently as responses or correctives to realism. From the perspective of comparative politics, realism is noteworthy for the ways it does *not* examine the internal politics of nation-states and finds relatively little room for domestic and comparative politics in international relations. The realist literature treats states in the international system largely as **unitary rational actors**—those capable of making reasoned decisions on the basis of national self-interest. This model holds that the main determinant of international action is self-interest, defined often in terms of survival and security.

unitary rational actor In international relations theory and especially realism, the idea that states act as if they were single individuals capable of making decisions on the basis of rational calculations about the costs and benefits of different actions.

This line of argument dates back to classical realists, most notably Thucydides in ancient Greece, Machiavelli in Renaissance Italy, and Thomas Hobbes, author of *Leviathan*, in seventeenth-century England.[25] These philosophers emphasized how human nature gave rise to conflict and necessitated seeking power to achieve security. The leading modern example of realist thinking in international relations can be found in the work of Kenneth Waltz.[26] Waltz's work is the foundation for much of contemporary realism and is known as "neorealism" to distinguish it from the classical realism of political philosophers of earlier centuries.

defensive realism A realist theory that holds that peace or cooperation can emerge under specific circumstances, namely, when it is easier to defend than to attack and when states can see clearly what other states' intentions are.

The conditions of anarchy and the balance of power are central to realism, but realism is a theory that contains many different perspectives. For example, **defensive realism** holds that a lack of conflict and even cooperation can emerge under specific circumstances, namely, when it is easier to defend than to attack and when states can see clearly what other states' intentions are.[27] On the other hand, **offensive realism** holds that states are never satisfied with the status quo (the way things are) and will seek to maximize their power whenever they can, striving toward the hegemonic position where possible.[28]

offensive realism A realist theory that holds that states will seek to maximize their power whenever they can.

Some of the work in realism features rational choice theory, discussed in previous chapters (such as the work of Timur Kuran in chapter 12 and David Laitin in chapter 13). Rational choice typically involves a formal model of strategic interactions between actors, often by conceiving of these interactions as "games" in which the "players" respond rationally to incentives and to the expected actions of other players, given their incentives. These games give rise to the name **game theory**: they are designed to simplify the problem to its essence to analyze the actions of the players.

game theory A set of approaches to the study of strategic interaction between actors, often relying on mathematical modeling and assumptions of the rationality of different actors.

The most famous illustration is the **prisoner's dilemma**. In this game, one imagines two prisoners being interrogated separately by a jailer. Each prisoner can choose whether to rat out his fellow prisoner or not, and what each says affects the sentence of both prisoners (see Table 16.2). Each prisoner's cell in the table has two possibilities—to not tell or to rat out the other prisoner—giving four possible outcomes in the table. These outcomes are known as the **payoff matrix** because they reflect the payoffs the players get depending on their choices. The prisoners would be better off if both refused than if both were to rat out the other, so we might expect them to cooperate and not tell. Yet the result will be that both defect and rat each other out. Why?

prisoner's dilemma (game) A model of a game in which two actors would benefit from cooperation, but each has individual incentives to defect from cooperation.

payoff matrix In game-theoretic models, the distribution of payoffs to players depending on the choices made.

INSIGHTS

Theory of International Politics
by Kenneth Waltz

Waltz's theory of realism holds that the actions of states can be explained by the structure of the international system and the distribution of power within it. The central fact that shapes the behavior of states is the *anarchy* of the international system in which there is no sovereign power. Given the anarchic system, the distribution of power within that system shapes how states act. States behave differently depending on whether the system has a single great power, two great powers, or multiple great powers. A *bipolar* world is one with two great powers, such as in the Cold War between the United States and the U.S.S.R. Waltz argued that this was the most stable arrangement. A *multipolar* system has many powers, such as in Europe in the nineteenth century and up to World War I. In a *unipolar* system, there is a single power, known as a *hegemon*. Waltz argued that the bipolar system would be especially stable because it enables countries to join with one power or the other to balance the efforts of the other to reach hegemony. This idea of the *balance of power* came to be one of the leading premises of realism.

Kenneth Waltz, Theory of International Politics. *Reading, MA: Addison-Wesley, 1979.*

Consider the situation from the perspective of prisoner 1 (called P1) by looking only at P1's payoffs. If P2 cooperates, P1 is better off defecting, because he will go free. If P2 defects, P1 is still better off defecting as well, because he gets five years instead of ten. No matter which strategy P2 chooses, P1 is better off defecting; put another way, no matter which row of the payoff matrix P1 finds himself in, he is better off in the "Defect" column. In the terms of game theory, P1 has a dominant strategy to rat out P2. By the same token, no matter what P1 decides, P2 is better off defecting and ratting out P1. So they both go to jail for 5 years, even though they both would have been better off had they cooperated.

In international relations, this logic can be used to model many kinds of behavior when one state does not know what another is doing. One major illustration is the idea of an arms race, and the phenomenon called the **security dilemma**.[29] The security dilemma arises in situations where each actor thinks that the other actor will be trying to maximize its advantage. Whatever the other actor does, a country is better off building up its own arms. So both defect from cooperation and produce more arms to protect themselves. Cooperation might be a much better outcome overall than an arms race, but each individual country's incentive is to defect from an agreement. Seen from a rationalist perspective, this is a version of the prisoner's dilemma.

security dilemma Dilemma in which each actor in the international system expects others to maximize their own security advantage and thus builds up power itself, leading to an arms race.

TABLE 16.2 The Prisoner's Dilemma

		Prisoner 1	
		Cooperate ("Don't Tell")	Defect ("Rat Out")
Prisoner 2	Cooperate ("Don't Tell")	P1 gets 1 year, P2 gets 1 year	P1 goes free, P2 gets 10 years
	Defect ("Rat Out")	P1 gets 10 years, P2 goes free	P1 gets 5 years, P2 gets 5 years

In rational choice, cooperation between actors is possible under certain circumstances, if the payoffs to each actor are best for them individually. This can often occur through repeated interactions.[30] For example, if the prisoner's dilemma happens with repeated interactions between the "players," then many more dynamic possibilities are opened up as players are able to signal their intentions to one another and to reward or punish one another over time. In addition, some scholars note that international institutions can be used to create circumstances for cooperation, as we discuss next under "Liberalism." Realism is the predominant approach, or paradigm, in international relations, but liberalism places greater emphasis on how domestic institutions and politics shape the behavior of states.

Liberalism

The most prominent school of thought to challenge realism in international relations has been **liberalism,** which holds that states can have different preferences and internal structures that lead them to behave in different ways. Liberalism pays greater attention to the role of domestic institutions in international relations, and it makes efforts to explain cooperation and peace between some states while also accounting for conflict in other circumstances. The liberal critique of realism holds that realism is best suited to explaining conflict and a lack of cooperation, but that it fails to account for more optimistic outcomes. As a leading scholar of liberalism puts it, "[t]he Realist model of international relations, which provides a plausible explanation of the general insecurity of states, offers little guidance in explaining the pacification of the liberal world."[31] Liberal scholars argue that domestic institutions and comparative politics matter more. For example, free-market democracies that value individual liberties highly may be expected to act differently from totalitarian dictatorships. Cooperation and lack of conflict can emerge when like-minded states interact, when states have incentives to trade and exchange with one another, or when states comply with different institutional norms.

There are several strains of liberal thought.[32] One, known as "commercial liberalism," is based on the idea that countries engaged in economic interactions with one another have more incentive to be peaceful.[33] This line of logic dates back to the eighteenth-century economist Adam Smith. Another strain of liberalism is "liberal institutionalism," which argues that international institutions—such as free trade blocs, international forums, and international financial institutions—can mitigate the effects of anarchy and make more cooperation possible than realists expect.[34] One of liberalism's strongest claims is the existence of a **democratic peace.** This theory seeks to explain why democracies (almost) never go to war with one another and have not done so since the first democracies emerged in the 1700s.[35] The reasons for the democratic peace may be numerous (see the Insights box on "Kant, Liberal Legacies, and Foreign Affairs"), including common values and the ability of democratic regimes to observe the domestic debates going on inside other democratic regimes.

Several arguments in international relations focus on the importance of domestic politics. Some of these show how foreign policy decision making does not come only from a calculation of a state's interest but also depends on the actors and interests involved in making the decision. When one looks inside the

liberalism In international relations, a theory that holds states can have different preferences and internal structures that lead them to behave in different ways, especially with regard to the conduct of states that hold liberal values of democracy and free market commerce.

democratic peace A phenomenon associated with liberalism that holds that democratic countries will rarely if ever go to war with one another.

INSIGHTS

Kant, Liberal Legacies, and Foreign Affairs
by Michael Doyle

Doyle is a leading contemporary proponent of democratic peace theory, and this book offers his synthesis of liberal theory along with treatments of other theoretical approaches. The treatment of liberalism traces the democratic peace to the philosopher Immanuel Kant, who argued a "perpetual peace" would emerge between liberal republics. Doyle notes that democracies regularly go to war, but almost never against other democracies. Thus, democratic peace holds *between* democracies but not between a democracy and an authoritarian regime. The reasons for this are numerous. First and foremost, in liberal regimes, the voting public must consent to the costs of war, and decisions to go to war will not be undertaken lightly.

Not being led simply by dictatorial rulers, liberal regimes deliberate carefully about war and do not enter it rashly. Second, democracies have an ability to observe one another's political processes and intentions rather transparently, and extend to one another respect and a presumption of accommodation. And third, the logic of liberal regimes typically extends over into commercial or economic interests, which adds material reasons to the moral commitments that prevent conflict between liberal states.

Michael Doyle, "Kant, Liberal Legacies, and Foreign Affairs." Philosophy and Public Affairs 12, No. 3 (1983): 205–235; and "Kant, Liberal Legacies, and Foreign Affairs, Part 2." Philosophy and Public Affairs 12, No. 4 (1983): 323–353.

government to see how a decision is actually being made, the "unitary rational actor" looks less clear. In addition to the presence of liberal institutions, the organizational processes for making decisions and the interactions between decision makers and their advisers may be especially important in the final decisions made by governments.[36]

Constructivism

The third leading school of thought in international relations today is **constructivism**. Constructivism is an approach arguing that decisions made by states need to be understood in their broader, constructed context of social and political interactions. In particular, states will not simply view one another as having purely aggressive intentions, even in a state of anarchy. The contexts in which states interact may range from competitive to cooperative, and states may respond in many different ways.[37] One might not necessarily interpret all military exercises by other countries as overtly hostile, for instance, even if they do heighten the sense of alert. Here, too, comparative politics has some role in shaping international relations: countries that have reason to trust one another may do so on the basis of histories or cultures that are partly shaped by domestic politics. One prominent formulation from constructivism holds that anarchy does not simply lead to conflict but rather depends on "what states make of it"[38] (see the Insights box on *Social Theory of International Politics*).

constructivism In international relations, a theory that holds that decisions made by states need to be understood in the context of social and political interactions, and that behavior is shaped by norms and values as well as narrowly defined interests.

Marxism

Prior to the emergence of constructivism, the other alternative explanation to realism and liberalism was **Marxism**. Marxism wielded considerable influence for many decades as an explanation for the behavior of actors in the international system. The peak of its appeal came during the Cold War, though new variations on Marxist theory have been proposed since. While the end of the Cold War

Marxism In international relations, a theory that emphasizes the role of social classes in shaping politics and highlights the role of capitalist accumulation as a prime driver in international affairs.

INSIGHTS   Social Theory of International Politics
by Alexander Wendt

For Wendt, the anarchy of the international system does not necessarily give rise to states conflicting with one another. At the most fundamental level, states may view other states as enemies, as rivals, or as friends. Where states expect one another to behave as enemies, war and conflict will be commonplace. Yet Wendt notes that recent centuries have often seen states treat one another as rivals rather than enemies. In these circumstances, states may compete and will not be at permanent war; they may develop a culture in which they often respect one another's sovereignty and do not represent existential threats to one another, though reversions to war are possible. Beyond this, states sometimes treat one another as "friends" and see themselves on the same team. Conflict is highly unlikely in these circumstances. Examples may be the United Kingdom and United States, or even contemporary France and Germany, which clearly view one another as partners today despite the horrific wars in their pasts. Wendt argues that states can internalize to different degrees these worldviews, and that these will give rise to different types of politics between them.

Alexander Wendt, Social Theory of International Politics. *Cambridge: Cambridge University Press, 1999.*

largely removed the prospect of communism as a viable way to address imperialism worldwide, Marxist theory persists in diagnosing how the global political economy functions, and especially who gains and who loses in this system. In general, Marxist theory emphasizes the role of social classes in shaping politics and highlights the role of capitalist accumulation as a prime driver in international affairs. Many of the manifestations of Marxism as it relates to international relations theory are in the area of international political economy, and we treated some of these—such as dependency and world-systems theory—in chapter 5 on development. Nonetheless, there are ways that Marxist analysis relates to questions of violence and conflict. Most notably, Vladimir Lenin, the founding leader of the Soviet Union, theorized that brutal imperialism and domination and exploitation of poor countries was the logical consequence of capitalism's international efforts at accumulation.[39] This formulation thus took a theory of society, economy, and comparative politics and scaled it up to the level of international relations.

THINKING COMPARATIVELY

KEY METHODOLOGICAL TOOLS

Levels of Analysis

In our discussion linking comparative politics and international relations, we are considering different levels of

The EU and Levels of Analysis

This chapter has touched on some of the leading issues in international relations that relate to comparative politics. The discussion of "Causes and Effects" highlights how different explanatory models in international relations reflect different perspectives on the importance of domestic politics and institutions on international relations. The range of topics in international relations is so vast that it is its own field, and this discussion in a text on comparative politics can only briefly mention a subset of the relevant issues.

Supporters of Catalan independence from Spain at EU offices in Brussels. In a global era, issues at regional, national, and supranational levels of analysis are often intertwined.

Yet examining certain topics will reveal many of the key themes that link comparative and international politics. The EU is the world's quintessential example of efforts at supranational governance in which countries have given away a degree of real sovereignty. As such, it poses many of the central analytical questions addressed herein. For example, the crisis over the euro that started around 2009 brought up a host of dilemmas in international cooperation. How can countries ensure that others do not freeride? Can states trust one another to cooperate, or will each behave in its own self-interest? At the same time, there are even more fundamental questions, such as "what is Europe?" Related to these questions, "what is the nation, and how does it relate to Europe?"

Is it a political unit that has overcome the challenge of anarchy by creating institutions? Is it a certain set of peoples, or is it changing definitively due to immigration, transnational movement of ideas, and the spread of globalization? There are more questions than answers when it comes to complex issues in international relations, as Europe illustrates. As we note in concluding, this uncertainty is important from the perspective of research in comparative politics: it means that the central questions are not resolved, and that research areas and agendas remain open to the curious and motivated analyst.

The EU also shows that the debates between theoretical perspectives are unresolved, as has been the case in our other chapters. The fact of European cooperation over sixty years may support the ideas of liberalism and constructivism: shared values, norms, and a common political adherence to democratic institutions may have facilitated peace and cooperation. On the other hand, each of the countries in the EU has valued its own self-interest over integration on many

THINKING COMPARATIVELY

occasions. This observation might seem to support realist theory, though a variety of interpretations is possible. While cooperation may support one or more of these theoretical perspectives, so too can the seeming breakdowns in cooperation give ammunition to realism, liberalism, constructivism, Marxism, or other theoretical frameworks. Here, too, the example of the EU generates major debates that are not easily resolved except through further contestation of ideas.

The fundamental difference between comparative politics and international relations is that the former looks primarily at politics within countries while the latter looks primarily at politics between countries. We have noted in this chapter (and in previous chapters) that politics within countries affects politics between countries, and vice versa: international forces sometimes shape phenomena such as democratization, development, nationalism, and revolutions. The EU shows how these **levels of analysis** interact (see the "Key Methodological Tool" discussion in the margin). In the EU, decisions made by the European Central Bank regarding the fate of the euro will have significant effects on politics in Germany and Greece, at the same time that politics in Germany and Greece have major effects on the euro and on the decisions of the European Central Bank. Paying attention to the different levels of analysis in such situations is useful for developing a clear sense of how comparative politics and international relations each contribute to the study of politics globally.

We cannot resolve the fundamental issues of comparative politics and international relations here, of course. Even a start at doing so requires the combined efforts of thousands of social scientists and academics, diplomats and statespersons, members of advocacy and activist groups, not to mention millions (or even billions) of citizens. It requires a collective enterprise in seeking knowledge that is based both on collaboration and on disagreement and debate. We reiterate that the domestic politics of countries affects international politics, and that international politics affects domestic politics as well, and we encourage you to further explore the major themes of these fields. We hope you will use the tools from this chapter and the text as a whole to participate in this exploration, making your own contributions to the knowledge that scholars of comparative politics continue to seek.

levels of analysis In international relations, the different levels that can be the context of a study, including the individual level, the nation-state level, and the level of the international system.

Chapter Summary

Concepts

- Comparative politics focuses largely on politics within individual countries, while international relations focuses on relations between countries.

Issues

- There are a large number of issues that link comparative politics and international relations,

including globalization and trade, international integration immigration, transnational networks, nuclear and terrorist threats, and the question of environmental sustainability.

Causes and Effects

- There are several main schools of thought in international relations, including realism, liberalism, and constructivism, and Marxism once featured prominently as well.

- Contemporary realism emphasizes the anarchy of the international system and the efforts of each nation-state to make itself secure in this system, which leads to frequent conflict.
- Liberalism emphasizes the effects of political institutions and domestic politics more than realism and finds more factors that mitigate the likelihood of conflict.

- Constructivism emphasizes the social context in which international interactions happen and argues that anarchy does not necessarily lead to conflict.

Thinking Comparatively

- International relations often operates at a different level of analysis from comparative politics by looking at the international system, but the levels of analysis can interact.

Thinking It Through

1. We discussed the problem of global climate change in this chapter as a major issue facing the international community. Imagine that you are the head of an international commission charged with coming up with a plan to address the problem. You have been told to prepare three proposals, one based on realist assumptions about international relations, one based on liberal assumptions, and one based on constructivist assumptions. How would your three proposals differ?

2. Substitute the problem of nuclear proliferation for climate change in the previous question. How would your three proposals differ? Now compare your answers to these questions. Does theoretical perspective impact these problems of international politics in the same way across different issues or in different ways?

3. Take a main phenomenon discussed in any of the institutional chapters in this book (chapters 8–11), such as presidentialism versus parliamentarism, proportional representation versus district systems, federalism versus unitarism, or multiparty systems versus two-party systems. How might these variations in

institutional design impact the likely behavior of different states in the international system?

4. The foreign policy doctrine of U.S. President George W. Bush from 2001 to 2009 was based on the ideas that the United States was an indispensable leader as the world's hegemon, and that it should act unilaterally and preemptively as necessary to prevent threats from arising. It also held that U.S. action should promote regime change in favor of democracy to enhance American security. Does this sound like a realist doctrine, a liberal doctrine, or a constructivist doctrine? Why?

5. The European Union has achieved significant economic integration in recent decades, but it still makes many of its major decisions by unanimous consent. One of the dilemmas of the EU has been the trade-off between "broadening" the Union to more members and "deepening" the integration among existing members. Why might these two goals be seen as potentially contradictory? If you were a government leader in France or Germany, which of these two directions would you want to see the EU favor, and why?

Brazil

Key Features of Contemporary Brazil

Population:	207,353,391 (estimate, July 2017)
Area:	8,515,770 square kilometers
Head of State:	Michel Temer (president, 2016–present)
Head of Government:	Michel Temer (president, 2016–present)
Capital:	Brasilia
Year of Independence:	1822
Year of Current Constitution:	1988
Languages:	Portuguese (official), many indigenous languages
GDP per Capita:	$15,200 (*CIA World Factbook* estimate, 2016)
Human Development Index Ranking (2016):	79th (high human development)

Sources: *CIA World Factbook*; World Bank World Development Indicators; United Nations *Human Development Report 2016*.

Introduction

Brazil has always been of interest to comparative political analysts, probably now more than ever. The country has in recent years achieved considerable economic growth and consolidated its democracy, after years of alteration between democratic and authoritarian rule in which the latter was predominant. It has also exercised more global influence than ever before—a long-standing ambition—with one symbolic manifestation of its expanded global role being that it hosted the 2016 Summer Olympics. Scholars are eager to understand how Brazil has achieved these successes. At the same time, recent Brazilian governments have been wracked by corruption scandals, and many Brazilian citizens are disenchanted with current political developments. Scholars are interested in understanding these trajectories and predicting the path that Brazil is likely to take in the future.

Brazil also stands out in Latin America for several important reasons. First, it is the only Portuguese-speaking country in the region (though its population comprises a hefty chunk of the total Latin American population, meaning a large share of Latin America speaks Portuguese). Second, it emerged from colonialism as an intact unit, despite its strong

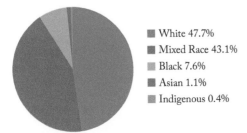

- White 47.7%
- Mixed Race 43.1%
- Black 7.6%
- Asian 1.1%
- Indigenous 0.4%

Ethnic Groups in Brazil
Source: CIA World Factbook.

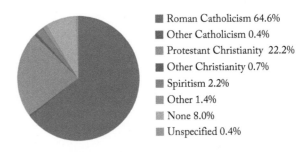

- Roman Catholicism 64.6%
- Other Catholicism 0.4%
- Protestant Christianity 22.2%
- Other Christianity 0.7%
- Spiritism 2.2%
- Other 1.4%
- None 8.0%
- Unspecified 0.4%

Religious Affiliation in Brazil
Source: CIA World Factbook.

COLOMBIA

VENEZUELA

GUYANA

SURINAME

French
Guiana
(FRANCE)

Boa Vista

*NORTH
ATLANTIC
OCEAN*

Equator

Amazon

Belém

São Luís

Manaus

Amazon

Fortaleza

Teresina

Natal

Rio Branco

Recife

PERU

Palmas

Maceió

B R A Z I L

Salvador

Brasília
★

BOLIVIA

Campo
Grande

Rio Grande

Belo
Horizonte

PARAGUAY

Vitória

CHILE

São Paulo

Rio de Janeiro

*SOUTH
PACIFIC
OCEAN*

ARGENTINA

Curitiba

Santos

Porto Alegre

*SOUTH
ATLANTIC
OCEAN*

URUGUAY

0	200	400 Kilometers
0	200	400 Miles

regional tensions, whereas Spanish America split up into many smaller countries. Third, and related to this, Brazil gained its independence without a war, but, in essence, with the help of the Portuguese royal family. This and subsequent events have led some to describe Brazil as a non-revolutionary society in which gradual change is predominant. Slavery lasted longer in Brazil than in most societies, and the country entered the twentieth century with an agrarian economy and a highly unequal social order (Roett 2011; Skidmore 2010). It did, however, have more success than many other Latin American countries in achieving partial industrialization in the twentieth century.

Brazil is characterized by pronounced regional differences. The country is geographically enormous, and settlement patterns and economic bases in different regions vary considerably. The large cities of the southeast, such as São Paulo and Rio de Janeiro, include huge populations and are more closely linked to the global economy, especially São Paulo. While this area can be viewed as a "region," historically, there were tensions *between* these cities, with Paulistas and residents of Rio sometimes vying for national influence. More striking contrasts, however, are found between this and other regions, including the relatively poor and isolated Amazonian region, where a larger Amerindian population is present; and the northeast, where some of the earliest settlement was established on the basis of sugar cultivation. This area, too, remains relatively poor when compared to the southeast.

Race and ethnicity are complicated in Brazil (as they are everywhere!). It is very important to not view race and ethnicity through a U.S.-style racial template. In the traditional U.S. culture of race and ethnicity, racial and ethnic categories are often imagined to be more rigid than they typically are in Brazil. However, one does not want to fall for what scholars have called the Brazilian "myth of racial democracy." That is, social-scientific evidence strongly indicates that racial and ethnic discrimination do take place in Brazilian society. One question worth thinking about is whether the Brazilian way of "doing" ethnicity and race makes addressing this discrimination easier or more difficult (see discussion in Marx 1998). In any case, keep in mind that categories like "white" or "black" can mean different things in different societies.

In religious terms, Brazil remains a society of high vitality. The Catholic Church is still important to a large share of the population, and Brazil has contributed notably in past decades to theological developments like liberation theology and the establishment of ecclesiastical base communities. At the same time, Brazil also has one of the highest rates of Protestant adherence in Latin America. Some even see Protestant strength as causally related to Catholic innovation (because of competition) in countries like Brazil (see Gill 1998). Pentecostal forms of Protestantism have been particularly important, especially among poorer populations.

Historical Development

Brazil began its colonial history as a quintessentially agricultural society, with early inroads by both Dutch and Portuguese colonialists (on the colonial period, see Fausto 1999 and Skidmore 2010). In the end, it became the principal colonial possession of the Portuguese crown, which had played a crucial role in early European navigation and exploration, much out of proportion to its influence and power within Europe otherwise. Prior to its colonization, Brazil was home to numerous Amerindian cultures. These were fascinating and important, but they tended not to be large-scale state societies, unlike the Inca, Maya, and Mexica (or Aztecs) in different parts of the Spanish Empire. This has implications for the colonial political and social structures that developed. The economic model that emerged in colonial Brazil was based fundamentally on plantation agriculture, with the initial focus in the northeast, where sugar cane was the main product for export. Later in the

colonial period, this was supplemented by mining. In colonial Spanish America, mining tended to "go with" complex Amerindian organization and to produce initially somewhat "indirect colonialism," with high levels of administration carried out, in part, through existing social structures (Mahoney 2010). These areas became the "cores" of the colonial system, whereas agricultural production for export was largely confined to the colonial "periphery" like Argentina and Venezuela (areas that only much later grew in prominence). Brazil, interestingly, seems to deviate from this general regional pattern. In this respect, perhaps, it more closely resembles early English colonialism in places like Barbados, where highly lucrative sugar cultivation was also practiced, with a social structure based mostly on slavery.

The eighteenth-century expansion of mining activities, especially in Minas Gerais, had important implications for the political structure of the Portuguese colonies and for

Historical Development

Timeline

1500	Portuguese mariner Pedro Alvares Cabral is the first European to explore Brazil.		1960	President Juscelino Kubitschek moves capital to new city of Brasilia.
1500s	Portuguese crown attempts to colonize Brazil by granting Captaincies (*Capitanias*) to nobles, but few successful outposts are established.		1964	Military overthrows President João Goulart in coup d'état.
1600s	French and Dutch excursions establish inroads along Brazil's coast but depart by mid-1600s.		1964–1982	Military rules Brazil in "bureaucratic-authoritarian" style; industrialization deepens.
1808	The Portuguese monarchy flees Portugal and establishes residence in Brazil.		1982	Massive street protests for direct elections (*Diretas Ja!*), with trade union leader Luiz Inácio Lula da Silva a prominent figure; democratic elections are held for governors.
1821	Portuguese monarchy returns to Portugal.			
1822	Dom Pedro, a prince and son of Portugal's king, declares Brazilian independence from Portugal and remains in Brazil as Emperor.		1985	Presidential election is held; Tancredo Neves is elected but dies before taking office; José Sarney becomes president.
1888	Princess Isabel abolishes slavery by decree while Emperor Dom Pedro II is away in Europe.		1988	Constitution is passed by Brazil's Constituent Assembly.
1889	The military deposes Emperor Dom Pedro II and establishes a republic, now known as the Old Republic (*República Velha*); constitutional democracy is largely limited to land-owning males.		1988–1994	Growing inflation problems and economic crisis
			1992	President Fernando Collor (1990–1992) resigns amid corruption scandal.
1880s–1920s	Economic boom based on agricultural exports (coffee, sugar, etc.) to Europe		1995–2003	Presidency of Fernando Henrique Cardoso (a sociologist) ends economic crisis, begins to see economic growth, better social services, and declining inequality.
1930	General Getúlio Vargas takes presidency.			
1930s	Great Depression interrupts world trade, cuts off imports, and harms the economy; this gives impetus to Brazil's fledgling industrialization in the medium term.		2003–2011	Presidency of Luiz Inácio Lula da Silva, a former Marxist trade union leader and head of the Workers' Party (PT); continued economic growth and declines in inequality, as well as an expanding international role for Brazil
1937	President Vargas proclaims "New State" (*Estado Novo*) along fascist lines.		2011	Dilma Rousseff of the PT becomes Brazil's first female president.
1946	Brazil returns to democratic rule.		2015	Rousseff begins her second term.
1954	Vargas commits suicide while president (1951–1954), having been elected some years after his previous removal.		2016	Rousseff is impeached and removed from office in the midst of a corruption scandal; Michel Temer takes over as interim president and then as president.

Brazil's future. Perhaps the most important effect was the shift in regional elite power and in colonial administration, as the northeast city of Salvador ceased to be the main colonial port, with Rio de Janeiro taking over that role. Rio was also the capital until it was moved to the new planned city of Brasilia in 1960.

As noted in the brief introduction, the transition to independence in Brazil was relatively peaceful. There had in the late colonial years been a couple of minor rebellions (Fausto 1999), including the Inconfidência Mineira, but nothing that threatened the regime. The royal family, under Dom João, moved the Portuguese court to Rio de Janeiro in late 1807 (arriving in 1808) when the French Emperor Napoleon invaded Portugal. Dom João remained there until 1821, when a liberal revolt back home forced him to

return to Lisbon. Approximately a year after his return, his son Pedro, who had been sent as regent, declared independence. He was soon named Emperor. Between the rule of Pedro I, the long rule of Pedro II, and a regency in between, the Brazilian empire would last until the 1880s. It was as such the only modern empire of significant duration in the Americas. Brazil's empire was quite conservative in numerous ways—the critical alliance was between the government, the Catholic Church, and agricultural elites—but it was a constitutional monarchy (Roett 2011: 26–27).

Over the course of the nineteenth century, the nature of Brazilian exports changed, but its key economic activity remained the export of primary products. Coffee was ascendant, and on the basis of coffee production and export, again the regional balance of power and status shifted a bit, to the benefit of the São Paulo elite. Dependence on coffee, though, was notoriously problematic for Latin American countries. Coffee prices had a tendency to fluctuate widely, meaning that business was hard to predict and sometimes ruined farmers. This also contributed, without a doubt, to the relative weakness of the Brazilian state, as it did to numerous other states in Latin America involved in the export of coffee and other agricultural and mineral goods. Just the same, Brazilian politics remained surprisingly stable in this period, and the country was not wracked by the relentless civil wars that troubled its neighbors. Brazil *was* involved, though, in the most infamous international war of Latin American history, the "War of the Triple Alliance," which pitted Brazil, Argentina, and Uruguay against Paraguay and resulted in the devastation of the latter country and killed so many of its men as to produce unusual demographic problems. Brazil also suffered heavy losses, however, and experienced fiscal difficulties as a result of its involvement.

Another important nineteenth-century development (Skidmore 2010: 71–72) was the heavy importation of a philosophical belief system known as "positivism" (the slogan on the Brazilian flag, "Order and Progress," is a mark of the influence of this philosophy). In a nutshell, positivism claimed that human history moves from "religious" to "metaphysical" to "positive" stages as culture becomes more rational and scientific. This philosophy had great appeal to intellectuals in places like Brazil and Mexico, where it seemed to offer a diagnosis of the sources of the country's alleged "backwardness" and also a treatment program: economic and cultural modernization, including the establishment of railroads and other infrastructure as well as the expansion of education. Of course, the implications of this view for old-fashioned concepts like "Empire" were not too "positive." Positivism, scientism, republicanism, and other ideas about modernization caught on more and more among Brazilian elites. The trouble was that the society was still based on plantation agriculture for export, and thus, important actors were opposed to full political modernization. All bets were off, though, after the abolition of slavery in 1888 and after Pedro II was deposed a year later. Paradoxically, a number of the republicans who favored the abolition of monarchy had previously been staunch conservatives, which seems to show the centrality of interest in their calculations (Fausto 1999). Presumably, they hoped to exert greater influence in a republic. And indeed, the republic that was created was for many years disproportionately responsive to elite interest. From this point on, in certain respects, Brazil started to resemble the more typical Latin American pattern, with political instability and weak institutions serving as obstacles to development.

The next major development in the political history of Brazil was the coup d'état that brought Getúlio Vargas to power in 1930. Vargas was a populist, and he largely worked to undercut the influence of the regional oligarchies that had exerted disproportionate influence over the country in the previous decades, though he did retain ties to some elite groups (Roett 2011; Skidmore 2010). Vargas encouraged industrial magnates and labor alike, and the latter became an increasingly important force in Brazilian politics in this period. Vargas was also a state-builder and a centralizer. The Brazilian state he helped to develop was also one with militaristic features. Vargas built on earlier efforts to inculcate strong nationalism in the Brazilian people and linked this nationalism to his efforts to further industrialize and modernize the country. Beyond noting his nationalism and populism, it is hard to pin Vargas down ideologically. Some have viewed him as having some left-wing tendencies, and many have interpreted him as toying with something close to fascism. By the end of this period, he had become dictator; and while Brazilian troops fought with the allies in World War II, Vargas was deposed following the end of the war.

In the coming years, political instability continued—Vargas was even brought back in 1951, though he killed himself in office rather than be deposed again in 1954—but amidst the disorder, Brazil continued with a program of economic nationalism and import substitution industrialization (ISI). The country's record in this connection was mixed. Growth was irregular and often slow, and inequality remained notoriously high, but the country had a more diversified industrial base than did many of its neighbors. Under Juscelino Kubitschek (1956–1960), the modernist capital of Brasilia was established. In 1964, following a military coup, the country succumbed to the wave of "bureaucratic-authoritarianism" that was to dominate the region for some years (O'Donnell 1973; Stepan 1971).

This military regime sought to take an active role in shaping the development process and deepening industrialization (O'Donnell 1973). It saw Brazil's strong unions and demands for worker advantages as factors that prevented the accumulation of capital needed to become an advanced, industrial society. Accordingly, it centralized power and repressed dissidence, most notably after it decreed Institutional Act #5 (*Ato Institucional No. 5*) in 1968, which banned assembly and the holding of union elections. The military promoted industrial investment from foreign and domestic sources in an attempt to convert Brazil's industry from making the likes of textiles and sugar to making more sophisticated products like steel and automobiles for consumption in Brazil itself. The military partially succeeded, presiding over some deepening of industrialization that represented a substantial portion of the "Brazilian Miracle" after World War II (Evans 1979; Cardoso and Faletto 1979). Ultimately, however, making the necessary investments required more and more state spending and debt. In the long run, the borrowing culminated in the 1980s debt crisis. Growing pressures for political liberalization signaled the exhaustion of military rule.

The military controlled the process of liberalization in the initial stages but found itself pushed to make greater moves toward full democracy (Haggard and Kaufman 1995). Political pressure for democratization came from many political actors. Several politicians from São Paulo and other large states pressed the regime to grant more authority to the states. By the mid-1980s, millions took to the streets to demand elections, with many led by trade union leader and political hopeful Luiz Inácio Lula da Silva. The protests led to massive rallies in the 1980s calling for "Direct Elections Now" (*Diretas já!*), which the business community increasingly supported. As the military regime recognized its loss of power, it agreed to elections for state governors in 1982, followed by national elections in 1985.

Democratic elections resulted in a massive victory for Tancredo Neves, who defeated the military-backed candidate convincingly. Neves died before assuming office, however, leaving Vice President José Sarney to assume the presidency. In 1990, Fernando Collor became the first directly elected president of Brazil after the military regime. His presidency was marked by scandals and a failed economic policy that led to impeachment in 1992; Vice President Itamar Franco governed until the next elections in 1994.

The next two presidents governed Brazil for two terms each, for a total of sixteen years, and these years saw relative improvements in addressing Brazil's economic and social challenges (Roett 2011). Fernando Henrique Cardoso's government (1995–2003) consolidated a new economic policy—The *Plano Real*—together with a new currency (the *real*) that brought a relatively stable economy and the beginnings of a decline in inequality. This was followed by two terms of Luiz Inácio Lula da Silva (2003– 2011), known simply as Lula. He was a founding member of the Workers' Party (*Partido dos Trabalhadores*, PT) and union leader who was once a Marxist but governed in a centrist fashion. Dilma Rousseff of the PT was elected in 2010 as Lula's successor. She narrowly won re-election in 2014, but her administration soon fell apart due to a massive corruption scandal involving the state owned oil company Petrobras. She was impeached in 2016 and removed from office. Her (unelected) successor, Michel Temer, soon came under scrutiny himself for corruption and narrowly survived an impeachment vote in 2017; the country's political elite is in a moment of high turnover amid public frustration.

Regime and Political Institutions

The executive in Brazil's federal system is directly elected, with the vote tally for the presidency based on the national popular vote. If no candidate receives a majority in the first round, a second-round runoff election is held between the two leading candidates. In both rounds, voting is obligatory for all citizens, though the secret ballot gives citizens the opportunity to "spoil" their ballot or leave it blank. This virtually guarantees that the elected president will have been voted into office with a majority mandate. The term of office is four years (except in cases of impeachment and early removal), and the president is limited to two terms.

According to the Constitution, the president has considerable powers, including the ability to decree certain laws for a limited time (thirty days), with the so-called provisional measure (*medida provisória*). Yet despite these formal powers, the fragmented nature of the party system limits the president's power over the national legislature. The president can often count on less than one-third of the Congress being co-partisans. Even these co-partisans are primarily concerned with satisfying their own constituencies in their states and not with pleasing the national party leaders. While formal powers are useful, most presidential prerogatives of significance can be consolidated only by extensive negotiating and bargaining with other parties, individual legislators, and the state governors and city mayors who support these legislators. This process typically involves a more or less explicit trading of favors and resources (and often outright corruption) that makes it costly to change the *status quo*.

The judicial power in Brazil has as its most important instance the Federal Supreme Court (*Supremo Tribunal Federal*—STF), which has the authority to pronounce on the constitutionality of law. The Constitution reserves substantial responsibilities, functions, and resources for the state governments as well.

Regime and Political Institutions

Regime	Federal republic, representative democratic elections
Administrative Divisions	Twenty-seven federal units: twenty-six states (*estados*) + Federal District of Brasilia
Executive Branch	President
Selection of Executive	Direct election by national popular vote; voting is compulsory; runoff between top two candidates if none receives 50 percent in the first round
Legislative Branch	Bicameral Congress (*Congresso Nacional*) Lower chamber: Chamber of Deputies (*Câmara de Deputados*) Upper chamber: Senate (*Senado Federal*)
Judicial Branch	Federal High Court (*Supremo Tribunal Federal*) has some power of judicial review
Political Party System	Multiparty system, with four to five prominent leading parties: PT (left/center-left), PSDB (centrist, technocratic), PMDB (centrist, traditional), Democrats (center-right, traditional)

Political Culture

In many ways, Brazilian society is renowned for bringing together elements of distinct traditions. In terms of its people, Brazil has large numbers of indigenous peoples, people of African descent, and descendants of migrants of European and Asian origin. Brazilian politics follows the national trend of blending and combining traditions. While unique, Brazil is also like many countries in processes of rapid modernization in that it presents a fascinating mixture of the traditional with the technocratic and "modern."

This complex culture can be seen, for example, in the combination of highly advanced centers of efficiency in certain aspects of the state, combined with old-fashioned, patronage-based bureaucracies (Evans 1989). Some diplomats in Brazil's Foreign Ministry and economists at its Central Bank are among the world's best, while many legislators, ministers, and judges (and some presidents) have been notoriously corrupt. Brazil is home to some of the world's most advanced industries—in petroleum exploration, aircraft manufacture, and mobile phone assembly, among other areas—but is also home to poverty that rivals the poorest countries on earth. As home to most of the Amazon, Brazil is a leader in global debates about environmental sustainability, while also winking and nodding at wealthy politicians who chop down huge swaths of pristine rainforest for their profitable cattle ranches. A cultural element that works its way into politics is the notion of *jeitinho*, or "finding a little way." This has a connotation of skillfulness and cleverness, but also of being conniving and evasive. At its best, it means creativity and inventiveness, whether in business or in Brazilians' renowned abilities in soccer. At its worst, it contributes to practices like tax evasion, corruption, and getting ahead at another's expense. The blend of modern and traditional can be seen among the many Brazilians who will condemn corruption among politicians, but who also pride themselves in avoiding payment of their tax share.

Brazil has changed over time, and often for the better. One example is the politics between leftists and industrial capitalists. As Brazil has moved into the twenty-first century, major political forces on both the left and the right have moderated. The Workers' Party (PT) moved from radical Marxism in the 1980s to more social-democratic policies in the 1990s. The PT and its leader, Lula da Silva, were unacceptable to the military and unelectable for most middle-class Brazilians into the 1990s; but by the 2002 elections, they had become mainstream. In fact, Lula won election and then reelection handily in 2006, earning the support of many in the middle class. During Lula's time in office, the government continued pro-market reforms, much to the relief of the business community, while also extending more benefits to the poor (see the following section, "Political Economy"). Meanwhile, the military and other conservatives tout Brazil's democracy, even when it results in the election of political rivals; and the traditional oligarchic politicians and bosses of Brazil's northeast have also updated their image, albeit slowly. Few revel openly anymore in the old approach of just delivering "pork" to constituents.

Brazil is thus home to a bewildering and sometimes contradictory political culture. Modern and sophisticated, but also complex and gritty, it seems a country on the move, yet also one sometimes stuck in time. A leading saying is that "Brazil is the country of the future, and always will be." Brazil is more democratic, equitable, and stable than just a couple of decades ago, but most Brazilians and Brazilianists would say it has a long road to travel in its development.

Political Economy

Brazil has spent many years in recent decades as one of the most dynamic economies in the developing world, but it is also characterized by shocking inequalities, extreme poverty, rampant corruption, high costs of doing business, and among the world's highest tax rates. While it still faces huge difficulties in integrating its diverse population into the modern economy, Brazil has developed dramatically from its export-oriented agricultural base in the nineteenth century, when the country was dominated by oligarchic plantation owners who exported coffee, sugar, and other products to Europe.

The country's economic history accounts for much of where Brazil is today. Brazil began to industrialize in earnest in the late nineteenth century, and this process accelerated through the 1920s, especially in the south and southeast of the country. The Great Depression and its collapse of world trade was initially a catastrophe for South America's agriculturally dominated economies, who lost their markets around the world. But the decline in trade led Brazil to produce more of its own industrial goods (such as textiles, cement, or processed foods) rather than relying on imports. This led to more advanced industrialization and the "Brazilian Miracle" after World War II (see the "Historical Development" section at the beginning of the profile). Under both democratic rule (1946–1964) and military rule (1964–1980s), Brazil moved from production of simple industrial goods to a much more intensive economy that produced appliances, automobiles, electronics, petrochemicals, and even airplanes. The industrialization extended wealth to a broader cross section of society, creating an urban middle class of workers, managers, and professionals. From 1968 to 1973, Brazil's GDP had an average growth of more than 10 percent a year, but economic collapse in the 1980s led to shuttered factories and sent millions out of work and into the less secure, informal economy of street vending and odd jobs. Soon thereafter, excessive government spending led to hyperinflation and further decline. Finally, in the 1990s, the country stabilized under President Fernando Henrique Cardoso (1995–2003) and grew impressively once again in the years under President Luiz Inácio Lula da Silva (2003–2011).

Poverty and inequality remain Brazil's greatest economic challenges. For years, Brazil was reputed to be the most economically unequal society on earth, with only a fraction of very wealthy people and huge numbers of people living in poverty in rural areas or in urban shantytowns known as *favelas*. As Brazil achieved considerable growth in much of the 21st century, at least until a prolonged downturn after 2014, inequality fell, but still remains at very high levels. The improvements have been helped along by policy changes, especially new and improved social programs. The governments of Cardoso, Lula, and Dilma Rousseff (2011–2016) created and expanded innovative social programs that provide modest cash benefits to low-income families that have their children vaccinated and stay in school. This reduces poverty while also improving Brazil's human capital for the next generation.

In terms of the contemporary economy, Brazil is a major exporter again, but now with an even more highly diversified economy. It features substantial sectors in agricultural exports, manufacturing, extractive industry (such as oil production), and services. At the same time, Brazil has struggled in recent years with inflation and slowing growth. From a growth rate of about 7.5 percent in 2010, Brazil declined over several subsequent years and experienced severe recession and economic contraction after 2014. To the extent that Brazil can combine growth with improved distribution of income, it is well positioned to be one of the leading economies of the twenty-first century. Alternatively, the country may continue to be characterized by the tongue-in-cheek curse in a renowned Brazilian saying mentioned previously: Brazil is the country of the future, and always will be.

CASE STUDIES

Does the Global Economy Help or Hurt Developing Nations like Brazil?

CHAPTER 5, PAGE 113

For centuries, Brazil has been one of the most important countries to consider on the question of whether opening up to the global economy helps or hinders development. Depending on perspective and the moment in history, openness to the outside world has helped Brazil advance economically and has contributed to economic challenges; closing off to the global economy seemed both to help and to hurt as well. Can Brazil help us understand under what conditions other developing countries should open or close themselves off to trade with the advanced economies?

Brazil's earliest interactions with the global economy were based on the notorious slave trade, which brought slaves from west Africa to harvest agricultural products. Up until the 1880s, Brazil relied on slave labor. While this period saw some agro-export success, the economic gains were obviously distributed primarily to the oligarchic elite and not to workers. This early pattern formed the basis of Brazil's tremendous inequality, so the overall effect on the economy is open to interpretation. Brazil did continue to grow its economy after slavery was abolished and up to the 1920s, and it did so in large part through agricultural exports to industrialized countries.

As noted in the section on "Political Economy," ties to the global economy in the 1930s had ambiguous effects on Brazil. The Great Depression hit Brazil and Latin America hard, as it cut off the trade with the outside world on which the economy had come to depend; this suggests that being deprived of global markets hurt Brazil. On the other hand, Brazil deepened its industrialization in the wake of the Depression as it shifted to domestic production for domestic markets; this suggests that looking inward actually helped. The ambiguities extend further with the era known as bureaucratic-authoritarian rule under the military from 1964 to the 1980s. During this period, Brazil continued to protect domestic industry by raising barriers to foreign corporations, but with a caveat: the government in Brasilia also invited foreign corporations to establish factories in Brazil and serve the domestic market (Evans 1979). The deepening of industrialization that followed might suggest that Brazil benefited from either closing off to foreign capital or opening up to it, depending on the interpretation.

The pro-market, neoliberal era of the 1980s and 1990s gave additional fodder for debate about the merits of international economic linkages. A consensus emerged in the early 1980s that Brazil's indebted economy needed to be stabilized and reformed, but the consensus also took on a more assertive form with the argument that countries like Brazil needed to get the government out of the economy. Major U.S.-based institutions pushed a "Washington Consensus" that demanded privatization, deregulation, and less spending by Latin American governments. This set of policies undoubtedly contributed to a downturn in the short term, but whether it created the basis for Brazil's longer term success is subject to debate.

Recent years have repeated the pattern of Brazil both benefiting from globalization and being challenged by it. The country has seen a commodity boom and rising incomes from exports, but is also facing increasing competition from China, for example, in a variety of areas. In short, one cannot simply see Brazil's interaction with the global economy as good or evil. Connections to the global economy must be seen as partly (but not wholly) responsible for many of Brazil's booms and busts alike, and responsible for many opportunities as well as many inequalities. Nor can one look at it just at a single moment in time. The recent era of neoliberalism and free market economics is one period in which openness shaped the political economy of the country, but a longer historical perspective would suggest that this is an incomplete picture. Linkages to the global economy must be seen more broadly and in historical terms as one of the key tensions in Brazilian economic trajectory.

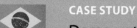

Brazil has moved back and forth between authoritarianism and democracy for much of its existence as an independent country. The country was an empire for the period from 1822 to 1889, followed by a Republic from 1889 to 1930. Both of these had some formal democratic institutions including elected legislatures and relatively liberal laws that enfranchised large numbers of people by nineteenth-century standards, but both were in practice dominated by landowning elites (Graham 1990). The twentieth century saw a coup leading to military rule from 1930 to 1945, followed by a democratic republic from 1945 to 1964, which in turn fell to another military coup. Brazil's military regime fell under the category known as bureaucratic-authoritarian (see chapter 7) from 1964 to the 1980s. A gradual transition to the current democratic republic began in 1982, resulted in a presidential election in 1985, and was codified in the Brazilian Constitution of 1988.

Brazil's numerous experiences with regime change feature prominently in studies of democratization and democratic breakdown, partly because it is a large and important country in Latin America and partly because the historical evidence can provide support for several different theories of regime change. There is evidence, for example, that individual groups of political actors played a major role in transitions, and that prevailing ideas in the military shaped its willingness to wield authority, but also that the progressive modernization of the economy played a major role in

Brazil's political changes (O'Donnell, Schmitter, and Whitehead [1986] 1993; Stepan 1971; O'Donnell 1973; Evans 1979).

The study of democracy in Brazil goes beyond the question of transition from one regime type to another. Perhaps the most important issues today for those studying Brazilian politics are about democratic consolidation. Since 1988, Brazil's democracy has achieved some consolidation, with repeated elections that have seen incumbents voted out of office and the election of Lula da Silva, whose candidacy was at one point unacceptable to the military. The country has protections for civil liberties as well, and a return to outright authoritarian rule seems quite unlikely in the near future. Yet that does not mean Brazil has created effective representation or equal opportunity for all citizens. The rule of law does not extend equally to everyone everywhere in Brazil: some areas (both remote rural areas and parts of major cities) are almost lawless and ruled by criminals, while corruption is considerable in the police and in many political institutions. Indeed, Brazil has witnessed two removals of presidents from office in recent years, and even presidents who complete their terms have often come under scrutiny and threat of impeachment, often for reasons relating to corruption. Of course, looking at this in comparative perspective, it is possible to say that no country perfectly fulfills the ideal of a consolidated democracy.

One of the most interesting transitions in recent years has been a set of economic and policy changes that

have improved the well-being of the lowest-income people in Brazil. One of these changes is the overall growth of the Brazilian economy, which has been stable and solid after decades in which the country was known for its massive crises. In terms of government policies, the most famous is the *Bolsa Familia*, or Family Allowance. This program, known as a "conditional cash transfer," provides direct income from the government to poor families on the condition that they keep their children in school and keep their vaccinations up to date. The program predates the Lula presidency, but it was dramatically expanded on a nationwide basis under Lula. While economic growth and policies such as *Bolsa Familia* may seem to be largely an issue of economics, they can also bring political change. First, economic growth and "pro-poor" programs are credited with reducing inequality and poverty in recent years, and there is some evidence that low-income Brazilians with access to some disposable income participated actively in reelecting Lula (Zucco 2008). Second, such social policies suggest government that directly addresses problems facing the poor, which was not always the case under Brazilian democracies that were long considered elite led. Third, this set of changes brings poorer Brazilians into greater contact with state institutions, such as the education and health systems. This raises the prospect of strengthening relations between the state and society at large, which is one measure of what democratic consolidation is about.

Electoral Rules and Party (In)Discipline in Brazil's Legislature

Brazil has a bicameral legislature, like most federal systems. The upper chamber, called the Senate (*Senado*), is designed to represent the states (*estados*). Three senators represent each state in the Senate, for a total of eighty-one for the twenty-seven states of the federation, including the Federal District that comprises the capital, Brasilia. The lower chamber, known as the Chamber of Deputies (*Câmara dos Deputados*), nominally represents the population at large; but in Brazil's federal system, the electoral rules for the Chamber of Deputies guarantee that even the lower chamber takes on a localist flavor. One of the most pressing issues in Brazilian politics is how members of Congress come to represent the interests of certain localities over those of the country at large, even though Deputies are not elected in specific districts.

Representatives in the Chamber of Deputies are elected by an arrangement known as open-list proportional representation (or open-list PR). Deputies are elected on a state-wide basis, and not from specific local districts. There may be as many as seventy deputies from a state (as in the case of São Paulo) and as many as 513 deputies in all, with the number from each state depending on population. In elections to the Chamber, voters choose their most preferred candidate from a long list of options; that candidate is affiliated with a political party, and there are many parties in Brazil, both large and small. The open-list PR system allocates a state's seats in the Chamber of Deputies based on the total number of votes a party receives in each state from all its candidates. Thus, if the state of Paraná is

entitled to thirty seats in the Chamber, and all of the candidates from the Worker's Party in Paraná together earn one-third of all the votes in the state, then the PT earns ten seats in the Chamber from the state of Paraná. This makes it a form of proportional representation that reflects the votes for different parties.

But which ten members of the Worker's Party would be sent to Congress from Paraná in this example? This is determined by which candidates received the most individual votes. This "open-list" feature means voters have more say over which candidates go to Congress, as contrasted with conventional PR systems in which party leaders rank their preferred list of representatives that will go to the legislature depending on the party's share of the vote. Obviously, candidates seeking election want their party to garner a lot of seats (since that gives a greater chance of being elected), but they must also gain considerable individual name recognition to separate themselves from the pack. Individual candidates thus prioritize making a name for themselves in certain cities and towns, carving out electoral support, while also seeking to join parties that they think will give them the best shot at election. What they do not necessarily prioritize is following the wishes of their party's leaders. This weakens the cohesion of parties and makes those political parties difficult to "discipline."

Open-list PR thus has certain intuitive advantages, such as combining proportionality with votes for individual representatives, but it has also contributed to problems in governing in a Congress that was chaotic for many years (Power 2000).

One result was a large number of parties represented in both chambers, and for a long time a great deal of "floor crossing," as deputies moved from party to party (call it "party hopping") in an attempt to jockey for the best position for future elections. It also led party leaders to attempt to "bribe" legislators in their party to secure their votes on important legislation; sometimes this happened with patronage or "pork" for a legislator's home district or electoral base, and sometimes the bribes were literal. As Brazilian governance grew somewhat less chaotic over the period from 1994 to the present, the problems associated with open-list PR were seen as somewhat less troubling: more legislators stuck with their presidents and with their parties, though the trends of "party indiscipline" continued.

Brazil's electoral system offers an illustration of how institutions must be understood in relation to one another, and how diverse institutional arrangements can be. In this case, the functioning of the legislature depends on both electoral systems (as examined in chapter 9) and party systems (examined in chapter 11). Many analysts of Brazil have argued that the way deputies favor their own states leads to patronage politics rather than a legislature that looks out for the national interests. The debate about consequences is ongoing, but one common academic suggestion to reform Brazilian politics has been the modification or elimination of open-list PR, with the argument usually favoring more traditional ("closed-list") PR that would give party leaders greater leverage over their rank-and-file members in Congress.

CHAPTER 12, PAGE 285

CASE STUDY
Brazil's Landless Movement

As noted already, Brazil has often been seen as a society where social change comes about not through revolutions but through gradual transitions, yet some important transformative movements have come out of Brazil. Like the rest of Latin America, Brazil has long been characterized by high levels of poverty and inequality. One form of this inequality has been in patterns of land ownership. This is important, of course, because many Brazilians value social equality and would like to see fair opportunities for all citizens. It is also important, though, because comparative analysis shows that high levels of inequality are bad for other things that people value, like democracy. While Brazil has not seen land reform on the scale of those produced by major social revolutions such as China, Russia, or Cuba, it has, in recent years, seen notable efforts to distribute some land to the poor, land both privately owned and

held by the state. This land redistribution would have been very unlikely without the Landless Movement.

The movement began in the 1970s with the main aim of encouraging groups of activists to occupy and distribute land and to pressure the state to sanction this. Efforts began in the south but spread to various parts of the country. Social movement theory would predict that organizations would be needed if this movement were to develop. Sure enough, in 1984, a formal organization, the MST (the Movement of Landless Rural Workers), was created.

The activities of this movement have shifted and varied over time (Ondetti 2008). The movement first appeared in the 1970s, had mixed experience in the 1980s and early 1990s, and then had considerable success during the first administration of Fernando Henrique Cardoso (1995–1999), who implemented a major land reform program. The movement

had renewed success under the administration of Luiz Inácio Lula da Silva (2003–2011), although the MST was somewhat critical of Lula because of expectations raised by his perceived ideological affinity with the movement and also the associations between his Political party—the Workers' Party (PT)—and the MST.

Why is the Landless Movement considered a social movement rather than a revolution? It is important to remember that our categories of contention are "ideal types." It may be possible to argue that the Landless Movement is revolutionary, since it does clearly aim to transform the Brazilian social structure. However, most see it as a social movement because it does not aim to directly capture the state and because it is focused on the specific issue of land reform rather than a total transformation of politics and society, even though many of its activists and supporters do have such hopes for a total transformation.

CASE STUDY
Gender and Political Representation in Brazil: Where Has Progress Come From?

CHAPTER 14, PAGE 340

Like most modern societies, Brazil has struggled to provide gender equity. Also like most modern societies, it still has a ways to go on this issue. That said, the country has made considerable progress in recent years, especially since the 1990s, perhaps symbolized by the fact that the country recently had a globally prominent female president, Dilma Rousseff—though it should be noted that her administration ended in a corruption scandal. Comparative

political analysts ask how and why this progress has been made, in part because understanding the sources of both progress and failures may help future organizers and party leaders to make further progress, both in Brazil and elsewhere.

Some of the political successes of the Brazilian women's movement include the following:

1. Women's suffrage in 1932, though this proved moot in the

Estado Novo (1937–1945, when women were equally *unable* to vote) and in later authoritarian governments.

2. The decriminalization of divorce in 1977, with reforms in the late 2000s making divorce easier to obtain. This is important because typically women without the right to divorce are more likely to be stuck in dangerous situations like ongoing domestic violence,

CASE STUDY (continued)

Gender and Political Representation in Brazil: Where Has Progress Come From?

CHAPTER 14, PAGE 340

and it is widely held in today's world that people should be free to enter into and exit relationships consensually.

3. Creation of the *Conselho Nacional dos Direitos da Mulher* (CNDM, The National Council on Women's Rights) in 1985 and the *Secretaria Especial de Políticas para as Mulheres* (SEPM) in 2003. This was a consequence of important women's movement activism in civil society, and it essentially coincided with the re-emergence of Brazilian democracy. The CNDM has been involved in numerous important feminist initiatives (Macaulay 2006: 48).

4. In 1996, the passage of a law proposed by the PT (Workers' Party) establishing minimal candidate quotas of 30 percent for both men and women. This

means that parties are required to run slates of candidates at least 30 percent of whom are women.

5. Dilma Rousseff's election in 2010.

Fiona Macaulay (2006: 39) notes that an interesting feature of recent Brazilian experience is that advances on gender issues at the national level have not often come from the state but rather from the Partido dos Trabalhadores (the party of both Rousseff and Lula da Silva), though some proposals have come from actors from a variety of parties, even though gender has not historically been an axis of "party system cleavage" in Brazil. This latter point is not especially surprising, particularly given that gender-based parties, unlike ethnicity-based parties, are rare for reasons discussed in chapter 14 (see Htun 2004; Htun and Power 2006). More interesting is the fact that PT has, in comparative terms, nominated many more female

candidates than other parties and has more consistently focused on gender issues. Macaulay's analysis suggests that this is partially due to the role that female activists and party operatives have played within the PT.

Macaulay further points to the fact that Brazil has a fairly decentralized federal political system, and that local and state-level reforms have also been beneficial to women in some areas (Macaulay 2006: 35). The downside of this, of course, is that women's rights and their enforcement vary from area to area as well. Despite substantial progress on issues of gender and politics in Brazil, serious problems remain, including limited representation of women's issues, a higher rate of poverty for women than men, and a notably high rate of domestic violence. Many would also point to Brazil's strong restrictions on abortion in this connection.

Research Prompts

1. We have noted that Brazil is sometimes considered a "non-revolutionary" society in which transitions are gradual. Be this as it may, it is demonstrable that Brazil stands out in the Latin American context for the degree to which its transition to independence was peaceful. Why might this be? What would major theories of revolution say about this, and how might this case (in comparative Latin American perspective) help us to consider the relative merits of those theories?

2. For decades, Brazil has alternated between periods of impressive economic growth and serious economic crises. What would the major theories of development considered in chapter 5 say about this case? What can Brazil's experience tell us about those theories?

3. Describe the nature of Brazil's electoral system. If this system were adopted in the United States, what would its consequences

for politics likely be in the short, medium, and long terms? Why must we be cautious and tentative in asking such hypothetical questions?

4. A question is raised in the case study herein about whether the Brazilian Landless Workers' Movement is a social movement or a revolution. How would *you* define it based on the description offered here? What are the implications of your choice for *your* theoretical approach to contention?

5. Brazil has oscillated between democracy and authoritarianism for some time, with a strong authoritarian tradition. More recently, it has had notable democratic success. Is this likely to last? Why or why not? Be sure to draw both on facts about Brazil and on theories of democratic consolidation in your response.

China

Key Features of Contemporary China

Population:	1,379,302,771 (estimate, July 2017)
Area:	9,596,960 square miles
Head of State:	Xi Jinping (president, 2013–present)
Head of Government:	Li Keqiang (premier, 2013–present)
Capital:	Beijing
Year of Independence:	Never formally colonized, with the exception of Hong Kong, despite European imperial involvement in the nineteenth century. People's Republic of China established in 1949.
Year of Current Constitution:	1982
Languages:	Mandarin is the majority language. There are numerous dialects and minority languages.
GDP per Capita:	$15,400 (*CIA World Factbook* estimate, 2016)
Human Development Index Ranking (2016):	90th (medium human development)

Sources: *CIA World Factbook*; World Bank World Development Indicators; United Nations *Human Development Report 2016*.

Introduction

For a comparative politics scholar, China is one of the most fascinating countries. It raises numerous questions and issues, as we shall see, about economic development, democracy, the relationship between political parties and the state, and the causes and consequences of social revolutions, among many others. We shall explore some of these here, and you can use the theories that you have acquired in the thematic chapters of this book to compare and contrast China with other cases.

Of course, a leading issue in the politics of China is the question of how it has rapidly become the world's second-largest economy and a major global power, just a few short decades after being characterized by extreme poverty (though many Chinese citizens remain very poor). It has done so in a non-democratic, one-party state that restricts many basic freedoms. China thus presents a challenge to the so-called "Western model" of politics and economics based on liberal democracy and free markets. The implications of China's rise for the future are massive, both within China and around the world. We examine these issues of political economy and the regime in this profile.

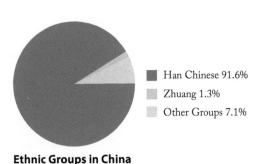

Ethnic Groups in China
Source: CIA World Factbook.

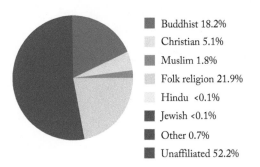

Religious Affiliation in China
Source: CIA World Factbook.

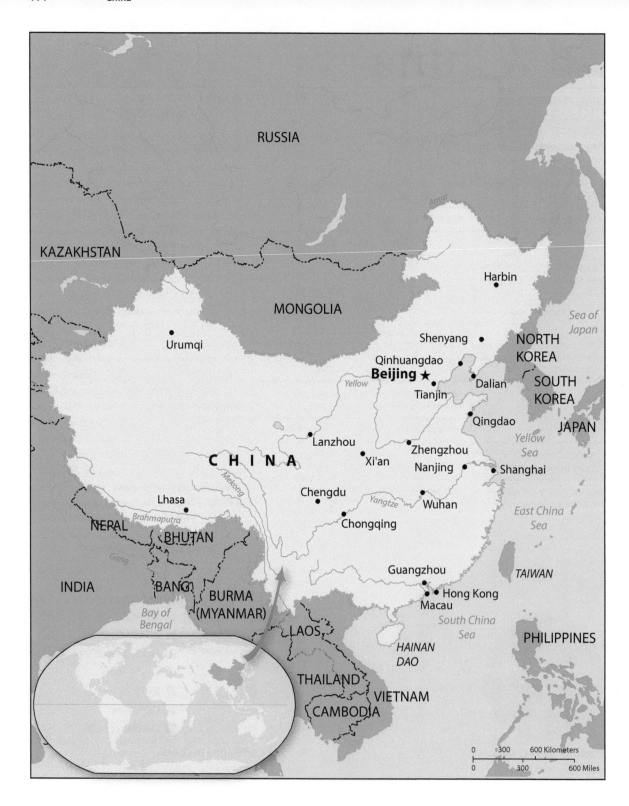

Another striking thing about China from the point of view of political science is the degree of political, economic, and cultural unity that it has managed to achieve despite its enormous size (in terms of both geography and population) and its diversity. China is among the most geographically diverse countries in the world. Its land mass encompasses over 9.5 million square miles. Parts of southern China are tropical and subtropical, whereas in the north, winters can be quite cold. Rainfall also varies considerably, being ample near the coast and minimal in the enormous Gobi Desert. The world's largest mountains—the Himalayas—are shared by China, but other regions are largely flat, and the Turfan Depression lies below sea level. China even has rainforests in the south.

China's population currently stands at around 1.4 billion, making it the largest country in the world in population terms. Demographers expect Chinese population growth to slow in the coming decades, and some suggest that India's population will overtake China's, though the accuracy of this forecast remains to be seen. China's demography has historically been shaped by state policy. Population growth was partially shaped by the efforts of the state to expand population under Mao Zedong. In the late 1970s, in an effort to slow population growth, the "One Child Policy" was established. This policy imposed penalties on families with two or more children, though this rule was not supposed to apply to ethnic minorities and other groups under some circumstances. One major development that was at least partially an unintended consequence of this policy is that many families used sex-selective abortion, and in some cases even infanticide, in their efforts to ensure that their one child would be male. As a result, today's population in China is unbalanced in terms of gender.

The population of China may seem homogeneous to many observers, but only at first glance. Over 90 percent of the population falls into the Han ethnic category. Yet the remaining 8.5 percent of the population falls into numerous groups (small in percentage terms, because of China's large population, but still numerous in absolute terms). These categories include the Manchu (the ethnic group that was dominant during the Qing Dynasty), Tibetans, Mongols, Zhuang, and Uighur, among others.

In terms of religion, China's state is officially atheist in character, owing, in part, to the legacy of Marxism, which holds that religion is a form of "false consciousness." Another factor is the sense that the past activity of religious missionaries, especially in the nineteenth century, was disruptive. Just the same, vibrant religious communities remain in China, and religion has historically played an important role in social conflict (see, in particular, discussion of the Taiping Rebellion later in these country materials). The preceding chart shows the percentage of the population that professes allegiance to several major religions. Students should keep in mind that some scholars estimate higher levels of religious belief and practice than these data suggest (see Pew Forum 2008).

In short, China is a large, complex, heterogeneous society in which one major ethnic group (Han Chinese) predominates. The state is officially secular, but underneath this surface, a number of citizens are religious (Weiming 1999). It has a varied geography and some striking demographic patterns. These basic features form the context through which we try to understand China's political development.

Historical Development

China stands out among most modern countries for how long it has existed as a large-scale and more or less unified civilization. Indeed, China has been a distinct geopolitical entity for *millennia*. As we shall see, however, this does not mean that it does not change, or that it is not changing now. The beginning of the history of Imperial China is conventionally dated at 221 BCE, and historians have traced the sequence of imperial regimes that followed. The history of *modern* China, however, begins in the later years of the Qing Dynasty (1644–1912). The Qing Dynasty entered into difficulties in the nineteenth century due to several key factors: foreign intervention, fiscal challenges, internal instability, and a changing geopolitical environment (for an overview of this period, see Spence 1990; Fairbank and Goldman 2006).

China in the nineteenth century faced increasing foreign intervention. Western nations imposed their own "rights" to trade with China, using force when they judged it necessary. This even included British merchants' introduction (smuggling) of opium to the Chinese market. When China tried to resist the imposition of the sale of this drug, they were twice militarily coerced (in the 1840s and 1850s); and among other things, Hong Kong became a crown colony of the British Empire. Beyond direct interference of this sort within China proper, European powers also interfered in China's traditional sphere of influence, particularly in so-called French IndoChina (a French colonial project in Southeast Asia). It is important to understand that China considered itself, not without evidence, to be one of the world's great civilizations, and their relative weakness in the face of European powers was experienced as humiliating. At the same time, the Qing Dynasty found itself in serious fiscal difficulties. It was unable to consistently raise the revenues that were required to protect itself and to maintain internal order (Fairbank and Goldman 2006: 187; Spence 1990). Partially as a result, the country witnessed serious internal disturbances.

Among these were the Taiping Rebellion of the 1850s and 1860s, which was led by Hong Xiuquan, who claimed to be the brother of Jesus Christ and who wanted to displace the Qing and impose a quasi-religious regime. The ensuing conflict killed many millions before the Qing eventually put it down. This was only the most important of a series of nineteenth-century rebellions against the Qing. Finally, it is important to note that during this same period of the late nineteenth century, China's neighbor Japan underwent dramatic changes, and by the end of the century emerged as a major regional power, defeating China itself in the Sino-Japanese War of 1894–1895 and then defeating Russia in the Russo-Japanese War of 1904–1905.

Historical Development

Timeline

1644–1912	Qing Dynasty
1839–1842	First Opium War (with Britain)
1842	Treaty of Nanking; Britain takes Hong Kong and imposes trading rights for itself.
1850–1873	Taiping (1850–1864), Nien (1853–1868), and Panthay (1855–1873) Rebellions
1856–1860	Second Opium (or "Arrow") War with Britain and France
1860	Convention of Peking imposes humiliating conditions on China
1894–1895	Sino-Japanese War (China defeated)
1898	Hundred Days' Reform, ended by coup d'état
1899–1901	Boxer Rebellion, ended by foreign intervention (eight foreign powers)
1911–1912	Revolution of 1911
1912	Fall of the Qing Dynasty, foundation of Guomindang (GMD or Nationalist Party), establishment of the Republic of China, which then falls into disorder and civil conflict
1920–1921	Chinese Communist Party founded
1925	Death of Sun Yat-sen, founder of the Guomindang
1926	Chiang Kai-Shek leads "Northern Expedition," achieving partial political unification.
1931	Japanese invasion of Manchuria
1934–1935	The "Long March" of the Communists, who face repression at the hands of the Nationalists; the march facilitates Mao's rise within the group and the move toward the countryside.
1936	Beginning of the "Anti-Japanese War," which can be thought of as the beginning of the Second World War in China.
1937	Japanese invasion of Manchuria (Northeast China) in lead-up to World War II
1946–1949	After end of World War II, Civil War between Nationalists and Communists continues.
1949	Communists victorious, Nationalists exiled to Taiwan.
1949	People's Republic of China is proclaimed.
1950–1952	Major land reform is carried out.
1950–1953	Korean War, in which China backed North Korea against U.S.-backed South Korea
1955–1956	Major agricultural collectivization is carried out.
1957	The "Hundred Flowers Campaign" in which dissent is encouraged but then punished
1957, 1959	The "Anti-Rightist" Campaigns in which alleged enemies of the revolution are repressed
1958–1960	The "Great Leap Forward"—An effort to force industrialization and meet often unrealistic production goals; among other things this produces a famine that leads to millions of deaths, some say as many as twenty million or more.
1966–1969	The "Cultural Revolution" and massive political repression, especially in the late 1960s, though some think this period lasts until Mao's death; the government encourages students to root out alleged enemies of the revolution. Among others, Deng Xiaoping loses his position, only to be rehabilitated in 1974.
1976	Arrest of the "Gang of Four," prominent Communist leaders of the Cultural Revolution
1976	Mao Zedong's death

Timeline (*Continued*)

1978–1979	Deng Xiaoping consolidates his dominance in the post-Mao transition. Deng Xiaoping reforms begin, which open China to greater private enterprise and foreign trade and begin to dismantle the collectivization of agriculture, leading to greater agricultural productivity.	2001	China becomes member of World Trade Organization (WTO).
		2003	Hu Jintao assumes presidency.
		2008	Beijing Olympics are taken by many as a sign of China's ascendancy.
1989	Tiananmen Square assault by military on protesters centerpiece of repression of movement for political reform	2007–2010	China becomes world's second-largest economy, largest exporter, largest holder of foreign currency reserves, and largest polluter.
1993	Jiang Zemin assumes presidency.	2013	Xi Jinping becomes president and Li Keqiang becomes premier.
1997	China officially takes over Hong Kong from United Kingdom.		

Not surprisingly, many in China were not pleased by this constellation of factors. It is not hard to see why this led to an upsurge in Chinese nationalism (Harrison 2001). Some decided that greater openness to both Japan and the West would be needed, in terms of both technology and political ideas. By the first decade of the twentieth century, the Qing regime was embracing reforms and even toying with constitutionalism. However, this was not enough to stop the growing discontent; and a political revolution (the "Chinese Revolution of 1911") toppled the Qing in 1912. The most important leader in this movement was Sun Yat-sen.

Unfortunately, this revolution did not bring about stable, constitutional government (on this period, see Fairbank and Goldman 2006; Spence 1990). Rather, China descended into what scholars refer to as the period of "Warlordism" (Schoppa 2010: 47–48). In short, the existing state broke down, and local power brokers were responsible for much of the order that remained. It was in this context that some of the political forces that still shape China were created. In the 1920s, Chiang Kai-shek, leader of the Nationalist Party (the Guomindang or GMD), successfully established central political order in much of China. Yet this victory was never absolute. The Communist Party had been established in the early 1920s, with the earlier groundwork being set by the "May Fourth Movement," and the Nationalists and Communists existed in tension. At times, the Communists followed Comintern orders to cooperate with the Nationalists, and at other times not. Likewise, Chiang Kai-shek and the Nationalists alternated between cooperation with and coercion of the Communists. Moreover, there was even sustained violent confrontation *within* the GMD in

the late 1920s. During the long resistance to Japan in the 1930s and 1940s, there were periods in which the Nationalists were forced to temporarily cooperate with the Communists, but this didn't last. After the war, the Communists, under the leadership of Mao Zedong, gradually defeated the Nationalists, who retreated along with Chiang Kai-shek to Taiwan. In accomplishing this, the Communists were greatly aided by the work they had done in organizing peasant communities.

In 1949, Mao declared the People's Republic of China (PRC). At first, the new regime was very much in line with the Communist regime in the Soviet Union, but over time they took a different course (Teiwes 2010). A key emphasis on the PRC was to encourage the collectivization of agriculture and forced industrialization. In 1958, Mao declared the "Great Leap Forward." This is often thought of by scholars as one of the clearest examples of the "voluntarism" of Maoist thought. Whereas traditional Marxism had emphasized that underlying structural conditions would determine the sequencing of revolutionary processes, Maoism held that through a great act of the collective will, China could *force* modernization. Unfortunately, the "Great Leap Forward" produced famine rather than modernization. The main reason was that agricultural collectives felt obligated to exaggerate their productivity, and the state in turn demanded so-called excess grain production (Fairbank and Goldman 2006: 368–374). Millions died.

Politically, China under Mao was a party dictatorship, one in which the party was clearly personally controlled by Mao himself. The party and the state were organizationally interpenetrated at every level. Although there were some minimal "democratic" features internal to the party at certain levels, the party was understood to have a monopoly on guiding the state. The rationale for this was that the party was said to truly represent the workers, and any other party, therefore, would necessarily represent class enemies and be on the wrong side of history.

Mao was always on the lookout for China's turn away from revolution. He thought that revolution needed to be "permanent" and that the bourgeois "class enemies" of the workers could be anywhere, potentially threatening the revolution. For this reason, he encouraged "self-criticism." Indeed, in the late 1950s, he initiated the "Hundred Flowers" campaign (Spence 1990: 569–573). The idea was that intellectuals and others would criticize and thus improve the revolution. However, Mao was less than satisfied when his own policies became the object of criticism. He and others soon denounced these critics as "rightists." This phenomenon was even clearer in the "cultural revolution" of the late 1960s (Spence 1990: 602–617; Fairbank and Goldman 2006: 383–405). Mao tried to organize a movement to target "rightists" and alleged enemies of the revolution, but soon the student "Red Guard" groups escaped his control. Many were attacked and killed, and still others lost their jobs and were imprisoned or sent to work with the peasants in the countryside. Purges touched all levels of the society, including future leader Deng Xiaoping.

Mao died in 1976, and after a brief period, a new, reformist generation came into leadership (Gilley 2010). Deng himself was the central figure here. The new leadership slowly allowed some limited criticism of Mao and Maoism. Greater intellectual freedom was allowed, though there were still some important limitations in this connection. Perhaps most impactfully, the regime began to make economic reforms. At first, many of these were concerned with agricultural policy. Agricultural workers were allowed to profit individually (though most land was still state-owned), changing the incentive structure of the agricultural economy, in turn producing greater productivity. China slowly and strategically privatized some state firms, moving toward a model of "market socialism." The country also skillfully increased its integration with the global economy. China's growth in recent decades has been truly astonishing, with hundreds of millions lifted out of poverty.

Politically, the reforms have been less noteworthy. The central goal seems to have been the preservation of the power of the Communist Party, which has been quite ideologically flexible. Just the same, the party continues to describe itself as Maoist; and, at least ostensibly, capitalist reforms in the economic sphere are presented as preparing the way for fuller socialism in the future. The regime has expanded the role that citizens can play in local politics, and internal party politics are no longer just the product of the deliberation of a single individual—this became especially clear under the leadership of Jiang Zemin—but for the most part, important decision making remains securely walled off from "the people."

Many expect the twenty-first century to be "China's century," and China has recently become the world's second-biggest economy. However, as we discuss herein, some questions and pressures remain. Can China maintain its high level of economic growth without the economy overheating and high inflation eroding citizens' gains? Will China democratize, or will the party continue to resist pressures to allow this? Can Chinese growth be made more compatible with the ecological interests of the country (and the world)? Will China continue to expand its geopolitical influence and, if and to the extent that it does so, how will this impact the Pacific region and the wider world?

Regime and Political Institutions

The central feature of the Chinese regime is the single-party system, and decision making effectively rests with a small group of Communist Party of China (CPC) elites in the top state organ known as the Politburo. The legislature, or National People's Congress (NPC), is elected by intricate systems that ensure both Communist Party dominance and top-down control. It is indirectly elected by lower-level assemblies that stretch down to localities: village-level assemblies choose representatives in *towns*; who select representatives in turn to larger *counties*; and the indirect elections continue upward to the levels of *prefectures*, *provinces*, and finally up to the NPC at the top. At each level, the CPC dominates and ensures that only its party members are selected for the higher levels of the legislature.

Regime and Political Institutions

Regime	Authoritarian
Powers in Constitution	Unitary system; written constitution; officially socialist
Administrative Divisions	Twenty-two provinces (and China claims Taiwan as twenty-third) Five autonomous regions (including Tibet) Four municipalities (Beijing, Shanghai, Tianjin, and Chongqing) Two special administrative regions (Hong Kong, Macau)
Executive Branch	Three top positions with executive functions: President of People's Republic of China; Secretary-General of Communist Party; and Chairman of Central Military Council Politburo is executive committee of the Communist Party, and includes top leaders of the party Head of government is the premier, recommended by president and approved by legislature; leads the State Council that oversees administration
Legislative Branch	National People's Congress (NPC); elected in indirect elections from village level up to NPC
Selection of Executive	Indirect; president selected by NPC
Judicial Branch	Supreme Court elected/appointed by NPC and its committees
Political Party System	Single dominant party: Communist Party of China (CPC)

The executive branch has several prominent positions, as examined further in the case study "Who Governs China?" and as noted in the regime chart. The president is the formal head of state, while the secretary-general leads the CPC. In practice, a single person often holds both positions, along with the role of commander in chief, and is known as the "paramount leader." The premier, who is responsible for the ongoing operations of the government and for implementing laws, is nominated by the president and approved by the NPC. This system ensures that policies set by the Politburo and the executive pass into law.

Political Culture

Political cultures are complex and multifaceted, located both in the minds of individual members of society and in publicly established symbols and structures. As such, mapping political culture is a complex task, above all in a large society like China. A typical strategy is to focus on important features or currents of a given country's political culture. Here, we briefly focus on two of the most important currents in Chinese political culture: Confucianism and Maoism.

Confucianism is traced back to Confucius, a philosopher who lived from around 551 to 479 BC. For the study of political culture, the particulars of his philosophy are not the important thing. Rather, we are interested in how generally Confucian ideas were picked up and carried along culturally over many years, and we are also interested in the consequences of these ideas. Confucianism as established emphasized formal education, the importance of public ritual, a strict code of ethical responsibility, and piety toward one's family and ancestors (Harrison 2001). While many find these ideas intrinsically appealing and interesting, as social scientists, we believe that they became influential in part because the Chinese imperial state employed them for many centuries in its efforts to maintain its legitimacy and staff itself. Imperial examinations based on Confucianism determined who would be able to hold which official jobs. This enhanced and maintained Confucianism's prestige in pre-modern China, as it was associated with both the state and high social status.

Confucianism is often used by theorists (sometimes, perhaps, functioning as a cultural stereotype) who emphasize culture in their efforts to explain several political and economic phenomena observable in China and other countries with strong Confucian heritage, such as Japan, Korea, Singapore, and Vietnam. Some argue, for example, that Confucian political culture underlies—and, according to some, justifies—authoritarian politics. This idea was actively promoted by Lee Kwan Yew in Singapore, for example. Others, as pointed out in chapter 5, have tried to use Confucian culture to explain both (1) the economic underdevelopment experienced by China until recently *and* (2) its recent growth.

Maoism attempted to replace Confucianism in the sphere of political culture, viewing this as necessary to modernization. For this reason, many analysts are suspicious of claims about the contemporary consequences of traditional Confucianism, since they argue that there is little continuity between pre-modern Confucianism and contemporary Chinese political culture.

Maoism—in China often called "Mao Zedong Thought" (Joseph 2010a: 135–150)—is a variant of Marxism. As such, it emphasizes the importance of class struggle, sees history as the story of class exploitation, and calls for a future in which the division of labor and associated exploitation will be reversed. However, Mao made major revisions to previous versions of Marxism. The two most important are (1) the centrality of the peasantry in Maoist thought and (2) Maoism's voluntarism.

Marx was skeptical of peasants as revolutionaries. He thought that they were inherently conservative. It was the urban, industrial workers—the proletariat—that were most fully alienated and that, therefore, had the greatest revolutionary potential. Scholars have often noted the irony that Marxism ended up being most successful in places like Russia, China, and later the so-called Third World where and when industrialization and urbanization were less established (though industrial workers did play an important role in the Russian Revolution). Some would argue that Maoism is more consistent with what actually happened in the twentieth

century. Mao emphasized the revolutionary potential of peasants and concentrated his organizing among them. He regarded them as virtuous, often punishing wayward elites, sending them to work with peasants for "re-education."

When we say that Maoist thought emphasizes "voluntarism," we mean that Mao thought that through a great act of will, a collectivity could "leap" out of the structured determination of history (Joseph 2010a: 141–142). Thus, a people could heroically exceed the economic productivity of which conventional analysis would expect them capable. Critics would point to the disastrous consequences of the "Great Leap Forward" as showing the dangerousness of this idea.

In the years following Mao's death, Maoism has become more open and flexible. It remains, at least formally, the core ideology of the state. Just the same, some wonder if Maoist "market socialism" is really socialism—or Maoism—at all. Confucianism, which was officially to have been replaced, has been gradually endorsed as well by China's elites. Some students of culture would argue that the Confucian legacy, despite Mao's opposition to it, had never really disappeared in any case. Thus both of these key strands of Chinese political culture remain important in today's China, as intellectuals work to revise aspects of each that are viewed as inconsistent with the modern world (e.g., traditional Confucianism's critical stance toward commerce).

At the same time, China has many of the features of industrialized societies, and a growing question is how middle-class consumers (especially in cosmopolitan urban areas) will coexist with Confucian or Maoist views in an increasingly entrepreneurial society. In recent years, much of China's elite and masses alike have embraced a vision that "to become rich is glorious." The country has embraced many aspects of capitalism, even as the government tightly limits political rights and intervenes heavily in the economy. China's political culture thus draws on multiple strains of longstanding philosophy "made in China," even while taking on some of the cultural features of other contemporary societies in an age of global communications and exchange.

Political Economy

Despite a long and rich history and culture, China spent centuries in a state of economic stagnation that continued up to the 1980s. Through the mid-twentieth century and Mao's Communism, China witnessed poverty and even famine on a massive scale, both of which were exacerbated by the policies of the Communist Party leadership. China's economic model changed

dramatically, however, after the rise of Deng Xiaoping in 1978. Deng instituted reforms that opened China up to greater capitalism, with the most prominent changes being opening agriculture and industry to private ownership.

China's recent embrace of greater openness to market forces has had dramatic effects. Industry flourished, especially along the coast, as China pushed economic growth based on cheap exports and became the "workshop of the world." Agricultural productivity improved as well, and reinforced industrialization: as productivity improved in rural areas, fewer people were needed to produce the same amount of food, and many rural dwellers migrated to urban areas to become factory workers. Wages were (and remain) low by Western standards, but often represented significantly increased income from that which was available in rural areas. It may be that since the reforms were passed, more than *half a billion* people (often estimated at 600 million) have come out of poverty. China has become the world's leading exporter and second-largest economy, based in part on export-led growth in manufacturing and related investment. It has gone from being one of the world's poorest countries to middle-income status in just three decades.

Despite the apparent success of market-friendly reforms, China is far from purely capitalist. The state continues to play a major role in the economy, including in ways that some global competitors say gives China "unfair advantage." For instance, China has required that major foreign investors wishing to invest in China must partner with Chinese companies in "joint ventures." This ensures that Chinese companies benefit from investment and the transfer of skills, knowledge, and technology. These and other state interventions are in addition to controlling the currency to promote exports.

China's political economy still faces several major challenges. One of the most pressing for most Chinese is the continued poverty of rural areas, and the related problem of high and growing inequality. Urban areas along the coast have benefited the most from China's boom, along with some cities along major waterways. Despite efforts to develop the interior, China still has high levels of poverty in rural areas. Second, China's environment is degraded due to pollution that has come with industry. Many cities have heavily polluted water supplies and awful air quality from factory emissions and the shift from bicycles to ever more cars for transportation. Third, China faces a demographic challenge that many wealthy countries face, but even more so: Its "One Child" policy limited the birth rate for many years, but it also means a rapidly aging population that may struggle in the future to care for its growing number of elderly citizens. A final major challenge is the rule of law for intellectual property, as China has been a haven for digital piracy and "ripping off" patents and copyrights of major international companies. This is not just a problem for Disney, Levi's, or the pharmaceutical company Pfizer, but also for China's ambitions to become a world leader in the research and development that lead to a more value-added economy. At the same time, some would argue that this way of looking at things privileges the point of view of the wealthiest countries, asking developing countries to play by a different set of rules than they did while they themselves were developing.

China's political economy is explored further in the following case study, "How Did China Become an Economic Power?"

CASE STUDIES

CASE STUDY
How Did China Become an Economic Power?

CHAPTER 5, PAGE 107

China is seen today as the greatest challenger to the global economic power of the United States, yet just over thirty years ago it was one of the world's poorest countries. This slow development came despite the country's ancient history as a leader in world trade and technological innovation. Starting in 1949, the Communist Party increased the state's role in the economy. Mao and the Communists collectivized agriculture (prohibiting private farming) and tried to promote heavy industry such as steel production. From the 1950s to the 1970s, Mao attempted major economic overhauls in the so-called "Great Leap Forward"—which resulted in a catastrophic famine—and the so-called "Cultural Revolution." In 1978–1979, China began economic reforms under a new leader, Deng Xiaoping. These reforms facilitated private enterprise and gave more flexibility to local officials. Critically, the reforms were gradual and strategic: China didn't open all areas of its economy immediately to international market forces. China seized advantage of growing globalization and adopted an export-led growth model based on selling goods to the world's wealthiest countries.

How Did China Become an Economic Power?
CHAPTER 5, PAGE 107

The last thirty years have seen spectacular growth of about 10 percent per year, a rate at which the size of the overall economy doubles about every seven years (though in the most recent years, annual growth has been closer to about 7%). With growth has come economic power, but also a rising tide of inequality (especially between the relatively wealthy coastal regions and the rural interior of the country) and significant environmental degradation. Recent years have seen some disputes with the United States over trade and the value of the Chinese currency, which Washington asserts is unfairly "undervalued" to favor Chinese companies by making Chinese goods cheaper to Americans and American goods more expensive in China. Others, though, suggest that China should attempt to shape the value of its currency in the pursuit of its own interests and not those of the United States or other countries. This policy, which in part involves China using the proceeds from sales of exports to buy American government bonds, is controversial. It is seen by some as the United States and other countries "borrowing from China to buy from China."

Nonetheless, from the perspective of the developing economy, keeping the currency at a low value seemed to work very well for countries such as South Korea as they industrialized and modernized. It meant people in these Asian countries had to defer the chance to consume as they grew wealthier, sometimes for a generation. In the end, however, the willingness to save and lend instead of borrow and consume contributed to development. Whether this tendency is a matter of culture and society, of economic policy, or of political regime remains a matter of debate. Some say it reflects a culturally "Asian" willingness to defer gratification (or, one could argue, a contemporary Western inability to defer gratification). Others suggest that only rather authoritarian regimes can manage such approaches and that such theories about cultural tendencies approach being mere stereotypes. Still others might say that China's willingness to forego consumption in the short term is simply a matter of astute economic policy.

China's developmental success has been astounding, but it also has problems. The most conspicuous may be an increasing challenge of sustainability, as China has passed the United States to become the world's largest polluter in absolute terms (though the United States remains a much larger polluter per capita than China). In addition, China's development model may have the "opposite" challenge of the United States today. China as a country saves a great deal of money and consumes relatively little, given its size and income. The country's earnings depend heavily on exports, as well as on increasing investment in infrastructure ranging from railroads to coal-fired power stations to apartment buildings. While China scolds the United States for spending beyond its means and borrowing too much, others might criticize China for an economy that saves, invests, and lends too much.

We can learn from China's successes and problems to address questions that interest peoples around the world: Why does rapid economic development happen? Is China's success evidence that the free market promotes development, or that the state drives development, or both, or neither? Is recent economic success a consequence of Chinese culture? If so, how do we account for China's long economic stagnation before 1979?

Is China Destined for Democracy?
CHAPTER 6, PAGE 134

Is it possible to predict whether countries will become democracies? Some will say yes and others no, but political scientists are generally interested in the *predictive power* of their theories for the future, even if these theories are based on evidence from the past. For instance, a political scientist who argues that economic development leads to democracy might make this argument using existing evidence and building on the modernization theory seen in chapter 6. At the same time, this theorist would also be making a theoretical prediction: poor countries that grow and modernize economically are predicted to democratize in the future. If a theory is accurate and powerful, it will often help us to predict future events, even if they are based on readings of the past. The question of whether China will become a democracy presents a useful example of how theories make predictions, and how empirical evidence supports or challenges theories.

Imagine three theorists who are asked about the future of China. The first is a modernization theorist, as noted earlier. What would a modernization theorist predict about democracy in China's future, given China's rapid economic growth? A second theorist is a certain kind of culturalist who believes that a country's regime type (whether democratic or authoritarian) is rooted in deep cultural values. What would this theorist expect, if China has never had a "political culture" of democracy? A third theorist might argue that democratization depends on the actions of specific individuals. Would this theorist be able to make predictions about the future?

Observing China's rapid economic growth and emergence of an urban middle class, the modernization theorist might predict that China will move inexorably toward democracy in the coming years. As China develops economically and urbanizes, a middle class is emerging. Modernization theorists would likely predict that China will follow the path of other countries that have developed: countries that modernize regularly progress toward more rights (such as property rights) and a middle class more willing to use its economic and political power to demand and protect these rights. Economic development leads to democracy, so if China sees development, democracy should follow.

The culturalist theorist we mentioned might explain the lack of demand for democracy in China by deep and long-lasting tendencies in the population,

the political system, or the political culture. For example, one argument about the polities of East Asia suggests that cultures in the region accept the importance of state authority and may tolerate a lack of rights as a result; this is sometimes seen as a Confucian heritage, drawing on the works of the philosopher Confucius discussed briefly in the "Political Culture" section earlier in the chapter. While not all culturalists would adopt this perspective, and this interpretation of Confucianism is highly contestable, our hypothetical culturalist might say that China's cultural heritage will work against democratization.

The third theorist may compare transitions to democracy in other countries and conclude that these really depended on the decisions of a small handful of very important individuals. The experience of South Africa and Presidents Nelson Mandela and F. W. de Klerk in the early 1990s might be such an example, as would many other cases around the world. This theorist would only be able to make more ambiguous predictions about China's future, and might conclude that "it depends on leaders" more than forces like economic change or culture; it would thus be difficult for this theorist to predict in advance how movements toward democracy in China will play out, since "it depends" on individuals and their choices.

The modernization theorist would likely predict that China is on the road to democracy, and that democracy is all but inevitable as China grows richer. Our example of a culturalist would likely be skeptical about the prospects for democracy. And the theorist focusing on leadership would probably caution both of the others that their predictions are

quite uncertain. The first two theories have the merit of making clear predictions in advance. They can be falsified for the Chinese case if they get it wrong (though probabilistic predictions are hard to falsify with a single case). If we fast-forward thirty years, either the modernization theorist or the culturalist is likely to have been shown wrong, at least for this case, and the other theory may well have some evidence supporting it.

The third theory, about leaders, may have more difficulty making clear predictions about whether China will become a democracy at a certain point in time, but it does make an important theoretical prediction of its own: if and when China does democratize, it will be primarily because of the leadership and decisions of individuals. This too can be falsified, if it is shown that large groups of people or impersonal forces drove the outcomes in China more than selected leaders. The theory might say that democratization is more unexpected in some places than others. Someone who traces democratization to economic modernization will expect that they can "see democracy coming," even if they cannot pinpoint the moment it will occur.

Consider whether one or more of the three hypothetical theorists makes the most intuitive sense to you. Some emphasize political economy, some emphasize culture, and some emphasize individuals, among other possibilities. Your preference will give you some ideas about what you would predict for China. More generally, if you find yourself coming back to similar kinds of predictions across different chapters, this may give you some insight into the type of comparativist and thinker you are.

CASE STUDY
Who Governs China?

CHAPTER 10, PAGE 239

Understanding who really leads China and holds power there requires careful examination of leadership positions as well as the informal influence of different individual politicians and groups. This authoritarian, single-party country has over a billion people and multiple influential institutions that feature prominently in government, yet power often comes to be associated with individual leaders. How does this work? As suggested previously under the "Regime and Institutions" sections of this country profile, China's system formally features three different top executive positions, plus a head of government called the premier that presides over the legislature. There are also two major councils that bring together top leaders, one for the state government called the State Council and one for the Communist Party known as the Politburo.

The three top executive positions are the President of the People's Republic of China (the formal head of state), the Secretary-General of the Communist Party (the head of the governing party), and the Chairman of the Central Military Council (the commander-in-chief, as it were). At present, Xi Jinping has consolidated all three authorities in his person, so there is little doubt about who leads the executive branch. Moreover, at the time of this writing, in 2018, he is moving to end term limits, suggesting he plans to hold onto power for a considerable period. Meanwhile, to use the terms of chapter 10, the premier is a head of government similar to a prime minister; he is appointed by the president and approved by the legislature, the National

People's Congress. Li Keqiang is currently in this post. There are also other members of the Politburo that are politically prominent, and some of them jockey for position to be the next generation of Chinese leaders.

It is common to talk about major periods in recent Chinese history that are associated with a single "paramount leader," regardless of these many different official leadership posts. The paramount leaders sometimes have held the official executive leadership positions, but not always. Recent leaders, including Xi Jinping, have held the three key offices of head of state, head of the Communist Party, and head of the military, and this trifecta can be taken as a clear indicator of their "paramount" status. They have been president, party leader, and commander-in-chief all in one, leaving little doubt about who is the top decision maker. Yet the previous paramount leaders, Mao Zedong (1949–1976) and Deng Xiaoping (about 1978–1992), could be seen as the leaders of their eras because of their ability to wield influence over party and state institutions in slightly different ways. Mao's control was most direct: he was the chairman of the various committees, commissions, and major decision-making bodies of his era; it is for this reason that he is often referred to as "Chairman Mao" and not "President Mao." Deng Xiaoping, by contrast, did not hold all of the top positions himself, yet there was also little doubt who the decision maker was during his time as paramount leader. Deng held certain posts as the head of the administration in the State Council, and

he presided over the military at certain times, but these were not the true source of his leverage. Rather, he exercised authority through the individuals who served as "figureheads" in the top three posts and through his predominance among the members of the Politburo and other organs of state and party.

Paramount leaders have governed and wielded power in very different ways. Mao Zedong pushed ambitious economic plans and attempts to modernize China in a very top-down, authoritarian fashion. These included the so-called Great Leap Forward and the Cultural Revolution, which over the long run were responsible for the famine, stagnation, and repression associated with Mao's rule. Deng Xiaoping became paramount leader at the end of 1978 and remained so into the 1990s. Deng became known as the leader who set China on the path to economic dynamism with major reforms, but he was also responsible for the violent crackdown in Tiananmen Square in 1989. After Deng's passing from the scene, Jiang Zemin, Hu Jintao, and Xi Jinping continued Communist Party control with economic reform. All can be seen in different ways as pragmatists who have attempted to increase China's engagement with the world and further development by engaging more people in the process, all while retaining the tight grip of the Communist Party.

The image of Chinese executive leadership is one in which top politicians accumulate power informally within the Communist Party and interlocking state institutions, often making alliances as needed with other key players while

CASE STUDY (continued)

Who Governs China?

CHAPTER 10, PAGE 239

gaining in seniority. In contemporary China, we might say that accumulating power within the party and state has led to the top executive positions, rather than the power coming from the positions themselves. The presidency has little formal power attached to it, for example, though the president is the head of state. Yet becoming president is a clear sign of power. The election of the president is dominated by the Communist Party in the legislative branch (National People's Congress), but upon the recommendation of a single candidate by the Politburo, the leading decision-making organ within the Communist Party. In short, the one candidate selected by the CPC elites is almost guaranteed to be president. It may not be surprising that the party will often select its own leader, or the person it wishes to become its leader, to the position. China's intricate set of governing mechanisms makes the Politburo and other leadership organs the leading sources of executive power in the world's most populous country.

CASE STUDY

The Chinese Party System

CHAPTER 11, PAGE 262

China is the most influential and important dominant-party system in the world today. The country functions essentially as a single-party system, though some other parties are nominally allowed. China's Communist Party has held onto power for over six decades through a combination of factors. The various mechanisms for ensuring the dominance of the Communist Party are useful to understand, especially since the meaning of "Communist" in Communist Party has shifted so dramatically with the many changes in China over the last several decades.

The first and most obvious factor is the tight linkage between the Communist Party, the Chinese state bureaucracy, and the military. The Communists control the state apparatus and can call on the military as needed to protect the regime. Through years of Communist dominance, the state and military have contributed to single-party rule. This has sometimes taken place with violent repression by the military, as in Tiananmen Square in 1989 and in purges by leader Mao Zedong in previous decades. It has also happened on an ongoing basis through the use of state organs to harass certain opposition forces that might pose a threat, imprison prominent dissidents, and control the media (including new media such as Google's China-based search engine and social media). Many of these efforts to minimize opposition have been passed by the National People's Congress (NPC), but they rely on the state for enforcement.

A second factor is the electoral system, which provides built-in advantages for the Communist Party. The most important feature is the indirect election process, by which local councils elect members of governing councils at higher levels, and so on, up to the NPC. For instance, national-level legislators are selected by provincial legislators, who are in turn selected by council members at lower levels. The result of this indirect election process is absolute dominance for the Communists at the national level in Beijing. Although it is possible for independents and even some members of other small parties to elect a single delegate or two at the local level, it is exceedingly difficult for enough independents to be elected to get an independent or member of another party at the next level up. The well-established, well-resourced Communists are present in every local election throughout the country and dominate the indirect elections to higher levels; this means a virtual single-party state at the national level, with the only exceptions being other parties that are closely "allied" to the Communists and basically under Communist control.

A third set of factors has to do with the Communist Party's legitimacy, including its actual performance in government. China's economic growth under Communist Party rule has been very strong in recent years. While it is difficult to get

CASE STUDY (continued)
The Chinese Party System
CHAPTER 11, PAGE 262

an independent view of Chinese public opinion, even international news reports suggest that many Chinese are relatively satisfied with government performance and are thus not pressing for immediate moves toward a multiparty system. This idea that a government's legitimacy can be based on economic performance has often been tested in a democracy, and it also seems to have held in some authoritarian and exclusionary systems (Epstein 1984). Legitimacy can also be based on factors other than economics. The Chinese Communist Party has made significant efforts over the years to associate itself with a variety of ideas that it has used to trumpet the regime's ability to represent the Chinese people. These have included the claim that the Communists can uniquely represent the working class and peasants, but they have also included touting Chinese nationalism. The Chinese Communists have focused on trumpeting China's greatness and rise to power, and opposition to foreign (especially Western and Japanese) influence. This has flourished through the Communist period (even though Communist ideology is traditionally seen as formally opposed to nationalist sentiment). This cluster of factors shows several ways that an authoritarian, single-party system can persist even in the presence of elections.

CASE STUDY
The Chinese Revolution
CHAPTER 12, PAGE 297

The case of China allows us to consider two issues of concern to us in the study of contention and revolutions. First, it highlights the question considered in the chapter about how to define revolutions and even subtypes like "political revolutions" and "social revolutions." Second, it focuses attention on the importance of mobilization in successful revolution, a factor highlighted by resource mobilization and political opportunity theories. Interestingly, the case of China considered alone gives at least some support to *all* of the theories considered in chapter 12.

The reason that China highlights the definitional issue is that the country went through a long process of social change, and it is therefore difficult to precisely date when revolution began. As discussed in the preceding historical narrative, China saw major changes over the course of the nineteenth century, including foreign intervention, domestic revolts (some of which, like the Taiping Rebellion, were revolutionary in intention), and fiscal problems. This led many to seek the modernization of both state and society. At the same time, the state came to be perceived as weak, because of those very same fiscal difficulties, the trouble it had in maintaining domestic order, and in particular its loss in the Sino-Japanese War. State weakness—sometimes called "state breakdown"—is seen by many scholars as an essential precursor to revolution. The late Qing state responded by implementing an ineffectual reform program, a factor sometimes stressed by relative deprivation theories of revolution.

In 1911 and 1912, contention reached a level most scholars would consider revolutionary, and yet what took place at that time was not a "social revolution" in the sense defined in chapter 12. The fundamental emphasis was on the transformation of political structures: the end of the Qing Dynasty and the creation of a republic. Of course, as our brief historical narrative shows us, the republic was weaker than expected, and China descended into the period of "Warlordism." Now this certainly had consequences for social structures (just as the successful creation of a strong republic would have), but these consequences were indirect.

It was within this context that the rival parties involved in the next stage of the revolutionary process developed, the Nationalists (heirs to the early republicanism) and the Communists (Averill 1998). As the reader knows from the previous historical narrative, the Communists were ultimately triumphant. The most important factor that scholars have used to explain this difference is their advantage in mobilization capacity (Skocpol 1979: 252–262). While the Nationalists were in power, they were often ineffective, and some of their members acquired a reputation

CASE STUDY (continued)

The Chinese Revolution

CHAPTER 12, PAGE 297

for corruption (Schoppa 2010:59), although some recent scholars argue that the Nationalists were more capable state-builders than traditional accounts suggest (see a brief discussion of these and related issues in Edmonds 1997). In the rural areas controlled by the Communists during the conflict, they were focused on the establishment of peasant organizations, indeed, as early as the late 1920s. This strategy—which is linked to Maoism's emphasis on peasants as revolutionary actors, which Marx would have rejected—paid enormous dividends in the 1940s when peasants helped the Communists defeat the Nationalists once and for all. Of course, proponents of other theories of revolution could point to other factors that might help to explain the Communists' success. Cultural or framing theories could point to the salience of Maoist ideology. Relative deprivation and political opportunity theories could point to the ongoing weakness of the state.

Finally, it is important to note that the Chinese Revolution did not end in 1949. Mao was a proponent of "permanent revolution." Indeed, at least ostensibly, it is still going on today. More realistically, perhaps, we could say that it was carried out in stages during Mao's rule. Collectivization of agriculture, the "Great Leap Forward," and the "Cultural Revolution" (Perry 1998) were all key episodes in the Maoist effort to remake the underlying structures of Chinese society.

Research Prompts

1. Consider the discussion of economic development and democracy in China that you have read in these country case materials. Alongside it, review the discussion of these same themes in the country case materials on India. Both societies have been "modernizing" rapidly in recent decades, but they have done so in very different terms. India first embraced democracy and only more recently has achieved rapid economic growth. China has achieved dramatic growth, but so far has seen very little democratization. What accounts for these different trajectories? Which theories can you draw on from the thematic chapters of this textbook to explain the variation between these two cases? How might we empirically test the hypothesis that you generate?

2. The case study on democratization in China (which connects to chapter 6) asks you to think about what several major theories of democratization would predict with respect to the Chinese case in the coming years. Bring the thought experiment to its conclusion: which theory do you find most plausible with respect to China, and why? How could we get an empirical answer to this question?

3. Compare the Chinese Revolution to the Russian Revolution, discussed in the country case materials on the Russian Federation. Both were intended to be Marxist revolutions, but they exhibited notable differences. How were these revolutions different, and how might a social scientist *explain* their differences?

4. Compare the overview of Chinese political history with our overview of Mexican political history in the Mexico country case materials. Both societies have had long-standing, highly complex civilizations stretching back centuries. However, Mexico experienced direct colonialism, whereas China's brush with European imperialism was largely indirect. What are the major implications or consequences of this difference for Chinese and Mexican political development? How could one use major theories of comparative politics to begin generating ideas in response to this question?

5. The chapter 11 case study shows that China is governed through a complex set of political institutions. Compare and contrast this with Iran, especially the box on Iran's judiciary. Can you hypothesize about why authoritarian regimes might have such intricate sets of governing institutions? Do these compare or contrast with any other countries that have witnessed authoritarian rule in the twentieth century—such as Brazil, Germany, Mexico, Nigeria, Japan, or Russia? What selection of cases might best enable you to test your preliminary hypothesis?

France

Key Features of Contemporary France

Population:	67,106,161 (estimate, July 2017)
Area:	643,801 square kilometers
Head of State:	Emmanuel Macron (president, 2017–present)
Head of Government:	Edouard Philippe (prime minister, 2017–present)
Capital:	Paris
Year of Independence:	France was never formally colonized. Many date the consolidation of the French state to the era of Louis XIV (1643–1715) and the birth of modern France to the French Revolution of 1789.
Year of Current Constitution:	1958
Languages:	French
GDP per Capita:	$42,300 (CIA World Factbook estimate, 2016)
Human Development Index Ranking (2016):	21th (very high human development)

Sources: *CIA World Factbook*; World Bank World Development Indicators; United Nations *Human Development Report 2016*.

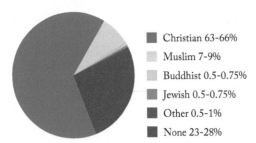

- Christian 63-66%
- Muslim 7-9%
- Buddhist 0.5-0.75%
- Jewish 0.5-0.75%
- Other 0.5-1%
- None 23-28%

Religious Affiliation in France

Source: CIA World Factbook.

Introduction

France has historically been situated at the center of Western Europe. This is true not only geographically but in terms of France's identity and culture. At least since Charlemagne united significant portions of Western Europe in the eighth and ninth centuries, presenting himself as heir to the Roman Empire, many have considered France the central carrier of European civilization.

Geographically, France extends from the English Channel in the north to the Mediterranean in the south. The Pyrenees divide it from Spain (and the tiny mountain country of Andorra) in the southwest, and it shares its eastern border with Belgium, Luxembourg, Germany, Switzerland, and Italy. In addition to its mountainous areas (both the Pyrenees and the Alps as well as the smaller Jura and Massif Central), it has good farmland, being most famous for the production of grapes and cereals. French agriculture has historically excelled in the production of wine, cheese, and other items considered by international consumers to be luxurious.

Today's France is interesting to scholars of comparative politics for numerous reasons. France's passage to political modernity was extraordinarily rocky, with what many consider the first modern revolution. France also played out in striking fashion the contrast between democratic-republican and authoritarian centralist forms of politics, settling on a "mixed presidentialist" system in the Fifth Republic (which still goes on today) that continues to stimulate much debate. France also showed us what conflict between civic republicanism and a monopolistic church could look like, pioneering a certain kind of secularism, often called *laïcité*.

It is difficult to estimate the relative share of the population comprised by different ethnic groups in France. This is because France places restrictions on national statistical surveys that document the ethnic and racial identities of respondents, in part because of a strong cultural tradition proscribing such questions. The *CIA World Factbook*, the main

source we have used here for data on the ethnic composition of the other countries considered in this book, does not list estimated percentages of ethnic groups in France. It notes simply that French ethnic groups include "Celtic and Latin with Teutonic," as well as "Slavic, North African, Indochinese, and Basque minorities." Of these groups, the North African minority—many from France's former colony of Algeria—and sub-Saharan Africans may be the most politically important.

Many in this group may list Islam as their religion, though the majority are probably non-practicing. We can only estimate the relative share of the French population who are officially Muslims. Adherents of Islam probably constitute somewhat less than 10 percent of the French population: a recent report from the Pew Research Center estimates that 7.5% of the French population practices Islam (Hackett 2016). In recent years, there have been many questions about their assimilation (as well as about discrimination that they face). The majority of the French population is at least nominally Catholic; but, as in much of Europe, most in the nominally Christian category are not regular church attendees, and as in much of Western Europe, the proportion of the population without religious affiliation is growing. Some sources (e.g., Kuru 2009: 244) estimate that just more than half of the French population (55 percent) adheres formally to a religion.

Historical Development

As noted, France has traveled a rocky road to political modernity. In 1789, France gave us what many consider the first modern revolution (Arendt 1963; Furet [1988] 1995), deposing the Bourbon monarchy, establishing a Republic, abolishing the nobility (noblesse), and opposing the power of the Roman Catholic Church and ultimately repressing it. The revolution even created a new calendar, with the beginning of the revolution the starting point from which future years would be counted. This revolution is discussed further in a case study later in the France country materials.

After a decade of radicalization and increasing confusion, Napoleon Bonaparte took power (see the discussion in Parry and Girard 2002: 7–24). Napoleon was an early example of what modern authoritarianism (with lots of references to "the people" and even plebiscites and other elements of democracy) might look like. He further spread modern politics through conquest, centralizing political authority and imposing Napoleonic law in numerous countries—it still serves as the basis for law in much of the world today—and also raising nationalism in the resistance he engendered. Ever since the time of Napoleon's domination, people have debated whether his regime consolidated or reversed the revolution. The best answer is probably to say that it did both. On one hand, he re-established order, proclaiming himself emperor, making a Concordat with the Church, and creating a new "nobility" that was distinct from the hereditary noblesse of the prior regime. On the other hand, he spread many of the revolution's achievements to the rest of Europe and beyond.

Napoleon was once deposed after military defeat and sent to an island exile, but he escaped and briefly resumed his efforts before being defeated again at Waterloo. Following Napoleon's demise, France saw the restoration of the old Bourbon monarchy that had lost power in the great revolution of 1789. Louis XVIII and Charles X governed as constitutional monarchs (Furet 1995: 270–272), however, even if they and some of their supporters might have preferred absolutism. In other words, there was no full return to the political and social system from before the revolution.

In 1830, Charles X was replaced by Louis-Philippe (also a Bourbon but from the more liberal Orleans branch of the family) in the "July Revolution" (see Parry and Girard 2002: 55–59). Called the "Citizen King" because of his stronger and more consistent support for the "constitutional" in "constitutional monarchy," Louis-Philippe would hold the throne until 1848, when a revolutionary wave shook Europe. In France, this brought about the "Second Republic." By the end of the year, Louis-Napoleon Bonaparte was elected president. The nephew of the former Emperor, he declared *himself* Emperor Napoleon III in 1851, ending the Second Republic and ushering in the Second Empire. Napoleon III was known for encouraging industrialization and economic modernization, and Paris was redesigned under his watch, producing much of the infrastructure and plan for the city as it is known today (Parry and Girard 2002: 63–69; Schwartz 2011: 60–61). This was also a time of increasing French geopolitical ambitions, as Napoleon III waged military campaigns, increased French colonial activity, and invaded Mexico, installing a member of the Hapsburg family as Emperor Maximilian there in the 1860s. Eventually, though, military activity was Napoleon III's downfall. He was defeated by Bismarck's Prussia in the Franco-Prussian War of 1870 and almost immediately lost power in France. This transition marked the beginning of France's Third Republic.

The Third Republic—which would last up until World War II—is considered by some to have been a French "golden age," the "Belle Epoque," as it is often called (Parry and Girard 2002: 74). It was a period of great flowering in the arts and literature, but it also saw a great deal of political and social activity and controversy, and has been seen by many in France as a period of instability. Perhaps most famously, it witnessed the "Dreyfus Affair" in which a Jewish officer was falsely accused of spying for Germany. It is hard to exaggerate how important this event was for intellectuals and politicians, who saw it as about more than just the guilt or innocence of one man, but rather about the nature of French culture and identity. Dreyfus's accusers were thought of as conservative, even reactionary, often Catholic, and in some cases anti-Semitic. Some viewed them as heirs to the supporters of monarchy and empire from previous centuries. Dreyfus's supporters were thought of as secular, and often socialists. Some viewed them as the heirs of the Republican tradition (for more on the Dreyfus Affair, see Begley 2009).

France was badly shaken by World War I. Like the rest of the participants in other countries, neither the army, nor the politicians, nor the citizens of France fully anticipated the nature of trench warfare, with its enormous loss of life, terrible conditions, and seemingly infinite stalemates. The country was eventually among the victors, but the conflict played an important role in producing the next European crisis. France insisted that Germany pay huge indemnities, and its preparatory strategy for the next possible war with Germany was based on its experiences in World War I, preparing a single, supposedly impregnable, line of defense called the Maginot line.

The indemnity imposed on Germany contributed to the economic and social problems that conditioned Hitler's rise to power. While Hitler rose in Germany, France saw a different pattern, most notably with the left-wing "Popular Front" government headed by Leon Blum, which was formed in 1936 (Parry and Girard 2002: 163–169). The short-lived government was accompanied by strike and labor mobilization; but France was highly polarized in this period, and the Popular Front government was over by 1938. When war came, Germany bypassed the Maginot Line with relative ease. The French state collapsed, and the Vichy Government was established under Marshall Philippe Pétain, one of the leaders of the army that had just failed so miserably in stopping the German assault. This government was long seen as essentially a puppet of the German occupiers, though more recent historical evidence suggests that the Vichy government played an active role in decision making and collaborated more willingly with the Nazis, even participating in the deportation of Jews. At the same time, many thousands of French men and women participated actively in the resistance, as well as in the Free French, led by Charles De Gaulle.

After the allied victory, De Gaulle would become president of the "Fourth Republic." During this period, France focused on reconstruction and economic development, assisted by the United States' Marshall Plan. De Gaulle soon left power, but he was called back in 1958, in the midst of crisis over French colonial affairs in Algeria. The new (and current) constitution was written, and France's contemporary "mixed presidentialist" system was established. France went through several decades of strong economic performance and *relative* political stability. In this same period, France lost most of its imperial possessions, especially with decolonization in Africa in 1960.

A prominent feature of France's post-war politics has been the process of European integration, which has often been led by France in tandem with democratic Germany. The early years of integration were especially dramatic because the two countries had been the central belligerents in continental European wars from Napoleon to Hitler. Beginning in 1950, France and Germany—along with Italy, Belgium, the Netherlands, and Luxembourg—agreed to free and open trade in coal and steel. This was seen as economically significant, but even more important symbolically and politically, as it meant the two countries would be openly trading the raw materials needed for war. Further integration came in 1957, when the Treaty of Rome extended the economic cooperation to create a European Economic Community. Further extensions of the European project came with expansion to many other countries (now twenty-seven), and the deepening of integration through free trade, free flows of labor and capital, and the creation of today's common currency, the euro. The former European Coal and Steel Community of 1950 has now become the broader and deeper European Union (EU).

Today France is considered to be, with Germany, one of the two most powerful state-level actors in the EU. Yet it faces a number of significant questions. Several of these are policy questions, and one is about politics itself. First, has its system of immigration and assimilation broken down? Second, what will happen to the French welfare state? Is it in need of reforms, and if so, which reforms, and will it be politically possible to produce them? Finally, what will France's role be in the Europe of the future, given the enormous questions that the EU now faces as it struggles to coordinate region-wide monetary policy with state-level fiscal policy? One of the intriguing facts about contemporary France is the degree to which many of these policy decisions will be made at a European level.

Historical Development

Timeline

800	Charlemagne consolidates rule in much of Western Europe.
1000s–1700s	Rivalry between France and Britain through Middle Ages includes numerous wars.
1334–1453	Hundred Years' War between France and Britain
1643	Louis XIV becomes King of France, rules for over 70 years.
1789	French Revolution begins with the storming of Bastille prison; self-proclaimed National Assembly issues Declaration of the Rights of Man and Citizen.
1793	The most violent part of the French Revolution begins, known as the Reign of Terror; King Louis XVI executed by guillotine.
1799	Napoleon's Seizure of Power
1804	Napoleon's Coronation as Emperor
1812	Russian invasion
1814 1815	Napoleon's defeat and imprisonment; Napoleon returns, but is soon defeated by British at Battle of Waterloo.
1814–1830	Bourbon Restoration of Louis XVIII (1814–1824) and Charles X (1824–1830)
1830	July Revolution
1830–1848	July Monarchy of Louis-Philippe ("Citizen King")
1848–1852	Revolution of 1848 and the Second Republic
1848	Louis-Napoleon Bonaparte elected President of the Republic
1852	Louis-Napoleon Bonaparte named Emperor Napoleon III, beginning the "Second Empire" (1852–1870)
1870–1871	Franco-Prussian War, in which France is soundly defeated
1870	The Second Empire ends shortly after Napoleon III's forces are defeated by Prussia (under Bismarck) at the Battle of Sedan in September 1870.
1870–1940	Third Republic
1871	Paris Commune
1894	Conviction of Alfred Dreyfus
1906	Dreyfus declared to be innocent
1914–1918	First World War
1936	Short-lived "Popular Front" government
1939–1945	Second World War
1940–1944	Vichy Government, which collaborates with the Nazis
1944–1946	After the fall of the Vichy government, a provisional government is in place.
1946–1958	Fourth Republic
1954–1962	War in Algeria, culminating in Algerian independence in 1962
1958–Present	Fifth Republic
1958	Constitution establishes "Mixed Presidentialist" system
1966	France leaves NATO
1968	Major student protests in Paris (and numerous other countries)
1981	François Mitterrand is elected president (the only Socialist elected to this post during the Fifth Republic) and governs until 1995.
1995–2007	Presidency of Jacques Chirac
1999	France adopts the euro.
2007–2012	Presidency of Nicolas Sarkozy
2009	France returns to NATO.
2017–present	Presidency of Emmanuel Macron

It should be noted, though, that France (like other countries in the EU) has a national veto on most important matters.

In terms of politics, France today faces a version of a question faced by many other countries as well: what will become of its populist movement amidst the declining popularity of traditional parties and seeming realignment of old electoral coalitions? The Socialist Party can no longer count on the support of so-called working class voters, a number of whom now support the National Front and its allies. The 2017 election of Emmanuel Macron was interpreted by many as a rejection of the populist right, but he himself was not a member of an established party and represents a kind of discontent with those traditional parties.

Regime and Political Institutions

France has a *semi-presidential* system of government, also called a *presidential-parliamentary* system. This hybrid has both a directly elected president and a prime minister, with the former the head of state and the latter the head of government. Presidential elections are followed by elections to the legislature, after which the president nominates a prime minister to run the government. However, prime ministers serve at the discretion of the legislature, and the lower house (the *Assemblée Nationale*, or National Assembly) may force resignation of the government at any time by a simple majority voting for censure. In practice, this has meant that the president appoints a prime minister only after consulting the leader of the largest party in the legislature to determine the latter's wishes.

The upper legislative chamber, the Senate, has nearly coequal powers with the National Assembly, but the National Assembly takes the lead on most legislative debates and legislation. A sophisticated system of checks and balances includes the president's ability to dissolve the legislature and call new elections, but no more than once in any given year. By convention, the prime minister has greater power over domestic politics and the president more power over foreign affairs; but these lines can be blurred, especially when the president and the legislative majority are from different parties, a situation known as *cohabitation*.

Regime and Political Institutions

Regime	Republic, democratic
Administrative Divisions	Eighteen regions (of which thirteen are in "metropolitan France" and five are overseas); smaller divisions are departments, arrondissements, cantons, and communes
Executive Branch	Semi-presidential; president and prime minister
Selection of Executive	Direct election of president, in two rounds, with second-round runoff between top two candidates, appointed prime minister
Legislative Branch	Bicameral Lower chamber: National Assembly (*Assemblée Nationale*); Upper chamber: Senate (*Sénat*)
Judicial Branch	Several top authorities: Court of Cassation (*Cour de cassation*) as court of final appeal for individuals; appointed Constitutional Council (*Conseil constitutionnel*) has authority to rule laws unconstitutional and invalid
Political Party System	Multiparty system with several parties in Parliament, generally with one large party on the center-right (the Union for a Popular Movement, UMP) and the Socialist Party on the center-left; also the National Front (far right), Communist Party (far left), and other moderate and fringe parties

Finally, a judicial body known as the Constitutional Council has the power to review major laws before their passage and can rule them unconstitutional and thus invalid; this council may also hear appeals to laws and similarly rule on constitutionality. The Council is composed of nine members, three each appointed by the president and the leaders of the two legislative houses, as well as all former French presidents not actively involved in politics.

Political Culture

Probably the most distinctive feature of French political culture is the historical divide between a left-wing, secularist, republicanism and a more conservative and less egalitarian alternative, often associated with Roman Catholicism. We do not wish to caricature the distinction between these two strands of French political culture. They have each changed a good deal over time, and their underlying political coalitions have been in flux in recent years. For example, few on the French left today favor the direct assault on the church that many eighteenth- and nineteenth-century revolutionaries did; and the French right is no longer royalist. Moreover, both traditions have favored political centralism, and some would say authoritarian centralism. Nevertheless, here follow ideal-typical sketches of the two traditions.

Both right- and left-wing thought in France had origins among the eighteenth-century *philosophes*, and the very designations "left" and "right" emerged in the French Revolution. From the beginning, the French left radically opposed hierarchy and royalty, promoting democracy and republicanism as alternatives. Viewing the Roman Catholic Church as linked to royal politics and the nobility (and indeed being the "First Estate" prior to the Revolution), and noting its substantial control over land, schooling, and much lawmaking, a radical left aimed to eliminate these "regressive" social actors. This tradition was largely critical of Napoleon as well as the Second Empire of Napoleon III (1852–1870). Over the course of the nineteenth century, many of its proponents turned to socialism and communism. Although by the middle of the twentieth century, it was clear that communism on the Soviet model was not a viable option for France, the communists were important in the resistance against Hitler. Many communists were seen as national heroes of the Resistance, and aspects of communist ideology remained popular with intellectuals and the working classes. After World War II, the larger French left favored social democracy and helped to construct the French welfare state.

The right-wing tradition is also quite heterogeneous and has also changed over time. Some of the supporters of the restoration monarchies of Louis XVIII and Charles X were out-and-out royalists, but even they were relatively few. In the nineteenth century, the French right favored maintaining and even expanding the privileges of the Catholic Church. Supporters included not only the remnants of the old nobility but also wealthy industrialists. More than anything, they favored the maintenance of social order.

Over the course of the late nineteenth century, a nationalism of the right grew in France (Brubaker 1992: 11-12), suspicious of "cosmopolitanism" and often anti-Semitic. Though most scholars think this was confined to a minority, it became important by the early years of the twentieth century. This tradition may have witnessed its most extreme expression in the collaborating Vichy regime during World War II. It lives on in the National Front party of Jean-Marie Le Pen (now run

by his daughter, Marine Le Pen), a xenophobic party that is above all preoccupied with immigration, especially immigration by Muslims, while also having a history of anti-Semitism. This group was for many years politically marginal; though the elder Le Pen did finish in second place in the presidential elections of 2002, the vast majority voted against him. Marine le Pen did well in the first round of the 2012 elections, however; and, indeed, Nicholas Sarkozy moved to the right on immigration issues in the final round in an effort to attract her supporters. (Many commentators viewed this move as a strategic mistake, contributing to Hollande's 2012 victory.) Perhaps even more surprising, the National Front did very well in the 2014 EU Parliament elections, shocking many observers, both in France and internationally. It is worth noting, though, that this was not a specifically French development; right-wing parties did very well in the 2014 European parliamentary elections more generally. In still more recent years, the National Front's influence has grown. Marine Le Pen came in second in the first round of the 2017 presidential election and faced Emmanuel Macron in the second round, losing, but garnering approximately 34 percent of the votes. Remarkably, the Socialist Party candidate won only about 6% of the votes in that election. Macron stands outside of the traditional party structure. His party, "On the March," presents itself as a technocratic alternative to traditional parties. Analysts debate the extent to which he stands outside the traditional clash of ideologies discussed in this section.

Over the years, French political culture has developed a strong center that builds on a compromise between the two traditions noted here. Historically, both the socialists and the leading right-of-center parties have supported maintaining the welfare state, status quo in terms of church–state relations, though they disagree about some of the details. As in much of the post-industrial world, though, analysts now wonder about the stability of that traditional consensus.

Political Economy

France has one of the most advanced economies, and has had for some time. Measured in terms of the Human Development Index, its citizens live in one of the twenty best-off economies in the world. The French economy is among the ten largest in the world, whether this is measured in terms of simply income or in terms of what income can buy, and it has one of the highest GDPs per capita in the world. Moreover, citizens benefit from relatively generous welfare state benefits that are discussed

further a bit later in this section. They also pay higher taxes than citizens in countries with less generous welfare states: indeed, government revenues amount to nearly 50 percent of GDP.

The French economy has historically privileged an important role for the state, through regulation, government ownership of firms, and redistributive efforts. In recent years, as societies with welfare states entered into a period of "retrenchment" following the economic crises of the 1970s, there were some efforts to scale back this state involvement, particularly under conservative presidents Jacques Chirac and Nicolas Sarkozy. The state has partially divested itself from some of its holdings, though it has had a bit more trouble freeing itself from welfare obligations and deregulating the labor market, as it has faced public resistance when it has attempted to do so.

The French economy in some ways is a typical "post-industrial" economy. Note that this does not mean that there is no industry, but rather that services are dominant. Indeed, industry accounts for 19.6 percent of GDP. Agriculture only accounts for 1.6 percent, with services accounting for a full 78.8 percent of GDP (2016 estimate, per *CIA World Factbook*).

France has relatively low income inequality, near the average for eurozone countries. Its Gini index is 29.2 (2015 estimate reported in the *CIA World Factbook*), where 0 would mean perfect equality and 100 would mean perfect inequality. To put this in perspective, the United States has a Gini index of over 40, and some countries have figures around 70! France also has relatively low poverty. Historically it has suffered from relatively high levels of unemployment, which some analysts have attributed to the rigidity of its highly regulated labor market. Some would argue that this is due to the French state's ongoing involvement in the economy. However, other advanced economies have, sadly, "caught up" with France in unemployment. Some, notably its neighbor to the south, Spain, have far more serious unemployment problems.

The French welfare state has been resilient in the face of efforts to roll it back (Prasad 2006). It has, as noted previously, seen considerable privatization, and there have been pushes toward deregulation; but the state continues to play an enormous role in the French economy, employing numerous citizens and capturing a large share of the GDP. Moreover, state services continue to be fairly generous in comparative terms. Comparative analysts have identified several reasons for this. First, there is the French tradition of statism that we have mentioned. Second, while the modern French welfare state had roots in the leftist *Front Populaire* alliance in the late 1930s, it is important to note that some important features of the French welfare state were created, expanded, and maintained by conservatives. In the Fifth Republic, De Gaulle established a long tradition of conservative electoral success. Indeed, while in the United Kingdom and the United States, the 1980s saw attacks on the welfare state as conservative parties returned to power, in France, the Socialists finally took power in 1981 when François Mitterand was elected (1981–1995). Thus, on one hand, the conservatives were identified with the welfare state; and on the other, during the moment when the right was attempting to dismantle aspects of the welfare state in other countries, the left held power in France.

Another key feature of the French welfare state that may help to preclude attacks on it is that (1) many of its benefits are not radically redistributive (Esping-Anderson 1990: 27) and (2) a significant portion of state revenues come from a consumption tax called a Value-Added Tax (or VAT, similar to state-level sales taxes found in the United States). Why would this matter? According to some scholars (Prasad 2006), consumption taxes are less likely to be perceived as unfair by political opponents of the welfare state, and thus less likely to generate strong opposition.

CASE STUDIES

CASE STUDY

The State in France

CHAPTER 3, PAGE 60

Within the comparative European context, France is thought of as having historically had a strong state. While we would not recognize the French state of the seventeenth century as "strong" in the twenty-first-century world, in its time it was more unified and it more consistently controlled its territory than many of its competitors.

For this reason, many historians have thought of the French state of Louis XIV as serving as the epitome of European absolutism. It is perhaps as a result of this strong absolutist state that the modern French state has been so centralist. The French Revolution had a well-institutionalized, if fiscally unsound, state to transform, and

in the post-revolutionary years the state was expanded, with new layers of administration added. Over the course of the nineteenth century, the state's reach and dominance over local society increased slowly but surely (Weber 1976).

The French economy has featured a prominent role for the state for many years, especially when contrasted with Great Britain and the United States. This has been true at least since the time of Jean-Baptiste Colbert, a seventeenth-century economic thinker. France was one of the earliest of economic modernizers and was a great economic power in the eighteenth century. The modern French economy with its significant state involvement—known as *dirigisme*—is a product of the immediate aftermath of the Second World War. President Charles de Gaulle nationalized key industries and used the state to promote recovery from the damage of the war, while American aid in the form of the post-war Marshall Plan contributed to reconstruction. The program was successful: France achieved solid growth and marked improvements in the standard of living in the three decades from about 1945 to about 1975, known as the *trente glorieuses* ("glorious thirty").

Under recent president Nicolas Sarkozy, there was great debate about the role that the state would continue to play in the economy. On one hand, there is the question of whether future economic competitiveness can coexist with the general support of workers' rights that state regulation makes possible. On the other hand, there is the ongoing question of the state's ability to make economic policy. Monetary policy is already carried out at the EU level, and there is now some talk of the centralization of European fiscal policy as well, though it is too early to tell whether this will take place.

Heir to a revolutionary tradition that figures prominently in its national consciousness, the French state has often aimed to present itself as the defender of "the people," including workers. The French state has heavily regulated the labor market, for example, by implementing a thirty-five-hour work week and by establishing strong protections against layoffs and firings. The state directly employs a relatively large proportion of the workforce, totaling 5.4 million workers and over 20 percent of the total workforce as of the end of 2014 (DGAFP *Annual Report 2014*). It has also provided generous stipends to the unemployed. Perhaps as a result, France has often struggled with higher levels of unemployment than some other developed countries. Former president Sarkozy tried to overturn some of these regulations but was stymied by public protests.

The French state has historically played a critical role in French national consciousness. Citizenship, understood as a kind of relationship that an individual has with the state, has historically been key to French national identity (Brubaker 1992; Greenfeld 1992). This is reinforced by the strongly centralist institutional structure of the French state. Loyalty is owed to the central state as the institutional embodiment of the nation and not to other identities or institutions that mediate between citizens and the state.

Nobody doubts France's democratic credentials. In the late twentieth and early twenty-first centuries, it was among the world's leading democracies. Moreover, its 1789 revolution was and remains a source of inspiration to pro-democracy forces everywhere (even if it did not immediately culminate in a democracy). Indeed, it is precisely because of the country's democratic achievements that it is worth reflecting on the challenges that France faced in institutionalizing its democracy. If France, of all countries, encountered such difficulties, should we expect anything less for today's democratizers? In short, the French case underscores the difficulty of democratic consolidation.

We will not repeat the sequence described in the "Historical Development" section of the country profile. It is enough to note that the revolution, which deposed the monarchy, passed through a republican period, to the "terror," and eventually to Napoleon's rule, which was despotic by any modern definition. This was followed by the restoration of

Authoritarian Persistence in Nineteenth-Century France   CHAPTER 7, PAGE 160

the previous monarchy; and then the "July Monarchy" of the "Citizen-King," Louis-Philippe; and finally, by the Second Republic (1848–1852). The Second Empire (of Napoleon III) lasted from 1852 to 1870, when, following France's defeat in the Franco-Prussian war, the "Third Republic" began (for an authoritative overview of this period, see Furet [1988] 1995). Indeed, even in the twentieth century, France saw considerable conflict between democratic and authoritarian tendencies, finally put to rest in the post–World War II period.

In short, French political history in the nineteenth century presents us with a range of political and social models, instability, and considerable authoritarian persistence. Why did these occur? One hypothesis might be the collapse of the existing order. Perhaps the elimination of well-established, if flawed, political models left the political arena too open

to contestation. Indeed, if the monarchy could be abolished, was anything beyond question, negotiation, or dispute?

Another idea comes from Alexis de Tocqueville, the great observer of both American and French society. As we saw elsewhere in this book, he found much to admire about the participatory-democratic habits and decentralization of American politics. In contrast, he thought that a key problem in France was the lack of these habits (because institutions had not encouraged them) alongside a centralized state and a revolution that had awakened a passionate distrust of all inequalities without providing opportunities for French citizens to develop democratic freedoms (see Tocqueville [1856] 2002, esp. pp. 310–311).

Another approach might emphasize the legacies of inequalities themselves: the revolution aimed to abolish the

nobility, but of course privilege lived on; and both old and new social elites and the church did what they could to protect their interests as they saw them (for one variation of this argument, see Marx [1852] 2007). If it was clear to such actors that their opponents meant for their elimination, this would have major implications for their strategic decisions. The same is true of their opponents.

Think about how a rational-choice approach (e.g., that of Lichbach 1995, or Kuran 1991) might model the situation in which these actors found themselves and how such an approach might try to explain the sequence of unstable politics found in nineteenth-century France. Then think about the implications of the French case for contemporary democratizers. Can we compare such cases over time? And, if so, are there any limits on our ability to do so?

Electing the French President: What Do Runoffs Do?   CHAPTER 10, PAGE 234

In France in 2002, most voters were shocked as the results came in for the first round of presidential voting. In the first round of French elections, the nationwide popular vote is tallied for the many candidates, and a candidate is elected only if he or she secures an outright majority, which is uncommon. In the absence of a majority, the top two candidates have a runoff to determine the winner. This system allows citizens to vote for their most preferred

candidate in the first round, then vote for an "electable" candidate in the second round. Typically, the runoff had amounted to a showdown between the leading candidate of the center-right (often called the "Gaullist" candidate after French war hero and later president Charles de Gaulle) and the candidate of the center-left Socialist Party. But in 2002, with the first-round vote split between many candidates on the left, the Socialist performed poorly and came

in third with 16 percent, behind center-right candidate Jacques Chirac (just under 20 percent) and the far-right candidate, Jean-Marie Le Pen, leader of the National Front, who took just under 17 percent of the vote. The runoff came down to the right versus the far right.

For some, Le Pen's first-round success served as a condemnation of the French practice of having elections with a "runoff" between the top two candidates: it gave a huge platform and political spotlight to a candidate on the fringe (though the National Front has done surprisingly well in subsequent elections). What happened next had the opposite effect, though it was predictable: Jacques Chirac won 82 percent of the vote in the runoff, and Le Pen won less than 18 percent. Chirac thus took nearly all of the vote that had gone to all other candidates in the first round and won the presidency overwhelmingly, and Le Pen barely increased his tally at all despite the elimination of all other candidates. Turnout also increased in the second round, despite the fact that Chirac's win was near certain, as French voters turned out overwhelmingly (while also taking to the streets in protest) to vote against Le Pen.

When *Marine* Le Pen ran in 2017, many observers were less surprised when she, like her father before her, came in second. By this time, a global wave of populist candidates had already drawn a great deal of media attention, and Le Pen's candidacy caused considerable anxiety among those opposed to that populist wave. Again, opponents of the right coalesced around the other candidate, but this time Le Pen won almost 34% of the second round vote. Moreover, overall turnout this time did not increase in the second round, but dropped by almost 5 million votes.

This raises the issue of whether runoffs are good or bad for representation and democracy. Some regarded the 2002 Le Pen result in the first round as an anomaly, and proponents of the system can argue that it performed exactly as intended: it allowed French voters to express their initial preference, then weeded out the more extreme candidate. It also signaled the frustration of voters with the Socialist Party, which could have allowed that party to reshape its platform for the future rather than simply resting on its laurels as the presumptive leader of the left. One might argue that the 2017 election showed the same lessons. Macron still won in a landslide, though not as dramatically as had Chirac. Others could worry, though, that the top four candidates all had very similar vote totals in the first round (all around 20–25 percent of the total votes). Could a future election lead to a second round in which both candidates were judged to be extreme and non-representative by the majority of the electorate?

It is also important to note that in both cases, the runoff ensured that the individual elected president ultimately received more than 50 percent of the votes in a presidential election, which would not be true if the victory were awarded to whoever won a plurality in the first round. That is, in a runoff system, the president ends up with a clear mandate of over half of French voters electing him or her. This contrasts with the American model, for example, in which it is relatively common for presidents to win the presidency with less than 50 percent of the popular vote (a list that includes, in recent memory, Bill Clinton, George W. Bush, and Donald Trump). It should also be noted that voter turnout is much higher in French elections than in the United States and many other countries, at about 80 percent in most presidential elections and 60 percent in parliamentary elections (International IDEA 2011).

For these reasons, runoffs are currently used in elections in a large number of countries, including for parliamentary districts in France itself. The runoff features frequently in elections in Latin America and Africa, where presidentialism is common. In these countries, there are particular historical and social reasons that can make the runoff appealing. In Chile in 1970, the Marxist Salvador Allende was confirmed president by Congress after receiving less than 37 percent of the vote; three years later, a military coup to overthrow the elected president resulted in nearly two decades of brutal dictatorship. And in Africa, presidential elections can result in voting along ethnic lines in the first round but broader coalition building across ethnic lines to win in the second round. It is worth considering how history might have been different—and whether violence and democracy would be affected—if a French-style runoff system had existed in Chile in 1970 or did not exist in some African countries today.

CHAPTER 12, PAGE 289

CASE STUDY
The French Revolution

The French Revolution took place amid major structural problems in eighteenth-century French society (Furet 1995; Doyle 2003). In this period, France, like much of early modern Europe, remained an "estate society," divided into three groups: a nobility with special privileges, the clergy, and commoners. The social status of the nobility, however, was weakened by the ongoing efforts of the centralizing, absolutist crown. As the monarchy and its state grew stronger, the nobility felt increasingly marginalized. At the same time, the French absolutist state, largely through its involvement in foreign wars (especially the American Revolution), faced major fiscal difficulties (Doyle 2003). Indeed, by the late eighteenth century, it was nearly bankrupt. Meanwhile, periodic problems in food distribution and rural poverty ensured that much of France's rural population felt discontent. Finally, the spread of the Enlightenment and of nationalism provided the bases for an intellectual critique of the old regime (Greenfeld 1992; Bell 2001).

The revolution began as a series of efforts to reform the French state. The crown called an "Assembly of Notables," but the assembly declared that the Estates General, which had not met since the early seventeenth century, needed to be called. When the Estates General convened, it was divided in the customary manner into the three estates mentioned previously. However, before long, politics and propaganda forced representatives of the first two estates to join the latter one, the core idea being that the French nation shouldn't be divided by estates because all of its members should be equal. The third estate *was* the nation, as Sieyes declared (Furet 1995: 45–51). In other words, the Estates General was reinterpreted as being something like a modern, national legislature (though the leaders of the Estates General remained bourgeois and nobles, along with some clergy, and not "popular" actors).

Reform quickly devolved into a novel form of collective behavior that was surprising even to its most central participants and those who attempted to lead and control it. Street actions began, and mobs attacked the Bastille prison on July 14, 1789, wishing to destroy a reviled symbol of the arbitrary authority of the monarch to imprison opponents at will. By 1792, the monarchy had fallen amid increasing violence—much perpetrated by mobs known as the "*sans culottes*"—opening a period known as the "Terror" in which perceived enemies of the revolution were murdered in large numbers. Robespierre was a key figure in this period, perpetrating the paranoid violence that ultimately consumed him. This was followed by a period of relaxation known as the "Thermidorian reaction," and, finally, by the rise of Napoleon. On one hand, Napoleon appears a conservative figure, since, for example, he declared himself emperor. But on the other hand, he can be viewed as a revolutionary whose mission was to spread the French Revolution to the rest of Europe, through an imperial war.

What struck so many contemporaries was the Revolution's *destructive* nature. It seemed intent on an eradication of the old society and the replacement of all of its forms by new, "revolutionary" ones. This included the creation of a new, revolutionary calendar, the efforts to destroy the Church and its teachings, the war on the nobility, the destruction of many architectural sites, and so forth. The French revolution subsequently became the model for many later revolutionaries and its ideals inspirational for nationalists and republicans everywhere. At the same time, it surprised nearly everyone involved, and those who attempted to control it quickly learned that they had helped to unleash social forces beyond their ability to lead (Arendt 1963).

CHAPTER 15, PAGE 363

CASE STUDY
Religion and Secularism in France

France is the society most closely associated with the idea of *laïcité*, though one encounters it prominently in a number of other societies as well, including parts of Latin America (Blancarte 2008). France was historically a Catholic society. For a time, there had been a relatively large Protestant minority (the "Huguenots"), but they were repressed and most fled after 1685, when Louis XIV revoked the Edict of Nantes that had granted freedom of conscience and practice to Protestants. France's Catholicism was central to its early modern identity.

Most scholars see French secularism as having its origins in the eighteenth century. Religion and politics had been closely linked in continental Europe for a long time, but the church and the state had experienced considerable tension at certain points in the history of their relationship. As the French absolutist state rose, a theological position known as Jansenism, and a political theory known as Regalism, helped the king to exert greater control over the church. After the French Revolution began in 1789, republicans and revolutionaries identified the church with the "old regime" (Kuru 2009) and thus repressed it, murdering many priests. The French Revolutionary regime tried to create its own, secular religion and to replace religious symbols with its own, secular ones. This was changed by Napoleon, who concluded an agreement (known as a "concordat") with the church; but even then, the state dominated the church, and the church never returned to its former powers. Subsequent French history witnessed multiple struggles between monarchy/empire and democratic republicanism (Furet 1995), with the former being more closely associated with a pro-Church position. Democratic republicanism was eventually triumphant, though; and over time, French Catholicism (along with other, minority religions) was "privatized" (on privatization, see Casanova 1994). In today's France, the view that the Catholic Church should have an expanded rule in politics is marginal.

In recent years this has been linked to great controversy, particularly because immigration has notably increased the Islamic share of the French population. Great debates have been held over whether religious garb (in particular, the Muslim *hijab*) can be worn in schools and other public organizational spaces (Scott 2007; Zaretsky 2016). Opponents of traditionally Islamic symbolism in public have drawn on long-standing national mythology about *laïcité*, though their critics suggest that this is a cover for unspoken ethnic discrimination; and recent, careful, social scientific work by Adida, Laitin, and Valfort (2016)—discussed in an Insights box in chapter 15—suggests that religiously based discrimination against Muslims is notable in contemporary France. The fundamental conflict has concerned not whether members of religious groups should be able to practice their religion, but whether they should be able to engage in religious expression (including clothing) in public settings. It is worth noting further that to some extent, this issue cuts across the French political spectrum.

France's relationship with globalization has been complex. In the late nineteenth century, France was a lead "globalizer." If you travel in the developing world today, you may learn that the architecture built in the nineteenth century had a marked French style; this is a visible indicator of French influence at one point in time. French ideas were extraordinarily popular around the globe in this period, at least in more cosmopolitan social sectors in many societies. Especially influential was the idea of positivism, that science and reason could contribute to the betterment of society. In the late nineteenth century, the culture with the broadest global reach was almost certainly French, though the British Empire ensured global expansiveness for British culture as well.

In the twentieth century, though, France grew more ambivalent about globalization. Perhaps this is because rather than being a net exporter of cultural forms, it began to import them. France continued to be influential in global culture, especially in its former colonies; but in many ways, its leading position was overtaken by the United States. Globalization has taken on new forms and grown, with new media and new patterns of communication, and the influence of American ideas and culture has spread. One indicator of this rise of "Anglo-Saxon" culture has been the replacement of French, which was long the language of diplomacy, with English as the dominant language in international affairs. Less formally, but perhaps more consequentially, cultural forces from Hollywood to hip hop have reshaped French film, literature, music, and the arts.

French ambivalence about globalization also reflects economic ideas, especially about global capitalism. This dates back centuries. In the early modern period, royal ministers exhorted nobles to engage in commerce; but many rejected this idea, convinced that commerce would "disparage" (*déroger*) nobility (Furet 1995; Greenfeld 2001). Important early socialist works, many of which predated and anticipated Marx, developed in France. In the late eighteenth century, Rousseau and others developed the critique that modern social relations were corrupting; this later found expression on both left and right, and in both radical democratic movements and with more extreme opposition to capitalism and democracy. Within the French economy itself, there has often been an emphasis on craftsmanship and small-scale production. At the same time, France in the twentieth century did establish major corporations, but often did so with state

support; examples of major French companies that were state-owned or nationalized at one time include the car company Renault, the oil giant Total, and several major banks and utilities.

A common refrain in France has been the need to develop in a "French way," resisting Americanization and globalization. Economically, this is linked to common tropes in French culture: societies fully immersed in global capitalism "live to work," whereas some French citizens would argue that the French "work to live." France has thus been somewhat skeptical of multinational businesses and of the consequences of international trade agreements, and it has even tried to limit the spread and use of English words in French business. This is not simply a matter of the French government but important segments of the citizenry as well. One example is José Bové, an activist and "farmer" who destroyed a McDonald's restaurant under construction in 1999. This action was well received by many members of the French public, and Bové is a well-known figure in France, though his popularity has its limits; when he later ran for president, he received less than 2 percent of the vote. On the other hand, he is not a typical "French farmer." His parents were university researchers, and he spent part of his childhood in California. In any case, some took his stance to be a fairly extreme expression of a common sentiment.

While ambivalent about some aspects of globalization, France has also been a key mover of deeper integration in continental Europe in the period since

World War II. It has sought to develop strong economic ties to Germany and other economies while developing in a way that relies heavily on elements of free markets yet continues to guarantee an active role for the state in the economy. It has been a strong supporter of the EU; and in 2011, France, along with Germany, exercised a considerable influence over how the EU responded to the fiscal crises in Greece and Italy and worries over Portugal and Spain as well. Marine Le Pen's 2017 election campaign, though, gave voice to Euroskepticism; and there is no guarantee that France will continue to promote deeper European integration in the coming years.

France also retains major global linkages to former colonies, particularly in North Africa and sub-Saharan Africa. North African migrants—especially from Algeria and Morocco—constitute an important group in French society, one that pushes the boundaries of cultural change, given that some members of that group are perceived to be less than receptive to traditional French notions of *laïcité* (see the Introduction and the "Religion and Secularism" case study for more information on this).

Together, these debates about economics and cultural identity suggest a society that has conflicting and perhaps contradictory views about the desirability of globalization; in this, France shares many challenges with other countries—including the United States—that grapple with the tough issues of how to respond as nations in an international twenty-first century.

Research Prompts

1. France has runoff elections, and the United States does not. What are the major consequences of this difference? Would you expect the consequences of this difference to play out in the same way in a wider range of comparative cases? Why or why not?

2. France is a society that has had many revolutions, and one in which revolution has become a key idea in the culture. Brazil is a society that, despite promoting social change in important, novel, and influential ways, has largely been free of revolutions as such. Can you explain this difference?

3. The French state captures as revenue a considerably larger share of its GDP than many other countries. Why might this be?

4. The French welfare state has survived "retrenchment" more successfully than a number of others, despite some changes, including the privatization of a number of formerly state-owned enterprises. How do you explain its staying power? Will it likely remain strong in the future?

5. The United Kingdom has a fairly small extreme, xenophobic right wing (represented by the British National Party, though note the success of the Brexit referendum, which drew support from the xenophobic right and from others); whereas in France, this group may be a bit larger, at least as judged by the recent electoral showings of the National Front. Is this difference due to different ideas of nationhood, different historical experiences, different patterns of decline of traditional left-wing parties, different political institutions, or something else?

Germany

Key Features of Contemporary Germany

Population:	80,594,017 (estimate, July 2017)
Area:	357,022 square kilometers
Head of State:	Frank-Walter Steinmeier (president, 2017–present)
Head of Government:	Angela Merkel (chancellor, 2005–present)
Capital:	Berlin
Year of Independence:	Unification achieved in 1871; reunification in 1990
Year of Current Constitution:	1949
Languages:	German
GDP per Capita:	$48,100 (*CIA World Factbook* estimate, 2017)
Human Development Index Ranking (2016):	4th (very high human development)

Sources: *CIA World Factbook*; World Bank World Development Indicators; United Nations *Human Development Report 2016*.

Introduction

Germany is a country of enduring interest to political scientists for a number of reasons. Its historical state-building process draws attention, both because of the early success of Prussian state-builders and because of the relatively late development of the unified German state (1871), after years of decentralization and nationalist aspiration. Germany is also of interest because of its development trajectory, as it achieved relatively rapid industrialization and economic growth in the mid to late nineteenth century, and came to be perhaps the preeminent European power shortly after its political unification. The country, as we will see, is frequently cited as a prototypical case of ethnic nationalism, meaning that boundaries between Germans and others are typically understood in ethnic terms rather than determined by citizenship. As such, Germany is frequently contrasted with France, and a robust social-scientific literature seeks to explain this difference (though others critique the distinction). Moreover, there are major debates about whether German political culture is changing or has changed in this connection.

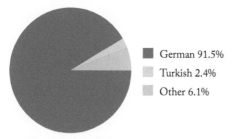

German 91.5%
Turkish 2.4%
Other 6.1%

Ethnic Groups in Germany
Note that most of those in the "other" category are from or descend from citizens of other European societies, including Russia.
Source: CIA World Factbook.

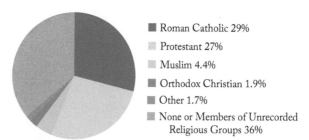

Roman Catholic 29%
Protestant 27%
Muslim 4.4%
Orthodox Christian 1.9%
Other 1.7%
None or Members of Unrecorded Religious Groups 36%

Religious Affiliation in Germany
Source: CIA World Factbook.

Germany is also of interest as a society that has witnessed rapid and consequential political transitions. It has seen authoritarianism (with some democratic features) under Bismarck and Kaiser Wilhelm II, and then democratization in the wake of World War I. Democratic consolidation, however, failed in that period, and the Weimar Republic collapsed by 1933. The country then witnessed the rise of a totalitarian regime. Finally, after Germany's defeat in World War II, it has seen the successful consolidation of a representative democracy, initially in the West but continuing in all of Germany with reunification after the collapse of Soviet power. Indeed, many see potential lessons in the success of this democratic consolidation. Today Germany is a European and global leader, with robustly democratic politics, a strong economy (a highly advanced one that has managed to maintain strength in the export of manufactured goods), and a return to international influence.

Germany's geography has historically been shaped by political division, most notably in the forced separation between East and West Germany after World War II. Previously, much of its long-run history of political disunity caused the region to be dominated by Prussia in the east and Austria (today not a part of Germany) in the south, with smaller states in the west. Religious variation exacerbated subregional differences, with southern parts of the German region having large Catholic populations (in Austria and Bavaria, for example) and with the north tending toward Protestantism. As is the case in much of Western Europe, German society has seen noteworthy secularization. The majority of the country is still nominally Christian, but rates of church attendance are low. There is an increasing Muslim population. Historically many of the Muslims in Germany were Turkish migrants or of Turkish descent. In recent years, immigration from majority-Muslim countries has increased, notably refugees from war in Syria (for more demographic information on Muslims in contemporary Germany see Pew Research Center 2017). The question of how immigrants—including but not limited to religious minorities—will be incorporated into German society remains an important issue of some interest to scholars. Despite secularizing trends, religion still matters in Germany (see discussion in Fetzer and Soper 2005).

Historical Development

Germany's modern history is extraordinarily complex, owing in part to the many political units that composed the state up to the late nineteenth century. Indeed, until 1871, there was no "Germany" in the sense of a single nation-state but rather a complex configuration of smaller states and principalities as well as free towns. Prussia stood out as a strong early state against this background. Moreover, it is not that there was a clear and recognizable "German nation" that was simply awaiting political unification (Berger 2004). Indeed, as historians point out, many residents of Prussia did not speak German, numerous Swiss did (and still do), and there was little consensus about what exactly qualified one as a German (Kitchen 2006: 9; Berger 2004). At the same time, a vague sense of German identity had developed over the course of the eighteenth century. At first, this identity was very "cosmopolitan" and focused on the idea of Germany as a cultural community (Greenfeld 1992; Berger 2004). However, the Napoleonic invasions transformed German identity, leading to efforts to define Germanness *against* what French civilization was taken to represent (Kitchen 2006; Greenfeld 1992).

In the post-Napoleonic years, aspirants to a German nation-state would have to make do with a loose confederation of existing units, established at the Congress of Vienna, with both Austria and Prussia exerting leadership. The period of the confederation was one of modernization and its attendant uncertainties and conflicts: Germany began industrialization, while modern liberals and traditionalists squabbled. There were periods of street contention, most notably in 1848, a year in which many European countries experienced attempted revolutions. More generally in this period, intellectuals and artists developed ideas of German nationhood, and many hoped to see them made into a reality (Berger 2004; Greenfeld 1992). Conflict between these contenders for dominance of the confederation issued in the Austro-Prussian War (1866) in which Austria was defeated. The German Confederation was replaced by a smaller confederation, led by Prussia and excluding Austria and parts of Southern Germany.

The German state would achieve unification in the wake of Prussia's defeat of France in the Franco-Prussian War, sealed at the Battle of Sedan in 1871, which led to the fall of Napoleon III (for a good overview of this period, see Kitchen 2006). The united Germany—which excluded Austria—was organized as an Empire, referred to as the "Second Reich." Otto von Bismarck, a Prussian "Junker" who is considered the architect of unified Germany, and who had led Prussia and the North German Federation in the years prior, was named chancellor, a post that he would hold until 1890.

Bismarck is important not just because of Germany's unification and the way in which Germany's unification influenced European power politics—following the Franco-Prussian War Germany emerged as Europe's central power—but also because of the way he managed domestic politics. Germany was divided between conservatives who supported monarchy, liberals, and socialists and social democrats. Political parties and intellectual groups proliferated, and there were many subtypes of these categories ("old" vs. "new" liberals, etc.). Bismarck governed largely as a conservative but made use of some ideas from the moderate left. Perhaps most important is the establishment of incipient welfare state functions—disability, unemployment, and health insurance, as well as pensions—in the 1880s (Esping-Andersen 1990: 24), to be expanded in the twentieth century (Mares 2001: 60–63; Hentschel 2008: 793–801). These programs were not as generous as later welfare state programs would be, nor as generous as the social democrats wanted. The German imperial state also extended suffrage to all males.

Historical Development

Timeline

1648	Treaty of Westphalia signals rise of modern nation-state system; present-day Germany governed by many principalities.
1815	End of Napoleonic Wars; Congress of Vienna gives rise to loose Germanic Confederation led by Prussia (present-day northern Germany) and Austria.
1834	Establishment of the Zollverein (Customs Union) in the Confederation
1848	Revolutionary upheaval in Europe, including in German states
1864	German-Danish War over Schleswig-Holstein
1866	Led by Chancellor Otto von Bismarck, Prussia defeats powerful Austria in Austro-Prussian War.
1870	Prussia defeats France in Franco-Prussian War.
1871	Unification of Germany under Prussian leadership
1914–1918	World War I. Germany joins Austria-Hungary and Ottoman Empire as Central Powers vs. Great Britain, France, and Russia as Allies; United States enters war on side of Allies in 1916.
1918	Armistice ends World War I, with Great Britain and France demanding reparations from Germany and demilitarization of Rheinland.
1919–1933	Weimar Republic presides over hyperinflation and Great Depression.
1933	Hitler elected chancellor as head of National Socialist (Nazi) Party, establishes "Third Reich."
1939	Germany invades Poland; Great Britain and France declare war on Germany.
1939–1945	World War II. The Holocaust, led by Adolf Hitler and the Nazi Party, results in the extermination of 6 million Jews as well as members of many other groups. Germany invades and occupies much of western Europe, bombs Britain extensively, and invades Russia, but ultimately retreats. Retreat from Russia in 1943 and D-Day in 1944 (Allied invasion of occupied France) signal beginning of the end of Third Reich.
1945	Allies (including Soviet Union, Great Britain, United States, France) take Berlin. Third Reich Falls; Hitler commits suicide. Soviets occupy East Germany; Americans, British, and French occupy West Germany.
1945–1989	Germany divided into Communist East Germany and democratic/capitalist West Germany; major repression in East Germany.
1948	Berlin Airlift
1950	Treaty of Rome begins integration in western Europe of European Community, with West Germany and France leading.
1961	Berlin Wall raised overnight by Soviets and East German regime.
1989	Fall of the Berlin Wall signals end of Communism.
1990	Reunification of East and West Germany as Federal Republic of Germany (Helmut Kohl, chancellor)
1980s–1990s	European integration accelerates (Single European Act, 1987; Maastricht Treaty, 1992 through 1999).
2002	Euro begins circulating as new currency, with Deutschmark phased out.
2005	Angela Merkel becomes Germany's first female chancellor (re-elected most recently in 2017).
2011–2015	Countries in the eurozone face the need for financial bailouts, which are resisted in Germany.
2015	Under the leadership of Angela Merkel, Germany accepts hundreds of thousands of refugees.
2017-2018	Elections led to protracted negotiations that finally culminated in a coalition government with Merkel beginning to serve as chancellor for a fourth term.

In economic terms, late nineteenth-century Germany saw continued industrialization and growth. The country came to rival Britain in many respects (Kitchen 2006). Its economy was particularly strong in some areas such as chemical engineering. Its research universities were important as well, and were emulated elsewhere, including in the United States.

In terms of foreign policy, the state rushed to compete with more established colonial powers in the "scramble for Africa," though Germany never successfully established a large colonial system (Kitchen 2006: 168–169). Bismarck, having alienated France not just through defeating them in the Franco-Prussian War but in taking Alsace-Lorraine as part of the peace settlement, essentially built his foreign policy around manipulating alliances such that France would be unable to make common cause with Russia, Austria, and/or the United Kingdom against the new German state. Perhaps surprisingly, he was able to do so with success, though historians tend to see the settlement of the Franco-Prussian War and the subsequent diplomacy of binding alliances as critical to the development of the First World War.

Leadership was less capable following Bismarck's departure from office in 1890 (Kitchen 2006). After a Serbian nationalist linked to some figures in the Serbian government killed Archduke Franz Ferdinand of Austria, war began, and Germany joined Austria (Davies 1996: 875–895). Russia backed Serbia, and France and the United Kingdom allied with Russia. The United States would soon join the allies as well. World War I was a brutal conflict in which trench warfare was predominant. While some foresaw the implications of new military technology and strategy, many of the combatants and citizens on both sides were shocked by the tragedy of webs of alliances and concerns over national honor leading to years spent in the mud, with millions of deaths in a war that was basically at a stalemate for much of its duration (Weber 1972: 363–370). Its global consequences were far-reaching. As we shall see, it changed German politics forever, but it also produced the circumstances of the Russian Revolution, which led to the formation of the Soviet Union.

Germany's defeat meant the end of the Empire. A new, republican government was formed. The new form of the German state, known as the Weimar Republic because its constitution was established in the city of Weimar, was hampered from the start by a series of difficulties (Fulbrook 1990: 155). Despite great hopes, it would only survive for a bit more than a decade, collapsing as the Nazis ascended to power.

Some of the major problems were consequences of the Treaty of Versailles, which ended World War I. Despite the objections of some if its allies, France insisted on disabling indemnities for Germany to pay indefinitely. This condition generated discontent and provoked resentment among the German population that would later feed into critiques of the Weimar Republic's liberal order, and it also weakened the state's economic position (Fulbrook 1990: 163–164).

The situation was exacerbated when the global depression spread to Germany (James 2009). Society polarized politically, and institutional alterations to the Weimar Republic could not help. The Nazi party did well in the 1930 and 1932 legislative elections, and Hitler came in second, with approximately 37 percent in the presidential elections of 1932 (Kitchen 2006: 249, 251). In 1933, Hitler was appointed chancellor, the position from which he would dismantle the Weimar order and, with it, German democracy.

This brings our short narrative to the infamous period of the Nazi Party's dominance of Germany. Under Hitler, the Nazis quickly moved to undermine the rule of law and the existing constitutional order. They did so both through formal institutional means (e.g., the "Enabling Law" of 1933) and informally, such as during the "night of the long knives" in which the Nazis purged political elites (Fulbrook 1990: 178–187). Germany became a totalitarian police state.

Most alarming of all, the anti-Semitism that had been present in Germany for years (Kitchen 2006: 133–138), and been a prominent part of Hitler's rhetoric, came fully out into the light of day (Fulbrook 1990: 196–203). Jewish identity was legally defined, and a series of discriminatory laws were passed, which increasingly circumscribed German Jews' movement within the society. Violence against Jews became increasingly common, notably the mass violence of the Kristallnacht of 1938. Even more chillingly, the regime aimed to sequester Jews in concentration camps with ultimately genocidal purposes. Historians estimate that around 6 million Jews were murdered by the Nazis. This religious minority suffered more than most, but other groups, such as Poles, Soviet Citizens, Roma, LGBTQ people, and even some Christian religious actors, as well as political activists opposed to the Nazis, were also oppressed and murdered in great numbers.

Hitler's foreign policy was expansionary (Fulbrook 1990: 187–195), and Germany's territorial ambitions led to the Second World War. Germany took Czechoslovakia in 1938 after the famous attempt by Neville Chamberlain to "appease" Hitler at Munich. In 1939, Germany invaded Poland, and World War II began. At first the Soviet Union was not part of the hostilities, Stalin and Hitler having signed a non-aggression pact, but the Nazis had no intention of long-term coexistence with a major socialist power (Kitchen 2006: 297–298, 301–304). While France quickly fell to Germany, the collaborating Vichy regime put in place, Britain and later the Soviet Union fought persistently. They were joined by the United States after Japan's attack on Pearl Harbor in December of 1941. It took until 1945, but the Allies were eventually triumphant, and Germany was partially destroyed in the process.

The effort to reconstruct Germany—economically, politically, and socially—was daunting. The Soviet Union had occupied the eastern portion of the country while the United Kingdom, France, and the United States occupied the west. These would become two distinct states, the Federal Republic of Germany (West Germany) and the German Democratic Republic (East Germany). West Germany embraced liberal democracy and a mixed economy, with strong support for social democracy and a relatively robust welfare state. East Germany became a satellite state of the Soviet Union. Economic reconstruction of West Germany was greatly aided by funds from the United States in the form of the Marshall Plan (Davies 1996: 1080).

Cultural reconstruction was perhaps just as complicated, if not more so. Successive generations of Germans had to redefine their identity after the historical crimes of the Nazis (see discussion in Olick 2005), trying to rehabilitate a sense of Germanness that was not implicated and that would not be likely to issue in a return to militant xenophobia. Against the skeptics, West Germany had success in building a largely tolerant, functional, democratic society, one that has largely been economically successful to boot. A stable party system developed (Davies 1996: 1074), with the Christian Democratic Union Party and the Social Democratic Party being the most important (and they remain as such today in unified Germany). Unlike in the Weimar Republic (Kitchen 2006), post-war Germany was not damaged by relentless conflict between small parties. Moreover, key leaders of both parties, like Konrad Adenauer (a Christian Democrat) and Willy Brandt (a Social Democrat), played key roles in the ongoing democratic consolidation of West Germany. The East German state, perhaps owing to its status as a satellite, was judged by most to be less successful, with poor economic performance over many years.

As part of the wave of revolutions that swept Central and Eastern Europe and brought the Soviet Union to an end, the Berlin Wall fell in 1989, and East and West Germany were unified in 1990. East Germany, owing to decades spent as a command economy and with political subordination to the Soviet Union, had a lower level of socioeconomic development. The reunification of Germany resulted in major transfers of resources from west to east. Despite the fact that this has partially redressed the imbalances in economic development, differences are still visible.

Throughout recent decades, Germany has been a leader in the creation and expansion of the European Union. It was an initiator of the project of European integration, beginning in the 1950s with free trade in coal and steel, and then moving to a common market, common trade policies, and ultimately to a common currency and open borders within parts of the continent. While the process of European integration has been remarkable, the region has fallen on more difficult times even as Germany has boomed economically. Two challenges to the European project are noteworthy: the financial and monetary challenges to the Euro, and the recent trend of increasing nationalism and populism with the EU. With respect to the Euro as a currency, Germany has faced the dilemma of either supporting governments in financial difficulty (especially Greece) or risking the collapse of the currency. This challenge seems to have abated as of early 2018, but could resurge again. In terms of nationalism and populism, many countries in the EU have had governments that oppose further integration or want to restrict movements of people within the Union. This was seen in the United Kingdom (with the so-called Brexit), but can also be seen with the recently elected governments of Austria, Hungary, and Italy, among others. Germany remains the motor of European integration, but it is leading a process whose next steps are uncertain.

Regime and Political Institutions

The head of government in the Federal Republic of Germany's parliamentary system is the chancellor, a position comparable to a prime minister. The chancellor is selected by the lower house of the legislature, the Bundestag (see the chapter 9 case study, "Institutional Design: Germany's Bundestag and Bundesrat") after legislative elections. Since no single party is usually able to attain a majority of seats in the Bundestag, Germany's chancellor regularly governs at the head of a coalition of two or more parties. The chancellor is almost always either from the Christian Democratic Union Party (CDU, an example being current chancellor Angela Merkel, or, in earlier years, Helmut Kohl or Konrad Adenauer) or the Social Democratic Party (SPD, with examples like Gerhard Schroder or Willy Brandt). The chancellor's power is limited by Germany's federalism, which empowers representatives of the states (Länder) in the upper house (Bundesrat) to vote on all legislation affecting the states.

Regime and Political Institutions

Regime	Democratically elected federal republic
Administrative Divisions	16 Länder (states)
Executive Branch	Chancellor (head of government), President (head of state, ceremonial)
Selection of Executive	Selected by Bundestag
Legislative Branch	Bicameral Lower chamber: Bundestag; members elected by mixed system of districts, proportional representation Upper chamber: Bundesrat; members selected by Länder (state) governments
Judicial Branch	Constitutional Court with powers of judicial review
Political Party System	Multiparty, with frequent coalitions Main parties: CDU (center-right), SPD (center-left), Greens (left), Liberals (right), Left. Of these, the CDU and the SPD have historically been predominant.

Though limited by coalition politics and federalism, chancellors and their cabinets can rely on considerable party discipline to pass legislation (see the chapter 11 case study on "Consensus-Based Politics in Germany"). In addition, Germany is arguably the central player in Europe, and its government has a major role in shaping the actions and policies of the broader European Union. In particular, the European Central Bank is a Europe-wide institution that presides over the common currency known as the Euro, but it is located in Frankfurt and is seen as shaped by German economic policies. (See chapter 16 for a longer discussion of the European Union.)

Political Culture

Much attention has been focused on nationalism as a key feature of German political culture, with considerable preoccupation, very understandably, with the Nazi regime of the 1930s and 1940s. A whole industry of scholarship attempts to unpack the relationship between that regime and the long-run German political-cultural tradition (see, e.g., discussion in Greenfeld 1992; Goldhagen 1996; Browning 1992; as well as in Berger 2004). Precisely because this important conversation has received so much attention, we focus less centrally on it here.

Rather, we will note that a key question of German political culture—both East and West before reunification—has centered on how German identity could be reconstituted following that shameful episode in the nation's history. Indeed, this has perhaps been *the* central question of German political culture since the Second World War. The political right in Germany was so de-legitimated by association with the Nazis as to render a conservative nationalism almost impossible. The center-right (led by Adenauer and the Christian Democrats) was dominant in the early years, but this was not a right-wing ideological group but rather a moderate regime that focused on reconstruction and stabilization of the society (Kitchen 2006: 316–345; Davies 1996: 1072). Later, the Social Democrats would have great success, particularly during the chancellorship of Willy Brandt, under whose leadership Germany aimed to both maintain its alliances with the other Western democracies and achieve a partial rapprochement with the Soviet Union (Kitchen 2006: 354–361; Davies 1996: 1114). More generally, both parties have stuck to a relatively safe position in support of the welfare state. In short, Germany's experiences with political instability in the Weimar years and with totalitarianism in the 1930s and 1940s seem to have led the country to be healthily wary of radical polarization (though the right wing Alternative for Germany party won about 12% of the vote in the 2017 election, raising concern among many observers of German politics).

On the other hand, Germany has sometimes been at the forefront of efforts to experiment with direct democracy and related ideas. For example, a number of its states, particularly Bavaria, stand out for their frequent use of referenda. Perhaps more quixotically, a number of German localities have issued local currencies, at least some of them hoping to resist excess "commodification" and to retain local control of economic processes by doing so. Finally, the Green party has done well in Germany (indeed, Germany has had a strong environmental movement more generally), another example of innovative, broadly social-democratic tendencies.

There is another related question of political culture and Germany's adaptation to the post-war world. This is the role of Germany as a prime mover in European unification. Much of the political innovation of the period after 1945 in Europe has come with the creation of new supranational institutions at the European level. Germany and France have been the pillars of this long experiment from the beginning, along with Italy and the smaller Benelux countries of Belgium, the Netherlands, and Luxembourg. At its origins, the European Union (which was known previously by different names such as the European Community) was widely seen as an effort by the continental powers to preclude future wars through economic, social, and political cooperation. As of 2018, many commentators are left wondering about the future of this initiative, due to financial problems in a number of eurozone countries and increasing Euroskepticism in many European electorates, not to mention the planned withdrawal of the United Kingdom from the EU.

Political Economy

Germany is by most counts the world's fifth-largest economy, coming behind only the United States, China, Japan, and India (on the basis of purchasing power). The industrial powerhouse was the world's largest exporter for some years, before ceding that honor to China more recently. By virtue of its size and prominence, Germany is the engine of the European Union, the world's largest economic free trade area, which has a combined economy somewhat larger than that of the United States. The country's economic model contains many free market elements, but also features an active state role in investment, in building human capital, and in providing support for the vulnerable. Economic decision making since World War II has prioritized consensus between major economic actors, including corporations, labor unions, and the state. At the same time, it has shown less willingness to engage in Keynesian countercyclical spending (Allen 1989) than other major advanced industrial societies, remaining fiscally cautious.

The history of the German economy is one of the most intriguing and most closely studied in the area of development. At the time of the nineteenth-century Industrial Revolution, Germany fell behind Great Britain as the leading economic power, but it soon grew powerful by developing a steel industry, heavy industry, and railroads. In contrast with a British economic model that was relatively free-trade and free-market oriented and based on private investments of moderate size, the German experience was more based in investment from major sources of capital, such as industrial investment banks and the state itself (Kurth 1979), though scholars debate the *extent* to which state involvement was a factor (Hentschel 2008: 753). Germany's ability to catch up to the likes of Britain even led to the development of theories that there could be "advantages to backwardness," as relatively less-developed countries would create the large institutions needed to push development forward and leapfrog the leader (Gerschenkron 1962). By the early twentieth century, Germany was one of the world's industrial and economic leaders. The twentieth century brought massive upheaval, especially after Germany's defeat in World War I. After the war, Germany went through the horrors of the Great Depression, during which the country suffered hyperinflation.

This sequence of events contributed to the rise of the Nazis and Adolf Hitler; World War II then brought destruction to much of Europe, and ultimately to Germany itself. From 1945 to 1990, the country was split into the capitalist West and the Communist East, with the latter falling far behind West Germany economically. West Germany was quite successful after the war, as was Japan, which led to the theory that the loss in the war had eliminated the many "special interests" in politics that complicate reform; this would explain success relative to victors such as the United Kingdom and the United States (Olson 1984). After the fall of the Berlin Wall signified the end of the Cold War in 1989, Germany reunified in 1990 and resumed its place as one of the world's leading economies.

Per estimates for 2016, 30.3 percent of Germany's GDP comes from industrial production, 69.1 percent comes from the service sector, and only 0.6 percent comes from the agricultural sector (*CIA World Factbook*). Germany's unemployment rate was estimated at 4.2 percent (2016 estimate per *CIA World Factbook*), which is quite low by European standards, especially since the economic crisis that began in 2008. Germany's Gini index was 28.9 in 2015, according to OECD (Organisation for Economic Co-operation and Development) estimates (http://www.oecd.org/social/income-distribution-database.htm), which makes the German income distribution fairly egalitarian by comparative standards.

Since 2011, a big question for Germany's economy has been whether the eurozone will hold together. The question

has arisen as several southern European economies (most notably Greece, but also Spain and Portugal, among others) have lagged behind Germany and northern Europe in terms of productivity. This situation has raised the prospect that some countries might need to drop the euro as a currency to regain their competitiveness. From the perspective of many Germans, their southern neighbors had lived beyond their means for years and had to make the painful adjustments necessary to compete. However, this is not a simple morality tale of German frugality and southern European laziness. In fact, Germany's economy has depended on its southern neighbors as well, both as markets for its exports and as destinations for a good deal of the capital in its banking sector. Perspectives critical of Germany suggest that the German obsession with inflation has led it to force other European countries to make painful cuts to public services and wages. This situation shows the interdependence of international economies now, and especially in Europe. As of 2018, debates about the eurozone's future (and that of the EU in general) continue, with Germany playing a leading role.

CASE STUDIES

CASE STUDY

The German State: Unification and Welfare

CHAPTER 4, PAGE 88

The story of the unification of the German state is a complex one for the major theories of state formation considered in chapter 3. Judged against European benchmarks, the German state developed late (1871), though Prussia developed a strong state in the eighteenth century (Anderson 1974). The question of why Germany was so late to modern state-building is a difficult one to answer, and in part will depend on which theory of state formation one finds most plausible. Most would agree that at certain critical junctures (e.g., the aftermath of the Protestant Reformation) divisions between small-scale political and cultural units were reinforced. Others would likely place emphasis on the rivalry between Prussia and Austria (first the remnant of the Holy Roman Empire): rather than a single German center of power there were two, and neither was sufficiently strong to decisively vanquish or incorporate the other. Still others would focus on local traditions of dependence in smaller states like Bavaria, and pressure from other powers (to take just one example, after the Hanoverian succession, the British Crown was eager to ensure that Hanover remained their possession and was not swallowed up). Some would argue that the very question is confused: with something like state formation, perhaps we should not ask why it didn't happen when and where it didn't but why it *did* happen when and where it *did*.

So why did the state finally develop? Arguments could be made in support of each of the major theories of state formation considered in chapter 3. Proponents of the cultural theory might point to the prior development of German nationalism (discussed further in the Case Study "Ethnic Boundaries of the German Nation?"). Its emergence among some German elites predated unification by about a century, though even at unification not all residents of the German state would be committed German nationalists. Given that national identity demands that the nation be sovereign, and

CASE STUDY (continued)

The German State: Unification and Welfare

CHAPTER 4, PAGE 88

given the challenges inherent in exercising such sovereignty without a unified state, proponents of this theory would suggest that it explains state formation by pointing to the collective *motive* to form a state. The Bellicist theory would focus on war making, noting the centrality of interstate conflict to the rise of Prussia and to its eventual displacement of Austria. Its proponents would further stress that Prussia's defeat of France was the decisive element in establishing the formation of a broader German state. Economic theories of the state would focus on efforts by Friedrich List and others to industrialize Germany. From this point of view, we should be attentive to the fact that one of the earlier organizations that produced some unity was the Zollverein (Hentschel 2008: 762), which managed customs on trade within Germany. Finally, diffusion and

systems theories would point to the fact that, from at least 1648 on, Europe was governed by a "state system." Tendencies toward organizational imitation might be taken to explain the rise of the German state. Think a bit about how one might try to gain some empirical leverage in testing these theories of German state formation.

Germany is also of interest because—despite its later problems—it was one of the first states to move toward welfare functions. Here Bismarck was again important. Bismarck was a junker (junkers were often relatively poor but proud nobles from eastern Germany who traced their noble status back to the medieval period), and members of his social class tended to be quite conservative. Conservatives strongly opposed the socialist and social democratic activists, like Marx (exiled to England) and Lasalle, who

were active or influential in the period. In what some have considered a brilliant political move, Bismarck co-opted some social democratic demands by authorizing a system of social insurance (Esping-Andersen 1990: 24; Hentschel 2008: 793). This was no twentieth-century welfare state, but it did provide disability and health care insurance as well as retirement benefits. Some would argue that the German Empire's early welfare state construction was critical to the success of its state formation. One question you might ask is why welfare state construction was so closely linked to state formation more generally in this case. Come back to this case study when you have finished reading all of chapter 3 (if you have not already finished that chapter), and think about the implications of each theory of welfare state formation you find there.

CASE STUDY

Democracy and Authoritarianism in Germany

CHAPTER 7, PAGE 159

Many people know of German Nazism (1933–1945) as the epitome of twentieth-century totalitarianism, with its denial of basic human rights and its culmination in the atrocities of the Holocaust. But it is important to consider German history in the twentieth century as a set of shifts between democratic and authoritarian rule. In other words, Nazism is not the whole story in Germany. This is a country that has seen oscillations between democracy and democratic breakdown,

culminating in democratic consolidation over the last fifty years such that virtually no observers worry about the ongoing democratic status of contemporary Germany.

In the German Empire after unification there were democratic elements, most notably that suffrage was extended to all males for voting in legislative elections. Yet few would describe this system as "democratic," since the chancellor (Bismarck until 1890) and the Kaiser (Wilhelm

I and II) held disproportionate power. After the collapse of this system as a result of the First World War, the country embarked on an experiment with a democratic republic. Great effort was expended on the constitution of this Weimar Republic, but it would be for naught (for more on this fascinating period, see the essays in McElligott 2009). Serious economic problems, resulting from both the Treaty of Versailles and, later, the Great Depression, compounded the existent political polarization of German society. Political parties proliferated; and despite institutional changes meant to quell disorder, Hitler and the Nazis would eventually take power. It is unclear how long and in what form the Nazi regime would have lasted if it were not for the Second World War, but in any case, military defeat brought the Nazi era to a close. This led to an externally imposed transition in East and West Germany.

Here, as discussed in the Germany country profile, Germany's political history bifurcates until 1990. During the Cold War, Germany was divided into a democratic West Germany and a Communist East Germany. Thus the eastern part of today's Germany experienced both of the twentieth century's most

infamous forms of totalitarian rule: Nazism and Soviet Communism. The two most important stories here, from the perspective of democratization theory, are (1) the re-establishment of democracy in West Germany after the Second World War (Schmidt 2008: 58–59) and (2) the successful reunification of Germany and the continuation of the country's robust democracy in the face of reunification.

The case of West German democratization is fairly singular. In other words, the degree to which it can serve as a model for other regimes seeking to make a democratic transition is limited. First of all, the authoritarian regime fell because it was defeated by foreign powers. Second, those powers helped

to shape the transition, both in political and especially in economic terms. Third, the nature of the authoritarian regime demanded such thoroughgoing repudiation that democracy's legitimacy was high (indeed, in general, the defeat of the axis powers was linked to a global wave of democratic prestige).

The case of unification is a bit more useful for comparative analysis, if for no other reason than not all of the aforementioned conditions apply to the case. So far at least, unified Germany has defied fears that it would come to dominate Europe or revert to the authoritarian impulses that surfaced at various points in the country's history. Indeed, to most observers, unified Germany appears to be a highly stable and successful democracy.

There are many ways to structure legislatures, and the German model is an intriguing one for other countries. Germany is a federal country in which the sixteen states (Länder) have considerable authority, and it has a bicameral legislature with a chamber known as the Bundesrat to represent the states. The country also has a blend of different electoral systems for its lower house, known as the Bundestag. The mixed system is a case of careful institutional engineering that incorporates many different features.

In the Bundestag, the electoral system features elements of both district-based representation and proportional representation (PR). At each election, every German has two votes: one for a preferred candidate from the district and one for a preferred party; this is similar to the New Zealand example, also discussed in chapter 9. The district-based vote for a candidate means that each geographic constituency in Germany has its own representative, just like in district systems elsewhere in the world. But

the party vote is tallied to ensure that the overall distribution of seats in the Bundestag reflects the partisan preferences of the country as a whole. After all the district representatives are calculated, the party vote is used to add "at-large" seats as necessary to the Bundestag. For example, a party that gets 24 percent of the overall party vote but only earns 18 percent of the district seats would be "compensated" with additional at-large seats to make its overall representation in the parliament proportional to its

Institutional Design: Germany's Bundestag and Bundesrat

CHAPTER 9, PAGE 215

support. This gives the proportionality in the legislature associated with PR, even while giving each constituency its own representative as in district systems. All members of the Bundestag vote to elect a chancellor as the head of government.

The legislature also has another innovation: a modified version of the vote of no confidence. As with other parliamentary systems, Germany's chancellor and government can be dismissed by a vote of no confidence, but the form is known as a "constructive vote of no confidence." The twist in Germany is that those proposing to bring down the government must simultaneously present and support a new governmental majority coalition that will go into effect. This prevents opposition parties from reducing the government to permanent gridlock by bringing down governments without being able to propose a viable governing alternative.

Germany also has features that protect the sixteen states in the federal system, mainly through the Bundesrat.

The members of the Bundesrat are appointed by the respective state governments to represent the interests of that state. Each state's delegation to this upper chamber must vote as a bloc, otherwise its votes are not counted. With regard to powers, the Bundesrat has the right to vote on any matter that materially affects the sixteen Länder, including matters of budgets and administration. While the powers thus have some constitutional limits, the amount of legislation deemed to affect the states is considerable, which gives the Bundesrat substantial authority. On issues that do not have special bearing on the states, the Bundesrat can still review legislation and offer objections, which can be overturned by the Bundestag.

In addition to these legislative arrangements, Germany has a ceremonial president, who has relatively few powers beyond those of a figurehead. Germany's presidential selection is undertaken by a body that brings together the elected legislators of the Bundestag along with

representatives of Germany's sixteen Länder. The president is deemed to be impartial, and nominees are typically selected for their reputation for being non-partisan.

In combination, the various aspects of the German political system are intended to balance and distribute power in several ways. The party vote has the effect of ensuring that the most successful parties have a mandate to govern, while the constituency vote allows each geographic area to be represented by its preferred candidate. The constructive vote of no confidence allows for an unpopular government to be overturned while also placing a premium on governability. Finally, the delicate balance of powers between the Bundestag and Bundesrat is designed to ensure that federalism is protected, but so are the prerogatives of the parliamentary majority. This set of institutional designs shows that there is a nearly endless variety of possible models for structuring political systems.

Consensus-Based Politics in Germany

CHAPTER 11, PAGE 265

Germany is a country that exhibits many of the features of consensus-based politics. Through two main mechanisms highlighted in chapter 11, Germany's politics typically includes multiple political perspectives in the government (Lijphart 1999). The first is the multiparty

parliamentary system, which relies often on coalitions to form governments, even though it is common for certain leading parties to wield most of the influence. The Social Democratic Party (SPD) and the Christian Democratic Union (CDU) have been the major players for years,

though several other smaller parties have retained influence and sometimes been in government coalitions. Moreover, in recent years, support for the SDP has declined (as it has for many traditional parties in Europe). One of the beneficiaries of this decline has been the Alternative

Consensus-Based Politics in Germany
CHAPTER 11, PAGE 265

for Germany (AfD), a right-wing populist party, which garnered 94 seats in the 2017 elections to the Bundestag.

The second mechanism from chapter 11 highlighted in the case of Germany is that German politics has featured a form of corporatism that institutionalizes cooperation between major interest groups.

The factors contributing to the multiparty system relate to the electoral system noted in the preceding box, "Institutional Design." While some larger parties tend to do well in the district elections, the smaller parties benefit from the proportional representation seats in the Bundestag. German legislatures have recently had five or six parties represented, and governments have generally required a coalition of two or more parties. There have been coalitions made up of parties on the left and coalitions comprised of parties on the right, as well as a "Grand Coalition" that brought together the country's two leading parties for several years. All of these cases have necessitated political bargaining between governing parties, and some distribution

of cabinet seats. German governments have been relatively stable since World War II, with many governments seeing out their terms of office, and the country has had a relatively small number of chancellors.

Germany is also a case of consensus formation in political negotiation between interest groups. That is, Germany has a form of corporatism. Corporatist arrangements bring together labor, business, and government to make decisions about the economy and wages, regardless of who is in government. This can moderate the economic consequences of political shifts from left to right, since the same actors are expected to bargain with one another on a sustained basis. This is common in northern Europe, including countries such as the Netherlands, Austria, and the countries of Scandinavia (Siaroff 1999). It has been argued that German corporatism is of a special character insofar as it also includes a fourth actor: the major banks that finance investment (Siaroff 1999, citing Hicks 1988). This inclusion of the

banks as major corporatist actors is seen as distinct from the more "social democratic" corporatism seen in other parts of northern Europe where labor may have a stronger voice relative to capital.

There is a unifying theme that links multiparty systems and corporatist systems in countries like Germany: an emphasis on consensus that tends to accommodate a range of actors in decision making. This contrasts with more majoritarian rule in countries such as the United Kingdom, where governments often consist of a single party, and relations between governments and interest groups are more arms-length. Whether this has contributed to social stability in Germany since World War II—through the partition and reunification of the country and its emergence as the economic powerhouse of the Eurozone—is a topic for further consideration. As Europe faces continued conflict around globalization and regional integration, immigration, and other issues, we will see whether German politics can manage more consensus than comparative cases.

Ethnic Boundaries of the German Nation?
CHAPTER 13, PAGE 315

As noted in chapter 13, France is often taken to exemplify the "civic" nationalist tradition, while Germany is frequently held up as the clearest example of the "ethnic" tradition (Brubaker 1992; Greenfeld 1992; Berger 2004). This can mean different things, but at a minimum it

suggests that the "symbolic boundaries" (Barth 1969; Lamont and Molnar 2002) that tend to be used when German nationalists speak about their identity have often emphasized ascriptive characteristics imagined to be biological or quasi-biological.

The national identity that developed in Germany in the early nineteenth century spread in the context of French domination of German territories under Napoleon (Kitchen 2006). Some scholars have argued that it was characterized by "ressentiment" against the French, and

CASE STUDY (continued)
Ethnic Boundaries of the German Nation?
CHAPTER 13, PAGE 315

that as a result it was defined *against* French notions of national membership as linked to citizenship and related Enlightenment ideals (Greenfeld 1992). Others have noted that German national identity developed in the context of political divisions: the boundaries of the territorial state could not serve as the boundaries of membership, since there was no German territorial state at the crucial moment of the formation of the national identity (Brubaker 1992).

Few dispute that German nationalism has historically drawn ethnic boundaries. Rather, debates center on several related issues about the *extent* to which this has been the case and its main implications (Berger 2004). With regard to the first issue, some assert that what appears to be ethnic nationalism is more of a "cultural nationalism," suggesting that not all Germans have historically divided themselves from others on the basis of racial ideas, but adherence to cultural traditions. Just the same, most would acknowledge that at key points in German history, ethnic boundaries have come to the fore. With regard to the second issue, the major controversy concerns the relationship between German ethnic nationalism and the Nazi atrocities. Some scholars (Greenfeld 1992; Goldhagen 1996) argue that there is a direct linkage between the ethnic nationalism formed in the nineteenth century and the Holocaust and that a majority of German citizens were complicit in these acts. Others, though, wish to emphasize a narrative about a more heterogeneous German culture of identity, one that has historically included not just xenophobia but alternative strands emphasizing liberal tolerance. Analysts continue to debate these issues; and in recent years, German citizenship laws have undergone some partial, liberalizing reforms.

Think about how each of the major theories of ethno-national conflict and violence discussed in chapter 13 would apply to this case. What sorts of features of German identity would those focused on cultural boundaries point to? How might proponents of instrumentalist and social-psychological theories approach this case?

Research Prompts

1. What would major theories of democratization and democratic consolidation say about the pattern of authoritarianism and democracy that Germany witnessed in the late nineteenth and twentieth centuries? What are the implications of the German case for those theories?

2. As discussed in several of the case studies, Germany has often been considered a prototypical case of ethnic nationalism and, moreover, its nationalism has often been causally linked to its twentieth-century totalitarian regime. Design a comparative analysis—drawing on several cases—that would allow us to examine this claim. Is yours an MSS or MDS design? Why?

3. Some argue that Germany is a case of state-led development. Others argue that market forces have played a central role in Germany's historical economic performance. How can these claims be reconciled? To what extent is either or both of these claims true?

4. What are the pros and cons of the institutional structure of Germany's government? Besides the fact that it seems complicated at first glance, what is the strongest argument you can make against the German two-vote system, which combines district-based elections with overall proportionality in the Bundestag? What is the strongest argument that you can make *for* it?

5. Germany was in certain respects a "late modernizer" within the European context. In particular, it is noteworthy that the country only achieved political unification in 1871. Situating Germany in its comparative European context, analyze the main consequences of this modernization pattern.

 # India

PROFILE

Key Features of Contemporary India

Population:	1,281,935,911 (estimate, July 2017)
Area:	3,287,263 square kilometers
Head of State:	Ram Nath Kovind (president, 2017–present)
Head of Government:	Narendra Modi (prime minister, 2014–present)
Capital:	New Delhi
Year of Independence:	1947
Year of Current Constitution:	1950
Languages:	English, Hindi; other major languages include Bengali, Tamil, Urdu
GDP per Capita:	$6,600 (*CIA World Factbook* estimate, 2016)
Human Development Index Ranking (2014):	131st (medium human development)

Sources: *CIA World Factbook*; World Bank *Development Report 2014*. World Development Indicators; United Nations *Human Development Report 2016*

Introduction

India is the world's largest democracy, and a surprising one by most accounts. It is a diverse society of over one billion people, divided into different major religions, languages, and social groups (see the charts that follow). This diversity was perhaps even more striking under British colonial rule prior to 1947, as British India also contained both present-day Pakistan and Bangladesh, two Muslim-majority countries that together combine for over 325 million people today, more than the United States. Prior to colonialism, India was largely decentralized, with the territory being ruled by many regional or local princes. The creation of the Indian nation-state as we know it today was part and parcel of the process of Indian decolonization.

Much of the country was characterized for centuries by a rigid caste system that stratified the population by professions and by social standing. Along these many sources of

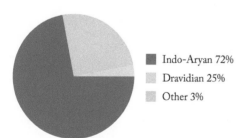

Ethnic Groups in India

Note that while the CIA World Factbook includes only three main groups, which are really language families that overlap with ethnicity, these categories include many smaller groups. Note, too, that caste distinctions in India are sometimes treated as similar to ethnic distinctions.
Source: CIA World Factbook.

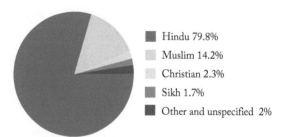

Religious Affiliation in India

Note that Hinduism is used as an umbrella term to cover a wide range of religious groups with different traditions, practices, and beliefs. Many of these groups would reject the characterization of being Hindu. In constitutional terms, even well-established groups such as Jains and Buddhists are nominally considered Hindu.
Source: CIA World Factbook.

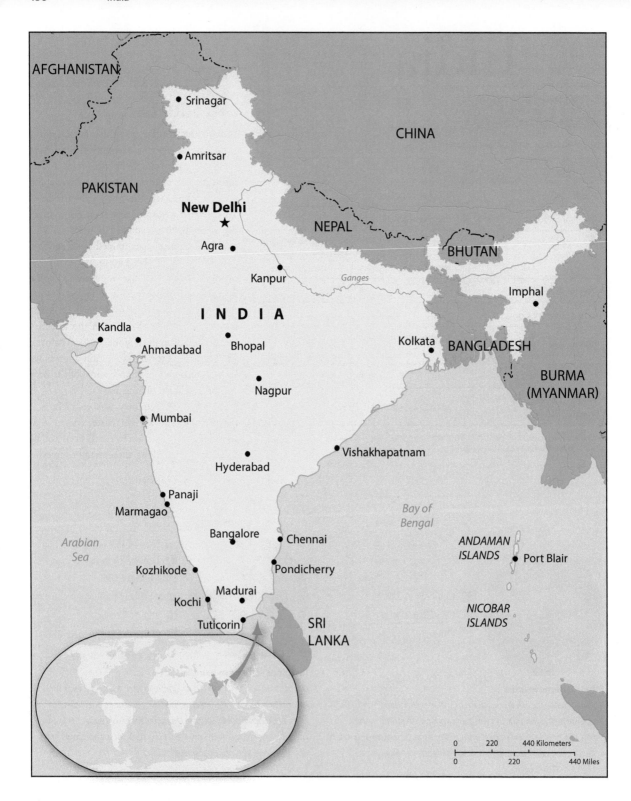

diversity and potential conflict, India was one of the poorest countries on earth throughout the twentieth century. It is a source of inspiration to many that India has retained its democracy for almost all of its two-thirds of a century of independence, despite the ravages of poverty and hunger, social inequality, and a multitude of cultures and beliefs densely packed into the South Asian subcontinent.

Even with its many social problems, India today is likely to be seen as a thriving hub of the future, renowned for technological innovation, engineering prowess, and entrepreneurial spirit. It has grown rapidly in recent years and has become a global leader in technology, science and engineering, and the service industry. It is likely to become the world's most populous nation in the next decades; and if much of that population can come out of poverty and into the middle class, it will, along with China, become one of the leading global powers as the twenty-first century progresses.

Historical Development

India is home to some of the world's most historic civilizations and is the source of several of the world's great religions, most notably Hinduism, which remains its majority religion, and Buddhism, which continues to have a tremendous influence in numerous East and Southeast Asian countries, though it is of less importance in contemporary India. The country's recorded history dates back millennia and consisted for centuries of a range of empires, small states, and principalities. It was for many centuries a crossroads of peoples, where cultures came together and new ones were created, and where trade networks linked together. India's past involves some of recorded history's most compelling characters, including the emperor Ashoka, who in the four decades before his death in 232 BCE nominally united much of the region known as the Indian "subcontinent" and ordained a legal code that emphasized sectarian and ethnic tolerance in the heterogeneous territory. The subcontinent witnessed Greek invaders from the west under Alexander the Great and Turkic raiders from the north. Turks established states in north India by the early 1200s. The region was settled by Muslims, as well as Hindus and Buddhists, and was crisscrossed by merchants as it became a linchpin of the spice trade that connected the East and West. Many of South Asia's Muslims today are descendants of those who converted to Islam at this time. Much of India was then united under the Mughal Empire up to the 1700s. The Mughal reign was an important centralizing period and helped to create what we know today as modern India, but the subcontinent remained a diverse and heterogeneous empire under the Mughals, and not a modern nation-state.

Despite its exceedingly rich prior history, the formation of modern India is often seen as beginning with the advent of European colonial rule, which began in the seventeenth century and lasted up to 1947. India was gradually colonized by many European powers over several centuries, though over time, British colonialism came to dominate. Small portions of the coast were first taken by Portugal; and then in the seventeenth and eighteenth centuries, French and English companies progressively colonized much of the subcontinent. British colonial rule did not begin with outright conquest but rather with the establishment of trading posts under the British East India Company (on the East India Company and the growth of colonialism, see Metcalf and Metcalf 2006). The Company had a charter from the British monarch to establish a monopoly trade in India for products that included cotton and silk, tea, and opium: indeed, these same British interests forced Chinese authorities to open their markets to opium sales in the nineteenth century, which led to drug addiction and destabilizing and humiliating international conflicts for the Qing Dynasty. Given the richness of trade, British India came to be seen as the crown jewel of all European colonial possessions. It eventually encompassed present-day India, Pakistan, and Bangladesh and became central to the aims and aspirations of the British Empire.

After eighteenth-century conflict between England and France, the British East India Company gained colonial control over much of today's India, Pakistan, and Bangladesh. British colonialism gradually became more direct and intense over time. It met with resistance at various points but succeeded in part through playing various Indian actors against each other. The most serious nineteenth-century resistance against the British was the revolt of 1857–1859 (sometimes called the "Sepoy Rebellion"), after which the British state took over control from the East India Company and ruled India directly. Scholars debate whether, to what extent, and how the empire truly served Britain's economic interests

Historical Development

Timeline

−1600s	Territory today encompassed by India was, by the fifteenth century, home to large numbers of empires, states, and religious traditions, including Hinduism, Buddhism, and Sikhism.
1498	Portuguese explorer Vasco da Gama reaches India and the Portuguese establish a small state by 1505.
1600s	British East India Company begins trading in India and eventually consolidates control over most of the subcontinent, prevailing over French and Dutch competition.
1857	Major rebellion against rule of the British East India Company
1858	Britain asserts direct crown control over most India, and rules parts of India indirectly through "Princely States" of local nobles.
1915–1930s	Mohandas Gandhi becomes leader of the Indian National Congress and leads protests against British rule, demanding home rule and eventually independence.
1919	Massacre of several hundreds of unarmed Indians at Amritsar by British troops under General Reginald Dyer
1930s–1940s	Anti-colonial movement accelerates with mass strikes and mobilizations, led by Gandhi and Jawaharlal Nehru of the Congress Party, and Muhammad Ali Jinnah of the Muslim League.
1947	Independence and partition of British India into India and Pakistan (with Pakistan including East Pakistan, or present-day Bangladesh); tensions and conflict emerge between Hindus and Muslims over partition, culminating in war and massive refugee flows of Indian Muslims to Pakistan and Pakistani Hindus to India.
1948	Mohandas Gandhi is assassinated by Hindu fundamentalist who rejected Gandhi's calls for peace between Hindus and Muslims.
1950	India ends its symbolic links to Great Britain with adoption of new constitution that establishes a republic; India's "princely states" are incorporated into the nation's states and territories.
1962	War with China centered on a border dispute.
1964	Death of Jawaharlal Nehru
1966	Indira Gandhi (daughter of Nehru and no relation to Mahatma Gandhi) becomes prime minister and continues most policies set by Nehru.
1971	India and Pakistan go to war over East Pakistan; former East Pakistan separates from West Pakistan and becomes Bangladesh.
1974	India explodes a nuclear device.
1975–1977	"The Emergency": martial law under Indira Gandhi, who rules by decree and imprisons opposition leaders
1977	Congress Party loses power for the first time.
1979	Indira Gandhi returns as prime minister.
1984	Indira Gandhi is assassinated by her Sikh bodyguards; riots ensue in which several thousand members of the Sikh minority are killed; Rajiv Gandhi (Indira's son) becomes prime minister.
1989	Protests increase in Kashmir, a Muslim majority area administered by India on the border between India and Pakistan.
1991	Rajiv Gandhi is assassinated by militants seeking a separate homeland for Sri Lankan Tamils and angry at India's intervention in the conflict.
1991	Pro-market economic reforms begin under finance minister Manmohan Singh (later prime minister), under pressure from the International Monetary Fund and the World Bank.
1992	Hindu nationalists destroy a mosque in Ayodhya that is of historical importance to some Muslims, but also is in a location sacred to some Hindus.
1996	Atal Bihari Vajpayee becomes prime minister as head of the Hindu nationalist Bharatiya Janata Party (BJP); governs only briefly, but returns from 1998 to 2004.
2000s	India's economy booms, with growth rates occasionally reaching near 8 percent.
2004	Congress Party voted back into power with Manmohan Singh as prime minister.
2008	Islamist militants from Pakistan stage simultaneous terror attacks in Mumbai.
2014-present	Government of Prime Minister Narendra Modi of the BJP

(Balakrishnan 2010), but there is little doubt that it enhanced Britain's international standing, power position, and sense of prestige—and many argue that it "deindustrialized" India (e.g., Allen 2011). There is also no doubt that it was not desired by most of the subjugated population and that it was a strikingly "illiberal" set of institutions for such a self-consciously "liberal" society to adopt.

In the early twentieth century, Indian resistance to British rule grew, with the Indian Congress Party leading the anti-colonial movement. Its key leader was Mohandas Gandhi (often known as Mahatma, or "great soul"), who led peaceful demonstrations, marches, and protests demanding home rule. Gandhi's methods pioneered non-violent resistance—later used by the likes of Martin Luther King in the United States—and were known in India as *satyagraha*. Gandhi's charismatic appeal to many millions of Indians was enhanced by his decisions to eat and dress simply rather than following the expectations of British culture (and, in part, due to religious reasons). The other main political leader of Congress was Jawaharlal Nehru; also making common cause with them in the eventual demands for independence was Muhammad Ali Jinnah of the Muslim League.

Gandhi, Nehru, and Jinnah pressed for Indian independence from Britain, and the move to decolonization accelerated after World War II; but as independence approached, Jinnah and the Muslim League insisted on a partition of India with an independent state for Muslims. (British colonialism, of course, played a critical historical role in exacerbating such divisions.) On August 15, 1947, India became independent but had split into a majority-Hindu India and majority-Muslim Pakistan. Pakistan included West Pakistan (present-day Pakistan) and East Pakistan (present-day Bangladesh), which were on opposite sides of India. If combined, these three countries today (India, Pakistan, and Bangladesh) would have a total of over 1.5 billion people and would easily be the most populous nation on earth. As it is, their actual division has been consequential, with conflict between India and Pakistan being a major source of instability. The 1947 partition led to thousands of deaths and millions of refugees as Hindus left Pakistan for India and Muslims left India for Pakistan (both groups often walking on foot), with conflicts and massacres between the groups occurring in the process. Tensions continued after the assassination of Gandhi in 1948 by a Hindu fundamentalist who objected to Gandhi's efforts to reconcile and promote tolerance between Hindus and Muslims.

Indian politics in the first decades after independence were dominated by the Indian Congress Party. As India's first prime minister, Nehru led the country from 1947 to his death in 1964. His governments developed many lasting features of the Indian state and economy, most notably creating a very active and interventionist state. While some economic production remained in private hands, the state owned many large enterprises and regulated the economy heavily. A central Planning Commission was tasked with organizing the economy, and the government proceeded on the basis of Five-Year Plans modeled on Soviet planning. In this mixed economy, India achieved some modest growth and developed strong educational programs in science and engineering while also working to improve agriculture. However, the statist approach also lent itself to corruption and inefficiency, given the need of businesses to secure permits and licenses from administrators and bureaucrats.

Indira Gandhi ascended to the role of prime minister in 1966 and governed for over a decade. She largely followed the policies set in place by her father, Jawaharlal Nehru, and built on these with efforts to increase agricultural production in rural areas. On the international front, her government supported residents of East Pakistan who militated for independence from Pakistan in 1971; this led to a war with Pakistan that resulted in the independence of East Pakistan as the new nation of Bangladesh. Indira and her followers were accused of electoral fraud in the 1971 election by an increasingly restive opposition; and in response, the government declared martial law in 1975. Known as "The Emergency," this period lasted nearly two years, until 1977, and can be seen as the only period in which democracy suffered a setback in independent India. The Emergency ultimately ended in 1977, costing the Congress Party control of the government for the first time, as the Janata Party (under Prime Minister Morarji Desai) took over the government until 1980. Indira Gandhi and the Congress returned to power in 1980, and the prime minister herself was assassinated by her bodyguards—of the Sikh minority—in 1984. This resulted in deadly anti-Sikh riots. In the meantime, the post of prime minister passed to Rajiv Gandhi, Indira's son and the next generation of the "Nehru-Gandhi dynasty" in the Congress Party. Rajiv himself was assassinated by a Sri Lankan Tamil separatist in 1991.

Through the 1990s and 2000s, India has witnessed several sources of violence and instability. The most important international conflict has been with Pakistan, especially as the two nuclear-armed powers contest the disputed region along their shared border. The Indian-administered province of Jammu and Kashmir has a Muslim majority, much of which wishes to come under Pakistani sovereignty, with another contingent advocating independence. Conflict erupts sporadically and was most tense when the two countries tested nuclear devices in a standoff in 1998. Sectarian conflict has a domestic component as well, with conflicts ongoing between Indian Hindus and the significant minority of Indian Muslims. A most dramatic conflict came when mobs of Hindu nationalists demolished a holy Muslim mosque by hand in Ayodhya in 1992, on the grounds that it had been built on the site of a temple marking the birthplace of the Hindu divinity Rama. Tensions mounted further when the BJP governed in the period from 1998 to 2004, as the party promoted Hindu nationalist ideals while attempting to court some Muslim and Christian voters. The party maintained that Hindu should be India's leading cultural identity and should be fostered by state institutions.

Violence and conflict continue in contemporary India. In 2008, the international and domestic aspects of India's sectarian divide came together tragically when coordinated bombings and suicide attacks on prominent sites in the metropolis Mumbai resulted in several hundred deaths. In addition to these conflicts between Muslims and Hindus, India has also witnessed insurgencies by radical leftists known as Naxalites, who are inspired by Maoist doctrine. Violence also takes on various daily forms that amount to more deaths, but these appear less in the news: India has high levels of social violence against women, with deadly abuse remaining common. An increasing phenomenon is sex-selective abortion, which has resulted in many "missing girls."

India has been led by reformist governments and prime ministers in recent years, and amid many uncertainties has emerged economically in the last two decades, as discussed in the "Political Economy" section later in the chapter. Prime Minister Manmohan Singh (a Sikh, and the first non-Hindu to hold the post) governed from 2004 to 2014 and was formerly the finance minister that initiated important economic reforms in 1991. In 2014, Narenda Modi of the BJP was elected. Some economic analysts responded to his election with enthusiasm, given the economic successes in the state of Gujarat under his watch. Economic growth has been steadily high in India under Modi, ranging between 6 and 8 percent. India is still rife with extreme poverty and startling inequality, but it is increasingly viewed as a world economic leader and one of the keys to the economy of the twenty-first century. As the world's largest democracy and a highly heterogeneous country, it faces massive challenges, but opportunities as well.

Regime and Political Institutions

India is a federal parliamentary system with two chambers of parliament: the lower house, called the Lok Sabha (with about 550 members, though the number varies), and the upper house known as the Rajya Sabha (with no more than 250 members), which represents the states. The Lok Sabha has the greater powers of the two: it elects the prime minister and can vote out the government with a vote of no confidence; the government is thus accountable to the Lok Sabha. The Lok Sabha also is the final authority on "money bills" regarding taxation and spending appropriations. In some cases, a government minister introduces legislation in the Lok Sabha, while in other cases individual members of the Lok Sabha introduce bills. Except for money bills, the Rajya Sabha has a role after bills pass the lower chamber. If the Rajya Sabha votes against a bill, a joint committee of the two houses is formed, with a majority prevailing. Since the Lok Sabha is more numerous, it has the advantage in such votes.

Other branches and powers of government also have roles. India has a formal, written constitution and a Supreme Court responsible for deciding on the constitutionality of law. As a federal system, important parts of Indian law are made at the state level. States have their own High Courts (with some states grouping together to share a High Court) and their own legislatures and executives. The state assemblies select most of the members of the national Rajya Sabha. The president is largely ceremonial but must assent to parliamentary bills for these to become law. Occasionally, the president may offer an objection to a bill and send it back to the legislature; but if it passes a second time, the president is constitutionally required to assent. On very rare occasions, the president may exercise a "pocket veto" by neither assenting to a bill nor returning it to the parliament. On most occasions, presidents assent to the wishes of parliament.

Regime and Political Institutions

Regime	Federal representative democracy; parliamentary system
Administrative Divisions	Twenty-nine states and seven union territories
Executive Branch	Prime minister as head of government (in Parliament) President with largely ceremonial powers
Selection of Executive	Prime minister selected by Parliament President elected by electoral college of Parliament and state legislators
Legislative Branch	Bicameral Parliament Lower chamber: Lok Sabha (House of the People) Upper chamber: Rajya Sabha (Council of States)
Judicial Branch	Supreme Court of India
Political Party System	Multiparty system, with two major parties leading coalitions at the national level: Indian Congress Party (United Progressive Alliance) and Bharatiya Janata Party (National Democratic Alliance)

Political Culture

There are a number of noteworthy features of India's political culture, several of which are discussed in detail in the case studies that follow. We will try to single out and briefly comment on these here. Perhaps the most singular feature of Indian political culture is its diversity. India is a strikingly heterogeneous and culturally complex society. As discussed previously, it is the point of origin for two of the most important world religions: Hinduism and Buddhism. The latter is now practiced by a very small minority of the Indian population, but India has an enormous Muslim population and notable Sikh and Christian populations, as well as other religions like Jainism. India is similarly a country of great ethnic diversity, and regional identities vary considerably as well. Religious, ethnic, and geographical categories overlap, but they are not identical.

India is also a society that has exhibited a high degree of inequality and stratification. This can be measured in terms of income, for example, as India has relatively high income inequality, but cultural sources of inequality are also notable. The most controversial has been that of caste. Caste is a source of controversy both in India proper and among scholars. It is controversial among scholars because it used to be asserted that caste was a long-standing tradition of Indian culture (Dumont [1966] 1981). While most historians argue that caste had featured in Indian life before the advent of British colonial rule, some recent historians (e.g., Dirks, 2001) have argued that caste as we know it was at least partially a function of colonialists having used such distinctions to aid in subjugating and ruling India. Whatever the historical sources, caste distinctions have been important features of contemporary Indian politics, with political parties sometimes coinciding with castes (see Case Study on "Ethnicity and Political Parties in India"), and with some groups being favored over others.

Another notable feature of modern Indian political culture—which exists in tension with the previously noted characteristic—is India's democracy. As is discussed in more detail in a Case Study, "Democracy's Success in India," India is notable for being the world's largest democracy, and it achieved this well before its recent gains in economic development. Indeed, the country remains relatively poor and yet has largely been a democratic success. This is an important phenomenon in many ways. Indians treat political and civil liberties as rights and entitlements, and this has given rise to social movements and protests, alternations in government, and a wide range of political parties, including important communist parties being elected to run some states (and performing quite well by many measures in the famous case of the state of Kerala).

India is known for its remarkable contradictions when it comes to how the political culture interacts with the economy. The country has tremendous entrepreneurial energy, yet also was known for decades as having a hidebound state. The state itself is also contradictory. The country has a famously strong administration and civil service, in the sense that top-ranking officials are accomplished, well-educated, and admired. On the other hand, the Indian state has been characterized by massive amounts of corruption, with bribes being expected from the lowest official up the chain to higher ranking superiors. The result has been a state that has technical competence at the top, but historically has failed to deliver needed services to the beneficiaries in the population. This contradictory nature of the political culture plays a role the persistence of extreme poverty.

Political Economy

India's political economy is seemingly a study in contrasts, as is the case with many developing countries. The country's economic history has witnessed a combination of stagnation, modest growth, and more recent success. Under state planning and state-led development for much of its post-independence period from the 1940s through the 1980s, India had a middling level of economic success (Kohli 2004). Yet it was clear that the challenges remained as of the 1990s. One of the key features of the Indian political economy was noted earlier: the use of extensive government planning, intervention, and regulation. A leading manifestation of this was what came to be known as the "license raj," or the complex system of regulations—often in the form of required licenses and permits—that businesses needed to follow. This system was nominally supposed to ensure coordination, planning, and protections for workers, but it came to represent bureaucratic inefficiency that stifled innovation.

By the 1990s, the Indian state was seen as increasingly meddlesome, dysfunctional, corrupt, and much in need of reform. As one leading scholar of India put it, the state was "highly centralized and interventionist, and yet seem[ed] powerless" (Kohli 1990: 8). A major response came in 1991 with a set of reforms that opened up India's economy somewhat and began to dismantle the license raj. While India did not undertake any massive transition to free-market principles, the changes were significant by Indian standards. The change coincided with the end of the Cold War, when the Soviet Union collapsed, having once been the command economy model that India (while remaining democratic) had sought to follow.

India's growth soon accelerated, though this is not attributable to the reforms alone (see the Case Study box "What Explains India's Recent Growth?"). The country has grown rapidly in the years after 2002, averaging in the range of 6-8 percent per year in recent years. This is even more impressive given that population growth has slowed in the country to closer to 1 percent, meaning the growth per capita has accelerated. From an economy that was hidebound and rather inefficient, modern enterprise has emerged in various forms, ranging from some of the most successful multinationals in the world (such as the Tata conglomerate) to remarkably innovative small-scale enterprises popping up as survival strategies in dirt-floor homes in the Mumbai slum of Dharavi. Much of India's growth has come in the diverse service sector, not only in manufacturing. Despite this, agriculture still employs about half of all Indians, often in the form of small-scale or subsistence agriculture on family plots.

Of course, the boom in the GDP growth rate does not imply that India's economic problems are solved. A leading feature to note in India is high levels of extreme poverty, prevalent in rural and urban areas alike. The countryside, where land is relatively scarce given the population density, remains home to some of the world's most chronic situations of malnutrition and undernourishment. Despite the decades since the end of princely titles and the abolition of caste discrimination, there are powerful landed elites that control much of the wealth, while incomes for the poor are tiny and fragile. Equally striking juxtapositions are found in the massive and growing inequalities in India's major cities. Mumbai has become a classic example of this, being a center both of the aforementioned corporate boom—with high-end real estate and a wealthy financial district—and of overcrowded slums (Mehta 2004). Regardless of innovation and entrepreneurship, work among the urban poor remains largely in the informal sector, with no benefits, much uncertainty, and often hazardous working and living conditions.

CASE STUDIES

CHAPTER 5, PAGE 100

CASE STUDY

What Explains India's Recent Growth?

For many years after its independence from Britain in 1947, India achieved relatively slow growth on the order of about 4 percent per year. Growth was hindered by extensive regulations and the "license raj" that required many licenses and approvals to conduct business. Under this system, state policy often favored the well connected rather than making decisions based on economic rationality and efficiency. Economic improvements have been more dramatic in recent years, and this change has followed the implementation of pro-market economic reforms in 1991 at the direction of Manmohan Singh, who at the time was finance minister and later served as Prime Minister. But what is India's development path, and does openness to the market alone explain its recent success?

There are a number of distinctive features of India's development. One is that India established a robust democracy *before* achieving a modern economy, whereas many theories lead us to expect the opposite sequence. This makes India a very interesting case for scholars who want to study how politics shapes economic performance. India's state action has long been shaped by the government's need to respond to the expectations of important economic actors and the populace at large, which makes it different from development initiatives attempted by authoritarian regimes that could have more closed patterns of decision making (Kohli 2004).

India's recent growth has also been very interesting as a contrast to other developing countries, especially China. While China has achieved much of its rapid growth on the basis of investment in manufacturing, India has seen extensive growth in services as well and has boomed in part due to the growing consumption of its middle class, as opposed to investment for exports to foreign countries. While India and China have highly skilled professional sectors, a difference is in the caricature of each development model: China is the "world's workshop," making plastic toys and simple electronics on the factory floor, while India is the world's "back office," home to many "call centers" that provide customer service and other support, as well as engineering, computing, and other services (see Friedman 2005 for a popular version of this argument). The reality is much more nuanced, but the distinction illustrates some features of the respective paths.

An additional striking feature of Indian development is that high levels of extreme poverty have still accompanied its growth over the last two decades. While poverty has been reduced, hundreds of millions are still extremely poor in India. Scholars debate why extreme poverty persists in the country, with many stressing more growth as the remedy and others saying that only growth coupled with better governance, improved agricultural performance, and more effective investment in human capital will work (Sen 1999 Balakrishnan 2010).

As for the causes of the boom, a common argument is that the liberalization of the economy after 1991 was the key factor. This can certainly be supported by the timing of the boom, which began after the reforms had taken root, though critics could argue that the boom did not happen immediately following the reforms. Policy reform is not the only factor, however. Careful attention should be paid to the deeper historical origins of the contemporary Indian economy. In particular, the long emphasis on education under Nehru in such areas as science and technology has likely paid important dividends in subsequent decades as the beneficiaries of investments in education have entered the labor force (see Kohli 2004). The favorable international context has also mattered, including technological advances in telecommunications and information sharing that facilitated offshoring of service jobs to India's booming technology sector (Friedman 2005). In other words, while market reforms may have been a component of India's changing economic fortunes, the correlation between the two is not the same as proof of causation.

CASE STUDY
Democracy's Success in India: What Can We Learn from a "Deviant Case"?

CHAPTER 6, PAGE 136

How does modernization theory account for low-income democracies such as India? As discussed in chapter 6, modernization theory predicts that economic development will lead to democratization and democratic consolidation. Indeed, this relationship generally holds. More often than not, increasing economic development increases the probability that any given society will have democratic politics. India, however, poses a major anomaly for some versions of modernization theory. Given that India's population is approximately one-seventh of the world's population, this anomaly is not easily dismissed.

Why does India constitute an anomaly or "deviant case" for modernization theory? India only recently began to see notable economic development; and for most of the twentieth century, the country was profoundly poor. Modernization would lead us to suspect authoritarian governance under these conditions. Yet after decolonization, India defied pessimists and built the world's largest democracy, one that has now endured for decades. There are several conclusions that one could draw from this. We could decide that this anomaly disproves or

refutes modernization theory, and turn to some other theory of democratization. For example, we could turn to institutional theories of democratization as an alternative. Perhaps something about the parliamentary form of government rather than presidential government contributed to India's rather successful democracy (as is discussed in chapter 10); one could consider the Indian case to test this hypothesis. For example, has the parliamentary system with its multiparty coalitions and governments that are accountable to the legislature resulted in more power-sharing and less "winner-take-all" politics? Has it resulted in a prime ministerial "style" that is less centralized than in presidential systems? There is evidence both for and against the argument that parliamentarism has been a cause of India's democratic success.

Another alternative, though, would be to use a deviant case like India's democracy to amend or clarify the nature of the original theory. What if modernization theory is not making the law-like generalization that development leads inevitably to democratization, but rather a "weaker" claim that economic

development *facilitates* democratization and democratic consolidation? Why would this be different? Because the theory would now say that it is *unlikely* that India could successfully democratize without first achieving a higher level of economic development, but not that it is *impossible*. A more flexible theory of modernization might be compatible by including insights from other theories. For example, perhaps modernization theory could be linked to institutional theories, like the one on parliamentarism mentioned previously. Maybe parliamentarism is particularly called for as a form of institutional design when the society in question has a relatively low level of economic development. We are speculating here for the sake of argument and not proposing this theory; India's history of development and democracy does not and cannot prove this assertion. Rather, it might suggest this hypothesis, which we could then test through the examination of other well-selected cases. In general, deviant cases are useful. We should be pleased when we find them, as they help us to critically assess existing theories, modifying or rejecting them as appropriate.

CASE STUDY
Federalism and Differences in Development in India

CHAPTER 8, PAGE 192

One of the main advantages of federalism is purported to be its impact on economic and social development. As noted in chapter 8, federal systems may allow different states to engage in healthy

competition with one another while also ensuring that government decisions about taxes and services are "closer to the people," and thus more responsive. A country like India, the United States, or

Brazil can have different policies in different states, each adapted to local needs and demands. Yet this key advantage of federalism and decentralized government is also one of its disadvantages:

CASE STUDY (continued)
Federalism and Differences in Development in India
CHAPTER 8, PAGE 192

allowing states to do things differently can mean some may do better and some worse than others.

India has highly varying levels of development and economic well-being, and some of the variations are by state. In recent years, federalism has been complemented by decentralization to a more local level, as major reforms transferred significant development responsibilities from the central government to local institutions, a system of decentralization known as the *panchayat raj*. For comparativists studying a country as huge and complex as India, a comparison across states or across local communities can be as fruitful as efforts to compare India to another country (Kohli 1990, Mullen 2011, e.g.).

Some Indian states have witnessed very high performance, with some of the best outcomes found in relatively unlikely places. The state of Kerala, for example, was renowned for a period of time as a place where significant improvements

in development indicators were realized without rapid economic growth but rather through strategic interventions in providing public services made by the Communist Party that governed in the state (Sen 1999). In West Bengal as well, surprising achievements happened in rural areas as Communists with few links to the landed elite were able to reach out to the poor in the countryside and incorporate them into politics (Kohli 1989). Yet other states—such as the poor states of Bihar and Orissa—have lagged behind considerably. In terms of India's economic boom, advances have been clearest in some of the areas where high-tech industries and firms have clustered, such as around the metropolitan cities of Delhi and Mumbai, as well as Bengaluru (formerly Bangalore) in the state of Karnataka and Hyderabad in the state of Andhra Pradesh.

Are federalism and decentralization of power thus "good" for development because they allow the better-performing states to get ahead and set the model for

the worse performers, or are they "bad" for development because they allow the worse-performing states to fall behind? There is no simple answer to this question. One thing that is certain is that poorly governed states do not always automatically adopt models as demonstrated by well-governed states. Politics, history, and other institutions shape policy responses and do not always easily allow the "right" policy to be chosen (see Kohli 1989, Mullen 2011). The states that are poorly governed often remain that way, to the detriment of their populations, regardless of being able to observe better performance in other places. On the other hand, federalism and decentralization can be seen as providing opportunities for those states with healthier institutions and political cultures to be able to benefit their own populations, even if governance elsewhere in the country is poor. The pros and cons of federalism are thus both on display in highly uneven political economies like India.

CASE STUDY
Ethnicity and Political Parties in India
CHAPTER 14, PAGE 344

Indian society was historically divided into "castes," and many have viewed these divisions as long-standing (e.g., Dumont 1981), though more recently some historians have argued that the caste "system" as such only developed during the period of British colonialism (Dirks 2001). The proponents of the latter view are not saying that caste did not exist before colonialism, but rather that

the British used it as an instrument of colonial rule and in doing so, universalized and rigidified it. Depending on how one defines ethnic groups, populations defined as castes can be thought of as falling into this category. The question is a bit complicated, since caste groups are understood to form bases in the society's stratification system rather than culturally distinct groups that exist side

by side (in other words, caste's linkage to the class structure is more direct than the general correlation between class and status group that we find in some other societies). It is also debatable whether the Hindu nationalist party Bharatiya Janata Party (BJP) should be considered an ethnic party: it is ostensibly organized around religion, but ethnic and religious differences are often closely associated.

CASE STUDY (continued)
Ethnicity and Political Parties in India

CHAPTER 14, PAGE 344

The Bahujan Samaj Party (BSP) stands out for its relative success in recent years in some states. This party aims to represent low-caste individuals. Kanchan Chandra (2004), in an important book on the subject, refers to these groups as the "scheduled castes" rather than the "untouchables," a label you might have heard but one that is considered offensive by many. Chandra seeks to develop a general theory of the success of ethnic parties based largely on the analysis of the BSP. This theory is limited to "patronage democracies" in which the spoils of the state are the main objects of political competition, and political parties are, at least in part, vehicles through which groups aim to capture those spoils.

Chandra's basic contention is that parties will be successful at capturing a high percentage of the vote of the ethnic group or groups they claim to represent when two criteria are met. The first is that the internal party structure must allow members of the group in question to move up within the party. This is because potential voters need to be able to see that group members will actually be able to hold some power and, presumably, access spoils. The second major criterion is that the party must stand a reasonable chance of actually winning a share of power. Again, the presumption is that it would be irrational to cast one's vote for a party that stands no reasonable chance of winning. This is shaped by (1) the relative size of the group or coalition of groups in question, (2) the perceived likelihood that members of those groups will vote for the party, and (3) the nature of the electoral system. As you think about Chandra's approach to the analysis of ethnic parties, consider how well it might explain other cases mentioned in chapter 14.

CASE STUDY
India in the Twenty-First Century: Domestic Politics, Identity, and Security

CHAPTER 16, PAGE 391

In India, domestic and international politics are deeply intertwined. This is true on questions of security as well as in the economy. Especially important is the country's relationship with neighboring Pakistan and how this reflects relations between Indians domestically. The challenge of India–Pakistan relations affects questions of nationhood, identity, violence, and government in India; in short, international relations affect most everything addressed in the chapters of this book. On the flip side, India's domestic politics also affects its international relations. Comparative politics and international relations may be two subfields of political science, but they are not totally separable.

India's long and contested border with Pakistan is often called the "world's most dangerous border." It has been a source of conflict for more than sixty years, since the partition of India at independence in 1947; that division left millions of Muslims in India and millions of Hindus in Pakistan that wanted to change their nationhood and generated flows of refugees across the borders in both directions. Religious differences, both within India and between the two countries, have been important ever since. One of the most contentious points has long been the disputed region of Kashmir, which is claimed by Pakistan but currently administered by India. The border between Pakistan and India is notoriously tense and is clouded by the prospect of nuclear standoff or even possible use of nuclear weapons. In 1998, Pakistan's testing of an atomic device resulted in India testing its own devices just days later; both tests were widely seen as provocative signals to the opposite country. Indeed, the development of nuclear weapons in Pakistan was fueled in large measure by historical animosity toward India, which was a nuclear power as of the 1970s. The fact that both have nuclear weapons heightens the stakes of war and peace in the region.

Relations between the countries affect the domestic politics of each in many ways. To consider just India here, a key issue in domestic politics is, of course, how to handle relations with Pakistan. But this is more than just a policy issue: it enters into the many topics we have discussed throughout the chapters of this book. For example, the very question of Indian nationhood and identity, the political party system, and the resulting policymaking in the Indian parliament have been affected by the question of Islam and the resulting rise of Hindu nationalist sentiment. This was at the origin of some of the popularity of the Hindu nationalist BJP, which governed from 1998 to 2004 and again from 2014 to today, though the party addresses issues other than Hindu nationalism. Distrust between groups is fed by such events as the 2008 bombings in the metropolis of Mumbai by Pakistani militants, though it should be noted that most Hindus and Muslims in India live side by side peacefully; indeed, many Muslim groups spoke out against the attacks, and there was relatively little recrimination against Indian Muslims generally.

In this connection, it is worth remembering that India itself has a large Muslim population. A decade ago India had approximately 160 million Muslims, which was a minority of the country's population but still represented over 10 percent of the world's Muslims and the third-largest Muslim population in the world after those of Indonesia and Pakistan (Pew Forum 2009). The Pew Research Center expects that Muslim population of India to continue to grow, estimating that it will reach 311 million by 2050, and if Pew's projections are correct India will at that time be the country with both the largest Hindu and the largest Muslim populations in the world (Pew Research Center 2015).

The international relationship between the two nuclear powers of India and Pakistan also affects the domestic politics of other countries around the globe. The United States, for instance, debates its relationship with Pakistan, which seems a necessary yet challenging one. There is distrust between the countries, with the United States accusing Pakistan of a duplicitous intelligence and security services that seek to harbor

Islamic fundamentalist terror groups rather than hunt them down; the most obvious example came after the death of al Qaeda leader Osama bin Laden, who was found living very close to a major Pakistani military academy. Yet a common analysis is that Pakistan is primarily concerned about its relationship with India and dedicates its security and intelligence forces toward India rather than toward Afghanistan and al Qaeda.

The fact that there are some tensions around religious differences and geopolitical rivalry with Pakistan does not suggest in any way that Islam is a "problem" that drives Indian politics. India has persisted for over six decades as a democracy with basic rights for all, and most Indians of different religions live peacefully alongside one another. The country also has many other hot issues of identity and nationhood, such as traditional social segregation by class or caste, for example. The relevance of these issues simply illustrates how international factors feed into domestic politics, and vice versa.

Research Prompts

1. As a low-income democracy, India is seen as a deviant case for modernization theory when it comes to democratization. What comparative analyses could you set up to test hypotheses about the reasons behind India's democratic success? Would you prefer another low-income democracy elsewhere, such as Ghana in Africa? Or a low-income country neighboring India that shares a region and some history but is not democratic, such as Pakistan? What would be the merits of your research design?

2. Do a brief search of the literature to find two or more states of India to compare on the question of economic development. What do you find are some of the main factors that emerge to account for why certain states have done better or worse than others?

3. India has developed economically at a much faster rate since making economic reforms beginning in 1991. What is the best argument you can make that India's economic boom of the last

two decades has been based on something *other than* this set of reforms? What is the evidence you have to make this other claim?

4. If relations between India and Pakistan are deeply rooted in identity issues and history, what are the implications for policymaking that might contribute to peace going forward? Are there any factors that can be changed (unlike the demographics and history of the countries) that can contribute to a more optimistic outcome?

5. The end of British colonialism in India was led by remarkable historical figures such as Mahatma Gandhi, who was seen as a national hero. Yet independent India (while democratic) was neither peaceful nor just: it has witnessed significant sectarian violence, political assassinations, ongoing social inequalities, and state corruption. Does this imply that the efforts of individuals such as Gandhi are ultimately unable to transform the quality of governance, and that politics depends more on cultures and structures that individuals cannot change? If not, why was someone like Gandhi unable to create lasting change in these areas? If so, on the other hand, how can one account for the decolonization of India itself without reference to individuals and their actions?

Iran (Islamic Republic of Iran)

Key Features of Contemporary Iran

Population:	82,021,564 (estimate, July 2017)
Area:	1,648,195 square kilometers
Head of State:	Ali Hoseini-Khamenei (Supreme Leader, 1989–present)
Head of Government:	Hasan Ruhani (president, 2013–present)
Capital:	Tehran
Year of Independence:	The Islamic Republic was founded in 1979, but Iran was never fully colonized and had been a distinct geopolitical entity in a variety of forms for centuries.
Year of Current Constitution:	1979
Languages:	Persian is the majority language. Other important languages include Turkic, Azeri, Kurdish, and Luri, among others.
GDP per Capita:	$18,100 (*CIA World Factbook estimate*, 2016)
Human Development Index Ranking (2016):	69th (high human development)

Sources: *CIA World Factbook*; World Bank World Development Indicators; United Nations *Human Development Report 2016*.

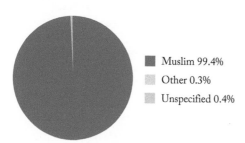

- Muslim 99.4%
- Other 0.3%
- Unspecified 0.4%

Religious Affiliation in Iran

A large majority of Muslims in Iran practice Shia Islam.
Source: CIA World Factbook.

Introduction

Iran is of interest to many political analysts because of its revolutionary regime and because of its foreign policy. Many international relations thinkers see Iran as potentially threatening to the West, and in particular to American policy in the Middle East, as well as to Israel. Given that in 1979, Iran witnessed a revolution against an authoritarian regime backed by the United States, yielding a strongly religious, anti-American regime; and given further that the United States has backed authoritarian governments in other Islamic societies in an effort to prevent governments like that in Iran from taking power there, much attention has been focused on explaining contemporary Iranian politics. And indeed these are important considerations. However, it is important that we not think of Iran *solely* in terms of the foreign policy interests of the West. Rather, we, as comparative political analysts, need to treat it like any other case, posing empirical questions about why the country's politics has the features that it does.

The "revolutionary" character of the regime is itself a source of considerable interest. While in some respects the Iranian revolution resembled other major revolutions, it differed from many in that it did not clearly lean toward the political left, though some elements in the revolutionary coalition did (Parsa 2000; Kurzman 2004; Salehi-Isfahani 2009: 32–33). Indeed, it is hard to place the Iranian revolution in ideological terms. In certain respects, it is very conservative, and it often is described as such. Yet secular Marxists were part of the revolutionary coalition that helped to bring down the Shah, and even today there are features of the Iranian government that are left-leaning. Thus, Iran has the potential to unsettle some of our preconceived notions about how politics works.

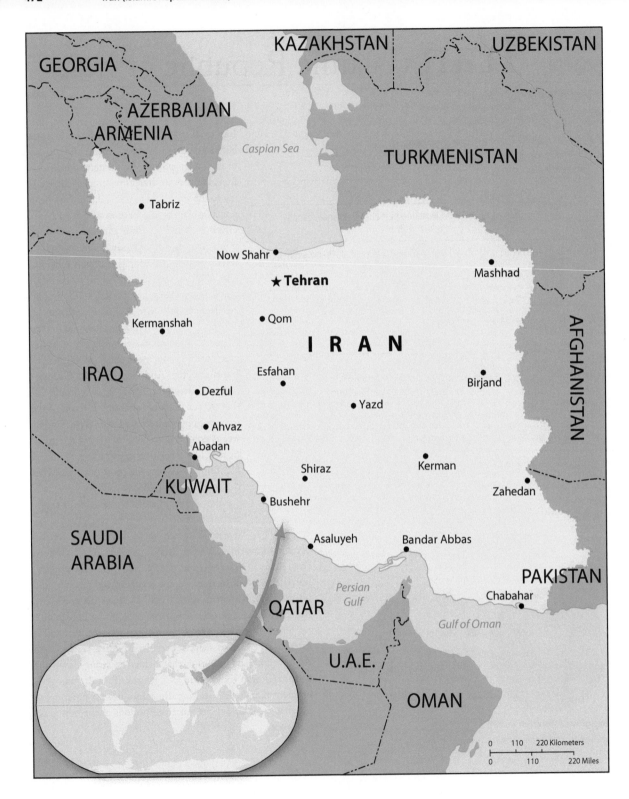

Historical Development

Iran has a long and fascinating history, dating back to the great Persian Empire (and earlier). Here we are interested in its contemporary history, which means that we need to begin with the twentieth century. Our goal is to understand how Iran developed such that the Islamic Revolution could take place in 1979.

It is critical to understand that although Iran had not been formally colonized, it had been at the mercy of two imperial powers, Great Britain and Russia (and later the Soviet Union), for some years (Hambly [1991] 2008a, [1991] 2008b). This weakened the Qajar Dynasty, which had held power since 1795 in a monarchical system. Iran was largely a traditional religious society in which Shari'a law was practiced, and the clergy exercised some state-like functions (Keddie [1991] 2008: 179), but Western-derived ideas of nationalism and modernization had begun to seep into the country by the late nineteenth century (Moaddel 2005). In 1905–1906, contentious action forced the Qajar to adopt a constitutional monarchy (Keddie [1991] 2008: 202–203). This is not to say that the Qajar regime was happy about such a development (Keddie [1991] 2008: 205–207), and the Shah in 1908 attempted to circumvent constitutionality but was forced from office. He would make a failed attempted to reestablish his authority two years later. The turn to constitutional monarchy did not, however, make the British and Russians any less likely to intervene in Iran; and in 1907, at the Anglo-Russian Convention, they had essentially agreed to divide the country into zones where one or the other power would exert predominant influence (Keddie [1991] 2008: 205). Foreign intervention continued during the First World War. After the war, the government made an agreement with the United Kingdom that would have expanded that country's influence in Iran; but the agreement was not implemented, and its contents generated discontent when they became public (Hambly [1991] 2008b: 215–217).

In 1921, Reza Khan helped to organize a coup d'état, with Sayyid Ziya al-Din Tabatabai emerging as Prime Minister and Reza Khan as Minister of War (Keddie [1991] 2008: 210–212; Hambly [1991] 2008b: 219–221). Reza Khan would become Prime Minister himself in 1923 and then, in 1925, he would become the country's monarch (Hambly 2008b: 224–225), as Reza Shah Pahlavi, inaugurating the Pahlavi Dynasty, which would last until 1979. Reza Shah, like his son and successor, Mohammad Reza Shah (often referred to simply as "the Shah"), was secular, Westernizing,

and modernizing in orientation. Notable projects included the establishment of a Western-style legal system, the expansion of the state bureaucracy, and the creation of the Trans-Iranian Railway. Reza Shah also tried to force his subjects to wear Western clothing, among other symbolic mandates (Hambly [1991] 2008b: 225–226, 230–232).

The Shah established close ties with Germany in the 1930s (Hambly [1991] 2008b: 241–243). While this may have owed more to interest (achieving a counterweight to the Soviet Union and the United Kingdom) than to ideological affinity, the association would later prove problematic for him. During the Second World War, he attempted to maintain formal neutrality, but the Allies would not accept this, in part because they wanted to use the Trans-Iranian Railway to send supplies to Russia. As a result, Soviet and British troops occupied the country, and in 1941, the Shah resigned. This placed his son, Mohammad Reza Shah, on the throne. Not being formally associated with his father's links to Germany, the new Shah could weather the diplomatic and political storms. After some years, the Shah would be known as a strongly authoritarian ruler who used systematic violence to quell opposition.

A crisis would develop in the early 1950s after Mohammad Mosaddeq became Prime Minister (Hambly [1991] 2008a: 251–263). Mosaddeq, among other things, sought to nationalize Iran's oil industry (as had been done, for example, by Mexico with its own some years earlier). A coup d'état was launched, with support from both the United Kingdom and the United States, who wanted to ensure continued Western control over Iranian natural resources (Keddie [1991] 2008). There is no telling what would have happened had foreign intervention not brought down this government (Hambly [1991] 2008a: 254), but it is conceivable that Mosaddeq could have built on successful nationalization to expand Iranian democratization. In any case, this was not to be, and the Shah's authoritarian government negotiated generous terms for multinationals involved in the extraction of Iranian oil, such that nationalization would not dramatically impinge on the interests of the oil companies (Hambly [1991] 2008a: 265).

The Shah's regime was basically an authoritarian developmentalist state (Foran 2005: 75–81). Mohammad Reza Shah, in a series of economic plans, aimed to continue the process of industrialization and modernization that had been started under his father, using oil revenues as a principal source of funding. In this he was fairly successful: Iran

Historical Development

Timeline

1795–1925	Qajar Dynasty
1906	Constitutional monarchy established after the "Constitutional Revolution"
1907	Anglo-Russian Convention, used to justify English and Russian spheres of influence within Iran and periodic intervention
1908	Mohammad Ali Shah tries to undo the constitutional order but is forced from power.
1919	Anglo-Iranian Agreement, never implemented, but upon becoming public generates considerable discontent
1921	Reza Khan becomes Minister of War after helping to bring a coup that places Seyyed Zia'eedin Tabatabaee as Prime Minister (still under the Qajar Dynasty).
1923	Reza Khan (later to be Reza Shah) becomes Prime Minister.
1923	Ahmad Shah leaves the country, showing Qajar Dynasty's weakness.
1923	Major political reforms
1925	Reza Shah Pahlavi becomes monarch (beginning of Pahlavi Dynasty)
1925–1926	Establishment of European-style legal system
1938	Completion of Trans-Iranian railway
1941	Reza Shah resigns following the country's occupation by the United Kingdom and the Soviet Union (part of World War II), leaving Mohammed Reza Shah in power.
1942	Formal alliance is formed between Iran, the United Kingdom, and the Soviet Union in the struggle against the Nazis.
1944	Death of Reza Shah
1951–1953	Tumultuous period in which the elected government of Mohammad Mosaddeq holds power, including efforts to nationalize the Iranian oil industry.
1953	Coup d'état, with backing from Britain and the United States, brings down the Mosaddeq government.
1954	Settlement of the oil industry question, with favorable terms for multinational corporations

1963	The "White Revolution" is announced, and includes a number of reforms such as agrarian reform and women's suffrage.
1963	Exile of Ayatollah Khomeini
1973	Spike in global oil prices benefits Iran in the short term.
1978–1979	Increasing social conflict, Iranian Revolution, and the return of Ayatollah Khomeini; the Shah departs Iran.
1979	Foundation of Islamic Republic; by the end of the year, religious leaders had come to dominate, and a new constitution was passed.
1979	Beginning of Iranian hostage crisis
1980	Abolhassan Bani-Sadr is elected as president, but is impeached the following year.
1980–1989	Iran–Iraq War
1981	Release of American hostages shortly after Ronald Reagan takes office
1981	Bani-Sadr forced from power by Khomeini, further cementing the position of religious leaders in the revolutionary regime.
1981	Mohammad-Ali Rajai elected president but killed within a month; Ali Khamenei, future Supreme Leader, assumes the presidency.
1988	Iran Air flight 655 is shot down accidentally by the United States, killing 290 passengers and crew members.
1989	Death of Ayatollah Khomeini; rise of Ayatollah Khamenei; election of Akbar Hashemi Rafsanjani to the presidency
1997	Election of Mohammad Khatami to the presidency (perceived as more liberal, raising hopes of reform in both Iran and the West)
2005	Election of Mahmoud Ahmadinejad to the presidency (perceived as a hardliner, dampening hopes for reform)
2009	Ahmadinejad's re-election, apparently fraudulent, provokes major protests.
2013	Hassan Rouhani is elected president.
2015	Joint Comprehensive Plan of Action (JCPOA) on nuclear weapons program reached between Iran and the United States, China, France, Germany, Russia, and the United Kingdom.

modernized somewhat rapidly, built a middle class with a cosmopolitan orientation, and established a notable higher education infrastructure. In political terms, the Shah was largely regressive, though he was willing to make reforms when he thought this would enhance his position. Thus the "White Revolution" of 1963 distributed land, extended suffrage (most notably to women), and made a number of other reforms (Hambly [1991] 2008a: 279–283). This should not be understood as purely benevolent largesse, however: The Shah faced civil discontent and protests, and his "White Revolution" was accompanied by efforts to repress his critics. For example, the Ayatollah Khomeini, a prominent cleric, was forced to leave the country in 1963. More generally, the Shah's state was highly repressive, and the security forces (the SAVAK) were notorious for torturing and murdering dissidents (Foran 2005: 77; Hambly [1991] 2008a: 290–291). It is worth further emphasizing that this regime was supported by Western powers like the United Kingdom and the United States, largely because of Cold War concerns. Indeed, when President Jimmy Carter began to emphasize human rights as a major criterion in U.S. foreign policy in the late 1970s, this helped to weaken the Shah's position (Foran 2005: 78; Kurzman 2004: 22–23). This occurred during an economic downturn, further weakening the Shah.

Just the same, the revolution took many by surprise. According to Charles Kurzman, it was "unthinkable," both in the sense that few predicted it and because social-scientific theories have had some difficulty in accounting for it (Kurzman 2004). It is important to emphasize that in 1978 and 1979, actors demanding change spanned the political spectrum and the religious–secular divide: it was by no means obvious to all that a conservative religious regime would emerge victorious from the Iranian Revolution, at least initially; though it is also clear that the religious component of the revolution was absolutely central to its success, as Khomeini was the one actor who seemed capable of unifying diverse revolutionary elements (Arjomand 2009). Secular Marxists were important in the opposition to the Shah's regime; and over time, the middle class got on board as well. As often happens in revolutions, various groups likely felt that they would be able to control the process, and the secular allies of the clergy undoubtedly did not envision the regime that emerged. Scholars who are interested in the role of culture in explaining revolutions often point to this case, drawing attention to the importance of Twelver Shi'ism in Iran, which facilitated the rise of the clergy to political leadership, particularly on Khomeini's interpretation of the nature of sacred authority (Arjomand 2009: 16–35). The clergy's consolidation of their power only took place over the first couple of years of the regime, during and after the conflict with Bani Sadr. Even in the constitutional order that was established, which places ultimate authority with the clergy (discussed further in the case studies that follow), some democratic forms are present, with elections held for the presidency and the parliament.

It would not be an exaggeration to say that the Iranian Revolution shocked the world. What to make of a revolutionary regime that was radically anti-Western but not also secular and socialist on the model of China and the Soviet Union? At the very least, this dramatically complicated the modernization narratives that underlay both Soviet and Western capitalist development. When American hostages were taken by revolutionary sympathizers, this did little to ease the shock. An effort to rescue them authorized by Jimmy Carter was unsuccessful, and they would only be released after Ronald Reagan took office.

During the post-revolutionary era, we could divide Iranian presidential politics into five main periods. The first is the instability of the early years. The second is the period of Khamenei's presidency during which clerical authority was consolidated and the war with Iraq took place. The third is the period of Rafsanjani's presidency, after 1989, during which, as Arjomand notes (2009: 7), the system of "dual leadership" between the Supreme Leader and the president fully developed. Rafsanjani's presidency is also notable for efforts to rebuild the Iranian economy, which included some capitalist reforms. The fourth period encompasses Mohammad Khatami's reformist presidency beginning in 1997, which raised hopes for many that the regime would liberalize. Finally, the 2005 election of Mahmoud Ahmadinejad opened a period of conservative retrenchment.

Some expected that revolutionary Iran would not last, particularly given international pressures that it faced, including the Iran–Iraq War (1980–1989) but also the country's relative diplomatic isolation. Yet the regime consolidated its control and it has remained in power since. The transition after Khomeini's death in 1989 was particularly important. Arjomand (2009) describes what followed, in the language of Max Weber, as the "routinization" or "institutionalization" of the "charismatic authority" of Khomeini, meaning that the revolution had to face the classic problem of going on without its mystical leader and turning the revolution into something that did not depend on that leader. Major constitutional reforms removed the office of Prime Minister, making the system more presidentialist; and in many ways, the reforms also solidified the clergy's power and authority. Sayyed Ali Khamenei took over as the new Supreme Leader, a post he still holds at the time of this writing. With the election of the relatively liberal Mohammad Khatami in 1997, some observers both in Iran and abroad felt that the regime might be opening to greater democratization, but these hopes were dashed after the election of Ahmadinejad in 2005. Ahmadinejad was both a hardliner *and* a populist whose demagoguery appealed to many of Iran's worse off. Just the same, he faced opposition, and his re-election in 2009 was denounced by many as fraudulent. This led to major protests against the regime, in the so-called "Green Revolution" (discussed further in the Case Study "Iran's Islamic Revolution and 'Green Revolution'?"), supported by many prominent former leaders. Again, it seemed for a time like the regime might need to make major concessions, but the use of force brought the protests to a halt. Some have seen the 2013 election of Hassan Rouhani as signaling a partial move back toward the center, and some were hopeful about his election leading to a potential thawing of Iranian–Western relations. It is possible to interpret the 2015 JCPOA agreement—the so-called Iran nuclear deal—between Iran and major western powers against this background. At the same time, the fate of that agreement is unclear, and the relationship between Iran and the West remains conflictual.

It should also be noted that Iran has fraught relations with many neighbors. It has supported the brutal regime of Bashar al-Assad in Syria and has long posed a threat to Israel. Beyond this, it has a major regional rivalry with Saudi Arabia (a Sunni-led country). One manifestation of this rivalry has been the conflict by proxy in Yemen, where Saudi Arabia has accused Iran of backing a group of rebels known as the Houthi.

Regime and Political Institutions

Iran's policymaking process is very complex, as both elected and non-elected officials play major roles in setting policy. The regime has a dual nature, as the elected features of a republic mix with the institutions of theocratic rule by Muslim clerics. On one hand, Iran is a presidential system with a popularly elected president that governs with the cabinet. The parliament, known as the Majlis, is also elected, and it exerts some checks on presidential power. However, another important policymaking body is the Guardian Council, a group of twelve clerics that have a range of important powers. They can approve or reject candidates for the presidency, for parliament, and for ministerial positions. They can also veto legislation made by the Majlis if they deem it not to fit with Islamic law or the Iranian Constitution. Finally, the Supreme Leader is perhaps the central figure in Iranian politics. He too is a cleric (a high-ranking *ayatollah*), and he appoints half of the members of the Guardian Council as well as the head of the judiciary; the Supreme Leader also indirectly controls who is eligible for the other six posts in the Guardian Council, since the head of the judiciary nominates these for consideration by the Majlis. The Supreme Leader, not the president, has authority over the military. Moreover, the Supreme Leader must officially affirm the election of the president. Many commentators thus conclude that power lies ultimately with the clergy and not with the more "democratic" bodies in Iran, though these elected bodies are not mere puppets. Finally, there are additional consultative bodies in Iran: An Expediency Council advises the Supreme Leader, and an Assembly of Experts is empowered to elect the Supreme

Regime and Political Institutions

Regime	Theocratic state, but with some features of presidential and parliamentary democracy
Administrative Divisions	Unitary state; thirty provinces + capital province of Tehran
Executive Branch	President and cabinet, but with a number of executive functions held by the Supreme Leader (non-elected) and the Guardian Council
Selection of Executive	Election from within a set of candidates approved by the Guardian Council
Legislative Branch	Elected Parliament, called the Majlis; the Guardian Council can veto legislation.
Judicial Branch	Politicized judiciary controlled by religious conservatives, with Islamic law the basis of the system. Supreme Court and Judicial High Council are top bodies.
Political Party System	Multiparty system but with restrictions

Leader after his predecessor dies, resigns, or is incapacitated; the Assembly of Experts is nominally empowered to review the Supreme Leader, but has not done so in practice, perhaps in part because its composition is indirectly controlled by the Supreme Leader. These arrangements are discussed in more detail in the case studies that follow.

Political Culture

One feature of Iranian political culture is the extent to which religiosity, ideological orientation, political traditionalism, and worldview correspond to position in the Iranian class structure. Of course, cultural orientation everywhere is linked to social class, as generations of sociologists have shown, but this tends to be very pronounced in countries like Iran. Part of this has to do with the fact that Iran, like its neighbor, Turkey, went through an effort at Westernization and modernization "from above." Reza Shah in Iran, and Kemal Ataturk in Turkey, each attempted to not only modernize the economy, the state bureaucracy, and the infrastructure of their countries, but to Westernize their populations culturally. This meant, in part, accepting a particular Western conception of what modernity is, one that privileges the secular. Both regimes attempted to impose a Western cultural program as a sort of total way of life, regulating, for example, the clothing of their populations (as a number of other countries, starting at least with Russia under Peter the Great, had done). In both countries, this program was most successful among those groups that benefited most from modernization. It is not surprising that middle-class persons in Iran would be more likely to adopt a Western cultural style, both because of the benefits they derived and because institutions in which they were embedded, such as the universities and the state bureaucracy, reinforced this style. Those groups that benefited less, though, and that were less organizationally wedded to a Westernized cultural style, did not undergo the same change to the same extent. As a result, poorer and more rural actors remained more religious and traditional in their orientation (as, indeed, poorer and more rural populations tend to do in general). This difference lives on in contemporary Iran, though we would not wish to exaggerate it.

Related to this is the character of Iranian nationalism. In many, and perhaps most, countries, nationalism has a secular character (Greenfeld 1992), perhaps because the idea of the sovereign authority of the people has the potential to undercut religious organizations. This was certainly true in Iran under the Shah, and even earlier, when a secular brand of nationalist discourse was used as an alternative to Islam (Moaddel 2005). In this respect, Iran was similar to many of the Arab states—such as Iraq, Egypt, and Syria, among others—which also saw secular nationalism juxtaposed to Islam. Yet Iran saw the emergence of an alternative, religious nationalism, which defined itself *against* this secular nationalism (Juergensmeyer 1993). This alternative nationalism could present itself as authentically Islamic and could present its secularist alternative as a foreign import, possibly even colonial. In any case, religious nationalism of this sort has been and remains an important feature of Iranian political culture.

Political Economy

One of the most striking features of the Iranian Revolution and its aftermath is the damage that was done to the economy. Economic growth dropped dramatically in the years after 1979, with GDP per capita dropping by 50 percent over the revolutionary regime's first decade before gradually recovering to around pre-revolutionary levels (Salehi-Isfahani 2009: 6–7). Part of this has to do with the fact that Iran is a major oil producer, and the international oil market hit all oil exporters hard in the 1980s, with lower commodity prices in general contributing to the debt woes of much of the developing world in that period. As Salehi-Isfahani notes (2009: 7), bad policy and the long-standing war with Iraq also played major roles in the country's poor economic performance in this period. Not surprisingly, when Hashemi-Rafsanjani was elected in 1989, he embarked on economic reforms (Arjomand 2009: 56–58), including privatization of some enterprises—though these were minimal, and public sector employment remained high—and changes made to financial markets. Economic performance in the 1990s was mixed; but with the oil boom of the 2000s, Iran achieved notable growth and accompanying improvements in well-being (Salehi-Isfahani 2009: 8).

The most important problem that Iran faces, like that of other oil producers, is managing to achieve sustainable growth while easing its own dependence on oil. For a time, sanctions that had been placed on Iran had negatively impacted their oil exports, but after JCPOA, the oil industry has recovered somewhat (CIA World Factbook, https://www.cia.gov/library/publications/the-world-factbook/geos/print_ir.html). Nonetheless, Iran's economy suffers from some of the known challenges faced by other major oil producing countries (see discussion in Chapter 5 and in the Nigeria country materials).

For the oil that stays in the country, the government has traditionally provided massive subsidies for energy consumption that were declared to be in the range of $100 billion per year up to 2010. The country's oil dependence is visible if we look at various economic sectors' share of GDP: as of 2016, agriculture stands at 9.8 percent, with industry at 34.3 percent and services at 55.9 percent (*CIA World Factbook*). In addition to the problem of oil dependence and questions of the "resource curse" discussed in the Nigeria case, Iran's broader economy was damaged by sanctions prior to the JCPOA nuclear agreement. In 2015, the country's currency (the *rial*) was worth only about one-third in dollar terms of what it was worth in 2012. The Iranian economy has improved somewhat since the nuclear deal, but not to the extent that many in Iran had hoped (Laub 2017).

Finally, like many developing countries (and some "developed" countries, notably Spain), Iran has a growing problem with youth unemployment. The country's general unemployment rate as of 2016 stood at an estimated 12.5 percent (*CIA World Factbook*), with youth and young adult unemployment considered to be notably higher. These figures are according to the Iranian government, and they may understate the true degree of unemployment in the country. Stronger growth would, of course, reduce these numbers some, but there is clear evidence that unemployment has become a structural part of Iran's economy.

CASE STUDIES

CASE STUDY

Democratic Features of Authoritarian Systems? The Case of Iran

CHAPTER 7, PAGE 152

We saw in chapter 6 that democracy and democratization are "moving targets" in the sense that standards and critical thresholds for democratic practice change over time. The United States of America in 1800, for example, would not be judged very democratic in today's world, though at the time, it was one of the democratic pioneers. So what do we make of countries that have some democratic features but that retain strong authoritarian characteristics as well? We saw in chapter 7 that one example of this can be found in the so-called "hybrid" or "competitive authoritarian" regimes that scholars have discussed in recent years, such as Venezuela. In these instances, the following pattern is common: a democratic system becomes *more* authoritarian over time as one set of actors becomes adept at manipulating institutions to maintain and augment their political interest. For the most authoritarian of such regimes, democratic competition becomes a farce that can be used to try to shore up the regime's legitimacy, but the underlying logic of the system is nearly fully authoritarian.

Iran, though, is a different sort of case. While very few commentators would regard the Iranian regime as *democratic*, it has some clear democratic *features*, and it is possible to argue that it is as democratic as the dictatorship of the Shah that preceded it (which had the support, incidentally, of the Western democracies). As noted in the preceding text, Iran does have an elected president and an elected legislature, the Majlis. Religious leadership can restrict individuals from running for these positions (and from serving in the Cabinet as well), and it does so with regularity. However, Iranian voters are nevertheless often faced with real choices in these elections. The reform movement associated with Mohammad Khatami, elected in 1997, discussed in the "Historical Development" section earlier in the chapter, gives clear indication of this, as does the shift that came with Mahmoud Ahmadinejad's election in

CASE STUDY (continued)

Democratic Features of Authoritarian Systems? The Case of Iran

CHAPTER 7, PAGE 152

2005. However, subsequent events make clear that not only do existing institutions work to limit and even exclude change, but institutional norms can be violated if necessary to preserve the status quo. Widespread perceptions of fraud in the 2009 re-election of Ahmadinejad led to protests that the regime quelled with violence.

Voters also have the ability to indirectly shape clerical rule. This is done through two institutional mechanisms. First, the elected Majlis can exert some influence over who is appointed to the Guardian Council. Second, the Assembly of Experts is actually an elected body. However, there is a catch. Only clergy can run in elections for this Assembly. Just the same, the electorate can indirectly exert *some* influence through this mechanism. Of course, complex systems of indirect influence produce collective action problems for individuals seeking to make far-reaching changes.

So it does little good to characterize the Iranian regime as just a dictatorship (Arjomand 2009: 4) or as "medieval." It seems to be something else. Culturally, at the root of this lies a conflict over the nature of sovereignty. Traditional, religious regimes historically have insisted that sovereignty was divine and thus could only be discerned or exercised by religiously legitimated authorities. Most modern democratic states—even constitutional monarchies—tend to view sovereignty as vested in the people (this change owed greatly to the global spread of national identity). The institutional structure of the Iranian state, though, seems to imply a sort of dual sovereignty of the people and a deity, with the latter (whose will, again, can only be discerned by religious elites) exerting ultimate authority. This set of arrangements is itself a function of the conflictual nature of the process that produced the current regime. Some

clerical actors were and are proponents of theocracy. Some other actors are proponents of popular sovereignty. The result is a sort of hybrid.

Many other states had historical periods in which sovereignty was blurred in this way. Prominent examples might be England in the seventeenth century and Japan after the Meiji Restoration, among many others. This could be taken to give optimism to those who hope for a more democratic Iran. However, we should not assume without further evidence that mixed sovereignty is a stage on a progressive, linear development. The fact that popular sovereignty and fully constitutional governance came to triumph in much of the world does not mean this will necessarily take place in Iran. In the meantime, we can only conclude, with Arjomand (2009: 6), that "theocratic government, participatory democracy, and populist social justice" exist in tension in Iran's post-revolutionary regime.

CASE STUDY

Constitutional Design: Theocracy in Iran

CHAPTER 8, PAGE 188

In Iran, Muslim clerics have very important roles in constitutional interpretation at the pinnacle of the political system, and indeed at lower levels of government as well. In this country where powerful clerics act as judges who interpret the constitution, the style of government has been seen as emblematic of the idea

of "theocracy," or rule by a religious hierarchy. To understand how this Islamic Republic works in practice requires an understanding of the mix of "Islamist" and "republican" implicit in the name.

Iran's governing structure was noted earlier in the "Regime and Political Institutions" section, but we review

certain aspects here that illustrate how the power of religious clerics operates. Iran has an elected president and an elected legislature (Majlis), but both are quite weak in certain aspects due to Iran's power structure. At the pinnacle of the political system, above the president, is the Supreme Leader, a cleric who is constitutionally empowered to ensure that Iran is governed in accordance with the principles of the Islamic Revolution. This head cleric appoints the judiciary (which enforces Islamic Shari'a law) and the leaders of the major media outlets, and has the authority to veto presidential candidates and/or remove elected presidents. This rule by religious leaders is buttressed by the Guardian Council of twelve clerics, the final authority on most matters. It has considerable powers, including a right to veto any law passed by the Majlis and the power to approve or veto any candidate for the presidency or legislature. It thus has more extensive powers than most constitutional courts or supreme courts.

The clerics of the Guardian Council are not directly elected. Instead, six of them are appointed by the Supreme Leader and six are selected by the Majlis, though the six chosen by the latter method are also subject to nomination by the judiciary. In effect, elected politicians and the policies they make are subject to review by clerics whose powers are judicial in nature, but they also have characteristics of legislative or executive power. The checks on the judiciary are more indirect and come with appointment of new clerics to the posts by political leaders. In a sense, this is similar to life appointments to constitutional courts in other countries: interpreters of

the constitution in countries such as the United States are appointed to life terms by the elected branches and are thus supposed to be free from political pressures. In Iran, however, those who do the appointing are not elected by conventional democratic means, which makes the notion of "checks and balances" more challenging to interpret.

The power of Supreme Leaders has shaped modern Iran. Ayatollah Ali Khamenei has been Supreme Leader since 1989 and is the successor to Ayatollah Ruhollah Khomeini, the leader of the Islamic Revolution that took power in 1979. Both of these Supreme Leaders have adhered to a strict interpretation of Shia' Islam and a conservative political stance that has resisted political reforms. Examples have included pushes for a strict adherence to Islamic law, a conservative dress code for women, and intolerance of critiques of the electoral process.

While the theocratic elements of the Iranian regime are prominent, we must not overlook the aspects of Iran's politics that are more "republican"—that is, that relate to elected officials. While elected officials are circumscribed by the power of the clerics, each elected government has made its imprint. The former president Mahmoud Ahmadinejad (2005–2013) was a fiery conservative who adopted a strongly anti-American and anti-Israel foreign policy that

distinguished his government from that of the president, Hassan Rouhani, who, as noted earlier, is seen as somewhat more reformist. Former president Ali Akbar Hashemi Rafsanjani (1989–1997), seen as a more mainstream conservative by Iranian standards, continued to wield influence chairman of the Assembly of Experts for some years and, until his death in 2017, as head of the Expediency Council, two bodies noted previously.

Iran is a challenging case that can help observers define the boundaries of what is a democracy and what is not, especially when it comes to the power of unelected officials and the nature of who chooses political leaders and how. From one perspective, Islamic countries may plausibly have different political legal systems than countries whose founders were of European origin and still have some features of a constitutional republic or a democracy. From another, basing law on religious texts interpreted by clerics will by definition constrain rights and liberties to an extent that democracy is not possible. In Iran, the judiciary seems to be an especially powerful branch of government, but the clerics also seem to have powers that go beyond those of a typical judicial branch. There is much to interpret in the question of whether Iran is a theocracy, a republic, or both, and whether it is dominated by the judiciary, the executive, or both.

In 1979, many observers were surprised by the Iranian Revolution. A coalition of actors including secular Marxists, students, everyday people, and especially religious readers like the Ayatollah Khomeini and their followers successfully deposed the Shah who had governed for decades. They then implemented an Islamic revolutionary regime. This case has fascinated scholars of revolution. It seems to problematize structuralist accounts of revolution, and scholars who seek to explain it have emphasized charismatic leadership (Arjomand 2009) and cultural or ideological frames (Foran 2005: 80–87; Parsa 2000) alongside structural factors. Indeed, one major theorist argues that social science simply cannot satisfactorily explain the Iranian Revolution (Kurzman 2004). It begs for comparison with other societies in the Muslim world where secular authoritarian dictatorships did *not* see successful Islamic revolutions (the comparison with Egypt, which became a center of Islamist *ideology*, is perhaps the most instructive). Scholars have considered a number of potential explanatory factors in this connection, one of the most promising being the potential political role of the clergy in Shi'ism, whereas Sunni Islam has a tradition of separation between religious and political leaders. Just the same, this is not a total explanation, since Sunni Islam is certainly compatible with regimes that legitimate themselves in religious terms and enforce religious law, with Saudi Arabia being just one notable contemporary example.

Ever since the revolution, the Iranian regime has been hard to classify. On one hand, it attempts to use the state's oil wealth to address social issues, and leaders like Mahmoud Ahmadinejad formed alliances with leaders of the international left, like Hugo Chávez in Venezuela. On the other hand, the regime is staunchly conservative, restricting behaviors it regards as immoral and upholding religious law, thus appearing to many to be reactionary. As has been noted, a religious council is the country's ultimate authority. Despite the successful consolidation of the revolution and the authoritarian nature of the regime it produced, post-revolutionary Iran has witnessed contention. Over the three decades in which this regime has held power, more moderate "reformers" like Mohammad Khatami have struggled against more radical figures like Ahmadinejad. Reformers have pushed for more pluralism, greater freedoms, and less hostile relationships with the West. In the 1990s, it looked like they might succeed, but they have since met with a number of setbacks.

In June of 2009, Ahmadinejad was reelected as president of Iran. His reelection was denounced as fraudulent by observers both internationally and in Iran. Protesters engaged in a series of massive street rallies, famously organizing themselves, in part, via new social media like Twitter and Facebook. Some began to speak optimistically of these protests as a "Green Revolution" that would usher in a less authoritarian, more democratic system. After some hesitation, the state used considerable force to repress these rallies, killing some of the protesters and making it clear that further protests would be met with greater violence. Leaders of the opposition—and some foreigners alleged to be in league with them—were arrested. Resistance to the regime went underground; and so far, at least, no "Green Revolution" has taken place. Scholars are still trying to sort out all of the reasons why the revolt was ultimately unsuccessful.

Some would stress the continued strength of the Iranian state, arguing that so long as a state is willing to violently repress protests and is capable of doing so, proponents of social change have little hope. Others argue that the lack of concrete international support doomed the protesters. Still others suggest that the protesters were only one among several major groups in the society and that the regime still has many supporters. Two key recent factors that add to the complicated prospects for collective action are the 2013 election of the more reformist Rouhani and the drop in global oil prices that took place earlier this decade. If the latter continues indefinitely, this could put pressure on the regime. The successes and failures of revolutions and social movements such as those in Iran are the subject of major debates; and indeed, in the long wake of the "Arab Spring," a process the Iranian regime has found worrisome, interest in these questions has only increased.

CASE STUDY

Gender in Post-Revolutionary Iranian Politics

CHAPTER 14, PAGE 337

Iranian society is notorious for gender inequality. It was hardly an egalitarian society in this respect before the 1979 revolution; and for most of the post-revolutionary period, religious elites have favored policies and views that many would consider discriminatory. The consequence and legacies of this show up clearly in the quantitative data. In terms of women's political representation in the legislature, Iran is near the bottom: it recently ranked 134th internationally, with 3.1 percent of seats in the Majlis held by women (Inter-parliamentary Union 2018). Similarly, its global Gender Empowerment Measure rank has the country in the 103rd position. The World Economic Forum's Gender Gap Index for 2016 ranks Iran 139th (out of 144). The country scores particularly badly in terms of "economic participation and opportunity" and "political empowerment." In recent years, Iran's performance in terms of gender equality/inequality in the

areas of "educational attainment" and "health and survival"—the other main components of the index—were also poor, though not as bad as the first two (World Economic Forum 2016). Moreover, feminist activists have been repressed (Haeri 2009: 125–126).

At the same time, some scholars have argued that the picture is more complicated than these data suggest. Ziba Mir-Hosseini (1999) has argued that in some areas, women's participation in public life has improved, notably in the educational system, and particularly in universities. Mir-Hosseini (1999: 7) points out that this may even be a function of religious traditionalism in a certain sense, since "the enforcement of hejab became a catalyst . . . [and] by making public space morally correct in the eyes of traditionalist families, it legitimated women's public presence." In recent years, females are near parity with males in terms of primary and secondary educational enrollment, and women's enrollment in

tertiary education *exceeds* that of men (Hausmann et al. 2010: 165). Mir-Hosseini further points to more gender-centered and even feminist trends in some areas of intellectual, cultural, and institutional life under the post-revolutionary regime, such as changes in divorce laws after 1992 and even the appointment of some female judges (1999: 7–8). Moreover, Shahla Haeri (2009) stresses an incipient women's movement in Iran, suggesting that expanding women's participation helped to fuel the reform agenda during the Khatami presidency and that women continue to organize.

Nobody would argue that the post-revolutionary regime in Iran is a feminist one, just as no proponent of liberal democracy would argue that Iran in 2015 was a democratic society. However, scholars remind us that beneath repressive surfaces, women and others work to expand women's rights in even the most difficult of circumstances.

CASE STUDY

Religion and Politics in Iran

CHAPTER 15, PAGE 364

Iran is a very interesting case to contrast with France with respect to the question of religion and politics. Like much of the Islamic world, Iran saw the rise of a twentieth-century regime that embraced secular nationalism. The Shah's regime constructed historical memories about the great Persian civilization of the past and tried to marginalize Islam.

The government of the Shah repressed religious leaders it considered a threat. In short, the Shah's regime aimed to conduct itself in accord with Western-derived notions of secular modernity (and, indeed, with the concrete backing of Western powers). In this it was roughly parallel to modernization in many predominantly Sunni parts of the Islamic

World: in places like Egypt, Iraq, and Syria, secular nationalist regimes predominated (for comparative discussion, see Moaddel 2005).

In many Muslim-majority countries, these secular-nationalist regimes were met with religiously organized resistance (Juergensmeyer 1993), though in most of the Islamic world, this resistance

CHAPTER 15, PAGE 364

CASE STUDY (continued)
Religion and Politics in Iran

was not successful in its ultimate objective of taking power. In Iran, this resistance *was* successful, and a religious regime captured the state in the revolution of 1979. Comparative analysts have debated the best explanation for the success of religious actors in Iran, but one of the most convincing theories is that Shi'a, rather than Sunni, Islam is dominant in Iran; and the clergy is historically more powerful and independent in Shi'a Islam, facilitating their serving as

political actors in the revolution. While this is not a total explanation—the presence of a strong clergy is not a necessary and sufficient condition for successful revolution—analysts believe that it *helps* us to understand why successful religious revolution might have been more likely in Iran.

The revolution produced a religious state that is nevertheless modern. Contemporary Iran is a highly differentiated society with extensive enrollment in

higher education, a complex state, and many of the other features we would typically consider key to modernity. But the state is understood to be legitimated in religious terms and to ultimately serve religious ends. As discussed in chapter 15, a number of scholars now argue that Western secular modernity is only one of a number of possible varieties. Modern Iran is a case in point. While some media depictions present it as a "backward" society, this is potentially deceiving.

CHAPTER 16, PAGE 390

CASE STUDY
Iran and the Politics of Nuclear Proliferation

Iran has a foreign policy that puts it in conflict with that of the United States, and the two countries have been in heated diplomatic conflict for years over Iran's "nuclear ambitions" and its apparent desire to develop a nuclear weapon. One leading American concern is that Iran will target its regional neighbor Israel, a key American ally in the volatile Middle East. Along with the United States, a number of other countries have hoped to prevent Iran from developing nuclear weapons technology. Iran has historically claimed to be developing its nuclear technology for peaceful purposes and as an energy source, but international observers have been skeptical of this claim and have urged Iran to stop processing radioactive material for nuclear fuel. The country has thus been at the forefront of contemporary debates about foreign policy and the question of

nuclear proliferation and thus serves as a useful illustration of some of the leading dilemmas in international relations.

For those hoping to prevent nuclear proliferation, one of the central challenges is preventing new countries from attaining nuclear weapons when they may have real incentives to develop them. Why would a country wish to have nuclear weapons? One simple answer of long standing in international relations theory is that the country thinks it will be more secure with nuclear weapons than it was without them. Applied to the case of Iran, it may believe it can deter an American or Israeli attack if Iran has a nuclear weapon it can use in retaliation. There may also be domestic reasons for building nuclear weapons, such as if the public, the military, and the energy industry push for it, for example (Sagan 1996). In normative terms, those seeking

nuclear technology also note a double standard among those who have nuclear weapons yet seek to deny others the right to develop them.

Other actors—especially the United States and Israel—have sought to compel Iran to cease its advancement toward nuclear status. They implemented economic sanctions against Iran. Then, in 2015, a major diplomatic effort led to an agreement—the Joint Comprehensive Plan of Action—that would include inspections, limiting Iranian nuclear activity to peaceful uses and reducing sanctions. More recently, United States president Donald Trump has signaled an intention to undo or renegotiate the agreement with Iran, arguing that it is ineffective and endangers U.S. allies such as Israel. In early 2018, it was unclear what would become of this international agreement and the Iranian nuclear program.

Research Prompts

1. Do some background reading on the Iranian revolution and on Egypt, and compare Iranian society in politics on the eve of the revolution to the society and politics of Egypt in the same period. Can you come up with a theory of why a revolution took place in Iran but not in Egypt at that time? How might you go about testing your theory? Now bring Turkey into the mix.

2. Compare the "Green Revolution" in Iran to the Arab Spring movements discussed in the "Thinking Comparatively" section at the end of chapter 12. How does this case fit into the comparative framework discussed there?

3. Chapter 6 on democracy and regimes discusses the conceptualization of democracy and democratization at great length. As discussed here, Iran is a complex case in this connection. To what extent do you judge contemporary Iran to be a democratic society? What does Iran suggest about the general relationship between authoritarianism and democracy in modern societies?

4. Iran is a major oil producer and exporter. How do you think this has impacted Iran's political history in recent decades? Did Iran's status as an oil producer increase the likelihood of a revolution taking place against the Shah or reduce that likelihood? And has it been an aid or a hindrance in the efforts of the revolutionary and post-revolutionary regime to consolidate its gains?

5. Is Iran a traditional society or a modern society? Or does the country give us reason to question this binary pair?

Japan

Key Features of Contemporary Japan

Population:	126,451,398 (estimate, 2017)
Area:	377,915 sq km
Head of State:	Emperor Akihito (1989–present)
Head of Government:	Shinzo Abe (prime minister, 2012–present)
Capital:	Tokyo
Year of Independence:	Never formally colonized, though occupied by the Allies after World War II
Year of Current Constitution:	1947
Languages:	Japanese
GDP per Capita:	$41,300 (World Bank estimate, 2016)
Human Development Index Ranking (2016):	17th (very high human development)

Sources: *CIA World Factbook*; World Bank World Development Indicators; United Nations *Human Development Report 2016*.

Introduction

Japan has long been a country of interest to comparative political analysts working on modernization processes. This is because Japan was, in many ways, the first non-Western society to "modernize," in the sense of developing a growth-oriented, industrial economy, a modern state, a modern national identity, and system of social stratification based predominantly on economic class rather than ascriptive status-group membership. Japan's culture had been largely insular—as a matter of official policy—for several centuries until the middle of the nineteenth century. However, in the closing decades of the nineteenth century and throughout the first part of the twentieth century, it achieved dramatic social transformation, becoming a modern state almost overnight. Scholars have long been intrigued by this pattern. On one hand it is intrinsically interesting from an intellectual point of view. On the other hand, many have hoped that Japan would hold the key to development that other nations could follow. Indeed, many of the "Asian Tigers" that achieved economic modernization in recent decades took several pages from Japan's playbook.

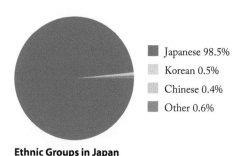

■ Japanese 98.5%
■ Korean 0.5%
■ Chinese 0.4%
■ Other 0.6%

Ethnic Groups in Japan
Source: CIA World Factbook.

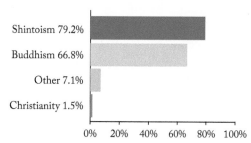

Shintoism 79.2%
Buddhism 66.8%
Other 7.1%
Christianity 1.5%

0%   20%   40%   60%   80%   100%

Religious Affiliation in Japan
Note that according to these data the majority of the Japanese population adheres to both Shintoism and Buddhism, exceeding 100 percent.
Source: CIA World Factbook.

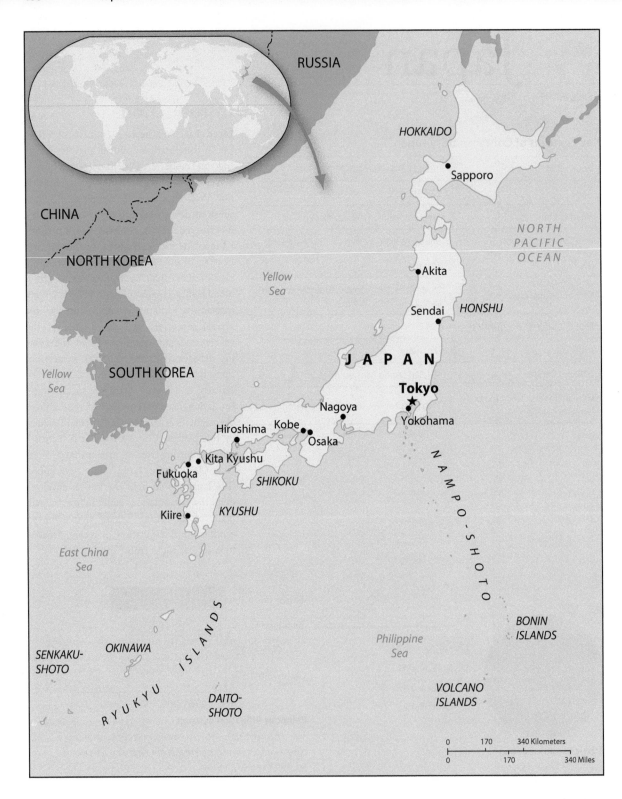

RUSSIA

HOKKAIDO

●Sapporo

NORTH
PACIFIC
OCEAN

CHINA

NORTH KOREA

Yellow
Sea

●Akita

Sendai● HONSHU

Yellow
Sea

SOUTH KOREA

J A P A N

Tokyo
★

Nagoya●

●Yokohama

Hiroshima● Kobe●
●Osaka

Kita Kyushu●

Fukuoka●

SHIKOKU

N A M P O - S H O T O

Kiire● KYUSHU

East China
Sea

Philippine
Sea

BONIN
ISLANDS

SENKAKU-
SHOTO

OKINAWA

R Y U K Y U   I S L A N D S

DAITO-
SHOTO

VOLCANO
ISLANDS

| 0 | 170 | 340 Kilometers |
| 0 | 170 | 340 Miles |

Japan's geography only adds to the interest of this case. Japan is not especially resource rich, and its land is not abundant relative to its modern population. As such, when the Japanese economy modernized, the state looked abroad in its search for natural resources, one of the principal factors leading to the country's disastrous involvement in the Second World War (Nakamura [1988] 2008: 485). Japan is small in relative terms, a series of mostly mountainous islands. This impacted the country's early development in important ways, helping to protect it from constant threat of invasion (Gordon 2009: 3–4) and aiding in the Tokugawa efforts to maintain cultural isolation. It has also meant that Japan has faced unique problems with land scarcity as its population has grown.

Japan is largely ethnically homogeneous, though not entirely so. According to the *CIA World Factbook*, 98.5 percent of the population is ethnically Japanese. Perhaps not surprisingly, most students of Japanese national identity note that the Japanese nation tends to define its boundaries in ethnic rather than civic terms. In the religious field, some caution is in order when comparing Japan (like China) to some of our other cases. Western populations tend to view religious affiliations as mutually exclusive. Not all Eastern religions *necessarily* see things this way (though some do, and there are religious clashes in Asian countries as well). However, religions like Buddhism, Shintoism, or Confucianism can sometimes coexist with others even in the allegiance of a single individual because these religions have more ritualistic rather than creedal tendencies (though we would not wish to exaggerate the extent of this difference in tendency). In other words, some varieties of these religions are less focused on the content of theological belief than on a series of values and practices. Thus you will notice in the religious affiliation chart that, according to at least one source, majorities of the Japanese population claim affiliation with both Buddhism and Shintoism.

Historical Development

Japan was governed from the beginning of the seventeenth century until 1868 by the Tokugawa regime, sometimes referred to as the Tokugawa shogunate. This was an oligarchical system in which the upper nobility (or Daimyo) displaced the emperor and governed through a military leader (shogun) and his state (known as the Bakufu). A characteristic feature of Tokugawa Japan was its closedness to the rest of the world, and to the West in particular. Tokugawa Japan was an essentially agricultural society with a large peasant class, a relatively large military nobility (the Samurai), and a smaller upper nobility (the aforementioned Daimyo). The relationships between these groups were superficially similar to the feudal arrangements that prevailed in medieval Europe. As in feudal Europe, commerce was not a highly regarded activity and was essentially tolerated as necessary: pains were taken to avoid trading with other societies. Status distinctions were rigid and linked to differences in political and personal rights.

This all began to change by the middle of the nineteenth century (Gordon 2009: 22). European powers had expanded their colonial adventures in Asia. India was becoming more formally colonized than ever before, and foreign powers intervened decisively in China, in particular during the two "opium wars." European societies sought sources of materials but also markets for the sale of their goods. While Japan was not colonized, foreign powers began to pressure it to open to trade. For a while it resisted, but despite the country's proud martial traditions, it was clear when Commodore Matthew Perry sailed into Japanese waters in 1853 and 1854 that Japan could not match the West's military technology (Gordon 2009: 49–50). The Tokugawa government reluctantly and slowly opened to Western trade. This was damaging to their interests in several ways. First, greater openness meant more access to new ideas, like democracy, constitutional monarchy, and nationalism (Greenfeld 2001). Second, these ideas seemed to be linked to capacities that the Japanese state lacked. Finally, capitulating to Western demands suggested weakness, which is always bad for a state but was likely especially so for a state for whom the military nobility was so important. It did not take long for discontent to spread. As cultural or framing theorists of revolution would note, the toppled emperor remained as an alternate object of loyalty to those dissatisfied with the Tokugawa regime. Radicalized and traditional actors alike came to see the emperor as a potentially unifying figure. For the traditionalists, the return to a state based on the emperor was presented as a "restoration," in this instance the "Meiji Restoration" of 1868. The next several decades were somewhat tumultuous, as the new regime unraveled Japan's semi-feudal system (Gordon 2009: 62–64) and began building a modern state. There was a marked turn toward Western learning, and a growing push for more popular responsiveness on the part of the government. The Meiji constitution was passed in 1889. By modern standards, this was not an especially democratic document, with only a tiny fraction of the population eligible to vote (Gordon 2009: 91, 125) and given that it declared the emperor to be ultimately sovereign (Mitani [1988] 2008: 59). Subsequent democratization was yet to come, and universal suffrage (including the vote for women) would not be established until after World War II.

Historical Development

Timeline

1600–1868	Tokugawa regime
1853	Commodore Perry (from the United States) arrives, demanding that Japan open itself to trade with the West.
1867–1868	Meiji Restoration, which is ostensibly conservative but will produce a program of modernization and Westernization.
1870–1873	Major reforms
1877	Satsuma revolt
1889	Meiji Constitution, which establishes constitutional monarchy and limited parliamentary system
1890	Elections held under the Meiji Constitution
1894–1895	Sino-Japanese War; Japan occupies Taiwan by 1895.
1904–1905	Russo-Japanese War
1910	Japan colonizes Korea, signifying expansionist phase of Japanese Empire
1914–1918	Japan is a combatant in the First World War, allied with Britain, France, the United States, and Russia.
1923	Japan suffers the deadliest earthquake in its history.
1931	Japan invades Manchuria on Chinese mainland, establishes Manchukuo government.
1937–1941	Second Sino-Japanese War
1941	Japanese bombing of Pearl Harbor begins Japan's involvement in the Second World War, on the side of Axis powers Germany and Italy.
1941–1945	War in the Pacific, with Japan fighting the United States and other Allies on islands, atolls, and in regions from the Philippines to near Japanese coastline.
1945	The United States drops atomic bombs on Hiroshima and Nagasaki; Japan surrenders.
1947	Constitution of 1947 is proclaimed, re-establishing democracy, and including women's suffrage.
1953–1970s	"Japanese Miracle," a period of dramatic economic expansion
1991–2001	Economic crisis and the "Lost Decade"
1993–1994	The Liberal Democratic Party (LDP) briefly loses power but remains the largest party in Diet; coalition government initiates electoral reforms.
1995	Aum Shinrikyo cult/terror organization releases deadly sarin gas in Tokyo subway; thirteen people are killed and many more are injured or incapacitated.
2009	LDP loses control of government as DPJ wins general election.
2011	Massive earthquake and resulting tsunami results in over 15,000 deaths and reactor meltdowns at the Fukushima nuclear power plant.
2012	Shinzo Abe elected Prime Minister as LDP regains control of government (re-elected in 2017, with LDP retaining control of government).

Japan went through many striking changes in the period from the 1880s to the Second World War, modernizing its economy, society, and state. The country transformed its social structure by doing away with samurai status differences and built a modern state (Gordon 2009: 64–66). It also began to achieve rapid economic development (Crawcour 2008: 386–387) during and after the First World War. In the same period, from 1890 to 1910, Japan began to flex its military muscle outward in Asia. It first won a major war against China (1894–1895) and claimed present-day Taiwan as a colony. It then won a war with Russia (1904–1905) and later claimed Korea as colony (1910), among many other islands and territories. In a matter of decades, the country moved from being a predominantly agricultural society to being one of the world's major economic and military powers.

A distinguishing feature of this process was the strong role that the state played in allocating capital for productive use as it industrialized. The state owned or controlled many firms, and the state linked itself to private firms that received state assistance in accessing capital and in other ways (Crawcour 2008: 414). In some areas, like heavy industry, the state maintained its involvement for strategic reasons even though it took decades to achieve profitability (Crawcour 2008: 422, 435). The state also played an important role in the development of railways, Japanese shipping, and other infrastructural developments (Crawcour 2008: 393–399) as well as through creating a system of commercial law (Gordon 2009: 95), a factor that institutional economists would emphasize (e.g., North 1990). The Japanese economy took off during World War I because Japanese producers for export could take advantage of the disruption of existing supply chains to access markets. Economic historians consider Japanese economic performance to have been strong in relative terms throughout not just the 1920s but also the 1930s, though the country did experience frequent financial crises, and the effects of the Great Depression were notable (Nakamura [1988] 2008).

Japanese economic and military expansion took place under an increasingly aggressive, militaristic, and nationalistic regime. Japan invaded Manchuria on the Chinese mainland in 1931 and attempted to establish control of much of the Pacific in subsequent years. When World War II came about, Japan allied with Nazi Germany and fascist Italy. In 1941, Japan's attack on Pearl Harbor, Hawaii, brought the United States into the war that had begun in 1939. After more than three years of total war fought across the Pacific Ocean, American forces closed in on Japan and prepared for invasion. In 1945, however, American forces established air supremacy over Japan and firebombed Tokyo and other Japanese cities, leaving hundreds of thousands dead. President Harry Truman then authorized the dropping of two atomic bombs on the Japanese cities of Hiroshima and Nagasaki on August 6 and 9, 1945. Japan surrendered six days later.

After the tragedies of World War II, Japan began economic and political reconstruction under American-led Allied military occupation until 1952. A lasting impact of post-war reconstruction was the beginning of Japan's remarkable economic performance; it is estimated that the Japanese economy grew at the tremendous rate of almost 10 percent per year between 1945 and 1973 (Kosai 2008: 494). Again, the state played a large role in the economy: as Japan recovered from the war, the government strategically supported the redevelopment of the coal and steel industries, utilizing the so-called priority production method (Kosai 2008: 500–501). The state, in cooperation with private enterprise, later implemented "rationalization plans" for key industries (Kosai 2008: 516–518). Beginning in the early 1960s, the government relaxed regulations on foreign trade, which helped Japanese exports in their subsequent boom (Kosai 2008: 522–527).

Democratization progressed along with economic growth in the years during and after the Allied occupation, with a series of new constitutional guarantees in the constitution of 1947 (Fukui [1998] 2008: 156). This owed both to the occupation authorities insisting on democratization *and* to Japanese efforts. Japan's democratization over this period also may be due to the Japanese economic success of the post-war years: as a number of theories in chapter 6 would suggest, strong economic growth and the emergence and development of a middle class, which clearly took place in post-war Japan (Fukui [1998] 2008: 204), are associated with democratic consolidation. One lasting aspect of the peace was a constitutional commitment not to deploy its military overseas.

Post-war Japan became a democracy, albeit one with a notable limitation: it was dominated by a single party, the Liberal Democratic Party of Japan (LDP), for most of the post-war period. The LDP's hegemony is a bit more complex than it appears at first glance, and this was not simply a single-party system. During the early years after Allied occupation, a multiparty system developed; but by the 1960s, the LDP had come to win majority governments consistently. Japan was still technically a pluralistic and competitive political environment, but the LDP managed to defeat its (socialist and other) opponents and to regularly win legislative majorities, thus not needing to form coalitions. Many commentators and citizens felt that this reduced responsiveness to citizen concerns. A system developed in which representatives established local ties and worked to enhance the interests of local constituencies, organized partially through exclusive sets of social networks called *koenkai* (Kabashima and Steel 2010: 3–4, 15–17). This was, many analysts believe, reinforced by Japan's electoral system, as discussed in the chapter 11 Case Study. In Japan's system, voters voted for one individual within a district, but often multiple LDP candidates were running within the district. To differentiate themselves from other LDP candidates, politicians sometimes turned to personal networks and even corruption (Kabashima and Steel 2010: 15–17). This led to complex factionalism and divisions within the LDP. While the LDP exerted near hegemony for decades, they occasionally had to form coalition governments as well; and the (now-defunct) Democratic Party of Japan (DJP) in particular remained an electoral adversary.

Beginning in the late 1980s, it became clear that the LDP's grip on power was weakening, and it had to form coalitions to govern in the 1990s, as many voters became disenchanted with parties more generally (LeBlanc 1999: 5). The party fell out of power briefly in 1993–1994, though it remained the largest party in the Diet. During the 1990s, difficulties and frustrations mounted as the country experienced financial crisis and a prolonged period of stagnation. Some have suggested that this ended the implicit bargain in Japan's post-war democracy in which the LDP governments were continually returned to power in exchange for sustained economic growth.

Another factor in the LDP's long dominance was the fragmentation of the opposition, but this was finally, if temporarily, overcome when the DJP took over the government after a resounding win in elections in 2009. From the point of view of some democratic theorists, alternation in power constitutes an advance, as it suggests the possibility of increased pluralism and competition. Many commentators did not view the DJP government as successful; and in 2012, the LDP returned to power. In late 2017, Abe and the LDP were re-elected once more. Observers may wonder whether the DJP victory in 2009 was just a temporary exception or whether Japan will in the coming years see greater interparty competition. At present, the major competitors to the LDP are new parties, and it is unclear how stable the current party system is in Japan.

Regime and Political Institutions

Japan has a parliamentary system with a ceremonial emperor. The bicameral parliament has a lower chamber in which 300 of 480 seats are elected by district constituencies, and the remaining seats are elected by proportional representation in different "blocks" or regions of the country. The upper chamber has most of its members elected in their respective prefectures, with a remainder voted in by proportional representation as well. The House of Representatives is the more powerful body, being able to overrule the House of Councillors on budget and finance matters, and override the House of Councillors with a two-thirds majority on other matters. In the late twentieth century, perhaps the most distinguishing feature of the policymaking process in Japan was the dominance of the LDP. Because of the extent of this dominance, and perhaps because of the nature of the Japanese electoral system (Kabashima and Steel 2010: 15–17), the LDP did not need to be fully responsive to the wishes of the electorate. Rather, the state was a place in which political elites worked with the business community to manage Japanese economic performance. Following the rise of coalition governments, though, and accelerating through the DJP's success in 2009, some wondered whether we might be seeing an increase in responsiveness to citizens (Kabashima and Steel 2010). On one hand, commentators note a decline in public trust of political parties. On the other hand, a number of population segments are involved in civil society. All else being equal, political activity among the citizenry and pluralist competition between parties could be expected to increase accountability.

Regime and Political Institutions

Regime	Constitutional monarchy (parliamentary democracy with ceremonial emperor)
Administrative Divisions	Centralized, unitary government; forty-seven prefectures
Executive Branch	Prime minister and cabinet
Selection of Executive	Selected by Parliament, ceremonially appointed by emperor
Legislative Branch	Bicameral parliament (Diet) Lower chamber: House of Representatives Upper chamber: House of Councillors
Judicial Branch	The Japanese Supreme Court (which has fourteen Justices and one Chief Justice) is the ultimate judicial authority in the country.
Political Party System	Multiparty system that has been in flux in recent years. Dominated by the LDP for decades, though the DJP governed 2009–2012; political environment is formally one of pluralistic competition, with the LDP seemingly returning to dominance and new parties making up the main opposition.

Political Culture

Scholars interested in Japanese culture have emphasized a number of themes, but perhaps the most relevant one to comparative politics is the allegedly collectivistic and egalitarian character of Japanese beliefs and practices (Kunio 2006), particularly with regard to their manifestation in Japanese *economic culture*. Japan has relatively low levels of income inequality (Kosai 2008: 512). Some assert that this might be partially due to the cultural foundations of business management in Japan. Yoshihara Kunio goes so far as to add alleged cultural orientations toward materialism, savings, high valuation of educational attainment, and a strong work ethic as key components of Japanese economic culture (Kunio 2006: 83), even as he stresses the institutional dimensions of Japan's economic performance as well. It should be recognized, however, that these low levels of inequality and high savings are most noteworthy in the post-war era and not as true for earlier periods.

Much has been made of Japanese corporate governance as a lens into Japanese culture. Japanese firms seem to differ from Western firms in key respects. Major Japanese industrial firms have relationships with their (especially male) employees that many define as paternalistic, providing extensive benefits and nearly guaranteeing lifetime employment for good conduct. The notion that all are part of a "team" or even a "family" is relatively strong. Japan is a market economy, but the tendency to change jobs over the course of one's lifetime that has become common in places like the United States has not hit Japan to the same extent. Within Japanese firms, one tends to see a strong sense of solidarity, while status differences are mitigated by cultural norms that discourage massive income inequality within the firm. In a typical corporation in the United States, the salaries of executives dwarf those of entry-level employees; but in Japan, the ratio of executive to entry-level employee salaries tends to be notably lower.

Of course, this is not a perfect system. Relations between workers and management may be less conflictual than in many other countries, but labor has a relatively weak position vis-à-vis corporations: workers have difficulty establishing industry-wide organizations and demanding change rather than pursuing institutionally structured negotiation. This was at least partially a product of the LDP's policy of reducing union strength (Manow 2001: 44). In addition, strong cultural norms of employment security and relative equity might impact the competitiveness of Japanese firms over the long haul. Moreover, the alleged collectivism and "team orientation" of Japanese firms may be a factor in the notably high rates of discrimination against women (including lack of equal participation in the benefits of employment and sexual harassment) that exists in Japanese workplaces. Finally, the culture of Japanese firms has sometimes been seen as a hindrance, requiring reform. The firms that developed in the early years of Japanese industrialization—the *zaibatsu*—were highly concentrated and monopolistic (Gordon 2009: 96–97). They would later be partially broken up in the post-war years, but large conglomerates known as *keiretsu* persisted, with an example being Mitsubishi. Centered around huge banks, these were an integral part of post-war industrialization, but they later came to symbolize the possibility of crony capitalism, with cozy relationships between economic and political elites.

These aspects of economic culture—with an emphasis on continuity and outward collective harmony—can be seen reflected in politics more narrowly defined. The LDP governed without interruption for decades and attempted to represent Japan's diverse interests; but the party was also divided by fierce internal factionalism that contributed substantially to its eventual losses, as party members disagreed over how to respond to constituent demands and needs. For more on various aspects of Japan's rich political culture—including the LDP, the state, and gender issues—see the more detailed country case studies later in these materials.

Political Economy

So far in this country profile, we have discussed the long-run development history of Japan, and we discuss the state's role in the Japanese economy in the following case study. Here, in contrast, we will focus on recent history and the contemporary state of Japanese political economy. Japan, as we have noted, was the first non-Western society to develop sustained economic growth, in many ways establishing a path that has been followed, with variations, by the so-called Asian tigers (e.g., South Korea, Singapore) and, more recently, even China. This it did, in part, through state coordination. This does not mean a Soviet-style command economy but rather the state strategically favoring certain sectors and helping to coordinate the deployment of capital for productive purposes: in other words, state *management* of the economy but not large-scale state *ownership*. The Japanese state had a history of working well with the large, industry-spanning corporations that were so important to Japanese growth in the twentieth century (see Evans 1989).

Japan was one of the world's great economic success stories of the twentieth century. While economic development picked up during the interwar period, it was especially following reconstruction and American occupation after World War II that Japan built major global enterprises and became an export powerhouse, with examples of leading firms including Toyota and Honda in the automobile industry and Sony and Toshiba in electronics. The tradition of strong growth slowed by the 1980s and went into crisis in the early 1990s. The causes of the crisis were complex, but they included an overheated real estate market that collapsed and serious problems spreading throughout the financial system (much like in the United States in 2008). The government responded very slowly and only "bailed out" the banking system toward the end of the decade. Japan's economy has never completely recovered. A number of analysts have concerns today about Japanese competitiveness and the competition posed by China and other countries to Japan's position as a preeminent economic power. Notably, in this case, the concern also extends to geopolitics, and China's increasing ambitions in the Pacific Rim may be expected to come at the expense of Japan's influence.

In recent years, there has been considerable debate over the country's current economic policy of Prime Minister Shinzo Abe. After nearly two decades of low growth, Abe promised a set of dramatic policies (commonly referred to as "Abenomics") to jumpstart the economy. These included increased government spending and loose monetary policy that lowers interest rates; it was hoped that this would encourage consumers to spend after many years of stagnation (and that this would helpfully raise prices after many years of price declines that had discouraged spending). Abe has also promised structural reforms that would encourage easier hiring and firing, thereby making the labor market more flexible. Indicators have been mixed: the Japanese stock market valuation has increased greatly since Abe took office, but growth has been relatively low, and the country's debt has continued to increase to very high levels (for more on contemporary Japanese political economy, see McBride and Xu 2017).

Despite some concerns about Japanese economic performance in recent years, many of the country's basic economic indicators are still sound. According to the *CIA World Factbook*, the country's unemployment rate stood at an enviable 3.1 percent in 2016. (It should be noted that the unemployment rate is calculated on the basis of the number of people in the labor force as the denominator, so Japan's large elderly population that is out of the labor force may affect this number.) GDP per capita stood at $41,200 in 2016 per the *CIA World Factbook*; and in terms of Human Development indicators, Japan is among the global leaders. The Japanese economy accomplishes this while maintaining a level of income inequality better than that found in the United States and comparable to that of the Western European welfare states (though these states slightly outperform Japan in terms of this indicator). Its Gini level stood at 33 in 2015, according to the OECD (http://www.oecd.org/social/income-distribution-database.htm).

Japan was famous for its manufacturing for export, which stood at the heart of the "Japanese Miracle" that ran from the 1950s to the 1970s; but today services are predominant, accounting for 69.4 percent of GDP in 2016, with industry accounting for 29.6 percent and agriculture 1.1 percent (as reported by *CIA World Factbook*).

CASE STUDIES

As noted in the "Historical Development" section at the beginning of this profile, Japan has shown remarkable economic performance since the late nineteenth century. It has done so, many scholars believe, because of the adroit way in which the state has managed economic development. As noted earlier, Japanese economic development began shortly after efforts to create a modern state, one that quickly expanded its tax base and, among other things, invested in human capital by ensuring that a high and growing percentage of the population received at least elementary education (Gordon 2009: 67–68, 70).

The Japanese state did not achieve this by establishing a Soviet-style command economy. Rather, it worked as a coordinating agent (Hall and Soskice 2001) that could help the economy avoid a series of problems, such as the lack of capital, the establishment of basic infrastructure, the development of heavy industry, and other achievements that might have been more difficult without coordinated effort. As one historian puts it, "in its macroeconomic policy the [Japanese] government followed the principle of balanced budgets, but at the same time in its micro-economic or sectorial policy, it followed government interventionist principles, by providing special tax measures for and fiscal investment in particular industries" (Kosai 2008: 535). The state remained a major player in planning and even in operating enterprises. One of the leading institutions in the Japanese government was the Ministry of International Trade and Industry (MITI), which took on major roles in planning and coordination of the economy, in a style has been termed "plan-rational" development (Johnson 1982). This Japanese model of the developmental state was subsequently emulated by other "East Asian tigers" such as Korea, Singapore, and Taiwan. In other words, the Japanese state remained relatively lean and did not promote growth through widespread state ownership, but rather it aimed to help to shape the economic environment in a way that would be good for Japanese businesses.

In achieving this balance, it was likely aided by the fact that labor unions tend to be specific to firms in Japanese culture (think of them as vertically integrated within firms) rather than tied to classes of workers as such as in other societies (think of these as horizontally integrated, cutting across firms; Hall and Soskice 2001: 34–35). This likely reduced pressure for state expansion because it reduced the likelihood of class-based organizing. At the same time, it is worth remembering, as noted in the "Political Culture" section, that government policies influenced union weakness: the LDP, which was strongly opposed to robust union organization, reduced freedom to organize and strike and required arbitration in case of labor disputes (Manow 2001: 44). Finally, Japan's rapid economic growth made possible a distribution of the gains that kept most actors satisfied: pay increases were possible while firms remained profitable.

At the same time, the paternalistic features of Japanese firms and their tendency to provide lifetime employment likely reduced potential welfare costs for the state. This links to issues of gender and politics discussed in the next case study: paternalism extended to expectations for families in providing care for children and others, and this often means women's unpaid labor (Kabashima and Steel 2010: 19), as families in the "private sphere" take on a relatively important role in the provision of "welfare" service (Esping-Anderson 1997: 181).

In the 1970s, the Japanese state aimed to take on more welfare functions (Kosai 2008: 536), as discussed earlier in the "Political Economy" section. Some have argued that Japan evidences a distinct type of welfare state formation, but the most important analyst of welfare states, Esping-Anderson (1997), argues that the Japanese welfare state is a "hybrid" of conservative and liberal approaches to welfare state formation and functioning. It combines low levels of social spending with state policies to maintain full employment, strong cultural expectations of family provision, and company-based (i.e., private-sector) provision of social insurance (there is a public system, but it is supplementary).

The Hybrid Electoral System of the Japanese Diet

CHAPTER 9, PAGE 213

Japan's parliament, called the Diet, is bi-cameral, having been established in its current form by the Constitution of 1947, which was crafted under the American occupation that followed Japan's surrender in World War II. Yet electoral procedures for the Diet have changed, most substantially in the electoral reform of 1994 that dramatically altered Japanese politics. The Diet is now elected by a hybrid system that includes features of both district-based and proportional representation.

The lower (and more powerful) chamber in Japan is called the House of Representatives and was modeled in part on the American chamber of the same name and in part on the British House of Commons. Currently, this lower house is comprised of 475 representatives elected by a system that mixes single-member districts (like the U.S. House of Representatives) with proportional representation (more common in continental European democracies). Of the 475 representatives, the majority win seats in specific district elections, and an additional 180 are chosen based on party lists in eleven different regions around the country. All representation thus has a territorial component, though the 180 seats attempt to introduce proportionality into the system. The House

of Councillors is the upper chamber, with the majority of its members selected from Japan's forty-seven prefectures, while an additional group of members are directly elected at a national level (in a single nationwide district). The legislative chambers are not symmetric in their powers, as the House of Representatives has the authority to overrule the House of Councillors and also selects the prime minister. Most laws gain approval from both chambers to pass, but a two-thirds majority in the House of Representatives can pass legislation even over the negative vote of the House of Councillors.

The system is notable not only for its hybrid structure but also for how it reformed a previous system. From 1947 to 1994, the electoral system consisted of districts that would elect three to five representatives, according to whichever candidates received the most individual votes. The old electoral system for the House of Representatives, called the "single non-transferable vote" (SNTV) system, has been argued to be more proportional than majoritarian systems with single-member districts; but in Japan, it seemed to favor the long-dominant Liberal Democratic Party (LDP), for reasons seen later in the Case in Context box titled "How has Japan's

Dominant Party Won for So Long?" for chapter 11 (Cox 1996). The LDP attempted on multiple occasions to move toward single-member districts, which would give it even larger majorities, but opposition parties successfully resisted these changes.

The reformed system finally came about in 1994. At that time, the LDP had at last lost governing power, though it remained the largest party in parliament. The reform of 1994 was intended to change a party system that had for a long time been characterized by individual politicians cultivating support from local networks; this system was to be replaced with one in which parties would take more programmatic stances (Horiuchi and Saito 2003: 672). Another consequence of the 1994 reform was to reduce the power of rural areas, which had been overrepresented for decades, and give more equal representation to urban areas. Over the long run, the effects of the reform seemed to contribute to the eventual defeat of the LDP and the temporary rise of the Democratic Party of Japan (DPJ), which held a clear majority of more than three hundred seats in the House of Representatives between 2009 and 2012. As noted previously, the LDP has since returned to power and remained there.

How Has Japan's Dominant Party Won for So Long?

CHAPTER 11, PAGE 263

Japan has been ranked as a "Free" country by the independent organization Freedom House for every year since it began keeping track of democracy

around the world. Yet for most of that period up to recent years, Japan has been dominated by the Liberal Democratic Party (LDP). The LDP governed from

1955 to 2009, except for a brief interlude in 1993–1994, and has again governed since 2012. Throughout the long period of its dominance, the system legally allowed and enabled other parties to participate, though the LDP rarely faced serious party competition. The country had the free elections expected of a multiparty democracy, and was not a single-party state, but it had one party that dominated elections. How a dominant party—albeit one riddled with factionalism—coexisted with democracy was one of the key questions of Japanese politics. What accounts for the continued victories of the LDP over so many years?

There are several possible explanations for this. One could be based on interest group representation in Japan, as well as economic performance. Japan's LDP presided over a form of corporatism that may have helped the party continue its victories, not least due to economic achievements for several decades up to the 1980s. During most of the LDP's rule, the government reached out to business as well as other interest groups as it made its decisions about planning and guiding certain aspects of the economy (Evans 1989). Japan had well-structured relationships between government policymakers and economic stakeholders; companies could expect to give input to the policy process, and some would receive advantages to boost production, but these would only persist as long as performance was good. Government leaders kept very close ties to top business executives, and thus they knew what business required to build and expand; it seems many of these ties went back to personal relationships at the highly prestigious Tokyo University Faculty of Law (Evans 1989). Despite this close relationship, the LDP government also had some "autonomy" from the

corporations and conglomerates; government did not simply do the corporations' bidding. A result was economic success, which may have favored the LDP's dominance. Perhaps surprisingly, some scholars have even argued that Japan's loss in World War II was part of the reason for this more cooperative arrangement; by contrast with the United Kingdom, in which special interest groups survived the war and continued their demands when the war ended, Japan had a new political system, a reconstructing economy, and a rapidly changing society (Olson 1984). This relationship between government and business was presumed healthy for a time, but as Japan went through the "lost decade" of the 1990s with little growth and evidence accumulating that the country's economic bubble had burst, the constructive engagement between state and business was recast as "crony capitalism," a system of favors to insiders that caught up with Japan in the long run. This coincided with the LDP's increasing weakness.

There are also several arguments relating to the electoral system, the internal workings of the LDP, and Japan's unique political culture. As noted in the previous Case Study, "The Hybrid Electoral System of the Japanese Diet," Japan long had an electoral system for the House of Representatives based on a single, nontransferable vote (SNTV), in which LDP politicians often competed against one another for the seats within a certain constituency. (This system is still used for the upper chamber but has now been replaced in the lower house.) A key feature of the LDP years was factionalism inside

the party: while the party presented a common banner, it was riddled with internal divisions often centered around individual leaders or small groups of politicians. In this system, LDP incumbents benefited from the mobilization by informal "support groups" from certain neighborhoods or communities in the constituencies. These groups were known as *koenkai*, and they supported favored politicians in the expectation of favoritism in return. Since the LDP had the advantages of incumbency, it was able to win a large proportion of seats by distributing benefits to local constituencies (Cox 1996). In addition to the *koenkai* and the patronage that helped the LDP, the electoral system also disproportionately favored rural areas, where the LDP had its strongest base. Finally, the electoral system fragmented the opposition such that the LDP commanded majorities in the seats in the Diet even when it was unpopular and failed to gain a majority of votes (Scheiner 2006). In this context, the LDP became a powerful machine without being ideologically coherent, and its flexibility seemed to allow it to co-opt or incorporate other actors that emerged from other parties.

Electoral reform in 1994 eventually gave an opening to other parties. One argument that purports to explain both the persistence and the (temporary) fall of the LDP thus finds that the LDP benefited from the electoral system for many years, but the party's decline was assured as other parties adapted to the new electoral system. In this logic, the LDP's ability to hang on for another decade and more after 1994 was attributable in

CASE STUDY (continued)

How Has Japan's Dominant Party Won for So Long?　　CHAPTER 11, PAGE 263

part to the particularly charismatic Prime Minister Junichiro Koizumi (Krauss and Pekkanen 2011). The LDP's resurgence since 2012, however, may cast this interpretation into doubt.

There are other possible explanations besides the preceding ones for the LDP's long hegemony. In general, it can be said that any number of the variables seen in previous chapters—from

development and the role of the state to the functioning of electoral systems in the legislature—can be posited to contribute to the dominant-party system that governed Japan for half a century.

CASE STUDY

Importing National Identity in Japan?　　CHAPTER 13, PAGE 313

Japan—much like China—had a strong sense of identity and civilizational uniqueness for centuries. Indeed, there is much that resembles modern nationalism in the Tokugawa regime's hostility to foreign influence and sense of Japanese cultural superiority. However, most scholars of national identity do not see Tokugawa Japan as a national society (Greenfeld 2001; Gordon 2009: 51) because however salient Japanese identity was, it was not tied to the idea of the Japanese as a sovereign and equal people. Rather, estate-based divisions were of critical importance, with a huge gap between the nobility and commoners, and political authority was not seen as a reflection of the will of any unified "nation."

Nationalism as such, therefore, was imported to Japan (Doak 2006; Greenfeld 2001). It happened in the nineteenth century, during and after the opening of the society to the West. It is worth noting that nationalism as a type of identity spread globally in this way into virtually all of today's societies: in other words, Japan is not unusual in this respect, though it is an exemplary case of this

phenomenon. Why would an identity like this spread? Who would gain from it?

Scholars who are interested in explaining Japan's turn to nationalism can focus on several different types of interests. First, some note that nationalism provided a language that articulates a critique of the Tokugawa regime and that demanded a response to the military and economic superiority of foreign powers. Second, some note that nationalism served the interest of the Meiji state in inculcating national sentiment in its citizens: as elsewhere, the state endeavored to use nationalism to influence the behavior of its citizens (Gordon 2009: 135–137). Third, some emphasize the importance of the status-inconsistency of elite groups—in particular the large class of samurai—a variable that has been linked to the importation of national identity in numerous other cases (Greenfeld 2001). Note that the first two explanatory strategies focus on the relationship between national identity and the state, whereas the latter one focuses more on what's happening within society, outside of the state. See if you can find ways in which these explanatory strategies could be blended together.

In any case, by the close of the nineteenth century, a significant portion of Japanese society thought of that society in national terms. Moreover, there was a strong sense that the nation needed to assert itself internationally, as it did in both the Sino-Japanese War and the Russo-Japanese War, before adopting a still more expansive policy in the twentieth century, culminating in its involvement in the Second World War. After Japan's defeat in that conflict, Japanese nationalism has found less militaristic expression, with a strong focus on economic competition as an avenue for the realization of the nation's status.

So, did Japan (and other countries) really "import" national identity? It seems clear that the general concept of national identity, linked to popular sovereignty and idealized equality of membership, did diffuse globally over recent decades and centuries, and in this sense the idea of the nation was imported to Japan. But what Japanese citizens *made* with this identity is a different story: Japanese nationalism was fashioned in the mold shaped by its members, as in every other nation in each's unique way.

CASE STUDY
Gender Empowerment in Japan?

CHAPTER 14, PAGE 338

Historically, women's participation in Japanese politics has received little emphasis, both in popular discussion and in the academic literature, in part because of discrimination and in part because of the (male) elite-centeredness of much work in political science (LeBlanc 1999).

What scholars have uncovered has largely not been good. Japan stands out, when compared to its peers in terms of socioeconomic development, for the relatively low political empowerment of women. For example, despite having the world's seventeenth best HDI in 2015, as well as the seventeenth best Gender Development Index value, women are less well represented in Japanese politics (United Nations Development Programme 2016). In terms of women's legislative representation, Japan recently stood at 158th (Interparliamentary Union 2018). Similar trends have been visible in subnational representative bodies. As Sherry L. Martin (2008: 125) puts it, "the extent of women's underrepresentation in elected offices makes Japan an outlier

in comparative studies of women and politics," though Martin acknowledged some progress at the time of that writing.

The political ethnographer Robin LeBlanc (1999) has emphasized that Japanese women do have agency, and that narratives about their participation in political life that are focused on elite politics often miss the ways in which women can mobilize a "housewife" identity and build on social networks to pursue their chosen ends. This is not to say that women and men have achieved political equality in Japan (or elsewhere, for that matter), but that there is more to Japanese women's political participation (and women's participation in politics in other societies as well) than can be revealed through a traditional political science lens.

Beyond questions of political representation, it is worth noting that Japan stands out as a country where gender discrimination in employment and everyday life is quite high (World Economic Forum 2017). Japan's Gender Gap Index ranks it 114th globally. Japan does very

well in terms of one of the four subindices ("health and survival"), but abysmally in terms of "political empowerment," ranked 123rd overall (World Economic Forum 2017: 11–12). It is ranked just 114th in terms of "economic participation and opportunity" and 74th in terms of educational attainment (World Economic Forum 2017: 11–12). In the latter case, Japan does well in all but one item of which the index is composed: women's enrollment in tertiary education, though the society is making progress on this measure (World Economic Forum 2017: 17, 190).

This is all, of course, of concern to women and others who are opposed to inequality. But the ramifications of gender discrimination extend beyond such concerns as well. Indeed, some evidence indicates that Japanese economic performance suffers notably *because* of gender inequity, suggesting that with "economic gender parity," Japan's GDP might be $550 billion greater (finding cited in World Economic Forum 2017: 27).

CASE STUDY
Resource Management in Japan

CHAPTER 16, PAGE 388

There are two highly symbolic illustrations from Japan that show the challenge of environmental sustainability and the importance of the "tragedy of the commons" discussed in chapter 16. One is the fishing of the world's oceans, and the other is the question of climate change. Many situations involving the global environment are situations where

multiple countries draw on resources that are used by all, and the earth's atmosphere and its oceans are two leading examples. The atmosphere has an ability to hold carbon dioxide and other greenhouse gasses, but growing levels of pollutants have been associated with global climate change. A lack of attention to this common pool resource will make

everyone worse off. In a similar sense, the oceans have a fish stock on which many countries rely, yet there is clear evidence of overfishing and a lack of coordination or adequate provision for sustainability over the long run.

One aspect of the challenge arises from the lack of a clear governing authority for these international common

CASE STUDY (continued)
Resource Management in Japan

CHAPTER 16, PAGE 388

pool resources. There is no overarching world government to require states to behave in certain ways; the United Nations does not have significant authority, and the world's sovereign nations have little incentive to give up their powers to some world government. Certain states—especially smaller or weaker states—may be compelled to behave in certain ways by threats of war, economic sanctions, or diplomatic pressure; but in international relations terms, the system has an anarchic structure in which each state is sovereign. This gives rise to the collective action problems at the international level.

Japan is one of world's great offenders when it comes to overfishing the oceans, though by no means the only one. Japanese fishing (and whaling) has been thus one of the clearest illustrations of how the tragedy of the commons operates. The example of Atlantic bluefin tuna is illustrative. Japanese consume as much as three-fourths of all the Atlantic bluefin tuna caught in the world, eating it mostly raw as sashimi (Blair 2010). The stock of the fish is severely depleted, and there is a risk that it will be fished to extinction; this depletion happened especially after the 1970s, when bluefin tuna consumption took off in Japan (Kolbert 2010). Yet Japan celebrated when an international body opted not to prohibit international trade in the species (Kolbert 2010). As with other cases of extinction and endangerment of species, the example shows how quickly irreversible change can occur when resources begin to decline.

Another issue links Japan symbolically to the question of sustainability, though it is hardly a "Japanese issue" alone. This is the Kyoto Protocol, an international agreement to address the issue of climate change. The protocol was agreed to in the Japanese city of Kyoto in 1997 and subsequently was ratified by legislatures of the many countries that signed it, with the exception of the United States. It was designed as a global response to climate change that would commit all signatory countries to reduce global emissions to levels below those from 1990. Yet the Kyoto Protocol faced challenges from the start. The United States was the world's largest polluter when its congress rejected the protocol. Meanwhile, major developing countries were not required to reduce emissions under the agreement, though China is now the world's largest polluter. More recently, Russia and Japan itself declined to sign onto future reductions, while Canada pulled out of the protocol at the end of 2011. As with overfishing, the lack of collective action is indicative of the challenges present in issues of international environmental protection.

Research Prompts

1. Compare the modernization paths of China and Japan. In what ways are they similar, and in what ways are they different (in terms of both politics and economics)? Using theories from chapters 3–7 (and, possibly, chapters 12 and 13 as well), develop hypotheses to explain the variation that you noted in response to the first part of this prompt.

2. Compare the period of LDP hegemony in Japan to the experience of Mexico under the PRI. How did each party cement its control? To what extent did the nature of single-party dominance vary? What similar and different causes lay behind single-party dominance? How has each recovered in the years since the end of their previous hegemony? Then bring China into the comparison. What might this comparison suggest about what seem to be the main factors that influence types of single-party dominance in more and less democratic societies?

3. Compare long-run economic development in the United Kingdom, Germany, and Japan. Be especially attentive to the role of the state in these cases. How do the cases contrast? What are the implications of your comparison for the theory that state involvement is bad for economic development?

4. In chapter 15, we introduced the concept of "multiple modernities" that scholars like S. M. Eisenstadt have developed. Japan is often regarded as a Western-style modernizer. Is Japanese modernity "Western," or does it have its own distinct characteristics?

Mexico

PROFILE

Key Features of Contemporary Mexico

Population:	124,574,795 (estimate, July 2017)
Area:	1,964,375 sq km
Head of State:	Enrique Peña Nieto (president, 2012–present)
Head of Government:	Enrique Peña Nieto (president, 2012–present)
Capital:	Mexico City
Year of Independence:	Often cited as 1810, when the movement for independence began, but actual independence was established in 1821.
Year of Current Constitution:	1917
Languages:	Spanish; Nahuatl; Mayan; other Amerindian languages.
GDP per Capita:	$18,900 (*CIA World Factbook estimate*, 2016)
Human Development Index Ranking (2016):	77th (high human development)

Sources: *CIA World Factbook*; World Bank World Development Indicators; United Nations *Human Development Report 2016.*

Introduction

Mexico is a country that receives a great deal of attention from political scientists for numerous reasons. One of the most important is that it is a large country bordering on one that is culturally very different with a contrasting political and economic history (Camp 2007: 1–9), thus facilitating comparisons. Another is that its economic and political histories are fascinating and set up many other potential comparisons that allow us to gain some leverage over a number of theories of comparative politics. In economic terms, it has alternated between periods of growth and stagnation, and the state's economic policy has shifted on numerous occasions over the decades. Since 1994, it has been economically integrated with the rest of North America via the North American Free Trade Agreement and has more generally increased its global economic integration in recent years. Along with Brazil, it has had moderate success in recent decades in establishing a diversified industrial base. Yet severe poverty is a persistent problem, and economic difficulties are linked to serious political challenges.

In political terms, Mexico has occasionally been thought of as having a strong state, since the state has often been interventionist

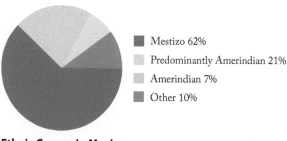

- Mestizo 62%
- Predominantly Amerindian 21%
- Amerindian 7%
- Other 10%

Ethnic Groups in Mexico
Source: CIA World Factbook.

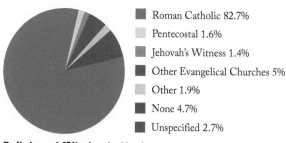

- Roman Catholic 82.7%
- Pentecostal 1.6%
- Jehovah's Witness 1.4%
- Other Evangelical Churches 5%
- Other 1.9%
- None 4.7%
- Unspecified 2.7%

Religious Affiliation in Mexico
Source: CIA World Factbook.

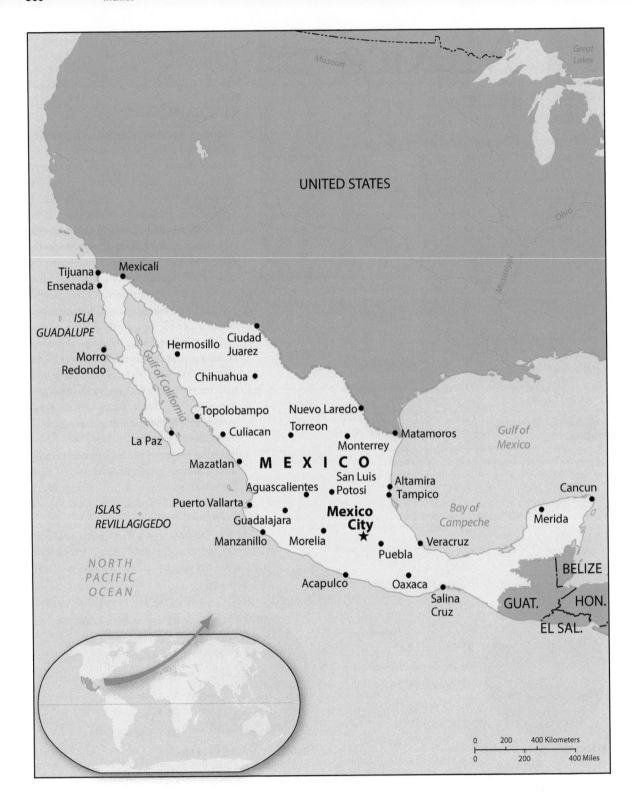

UNITED STATES

Missouri

Great Lakes

Ohio

Mississippi

Tijuana • • Mexicali
Ensenada •

ISLA
GUADALUPE

Morro
Redondo •

Hermosillo •   Ciudad
                Juarez •

Chihuahua •

Gulf of California

Topolobampo •   Nuevo Laredo •

La Paz •   Culiacan •   Torreon •   Matamoros •   *Gulf of*
                                                                Mexico

Mazatlan •   **M E X I C O**   Monterrey •

Aguascalientes •   San Luis   Altamira •
                          Potosi •   Tampico •

ISLAS   Puerto Vallarta •   *Bay of*   Cancun •
REVILLAGIGEDO   **Mexico**   *Campeche*
                 Guadalajara •   **City**   Merida •

Manzanillo •   Morelia •   ★   BELIZE

                              Puebla •   Veracruz •

NORTH
PACIFIC
OCEAN   Acapulco •   Oaxaca •   GUAT.   HON.

                              Salina   EL SAL.
                              Cruz

                                        0   200   400 Kilometers

                                        0   200   400 Miles

in Mexico's history. In terms relative to the rest of Latin America at the time, the decades of late-nineteenth-century dominance by Porfirio Díaz, called the "Porfiriato," saw fairly strong development (Mörner 1993:6) in which the state encouraged foreign capital to build railroads and to transform the countryside, promoting a more commercial agricultural model and beginning to establish industrial activity in the cities (Meyer and Sherman 1987: 431–479; Krauze 1997: 218). Likewise, the state that emerged from the Mexican Revolution (which began in 1910), after serious instability and around one million deaths, was a state that came to intervene actively in the economy, for example, in Mexico's early nationalization of oil (1938). The post-revolutionary regime also acted strongly against the Roman Catholic Church, dramatically reducing its capacity to act in politics (Blancarte 1992). So, on one hand, at key periods in its history, the Mexican state appears to be strong. On the other hand, however, we must consider that the state was for many decades prone to instability and irregular transfers of power; that even in the years of relative stability promoted by the Institutional Revolutionary Party's (*Partido Revolucionario Institucional,* or PRI) dominance for much of the twentieth century, authoritarianism was the norm (Mexico in most of that period was, as we shall see, a variation on the "party dictatorship" model); and that in very recent years, the country has struggled with serious problems of organized crime and drug trafficking, prompting some analysts to worry (somewhat hyperbolically, we think) about the possibility of a Mexican "failed state" on the U.S. border (for a more reasonable view, see O'Neil 2009). These issues are discussed in more detail in the chapter 3 Case Study, "The Mexican State and Rule of Law."

Perhaps these challenges should not be surprising when we consider (1) that modern Mexico is geographically diverse; (2) that it is a highly unequal society with considerable heterogeneity and cultural diversity; and (3) that it emerged from a highly conflictual and unequal post-colonial society in which multiple exogenous shocks disrupted the traditional social structure. In terms of geographical and cultural diversity, the sharpest contrast is between the drier, northern portion of the country, which is the center of most industrial activity; and the southern portion of the country, which has a tropical climate and is poorer, with a larger indigenous population. Exogenous shocks to Mexican development included numerous foreign interventions that both changed domestic politics and, in the most extreme instance of war with the United States in the 1840s, led to massive loss of territory. To this list we could add the impact of foreign capital during the Porfiriato and the social dislocation experienced by the rural, largely indigenous population, and it is not hard to understand why important groups of rural poor were willing to follow leaders like Pancho Villa and Emiliano Zapata during the Mexican Revolution (Womack 1968; Knight 1990a). That revolution, like the events that caused it, would prove to be a destabilizing force, even as a new order emerged that claimed to govern in its name.

Historical Development

Mexico was arguably the most important of Spain's colonies in the "New World" (Thomas 1993). This was mainly due to its economic value, which had two main sources. First, it had mining wealth, and Spain was a mercantilist power, meaning that it viewed the maximization of holdings of gold and silver ("bullion") as fundamental to state power and the key measure of economic performance. Second, Mexico had a large, complex Amerindian civilization before the arrival of Europeans (in fact it had numerous indigenous groups and cultures, perhaps most notably the Maya in the South, though their complex society had entered into decline some time before European contact; and the empire of the Mexica, often called the "Aztecs," centered in today's Mexico City). This meant that state-like structures could be built "on top of" the existing political and social institutions in the society (Mahoney 2010). This was similarly the case in the area around today's Peru, for the same reasons (in this case, the Inca civilization was the relevant one). Thus, both Mexico and Peru famously became "cores" of the Spanish colonial system, while areas like the Southern Cone (today's Argentina and Chile), Venezuela, and parts of Central America remained "peripheral" to that system until the closing years of Spanish colonialism (Halperín Donghi 1993).

Being a colonial core meant that the central power paid lots of attention to Mexican society (Mahoney 2010). Colonial Mexico had more colonial bureaucracy than peripheral regions, and it had a more complex social structure, in part because of the society's relative cultural diversity but in large measure because the amount of wealth generated by mining, and thus the rents that could be siphoned off by multiple actors, facilitated this. Perhaps not surprisingly, its efforts to achieve independence followed a path that differed in certain key respects from the pattern witnessed in more peripheral areas. In places like Buenos Aires and Caracas, local elites tended to be strong supporters of independence (Lynch 1973). In places like Mexico, such elites were less sure, and the first stages of the revolt against Spain came out of the Mexican periphery. Indeed, Mexico only became independent when a *liberal* revolt in Spain caused some Mexican conservatives, most notably Augustin de Iturbide, to change sides, favoring a conservative government at home versus a liberal government from Europe (Meyer and Sherman 1987: 294–308; Anna 1998). At first, Mexico tried an imperial system, with Iturbide the emperor. This lasted only a matter of months before the country became a republic. The import of this, for comparative politics, is that this process both indicated and reinforced a strong traditionalist or conservative strain in the politics of independent Mexico.

In all of Latin America, politics in the nineteenth century was divided between conservatives and liberals; but the conservatives were both stronger and more conservative in Mexico than in many other places (on nineteenth-century Mexican conservatism, see Krauze 1997). Perhaps most important, Mexican conservatives helped the Roman Catholic Church maintain throughout a good portion of the nineteenth-century strength and privileges that were almost without parallel in the region, two of the most important being the Church's enormous landholding and the fact that it was allowed to operate a parallel legal system through which its clergy could be tried (Lynch 1986; Gill 2008). This ongoing polarization was an important factor in the War of the Reform in the 1850s and the revolution beginning after 1910, as well as the subsequent Cristero Rebellion in the 1920s.

Historical Development

Timeline

1810	"Grito of Dolores" marks beginning of independence movement.
1821	Plan of Iguala and its "Three Guarantees" and the establishment of Mexican independence
1833–1834	Valentín Gómez Farías attempts anti-clerical and other reforms. Santa Anna displaces Gómez Farías, prompting a period of conservative rule.
1836	Independence of Texas
1838–1839	The "Pastry War" (French invasion)
1846–1848	U.S. War with Mexico, which leads to the United States seizing a considerable portion of Mexican national territory including much of present-day Arizona, California, Colorado, Nevada, New Mexico, and Utah
1853	Gadsden Purchase transfers more Mexican land to the United States.
1855	Ley Juárez introduces anti-clerical reforms.
1856	Ley Lerdo forces alienation of Church Lands.
1857	Liberal constitution of 1857
1858–1861	War of the Reform
1862	European intervention, led by France
1864–1867	Rule by Emperor Maximilian, imposed by French forces
1867	Return to liberal government under Juárez
1876–1911	The Porfiriato, during which Porfirio Díaz dominates Mexican politics
1910	Díaz "defeats" Madero in a fraudulent election that is the opening scene of the Mexican Revolution.
1911–1913	Presidency of Francisco Madero
1913–1914	Presidency of Victorino Huerta, which begins with a coup d'état and the murder of Madero
1914–1920	Presidency of Venustiano Carranza, proponent of "constitutionalism"
1920–1924	Presidency of Alvaro Obregón
1924–1928	Presidency of Plutarco Elías Calles, who creates the party that later becomes the PRI
1926–1929	Cristero Rebellion
1928–1934	Period in which Calles dominates but does not hold the presidency
1929	Founding of PRI (at the time called the PNR)
1934–1940	Presidency of Lazaro Cárdenas, which includes nationalization of oil in 1938 as well as major agrarian reforms
1968	Major student protests quelled with violence.
1988–1994	Presidency of Carlos Salinas de Gortari, known for its liberal economic reforms
1994–	North American Free Trade Association (NAFTA) enters into effect.
1994	Beginning of Zapatista National Liberation Army (EZLN) activities under Subcomandante Marcos
1994–2000	Presidency of Ernesto Zedillo
1994	Peso crisis, resolved with major aid from the United States under Bill Clinton
2000	Election of Vicente Fox of the Partido Acción Nacional (PAN) signals the end of PRI hegemony in Mexico, and progress for Mexican democracy.
2006–2012	Presidency of Felipe Calderón
2012–present	Presidency of Enrique Peña Nieto

In the early years of the republic, Mexico descended into what scholars call "caudillismo," which essentially means rule by strongmen. You will recognize from chapter 3 that this would be a symptom of relative state weakness: the Mexican state was at least partially a vehicle for the pursuit of the private interest of a "predatory" elite rather than an organization in which rule of law, equal access, and institutional legitimacy were established. While the institutional trappings of a liberal republic were in place, the holder of the presidency ultimately answered to a military elite—and in Mexico this meant Antonio López de Santa Anna. Santa Anna famously switched sides in Mexican politics, alternating between the conservatives and the liberals (Meyer and Sherman 1987; Bazant 1985: 436–444), sometimes assuming the presidency himself, but even then often vacating the office to retire to his private estate while a designee handled the government's day-to-day affairs. His authority rested essentially on his reputation as a great warrior and his ability to establish a private army to outcompete potential domestic rivals. Of course, there is one easy way to lose legitimacy in a system of this sort, which is to fail in military terms. Santa Anna lost power after the unsuccessful effort to stop the declaration of the independent Republic of Texas. He would temporarily gain it back after heroic service against the French in the "pastry war," and then lose power again in subsequent years; gaining it again during the U.S. invasion of Mexico and losing power for good in 1855, when the Revolution of Ayutla (1854–1855) brought the liberals to power (Hamnett 1994).

After so many years of political instability and protection of conservative interests, the liberals were eager to dramatically remake Mexican politics (Krauze 1997: 157–159). This they attempted to do in the Constitution of 1857 and in two major reforms, known as the Ley Juárez and the Ley Lerdo (after their authors). These laws expanded civilian power over the clergy and forced the Church to sell its massive properties. However, the Church's conservative allies were unwilling to accept the new order, and a major civil war, known as the War of the Reform (1858–1861), broke out (Hamnett 1994). Eventually the republic was able to defend itself against conservative insurgents. At the same time, Mexican conservatives, led by Juan Almonte, successfully convinced Napoleon III to invade France and to impose a European monarch, Archduke Maximilian, as Emperor of Mexico (Meyer and Sherman 1987: 391–401). Ironically, Maximilian had liberal sympathies and did not roll back the reforms and otherwise pursue the policies that his conservative supporters would have liked. As a result, he soon had relatively little backing. As long as French troops remained in Mexico, he was able to withstand Juárez's resistance movement. But after the close of the American Civil War, with the United States sending troops to the Mexican border and threatening intervention in favor of Juárez and the liberals, French troops withdrew, and Maximilian's regime ended soon thereafter.

This meant a (brief) return to liberal, civilian government. However, in 1871, Porfirio Díaz ran on a campaign of "no re-election." Having lost, he began a revolt that culminated in his taking power in 1876. In certain respects, this signaled a return to caudillismo, as he would govern, though not always formally holding office, until 1910. However, some important differences separate the "Porfiriato" from the style of rule developed by Santa Anna in the first half of the century. First, Díaz aimed to use his power to force the modernization of the country (as he and his advisers understood this process). As in Brazil, "positivism" played a key role in forming Mexican ideas of progress and modernization (Camp 2007: 36–38). Díaz courted foreign investment and presided over some growth in manufacturing, the construction of a notable system of railroads, and the transformation of agriculture (Meyer and Sherman 1987: 431–479; Krauze 1997). All of these developments would have important implications for subsequent politics, as they produced some dislocation and upset traditional ways of doing things. Perhaps agricultural changes were the most important because they broke up traditional local landownership patterns and helped to concentrate land in the hands of a small elite (Camp 2007: 38), and introduced wage labor as the basis of the rural economy in at least some areas. As many scholars have pointed out, this, and social inequality more generally, would play a major role in the discontent that fueled the Mexican revolution beginning in 1910 (Camp 2007: 42; Knight 1990a). In particular, Emiliano Zapata's insurgency was focused, above all, on landownership (Womack 1968).

The revolution had as its proximate cause the revolt of Francisco Madero, who had run against Díaz and lost in a fraudulent election (for a definitive account of the revolution, see Knight 1990a, 1990b). Madero was essentially a northern elite and a liberal. He was soon joined in his efforts by distinct social groups, the most important of which were led by Francisco ("Pancho") Villa in the north and Zapata. Ideologically, these groups went well beyond Madero's liberalism: though historians disagree about what exactly they stood for, it is agreed that they sought to redress problems of economic inequality and not just political issues. Scholars disagree about when, precisely, the revolution ended, and we cannot trace here all of its twists and turns. Note, though, that Madero governed until he was assassinated by Victoriano Huerta in 1913. Huerta was in turn displaced by Venustiano Carranza in 1914. It was under Carranza that the revolutionary constitution of 1917 was passed. Carranza was forced out in a revolt in 1920 led by Álvaro Obregón, and Obregón would himself assume the presidency. Several years later, Obregón would be followed by Plutarco Elías Calles, who would found the party that would become the PRI and who would dominate Mexican politics—both directly and indirectly (Krauze 1997: 404–437)—until Lázaro Cárdenas was elected in 1934. Elías Calles is best known for consolidating the system of PRI-party dominance that would endure until 2000 and for presiding over the period of the Cristero Rebellion: a major civil war in which insurgents aimed, unsuccessfully, to defend the Roman Catholic Church from the state's alleged depredations (Blancarte 1992). Cárdenas is best remembered for his populist politics, for his role in further solidifying Mexican corporatism, for the nationalization of Mexican oil, and for his efforts at agrarian reform (Krauze 1997: 438–480).

There is much to debate about the extent to which this broader process was revolutionary. It clearly generated some important changes in politics, social life, and even religion. Yet the regime that it ended up producing by the middle of the twentieth century looked in certain ways like those found in many other Latin American societies at the time. The most obvious difference was that authoritarian politics in Mexico was so clearly dominated by one political party, the PRI. The most obvious similarity would be the turn to import substitution as a development strategy. In Mexico, for a time at least, many judged this approach to be successful, yielding the so-called "Mexican miracle" (Basáñez 2006: 297) of medium-term sustained economic growth. Economically, though, the country entered into crisis—like most of Latin America—in the 1980s. By the early 1990s, President Salinas de Gortari introduced important liberal economic reforms. Scholars debate the relationship between these reforms and the subsequent economic turbulence, including the peso crisis of 1994. Also in the early 1990s, Mexico witnessed the beginning of an insurgency in the southern state of Chiapas, protesting liberal reforms and "globalization" more generally. In later years, Mexico's citizens became more and more interested in breaking the PRI's stranglehold on power. The National Action Party (*Partido Acción Nacional, or* PAN) successfully won the presidency with Vicente Fox in 2000. PAN is a center-right party that tends to be less anticlerical than the PRI (indeed, the Catholic Church played a role in Mexican democratization, as it did elsewhere during "third wave" democratization). It has also continued with economic liberalization. Fox was succeeded by President Felipe Calderón. Calderón had some success but faced difficulties generated by his efforts to control drug gang activity, especially in border states. In some areas, the state's ability to exert its Weberian "monopoly on the legitimate use of force" was totally called into question. PRI candidate Enrique Peña Nieto won the 2012 presidential elections. As of late 2017, Peña Nieto was historically unpopular (Pew Research Center 2017)—due to a number of factors, including perceptions of corruption and government competence, as well as ongoing crime and human rights abuses, most notably the unresolved disappearance of 43 university students in 2014, presumed murdered (the remains of several have been identified): and many wonder whether the PRI will be able to retain its hold on power. Presidential elections are scheduled for summer, 2018; and at the time of this writing, the most popular candidate is Manuel López Obrador, a leftist from outside the traditional party structure (Reuters 2017; see also Bloomberg's coverage of the Mexican election https://www.bloomberg.com/graphics/2018-mexican-election/, accessed March 26, 2018).

Regime and Political Institutions

Mexico's political system is strongly presidentialist, though it has become less so in recent years as multiparty competition has become a reality (Camp 2007: 181–183). In the years of PRI dominance this was highlighted by the extraordinary power that the president had both within the institutional framework of the state *and* within the party. The executive branch plays a critical role not just in the administration of the state but also in conceiving and proposing legislation. Indeed, historically, the extent to which legislation is proposed by the executive in Mexico has been significant (Camp 2007: 181–182). Camp notes two additional sources of the legislature's relative weakness (2007: 187–188). First, representatives cannot be re-elected immediately after serving a term. Second, the research staff of the legislature is small and poorly funded, whereas the executive's staff is robust.

The judicial system has also suffered historically from relative weakness and lack of independence, though this

Regime and Political Institutions

Regime	Federal republic, democratic (more fully so in recent years, especially since PAN victory in 2000 presidential election)
Administrative Divisions	Thirty-one states as well as the Federal District of Mexico City
Executive Branch	President
Selection of Executive	President is elected by popular vote. Note that presidential selection has changed notably in recent years (see Case Study box, "Mexico's 'Perfect Dictatorship' and Its End," later in these country materials).
Legislative Branch	Bicameral Congress Lower chamber: Chamber of Deputies (*Cámara de Diputados*) Upper chamber: Senate (*Senado*)
Judicial Branch	Supreme Court of Justice, composed of eleven justices (one the "president" of the supreme court). Justices are nominated by the executive and approved by the legislature.
Political Party System	Multiparty system, though for much of the twentieth century Mexican politics was completely dominated by the PRI. The PAN broke this monopoly in 2000; but as of this writing, a PRI member again holds the presidency, with many expecting it to lose power in elections scheduled for 2018.

has changed somewhat in the wake of reforms passed in the 1990s (Camp 2007: 189–192). After the defeat of the PRI in 2000, there has been greater competitiveness in the electoral system.

Political Culture

Mexico is a country where scholars have focused a good deal of attention on questions of political culture. Classic accounts of the "culture of poverty" by anthropologists (Lewis 1961) and of the "civic culture" by political scientists (Almond and Verba 1963) looked at Mexico as a prominent case. These accounts tended to view Mexico in negative terms, or to treat its culture as problematic or as contributing to perceived economic or political deficits. Thus Lewis aimed to explain multigenerational poverty in the Tepito neighborhood of Mexico City (though generalizing about persons in poverty more generally), arguing that it was transmitted through cultural traits like authoritarianism, a tendency toward interpersonal violence, misogyny, and poor education (it is important to note here that Lewis was not claiming that Mexicans possessed these traits more than other populations). Almond and Verba, in contrast, relied on more representative surveys of a sample of the Mexican population as they compared Mexican political attitudes and orientations to those held in other countries like England, Germany, Italy, and the United States. Their general conclusion was that the Mexican population had a less democratic cultural orientation than the populations of other countries. This sort of argument has generated a robust debate in the social sciences and in policy debates about the relationship between culture, poverty, and democracy more generally.

Let us focus on the political culture example for a moment. That Almond and Verba's (1963) data showed less democratic attitudes and orientations (as they were defining them) is clear. This is not the source of any controversy among social scientists. Where the argument gets more complex is when causal claims are made about the relationship between these values and political outcomes. Almond and Verba's study was conducted at the height of the PRI party dominance in Mexico. Some scholars want to argue that political culture "trickles up" and shapes institutions (Inglehart and Welzel 2005). Others want to argue that political institutions produce cultures. So from one point of view, Mexican authoritarianism was a response to a more authoritarian political culture. From another point of view, the observed cultural tendencies in that period were reasonable adaptations to an authoritarian political environment. Note that this is a general debate in comparative politics and that Mexico is just one particularly interesting case in this connection.

Can you think of ways in which we might be able to make progress on this debate rather than having each side repeatedly assert its theoretical point of view? One strategy would be to focus on Mexico's democratic transition. If the first theory is right, it should have been driven largely by cultural change. That is, Mexican political culture should have become more "democratic," with institutional change and formal democratization following. If the second theory is right, we would expect elite bargaining and institutional change to come first, with cultural changes to follow, if at all.

While this is a good strategy, as is often the case the empirical data do not immediately resolve the conflict between these rival theories, there is evidence to support both views. It is pretty hard to explain the Mexican transition without focusing on internal party dynamics in the PRI, organizing in the PAN, and the crises and economic dislocations of the 1980s and 1990s that undercut one of the PRI's main pillars of legitimacy. On the other hand, there is evidence (Camp 2007) that Mexican political culture in this period changed notably (simply speaking, becoming more democratic), in one account "converging" a bit with the political cultures of Canada and the United States, just as Mexican economic culture notably shifted through modernization (Basáñez 2006).

Political Economy

Mexico is an important emerging economy, increasingly integrated with the broader global economy. Its economic history has been mixed, alternating between periods of growth and crisis. As discussed previously, it was, in economic as well as political terms, one of Spain's most important colonial possessions. In the nineteenth century, political instability caused economic problems, since a predictable political and economic environment is necessary for investors and other economic actors to act optimally. In the later nineteenth century, modern economic infrastructure was built during the Porfiriato, but the social dislocations caused in part by this process yielded later instability. The Mexican Revolution ushered in another period of instability that likely held economic performance back, though it is arguable that the fruits of development in subsequent years were somewhat more equitable as a result of this process. Finally, as in much of Latin America and the rest of the developing world, Mexico turned to import substitution as its development strategy in the middle of the twentieth century. This set of policies coincided with fairly consistent and strong economic growth for several decades—though even at the end of this process, Mexico was left with high inequality and notable poverty.

Today's Mexican economy is dominated by services (63.4 percent of GDP) and industry (32.2 percent), with agriculture accounting for under 4 percent of GDP (2016 estimates, *CIA World Factbook*). Unemployment is at least formally quite low at present, estimated at 3.9 percent (2016 estimate, *CIA World Factbook*). As the *CIA World Factbook* notes, Mexico has a high rate of *underemployment*, however. What this means is that many Mexicans do not have satisfactorily remunerative jobs, and a large percentage (around a quarter of the labor force) works in the informal economy. This is very common in the developing world, and it is worth keeping in mind because it impacts the extent to which unemployment rates in developed and developing societies are comparable measures. Mexico does continue to suffer from high income inequality. Its Gini coefficient stands at 48.2 (2014 estimate, per *CIA World Factbook*). This is somewhat worse than the Gini coefficient for the United States, itself known as a country with relatively high income inequality.

The Mexican state has historically played an important role in economic management. As noted previously, during the Porfiriato, the state endeavored to attract and protect capital. Its role in the economy grew after the revolution and under the PRI (Camp 2007: 45), particularly beginning in the 1930s and 1940s. Mexico practiced state-led development, nationalizing enterprises like oil (creating the giant PEMEX firm) as well as railroads, engaging in land reform (which generally tended toward the distribution of relatively small landholdings), and adopting a strategy of import-substituting industrialization, protecting domestic industries. It invested heavily in infrastructure as well. This was the period of the "Mexican miracle" (Basáñez 2006: 297), which produced steady growth, relatively low inflation, and rapid industrialization. Unfortunately, Mexico suffered, along with the rest of Latin America, from the debt crisis of the 1980s, related here to the dramatic decline in oil revenues, which, along with other factors, exacerbated the state's difficulties in paying its debts. Consequently, the country faced serious economic difficulties—including an increase in poverty and the expansion of the informal economy—and Mexico slowly turned toward reform. Mexico followed prescriptions to privatize a number of industries, including banks that had undergone emergency nationalization in 1982, though the state continues to own PEMEX, CFE (a major power company), and other enterprises. The Mexican economy has also seen the growth of agribusiness in recent years. Mexico has come to be more integrated with the global economy, particularly through NAFTA (which came into effect in 1994), aiming to bolster growth through industrial exports. This strategy has produced gains, though it has also left the country vulnerable to global economic forces, including the peso crisis of 1994 and the country's serious exposure to the global economic crisis beginning in 2008. The election of Donald Trump to the presidency of the United States has also raised questions about the future of NAFTA, as the American president has promised to renegotiate its terms.

CASE STUDIES

CASE STUDY
The Mexican State and Rule of Law

CHAPTER 3, PAGE 57

As discussed in chapter 3, one of the distinguishing features of modern states (in addition to their relative autonomy, bureaucratic mode of organization, and so forth) is that they have established the *rule of law*. This means that, at least theoretically, a fully functioning modern state (1) has a legal-rational framework for resolving conflict; (2) enforces that framework transparently; and (3) enforces it equally, rather than privileging one or another set of actors based on network ties or some other sort of affiliation.

The Mexican state has done this at various times in its history with varying degrees of success. As Mörner (1993: 6) notes, the state was relatively weak after independence and then grew in strength during the Porfiriato, entering a period of weakness during the revolution and its immediate aftermath before gaining capacity again in the middle of the twentieth century. In very recent years, there has been a great deal of concern in Mexico and abroad, particularly in the United States, about increasing levels of violence, drug trafficking, ongoing corruption, and the seeming inability or unwillingness of components of the Mexican state (army, police, and the judicial system) to curb criminal activity. Some areas of Mexico, it is alleged, largely lie outside of the state's real jurisdiction. In some towns in parts of the country, drug gangs essentially exercise state-like functions, resolving disputes and maintaining order of a certain sort.

How could we explain the presence and influence of powerful criminal organizations that make a mockery of the state's "monopoly on the legitimate use of force"? Several basic factors are likely decisive. First, there must be gains to be made above those made in licit activity for an important segment of people. Otherwise, there would be little incentive to *engage* in illicit activity. This would suggest that continued economic development would help to reduce organized, nonstate violence (of course, organized nonstate violence makes economic development more difficult to achieve). Second, the risks must not be so high as to discourage a large number of criminals from participating in illicit activity. In contemporary Mexico, as in many parts of the developing world, the risks that state enforcement poses to criminals is relatively low because of high rates of *impunity*. The state cannot or will not enforce the law in certain areas, dramatically reducing the cost (in terms of risk) for illicit activity. Finally, illicit groups must have the resources necessary to seek their chosen ends, and these resources can be both material and organizational. Material resources include both guns, which in the case of Mexico are often trafficked from the United States where there is little gun control, and money, again from the United States, as it is estimated that cross-border drug trade sends between $15 billion and $25 billion to Mexico each year (O'Neil 2009: 70). Organizational resources include the ongoing existence of criminal gangs, as well as their established ties, via corruption, to state actors.

Interestingly, a number of commentators have tied the escalation in Mexican drug violence to reform. Some of this has to do with the fact that the PRI historically sometimes worked *with* criminal networks rather than aiming to squash them (O'Neil 2009: 65). Moreover, at lower levels of the organizational structure of the state, police corruption was common under the PRI (Davis 2006), and remains so. Where and when the PAN came to hold office, linkages between the PRI and drug traffickers were broken, producing non-institutional (and thus often violent) responses (O'Neil 2009: 65). In essence, whereas the PRI had allowed the continued existence of illicit organizations but had co-opted them and used them for their purposes, after the emergence of democratic pluralism, these organizations faced higher risks and thus sought new techniques to maintain and protect their autonomy and interests. Exogenous factors were important as well, including U.S. efforts to restrict the flow of trafficking in the Caribbean region. If the costs of one path get too high, traffickers will look for another path, and trafficking through Mexico rose dramatically in response

to changing patterns of U.S. enforcement (O'Neil 2009: 66; Davis 2006: 62). Of course, this necessarily bolstered the position of Mexican illicit organizations. Thus, at the same time, Mexican criminal organizations had greater profits, more autonomy, and a reason to become more independent. Then the Mexican government attempted to stamp them out. At this point, the organizations had little choice but to fight back. In addition, it is possible that successful efforts to repress these criminal organizations can, for a time, produce greater violence. When leaders of the criminal organizations are captured, the members of those organizations may fight with each other to replace them.

It is worth noting that some of the same commentators cited previously have seen linkages between Mexican

democratization (O'Neil 2009; Davis 2006) and rising crime in Mexico (this is perhaps not surprising since reform and democratization have been so closely linked). Indeed, the rise in crime witnessed in Latin America from the 1980s on did roughly mirror the pattern of regional democratization. Could it be, as some authors have asked, that democratization and rule of law don't always go hand in hand? Others (Magaloni and Zepeda 2004) have looked at economic data, though, and argued that while democratization *seems* the culprit, its near simultaneity with rising crime is largely coincidental, and that the most important variables associated with rising crime are income inequality and economic difficulties. This is an ongoing debate in the field.

In Mexico in 2000, a remarkable thing happened to the *Partido Revolucionario Institucional* (the PRI): it lost. The PRI ruled Mexico from 1929 to 2000, a period of seventy-one years that equaled the amount of time the Communist Party ruled the former Soviet Union. Throughout that time, the PRI held elections, and it routinely won them. The party's dominance was so complete that a leading Latin American intellectual, the Peruvian Nobel Prize–winning novelist Mario Vargas Llosa, called Mexico "The Perfect Dictatorship." How did the PRI

dominate for so long, and conversely, why did this finally come to an end?

The PRI's electoral invincibility was built on several pillars, and including both "carrots" and "sticks." The "carrots" included the successful incorporation of many diverse interest groups into the party's governing structure; we note this later, in the Case Study box, "The PRI and Corporatism in Mexico" from chapter 11, where we discuss corporatism under the PRI. In addition, PRI rule included many "sticks," though oppression was not constant and not always overt. The most

dramatic event came in 1968 when the government cracked down on student protesters in a plaza in Mexico City in what came to be known as the Night of Tlatelolco (Krauze 1997: 717–726). Official figures at the time were that four people were killed; but other estimates were much higher, ranging as high as 3,000.

The PRI's eventual decline was accelerated by a range of factors and by several events. In particular, the government's legitimacy suffered when it presided over major economic turmoil in 1982. In that year, Mexico hit a debt

CASE STUDY (continued)
Mexico's "Perfect Dictatorship" and Its End
CHAPTER 7, PAGE 157

crisis that left it unable to pay back foreign debt, and this signaled the end of the "Mexican Miracle" of growth that it had achieved for several decades. During the 1980s, support from peasants and labor unions began to shift to opposition parties, including the PRD and the PAN. Around this time, opposition parties first built their political base by winning elections in Mexico's states and cities, with numerous governors being elected from other parties from 1989 through the 1990s. As this happened, it became costlier and more difficult for the PRI to rig a national election just as the economic crisis depleted the government's resources (Levy and Bruhn 2006). Even less political events seemed to contribute further to the PRI's decline. A major earthquake in Mexico City in

1985 was handled with incompetence by the government, yet other NGOs responded effectively, which undermined the PRI's claim that it alone was capable of addressing public needs (Haber 2006: 74–76).

The declining legitimacy of the PRI came to a head when it used less-than-subtle tactics to win the 1988 presidential election. In that year, the party-controlled electoral council infamously announced that all of its computers tragically crashed just when it appeared the popular opposition candidate Cuauhtémoc Cárdenas of the PRD party (and son of PRI founder Lázaro Cárdenas) would win the presidential election. When the computers turned back on, PRI nominee Carlos Salinas de Gortari miraculously found himself with

an insurmountable lead over Cárdenas. The ballots from this 1988 election were later burned, but the result contributed further to the collapsing legitimacy of the party.

The PRI managed to hold on for one more election in 1994, but it lost the presidency at last in 2000 (for more detail on the transition, see the essays in Middlebrook 2004). It returned to power with the 2012 election of Enrique Peña Nieto, but many observers would argue that it will not (and perhaps does not aim to) recover its traditional form of dominance. Indeed, at the time of this writing, Peña Nieto is extremely unpopular and many expect either Manuel López Obrador or the candidate for PAN to win the presidential elections scheduled for 2018.

CASE STUDY
The PRI and Corporatism in Mexico
CHAPTER 11, PAGE 269

As noted previously, Mexico was once called "The Perfect Dictatorship." Part of the reason for this name was the ability of Mexico's PRI party to bring major interest groups under its banner. This included labor, business, the state bureaucracy, as well as the peasantry. At the same time, the PRI successfully marginalized from politics the military and the church, two other major forces in Latin America that could threaten the basis for rule (Stevens 1977: 253). The broad-based form of corporatism that took in Mexico's major institutions made it very difficult for competitors to defeat the PRI,

and the party governed uninterrupted from the 1930s to 2000.

The PRI in Mexico managed the representation of different interest groups by incorporating these various forces into the dominant party's decision-making structures. Under most circumstances, it would be challenging for a single party to be the party of both labor and business, yet Mexico's corporatism developed a symbiotic relationship for the interest groups and the governing party. The labor movement was represented mainly by the Confederation of Mexican Workers (CTM), which received

state sponsorship and whose leadership maintained close relations with the political leadership of the PRI. A similar relationship emerged between the PRI and the National Peasant Confederation (CNC). In the cases of labor and peasant groups alike, organizations that joined the government-sponsored confederation received particular economic benefits (such as wages or subsidies) that unaffiliated groups did not (see Levy and Bruhn 2006: 73–83). Meanwhile, business groups were more formally independent from the PRI, but they received considerable support from the party in the form

CASE STUDY (continued)
The PRI and Corporatism in Mexico

CHAPTER 11, PAGE 269

of policies and preferential treatment, such as subsidies, tax breaks, loans, protections from foreign competition, and pro-business state investment (Levy and Bruhn 2006: 84). In return for this set of policies that favored the broad array of interest groups, Mexico's unions and business leaders were expected to turn out the vote for the PRI. This state corporatism worked in different ways in other countries in Latin America, as well as in Europe, due to the long-standing dominant party system.

However, the PRI eventually lost its control in Mexico. Some of these reasons were highlighted in the chapter 7 Case Study, "Mexico's 'Perfect Dictatorship' and Its End," but an important component of the end of the dominant party system was the decline of the PRI's corporatist strategy. Over time, pressures on the PRI increased, partly due to faltering economic performance, especially after the debt crisis of the early 1980s. When the PRI lost its ability to command support from peasants, laborers, and business, it lost not just voters but also the institutional underpinnings of its rule.

Key moments in Mexico's political economy came in the 1970s, when business groups grew disenchanted with the increasingly populist strategies employed by presidents Luis Echevarría and Jose López Portillo from the 1970s to 1982 and based in part on the discovery of new oil reserves. Increased government spending and indebtedness resulted in a debt crisis in 1982, during which Mexico devalued the peso and moved much more toward a neoliberal economic model emphasizing markets and free trade. This in turn alienated the other part of the PRI's political base—labor and peasants—and signaled the beginning of the end of the party's traditional form of dominance.

CASE STUDY
Industrialization, Modernity, and National Identity in Mexico

CHAPTER 13, PAGE 312

As mentioned in chapter 13, one major theory of nationalism holds that it is a product of industrial capitalism. Recall that this theory is functionalist in that it takes nationalism and national identity to emerge because industrial capitalism needs it, or at least needs some functional equivalent, to do so. The idea here is that nationalism's emphasis on equality and the importance of vernacular language, as well as the inherent similarity and fraternity between conationals from different localities, helps to break down barriers to geographic and social mobility; and that an industrial economy with its urbanization, shift to wage labor, and so forth cannot function if cultural barriers prevent it.

This argument, as noted in chapter 13, is plausible.

However, when applied to the empirical case of Mexico, it becomes difficult to sustain. Mexico begins to see at least some of its residents acquiring national consciousness in the years after and around 1810. Even the Plan of Iguala (1821), in many ways a conservative document, uses the language of nationalism, referring to Mexico in several passages as "La nación." (The Plan de Iguala is available online via Rice University: https://scholarship.rice.edu/handle/1911/9226.) In short, there is no doubt that nationalism was *present* in the country during the independence struggles and even a few years before.

This does not mean, by any stretch, that national identity had established "hegemony" in Mexico in this period. In other words, it does not follow from the fact that official documents used national language (1) that all Mexicans thought of themselves as members of the nation or (2) that those who did all had the same idea of the nation (Anna 1998). Some elites in the early independence years likely continued to try to hold on to the sort of identity that had predominated in the colonial period. Many subaltern persons likely thought of themselves in terms of predominantly local identities, though careful research by historians has shown that some subaltern actors did quickly begin to make

CASE STUDY (continued)
Industrialization, Modernity, and National Identity in Mexico
CHAPTER 13, PAGE 312

use of national identities to make political claims on elites in Latin America once these became available (Mallon 1995). In any case, given that Mexican industrialization does not get underway in any meaningful sense until the Porfiriato, it is essentially impossible to argue that *industrial* capitalism precedes and therefore causes the spread of national identity in this case. Some might argue that an agriculture- and mining-based *commercial* capitalism was tied to the development of nationalism in Mexico, but this is a different argument and would require considerable evidence.

Does this mean that we should throw out arguments about industrial capitalism causing national identity to emerge or that this case refutes them categorically? Not necessarily. First of all,

Mexico may turn out to be exceptional in this regard, and a scholar cannot know until he or she examines other cases. In other words, maybe industrial capitalism giving rise to nationalism as seen in Ernest Gellner's theory (discussed in chapter 13) is a *common* path but not the only possible one. Second, even if industrial capitalism did not cause national identity's *emergence*, it still played an important role in the story of nationalism in Mexico. It's just that its main role in this connection comes later, when nationalism is an important ideology in the twentieth century—for example, during the administration of Lazaro Cárdenas. Nationalism is closely linked to Cárdenas's populist rhetoric and his corporatist mode of interest mediation (see the preceding case study discussion),

which itself is closely linked to the emergent industrial order (given that urban workers, along with agricultural workers, are among the most important corporate groups). Indeed, populist politicians like Cárdenas (and like Gaitán in Colombia, and, more recently, Hugo Chávez in Venezuela, at least until 2005) used nationalism rather than orthodox Marxism as the language through which they aimed to mobilize both industrial workers and peasants. Proponents of this industrial-capitalism-centered theory of national identity might be able to reconstruct a more modest version of the theory by focusing on this later juncture. However, in doing so, they will be focusing on something causally downstream from the actual emergence of Mexican nationalism.

CASE STUDY
Why Aren't There Major Ethnic Parties in Mexico?
CHAPTER 14, PAGE 343

Mexico had a complex indigenous population—indeed, one of the great human civilizations—prior to European contact. In subsequent years, people of European descent have on average fared better in Mexico than persons of indigenous descent, even though the majority of the Mexican population is of mestizo background and the next largest group is of predominantly Amerindian ancestry. Given the country's history of inequality and ethnic discrimination, why have indigenous groups not organized via ethnic political parties in Mexico?

This sort of question cannot be answered definitively, because it is asking, in essence, about a counterfactual. In other words, logically, the question is indistinguishable from the question "What would have caused ethnic political parties to have formed in Mexico?" The best way to provisionally answer such a question is to generate potential causes that plausibly would have increased the probability of the formation of such parties, but there is clearly no formula such that "if characteristic X had been present in

Mexican society, ethnic parties *would* have developed."

What sorts of features might have encouraged the formation of ethnicity-based parties in Mexico? Among others, we might expect (1) salient and impermeable boundaries between ethnic groups; (2) the lack of other frameworks for mobilization of the subaltern population; and (3) the opening of political space within which such parties could form and have some prospect of electoral success (since, from certain points of view, party organization is irrational if it cannot lead to increasing a group's power).

Historically, in Mexico, these conditions tended not to apply. While inequality has been a pervasive feature of Mexican society, and while ethnicity has been a major dimension of inequality, the boundaries between ethnic groups have historically been fluid (Camp 2007: 26). The majority of the country, as noted before, is of mestizo background (Krauze 1997; Camp 2007: 81), which could facilitate some freedom in self-identification. In addition to the fact that the cultural boundary between the categories "indigenous" and "mestizo" is permeable (as is, to a more limited extent, the boundary between "mestizo" and "white"), the very predominance of mestizos in the society undercuts the likelihood of a party linked to mestizo or indigenous identity. Moreover, other frameworks—frameworks that preclude mobilization around specific ethnic identities—have been salient in Mexican political history. Mexican national identity, at least since the early twentieth century, has been marked by the idea of ethnic mixing, most notably in José Vasconcelos's ([1925] 1997) famous idea of the "cosmic race," produced by the mixing of persons of African, indigenous, and European

descent. Mexican immigrants in the United States will sometimes use the word "raza" to refer to their identity as Mexican or Chicano/a. In addition to this sort of national frame, Mexico's revolutionary tradition tended to frame dissent in relation to class. Thus Zapata's insurgency during the Revolution, which included many mestizo and indigenous actors, largely privileged a peasant or rural laborer identity rather than an indigenous identity as such. Further, the corporatist mode of interest mediation developed under the PRI (particularly under Cárdenas) likely cut against ethnic affiliation because it again organized people in relation to their economic activity rather than their ethnic status. Finally, major political ideologies like Marxism and liberalism tend to oppose ethnic mobilization: to the extent that these were historically operative in Mexico, they likely mitigated any potential for ethnic mobilization via political parties.

Finally, Mexican parties were established at certain critical junctures in which conditions likely did not favor ethnic mobilization as the basis for party affiliation. This should be obvious with respect to the PRI. The other two major parties (the PRD, a leftist party composed of a splinter group formerly of the PRI and a coalition of communists and

socialists; and PAN, which is a center-right party with affinities for Christian Democratic parties) did not concentrate supporters of a particular ethnic group at their founding or in subsequent history. The political closure characteristic of Mexico during the years of the PRI's dominance also did little to increase the likelihood of the establishment of ethnicity-based political parties.

Does this all mean that ethnicity is unimportant in Mexican politics? Not at all. Indigenous communities have mobilized in numerous ways (Hernández Navarro and Carlsen 2004), and it is always possible that more influential ethnic parties will emerge in the future. Factors that might contribute to this possibility could include the much-documented role of international NGOs in helping to organize ethnicity-based political mobilization, the modeling effects of such organization in other parts of Latin America in recent years, and the ongoing effects of political opening and democratic consolidation in Mexico. One might expect this sort of outcome to be more likely in areas like Chiapas, where a larger portion of the population is indigenous; where historical discrimination, inequality, and poverty have been especially high; and where the EZLN ("Zapatista") insurgency has been based.

Research Prompts

1. The "Mexican Miracle" was achieved, in part, through policies of import substitution. In more recent years, the country has taken a more market-friendly approach. What would our theories of development from chapters 4 and 5 say about this sequence?

2. Think about the years of the PRI's dominance in Mexico. The regime was clearly authoritarian, but it had some democratic elements. How would you classify it in terms of the ideas of democracy and authoritarianism discussed in chapters 6 and 7?

As you conduct research, what do you find other scholars saying about this issue?

3. Do a little outside research to compare the development of national identity in Mexico to other cases (good choices for comparison might be Argentina, Chile, Colombia, and Venezuela). What, if anything, is distinctive about the Mexican case?

4. In the preceding Case Study on "Why Aren't There Major Ethnic Parties in Mexico?" you learned that Mexico's political parties have not been organized predominantly along the lines of ethnicity. Do some research and find a Latin American case where ethnicity *has* been a key basis of political organizing. What accounts for the difference?

Nigeria

Key Features of Contemporary Nigeria

Population:	190,632,261 (estimate, July 2017)
Area:	923,768 sq km
Head of State:	Muhammadu Buhari (president, 2015–present)
Head of Government:	Muhammadu Buhari (president, 2015–present)
Capital:	Abuja
Year of Independence:	1960
Year of Current Constitution:	1999
Languages:	English (official), Hausa-Fulani, Yoruba, Igbo, many others
GDP per Capita:	$5,900 (*CIA World Factbook* estimate, 2016)
Human Development Index Ranking (2016):	152nd (low human development)

Sources: *CIA World Factbook*; World Bank World Development Indicators; United Nations *Human Development Report 2016.*

Introduction

Nigeria is the largest country in Africa and has been subject to enduring interest among political scientists for several reasons. Of these, the two most important are that (1) it is a prominent example of the perils of oil dependence (Karl 1997), and (2) it has been the site of considerable interethnic conflict. Indeed, these issues, discussed herein, are not unrelated. Also related are the relative weakness of Nigerian institutions, development problems the society has faced, and the lessons that Nigeria might offer about how political modernization can take place in a post-colonial society.

Yet Nigeria is much more than this. A country of great cultural diversity, Nigeria has provided the world with Nobel laureates and other artists, writers, and musicians. It is the largest society in Africa, and many believe that if it can overcome its history of underdevelopment and ethnic conflict, it would have great potential. Indeed, though there are many concerns, the country has been democratic for well over a decade, a source of considerable optimism.

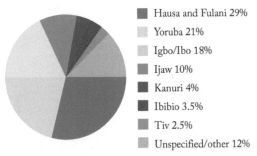

Hausa and Fulani 29%
Yoruba 21%
Igbo/Ibo 18%
Ijaw 10%
Kanuri 4%
Ibibio 3.5%
Tiv 2.5%
Unspecified/other 12%

Ethnic Groups in Nigeria
Note that the Nigerian population includes hundreds of ethnic groups, but these are the most numerous.
Source: CIA World Factbook.

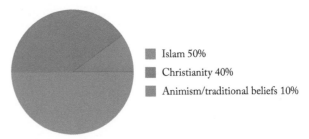

Islam 50%
Christianity 40%
Animism/traditional beliefs 10%

Religious Affiliation in Nigeria (estimates)
Source: CIA World Factbook.

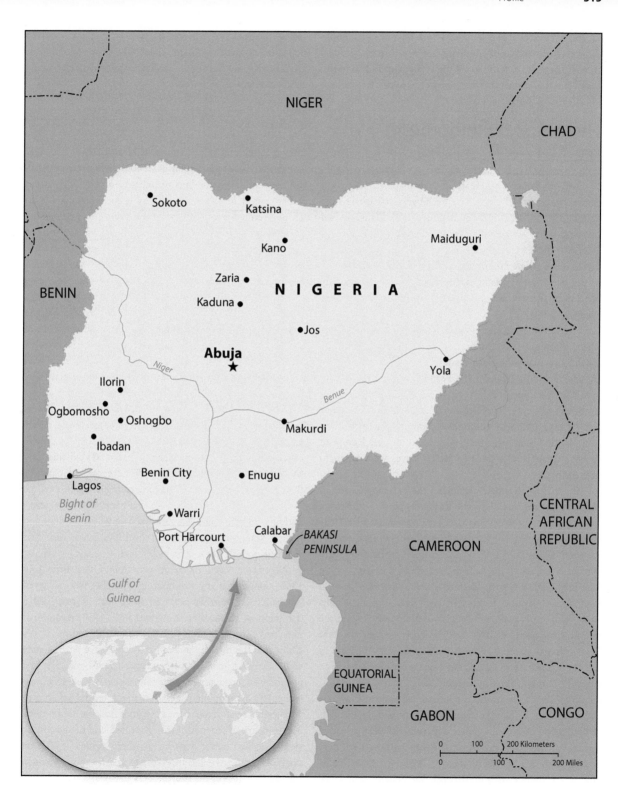

NIGER

CHAD

Sokoto

Katsina

Maiduguri

Kano

BENIN

Zaria

N I G E R I A

Kaduna

Jos

Niger

Abuja
★

Yola

Benue

Ilorin

Ogbomosho

Oshogbo

Makurdi

Ibadan

Benin City

Enugu

CENTRAL
AFRICAN
REPUBLIC

Lagos

*Bight of
Benin*

Warri

Port Harcourt

Calabar

*BAKASI
PENINSULA*

CAMEROON

*Gulf of
Guinea*

EQUATORIAL
GUINEA

GABON

CONGO

0	100	200 Kilometers
0	100	200 Miles

Nigeria's diversity encompasses both religious and ethnic difference. In terms of ethnicity, there are many groups, though the most prominent are the Hausa and Fulani in the north and the Yoruba and the Igbo in the south. In religious terms, the society is diverse as well, with about half the population practicing Islam, about 40 percent adhering to Christianity, and the remainder mostly practicing traditional African religions.

Historical Development

Before British colonial rule, Nigeria had a variety of different indigenous state structures (Falola and Heaton 2008). In northern Nigeria, where Islam had made its way from Arabia centuries earlier, there were relatively well-established states. Among the large population of the Hausa-Fulani ethnic groups—which today are the largest ethnic group in Nigeria—there were rather large and militarily capable units. In the south, where the Yoruba and Igbo peoples predominate in the southwest and southeast, respectively, people generally lived in smaller political groups such as villages or clusters of villages.

Interaction with Europe and the global economy took shape through early explorations by Europeans and the establishment of the slave trade along the coast of West Africa, including Nigeria. The Portuguese were the first to establish a trading post in the late 1400s, and several other countries were later involved along the Nigerian coast. After establishing authority through a combination of military intimidation and bargaining with local groups, European powers established a trade in which slaves were taken to the Americas.

The British ultimately became the principal force in Nigeria when in the 1800s the European powers undertook what came to be known as the "Scramble for Africa." The scramble was largely a land grab and a geopolitical contest between Great Britain, France, Portugal, and Belgium, who staked their claims to dominate most of the territory on the continent; Germany claimed several territories as well; and Spain played a lesser role, with Italy staking claims only in the early twentieth century. These powers met at the Berlin Conference in 1884–1885 and divided the continent into colonial states. Many of the British colonies were in southern and eastern Africa, but Nigeria was the largest and most important colony in western Africa.

Over the course of the late nineteenth and early twentieth centuries, Britain increased the extent and depth of its colonization of Nigeria, slowly asserting authority over the vast land. This happened through a combination of military subjugation and negotiation with Nigerian leaders willing to collaborate with the British. The system came to be known as indirect rule (Falola and Heaton 2008: 110–116; Lange 2009; Dorward 1986: 402–404), because the British did not send large numbers of forces to occupy Nigeria but rather sought to exert authority by using indigenous leaders as intermediaries with local populations; in a perversion of indigenous African forms of rule, this often involved the appointment of village chiefs and other customary leaders by the British administrative authorities. The system served the interests of the colonizers, but it set the tone for a long run of unaccountable government across much of Africa (cf. Mamdani 1996). By the time of the First World War, the Commissioner Frederick Lugard had established a form of indirect rule over nearly all of present-day Nigeria. He unified the northern and southern colonies into a single political unit, which formed the basis for today's nation-state, with its large size and its conflicts between regions.

As World War II came to an end, the European powers had increasing difficulty justifying their colonization in moral, economic, or political terms. Nationalists gained in prominence in most of the colonies (see discussion in Williams 1984 and Falola and Heaton 2008: 136–157), empowered in part by their learnings in Europe and the increasing recognition of the contributions Africans had made in the war. One of Nigeria's leading nationalists was Nnamdi Azikiwe, whose writings first became known in the 1930s. By the 1950s, it was clear that colonialism in Africa was on its last legs.

Nigeria achieved independence from Great Britain in 1960, alongside many neighboring countries who achieved independence from France that same year. It remained a dominion of the United Kingdom until 1963, meaning it remained part of the British Commonwealth and nominally considered the British monarch as a ceremonial head of state while retaining political independence and self-rule. The first postindependence government followed a British-style parliamentary system, but Nigeria became a federal republic in 1963, with the aforementioned Nnamdi Azikiwe as president. The principle of federalism was instituted, and the governing system divided power between the three regions of Nigeria: the Northern region and the Western and Eastern regions in the southern half of the country.

Historical Development

Timeline

1500s–1800s	Period of slave trade along the coast of West Africa, including Nigeria; slaves are taken to the Americas	1995	Abacha regime executes political activist and author Ken Saro-Wiwa.
1800s–	Period of initial establishment of British colonies in present-day Nigeria; Sokoto Caliphate governs many of the Hausa-Fulani groups in the north; smaller groups govern among Yoruba, Igbo, other groups in the south.	1998	Abacha dies suddenly in office, followed soon after by the sudden and suspicious death of civilian rival Moshood Abiola.
		1999	Nigeria returns to civilian rule under former general Olusegun Obasanjo.
1850s–1900	Increasing colonization of Nigeria by Great Britain	2003	Obasanjo is reelected for a second term.
1900–1919	Era of Lord Frederick Lugard, British administrator who establishes indirect rule using traditional authorities as intermediaries and unifies colonies of Nigeria	2007	Umaru Yar'Adua is elected president but is in grave health for most of his presidency.
1960	Independence from Great Britain	2008–2011	Tensions worsen between northern Muslims and southern Christians.
1966	Military coup overthrows civilian government.	2010	As many as one thousand people are killed in clashes between Christians and Muslims in the city of Jos and elsewhere in central Nigeria.
1966–1975	Presidency of military leader Yakubu Gowon		
1967–1970	Biafra War		
1976	Assassination of military leader Murtala Mohammed (president, 1975–1976)	2010	Yar'Adua dies of natural causes; Vice President Goodluck Jonathan becomes president.
1979	Military leader Olusegun Obasanjo (1976–1979) turns power over to civilian Shehu Shagari.	2011	Goodluck Jonathan is elected to full presidential term.
1983	Military takes control again under Gen. Muhammadu Buhari.	2011-present	Increased terrorist activity by Islamist extremist group Boko Haram, including deadly bombing of a UN compound in Abuja, kidnapping of schoolgirls, and massacres in several towns across northern Nigeria, and other attacks.
1985–1993	Presidency of military leader Ibrahim Babangida; human rights abuses worsen.		
1993	Military holds elections but annuls them after apparent victory of businessman Moshood Abiola.	2015	Muhammadu Buhari, a former military dictator, is elected president, defeating incumbent Goodluck Jonathan.
1993–1998	Presidency of Gen. Sani Abacha; corruption and human rights abuses reach their worst levels, with regular torture and execution of dissidents.		

Ethnic and regional tensions emerged early on, as the populous north came to dominate the parliament in a vote split almost purely along regional and ethnic lines, and this resulted in a coup by elements of the military from the Igbo ethnicity in the Eastern region. The coup came to be known as the "Igbo coup." This characterization has been disputed, but the name stuck and signaled the increasing alienation of the Igbo from the northern Hausa-Fulani as well as the western Yoruba. Though the eventual military leader chosen as president, Yakubu Gowon, was from central Nigeria and was seen as a compromise selection, the tensions between Igbos and other groups worsened.

In 1967, the Nigerian Civil War (also known as the Biafra War) broke out, pitting the Eastern region and its Igbo majority against the federal government (Falola and Heaton 2008: 175–180). The conflict was over autonomy, with the Igbo seeking to establish the independent state of Biafra, but the hostility was lubricated by oil. Much of Nigeria's oil is found in the southeast, and the Igbo in the region argued that more of the resource should be turned into local development rather than being redistributed to other parts of Nigeria. The federal government, meanwhile, wanted to retain the union but also the resources that oil guaranteed. After three years of bloody conflict in which over one million people died—mostly on the Igbo side—the federal government won the war, and Nigeria remained a single country.

The 1970s saw another succession of military rulers, with power passing to presidents Murtala Mohammed (a northerner), who was assassinated, and then Olusegun Obasanjo (a southwestern Yoruba). Obasanjo ultimately proposed free elections and the establishment of a new republic and turned power over to civilian leader Shehu Shagari, a northern

Muslim. Shagari and the republic did not see out their term, however, as the military seized control again under General Muhammadu Buhari, citing extensive corruption and fraud under Shagari. Military rule continued under President Ibrahim Babangida, who ruled from 1985 to 1993, but governing conditions did not improve. In particular, corruption continued unabated despite the imprisonment of several high-ranking officials and the execution of violent criminals. While Babangida was initially popular, he came under pressure to redemocratize as a wave of democracy swept across Africa in the early 1990s.

The military held elections in 1993, but when prominent businessman Chief Moshood Abiola looked to be the victor, the military annulled the results. This paved the way for the presidency of military General Sani Abacha (for an overview of this period, see Falola and Heaton 2008: 229–234), who earned the dubious distinction of being the worst dictator in Nigeria's less-than-proud history of corrupt and authoritarian presidents. Corruption and human rights abuses reached their worst levels under Abacha. The regime stood accused of engaging in torture on a regular basis. It also executed dissidents, most notably the author Ken Saro-Wiwa and his colleagues, who had become prominent political activists of the Movement for the Survival of the Ogoni People, an environmental movement declaiming the degradation of air, water, and land in Nigeria's oil-rich Niger Delta. During his reign, Abacha and his family were rumored to have accumulated several billion dollars in assets, though the exact amount squirreled away overseas has not been determined. In 1998, Abacha's rule came to a sudden end when he died in office. Rumors soon emerged that he was poisoned; the rumor gained in popularity when his death was soon followed by the sudden and suspicious death of Chief Moshood Abiola, the presumptive winner of the 1993 elections.

After Abacha, a transitional military government under General Abdulsalami Abubakar moved to draft a new constitution, establish a new republic, and return Nigeria to civilian rule by 1999. In elections that year, former general and one-time military president Olusegun Obasanjo won the presidency handily. This Christian southerner selected a Muslim northerner as vice president and governed at the head of the People's Democratic Party (PDP), which crafted a cross-ethnic coalition. Obasanjo remained relatively popular in Nigeria's challenging political environment and was reelected for a second term in 2003. He then ceded power

in 2007 to another PDP president, the Muslim northerner Umaru Yar'Adua. Yar'Adua was ill for most of his presidency, and authority was largely exercised by Vice President Goodluck Jonathan after 2009. In 2010, Yar'Adua died and Jonathan became president; he later won a full term of office running as an incumbent in 2011.

One political challenge that emerged is the fact that Jonathan is a southerner. This has led some northerners to object that the south had two turns at having recent presidents, with Obasanjo and Jonathan, while the north had only one president in Yar'Adua, and that for less than one term. This is seen by some as breaking an unwritten rule that power should be systematically alternated between north and south to ensure stability. In this tense issue, it should be noted that Jonathan is a member of the Ijaw ethnic group, and not of the more numerous Yoruba or Igbo groups.

Ethnic and regional tensions have come to the fore again in recent years in Nigeria with a string of clashes between Christians and Muslims and with the emergence of Islamist fundamentalist groups. Much of the violence has occurred along the central belt of Nigeria, along the fault line between the Muslim-dominated north and the Christian-dominated south. In central states such as Plateau and Bauchi, more than one thousand people were killed in clashes in 2010. The city of Jos, capital of Plateau State, has been the biggest flashpoint, but killings have happened in other cities, towns, and villages. Over these same years, the Islamist extremist group Boko Haram has emerged as a significant threat to stability, having coordinated and led deadly bombings and attacks of markets, police stations, polling stations, and international agencies in cities such as Bauchi and the capital Abuja—over recent years killing thousands of people and becoming internationally notorious for its mass abduction of schoolgirls in 2014. The group calls for stricter enforcement of Islamic Sharia law in Nigeria, where it is applied to some extent in the northern states, and for the outright rejection of modern education, and has claimed an affiliation with ISIS.

Nigeria's history thus includes long-standing tensions between ethno-regional groups, with religion overlapping this conflict. It also includes a long history of corrupt, inefficient, and ineffective government, though most indications are that this has slowly improved in the new republic since 1999. The continuation of these two basic issues shapes much of the rest of Nigeria's politics.

Regime and Political Institutions

According to its constitution, Nigeria now follows the policymaking processes that exist in many other presidential systems, and the system should sound familiar to students who are knowledgeable about American lawmaking. The legislature passes bills through both houses—the National Assembly and the Senate—and the president signs the bill into law or vetoes it. In the case of a veto, the National Assembly can override the president by a vote of two-thirds in both chambers. Laws are subject to constitutional review by the independent Supreme Court. And, as a federation, Nigeria has states that exercise considerable authority as well, in a way that is semi-autonomous from the central government.

Regime and Political Institutions

Regime	Federal republic, democratically elected since 1999
Administrative Divisions	Thirty-six states + Federal Capital Territory (Abuja)
Executive Branch	President
Selection of Executive	Direct election by national popular vote; runoff among top two candidates if none secures 50 percent in first round; to win in first round, candidate must also secure at least 25 percent of the vote in at least two-thirds of the states.
Legislative Branch	Bicameral Lower chamber: House of Representatives Upper chamber: Senate
Judicial Branch	Supreme Court, appointed by president, confirmed by Senate
Political Party System	Multiparty, but with leading/dominant party Dominant party: People's Democratic Party (PDP)

However, there are two features of Nigerian politics that draw the attention of most outside observers and that affect the making of law and policy. One is the pervasive corruption in the system, which has famously involved bribes to lawmakers and theft of state assets by political elites. Politicians have long received "kickbacks" on contracts and shared in the profits of companies that receive government favors. This is instrumental in lawmaking and is part of the "process." This has happened under both civilian and military regimes. The second issue of note is the role of ethnicity and potential ethnic conflict. On one hand, concerns about ethnicity have led national decision makers to "balance" certain decisions and try to incorporate different regional groups into decision making, for instance through the structure of the leading PDP. On the other hand, ethnicity and kinship also relate to the issue of use of state resources for personal gain. Political elites are expected to bring "rents" home to "their people." A common view has been that an ethnic group having a prominent representative in office means a chance to "eat" (or "chop" in Nigerian parlance) from the national plate.

Political Culture

For many observers, the watchword for Nigeria's political culture has been *corruption*. The country routinely appears among the worst on lists by Transparency International when it ranks the most corrupt countries on earth. Politics has been plagued by corruption for decades, under military and civilian regimes alike. The phenomenon reaches from relatively low-level public servants, such as traffic police who stop cars on trumped-up charges looking for a small bribe, to presidents and other top officials. Former president Sani Abacha, a military leader, was rumored to have several billion dollars stashed away in international bank accounts from his four years in office when he died suddenly in 1998.

The issue of corruption is linked to the distribution of spoils to different groups. Groups of people in Nigeria often view elected representatives from their group as being responsible for providing for an "extended family," and a whole ethnic group can sometimes be seen as just such an extended family. As the saying goes in west Africa, when a group has elected one of its own as a prominent public figure, then "*it is our turn to chop*," where, as noted before, to "chop" means to eat. A similar proverb is that a "goat eats where it is tethered," which means that people will make the best for themselves out of whatever resources they can reach; by extension, those working inside the state will use the state for the benefit of themselves or their extended families. Prominent books in the 1990s held that "Africa works" in its own way for those linked to power and that a common approach is the "politics of the belly" (Bayart 1993). This does not mean that Nigerian (or African) citizens approve of corruption and impunity. Rather, it is to say that the complex patron–client systems involve broader communities than just a handful of corrupt elites.

While corruption has been an enduring problem, this does not capture all of Nigerian political life. Nigeria features a great deal of mobilization, and the citizenry has often taken on the central government in various ways. The country witnessed significant movements for autonomy in the 1990s, not to mention a major civil war in the 1960s over regional autonomy. Many movements have emerged in the Niger Delta, the locus of much of Nigeria's oil that is also one of the poorest and most polluted regions of the country. Resistance there has ranged from non-violent citizens' protests to the emergence of armed separatist groups, as well as criminal gangs seeking profit from kidnappings or banditry.

While there are certain "Nigerian" political characteristics, there are also many different Nigerias, and the country is not a conflict-ridden den of thieves. There are at least three kinds of variation here. The first is across different institutions, some of which have reputations for working quite effectively. The Supreme Court, for instance, is relatively independent and reputable (Suberu 2008). So too is the new electoral commission that was responsible for holding free and fair elections in 2010, in a country where doing so is very challenging. This contrasts with the worse track records of many elected officials and other institutions. The second variation is across different states, some of which have developed reputations for effective governance, often under especially dynamic governors. This has been particularly conspicuous most recently in Lagos State, where the country's largest city (Lagos) is located. Tension and conflict also differ by state, being higher in the central-north of the country, along the fault line between Christians and Muslim populations, and in the Niger Delta. The final variation is change over time. There are some indicators that corruption in Nigeria is receding ever so slightly, while ethnic and religious violence may be worsening once again. Nigeria's politics is never static, but always shifting.

Political Economy

Nigeria has a low average income compared to many of the countries profiled in this book. Yet the country is an economic giant by African standards, due to its large population and a petroleum industry that is the source of much of the nation's revenue. In recent years, it and South Africa have alternated as the largest economy in Africa south of the Sahara. Nigeria is thus seen as a particularly important country in sub-Saharan Africa, but it is also seen as representative of the continent with its poverty and other challenges.

The most important single sector in Nigeria's economy is petroleum extraction. Oil revenues account for over 90 percent of export earnings and over three-fourths of the government's revenues. This affects incomes and taxes: the country brings in large amounts of money and relies on natural resources rather than broad-based taxes to support government spending.

Oil shapes the country's patterns of economic growth and inequality. In terms of economic growth, the country's performance depends in part on the international price for oil, though Nigeria's dysfunctional political economy has repeatedly resulted in the squandering of revenues when the price for Nigeria's main export is high. The squandering of resources links to the fact that oil revenues are distributed in a very unequal and inequitable fashion. Oil-producing regions are some of the poorest in Nigeria, which has led to conflicts and demands for autonomy (as the boxes in this chapter note). Apart from regional differences, perhaps the most striking inequalities are between those individuals who are linked to the state patronage network and those who are not. State elites have siphoned off a large proportion of national revenues for decades, with top elites socking away millions of dollars while a large number of Nigerians live on less than a dollar a day. While patronage and corruption are not the only reasons for this, the state figures prominently in shaping the distribution of income. Nigeria's political economy thus relates to its political culture.

The running theme in Nigerian politics has been corruption and the misuse of state resources. In Nigeria and in Africa more generally, the particular style of political economy has given rise to new terms, such as "neopatrimonialism" (Bratton and Van de Walle 1997). The main implication of these terms is that those in state office view the resources of the state as available for their own personal use rather than for public services. State officials at all levels make use of government funds to favor themselves and their own families, ethnic groups, or other favored constituents. The system views the officeholder as a "patron" and these recipients of resources as "clients," from which come the terms *patron–client relations* and *clientelism*.

Apart from the extraction of petroleum (and now natural gas) and the rents these generate, Nigeria is a large and relatively advanced economy by African standards. The country does have a developed industrial sector, and it is the leading manufacturer in west Africa, though it is not a world leader in industrial technology: many products are simple consumer goods such as processed foods and beverages, textiles, and basic household products. Agriculture, meanwhile, still employs an estimated 70 percent of Nigerians and accounts for over 20 percent of the GDP (*CIA World Factbook*, 1999 and 2017 estimates, respectively). In urban areas, large numbers of Nigerians work in what is known as the informal sector, the largely unregulated part of the economy in which workers try to eke out a modest living without formal contracts or guaranteed wages. Among the many millions working in Nigeria's vast and dynamic informal sector are street vendors, hawkers, small merchants, and providers of a range of services, from messengers and couriers to mechanic shops on the side of the road to ambulant shoe-shine workers. Finally, Nigeria is an African leader in communications, with major industries ranging from mobile phone networks to "Nollywood," the Nigerian film industry that distributes movies across Africa at a rate faster than Hollywood itself.

CASE STUDIES

CASE STUDY

What Is a Weak State, and Can It Be Changed? The Case of Nigeria

CHAPTER 3, PAGE 64

Nigeria is one of the world's paradigmatic cases of a weak and dysfunctional state. It is seen as a direct contrast to more successful and stronger states in East Asia, such as South Korea or Taiwan (Evans 1995; Kohli 2004). But what does it mean to have a "weak state," especially in a country that has long been dominated by the military and has stood accused of repression and corruption? Are these not indicators that the state is overbearing rather than weak? And if a state like Nigeria is weak, can anything be done to change it?

Weak states can be defined as those that fail to establish decision-making autonomy from actors in society. Weak states are not autonomous but instead succumb to private interests. Their actions are permeated and infiltrated by private actors seeking special advantages, often called rents. These "special interests" can take a range of forms. They may be industrialists and investors that want preferential treatment to ensure their monopoly advantages or government contracts (see Bates 1981). Or they can be from the ethnic group of the president that expects government to shower favors on the president's home region (Chabal and Daloz 1999). The use of public monies to serve private interests is a sign of permeable boundaries between the state and society itself. Where there is a lack of a clear distinction between public and private, it becomes possible to use public power for private gain, which results in a "criminalization of the state" (Bayart, Ellis, and Hibou 1999). If a state is "strong," by contrast, it has the ability to stand up to special interests and private actors on a regular basis to make decisions that benefit the whole of society more broadly.

The term *state capacity* is also often used in a similar vein. When a state lacks capacity, this does not mean the state is incapable of doing things such as engaging in theft, abusing human rights, or rigging elections. Rather, a weak state with little capacity often does these things. It takes a state with strong capacity to implement more challenging and productive public services, like vaccination campaigns in remote villages, nationwide educational investments, or establishment of a rule of law. Thus, a strong state is defined by its ability to make autonomous decisions on behalf of society at large, not by its ability to resort to violence and crack down on dissent.

Some of the most important reforms for Nigeria's development would be improvements in governance and strengthening of the state. But can this be done? There are several impediments. Ending corruption and impunity, and making public officials more accountable to the citizenry, is a daunting task. The oil resource curse (see the Case Study box on chapter 5, "Why Are Natural Resources Sometimes a Curse?") also compounds the problem. As suggested by a range of

scholars, the easy money that comes with natural resources can weaken a state in certain contexts (see Karl 1997; Dunning 2008).

The answer to whether Nigeria can develop a strong state will draw different responses from comparativists with different theories of the state. Those more inclined to think that the state can be rationally engineered to work correctly will emphasize the political institutions that can be put in place and the incentives these will provide for actors to respond accordingly. Others who believe in the importance of individual actors will note that good performance of an institution like the state depends on the people who comprise it; finding the right set of leaders and officials should turn an institution around in a relatively short period of time. By contrast, those with a more structural, cultural, or historical bent will emphasize that institutions are embedded in a set of conditions that

make rapid change difficult: Nigeria is a highly unequal society with a long history of corruption at this point, and these will slow any change, preventing the development of a strong state "overnight."

There is surely some truth in all of these elements when it comes to building a strong state: history and culture matter for how most individuals perceive the state and its possibilities, and thus condition outcomes strongly, but better designs and better leaders will contribute to more effective governance than poorly designed systems and weak leaders. And most analysts would not adopt extreme views that deny the importance of several factors: rationalists understand that culture matters, and culturalists understand that people respond to incentives, for example. Yet the analysis of which factors are most important will condition whether one thinks transforming the state is feasible in a given span of time, and what steps can be recommended to get there.

Nigeria has the largest population and either the largest or second-largest economy in sub-Saharan Africa, but it is not a success story. Instead, Nigeria—a major oil producer—is often held up as an exemplary case of the "resource curse." You would expect that discovering oil would be very good for an economy, and

in some cases it can be, especially if the economy is already robust and diversified when oil is discovered. But often oil and similar high-value commodities produce unanticipated problems. The first is called the "Dutch Disease." Exporting oil brings in lots of foreign currency. The ready supply of, say, dollars means

dollars are not seen as valuable relative to the national currency; the domestic currency rises in value, and this hurts other exports because these goods are expensive for foreigners in dollar terms. Along the same lines, the potential profitability of oil makes it a magnet for big capital investment, thus crowding

Why Are Natural Resources Sometimes a Curse? The Nigerian Case

CHAPTER 5, PAGE 102

out investment in other industries. Oil-producing countries thus often see other areas of their economies decline.

Equally important, the global price for oil is cyclical. Economies like Nigeria tend to see boom and bust cycles that prevent them from achieving development. High prices at one point in time can leave a country vulnerable to downturns in the price of its main export commodity. Nigeria boomed during the 1970s when oil prices were high, but it declined during the period of low prices in the 1980s (Kohli 2004: 351). More recently, growth has increased again as oil prices have risen again, but Nigeria remains quite dependent on a single product.

Oil dependence also affects politics, and often for the worse (Karl 1997; Herbst 2000: 130–133). The easy access to oil money has a rather subtle effect: it stunts the growth of important relationships between the state and the society

at large. Politicians can have incentives to make bad policy in oil-rich countries. "Easy money" from oil can make states such as Nigeria more likely to simply offer handouts to their "clients" and to the populace during boom times. States with substantial cash flows from oil often do not develop a capacity to tax the population. This may sound like a low-tax paradise, but without taxation, the populace is less likely to see the government as a set of institutions to be held accountable for its governing performance. Rather, citizens become accustomed to government simply distributing benefits. This can result in a destructive relationship between state and society, especially in oil-producing countries. Such a counter-productive relationship is not universal, but may be most likely in places such as Nigeria with high prior levels of inequality (cf. Dunning 2008).

In addition to domestic challenges, the politics of oil and natural resources

also involves international actors such as oil companies. This is because developing countries themselves often lack technical capacity in areas that require advanced technology, and they may also lack the capital needed for investment, at least at early stages. Such countries thus commonly rely on licenses to foreign companies, or the use of foreign advisors, or joint ventures between major multinational companies and relatively weak states (Kohli 2004). This leaves another form of dependence. The impacts of interactions with foreign actors are hotly debated, but in Nigeria, low state capacity, partially dating back to weak state development under British colonialism, seems not to mix well with oil. In short, despite the enormous wealth that Nigerian oil has created for some, it has left the country with high levels of poverty and inequality and with institutional problems that will make overcoming these challenges difficult.

Federalism and the States in Nigeria: Holding Together or Tearing Apart?

CHAPTER 8, PAGE 190

Nigeria is a crucial case in examining whether constitutional engineering and design, particularly with regard to federalism, can contribute to stability and democracy. Federalism has been essential to efforts to address one of Nigeria's leading political challenges: ethnic and regional divisions. As noted earlier, in

the "Historical Development" section, the subject of federalism and autonomy came to the fore most dramatically with the Nigerian civil war from 1967 to 1970.

A principal tactic of the central government to hold the country together has been to increase the number of states, which have gone from an original

three regions at independence to thirty-six today. This happened in a series of steps. Independent Nigeria began with three regions—Northern, Western, and Eastern—each of which was associated with a particular dominant ethnic group: the Hausa-Fulani, Yoruba, and Igbo, respectively. The Mid-Western Region

CASE STUDY (continued)

Federalism and the States in Nigeria: Holding Together or Tearing Apart?

CHAPTER 8, PAGE 190

was added in 1963. In the lead-up to the Nigerian Civil War (see also the Case Study box on the civil war that follows: "The Nigerian Civil War or Biafran War"), the central government moved to reorganize the four regions into twelve states. The Civil War then pitted the Eastern region against the rest of Nigeria; and after the rebels surrendered, the military government responded by creating seven more states in 1976, and two additional states in 1987. In 1991, President Babangida announced that the number of states would increase to thirty, and six more states were added in 1996 (Suberu 2001: xxiv–xxvi). The numbers thus went from three to four regions, then to twelve states and on to nineteen to twenty-one to thirty and finally to thirty-six states.

Why would subdividing the states and increasing their number matter for stability? The approach has been largely about ethnic arithmetic (see Suberu 2001). In Nigeria, the central government has used the creation of new states in an attempt to multiply the number of administrative divisions in Nigeria. The theory was that this would eliminate the big divisions between the largest ethnic groups as an important factor in Nigerian politics and would substitute for this new administrative boundaries that citizens would focus on. At the same time, those living in the newly created states often favored the proposals for two reasons. First, the smaller ethnic groups in Nigeria sought their own states to avoid domination by the Hausa-Fulani, Yoruba, and Igbo. Second, the creation of states in a particular area meant they

would share in the distribution of the country's revenues. This gave incentives for many groups to favor new states, though at different times Nigeria's dominant ethnicities have opposed plans they believed would weaken them in the delicate balance of power.

Most new states were created by the military governments rather than through public consultation, and the justifications have ultimately been about national stability (see Suberu 2001: 80). The creation of states in the 1960s was based on the idea of balance: no region should be able to dominate the federation. As the Civil War approached and the Igbo-dominated Eastern Region threatened to secede, the military in power gained some support from non-Igbos in that region by offering to grant them new states (Suberu 2001: 87–89). Similarly, a panel in the 1970s argued that Nigeria would not remain stable without further subdivision; this resulted in the nineteen states as of 1976 (Suberu 2001: 90–91). The logic played out in slightly different ways in subsequent divisions, but always with an eye toward governability. Beyond creating states, the federal government has taken a number of other steps that supports them, most notably guaranteeing substantial revenues to the state and local governments. At the same time, while creating these states, the central government has also attempted to centralize many powers.

Giving different ethnic and regional groups their own authority and resources could either improve stability and increase the likelihood of democracy or harm those prospects. It could help by allowing each group some say in its own

affairs and some role in government, preventing winner-takes-all politics in national elections. Or it could draw such stark dividing lines between groups that it might give rise to secessionism or civil war. The Nigerian approach has been to give more small groups additional say, and to blur (or redraw) the lines between the large groups.

Has it succeeded? The evidence can be interpreted in different ways. On one hand, Nigeria has remained intact after the Civil War of the late 1960s, which is a non-trivial achievement in a society that is so fractured along ethnic, religious, and regional fault lines. On the other hand, the creation of new states has not ended ethnic or sectarian tensions. Politics in Nigeria is still centered around the division between the north, the southwest, and the southeast that troubled the country at independence. The 2015 presidential election, for instance, had an electorate divided geographically, with the victor Muhammadu Buhari winning the north and the southwest, while the defeated incumbent Goodluck Jonathan won in his native southeastern region. The creation of states has created new divisions in Nigerian politics but has not overcome the old divisions (Suberu 2001: 110). Nigeria still witnesses a spiral of intergroup conflict. Demands for more states or greater federalism are unlikely to mitigate conflict at this point, and may only serve to appease different groups clamoring for the resources that come with getting a state. Federalism might have changed the nature of conflict, but it has not necessarily stopped it.

The Presidency in Nigeria: Powers and Limitations

Over time, Nigeria's presidencies have seen their powers increase and decrease in different ways, and a brief comparison can provide insight into what has and has not changed in the country between military and civilian rule. Nigeria has elected civilian presidents since 1999, when a period of military rule came to an end. Prior to this, Nigeria had a parliamentary system in place from 1960 to 1966, followed by military rule for all but four years from 1966 to 1999, during which the country lived under several brutal and corrupt dictators, such as General Sani Abacha (1993 to 1998).

The civilian presidents since 1999 have included one-time military leaders Olusegun Obasanjo (1999–2007) and current president Muhammadu Buhari, as well as Goodluck Jonathan, who was president from 2010 until his defeat in 2015. They have earned better reputations for civil liberties than the military regime, and the presidents themselves have not stood directly accused of the titanic forms of corruption seen previously. While they have not eradicated abuses and corruption, they are widely viewed as an improvement on military rule.

Despite some improvements, Nigeria's core governance problems persist under the new presidencies, and this shows how these challenges remain embedded in the political culture and society. As noted in several instances earlier in this profile, Nigeria is one of the most corrupt nations on earth despite some earnest presidential efforts to tame this problem; the presidencies have not proved capable of dramatic advances, but rather modest and incremental steps that will leave corruption endemic for some time to come.

Corruption pervades much of the state bureaucracy over which the executive presides. For many years, positions in the bureaucracy have been seen as rewards for kin and supporters, for the salaries and more importantly for the corruption opportunities these positions provide. This form of patronage and clientelism remains prominent in Nigerian politics, part of the calculus of retaining power. Patronage and corruption cut both ways, giving the executive the opportunity to buy support but also a sense that it cannot control the actions of bureaucrats and is as much a prisoner of the system as a beneficiary of it.

The Nigerian presidency has formal powers attached to it, such as the power to assent to legislation or send it back to the legislature, where a two-thirds majority is required to pass a law without presidential assent. Yet there are also major limitations to presidential action, and some of these reflect the need to address Nigeria's other big challenge besides corruption: ethnic and regional tension. To be elected, the president is required to win a majority of the vote nationally, but the president also must win at least 25 percent of the vote in two-thirds of the states. Formal and informal requirements hold that political parties should represent the nation's federal character, especially the division between the mostly Christian south and mostly Muslim north.

The president is also not completely free to establish his own cabinet, though no written rules put it this way. The president is "expected" to choose a vice-president and ministers from the opposite region of the country to his place of origin. Also on this question of federalism, constitution and legal provisions require the federal government to send a large portion of its revenues to the states and local authorities (Suberu 2001). This latter point has important effects on governance: because states and local authorities control so much of the national revenue, the quality of governance can vary a great deal from place to place across the country. Some states will govern better and others worse, and the president has less leverage over this than might be the case in other countries.

All presidents from 1999 to 2015 were from People's Democratic Party (PDP), though the party was defeated by Buhari and his All Progressives Congress (APC) in 2015. Each president (of the PDP or APC) has had a legislative majority, which gives a degree of partisan power as well. Yet this too cuts both ways; the entrenchment of co-partisans makes it hard to shake up governance: presidents must reckon with governors and legislators who have strong bases in their respective states. And, to close the circle, this means that patronage and clientelism persist.

With its persistent tendency for patronage and the need to balance the precarious relationship between north and south, Nigeria shows that social context greatly affects the environment in which presidents operate, regardless of constitutional powers. Presidents since the military leader Sani Abacha may be better than their military predecessors, but governance has not been fully cleaned up, nor will it be for some time regardless of good or bad presidential intentions.

CASE STUDY

The Nigerian Civil War or Biafran War: Nationalism and Ethno-National Conflict in a Post-Colonial Society

CHAPTER 13, PAGE 320

Nigeria is an excellent example of a country where the state-linked national identity needs to compete with other, perhaps more deeply established, identities and interests that precede the rise of the national state (Falola and Heaton 2008). Of course, every case of state-sponsored national identity experiences this conflict to some extent—national identity can conflict with other identities like religion, ethnicity, clan, tribe, or locality—but the problem has often been acute in post-colonial situations where the state is left to create a nation out of groups that do not necessarily identify with each other.

Nigeria was a colony of Great Britain. It had been the site of many different social groups before colonialism, most notably the Hausa-speaking Islamic population of the northern region, the Yoruba of the west (many of whom practice traditional animistic religion), and the Igbo of the east (who are predominantly Christian). British colonialism drew all of these groups together and artificially constructed a political boundary around them. This issued in considerable tension that continues today.

The importance of British colonialism does not mean Nigerians had no agency in the creation of the Nigerian nation-state and Nigerian nationalism. Indeed, many important Nigerian intellectuals and political actors from at least the late nineteenth century sought to escape from British colonialism and to create an independent state (or independent states). But it is clear that the idea of "Nigeria" as a nation was not the single basis for national loyalty among these nationalists (Falola and Heaton 2008: 136–157). Some were Pan-African nationalists and hoped to craft an identity for a nation much larger than present-day Nigeria. Others had their strongest affiliation with their more local groups, expressing interest in, say, the Yoruba nation.

British colonial West Africa saw a relatively peaceful transition to post-colonial regimes. But in Nigeria, once the colonial authority was gone, jealousies and conflicts became more problematic. Ethnic, religious, and regional tensions—which had been present all along—spilled over into open violence and conflict (as noted previously). Two coups d'état in 1966 were related to these tensions, and the second of these issued in anti-Igbo violence. In 1967, the mostly Igbo eastern region declared itself the independent state of Biafra. The central government did not accept the legitimacy of this action, and a bloody civil war lasted until 1970. The central government was victorious, and the Igbo-dominated east remains to this day part of Nigeria. The war cost many thousands of lives directly, and produced many more deaths as a result of the economic dislocation and famine it generated, with estimates ranging from one to three million (Falola and Heaton 2008: 158). In terms of human life and suffering, it was catastrophic.

Some theories of ethno-national violence would stress the strong ethnic boundaries and, perhaps, religious markers of identity difference here. Others would stress the tit-for-tat nature of the conflict: Igbo people rebelled, this theory would suggest, because oppression from the north led them to draw the rational conclusion that they would be safer as an independent state. Instrumental theories would stress that Nigerian oil reserves are heavily concentrated in the country's southeast, noting that the stakes for both groups extended beyond ethnic conflict and rivalry and concerned access to and control over Nigeria's most important natural resource and the basis for its economy and for the state's revenues.

Debates remain about how to classify or characterize events like this conflict. Proponents of the Biafran independence effort would likely classify these events as a political or even anti-colonial revolution, arguing that the central government was an oppressive external imposition from which they were attempting to liberate themselves. Others consider this conflict to be a civil war, since it took place within an existing nation-state, regardless of whether that state itself was constructed from the outside.

Religious Difference and Conflict in Nigeria: Disentangling Ethnicity and Religion?

CHAPTER 15, PAGE 356

As noted in the previous case study, Nigeria's boundaries and structure were shaped by European colonialism. The British brought together groups and regions that likely would not have been politically unified, at least not in the short run, if not for European involvement. This has often produced rivalries and tensions, the most notorious of which was the calamitous Biafran War described previously. The Nigerian state retained control over all of these groups, however, and does to this day, though the society has seen considerable ethno-religious conflict. One of the major questions of comparative politics highlighted by this case is how, if it all, we might disentangle ethnicity and religion in terms of their effects on politics. In other words, are these conflicts about religion, or are they about ethnicity, or both?

Nigeria has attempted to address its diversity through federalism. In terms of religion, while the federal government maintains formal separation of church and state, religion finds its way into government at the state level (Fox 2008: 272–273). Sharia law is practiced in northern majority-Muslim states, though some of its more radical provisions have not been exercised. At the same time, people in non-majority-Muslim states are not subjected to these laws. In today's Nigeria, as noted earlier, it is estimated that about half of the population is Muslim and two-fifths Christian, with most of the balance professing a traditional animistic faith. Religious conflict remains common,

and the government has struggled in its efforts to restrain it. Paradoxically, perhaps, intergroup violence has increased under nonmilitary governments that have held power since 1999. To some, this suggests that federalism is not an effective solution, while others argue that this is a simplistic conclusion to draw on the basis of limited evidence (see Suberu 2001).

Ethno-religious violence in Nigeria is difficult to sort out, in part because it probably should not all be classified in similar terms. Conflicts in the area where Hausa-Fulani (predominantly Islamic) populations are contiguous with Igbo (predominantly Christian) involve both material interests and, sometimes, ethnic and religious dimensions. Some of the violence by minority ethnic groups in the Niger Delta, however, such as attacking oil pipelines, has little to no religious component.

Some of the most significant events in Nigeria's recent timeline have to do with sectarian or religious strife. As noted in the "Historical Development" section, conflict has emerged in many of the states and cities along the dividing line between the majority-Muslim north and the majority-Christian south. The city of Jos, for one, has witnessed numerous riots and clashes. The deadliest acts have been perpetrated by Boko Haram, a group of Islamist fundamentalists whose name means "Western education is sinful." They have claimed responsibility for numerous bombings and coordinated gun and grenade attacks in several states

in central and northern Nigeria, most notably Plateau State and Bauchi State. Boko Haram bombed the United Nations compound in the capital, Abuja, in 2011. This was followed by news reports that it seeks to collaborate and integrate more with al Qaeda and other related Islamic fundamentalist groups such as al-Shabaab in Somalia and, more recently, with ISIS. Boko Haram's violence has increased in recent years and, as noted previously, includes not just mass killings but also mass kidnappings. Amnesty International notes that both Boko Haram and the state have committed human rights abuses in the ensuing conflict (Amnesty International, 2017/2018 Nigeria Report, https://www.amnesty.org/en/countries/africa/nigeria/report-nigeria/). In light of the tensions in Nigeria, is important to note that the relationship between instrumental, ethno-national, and religious militancy is potentially dynamic. Religious frames may come to be more or less important depending on the context.

Religion is a crucial element in the balancing act among Nigerian political elites, as with the PDP. Former president Goodluck Jonathan (a southern Christian) faced some opposition in the north, and current president Muhammadu Buhari (a northern Muslim) may similarly face some opposition in the south. Yet one of the important questions is how these efforts at the top to manage the institutions relate to the identities, sentiments, and behaviors of people in society.

Research Prompts

1. British colonialism in Nigeria ended over fifty years ago. To what extent does the legacy of colonialism still affect the politics and economy of Nigeria today? How can we determine what contemporary outcomes are the result of historically distant factors like colonialism as opposed to more recent factors such as the events of the late 1990s?

2. Nigeria is used by scholars of development as a quintessential example of economic failure and underperformance. Viewing the history of Nigeria's political economy, does Nigeria's weak economic performance over the decades give more credence to proponents of market-led development or state-led development? What would be the recommendations from both market-led and state-led development advocates for Nigeria?

3. Compare and contrast Nigeria's development experience with one of the other developing countries mentioned in chapter 5: Brazil, China, or India. What do you learn from the comparison, and are there any comparative lessons that you can draw for why development does or does not happen?

4. Consider several of Nigeria's troubles—such as economic stagnation, corruption, or conflict—and select one issue of greatest interest to you. Examine to what extent Nigeria's challenge applies in another African country, and address how generalizable Nigeria's experience may be to the continent of Africa as a whole.

In what ways is Nigeria distinctive (or "most different") from one or more other African countries, and in what ways is it comparable (or "most similar")? If you examine another sub-Saharan African country and determine that it faces similar problems or does not face similar problems, which variables does your finding point to as helping to shape Nigeria's outcomes?

5. One key element of Nigeria's political life seems to be corruption. Can we say this corruption is caused by culture and society? Or by economic realities? Or political institutions? Which of these do you find to be the leading the cause, and how can you know?

6. Conflict in Nigeria has at least three components: ethnic, religious (or sectarian), and regional. Which of these divisions in Nigerian society is the primary cause of the conflict? Can you trace the historical evolution of conflicts in Nigeria to determine which of these is the leading causal factor?

7. Nigeria has implemented numerous institutional reforms to limit violence and conflict. These include the creation of more states in the federation and provisions requiring presidents to win a substantial proportion of the vote across many states. Is it possible to determine what the effects of these reforms have been on conflict and ethnic tension? How might you approach this question and research it to be able to offer an answer? How might comparative study help?

Russia (Russian Federation)

Key Features of Contemporary Russia

Population:	142,257,519 (estimate, July 2017)
Area:	17,098,242 sq km
Head of State:	Vladimir Putin (president, 2012–present)
Head of Government:	Dmitry Medvedev (premier, May 2012–present)
Capital:	Moscow
Year of Independence:	The Russian Empire dates back to 1721, and independent states comprising much of Russia predate that founding. The current state became independent of the Soviet Union in 1991.
Year of Current Constitution:	1993
Languages:	Russian is spoken by most citizens; there are more than one hundred other languages in the Russian Federation: Tatar and Ukrainian are among the most important.
GDP per Capita:	$26,500 (*CIA World Factbook* estimate, 2016)
Human Development Index Ranking (2016):	49th (very high human development)

Sources: *CIA World Factbook*; World Bank World Development Indicators; United Nations *Human Development Report 2016*.

Introduction

The Russian Federation is, in geographic terms, the largest country in the world. Its land is highly varied, stretching from temperate areas to the Arctic, and from Western Europe to the Sea of Japan. Its people and their culture are varied as well. Both its people and its expanse of land have captured the imagination of writers for generations, and many have felt that there is something ineffable about Russia. However, what is of still greater interest about Russia to comparative political analysts is the country's tumultuous political and economic history. Russia, as we will see, has over the last century gone from being a reactionary Czarist regime, to creating the Soviet Union—during which it aimed to completely remake the society and to spread socialist revolution around the globe; to watching the Soviet Union collapse; to being replaced by a relatively weak government; and finally, under Vladimir Putin, to the restoration of centralized authority. Contemporary Russia is Exhibit A in political scientists' efforts to describe so-called hybrid or "competitive

- Russian 77.7%
- Tatar 3.7%
- Ukrainian 1.4%
- Bashkir 1.1%
- Chuvash 1%
- Chechen 1%
- Other 10.2%
- Unspecified 3.9%

Ethnic Groups in Russia
Source: CIA World Factbook.

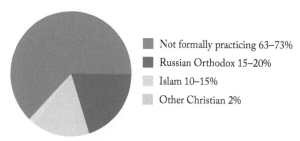

- Not formally practicing 63–73%
- Russian Orthodox 15–20%
- Islam 10–15%
- Other Christian 2%

Religious Affiliation in Russia, 2006 Estimates of *Practicing* Religious Populations
Note that some of those counted as "Russian Orthodox" may be only nominally so.
Source: CIA World Factbook.

authoritarian" (Levitsky and Way 2010) regimes discussed in chapter 7 of this volume.

Russia's 1917 revolutions—both the one that removed the tsar from power and the subsequent one, which gave the Bolsheviks control of the state—inspired waves of imitators. The Soviet Union formed one of the two poles in the Cold War that structured global affairs for half a century: it would be difficult to exaggerate the extent of this long conflict's impact, especially on the populations of those countries where proxy wars between the poles were fought. At the same time, the Soviet Union's brutality, particularly under Joseph Stalin, pushed many global political actors away from socialism and toward liberalism and social democracy. Russia is also of interest to students of political identities. Debates abound concerning the nature of Russian national identity and the timing and causes of its emergence and spread. These questions become particularly complicated in the Soviet years. As a Marxist regime, the Soviet Union was officially internationalist, but a number of observers see it as having been a vehicle for Russian national aims, and Stalin himself was a theorist of nationalism (Stalin 1994). Russian nationalism has often been considered to fall into the ethnic type (Greenfeld 1992), and Russian history gives numerous examples of repression of ethnic minorities.

Russia's post-communist transition is of particular interest to comparative analysts, in part because of the pattern of authoritarian persistence that it reveals. For some reason, Russia has never developed a sustainable, fully functioning democracy. There is much grist here for the mill of democratic theory.

Historical Development

Many accounts of modern Russia begin with Peter the Great, who in the late seventeenth century attempted to forcibly modernize the country. Peter was not the first notable ruler of Russia, but he is well known for the degree to which he centrally imposed reforms on his society (Bushkovitch 2012: 79). Some of these reforms changed the social structure in important ways. For example, he imposed a "Table of Ranks" that re-engineered the Russian social hierarchy, making noble status dependent on state service and creating the possibility to *achieve* nobility through partially meritocratic competition (Ascher 2009: 63; Greenfeld 1992). He personally studied Western techniques for shipbuilding and other technologies that he expected would increase Russia's power and prestige, and he brought foreign experts to Russia in large numbers (Ascher 2009: 58–65). Some of his reforms were more symbolic as well and invited a cultural turn to the West (Hughes 2008: 68–77; Bushkovitch 2012: 82–83, 94–98). For example, he forbade nobles to wear their customary beards and demanded changes in dress. Not all of these moves were popular, but there was little doubt that Russia under Peter was stronger than it had been in previous years. Russia played a central role in the Great Northern War that dramatically reduced Swedish power, much to Russia's benefit (Ascher 2009: 61–62).

Subsequent years saw some decline (Ascher 2009: 66–67), but Russia encountered another strong leader in Catherine the Great, who seized the throne in a coup d'état in 1762. Catherine was known as a patron of the European Enlightenment (on Russian culture under Catherine, see Hughes 2008: 81–88). In this, as in other things, there was an affinity between her rule and that of Peter, as again she turned to Western models as she aimed to increase Russia's power and status. She increased the administrative reach and centralization of the state, and continued to assert Russia's role as a geopolitical power. Moreover, she spread Western ideas throughout Russia and even patronized them in Western Europe (supporting French intellectuals, for example, even when they were not fully supported in their home country).

The first half of the nineteenth century saw the rule of Alexander I and Nicolas I. Alexander is best remembered for leading Russia as it defeated Napoleon in his famous invasion (in which the French occupied Moscow but were eventually defeated by Russian resistance and the harsh Russian winter). Both Nicolas I and Alexander I, though, presided over a period in which Russia failed to continue its path of modernization (Ascher 2009: 80–81). Much of this changed beginning in the 1860s under Alexander II, who implemented a number of reforms. The most important was the emancipation of the serfs (Bushkovitch 2012: 188–193) and state peasants, which commenced between 1861 and 1866 (the precise dating is dependent on whether one was a serf or state peasant). Material conditions of peasants, though, in many cases did not improve over the several decades that they paid for the land they received.

The formation of the Russian state and the way in which state service and the educational system linked to the stratification system had important implications for Russia's future, exacerbated by late-nineteenth-century reform. One, perhaps unintended, consequence of the long series of reforms that ran from Peter the Great's years onward was that educational attainment was very closely linked to status attainment: to be an intellectual was very desirable. This made educational attainment a major draw for talent; and sociologically, a society with an agrarian economy and relatively few prospects outside of state service (including the military) and an important, if numerically small, segment of highly educated persons is potentially explosive (Greenfeld 1992). Russian nationalism spread as Russian literature and cultural production grew. Moreover, that nationalism acquired a strongly populist component, epitomized in the Narodnik, or "To the People," Movement in the early 1870s (Service 2009: 17–18). Among other things, Russian intellectuals went to live with poor peasants in hopes of helping to lead a movement, which met with little success. However, discontent and agitation would continue. Most notably, Tsar Alexander II was assassinated

Historical Development

Timeline

1682–1725	Reign of Peter the Great, seen as Western-oriented modernizer of Russia
1762–1796	Reign of Catherine the Great, another Westernizer, patron of philosophers and other intellectuals, but nevertheless autocratic and a critic of the French Revolution
1812	Invasion of Russia by Napoleon of France; French reach Moscow, but then retreat and Napoleon is defeated
1815	Congress of Vienna
1853–1856	Crimean War pits Russia against France, Great Britain, and the Ottoman Empire
1861–1866	Beginning of the process of emancipation of the serfs and state peasants
1881	Assassination of Tsar Alexander II
1905	1905 Revolution (brings about constitutional monarchy)
1917	Russian Revolution(s) that topple the tsar and bring the Communists to power
1918–1921	Russian Civil War
1921	Vladimir Lenin's New Economic Policy (NEP)
1924	Death of Lenin, which leads to Joseph Stalin's rise to prominence
1928–1933	First Five Year Plan and introduction of a command economy
1929	Consolidation of Stalin's authority; Leon Trotsky is forced into exile
1933–1937	Second Five Year Plan
1935–1938	Period Notable for Stalinist Purges, including 1937–1938 mass executions (the "Great Terror")
1938–1941	Third Five Year Plan (ends prematurely due to the Second World War)
1939	Soviets sign Non-Aggression Pact with Nazi Germany, including secret agreement to divide up Europe; World War II begins in Europe
1940	Trotsky is murdered in Mexico
1941	Germany invades Soviet Union
1941–1945	Soviet involvement in World War II, in which more than 20 million Soviets die; Hitler invades the Soviet Union, but ultimately retreats in a major turning point in the war in Europe
1945	Soviets occupy Berlin with the fall of Hitler
1946–1989	Cold War, an ideological, military, and economic rivalry between the Communist world led by the Soviet Union and the capitalist, democratic world led by the United States
1949	Soviets test atomic bomb
1953	Death of Stalin
1956	U.S.S.R. cracks down on dissent in Hungary with invasion
1957	U.S.S.R. launches Sputnik satellite
1961	Berlin Wall erected; Soviet Union becomes first country to send man into space
1968	U.S.S.R. crushes "Prague Spring" movement in Czechoslovakia
1972	SALT I treaty as policy of détente between the U.S.S.R. and the United States commences
1989	Fall of Berlin Wall and collapse of Soviet-led communism in Eastern and Central Europe (Poland, Czechoslovakia, East Germany, Hungary, Bulgaria, Romania); Soviet Union begins to unravel
1991	Communist hardliner coup to replace Mikhail Gorbachev results in street mobilizations for further reform; U.S.S.R. collapses and divides into fifteen countries; Boris Yeltsin becomes president of independent Russia
2000	Vladimir Putin is elected president
2008	Dmitry Medvedev is elected president, with Vladimir Putin as prime minister
2012	Vladimir Putin is re-elected president amid allegations of electoral irregularities and widespread public protests; Putin nominates Dmitry Medvedev as prime minister
2014	Russia annexes the Crimean peninsula, a Russian-majority region in neighboring Ukraine, and Russian-backed separatists in eastern Ukraine seek to join with Russia
2018	Vladimir Putin is re-elected once more, in a contest that few political scientists would regard as fair and democratic

in 1881. His successor, Alexander III, endeavored to undo many of the reforms of the previous decades (Ascher 2009: 125–130).

Demands for change came to a head in the first years of the twentieth century. Note that Russia was relatively exceptional in this period (in the European context) for still being a non-constitutional monarchy. Russia's highly educated, literate, and partially Westernized nobility, along with non-noble intellectuals, were painfully aware of this sign of "backwardness." The country had begun state-led industrialization (Service 2009: 4–5); and while industrial workers were only a tiny fraction of the overall population, they were important agitators concentrated in the largest cities in what would be called the Revolution of 1905 (Carr [1979] 2004: 2; Fitzpatrick 1994: 33–34). Another critical factor was Russia's poor showing against Japan in the Russo-Japanese War, which seemed to signal state weakness and the need for reform. The revolution itself consisted largely of a series of strikes and other actions (Fitzpatrick 1994: 32–33). It also, lamentably, unleashed a series of pogroms. The goals of the "revolutionaries" varied considerably. Some were simply disaffected peasants and urban workers. Others were committed ideologues, most notably the Petersburg Soviet, which was a harbinger of things to come. The revolution ended with Russia becoming a constitutional monarchy. For many Marxist commentators, this marked it as a "bourgeois revolution," potentially setting the stage for the next revolutionary sequence, which they hoped would issue in communism.

They would not have to wait long, as "the" Russian Revolution would emerge in 1917 (Fitzpatrick 1994; Carr [1979] 2004). The years after the 1905 revolution saw agrarian reform that would increase private landholding as well as other changes. However, the decisive event that helped to trigger the Revolution of 1917 was the First World War. Russia suffered heavy losses, and its troops faced difficult conditions. The war lost public support, and the relative military weakness of the state that had lost the Crimean War and the Russo-Japanese War was again exposed. The year 1917 was the key year, with two critical revolutionary stages. In March, street protests led to the fall of the tsar and his government. A provisional government was formed by the legislature (the Duma), but it was soon rivaled by "Soviets," (councils) of workers, peasants, and general military personnel in other parts of the country. In short, it was not entirely clear who was in charge of Russia. Before long, the Bolsheviks, a radical socialist group, took over the Soviets, and the Provisional Government fell, leaving the Soviets in charge. This would be followed by withdrawal from World War I early the next year and ongoing civil war between Bolsheviks (who renamed themselves the Communists) and

Mensheviks. Contrary to Lenin's expectations, the rise of the Soviet Union did not trigger a wave of successful proletarian revolutions throughout Europe (Ascher 2009: 167–168). The new government soon began to increase the already notable role of the state in the Russian economy, and it began agrarian reforms, pitting poorer peasants against those who were better off. Some of this was relaxed with Lenin's more pragmatic "New Economic Policy," beginning in 1921 (Service 2009: 123–149; Bushkovitch 2012: 318–319). Lenin died in 1924, setting off a struggle within the party for supremacy. The main contenders were Joseph Stalin and Leon Trotsky. By 1929, Stalin had consolidated his authority, and Trotsky was forced into exile (Ascher 2009): he would be murdered by Stalin's agents, in Mexico, in 1940. Particularly beginning in the 1930s, Stalin became famously paranoid, and the Stalinist regime purged numerous alleged opponents, often using "show trials" and forced confessions in an effort to maintain the appearance of legitimacy. This behavior would continue after the war. Millions died or were imprisoned under Stalin.

The Stalinist regime set out to extend socialist revolution. The first Five Year Plan (1928–1933) aimed to both force rapid industrialization and to collectivize agriculture (Fitzpatrick 1994: 129–141). It was somewhat successful with regard to the former goal, but the latter goal was largely a failure in economic and human terms, costing millions of lives (Service 2009: 181). The Second (1933–1937) and Third (1938–1941) Five Year Plans continued Stalin's efforts to achieve state-led full industrialization. The last of these efforts was disrupted by the invasion of Nazi Germany. For the first two years of that war, the Soviet Union remained uninvolved because of a non-aggression pact that Hitler and Stalin had signed in 1939 (Kitchen 2006: 297–298, 301–304). But in 1941, Hitler changed course and invaded the Soviet Union (Bushkovitch 2012: 378–382). The fighting on the eastern front (Germany fought the Soviet Union in the east and the other allies in the west) was brutal and the loss of life enormous. While the allies emerged victorious, the process was very costly for the Soviet Union. At the same time, it ended up greatly expanding the territory controlled by the Soviet Regime, notably Eastern Europe and much of Central Europe, which in the years after the war became Soviet satellite states.

The settlement at the end of World War II set the stage for the Cold War. The Soviet Union and the United

States—thought of as representatives of two, inconsistent, visions for how to organize society—jostled for global influence, and proxy wars were fought in a number of developing countries, causing considerable suffering and loss of life. For both sides, fears of the prospect of nuclear war were part of daily life. Stalin died in 1953, and was followed by long terms for two consecutive leaders, Khrushchev and Brezhnev. Khrushchev aimed to "de-Stalinize" the country, repudiating the purges and other forms of oppression that had claimed so many, and making a number of reforms. Five year plans continued, however, and neither of these leaders seriously considered a non-socialist model in economic policy. The fact that they criticized Stalin's atrocities should not lead us to conclude, however, that they were not willing to repress civilians themselves, as a number of citizens of Russia and of Soviet satellite states were to learn (Davies 1996: 1102–1104; Service 2009: 435–500).

After Brezhnev's death in 1982, there was a series of short-lived, inconsequential leaders until Mikhail Gorbachev was selected in 1985. Gorbachev embarked on a series of reforms (Davies 1996: 1121; Bushkovitch 2012: 448–451). In the economic sphere, this involved trying to expand the role of markets, so as to preserve socialism through enhancing productivity and efficiency. It was clear to all in the Soviet world that change was afoot; and once it became clear that Gorbachev would not repress protest in Central and Eastern Europe with the force that previous Soviet leaders had used, those countries began to seek independence. Poland was the initial leader, and its Solidarity Movement struggled for years in its efforts to bring about a transition, with a successful and peaceful revolution taking place in 1989, followed shortly thereafter by a wave of similar ones throughout the region (Ash 2002). Communist elites in the Soviet Union were alarmed, not surprisingly. Eventually some of them launched a coup d'état against Gorbachev in an effort to restore centralized control: the plan backfired, and when the dust settled, Boris Yeltsin was in charge of the Russian Federation (the Soviet Union was gone).

Gorbachev had hoped to save the dream of communism: Yeltsin moved to end it. He presented himself as a democrat, though his governing style was somewhat autocratic. He was able to inaugurate a new, more democratic constitution for the Russian Federation after taking advantage of a conflict with the Supreme Soviet, which had been elected before the collapse of the Soviet Union (Service 2009: 522–528). From the beginning, Yeltsin embraced radical free-market reform (McFaul 2008: 359–361), quickly privatizing key industries and helping to create what commentators now sometimes refer to as Russia's "crony capitalism." A relatively small group of wealthy individuals benefited disproportionately from privatization schemes, and economic performance was consistently poor for a number of years, yielding an increase in poverty (Ascher 2009; Service 2009: 518–519, 540–541). Rule of law declined precipitously as well (Service 2009: 519, 534; Bushkovitch 2012: 452–453). Economic problems were exacerbated by the disappearance of Soviet social entitlements, however imperfect these may have been. Euphoria gave way to frustration and, for some, to nostalgia (Service 2009: 529). Yeltsin's inconsistent leadership did not help matters, nor did the war in Chechnya. In 1999, Yeltsin elevated Vladimir Putin, first to the post of prime minister and then acting president, and Putin was then elected president in 2000.

Russia under Putin has been frustrating to those who hoped that the post-Soviet transition would lead to a liberal, representative democracy and a fully capitalist economy. Putin's key goals seem to have been to (1) solidify his own power base; (2) centralize authority (Service 2009: 552); (3) strengthen the state; (4) curb the influence of the business leaders or "oligarchs" who might oppose him and his allies; and (5) resume a more assertive foreign policy. Under Putin, Russia has reasserted control over its traditional spheres of influence. Notable examples are Russia's decisive victory over Georgia in 2008 and its military involvement in neighboring Ukraine, including Russia's annexation of Crimea in 2014. In recent years tensions with the West have been exacerbated by allegations of Russian meddling in democratic elections (including in the United States) and by the 2018 poisoning of former Russian spies on British soil.

Putin has solidified personal control of Russian politics. While the government has formally independent branches, few doubt his authority. This is perhaps clearest in electoral politics, where Russia is a case of so-called "competitive authoritarianism" (Levitsky and Way 2010). Putin has formally satisfied the rules regarding term limits, moving to the position of prime minister while a protégé, Dmitry Medvedev, ascended to the presidency. For a time, commentators wondered whether and to what extent Medvedev would stake out an independent line. However, it soon became clear that Putin would remain the central figure in Russian politics. Putin was re-elected to the presidency in 2012, with numerous allegations of electoral irregularities and widespread public protests, and again in 2018. The authoritarian character of the contemporary Russian regime is also revealed by the government's selective targeting of political opponents for prosecution (Service 2009: 550). Many accuse the Russian government of attempting to aid potential competitive authoritarian regimes across Europe and the wider world and to impede the smooth functioning of other democracies.

Regime and Political Institutions

From an institutional perspective, Russia is a semi-presidential system. The president and the prime minister both have considerable powers. However, in reality in recent years, institutions are not as strong and independent as a review of their formal features might lead us to suppose (as can be seen in several of the case study boxes that follow). Most observers believe that even in his years as prime minister, current president Vladimir Putin was the true decision maker on key issues, not then-president Dmitri Medvedev. Optimists might argue that some degree of institutionalized democracy persists through this pattern. After all, Putin did not attempt to ignore the constitutional rule that would have prevented him from holding another consecutive presidential term. Pessimists, though, would note that his personal decision to run again for president even while his ally,

Medvedev, had another term of eligibility—and the fact that Medvedev did not publicly contest this—indicates that the informal and backstage exercise of power was fundamental here. Presidential powers are strong on paper. The president can even veto no-confidence votes in the legislature, though these are subject to override in the Duma. In practice, though, in the current system, Putin's personal authority seems more important than formal powers (see further discussion in the Case Study for chapter 10 titled "Executives in Russia: Formal and Informal Powers"). Personalism is not restricted to the executive itself: political parties have come to be associated with leading individuals in several cases. In short, contemporary Russian politics still has some minimal democratic features, but few observers now regard it as a functioning democracy.

Regime and Political Institutions

Regime	Federal Republic
Administrative Divisions	Eighty-three or eighty-five units in the Federation, of which twenty-one (or twenty-two) are formally republics; since annexation in 2014, Russia has claimed Crimea as a constituent republic and the Crimean city of Sevastopol as a federal city, but many Western countries do not diplomatically recognize this change.
Executive Branch	Semi-presidential: president and prime minister
Selection of Executive	President is elected and appoints the prime minister.
Legislative Branch	Bicameral Lower chamber: State Duma Upper chamber: Federation Council
Judicial Branch	Supreme Court is the highest judicial authority. A Constitutional Court is responsible for judicial review. There is a separate Superior Court for economic issues, called the Supreme Arbitration Court of the Russian Federation.
Political Party System	Russia's is a multiparty system, though some doubt the independence and efficacy of some of the parties. Important parties include United Russia (the party of Putin); the Communist Party; and the Liberal Democratic Party of Russia.

Political Culture

As noted in the "Historical Development" section of these country materials, Russia has long struggled with its relationship with Western Europe. One strong political cultural tendency has been toward Westernization and modernization. This has meant different things at different times and for different constituencies, including constitutional monarchy, democratization, economic development, literary and artistic achievement, and even the turn to socialism. Another tendency, though, has pulled in the opposite direction, emphasizing the idea of a distinctively Russian, Slavic, or Orthodox identity that is different from, and perhaps superior to, Western European culture.

Linked to this has been Russia's historic ability to dominate the nations in its periphery, which has lent the country a sense of important geopolitical status. Thus it is hardly surprising that Russian political culture after the fall of the Soviet Union showed signs of frustration and loss, bordering on what sociologists call "status-inconsistency," as Central and Eastern Europe withdrew and moved into the orbit of Western Europe and the United States. Indeed, Russia's concerns about some of these countries' entry into NATO can only be partially explained in terms of national security interest, as this interest is blended with concerns about national pride and the sense that Russia has a natural or historically established "right" to dominate these countries. More generally, Russia underwent a transition from being a society that saw itself as being on the "right side of history," with allegedly scientific certainty of eventual triumph, to one that saw

much of the globe view the society's political and economic structures as backward (a judgment that, as the preceding historical narrative shows, the country has long been trying to escape). These tendencies have no doubt facilitated the authoritarian features of the Russian government in the Putin years, as he presents himself as the one person capable of restoring Russia's "rightful" place in the international status hierarchy (on the importance of restoring Russia's image, see Service 2009: 549). Putin can also draw on notions mentioned earlier of Russia as "different" from Western Europe and special, arguing that Russian democracy is likewise different from the democracy of other countries. At the same time, some scholars have pointed to supposed high levels of Russian support for democratic values as a counterweight to this sort of narrative (Brown 2006: 393–394).

Another key feature of Russia's political culture in recent years has been widespread corruption. As a feature of political culture, corruption acts both directly and through perceptions. In other words, the actual corruption produces certain consequences, but perceptions of corruption facilitate certain kinds of politics. Many commentators, both in Russia and abroad, allege that Russian economic liberalization was mismanaged, leading to oligarchical politics in the 1990s. Supporters tried to justify Putin's more authoritarian turn as a necessary response to such developments; yet in certain respects, it has led to weak rule of law and ongoing corruption in both economics and politics, even while order was restored (Brown 2006: 395).

Political Economy

Russia is a fascinating case for political economists because it has witnessed a shift from a largely agrarian economy, to state-led industrialization and central planning under the Soviet Union, to a bumpy transition to a market economy. The Soviet system was a command economy. This means that the state was responsible for major decisions about investment, production targets, and the social organization of economic life. From the perspective of contemporary economics, this leads to inefficiencies, since markets are judged more capable than state functionaries of handling the complex arrays of information about pricing, supply, and demand. Over the long haul, the Soviet Union did not match the economic performance of the advanced capitalist

societies. It did, however, have periods of strong growth and clearly was successful in achieving industrialization (though the human costs of this were very high). Some would allege that the Soviet system failed because it does not give sufficient incentive to entrepreneurial activity and encourages a culture of dependency. It is hard to know how true this is of the Russian case. On one hand, popular dissatisfaction with the market reforms of the 1990s *might* be taken to indicate a sense of citizen entitlement of this sort. On the other hand, the "shock therapy" strategy of Russian privatization and the political and economic corruption that followed might be to blame for this reaction. Perhaps more measured economic reforms—with less tumultuous economic and social consequences—would have mitigated the impact of changes.

The Russian economy saw relatively strong performance in the first part of this century. Russia saw high GDP growth in the 2000s, owing in part to high oil prices. The global recession hit Russia hard in 2009; and after a brief recovery, growth was estimated at -0.2% in 2016 and then returned to a positive number in 2017 at 1.8% (*CIA World Factbook*). At present, with oil prices lower than they were earlier in the decade, Russia faces economic challenges, exacerbated by international sanctions against Russian banks and companies following Russia's incursion into Ukraine in 2014. As of 2015, the country's Gini coefficient stood at 41.2 (*CIA World Factbook*), with a slightly more equal income distribution than the United States, though more unequal than most of Western Europe. Russia remains a society with a relatively high level of industrialization. Of its GDP, 4.7 percent is produced by the agricultural sector and 32.4 percent by industry, with the service sector accounting for 62.3 percent or so (*CIA World Factbook*, 2017 estimates). The oil and natural gas industries are particularly important components of the Russian economy, and the country depends on the proceeds of its exports to Europe.

Russia faces a series of social problems linked in different ways to its economic fortunes, including high rates of alcoholism and drug addiction, a high crime rate, relatively low life expectancy, and a very low birth rate—particularly among ethnic Russians—producing challenging demographic issues. Alcoholism has long been a problem in Russia, but it seems to have increased during the tumultuous years following the collapse of the Soviet Union. The same is true of life expectancy, which fell notably as economic problems mounted in the years after the transition. Poverty jumped dramatically, and as criminologists would predict, all else being equal this leads to increasing crime. Yet here, as with other major social problems faced by the Russian state today, the explanation cannot *just* turn to economics. Rather, the failure of the state to establish rule of law and the resulting corruption, cronyism, and impunity mentioned previously are no doubt also implicated in ongoing high rates of crime. The decline of the ethnic Russian population is potentially quite problematic, particularly given the high levels of xenophobia and nativism among ethnic Russians: if the demographics do not change, Russia will need to depend more on immigrant labor; but given Russia's traditions, this might generate further problems.

CASE STUDIES

CASE STUDY
Oligarchy, Democracy, and Authoritarianism in Russia   CHAPTER 7, PAGE 156

Russia's political development has been mixed since the fall of the Soviet Union in 1991. An optimistic burst of activity in the early 1990s pushed the country from Soviet rule toward a greater emphasis on individual rights, but the country is now widely considered to be under authoritarian rule, or at least to be moving decisively toward centralization. At best, Russia can be seen as a hybrid regime with many authoritarian features that blend in some elements of electoral democracy. Russia's trajectory since 1991 is one in which a democratizing moment

has been followed by a return to more centralized power and decision making by a closed set of economic and political elites, with repression of political opponents..

In the early 1990s, as the former Soviet Union crumbled, Russia moved toward more open and democratic rule under the erratic president Boris Yeltsin. The country also moved to a more open economy as privatization turned state enterprises over to private hands. Despite the excitement of the reforms, the strongest lasting image of

this period is probably the dysfunctional transfer of economic power in which Russia developed only weak state institutions and lacked a rule of law. This gave rise to a corrupt network of "oligarchs," newly wealthy tycoons that operated in a style reminiscent of the mafia, especially in the areas of oil and natural gas. Privatization was seen going in step with democratization by giving individuals more freedoms, but the practice led to the creation of mega-rich corporate bosses that came to dominate the economy due to privileged

CASE STUDY (continued)
Oligarchy, Democracy, and Authoritarianism in Russia   CHAPTER 7, PAGE 156

connections to the state at the time of privatization. The result was a massive concentration of wealth in the hands of a few elites who were well connected to the state. As one observer noted, "an oligarch's success, in other words, almost always depended on his connections to the government officials in charge of privatizing the country's rich energy and mineral deposits" (Goldman 2004: 36). The oligarchs exercised considerable control in Russian politics under Yeltsin and contributed to the breakdown of the rule of law, even bankrolling Yeltsin's campaign in exchange for options to purchase state assets at favorable prices (Rose, Mishler, and Munro 2006: 64).

While the emergence of the oligarchs thus undermined the rule of law under Yeltsin in the 1990s, cracking down on them also compromised democracy and facilitated the rise of new authoritarianism under Vladimir Putin. During his presidency, Putin used state power to suppress powerful adversaries, most notably certain oligarchs (though he has aligned himself with other wealthy business owners). A key period was 2003 to 2005. In that

time, the Putin government jailed Russia's wealthiest oligarch, the outspoken Mikhail Khodorkovsky, and prosecuted him on charges of tax fraud. The Putin administration renationalized his oil firm Yukos, transferring the resources to the Russian state, in what was widely seen as a deliberate attack on the power of oligarchs who might get out of line (e.g., by funding political opponents of Putin and his allies). The move signaled that Putin would allow no dissent, though the government would work with oligarchs that supported Putin and his version of "managed democracy" (Colton and McFaul 2003; Goldman 2004: 36). Many of the wealthy beneficiaries of Russia's 1990s privatization have either learned to work closely with the state or have been harassed by the state. The oligarchy has thus increasingly come under state pressure or state control.

Putin's centralization of authority has taken on several forms, and the year 2004 was important on many fronts besides the crackdown on Khodorkovsky. A major tragedy altered Russian politics when separatists in the Caucasus region attacked a school and massacred

more than three hundred people, mostly school children; this terror attack plugged into Putin's claims that the rule of law and security required a strong central hand. Putin abolished gubernatorial elections in 2004 and increasingly cracked down on NGOs over time (Sharafutdinova 2011: 5; Freedom House 2011).

One of the key features of Russia's authoritarian rule has thus been the removal of alternative sources of power. The moves to sideline those oligarchs who were critical of Putin's rule have been part and parcel of a broader centralization of power and control. One leading commentator notes that Russia is actually quite similar to other authoritarian regimes in middle-income countries: It is not a totalitarian dictatorship, but "Putin has reduced the role of parliament, increased state control over the media, and overseen the renationalization of two major oil companies" (Treisman 2011: 342). The assertion of power over political institutions has gone hand in hand with the state's establishment of control over the economy. We return to Putin and his style of rule in the case studies that follow.

CASE STUDY
Executives in Russia: Formal and Informal Powers   CHAPTER 10, PAGE 237

In the 2012 elections, Vladimir Putin returned to Russia's presidency, after having previously been president from 2000 to 2008. What is especially striking about the previous years, however, is the way Putin exercised substantial executive power while he was *not* the president.

In fact, President Dmitry Medvedev (2008–2012) was seen by many as a near-puppet who never emerged from Putin's shadow. Medvedev was widely viewed as Putin's protégé and as owing his political career to his predecessor. This case raises the issue of the formal and informal

sources of executive power. Putin created a presidency that has strong formal powers, but it is clear his informal powers and control over much of Russian politics are even more significant.

Medvedev's relative weakness compared with Putin was not for a lack of

Executives in Russia: Formal and Informal Powers
CHAPTER 10, PAGE 237

formal powers of the presidency. The prime minister is appointed by the president with the consent of the legislature, the Duma. The prime minister is thus responsible both to the president and to the Duma, and can be dismissed by either. Under normal circumstances, the president would seem to have considerable authority over the prime minister. In fact, the dominance of the presidency was clear during Putin's first two terms (2000–2008), but power seemed to remain more with Putin than with the office of the presidency once Russia's strongman changed offices.

During his first two terms as president, Putin concentrated authority over security decisions, the budget, and policymaking, especially relative to Russia's first elected president, Boris Yeltsin (1991–1999). Yet Putin seemed to carry similar power over to the position of prime minister, presiding over the State Duma in the legislative branch. In a Russia where democracy has been under increasing authoritarian pressures, Putin has wielded extraordinary power over both the executive and legislature, first as president and then as prime minister. The peculiarity is that Putin for a time wielded his power as prime minister in a system in which he concentrated so much power in the presidency.

Putin's apparent dominance of the political system in the period in question was not spelled out in the constitution. Rather, the underpinnings of his power were (and remain) more numerous and less explicit. He is, for instance, a former head of the intelligence services (formerly the KGB under Soviet rule) and tightly linked to the security apparatus. He also has close linkages to businesses owned or supported by the state, some of which are corrupt and rely on Putin's power apparatus for their power and wealth. Putin exercises leverage over appointments in the media and judiciary. These informal sources of power—which are more based on the individual's leverage than the constitutional post that he holds—enabled him to retain effective control in Russia even while outside of the presidency. Indeed, the effects of this can be seen even in the process that led to Putin's return to the presidency. Putin maneuvered in such a way that the incumbent president declared that Putin should reclaim the post, even though Medvedev was eligible to run for a second term. Indeed, Medvedev signed a law extending the next presidential term from four years to six, with the full knowledge that Putin was likely to run once again.

One thing is clear: for the period from 1999 to the present, one man has dominated Russian politics, even though he has held different political leadership positions during that time.

Personalism and the Party System in Russia
CHAPTER 11, PAGE 268

Russia illustrates the challenge and importance of party system institutionalization. During the Soviet period from 1918 to 1991, the party system was focused on the single party, the Communist Party. After the collapse of the Soviet Union, Russia became a country where the political party system lost much of its structure. Russia saw some major parties emerge—and the Communists remained a minority party—but many of these came and went. In more recent years, Vladimir Putin has accumulated more power, but not through constructing a well-institutionalized party to contest democratic elections. On the contrary, Russia's poorly institutionalized party system has facilitated authoritarian tendencies even in the absence of single-party rule.

To continue building on the themes of the previous boxes, the Putin years have seen significant centralization of power. But the United Russia party that has backed Putin has taken a back seat to a more personal system of rule. As Kathryn Stoner-Weiss (2006: 114) describes Putin's presidency through his first term, he had "assiduously avoided any official affiliation with any national political party, preferring instead to rule in a non-transparent fashion through family members and longtime friends."

CASE STUDY (continued)
Personalism and the Party System in Russia

CHAPTER 11, PAGE 268

Personalism is not limited exclusively to Putin and the United Russia party. Another leading party (which in early 2018 holds 40 seats in the Duma) has also become associated with their particular leadership: the Liberal Democratic Party under the erratic and unpredictable xenophobe Vladimir Zhirinovsky. Perhaps more significantly, Russians felt little affinity for parties even after the transition from Soviet rule to a multiparty system in the 1990s (Mainwaring 1998). President Boris Yeltsin was nominally an independent during his time in office. This meant that the political party system never institutionalized before the Putin years; instead, Russians generally expressed dissatisfaction with the emergence of party options, which may have contributed to a desire for a strong central hand in the long run (Sharafutdinova 2011). In other words, the weak institutionalization of parties—with their weak links to society and lack of consistent programmatic alternatives—facilitated the rise of powerful actors such as Putin who work around institutions.

This prevalence of personalism in Russian politics is a clear demonstration of how political development and political institutions interact. The previous case study on oligarchy, democracy, and authoritarianism shows how Russian authoritarianism consists of centralized decision making that is tightly linked to the personalism of the president. Similarly, the legislature has been reshaped in a way that facilitates central control, while the structure of the executive seen in chapter 10 clearly facilitates personalism. In short, the various features of Russian politics work together to create a top-down system. Personalism is thus a theme that shows how the various institutions of government link to other features of a society's political culture.

CASE STUDY
The Russian Revolution

CHAPTER 12, PAGE 295

Karl Marx expected that the great revolution against capitalism would come in a highly developed capitalist society like Britain. If he had lived long enough to see it, he might have been surprised that it was in *Russia* where the most iconic revolution in his name would be made (Fitzpatrick 1994: 26–27).

The setting for the Russian Revolution of 1917 was made over many years. By the late nineteenth century, it was clear that the Czarist regime (Russian monarchs were called czars) was falling behind the rest of Europe and needed reform. In 1905, this produced Russia's so-called liberal revolution, which ended with a weak constitutional monarchy. However, this did not stop political agitation. Though Russia was a largely agrarian society, figures like Leon Trotsky (and Vladimir Lenin, though he was in exile for many years) as well as lesser-known figures, led or influenced socialist organizing in the face of ongoing repression. Lenin in particular is famous for insisting on party discipline (Fitzpatrick 1994: 30–31): though his group was numerically smaller than some other groups demanding change, their organization and unanimity may have been key to their success. Russia's involvement in the First World War weakened the state's position in society, and the Czar fell in early 1917. In the fall, the provisional government collapsed and the Soviets, largely controlled by the Bolsheviks, assumed increasing authority. Russia withdrew from the First World War in early 1918, and civil war broke out between groups of "red" and "white" Russians. This conflict lasted several years, but in the end the Bolshevik forces were victorious.

Through this process the Soviet Union was born. Until its demise in 1991, the Soviet Union declared itself to be a Marxist revolutionary regime. Among other things, it aimed to ultimately collectivize all of the "means of production," doing away with the capitalist division of labor. That is, the state looked to take over economic activity, from industrial factories to agriculture to shops. According to Marxist theory, this would do away once and for all with exploitation and other classes beyond the working class. Eventually, there would be no more need for a coercive state. This is not what happened in practice. While the regime was indeed somewhat successful in redistributing wealth, it was very authoritarian. Indeed, the state became highly coercive and totalitarian, attempting to control not just the economy but even political thought. Especially under Joseph Stalin, the Soviet Union's human rights abuses were legion (Service 2009: 220–229). Millions were killed by the state. The regime also came to dominate much of Central and Eastern Europe.

The Russian Revolution was, however, without a doubt one of history's most dramatic social revolutions. It radically transformed not just the structure of politics in Russian society but the state's role in the economy and the nature of social stratification both within that society and in the world outside of it. In fact, by becoming the leading example of communism, it had a transformative effect on politics around the world.

CASE STUDY
Communist Ideology in Practice: Russia and the Soviet Union
CHAPTER 15, PAGE 360

A number of societies turned to socialism in the twentieth century, but the most iconic exemplification of this ideology was the Soviet Union, brought into being by the great Russian Revolution discussed in the previous case study.

It is important to recognize that however much the society violated these claims, the Soviet Union claimed to be democratic, indeed, *more* democratic than the capitalist West. In essence, defenders of this view can draw on early ideas of Marx's, that representative democracy is not enough, given that unfreedom is not just a lack of political representation but more fundamentally *alienation* produced by the division of labor. Given the Marxist view of history as class struggle moving inexorably forward, it was not felt that the "bourgeoisie" or individuals thought to have bourgeois values and interests at heart *ought* to be given representation in a democracy. Rather, the proletariat was imagined to be the demos, and methods and practices many observers would regard as authoritarian and antidemocratic were said to be justified in relation to serving their alleged "class interest." It is, of course, not hard to see how such an argument could be exploited by authoritarian party leaders to their advantage.

The Soviet Union had a number of aims. While Russia was dominant, and Americans often thought of the Soviet Union as "the Russians," the Soviet Union claimed to be multinational and based on class rather than national identity. It came to incorporate many other societies. It tried, with considerable success, to force the ongoing industrialization of its underlying societies. It tried, with mixed success, to transform agricultural productivity. Perhaps most important, it aimed to serve as the vanguard in a global revolution that would end capitalism everywhere. We would not want to exaggerate the extent of ideological uniformity in the Soviet Union, especially in the early years. First, it is worth noting that Leninism differed on certain points from Orthodox Marxism, at least as understood by some others. In particular, some doubt whether Marx would have thought Russia, with its relatively brief period of industrialization and its only very recent turn to constitutional monarchy (in its "bourgeois revolution" of 1905), to be the appropriate site for revolution, as mentioned in the previous case study—though Marx and Engels did allude to this possibility in a late, Russian-language edition of the Communist Manifesto. Lenin, however, saw conditions as propitious. Moreover, Lenin emphasized the efficacy of a strong "vanguard" party leading the revolution (there were some textual sources in Marx for this idea, but it is recognized that Lenin took it further).

CASE STUDY (continued)

Communist Ideology in Practice: Russia and the Soviet Union

CHAPTER 15, PAGE 360

Beyond variation in ideology between Lenin and Marx, it is worth noting that, particularly in the early years, there were ideological differences among the leaders of the Soviet Union, most famously reflected in the conflict between Stalin and Trotsky (who was forced into exile in Mexico and later killed there). Stalin's repression of dissent temporarily reduced the public expression of ideological dissent, but his successors partially repudiated some of his initiatives.

The ideological conflict between socialism and liberalism in the post-war period issued in the "Cold War," a period of intense but indirect conflict between the Soviet Union and its allies, on one side, and the United States and its allies on the other. It may seem hard to imagine now, but it was by no means clear to all observers that the United States or liberalism would triumph.

The Soviet Union committed mass atrocities, especially under Stalin. This caused many international observers who were previously sympathetic to turn against the regime. Indeed, following the Soviet Union's weakening and collapse over the course of the late twentieth century, many considered the broader ideology of socialism to be totally discredited, though this judgment has been disputed by those who argue that the Soviet Union was not a true and accurate test of socialist ideology.

Research Prompts

1. Russia has a notable tradition of authoritarian politics. How would you account for authoritarian persistence in Russia? What would the major theories from chapter 7 say about this case?

2. Compare the reforms of Gorbachev to the reforms of Deng Xiaoping in China. What is similar about the circumstances they faced, and what are the major differences in this respect? What was different about their respective strategic approaches to reform? To what extent can the recent political and economic trajectories of these two societies be traced to different approaches to and processes of reform?

3. The Russian Revolution of 1917 produced a dramatic series of political, social, and economic changes. Compare that revolution to the French and Chinese Revolutions. Can a common causal framework explain all three? What if we add the Iranian Revolution to the mix?

4. Russia is a useful case for proponents of the idea that the contemporary world is increasingly populated by "hybrid," "gray zone," and "competitive authoritarian" systems. What does Russia show us about the democratic status of such systems? Is a "hybrid" regime half democratic? Or is democratization a threshold status of which hybrid regimes fall short?

5. Russian politics is characterized by personalism and a high degree of centralization and authoritarian decision making. This is reflected in various institutions, as seen in the various case studies just presented. Would reforming one of these institutions alter the Russian political culture or would changing institutional designs be ineffective without a deeper change in the culture? If institutional reform would be helpful, what institution would be the most useful one to change? Since your answer will be forward-looking and speculative, what sorts of evidence could you find from comparative study or from within-case comparison to support your claim?

United Kingdom

Key Features of the Contemporary United Kingdom

Population:	64,769,452 (estimate, July 2017)
Area:	243,610 sq km
Head of State:	Queen Elizabeth II (1952–present)
Head of Government:	Theresa May (prime minister, 2016–present)
Capital:	London
Year of Independence:	Never colonized. Political arrangements linking Northern Ireland, Scotland, Wales, and England have changed over time.
Year of Current Constitution:	Common law system; there is no formal constitution, though the Magna Carta dates back to the thirteenth century.
Languages:	English is the majority language. Other languages include Scots, Scottish Gaelic, Irish, and Welsh.
GDP per Capita:	$42,500 (*CIA World Factbook* estimate, 2016)
Human Development Index Ranking (2016):	16th (very high human development)

Sources: *CIA World Factbook;* World Bank World Development Indicators; United Nations *Human Development Report 2016.*

Introduction

It is often noted that the United Kingdom is an island society, and that this has had important implications for its development. It is relatively small, comprising only about 244,000 square km, and yet in several important ways, it pioneered key features of modern politics. While it lacks a formal, written constitution, it was perhaps the society in which the idea of a "constitutional order" first emerged. Its parliament survived the rise of absolutism (or, as some would put it, Britain never saw full-scale absolutism at all), and constitutional monarchy was established early, with the "Glorious Revolution" of 1688–1689. Moreover, many scholars consider it to have been among the first societies, and possibly the first, to establish modern national identity (Hastings 1997; Greenfeld 1992; Kohn 1944). Finally, Britain was a lead colonizer, spreading many of its political practices abroad. There is a lively discussion among political scientists about whether British colonialism produced democratic independent societies following decolonization (e.g., Bernhard, Reenock, and Nordstrom 2004).

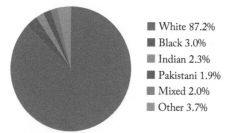

Ethnic Groups in the United Kingdom

- White 87.2%
- Black 3.0%
- Indian 2.3%
- Pakistani 1.9%
- Mixed 2.0%
- Other 3.7%

Note that within the category "white," more than 80 percent consider themselves English, with the bulk of the remainder being groups that consider themselves Scottish, Welsh, and Northern Irish.
Source: CIA World Factbook.

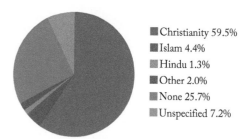

Religious Affiliation in the United Kingdom

- Christianity 59.5%
- Islam 4.4%
- Hindu 1.3%
- Other 2.0%
- None 25.7%
- Unspecified 7.2%

Source: CIA World Factbook.

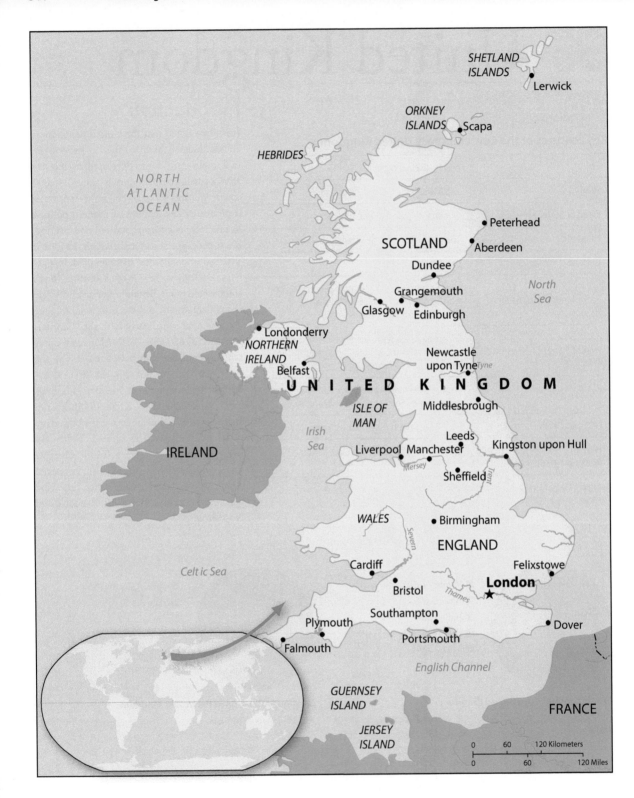

SHETLAND ISLANDS
• Lerwick

ORKNEY ISLANDS
• Scapa

HEBRIDES

NORTH ATLANTIC OCEAN

SCOTLAND

• Peterhead
• Aberdeen
• Dundee
• Grangemouth
Glasgow • • Edinburgh

North Sea

• Londonderry
NORTHERN IRELAND
• Belfast

UNITED KINGDOM

Newcastle upon Tyne
Tyne

ISLE OF MAN

• Middlesbrough

Irish Sea

IRELAND

Liverpool • • Manchester
Mersey
• Leeds
• Kingston upon Hull
• Sheffield
Trent

WALES
Severn
• Birmingham

ENGLAND

Celtic Sea

Cardiff •
• Bristol
Thames
• Felixstowe
London ★

Southampton
Plymouth •
• Dover
• Portsmouth
Falmouth •

English Channel

GUERNSEY ISLAND

FRANCE

JERSEY ISLAND

0   60   120 Kilometers

0   60   120 Miles

While the United Kingdom was historically a lead society in many of these areas, it is now often viewed as highly traditionalistic. Unlike France, it still has a constitutional monarchy, though Queen Elizabeth's role is largely symbolic. Moreover, its legal system is a common law system in which traditional practice is determinative of outcomes.

The United Kingdom, along with the United States, has been a key promoter of the modern ideology of liberalism, holding that individual rights; representative, democratic government; and market-driven economics are the keys to political modernity. This is not to say that it has lacked a tradition of left-wing organizing, and the left in Britain has historically had a number of successes, most notably in the decades immediately following the Second World War (Clarke 2004: 221–224). Among other things, the British left played a key role in the construction of the United Kingdom's relatively robust welfare state, including the highly popular Health Service (the United Kingdom's single-payer health care system).

In religious terms, the largest group in the United Kingdom, at nearly 60 percent, is Christian (2011 estimate, per *CIA World Factbook*). However, it is worth keeping several things in mind when you interpret this. First, the largest population within this group is the Anglican Church, which is the established Church of England. Second, the other major groups would include both other Protestant denominations as well as Roman Catholics. Finally, a large share of this nearly 60 percent is understood by social scientists to be only nominally Christian. Indeed, it is often claimed that more Muslims than Anglicans attend religious services in the United Kingdom each week (a fact that, if true, points both to low levels of religiosity among Anglicans and high religiosity among British Muslims). In any case, it is clear that the United Kingdom is now a religiously diverse society, and one in which secularization has been extensive (Berger, Davie, and Fokas 2008; Bruce 2004).

Historical Development

As noted already, the United Kingdom (or Great Britain, and before the union with Scotland and Ireland, England itself) is often viewed as an "early modernizer." It was among the first growth-oriented, modern economies and, relatedly, among the first "commercial societies" (Greenfeld 2001). It was the first Western European society to break from the dominance of the Roman Catholic Church. It was among the first with a constitutional order, though it has no formal, written, constitution. Its parliament helped it to resist royal absolutism in the seventeenth century, though the cost of this was civil war. Indeed, in the middle of the seventeenth century, it existed as a republic, before the Restoration of the Stuart monarchy in 1688. Some scholars argue that England was the first society to establish a modern national identity (Hastings 1997; Kohn 1944; Greenfeld 1992). Finally, according to some scholars (e.g., Pincus 2009), its "Glorious Revolution" of 1688–1689 was the first modern revolution.

Yet this should not lead us to suppose that the United Kingdom suddenly came to assume all of the features that we associate with political modernity some centuries ago. Rather, the political history of the British Isles is a story of gradual change with several key moments of "punctuated" and more rapid transformation. In this section, we will very briefly survey some of the key political developments of the seventeenth, eighteenth, nineteenth, and twentieth centuries.

In much of the rest of Europe, the seventeenth century was the century of royal absolutism. The state grew as the centralizing monarch marginalized his noble and religious opponents. In England, however, things were different (for an excellent overview of this highly complicated period, see Kishlansky 1996). Parliament remained powerful, and could on occasions effectively resist royal efforts to collect taxes. Moreover, religious dissent was common. When the king tried to enforce religious orthodoxy and then to force Parliament to consent to taxation, the Civil Wars, which pitted the "Roundheads" against the royalist "Cavaliers," broke out. The King, Charles I, was deposed and eventually executed in 1649. Oliver Cromwell dominated English (and Scottish and Irish) politics until his death (Kishlansky 1996: 187–212). Once Cromwell was gone, though, the country turned back to the Stuarts, and Charles II was crowned in the Restoration. He was followed by James II, who was criticized because of his Catholic leanings. Perhaps more important, James II set about to dramatically strengthen the state, including building a larger navy and a standing army (Pincus 2009). With the support of some well-placed Britons, however, the Dutch Stadtholder, William of Orange, invaded. He faced almost no resistance; and he and his wife, Mary (who was a Stuart), were crowned King and Queen in the "Glorious Revolution." In general, this period witnessed

Historical Development

Timeline

1215	Magna Carta		1949	Independence of Ireland (except Northern Ireland)
1530–1534	Break from Rome		1951–1955	Second Churchill Government (Conservative); conservative governments will continue until 1964.
1580s–1700	First Wave of English Colonialism			
1600	Establishment of East India Company		1956	Suez Crisis
1642–1651	Civil Wars		1964–1970	James Harold Wilson Government (Labour). Labour governments will succeed each other until 1979, with the exception of the 1970–1974 (Heath) Conservative government.
1649–1659	Cromwell and the Protectorate (1653–1659)			
1660	Restoration (Charles II)			
1688–1689	Glorious Revolution (William and Mary)			
1694	Creation of the Bank of England		1973	United Kingdom joins the Common Market (EC).
1707	Act of Union (England and Scotland)		1975	Referendum on Common Market (EC) Membership (Approved)
1714	Hanoverians inherit the throne (George I)			
1756–1763	Seven Years War		1976–1979	James Callaghan Government (Labour)
1776–1783	American Revolution		1979–1990	Margaret Thatcher Government (Conservative); some efforts to reduce the scope of the welfare state, including notable privatizations
1798	Major Irish revolt led by Wolfe Tone and the United Irishmen			
1801	Act of Union		1982	Falkland Islands/Malvinas War
1807	Slave Trade Act		1990–1997	John Major Government (Conservative)
1832	Reform Act of 1832		1991	First Iraq War
1833	Slavery Abolition Act		1997	Hong Kong passes from United Kingdom to China.
1867	Voting rights extended		1997	Scottish and Welsh voters choose to create their own legislatures.
1911	National Insurance Act (early, very limited welfare state development)			
1914–1918	World War I		1997–2007	Tony Blair Government (Labour)
1918	Limited women's suffrage		2002	Eurozone begins, but the United Kingdom opts not to participate.
1921	Emergence of Irish Free State			
1930	Women's suffrage		2003	Beginning of Second Iraq War
1938	Munich Pact		2007–2010	Gordon Brown Government (Labour)
1939–1945	World War II		2010–present	David Cameron Governments (Conservative/Liberal Democrats Coalition from 2010 to 2015; Conservative majority after 2015 election)
1942	Beveridge Report (very influential in subsequent welfare state development)			
1940–1945	Churchill government		2014	Scotland referendum on independence fails, with 45% voting for independence and 55% for remaining in the United Kingdom.
1945–1951	Labour Government with Clement Atlee as prime minister; creation of British welfare state, including National Health Service (1948)			
1947–1960s	Waves of decolonization in India, Africa, the Caribbean, and elsewhere		2016	United Kingdom votes to leave the European Union in a referendum commonly called "Brexit." Cameron steps down as prime minister; Conservatives again win electoral majority under Theresa May.

heightened political activity, with lots of coffeehouse discussion and pamphlet writing, which some have argued led to the creation of the first modern "public sphere" (Habermas 1989). It also witnessed the development of the two parties, the Whigs (more liberal) and the Tories (more conservative), who would dominate British politics for many years (Kishlansky 1996: 313–335).

The eighteenth century largely witnessed a return to stability (Langford 2010). Political stabilization was evidenced by the end of Jacobite "pretenders" (people who claimed to be the true heirs to the Stuart line) and the transition to the House of Hanover. Prime Minister Robert Walpole practiced a sort of machine politics, and many think of the eighteenth century as one in which a kind of new, commercial aristocracy established itself. Throughout the century, Britain had notable military success, both in the War of the Spanish Succession (1701–1714) and in the Seven Years War (1756–1763), though it failed in its effort to hold onto the colonies that became the United States. Commercial society grew, and in the second half of the century, Britain saw the beginnings of the Industrial Revolution in which technologically adapted manufacturing, especially of textiles, dramatically expanded productivity (Harvie 2010: 475–481). This had numerous consequences, as it made new fortunes, slowly but surely changed the nature of labor, and led eventually to the urbanization of British society. At the same time, there is evidence that all of these changes were experienced by some as disorienting. The literature and art of the eighteenth century shows this, and there was a heightened concern for social problems like poverty and starvation, perhaps because these were increasing (Langford 2010: 424–438). In the religious field, new forms of Protestantism emerged and spread, especially Methodism, which would play a critical role in the abolition (of the slavery and the slave trade) and reform movements (of British politics) that began to develop by the end of the century.

The nineteenth century, for much of which Queen Victoria held the throne, was a time of expanding liberalism, the extension of suffrage, and the solidification and expansion of British colonialism (Harvie 2010; Matthew 2010). Beginning in the mid-to-late eighteenth century, and accelerating in the nineteenth, some British leaders (often Whigs but also some Tories) advocated expanding the electorate and updating parliamentary representation to make it more representative of the industrializing and urbanizing society that Britain had become. At the same time, popular actors came to make more demands on government (Tilly 1997). The Reform Act of 1832 expanded the vote, though one still needed to have property to vote even after this act. However, social movement activity began to develop, perhaps most notably the "Chartist movement," which drew on industrial workers and used strikes and demonstrations in its effort to expand suffrage and representation (Harvie 2010: 498–499). Further voting reform took place in 1867, where suffrage was extended, though only to (some) males and in a way that by today's standards would still be considered highly restricted.

Britain's twentieth-century experience (like that of other advanced industrial societies of the time) was largely shaped by the two world wars and the Great Depression (Morgan 2010a; Clarke 2004). World War I was enormously costly in terms of both lives and resources, but Britain and its allies emerged victorious. Voting rights were further extended in the post-war years, notably to women. As of 1918, women over thirty who met certain conditions could vote; and after 1928, all men and women over twenty-one were able to exercise this right. Britain, like most of the world, suffered serious economic difficulties in the late 1920s and the 1930s. The country aimed to stay out of World War II, and Prime Minister Neville Chamberlain famously appeased Hitler at Munich, but they were eventually forced to participate in the war after Germany invaded Poland. While not as many British soldiers died in World War II as in World War I, fighting was intense, and Britons had to face constant German air raids, which killed an estimated sixty thousand civilians (Morgan 2010a).

As we discuss further later in this profile, in the post-war years the Labour Party was ascendant, and it worked to construct the British welfare state (Clarke 2004: 216–247). This welfare state has been somewhat reduced in subsequent years, especially in the administration of Margaret Thatcher (1979–1990), but important components of it have been remarkably resilient (Prasad 2006). Another, major, twentieth-century development was the shrinking and eventual disappearance of the British Empire (Clarke 2004). Once it had stretched across the globe, but in the mid to late twentieth century, almost all of the United Kingdom's colonies achieved independence, though most retained some ties to Britain and to each other through the Commonwealth of Nations (initially called the British Commonwealth). The United Kingdom also slowly achieved partial, if controversial, integration with Europe, joining the European Community (later the European Union) in 1973, though it decided not to adopt the euro. This integration underwent a stunning reversal in 2016 when the United Kingdom voted in a referendum to exit the European Union (the so-called Brexit). While the country retains considerable social and cultural overlap with Europe (most visibly in the highly cosmopolitan city of London), its future degree of economic and political integration with the continent is an open question. At the same time as integration into Europe has fluctuated, the United Kingdom has experienced challenges to the state from below. Scotland and Wales both had powers devolved to their legislatures in the 1990s, and Scotland had a relatively close vote on independence in 2014.

Regime and Political Institutions

Government in the United Kingdom is based on the principle of parliamentary sovereignty, which holds that Parliament (and particularly the House of Commons) is the supreme law-making body, and that whatever it votes into law is deemed constitutional. Acts of Parliament are not subject to judicial review and can be overturned only by subsequent acts of Parliament. While the legislature is supreme, the executive branch of government is powerful, being led by a prime minister who is selected by majority vote of the House of Commons.

The prime minister is routinely the leader of the party winning the most seats in the parliamentary elections, and he or she in turn selects a cabinet that proposes and presents most bills for passage into law by the broader House. This government remains in office for a term of up to five years, as long as it maintains the "confidence" of the House of Commons; elections must be held at least every five years, and the executive can be re-elected for multiple terms. Parliament has the power to "bring down" the prime minister's government by a majority vote of no confidence (or by defeat of a major bill, which is often interpreted as a vote of no confidence), while the prime minister has the power to dissolve Parliament and ask the monarch to call for a new election. Dissolution may happen either when the executive believes Parliament is unable to govern, or when the prime minister senses an electoral advantage in calling an election. In general, bills proposed by the prime minister's government are passed by the House of Commons, due to strong discipline within political parties.

Despite the principle of parliamentary sovereignty, there are some practical limitations on Parliament. Nominally, the monarch calls elections and invites winning parties to form

Regime and Political Institutions

Regime	Constitutional monarchy, with parliamentary democracy
Powers in Constitution	No formal written constitution, but widely considered to include certain established laws and rights that are assumed to have constitutional status
Administrative Divisions	Great Britain (includes England, Scotland, and Wales) and Northern Ireland; three island dependencies (Isle of Man, Jersey, Guernsey); over a dozen overseas territories (British Virgin Islands, Cayman Islands, Gibraltar, Falkland Islands, etc.)
Executive Branch	Prime minister (and cabinet)
Selection of Executive	Elected by House of Commons
Legislative Branch	Bicameral Parliament Lower chamber: House of Commons Upper chamber: House of Lords
Judicial Branch	Interprets statutes, but has no right of judicial review
Political Party System	Two-party to three-party system; Conservatives (Tories) and Labour are two main parties; Liberal Democrats are third party.

government, though the monarch's role is almost exclusively ceremonial rather than political. More substantively, Parliament itself is governed by traditions, customs, and constitutional interpretations: though Parliament could theoretically pass any law it wants, it routinely stays within the bounds of common interpretations of the British constitution. A final restraint on Parliament in recent years has seen some devolution of power from the U.K. Parliament to assemblies in the regions or "countries" of the United Kingdom (the Scottish Parliament and the Welsh Assembly), as well as some recognition of the powers of the European Union to legislate on certain matters that are binding on British law, though the latter will cease to be operative when the UK definitively exits the European Union in 2019.

Political Culture

Political culture in the United Kingdom, like in other countries, is heterogeneous and dynamic and therefore hard to pin down. The classic comparative study of Almond and Verba (1963) treated the United Kingdom as possessing a vibrant "civic culture." Several themes, though, have been particularly important in the political culture of late twentieth-century and twenty-first-century Great Britain and are, therefore, worth special mention.

The first theme concerns the shifting nature of liberalism and the relationship between class affiliation and party loyalty. A highly stratified society, the United Kingdom in the early to mid-twentieth century saw a strong relationship between working-class membership and Labour Party support. By the 1970s, however, this had begun to change (Morgan 2010a). On one hand, this change might be attributed to the stagflation the British economy faced in that decade. On the other hand, the United Kingdom witnessed a familiar pattern in the political-cultural development of post-industrial societies. Rising incomes and a major shift in the composition of the labor market—a move away from manufacturing and toward services—have generally been found to change political culture, rendering it more individualistic and less tied to communities and classes (Inglehart and Welzel 2005). By the 1970s, Labour was in crisis, and it would not take power again until it had come to represent the interests, and match the cultural style, of middle-class service sector workers (Morgan 2010a; Clarke 2004: 401–439). This "New Labour" has had to contend with a resurgent free market approach, which preceded it in the form of the reforms of Margaret Thatcher's governments (1979–1990) and, to a lesser extent, the government of her successor John Major (1990–1997); but also, more recently, following the electoral success of Prime Minister David Cameron of the Conservative Party, which governed with a majority in 2015-2016. Cameron and his associates, in addition to scaling back aspects of the welfare state, explicitly spoke of transforming British political culture, hoping to create what they called the "Big Society" in which voluntarism and community activity partially replace the actions of the state. Cameron left office in 2016, resigning after the Brexit vote.

Another major theme in the changing political culture of twentieth-century Britain was the redefinition of British identity in the wake of the collapse of the British Empire. "Empire" had been a key aspect of the identity of subjects of the United Kingdom for at least the late nineteenth and early twentieth centuries (this is not to say that empire was unimportant before this but that the imperial nature of Britishness became especially salient at this time). Relatedly, the role of the monarchy in British political culture has gradually changed. The Queen is still important, but the royal family has for some time now been much more discussed in gossip tabloids than in political newspapers (Morgan 2010b: 674; Clarke 2004: 388, 418–419). Their role is largely symbolic, and even still they are not typically treated with the same deference as their (also symbolic) forebears from the early to mid-twentieth century were. As is discussed later, in the Case Study "National Identity in the United Kingdom," to some extent these changes have coincided with other changes in British identity, including a growing resurgence of regional-national identities and the growth of a multicultural understanding of citizenship (Modood 2007). However, this should not lead us to suspect that Britishness has ceased to be an important feature of political culture in the United Kingdom. The population of the United Kingdom has been noted for its relatively high level of "Euroskepticism." This cultural feature of the population has important policy consequences: for example, the United Kingdom has never joined the Eurozone and, as noted previously, in 2016 voted to leave the EU.

Political Economy

As mentioned in other sections of this country profile and as discussed in the case studies that follow, the United Kingdom has had a central role in the history of global political economy. It was the site of origin for many ideas about free trade (even if the country did not always practice them if unsuited to its interests); it had arguably the first modern, growth-oriented economy; it was the launching point for the industrial revolution; and it played an important role in constructing the global economy through its formal colonialism and informal efforts to trade with other parts of the world. It is worth keeping in mind, though, the United Kingdom's political economy in the post-war world, as the country underwent enormous changes in that period. The two most important in this connection are (1) the decolonization of many of its overseas possessions and the accompanying re-calibration of Britain's role in both global politics and the global economy; and (2) the creation of the British welfare state. The latter development is discussed further the case studies below.

Like many other countries that industrialized early, Britain has become a post-industrial economy, meaning, in essence, that services (which account for 80.4 percent of GDP) dramatically outstrip manufacturing (19 percent) in economic importance. Britain is also notable for the small share that agriculture plays in its GDP, constituting only 0.6 percent (*CIA World Factbook*, 2017 estimates). The country is among the wealthiest countries in terms of GDP per capita in the world (2017 estimate from *CIA World Factbook*: $43,600); and per the same source its estimated unemployment rate as of 2017 stood at 4.4 percent. Its Gini index (which mea-sures income inequality) stands at 38.0, which is around the average for Western European societies with redistributive

welfare states (World Bank 2013 estimate). In recent years it was estimated to have a poverty rate of 15 percent, which is comparatively quite high (CIA 2013 estimate).

As is discussed in more detail in the case studies that follow, the welfare state in the United Kingdom has faced po-litical opposition since the early 1980s. As such, it makes an interesting comparison with France, which saw no Margaret Thatcher arise in that decade (see further discussion in the French case). One major theory focuses on the politics of re-trenchment, noting that in places like the United Kingdom (and the United States), the welfare state was created by par-ties on the left in response to the crises of the middle of the twentieth century (the Great Depression and World War II). This creates the possibility of a strident opposition from across the spectrum (Prasad 2006; Huber and Stephens 2001).

Sources for economic data in this discussion: CIA World Fact-book; World Bank World Development Indicators.

CASE STUDIES

CASE STUDY
The State in the United Kingdom

CHAPTER 3, PAGE 63

As with many other aspects of the politics in the United Kingdom, the state in this case had strong early development and then, in some ways, did not later grow as rapidly thereafter. Scholars who study the rise of the state point to late medieval England as a place where the modern state first started to come into view (Strayer 1970: 35–48). England was likely aided in this by several factors. First, it is a relatively small island, facilitating central-ized rule. Second, historically, the English nobility was in certain respects not as strong as its peers on the continent; and by the time of the rise of the Tudor mon-archy (late fifteenth century), it had badly damaged itself through internal conflict, most notably in the "War of the Roses." In terms of the actual mechanics of English state-building, Strayer (1970: 37–38), in

his classic account, stresses the late me-dieval rise of royal officials, the royal court system, and the emergence of the Exche-quer as key in this connection. All of these institutions either increased the king's role as an arbiter of domestic disputes (thus moving in the direction of the We-berian "monopoly on legitimate force") or expanded the state's ability to record information and, in essence, to monitor localities and its dealings with them.

As noted previously, England never fully embraced royal absolutism, which, in places like France, was a key stage in modern state-building. In France, the modern state emerged, in part, as suc-cessive kings managed to expand their power vis-à-vis the nobility. At first glance, it looks like the English kings of the seventeenth century failed in this

endeavor. But there is more here than meets the eye. While it is true that Par-liament successfully resisted royal ini-tiatives, it was not simply an organ that represented the upper nobility. Indeed, many of the upper nobility in the sev-enteenth century sided with Charles I rather than Parliament and Cromwell, though this was by no means universal. When Charles II and especially James II, after the Restoration, set about building a more modern state, with a more com-plex bureaucracy, a greater ability to ex-tract resources from its citizens, and with a modern military, there was resistance in the form of the Glorious Revolution (Pincus 2009)—but this did not stop the effort. Subsequent monarchs continued James's state-building efforts in impor-tant ways (Kishlansky 1996).

CASE STUDY (continued)
The State in the United Kingdom
CHAPTER 3, PAGE 63

One of the great tensions in the history of British state-building is that the society produced a relatively strong state but also, as discussed elsewhere in this text, an ideology—liberalism—that seems very suspicious of strong states. More generally, the British welfare state is probably best viewed as an organization that developed because of factors external to British politics writ narrow: two world wars, the Great Depression, and the changing British class structure. Note that many of its features, as in the United States, only developed around World War II (indeed, in the Labour government that was elected in 1945), though there were precedents in the early twentieth century (Clarke 2004: 59–60). In France, typical arguments against preserving the welfare state in its entirety focus largely on questions like the efficiency of labor markets and economic competitiveness. In places like the United Kingdom (and the United States), there is an alternative, liberal critique of the welfare state as a result of this tension.

CASE STUDY
Political Economy of Britain
CHAPTER 4, PAGE 79

The United Kingdom may be seen as the birthplace of the modern world economy. While not considered a "developing country" today, the British experience has been the basis of many of the most enduring research questions in the study of development, precisely because it is the country where the massive economic expansion of the last two centuries started. It was here, from the late 1700s to the mid-1800s, that the Industrial Revolution began, giving rise to the explosion in productivity and rising incomes that have set the last two centuries apart from any other period of human history.

The desire to understand why the Industrial Revolution happened here rather than somewhere else was the beginning of the comparative study of modern economic development, and analysts have put forward numerous theses. The Industrial Revolution consisted of a cluster of technological innovations that drove down costs of production and brought about rapid industrialization: new inventions (such as the steam engine), new factory techniques (including greater use of machinery), and improved infrastructure (such as railways and improved shipping). Other factors helped make this set of innovations work especially well in Britain. Some argue that the availability of coal mattered, while others argue that the country was relatively urbanized. Yet others suggest that development happened here due to attitudes and culture, whether in the populace at large or in the relatively liberal government with its orientation toward individual economic rights. Also in the 1800s, Great Britain consolidated its imperial control over colonies ranging from Africa to India to the Caribbean, though it had lost control of America by 1783. As the Industrial Revolution spread, the United Kingdom became a leader in the globalization that transformed the world economy from the late nineteenth century up to the Great Depression of the 1930s.

Britain was a leader in promoting the *laissez-faire* or liberal economic policies that had been dominant in years before the Great Depression; but it also was the home of economist John Maynard Keynes, who offered a twentieth-century approach to preventing an economic depression and taming the business cycle: countercyclical government spending. A central idea of Keynesian economics is that recessions and depressions are self-reinforcing because demand drops as employment falls and assets lose their value—and that government spending can halt or reverse this process by stimulating demand. In theory, governments could build up surpluses in good times and spend as necessary to soften or stop downturns. This theory was (and remains) hugely influential, as over the course of the century, the state intervened more in the economy in Britain and beyond.

After surviving the two world wars without defeat, the United Kingdom has remained one of the linchpin economies of the global order. State involvement in the economy increased notably after

CASE STUDY (continued)

Political Economy of Britain

CHAPTER 4, PAGE 79

World War II. The Labour Party, under the leadership of Clement Atlee, won a plurality for the first time in 1945, displacing the Conservative Party from which both Neville Chamberlain and Winston Churchill had governed. The British welfare state was relatively underdeveloped up to this point, but it grew notably in the post-war years, particularly through the establishment of the National Health Service and the expansion of public housing initiatives (called "council houses"), as well as social insurance (Clarke 2004: 216–231).

As in many other advanced industrial societies, Britain did relatively well in the post-war years, but by the 1970s had entered into recession and "stagflation"

(inflation accompanied by stagnation in economic growth and wages). This prompted some rethinking, and one of the major changes in the country's economic policy took place beginning in 1979, when the newly elected Prime Minister Margaret Thatcher (the "Iron Lady") pushed the economy toward free-market principles by privatizing state-owned enterprises (including many council houses, increasing homeownership rates in the process, but also business organizations), reducing government spending, and deregulating the economy (Clarke 2004: 358–400). Notably, the Thatcher government (1979–1990) barely attempted to scale

back some key aspects of the welfare state, such as the National Health Service, given their high levels of public support (Prasad 2006). Following the era of Thatcher and her Conservative successor John Major (1990–1997), the government of Tony Blair (1997–2007) brought in an era of "New Labour" that largely retained a pro-market orientation. Today, the British economy is actively plugged into world trade, especially in services, where the City of London is a top financial center in the global economy. Commentators wonder, though, how Brexit will alter London and the UK's global role.

CASE STUDY

No Constitution? No Supreme Court? Constitutionality in the United Kingdom

CHAPTER 8, PAGE 184

For two countries that are so historically and culturally intertwined, the United Kingdom and the United States have dramatically different democracies. The United Kingdom is a constitutional monarchy with no single constitutional document, no judicial review of the constitutionality of laws, a prime minister elected chief executive by the legislature, and a principle of legislative supremacy; this contrasts with the American republic, centered around a Constitution, separately elected legislatures and executives, a Supreme Court, and a set of checks and balances and separations of powers between government actors.

Many countries follow certain aspects of the British model, but the aspect

most unique to the United Kingdom is probably the lack of a single constitutional document. Rather than one core written charter that is amended periodically (as in most countries), the United Kingdom deems several documents to have constitutional significance. As the country developed its unified political system over the course of many centuries, several major acts shaped British political tradition. The constitutional documents include the Magna Carta of 1215, but also a range of other laws of great significance and stature. These include the Bill of Rights of 1689, which emphasized certain limitations on the power of the monarchy, and the Acts of Settlement of 1701, which established

patterns of succession to the throne. In a sense, it may be said that the United Kingdom has a "written" constitution, but one that relies on a range of written documents rather than a single one. More generally, the "British Constitution" is partly shaped by tradition, custom, and a common cultural understanding of basic laws, powers, and functions of different political actors.

The British Constitution is one of the most flexible in the world, at least according to the law. This is not solely because the United Kingdom has an "unwritten" constitution, though this certainly relates to the question of how the constitution can be changed. Rather, the flexibility comes from the fact that

No Constitution? No Supreme Court? Constitutionality in the United Kingdom

CHAPTER 8, PAGE 184

in the British system, Parliament is sovereign. What does this mean? When Parliament passes a law, it is by definition constitutional, as the legislating body is the highest political and legal authority in the land. Contrast this with the United States, in which the Constitution is the ultimate sovereign authority: even Congress and presidents as must act in accordance with its principles.

So why does Parliament not simply overturn long-standing parts of the British constitution on a whim? Why has there not been massive "zigzagging" in terms of what the constitution means, from one election to the next, as new parties take power and lose power? In reality, custom and tradition prevent Parliament from overturning the founding laws of the polity. Much as American political parties would probably not envision getting rid of core elements of the Constitution such as the Bill of Rights, even if they had the supermajority they would need, so too does the British system exhibit constitutional stability from one elected government to the next.

The unwritten constitution and the fact of parliamentary sovereignty have one more implication for constitutionality in the United Kingdom: there is no role for the judiciary in ruling on whether a law is constitutional. In most countries, some judicial body has the power to rule on whether laws passed by the legislature are compatible with the written constitution. If that judicial body, such as the Supreme Court in the United States, finds a law unconstitutional, it may strike it down. But if Parliament is sovereign and there is no single constitution, there is no place for judicial review. Thus, the United Kingdom had no real "Supreme Court" until the 2000s, and even now its powers are limited to specific questions relating to issues of devolution of power to Scotland and Wales, along with very restricted responsibilities in the area of legal revision.

This limited judiciary should be of interest to Americans accustomed to a different system with its own controversies, especially the debate in the United States about whether unelected judges make law from the bench. This is referred

to as "judicial activism," and there is one clear way to end it: end judicial review. One argument against extensive use of judicial review is that judiciaries remove contentious issues from the public arena. According to this argument, debates about the most fundamental issues in a democracy are now increasingly fought out by ideologues and advocates in front of unelected judges. These issues are thus examined and decided on by small groups and powerful individuals and may not be reflective of broader public opinion. Those arguing against judicial activism would often prefer to have society's most contentious issues decided in legislatures rather than in courts. The United Kingdom prevents judicial activism by granting Parliament unambiguous supremacy over the judiciary. One question for opponents of judicial activism is thus whether they would be willing to sacrifice judicial review. Put another way, judicial review and some judicial activism are the "flip side" of the checks and balances between branches of government: the U.K. system forgoes most of these checks and balances.

The Mother of Parliaments: The United Kingdom and the Westminster Model

CHAPTER 9, PAGE 209

The United Kingdom is called the "Mother of Parliaments," as its Parliament dates back to at least the thirteenth century, when King John convened the nobility of England as an advisory council that controlled the economy. In 1215, the

nobility sensed the King's weak position and need for the support of nobles to raise revenue for the crown, so they insisted on a "Great Charter"—the Magna Carta—and thereby secured various rights with respect to property and

requirements for royal consultation of the nobles. Since that time, Parliament has steadily gained power relative to the monarch, most notably beginning in the seventeenth century with the English Civil Wars and their aftermath

CASE STUDY (continued)

The Mother of Parliaments: The United Kingdom and the Westminster Model

CHAPTER 9, PAGE 209

(1642–1660), and with the Glorious Revolution of 1688. Initially comprised of nobles (lords) and later also of commoners, these Parliaments evolved from advisory councils to become powerful legislatures that eventually asserted their sovereignty over the monarch. These origins can still be seen today in the existence of the House of Commons and the House of Lords.

From these origins has come the system known worldwide as the Westminster system, after the London neighborhood where the government resides. Parliament is considered the country's supreme and sovereign political power (see preceding section on "Regime and Political Institutions"). While parliamentary sovereignty is the central fact of the United Kingdom's political system, a variety of institutional mechanisms gives the executive substantial power to push legislation through Parliament. The legislature votes, but the cabinet and the prime minister forward most legislation, on the assumption that the "backbenchers" in the governing party will support the government's proposal. This model of parliamentary democracy has been

used by countries around the world, not least because of the influence of Britain's colonial empire on many of today's independent countries, from the giant India to tiny islands in the Caribbean.

In the British parliamentary model, the House of Commons is now the dominant chamber. It houses the executive branch of the prime minister and the cabinet and has almost sole responsibility for passing laws, approving budgets, and holding the executive accountable; it can cause the government to fall by a vote of no confidence. Members of the House of Commons are chosen in single-member districts, in a "first-past-the-post" system in which the largest number of votes in a district suffices to elect a member of parliament (MP), even if this is only a plurality and not a majority. This electoral system is widely viewed as favoring the largest parties and punishing smaller parties.

The House of Lords is marginal by contrast, as is the monarchy. Though they were the founding body of Parliament, Lords progressively lost power to Commons over the centuries as the United Kingdom modernized and expanded

the franchise. Lords now possess some limited ability to slow Commons' policymaking process by requesting further review. Major reforms in 1999 dramatically reduced the number of hereditary lords, and debate continues about eliminating hereditary peerages entirely. The queen or king, meanwhile, retains powers to invite parties to form a government or accept a resignation, but these are almost purely ceremonial.

This Westminster parliamentary system is partially emulated in many other countries, though some countries established their own parliaments and assemblies independently of the United Kingdom in their early histories. While the United Kingdom and its Parliament may have been the Mother of Parliaments, there are few other places that precisely follow the House of Commons/ House of Lords model; in most places with bicameral legislatures, the role of the upper chamber is more explicitly territorial, representing states, provinces, or regions. The lower chambers around the world, meanwhile, are elected in a variety of different electoral processes, as chapter 9 shows.

CASE STUDY

National Identity in the United Kingdom

CHAPTER 13, PAGE 311

Many scholars see English nationalism as having developed early. Indeed, some see England as the first national society (Hastings 1997; Greenfeld 1992).

Others see it as the first *modern* nationalism (Kohn 1944). Still others see English nationalism as developing rather late (Kumar 2003). As in all cases, this

depends on how one defines "nationalism." Those who see English nationalism as developing early see it as linked to a number of prominent features of early modern English society, especially the distinctively modern political philosophy produced in the seventeenth century as well as the civil wars and the "Glorious Revolution" discussed earlier.

According to one major argument, English nationalism emerged in Tudor England and helped to resolve the status-inconsistency of upwardly mobile English persons favored by the Tudor monarchs (Greenfeld 1992). Before this, the word *nation* had referred to elite groups. Basically, defining England as a nation amounted to bestowing a kind of status on socially mobile English persons as a result of their membership. English nationalism was helped and hindered by a variety of actors. Queen Elizabeth seems to have promoted it, and Mary to have opposed it. English Protestantism contributed to its spread across society and down the social hierarchy.

Nationalism was clearly institutionalized as one of the main ways in which the state would legitimate itself by the establishment of constitutional monarchy in the late seventeenth century. One thing that had not been decided once and for all, though, was the composition of the body of the nation itself. Over the course of the "long eighteenth century," British, rather than English, nationalism was broadened to include the Scottish and Northern Irish (Colley 1992). In institutional terms, this was accomplished when union was established in 1707. In cultural terms, though, it is unclear to what extent it was successful.

Irish nationalism gained strength with the movement of the United Irishmen in the late eighteenth century and

underwent another revival in the late nineteenth and early twentieth centuries. Ireland was granted "home rule" status in 1912, but civil conflict developed, as the society was divided between those who favored an independent, Catholic Ireland and those (often Protestant) who favored continuing political ties to Britain. An insurrection led, finally, to the establishment of the (still dependent) Irish Free State in 1921, with its 1937 constitution to follow and its achievement of full independence, as the Republic of Ireland, in 1949.

However, Northern Ireland remained (and remains to this day) part of the United Kingdom. Throughout the late twentieth century, considerable violence was perpetrated by supporters of unification of the north with the Republic and supporters of continued ties to England. The Irish Republican Army (IRA) carried out terrorist bombings both in Northern Ireland and in England itself, and both sides carried out targeted assassinations and torture. A peace process was initiated in the 1990s and yielded agreements in the 2000s. It has been largely successful in ending the violence.

Scottish and Welsh national identities also underwent resurgence beginning in the late nineteenth century. Initially, many of these efforts were focused on the preservation of cultural traditions, styles of life, and language. Some came to view British identity as the imposition of English "internal colonialism" (Hechter 1975). In recent years, resurgent regional (or perhaps national) identities among some of these groups, particularly the Scottish, have led to efforts to decentralize authority and to establish

some degree of regional autonomy (a process that bears useful comparison with somewhat similar developments in Spain). Scotland voted to create its own parliament and Wales its own assembly in 1997. In 2014, a referendum on Scottish independence failed, but many had expected it to succeed. There is some question about whether pushes toward greater autonomy or independence will surge again in Scotland and Northern Ireland in the wake of the decision by the United Kingdom to leave the European Union, since those regions of the country (along with much of Metropolitan London) voted strongly in favor of remaining in the EU.

The predominant tradition of nationalism in the United Kingdom, according to most analysts, has been civic. This, however, should be qualified. In the early modern period, national membership might have been civic in the sense of being open to some, but there were clear boundaries established between English nationals and members of "outgroups"—most notably the Irish, American Indians, and African slaves. English nationalism's civic character, according to many analysts, was on display in the gradual process via which Great Britain or the United Kingdom was formed. That is, an ideal of "Britishness" developed that was inclusive of (at least some) Welsh, Scottish, and Northern Irish persons. Its civic character was also on display, paradoxically, in the United Kingdom's imperial identity. The empire, it was important to note, like all of European colonialism, was an important carrier of national identity, and a spur to the development of modern national identities in much of the colonial world.

National Identity in the United Kingdom
CHAPTER 13, PAGE 311

It spread national identity through providing an example, but also through fomenting resistance (Calhoun 1997: 108–110).

Among other things, the British case demonstrates that civic nationalism, while existing in tension with racism, is nevertheless compatible with and can reinforce ethnic hierarchies of various kinds. More recently, as in a number of other countries whose national identities have been understood to be civic, there has been some discussion of whether civic identity is being replaced by a multicultural model. Some have maintained that multiculturalism *is* civic or is broadly consistent with civic political traditions (Modood 2007).

In addition, as in most cases of civic nationalism, one sees countercurrents that dispute the civic conception of nationhood and propose an ethnic one in its place. In recent years in Britain, this is best exemplified by the British National Party, with its sense of "Englishness" as an ethnic category and its xenophobic attitude toward immigrants, particularly Muslims and those from South Asia and the Caribbean. Fortunately, this party remains marginal.

CASE STUDY
Liberal Ideology in the United Kingdom
CHAPTER 15, PAGE 358

The United Kingdom is considered by many to be the birthplace of liberalism. The earliest architects of the ideology, such as John Locke and the Earl of Shaftesbury, wrote and acted in Britain in the tumultuous seventeenth century. Later British thinkers like Adam Smith and David Ricardo developed liberalism's core economic doctrines. In the nineteenth century, the British philosopher John Stuart Mill produced what many consider to be the most forceful and coherent articulation of liberal doctrine: providing clear rationales for both its political dimensions, such as respect for the rights of the individual and representative government, and its economic dimensions, which above all involve reducing state involvement in the economy.

Some argue that the United Kingdom played an important role not only in developing liberalism but also in *spreading* it. British colonialism transmitted liberal ideas to elites in colonial societies. This is very clear in the cases of settler colonialism like today's United States—which is considered liberalism's "lead society" in today's world, essentially replacing the United Kingdom in this connection—as well as British Canada, Australia, and New Zealand but may also be visible in societies like India and in the former British colonial possessions in Africa and East Asia.

Some would argue that after the Second World War, liberalism went into partial retreat in Britain. It is true that the Labour Party, which dominated for several decades, blended liberalism and socialism into "social democracy." Perhaps the most notable change was the establishment of the National Health Service in 1948. Old-fashioned liberals criticized the creation of a universal health care system as paternalistic and threatening to individual choice. More progressive liberals, though, argued that investments in human capital and the maintenance of basic protections against serious deprivation are perfectly consistent with and even help to fulfill the goals and aspirations of a liberal and democratic polity.

Liberals closer to the right of the political spectrum typically would view social democracy as a betrayal, or at least a watering down, of liberal principles. Those on the radical left, however, view the liberalism of the Labour Party as conservative and reactionary. Beginning in the 1990s, with the rise of Tony Blair's "Third Way" leadership strategy in the Labour Party, the British social democrats showed themselves to remain clearly in the liberal camp. In more recent years, under Jeremy Corbyn's leadership, Labour has moved to the left, and ideological debate continues in the Labour Party (and in the UK more generally).

Research Prompts

1. Compare and contrast state formation in the United Kingdom and France. What is similar and what is different about the timing and nature of state-building in each case?

2. Compare and contrast the United States, the United Kingdom, and one other case on the question of judicial review. Be attentive to *why* you select that other case. In the cases you chose, what are the relative consequences of having or not having judicial review? What conclusions can you draw about the costs and benefits of judicial review?

3. Analyze in comparative perspective the construction of the welfare state in the United Kingdom after the Second World War. What are the major implications of the fact that it was the Labour Party that constructed it? How does this compare to the American and French cases?

4. What are the major implications of Britain's development history for *today's* developing countries? Can these countries simply repeat Britain's steps? Why or why not?

5. Some scholars say national identity in the United Kingdom developed in the sixteenth century, others the seventeenth, others the eighteenth, and some even later. As comparative political analysts, how do we decide? Stake out an argument for a definition of national identity, and design a project exploring when this identity emerged in the United Kingdom.

United States

Key Features of the Contemporary United States

Population:	326, 625, 791 (estimate, July 2017)
Area:	9,833,517 sq km
Head of State:	Donald J. Trump (president, January 20, 2017–)
Head of Government:	Donald J. Trump (president, January 20, 2017–)
Capital:	Washington, DC
Year of Independence:	1776/1783
Year of Current Constitution:	1787 (ratified 1788)
Languages:	English; many others, including most prominently Spanish, other Asian and European languages
GDP per Capita:	$57,400 (*CIA World Factbook* estimate, 2016)
Human Development Index Ranking (2016):	10th (very high human development)

Sources: *CIA World Factbook;* World Bank World Development Indicators; United Nations *Human Development Report 2016.*

Introduction

If you were taking this course several decades ago, you would likely find the institutions and political culture of the United States held up as the benchmark against which the politics of other countries could be compared (and, perhaps, judged). On one hand this is understandable. If you are a student in a university in the United States, there is a reasonably high likelihood that you already have some familiarity with the basic political features of this society. If this is the case, it is natural that you would use this knowledge as you make comparisons. At the same time, we need to be careful to not implicitly assume that U.S. politics is the model toward which other societies are (or should be) headed or the standard against which they should be judged. It is, of course, perfectly appropriate for us to draw whatever value judgments we like about such matters as citizens (pro or con), but as social scientists, our job is to bracket any such judgments.

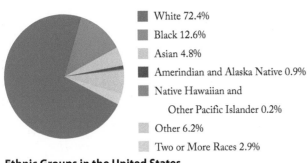

- White 72.4%
- Black 12.6%
- Asian 4.8%
- Amerindian and Alaska Native 0.9%
- Native Hawaiian and Other Pacific Islander 0.2%
- Other 6.2%
- Two or More Races 2.9%

Ethnic Groups in the United States

Note that Hispanics, not captured here as a group because of the categories used when data is collected in the United States, are estimated to constitute about 16.3 percent of the population. Most persons of Hispanic ancestry or ethnic identification show up here in either the "white" or "black" categories.
Source: CIA World Factbook.

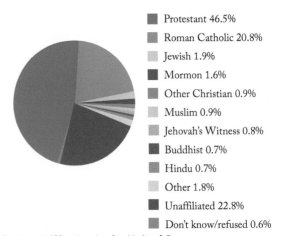

- Protestant 46.5%
- Roman Catholic 20.8%
- Jewish 1.9%
- Mormon 1.6%
- Other Christian 0.9%
- Muslim 0.9%
- Jehovah's Witness 0.8%
- Buddhist 0.7%
- Hindu 0.7%
- Other 1.8%
- Unaffiliated 22.8%
- Don't know/refused 0.6%

Religious Affiliation in the United States

Source: CIA World Factbook.

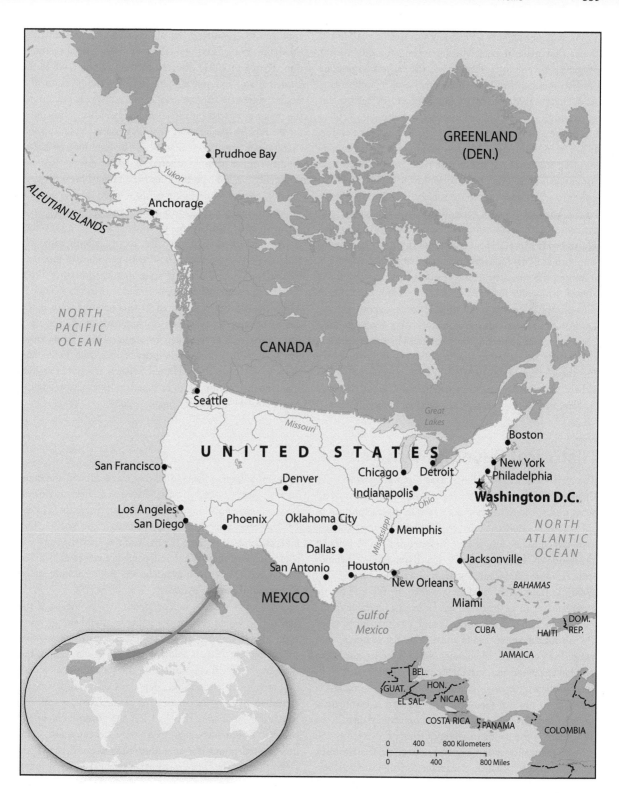

GREENLAND
(DEN.)

Prudhoe Bay

Yukon

Anchorage

ALEUTIAN ISLANDS

NORTH PACIFIC OCEAN

CANADA

Missouri

Seattle

Great Lakes

Boston

San Francisco

Chicago Detroit New York
Philadelphia

UNITED STATES

Denver Indianapolis

Ohio ★ Washington D.C.

Los Angeles

San Diego

Phoenix

Oklahoma City

Dallas

Memphis

NORTH ATLANTIC OCEAN

San Antonio

Houston

Jacksonville

New Orleans

Miami

BAHAMAS

MEXICO

Gulf of Mexico

CUBA

DOM. REP.

HAITI

JAMAICA

BEL.

GUAT.

HON.

EL SAL.

NICAR.

COSTA RICA PANAMA

COLOMBIA

Mississippi

0   400   800 Kilometers
0   400   800 Miles

As such, let us note several key features of the United States that make it especially interesting for the student of comparative politics. First, it was the earliest large-scale modern society to embrace democracy and republicanism. As such, it was viewed by its founders and by subsequent generations as a kind of experiment; and although it is no longer the only such experiment, we can still view it as one. It has been relatively stable, governed under a single constitution for centuries, and it rose from being a successful commercial and agricultural society to a major industrial power to a key "post-industrial" society. It is also, at present, largely without peers in terms of geopolitical power and influence. Second, as scholars since Tocqueville (see also Hartz 1955; Lipset 1963) have stressed, the United States was born as a "new" society, meaning that it only minimally inherited the social structural features that attenuated the rise of democracy for some time in the European context. This allows us to ask interesting questions about the relationship between historical factors (like long-standing patterns of landownership) and variables like democratization or the formation of liberal political culture, comparing the United States to "Old World" societies. Scholars debate whether and to what extent the United States is "exceptional" in its liberal democracy, its "denominational"

approach to organizing the place of religion in public life (Niebuhr 1929), and its relatively weak socialist tradition (Kaufman 2002). Related to the last point, while the United States has shared with its peers the creation of a welfare state over the last near-century, it stands out among the major advanced industrial and post-industrial societies for the relative weakness of its welfare state. (Note: It is not that its state is weak but that its welfare functions are not as robust as those of some others.)

Finally, while many societies are and have been net destination sites for immigration, the United States, both in its extent and the degree to which this is bound up with the country's identity, largely stands apart in the centrality of immigration in its history. The society is both ethnically and religiously heterogeneous. This periodically produces tension, and waves of large-scale immigration have often been met by waves of xenophobia and intolerance (Kennedy 1999: 14–15). Perhaps related to this heterogeneity is the degree of religious pluralism characteristic of the society, a feature that has been linked by some scholars to its comparatively high levels of religiosity (Iannaccone, Finke, and Stark 1997). Indeed, the United States is far more religious than one might expect it to be based on its level of economic development (Norris and Inglehart 2004).

Historical Development

Today's United States includes areas that were colonized by Spain, the Netherlands, France, and England. Contrary to what students in the United States might expect, for most of the colonial period, the thirteen colonies in North America were not considered the most important of Britain's colonial possessions. Caribbean societies like Barbados and Jamaica were far more significant as sources of wealth (Dunn [1972] 2000), as India later would be. However, by the mid to late eighteenth century, the crown was becoming increasingly interested in its North American colonies as both markets for British manufactured goods and a potential source of revenue. The population of colonial North America had some notable characteristics, varying by region (Fischer 1989). In the Northeast, the original settlers were largely seeking the freedom to practice their religion, and here a commercial society later developed. Land was more evenly distributed here than in the southern colonies (though there was still a lot of inequality), and there was no real quasi-aristocracy. In the southern colonies, plantation agriculture developed.

Here, more large-scale landholding was common, and elites lived a more aristocratic life. Moreover, their origins in Britain itself tended more toward aristocratic groups (Fischer 1989). While some slavery was practiced in the North before independence, it became the basis of much of the southern plantation economy. When independence was established in the United States, the movement was predominantly led by elites from these two regions.

Even after gaining independence, it was unclear if the new nation would survive as a polity or would simply prove vulnerable to disintegration. A number of views about what should replace British colonialism were in circulation, but the new country finally settled on the constitutional system that remains in place to this day; the Constitution was designed to correct the deficiencies of the "Articles of Confederation," a charter that had left the government of the thirteen original colonies excessively decentralized, with little central power (for an authoritative account, see Wood [1969] 1998). The U.S. Constitution established a division of

Historical Development

Timeline

1600s	Establishment of early colonial settlements at Jamestown, Virginia (1607); Plymouth, Massachusetts (1620); and other sites along the Atlantic coast
1754–1763	French and Indian Wars, conflict between English and French settlers, along with Native American allies in present-day United States and Canada
1775	Beginning of American Revolution after years of tension between colonies and British Crown over taxation and representation
1776	Signing of Declaration of Independence
1781	Articles of Confederation take effect as first attempt at independent American government.
1783	Surrender of British forces at Yorktown, Virginia, signifies end of American Revolution.
1787	Constitution drafted; ratified by states in 1788.
1791	Bill of Rights, the first ten amendments to the Constitution, takes effect.
1803	Louisiana Purchase
1812	War with Great Britain, ends in 1815
1820	Missouri Compromise attempts to balance power between northern free states and southern slave states.
1840s	Annexation of Texas and Mexican-American War greatly expand U.S. territory.
1850s	Rising tensions between North and South
1861	Civil War begins.
1863	Emancipation Proclamation
1865	End of Civil War; President Abraham Lincoln assassinated.
1870s	Reconstruction
1880s	Peak of the Gilded Age
1898	Spanish-American War
1916–1918	American involvement in World War I on the side of Allies
1920	Women's suffrage movement results in vote for all adults.
1929	Great Depression begins, lasts through 1930s.
1933–1945	Presidency of Franklin Delano Roosevelt, who champions the New Deal (including Social Security) and leads the United States through most of World War II
1941	United States enters World War II with Japanese bombing of Pearl Harbor, Hawaii.
1945	World War II ends with United States dropping atomic bombs on Japanese cities Hiroshima and Nagasaki.
1950s–1960s	Civil Rights movement, *Brown v. Board of Education* (1954) Supreme Court decision; Civil Rights Act (1964); Voting Rights Act (1965)
1963	Assassination of President John F. Kennedy
1963–1969	Presidency of Lyndon Baines Johnson, who both increases U.S. involvement in the Vietnam War and expands the welfare state via his "Great Society" programs
1969–1974	Presidency of Richard Nixon, which included continued war in Vietnam, partial rapprochement with China, and the decision to float the dollar on currency exchanges rather than pegging its value to gold; Nixon resigned in August 1974 as he faced impeachment for the Watergate Scandal.
1974–1977	Presidency of Gerald Ford, which included the end of the Vietnam War
1977–1981	Presidency of Jimmy Carter, with a renewed emphasis on human rights in foreign policy but economic problems domestically
1981–1989	Presidency of Ronald Reagan, which includes partial retrenchment of the welfare state and a more aggressive foreign policy
1989–1993	Presidency of George H. W. Bush, which includes war in Iraq and end of the Cold War
1993–2001	Presidency of Bill Clinton, which includes notable economic growth and the fiscal solvency of the state, the signing of the North American Free Trade Agreement, and welfare reform
2001–2009	Presidency of George W. Bush, which includes the September 11 attacks; wars in Afghanistan and Iraq; and the financial crisis of 2008, causing a major recession
2009–2017	Presidency of Barack Obama, which includes pass of the Affordable Care Act and ongoing economic difficulties followed by economic recovery.
2017-present	Presidency of Donald Trump

powers across three branches of government and a separation of powers between the central government and the states. The American Constitution became an emblematic example of a framework document that outlines the basic system of governance and establishes the principles of the rule of law that "constitutes" the basic political compact. It is, in a sense, an outline for politics. Comprised of just seven articles and a small number of sections, the entire document fits comfortably onto a handful of pages. Yet it has proved robust enough to withstand over two centuries of change with only twenty-seven amendments, despite major economic and political developments, and several wars that challenged the existence of the United States as a republic.

Some of the amendments to the Constitution have been substantial, and broader social change has altered the United States polity considerably over the years. Here we briefly highlight three main developments in that connection: the extension of suffrage and full participation in the life of the society to groups that were once excluded; the creation of the modern party system that has dominated American politics now for decades; and the growth of the state, and, in particular, of the welfare state in the twentieth century.

Let us begin with the gradual extension of full citizenship. On one hand, with its civic nationalism and its founding declaration that "All men are created equal," the early United States was an example of equality and freedom (Wood [1969] 1998). On the other hand, judged by today's standards, a great deal of exclusion and inequality remained. The constitutional convention failed to ban slavery, leaving such matters, like so much else, up to the states, setting up a major showdown later over this issue. The Amerindian population was largely consigned to the least productive land, and the "rules of the game" were repeatedly changed on them as the United States consistently failed to abide by previous treaty agreements. Women's civil rights were also narrowly circumscribed. Of course, inequality was felt by other groups in other ways, including class inequality, but we focus here very briefly on the experience of African Americans.

Over the course of the nineteenth century, tension built over the persistence of slavery. Abolitionists campaigned against it, while slave owners and their supporters justified it. Presidents and congressmen worked to balance power such that the status quo could persist—in which southern states could continue slavery and northern states could meekly oppose it—but eventually this became impossible. The country's defining event of the nineteenth century, the Civil War (1861–1865), was fought over this issue (for an overview, see McPherson 1988). After four calamitous years, the Union was victorious. In the initial post-war years, African Americans had social and electoral success in a number of southern regions. But much of this depended on the presence of northern troops during Reconstruction, which ended in the late 1870s. After the end of this period, local majority-group actors in the South used force to reestablish exclusive control over political organizations and then wrote explicit racial discrimination into law, creating what was called the "Jim Crow South" with its sharp racial segregation and, in some localities, the threat of non-official (but tolerated) violence against African Americans who in any way seemed to threaten this order.

At the same time, African Americans who moved to northern cities in the "Great Migration" often discovered that discrimination was also present there (for an evocative account, see Wilkerson 2010). Jim Crow segregation only fell in the face of social organizing, social movement activity, and extensive litigation. Indeed, when the federal government, under pressure, began to enforce equal access to voting, education, and other rights in the 1960s, it faced resistance from some southern populations and even from state-level leaders like George Wallace (Patterson 1996: 579–589). It would be a stretch to say that these struggles are over, though tremendous progress has been made, largely as a result of the civil rights movement. Social scientists point to ongoing evidence of job discrimination, substantially lower incomes and asset levels, substantially poorer public health indicators, and higher incarceration rates among African Americans as evidence that both historical legacies and ongoing discrimination remain issues in the country (Brown et al. 2003).

You may be surprised to see that the evolution of the modern party system in the United States is linked to these developments. On one hand, the fact that the United States has a two-party system is partially a function of its "winner take all" approach to elections; but this does not, in and of itself, explain why the two parties have developed as they have and linked themselves to the interests and support of the groups that they have. In the initial years of the republic, the major conflict was between so-called "federalists" and "democratic republicans." The former favored stronger central power (indeed, both groups were proponents of "federalism" as such), a national bank, and so forth; while the latter group felt more strongly about having a weak central government with stronger state and local governments. Over time, the federalists were essentially replaced by the Whigs. The Civil War, though, was a critical juncture. Abraham Lincoln, the candidate of the little-known Republican Party, was elected in 1860; and the party competition that emerged in subsequent years meant that the Democrats would be strong among predominantly white voters in the South and Republicans in the North. Moreover, African American political actors tended to be strongly Republican. This changed in the twentieth century (Kennedy 1999), particularly during the years of the Great Depression, where Franklin Delano Roosevelt's expansion of the welfare state appealed to many groups of minority voters, including many

African Americans, workers, and members of immigrant groups. For a time, there was considerable tension in the Democratic Party between more conservative, often southern, traditionalist party members and supporters of the more "liberal" (in the American sense) trajectory of the Democratic Party in the post-war years. More recently, following Richard Nixon's famous "Southern Strategy" (Patterson 1996: 702, 741–742), the Republicans have, quite ironically, established their strongest base in the South, and regions like the Northeast have become staunchly Democratic—indeed, in the 2008 congressional elections, New England sent *no* Republicans to the House of Representatives.

The welfare state in the United States is not especially robust if you compare it to those found in other advanced industrial societies such as France, Germany, or the Scandinavian countries. Proponents of the welfare state in the United States could, however, point to certain notable achievements. While there had been previous efforts at regulation and improving the conditions of workers and other populations, the American welfare state was really created in Franklin Delano Roosevelt's "New Deal" in the 1930s (Kennedy 1999). This is the period in which social security—the American form of social insurance that both provides retirement benefits and also support in the event of a wage earner's disability or death—was established, along with some forms of housing assistance, periodic relief programs meant to provide work and other forms of assistance during the Great Depression, and increased regulation of the labor market.

The second major period of construction of the American welfare state (Patterson 1996: 524–592) was during the presidency of Lyndon Baines Johnson (1963–1969). Here, major health care programs like Medicare (which provides health care to retirees) and Medicaid (which provides care to some individuals who otherwise could not afford it) were established, as were numerous other social welfare programs such as Head Start and Food Stamps (technically called the Supplemental Nutrition Assistance Program), among others. Beginning in the 1970s, as the U.S. economy faced "stagflation" and other difficulties, a movement known to scholars as "retrenchment" gathered steam, as in some other countries (Prasad 2006).

When Ronald Reagan took office in 1980, he did so after strongly opposing the welfare state features established by the New Deal and the Great Society programs. However, while he scaled back a variety of relief programs, key features of the welfare state persisted. Indeed, it was under the presidency of Democrat Bill Clinton that so-called "welfare"—the Aid to Families with Dependent Children (AFDC) program—was "reformed." That is, it was transformed into the more restrictive Temporary Aid to Needy Families (TANF) program, administered via block grants to the states and no longer classified as an "entitlement" (Patterson 2005: 374–376). This pattern of mid-century welfare state expansion followed by retrenchment beginning in the 1970s is common to other advanced industrial societies, even if the U.S. welfare state was relatively weak to begin with. Interestingly, though, recent politics has involved both the establishment of a major health care bill that would extend coverage to most of the U.S. population (something always conspicuously absent from the U.S. welfare state) *and* a renewed effort by other actors to reform those aspects of the welfare state that have, until now, largely been strongly defended by both parties: Medicare and Social Security. In short, the issues that have animated the debate about the American welfare state are still very much part of public discussion.

Regime and Political Institutions

The predominant feature of the American political system is the separation of powers among various levels and institutions of government. This includes not only the set of "checks and balances" between the legislature, the executive, and the judiciary, but also the separation of power between the federal government and the fifty states. At the federal level, the United States Congress is a bicameral legislature comprised of a House of Representatives and the Senate; the Representatives in the House are selected in one of 435 districts around the country, with each district representing over a half-million Americans. Every state has a minimum of one seat for a Representative in the House, and the number of districts per state ranges from one in the least populous states (such as Wyoming) to fifty-three in California. This representation in the House, which is roughly proportional to a state's population, is counterbalanced by the two Senators for each state. Either chamber can propose bills it wishes to see become law, but the bill must pass both houses of Congress, then be signed into law by the president. Alternatively, the president can choose to veto the bill, which can then be overturned only by a two-thirds majority vote in both houses of Congress. In addition, the federal judiciary can strike down laws it deems unconstitutional. This provides the judicial check on the other branches; the check on the judiciary in turn is

Regime and Political Institutions

Regime	Federal republic, democratically elected
Administrative Divisions	Fifty states, each of which has counties, cities, towns, etc. Also District of Columbia (federal capital) and several overseas territories and dependencies.
Executive Branch	President
Selection of Executive	Elected by "electoral college," with delegates awarded depending on popular vote in each state or electoral district
Legislative Branch	Bicameral Congress House of Representatives (lower chamber) elected in single-member districts Senate (upper chamber), two senators per state
Judicial Branch	Federal court system led by Supreme Court with powers of Constitutional review
Political Party System	Two-party system: Democratic Party, Republican Party

that its judges are nominated by the president and approved by the Senate.

Alongside these checks and balances in the policymaking process, the United States also exhibits a separation of powers between the federal (central) government and the states. The United States was an early leader in establishing the principle of federalism, in which both levels of government have significant constitutional authority. One of the key aspects of the Constitution is the reservation of "residual" powers to the states, meaning the states have authority over issues not expressly granted to the federal government. This question of "states' rights" relative to federal law was the crux of the issue of slavery up through the Civil War, and to this day many of the biggest debates in American politics are over whether issues ranging from welfare to abortion law should be the responsibility of the federal or state governments. States and local governments have a great deal of responsibility in social services. States do much of the work in administering programs for the poor (such as Medicaid and income support), while localities have especially significant responsibilities in education. More people participate in elected offices on school boards than any other position. Local executives such as mayors also oversee services such as local roads, sanitation, and the police.

Political Culture

American political culture, like political culture everywhere, has multiple streams and features. However, certain key themes stand out and have been discussed at length by scholars interested in this case. These include a tradition of skepticism of governmental authority, which extends back at least to the revolutionary era (though Americans have often pursued governmental action as well); so-called "rugged individualism"; the much-discussed American "frontier mentality"; an isolationist tendency with respect to foreign policy, but alongside an important militarist strain; and the idea of the "American dream" with the associated idea of meritocratic equality. Almond and Verba (1963) argued that the United States was a case exhibiting strong "civic culture," though in recent years some have worried about whether this is still true (Putnam 2000).

The tradition of skepticism of governmental authority may, to some extent, have its origins in the early stages of colonialism. In the New England colonies in particular, the population was, in the initial stages, largely there for reasons of religious intolerance back home. They lived in fear of English authorities, and they established strong traditions of community reliance and local self-governance. At the very least, later Americans could look back to thinkers like Roger Williams and see them as anticipating their own skepticism of government involvement in private life (Miller [1953] 1983a, [1954] 1983b). This was certainly true of key members of the revolutionary generation, who objected not only to taxation without consent but also to the use of force British authorities exercised in suppressing their protests. (Some accounts of the revolution, such as Nash 1979, stress additional grievances and point to differences in social class.) When the country became independent, its founders clearly did have in mind "limited government," and government powers expanded in several key stages and in response to crises and changing conditions in subsequent years. Still, having founding documents and traditions that so clearly express skepticism of government means that the political culture, no matter how much it changes, always has these points of reference. As anyone who even distantly follows American politics could attest, these issues remain much discussed.

Several of the other commonly cited features of American political culture noted previously are related to this idea. The notion of "rugged individualism" carries the image of single persons and small families struggling, without aid, against nature. In general, comparative researchers find a strong individualist tendency in American political culture. This links to Americans' understanding of the meritocratic character of the American class structure. Americans, unlike Europeans, tend to believe that individuals are largely responsible for where they end up in life: society is basically fair, and everyone who

is talented and works hard has a good chance of getting ahead. Indeed, Americans often believe that this alleged quality of the American class structure is what sets the country apart (thus the "American dream"), even though considerable research shows that, at least in recent years, the American class structure is no more open than the class structures of most Western European countries (Haskins, Isaacs, and Sawhill 2008). The notion of the "frontier mentality" was much discussed after a famous argument put forward by historian Frederick Jackson Turner (1921) in the late nineteenth and early twentieth centuries. Turner and those influenced by him worried about what would become of Americans' energies now that the frontier was gone (because westward expansion was completed). This idea is based on the recognition that Americans have historically thought of themselves in relation to founding myths about struggle against nature; making bountiful an (allegedly) unpopulated land; and, again, relying on themselves in this struggle. The isolationist impulse, discussed more in one of the case studies that follow ("The United States and the World"), also is related and also has long historical roots.

Political Economy

The United States is the world's largest economy as of 2017, despite recent challenges and the rise of China. The twentieth century was a time of dramatic expansion of American manufacturing, epitomized by the rise of the automobile industry (Kennedy 1999: 20–21). As the United States became the undisputed industrial leader of the free world after World War II, it also became the world's leading voice for capitalism. Economic setbacks came with the Great Depression of the 1930s, the oil crises of the 1970s, and the global financial crisis of 2007–2009, but the American economy continues as a world leader. By the twenty-first century, the economy had shifted away from low-skilled, labor-intensive manufacturing, due to automation and increasing imports of products built overseas (and, therefore, the outsourcing of much industrial work to developing countries). The economy has become more "service-oriented," including many professionals with college degrees and many working in retail sales. Inequality has increased notably as these trends have unfolded (Patterson 2005: 351–353).

The United States does not have the highest GDP per capita, as it lags behind several small countries that are banking centers and several oil-exporting countries with small populations. Moreover, inequality in the United States is high compared to other wealthy countries, and more than

10 percent of the population falls below the poverty line. This suggests that by many measures, the issue of development is relevant even in this seemingly powerful economy. Health indicators and education lag behind many countries in both Europe and Asia; and the United States now faces a major challenge in the so-called "opioid epidemic," with high and increasing rates of addiction to dangerous drugs.

In addition, the society faces challenges of social and economic inequality. Some minority groups, such as African Americans, have economic and social indicators that are much worse off than the national average. This is also clear with respect to social class. For example, education level—a proxy for class—is negatively correlated with the likelihood that Americans will die from chronic disease or even suffer injuries (Berkman 2004).

The American economy has now significantly recovered from the deep recession of 2007 to 2009. Unemployment has returned to reasonable levels (4.9% in 2016, according to the *CIA World Factbook*). There is some cause for concern about the size and sustainability of the national debt, particularly after recent tax cuts, and some are concerned that the imbalance may worsen as a result of continued low taxes and increased spending for an aging population in the coming years.

Despite these many challenges, the American economy is diversified and robust in many areas, and it remains the envy of many countries around the world. It is home to many of the largest and most successful corporations in the world and is a leading center of technological innovation and finance. The United States also features countless small businesses and is renowned for its culture of entrepreneurship. Finally, the country is widely seen as having much of the "soft infrastructure" that makes for a resilient and vibrant economy: protection of property rights, deep labor and capital markets, and clusters of innovation and knowledge. As a result, the United States continues to draw talent and capital investment from around the world, and it looks set to remain a global economic powerhouse into the future.

CASE STUDIES

CASE STUDY
Did Free Markets Help the United States Get Rich? Will They in the Future?

CHAPTER 4, PAGE 73

Development is a process that unfolds over time, and it can be helpful to consider a range of different cases in comparative perspective, whether these are different countries at the same point in time, the same country at different points in time, or other possibilities. As a thought experiment, consider this statement about the usefulness of tariffs (taxes on foreign goods) and subsidies (or government support for domestic producers), and guess in which country the government published this report advocating for state intervention:

> [We should] place tariffs on foreign goods of those products we wish to encourage, and to apply the proceeds of that tariff as a subsidy on the production or manufacture in [this country]. In this way, our companies have every advantage in their production.

Notice the anti-free-market tone. Is this a statement from Russia? Communist China? Actually, this excerpt (slightly modified for clarity) is from one of the Founding Fathers of the United States:

Alexander Hamilton ([1791] 1828: pp. 110–111). Why would Hamilton argue against free markets and for protectionism and active government promotion of industry? Because the United States was a backward country when he was writing in 1791. The world's leading economy was Great Britain, which had led the world into the Industrial Revolution. In fact, powerful Britain was the leading advocate for free trade in the nineteenth century.

Partly due to the protectionist logic laid out by Hamilton, the United States relied heavily on tariffs for government revenues through the nineteenth century and up to the 1930s. As early as the 1800s, northern industry in the United States sought to protect its production by imposing higher tariffs on imported goods. This culminated in the sky-high Tariff of 1828, the highest rates in American history. The southern states abhorred the tariffs, which raised prices of imported goods, and called it the "Tariff of Abominations." The resulting dispute contributed to rising tensions before the Civil War. While tariff rates later declined, the United States passed the Smoot–Hawley tariff a century later,

which was interpreted as contributing to the Great Depression.

The United States became the leading advocate for free trade only after World War II. That is, the United States pushed for free trade when it was the preeminent economic power in the world. One theory is that wealthy countries like to "kick away the ladder" after they have climbed it. That is, the United States and other wealthy countries succeeded under protectionism, but once they became dominant powers, they sought to establish rules that favor the powerful and make everyone else live by them. This would explain not only the American conversion to a pro-free-trade stance, but also the British preference for free trade in the nineteenth century.

Contemporary American economic policy still features a protectionist streak and heavy government spending in several areas, and not only due to the financial crisis of the late 2000s. For example, the defense industry depends heavily on government contracts, and the government is a major consumer of pharmaceuticals and medical devices

CASE STUDY (continued)

Did Free Markets Help the United States Get Rich? Will They in the Future?

CHAPTER 4, PAGE 73

through its Medicare program that provides health care to senior citizens. The U.S. protectionist impulse can be seen especially in debates over the rise of China, which is often accused of unfair trade practices. American policymakers and voters routinely lament the low wages, lack of worker protections, and environmental abuses of Chinese production, all of which lower the prices of Chinese goods and can make American goods less competitive. A common response is to advocate for protection of American jobs by putting barriers on Chinese goods.

Countries change their development strategies over time, with some periods involving much more state intervention and other periods less so. Perspectives on free trade also tend to change depending on a country's economic circumstances. It is worth remembering that the United States was not always a paragon of free markets, and it is possible that in the future too it may have a much less favorable view of whether free markets are the road to wealth.

CASE STUDY

Is American Democracy in Trouble?

CHAPTER 6, PAGE 142

Many of today's most robust democracies have had tumultuous histories. Think, for instance, of Germany or France, which over the last two centuries have seen both democratic and authoritarian regimes (and, in the former case, perhaps the most notorious totalitarian regime in modern history). Other countries, though, saw slow and steady democratization over time. The United Kingdom and the United States are sometimes thought of as examples of the latter pattern. This means that polities like the United States are securely democratic, right?

Relatively few political scientists probably fear the imminent demise of American democracy, but scholars do vary considerably in terms of *how* safely institutionalized they consider that democracy to be. Think, for a moment, about what the different theories of democracy discussed in chapter 6 might

suggest about this case. What are the implications of each theory for the *survival* of democratic regimes? What risk factors might increase the probability of democratic decay?

One worry that some scholars have voiced concerns rising income inequality (e.g., Hacker and Pierson 2010). The gap between rich and poor Americans is much wider today than it was several decades ago. According to scholars like Pierson and Hacker, this change has dangerous implications, and we might expect it to be self-reinforcing because the "beneficiaries" of expanding income inequality exert disproportionate influence in the political process and might block efforts to reduce inequality. This concern links to traditional "modernization" theories of democracy like that of Lipset (1959, 1960) discussed in chapter 6. Recall that Lipset saw a strong middle class as the backbone of democratic regimes, seeing economic

development as, in part, acting indirectly to promote democratization through creating and sustaining a middle class. If the middle class shrinks or its position weakens, an implication of the theory would be that one of democracy's "social requisites" is in decline.

Another worry links to a different theory of democratization discussed in the chapter, the "cultural" theory. Some years ago, political scientist Robert Putnam (2000; for a similar set of concerns see Bellah, Madsen, Sullivan, Swidler, and Tipton 1985) published a book called *Bowling Alone* in which he argued that the habits, tastes, and modes of participation that had been operative in the United States since its founding, and which had been documented by Alexis de Tocqueville in the nineteenth century, were in decline. According to Putnam, the voluntary tendencies that were conducive to robust civic participation were giving way to individualism. The implication, again, is that the failure to practice democratic habits—or to maintain a democratic culture of civic participation—could undermine democratic institutions.

A third worry, which may overlap with the first two, concerns the rise of party sorting or "partisan sorting," often labeled "political polarization." As political scientists have documented (Fiorina and Abrams 2008; Mason 2015), in recent decades the American public's ideological preferences more closely mirror those of the parties with which they identify. One consequence is that there may be less ideological variation within parties than there used to be. Another may be that people (individual voters as well as politicians) may be more likely to adopt policy preferences (or vote for candidates) merely on the basis of party. In other

words, it is possible that more people now think "what is my party, what is my party's position, I'll adopt that position" rather than "what is my position, which party or candidate should I support in this election?" In addition, some worry that people are increasingly disproportionately likely to know and discuss politics with those who share their views.

These worries are not shared by all scholars (for a critique of Putnam's argument, e.g., see Ladd 1999). Some argue for the resilience of American democratic institutions in the face of these changes; and some, in fact, suggest that scholars like Hacker, Pierson, and Putnam exaggerate the trends in question. Increasingly, though, many political scientists have expressed concerns about the ability of institutions to stand up to executives with authoritarian tendencies (globally, as

with many cases of contemporary populism discussed in chapter 15, but also in the contemporary United States). In an important recent book, Levitsky and Ziblatt (2018) study cases where democratic regimes have given way to authoritarian ones *not* via military takeover but through democratic institutions themselves. They argue that constitutional checks and balances aren't enough to ensure the continued vitality of democracy. Instead, political parties need to work as gatekeepers to keep extremists from capturing the executive, and certain basic political norms need to be maintained to prevent would-be authoritarians, once in power, from capturing institutions and harassing opponents, a requirement likely to be more difficult to meet in the context of high partisan polarization and a fragmented media landscape.

The federal judiciary in the United States has a significant role in the interpretation of law and in ruling whether laws are constitutional. This role has led to accusations of "judicial activism." Because judges can invalidate laws or add new interpretations to laws passed by Congress, some argue that the judiciary is too powerful and that "unelected judges are legislating from the bench." Examples of controversial judicial decisions can be found in the federal courts,

but they are not limited to these; they also happen at the state level as well, such as when the top courts in states such as Massachusetts, Iowa, and New Jersey ruled that the state must extend same-sex marriage rights or equivalent benefits to gay couples.

Over the years, certain key rulings by the United States Supreme Court have proven especially noteworthy. The first of these, and the one decision that gave power to subsequent decisions, was

Marbury v. Madison in 1803. This ruling asserted the power of judicial review, a power the Supreme Court found to be implicit in the structure of government established in the Constitution. Several other key decisions in United States Supreme Court history can shed light on the question of judicial activism.

One of the leading decisions in which judicial action preceded legislative action was the famous *Brown v. Board of Education* (1954) decision. This unanimous

CASE STUDY (continued)
Is Judicial Activism in the United States a Problem?

CHAPTER 8, PAGE 195

(9–0) decision outlawed official racial segregation in public schools. The ruling predated and anticipated the civil rights achievements of the 1960s, with the Supreme Court reflecting a growing social consensus among a majority of Americans that racial segregation should be outlawed. This ruling had several elements of judicial activism: it took action when Congress had not done so, it substantially limited the extent to which states could make their own determinations about education, and it also essentially overturned the longstanding precedent of one of the Supreme Court's most notorious decisions: *Plessy v. Ferguson* (1896), which had established that "separate but equal" provisions for different races were constitutionally permissible. This had allowed racial segregation to persist. While arguably a textbook instance of judicial activism, *Brown v. Board of Education* is also widely seen as one of the Supreme Court's proudest moments.

Other controversial rulings in the history of the U.S. Supreme Court have also raised the question of judicial activism on hot-button issues such as slavery in the nineteenth century, and in the twentieth century issues of contraception, abortion, and affirmative action. The case *Griswold v. Connecticut* (in 1965) was concerned with contraception laws; the Supreme Court ruled that individuals have a constitutional right of privacy, based on a combined reading of a number of amendments to the Constitution. No specific "right to privacy" is found there, but the ruling stated that this right could be inferred from the "penumbras and emanations" of other foundational rights. Critics saw this as a case of an activist court run amok, inventing or "discovering" rights that were not explicitly established in the Constitution. Less than a decade later, *Roe v. Wade* (in 1973) ruled that women have a conditional right to abortion, depending on the trimester of pregnancy—with few restrictions in the first three months, case-by-case consideration in the second three months, and significant restrictions (such as jeopardizing the life of the mother) in the final three months. Another case that drew mixed reactions was *Bush v. Gore* (in 2000), which ruled that the state of Florida must stop its recount of the vote tally from the razor-thin 2000 presidential election between George W. Bush and Al Gore. This effectively ended the election dispute and resulted in George W. Bush's inauguration as president.

In essence, most major Supreme Court decisions of great consequence are likely to have elements of judicial activism, depending on one's definition of the term. In fact, many critics of judicial activism do not wish to criticize all court action, and would often be happy with courts taking consequential decisions that overturn laws and statutes. Rather, critics often have an interpretation of the Constitution in mind, and wish judges would rule according to that interpretation. Perhaps they view the Constitution as allowing only quite limited government and lament courts that read new rights into the Constitution. Or perhaps they view the Constitution as enabling many tacit rights for individuals (such as privacy, e.g.) and regret courts that make decisions they perceive as limiting these rights. That is, many critics of judicial activism in some decisions may look for an active judiciary in other areas; the debate is as often over conceptions of rights as it is over what the judiciary should and should not do.

CASE STUDY
The United States Congress: Dysfunctional or Functioning by Design?

CHAPTER 9, PAGE 220

The "Founding Fathers" of the United States developed an intricate political compromise designed to satisfy both the larger and smaller of the thirteen original colonies that came together to create the new nation. Led by James Madison, considered the "Father of the Constitution," the founders reserved considerable rights to those states that the central government could not infringe on and backed up these rights in the form of a Senate where each state was to have equal representation, regardless of population. While the idea of compromise between central and state power was crucial in the early development of the country, the balance of that power has been controversial for the entire history of the republic. Long after the acrimonious battles at the founding over states' rights, and long after the Civil War settled the question of state attempts to nullify federal law, the debate continues.

Some of the leading debates about how representative democracy truly is in the United States focus on the functioning of Congress, and especially the Senate. Consider one question: would it seem democratic if elected officials representing about 12 percent of the population could block legislation that the other 88 percent wants? Probably not, assuming the law in question does not violate any basic civil rights. Yet this could happen in the United States, at least in theory. The Senate features significant malapportionment and provides major leverage to smaller and less populous (often rural) states. There are historical reasons for this, of course: the "Great Compromise" at the founding of the American republic created a bicameral congress and gave the more populous states more representation in the House of Representatives, while protecting the interests of the less populous states by creating a Senate in which each state would have two Senators.

The power of a minority in the Senate can be further enhanced by certain rules that have been applied with increasing frequency. For instance, even a minority of Senators can block legislation, given the use of such rules as the "filibuster" (or more

formally, a cloture vote), which requires a supermajority of sixty out of one hundred senators to end a debate and move to a vote on a bill. In the most extreme scenario, legislation in the United States could be stopped by forty-one senators representing only about 12 percent of the country's population. While this particular configuration is unlikely, it is clear that groups of as few as forty senators representing well under half the population have blocked legislation favored by senators representing a large majority of the population. In a sense, tolerating the possibility of gridlock and inaction is the flip side of encouraging extensive negotiation and requiring supermajorities to pass legislation.

Representation in the House of Representatives is also subject to maneuvers that can distort representation. The districts for elections depend on the results of the Census, which takes place every ten years. As states grow in population, they may be awarded additional seats among the 435 in the House, while these seats are taken away from states declining in population. This realignment gives rise to redistricting, or the drawing of new maps that define the boundaries of congressional districts. The shape of districts is a hotly contested issue since it shapes the likelihood of who is elected to office. For instance, imagine an urban area shaped like a big circle that is large enough to merit two congressional seats. Say the population of the whole area is comprised of 40 percent Democrats, mostly located in the urban center, and 60 percent Republicans, mostly located in the suburbs that ring the city. Should the mapmakers draw districts

that cut the circle in half along its diameter with a straight line? Or should they create one congressional district for the urban center and one for the suburbs? The "straight line" solution might well give two Republican seats (since Republicans would outnumber Democrats by a ratio of 3:2 on either side of the dividing line), while the "center and ring" solution would probably give one seat in the House to each party (since the Democrats would dominate in the inner city and the Republicans in the district in the suburbs). The chosen solution may be determined by which party (if either) controls the redistricting process. In some instances, the mapmaking becomes an elaborate process known as "gerrymandering" in which incumbents who see an advantage in drawing a map a certain way create districts with bizarre shapes designed to help themselves and/or hurt their political opponents.

The design of the two chambers of Congress was thus deliberate and useful, but it has also permitted results that have led some to say the institutions are dysfunctional (see Mann and Ornstein 2008). Representation in the United States Congress was conceived to protect the rights of individuals and political minorities as well as the principle of federalism, but the institutions designed to do so also have certain features that advantage incumbents and promote partisanship. Most recently, major legislation—such as the Affordable Care Act of 2010 (so-called Obamacare) and the tax cuts of 2017—were passed without a single vote from a member of the opposition party.

"The Most Powerful Person in the World"?
Checks on American Presidents

CHAPTER 10, PAGE 234

While the president of the United States has long been considered the "Leader of the Free World," these presidents are part of a system of formal checks and balances between executives and the other branches. In fact, while presidents have the advantage of the "bully pulpit" of the office and can push for policies they prefer, they are quite constrained by the institutional environment in which they operate. Congress has responsibility for proposing legislation, and while the president can choose to sign bills into law or opt to veto a bill, the president cannot secure passage of any law without the backing of a majority in both houses of Congress. By contrast, the Congress can override the president's veto with a two-thirds majority in both houses. Congress also controls the "purse" and can revoke the spending authority of the executive branch in some circumstances, and it is responsible for executive oversight; for example, it can demand that executive branch employees appear to testify before the legislature. Finally, the Congress can impeach the president and bring him or her to trial, with the possibility of removing the president from office.

Thus, the word of "the most powerful person in the world" is not always final. This has given rise to several historical oddities. One was the diplomatic work of President Woodrow Wilson while overseas after World War I to establish an international League of Nations, only to have Congress vote down American membership upon his return. A similar result happened with the Kyoto Protocol

on greenhouse gas emissions in the late 1990s. On a more domestic note, the frequent fact of divided government regularly frustrates presidential intentions. For instance, President Barack Obama (2009–2017) and his administration had difficulty passing most significant legislation through Congress, since it was controlled by the opposing party. Even when a president has a majority, passing preferred legislation can be difficult, given the use of institutional maneuvers such as the congressional "filibuster" (see the case study on "The United States Congress: Dysfunctional or Functioning by Design?").

Constraints on the executive also come from the judiciary, and not just from congressional resistance. An example was seen in the recent George W. Bush (2001–2009) administration, when the Supreme Court ruled in *Hamdan v. Rumsfeld* (in 2006) that the administration could not try detainees in certain military tribunals and deprive them of access to other courts; the Rumsfeld named on the losing side of the argument was the administration's Secretary of Defense and a member of the president's cabinet. President Obama and his administration experienced challenges in court to the major health care initiative—the Affordable Care Act—that the president backed and that was passed in 2010. The Supreme Court, though, ultimately found the law constitutional in a 5–4 vote. The judiciary interprets constitutional limitations to executive power that include prohibitions on the president usurping powers of state governments.

Apart from the other branches of government, many other—some less formal—factors also limit presidential authority. One of these is public opinion, to which presidents are responsive. In part, the influence of public opinion is mediated through Congress, with presidents aware that unpopular ideas or proposals have little chance of passing Congress. Public opinion matters in obvious ways for presidents who hope to be re-elected to a second term, but also for presidents in their second terms who are reputed to be thinking of their historical legacy. By way of example, efforts by George W. Bush to transform the popular Social Security program for senior citizens into a more privatized system were unsuccessful, as citizen responses came out against the proposal. Beyond public opinion, the influence of the markets and money also matters: if stock and bond markets lose confidence in the government, their declines can raise costs for government and give the president less latitude in policy options. Finally, the international system and current events beyond the president's control can set the tone for a presidency in unexpected ways: September 11, 2001, and the economic recession of 2008–2009 no doubt reshaped the last two presidencies in ways not initially intended by the respective presidents. Altogether, the checks and balances and other circumstances that limit American presidents make the job of the "most powerful person in the world" seem much more a task of accommodating others than imposing one's will.

CASE STUDY

The United States and the World:
A Love–Hate Relationship?

CHAPTER 16, PAGE 382

For many decades after the Second World War, the United States was viewed as one of the key proponents of globalization, and as one of the societies the culture and economy of which have most benefited from increasing global integration. To a considerable extent, we consider this impression to be correct, though the story behind how the United States came to be a key actor in globalization has some potentially surprising elements.

There has been a long-standing tension in American politics between shutting the United States off from the world and engaging with it. George Washington famously urged the United States not to get involved in foreign wars; and for many years, the United States had a very small standing army, owing to a strong "isolationist" tendency in American political culture, an isolationism no doubt facilitated by the country's geographical distance from many potential rivals. The country was relatively late to imperialism and did not join in the European powers' "scramble for Africa." Indeed, where it did seek influence, such as in the Americas (Schoultz 1998), it used a combination of soft and hard power (the sheer number of historical U.S. military interventions in Latin America and the Caribbean is astounding!) but in most cases without formally establishing colonies (see Puerto Rico and the Philippines for key exceptions, and many would judge its treatment of Cuba under the Platt Amendment

to blur the line here). As noted earlier, in the Case Study box for chapter 10 titled "The Most Powerful Person in the World"?, Woodrow Wilson was the driving force behind the creation of the League of Nations, and then the United States refused to join! Both President Wilson in World War I and President Roosevelt in World War II had to work very hard to convince the country to participate in those wars. However, through participating, the United States gradually began to serve a global role from which it would be difficult to extricate itself, and U.S. global involvement accelerated rapidly after World War II as it worked to help rebuild Japan and Europe, to counter the influence of the Soviet Union, and to restore international order in a manner consistent with its interests. Much of the responsibility for the enforcement of global order has continued to be shouldered by the United States, which was instrumental in creating NATO, the United Nations, and international economic actors like the World Bank and the International Monetary Fund. Further, after Britain's relative decline, the United States emerged as the most important state proponent of economic liberalism, and it has been instrumental in pushing for trade agreements like NAFTA and the General Agreement on Tariffs and Trade (GATT).

As it has assumed these roles, it has, not surprisingly, generated both admiration and resentment. Its position

as a preeminent global power and as a showcase of capitalist development can inspire efforts at emulation, envy, and anger. This has been especially true to the extent that the country has attempted to encourage or even impose its preferred solutions for other countries' problems.

Interestingly, some domestic actors within the United States argue not that the United States is exerting disproportionate influence on others but, rather, that global mechanisms threaten the sovereignty of the United States. Critics on both the right and the left sometimes oppose U.S. efforts to expand free trade, and some actors (typically on the right) have even pushed for the United States to withdraw from the United Nations. In short, while isolationism is not regarded as a viable policy option by most analysts, an isolationist stream in American political culture is still visible and, indeed, played a role in the 2016 presidential campaign of Donald Trump, with slogans like "America First" and "Make America Great Again."

It is likely that in coming years, the United States will face new pressures and challenges related to globalization and the changing global order. China's influence in the Pacific (and the wider world) will continue to rise, and both powers will need to be cautious as they gradually sort out how they will interact in the region. Diplomatic relationships in the Americas have changed as well, and the Organization of American

The United States and the World: A Love–Hate Relationship?

CHAPTER 16, PAGE 382

States seems more autonomous from the United States than in the past. Beyond these issues of power politics, themselves traditional in character, the United States will likely continue to face the following problems and challenges:

- Criminality, from drugs to piracy
- Terrorism

- Economic globalization and interdependence
- Immigration and demographics

Each of these issues is transnational in nature. They are about phenomena that cross borders and affect the domestic politics of different nation-states. The rising prevalence of such issues shows

that the twenty-first century will likely be an era in which comparative politics that looks at politics within countries will become ever more integrated with the study of international relations between countries.

Research Prompts

1. Consider the discussion of basic American political institutions in this country profile and its accompanying case studies, and then consider these materials alongside the discussion of the same institutions in the materials on France and the United Kingdom. What are the major differences in political institutions in the countries? What would any large-scale comparative analysis of political institutions in the three countries need to explain?

2. The "institutional chapters" in this volume have asked you to move beyond the United States and the United Kingdom in terms of your thinking about political institutions. In the other country profile materials, find three cases that differ from the United States in some important way in terms of political institutions. Why are these models so different? What are the advantages and disadvantages of each for politics in the respective countries?

3. Look in the country profiles at discussions of the welfare state in France, the United Kingdom, Germany, and the United States. You will see that different welfare states developed at different paces and with different consequences (e.g., some spend more than others). How might you explain these variations?

4. Both the United States and the United Kingdom have, at different points in their history, been proponents of protectionism and then free trade. Based on your reading of these cases and

their profiles, do you expect that we will see the same pattern in China? Why or why not?

5. Compare and contrast the key points of the politics of ethnicity in the United States and India. Both countries have pasts that include racial and ethnic discrimination, and empirical evidence suggests that both legacies of past discrimination and ongoing concerns continue to disadvantage some groups in each society. Does this take place in the same way? Why are there differences in how ethnic diversity is reflected in patterns of political representation in the two countries?

6. In recent years, the United States has largely promoted globalization while France has been ambivalent. Explain this difference.

7. From the Case Study box on free markets ("Did Free Markets Help the United States Get Rich?"; pp. 566–567), what might Alexander Hamilton advise today for a country whose economy is based on producing (e.g.) bananas for export? Or, if you were an American diplomat and someone from a developing country made a case for protectionism, how might you reply if you wished them to open their markets to American goods? In the study of development, it is clear that countries—including the United States—have much to learn from debating the merits of causal arguments and from examining the cases studies of one another's experiences. What economic lessons can the United States learn from other countries?

CHAPTER 1

1. Of course, we are always curious to know greater historical detail, such as about who Columbus was, or about fifteenth-century Spain, or about the first encounters between Europeans and the indigenous peoples of the Americas. And there will remain some debate about whether the Americas were previously "discovered" by other peoples. Learning new facts will often force us to reinterpret our histories and to understand events differently. Therefore, attention to factual information is part of our analysis and a source of our intellectual curiosity. Yet there is a fundamental difference between *why* questions and the closed-ended questions easily answered through memorization or a quick search.

2. We emphasize *why* questions here for heuristic purposes—to help you learn and discover for yourself. Well-posed *why* questions very often lead to social-scientific explanations. However, as Jon Elster 2007 reminds us, we should not *equate* good explanations with the answers to *why* questions. Furthermore, in actual social science, the place where a *why* question ends and a *how* question begins can sometimes be difficult to say.

3. This example, which is discussed further in chapter 13, is adapted from Fearon and Laitin 2003.

4. If one is primarily interested in the causes of education policy in different countries, the safest way to formulate the question may be "What are the causes of education policy?" or "Why does education policy vary across countries?" If one is primarily interested in the consequences of systems of government, one might ask, "What are the consequences of systems of government for policy?"

5. There are caveats to this claim about the lack of laboratories in comparative politics. In certain circumstances, it is possible to set up controlled experiments, and statistical methods make it possible to control for many factors. Our emphasis here is on introducing qualitative comparative politics, where such experiments and the kinds of advanced statistical methods used to make causal inferences with observational data are not assumed to be available or are otherwise inapplicable.

6. So too, for that matter, do other physical and natural scientists rely on interpretations, it should be noted, but the social sciences deal with many facts that are not "laws of nature" or "laws of physics." See the discussion in Lieberson and Lynn 2002.

7. Others, called "Bayesians," use no such thresholds but instead try to precisely quantify the certainty or uncertainty we can have in the statistical associations we find in our samples. For a discussion of Bayesian and "frequentist" statistics in political science, see Jackman 2004.

8. For a sophisticated and classic discussion of these issues, see Weber 1949.

9. Gerring 2001.

10. Collier and Levitsky 1997; Collier and Adcock 1999.

11. There is much debate about how standardized concepts should be in political science. Some argue that concepts should be standardized and agreed on to mean the same thing from one work of scholarship to the next. Others argue that since no concept is perfect, scholars should be free to offer conceptual innovations depending on their specific projects, so long as they are clear.

12. Conceptualization is also challenging for several additional reasons. It is bound up with our own values, making it challenging to define issues such as democratization, gender, or revolutions without bringing to mind lots of connotations. In addition, while ordinary language is precise enough for daily life, it is often riddled with internal contradiction and lack of conceptual clarity. Many concepts have multiple and distinct meanings across different contexts and from person to person, leading to confusion and miscommunication.

13. In chapter 13, we discuss specific conceptualizations of nationalism and national identity put forward by various scholars.

14. Berlin 1958.

15. This is also sometimes referred to as Sartori's "ladder of generality." See Sartori 1970; Collier and Levitsky 1997.

16. In ordinary life, the ambiguity of words and concepts has some advantages. For example, in political discourse (e.g., presidential speeches) the very generality of the word "freedom" allows it to serve as a collective symbol for almost everyone, because even individuals with very different notions of what it means to be free can reach public, symbolic consensus. Yet this is not how we want social science to proceed, given that its goals are very different from those of forming and maintaining a political community or establishing consensus in conversation.

17. Gerring 2009.

18. These terms date back to the work of the political theorist John Stuart Mill in the nineteenth century.

19. Lipset 1959.

20. It was true historically in West Africa that urban residents had greater political freedoms, and one could make a similar case for contemporary China, for example, where economic liberties and political participation are greater along the coasts than in the interior.

21. That is, as noted previously, some argue that social science offers probabilistic rather than deterministic explanations. For an example, again see Lieberson and Lynn 2002.

22. Dunning 2012.

23. King, Keohane, and Verba 1994.

24. Przeworski and Teune 1970.

CHAPTER 2

1. Nossiter 2014.

2. As noted elsewhere in the text, a clue that further explains what a hypothesis is can be found in the word itself, whose etymology includes the prefix *hypo*, meaning "less than." This suggests that a hypothesis is an idea that is "less than a thesis" until it receives some evidence to support it.

3. We thank one of our anonymous reviewers for this formulation.

4. If you are interested in understanding in more detail *why* this may be the case, you might want to read a classic book by Karl Popper (1963) called *Conjectures and Refutations*. Popper argues that scientists should actually *try* to *disprove* their hypotheses or conjectures.

5. A long tradition of work in the history and philosophy of science since at least Kuhn (1962) gives us reason to be suspicious of such idealized portrayals as descriptions of how theories actually change, but most social scientists think that we should *aspire* to these ideals.

6. The quantitative approach requires some knowledge of key descriptive statistics and how to formulate and test hypotheses in a general sense, but it also depends on knowledge of rules of probability and probability distributions. Statistical methodologies formalize the process of testing hypotheses and allow researchers to speak with numerical confidence about the precision of their findings.

7. The most important work making this argument is King, Keohane, and Verba 1994 (or KKV, as it is often called).

8. Brady and Collier 2004; Van Evera 1997.

9. Or, alternatively, "What does country A have *more* of than country B?" For example, it may be that variable levels of human capital and education impact development. Country B is not presumably totally lacking in education and human capital, but has generally lower levels of these things.

10. This is partially adapted from Staffan Lindberg's work on democratization in Africa (2006: 118).

11. Even more troubling are cases where we could use another mathematical identifier and say X ≡ Y, that is, X is defined as being equal to Y. (To continue the logic using mathematical notation for a moment, even X ≈ Y can be a problem. This is because there is so little separating cause and effect that the argument becomes uninteresting.)

12. Endogenous comes from *endo-*, meaning "within," and *-genous*, meaning "origin," suggesting that the origin of a phenomenon comes from within the phenomenon itself. So if X causes Y, but Y also causes X, then X is causing itself.

13. See, for example, Babbie (2010: 95), who writes of a closely related example of a statistical association between ice cream sales and drowning rates.

14. Leinweber 2007.

15. See Lipset 1959.

16. For an overview, see Cassidy 2013.

17. One example that was hypothesized to exist for a long time was the supposed "Bradley effect" in which some American voters would profess to pollsters a preference to vote for an African American candidate but would then vote for a white opponent when alone in the voting booth. The hypothesized reason was that some of those surveyed would not want to seem to the pollster that they had a racial preference, even if they really held one. The result would be an overestimation of the number of voters favoring the black candidate. It is unclear whether the bias ever actually existed (or, if so, continues to exist), and it was not found in the 2008 presidential election between Barack Obama and John McCain, but the example serves to show the challenges of collecting reliable data.

18. Centeno 2002.

CHAPTER 3

1. Morgan 2007.

2. Anthropologists and historians have noted many kinds of states, going back thousands of years. Most comparative political analysis, however, is focused on the *modern* state, and thus we focus exclusively on this form here. Throughout the chapter, we use the term *state* to refer to the "modern state."

3. Weber 1946: 78.

4. Strayer ([1970] 2005), in a classic study, sees the state as originating in medieval Europe, particularly in England and France, but his argument is really that some of the key characteristics of modern states were established in this period. Few political scientists would see twelfth- or thirteenth-century France or England as modern states.

5. Over time, a number of actors, especially elites, did increasingly seek the king's protection. See Strayer [1970] 2005. See also North, Wallis, and Weingast 2009.

6. Strayer stresses the importance of early efforts of the crown in France and England to establish control over the law in establishing state structures. Strayer [1970] 2005: 26–33.

7. Tilly [1990] 1992: 69.

8. North, Wallis, and Weingast 2009.

9. For an engaging overview of the decline of interpersonal violence in recent human history, see Pinker 2011.

10. For a discussion of some of these issues, see Giddens 1987.

11. In referring to the goals of the state, we are using a kind of shorthand. The state, as such, does not have goals. Rather, the individuals and groups that compose it and make claims on it have goals. However, sometimes such goals become "institutionalized" over time, and states carry them on even when nobody is actively campaigning for them.

12. Tilly 1992; Levi 1988.

13. Levi 1988: 2.

14. On the concept of stateness, see Evans 1997 and Fukuyama 2004.

15. On "state breakdown" as a precondition of revolution, see Tocqueville 1983; Skocpol 1979.

16. Pérez Díaz 2011.

17. Putnam 1993.

18. Migdal 1988.

19. Ostrom 1990: 41.

20. See Migdal 1988; Putnam 1994.

21. Weber 1978: 956–1003. On bureaucracy and the state, see also Poggi 1990.

22. Poggi 1990: 74–75; Greenfeld 1996.

23. As Strayer ([1970] 2005: 58) puts it, "Sovereignty requires independence from any outside power and final authority over men who live within certain boundaries."

24. Sahlins 1991.

25. Huntington 1957.

26. Weingast 1997.

27. Moreover, it does so unequally. See Pettit and Western 2004 and Western 2006.

28. Foucault 1977.

29. Note that this does not mean that strong states necessarily tax a *lot*, but just that they tax successfully and regularly.

30. The quintessential example may be England's "Glorious Revolution." See Pincus 2009.

31. For example, see Karl 1997.

32. Scott 1999.

33. Loveman 2014.

34. Hardin 1997.

35. Hobbes [1651] 1996.

36. For an example of a theory that focuses on predatory elites, see Levi 1988.

37. On weak states as being failures to contain predation, see Bates 2008. See also North, Wallis, and Weingast 2009, discussed in the next section.

38. Tilly 1992; Centeno 2002.

39. Tilly 1992; W. H. McNeill 1982. See also Downing 1992.

40. Spruyt 2007.

41. J. R. McNeill and McNeill 2003; Chirot 1994.

42. Tilly 1975: 42.

43. Tilly 1992: 30.

44. Centeno 2002.

45. Herbst 2000.

46. Marx 1978: 187.

47. Evans, Reuschemeyer, and Skocpol 1985.

48. Gorski 2003; Greenfeld 1996.

49. Gorski 2003; Foucault 1977; see also Taylor 2007.

50. Among others, Greenfeld (1996) emphasizes nationalism as a critical prerequisite for the development of the modern state. As we shall see, other scholars see the state as the source of national identity. It is probably closer to the mark to see the development of the state and national identity as endogenous, as defined in chapter 2.

51. Gorski 2003: xvi.

52. In making this argument, Gorski is partly following in the footsteps of the French social theorist, Michel Foucault.

53. Gorski 2003: 36.

54. Strayer [1970] 2005.

55. Spruyt 1994; Wallerstein [1974] 2011; Meyer et al. 1997.

56. Lenin 1939.

57. Wallerstein [1974] 2011.

58. DiMaggio and Powell 1983.

59. Meyer and Rowan 1991.

60. For a partly critical perspective, see Wimmer and Feinstein 2010.

61. Strayer [1970] 2005.

62. North, Wallis, and Weingast 2009.

63. Colley 1992.

64. Pincus 2009.

65. Greenfeld 1992.

CHAPTER 4

1. There is another sense in which scholars also use the phrase "political economy" that is beyond the scope of our text. For some, it refers to using the methods of economics—especially formal algebraic models of decision making and strategic interaction—and applying these to political problems. We occasionally make reference to these sorts of approaches throughout the text, especially when we draw on "rational choice" or "rationalist" theories; but for the sake of clarity, we do not use "political economy" in that context.

2. The Gini Index is a measure very similar to the Gini coefficient that varies from 0 to 100 instead of from 0 to 1.

3. This argument, which can be found in most basic economics textbooks today, dates originally to Ricardo 1817.

4. See Weingast and North 1989; North 1990.

5. For a concise version of this, see Friedman 1990.

6. Buchanan 1984: 11.

7. Bell 2001.

8. Greenfeld 2001.

9. Esping-Andersen 1990.

10. For a critical view, see Wilensky 1975.

11. Arendt 1963; Foucault 1977; Taylor 2007.

12. See discussion in Pierson 2006: 12–14.

13. Hayek [1944] 1994.

14. Esping-Andersen 1990; Huber and Stephens 2001.

15. Ibid.

16. Howard (2007) argues that the U.S. welfare state is not so much small or weak as it is poorly designed.

17. Prasad 2006.

18. Mettler 2011.

19. Esping-Andersen 1990: 29.

20. "Asia's Next Revolution," *The Economist,* September 8, 2012.

21. Goodman and Peng 1996.

CHAPTER 5

1. Sen 1999.

2. Poverty may also be understood as occurring when people are deprived of certain capabilities, as we discuss later (Sen 1999).

3. Pogge 2008: 103; Collier 2007. For an overview of recent estimates, see http://www.worldbank.org/en/topic/poverty/overview, accessed December 13, 2017.

4. As noted above, the World Bank publishes comparable data about poverty for all countries, aiming for consistent data collection and using a standard strategy for measurement. http://www.worldbank.org/en/news/feature/2016/01/13/principles-and-practice-in-measuring-global-poverty. More recently, the World Bank has started to publish additional poverty lines specifically for middle income countries: http://www.worldbank.org/en/topic/poverty/brief/global-poverty-monitoring-recommendations-of-the-atkinson-commission-on-global-poverty-faqs. Data collection here still aims to be consistent. The threshold for who is considered to be in poverty, though, is higher.

5. See the website of the U.S. Department of Health and Human Services: https://aspe.hhs.gov/poverty-guidelines.

6. See Sen 1999 on how this process has happened in Kerala and in the country of Sri Lanka.

7. This distinction was made persuasively by Sen 1999.

8. In many societies, women bear greater work burdens (both outside and inside the home) yet see fewer of the benefits of economic development. We discuss this in chapter 14.

9. See Escobar 1995.

10. Stiglitz, Sen, and Fitoussi 2010.

11. Rosenstein-Rodan 1943.

12. See Weingast and North 1989.

13. See Mahoney 2010, and Pierson 2004, among many others.

14. Tocqueville 1988: 513.

15. On how this can contribute to the performance of government institutions, see Putnam 1995.

16. On "bonding" and "bridging" capital, see Putnam 2000. On "structural holes" see Burt 1992.

17. We discuss religion in politics in chapter 15 (and note the possible relationship between religion and regime type in chapter 6),

but the link between religion and development merits some comment here.

18. Noland and Pack 2004.

19. For a general discussion of this and related issues, see the World Bank's World Development Report 2015: Mind, Society, and Behavior, http://www.worldbank.org/en/publication/wdr2015

20. Almond 1991.

21. Lenin 1948 [translated from Russian edition of 1917].

22. Representative and influential works included André Gunder Frank's *Capitalism and Underdevelopment in Latin America: Historical Studies of Chile and Brazil* (1967) and Walter Rodney's *How Europe Underdeveloped Africa* (1981).

23. Prebisch 1950.

24. Wallerstein 2011[1974].

25. Cardoso and Faletto 1979; Evans 1979.

26. See World Bank 1997. One of the authors behind the World Bank's 1997 *World Development Report* was Peter Evans, who was a leading figure in the revised version of dependency theory. Another leading dependency theorist, Fernando Henrique Cardoso, went on to become president of Brazil (1995–2003), where he undertook many pro-market reforms but also presided over efforts to build state capacity and strength.

27. Collier 2007.

28. For a sophisticated historical interpretation of this, see Acemoglu, Johnson, and Robinson 2001, as outlined in the "Insights" box.

29. The World Values Survey, available online: http://www.worldvaluessurvey.org.

30. Such questions were asked in slightly different forms in Evans 1995 and Kohli 2004.

31. Kohli 2004.

32. See Amsden 1992; Kohli 2004.

33. Amsden 1992.

CHAPTER 6

1. Indeed, important work on conceptualizing, defining, and measuring democracy and democratization is ongoing in today's political science. See, for example, Coppedge et al. 2011.

2. While this distinction between procedural and substantive definitions is conventionally drawn and important, we wish to emphasize that there is a grey area between them. Gerardo Munck, for example, following Robert Dahl, defines democracy as procedural but sees it as a substantive good; Munck 2009: 129.

3. See Dahl 1971, and Schmitter and Karl 1991, for a concise summary.

4. On competitive authoritarianism, see Levitsky and Way 2002, 2010 (discussed in chapter 7). On the related concept of electoral authoritarianism, see Schedler 2006.

5. Schmitter and Karl 1991.

6. Huntington 1991; Markoff 1996.

7. Linz and Stepan 1996.

8. See the discussion in the country materials at the back of this book.

9. Ash 1993: 78.

10. On the concept of democratic consolidation, see Schedler 1998.

11. Linz and Stepan 1996: 5.

12. Lipset 1959, 1960; Inglehart and Welzel 2005; Rueschemeyer, Stephens, and Stephens 1992.

13. Almond and Verba 1963; Putnam 1993.

14. Huntington 1991; Markoff 1996; for an alternative sort of structural/systemic approach, see Bollen 1983.

15. Linz 1990a, 1990b. Stepan and Skach 1993.

16. An actor-centered theory can be found in the four-volume series edited by O'Donnell, Schmitter, and Whitehead (1986). See in particular volume 4, by O'Donnell and Schmitter, entitled *Transitions from Authoritarian Rule: Tentative Conclusions About Uncertain Democracies*.

17. For a discussion of the debate about whether institutional change and democratization is a cause or a consequence of economic development, see Glaeser, La Porta, Lopes de Silanes, and Shleifer 2004.

18. For more on causal mechanisms in social science, see Elster 2007.

19. Lipset 1959, 1960.

20. Inglehart and Welzel 2005.

21. The best known comparative study of this sort is probably still Almond and Verba 1963.

22. For a scholarly discussion of some of these issues, see Fukuyama 1995.

23. Wiarda 2001; Véliz 1980.

24. For one of the better examples, see Woodberry 2011, and Woodberry and Shah 2004.

25. Huntington 1991.

26. Ibid: 100–106.

27. Meyer et al. 1997.

28. Stepan 1999.

29. Linz 1990a, 1990b.

30. The broader social theory question underlying this issue is often called the "structure–agency problem," and the main idea is that it is often difficult to sort out how much of a social or political process is due to the intentional behavior of individuals and how much of it is due to social structures or institutional constraints.

31. For one well-known view on variables and "proper names" in research, see Przeworski and Teune 1970.

32. O'Donnell, Schmitter, and Whitehead 1986.

33. Huntington 1991.

34. For example, see Putnam 2000.

35. Collier, Mahoney, and Seawright 2004.

36. George and Bennett 2005.

CHAPTER 7

1. Adorno et al. 1950.

2. According to anthropologists and historians, there is astonishing variability in the political systems of hunter-gatherer societies in which we spent most of our evolutionary history; but in general, these were more egalitarian than the more complex societies that emerged after the development of settled agriculture and the creation of premodern states. See McNeill and McNeill 2003.

3. On the democratic wave, mentioned in chapter 6, see Huntington 1991. On contemporary authoritarianism, see Levitsky and Way 2010.

4. For classic treatments of democratic breakdown, see Linz and Stepan 1978, and Valenzuela 1978.

5. For a thoughtful consideration of hybrid regimes, see Diamond 2002.

6. For a seminal treatment of totalitarian rule, see Arendt [1958] 2004.

7. See some discussion of these issues in the country profile materials at the back of this book.

8. See, for example, Žižek 2002.

9. See, for example, Linz 2000 and the informative discussion in Brooker 2009.

10. On "sultanistic regimes," see Chehabi and Linz 1998.

11. For one example, see Vallenilla Lanz 1991.

12. On Africa's personalistic dictatorships, see Jackson and Rosberg 1982 and Decalo 1985.

13. Verbitsky 1996.

14. O'Donnell 1973.

15. Levitsky and Way (2010: 3) add to this the fall of the Soviet Union and its consequences.

16. Collier and Levitsky 1997.

17. Zakaria 2003.

18. O'Donnell 1994.

19. Schedler 2006.

20. Levitsky and Way 2002, 2010.

21. This quote has been attributed to de Soto for many years, and can be found in the Hans Morgenthau Lecture of the Carnegie Council in 2002: http://www.carnegiecouncil.org/publications/archive/morgenthau/99.html (accessed March 18, 2018).

22. Levitsky and Way 2010.

23. See Brownlee 2007 and Levitsky and Way 2010 on this issue.

24. For this reason some scholars have emphasized the importance and potential difficulty of transitioning away from clientelism as societies democratize. See the discussion in Fox 1994.

25. Corrales and Penfold 2011; Smilde and Hellinger 2011; Levitsky and Way 2010.

26. See the many excellent essays in Mahoney and Thelen (2010) on historical institutionalism.

27. On coalitions and institutions, see Hall 2010.

28. Skocpol 1973.

29. This is an implication of a number of the findings of Inglehart and Welzel 2005.

30. The attentive reader will recognize this as key to Inglehart and Welzel's neo-modernization theory of democratization, discussed in chapter 6; Inglehart and Welzel, 2005.

31. North, Wallis, and Weingast 2009.

32. Paige 1997.

33. Roberts 1995.

34. See, for example, Migdal 1988, discussed briefly in chapter 3.

35. Bates 2008.

36. See Jackson and Rosberg 1982.

37. Greenfeld 1997.

38. Véliz 1980.

39. Palmer 1980; Wiarda 2003.

40. Almond and Verba 1963; Inglehart and Welzel 2005.

41. For an overview, see Wintrobe 2007.

42. Olson 1965; Lichbach 1995. See also discussion of these issues in chapters 11 and 12.

43. Kuran 1991.

CHAPTER 8

1. For an exploration of constitutional design issues relating to the legislative and executive branches, two of the leading works are Sartori 1994 and Lijphart 1999.

2. Benjamin Franklin allegedly put his worries to an interested citizen in Philadelphia who asked what type of government the Constitutional Convention had established, saying the Founding Fathers built "a republic, if you can keep it."

3. This is sometimes referred to casually as the "fourth branch" of government, though most civil servants and administrators are technically part of the executive branch.

4. State-level rulings can be very significant not only for state residents (obviously) but also in broader national debates, as in recent years when the top courts in states such as Massachusetts, Iowa, and New Jersey ruled that the state must extend same-sex marriage rights or equivalent benefits to gay couples.

5. The high court may uphold lower court rulings by simply refusing to "hear the case" of a challenge or appeal.

6. Before 2009, the House of Lords was for a long time a quasi-judicial body that offered commentary on decisions by the House of Commons, but could not overrule it.

7. Depending on one's historical perspective, federalism may date back to the ancient world, when rulers such as Alexander the Great used decentralized authorities to govern distant parts of their far-flung empires. These rulers used local magistrates, representatives, or agents to ensure governability. At other points in history, small territories sought the advantages of uniting certain powers under common rule, even while they retained authority and autonomy locally. In many cases, these arrangements could be best characterized as *confederal*, with examples including different "leagues" of city-states and united provinces and principalities in Europe as the modern nation-states came into being.

8. On this, see Riker 1964; Stepan 1999.

9. There are several ways to specify the concept of federalism without specific reference to constitutions. For some scholars, federal countries are determined by other features: whether subnational governments have some representation at the national level, usually through an upper chamber in the legislature (such as a Senate) that is designed to defend the interests of the subnational units; or independent legislatures at the subnational level, such as state assemblies, which ensure democratically elected subnational government. See Wibbels 2005.

10. Examples of small federal island nations are Comoros and Federated States of Micronesia.

11. As a character in *Monty Python and the Holy Grail* once suggested with respect to the divine right of kings as opposed to constitutional government, "power is derived from a mandate from the masses, not from some farcical aquatic ceremony."

12. The most famous early example was the signing of the Magna Carta in England in 1215, when English nobles defeated the forces of King John and demanded that he approve a "Great Charter" that conferred rights to the nobility and required the participation of Parliament in certain decisions. This was by no stretch a full-blown democracy (as the rights were for the nobility and not for commoners), but it did establish an important principle that the ruler was at least partially constrained by the will of those governed.

13. Examples might be found in the Middle East, such as with the House of Saud in Saudi Arabia.

14. Of course, democratic regimes as well may fail to enforce certain constitutional rights, since these are regularly subject to interpretation and are not always perfectly implemented.

15. Hirschl 2010.

16. Riker 1964.

17. See Stepan 1999.

18. See Tiebout 1956.

19. Ibid.

20. Wibbels 2005.

21. Rodden, Eskeland, and Litvack 2003.

22. Rodden 2006.

23. See Oates 2005; Weingast 2009.

24. See Wibbels 2005; Rodden 2006; Rodden et al. 2003.

25. For an overview, see Kmiec 2004.

26. See Dworkin 1977, 1986.

27. Gewirtz and Golder 2005; Miles and Sunstein 2007.

CHAPTER 9

1. See, for example, the striking visualization of party polarization in the U.S. Senate in Moody and Mucha 2013.

2. The United States is an exception to the rule among democratic countries in that many presidents have not held elective office at the national level prior to their election, instead coming often from the governorship of a state. It is for this reason of political socialization that some scholars prefer parliamentary government—where the legislature chooses the executive—over a system where the president is directly elected: it weeds out "outsiders" unfamiliar with how the system works, and favors politicians who have come through the political system. Of course, a contrary argument can be found among those who find the political classes to be too insular and who want outsiders who are willing to "shake up" a political establishment that might be seen as lazy, or corrupt, or sclerotic.

3. Or, if retiring, they may work to ensure that their preferred candidate takes their place.

4. Mayhew 1974.

5. These qualifications may include getting a certain number of signatures on a petition to support the candidacy, or perhaps making a cash deposit (which may be refundable, if the candidate polls enough votes in the election). The reason for placing such restrictions on the ballot is to ensure that the electoral authorities can control the number of candidates and that elections are contested only by "serious" candidates and parties.

6. Many of the changes come down to how "remainders" are dealt with when it comes to assigning seats. The various methods include the D'Hondt method, the Sainte-Laguë method, and the largest remainder method.

7. See Power 2000.

8. In that chapter, we discuss the work of Duverger 1954.

9. See Cox and McCubbins 1993; Mezey 1979; Shepsle and Weingast 1981.

10. See the various chapters in Morgenstern and Nacif 2002 for an examination of party discipline using several Latin American cases.

11. There are limitations on votes of no confidence in many countries. As noted in the "Germany's Bundestag and Bundesrat" Case in Context box, a vote in that country must be a "constructive vote of no confidence," meaning that the members of the parliament proposing to bring down the government must simultaneously propose a new government to take its place. This is designed to discourage excessive "cycling" from one failed government to another.

12. https://www.bundestag.de/en/parliament/plenary/distribution ofseats

CHAPTER 10

1. Aberbach, Putnam, and Rockman 1981.

2. We emphasize *directly elected* presidents in this section, distinguishing them from prime ministers in the section on parliamentarism. But there are rare occasions, such as in South Africa, where a head of state is elected in an indirect fashion as a prime minister, yet is called a "president."

3. As noted previously, some parliamentary executives are even called by the confusing moniker of "President."

4. On political business cycles, see Nordhaus 1975.

5. This may seem self-evident, but there is a substantial literature documenting the importance of these institutional designs.

6. Examples may be the need for an expression of national unity at a time of war or national tragedy or sacrifice. Under these circumstances, several parties may agree to put certain aspects of political competition aside for the good of the nation. Another example is the desire to create a supermajority, as in South Africa, where the African National Congress had a strong majority and needed only the support of one or two very small parties to have the supermajority needed to amend the constitution.

7. This may be an explicit rule or a commonly accepted norm. In many cases, the ceremonial head of state (such as the king or queen) will call on the largest party to form the government.

8. Some of the most significant and influential ministries sought by coalition partners are the Ministry of Finance (or Economy) and the Ministry of Foreign Affairs, which correspond to the Secretary of the Treasury and the Secretary of State in the U.S. government, respectively. Coalition partners may prioritize control over other ministries depending on their interests. For example, a Green Party may seek the Ministry of the Environment, an anti-immigration party may want the Ministry for Home Affairs (or Interior), and a rural party representing farmers may seek to control the Ministry of Agriculture.

9. This exercise is a modified version of that used in Lijphart (1999).

10. Neustadt 1960.

11. Critics of the view that parliamentarism is preferable generally argue that the two forms are more or less equal in their effects, not that presidentialism is *better*.

12. See Geddes 1994.

13. See Geddes 1990.

CHAPTER 11

1. See Kirchheimer 1966; Kitschelt 1994.

2. Kirchheimer 1966.

3. See Michels [1911] 1962: 367.

4. Some African countries, such as Ethiopia or Tanzania, did indeed have highly ideological single-party systems, while many former French and Belgian colonies in west and central Africa had single-party regimes without strongly identifiable ideologies.

5. Zakaria 1994.

6. Lijphart 1999: 76–77.

7. See Ibid.

8. Laakso and Taagepera 1979.

9. Rae 1968.

10. See Mainwaring and Scully 1995.

11. Parties also differ in terms of how "disciplined" they are. That is, they differ on the extent to which party members follow the wishes of the party leadership. This was considered in chapters 9 and 10 on legislatures and executives.

12. Mainwaring and Scully 1995.

13. Collier and Collier [1991] 2002; Wiarda 1997: 73.

14. See Schmitter 1974.

15. Collier and Collier [1991] 2002; Katzenstein 1985.

16. Lukes [1974] 2005; Mills 2000 [1956].

17. We are thankful to an anonymous reviewer for suggestions on the discussion of authoritarian and democratic forms of corporatism.

18. There are hybrids and combinations of the two systems; see chapter 7 for further detail.

19. Véliz 1980; Zolberg 1966.

20. See Sartori 1976: 336.

21. The literature here is extensive, and it relates to issues of incumbent advantage, redistricting, and other issues beyond the scope of this chapter. A partial and early review of the question of safe seats can be found in Mayhew 1974.

22. Marx and Engels [1848] 1998; Lenin 1902.

23. See Fukuyama 1992, among others.

24. See Dahl 1989, among others.

25. Whether representatives should basically translate the will of the majority or should exercise independent judgment after being elected is a source of continuing debate, reflecting the so-called mandate–independence controversy mentioned in chapter 8.

26. See Evans 1995.

CHAPTER 12

1. Katz 1999; Martin 2008.

2. The basic distinction between class, status, and power as dimensions of social stratification can be found in Weber 1946.

3. Tilly and Tarrow 2007: 4–11.

4. Ibid: 5–6.

5. Scott 1985.

6. Alvarez, Dagnino, and Escobar 1998: 16–18.

7. Pérez Díaz 2014; Shils 1997: 320–325.

8. At the same time, it is important to remember that civil society is not autonomous from power and status. See Alvarez, Dagnino, and Escobar 1998: 16–18.

9. Tilly and Tarrow 2007.

10. Tarrow 2005.

11. Lindholm and Zúquete 2010.

12. *VOA News*, "Thousands Protest Globally Against Trump, Travel Ban," February 4, 2017, https://www.voanews.com/a/thousands-protest-globally-against-trump-travel-ban/3706760.html

13. See Ondetti 2008 for a detailed account.

14. Michels [1911] 1962: 342–356.

15. For a classic account of the U.S. civil rights movement from the perspective of social movement theory, see McAdam 1982.

16. Burns 1997: 4–5, 10–11, 15.

17. Tilly and Tarrow 2007: 108.

18. Ibid: 29–36, 108.

19. Some scholars even refer to contemporary societies as "social movement societies." See Tarrow 2011: 5–6, 117–118, and especially the essays in Meyer and Tarrow 1998.

20. It should be acknowledged that if this distinction holds, it is only a matter of degree.

21. See discussion in Pincus 2007: 398–399.

22. Huntington 1968: 264–266.

23. Brinton 1952: 41.

24. Skocpol 1994: 5.

25. Skocpol 1979: 4–5.

26. Not all scholars agree that the distinction between coups and revolutions is easily made. For more on conceptualizing and explaining coups d'etat, see Belkin and Schofer 2003; Johnson, Slater, and McGowan 1984; and Powell and Thyne 2011.

27. In his classic treatment, Huntington refers to these as the "eastern model" of revolution. Huntington 1968: 266–267.

28. Foran 2005.

29. Arendt 1963; Kumar 2005.

30. See Stathis Kalyvas's differentiation of civil wars from other forms of conflict on these grounds. Kalyvas 2007: 417.

31. Metelits 2009: 3.

32. Kalyvas suggests that revolutions are a type of civil war, but not everyone agrees; Kalyvas 2007: 417.

33. Centeno notes that they partially resembled civil wars; Centeno 2002: 47.

34. O'Leary and Silke 2007: 388–390.

35. Tilly 2004; Oberschall 2004: 26.

36. Sanderson 2010: 172.

37. Tilly 2004: 8–9.

38. Senechal de la Roche 2004: 1–2.

39. Black 2004: 17.

40. Senechal de la Roche 2004: 2; Black 2004: 16.

41. Ibid. 15, 23.

42. O'Leary and Tirman 2007: 6–7.

43. Gibbs 1989: 330. Bergesen and Lizardo 2004: 38.

44. Pape 2003: 345.

45. Sageman 2004: 140.

46. Hobsbawm 1981.

47. Scott 1985.

48. Ibid. xvi.

49. Smelser 1962: 1–12.

50. Tilly and Tarrow 2007: 9–10.

51. Some are further apart than others. Most social movements, for example, have not even the remotest connection to terrorism.

52. See the insightful discussion in Buechler 2004.

53. Smelser 1962.

54. Toch 1965.

55. Elster 1998: 58–60.

56. Brinton 1952: 33–36, 278.

57. Gurr 1970: 22–122.

58. McCarthy and Zald 1987. Doug McAdam, perhaps the most influential scholar in the "political process" or "political opportunities" school, presents this perspective as a critique of resource mobilization theories; McAdam 1982: 20–35. However, we consider them to fall into the same family of theories for our purposes in this introductory textbook.

59. Goldstone 1991.

60. See Goldstone 2001 for an overview of these and related theories.

61. Huntington 1968: 275.

62. Ibid. 277.

63. Some of these and other issues are reviewed in Goldstone 2001: 145–147. See also Parsa 2000.

64. The most important works on revolution from a rational choice perspective are Lichbach 1995, 1998. See also Coleman 1990: 489–502; Tullock 1971; and also Finkel, Muller, and Opp 1989.

65. Lichbach 1998.

66. Olson 1965; Lichbach 1995.

67. This example, which illustrates what Lichbach calls the "rebel's dilemma," follows the pattern of examples given in Lichbach 1995.

68. Of course, some political opportunity theorists *are* attentive to cultural factors. For example, see McAdam 1996: 25.

69. Hunt and Benford 2004: 437–438.

70. Melucci 1989; Castells, 2010.

71. On framing and "frame analysis," see Goffman 1974; Gamson 1992; and Benford and Snow 2000.

72. Kurzman 2005.

73. Greenfeld 1995.

74. Kumar 2005; Arendt 1963.

75. Tilly and Tarrow 2007.

76. Oliver and Johnston 2000.

77. Foran 2005.

78. A full analysis, of course, would question this assumption, looking at other indicators of development to be sure that high per capita GDP in the context of high inequality may not mask significant sources of economic discontent on the part of key populations.

79. McElreath 2016: 4-10.

80. Marc Lynch has made this point in a popular article (Lynch 2014) though it has been contested by Beehner (2014). On foreign intervention and civil wars more generally, see Regan 2002 and Elbadawi and Sambanis 2000.

81. Barth 1969.

CHAPTER 13

1. On all three cases, see the relevant sections of the 2017 Human Rights Watch World Report: https://www.hrw.org/world-report/2017. On the devastating conflict in South Sudan, see reports by Human Rights Watch and Amnesty International, such as this news release: https://www.amnesty.org/en/latest/news/2017/12/south-sudan-global-action-needed-to-end-human-rights-violations-and-humanitarian-crisis/. Some observers, including the British Secretary for International Development, have labelled this genocide: https://www.reuters.com/article/us-southsudan-war/uk-says-killings-in-south-sudan-conflict-amount-to-genocide-idUSKBN17E2TF. For allegations of ethnic cleansing in Myanmar against the Rohingya minority population, see the 2017 report, "They Tried to Kill Us All: Atrocity Crimes Against Rohingya Muslims in Rakhine State, Myanmar," prepared by the NGO *Fortify Rights* as well as the Simon-Skjodt Center for the Prevention of Genocide at the United States Holocaust Memorial Museum: http://www.fortifyrights.org/downloads/THEY_TRIED_TO_KILL_US_ALL_Atrocity_Crimes_against_Rohingya_Muslims_Nov_2017.pdf

2. Tajfel 1981; Stets and Burke 2000: 225; Brewer and Gardner 1996; Greenfeld and Eastwood 2007.

3. On symbolic boundaries, see Lamont and Molnár 2002.

4. Calhoun 1997: 2–3.

5. The author who has most clearly and consistently defined them in this way is Greenfeld 1992, 2001. For a partially overlapping definition, see Anderson [1983] 1991.

6. This typology was identified by Smith 1986.

7. On sociobiological and evolutionary psychology approaches, see discussion in Smith 1995: 32–35. See also Van den Berghe 1981 and Rushton 2005. Smith (1995: 33–34) identifies Clifford Geertz and Edwards Shils as examples of primordialists who take a cultural approach.

8. Gorski 2000; Hastings 1997.

9. Smith 1986. Greenfeld would date the origins of nationalism in sixteenth-century England, but considers this modern. See Gorski 2000 for a critique of other scholars' application of modernist definitions to European cases, arguing that by these definitions many early modern political identities were national. On conceptualization and timing of the development of national identity more generally, see Connor 2004.

10. Gellner 1983.

11. Greenfeld 1992.

12. Greenfeld 2001.

13. See, for example, Kohn 1944.

14. Again, a good example of this view is Kohn 1944.

15. For a partially critical perspective, see Brubaker 1999.

16. Smith 1986: 134.

17. Greenfeld 1992

18. Brubaker 1992; Greenfeld 1992

19. For a classic account of *jus soli* and *jus sanguinis* in France and Germany, see Brubaker 1992. For a critical perspective, see Weil 2001, who argues that approaches to citizenship do not fundamentally reflect ideas about national identity but instead are better explained by focusing on legal traditions and migration patterns.

20. As Deborah Yashar stresses, this does not mean that citizenship in the Americas is "ethnoblind" (Yashar 2005: 38–42).

21. See, for example, Weil 2001: 21.

22. Marx 2003; Hechter 2000: 6–7.

23. Bonikowski and DiMaggio 2016.

24. Harff and Gurr 2004; Fearon and Laitin 2003.

25. Laitin 2007.

26. Brubaker and Laitin 1998.

27. Brubaker and Laitin 1998; see also Varshney 2002.

28. Jowitt 2001.

29. Horowitz 1985; Varshney 2002.

30. Brubaker and Laitin 1998.

31. For one typology of such conflicts, see Chirot 2001: 7.

32. Harff and Gurr 2004.

33. Jowitt 2001. See also Greenfeld and Chirot 1994.

34. On "barricaded identities," see Jowitt 2001.

35. Akerlof and Kranton 2010.

36. Laitin 2007.

37. Laitin 2007 uses the term "cascading" to describe spreading participation in secessionist movements.

38. See related theories discussed in chapter 12. For the application of these theories to ethno-national conflict, see Horowitz, 1985, 2001.

39. In addition to Horowitz, see Greenfeld 1992 and Petersen 2002 on these issues.

40. See Fearon and Laitin 1996, 2003; Laitin 2007.

41. Cederman, Wimmer, and Min 2010.

42. For an accessible overview of research in this area, see Harff and Gurr 2004.

43. Some scholars of nationalism have urged caution about simple institutional policy recommendations such as democratization. For an interesting argument in this connection, see Snyder 2000.

44. For a classic discussion of consociationalism, see Lijphart 1977. For consideration of the relative performance of some consociational systems, see Lemarchand 2007.

45. Kaufman 2001; Pettigrew and Tropp 2011.

46. Varshney 2002.

47. For a discussion of the complexities involved in doing so, see Sikkink 2011; Teitel 2011; and Drumbl 2007.

48. Chirot 2001: 20–24.

49. See especially Harff and Gurr 2004.

50. For an example, see Harff 2003.

CHAPTER 14

1. We discuss immigration further in chapter 16.

2. On transnationalism, see Khagram and Levitt 2008; Ong 1999.

3. Barth 1969; see also the work by social identity theorists discussed in chapter 13.

4. American Anthropological Association website: *Race: Are We So Different?* http://www.understandingrace.org/home.html. See also Duster 2005.

5. Kimmel 2000.

6. Lovenduski 2005: 6.

7. See, for example, Sidanius and Pratto 1999. Costa, Terracciano, and McCrae 2001, though, find cross-cultural variation in gender role stereotypes, noting that this is a problematic finding for theories that argue for strong evolutionary shaping of gender roles. There is a vibrant debate about these issues in psychology.

8. England et al. 1994; Eccles 1987.

9. On the social construction of heterosexuality as the norm, see Katz 2007.

10. See Human Rights Campaign's online glossary of terms: https://www.hrc.org/resources/glossary-of-terms. Accessed December 22, 2017.

11. For a discussion of global comparative survey data on this question, see Pew Research Center 2013.

12. There is a growing comparative literature on LGBTQ movements in different global regions. For example, on LGBTQ movements in Latin America, see Corrales and Pecheny 2010 and de la Dehesa 2010.

13. American Anthropological Association website: *Race: Are We So Different?* http://www.understandingrace.org/home.html.

14. On the Irish and the racial category of "whiteness" in the United States, see Roediger 1999: 133–163. On race in Latin America, see Winn 1992: 271–307.

15. These categories were depicted in so-called casta paintings. See Katzew 2004. For a thorough discussion of ways in which concepts about race and ethnicity changed in Latin America via the institution of the population census, see Loveman 2014.

16. Cornell and Hartmann 1998: 22–23.

17. See, for example, Omi and Winant 1994.

18. Gans 2005.

19. Sorenson 2001.

20. Fredrickson 2003; Gans 2005.

21. See the overview of this history in Fredrickson 2003 as well as Pagden 2009, who stresses both the importance and the limits of racist and racist-like attitudes in colonial expansion; and Cañizares-Esguerra 2009, who suggests that the idea of race as justification for colonial domination was developed by overseas colonials rather than European actors.

22. Marx 1998.

23. Smith 1995: 57. Note that he refers to such groups as "ethnie."

24. Smith famously argues that national identities *grow out of* but are not fully reducible to ethnic identities.

25. For this reason, some distinguish between ethnicity and race on the grounds that ethnicity may be more a matter of choice, with multiple affiliations possible, whereas race may be more a matter of external ascription, and thus inescapable. This perspective is expressed in Fredrickson 2003, among many other works. For a fuller discussion of some of the differences between the concepts of race and ethnicity, see Cornell and Hartmann 1998: 25–35.

26. For discussion of some of these issues, see Tienda and Ortiz 1986; and Hirschman, Alba, and Farley 2000.

27. Posner 2005.

28. For two accounts of multiculturalism, one more supportive and the other partially critical, see Modood 2007 and Glazer 1997.

29. Gans 2005.

30. Indeed, some in the United States seek this as well.

31. For one example, see Loveman 2009, 2014.

32. Brown et al. 2003; Pettit and Western 2004.

33. Shapiro 2004.

34. Herring 2002. For an accessible recent overview of some ways in which we might track public opinion about race and racism in the United States, see Barry-Jester 2015.

35. Pager and Shepherd 2008: 182.

36. Brown et al. 2003.

37. On "audit studies," see Pager and Shepherd 2008: 184–187. Pager and Shepherd's review more generally is an excellent guide to the state of current research on discrimination.

38. Marx 1998.

39. Henderson and Jeydel 2010: 238–242; Roth 2006.

40. Moreover, according to some analysts, gender inequality seems to negatively impact societal-level economic performance. See Dollar and Gatti 1999.

41. On sexual harassment, see Henderson and Jeydel 2010: 124–130.

42. Henderson and Jeydel 2010: 116; Padavic and Reskin 2002: 121–147.

43. For a recent discussion of these and related issues, see Haveman and Beresford 2012.

44. For an interesting analysis of some of the cultural sources of such conflicts, see Blair-Loy 2003 as well as Haveman and Beresford 2012.

45. Padavic and Reskin 2002: 6–16. On consequences of this, see also Blau and Kahn 1992.

46. On health, education, and related arenas of inequality and disadvantage, see the extended discussion in Henderson and Jeydel 2010: 266–302.

47. Jaschik 2011.

48. On political underrepresentation, see Squires 2007: 22–24, 32; and Henderson and Jeydel 2010: 5–6.

49. Henderson and Jeydel 2010: 22–31.

50. Sainsbury 2005; Holli and Kantola 2005.

51. Here we use the concept of "capability" as developed by Amartya Sen (see chapter 5).

52. Indeed, some theories suggest that economic empowerment is fundamental. For example, see Blumberg 1984. For a partially contrasting view emphasizing culture and beliefs, see Ridgeway and Correll 2004.

53. For a critical perspective, see Izugbara 2004.

54. On the efficacy of conditional cash transfer programs, see Rawlings and Rubio 2005 and Handa and Davis 2006.

55. Weber 1946.

56. As noted before, political empowerment can take many forms, including women's representation in political institutions. On women's representation in legislatures, see Sawer, Tremblay, and Trimble 2006.

57. Htun 2004.

58. Lovenduski 2005: 4.

59. See the essays in Stetson and Mazur 1995, as well as Squires 2007: 32–38.

60. Henderson and Jeydel 2010: 37–64. For a model analysis of ethnic groups' social movement mobilization, see Yashar 2005.

61. Van Cott 2005.

62. Of course, some would argue that Michels' "iron law of oligarchy" (discussed in chapters 11-12) still applies in such cases.

63. Kriesi et al. 1992.

64. Castells 2010: xxviii.

65. Krook (2009) makes the same point with response to successful cases of quota system adoption. She draws on work by Charles Ragin and others that suggests that social and political outcomes are not just products of constant relationships between certain sets of variables but rather products of more complex interaction effects.

66. For one strong view on the relationship between the size of ethnic groups and group affiliation, see Posner 2005.

67. As noted in the Insights box (*From Movements to Parties in Latin America*), some of these factors are highlighted by Van Cott 2005.

68. For a review of these concepts, see chapter 12.

69. Van Cott 2005.

70. Indeed, proportional representation seems to lead to women's holding elected office at a higher rate, at least in more economically developed countries. See Matland 1998.

71. On the impact of cross-cutting affiliations on group party formation, in addition to Htun 2004, see Dunning and Harrison 2010. The latter work suggests that under some conditions, other forms of cross-cutting affiliation can weaken the potential for ethnic groups to form political parties.

72. On quotas and quota systems, see Franceschet, Krook, and Piscopo 2012; Krook 2009; and Squires 2007.

73. Krook 2009: 6–9.

74. Krook 2009. See also discussion of reserved-seat systems in general (not just for women) in Reynolds 2005. More generally, for an overlapping approach known as consociationalism, see Lijphart 1977.

75. For a more detailed discussion of different types of quota systems, see Krook 2009. Some scholars have argued that quotas are not as effective at changing attitudes and behavior as their advocates sometimes claim. See Zetterberg 2009.

76. Krook 2009: 7–9; Henderson and Jeydel 2010: 15.

77. On the effectiveness of quota systems more generally, see Krook 2009; Squires 2007: 53–60; and Franceschet et al. 2012.

78. Bernhard, Reenock, and Nordstrom 2004.

79. The measure referred to here was for a number of years calculated annually in the United Nations Human Development Reports, available at http://hdr.undp.org/en/reports/. See, for example, the 2009 report.

80. Hirway and Mahadevia 1996.

81. For a discussion of the Global Gender Gap Index, see World Economic Forum 2017. For the Gender Development Index and Gender Inequality Index, see United Nations Development Programme 2016.

82. South Africa, incidentally, is ranked tenth, but it is a special case.

CHAPTER 15

1. Bell [1960] 2000; for a more recent version of this sort of argument, see Fukuyama 1992.

2. Berger 1967.

3. Fox 2008.

4. Norris and Inglehart, *Sacred and Secular* 2004. Norris and Inglehart show the persistence of religious belief, but nonetheless *do* argue that religion declines when societies modernize.

5. Pew Research Center 2015.

6. Zarakol 2011.

7. Appadurai 1996; Coronil 1997.

8. On this point, see the writings of Partha Chatterjee, among others; for example, see Chatterjee 1993, 1997.

9. On the concept of "soft power," see the work of Joseph Nye 1990.

10. See the very interesting discussion of Islamic encounters with Western modernity in Moaddel 2005.

11. Though, as scholars like the anthropologist Talal Asad (2003) have pointed out, we do not always succeed in our efforts to avoid doing so.

12. For a classic statement of "modernization theory," see Inkeles and Smith 1974 as well as Berger, Berger, and Kellner 1973. For a more recent version, see Inglehart and Welzel 2005 and Norris and Inglehart 2004.

13. Eisenstadt 2000.

14. This means that not all political beliefs should be thought of as "ideology." For classic statements, see Geertz 1973a and Converse 1964. For a highly sophisticated discussion of the many ways in which the term has been used by political scientists, see Gerring 1997.

15. Karl Marx's followers go so far as to suggest that ideologies are simply reflections of underlying class interests. For Marx's own thoughts on these questions see especially Marx 1978a.

16. See, for example, Boli 1981.

17. Berger 1974.

18. Greenfeld 1996.

19. On viewing religion as a "cultural system," see Geertz 1973b. On transcendence as a key, substantive feature of religion, see Greenfeld 1996 and James 1902.

20. Asad 1993; Dubuisson 2003.

21. For an overview and relatively recent example, see Bruce 2002. For a summary of criticisms, see Gorski and Altinordu 2008.

22. Berger 1967.

23. Weber 1958.

24. Berger 1999; Berger, Davie, and Fokas 2008.

25. Stark 1999 argues that religiosity has increased over time. Putnam and Campbell 2010 document challenges faced by contemporary American religious organizations. Stark's perspective is reflection of the "supply side" or "economic" approach to religion. For other examples, see Finke and Iannaccone 1993; Gill 2008; and Warner 1993. Scholars with this perspective tend to argue that religious pluralism increases religious observance. Some, however, question this relationship between pluralism and religiosity (e.g., Chaves and Gorski 2001; Voas, Crockett, and Olson 2002).

26. Kaufmann 2010; Pew Research Center 2015.

27. As noted earlier, Norris and Inglehart (2004), using data from the World Values Survey, argue that societies undergo a shift toward a more secular worldview as they grow richer. Our point here is that the world as a whole could grow more religious even as, on average, societies grow more secular depending on (a) the relative population growth in more religious and more secular societies and (b) the speed at which societies grow wealthier (and more secular).

28. Casanova 1994.

29. Casanova 1994. See also relevant discussion in Bell 1977; Chaves 1994; and Martin 2005.

30. The concept of "privatization" has been most clearly discussed by Casanova 1994.

31. Niebuhr 1929.

32. Juergensmeyer 1993; Kepel 1994.

33. Fukuyama 1992.

34. For a brief, popular, discussion of neo-reaction, see Douthat 2016.

35. For a historical overview, see Payne 1995.

36. Marx 1978b and 1978c.

37. Fox 2008.

38. Ibid.

39. Blancarte 2008.

40. Brubaker 2016.

41. Adida et al. 2016.

42. On churches and sects, see the classic work of Weber (1969) and Troeltsch (1969). On denominationalism as a distinct category, see Niebuhr 1929 as well as Casanova 1994, 2007.

43. It is important to remember that these are all "ideal types" and that in the real world, we will find many exceptions and cases that do not neatly fit into one or another of these categories.

44. See José Casanova's (2007) thoughtful comparison of immigration and religious pluralism in Western Europe and the United States in this connection.

45. This is closer to Niebuhr's classic (1929) view.

46. See Lindholm and Zúquete 2010. On the left, see Levitsky and Roberts 2011.

47. See discussion of these issues in the essays in Smilde and Hellinger 2011.

48. Smilde and Pagan 2011.

49. For a partially overlapping argument, see Meyer, Boli, Thomas, and Ramírez 1997.

50. For a deep dive into the conceptualization of populism see Weyland 2001.

51. Mueller 2016: 2.

52. Ibid. 3–6.

53. Mudde 2004: 543–544.

54. Roberts 1995.

55. On populism in Venezuela, see especially Hawkins 2010.

56. Ostiguy and Roberts 2016.

57. Mudde and Rovira Kaltwasser 2013. For an accessible discussion that uses this distinction to critique comparisons of Donald Trump to Hugo Chávez, see Gill 2016.

58. For example, see Laclau 2005.

CHAPTER 16

1. On interdependence, see Keohane and Nye 1977.

2. See Friedman 2005.

3. See Wolf 2004.

4. Rogowski 1987.

5. For two leading perspectives on this debate, see Wolf 2004 for a perspective favoring the free market and Stiglitz 2002, 2007 for a critique of the international financial institutions.

6. Some of these "debates" may be explicit and take the form of dialogue, while other "debates" may be more implicit, with their implications revealed more in terms of decisions and behaviors of the immigrant groups.

7. For one of the recent major statements arguing in favor of assimilation to protect a national identity, see Huntington 2004. For a classic statement about the tendency to essentialize foreign cultures, particularly those of the Middle East, see Said 1978.

8. For an extended discussion of immigrant integration in Europe and the United States, see Alba and Foner 2015.

9. See BBC News Europe, "Merkel Says German Multicultural Society Has Failed," available at http://www.bbc.co.uk/news/world-europe-11559451 (accessed May 6, 2012).

10. For a review of recent research on this question, see Ousey and Kubrin 2017.

11. Sampson 2008.

12. Phillips 2006.

13. Modood 2007.

14. Huntington 2004.

15. Portes and Rumbaut 2006.

16. For reports on this issue, see the Intergovernmental Panel on Climate Change (IPCC) at http://www.ipcc.ch/.

17. See Singer 2004 for a discussion of the ethics of this debate.

18. On the characteristics that make for successful governance of the commons, see Ostrom 1990.

19. See Ostrom 1990.

20. Burke 2004.

21. See Naím 2003.

22. Keck and Sikkink 1998.

23. Ibid.

24. As of March 2018, the U.S. list of state sponsors of terrorism consisted of North Korea, Iran, Sudan, and Syria. See http://www.state.gov/j/ct/list/c14151.htm (accessed March 25, 2018).

25. Thucydides [n.d.] 1974; Machiavelli [1532] 1984; Hobbes [1651] 1996.

26. Waltz 1954, 1979.

27. Walt 1998: 31.

28. Mearsheimer 2001.

29. See Jervis 1978.

30. Axelrod and Hamilton 1981: 1392.

31. Doyle 1983a: 218.

32. See Walt 1998: 32.

33. Moravcsik 1997: 515.

34. Keohane 1984.

35. Doyle 1983a, 1983b, 1997.

36. Allison 1971.

37. Wendt 1992.

38. Ibid.

39. Lenin [1917] 1996.

40. Waltz 1954.

41. Putnam 1988.

42. Gourevitch 1978.

absolute deprivation A condition of being deprived of resources below some given threshold, as distinguished from *relative* deprivation.

absolute poverty A conception of poverty that involves setting a certain line below which people will be defined as poor, typically understood in terms of the inability to purchase a certain set of basic goods or services.

administration The bureaucracy of state officials, usually considered part of the executive branch, that executes policy.

alternative energy Energy sources, such as solar or wind power, that are not derived from fossil fuels.

alternative vote Voting system in which voters rank candidates and the votes of low-ranking candidates are reallocated until a winner is determined.

anti-colonial revolutions Revolutions brought by subjugated populations against colonial powers, typically with the purpose of removing them so that the society in question can achieve independence.

apportionment The process by which legislative seats are distributed among geographic constituencies.

argument The placement of evidence in logical form in support of a position or claim.

assimilation The practice of being integrated into another culture, especially with respect to immigration.

audit studies Research carried out by social scientists to measure the extent to which hiring practices are discriminatory.

authoritarian persistence The ongoing continuation of an authoritarian regime, such that democratic transition does not take place.

authoritarian regime A non-democratic regime.

authoritarianism A form of government or regime that is non-democratic.

bellicist theory Theory associated with scholars such as Charles Tilly, who argue that interstate wars were decisive in the creation of the modern state.

bias A preference for one idea or perspective over another, especially a preference that may result in unbalanced use of evidence or in analytical error.

bicameral legislature Legislature with two chambers, which may have equal or unequal powers.

biological determinism The view that a feature of social life, such as gender or ethnicity, is caused by underlying biology.

boundary Line drawn symbolically between groups of people.

brain drain The departure or emigration of skilled and educated members of a population, especially with reference to developing countries in the international system.

bureaucracy A form of organization that, in its ideal form, has individuals operating and working under established, specified, and complex rules. In government, the organization of unelected officials, often considered part of the executive branch, that implements, executes, and enforces laws and policies.

bureaucratic-authoritarian regime A type of authoritarian regime, common in Latin America and elsewhere in the mid- to late twentieth century, that was associated with control of the state more by a group of elites (often military) than by a single individual leader.

cabinet The group of senior officials in the executive branch, including ministers, who advise the head of government or head of state.

capital A factor of economic production consisting of accumulated wealth or financial resources available for investment.

case In comparative analysis, a unit or example of a phenomenon to be studied.

catch-all parties Political parties that are flexible on their ideological positions and aim to attract support from a broad range of interest groups and voters.

causation The property that obtains when one thing can be shown to cause another.

chamber An assembly or body of a legislature, often referring to one of two such bodies in a bicameral legislature.

citizenship A form of relationship between the state and individuals subject to its control, in which citizens have certain basic rights and are in some way represented in the state.

civic nationalism A form of nationalism that says that you are a member of the nation if you are a citizen of its state.

civil rights Rights of individuals to participate in civic life, including freedoms of assembly, speech, access to information, and equal access to institutions, among others.

civil society A space in society outside of the organization of the state, in which citizens come together and organize themselves.

civil wars Sustained military conflict between domestic actors.

class structure The ongoing and patterned relationships between "classes," typically understood as groups of individuals linked together by economic interest or activity.

clientelism The practice of exchanging political favors, often in the form of government employment or services, for political support.

climate change A set of changes to the earth's climate and the study of what causes these changes.

coalition A group of two or more political parties that governs by sharing executive power and responsibilities.

collective action Action undertaken by individuals and groups to pursue their ends in formally or informally coordinated ways, often in pursuit of some common or public good such as expanded civil rights or sustainable use of common resources.

collective action research program The name given to the rational choice theory of contention associated with the work of Marc Lichbach.

collective behavior A paradigm for understanding various forms of contention, popular for part of the twentieth century, that emphasized the irrational, social-psychological dynamics of protest.

committee In a legislature, a body composed of a group of legislators convened to perform a certain set of tasks.

comparative advantage In international trade, the idea that different countries or territories will have different relative advantages in the production of different goods and services, which forms the basis for gains from trade.

comparative checking The process of testing the conclusions from a set of comparisons against additional cases or evidence.

comparative politics The subfield of political science that aims to analyze multiple cases using the comparative method.

competitive authoritarianism A form of government or regime that allows some political competition but not enough to qualify as fully democratic.

concentration (of party system) Contrasting with fragmentation, the extent to which political power and representation in a party system are characterized by relatively small numbers of relatively large parties. (*See also* fragmentation)

concept An idea comparativists use to think about the processes we study.

conceptualization The deliberate process through which we create and select social-scientific concepts.

congress A form of legislature, typically associated with a presidential system in which there is a separation of powers.

consociational Systems that use formal mechanisms to coordinate different groups sharing access to power.

consociationalism An institutional approach to managing potential conflict in polities with multiple groups, one which involves ensuring that each *group* has political representation.

consolidation The process through which a new democratic order becomes institutionalized and therefore more likely to endure.

constituency A group of voters or a geographic district that legislators or other elected officials represent.

constitution Fundamental and supreme laws, usually written in a charter, that establish the basis of a political system and the basis for other laws.

constitutional design Features of constitutions that shape the basic features of the political system, such as separation of powers and responsibilities between levels of government and branches of government.

constitutional monarchy A political system in which a monarch such as a king, queen, or emperor plays a role as a head of state, but has powers limited by a constitution.

constitutional republic A polity without a monarch in which the basic rules of politics are laid out in a constitution.

constitutionalism The limitation of government through a constitution.

constructivism In international relations, a theory that holds that decisions made by states need to be understood in the context of social and political interactions, and that behavior is shaped by norms and values as well as by narrowly defined interests.

constructivism In nationalism studies, the view that nations are symbolic constructs and so place greater emphasis on the creative efforts of individuals and groups to define and redefine their identities.

contention The name, most associated with scholars like Sidney Tarrow and Charles Tilly, referring to the pursuit of collective goods largely outside of formal political institutions.

corporatism A system of interest group representation in which certain major groups are officially designated as representatives of certain interests, and have a more structured interaction with the government in power and with the state's administration.

correlation A relationship between two variables in which they tend to move in either the same direction (positive correlation) or in opposite directions (negative correlation).

coup d'état The use of force or threat of force, typically by the military or a coalition involving the military, to impose a non-electoral change of government.

critical race theory A movement in social, political, and legal theory that aims to discern the subtle effects of racism and related forms of prejudice.

decree An executive-made order that has the force of law, despite not being passed through a legislature.

deductive reasoning The process of moving from general claims or theories to specific observations or predictions about a phenomenon or set of cases.

defensive realism A realist theory that holds that peace or cooperation can emerge under specific circumstances, namely when it is easier to defend than to attack and when states can see clearly what other states' intentions are.

deflation Decline in the prices of goods and services, often associated with depressions or serious slowdowns in economic activity.

delegative democracy A hybrid form of regime that is democratic but involves the electorate "delegating" significant authority to a government.

democracy A form of regime associated with "rule by the people" that signifies rights and liberties for citizens, including political rights to participate in elections and civil liberties such as freedom of speech.

democratic breakdown The process through which a democratic regime partially or completely loses its democratic status.

democratic consolidation The process through which, after a transition from authoritarianism, a polity strengthens its democracy.

democratic peace A phenomenon associated with liberalism that holds that democratic countries will rarely if ever go to war with one another.

democratic regime A regime with predominantly democratic institutions, including basic civil rights and regular, free elections.

democratic transition The process through which a non-democratic regime becomes democratic.

democratization The process of a regime becoming more democratic, including both democratic transition and democratic consolidation.

denomination A type of religious organization, prevalent in the United States among other places, that is voluntary and accepts the principle of religious pluralism.

denominationalism A system or set of beliefs that privileges denominational forms of religious organization.

dependency A theory that argues that developing countries cannot simply embrace free trade because this will lead to ever-increasing wealth disparities between them and the advanced economies.

dependent variable In hypothesis testing, the dependent variable is the effect or outcome that we expect to be acted on (or have its value altered) by the independent variable.

development A process by which a society changes or advances, often measured in terms of economic growth, but also sometimes measured in terms of quality of life, standard of living, access to freedoms and opportunities, or other indicators.

deviant case (outlier) A case that does not fit the pattern predicted by a given theory; also known as a negative case.

differentiation The process through which institutions become increasingly autonomous from one another, including the reduction or other change in the linkages between religion and other institutions.

diffusion The process through which a practice or idea spreads locally, nationally, and globally.

direct democracy A conception of democracy that places great emphasis on direct citizen involvement in politics, especially involving plebiscites and/or citizen assemblies.

direct election With regard to executives, an electoral system in which voters cast a vote directly for the head of government or head of state.

dissolving the legislature The practice of a chief executive disbanding the legislature, often accompanied in a democratic regime by the calling for new elections.

district system An electoral system in which voters select representatives from specific geographic constituencies.

districting The process by which districts or other geographic constituencies are created for the purposes of elections.

dominant-party system Party system in which a country contains only one large political party that predominates politically, often controlling the legislative and executive branches of government.

Eastern nationalism An antiquated term for what is now often called "ethnic nationalism." (*See also* ethnic nationalism)

economic management States' efforts to shape the economic performance of their societies, especially in fiscal and monetary policy.

effective number of parties A measure designed to capture the number of meaningful parties in a party system that weights the number of parties represented by their size.

electoral authoritarianism A name applied to situations in which authoritarian regimes nominally compete in elections.

elite parties Political parties in which membership and scope were largely restricted to a small number of political elites.

empirical critique An effort to point to important evidence that does not support a conventional version of any given theory.

empirical Drawn from observations of the world.

employment Ongoing, regular access to paid work.

empowerment An increase in the social, political, or economic capabilities of an individual or group.

endogeneity The name given to any circumstance in which two variables exhibit mutual or reciprocal effects.

environmental sustainability The quality that one or another practice has with being compatible with the long-term health of the environment.

established religion Religion that is granted official status and support by the state.

ethnic group A group that identifies itself as having strong cultural commonality and a shared sense of long-run history, sometimes thinking of itself as a kind of kinship group.

ethnic nationalism A form of nationalism that says that you are a member of the nation because of your ancestry.

ethnicity The quality that one has by identifying with or being ascribed membership in an ethnic group.

European Union (EU) The political and economic union of many European states, numbering twenty-eight as of 2018.

everyday resistance Term coined by James Scott denoting efforts to resist or obstruct authority that are not clearly organized over time, such as work stoppages, slowdowns, and sabotage.

evidence A set of facts or observations used to support a proposition or hypothesis.

evolutionary psychology An approach to the analysis of human behavior that seeks to explain it almost exclusively on the basis of evolutionary theory. (*See also* sociobiology)

executive order An order made by a chief executive or top official to the bureaucracy that determines how the bureaucracy should enact or interpret the law.

executive The branch of government, or the individual(s) at the top of that branch, that executes or administers policies and laws in a country.

executive–legislative relations The set of political relationships between the executive branch of government, which executes laws/policies, and the legislative branch, which often has the authority to pass those laws/policies.

export-led growth A strategy for achieving economic growth dependent on sending natural resources or agricultural or industrial products for sale in foreign markets.

externality An economic phenomenon in which the gains and costs from a given activity do not accrue to the same actor.

falsifiability The testability of a theory or hypothesis. A good hypothesis could be logically demonstrated to be false by evidence.

fascism An authoritarian ideology associated with regimes like the Nazis and that of Italy's Benito Mussolini, favoring authoritarianism, militarism, and right-wing nationalism.

federalism System of government with constitutional design of separation of powers between central government and subnational governments.

feminism A social and intellectual movement that aims to ensure equal rights for women and men.

first-past-the-post Electoral system in which the candidate with the most number of votes is elected, regardless of whether a majority has been attained.

fiscal measure Measure of a government's revenues and/or expenditures.

fiscal policy Budget setting, which is dependent on generating revenue followed by government spending.

foreign policy The set of policies toward foreign nations made by a national government.

formal institutions Institutions that are governed by formal rules and typically linked to complex organizations like the state or corporations.

formal powers The powers possessed by a political actor, such as a chief executive, as a function of their constitutional or legal position.

fragile state A state that cannot or does not perform its expected functions, referred to by some scholars as a "failed state".

fragmentation (of party system) Contrasting with concentration, the extent to which political power and representation in a party system are characterized by relatively large numbers of relatively small parties. (*See also* concentration)

framing The way in which a given problem or situation is described and understood, with implications for how it might be addressed.

free rider Someone who benefits from a collective or public good without contributing to it.

functional definition Definition that aims to define a given phenomenon by what it *does* (as opposed to substantive definition).

game theory A set of approaches to the study of strategic interaction between actors, often relying on mathematical modeling and assumptions of the rationality of different actors.

gender Culturally constructed roles or identities one has by virtue of being ascribed the status of male or female, to be distinguished from biological sex.

generalizability The quality that a given theory, hypothesis, or finding has of being applicable to a wide number of cases.

genocide Efforts to diminish or destroy a people and/or culture.

gerrymandering Creation of districts of irregular shape or composition in order to achieve a desired political result.

Gini coefficient The most common measure of income inequality in any given population, usually expressed as a number between 0 and 1, with 0 being total equality and 1 being maximal inequality.

globalization The increasing interaction, both economic and cultural, among peoples and societies across national borders.

government In the context of executives, the set of top elected executive officials and high-level political appointees that shape and orient policy; also refers to the broader administrative apparatus of the state.

grand coalition A governing coalition composed of two or more major parties that hold a supermajority of legislative seats and represent a supermajority of the electorate.

greenhouse gases (GHG) Emissions of gases such as carbon dioxide and methane from industrial activity and consumption of fossil fuels that contributes to climate change.

gross domestic product (GDP) The total value of goods and services produced in a given country or territory; per capita GDP is divided by the population.

gross national income (GNI) A measure of the total income of all of a country's citizens, whether living in their home country or abroad.

guerrilla tactics Military techniques designed to produce ongoing stalemate, usually employed in situations of asymmetric military capability.

head of government The top executive official responsible for forming governments and formulating and implementing policies.

head of state A person with executive functions that is a country's symbolic representative, including elected presidents and unelected monarchs.

historical institutionalism An approach to theorizing that places emphasis on the power of institutions to shape the behavior of individuals, and how this operates over time.

Human Development Index (HDI) A composite measure developed by the United Nations to provide a broad view of annual development and well-being around the world, based on income, life expectancy, and literacy and school enrollments.

hybrid regime A class of regime that appears to be neither fully democratic nor fully authoritarian, such as electoral authoritarianism, delegative democracy, and illiberal democracy.

hyperinflation Exceedingly high inflation, which dramatically erodes the value of money over time.

hypothesis A specific prediction, derived from a theory, that can be tested against empirical evidence.

identity The social label ascribed to an individual or group that locates the individual or group in political society more broadly.

ideology A systematically coordinated and cognitively salient set of beliefs focused on politics.

illiberal democracy A polity with some democratic features but in which political and civil rights are not all guaranteed or protected.

immigration The movement of people to foreign countries.

impeachment A process by which a legislature initiates proceedings to determine whether an official, often a top-ranking executive official, should be removed from office.

impersonality A quality attributed by some scholars to modern states, which are presumed to be less likely to be identified with the personalities of their leaders.

independent variable In hypothesis testing, an independent variable is one that we expect to "act on" or change the value of the dependent variable.

indicator An element or feature that indicates the presence of an underlying factor.

indirect election Electoral system in which representatives are chosen by other elected officials, rather than directly by the citizenry at large. With regard to executives, an electoral system in which most voters never cast a ballot directly for the individual who becomes head of government.

individualization The treatment of problems as linked to the interests of individuals rather than as issues of common concern or interest.

inductive reasoning The process of moving from specific observations to general claims.

inequality In the social sciences, the differential distribution of access to goods like power, status, and material resources.

infant mortality A major public health indicator, which typically measures the number of infants per 1,000 born that do not survive until the age of one year.

inference The process through which we aim to test observable implications (often about cause and effect) of any given theory; also refers to conclusions reached through this process.

inflation Increase in the prices of goods and services.

informal powers Those powers possessed by an office holder that are not "official" but rather based on custom, convention, or other sources of influence.

institution A regularized or patterned activity that shapes the behavior of individuals and groups, including formal organizations like the state or political parties, as well as more informal institutions such as norms and values. Also, a social or political structure or set of practices, including government organizations, that shapes the behavior of individuals and groups.

institutionalism An approach to theorizing in comparative politics and related fields that places emphasis on the power of institutions to shape the behavior of individuals..

instrumentalism A type of explanation in social science that says that you can explain something by showing how its development or persistence is in the (usually material) interest of powerful individuals or groups.

insurgencies Contention with formalized military conflict.

integration In international relations, a process by which countries agree to collaborate economically or politically, to make some decisions collectively and to shape common strategies.

interdependence A relationship in which two or more actors (such as countries) are mutually dependent.

interest aggregation The process by which individuals' preferences are brought together to make collective decisions, often through political parties and the party system.

interest articulation The process by which political actors express their demands, needs, or wants in a political system, often through interest groups.

interest groups Organizations that make demands in the political system on behalf of their constituents and members.

intergovernmental organizations (IGOs) The set of international organizations that push for cooperation between countries and work for the prevention or mitigation of international conflicts.

international financial institutions (IFIs) Multilateral institutions, particularly the International Monetary Fund (IMF) and the World Bank, that have considerable leverage in international economy.

international political economy The study of how the economic relations between countries affect politics and how political relations affect economies.

international relations The study of relations between countries and between actors in the international system.

international security The study of issues of war and peace between nations and global security and conflict more broadly.

international trade The economic exchange of goods, services, and capital across international borders.

iron law of oligarchy The idea, developed by Robert Michels, that collective action always produces new elites.

isomorphism In institutional theory, the quality that two or more organizations have by virtue of being structurally very similar.

judicial activism Term used, often pejoratively, to characterize judicial actions that actively reinterpret legislation and thus imply exercising powers typically reserved for the legislative branch.

judicial review System of constitutional interpretation in which judges rule on the constitutionality of laws passed by legislature and executive.

judiciary The branch of government responsible for the interpretation of laws in courts.

laïcité The French name for the ideal of a lay state.

lay states States that establish a formal separation of religion and public life.

legislature Assembly or body of representatives with the authority to make laws.

level of analysis The level (e.g., individual, organizational, societal) at which observations are made, or at which causal processes operate. In international relations, the different levels that can be the context of a study, including the individual level, the nation-state level, and the level of the international system.

liberalism In political theory, an ideology that emphasizes individual freedoms, representative democracy, and the market economy. In international relations, a theory that holds states can have different preferences and internal structures that lead them to behave in different ways, especially with regard to the conduct of states that hold liberal values of democracy and free market commerce.

libertarianism A form of liberalism, strongly opposed to social democracy, that is especially concerned to minimize the role of government.

life expectancy The average age until which members of a society (or some group within society) live.

literacy rate The percentage of a population who can read.

lower chamber In a bicameral legislature, the house that typically has a larger number of legislators than upper chambers, and often represents the national vote either more proportionally or through smaller geographic constituencies.

malapportionment Apportionment in which voters are unequally represented in a legislature, such as through relatively greater numbers of legislators per capita for low-population areas and lesser number of legislators per capita for high-population areas.

market-led development An approach to economic management in which the state aims to control economic behavior as little as possible.

Marxism In international relations, a theory that emphasizes the role of social classes in shaping politics and highlights the role of capitalist accumulation as a prime driver in international affairs.

mass parties Parties consisting of large numbers of citizens as members and that undertake massive political mobilization.

measurement bias A measure is biased if it will not produce comparable results for all observations.

measurement error Either an episodic error, such as improperly recording data, or a systematic error, meaning that a measurement does not fully reflect what it is designed to measure.

measurement validity Whether a given measure effectively captures or represents what we are researching.

median voter The voter who is theoretically exactly in the middle of the distribution of voters.

minimum connected winning coalition A minimum winning coalition in which all parties in the coalition are "connected" or adjacent to one another on the political spectrum.

minimum size coalition A governing coalition that is closest to the threshold needed to govern, typically 50 percent of the legislative seats plus one seat.

minimum winning coalition A governing coalition that contains no surplus parties beyond those required to form a government.

mobilization The engagement of individuals and groups in sustained contention.

modern state A concept used to distinguish states in the modern world from earlier forms of political centralization; it includes features such as extensive bureaucracy, centralization of violence, and impersonality.

modernism The label applied by Anthony Smith to those theories of national identity that see it as exclusively modern.

modernity A contested term that refers to a type of society, typically one experiencing economic growth and with a relatively strong state, among other characteristics. (*See also* modernization)

modernization The process through which a society becomes "more modern," which is typically understood to mean having an advanced economy and, sometimes, a democratic polity.

modernization theory A theory that traces democracy to broad social changes, especially economic development and the changes that accompany it.

monarch A head of state in a monarchy, who usually inherits a position for life and may have either substantial political powers or very limited ceremonial powers.

monetary policy States' efforts to shape the value of a society's currency, often through the use of a central bank in the case of a modern state.

most-different-systems (MDS) A research design in which we compare cases that differ with respect to multiple factors but in which the outcome is the same.

most-similar-systems (MSS) A research design in which we compare cases that are similar with respect to a number of factors but with distinct outcomes.

multilateral In international relations, the actions of three or more countries working together.

multi-member district (MMD) Electoral system in which district constituencies have more than one representative.

multiparty democracy A democracy in which at least two parties compete for power.

multiparty system A political party system consisting of more than two significant parties that have opportunities to govern.

nation (the) A group thought of as sovereign and equal, typically comprised of a large, often geographically bounded population.

national identity An identity that locates one's social position in relation to national membership.

nationalism The view that the world is and should be divided into nations that are thought of by nationalists as sovereign and egalitarian.

nativism A political attitude that seeks to protect the interests of established groups of residents in a given country against the interests of more recent immigrants.

neoliberalism An ideological tendency that favors liberal democracy and market-led development.

new institutionalism The name given to the turn to institutional theory in the last several decades in economics, political science, and sociology.

nonstate actors In international relations, actors in international politics that are not nation-states; includes multinational corporations, transnational advocacy groups, and international criminal networks.

normative Concerned with specifying which sort of practice or institution is morally or ethically justified.

nuclear proliferation The expansion of the number of countries and other actors possessing nuclear technology.

offensive realism A realist theory that holds that states will seek to maximize their power whenever they can.

offshoring In international trade and business, the practice of an economic actor basing some of its services or processes abroad rather than in its domestic market. (*See also* outsourcing)

open-ended question A question that, in principle, is open to numerous possible answers.

open-list proportional representation Electoral system in which voters choose a candidate but votes are aggregated by political party to determine the allocation of seats across parties.

operationalization The process through which we make a concept measurable.

organization Institutionalized group such as a state, corporation, political party, social movement, or international body. Also, the ongoing coordination of collective action in the pursuit of common purposes.

outcome Typically used as a synonym for "effect," something that is produced or changed in any social or political process.

outsourcing In international trade and business, the practice of an economic actor contracting out to other actors, often overseas. (*See also* offshoring)

parliament A type of legislature, often associated with systems in which the legislators vote on the leadership of the executive branch and the formation of a government.

parliamentarism A system of government in which the head of government is elected by and accountable to a parliament or legislature.

parliamentary sovereignty System in which the constitutionality of laws passed by legislature and executive are not subject to constitutional interpretation by judiciary.

partisan powers The powers accruing to a government official, such as a chief executive, by virtue of the official's leverage or power over members of a political party.

party system institutionalization The degree to which a party system is stable and remains so over time, as measured by such characteristics as the persistence of parties, the stability of their ideologies, and the degree to which they are distinct from the specific individuals that lead them.

party system Patterns of party politics characterized by the number of relevant parties in a country.

path dependent The name given to historical processes in which future developments are shaped or partially determined by events at previous stages in those processes.

patronage The use of government favors, typically in the form of employment, to garner political support.

payoff matrix In game-theoretic models, the distribution of payoffs to players depending on the choices made.

peak organization Top associations, such as labor federations and large business organizations, that represent common interests by bringing together many like-minded organizations.

perennialism The label applied by Anthony Smith to those theories of national identity that see it as neither exclusively modern nor continuous with pre-historical forms of identity.

personalistic dictatorship A form of authoritarianism in which the personality of the dictator is highlighted.

pluralism A system of interest group representation in which groups compete openly to influence government decisions and public policy, and in which specific groups do not have official preferential access to decision making.

political culture The symbolically encoded beliefs, values, norms, and practices that shape the formal distribution of power in any given society.

political economy The interaction or interrelationship between politics and the economy in a given country or internationally, to include how politics affects economies and how economies affect politics.

political opportunities The availability of political options to redress grievances.

political party A political organization that seeks to influence policy, typically by getting candidates and members elected or appointed to public office.

political revolutions Revolutions, the main effect of which is to alter political institutions rather than social and economic structures.

political rights Rights of individuals to participate in political life, including the right to political speech, the right to vote, and the right to join political associations.

populism A political approach in which leaders, often heads of government and top executive branch officials, make direct appeals to "the people" and seek to develop direct political ties with the masses.

portfolio The set of duties and tasks that correspond to a given ministerial office.

poverty The state of being poor, as measured by low income, deprivation, lack of access to resources, or limited economic opportunities.

poverty line A specified threshold below which individuals or groups are judged to be in poverty.

president An executive leader that typically combines the functions of head of state and head of government, and is not directly responsible to a legislature.

presidentialism A system of government in which a president serves as chief executive, being independent of the legislature and often combining the functions of head of state and head of government.

prime minister A chief executive in a parliamentary system of government.

primordialism The label applied by Anthony Smith to those theories of national identity that see it as continuous with pre-historical ("primordial") forms of identity.

prisoner's dilemma (game) A model of a game in which two actors would benefit from mutual cooperation, but each has individual incentives to defect from cooperation.

privatization In the context of the economy, the transfer of control (of a business, industry, or service) from public to private. In the context of the social scientific study of religion, this refers to the process of religious practice being confined to the private sphere.

procedural definition of democracy A conception of democracy, contrasted with a substantive definition, that emphasizes the minimal standards, procedures, or rules that a country should have in place to govern political life.

proportional representation (PR) In its pure form, an electoral system in which voters choose a preferred party and seats are allocated to parties according to the percentage of the vote the party wins.

protectionism In international trade, the practice of a country protecting or giving favor to its own domestic producers.

public goods Goods or services, often provided by a government, for use by all members of a society and for which one person's use of the good does not compromise anyone else's use of the good. Examples include national defense, basic infrastructure, and a healthy environment.

public sphere The space in which public life and deliberation take place (as opposed to the "private sphere").

purchasing power parity (PPP) An adjustment made to income measures to account for differences in cost of living.

qualitative A form of analysis that aims to discern relationships between events or phenomena as described in narrative form, such as an account of an historical process.

quantitative Quantitative analysis aims for the mathematical discernment of relationships between variables, typically involving a large number of cases or observations.

race The idea that human beings are divided into different groups, often thought of (erroneously) as biological categories.

racial formation A concept developed by Omi and Winant (1994) that describes the process through which ideas of race are constructed and develop over time.

racialization The historical process through which social relations become interpreted in terms of racial categories.

rational institutionalism An approach to theorizing in comparative politics and related fields that places emphasis on the power of institutions to shape the behavior of individuals, one which often focuses on implications of institutions for individuals' strategic choices.

realism In international relations, a theory that treats states in the international system largely as acting on the basis of national self-interest, defined often in terms of power, survival, and security.

referendum A popular vote on a specific issue.

regime A form or type of governmental system, with an emphasis on institutions and rules.

regime change Any major change of regime type, including democratization, democratic breakdown, or certain types of authoritarian persistence in which one type of authoritarian regime gives way to another.

regime type The form of a political regime, such as democratic versus authoritarian, as well as subtypes, such as personalistic dictatorships or totalitarian regimes.

relative deprivation The state of having or feeling that one has less than other members of one's reference group (including one's own group over time).

religious monopoly The situation in which one major religion dominates the religious landscape within a given society (the opposite of religious pluralism).

religious pluralism The situation in which there are multiple religious organizations within a given society (the opposite of religious monopoly).

religious states States in which religion is a key part of official politics, often involving religious establishment, religious legitimation of the state, and restrictions on religious minorities.

remittances Cash or resources sent to a home country, often to family and friends, by emigrants.

representation In legislatures, the process by which elected legislators reflect the interests and preferences of voters in their constituencies.

representative democracy A conception of democracy in which politicians and institutions are understood to represent the electorate, who nevertheless can constrain their behavior through periodic elections and other forms of participation.

revolution A form of collective action in which some large-scale, structural change is either attempted or accomplished.

rule of law A system that imposes regularized rules in a polity, with key criteria including equal rights, the regular enforcement of laws, and the relative independence of the judiciary.

runoff Electoral system in which the top candidates after a first round of voting compete in one or more additional rounds of voting until a candidate receives a majority.

Sartori's ladder of abstraction The idea that we can organize concepts on the basis of their specificity or generality.

scope conditions The conditions or range of cases for which an argument works.

secularism The ideological complex that favors secular culture (the term is also sometimes used as a synonym for secular culture more generally).

secularization The process through which (according to some theories) societies become less religious as they become more modern.

security dilemma Dilemma in which each actor in the international system expects others to maximize their own security advantage, and thus builds up power itself, leading to an arms race.

semi-presidential system A mixed or hybrid system combining aspects of presidentialism and parliamentarism.

separation of powers The division of powers in a government system between branches of government or between levels of government.

single transferable vote (STV) Electoral system in which voters rank candidates and the winners' surplus votes are reallocated to other, lower-ranking candidates until a slate of representatives is chosen.

single-member district (SMD) Electoral system in which voters choose a candidate and the winner is elected by the most votes earned or through winning a runoff vote.

single-party system An authoritarian system in which parties besides the single dominant party are banned or disallowed.

social capital Advantage that individuals or groups hold by virtue of their social relationships.

social construction The process through which socially shared meanings and definitions are established and maintained.

social democracy An ideological movement that favors both representative democracy with respect for basic individual rights and state action to promote relative economic and social equality, viewed by some as a variety of socialism but by most as a variety of liberalism.

social identity theory An important theory in social psychology that sees personal identities as linked to and partially derived from group identities and roles.

social movement organization An organization that has been created to help maintain and lead social movement activity over time.

social movements Ongoing, organized collective action oriented toward a goal of social change.

social networks Structures of social ties and connections among individuals.

social revolutions Revolutions that dramatically change social structures.

socialism An ideology (or family of ideologies) that emphasizes economic equality as a key goal, to be pursued in large measure through state action.

sociobiology An approach to the study of societies that sees human society as governed by the same (evolutionary) principles as animal societies.

sovereignty The key way the authority of the modern state is conceptualized: states are understood to be the ultimate authority within their specifically demarcated territories.

state The most important form of political organization in modern politics, which, in its ideal form, is characterized by centralized control of the use of force, bureaucratic organization, and the provision of a number of public goods.

state breakdown Dramatic decline in state capacity.

state capacity The ability of the state to achieve its objectives, especially the abilities to control violence, effectively tax the population, and maintain well-functioning institutions and the rule of law.

state interventionism An approach to economic management in which the state plays a central role, not just through enforcing contracts and property rights but through active interventions such as coordinating investment, supplying credit, and, in many instances, through the establishment and running of state-owned enterprises.

state of emergency A condition allowed by some constitutions in which guarantees, rights, or provisions are temporarily limited, to be justified by emergencies or exceptional circumstances.

state system The condition that many of the most important actors in international relations are states, which can be understood as systemically linked to one another.

state-led development An approach to economic management in which the state plays a prominent role in coordinating the behavior of economic actors and intervening in the economy.

strain theory A theory suggesting that major social change causes social "strain" or conflict which increases demand for revolution.

strategic voting Voting in a way that does not reflect a voter's ideal preference, so as to prevent a less-desired outcome.

structuralism A view in social and political theory holding that social structures, rather than agents or culture, make most of the difference.

structuralism An approach to nationalism studies that sees big, difficult-to-change parts of society as determining what really matters about national identity.

subaltern Occupying lower rungs in a hierarchical system.

substantive definition Definition that aims to define a given phenomenon by what it *is* rather than by what it does (as opposed to functional definition).

substantive definition of democracy A conception of democracy, contrasted with a procedural definition, that views a polity's democratic status as dependent on the satisfaction of certain substantive ends, such as the extension of broad rights or the reduction of income inequality.

sustainability The notion, especially used with regard to the environment, that a resource is capable of being sustained for use or enjoyment by future generations.

term limit Restriction on the number of times or total amount of time a political official can serve in a given position.

territorial nationalism According to some scholars, a type of nationalism that closely resembles civic nationalism, in that membership is fundamentally determined by where one is born or where one resides rather than one's ancestry.

terrorism The use of violence to achieve political ends through psychological impacts on a civilian population.

theocracy An authoritarian state controlled by religious leaders, or a state with very strict religious restrictions that uses religion as its main mode of legitimation.

theoretical critique An effort to show that a given theory has logical limitations.

theory A general set of explanatory claims about some specifiable empirical range.

thesis A statement for which one argues on the basis of evidence.

Third-World revolutions A concept developed by John Foran holding that revolutions in the developing world have special characteristics.

Tocqueville effect The name given by some scholars to Tocqueville's observation that changing relative status positions were an important factor in some groups participating in the French Revolution.

totalitarian regime A form of authoritarian regime that aims to control everything about the lives of its subject population, such as in the Soviet Union and Germany under the Nazis.

transgender An identity in which one's gender does not conform to conventional matching with biological sex.

transition The movement from an authoritarian regime to a democratic one.

transnational Issues or institutions that cross international borders.

transnational network A network of nonstate actors working across state borders.

trust The extent to which an individual has confidence in the reliability or good conduct of others.

twenty-first-century socialism The name given to supporters of governments in some contemporary societies (e.g., Venezuela, Bolivia) that aims to emphasize their allegedly more participatory and democratic features.

two-party system A political party system consisting of two significant parties that have a duopoly on opportunities to govern.

underemployment When workers are employed less than they wish to be or below their skill level.

unemployment The lack of ongoing, regular access to paid work.

unicameral legislature Legislature with a single chamber.

unitarism System of government in which central government is predominant and the powers of subnational governments are limited to those delegated by the center.

unitary rational actor In international relations theory and especially realism, the idea that states act as if they were single individuals capable of making decisions on the basis of rational calculations about the costs and benefits of different actions.

United Nations The major international organization whose membership consists of most of the countries in the world, that has the aim of preventing and managing conflict and establishing multilateral cooperation on matters of international law, economics, and human development and well-being.

upper chamber The chamber in a bicameral legislature that is usually smaller in number of legislators, often representing larger geographic constituencies such as states or provinces.

utility The value that people derive from resources to which they have access.

variable An element or factor that is likely to change, or vary, from case to case.

variation Difference between cases in any given study of comparative politics.

veto An act of executive power in which an executive rejects a law passed by a legislature.

vote of no confidence A vote taken by a legislature that expresses a lack of support for the government or executive, which, if successful, often results in the dissolution of the government and the calling of new legislative elections.

welfare state A state that aims to provide a basic safety net for the most vulnerable elements of its population, often accomplished through social insurance, public health care plans, and poverty relief.

Western nationalism An antiquated term for what is now often called "civic nationalism." (*See also* civic nationalism)

within-case comparison The comparative analysis of variation that takes place over time or in distinct parts of a single case.

world society theory A theory associated with scholars such as John Meyer, who argue that basic organizational features of the state system are cultural and have diffused globally.

References and Further Reading

CHAPTER 1

Berlin, Isaiah. 1958. *Two Concepts of Liberty: An Inaugural Lecture Delivered Before the University of Oxford*. Oxford: Clarendon Press.

Brady, Henry, and David Collier, eds. 2004. *Rethinking Social Inquiry: Diverse Tools, Shared Standards*. Lanham, MD: Rowman and Littlefield.

Collier, David, and Robert Adcock. 1999. Democracy and Dichotomies: A Pragmatic Approach to Choices About Concepts. *Annual Review of Political Science* 2:537–565.

Collier, David, and Steven Levitsky. 1997. Democracy with Adjectives: Conceptual Innovation in Comparative Research. *World Politics* 49(3): 430–451.

Dunning, Thad. 2012. *Natural Experiments in the Social Sciences: A Design-Based Approach*. New York: Cambridge University Press.

Elster, Jon. 2007. *Explaining Social Behavior: More Nuts and Bolts for the Social Sciences*. New York: Cambridge University Press.

Fearon, James D., and David D. Laitin. 2003. Ethnicity, Insurgency, and Civil War. *American Political Science Review* 97(1): 75–90.

Gerring, John. 2001. *Social Science Methodology: A Criterial Framework*. Cambridge: Cambridge University Press.

Gerring, John. 2009. The Case Study: What It Is and What It Does. In *Oxford Handbook of Political Science*, ed. Robert E. Goodin, 1133–1166. New York: Oxford University Press.

Jackman, Simon. 2004. Bayesian Analysis for Political Research. *Annual Review of Political Science* 7: 483–505.

King, Gary, Robert Keohane, and Sidney Verba. 1994. *Designing Social Inquiry: Scientific Inference in Qualitative Research*. Princeton, NJ: Princeton University Press.

Lieberson, Stanley, and Freda Lynn. 2002. Barking Up the Wrong Branch: Scientific Alternatives to the Current Model of Sociological Science. *Annual Review of Sociology* 28: 1–19.

Lipset, Seymour Martin. 1959. Some Social Requisites of Democracy: Economic Development and Political Legitimacy. *American Political Science Review* 53(1): 69–105.

Mahoney, James, and Dietrich Reuschmeyer, eds. 2003. *Comparative Historical Analysis in the Social Sciences*. Cambridge: Cambridge University Press.

Mill, John Stuart. 1846. *A System of Logic, Ratiocinative and Inductive*. New York: Harper.

Przeworski, Adam, and Henry Teune. 1970. *The Logic of Comparative Social Inquiry*. New York: Wiley-Interscience.

Sartori, Giovanni. 1970. Concept Misformation in Comparative Politics. *The American Political Science Review* 64(4): 1033–1053.

Weber, Max. 1949. Objectivity in Social Science and Social Policy. In *The Methodology of the Social Sciences*, ed. and trans. Edward A. Shils and Henry A. Finch, 49–112. New York: The Free Press.

CHAPTER 2

Babbie, Earl. 2010. *Methods of Social Research*. 12th ed. Belmont, CA: Wadsworth, Cengage Learning.

Brady, Henry, and David Collier, eds. 2004. *Rethinking Social Inquiry: Diverse Tools, Shared Standards*. Lanham, MD: Rowman and Littlefield.

Cassidy, John. 2013. The Reinhart and Rogoff Controversy: A Summing Up. *The New Yorker*, April 26.

Centeno, Miguel Angel. 2002. *Blood and Debt: War and the Nation-State in Latin America*. University Park: Pennsylvania State University Press.

Collier, David, and Steven Levitsky. 1997. Democracy with Adjectives: Conceptual Innovation in Comparative Research. *World Politics* 49(3): 430–451.

Haig, Brian. 2003. What Is a Spurious Correlation? *Understanding Statistics* 2(2): 125–132.

King, Gary, Robert Keohane, and Sidney Verba. 1994. *Designing Social Inquiry: Scientific Inference in Qualitative Research*. Princeton, NJ: Princeton University Press.

Kuhn, Thomas. 1962. *The Structure of Scientific Revolutions*. Chicago: University of Chicago Press.

Leinweber, David. 2007. Stupid Data Miner Tricks: Overfitting the S&P 500. *The Journal of Investing* 16(1): 15–22.

Lindberg, Staffan. 2006. *Democracy and Elections in Africa*. Baltimore: Johns Hopkins University Press.

Lipset, Seymour Martin. 1959. Some Social Requisites of Democracy: Economic Development and Political Legitimacy. *American Political Science Review* 53(1): 69–105.

Nossiter, Adam. 2014. Fear of Ebola Breeds a Terror of Physicians. *New York Times*, July 28.

Popper, Karl. 1963. *Conjectures and Refutations: The Growth of Scientific Knowledge*. London: Routledge and K. Paul.

Van Evera, Stephen. 1997. *Guide to Methods for Students of Political Science*. Ithaca, NY: Cornell University Press.

CHAPTER 3

Anderson, Perry. 1974. *Lineages of the Absolutist State*. New York: Verso.

Bates, Robert. 2008. *When Things Fell Apart: State Failure in Late-Century Africa*. New York: Cambridge University Press.

Centeno, Miguel Angel. 2002. *Blood and Debt: War and the Nation State in Latin America*. University Park: Pennsylvania State University Press.

Chirot, Daniel. 1994. *How Societies Change*. Newbury Park, CA: Pine Forge Press.

Colley, Linda. 1992. *Britons: Forging the Nation*. New Haven, CT: Yale University Press.

DiMaggio, Paul J., and Walter W. Powell. 1983. The Iron Cage Revisited: Institutional Isomorphism and Collective Rationality in Organizational Fields. *American Sociological Review* 48:147–160.

Downing, Brian. 1992. *The Military Revolution and Political Change*. Princeton, NJ: Princeton University Press.

Elliott, John Huxtable. 2002. *Imperial Spain, 1469–1716*. 2nd ed. New York: Penguin.

Ertman, Thomas. 1997. *Birth of the Leviathan: Building States and Regimes in Medieval and Early Modern Europe*. New York: Cambridge University Press.

Evans, Peter. 1997. The Eclipse of the State? Reflections on Stateness in an Era of Globalization. *World Politics* 50(1): 62–87.

Evans, Peter B., Dietrich Reuschemeyer, and Theda Skocpol. 1985. *Bringing the State Back In*. New York: Cambridge University Press.

Foucault, Michel. 1977. *Discipline and Punish: The Birth of the Prison*, trans. Alan Sheridan. New York: Vintage Books.

Fukuyama, Francis. 2004. *State-Building, Governance, and World Order in the 21st Century*. Ithaca, NY: Cornell University Press.

Giddens, Anthony. 1987. *A Contemporary Critique of Historical Materialism: Vol. 2: The Nation-State and Violence*. Berkeley: University of California Press.

Gorski, Philip S. 2003. *The Disciplinary Revolution: Calvinism and the Rise of the State in Early Modern Europe*. Chicago: University of Chicago Press.

Greenfeld, Liah. 1992. *Nationalism: Five Roads to Modernity*. Cambridge, MA: Harvard University Press.

Greenfeld, Liah. 1996. Nationalism and Modernity. *Social Research* 63(1): 3–40.

Hardin, Russell. 1997. Economic Theories of the State. In *Perspectives on Public Choice: A Handbook*, ed. Dennis C. Mueller, 21–34. New York: Cambridge University Press.

Herbst, Jeffrey. 2000. *States and Power in Africa: Comparative Lessons in Authority and Control*. Princeton, NJ: Princeton University Press.

Hobbes, Thomas. [1651] 1996. *Leviathan*, ed. Richard Tuck. New York: Cambridge University Press.

Huntington, Samuel. 1957. *The Soldier and the State: The Theory and Politics of Civil–Military Relations*. Cambridge, MA: Belknap/Harvard University Press.

Karl, Terry Lynn. 1997. *The Paradox of Plenty: Oil Booms and Petro-States*. Berkeley: University of California Press.

Lenin, Vladimir. 1939. *Imperialism, the Highest Stage of Capitalism: A Popular Outline*. New York: International Publishers.

Levi, Margaret. 1988. *Of Rule and Revenue*. Berkeley: University of California Press.

Loveman, Mara. 2014. *National Colors: Racial Classification and the State in Latin America*. New York: Oxford University Press.

Lynch, John. 1994. *The Hispanic World in Crisis and Change*, 1598–1700. Malden, MA: Wiley-Blackwell.

Marshall, T. H. 1965. *Class, Citizenship, and Social Development*. New York: Anchor Books.

Marx, Karl. 1978. The German Ideology: Part I. In *The Marx-Engels Reader*, 2nd ed., ed. Robert C. Tucker New York: W. W. Norton and Company.

McNeill, J. R., and William H. McNeill. 2003. *The Human Web: A Bird's Eye View of World History*. New York: W. W. Norton and Company.

McNeill, William H. 1982. *The Pursuit of Power: Technology, Armed Force, and Society Since A.D. 1000*. Chicago: University of Chicago Press.

Meyer, John W., John Boli, George M. Thomas, and Francisco O. Ramírez. 1997. World Society and the Nation-State. *American Journal of Sociology* 103(1): 144–181.

Meyer, John W., and Brian Rowan. 1991. Institutionalized Organizations: Formal Structure as Myth and Ceremony. In *The New Institutionalism in Organizational Analysis*, ed. Walter W. Powell and Paul J. DiMaggio, 41–62. Chicago: University of Chicago Press.

Migdal, Joel S. 1988. *Strong Societies and Weak States: State-Society Relations and State Capabilities in the Third World*. Princeton, NJ: Princeton University Press.

Morgan, Glyn. 2007. *The Idea of a European Superstate: Public Justification and European Integration*. Princeton, NJ: Princeton University Press.

North, Douglass C., John Joseph Wallis, and Barry R. Weingast. 2009. *Violence and Social Orders: A Conceptual Framework for Interpreting Recorded Human History*. New York: Cambridge University Press.

Ostrom, Elinor. 1990. *Governing the Commons: The Evolution of Institutions for Collective Action*. New York: Cambridge University Press.

Payne, Stanley. 2011. *Spain: A Unique History*. Madison: University of Wisconsin Press.

Pérez Díaz, Victor. 2014. Civil Society: A Multi-Layered Concept. *Current Sociology* 62(6): 812-830.

Pettit, Becky, and Bruce Western. 2004. Mass Imprisonment and the Life Course: Race and Class Inequality in U.S. Incarceration. *American Sociological Review* 69(2): 151–169.

Pincus, Steve. 2009. *1688: The First Modern Revolution*. New Haven, CT: Yale University Press.

Pinker, Steven. 2011. *The Better Angels of Our Nature: Why Violence Has Declined*. New York: Viking.

Piven, Frances Fox, and Richard A. Cloward. 1993. *Regulating the Poor: The Functions of Public Welfare*. 2nd ed. New York: Vintage.

Poggi, Gianfranco. 1990. *The State: Its Nature, Development, and Prospects*. Stanford, CA: Stanford University Press.

Polanyi, Karl. 2001. *The Great Transformation: The Political and Economic Origins of our Time*. 2nd ed. Boston: Beacon Press.

Putnam, Robert. 1994. *Making Democracy Work: Civic Traditions in Modern Italy*. Princeton, NJ: Princeton University Press.

Sahlins, Peter. 1991. *Boundaries: The Making of France and Spain in the Pyrenees*. Berkeley: University of California Press.

Schumpeter, Joseph. 1962. *Capitalism, Socialism, and Democracy*. 3rd ed. New York: Harper Perennial Modern Classics.

Scott, James. 1999. *Seeing Like a State: How Certain Schemes to Improve the Human Condition Have Failed*. New Haven, CT: Yale University Press.

Skocpol, Theda. 1979. *States and Social Revolutions: A Comparative Analysis of France, Russia, and China*. New York: Cambridge University Press.

Spruyt, Hendrik. 1994. *The Sovereign State and Its Competitors*. Princeton, NJ: Princeton University Press.

Spruyt, Hendrik. 2007. War, Trade, and State Formation. In *Oxford Handbook of Comparative Politics*, ed. Carles Boix and Susan Stokes, 211–235. New York: Oxford University Press.

Strayer, Joseph R. [1970] 2005. *On the Medieval Origins of the Modern State*. Princeton Classic ed. Princeton, NJ: Princeton University Press.

Tilly, Charles. 1975. Reflections on the History of European State-Making. In *The Formation of National States in Western Europe*, ed. C. Tilly, 3–83. Princeton, NJ: Princeton University Press.

Tilly, Charles. 1992. *Coercion, Capital, and European States, AD 990–1992*. Oxford: Blackwell. (Orig. pub. 1990.)

Tocqueville, Alexis de. 1983. *The Old Regime and the French Revolution*, trans. Stuart Gilbert. New York: Anchor Books.

Wallerstein, Immanuel. [1974] 2011. *The Modern World System: Capitalist Agriculture and the Origins of the European World Economy in the 16th Century*. Berkeley: University of California Press.

Weber, Max. 1946. Politics as a Vocation. In *From Max Weber: Essays in Sociology*, ed. H. H. Gerth and C. Wright Mills, 77–128. New York: Oxford University Press.

Weber, Max. 1978. *Economy and Society*, Vol. 2, ed. Guenther Roth and Claus Wittich. Berkeley: University of California Press.

Weingast, Barry R. 1997. The Political Foundation of Democracy and the Rule of Law. *American Political Science Review* 91(2): 245–263.

Western, Bruce. 2006. *Punishment and Inequality in America*. New York: Russell Sage Foundation.

Wimmer, Andreas and Yuval Feinstein. 2010. The Rise of the Nation State Across the World, 1816–2001. *American Sociological Review*, 75(5): 764–790.

CHAPTER 4

Arendt, Hannah. 1963. *On Revolution*. New York: Viking Press.

Bell, David A. 2001. *The Cult of the Nation in France: Inventing Nationalism, 1680–1800*. Cambridge, MA: Harvard University Press.

Buchanan, James. 1984. A Sketch of Positive Public Choice Theory and Its Normative Implications. In *The Theory of Public Choice*, Vol. 2, ed. James Buchanan and Robert Tollison, 11–22. Ann Arbor: University of Michigan Press.

"Asia's Next Revolution," *The Economist*, September 8, 2012.

Esping-Andersen, Gøsta. 1990. *The Three Worlds of Welfare Capitalism*. Princeton, NJ: Princeton University Press.

Evans, Peter. 1995. *Embedded Autonomy: States and Industrial Transformation*. Princeton, NJ: Princeton University Press.

Foucault, Michel. 1977. *Discipline and Punish: The Birth of the Prison*, trans. Alan Sheridan. New York: Vintage Press.

Friedman, Milton. 1962. *Capitalism and Freedom*. Chicago: University of Chicago Press.

Friedman, Milton. 1990. Using the Market for Social Development. *Cato Journal* 8(3): 567–579.

Gerschenkron, Alexander. 1962. *Economic Backwardness in Historical Perspective*. Cambridge, MA: Harvard University Press.

Goodman, Roger, and Ito Peng. 1996. The East Asian Welfare States: Peripatetic Learning, Adaptive Change, and Nation-Building. In *Welfare States in Transition: National Adaptations in Global Economies*, ed. Gøsta Esping-Andersen, 192–225. Thousand Oaks, CA: Sage.

Greenfeld, Liah. 2001. *The Spirit of Capitalism: Nationalism and Economic Growth*. Cambridge, MA: Harvard University Press.

Hamilton, Alexander. [1791] 1828. Report on Manufactures. In *Reports of the Secretary of the Treasury of the United States*, 78–133. Washington, DC: United States Senate [Printed by Duff Green].

Hayek, F. A. [1944] 1994. *The Road to Serfdom*. 50th anniversary ed. Chicago: University of Chicago Press.

Howard, Christopher. 2007. *The Welfare State Nobody Knows: Debunking Myths about U.S. Social Policy*. Princeton, NJ: Princeton University Press.

Huber, Evelyn, and John D. Stephens. 2001. *Development and Crisis of the Welfare State: Parties and Policies in Global Markets*. Chicago: University of Chicago Press.

Marx, Karl. [1867] 1996. *Das Kapital: A Critique of Political Economy*. Washington, DC: Regnery Publishing.

Mettler, Susan. 2011. *The Submerged State: How Invisible Government Policies Undermine American Democracy*. Chicago: University of Chicago Press.

North, Douglass. 1990. *Institutions, Institutional Change, and Economic Performance*. New York: Cambridge University Press.

Pierson, Christopher. 2006. *Beyond the Welfare State? The New Political Economy of Welfare*. Malden, MA: Polity Books.

Prasad, Monica. 2006. *The Politics of Free Markets: The Rise of Neoliberal Economic Policies in Britain, France, Germany, and the United States*. Chicago: University of Chicago Press.

Ricardo, David. 1817. *On the Principles of Political Economy and Taxation*. London: John Murray.

Smith, Adam. [1776] 2003. *The Wealth of Nations*. New York: Random House Books.

Taylor, Charles. 2007. *A Secular Age*. Cambridge, MA: Belknap Press/Harvard University Press.

Weingast, Barry, and Douglass North. 1989. Constitutions and Commitment: The Evolution of Institutions Governing Public Choice in Seventeenth-Century England. *Journal of Economic History* 49(4): 803–832.

Wilensky, Harold L. 1975. *The Welfare State and Equality: Structural and Ideological Roots of Public Expenditure*. Berkeley: University of California Press.

CHAPTER 5

Acemoglu, Daron, Simon Johnson, and James A. Robinson. 2001. The Colonial Origins of Comparative Development. *American Economic Review* 91:1369–1401.

Almond, Gabriel. 1991. Capitalism and Democracy. *PS: Political Science and Politics* 24(3): 467–474.

Amsden, Alice. 1992. *Asia's Next Giant: South Korea and Late Industrialization.* New York: Oxford University Press.

Balakrishnan, Pulapre. 2010. *Economic Growth in India: History and Prospect.* New York: Oxford University Press.

Bates, Robert. 1981. *Markets and States in Tropical Africa: The Political Basis of Agricultural Policies.* Berkeley: University of California Press.

Berkman, Lisa F. 2004. The Health Divide. *Contexts* 3(4): 38–43.

Burt. Ronald. 1992. *Structural Holes: The Social Structure of Competition.* Cambridge, MA: Harvard University Press.

Cardoso, Fernando Henrique, and Enzo Faletto. 1979. *Dependency and Development in Latin America.* Berkeley: University of California Press.

Chang, Ha-Joon. 2003. *Kicking Away the Ladder: Development Strategy in Historical Perspective.* London: Anthem Press.

Collier, Paul. 2007. *The Bottom Billion: Why the Poorest Countries Are Failing and What Can Be Done About It.* New York: Oxford University Press.

Diamond, Jared. 1997. *Guns, Germs, and Steel: The Fates of Human Societies.* New York: W. W. Norton.

Escobar, Arturo. 1995. *Encountering Development: The Making and Unmaking of the Third World.* Princeton, NJ: Princeton University Press.

Evans, Peter. 1979. *Dependent Development: The Alliance of Multinational, State, and Local Capital in Brazil.* Princeton, NJ: Princeton University Press.

Frank, André Gunder. 1967. *Capitalism and Underdevelopment in Latin America: Historical Studies of Chile and Brazil.* New York: Monthly Review Press.

Fukuyama, Francis. 1995. *Trust: The Social Virtues and the Creation of Prosperity.* New York: Free Press.

Harrison, Lawrence. 2000. *Underdevelopment Is a State of Mind: Reflections on the Latin American Case.* Lanham, MD: Rowman & Littlefield.

Inglehart, Ronald, Roberto Foa, Christopher Peterson, and Christian Welzel. 2008. Development, Freedom, and Rising Happiness. *Perspectives on Psychological Science* 3(4): 264–285.

Kohli, Atul. 2004. *State-Directed Development: Political Power and Industrialization in the Global Periphery.* Cambridge: Cambridge University Press.

Kurth, James. 1979. The Political Consequences of the Product Cycle: Industrial History and Political Outcomes. *Industrial Organization* 33(1): 1–34.

Lenin, Vladimir Ilych. [1917] 1948. *Imperialism: The Highest Stage of Capitalism.* London: Lawrence and Wishart.

Mahoney, James. 2010. *Colonialism and Postcolonial Development.* New York: Cambridge University Press.

Noland, Marcus, and Howard Pack. 2004. Islam, Globalization, and Economic Performance in the Middle East. *SAIS Review* 24(2): 105–116.

Olson, Mancur. 1984. *The Rise and Decline of Nations: Economic Growth, Stagflation, and Social Rigidities.* New Haven: Yale University Press.

Pierson, Paul. 2004. *Politics in Time: History, Institutions, and Social Analysis.* Princeton, NJ: Princeton University Press.

Pogge, Thomas. 2008. *World Poverty and Human Rights.* 2nd ed. Cambridge, England: Polity.

Prebisch, Raul. 1950. *The Economic Development of Latin America and Its Principal Problems.* New York: United Nations.

Putnam, Robert. 1995. *Making Democracy Work: Civic Traditions in Modern Italy.* Princeton, NJ: Princeton University Press.

Putnam, Robert D. 2000. *Bowling Alone: The Collapse and Revival of American Community.* New York: Simon and Schuster.

Rodney, Walter. 1981. *How Europe Underdeveloped Africa.* Washington, DC: Howard University Press.

Rosenstein-Rodan, Paul. 1943. Problems of Industrialization of Eastern and South-Eastern Europe. *The Economic Journal* 53 (210/211): 202–211.

Sen, Amartya. 1999. *Development as Freedom.* New York: Anchor Books.

Stiglitz, Joseph, Amartya Sen, and Jean-Paul Fitoussi. 2010. *Mismeasuring Our Lives: Why GDP Doesn't Add Up.* New York: The New Press.

Tocqueville, Alexis de. 1988. *Democracy in America.* New York: HarperPerennial.

United Nations Development Programme (UNDP). 2014. *Human Development Report.* New York: UNDP. [Published annually, available at http://hdr.undp.org/en/content/human-development-report-2014]

Wallerstein, Immanuel. 1974. *The Modern World System.* New York: Academic Press.

Weber, Max. 1958. *The Protestant Ethic and the Spirit of Capitalism.* New York: Charles Scribner's Sons.

Weingast, Barry, and Douglass North. 1989. Constitutions and Commitment: The Evolution of Institutions Governing Public Choice in Seventeenth-Century England. *Journal of Economic History* 49(4): 803–832.

Williamson, John. 1990. What Washington Means by Policy Reform. In *Latin American Adjustment: How Much Has Happened?*, ed. John Williamson, 7–20. Washington, DC: Peter G. Peterson Institute for International Economics.

World Bank. 1997. *World Development Report: The State in a Changing World.* Washington, DC: World Bank.

CHAPTER 6

Almond, Gabriel A., and Sidney Verba. 1963. *The Civic Culture: Political Attitudes and Democracy in Five Nations.* Princeton, NJ: Princeton University Press.

Ash, Timothy Garton. 1993. *The Magic Lantern: The Revolution of '89 Witnessed in Warsaw, Budapest, Berlin, and Prague.* New York: Vintage Books.

Boix, Carles, and Susan C. Stokes. 2003. Endogenous Democratization. *World Politics* 55(4): 517–549.

Bollen, Kenneth. 1983. World System Position, Dependency, and Democracy: The Cross-National Evidence. *American Sociological Review* 48(4): 468–479.

Bratton, Michael, and Nicolas van de Walle. 1997. *Democratic Experiments in Africa: Regime Transitions in Comparative Perspective.* Cambridge: Cambridge University Press.

Collier, David, and Steven Levitsky. 1997. Democracy with Adjectives: Conceptual Innovation in Comparative Research. *World Politics* 49(3): 430–451.

Collier, David, James Mahoney, and Jason Seawright. 2004. Claiming Too Much: Warnings About Selection Bias. In *Rethinking Social Inquiry: Diverse Tools, Shared Standards,* ed. Henry Brady and David Collier, 85–102. Lanham, MD: Rowman and Littlefield.

Coppedge, Michael, and John Gerring, with David Altman, Michael Bernhard, Steven Fish, Allen Hicken, Matthew Kroenig, Staffan I. Lindberg, Kelly McMann, Pamela Paxton, Holli A. Semetko, Svend-Erik Skaaning, Jeffrey Staton, and Jan Teorell. 2011. Conceptualizing and Measuring Democracy: A New Approach. *Perspectives on Politics* 9(2): 247–267.

Dahl, Robert A. 1971. *Polyarchy: Participation and Opposition.* New Haven, CT: Yale University Press.

Dahl, Robert A. 1991. *Democracy and Its Critics.* New Haven, CT: Yale University Press.

Diamond, Larry. 1999. *Developing Democracy: Toward Consolidation.* Baltimore: Johns Hopkins University Press.

Elster, Jon. 2007. *Explaining Social Behavior: More Nuts and Bolts for the Social Sciences.* New York: Cambridge University Press.

Fukuyama, Francis. 1995. Confucianism and Democracy. *Journal of Democracy* 6(2): 20–33.

George, Alexander L., and Andrew Bennett. 2005. *Case Studies and Theory Development in the Social Sciences.* Cambridge: MIT Press.

Glaeser, Edward L., Rafael La Porta, Florencio Lopez de Silanes, and Andrei Shleifer. 2004. Do Institutions Cause Growth? *Journal of Economic Growth* 9(3): 271–303.

He, Baogang, and Mark E. Warren. 2011. Authoritarian Deliberation: The Deliberative Turn in Chinese Political Development. *Perspectives on Politics* 9(2): 269–289.

Huntington, Samuel. 1991. *The Third Wave: Democratization in the Late Twentieth Century.* Norman: University of Oklahoma Press.

Inglehart, Ronald. 1997. *Modernization and Postmodernization: Cultural, Economic, and Political Change in 43 Societies.* Princeton, NJ: Princeton University Press.

Inglehart, Ronald, and Christian Welzel. 2005. *Modernization, Cultural Change, and Democracy: The Human Development Sequence.* Cambridge: Cambridge University Press.

Kuran, Timur. 1991. Now Out of Never: The Element of Surprise in the East European Revolution of 1989. *World Politics* 44(1): 7–48.

Levitsky, Steven, and Lucan Way. 2002. The Rise of Competitive Authoritarianism. *Journal of Democracy* 13(2): 51–65.

Levitsky, Steven, and Lucan A. Way. 2010. *Competitive Authoritarianism: Hybrid Regimes After the Cold War.* New York: Cambridge University Press.

Linz, Juan. 1990a. The Perils of Presidentialism. *Journal of Democracy* 1(1): 51–69.

Linz, Juan. 1990b. The Virtues of Parliamentarism. *Journal of Democracy* 1(4): 84–91.

Linz, Juan, and Alfred Stepan. 1978. *The Breakdown of Democratic Regimes.* Baltimore: Johns Hopkins University Press.

Linz, Juan, and Alfred Stepan. 1996. *Problems of Democratic Transition and Consolidation: Southern Europe, South America, and Post-Communist Europe.* Baltimore: Johns Hopkins University Press.

Lipset, Seymour Martin. 1959. Some Social Requisites of Democracy: Economic Development and Political Legitimacy. *American Political Science Review* 53(1): 69–105.

Lipset, Seymour Martin. 1960. *Political Man: The Social Bases of Politics.* Garden City, NY: Doubleday & Company.

Markoff, John. 1996. *Waves of Democracy: Social Movements in Political Change.* Newbury Park, CA: Pine Forge Press.

Meyer, John W., John Boli, George M. Thomas, and Francisco O. Ramírez. 1997. World Society and the Nation-State. *American Journal of Sociology* 103(1): 144–181.

Moore, Barrington. 1966. *Social Origins of Dictatorship and Democracy: Lord and Peasant in the Making of the Modern World.* Boston: Beacon Press.

Munck, Gerardo. 2009. *Measuring Democracy: A Bridge Between Scholarship and Politics.* Baltimore: Johns Hopkins University Press.

O'Donnell, Guillermo. 1994. Delegative Democracy. *Journal of Democracy* 5(1): 55–69.

O'Donnell, Guillermo, Philippe Schmitter, and Laurence Whitehead, eds. 1986. *Transitions from Authoritarian Rule* (4 vols.). Baltimore: Johns Hopkins University Press.

Pincus, Steve. 2009. *1688: The First Modern Revolution.* New Haven, CT: Yale University Press.

Putnam, Robert D. 1993. *Making Democracy Work: Civic Traditions in Modern Italy.* Princeton, NJ: Princeton University Press.

Putnam, Robert D. 2000. *Bowling Alone: The Collapse and Revival of American Community.* New York: Simon and Schuster.

Przeworski, Adam, Michael E. Alvarez, José Antonio Cheibub, and Fernando Limongi. 2000. *Democracy and Development: Political Institutions and Well-Being in the World, 1950–1990.* New York: Cambridge University Press.

Przeworski, Adam, and Henry Teune. 1970. *The Logic of Comparative Social Inquiry.* New York: Wiley-Interscience.

Rueschemeyer, Dietrich, Evelyne Huber Stephens, and John D. Stephens. 1992. *Capitalist Development and Democracy.* Chicago: University of Chicago Press.

Schedler, Andreas. 1998. What Is Democratic Consolidation? *Journal of Democracy* 9(2): 91–107.

Schedler, Andreas, ed. 2006. *Electoral Authoritarianism: The Dynamics of Unfree Competition*. Boulder: Lynne Rienner Publishers.

Schmitter, Philippe O., and Terry Lynn Karl. 1991. What Democracy Is . . . and Is Not. *Journal of Democracy* 2(3): 75–88.

Stepan, Alfred. 1999. Federalism and Democracy: Beyond the U.S. Model. *Journal of Democracy* 10(4): 19–34.

Stepan, Alfred, and Cindy Skach. 1993. Constitutional Frameworks and Democratic Consolidation: Parliamentarianism Versus Presidentialism. *World Politics* 46(1): 1–22.

Tocqueville, Alexis. 2000. *Democracy in America*, trans. Harvey Mansfield and Debra Winthrop. Chicago: University of Chicago Press.

Véliz, Claudio. 1980. *The Centralist Tradition in Latin America*. Princeton, NJ: Princeton University Press.

Wiarda, Howard J. 2001. *The Soul of Latin America: The Cultural and Political Tradition*. New Haven: Yale University Press.

Woodberry, Robert D. 2011. Religion and the Spread of Human Capital and Political Institutions: Christian Missions as a Quasi-Natural Experiment. In *The Oxford Handbook of the Economics of Religion*, ed. R. McCleary, 111–131. New York: Oxford University Press.

Woodberry, Robert D., and Timothy S. Shah. 2004. Christianity and Democracy: The Pioneering Protestants. *Journal of Democracy* 15(2): 47–61.

Zakaria, Fareed. 2003. *The Future of Freedom: Illiberal Democracy at Home and Abroad*. New York: W. W. Norton & Co.

CHAPTER 7

Acemoglu, Daron, and James Robinson. 2006. *Economic Origins of Dictatorship and Democracy*. New York: Cambridge University Press.

Adorno, Theodor W., Else Frenkel-Brunswik, Daniel J. Levinson, and R. Nevitt Sanford. 1950. *The Authoritarian Personality*. New York: Harper Press.

Almond, Gabriel A., and Sidney Verba. 1963. *The Civic Culture: Political Attitudes and Democracy in Five Nations*. Princeton, NJ: Princeton University Press.

Arendt, Hannah. [1958] 2004. *The Origins of Totalitarianism*. New York: Schocken Books.

Bates, Robert. 2008. *When Things Fell Apart: State Failure in Late-Century Africa*. New York: Cambridge University Press.

Brooker, Paul. 2009. *Non-Democratic Regimes: Theory, Government, and Politics*. 2nd ed. New York: Palgrave MacMillan.

Brownlee, Jason. 2007. *Authoritarianism in an Age of Democratization*. New York: Cambridge University Press.

Chehabi, H. E., and Juan J. Linz, eds. 1998. *Sultanistic Regimes*. Baltimore: Johns Hopkins University Press.

Collier, David, and Steven Levitsky. 1997. Democracy with Adjectives: Conceptual Innovation in Comparative Research. *World Politics* 49(3): 430–451.

Corrales, Javier, and Michael Penfold. 2011. *Dragon in the Tropics: Hugo Chávez and the Political Economy of Revolution in Venezuela*. Washington, DC: Brookings Institution Press.

Decalo, Samuel. 1985. African Personal Dictatorships. *Journal of Modern African Studies* 23(2): 209–237.

Diamond, Larry. 2002. Thinking About Hybrid Regimes. *Journal of Democracy* 13(2): 21–35.

Fox, Jonathan. 1994. The Difficult Transition from Clientelism to Citizenship: Lessons from Mexico. *World Politics* 46(2): 151–184.

Greenfeld, Liah. 1997. The Political Significance of Culture. *The Brown Journal of World Affairs* Winter/Spring, 4(1): 187–195.

Hall, Peter A. 2010. Historical Institutionalism in Rationalist and Sociological Perspective. In *Explaining Institutional Change: Ambiguity, Agency, and Power*, ed. J. Mahoney and K. Thelen, 204–224. New York: Cambridge University Press.

He, Baogang, and Mark E. Warren. 2011. Authoritarian Deliberation: The Deliberative Turn in Chinese Political Development. *Perspectives on Politics* 9(2): 269–289.

Huntington, Samuel. 1991. *The Third Wave: Democratization in the Late Twentieth Century*. Norman: University of Oklahoma Press.

Inglehart, Ronald, and Christian Welzel. 2005. *Modernization, Cultural Change, and Democracy: The Human Development Sequence*. New York: Cambridge University Press.

Jackson, Robert H., and Carl G. Rosberg. 1982. *Personal Rule in Black Africa: Prince, Autocrat, Prophet, Tyrant*. Berkeley: University of California Press.

Kuran, Timur. 1991. Now Out of Never: The Element of Surprise in the East European Revolution of 1989. *World Politics* 44(1): 7–48.

Levitsky, Steven, and Lucan Way. 2002. The Rise of Competitive Authoritarianism. *Journal of Democracy* 13(2): 51–65.

Levitsky, Steven, and Lucan A. Way. 2010. *Competitive Authoritarianism: Hybrid Regimes After the Cold War*. New York: Cambridge University Press.

Lichbach, Mark Irving. 1995. *The Rebel's Dilemma*. Ann Arbor: University of Michigan Press.

Linz, Juan J. 2000. *Totalitarian and Authoritarian Regimes*. Boulder, CO: Lynne Rienner Publishers.

Linz, Juan, and Alfred Stepan, eds. 1978. *The Breakdown of Democratic Regimes*. Baltimore: Johns Hopkins University Press.

Mahoney, James, and Kathleen Thelen, eds. 2010. *Explaining Institutional Change: Ambiguity, Agency, and Power*. New York: Cambridge University Press.

McNeill, J. R., and William H. McNeill. 2003. *The Human Web: A Bird's Eye View of World History*. New York: W. W. Norton and Company.

Migdal, Joel S. 1988. *Strong Societies and Weak States: State-Society Relations and State Capabilities in the Third World*. Princeton, NJ: Princeton University Press.

Moore, Barrington. 1966. *Social Origins of Dictatorship and Democracy: Lord and Peasant in the Making of the Modern World*. Boston: Beacon Press.

North, Douglass C., John Joseph Wallis, and Barry R. Weingast. 2009. *Violence and Social Orders: A Conceptual Framework for Interpreting Recorded Human History*. New York: Cambridge University Press.

O'Donnell, Guillermo. 1973. *Modernization and Bureaucratic-Authoritarianism: Studies in South American Politics*. Berkeley: University of California Press.

O'Donnell, Guillermo. 1993. On the State, Democratization, and Some Conceptual Problems: A Latin American View with Some Post-Communist Countries. *World Development* 21(8): 1355–1369.

O'Donnell, Guillermo. 1994. Delegative Democracy. *Journal of Democracy* 5(1): 55–69.

O'Donnell, Guillermo, Philippe Schmitter, and Laurence Whitehead, eds. 1986. *Transitions from Authoritarian Rule* (4 vols.). Baltimore: Johns Hopkins University Press.

Olson, Mancur, Jr. 1965. *The Logic of Collective Action: Public Goods and the Theory of Groups*. Cambridge, MA: Harvard University Press.

Paige, Jeffery M. 1997. *Coffee and Power: Revolution and the Rise of Democracy in Central America*. Cambridge, MA: Harvard University Press.

Palmer, David Scott. 1980. *Peru: The Authoritarian Tradition*. New York: Praeger.

Roberts, Kenneth M. 1995. Neoliberalism and the Transformation of Populism in Latin America: The Peruvian Case. *World Politics* 48(1): 82–116.

Schedler, Andreas, ed. 2006. *Electoral Authoritarianism: The Dynamics of Unfree Competition*. Boulder, CO: Lynne Rienner Publishers.

Skocpol, Theda. 1973. A Critical Review of Barrington Moore's Social Origins of Dictatorship and Democracy. *Politics and Society* 4:1–34.

Smilde, David, and Daniel Hellinger, eds. 2011. *Venezuela's Bolivarian Democracy: Participation, Politics, and Culture Under Chávez*. Durham, NC: Duke University Press.

Valenzuela, Arturo. 1978. *The Breakdown of Democratic Regimes: Chile*. Baltimore: Johns Hopkins University Press.

Vallenilla Lanz, Laureano. 1991. *Cesarismo democrático y otros textos* [Democratic Caesarism and Other Texts]. Caracas, Venezuela: Biblioteca Ayacucho.

Véliz, Claudio. 1980. *The Centralist Tradition in Latin America*. Princeton, NJ: Princeton University Press.

Verbitsky, Horacio. 1996. *The Flight: Confessions of an Argentine Dirty Warrior*. New York: The New Press.

Wiarda, Howard J. 2003. *The Soul of Latin America: The Cultural and Political Tradition*. New Haven: Yale University Press.

Wintrobe, Ronald. 2007. Dictatorship: Analytical Approaches. In *Oxford Handbook of Comparative Politics*, ed. Carles Boix and Susan C. Stokes, 363–394. New York: Oxford University Press.

Zakaria, Fareed. 2003. *The Future of Freedom: Illiberal Democracy at Home and Abroad*. New York: W. W. Norton & Co.

Žižek, Slavov. 2002. *Did Somebody Say Totalitarianism? Five Interventions in the Misuse of a Notion*. New York: W. W. Norton.

CHAPTER 8

Breyer, Steven. 2006. *Active Liberty: Interpreting our Democratic Constitution*. New York: Vintage.

Dworkin, Ronald. 1977. *Taking Rights Seriously*. Cambridge, MA: Harvard University Press.

Dworkin, Ronald. 1986. *Law's Empire*. Cambridge, MA: Harvard University Press.

Gewirtz, Paul, and Chad Golder. 2005. So Who Are the Activists? *New York Times*, July 6. http://www.nytimes.com/2005/07/06/opinion/06gewirtz.html (accessed November 21, 2011).

Hirschl, Ran. 2007. *Towards Juristocracy: The Origins and Consequences of the New Constitutionalism*. Cambridge, MA: Harvard University Press.

Hirschl, Ran. 2010. *Constitutional Theocracy*. Cambridge, MA: Harvard University Press.

Kmiec, Keenan. 2004. The Origins and Current Meanings of "Judicial Activism." *California Law Review* 92:1441–1477.

Kymlicka, Will. 1995. *Multicultural Citizenship: A Liberal Theory of Minority Rights*. Oxford: Oxford University Press.

Lijphart, Arend. 1999. *Patterns of Democracy: Government Forms and Performance in Thirty-Six Countries*. New Haven, CT: Yale University Press.

Miles, Thomas, and Cass Sunstein. 2007. Verdict on the Supremes. *Los Angeles Times*, Oct 22. http://articles.latimes.com/2007/oct/22/news/OE-SUNSTEIN22 (accessed November 21, 2011).

Musgrave, Richard. 1959. *The Theory of Public Finance: A Study in Public Economy*. New York: McGraw-Hill.

Oates, Wallace. 1972. *Fiscal Federalism*. New York: Harcourt Brace Jovanovich.

Oates, Wallace. 2005. Toward a Second Generation Theory of Fiscal Federalism. *International Tax and Public Finance* 12(4): 349–373.

Riker, William. 1964. *Federalism: Origin, Operation, Significance*. Boston: Little, Brown, & Co.

Rodden, Jonathan. 2006. *Hamilton's Paradox: The Promise and Peril of Fiscal Federalism*. Cambridge: Cambridge University Press.

Rodden, Jonathan, Gunnar Eskeland, and Jennie Litvack. 2003. *Fiscal Decentralization and the Challenge of Hard Budget Constraints*. Cambridge, MA: MIT Press.

Rodden, Jonathan, and Erik Wibbels. 2002. Beyond the Fiction of Federalism: Economic Management in Multi-Tiered Systems. *World Politics* 54(4): 494–531.

Sartori, Giovanni. 1994. *Comparative Constitutional Engineering: An Enquiry into Structures, Incentives, and Outcomes*. New York: New York University Press.

Scalia, Antonin. 1998. *A Matter of Interpretation: Federal Courts and the Law*. Princeton, NJ: Princeton University Press.

Stepan, Alfred. 1999. Federalism and Democracy: Beyond the U.S. Model. *Journal of Democracy* 10(4): 19–34.

Tiebout, Charles. 1956. A Pure Theory of Local Expenditures. *Journal of Political Economy* 64(5): 416–424.

Volden, Craig. 2004. Origin, Operation, and Significance: The Federalism of William Riker. *Publius: The Journal of Federalism* 34(4): 89–108.

Weingast, Barry. 2009. Second Generation Fiscal Federalism: The Implications of Fiscal Incentives. *Journal of Urban Economics* 65(3): 279–293.

Wibbels, Erik. 2005. *Federalism and the Market: Intergovernmental Conflict and Economic Reform in the Developing World.* Cambridge: Cambridge University Press.

CHAPTER 9

Ames, Barry. 2001. *The Deadlock of Democracy in Brazil.* Ann Arbor: University of Michigan Press.

Amorim Neto, Octavio. 2002. Presidential Cabinets, Electoral Cycles and Coalition Discipline in Brazil. In *Legislative Politics in Latin America*, ed. Scott Morgenstern and Benito Nacif, 48–78. New York: Cambridge University Press.

Amorim Neto, Octavio, Gary Cox, and Mathew McCubbins. 2003. Agenda Power in Brazil's Câmara dos Deputados, 1989–1998. *World Politics* 55(4): 550–578.

Cox, Gary. 1997. *Making Votes Count: Strategic Coordination in the World's Electoral Systems.* Cambridge: Cambridge University Press.

Cox, Gary, and Matthew McCubbins. 1993. *Legislative Leviathan: Party Government in the House.* Berkeley: University of California Press.

Duverger, Maurice, 1954 [trans. Barbara and Robert North]. *Political Parties: Their Organization and Activity in the Modern State.* London: Methuen.

Eaton, Kent. 2002. *Politicians and Economic Reform in New Democracies: Argentina and the Philippines in the 1990s.* University Park: Pennsylvania State University Press.

Fiorina, Morris. 1992. *Divided Government.* New York: Macmillan.

International Institute for Democracy and Electoral Assistance. 2008. *Electoral System Design: The New International IDEA Handbook.* Stockholm: International IDEA.

Interparliamentary Union. www.ipu.org (links to all parliaments around the world).

Mayhew, David. 1974. *Congress: The Electoral Connection.* New Haven, CT: Yale University Press.

Mezey, Michael. 1979. *Comparative Legislatures.* Durham, NC: Duke University Press.

Moody, James and Peter Mucha. 2013. Portrait of Political Party Polarization. *Network Science.* 1(1): 119–121.

Morgenstern, Scott, and Benito Nacif, eds. 2002. *Legislative Politics in Latin America.* Cambridge: Cambridge University Press.

Norton, Philip, ed. 1998. *Parliaments and Governments in Western Europe.* Vols. 1–3. London: Frank Cass.

Pitkin, Hannah. 1972. *The Concept of Representation.* Berkeley: University of California Press.

Power, Timothy. 2000. Political Institutions in Democratic Brazil: Politics as a Permanent Constitutional Convention. In *Democratic Brazil: Actors, Institutions, and Processes*, ed. Peter Kingstone and Timothy Power, 17–35. Pittsburgh: University of Pittsburgh Press.

Samuels, David. 2003. *Ambition, Federalism, and Legislative Politics in Brazil.* New York: Cambridge University Press.

Shepsle, Kenneth, and Barry Weingast. 1981. Structure-Induced Equilibrium and Legislative Choice. *Public Choice* 37:509–519.

CHAPTER 10

Aberbach, Joel, Robert Putnam, and Bert Rockman. 1981. *Bureaucrats and Politicians in Western Democracies.* Cambridge, MA: Harvard University Press.

Chabal, Patrick, and Jean-Pascal Daloz. 1999. *Africa Works: Disorder as Political Instrument.* Bloomington: Indiana University Press.

Geddes, Barbara. 1990. How the Cases You Choose Affect the Answers You Get: Selection Bias in Comparative Politics. *Political Analysis* 2(1): 131–150.

Geddes, Barbara. 1994. *Politician's Dilemma: Building State Capacity in Latin America.* Berkeley: University of California Press.

Lijphart, Arend. 1969. Consociational Democracy. *World Politics* 21(2): 207–225.

Lijphart, Arend. 1999. *Patterns of Democracy: Government Forms and Performance in Thirty-Six Democracies.* New Haven, CT: Yale University Press.

Linz, Juan. 1990a. The Perils of Presidentialism. *Journal of Democracy* 1(1): 51–69.

Linz, Juan. 1990b. The Virtues of Parliamentarism. *Journal of Democracy* 1(4): 84–91.

Mainwaring, Scott, and Matthew Soberg Shugart. 1997. Juan Linz, Presidentialism, and Democracy: A Critical Appraisal. *Comparative Politics* 29(4): 449–471.

Nordhaus, William. 1975. The Political Business Cycle. *Review of Economic Studies* 42(2): 169–190.

Neustadt, Richard. 1960. *Presidential Power.* New York: John Wiley and Sons.

O'Donnell, Guillermo. 1994. Delegative Democracy. *Journal of Democracy* 5(1): 55–69.

Roberts, Kenneth. 1995. Neoliberalism and the Transformation of Populism in Latin America: The Peruvian Case. *World Politics* 48(1): 82–116.

CHAPTER 11

Becker, Gary. 1983. A Theory of Competition Among Pressure Groups for Political Influence. *The Quarterly Journal of Economics* 98(3): 371–400.

Carbone, Giovanni. 2008. *No-Party Democracy? Ugandan Politics in Comparative Perspective.* Boulder, CO: Lynne Rienner.

Collier, Ruth Berins, and David Collier. [1991] 2002. *Shaping the Political Arena: Critical Junctures, the Labor Movement, and Regime Dynamics in Latin America.* Notre Dame, IN: University of Notre Dame Press.

Cox, Gary, and Matthew McCubbins. 2007. *Legislative Leviathan: Party Government in the House.* Berkeley: University of California Press.

Dahl, Robert. 1961 *Who Governs? Democracy and Power in the American City.* New Haven, CT: Yale University Press.

Dahl, Robert. 1989. *Democracy and Its Critics.* New Haven, CT: Yale University Press.

Downs, Anthony. 1957. *An Economic Theory of Democracy*. New York: Harper and Row.

Duverger, Maurice. 1951. *Les Partis Politiques* [*Political Parties*]. Paris: A. Colin.

Evans, Peter. 1995. *Embedded Autonomy: States and Industrial Transformation*. Princeton, NJ: Princeton University Press.

Fukuyama, Francis. 1992. *The End of History and the Last Man*. New York: Free Press.

Kasfir, Nelson. 1998. "No-Party Democracy" in Uganda. *Journal of Democracy* 9(2): 49–63.

Katzenstein, Peter. 1985. *Small States in World Markets: Industrial Policy in Europe*. Ithaca, NY: Cornell University Press.

Kirchheimer, Otto. 1966. *The Transformation of Western European Party Systems*. Princeton, NJ: Princeton University Press.

Kitschelt, Herbert. 1994. *The Transformation of European Social Democracy*. Cambridge: Cambridge University Press.

Laakso, Markku, and Rein Taagepera. 1979. "Effective" Number of Parties: A Measure with Application to West Europe. *Comparative Political Studies* 12(1): 3–27.

Lenin, Vladimir Ilyich. 1902. What Is to Be Done? Burning Questions of Our Movement. Available at: http://marxists.org/archive/lenin/works/1901/witbd/index.htm (accessed November 1, 2011).

Lijphart, Arend. 1999. *Patterns of Democracy: Government Forms and Performance in Thirty-Six Countries*. New Haven, CT: Yale University Press.

Madison, James. [1787] 1961. No. 10: The Same Subject Continued: The Utility of the Union as a Safeguard Against Domestic Faction and Insurrection. In *The Federalist Papers*, ed. Clinton Rossiter, 77–83. New York: New American Library.

Mainwaring, Scott, and Timothy Scully, eds. 1995. *Building Democratic Institutions: Party Systems in Latin America*. Cambridge: Cambridge University Press.

Marx, Karl, and Friedrich Engels. [1848] 1998. *The Communist Manifesto*. New York: Verso.

Mayhew, David. 1974. *Congress: The Electoral Connection*. New Haven, CT: Yale University Press.

Michels, Robert. [1911] 1962. *Political Parties: A Sociological Study of the Oligarchical Tendencies of Modern Democracy*, trans. Eden and Cedar Paul. New York: Free Press.

Mills, C. Wright. 2000[1956]. *The Power Elite*. Oxford University Press.

Olson, Mancur. 1965. *The Logic of Collective Action: Public Goods and the Theory of Groups.* Cambridge, MA: Harvard University Press.

Olson, Mancur. 1982. *The Rise and Decline of Nations: Economic Growth Stagflation, and Social Rigidities*. New Haven, CT: Yale University Press.

Rae, Douglas. 1968. A Note on the Fractionalization of Some European Party Systems. *Comparative Political Studies* 1(3): 413–418.

Sartori, Giovanni. 1976. *Parties and Party Systems: A Framework for Analysis*. New York: Cambridge University Press.

Schmitter, Philippe. 1974. Still the Century of Corporatism? *The Review of Politics* 36(1): 85–131.

Sen, Amartya. 1997. Human Rights and Asian Values. *The New Republic* 217(2–3): 33–41.

Véliz, Claudio. 1980. *The Centralist Tradition in Latin America*. Princeton, NJ: Princeton University Press.

Wiarda, Howard. 1997. *Corporatism and Comparative Politics: The Other Great "Ism."* New York: M. E. Sharpe.

Zakaria, Fareed. 1994. Culture Is Destiny: A Conversation with Lee Kuan-Yew. *Foreign Affairs* 73(March–April): 113.

Zolberg, Aristide. 1966. *Creating Political Order: The Party-States of West Africa*. Chicago: University of Chicago Press.

CHAPTER 12

Alvarez, Sonia E., Evelina Dagnino, and Arturo Escobar. 1998. Introduction: The Cultural and the Political in Latin American Social Movements. In *Cultures of Politics, Politics of Cultures: Re-Visioning Latin American Social Movements,* ed. Sonia E. Alvarez, Evelina Dagnino, and Arturo Escobar, 1–32. Boulder, CO: Westview Press.

Arendt, Hannah. 1963. *On Revolution*. New York: Viking Press.

Barth, Fredrik, ed. 1969. *Ethnic Groups and Boundaries: the Social Organization of Culture Difference.* Boston: Little, Brown, and Company.

Beehner, Lionel. 2014. "What the Evidence on Interventions Really Tells Us About Syria," the Monkey Cage, *Washington Post*, August 18, 2014. https://www.washingtonpost.com/news/monkey-cage/wp/2014/08/18/what-the-evidence-on-interventions-really-tells-us-about-syria/?utm_term=.34dfa3254151

Belkin, Aaron, and Evan Schofer. 2003. Toward a Structural Understanding of Coup Risk. *Journal of Conflict Resolution* 47(5): 594–620.

Benford, Robert D., and David A. Snow. 2000. Framing Processes and Social Movements: An Overview and Assessment. *Annual Review of Sociology* 26: 611–639.

Bergesen, Albert J., and Omar Lizardo. 2004. International Terrorism and the World System. *Sociological Theory* 22(1): 38–52.

Black, Donald. 2004. The Geometry of Terrorism. *Sociological Theory* 22(1): 14–25.

Brinton, Crane. 1952. *The Anatomy of Revolution*. New York: Prentice Hall.

Buechler, Steven M. 2004. The Strange Career of Strain and Breakdown Theories of Collective Action. In *The Blackwell Companion to Social Movements*, ed. David A. Snow, Sarah A. Soule, and Hanspeter Kriesi, 47–66. Malden, MA: Blackwell.

Burns, Stewart, ed. 1997. *Daybreak of Freedom: The Montgomery Bus Boycott*. Chapel Hill: University of North Carolina Press.

Castells, Manuel. 2010. *The Power of Identity*. 2nd ed. Malden, MA: Wiley-Blackwell.

Centeno, Miguel A. 2002. *Blood and Debt: War and the Nation-State in Latin America*. University Park: Pennsylvania State University Press.

Coleman, James S. 1990. *Foundations of Social Theory*. Cambridge, MA: Belknap/Harvard University Press.

Elbadawi, Ibrahim A. and Nicholas Sambanis. 2000. *External Interventions and the Duration of Civil Wars. Policy Research Working Paper, No. 2433*. World Bank, Washington, DC. © World Bank.

https://openknowledge.worldbank.org/handle/10986/19794. License: CC BY 3.0 IGO.

Elster, Jon. 1998. A Plea for Mechanisms. In *Social Mechanisms: An Analytical Approach to Social Theory*, ed. Peter Hedstrom and Richard Swedberg, 45–73. New York: Cambridge University Press.

Finkel, Steven E., Edward N. Muller, and Karl-Dieter Opp. 1989. Personal Influence, Collective Rationality, and Mass Political Action. *American Political Science Review* 83(3): 885–903.

Foran, John. 2005. *Taking Power: On the Origins of Third World Revolutions*. New York: Cambridge University Press.

Gamson, William A. 1992. *Talking Politics*. New York: Cambridge University Press.

Gibbs, Jack. 1989. Conceptualization of Terrorism. *American Sociological Review* 54(3): 329–340.

Goffman, Erving. 1974. *Frame Analysis: An Essay on the Organization of Experience*. Cambridge, MA: Harvard University Press.

Goldstone, Jack. 1991. *Revolution and Rebellion in the Early Modern World*. Berkeley: University of California Press.

Goldstone, Jack. 2001. Toward a Fourth Generation of Revolutionary Theory. *Annual Review of Political Science* 4: 139–187.

Greenfeld, Liah. 1995. Russian Nationalism as a Medium of Revolution: An Exercise in Historical Sociology. *Qualitative Sociology* 18(2): 189–209.

Gurr, Ted. 1970. *Why Men Rebel*. Princeton, NJ: Princeton University Press.

Hobsbawm, Eric. 1981. *Bandits*. New York: Pantheon Books.

Hunt, Scott A., and Robert D. Benford. 2004. Collective Identity, Solidarity, and Commitment. In *The Blackwell Companion to Social Movements*, ed. David A. Snow, Sarah A. Soule, and Hanspeter Kriesi, 433–457. Malden, MA: Blackwell.

Huntington, Samuel. 1968. *Political Order in Changing Societies*. New Haven, CT: Yale University Press.

Johnson, Thomas H., Robert O. Slater, and Pat McGowan. 1984. Explaining African Military Coups d'État, 1960–1982. *American Political Science Review* 78(3): 622–640.

Kalyvas, Stathis. 2007. Civil Wars. In *Oxford Handbook of Comparative Politics*, ed. Carles Boix and Susan C. Stokes, 416–434. New York: Oxford University Press.

Katz, Mark. 1999. *Revolutions and Revolutionary Waves*. New York: St. Martin's Press.

Kumar, Krishan. 2005. Revolution. In *The New Dictionary of the History of Ideas*, Vol. 5, ed. Maryanne Cline Horowitz, 2112–2121. Detroit, MI: Charles Scribner's Sons.

Kurzman, Charles. 2005. *The Unthinkable Revolution in Iran*. Cambridge, MA: Harvard University Press.

Lichbach, Mark Irving. 1995. *The Rebel's Dilemma*. Ann Arbor: University of Michigan Press.

Lichbach, Mark I. 1998. Contending Theories of Contentious Politics and the Structure-Action Problem of Social Order. *Annual Review of Political Science* 1: 401–424.

Lindholm, Charles, and José Pedro Zúquete. 2010. *The Struggle for the World: Liberation Movements for the 21st Century*. Stanford, CA: Stanford University Press.

Lynch, Marc. "Would Arming Syria's Rebels Have Stopped the Islamic State?" The Monkey Cage, *Washington Post*, August 11, 2014: https://www.washingtonpost.com/news/monkey-cage/wp/2014/08/11/would-arming-syrias-rebels-have-stopped-the-islamic-state/?utm_term=.876e4a9aa1f9

Martin, William G., ed. 2008. *Making Waves: Worldwide Social Movements, 1750–2005*. Boulder, CO: Paradigm Publishers.

McAdam, Doug. 1982. *Political Process and the Development of Black Insurgency, 1930–1970*. Chicago: University of Chicago Press.

McAdam, Doug. 1996. Conceptual Origins, Current Problems, Future Directions. In *Comparative Perspectives on Social Movements: Political Opportunities, Mobilizing Structures, and Cultural Framings*, ed. Doug McAdam, John D. McCarthy, and Mayer N. Zald, 23–37. New York: Cambridge University Press.

McCarthy, John D., and Mayer N. Zald. 1987. Resource Mobilization and Social Movements: A Partial Theory. *American Journal of Sociology* 82(6): 1212–1241.

McElreath, Richard. 2016. *Statistical Rethinking: A Bayesian Course with Examples in R and Stan*. New York: CRC Press.

Melucci, Alberto. 1989. *Nomads of the Present: Social Movements and Individual Needs in Contemporary Societies*. Philadelphia: Temple University Press.

Metelits, Claire. 2009. *Inside Insurgency: Violence, Civilians, and Revolutionary Group Behavior*. New York: New York University Press.

Meyer, David S., and Sidney Tarrow, eds. 1998. *The Social Movement Society: Contentious Politics for a New Century*. Lanham, MD: Rowman and Littlefield.

Michels, Robert. [1911] 1962. *Political Parties: A Sociological Study of the Oligarchical Tendencies of Modern Democracy*, trans. Eden and Cedar Paul. New York: Free Press.

Oberschall, Anthony. 2004. Explaining Terrorism: The Contribution of Collective Action Theory. *Sociological Theory* 22(1): 26–37.

O'Leary, Brendan. 2007. IRA: Irish Republican Army (Oglaigh na hEireann). In *Terror, Insurgency, and the State: Ending Protracted Conflicts*, ed. Marianne Heiberg, Brendan O'Leary, and John Tirman, 189–227. Philadelphia: University of Pennsylvania Press.

O'Leary, Brendan, and Andrew Silke. 2007. Conclusion: Understanding and Ending Persistent Conflicts: Bridging Research and Policy. In *Terror, Insurgency, and the State: Ending Protracted Conflicts*, ed. Marianne Heiberg, Brendan O'Leary, and John Tirman, 387–426. Philadelphia: University of Pennsylvania Press.

O'Leary, Brendan, and John Tirman. 2007. Introduction: Thinking About Durable Political Violence. In *Terror, Insurgency, and the State: Ending Protracted Conflicts*, ed. Marianne Heiberg, Brendan O'Leary, and John Tirman, 1–17. Philadelphia: University of Pennsylvania Press.

Oliver, Pamela E., and Hank Johnston. 2000. What a Good Idea! Ideologies and Frames in Social Movement Research. *Mobilization: An International Journal* 4(1): 37–54.

Olson, Mancur, Jr. 1965. *The Logic of Collective Action*. Cambridge, MA: Harvard University Press.

Ondetti, Gabriel. 2008. *Land, Protest, and Politics: The Landless Movement and the Struggle for Agrarian Reform in Brazil*. University Park: Pennsylvania State University Press.

Pape, Robert A. 2003. The Strategic Logic of Suicide Terrorism. *American Political Science Review* 97(3): 343–361.

Parsa, Misagh. 2000. *States, Ideologies, and Social Revolutions: A Comparative Analysis of Iran, Nicaragua, and the Philippines*. New York: Cambridge University Press.

Pérez Díaz, Victor. 2014. Civil Society: A Multi-Layered Concept. *Current Sociology* 62(6): 812-830.

Pincus, Steven. 2007. Rethinking Revolutions: A Neo-Tocquevillian Perspective. In *The Oxford Handbook of Comparative Politics,* ed. Carles Boix and Susan C. Stokes, 397–415. New York: Oxford University Press.

Powell, Jonathan, and Clayton Thyne. 2011. Global Instances of Coups from 1950 to 2010: A New Dataset. *Journal of Peace Research* 48(2): 249–259.

Regan, Patrick M. 2002. Third-party Interventions and the Duration of Intrastate Conflicts. *Journal of Conflict Resolution* 46(1): 55–73.

Sageman, Mark. 2004. *Understanding Terror Networks*. Philadelphia: University of Pennsylvania Press.

Sanderson, Stephen K. 2010. *Revolutions: A Worldwide Introduction to Social and Political Contention*. 2nd ed. Boulder, CO: Paradigm Publishers.

Scott, James C. 1985. *Weapons of the Weak: Everyday Forms of Peasant Resistance*. New Haven, CT: Yale University Press.

Senechal de la Roche, Roberta. 2004. Toward a Scientific Theory of Terrorism. *Sociological Theory* 22(1): 1–4.

Shils, Edward. 1997. *The Virtue of Civility: Selected Essays on Liberty, Tradition, and Civil Society*, ed. Steven Grosby. Indianapolis, IN: Liberty Fund.

Skocpol, Theda. 1979. *States and Social Revolutions: A Comparative Analysis of France, Russia, and China*. New York: Cambridge University Press.

Skocpol, Theda. 1994. *Social Revolutions in the Modern World*. New York: Cambridge University Press.

Smelser, Neil J. 1962. *Theory of Collective Behavior*. New York: Free Press.

Tarrow, Sidney. 2005. *The New Transnational Activism*. New York: Cambridge University Press.

Tarrow, Sidney. 2011. *Power in Movement: Social Movements, Collective Action, and Politics*. 3rd ed. New York: Cambridge University Press.

Tilly, Charles. 2004. Terror, Terrorism, Terrorists. *Sociological Theory* 22(1): 5–13.

Tilly, Charles, and Sidney Tarrow. 2007. *Contentious Politics*. Boulder, CO: Paradigm Publishers.

Toch, Hans. 1965. *The Social Psychology of Social Movements*. Indianapolis, IN: The Bobbs-Merrill Company.

de Tocqueville, Alexis. 1955. *The Old Regime and the French Revolution*, trans. Stuart Gilbert. New York: Doubleday Books.

Tufekci, Zeynep. 2017. *Twitter and Tear Gas: the Power and Fragility of Networked Protest*. New Haven, CT: Yale University Press.

Tullock, Gordon. 1971. The Paradox of Revolution. *Public Choice* 11(1): 89–99.

Weber, Max. 1946. Class, Status, and Party. In *From Max Weber: Essays in Sociology*, ed. and trans. Hans H. Gerth and C. Wright Mills, 180–195. New York: Oxford University Press.

CHAPTER 13

Akerlof, George A., and Rachel E. Kranton. 2010. *Identity Economics: How Our Identities Shape Our Work, Wages, and Well-Being*. Princeton, NJ: Princeton University Press.

Amnesty International. South Sudan: Global Action Needed to End Human Rights Violations and Humanitarian Crisis, December 15, 2017. https://www.amnesty.org/en/latest/news/201712/south-sudan-global-action-needed-to-end-human-rights-violations-and-humanitarian-crisis/

Anderson, Benedict. [1983] 1991. *Imagined Communities: Reflections on the Origin and Spread of Nationalism*. New York: Verso.

Bates, Robert H. 2008. *When Things Fell Apart: State-Failure in Late-Century Africa*. New York: Cambridge University Press.

Biryabarema, Elias. UK Says Killings in South Sudan Conflict Amount to Genocide. Reuters, April 12, 2017. https://www.reuters.com/article/us-southsudan-war/uk-says-killings-in-south-sudan-conflict-amount-to-genocide-idUSKBN17E2TF

Bonikowski, Bart, and Paul DiMaggio. 2016. Varieties of American Popular Nationalism. *American Sociological Review* 81(5): 949–980.

Breuilly, John. 1994. *Nationalism and the State*. 2nd ed. Chicago: University of Chicago Press.

Brewer, Marilynn B., and Wendi Gardner. 1996. Who Is This "We"? Levels of Collective Identity and Self Representations. *Journal of Personality and Social Psychology* 71(1): 83–93.

Brubaker, Rogers. 1992. *Citizenship and Nationhood in France and Germany*. Cambridge, MA: Harvard University Press.

Brubaker, Rogers. 1996. *Nationalism Reframed: Nationhood and the National Question in the New Europe*. New York: Cambridge University Press.

Brubaker, Rogers. 1999. The Manichean Myth: Rethinking the Distinction Between "Civic" and "Ethnic" Nationalism. In *Nation and National Identity: The European Experience in Perspective*, ed. Hanspeter Kriesi, Klaus Armingeon, Hannes Siegrist, and Andreas Wimmer, 55–71. Zurich: Verlag Ruller.

Brubaker, Rogers, and David D. Laitin. 1998. Ethnic and Nationalist Violence. *Annual Review of Sociology* 24: 423–452.

Calhoun, Craig. 1997. *Nationalism*. Minneapolis: University of Minnesota Press.

Cederman, Lars-Erik, Andreas Wimmer, and Brian Min. 2010. Why Do Ethnic Groups Rebel? New Data and Analysis. *World Politics* 62(1): 87–119.

Centeno, Miguel A. 2002. *Blood and Debt: War and the Nation State in Latin America*. University Park: Pennsylvania State University Press.

Chirot, Daniel. 2001. Introduction. In *Ethnopolitical Warfare: Causes, Consequences, and Possible Solutions*, ed. Daniel Chirot and Martin Seligman, 3–26. Washington, DC: American Psychological Association.

Chirot, Daniel, and Martin Seligman, eds. 2001. *Ethnopolitical Warfare: Causes, Consequences, and Possible Solutions*. Washington, DC: American Psychological Association.

Connor, Walker. 2004. The Timelessness of Nations. *Nations and Nationalism* 10(1/2): 35–47.

Deutsch, Karl. 1953. *Nationalism and Social Communication: An Inquiry into the Foundations of Nationality*. Cambridge, MA: MIT Press and New York: Wiley and Sons.

Drumbl, Mark A. 2007. *Atrocity, Punishment, and International Law*. New York: Cambridge University Press.

Fearon, James D., and David D. Laitin. 1996. Explaining Interethnic Cooperation. *American Political Science Review* 90(4): 715–735.

Fearon, James D., and David D. Laitin. 2003. Ethnicity, Insurgency, and Civil War. *American Political Science Review* 97(1): 75–90.

Fortify Rights and the United States Holocaust Memorial Museum. 2017. They Tried to Kill Us All: Atrocity Crimes against Rohingya Muslims. http://www.fortifyrights.org/downloads/THEY_TRIED_TO_KILL_US_ALL_Atrocity_Crimes_against_Rohingya_Muslims_Nov_2017.pdf

Gellner, Ernest. 1983. *Nations and Nationalism*. Ithaca, NY: Cornell University Press.

Gorski, Philip. 2000. The Mosaic Moment: An Early Modernist Critique of Modernist Theories of Nationalism. *American Journal of Sociology* 105, No. 5 (March): 1428–1468.

Greenfeld, Liah. 1992. *Nationalism: Five Roads to Modernity*. Cambridge, MA: Harvard University Press.

Greenfeld, Liah. 2001. *The Spirit of Capitalism: Nationalism and Economic Growth*. Cambridge, MA: Harvard University Press.

Greenfeld, Liah, and Daniel Chirot. 1994. Nationalism and Aggression. *Theory and Society* 23:79–130.

Greenfeld, Liah, and Jonathan Eastwood. 2007. National Identity. In *Oxford Handbook of Comparative Politics*, ed. Carles Boix and Susan C. Stokes, 256–273. New York: Oxford University Press.

Guerra, Francois-Xavier. 2003. Forms of Communication, Political Spaces, and Cultural Identities in the Creation of Spanish-American Nations. In *Beyond Imagined Communities: Reading and Writing the Nation in Nineteenth-Century Latin America*, ed. Sara Castro-Klarén and John Charles Chasteen, 3–32. Baltimore: Woodrow Wilson Center Press/Johns Hopkins University Press.

Harff, Barbara. 2003. No Lessons Learned from the Holocaust? Assessing Risks of Genocide and Political Mass Murder Since 1955. *American Political Science Review* 97(1): 57–73.

Harff, Barbara, and Ted Robert Gurr. 2004. *Ethnic Conflict in World Politics*. 2nd ed. Boulder, CO: Westview Press.

Hastings, Adrian. 1997. *The Construction of Nationhood: Ethnicity, Religion, and Nationalism*. New York: Cambridge University Press.

Hechter, Michael. 2000. *Containing Nationalism*. New York: Oxford University Press.

Herbst, Jeffrey. 2000. *States and Power in Africa: Comparative Lessons in Authority and Control*. Princeton, NJ: Princeton University Press.

Hobsbawm, Eric. 1990. *Nations and Nationalism Since 1780: Programme, Myth, Reality*. New York: Cambridge University Press.

Horowitz, Donald L. 2000 [1985]. *Ethnic Groups in Conflict*. Berkeley: University of California Press.

Horowitz, Donald L. 2001. *The Deadly Ethnic Riot*. Berkeley: University of California Press.

Human Rights Watch. 2017. *World Report 2017*. https://www.hrw.org/world-report/2017

Hutchinson, John, and Anthony D. Smith, eds. 1994. *Nationalism*. New York: Oxford University Press.

Itzigsohn, José, and Matthias Vom Hau. 2006. Unfinished Imagined Communities: States, Social Movements, and Nationalism in Latin America. *Theory and Society* 35(2): 193–212.

Jowitt, Ken. 2001. Ethnicity: Nice, Nasty, and Nihilistic. In *Ethno-Political Warfare: Causes, Consequences, and Possible Solutions*, ed. Daniel Chirot and Martin Seligman, 27–36. Washington, DC: American Psychological Association.

Kaufman, Stuart. 2001. *Modern Hatreds: The Symbolic Politics of Ethnic War*. Ithaca, NY: Cornell University Press.

Kohn, Hans. 1944. *The Idea of Nationalism: A Study in Its Origin and Background*. New York: MacMillan.

Laitin, David. 2007. *Nations, States, and Violence*. New York: Oxford University Press.

Lamont, Michele, and Virág Molnár. 2002. The Study of Boundaries in the Social Sciences. *Annual Review of Sociology* 28:167–195.

Lemarchand, René. 2007. Consociationalism and Power Sharing in Africa: Rwanda, Burundi, and the Democratic Republic of the Congo. *African Affairs* 106(422): 1–20.

Lijphart, Arend. 1977. *Democracy in Plural Societies: A Comparative Exploration*. New Haven, CT: Yale University Press.

Marx, Anthony W. 2003. *Faith in Nation: Exclusionary Origins of Nationalism*. New York: Oxford University Press.

Meyer, John W., John Boli, George M. Thomas, and Francisco O. Ramírez, 1997. World Society and the Nation-State. *American Journal of Sociology* 103(1): 144–181.

Petersen, Roger D. 2002. *Understanding Ethnic Violence: Fear, Hatred, and Resentment in Twentieth-Century Eastern Europe*. New York: Cambridge University Press.

Pettigrew, Thomas F., and Linda R. Tropp. 2011. *When Groups Meet: The Dynamics of Intergroup Contact*. London: Psychology Press.

Rushton, J. Philippe. 2005. Ethnic Nationalism, Evolutionary Psychology, and Genetic Similarity Theory. *Nations and Nationalism* 11(4): 489–507.

Sassen, Saskia. 2006. *Territory, Authority, Rights: From Medieval to Global Assemblages.* Updated ed. Princeton, NJ: Princeton University Press.

Sikkink, Kathryn. 2011. *The Justice Cascade: How Human Rights Prosecutions Are Changing World Politics.* New York: W. W. Norton and Company.

Smith, Anthony D. 1986. *The Ethnic Origins of Nations.* Malden, MA: Blackwell.

Smith, Anthony D. 1995. *Nations and Nationalism in a Global Era.* Malden, MA: Polity Press.

Snyder, Jack. 2000. *From Voting to Violence: Democratization and Nationalist Conflict.* New York: W. W. Norton and Company.

Stets, Jan E., and Peter J. Burke. 2000. Identity Theory and Social Identity Theory. *Social Psychology Quarterly* 63(3): 224–237.

Tajfel, Henri. 1981. *Human Groups and Social Categories: Studies in Social Psychology.* New York: Cambridge University Press.

Teitel, Ruti. 2011. *Humanity's Law.* New York: Oxford University Press.

Tilly, Charles. 1975. Reflections on the History of European State-Making. In *The Formation of National States in Western Europe*, ed. Charles Tilly, 3–83. Princeton, NJ: Princeton University Press.

Tilly, Charles. 1992. *Coercion, Capital, and European States, AD 990–1992.* Malden, MA: Blackwell.

Tilly, Charles. 2005. *Identities, Boundaries, and Social Ties.* Boulder, CO: Paradigm Publishers.

United Nations Human Development Report. 2009. http://hdr.undp.org/sites/default/files/reports/269/hdr_2009_en_complete.pdf

Van den Berghe, Pierre L. 1981. *The Ethnic Phenomenon.* New York: Elsevier.

Varshney, Ashutosh. 2002. *Ethnic Conflict and Civic Life: Hindus and Muslims in India.* New Haven, CT: Yale University Press.

Weber, Eugen. 1976. *Peasants into Frenchmen: The Modernization of Rural France, 1870–1914.* Stanford, CA: Stanford University Press.

Weber, Max. 1958. *From Max Weber: Essays in Sociology*, ed. and trans. H. Gerth and C. Wright Mills. New York: Oxford University Press.

Weil, Patrick. 2001. Access to Citizenship: A Comparison of Twenty-Five Nationality Laws. In *Citizenship Today: Global Perspectives and Practices,* eds. T. Alexander Aleinikoff and Douglas Klusmeyer, 17–35. Washington, DC: Carnegie Endowment for International Peace.

Wilson, Edward O. 2000. *Sociobiology: The New Synthesis.* 25th anniversary ed. Cambridge, MA: Belknap/Harvard University Press.

Wimmer, Andreas. 2002. *Nationalist Exclusion and Ethnic Conflict: Shadows of Modernity.* New York: Cambridge University Press.

Yashar, Deborah. 2005. *Contesting Citizenship in Latin America: The Rise of Indigenous Movements and the Postliberal Challenge.* New York: Cambridge University Press.

Zubrzycki, Genevieve. 2006. *The Crosses of Auschwitz: Nationalism and Religion in Post-Communist Poland.* Chicago: University of Chicago Press.

CHAPTER 14

American Anthropological Association. *Race: Are We So Different?* (Project.) http://www.understandingrace.org/home.html

Barry-Jester, Anna Maria. 2015. Attitudes Towards Racism and Inequality Are Shifting. FiveThirtyEight.com, https://fivethirtyeight.com/features/attitudes-toward-racism-and-inequality-are-shifting/

Barth, Fredrik, ed. 1969. *Ethnic Groups and Boundaries: the Social Organization of Culture Difference.* Boston: Little, Brown, and Company.

Bernhard, Michael, Christopher Reenock, and Timothy Nordstrom. 2004. The Legacy of Western Overseas Colonialism on Democratic Survival. *International Studies Quarterly* 48(1): 225–250.

Blair-Loy, Mary. 2003. *Competing Devotions: Career and Family Among Women Executives.* Cambridge, MA: Harvard University Press.

Blau, Francine D., and Lawrence M. Kahn. 1992. The Gender Earnings Gap: Learning from International Comparisons. *American Economic Review* 82(2): 533–538.

Blumberg, Rae. 1984. A General Theory of Gender Stratification. *Sociological Theory* 2: 23–101.

Brown, Michael K., Martin Carnoy, Elliott Currie, Troy Duster, David P. Oppenheimer, Marjorie M. Shultz, and David Wellman. 2003. *Whitewashing Race: The Myth of a Color-Blind Society.* Berkeley: University of California Press.

Cañizares-Esguerra, Jorge. 2009. Demons, Stars, and the Imagination: The Early Modern Body in the Tropics. In *The Origins of Racism in the West*, ed. Miriam Eliav-Feldon, Benjamin Isaac, and Joseph Ziegler, 313–325. New York: Cambridge University Press.

Castells, Manuel. 2010. *The Power of Identity.* 2nd ed. Malden, MA: Wiley-Blackwell.

Cornell, Stephen E., and Douglas Hartmann. 1998. *Ethnicity and Race: Making Identities in a Changing World.* Thousand Oaks, CA: Pine Forge Press.

Corrales, Javier, and Mario Pecheny, eds. 2010. *The Politics of Sexuality in Latin America: A Reader in Lesbian, Gay, Bisexual, and Transgender Rights.* Pittsburgh: University of Pittsburgh Press.

Costa, Paul T., Jr., Antonio Terracciano, and Robert R. McCrae. 2001. Gender Differences in Personality Traits Across Cultures: Robust and Surprising Findings. *Journal of Personality and Social Psychology* 81(2): 322–331.

de la Dehesa, Rafael. 2010. *Queering the Public Sphere in Mexico and Brazil: Sexual Rights Movements in Emerging Democracies.* Durham, NC: Duke University Press.

Dollar, David, and Roberta Gatti. 1999. Gender Inequality, Income, and Growth: Are Good Times Good for Women? *World Bank PRR on Gender and Development Working Paper Series.*

Dunning, Thad, and Lauren Harrison. 2010. Cross-Cutting Cleavages and Ethnic Voting: An Experimental Study of Cousinage in Mali. *American Political Science Review* 104(1): 21–39.

Duster, Troy. 2005. February 18. Race and Reification in Science. *Science* 307(5712): 1050–1051.

Eccles, Jacquelynne. 1987. Gender Roles and Women's Achievement-Related Decisions. *Psychology of Women Quarterly* 11(2): 135–172.

England, Paula, Melissa S. Herbert, Barbara Stanek Kilbourne, Lori L. Reid, and Lori McCreary Megdal. 1994. The Gendered Valuation of Occupations and Skills: Earnings in 1980 Census Occupations. *Social Forces* 73(1): 65–100.

Franceschet, Susan, Mona Lena Krook, and Jennifer M. Piscopo, eds. 2012. *The Impact of Gender Quotas*. New York: Oxford University Press.

Fredrickson, George M. 2003. *Racism: A Short History*. Princeton, NJ: Princeton University Press.

Gans, Herbert J. 2005. Race as Class. *Contexts* 4(4): 17–21.

Glazer, Nathan. 1997. *We Are All Multiculturalists Now*. Cambridge, MA: Harvard University Press.

Handa, Sudhanshu, and Benjamin Davis. 2006. The Experience of Conditional Cash Transfers in Latin America and the Caribbean. *Development Policy Review* 5: 513–536.

Haveman, Heather A., and Lauren S. Beresford. 2012. If You're So Smart, Why Aren't You the Boss? Explaining the Persistent Vertical Gender Gap in Management. *The Annals of the American Academy of Political and Social Science* 639(1): 114–130.

Henderson, Sarah L,. and Alana S. Jeydel. 2010. *Women and Politics in a Global World*. New York: Oxford University Press.

Herring, Cedric. 2002. Is Job Discrimination Dead? *Contexts* 1: 13–18.

Hirschman, Charles, Richard Alba, and Reynolds Farley. 2000. The Meaning and Measurement of Race in the U.S. Census: Glimpses into the Future. *Demography* 37(3): 381–393.

Hirway, Indira, and Darshini Mahadevia. 1996. Critique of Gender Development Index: Toward an Alternative. *Economic and Political Weekly* 31(43): WS87–WS96.

Holli, Anna Maria, and Johanna Kantola. 2005. A Politics for Presence: State Feminism, Women's Movements, and Political Representation in Finland. In *State Feminism and Political Representation*, ed. Joni Lovenduski, 62–84. New York: Cambridge University Press.

Htun, Mala. 2004. Is Gender Like Ethnicity? The Political Representation of Identity Groups. *Perspectives on Politics* 2(3): 439–458.

Interparliamentary Union website. 2015. Women in National Parliaments (Situation as of March 1, 2015). http://archive.ipu.org/wmn-e/arc/classif010315.htm (accessed March 25, 2018).

Izugbara, C. Otutubikey. 2004. Gendered Micro-Lending Schemes and Sustainable Women's Empowerment in Nigeria. *Community Development Journal* 39(1): 72–84.

Jaschik, Scott. 2011, March 15. Worldwide Paradox for Women. *Inside Higher Ed*. http://www.insidehighered.com/news/2011/03/15/educators_consider_the_partial_progress_of_women_in_higher_education_around_the_world (accessed July 17, 2012).

Katz, Jonathan Ned. 2007. *The Invention of Heterosexuality*. Chicago: University of Chicago Press.

Katzew, Ilona. 2004. *Casta Painting: Images of Race in Eighteenth-Century Mexico*. New Haven, CT: Yale University Press.

Khagram, Sanjeev, and Peggy Levitt, eds. 2008. *The Transnational Studies Reader: Intersections and Innovations*. New York: Routledge.

Kimmel, Michael S. 2000. *The Gendered Society*. New York: Oxford University Press.

Kriesi, Hanspieter, Ruud Koopmans, Jan Willem Duyvendak, and Marco G. Giugni. 1992. New Social Movements and Political Opportunities in Western Europe. *European Journal of Political Research*, 22(2): 219–244.

Krook, Mona Lena. 2009. *Quotas for Women in Politics: Gender and Candidate Selection Reform Worldwide*. New York: Oxford University Press.

Lijphart, Arend. 1977. *Democracy in Plural Societies: A Comparative Exploration*. New Haven, CT: Yale University Press.

Loveman, Mara. 2009. The Race to Progress: Census Taking and Nation-Making in Brazil (1870–1920). *Hispanic American Historical Review* 89(3): 435–470.

Loveman, Mara. 2014. *National Colors: Racial Classification and the State in Latin America*. New York: Oxford University Press.

Lovenduski, Joni. 2005. Introduction: State Feminism and the Political Representation of Women. In *State Feminism and Political Representation*, ed. Joni Lovenduski, 1–19. New York: Cambridge University Press.

Marx, Anthony. 1998. *Making Race and Nation: A Comparison of South Africa, the United States, and Brazil*. New York: Cambridge University Press.

Matland, Richard E. 1998. Women's Representation in National Legislatures: Developed and Developing Countries. *Legislative Studies Quarterly* 23(1): 109–125.

Modood, Tariq. 2007. *Multiculturalism: A Civic Idea*. Malden, MA: Polity Press.

Nagel, Joane. 1996. *American Indian Ethnic Renewal: Red Power and the Resurgence of Identity and Culture*. New York: Oxford University Press.

Omi, Michael, and Howard Winant. 1994. *Racial Formation in the United States from the 1960s to the 1990s*. 2nd ed. New York: Routledge.

Ong, Aihwa. 1999. *Flexible Citizenship: The Cultural Logics of Trans-Nationality*. Durham, NC: Duke University Press.

Padavic, Irene, and Barbara Reskin. 2002. *Women and Men at Work*. 2nd ed. Thousand Oaks, CA: Pine Forge Press.

Pagden, Anthony. 2009. The Peopling of the New World: Ethnos, Race, and Empire in the Early Modern World. In *The Origins of Racism in the West*, ed. Miriam Eliav-Feldon, Benjamin Isaac, and Joseph Ziegler, 292–312. New York: Cambridge University Press.

Pager, Devah, and Hana Shepherd. 2008. The Sociology of Discrimination: Racial Discrimination in Employment, Housing, Credit, and Consumer Markets. *Annual Review of Sociology* 34:181–209.

Pettit, Becky, and Bruce Western. 2004. Mass Imprisonment and the Life Course: Race and Class Inequality in U.S. Incarceration. *American Sociological Review* 69(2): 151–169.

Pew Research Center. 2013. *The Global Divide on Homosexuality: Greater Acceptance in More Secular and Affluent Countries*. http://www.pewglobal.org/2013/06/04/the-global-divide-on-homosexuality/

Posner, Daniel N. 2005. *Institutions and Ethnic Politics in Africa*. New York: Cambridge University Press.

Rawlings, Laura B., and Gloria M. Rubio. 2005. Evaluating the Impact of Conditional Cash Transfer Programs. *The World Bank Research Observer* 20(1): 29–55.

Reynolds, Andrew. 2005. Reserved Seats in National Legislatures: A Research Note. *Legislative Studies Quarterly* 30(2): 301–310.

Ridgeway, Cecilia, and Shelly J. Correll. 2004. Unpacking the Gender System: A Theoretical Perspective on Gender Beliefs and Social Relations. *Gender and Society* 18(4): 510–531.

Roediger, David R. 1999. *The Wages of Whiteness: Race and the Making of the American Working Class*. Rev. ed. New York: Verso Press.

Roth, Louise Marie. 2006. *Selling Women Short: Gender and Inequality on Wall Street*. Princeton, NJ: Princeton University Press.

Sainsbury, Diane. 2005. Party Feminism, State Feminism, and Women's Representation in Sweden. In *State Feminism and Political Representation*, ed. Joni Lovenduski, 195–215. New York: Cambridge University Press.

Sawer, Marian, Manon Tremblay, and Linda Trimble, eds. 2006. *Representing Women in Parliament: A Comparative Study*. New York: Routledge.

Shapiro, Thomas M. 2004. *The Hidden Cost of Being African American: How Wealth Perpetuates Inequality*. New York: Oxford University Press.

Sidanius, Jim and Felicia Pratto. 1999. *Social Dominance: An Intergroup Theory of Social Hierarchy and Oppression*. New York: Cambridge University Press.

Smith, Anthony D. 1995. *Nations and Nationalism in a Global Era*. Malden, MA: Polity Press.

Sorenson, Aage. 2001. The Basic Concepts of Stratification Research: Class, Status, and Power. In *Social Stratification: Race, Class, and Gender in Sociological Perspective*, ed. David B. Grusky, 287–300. Boulder, CO: Westview Press.

Squires, Judith. 2007. *The New Politics of Gender Equality*. New York: Palgrave Macmillan.

Stetson, Dorothy McBride, and Amy G. Mazur, eds. 1995. *Comparative State Feminism*. Thousand Oaks, CA: Sage Publications.

Tienda, Marta, and Vilma Ortiz. 1986. "Hispanicity" and the 1980 Census. *Social Science Quarterly* 67(1): 3–20.

United Nations Development Programme. 2009. *Human Development Report 2009*. New York: United Nations Development Programme.

United Nations Development Programme. 2016. *Human Development Report 2016*. New York: United Nations Development Programme.

Van Cott, Donna Lena. 2005. *From Movements to Parties in Latin America*. New York: Cambridge University Press.

Weber, Max. 1946. Class, Status, Party. In *From Max Weber: Essays in Sociology*, ed. H. H. Gerth and C. Wright Mills, 180–195. New York: Oxford University Press.

Winn, Peter. 1992. *Americas: The Changing Face of Latin America and the Caribbean*. New York: Pantheon Books.

World Economic Forum. 2017. *The Global Gender Gap Report, 2017*. https://www.weforum.org/reports/the-global-gender-gap-report-2017

Yashar, Deborah J. 2005. *Contesting Citizenship in Latin America: The Rise of Indigenous Movements and the Postliberal Challenge*. New York: Cambridge University Press.

Zetterberg, Par. 2009. Do Gender Quotas Foster Women's Political Engagement? Lessons from Latin America. *Political Research Quarterly* 62(4): 715–730.

CHAPTER 15

Adida, Claire L., David D. Laitin, and Marie-Anne Valfort. 2016. *Why Muslim Integration Fails in Christian Heritage Societies*. Cambridge, MA: Harvard University Press.

Appadurai, Arjun. 1996. *Modernity at Large: Cultural Dimensions of Globalization*. Minneapolis: University of Minnesota Press.

Asad, Talal. 1993. *Genealogies of Religion: Discipline and Reasons of Power in Christianity and Islam*. Baltimore: Johns Hopkins University Press.

Asad, Talal. 2003. *Formations of the Secular: Christianity, Islam, Modernity*. Stanford, CA: Stanford University Press.

Bell, Daniel. [1960] 2000. *The End of Ideology: On the Exhaustion of Political Ideas in the Fifties*. Cambridge, MA: Harvard University Press.

Bell, Daniel. 1977. The Return of the Sacred? The Argument on the Future of Religion. *British Journal of Sociology* 28(4): 419–449.

Bellah, Robert. 1967. Civil Religion in America. *Daedalus* 26, No. 1 (Religion in America): 1–21.

Berger, Peter L. 1967. *The Sacred Canopy: Elements of a Sociological Theory of Religion*. New York: Anchor Books.

Berger, Peter L. 1974. Some Second Thoughts on Substantive Versus Functional Definitions of Religion. *Journal for the Scientific Study of Religion* 13(2): 125–133.

Berger, Peter L., ed. 1999. *The Desecularization of the World: Resurgent Religion and World Politics*. Grand Rapids, MI: Wm. B. Eerdmans Publishing Company.

Berger, Peter L., Brigitte Berger, and Hansfried Kellner. 1973. *The Homeless Mind: Modernization and Consciousness*. New York: Random House.

Berger, Peter L., Grace Davie, and Effie Fokas. 2008. *Religious America, Secular Europe? A Theme and Variations*. Burlington, VT: Ashgate Publishers.

Blancarte, Roberto, ed. 2008. *Los retos de la laicidad y la secularización en el mundo contemporáneo*. Mexico, D. F.: El Colegio de México, Centro de Estudios Sociológicos.

Boli, John. 1981. Marxism as World Religion. *Social Problems* 28(5): 510–513.

Brubaker, Rogers. 2016. A New "Christianist" Secularism in Europe. The Immanent Frame. http://blogs.ssrc.org/tif/2016/10/11/a-new-christianist-secularism-in-europe/ (accessed June 27, 2017).

Bruce, Steve. 2002. *God Is Dead: Secularization in the West*. Malden, MA: Blackwell.

Casanova, José. 1994. *Public Religions in the Modern World*. Chicago: University of Chicago Press.

Casanova, José. 2007. Immigration and the New Religious Pluralism: A European Union/United States Comparison. In *Democracy and the New Religious Pluralism*, ed. Thomas Banchoff, 59–84. New York: Oxford University Press.

Chatterjee, Partha. 1993. *The Nation and Its Fragments: Colonial and Postcolonial Histories*. Princeton, NJ: Princeton University Press.

Chatterjee, Partha. 1997. *Our Modernity*. Rotterdam/Dakar: SEPHIS/CODESRIA.

Chaves, Mark. 1994. Secularization as Declining Religious Authority. *Social Forces* 72(3): 749–774.

Chaves, Mark, and Philip S. Gorski. 2001. Religious Pluralism and Religious Participation. *Annual Review of Sociology* 27: 261–281.

Converse, Philip. 1964. The Nature of Belief Systems in Mass Publics. In *Ideology and Discontent*, ed. David E. Apter, 206–261. New York: Free Press.

Coronil, Fernando. 1997. *The Magical State: Nature, Money, and Modernity in Venezuela*. Chicago: University of Chicago Press.

Douthat, Ross. 2016. The Reactionary Mind. *New York Times*, April 23, 2016, https://www.nytimes.com/2016/04/24/opinion/sunday/the-reactionary-mind.html

Dubuisson, Daniel. 2003. *The Western Construction of Religion*, trans. William Sayers. Baltimore: Johns Hopkins University Press.

Eisenstadt, Samuel N. 2000, Winter. Multiple Modernities. *Daedalus* 129, No. 1 (Multiple Modernities): 1–29.

Finke, Roger, and Laurence R. Iannaccone. 1993. Supply Side Explanations for Religious Change. *Annals of the American Academy of Political and Social Science* 527 (Religion in the Nineties): 27–39.

Fox, Jonathan. 2008. *A World Survey of Religion and the State*. New York: Cambridge University Press.

Freston, Paul, ed. 2008. *Evangelical Christianity and Democracy in Latin America*. New York: Oxford University Press.

Fukuyama, Francis. 1992. *The End of History and the Last Man*. New York: Free Press.

Geertz, Clifford. 1973a. Ideology as a Cultural System. In *The Interpretation of Cultures*, ed. Clifford Geertz, 193–233. New York: Basic Books.

Geertz, Clifford. 1973b. Religion as a Cultural System. In *The Interpretation of Cultures*, ed. Clifford Geertz, 87–125. New York: Basic Books.

Gerring, John. 1997. Ideology: A Definitional Analysis. *Political Research Quarterly* 50(4): 957–994.

Gill, Anthony. 2008. *The Political Origins of Religious Liberty*. New York: Cambridge University Press.

Gill, Timothy. 2016. "People Are Comparing Donald Trump to Hugo Chávez. That's Mostly Wrong," Monkey Cage, *Washington Post*, October 17, 2016, https://www.washingtonpost.com/news/monkey-cage/wp/2016/10/17/people-are-comparing-donald-trump-to-hugo-chavez-thats-mostly-wrong/?utm_term=.5b307eaf34eb

Gorski, Philip S., and Ates Altinordu. 2008. After Secularization? *Annual Review of Sociology* 34: 55–85.

Greenfeld, Liah. 1996. The Modern Religion? *Critical Review: A Journal of Politics and Society* 10(2): 169–191.

Hawkins, Kirk A. 2010. *Venezuela's Chavismo and Populism in Comparative Perspective*. New York: Cambridge University Press.

Hobsbawm, Eric J., and Terence O. Ranger, eds. 1992. *The Invention of Tradition*. New York: Cambridge University Press.

Huntington, Samuel P. 1996. *The Clash of Civilizations and the Remaking of World Order*. New York: Simon and Schuster.

Inglehart, Ronald, and Christian Welzel. 2005. *Modernization, Cultural Change, and Democracy: The Human Development Sequence*. Cambridge: Cambridge University Press.

Inkeles, Alex, and David H. Smith. 1974. *Becoming Modern: Individual Change in Six Developing Countries*. Cambridge, MA: Harvard University Press.

James, William. 1902. *Varieties of Religious Experience: A Study in Human Nature*. New York: Longmans, Green.

Juergensmeyer, Mark. 1993. *The New Cold War? Religious Nationalism Confronts the Secular State*. Berkeley: University of California Press.

Kaufmann, Eric. 2010. *Shall the Religious Inherit the Earth? Demography and Politics in the Twenty-First Century*. London: Profile Books.

Kepel, Gilles. 1994. *The Revenge of God: The Resurgence of Islam, Christianity, and Judaism in the Modern World*. University Park: Pennsylvania State University Press.

Kuru, Ahmet T. 2009. *Secularism and State Policies Toward Religion: The United States, France, and Turkey*. New York: Cambridge University Press.

Laclau, Ernesto. 2005. *On Populist Reason*. London: Verso.

Levitsky, Steven, and Kenneth M. Roberts, eds. 2011. *The Resurgence of the Latin American Left*. Baltimore: Johns Hopkins University Press.

Lindholm, Charles, and Pedro Zúquete. 2010. *The Struggle for the World: Liberation Movements for the Twenty-First Century*. Stanford, CA: Stanford University Press.

Martin, David L. 2005. *On Secularization: Towards a Revised General Theory*. Burlington, VT: Ashgate.

Marx, Karl. 1978a. The German Ideology: Part I. In *The Marx-Engels Reader*, ed. Robert C. Tucker, 146–200. New York: W. W. Norton and Company.

Marx, Karl (with Friedrich Engels). 1978b. Manifesto of the Communist Party. In *The Marx-Engels Reader*, ed. Robert C. Tucker, 469–500. New York: W. W. Norton and Company.

Marx, Karl. 1978c. On the Jewish Question. In *The Marx-Engels Reader*, ed. Robert C. Tucker, 26–52. New York: W. W. Norton and Company.

Meyer, John W., John Boli, George M. Thomas, and Francisco O. Ramírez. 1997. World Society and the Nation-State. *American Journal of Sociology* 103(1): 144–181.

Moaddel, Mansoor. 2005. *Islamic Modernism, Nationalism and Fundamentalism: Episode and Discourse*. Chicago: University of Chicago Press.

Mudde, Cas. 2004. The Populist Zeitgeist. *Government and Opposition* 39(4): 541–563.

Mudde, Cas and Cristóbal Rovira Kaltwasser. 2013. Exclusionary vs. Inclusionary Populism: Comparing Contemporary Europe and Latin America. *Government and Opposition* 48(2), 147–174.

Mudde, Cas and Cristóbal Rovira Kaltwasser. 2013. *Government and Opposition* 48(2): 147–174.

Müller, Jan-Werner. 2016. *What is Populism?* Philadelphia: University of Pennsylvania Press.

Niebuhr, H. Richard. 1929. *The Social Sources of Denominationalism.* New York: Henry Holt and Company.

Norris, Pippa, and Ronald Inglehart. 2004. *Sacred and Secular: Religion and Politics Worldwide.* New York: Cambridge University Press.

Nye, Joseph. 1990. Soft Power. *Foreign Policy* 80:153–171.

Ostiguy, Pierre and Kenneth M. Roberts. 2016. Putting Trump in Comparative Perspective: Populism and the Politicization of the Sociocultural Low. *Brown Journal of World Affairs,* XXIII(I): 25–50.

Payne, Stanley. 1995. *A History of Fascism, 1914–1945.* Madison: University of Wisconsin Press.

Pew Research Center. 2015. The Future of World Religions: Population Growth Projections, 2010-2050 (April 2, 2015).

Putnam, Robert D. and David E. Campbell. 2010. *American Grace: How Religion Divides and Unites Us.* New York: Simon and Schuster.

Roberts, Kenneth. 1995. Neoliberalism and the Transformation of Populism in Latin America: The Peruvian Case. *World Politics* 48(1): 82–116.

Smilde, David, and Daniel Hellinger, eds. 2011. *Venezuela's Bolivarian Democracy: Participation, Politics, and Culture Under Chávez.* Durham, NC: Duke University Press.

Smilde, David, and Coraly Pagan. 2011. Christianity and Politics in Venezuela's Bolivarian Democracy: Catholics, Evangelicals and Political Polarization. In *Participation, Politics and Culture in Venezuela's Bolivarian Democracy,* ed. David Smilde and Daniel Hellinger, 317–340. Durham, NC: Duke University Press.

Stark, Rodney. 1999. Secularization, R.I.P. *Sociology of Religion* 60(3): 249–273.

Stepan, Alfred C. 2000. Religion, Democracy, and the "Twin Tolerations." *Journal of Democracy* 11(4): 37–57.

Tepe, Sultan. 2008. *Beyond Sacred and Secular: Politics of Religion in Israel and Turkey.* Stanford, CA: Stanford University Press.

Troeltsch, Ernst. 1969. Three Types of Christian Community. In *Sociology of Religion: A Book of Readings,* ed. Norman Birnbaum and Gertrude Lenzer, 310–314. Englewood Cliffs, NJ: Prentice-Hall.

Voas, David, Alasdair Crockett, and Daniel V. A. Olson. 2002. Religious Pluralism and Participation: Why Previous Research Is Wrong. *American Sociological Review* 67(2): 212–230.

Warner, R. Stephen. 1993. Work in Progress Toward a New Paradigm for the Sociological Study of Religion in the United States. *American Journal of Sociology* 98(5): 1044–1093.

Weber, Max. 1958. Science as a Vocation. In *From Max Weber: Essays in Sociology,* ed. H. H. Gerth and C. Wright Mills, 129–156. New York: Oxford University Press.

Weber, Max. 1969. Church and Sect. In *Sociology of Religion: A Book of Readings,* ed. Norman Birnbaum and Gertrude Lenzer, 318–322. Englewood Cliffs, NJ: Prentice-Hall.

Weiming, Tu. 2006. China's Cultural Renaissance. In *Developing Cultures: Case Studies,* ed. Lawrence E. Harrison and Peter L. Berger, 65–82. New York: Routledge.

Weyland, Kurt. 2001. Clarifying a Contested Concept: Populism in the Study of Latin American Politics. *Comparative Politics* 34(1): 1–22.

Woodberry, Robert D. 2011. Religion and the Spread of Human Capital and Political Institutions: Christian Missions as a Quasi-Natural Experiment. In *The Oxford Handbook of the Economics of Religion,* ed. R. McCleary, 111–131. New York: Oxford University Press.

Woodberry, Robert D., and Timothy S. Shah. 2004. The Pioneering Protestants. *Journal of Democracy* 15(2): 47–61.

Zarakol, Ayse. 2011. *After Defeat: How the East Learned to Live with the West.* New York: Cambridge University Press.

CHAPTER 16

Alba, Richard and Nancy Foner. 2015. *Strangers No More: Immigration and the Challenges of Integration in the North America and Western Europe.* Princeton, NJ: Princeton University Press.

Allison, Graham. 1971. *The Essence of Decision: Explaining the Cuban Missile Crisis.* Boston: Little, Brown.

Axelrod, Robert, and William D. Hamilton. 1981. The Evolution of Cooperation. *Science* 211: 1390–1396.

BBC News Europe. 2010, October 17. Merkel Says German Multicultural Society Has Failed. http://www.bbc.co.uk/news/world-europe-11559451 (accessed May 6, 2012).

Burke, Jason. 2004. Al Qaeda. *Foreign Policy* 142: 18–20, 22, 24, 26.

Carr, E. H. 1951. *The Twenty Years' Crisis: 1919–1939.* London: Macmillan & Co.

Churchill, Winston. 1947. "Speech in the House of Commons, 11/11/1947" in Hansard (The Official Report of the House of Commons). London: Government Printer.

Doyle, Michael. 1983a. Kant, Liberal Legacies, and Foreign Affairs. *Philosophy & Public Affairs* 12(3): 205–235.

Doyle, Michael. 1983b. Kant, Liberal Legacies, and Foreign Affairs, Part 2. *Philosophy & Public Affairs* 12(4): 323–353.

Doyle, Michael. 1997. *Ways of War and Peace: Realism, Liberalism, and Socialism.* New York: W. W. Norton.

Friedman, Thomas. 2005. *The World Is Flat: A Brief History of the Twenty-First Century.* New York: Farrar, Strauss, and Giroux.

Gilpin, Robert. 2001. *Global Political Economy: Understanding the International Economic Order.* Princeton, NJ: Princeton University Press.

Gourevitch, Peter. 1978. The Second Image Reversed: The International Sources of Domestic Politics. *International Organization* 32: 881–912.

Hardin, Garrett. 1997. Tragedy of the Commons. *Science 162* (3859): 1243–1248.

Hobbes, Thomas. [1651] 1996. *Leviathan*. Cambridge: Cambridge University Press.

Huntington, Samuel. 2004. *Who Are We? The Challenges to America's National Identity*. New York: Simon and Schuster.

Intergovernmental Panel on Climate Change (IPCC). 2007. *Climate Change 2007: Synthesis Report*. http://www.ipcc.ch/.

Jervis, Robert. 1978. Cooperation Under the Security Dilemma. *World Politics* 30(1): 167–214.

Kant, Immanuel. [1795] 1983. To Perpetual Peace: A Philosophical Sketch. In *Perpetual Peace and Other Essays*, trans. Ted Humphrey. Indianapolis, IN: Hackett Publishing Company.

Keck, Margaret, and Kathryn Sikkink. 1998. *Activists Beyond Borders: Advocacy Networks in International Politics*. Ithaca, NY: Cornell University Press.

Keohane, Robert O. 1984. *After Hegemony: Cooperation and Discord in the World Political Economy*. Princeton, NJ: Princeton University Press.

Keohane, Robert O., and Joseph S. Nye. 1977. *Power and Interdependence: World Politics in Transition*. Boston: Little, Brown and Company.

Krasner, Stephen. 1976. State Power and the Structure of International Trade. *World Politics* 28(3): 317–347.

Lenin, Vladimir I. [1917] 1996. *Imperialism: The Highest Stage of Capitalism*. London: Pluto Press.

Machiavelli, Niccolò. [1532] 1984. *The Prince*. New York: Bantam Books.

Mearsheimer, John. 2001. *The Tragedy of Great Power Politics*. New York: W. W. Norton.

Modood, Tariq. 2007. *Multiculturalism: A Civic Idea*. Cambridge, England: Polity.

Moravcsik, Andrew. 1997. Taking Preferences Seriously: A Liberal Theory of International Politics. *International Organization* 51(4): 513–553.

Moravcsik, Andrew. 1998. *The Choice for Europe: Social Purpose and State Power from Messina to Maastricht*. Ithaca, NY: Cornell University Press.

Morgenthau, Hans J. 1960. *Politics Among Nations: The Struggle for Power and Peace*. 3rd ed. New York: Alfred Knopf.

Naím, Moisés. 2003. The Five Wars of Globalization. *Foreign Policy* 134: 28–38.

Ostrom, Elinor. 1990. *Governing the Commons: The Evolution of Institutions for Collective Action*. Cambridge: Cambridge University Press.

Ousey, Graham C. and Charis E. Kubrin. 2017. Immigration and Crime: Assessing a Contentious Issue. *Annual Review of Criminology* (Review in Advance posted online at: http://www.annualreviews.org/doi/pdf/10.1146/annurev-criminol-032317-092026).

Phillips, Melanie. 2006. *Londonistan*. New York: Encounter Books.

Portes, Alejandro, and Rubén G. Rumbaut. 2006. *Immigrant America: A Portrait*. 3rd ed. Berkeley: University of California Press.

Putnam, Robert. 1988. Diplomacy and Domestic Politics: The Logic of Two-Level Games. *International Organization* 42: 427–460.

Rogoff, Kenneth. 2003. The IMF Strikes Back. *Foreign Policy* 134(1): 39–46.

Rogowski, Ronald. 1987. Political Cleavages and Changing Exposure to Trade. *The American Political Science Review* 81(4): 1121–1137.

Said, Edward. 1978. *Orientalism*. New York: Vintage.

Sampson, Robert J. 2008. Rethinking Immigration and Crime. *Contexts* 7: 28–33.

Singer, Peter. 2004. *One World: The Ethics of Globalization*. New Haven, CT: Yale University Press.

Stiglitz, Joseph. 2002. *Globalization and Its Discontents*. New York: W. W. Norton.

Stiglitz, Joseph. 2007. *Making Globalization Work*. New York: W. W. Norton.

Thucydides. [n.d.] 1974. *History of the Peloponnesian Wars*. New York: Penguin Books.

Walt, Stephen. 1998. International Relations: One World, Many Theories. *Foreign Policy* 110: 29–32, 34–46.

Waltz, Kenneth. 1954. *Man, the State, and War*. New York: Columbia University Press.

Waltz, Kenneth. 1979. *Theory of International Politics*. Reading, MA: Addison-Wesley.

Wendt, Alexander. 1992. Anarchy Is What States Make of It: The Social Construction of Power Politics. *International Organization* 46(2): 391–425.

Wendt, Alexander. 1999. *Social Theory of International Politics*. Cambridge: Cambridge University Press.

Wolf, Martin. 2004. *Why Globalization Works*. New Haven, CT: Yale University Press.

Country Profiles

Note: Information for the country profiles comes from the following sources.

CIA World Factbook. https://www.cia.gov/library/publications/the-world-factbook/index.html (accessed March 2, 2015).

United Nations *Human Development Report 2014*. http://hdr.undp.org/sites/default/files/hdr14-report-en-1.pdf.

World Bank World Development Indicators. http://data.worldbank.org/data-catalog/world-development-indicators/ (accessed March 2, 2015).

BRAZIL

Ames, Barry. 2001. *The Deadlock of Democracy in Brazil*. Ann Arbor: University of Michigan Press.

Cardoso, Fernando Henrique, and Enzo Faletto. 1979. *Dependency and Development in Latin America*, trans. Marjory Mattingly Urquidi. Berkeley: University of California Press.

Evans, Peter 1979. *Dependent Development: The Alliance of Multinational, State, and Local Capital in Brazil*. Princeton, NJ: Princeton University Press.

Evans, Peter B. 1989. Predatory, Developmental and Other Apparatuses: A Comparative Political Economy Perspective on the Third World State. *Sociological Forum* 4(4): 561–587.

Fausto, Boris. 1999. *A Concise History of Brazil*. New York: Cambridge University Press.

Gill, Anthony. 1998. *Rendering Unto Caesar: The Catholic Church and the State in Latin America*. Chicago: University of Chicago Press.

Graham, Richard. 1990. *Patronage and Politics in Nineteenth-Century Brazil*. Stanford, CA: Stanford University Press.

Haggard, Stephan, and Robert R. Kaufman. 1995. *The Political Economy of Democratic Transitions*. Princeton, NJ: Princeton University Press.

Htun, Mala. 2004. Is Gender Like Ethnicity? The Political Representation of Gender Groups. *Perspectives on Politics* 2(3): 439–458.

Htun, Mala, and Timothy J. Power. 2006. Gender, Parties, and Support for Equal Rights in the Brazilian Congress. *Latin American Politics and Society* 48(4): 83–104.

Kingstone, Peter R. 1999. *Crafting Coalitions for Reform: Business Preferences, Political Institutions, and Neoliberal Reform in Brazil*. University Park: Pennsylvania State University Press.

Macaulay, Fiona. 2006. *Gender Politics in Brazil and Chile: The Role of Parties in National and Local Policymaking*. New York: Palgrave Macmillan (in Association with St. Antony's College).

Mahoney, James. 2010. *Colonialism and Postcolonial Development: Spanish America in Comparative Perspective*. New York: Cambridge University Press.

Marx, Anthony. 1998. *Making Race and Nation: A Comparison of the United States, South Africa, and Brazil*. New York: Cambridge University Press.

O'Donnell, Guillermo A. 1973. *Modernization and Bureaucratic-Authoritarianism: Studies in South American Politics*. Berkeley: Institute of International Studies.

O'Donnell, Guillermo, Philippe Schmitter, and Laurence Whitehead, eds. [1986] 1993. *Transitions from Authoritarian Rule* (4 vols.). Baltimore: Johns Hopkins University Press.

Ondetti, Gabriel. 2008. *Land, Protest, and Politics: The Landless Movement and the Struggle for Agrarian Reform in Brazil*. University Park: Pennsylvania State University Press.

Power, Timothy J. 2000. Political Institutions in Democratic Brazil: Politics as a Permanent Constitutional Convention. In *Democratic Brazil: Actors, Institutions, and Processes*, ed. Peter R. Kingstone and Timothy J. Power, 17–35. Pittsburgh, PA: University of Pittsburgh Press.

Power, Timothy. 2008. Centering Democracy? Ideological Cleavages and Convergence in the Brazilian Political Class. In *Democratic Brazil Revisited*, ed. Peter R. Kingstone and Timothy J. Power, 81–106. Pittsburgh, PA: University of Pittsburgh Press.

Power, Timothy J., and Cesar Zucco, Jr. 2009. Estimating Ideology of Brazilian Legislative Parties, 1990–2005: A Research Communication. *Latin American Research Review* 44(1): 218–246.

Roett, Riordan. 2011. *The New Brazil*. Washington, DC: Brookings Institution Press.

Samuels, David. 2003. *Ambition, Federalism, and Legislative Politics in Brazil*. New York: Cambridge University Press.

Serbin, Kenneth. 2000. The Catholic Church, Religious Pluralism, and Democracy in Brazil. In *Democratic Brazil: Actors, Institutions, and Processes*, ed. Peter R. Kingstone and Timothy J. Power, 144–166. Pittsburgh, PA: University of Pittsburgh Press.

Skidmore, Thomas E. 2010. *Brazil: Five Centuries of Change*. 2nd ed. New York: Oxford University Press.

Stepan, Alfred C. 1971. *The Military in Politics: Changing Patterns in Brazil*. Princeton, NJ: Princeton University Press.

Zucco, Cesar. 2008. The Preside0nt's "New" Constituency: Lula and the Pragmatic Vote in Brazil's 2006 Presidential Elections. *Journal of Latin American Studies* 40(1): 29–49.

CHINA

Anderson, Benedict. [1983] 1991. *Imagined Communities: Reflections on the Origins and Spread of Nationalism*. New York: Verso.

Averill, Stephen C. 1998. Chinese Communist Revolution (1921–1949). In *Encyclopedia of Political Revolutions*, ed. Jack Goldstone, 78–83. Washington, DC: Congressional Quarterly, Inc.

Edmonds, Richard Louis. 1997. The State of Studies on Republican China. *The China Quarterly* 150: 255–259.

Epstein, Edward. 1984. Legitimacy, Institutionalization, and Opposition in Exclusionary Bureaucratic-Authoritarian Regimes: The Situation of the 1980s. *Comparative Politics* 17(1): 37–54.

Fairbank, John King, and Merle Goldman. 2006. *China: A New History*. 2nd ed. Cambridge, MA: Belknap Press of Harvard University Press.

Gilley, Bruce. 2010. Deng Ziaoping and His Successors: 1976 to the Present. In *Politics in China*, ed. William A. Joseph, 103–128. New York: Oxford University Press.

Harrison, Henrietta. 2001. *China: Inventing the Nation*. London: Arnold; New York: Co-published in the United States of America by Oxford University Press.

Joseph, William A. 2010a. Ideology and Chinese Politics. In *Politics in China*, ed. William A. Joseph, 129–164. New York: Oxford University Press.

Joseph, William A., ed. 2010b. *Politics in China: An Introduction*. New York: Oxford University Press.

Lin, Justin Yifu. 2009. *Economic Development and Transition: Thought, Strategy, and Viability*. New York: Cambridge University Press.

Perry, Elizabeth. 1998. Chinese Cultural Revolutions (1966–1969). In *Encyclopedia of Political Revolutions*, ed. Jack Goldstone, 83–85. Washington DC: Congressional Quarterly, Inc.

Pew Forum on Religion and Public Life. 2008. Religion in China on the Eve of the 2008 Olympics. http://pewforum.org/Importance-of-Religion/Religion-in-China-on-the-Eve-of-the-2008-Beijing-Olympics.aspx.

Schoppa, R. Keith. 2010. From Empire to People's Republic. In *Politics in China*, ed. William A. Joseph, 37–62. New York: Oxford University Press.

Skocpol, Theda. 1979. *States and Social Revolutions: A Comparative Analysis of France, Russia, and China*. New York: Cambridge University Press.

Spence, Jonathan D. 1990. *The Search for Modern China*. New York: W. W. Norton and Company.

Teiwes, Frederick C. 2010. Mao Zedong in Power (1949–1976). In *Politics in China*, ed. William A. Joseph, pp. 63–102. New York: Oxford University Press.

Weiming, Tu. 1999. The Quest for Meaning: Religion in the People's Republic of China. In *The Desecularization of the World: Resurgent Religion and World Politics*, ed. Peter L. Berger, 85–102. Grand Rapids, MI: William B. Eerdmans.

FRANCE

Adida, Claire L., David D. Laitin, and Marie-Anne Valfort. 2016. *Why Muslim Integration Fails in Christian Heritage Societies.* Cambridge, MA: Harvard University Press.

Arendt, Hannah. 1963. *On Revolution.* New York: Viking Press.

Begley, Louis. 2009. *Why the Dreyfus Affair Matters.* New Haven, CT: Yale University Press.

Bell, David A. 2001. *The Cult of the Nation in France: Inventing Nationalism, 1680–1800.* Cambridge, MA: Harvard University Press.

Blancarte, Roberto, ed. 2008. *Los Retos de La Laicidad y La Secularización En El Mundo Contemporáneo* [The Challenges of Secularism and Secularization in the Contemporary World]. Distrito Federal: El Colegio de Mexico.

Brubaker, Rogers. 1992. *Citizenship and Nationhood in France and Germany.* Cambridge, MA: Harvard University Press.

Casanova, José. 1994. *Public Religions in the Modern World.* Chicago: University of Chicago Press.

DGAFP *Annual Report 2014.* http://www.fonction-publique.gouv.fr/files/files/statistiques/chiffres_cles/pdf/chiffres_cles_2014.pdf.

Doyle, William. 2003. *Oxford History of the French Revolution.* 2nd ed. New York: Oxford University Press.

Esping-Anderson, Gøsta. 1990. *The Three Worlds of Welfare Capitalism.* Princeton, NJ: Princeton University Press.

Furet, Francois. [1988] 1995. *The French Revolution, 1770–1814.* Malden, MA: Blackwell Publishers.

Furet, Francois. [1988] 1995. *Revolutionary France, 1770–1880*, trans. Antonia Nevill. Cambridge, MA: Blackwell.

Greenfeld, Liah. 1992. *Nationalism: Five Roads to Modernity.* Cambridge, MA: Harvard University Press.

Greenfeld, Liah. 2001. *The Spirit of Capitalism: Nationalism and Economic Growth.* Cambridge, MA: Harvard University Press.

Hackett, Conrad. 2016. "5 facts about the Muslim population in Europe," Pew Research Center, July 19. http://www.pewresearch.org/fact-tank/2016/07/19/5-facts-about-the-muslim-population-in-europe/

International IDEA. 2018. Voter turnout data for France. https://www.idea.int/data-tools/question-countries-view/522/86/ctr (accessed on March 25, 2018).

Kuran, Timur. 1991. Now Out of Never: The Element of Surprise in the East European Revolution of 1989. *World Politics* 44(1): 748.

Kuru, Ahmet. 2009. *Secularism and State Policies Toward Religion: The United States, France, and Turkey.* New York: Cambridge University Press.

Lichbach, Mark I. 1995. *The Rebel's Dilemma.* Ann Arbor: University of Michigan Press.

Marx, Karl. [1852] 2007. The Eighteenth Brumaire of Louis Bonaparte. In *Classical Sociological Theory*, 2nd ed., ed. Craig Calhoun, Joseph

Gerteis, James Moody, Steven Pfaf, and Indermohan Virk, 112–121. Malden, MA: Blackwell Publishers.

Parry, D. L. L., and Pierre Girard. 2002. *France Since 1800: Squaring the Hexagon.* New York: Oxford University Press.

Prasad, Monica. 2006. *The Politics of Free Markets: The Rise of Neoliberal Economic Policies in Britain, France, Germany, and the United States.* Chicago: University of Chicago Press.

Schwartz, Vanessa. 2011. *Modern France: A Very Short Introduction.* New York: Oxford University Press.

Scott, Joan Wallach. 2007. *The Politics of the Veil.* Princeton, NJ: Princeton University Press.

Tocqueville, Alexis de. [1856] 2002. The Old Regime and the Revolution. Vol. 1: 1856. In *The Tocqueville Reader: A Life in Letters and Politics*, ed. Olivier Zunz and Alan S. Kahan, 278–319. Malden, MA: Blackwell.

Weber, Eugen. 1976. *Peasants into Frenchmen: The Modernization of Rural France, 1870–1914.* Stanford, CA: Stanford University Press.

Zaretsky, Robert. How French Secularism Became Fundamentalist. *Foreign Policy*, April 7, 2016, http://foreignpolicy.com/2016/04/07/the-battle-for-the-french-secular-soul-laicite-charlie-hebdo/

GERMANY

Allen, Christopher J. 1989. The Underdevelopment of Keynesianism in the Federal Republic of Germany. In *The Political Power of Economic Ideas: Keynesianism Across Nations*, ed. Peter A. Hall, 263–289. Princeton, NJ: Princeton University Press.

Anderson, Perry. 1974. *Lineages of the Absolutist State.* New York: Verso.

Barth, Fredrik, ed. 1969. *Ethnic Groups and Boundaries: The Social Organization of Culture Difference.* Boston: Little, Brown, and Company.

Berger, Stefan. 2004. *Germany: Inventing the Nation.* London: Arnold Publishers.

Browning, Christopher. 1992. *Ordinary Men: Reserve Police Battalion 101 and the Final Solution in Poland.* New York: HarperCollins.

Brubaker, Rogers. 1992. *Citizenship and Nationhood in France and Germany.* Cambridge, MA: Harvard University Press.

Davies, Norman. 1996. *Europe: A History.* New York: Harper Perennial.

Esping-Anderson, Gøsta. 1990. *The Three Worlds of Welfare Capitalism.* Princeton, NJ: Princeton University Press.

Fetzer, Joel S., and J. Christopher Soper. 2005. *Muslims and the State in Britain, France, and Germany.* New York: Cambridge University Press.

Fulbrook, Mary. 1990. *A Concise History of Germany.* New York: Cambridge University Press.

Gerschenkron, Alexander. 1962. *Economic Backwardness in Historical Perspective: A Book of Essays.* Cambridge, MA: Belknap Press.

Goldhagen, Daniel. 1996. *Hitler's Willing Executioners: Ordinary Germans and the Holocaust.* New York: Knopf.

Greenfeld, Liah. 1992. *Nationalism: Five Roads to Modernity.* Cambridge, MA: Harvard University Press.

Hentschel, Volker. 2008. German Economic and Social Policy, 1815–1939. In *The Cambridge Economic History of Europe*, Vol. 8, ed. Peter Mathias and Sidney Pollard, 752–813. New York: Cambridge University Press (Cambridge Histories Online).

Hicks, Alexander. 1988. Social Democratic Corporatism and Economic Growth. *Journal of Politics* 50(3): 677–704.

James, Harold. 2009. The Weimar Economy. In *Weimar Germany (The Short Oxford History of Germany)*, ed. Anthony McElligott, 102–126. New York: Oxford University Press.

Kitchen, Martin. 2006. *A History of Modern Germany, 1800–2000*. Malden, MA: Blackwell.

Kurth, James. 1979. The Political Consequences of the Product Cycle: Industrial History and Political Outcomes. *International Organization* 33(1): 1–34.

Lamont, Michele, and Virag Molnar. 2002. The Study of Boundaries in the Social Sciences. *Annual Review of Sociology* 28: 167–195.

Lijphart, Arend. 1999. *Patterns of Democracy: Government Forms and Performance in Thirty-Six Countries*. New Haven, CT: Yale University Press.

Mares, Isabela. 2001. Strategic Bargaining and Social Policy Development: Unemployment Insurance in France and Germany. In *Comparing Welfare Capitalism: Social Policy and Political Economy in Europe, Japan, and the USA*, ed. Bernard Ebbinghaus and Philip Manow, 52–75. New York: Routledge.

McElligott, Anthony, ed. 2009. *Weimar Germany (The Short Oxford History of Germany)*. New York: Oxford University Press.

Olick, Jeffrey. 2005. *In the House of the Hangman: The Agonies of German Defeat, 1943–1949*. Chicago: University of Chicago Press.

Olson, Mancur. 1984. *The Rise and Decline of Nations: Economic Growth, Stagnation, and Social Rigidities*. New Haven, CT: Yale University Press.

"The Growth of Germany's Muslim Population." Pew Research Center, Washington, D.C. (November 29, 2017) http://www.pewforum.org/essay/the-growth-of-germanys-muslim-population/ (accessed March 12, 2018).

Schmidt, Manfred G. 2008. Germany: The Grand Coalition State. In *Comparative European Politics*, ed. Josep M. Colomer, 58–93. New York: Routledge.

Siaroff, Alan. 1999. Corporatism in 24 Industrial Democracies: Meaning and Measurement. *European Journal of Political Research* 36(2): 175–205.

Weber, Eugen. 1972. *Europe Since 1715: A Modern Introduction*. New York: W. W. Norton and Company.

INDIA

Allen, Robert C. 2011. *Global Economic History: A Very Short Introduction*. New York: Oxford University Press.

Balakrishnan, Pulapre. 2010. *Economic Growth in India: History and Prospect*. New York: Oxford University Press.

Chandra, Kanchan. 2004. *Why Ethnic Parties Succeed: Patronage and Ethnic Head Counts in India*. New York: Cambridge University Press.

Dirks, Nicholas B. 2001. *Castes of Mind: Colonialism and the Making of Modern India*. Princeton, NJ: Princeton University Press.

Dumont, Louis. [1966] 1981. *Homo Hierarchicus: The Caste System and Its Implications*. Chicago: University of Chicago Press.

Friedman, Thomas L. 2005. *The World Is Flat: A Brief History of the Twenty-First Century*. New York: Farrar, Strauss, and Giroux.

Kohli, Atul. 1989. *The State and Poverty in India: The Politics of Reform*. New York: Cambridge University Press.

Kohli, Atul. 1990. *Democracy and Discontent: India's Growing Crisis of Governability*. New York: Cambridge University Press.

Kohli, Atul. 2004. *State-Directed Development: Political Power and Industrialization on the Global Periphery*. Cambridge: Cambridge University Press.

Mehta, Suketu. 2004. *Maximum City: Bombay Lost and Found*. New York: Alfred A. Knopf.

Metcalf, Barbara D., and Thomas R. Metcalf. 2006. *A Concise History of Modern India*. 2nd ed. New York: Cambridge University Press.

Mullen, Rani D. 2011. *Decentralization, Local Governance, and Social Wellbeing in India: Do Local Governments Matter?* New York: Taylor and Francis.

Pew Forum on Religion and Public Life. 2009. *Mapping the Global Muslim Population: A Report on the Size and Distribution of the World's Muslim Population*. Washington, DC: Pew Research Center. http://www.pewforum.org/2009/10/07/mapping-the-global-muslim-population/ (accessed April 17, 2015).

"By 2050, India to have world's largest populations of Hindus and Muslims." Pew Research Center, Washington, D.C. (April 21, 2015) http://www.pewresearch.org/fact-tank/2015/04/21/by-2050-india-to-have-worlds-largest-populations-of-hindus-and-muslims/ (accessed March 24, 2018).

Rudolph, Lloyd I., and Susanne Hoeber Rudolph. 1987. *In Pursuit of Lakshmi: The Political Economy of the Indian State*. Chicago: University of Chicago Press.

Russell, Malcolm B. 2003. *The Middle East and South Asia*. 37th ed. Harpers Ferry, WV: Stryker-Post Publications.

SarDesai, D. R. 2007. *India: The Definitive History*. Boulder, CO: Westview Press.

Sen, Amartya. 1999. *Development as Freedom*. New York: Alfred A. Knopf.

IRAN

Arjomand, Said Amir. 2009. *After Khomeini: Iran Under His Successors*. New York: Oxford University Press.

Foran, John. 2005. *Taking Power: On the Origins of Third World Revolutions*. New York: Cambridge University Press.

Gheissari, Ali, ed. *Contemporary Iran: Economy, Society, Politics*. New York: Oxford University Press.

Greenfeld, Liah. 1992. *Nationalism: Five Roads to Modernity*. Cambridge, MA: Harvard University Press.

Haeri, Shahla. 2009. Women, Religion, and Political Agency in Iran. In *Contemporary Iran: Economy, Society, Politics*, ed. Ali Gheissari, 125–149. New York: Oxford University Press.

Hambly, Gavin R. G. [1991] 2008a. The Pahlavī Autocracy: Muhammad Riżā Shāh 1941–1979. In *The Cambridge History of Iran. Vol. 7: From Nadir Shah to the Islamic Republic*, online ed., ed. Peter Avery, Gavin Hambly, and Charles Melville, 244–293. New York: Cambridge University Press.

Hambly, Gavin R. G. [1991] 2008b. The Pahlavī Autocracy: Riżā Shāh 1921–1941. In *The Cambridge History of Iran. Vol. 7: From Nadir Shah to the Islamic Republic*, online ed., ed. Peter Avery, Gavin Hambly, and Charles Melville, 213–243. New York: Cambridge University Press.

Hausmann, Ricardo, Laura D. Tyson, and Saadia Zahidi. 2010. *The Global Gender Gap Report, 2010*. Geneva: World Economic Forum, http://www3.weforum.org/docs/WEF_GenderGap_Report_2010.pdf (accessed August 13, 2012).

Interparliamentary Union website. 2015. Women in National Parliaments (Situation as of March 1, 2015). http://archive.ipu.org/wmn-e/arc/classif010315.htm, (accessed March 25, 2018).

Juergensmeyer, Mark. 1993. *The New Cold War? Religious Nationalism Confronts the Secular State*. Berkeley: University of California Press.

Keddie, Nikki. [1991] 2008. Iran Under the Later Qājārs, 1848–1922. In *The Cambridge History of Iran. Vol. 7: From Nadir Shah to the Islamic Republic*, online ed., ed. Peter Avery, Gavin Hambly, and Charles Melville, 174–212. New York: Cambridge University Press.

Kurzman, Charles. 2004. *The Unthinkable Revolution in Iran*. Cambridge, MA: Harvard University Press.

Laub, Zachary. 2017. *The Impact of the Iran Nuclear Agreement*. Council on Foreign Relations, OAD, www.cfr.org/backgrounder/impact-iran-nuclear-agreement (accessed March 24, 2018).

Mir-Hosseini, Ziba. 1999. *Islam and Gender: The Religious Debate in Contemporary Iran*. Princeton, NJ: Princeton University Press.

Moaddel, Mansoor. 2005. *Islamic Modernism, Nationalism, and Fundamentalism: Episode and Discourse*. Chicago: University of Chicago Press.

Parsa, Misagh. 2000. *States, Ideologies, and Social Revolutions: A Comparative Analysis of Iran, Nicaragua, and the Philippines*. New York: Cambridge University Press.

Sagan, Scott D. 1996. Why Do States Build Nuclear Weapons? Three Models in Search of a Bomb. *International Security* 21(3): 54–86.

Salehi-Isfahani, Djavad. 2009. Oil Wealth and Economic Growth in Iran. In *Contemporary Iran: Economy, Society, Politics*, ed. Ali Gheissari, 3–37. New York: Oxford University Press.

World Economic Forum. 2016. The Global Gender Gap Report 2016, http://reports.weforum.org/global-gender-gap-report-2016/economies/#economy=IRN (accessed March 24, 2018).

JAPAN

Berger, Gordon M. 2008. Politics and Mobilization in Japan, 1931–1945. In *The Cambridge History of Japan. Vol. 6: The Twentieth Century*, online ed., ed. Peter Duus, 97–153. New York: Cambridge University Press.

Blair, Gavin. 2010. Japan Sighs Relief as Bluefin Tuna Ban Fails. *The Christian Science Monitor*, March 19, http://www.csmonitor.com/World/Asia-Pacific/2010/0319/Japan-sighs-relief-as-bluefin-tuna-ban-fails (accessed August 13, 2012).

Bouissou, Jean-Marie. 1999. Organizing One's Support Base Under the SNTV: The Case of Japanese *Koenkai*. In *Elections in Japan, Korea, and Taiwan Under the Single Non-Transferable Vote: The Comparative Study of an Embedded Institution*, ed. Bernard Grofman, Sung-Chull Lee, Edwin A. Winckler, and Brian Woodall, 87–120. Ann Arbor: University of Michigan Press.

Christensen, Raymond V. 1994. Electoral Reform in Japan: How It Was Enacted and Changes It May Bring. *Asian Survey* 34(7): 589–605.

Cox, Gary W. 1996. Is the Single Non-Transferable Vote Superproportional? Evidence from Japan and Taiwan. *American Journal of Political Science* 40(3): 740–755.

Crawcour, E. Sydney. 2008. Industrialization and Technological Change, 1885–1920. In *The Cambridge History of Japan. Vol. 6: The Twentieth Century*, online ed., ed. Peter Duus, 385–450. New York: Cambridge University Press.

Doak Kevin. 2006. *A History of Nationalism in Modern Japan: Placing the People*. Leiden, Netherlands: Brill Publishers.

Esping-Anderson, Gøsta. 1997. Hybrid or Unique? The Japanese Welfare State Between Europe and America. *Journal of European Social Policy* 7(3): 179–189.

Evans, Peter B. 1989. Predatory, Developmental, and Other Apparatuses: A Comparative Political Economy Perspective on the Third World State. *Sociological Forum* 4(4): 561–587.

Fukui, Haruhiro. [1988] 2008. Postwar Politics: 1945–1973. In *The Cambridge History of Japan. Vol. 6: The Twentieth Century*, online ed., ed. Peter Duus, 154–213. New York: Cambridge University Press.

Gordon, Andrew. 2009. *A Modern History of Japan: From Tokugawa Times to the Present*. 2nd ed. New York: Oxford University Press.

Greenfeld, Liah. 2001. *The Spirit of Capitalism: Nationalism and Economic Growth*. Cambridge, MA: Harvard University Press.

Hall, Peter A., and David Soskice. 2001. An Introduction to Varieties of Capitalism. In *Varieties of Capitalism: The Institutional Foundations of Comparative Advantage*, ed. Peter A. Hall and David Soskice, 1–67. New York: Oxford University Press.

Horiuchi, Yusaku, and Jun Saito. 2003. Reapportionment and Redistribution: Consequences of Electoral Reform in Japan. *American Journal of Political Science* 47(4): 669–682.

Interparliamentary Union website. 2015. Women in National Parliaments (Situation as of January 1, 2018), http://archive.ipu.org/wmn-e/classif.htm (accessed March 25, 2018).

Johnson, Chalmers. 1982. *MITI and the Japanese Miracle: The Growth of Industrial Policy, 1925–1975*. Stanford, CA: Stanford University Press.

Kabashima, Ikuo, and Gill Steel. 2010. *Changing Politics in Japan*. Ithaca, NY: Cornell University Press.

Kolbert, Elizabeth. 2010. The Scales Fall. *The New Yorker*, August 2. http://www.newyorker.com/arts/critics/books/2010/08/02/100802crbo_books_kolbert?currentPage;eqall (accessed August 13, 2012).

Kosai, Yutaka. 2008. The Postwar Japanese Economy, 1945–1973. In *The Cambridge History of Japan. Vol. 6: The Twentieth Century*, online ed., ed. Peter Duus, trans. Andrew Goble, 494–537. New York: Cambridge University Press.

Kunio, Yoshihara. 2006. Japanese Culture and Postwar Economic Growth. In *Developing Cultures: Case Studies*, ed. Lawrence E. Harrison and Peter L. Berger, 83–100. New York: Routledge.

Krauss, Ellis S., and Robert J. Pekkanen. 2011. *The Rise and Fall of Japan's LDP: Political Party Organizations as Historical Institutions*. Ithaca, NY: Cornell University Press.

LeBlanc, Robin M. 1999. *Bicycle Citizens: The Political World of the Japanese Housewife*. Berkeley: University of California Press.

Manow, Philip. 2001. Business Coordination, Wage Bargaining, and the Welfare State: Germany and Japan in Comparative Historical Perspective. In *Comparing Welfare Capitalism: Social Policy and Political Economy in Europe, Japan, and the USA*, ed. Bernhard Ebbinghaus and Philip Manow, 27–51. New York: Routledge.

Martin, Sherry L. 2008. Keeping Women in Their Place: Penetrating Male-Dominated Urban and Rural Assemblies. In *Democratic Reform in Japan: Assessing the Impact*, ed. Sherry L. Martin and Gill Steel, 125–149. Boulder, CO: Lynne Rienner.

McBride, James and Beina Xu. 2017. Abenomics and the Japanese Economy. Council of Foreign Relations, https://www.cfr.org/backgrounder/abenomics-and-japanese-economy

Mitani, Taichiro. [1988] 2008. The Establishment of Party Cabinets, 1898–1932. In *The Cambridge History of Japan. Vol. 6: The Twentieth Century*, online ed., ed. and trans. Peter Duus, 55–96. New York: Cambridge University Press.

Nakamura, Takafusa. [1988] 2008. Depression, Recovery, and War, 1920–1945. In *The Cambridge History of Japan. Vol. 6: The Twentieth Century*, online ed., ed. Peter Duus, trans. Jacqueline Kaminsky, 451–493. New York: Cambridge University Press.

North, Douglas. 1990. *Institutions, Institutional Change, and Economic Performance*. New York: Cambridge University Press.

Olson, Mancur. 1984. *The Rise and Decline of Nations: Economic Growth, Stagflation, and Social Rigidities*. New Haven, CT: Yale University Press.

Scheiner, Ethan. 2006. *Democracy Without Competition in Japan: Opposition Failure in a One-Party Dominant State*. New York: Cambridge University Press.

United Nations Development Programme. 2016. Human Development Report 2016: Human Development for Everyone. New York: United Nations Development Programme.

World Economic Forum. 2017. *The Global Gender Gap Report, 2017*. http://www3.weforum.org/docs/WEF_GGGR_2017.pdf

MEXICO

Almond, Gabriel, and Sidney Verba. 1963. *The Civic Culture: Political Attitudes and Democracy in Five Nations*. Princeton, NJ: Princeton University Press.

Anna, Timothy E. 1998. *Forging Mexico, 1821–1835*. Lincoln: University of Nebraska Press.

Basáñez, Miguel. 2006. Mexico: The Camel and the Needle. In *Developing Cultures: Case Studies*, ed. Lawrence E. Harrison and Peter L. Berger, 287–303. New York: Routledge.

Bazant, Jan. 1985. Mexico from Independence to 1867. In *Cambridge History of Latin America. Vol. 3: From Independence to c. 1870*, ed. Leslie Bethell, 423–470. New York: Cambridge University Press.

Blancarte, Roberto. 1992. *Historia de la Iglesia Católica en México* [History of the Catholic Church in Mexico]. *Mexico*, DF: El Colegio Mexiquense/Fondo de Cultura Económica.

Camp, Roderic Ai. 2007. *Politics in Mexico: The Democratic Consolidation*. New York: Oxford University Press.

Davis, Diane E. 2006. Undermining the Rule of Law: Democratization and the Dark Side of Police Reform in Mexico. *Latin American Politics and Society* 48(1): 55–86.

Gill, Anthony. 2008. *The Political Origins of Religious Liberty*. New York: Cambridge University Press.

Haber, Paul. 2006. *Power From Experience: Urban Popular Movements in Late Twentieth-Century Mexico*. University Park: Pennsylvania State University Press.

Halperín Donghi, Tulio. 1993. *The Contemporary History of Latin America*, trans. John Charles Chasteen. Durham, NC: Duke University Press.

Hamnett, Brian. 1994. *Juárez*. New York: Longman.

Hernández Navarro, Luis, and Laura Carlsen. 2004. Indigenous Rights: The Battle for Constitutional Reform in Mexico. In *Dilemmas of Political Change in Mexico*, ed. Kevin J. Middlebrook, 440–465. London: Institute of Latin American Studies.

Inglehart, Ronald, and Christian Welzel. 2005. *Modernization, Cultural Change, and Democracy: The Human Development Sequence*. New York: Cambridge University Press.

Knight, Alan. 1990a. *The Mexican Revolution. Vol. 1: Porfirians, Liberals, and Peasants*. Lincoln: University of Nebraska Press.

Knight, Alan. 1990b. *The Mexican Revolution. Vol. 2: Counter-Revolution and Reconstruction*. Lincoln: University of Nebraska Press.

Krauze, Enrique. 1997. *Mexico, Biography of Power: A History of Modern Mexico*, trans. Hank Heifetz. New York: Harper Perennial.

Langston, Joy. 2006. The Birth and Transformation of the *Dedazo* in Mexico. In *Informal Institutions and Democracy: Lessons from Latin America*, ed. Gretchen Helmke and Steven Levitsky, 143–159. Baltimore: Johns Hopkins University Press.

Levy, Daniel C., and Kathleen Bruhn (with Emilio Zebadúa). 2006. *Mexico: The Struggle for Democratic Development*. 2nd ed. Berkeley: University of California Press.

Lewis, Oscar. 1961. *The Children of Sanchéz: Autobiography of a Mexican Family*. New York: Random House.

Lynch, John. 1973. *The Spanish-American Revolutions, 1808–1826*. New York: W. W. Norton.

Lynch, John. 1986. The Catholic Church in Latin America, 1830–1930. In *The Cambridge History of Latin America*, Vol. 4: c. 1870–1930, ed. Leslie Bethell, 527–595. New York: Cambridge University Press.

Mahoney, James. 2010. *Colonialism and Postcolonial Development: Spanish America in Comparative Perspective*. New York: Cambridge University Press.

Magaloni, Beatriz, and Guillermo Zepeda. 2004. Democratization, Judicial and Law Enforcement Institutions, and the Rule of Law in Mexico. In *Dilemmas of Political Change in Mexico*, ed. Kevin J. Middlebrook, 168–197. London: Institute of Latin American Studies.

Mainwaring, Scott, and Matthew Soberg Shugart, eds. 1997. *Presidentialism and Democracy in Latin America*. New York: Cambridge University Press.

Mallon, Florencia E. 1995. *Peasant and Nation: The Making of Postcolonial Mexico and Peru*. Berkeley: University of California Press.

Meyer, Michael C., and William L. Sherman. 1987. *The Course of Mexican History*. 3rd ed. New York: Oxford University Press.

Middlebrook, Kevin J., ed. 2004. *Dilemmas of Political Change in Mexico*. London: Institute of Latin American Studies.

Mörner, Magnus. 1993. *Region and State in Latin America's Past*. Baltimore: Johns Hopkins University Press.

O'Neil, Shannon. 2009. The Real War in Mexico: How Democracy Can Defeat the Drug Cartels. *Foreign Affairs*, July/August, 88(4): 63–77.

Pew Research Center. 2017. *Mexican Views of the U.S. Turn Sharply Negative: Widespread Dissatifaction with Economy and Political Leaders*, by Margaret Vice and Hanyu Chwe. http://assets. pewresearch.org/wp-content/uploads/sites/2/2017/09/13094516/ Pew-Research-Center_09.14.17_Mexico-Report.pdf

Reuters. 2017. Mexican Leftist Obrador Leads Ahead of 2018 Election: Poll, September 18, 2017, https://www.reuters.com/article/ us-mexico-politics/mexican-leftist-obrador-leads-ahead-of-2018-election-poll-idUSKCN1BT22G

Stevens, Evelyn P. 1977. Mexico's PRI: The Institutionalization of Corporatism? In *Authoritarianism and Corporatism in Latin America*, ed. James Malloy, 227–258. Pittsburgh, PA: University of Pittsburgh Press.

Thomas, Hugh. 1993. *Conquest: Montezuma, Cortes, and the Fall of Old Mexico*. New York: Simon and Schuster.

Vasconcelos, José. [1925] 1997. *The Cosmic Race: A Bilingual Edition*, trans. Didier Tisdel Jaén. Baltimore: Johns Hopkins University Press.

Weldon, Jeffrey. 1997. The Political Sources of *Presidencialismo* in Mexico. In *Presidentialism and Democracy in Latin America*, ed. Scott Mainwaring and Matthew Soberg Shugart, 225–258. New York: Cambridge University Press.

Womack, John. 1968. *Zapata and the Mexican Revolution*. New York: Vintage.

NIGERIA

Bates, Robert A. 1981 *Markets and States in Tropical Africa: The Political Basis of Agricultural Policies*. Berkeley: University of California Press.

Bayart, Jean-François. 1993. *The State in Africa: The Politics of the Belly*. New York: Longman.

Bayart, Jean-François, Stephen Ellis, and Béatrice Hibou. 1999. *The Criminalization of the State in Africa*. Bloomington: Indiana University Press.

Bratton, Michael, and Nicolas van de Walle. 1997. *Democratic Experiments in Africa: Regime Transitions in Comparative Perspective*. Cambridge: Cambridge University Press.

Chabal, Patrick, and Jean-Pascal Daloz. 1999. *Africa Works: Disorder as Political Instrument*. Bloomington: Indiana University Press.

Davidson, Basil. 1992. *The Black Man's Burden: Africa and the Curse of the Nation-State*. New York: Random House.

Diamond, Larry. 1988. *Class, Ethnicity, and Democracy in Nigeria: The Failure of the First Republic*. Syracuse, NY: Syracuse University Press.

Dorward, D. C. 1986. British West Africa and Liberia. In *Cambridge History of Africa. Vol. 7: From 1905 to 1940*, ed. A. D. Roberts, 399–459. New York: Cambridge University Press.

Dunning, Thad. 2008. *Crude Democracy: Natural Resources Wealth and Political Regimes*. Cambridge: Cambridge University Press.

Evans, Peter. 1995. *Embedded Autonomy: States and Industrial Transformation*. Princeton, NJ: Princeton University Press.

Falola, Toyin, and Matthew M. Heaton. 2008. *A History of Nigeria*. New York: Cambridge University Press.

Fox, Jonathan. 2008. *A World Survey of Religion and the State*. New York: Oxford University Press.

Herbst, Jeffrey. 2000. *States and Power in Africa: Comparative Lessons in Authority and Control*. Princeton, NJ: Princeton University Press.

Joseph, Richard A. 1987. *Democracy and Prebendal Politics in Nigeria: The Rise and Fall of the Second Republic*. New York: Cambridge University Press.

Karl, Terry Lynn. 1997. *The Paradox of Plenty: Oil Booms and Petro States*. Berkeley: University of California Press.

Kohli, Atul. 2004. *State-Directed Development: Political Power and Industrialization in the Global Periphery*. Cambridge: Cambridge University Press.

Lange, Matthew. 2009. *Lineages of Despotism and Development: British Colonialism and State Power*. Chicago: University of Chicago Press.

Mamdani, Mahmood. 1996. *Citizen and Subject: Contemporary Africa and the Legacy of Late Colonialism*. Princeton, NJ: Princeton University Press.

Suberu, Rotimi T. 2001. *Federalism and Ethnic Conflict in Nigeria*. Washington, DC: United States Institute of Peace.

Suberu, Rotimi T. 2008. The Supreme Court and Federalism in Nigeria. *Journal of Modern African Studies* 46(3): 451–485.

Williams, David. 1984. English Speaking West Africa. In *Cambridge History of Africa. Vol. 8: From c. 1940 to c. 1975*, ed. Michael Crowder, 331–382. New York: Cambridge University Press.

RUSSIA

Ascher, Abraham. 2009. *Russia: A Short History*. New ed. Oxford: Oneworld Publications.

Ash, Timothy Garton. 2002. *The Polish Revolution: Solidarity*. 3rd ed. New Haven, CT: Yale University Press.

Brown, Archie. 2006. Cultural Change and Continuity in the Transition from Communism: The Russian Case. In *Developing Cultures: Case Studies*, ed. Lawrence E. Harrison and Peter L. Berger, 387–405. New York: Routledge.

Bushkovitch, Paul. 2012. *A Concise History of Russia*. New York: Cambridge University Press.

Carr, E. H. [1979] 2004. *The Russian Revolution from Lenin to Stalin, 1917–1929*. New York: Palgrave Macmillan.

Colton, Timothy, and Michael McFaul. 2003. *Popular Choice and Managed Democracy: The Russian Elections of 1999 and 2000*. Washington, DC: The Brookings Institution Press.

Davies, Norman. 1996. *Europe: A History*. New York: Harper-Perennial.

Fitzpatrick, Sheila. 1994. *The Russian Revolution*. New York: Oxford University Press.

Freedom House. 2011. Country Report: Russia (2011), http://www.freedomhouse.org//report/freedom-world/2011/russia?page=22&country (accessed August 13, 2012).

Greenfeld, Liah. 1992. *Nationalism: Five Roads to Modernity*. Cambridge, MA: Harvard University Press.

Goldman, Marshall I. 2004. Putin and the Oligarchs. *Foreign Affairs* 83(6): 33–44.

Hoffman, David E. [2002] 2011. *The Oligarchs: Wealth and Power in the New Russia*. New York: Public Affairs.

Hughes, Lindsey. 2008. Russian Culture in the Eighteenth Century. In *The Cambridge History of Russia. Vol. 2: Imperial Russia, 1689–1917*, online ed., ed. Dominic Lieven, 67–91. New York: Cambridge University Press.

Kitchen, Martin. 2006. *A History of Modern Germany, 1800–2000*. Malden, MA: Blackwell Publishing.

Levitsky, Steven, and Lucan A. Way. 2010. *Competitive Authoritarianism: Hybrid Regimes After the Cold War*. New York: Cambridge University Press.

Mainwaring, Scott. 1998. Party Systems in the Third Wave. *Journal of Democracy* 9(3): 67–81.

McFaul, Michael. 2008. The Russian Federation. In *The Cambridge History of Russia. Vol. 3: The Twentieth Century*, online ed., ed. Ronald Grigor Suny, 352–380. New York: Cambridge University Press.

Rose, Richard, William Mishler, and Neil Munro. 2006. *Russia Transformed: Developing Popular Support for a New Regime*. New York: Cambridge University Press.

Service, Robert. 2009. *A History of Modern Russia: From Tsarism to the Twenty-First Century*. 3rd ed. Cambridge, MA: Harvard University Press.

Sharafutdinova, Gulnaz. 2011. *Political Consequences of Crony Capitalism Inside Russia*. Notre Dame, IN: University of Notre Dame Press.

Stalin, Joseph. 1994. The Nation. In *Nationalism*, ed. John Hutchinson and Anthony D. Smith, 18–20. New York: Oxford University Press.

Stoner-Weiss, Kathryn. 2006. Russia: Authoritarianism Without Authority. *Journal of Democracy* 17(1): 104–118.

Treisman, Daniel. 2011. *The Return: Russia's Journey from Gorbachev to Medvedev*. New York: Free Press.

The Long Life of Homo Sovieticus. 2011, December 11. *The Economist* 401(8763): 27–30.

UNITED KINGDOM

Almond, Gabriel A., and Sidney Verba. 1963. *The Civic Culture: Political Attitudes and Democracy in Five Nations*. Princeton, NJ: Princeton University Press.

Berger, Peter, Grace Davie, and Effie Fokas. 2008. *Religious America, Secular Europe? A Theme and Variations*. Burlington, VT: Ashgate Publishing.

Bernhard, Michael, Christopher Reenock, and Timothy Nordstrom. 2004. The Legacy of Western Overseas Colonialism on Democratic Survival. *International Studies Quarterly* 48(1): 225–250.

Bruce, Steve. 2004. The Strange Death of Protestant Britain. In *Rethinking Ethnicity: Majority Groups and Dominant Minorities*, ed. Eric P. Kaufmann, 116–135. New York: Routledge.

Calhoun, Craig. 1997. *Nationalism*. Minneapolis: University of Minnesota Press.

Clarke, Peter. 2004. *Hope and Glory: Britain 1900–2000*. 2nd ed. New York: Penguin Books.

Colley, Linda. 1992. *Britons: Forging the Nation, 1707–1837*. New Haven, CT: Yale University Press.

Greenfeld, Liah. 1992. *Nationalism: Five Roads to Modernity*. Cambridge, MA: Harvard University Press.

Greenfeld, Liah. 2001. *The Spirit of Capitalism: Nationalism and Economic Growth*. Cambridge, MA: Harvard University Press.

Habermas, Jurgen. 1989. *The Structural Transformation of the Public Sphere: An Inquiry Into a Category of Bourgeois Society*, trans. Thomas Burger. Cambridge, MA: MIT Press.

Harvie, Christopher. 2010. Revolution and the Rule of Law (1789–1851). In *The Oxford History of Britain*, ed. Kenneth O. Morgan, 470–517. New York: Oxford University Press.

Hastings, Adrian. 1997. *The Construction of Nationhood: Ethnicity, Religion, and Nationalism*. New York: Cambridge University Press.

Hechter, Michael. 1975. *Internal Colonialism: The Celtic Fringe in British National Development*. Berkeley: University of California Press.

Huber, Evelyne, and John D. Stephens. 2001. *Development and the Crisis of the Welfare State: Parties and Policies in Global Markets*. Chicago: University of Chicago Press.

Inglehart, Ronald, and Christian Welzel. 2005. *Modernization, Cultural Change, and Democracy: The Human Development Sequence*. New York: Cambridge University Press.

Kishlansky, Mark. 1996. *A Monarchy Transformed: Britain 1603–1714*. New York: Penguin Group.

Kohn, Hans. 1944. *The Idea of Nationalism*. New York: Macmillan Company.

Kumar, Krishan. 2003. *The Making of English National Identity*. New York: Cambridge University Press.

Langford, Paul. 2010. The Eighteenth Century (1688–1789). In *The Oxford History of Britain*, ed. Kenneth O. Morgan, 399–469. New York: Oxford University Press.

Matthew, H. C. G. 2010. The Liberal Age (1851–1914). In *The Oxford History of Britain*, ed. Kenneth O. Morgan, 518–581. New York: Oxford University Press.

Modood, Tariq. 2007. *Multiculturalism: A Civic Idea*. Malden, MA: Polity Press.

Morgan, Kenneth O. 2010a. Epilogue (2000–2010). In *The Oxford History of Britain*, ed. Kenneth O. Morgan, 677–710. New York: Oxford University Press.

Morgan, Kenneth O. 2010b. The Twentieth Century (1914–2000). In *The Oxford History of Britain*, ed. Kenneth O. Morgan, 582–676. New York: Oxford University Press.

Pincus, Steven. 2009. *1688: The First Modern Revolution*. New Haven, CT: Yale University Press.

Prasad, Monica. 2006. *The Politics of Free Markets: The Rise of Neoliberal Economic Policies in Britain, France, Germany, and the United States.* Chicago: University of Chicago Press.

Strayer, Joseph. 1970. *On the Medieval Origins of the Modern State.* Princeton, NJ: Princeton University Press.

Tilly, Charles. 1995. *Popular Contention in Great Britain, 1758–1834.* Cambridge, MA: Harvard University Press.

Tilly, Charles. 1997. Parliamentarization of Contention in Great Britain, 1758–1834. *Theory and Society* 26(2/3): 245–273.

Tilly, Charles, and Lesley J. Wood. 2009. *Social Movements, 1768–2008.* 2nd ed. Boulder, CO: Paradigm Publishers.

UNITED STATES

Almond, Gabriel A., and Sidney Verba. 1963. *The Civic Culture: Political Attitudes and Democracy in Five Nations.* Princeton, NJ: Princeton University Press.

Bellah, Robert N., Richard Madsen, William M. Sullivan, Ann Swidler, and Steven M. Tipton. 1985. *Habits of the Heart: Individualism and Commitment in American Life.* Berkeley: University of California Press.

Berkman, Lisa F. 2004. The Health Divide. *Contexts* 3(4): 38–43.

Brown, Michael K., Martin Carnoy, Elliott Currie, Troy Duster, David B. Oppenheimer, Marjorie M. Schultz, and David Wallman. 2003. *Whitewashing Race: The Myth of a Colorblind Society.* Berkeley: University of California Press.

Dawson, Michael C. 1994. *Behind the Mule: Race and Class in African-American Politics.* Princeton, NJ: Princeton University Press.

Dunn, Richard S. [1972] 2000. *Sugar and Slaves: The Rise of the Planter Class in the English West Indies, 1624–1713.* Chapel Hill: University of North Carolina Press.

Fiorina, Morris P. and Samuel J. Abrams. 2008. Political Polarization in the American Public. *Annual Review of Political Science* 11: 563–588.

Fischer, David Hackett. 1989. *Albion's Seed: Four British Folkways in America.* New York: Oxford University Press.

Hacker, Jacob, and Paul Pierson. 2010. *Winner-Take-All Politics: How Washington Made the Rich Richer—And Turned Its Back on the Middle Class.* New York: Simon and Schuster.

Hamilton, Alexander [1791] 1828. Report on Manufactures. In *Reports of the Secretary of the Treasury of the United States.* Washington, DC: Duff Green.

Hartz, Louis. 1955. *The Liberal Tradition in America: An Interpretation of American Political Thought Since the Revolution.* New York: Harcourt, Brace, and World, Inc.

Haskins, Ron, Julia B. Isaacs, and Isabel V. Sawhill. 2008. *Getting Ahead or Losing Ground: Economic Mobility in America.* Washington, DC: Brookings Institution Press.

Iannaccone, Laurence R., Roger Finke, and Rodney Stark. 1997. Deregulating Religion: The Economics of Church and State. *Economic Inquiry* 35: 350–364.

Kaufman, Jason. 2002. *For the Common Good? American Civic Life and the Golden Age of Fraternity.* New York: Oxford University Press.

Kennedy, David M. 1999. *Freedom from Fear: The American People in Depression and War, 1929–1945.* New York: Oxford University Press.

Ladd, Everett Carll. 1999. *The Ladd Report: Startling New Research Shows How an Explosion of Voluntary Groups, Activities, and Charitable Donations Is Transforming Our Towns and Cities.* New York: Free Press.

Levitsky, Steven and Daniel Ziblatt. 2018. *How Democracies Die.* New York: Crown Publishing Group.

Lipset, Seymour Martin. 1959. Some Social Requisites of Democracy: Economic Development and Political Legitimacy. *American Political Science Review* 53(1): 69–105.

Lipset, Seymour Martin. 1960. *Political Man: The Social Bases of Politics.* New York: Doubleday & Company.

Lipset, Seymour Martin. 1963 *The First New Nation: The United States in Historical and Comparative Perspective.* New York: Basic Books.

Mann, Thomas, and Norman Ornstein. 2008. *The Broken Branch: How Congress Is Failing America and How to Get It Back on Track.* New York: Oxford University Press.

Mason, Lilliana. 2015. "I Respectfully Disagree": The Differential Effects of Partisan Sorting on Social and Issue Polarization. *American Journal of Political Science* 59(1): 128–145.

McPherson, James M. 1988. *Battle Cry of Freedom: The Civil War Era.* New York: Oxford University Press.

Miller, Perry. [1953] 1983a. *The New England Mind: From Colony to Province.* Cambridge, MA: Belknap Press/Harvard University Press.

Miller, Perry. [1954] 1983b. *The New England Mind: The Seventeenth Century.* Cambridge, MA: Belknap Press/Harvard University Press.

Nash, Gary B. 1979. *The Urban Crucible: Social Change, Political Consciousness, and the Origins of the American Revolution.* Cambridge, MA: Harvard University Press.

Niebuhr, H. Richard. 1929. *The Social Sources of Denominationalism.* New York: Henry Holt and Co.

Norris, Pippa, and Ronald Inglehart. 2004. *Sacred and Secular: Religion and Politics Worldwide.* New York: Cambridge University Press.

Patterson, James T. 1996. *Grand Expectations: The United States, 1945–1974.* New York: Oxford University Press.

Patterson, James T. 2005. *Restless Giant: The United States from Watergate to* Bush v. Gore. New York: Oxford University Press.

Prasad, Monica. 2006. *The Politics of Free Markets: The Rise of Neoliberal Economic Policies in Britain, France, Germany, and the United States.* Chicago: University of Chicago Press.

Putnam, Robert D. 2000. *Bowling Alone: The Collapse and Revival of American Community.* New York: Simon and Schuster.

Schoultz, Lars. 1998. *Beneath the United States: A History of U.S. Policy Toward Latin America.* Cambridge, MA: Harvard University Press.

Turner, Frederick Jackson. 1921. *The Frontier in American History.* New York: Henry Holt and Co.

Wilkerson, Isabel. 2010. *The Warmth of Other Suns: The Epic Story of America's Great Migration.* New York: Random House.

Wood, Gordon. [1969] 1998. *The Creation of the American Republic, 1776–1787.* Chapel Hill: University of North Carolina Press.

Wuthnow, Robert. 2007. *After the Baby Boomers: How Twenty- and Thirty-Somethings Are Shaping the Future of American Religion.* Princeton, NJ: Princeton University Press.

Credits

PHOTOS

CHAPTER 1
p. 1: Photo by Guido Bergmann/Bundesregierung via Getty Images; p. 6: AP Photo/Francois Mori; p. 11: Kyodo via AP Images; p. 15: Copyright Piotr Redlinski/Corbis/AP Images; p. 17: AP Photo/Kwesi Osowu.

CHAPTER 2
p. 24: Photo by Robin Utrecht/Sipa USA (Sipa via AP Images); p. 29: TOLES ©2005 The Washington Post. Reprinted with permission of UNIVERSAL UCLICK. All rights reserved; p. 31: Imaginechina via AP Images; p. 36 AP Photo/Korean Central News Agency via Korea News Service.

CHAPTER 3
p. 47: ODD ANDERSEN/AFP/Getty Images; p. 59 Photo by Imagno/Getty Images.

CHAPTER 4
p. 71: AP Photo/Andrew Harnik; p. 76: Agencia Estado via AP Images; p. 80: John W Banagan/Getty Images; p. 84: Paula Bronstein/Getty Images; p. 92: Kyodo via AP Images.

CHAPTER 5
p. 97: AP Photo/Susan Walsh; p. 102: AP Photo/Saurabh Das; p. 111: YURI CORTEZ/AFP/Getty Images

CHAPTER 6
p. 121: LILLIAN SUWANRUMPHA/AFP/Getty Images; p. 127: CLAUDIO REYES/AFP/Getty Images; p. 130: AP Photo/ Stephen Wanderai; p. 136: SANJAY KANOJIA/AFP/Getty Images.

CHAPTER 7
p. 147: AP Photo/Tsvangirayi Mukwazhi); p. 155: AP Photo/Esteban Felix; p. 158: SERGEI SUPINKSY/AFP/Getty Images

CHAPTER 8
p. 174: Photo by Oryx Media Archive/Gallo Images/Getty Images; p. 177: AP Photo/STR; p. 182: 3 Agência Brasil; p. 188: AP Photo/ Martin Bureau, Pool; p. 194: AP Photo/Rodger Bosch.

CHAPTER 9
p. 201: AP Photo/Mark Baker; p. 206: AP Photo; p. 208: Press Association via AP Images; p. 215: Axel Schmidt/dapd/AP Images; p. 224 JACK GUEZ/AFP/Getty Images).

CHAPTER 10
p. 229: Press Association via AP Images; p. 237: AP Photo/RIA Novosti Kremlin, Yekaterina Shtukina, Presidential Press Service; p. 239: GREG BAKER/AFP/Getty Images; p. 240: AP Photo/ Michael Sohn; p. 247: Bettman/Getty Images.

CHAPTER 11
p. 254: AP Photo/ Ivan Sekretarev; p. 258: AP Photo/Eduardo Di Baia; p. 261: AP Photo/Themba Hadebe; p. 263: Kyodo via AP Images

CHAPTER 12
p. 280: Sipa via AP Images; p. 284: Sipa via AP Images; p. 286: AP Photo/Gene Herrick; p. 290: Bettman/Getty Images; p. 302: Sipa via AP Images

CHAPTER 13
p. 308: AP Photo/Michel Euler; p. 315: Chip Somodevilla/Getty Images; p. 318: JERRY LAMPEN/AFP/Getty Images

CHAPTER 14
p. 328: AP Photo/Pablo Martinez Monsivais; p. 330: William F. Campbell/Timepix/The LIFE Images Collection/Getty Images; p. 338: Alex Wong/Getty Images; p. 341: AP Photo.

CHAPTER 15
p. 351: GDA via AP Images; p. 355: Kaveh Kazemi/Getty Images); p. 359: DOMINIQUE FAGET/AFP/Getty Images; p. 362: AP Photo/Francois Mori; p. 368: CTK via AP Images.

CHAPTER 16
p. 372: Sipa via AP Images; p. 377: Bettman/Getty Images; p. 386: Imaginechina via AP Images; p. 397: Wiktor Dabkowski/ picture-alliance/dpa/AP Images.

FIGURES

PREFACE
pp. xxx–xxxvii: Cartography © Philip's

CHAPTER 2
p. 33: Map Courtesy FreedomHouse.org

CHAPTER 9
p. 227: Courtesy of New Zealand Electoral Commission

Note: Tables and figures are indicated by "*t*" and "*f*" following page numbers.